NELSON

A DREAM OF GLORY, 1758–1797

JOHN SUGDEN

A JOHN MACRAE BOOK
Henry Holt and Company | New York

Henry Holt and Company, LLC
Publishers since 1866
115 West 18th Street
New York, New York 10011

Henry Holt® is a registered trademark of
Henry Holt and Company, LLC.

Originally published in Great Britain in 2004 by Jonathan Cape,
an imprint of the Random House Group Ltd.

Library of Congress Cataloging-in-Publication Data
Sugden, John, 1947–
    Nelson : a dream of glory, 1758–1797 / John Sugden.—1st ed.
        p.   cm.
    "A John Macrae book."
    ISBN-13: 978-0-8050-7757-5
    ISBN-10: 0-8050-7757-X
    1. Nelson, Horatio Nelson, Viscount, 1758–1805. 2. Nelson, Horatio Nelson,
Viscount, 1758–1805—Childhood and youth. 3. Great Britain—History, Naval—18th
century. 4. Admirals—Great Britain—Biography. I. Title.
DA87.1.N4S84 2004
359'.0092—dc22
[B]   2004054057

Henry Holt books are available for special promotions and
premiums. For details contact: Director, Special Markets.

First American Edition 2004

Printed in the United States of America
1 3 5 7 9 10 8 6 4 2

This one is for my mother, Lily,
who told me that Nelson was *the* great man;

for Phil, who prefers James Cook;

and for Terri,
who alone of us has crewed aboard a tall ship

Hope revives within me. I shall recover,
and my dream of glory be fulfilled.
Nelson will yet be an admiral.

—Horatio Nelson, aged twenty-one,
shipped home with malaria, 1780

CONTENTS

LIST OF ILLUSTRATIONS

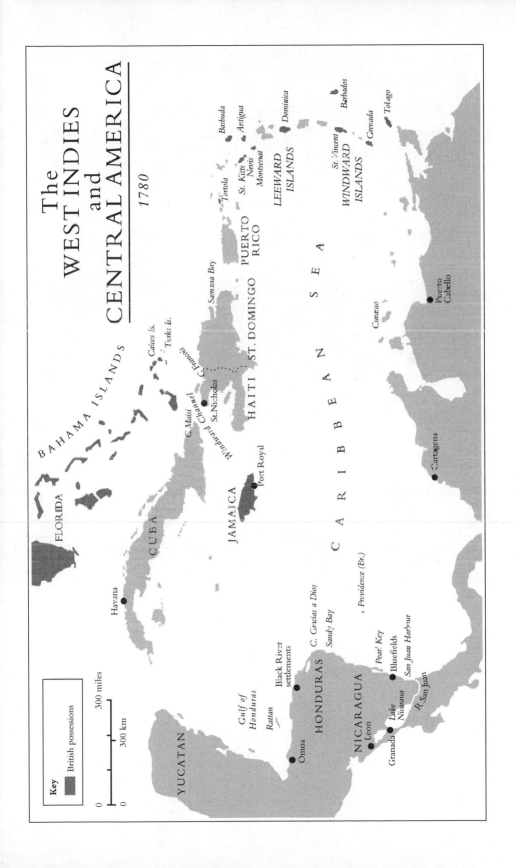

The
WEST INDIES
and
CENTRAL AMERICA

1780

Key
British possessions

300 miles

300 km

FLORIDA

BAHAMA ISLANDS

CUBA

Havana

C. Maisi

Caicos Is.
Turks Is.

Windward Channel

St. Nicholas

JAMAICA

Port Royal

Old Bahama Channel

Samana Bay

HAITI   ST. DOMINGO

PUERTO
RICO

Tortola

St. Kitts
Nevis
Montserrat

Barbuda

Antigua

Dominica

LEEWARD
ISLANDS

St. Vincent

WINDWARD
ISLANDS

Grenada

Barbados

Tobago

C A R I B B E A N   S E A

Curaçao

Providence (Br.)

Puerto
Cabello

Cartagena

YUCATAN

Gulf of
Honduras

Rattan

Black River
settlements

C. Gracias a Dios

Sandy Bay

HONDURAS

Omoa

NICARAGUA

Leon

Granada

Lake
Nicaragua

Pearl Key

Bluefields

San Juan Harbour

R. San Juan

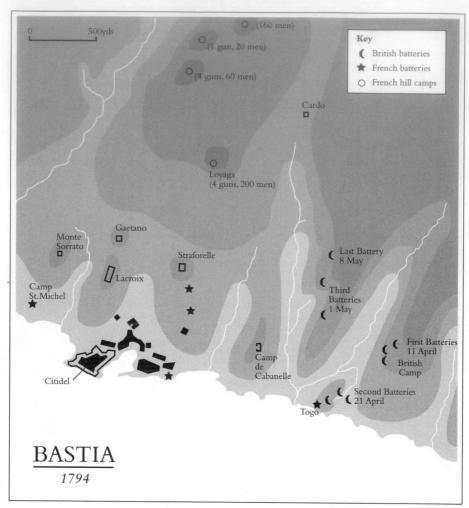

0   500yds

(160 men)

(1 gun, 20 men)

(4 guns, 60 men)

Key
☾ British batteries
★ French batteries
○ French hill camps

Cardo

Loyaga
(4 guns, 200 men)

Gaetano

Monte
Sorrato

Straforelle

Lacroix

☾ Last Battery
8 May

☾ Third
Batteries
1 May

Camp
St.Michel

☾ First Batteries
11 April

☾ British
Camp

Citidel

Camp
de
Cabanelle

☾ ☾ Second Batteries
21 April

Togo

BASTIA
1794

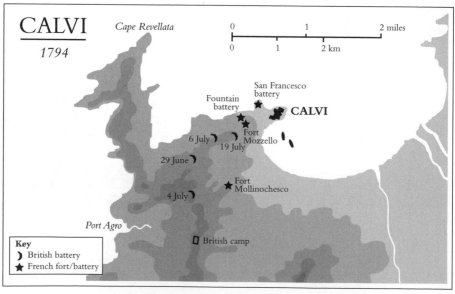

CALVI
1794

Cape Revellata

0   1   2 miles

0   1   2 km

San Francesco
battery

Fountain
battery

CALVI

6 July

Fort
Mozzello

19 July

29 June

4 July

Fort
Mollinochesco

Port Agro

Key
☽ British battery
★ French fort/battery

British camp

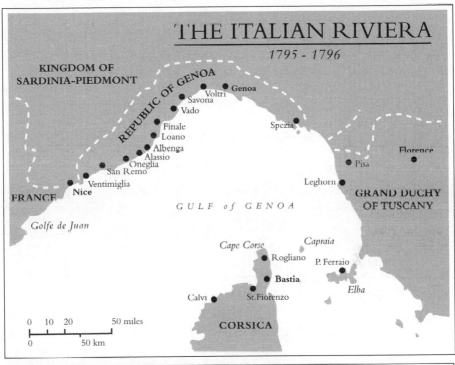

THE ITALIAN RIVIERA
1795 - 1796

KINGDOM OF
SARDINIA-PIEDMONT

REPUBLIC OF GENOA

Voltri
Genoa
Savona
Vado
Finale
Loano
Albenga
Alassio
Oneglia
San Remo
Ventimiglia
Nice

Spezia

Florence

Pisa

FRANCE

Leghorn

GRAND DUCHY
OF TUSCANY

GULF of GENOA

Golfe de Juan

Cape Corse

Capraia

Rogliano
P. Ferraio

Bastia

Elba

Calvi
St. Fiorenzo

CORSICA

0   10   20   50 miles

0   50 km

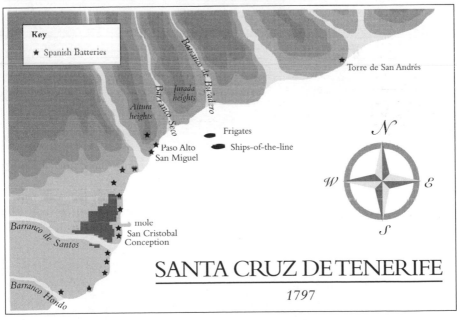

Key

★ Spanish Batteries

Barranco de Bufadero

Torre de San Andrés

Jurada heights

Altura heights

Barranco Seco

Frigates

Paso Alto
San Miguel

Ships-of-the-line

N

W   *E*

S

Barranco de Santos

mole
San Cristobal
Conception

Barranco Hondo

SANTA CRUZ DE TENERIFE
1797

BATTLE of CAPE ST.VINCENT

approximate positions at 12.10 pm

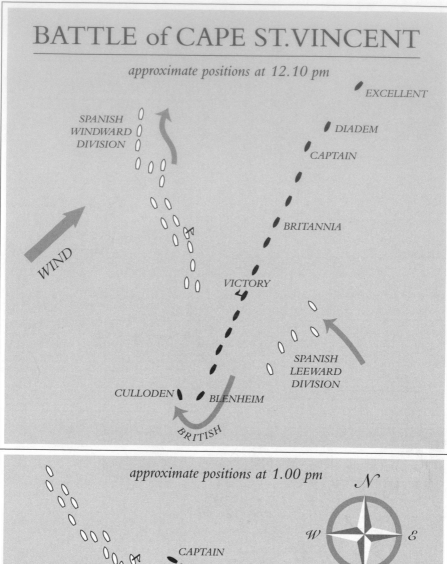

EXCELLENT

DIADEM

CAPTAIN

SPANISH
WINDWARD
DIVISION

BRITANNIA

WIND

VICTORY

SPANISH
LEEWARD
DIVISION

CULLODEN   BLENHEIM

BRITISH

approximate positions at 1.00 pm

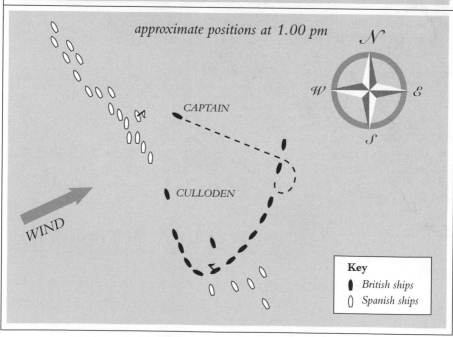

N

W   E

S

CAPTAIN

CULLODEN

WIND

Key

● British ships

◗ Spanish ships

INTRODUCTION

Nelson was once Britannia's God of War
And still should be so, but
The tide has turned;
There's no more to be said of Trafalgar.
'Tis with our hero quietly inturr'd.
                    Lord Byron, *Don Juan*

'NEVER,' recalled secretary John Barrow of the Admiralty, 'can I forget the shock I received on opening the board-room door the morning after the arrival of the despatches, when Marsden called out, "Glorious news! The most glorious victory our brave navy ever achieved – but Nelson is dead!"'[1]

To the British people, and many others fighting Napoleon, the death of Nelson in 1805 was one of those ineffaceable events that live as long as memory. The nation won its greatest naval victory and went into mourning. As Josiah Wedgwood the younger remarked, 'grief and regret' were 'so general and so strong as quite to check and abate the delight the victory would otherwise have created in all our bosoms'.[2]

Britons of every stamp remembered where they heard the news and the thoughts it inspired. The essayist Charles Lamb, no admirer of public persons, confessed to have been a follower of Nelson ever since he had seen him walking in Pall Mall 'looking just as a hero should look'. Now, he felt 'very much cut about it indeed' because 'nobody is left of any name at all'. The Wordsworths were in their native Lake District. Dorothy burst into tears, while her brother refused to believe that Nelson was dead until he had run into a Patterdale inn to confirm the tidings. A partially unreconstructed radical, William Wordsworth did not approve of all that Nelson had done, but reflected deeply enough to compose a poetic tribute to 'the happy warrior'.[3]

Coleridge was in Naples when the news reached him. 'When he [Nelson] died it seemed as if no man was a stranger to another, for all were made acquaintances in the rights of a common anguish,' he wrote. 'Never can I forget the sorrow and consternation that lay on every countenance . . . Numbers stopped and shook hands with me, because they had seen tears on my cheek and conjectured that I was an Englishman, and several, as they held my hand, burst themselves into tears.' But it was that other old pantisocrat, Robert Southey, who perhaps best captured the national mood. 'The death of Nelson was felt in England as something more than a public calamity,' he remembered from the perspective of another eight years. 'Men started at the intelligence and turned pale, as if they had heard of the loss of a dear friend. An object of our admiration and affection, of our pride and of our hopes, was suddenly taken from us, and it seemed as if we had never, till then, known how deeply we loved and reverenced him.'[4]

That huge sense of loss manifested itself in a torrent of memorabilia and a multiplicity of monuments. Horatio Nelson, the Norfolk commoner, was raised in stone like the heroes of antiquity. Great columns, arches and statues were erected in far distant places. Some, though weathered or crumbling, still stand as mute testimony to the great debt the British public felt they owed the man now dead.

More than thirty substantial monuments were created in a vast and enduring surge of grief and pride. State patronage contributed, but most of the memorials depended upon public subscriptions and private enthusiasm, and took many forms. Alexander Davison, Nelson's friend and prize agent, planted trees at Swarland in Northumberland to represent the positions of the ships in the battle of the Nile. A rough granite pillar, twelve feet high, was hauled on rollers from Aird's Bay in Scotland by local iron-workers and erected on a hill at Taynuilt in Argyll and Bute. Twelve hundred men of the Sea Fencibles (a kind of naval home guard) were reported to have thrown up a twenty-foot triumphal arch at Cork in Ireland in just five hours on 10 November 1805, and a high tower built on Portsdown Hill overlooking Britain's greatest naval base at Portsmouth was financed by veterans of the battle of Trafalgar.[5]

The history of these monuments is instructive. They did more than remind new generations of a dead hero. They represented the nation itself and an uncomplicated patriotism that for long sustained it. The citizens who raised those stones saluted a man who had rescued them from foreign domination. He stood for freedom and national endeavour. He was the very epitome of the greatness of Britain, a founder of its security and worldwide influence. Enemies certainly understood, whether rival powers or anti-colonialists. In 1940 Hitler talked about dismantling the famous column in Trafalgar Square and shipping it to Berlin as a concrete symbol of Britain's defeat, while twenty-six years later Irish republicans blew up the impressive pillar and statue that had been a focal point in Dublin for more than a century. Both Bridgetown in Barbados and Montreal in Canada have talked about moving their huge Nelson statues to obscurer locations, where they are less capable of offending nationalist sentiment.

Even in Britain changing political attitudes to the state have rebounded upon the Nelson memorials. During the nineteenth century, when the admiral enjoyed a tremendous popular appeal, the statues in Glasgow and Trafalgar Square became places of pilgrimage and venues for radical protest. But more distant and sceptical generations allowed many of the monuments to decay, and not so long ago the relatively unadorned statue unveiled in Birmingham in 1809 was threatened by doctrinaire city councillors. The city's first public statue, the Birmingham monument had been financed by a true cross section of the community, and even its triumphalism was moderated to appease local Quaker sentiment. But for these modern critics Nelson had become nothing more than an embarrassing war monger and the symbol of an unsavoury empire.

Biographies of Nelson are also monuments, and equally reflect shifting opinion. The first major biographies were largely compilations, often reproducing badly bowdlerised chunks of primary material with little in the way of synthesis or analysis to act as a guide. Like the stone pillars their duty was to commemorate, and most that put the hero in a poor light was exorcised. In the words of one of the more competent scribes, it was Nelson's 'ardent love of country, his fervent attachment to his profession, [and] his acute skill and accurate judgement in nautical affairs' that alone concerned the historian. So, at least for a time, also thought James Harrison, hired by Nelson's former mistress, Lady Hamilton, to produce the two-volume *Life of the Rt Honourable Horatio, Lord Viscount Nelson* in 1806. Information furnished by her ladyship and other associates of Nelson lent Harrison 'a considerable store of novelties', among which treasures were revealing love letters that the author subsequently published anonymously to his patron's disadvantage. But the biography itself, though impaired by a spite towards Nelson's wronged wife that led her to denounce it as 'the basest production that ever was offered to the public', generally eschewed controversial ground in favour of the story of a selfless patriot.[6]

It was James Stanier Clarke, librarian and chaplain to the Prince of Wales, and Dr John McArthur 'of Horndean, Hampshire' (as he signed himself) who supplied what came to be regarded as the standard life, however. Their ponderous twin tomes entitled *The Life of Admiral Lord Nelson* were published in 1809. Based upon contributions from many of Nelson's friends, colleagues and relations, as well as papers still held by his wife and brother, the book claimed great authority. The 'editors' were in a position to learn much about their subject. Noted for his skill with a sword rather than a pen, McArthur may have met Nelson as early as 1782 and certainly served him as prize agent in the Mediterranean during the 1790s. Both men had edited the *Naval Chronicle*, an on-going miscellania of matters afloat that had published a fragment of autobiography written by Nelson in 1799.

In that self-congratulatory fragment Nelson pointed the way for his biographers, representing his life as an exemplification of the maxim 'that perseverance in any profession will most probably meet its reward', and omitting most that did not relate to heroic deeds, stalwart service and public duty. His sketch exaggerated some of his achievements and denied the considerable nepotism that had lubricated his career. No self-effacing hero, Nelson had always played to his public, proclaiming himself its champion and inviting idolatry. As the epigraphs to the following chapters show, he did not mistake his constituency. The admiral had his critics but the British public responded rapturously.

The full biography by Clarke and McArthur was hardly more critical. Frequently analysis and coherent narrative were abandoned in favour of doctored selections from the admiral's correspondence. Although the authors professed to expose 'the private feelings and motives, as well as the great principles of his public and professional character', they trod warily – necessarily so when so many of the dramatis personae were still alive. McArthur probably knew about the mistress Nelson had abandoned in the Mediterranean, but saw no virtue in publishing what could only have been deeply repugnant to

Lady Nelson. When it came to the admiral's notorious affair with Emma Hamilton the plea of ignorance failed, so the authors merely declared the subject off limits. Henceforth, they said, their book would be 'exclusively devoted to his more splendid public character'.[7]

So eagerly was the heroic interpretation of Nelson's life embraced that for many years writers only ventured beyond it at their peril. When Thomas Joseph Pettigrew, an eminent medical man, antiquary and early Egyptologist, published his *Memoirs of the Life of Vice-Admiral Lord Viscount Nelson* in two hefty volumes in 1849 it was hissed out of print. Like his predecessors Pettigrew employed a documentary style of presentation, but his was an industrious, honourable and significant work. It had the inestimable advantage of following Sir Harris Nicolas's monumental seven-volume set of *The Dispatches and Letters of Vice Admiral Lord Viscount Nelson*, published in 1844–6, still, for all its omissions and suppressions, the single most important book on the subject. In addition Pettigrew consulted papers with the Admiralty, something few of his successors felt it necessary to do, and hung his narrative around six hundred original documents he had somehow purchased from a collection formerly owned by Lady Hamilton.[8]

Those new letters, which proved beyond question that Nelson's only surviving child was the progeny of an adulterous affair with Emma Hamilton, accounted for much of the violent reaction. Nelson's faithful admirers castigated Pettigrew for publishing 'letters written in his most unguarded moments' and stamping 'his memory with infamy'. Some even declared the letters forgeries, and Pettigrew died in 1865 with his reputation clouded. It was not until some of Pettigrew's Nelson papers were used by John Cordy Jeaffreson for *Lady Hamilton and Lord Nelson* (1888) and a number found their way into print as *The Hamilton and Nelson Papers* (1893–4) that the besmirched biographer was vindicated.[9]

By steering away from Nelson's questionable private life and through a succession of heroic deeds against ill-intentioned foreigners the early biographies polished his image for popular consumption. But the major works were inedible compositions, and it was the new poet laureate, Robert Southey, who interpreted the admiral's career for the nation in his classic *Life of Nelson*, endlessly reprinted since its first appearance in 1813. Southey admitted the difficulties naval history caused him. 'I walk among sea terms as a cat goes in a china pantry, in bodily fear of doing mischief, & betraying myself,' he wrote. Yet, though he added little new information his beautifully economic prose cemented the admiral's status as the authentic British hero.[10]

Shorn of indiscretions Nelson made an ideal patriotic hero. Like most men of modest means he was interested in prize money, but seldom made pecuniary gain alone the engine of his larger actions. In fact he risked financial ruin in the public service several times. Nelson was relentlessly self-seeking, but it was attention, recognition and applause rather than money that fascinated him. As he once famously said, he wanted his name to stand on the record when those of the money-makers had been forgotten. The rewards he sought were more readily compatible with selfless and dutiful patriotism.

Southey's Nelson was the ideal public servant who placed man above Mammon and 'resolved to do his duty, whatever might be the opinion or conduct of others'. Moreover, whereas the Duke of Wellington was an aloof patrician with scant regard for the rank and file, as well as an unpopular Tory premier, Nelson appealed to Everyman. He was a monarchist, but disdained the sectional interests of elites and strove for the good of the nation as a whole, and he was to a considerable extent protective of and beloved by all ranks. Fittingly, therefore, though (unlike Wellington) he was only stingily rewarded by government he was acclaimed by the people as their champion.[11]

While Southey claimed Nelson for the nation, he particularly directed his book to the budding naval officers who would protect Britain's control of the seas. The first important interpretative biographies of Nelson, published at the end of the nineteenth century, were even more conscious of his importance as a professional role model. Their interest was the admiral rather than the man, and they presented him as the ultimate exemplar of naval achievement. Nelson had inspired earlier sea officers, of course. His offensive spirit and belief in total victory had encouraged Hoste, Cochrane, Perry, Pellew and Codrington to win the last battles of the age of fighting sail. Nevertheless, it was not until the dawn of a new century that historians scrutinised Nelson's career in detail to distil lessons for the ironclad navies of another time.[12]

The interest during this period was hardly surprising. The empire was at its height and the mother country's massive economic power and global influence transparently rested upon naval muscle. It was also an age of awakening giants, such as the United States and Japan, and of international tension and imperial competition as the European powers divided into two armed camps and partitioned Africa. The

American theorist Alfred Thayer Mahan's seminal *Influence of Sea Power Upon History* (1890) was only the best known of several works that turned the eyes of ambitious nation-states towards maritime capability. Conflict was in the air, big battle fleets were building in Europe, America and Asia, and the British premier Lloyd George lobbied his electorate for a mandate on pensions and dreadnoughts. The Royal Navy saw off the German challenge during the First World War, but only just.[13]

Amid such 'navalism' the study of sea power flourished, and just as Clausewitz had ransacked the campaigns of Napoleon for his celebrated treatise on military principles, so emboldened naval historians turned to Nelson. Mahan's magisterial *Life of Nelson*, originally published in two volumes in 1897, was the first important synthetic biography of the English admiral. Detailed, mature and informed, it was also an articulate and well-crafted narrative and remains the foundation of all subsequent assessments of Nelson the commander.

But in no sense did Mahan and his associates offer a comprehensive portrait. Their gaze, like those of the first generation of Nelson scholars, remained fixed upon his professional career, and though they ploughed long and deep furrows in the letters published by Nicolas and Morrison few looked much further for information. Perhaps worse, they were unduly idolatrous. Mahan was upset at suggestions that his hero could make a false statement – though many will be instanced in our pages – while his British counterpart, Sir John Knox Laughton, would brook no stain on the professional judgement of a man he saw as the ultimate naval icon. Sir John was a bonny fighter, as his fiercely independent contributions to the *Dictionary of National Biography* cuttingly attest, but he charged too vigorously and enjoyed bayoneting the wounded. His savage dismissal of Pettigrew's book demonstrated not only his lack of interest in non-naval matters but also his capacity for forming hasty and ill-judged opinions.[14]

The generations confronting the Nazi war machine were probably the last to take the importance of the Royal Navy as read. To them it was still a shield about which there could be no complacency, and during the Second World War the image of Nelson remained a potent one. A remarkably wooden Laurence Olivier even portrayed the admiral in a British film designed to win American hearts to a crusade against the European dictators.[15]

It was at this time that the last full-dress biography of Nelson was published, first in the United States in 1946 and the following year in

Britain. The author was Carola Oman (Lady Lenanton), who had inherited from her father, the noted Oxford don Charles W. C. Oman, the taste and tools for history and a rarer recognition that even ground-breaking research needs to be turned into a literate and accessible text. Her prize-winning *Nelson* was admirable in its scope and proportions. Unlike her main predecessors, she tackled her subject in the round, the man as well as the commander, and cast a mature and balanced eye over manuscripts unused by previous scholars, including mush-rooming deposits at the National Maritime Museum and a rich collec-tion of Lady Nelson's papers made by Lady Llangattock. Both archives subsequently furnished material for George P. B. Naish's invaluable supplement to Nicolas – *Nelson's Letters to His Wife and Other Documents, 1785–1831* (1958). Today, almost sixty years after Oman completed her book, it stands with Mahan's as one of the two touch-stones against which all other biographies must be measured.[16]

By the 1960s a sea change in the nation's attitude to Nelson was becoming apparent. The admiral himself would not have been surprised at the growing indifference a securer generation was showing its naval heritage, for it had always been thus. In 1802 he had misquoted Thomas Jordan's ancient epigram:

> Our God and sailor we adore,
> In time of danger, not before;
> The danger past, both are alike requited,
> God is forgotten, and the sailor slighted.[17]

Moreover, the empire was imploding and in an introspective post-colonial world generated as much shame as pride. In Britain academe became more insular, increasingly absorbed with socio-economic and constitutional change, and naval history, which had once earned knighthoods for eminent practitioners, became at best unfashionable, and, among intellectuals recoiling from anything that smacked of mili-tarism, disreputable. As for Horatio Nelson, he was no longer sacred. His importance to our island story seemed uncertain, and the virtues for which he was synonymous – open-mouthed patriotism, public duty and personal courage – curiously outmoded. Amid growing cynicism common folklore and fiction focused ever more upon the admiral's sexual rather than naval conquests.

At least a way opened for a franker portrait of the man, but although valuable monographs treated aspects of Nelson's career few biographies in the half-century after the war took the subject very far. Professional historians had little interest, and popular writers satisfied themselves with well-known published sources and uncritical recapitulation. Only two quite different workers took their jackets off. The journalist Tom Pocock stubbornly refused to accept that there was nothing new to be said about Nelson and devoted a series of works to the subject during a particularly lean period. His books were undocumented and popular in style, but rested upon a substantial amount of fresh material, some of it from sources previously unexplored by any scholar. Pocock's *Horatio Nelson* (1987) was the most adventurous biography for forty years, but his most original contribution was *The Young Nelson in the Americas* (1980).[18]

Terry Coleman's *Nelson: The Man and the Myth* (2001) came from very different cloth. Nelson aficionados disliked the book, but it was a bravely irreverent work of commendable industry and added interesting facts and opinions. Regrettably, the author also ignored some of the recent research, and subjected Nelson's career to an uneven and occasionally vindictive criticism. In that he encapsulated the spirit of his age as surely as the hagiographers of the nineteenth century had reflected theirs. A belief that only pejorative judgements can be measured ones seems to have entrenched itself not only in sales obsessed journalism but also in academic worlds that once echoed to the clarion call of objectivity. As N. A. M. Rodger has written without total exaggeration, 'no modern university historian could possibly write the life of a famous hero and hope to preserve his reputation, unless he destroyed that of his subject'. But sound portraits of complex and changing individuals are no more produced by the selection and exaggeration of the negative than they are by the positive. While Coleman's book was refreshing in a tradition dominated by drum-beaters, it hardly offered a satisfying alternative.[19]

The need for a new full-dress biography has become increasingly evident. Much of the manuscript material remains relatively unexplored. The one hundred and fifteen volumes of Nelson papers in the British Museum, with other relevant deposits there, were closed during the war years, when Oman wanted to consult them, and no subsequent biography has shown systematic use. The Nelson collections at the National Maritime Museum have been considerably enriched over the years, and the Phillipps–Croker papers, originally preserved by Lady Hamilton and acquired as Oman's book was going to press, alone contained thousands of unpublished documents. Most notably of all, neither Oman nor any successor made more than marginal use of the labyrinthine files of the Admiralty, Foreign, Colonial, War and Home Offices in the Public Record Office – hundreds of volumes and boxes of first-hand material of every description. As recently as 2002 another collection of Nelson papers, preserved by the aforementioned Alexander Davison, came onto the market. The present biography is the first to be based upon a systematic and comprehensive trawl of these and the other primary sources, published and unpublished, bearing upon Nelson and his activities.[20]

Then, too, our knowledge of Nelson had grown through disparate books and journals. Among relatively recent studies transforming our understanding of his times and career N. A. M. Rodger's *The Wooden World* (1986), Brian Tunstall and Nicholas Tracy's *Naval Warfare in the Age of Sail* (1990) and Brian Lavery's *Nelson and the Nile* (1998) must be mentioned. For several years Colin White has been preparing a valuable supplementary volume of fresh Nelson letters for publication, and the Society for Nautical Research, the Nelson Society and the 1805 Club have contributed to a swelling body of revisionary material in the volumes of the *Mariner's Mirror*, the *Nelson Dispatch* and the *Trafalgar Chronicle*. A work of assessment and integration is obviously needed.

It is time to fill the gaps in Nelson's record, explain all its twists and turns and remove the persistent mythology. Some phases and facets of his career have been particularly neglected. The first thirty-five years, for example, though almost three-quarters of Nelson's life, detained a mere forty pages of Pettigrew's large two-volume biography and only twice as many of Mahan's. Even Oman devoted only 17 per cent of her text to that earlier period. Partly this reflects a notion that the admiral's final years as a history maker are the focus of public interest and need to be reached as hastily as possible, and partly the relative dearth of published sources for the career of the young Nelson which make it difficult to recover. Origins have a fascination of their own, however, and studies of human development have long alerted us to the vitally formative nature of early years. It is high time that Nelson's, with the experiences and individuals shaping them, were fully addressed.

Nelson's rise to prominence in the Mediterranean between 1793 and 1797 has only slightly been less underwritten, although it was during those years that he learned the art of an admiral and earned the recognition of his peers. In the present volume I have redressed these imbalances and provided the first comprehensive reconstruction of Nelson's earlier career. In the process fresh information has had to be complemented by the modification or deletion of some of the canonical stories about Nelson. He actively promoted his own legend, and was being lionised before his death. Embellishments, misconceptions and outright fictions have continued to flourish, and the need to trace stories to source and ground a new biography in a professional evaluation of credible primary evidence has become a major imperative.

There have been many Nelsons because there have been many writers, tailoring material to different purposes, but I stand with the Duke of Wellington when he espoused the balanced portrait. Wellington only met Nelson once, in the summer of 1805, when the rising but comparatively obscure general visited the secretary for war and colonies in London after his return from India. Finding himself waiting in an anteroom with the immediately recognisable figure of Horatio Nelson, Wellesley (as he then was) began to converse, 'if I can call it conversation, for it was almost all on his side and all about himself' and in 'a style vain and so silly as to surprise and almost disgust me'. But suspecting shortly that his audience was 'somebody', Nelson briefly left the room to investigate, returning 'a different man, both in manner and matter'. Now he spoke as an 'officer' and 'statesman', and in later life Wellington couldn't recall 'a conversation that interested me more'.

Reflecting, the general mused that 'if the secretary of state had been punctual and admitted Lord Nelson in the first quarter of an hour I should have had the same impression of a light and trivial character that other people have had, but luckily I saw enough to be satisfied that he was really a very superior man. But certainly a more sudden and complete metamorphosis I never saw.' Wellington's experience has been much quoted, but its warning about misleading abstractions is often forgotten. To understand Nelson it is necessary to see the whole of the man. In fact the triviality and the professionalism observed by Wellington were born of a common dynamic. They were both driven by Nelson's need for distinction and acclaim. It spurred him to extreme endeavour, and to theatrical vanity. Both were sides of a single coin.[21]

The sea and seafaring necessarily feature substantially in every biography of Nelson, but we must remember that he was also a Georgian, governed by the circumstances of his age and influenced by its beliefs and attitudes. The eighteenth-century England that moulded Nelson is often lost among the swelling sails, fierce cannonades and straining shrouds and stays. A product of modest 'middling' stock, he rose to become a peer of the realm, but throughout remained a quintessential late eighteenth-century man. Neither an autocrat nor a populist, Nelson adhered to his notion of a naturally hierarchical society in which deferential inferiors were bound to betters by a system of paternalism. It was this vision, with its emphasis upon mutual obligations between governors and governed, that shaped his exercise of authority as well as his political attitudes. When we put Nelson back into the society in which he lived many of his actions and reactions readily fall into place.

Nelson has suffered from much idolatry and some denigration, but readers deserve dispassionate judgements. The admiral walked noisily through history, seeking the applause of fellow travellers, but was flawed like the rest of them. He was inherently generous and humane, but hardened by war and capable of startling ruthlessness. He set great store by loyalty and duty, and rested matters of state upon them, but betrayed a good wife and deserted a mistress. Generally honest and relatively careless of wealth, his advance into middle age deepened a financial insecurity and sharpened acquisitive instincts, and he benefited from some of the pecuniary abuses of the day. Highly intelligent and sensitive, Nelson devoured newspapers and books, but never banished the powerful prejudices that occasionally marred his judgement. His experience of life only reinforced his suspicion of foreigners and a belief in traditional English government. Though he prided himself on honour, strength and independence of mind, he was easily flattered and manipulated by flatterers. A sound professional, thoughtful and painstaking in preparing for combat, he could be wrong-headed and reckless and a victim of his own powerful warrior spirit. His intentions were usually good, but not infrequently he acted badly.

As the full extent of the material for this project came into view, it was obvious that it would require more than a single volume. This book covers the least familiar period of Nelson's life, and traces him from childhood to the brink of international fame in 1797. We leave him looking as we all know him, a slim, sharp-featured, boyish admiral bedecked in the first of his honours, effectively blind in one eye and with an empty right sleeve, but with his last few and great years at the forefront of the European war still ahead.

This book was not written specifically for the bicentenary of

Nelson's death. The idea for it germinated decades ago, and serious research began at the beginning of the nineties, but the increasing interest in Nelson occasioned by the anniversary, with an attendant sharpening of literary cutlasses, has inevitably loomed over the last few years. To rush the research to fit some arbitrary date would defeat its object, however, and my own reflections upon the findings of the anniversary writers will have to await a succeeding volume of this biography. In the preparation of the first I have benefited from aid and kindness at every step, and am proud to record the names of my benefactors in the acknowledgements. Nevertheless, burdens imposed by a long-term project like this do not fall equally, and the people closest to me shouldered far too many. My dedication, therefore, is to those for whom Nelson, quite honourably and unwittingly, has also proven himself to be an efficient thief of time.

I

PROLOGUE: DUEL AT MIDNIGHT

Upon a terrace by the Thames
   I saw the admiral stand,
He who received the latest clasp
   Of Nelson's dying hand.

Age, toil and care had somewhat bowed
   His bearing proud and high,
But yet resolve was on his lip
   And fire was in his eye.

I felt no wonder England holds
   Dominion o'er the seas,
Still the red cross will face the world
   While she hath men like these.

Letitia Elizabeth Landon, *Tribute to Admiral Hardy*

1

IT was late in the evening of Monday 19 December 1796 and the sky promised a night of cloud and fresh squalls. The two fast British frigates bore northeastwards on the starboard tack, the Spanish Mediterranean coast out of sight to larboard, and the enemy port of Cartagena somewhere in the darkness ahead. The smaller of the frigates, the *Blanche* captained by D'Arcy Preston, was flung out on the inshore flank, and both ships were on full alert. For though this was not what Commodore Nelson on *La Minerve* called a fighting mission, it was a dangerous one nonetheless.

Only weeks before, the main British fleet under Sir John Jervis had quit the Mediterranean, and left it an enemy lake controlled by the combined forces of France and Spain. Now Nelson was going back with these two small ships. They were five days out of Gibraltar, almost alone in a hostile sea spotted with enemies.

Nelson's orders, dated nine days before, were to evacuate Britain's only remaining garrison in the Mediterranean, the handful of troops on the island of Elba, between Corsica and the Italian peninsula, with all artillery, baggage and stores. Some seventeen warships at Elba, the largest of them only frigates, were also to be extricated.

It was a difficult operation, but Sir John Jervis knew that if anyone could do it, it was Nelson. Expecting to fight the Spanish fleet in the Atlantic, the British commander-in-chief had been unable to spare a big ship of the line for the mission. It had to be frigates – smaller but faster vessels, able to avoid more heavily armed adversaries. Jervis had several fine frigate captains fit for the enterprise, but he was wary of arousing jealousies among them, and thought it wiser to entrust the expedition to an officer of greater rank, one respected by every captain in the fleet. It was thus that Commodore Horatio Nelson of the *Captain* ship of the line received instructions to shift his broad pendant to *La Minerve*, under Captain George Cockburn, and sail to Elba. 'Having experienced the most important effects from your enterprise and ability upon various occasions since I had the honour to command in the Mediterranean,' Sir John told him, 'I leave entirely to your judgement the time and manner of carrying this critical and arduous service into execution.'[1]

There was not a drop of flattery in the admiral's words, for he meant every one. He had the cream of the Royal Navy in his fleet. Men such as Troubridge, Miller, Collingwood and Saumarez. But at the age of thirty eight, and with a slight, delicate frame and shock head of hair that made him seem positively boyish, Nelson was its rising star. He had already won laurels for his previous commanders-in-chief, Hood and Hotham, and was now serially proving his worth to Jervis. But while the admiral owned that 'a more able or enterprising officer [than the commodore] does not exist', he was also discovering that Nelson's uses went much further than fighting. The commodore had worked effectively with different professionals, with diplomats, army officers and merchants as well as fellow naval officers, and arbitrated between men of disparate tempers and inclinations. Those qualities were needed now, and Jervis chose Nelson in the strong belief that his 'firmness and ability will very soon fix all the parts of our force, naval and military'. Indeed, the admiral was so sure that Nelson would discharge these new, dangerous and difficult duties with complete professionalism that he put the accompanying frigate under his own relative, Captain Preston, freshly arrived upon the station.[2]

Nelson had taken only a few of his personal following from the *Captain* to *La Minerve*. James Noble, his young signal lieutenant, was an American, the son of a revolutionary Loyalist (an American colonist sympathetic to the British), and had distinguished himself aboard the commodore's previous ship, the *Agamemnon*. He had been wounded by the French, and captured by them, but neither incident deterred him from volunteering for every service. With Nelson also came his secretary, John Philip Castang, a Londoner who had followed him for four of his twenty-nine years; a twenty-four-year-old seaman named Israel Coulson, duly rated yeoman of the powder room on *La Minerve*; and Giovanni Dulbecco, an Italian boy, also formerly of the *Agamemnon*.[3]

However, Nelson knew the entire crews of *La Minerve* and the *Blanche* well, for both ships had served under his command during much of the year. Captain Preston was a new appointment, but Cockburn of *La Minerve* was one of Nelson's favourite officers. A dour but dependable Scot, Captain Cockburn was a tight-lipped creature with few close friends, but he was talented and energetic, and would one day earn fame – or infamy – for his capture of Washington, the American capital, during the War of 1812. Now a rising captain in his twenties, he was flourishing under Nelson's supervision.

Hitherto the voyage had been uneventful. Buffeted by gales, they had nevertheless passed Cape de Gata earlier on the 19th, and seized a Genoese polacre. The republic of Genoa was in dispute with Britain, but Nelson released the ship after relieving it of eight bales of silk and a trunk that appeared to belong to the Spaniards, with whom his country was at war. Sold as prize, Nelson reckoned, the merchandise might at least give his seamen a drink. Then the frigates had sailed on, and as night fell penetrated the dangerous approaches to the Spanish naval base of Cartagena.[4]

At ten in the evening the *Blanche* signalled. Nelson ordered Cockburn to close with their consort, and Preston made his report. He had seen two Spanish frigates to leeward, bearing towards them. The British ships suddenly hummed with activity, as staccato drumbeats hastened the men to their quarters and the frigates were cleared for action.

In the dark the process was complicated as well as hurried, but the men were trained to work efficiently and silently. Pillars, partitions, hammocks and other impedimenta were stowed out of the way, inflammables such as canvas doused in water to resist fire, and decks sprinkled with sand to provide greater grip to running bare feet. Red-coated marines stood ready with their muskets, while gun crews cast the cannons loose. Mechanically men unplugged the threatening muzzles, cleared touchholes and levelled the pieces before hauling them to the opened ports. Lines of 'powder monkeys' formed to shift the cartridges, shot and wads from the magazines and powder rooms to the guns. Others prepared to receive rather than inflict damage. Carpenters and their mates braced themselves to stop any holes punched through the timbers below the waterline, while in the airless murk of the bowels of the ships, probably on the platforms below the gun decks, the surgeons and their assistants laid out their grisly tools.

Some historians have criticised Nelson's decision to fight on the grounds that it jeopardised his greater mission, the evacuation of Elba, but this is to miss the whole thrust of his experiences in the Mediterranean over the previous three to four years. As he ordered Cockburn to haul the ship's wind, cross the bows of the *Blanche* and pass under the stern of the largest of the enemy frigates, he had not the slightest fear of failure.

For times were changing and the French and Spanish navies were not what they had once been. Political turmoil, shortages of skilled sailors and experienced officers, and inefficient defensive tactics had taken their toll. However impressive or powerfully armed their ships, they were far outmatched in seamanship and gunnery by the British crews. In fact, while its rivals decayed, the Royal Navy had relent lessly improved, keeping the sea in all weathers and forging an awesome fighting efficiency under outstanding captains. Nelson had always been an opportunist, hungry for distinction, but he was one of several officers who understood the implications of those changing historical circumstances.

The traditional tactics of battle, which saw belligerent fleets in more or less parallel lines banging away at each other over distance, were defensive in character and keyed to a time when the competing navies had been more equally matched. But now Britain's superiority in battle was making the old safe and sure line-ahead formations increasingly obsolete. Risks might be taken to achieve decisive results, and the 'line' abandoned. When Nelson advised an admirer, the young Lord Cochrane (later the model for the fictional heroes of Marryat, Forester and O'Brian) to 'never mind manoeuvres, always go at them', he was not expressing a mindless and reckless enthusiasm for combat. As much as anyone he believed in rigorous training and careful planning. Rather he was acknowledging the massive battle superiority of the Royal Navy, and suggesting that its advantages were maximised in close-quarter actions with the enemy.[5]

That night off the Spanish coast he was set to prove it in a straight stand-up fight.

It was ten-forty before *La Minerve* slipped under the impressive stern of the *Santa Sabina*, the Spaniard's burning poop light and greater size marking it as the senior of the two enemy ships. The odds were roughly equal on the face of it, though Nelson had a slight superiority in the number of guns and weight of metal fired. *La Minerve* was a captured French prize. She carried forty-two guns, two of them carronades designed for close-range action, while the Spanish ship mounted forty: twenty-eight eighteen-pounder and twelve eight-pounder cannons. The manpower conferred few advantages either way. On the *Santa Sabina* Don Jacobo Stuart commanded some 286 men, whereas Nelson had 216 seamen and 25 marines, giving a total of 241, besides perhaps a score of 'supernumeraries'.[6]

But as Nelson knew full well it was teamwork and the skill with ships and guns that mattered. From the beginning he outmanoeuvred his opponent by running alongside the Spaniard's vulnerable stern, where the timbers were flimsier and there were few enemy guns to face. From that position he could 'rake' the *Santa Sabina* with his full broadside, hitting her end-on and smashing wood, dismounting guns and killing and maiming men along the entire length of her decks.

'This is an English frigate,' Nelson called, with his usual submersion of the other British nationalities. There was no answer, and *La Minerve* opened fire, the guns along her side spitting fire into the night as they bore upon their targets. Three minutes later the *Blanche* brought the other Spanish frigate, the forty-gun *Ceres*, to action, and all four ships were wreathed in the powder smoke of murderous point-blank volleys. The horror of a sea fight was like no other. Large round shot could smash through ship timbers more than two feet thick, and there was nowhere for men to run. Caged in a wooden hell, amidst the roar, smoke and stench of guns, and air filled with lethal flying debris, they knew that only inches of plank and sheathing divided them from the deep below. Men slaved silently at their pieces, and fell and suffered and died.[7]

Nelson's opponent, Don Jacobo Stuart, was not one to run away from a challenge. A descendant of the expelled James II of England, he was as proud as any Castillian *caudillo* and fought bravely, but he was simply outgunned and outsailed. Cockburn, who as captain of *La Minerve* was responsible for her management, handled his frigate beautifully. She wore this way and that to prevent her opponent escaping to leeward, and unleashed one broadside after another into her with mechanical precision. According to the Spaniards, the fire from Nelson's ship 'was a perfect hell'.[8]

While *La Minerve* and *Santa Sabina* manoeuvred and fought, as if partners in a macabre midnight dance, the *Blanche* vindicated the commodore's confidence by defeating the *Ceres* with little trouble. Preston, like Nelson, fired into the Spaniard's bow and stern when he could, raking her fore and aft. As usual the enemy fire was misdirected, largely flying up towards masts, spars, sails and empty air rather than into the British hull; it was also sluggish and poorly aimed. 'When they did fire their guns they were in such haste that their shot all went over us,' recalled an American seaman aboard the *Blanche*. After taking eight or nine broadsides in half an hour and suffering forty-five casualties the *Ceres* ceased firing. Her colours were hauled down and she called for quarter.[9]

Meanwhile, Nelson's battle with the *Santa Sabina* raged for two and a half hours, ending at about one-twenty in the morning when Don Jacobo hauled down his colours and declared he could fight no more. The masts of the Spanish frigate had all been damaged close to the decks, her mizzen was down, her hull riddled and her sails and rigging slashed to pieces. Many of her men were killed and wounded – probably many more than the fifty-six later admitted in Cartagena and fewer than the 164 claimed by Nelson. But she had not been crushed with impunity. *La Minerve* had suffered most aloft, due to the inefficient continental practice of trying to bring down masts and sails, but she had also sustained forty-six human casualties, including a midshipman and seven others killed. Lieutenant Noble had been showered in splinters and injured in six or seven places.

Jonathan Culverhouse, the first lieutenant of *La Minerve*, went aboard the prize and sent the Spanish captain on the opposite journey. Once on the quarterdeck of the British ship, Don Jacobo explained that he had lost all his senior officers and offered his sword, but Nelson generously declined to take it. While they talked Thomas Masterman Hardy, second lieutenant of the victorious ship, took a prize crew of twenty-four to the *Santa Sabina* to help Culverhouse secure the prisoners, clear wreckage and fix the ship for sailing as best they could. Speedy repairs were begun on both ships as they got underway towards the southeast, *La Minerve* towing her prize behind.

Elated by his victory, Nelson returned to his cabin to pen a candlelit report to Sir John Jervis. This was a dispatch obviously destined for the *London Gazette* and he was determined to do his men justice. No one fought more tenaciously for his followers than Commodore Nelson and he jumped at this new opportunity to advance Cockburn and his officers.

You are, sir, so thoroughly acquainted with the merits of Captain Cockburn [he wrote] that it is needless for me to express them, but the discipline of the *Minerve* does the highest credit to her captain and lieutenants, and I wish fully to express the sense I entertain of their judgement and gallantry. Lieutenant Culverhouse, the first lieutenant, is an old officer of very distinguished merit. Lieutenants Hardy, [William Hall] Gage, and Noble deserve every praise which gallantry and zeal justly entitle them to, as do every other officer and man in the ship. You will observe, sir, I am sure with regret, amongst the wounded, Lieutenant James Noble, who quitted the *Captain* to serve with me, and whose merits and repeated wounds received in fighting the enemies of our country entitle him to every reward which a grateful nation can bestow.

If the engagement had ended there, Nelson would have taken two Spanish frigates and scored a minor but striking and morale-lifting success. Unfortunately, it did not, and the fortunes of war had more in store for him.

At three-thirty in the morning another frigate materialised through the gloom. Nelson and Cockburn thought it was the *Blanche*, which had separated in her battle with the *Ceres*, but at four-fifteen they heard the newcomer hailing the *Santa Sabina* in Spanish. Then it flung a broadside into the crippled prize. Instantly, *La Minerve* cast off the tow line to allow Culverhouse and Hardy to shift for themselves, and turned upon their fresh adversary. Once again the weary men, their rest already stolen by the previous encounter, rushed to their stations. Once again the fire power and seamanship on Nelson's frigate told. After a mere thirty minutes the newcomer, the *Perla*,

had had enough. The Spaniards simply wore their ship to turn and
'run off'.

But now, victorious in three night combats, the British were dogged
with bad luck. The *Blanche*, further seaward, had long realised that
what they had taken to be isolated enemy warships were in fact lookouts for a much larger enemy force. In fact they belonged to the principal Spanish fleet under Don Juan de Langara y Huarte, bound for
Cartagena. At the beginning of his fight with the *Ceres*, Captain Preston
had noticed two more frigates to leeward, and by the time he had
defeated his opponent another ship was also visible. Fumbling to take
possession of his prize in squally weather, he eventually gave up as
enemy ships gathered right and left. With dawn filtering over the water
on the 20th, Preston counted six Spanish ships in the offing, apart
from the original pair, and two of them were ships of the line, far too
formidable for any frigate to engage. Some of the Spaniards were
already turning upon *La Minerve*, but a dozen miles lay between the
two British vessels and Preston was powerless to help. His duty now
was to save his ship and run.

Nelson was in deep trouble. *La Minerve* had started the battle
several men short of the full complement of three hundred, suffered
fifty-seven killed and wounded defeating the two enemy frigates, and
sent another twenty-six to her prize. In continuing bad weather the
remaining hands were straining every sinew to repair sails, rigging
and spars, and support battered lower masts when daylight revealed
the fresh antagonists astern. Of two enemy ships of the line visible,
one was the massive three-decked *Principe de Asturias* of 112 guns.
Like Preston, Nelson had no option but to flee. He fired some defiant
but futile shots into the advancing three-decker and turned tail.

It was then that an unusual act of heroism aboard the *Santa Sabina*
prize helped save *La Minerve*. Lieutenants Culverhouse and Hardy,
who commanded, were no strangers to derring-do. Culverhouse was
a West Country man from Glastonbury, with a home in Bideford.
About thirty-six years old, he was one of many able officers without
the social connections to achieve steady promotion, and had been a
lieutenant for nine years. A former shipmate thought him a 'very active'
and 'excellent signal lieutenant, a good sailor, an agreeable messmate,
and in every respect a very clever fellow'. He was popular too, 'full
of fun and drollery' and capable of entertaining all and sundry with
'humorous songs in the most comic style'. Hardy, a big square-
shouldered, large-featured man from Dorset, was a practical, business-

like officer. Though under thirty he had been at sea since the age of twelve, like Nelson himself, and knew most there was to know about managing a ship. Both men had followed Cockburn into *La Minerve* from his previous frigate, the *Meleager*, and had been earning Nelson's approval over the last eighteen months. Commanding the *Meleager*'s boats they had captured the *Belvedere* in July 1795, and both had won additional laurels during Nelson's attacks on Loano and Oneglia the following spring.[10]

Now in charge of the Spanish prize, they decisively intervened to spare their superior officers and old ship from capture. Rather like a female duck feigning injury to draw a predator from her young, the injured *Santa Sabina* limped away to the northeast, raising the English over the Spanish colours in a provocative gesture of defiance. That insult may have done the trick, for the enemy three-decker and a frigate turned upon the wounded ship. She had no chance, and at about nine-thirty, after her fore and main masts had been brought down, Culverhouse and Hardy surrendered.

But *La Minerve* made good her escape. Still pursued by a ship of the line and a pair of frigates, Nelson fled past Cartagena and eventually shook off his opponents as dusk fell at around six o'clock. He reached Porto Ferraio in Elba on 26 December, two days ahead of the *Blanche* and in time to attend a seasonal ball. It was his initial victory over the frigates, rather than the ignominious retreat, that was remembered, and the commodore was received at the festivities to the vigorous strains of 'Rule, Britannia!' and 'See the Conquering Hero'.

2

Nelson fought the midnight action off Spain on the eve of achieving national fame in the battle of Cape St Vincent and within months of his subsequent promotion to the rank of rear admiral. On the other hand he had been at sea since boyhood, and the engagement followed almost four years of continuous war experience in the Mediterranean. It reveals him to us, therefore, as a budding admiral with his apprenticeship thoroughly completed but with his great years ahead.

Almost all the qualities that would distinguish him were already in place, and some shine fiercely from the brush with the Spanish frigates. His zest for action and fame was certainly apparent. Contrary to normal practice Nelson personally wrote the account of the battle for the captain's log to ensure that the record was both correct and appreciative. In his letters he almost crowed with self-magnification. His action would be 'in the *Gazette*,' he told his father. 'Take it altogether, I may venture to say, it is the handsomest done thing this war. It was what I know the English like in a *Gazette*. I feel all the pleasure arising from it which you can conceive.' No less important, the skirmishes demonstrated that Nelson had already got the measure of his adversaries, and realised that historic opportunities were developing. The disparity between the performances of the Franco-Spanish navies on the one hand and the British on the other was growing and opening a path to decisiveness in battle. Risks that might have been unjustified in the past were becoming viable.[11]

Perhaps as much as anything, the midnight battle suggested a key to Nelson's exceptional powers of leadership. His magnetism was a complicated blend. Men followed him because they admired his professional qualities and were proud to share his glories. They felt at ease with his quiet but accessible manner, sensed sympathy and understanding, and were grateful for many boons spontaneously bestowed. Calculated self-interest also played its part, for Nelson was an old-fashioned paternalist. He was no egalitarian, and believed in the hierarchical society, but to him the bonds between those above and below were important. More than anything else loyalty was the glue that held the layers together. Nelson demanded unswerving allegiance from officers and men. But he responded with a fierce loyalty of his own, fighting vigorously for their welfare.

Many – very many – loved him for it. In a difficult and sometimes lonely world, followers were reassured by the thought that their leader was always fighting their corner, appreciating good service and using what favour and influence he had for their benefit. Dozens of devoted officers whose names barely appear in the books about Nelson followed him from ship to ship, men such as Bromwich, Bullen, Hinton, Andrews, Wallis, Weatherhead, Noble, Compton, Spicer and Summers. And ordinary ratings formed extraordinarily powerful attachments to a commander who discharged his duties to them with unusual care.

There was something else that drew Nelson to his men too, something that went beyond empathy, duty and symbiosis, something elemental that charged his relationships to followers with great emotion. He could never have disparaged them as the sweepings of the earth, as Wellington occasionally did his soldiers. To Nelson they were partners in a patriotic and sacred enterprise, and through the sharing of dangers formed with him an elite brotherhood.

No one expressed it more perfectly than Nelson's favourite writer, William Shakespeare. The sailor's interest in the bard has long been known, but only recently have we begun to appreciate its great extent. Nelson knew many of the plays well, committed passages to memory, and slipped telling Shakespearean phrases into his letters. *Henry V* was a particular inspiration, and the king's famous speech on the eve of the battle of Agincourt a favourite crib. In lines Nelson treasured Shakespeare beautifully encapsulated his attitude to the peculiar bonding that was bred in conflict:

> 'We few, we happy few, we band of brothers;
> For he today that sheds his blood with me
> Shall be my brother; be he ne'er so vile
> This day shall gentle his condition.'[12]

The men of the *Blanche* saw the almost familial interest he had in them when they arrived at Porto Ferraio after their flight from the Spaniards. 'When we came to an anchor,' a sailor recalled, 'Nelson came on board and ordered the captain to beat to quarters [call the men to their stations by a drumbeat], and as we were in a line before our guns, he came round the decks and shook hands with us as he went along . . . telling us he was rejoiced to find that we had escaped.' A small gesture, but immediately endearing to men who had fought and bled in his service, and knew they had been seen, valued and worried about.

As for the crew of *La Minerve*, Nelson's priority was to secure the liberation of those left on the *Santa Sabina*. On 24 December, en route to Elba, he wrote to the Spanish admirals at Cartagena, pointing out the excellent treatment he was according Don Jacobo Stuart, who was still his reluctant guest. He entreated the Spaniards to offer the like to 'my brave officers and men, your prisoners', and requested they be sent to Gibraltar for release in an early exchange. When *La Minerve* eventually reached Porto Ferraio, Nelson shipped every available Spanish prisoner to Cartagena under a flag of truce to facilitate the freedom of the unfortunate Britons. Even so it was not until February that Culverhouse and Hardy were returned to their own people.[13]

In the meantime Nelson did his best to secure them just rewards. To lieutenants struggling to reach the crucial rank of 'post-captain' Nelson was almost invariably a champion, and we have already seen him press the claims of Culverhouse, Hardy and Noble in his first dispatch about the capture of the *Santa Sabina*. In a second letter of the 20th, notifying Admiral Jervis of his unfortunate change of fortune, Nelson again insisted on 'justice to Lieutenants Culverhouse and Hardy' and paid 'tribute' to 'their management of the prize'.

These dispatches went to the commander-in-chief in the regular way, and it was up to him to decide whether to forward them to the Admiralty without comment or to endorse them with recommendations of his own. Nelson's relationship with Sir John Jervis was good, however, and the commodore's opinions were almost always received with enthusiasm. Nevertheless, Nelson slipped a reminder into his next letter four days later, enlarging a general observation about the 'good men' lost aboard the Spanish frigate with the remark that Captain Cockburn deserved 'every favour you are pleased to bestow on him'. As for the lieutenants, 'I take it for granted the Admiralty will promote Lieutenant Culverhouse, and I hope Lieutenant Noble will also be promoted.'[14]

As insurance, Nelson had lately developed the habit of addressing letters directly to the Admiralty, over the heads of his commanders-in-chief. In that way he was sure that his activities and opinions were always properly noticed in Whitehall. At the beginning of 1797 he took up the promotion of his officers with Earl Spencer, the first lord of the Admiralty, himself. He would not trouble the board with anything more about the engagement with the Spaniards, he said, 'but I cannot omit most earnestly recommending Lieut. Culverhouse, first of *La Minerve*, to your Lordship's notice. Lieut. James Noble, who left the *Captain* to serve with me, and who is grievously wounded – I presume to press his repeated wounds and merits on your Lordship's notice.' Not long afterwards the commodore was also impressing Spencer with the deserts of Cockburn, 'than whom a more able, gallant young captain does not serve His Majesty'.[15]

Though most captains protected their followers to some degree, Nelson was uncommonly generous and indefatigable in his praise and support. To understand why men such as Culverhouse, Hardy and Noble gave their best for Nelson, we must appreciate that theirs was a difficult and competitive service in which many fine officers failed simply because their merits went unsung. In Nelson they recognised an unusually attentive and effective patron.

And so he proved himself now. After spending almost ten years as a lieutenant and suffering considerable neglect, Culverhouse was deeply moved by the 'handsome manner' in which Nelson had put his name before the mighty. Suddenly, even greater guardians took notice. Culverhouse was promoted commander on 27 February 1797, and when he had to leave the fleet to attend to illness in his family, his commander-in-chief personally wrote to the first lord on his behalf, begging 'permission to place him under your lordship's protection'. Thus assisted, Culverhouse was able to proceed fairly quickly to the rank of post-captain in 1802, though his career tragically ended when he drowned with his wife in Table Bay at the Cape of Good Hope. Noble, who received his promotion to commander the same day as Culverhouse, could easily have been overlooked had it not been for Nelson's determination to advance him. Lieutenants Gage and Hardy, whom he had also named in dispatches, had to wait longer. Lieutenant Gage was the son of the late military commander-in-chief in North America and governor of Massachusetts, a man of considerable influence. His promotion seemed assured anyway, sooner or later. Nevertheless, when he was advanced to commander on 13 June 1797 it appears to have been largely at the behest of Nelson and Jervis. As for Hardy, by then he had made his promotion certain by capturing a French corvette in May.[16]

For Cockburn himself, who was already a post-captain and on the road to achieving his flag as an admiral, Nelson could do little except advertise his qualities and put him in the way of suitable commands. Indeed, the captain's transfer to La Minerve from a smaller frigate had itself partly rested upon Nelson's recommendation. But to the tributes the commodore had paid Cockburn in his dispatches he added one of those personal gestures that came so easily to Nelson. Without breathing a word to Cockburn, he wrote to London instructing his agents to commission the manufacture of a commemoration gold-hilted sword, which he intended to present to the captain as a mark of esteem. Whatever Nelson's superiors did or did not do for Cockburn, this was tangible testimony to the regard of one professional for another, a reminder of perils shared and a symbol of brotherhood in arms. Later, when Nelson became an international hero, we can imagine with what pride Cockburn treasured that sword.

If Nelson was fully fledged as a naval commander by 1797, so were the strengths and frailties he would soon show to the world. He exulted in acts of courage, and possessed an almost unbounded self-confidence and formidable sense of purpose. He was astute, persevering and energetic. No less was he vainglorious, petulant, opinionated and inclined to impetuosity and insubordination. Nevertheless, on the long, formative journey Nelson had made to reach this point he had won more friends than enemies. It had been a remarkable odyssey, played against a background of contrasts as great as his own. It had taken him from the Arctic wilderness to the Indian Ocean, and from the green shores of the Americas and pestilential Caribbean islands to the sapphire seas and rocky margins of the Mediterranean. He had ridden many storms, at sea and ashore, rising on the crests of intoxicating triumphs and pitching into depressing troughs. For Nelson life had run at a terrific pace, but it had been a roller coaster rather than a *tour de force*.

And it had begun deceptively quietly, on the remote, sparsely populated coast of Norfolk, where cold nor'easters occasionally stormed up tidal creeks and estuaries or swept dunes and salt marshes and where simple farmers and fishermen worked to time-honoured seasonal patterns. Predominantly it was a peaceful and predictable place, suited to the household of a God-fearing and gentle country clergyman.

BOOK ONE

THE PRELUDE, 1758–92

II

THE SMALL WORLD OF
BURNHAM THORPE

What day more fit the birth to solemnize
Of the greatest hero you can surmise?
'Tis that consecrated to the Prince of Hosts
Of whose strong protection each Christian boasts.
That noble Nelson on this day was born
Most clearly showed he would the world adorn,
The warrior of Heaven, hurl'd headlong from the sky.

Anon., *On the Birth Day of . . . Admiral Nelson*

1

EDMUND Nelson, the father of Horatio, was a country parson, born
into a family of modest but gentrified farmers accustomed to slotting
sons dislodged from the land or unsuited to its cultivation into the
Church. His paternal grandfather and two Nelson uncles lived off the
rich Norfolk soil; two of Edmund's cousins, offspring of the afore
mentioned uncles, became clergymen, and his father, Edmund Nelson
senior, was himself an ecclesiastic, educated at Eton and Cambridge.

Edmund senior enjoyed a number of Norfolk preferments in his
day, including the rectory of East Bradenham (where Edmund junior
was born on 19 March 1722); the vicarage of Sporle and rectory of
Little Palgrave, presented by Eton College in 1729; and the rectory
of Hilborough, acquired five years later. For the last he was indebted
to his father-in-law, a prosperous baker named John Bland, who had
purchased the benefice from the Hare family in 1718. Edmund senior
had married Mary Bland in London in 1717, and when her father

made him rector of Hilborough he surrendered his position at East Bradenham to live out his remaining years in the small village south-east of King's Lynn. Having attained the uncommon age of eighty-three, he was laid to rest in 1747, in the fourteenth-century church he had served for more than a dozen years.[1]

Mary (Bland) Nelson, his wife, lived even longer. Inheriting the patronage of the parish, she remained at Hilborough till her death on 4 July 1789 at the reputed age of ninety-one. Her grandson, Horatio Nelson, would remember her as small and frail, but she was said to have read small print and executed fine needlework into her final years.[2]

Edmund junior was one of eight children of Edmund and Mary Nelson. Despite the durability of their parents, the brood does not seem to have been a particularly strong one. Three died in infancy, not unre-markable at a time of high death rates, and Edmund junior himself was afflicted with 'a weak and sickly constitution' throughout life, something he duly passed to his son Horatio. Nevertheless, three sisters and a brother survived to become Horatio Nelson's paternal aunts and uncle. Mary remained single. Alice saluted the family tradition by marrying the Reverend Robert Rolfe, and Thomasine became the wife of a Norfolk shoemaker. The brother, John Nelson, did not amount to much. According to Edmund he 'enlisted as a soldier [and] after various unlucky circumstances and misconduct embarked for some foreign service about the year 1760' and was never heard from again.[3]

The younger Edmund Nelson may have been physically fragile but his mind was sharp enough and he passed through schools at Scarning, Northwold and Swaffham to reach Caius College, Cambridge, at the age of eighteen. With the aid of a college bursary he collected a bach-elor's degree the year Bonnie Prince Charlie landed in Scotland and a Master of Arts three years later, and he followed his father into the clerical profession. He worked as a curate, first for his father at Sporle, and then in 1747 for the Reverend Thomas Page at Beccles in Suffolk. When the elder Edmund Nelson died that year, his son succeeded to the livings of both Hilborough and Sporle. The positions were not lucrative, however. 'The whole profit of Hilborough I gave up for the purpose of paying my father's debts and the maintenance of my mother and her family,' Edmund recalled. 'Sporle's living is about eighty pounds per annum. I resided with my mother at Hilboro'.'

Still, in one respect the young parson was lucky, for at Beccles he married a good wife.

2

Horatio Nelson's parents were married on 11 May 1749, under the benevolent supervision of Edmund's old friend Thomas Page.

Like her husband's Catherine Suckling's father was a clergyman. She was the oldest child and only daughter of the Reverend Dr Maurice Suckling, rector of Barsham and Woodton and prebendary of Westminster. She had been born on 9 May 1725, in the rectory of Barsham, where the River Waveney wound through the green rolling hills of Suffolk. Dr Suckling had died when Catherine was only five and was buried in Barsham. His grieving widow, Ann, had then taken the family to nearby Beccles, where Catherine had met and been courted by her young Norfolk curate.

Catherine was twenty-four when she became Mrs Edmund Nelson. She was pleasantly featured, though hardly beautiful if we may believe a portrait that showed her at eighteen, rather austere of countenance, with dark hair and blue eyes. Little that is reliable about her has come down to us, but the marriage was a successful one, and Edmund always spoke of his wife with unusual devotion. There is no doubt that he married for love, but providentially it was Catherine who supplied the family with what eighteenth-century people called 'interest'.

Everyone knew what 'interest' meant: the ability to call upon influential people to improve one's life chances and prospects. After marrying Catherine, Edmund could milk the patronage of a powerful fraternity. Her father, Dr Suckling, came from a line of gentlemen, military men many of them, including the Cavalier poet Sir John Suckling. But it was Catherine's mother, Ann, who could boast by far the more impressive lineage. She was a daughter of Sir Charles Turner, a wealthy merchant of Lynn, and Mary Walpole of Houghton Hall, Norfolk – and the Walpoles were among the first families of the realm.

Ann's maternal aunts and uncles were indeed a formidable tribe. Dorothy was married to a powerful politician, Charles, second Viscount Townshend of Rainham, sometime secretary of state, but familiar to today's school children as 'Turnip Townshend' the agricultural improver. Galfridus Walpole had risen in the navy, and his brother Horatio became the first Baron Walpole of Wolterton Hall. Greater than even these distinguished siblings, however, was Sir Robert Walpole, first Earl of Orford, a Whig grandee who became the first minister of George I and George II. The 'interest' possessed by the Walpoles was awesome and labyrinthine, and their power to reward successively elevated their brother-in-law, Sir Charles Turner, to the boards of Trade, Admiralty and Treasury between 1707 and 1730. Time had moved on since then, and Sir Charles and Mary had both died before their granddaughter Catherine Suckling reached her fourteenth birthday. But, though less powerful than hitherto, the long arm of the Walpoles continued to exercise a benign influence upon her fortunes.

Catherine and her brothers, Maurice and William, owed their livelihoods to it. Before his death in 1745 Sir Robert Walpole had launched Maurice upon a successful naval career, while William was placed in the customs service as a boy. In 1772 he was appointed Deputy Collector of Customs in London, a post he held throughout his remaining years. There were dividends for Catherine too, bestowed upon her husband, the Reverend Edmund Nelson of Norfolk.

Soon after marrying, Edmund had taken his young bride to Swaffham, leaving his mother and aunts at Hilborough, and it was at Swaffham that the first of the couple's eleven children were born. Two boys died in infancy and were buried at Hilborough, the second of them Horatio, named for Lord Walpole, his godfather. Another son, born on 24 May 1753 and christened Maurice for his uncle, survived. After Maurice's birth the Nelsons moved to a rented house in Sporle, where Edmund still held a living, and had their first daughter, Susanna, on 12 June 1755. It was at this point that the Walpole arm reached out again.

Among the many properties at the disposal of the Walpoles were several in the village of Burnham Thorpe in west Norfolk. Indeed, the family held more land thereabouts than anyone else, and as late as 1796 land tax records assigned them no less than five dwellings within the tiny confines of the village itself. When Thomas Smithson, the rector of Burnham Thorpe, died in 1755 the Honourable Horace Walpole, Lord Walpole's heir, presented Edmund Nelson with the rectories of Burnham Thorpe and Burnham Sutton and the livings of Burnham Ulph and Burnham Norton. Thus equipped, Edmund was able to resign his positions at Hilborough and Sporle and allow his mother to bestow them upon her son-in-law, Robert Rolfe. Packing his belongings he made his way towards the cluster of hamlets that graced the River Burn as it flowed briskly northwards into the wild marshes of the Norfolk coast.

And so the Nelsons came to Burnham Thorpe – an unassuming parson, his well-connected wife and their son and daughter.

3

They occupied the rectory, situated less than a mile south of the village on a narrow road that ran to North Creake. A hill dominated it to the west, while, in the opposite direction, through a small gatehouse and across the road the Burn babbled between reedy banks, only some thirty yards away. Beyond, the land was open, with flat, wide fields stretching towards the horizon.

From above, the new home of the Nelsons appeared L-shaped. The longer wing may have been the original building, a two storey cottage with three square windows above and two flanking the door below. An attractive pitched roof of red tiles with two chimneys enclosed an attic room with its window peeping through the foliage scaling the gable end. In the smaller wing the rooms on the upper floor were lit by dormer windows. Outside there was a pump and a sixty-foot barn, built by Edmund's predecessor, as well as thirty acres of glebe land with a selection of climbable trees that gave ample space for children to play and Edmund to indulge his love of gardening.[1]

With a growing household Edmund may have been glad of the sanctuary of the church, reached by a mile-long amble north, past hedgerows which the seasons adorned with snowdrops, cow parsley and poppies. It was primarily a thirteenth-century edifice, though a picturesque eastern façade in stone and black and white flint chequers may have reflected the influence of the fifteenth-century knight, Sir William Calthorpe, who lay beneath a sombre effigy in the chancel. Walking to and from his workplace, the rector passed through the village, where he might have exchanged pleasantries with his flock. Burnham Thorpe was tranquillity itself, perhaps oppressively so. Even at the end of the century a mere 396 villagers, most of them illiterate, shared the seventy-three dwellings. Only four freeholds, one the rectory, were sufficient to warrant a vote in the county elections. There was a tavern, the Plough, and a cluster of flint cottages sandwiched between two long streets, but apart from the River Burn skirting the eastern flank of the village little stirred. Admiral Nelson remembered it as 'lonesome', and his father unquestionably agreed. 'All is hush at high noon as at midnight,' he remarked.[5]

Here in the rectory the younger Nelsons squalled into the world. William arrived on 20 April 1757, named for a paternal uncle and godparent, and on 29 September 1758 Horatio, the future admiral. Horatio was a weak child, and, fearing that he would not reach the public christening scheduled for 15 November, his parents had him privately baptised when he was ten days old. His sponsors, to whom he might look for 'interest' and protection, were the Reverend Dr Horace Hammond, who had married one of Catherine's cousins; Joyce Pyle, a connection of the Rolfes; and the thirty-five-year-old Horace, the newly installed second Lord Walpole, to whom this new Horatio owed his name.[6]

The last of the Nelson children were Ann, born on 20 September 1760, whose name honoured her maternal grandmother; Edmund, who arrived on 4 June 1762; Suckling, a boy, born 5 January 1764; and Catherine, the baby of the family, who appeared on 19 March 1767. Another son died in infancy.

The sponsors Edmund and Catherine found for these youngsters reflect the range of their acquaintances. They included members of both families. From Catherine's side came her mother and brothers, her mother's brother-in-law (John Fowle) and relatives such as the Lords Walpole, John Berney and Sir John Turner. Edmund supplied his uncles, mother and brother-in-law, Robert Rolfe. Local gentry were also recruited for the service, among them Dr Charles Poyntz, after 1760 the incumbent of North Creake but also a canon of Windsor and prebendary of Durham; a Dr Taylor; and Sir Mordaunt Martin, a baronet of Burnham Westgate. With what he eked from his glebe-land and preferments, Edmund knew his offspring would have little money to ease their passage, and that connections such as these would be necessary if they were to make 'a way to get through life in a middle station'.[7]

4

Horatio Nelson's first years were spent in Burnham Thorpe, close to the ceaseless groan of the waves. The River Burn stole northwesterly to the sea through sandhills and salt flats, and Burnham Thorpe was situated three or so miles inland, at the head of a finger-like marsh estuary that had once been navigable to barges at high tide. Around were the other little Burnhams, or 'homesteads by the sea' – Burnham, Burnham Norton, Burnham Ulph, Burnham Westgate and Burnham

Sutton to the west of the estuary, and Burnham Overy across to the east.

Little except Saturday markets and occasional fairs excited Burnham Thorpe, where agriculture remained the principal way of life. Children discovered simple pleasures. Standing on the coast young Nelson could see small windswept islands offshore to the left and Holkham Bay to the right, while ahead tossed the cold North Sea, now grey, now blue, and its multitude of craft. Overy Staithes, a small port near the mouth of the Burn, bustled with schooners and small vessels with alluring names. Horace, as he invariably called himself, saw barley being shipped to London for the brewing industry, manufactures, wines and foodstuffs coming in, and fishermen dealing in mussels and oysters.

Inland young Horace explored narrow paths that wove around low hills in all directions, passing fascinating barns, mills and brick and lime kilns. Burnham Thorpe itself radiated several minor thorough-fares. The main road through the village struck northwest to Burnham Westgate, by far the largest of the Burnhams, and slipped southeast and around the large Holkham estate which lay less than two miles east of the rectory. A byroad to Burnham Overy boasted Thorpe Hall, the home of the prestigious Crowe family, while another passed the Nelsons' home and the ruins of Creake Abbey to reach North and South Creake. To get to a town of any real size the Nelsons had to journey to Wells, situated on the coast on the eastern side of the Holkham estate.[8]

Horace spent much of his time skylarking with his older brothers Maurice and William, and such village locals as the Blacks, Bees and Jarvises. Early biographers echoed those adventures uncertainly. The most famous and least likely anecdote tells us that at the age of five or six the boy visited his grandmother, Mary (Bland) Nelson, at Hilborough. At the invitation of an older boy he went bird-nesting but failed to report at dinner time which occasioned the dispatch of anxious search parties. Finally, Horace was discovered beneath a hedge, examining the spoils of his expedition. 'I wonder fear did not drive you home?' scolded the grandmother when he was returned. 'Madam,' the boy is supposed to have replied stiffly, 'I never saw *fear*!' Given that Nelson's reputation for courage was so vastly enjoyed by contemporaries, we are entitled to dismiss this story, improbable in itself. Although much plagiarised since its debut in 1800, no credible witness stepped forward to vouch for it.[9]

Mythology, in fact, is the continual bane of the Nelson student. It steals insidiously into our sources at every turn, and is difficult to expunge because it was being created by contemporaries, including Nelson himself and his associates. After the admiral's death it multiplied. People who had known Nelson exaggerated their connections with him, and people who had never seen him said they had.

The legend of 'Nurse Blackett' is one of the commonest about Nelson at Burnham Thorpe. She is said to have lived at the rectory as a nanny to Horace and the younger Nelson children, but the story only comes to us second or third hand at the beginning of the twentieth century. Its source, a Mrs High, the wife of 'Nurse' Blackett's grandson, included a variation on the tale of Horace going missing. In this version the seven-year-old Nelson sneaks out of the rectory one night in search of a bird's nest, and is found asleep in the woods after Nurse Blackett raises a hue and cry. Again, the point of the anecdote is the boy's fearlessness and his indifference to the dark.

It seems likely that the Blackett material was a weave of fact and fantasy. Mary Blackett herself existed, and may have worked at the rectory one time or another, but she was born in or around Burnham Thorpe in 1754 or 1755 and was therefore too young to have acted the part described. Possibly she supervised the youngest Nelson children after Horace himself had gone to sea, or more probably worked at the rectory as a domestic when Nelson lived there with his wife in the 1790s, but whatever truth the stories contained appears to have grown in the telling.[10]

Biographer James Harrison, who drew upon close associates of the admiral, occasionally supplied genuine details of Nelson's career, but his story of the infant Horace also sounds like family folklore at best. According to this legend Mrs Nelson was asked to stop a fracas between Horace and his larger brothers, but declined with the words, 'Let them alone. Little Horace will beat them!' As it stands this further testimony to Nelson's embryonic pluck and determination rests upon no certain authority, and probably tells us more about the myth of 1806 than the boy of the 1760s.[11]

Because his mother died young, the dominant figure in Horace's early life was his father, the Reverend Edmund Nelson. Edmund's portraits, as well as the remaining fruits of his pen, largely document his later career, rather than those first years he spent as rector of Burnham Thorpe, but the materials are vivid and generalisations seem permissible. Dressed soberly in dark clothes, the reverend ventured abroad in long coats and tall hats, cane in hand. His hair fell loose and long over narrow shoulders, adding distinction to an expressive face with a high forehead, a long curved nose and a gentle but firm mouth with a pronounced underlip. Little interested in the 'dogs, guns, great dinners, claret and champaign' so beloved by the local gentry, but firm on 'Xtian duty', he deployed opinions freely. Horace was admonished to work hard and honourably, pray, keep himself clean and value good schooling, and to number snuff and alcohol among the common shortcomings of his elders.[12]

If a little strict, Edmund Nelson was a kind, modest and generous man, willing to reach into his pockets for those in need and to stand and be counted in times of trouble. He had a dry sense of humour. In 1790 he described himself as 'an odd whimsicall old man, who knows nothing of the present time and very little of any other'. His education had left him with a painfully convoluted writing style, poor spelling and a love of personification. Winter was a 'blooming Dowager' from which Nature emerged reluctantly. 'She is ashamed to come forth, half-naked in tattered clothes, exposed to the ridicule of every dirty boy.' Flowers such as primroses and violets, however, were 'forward lasses and regard not who pluck them'. Time, he told one daughter, was 'a subtle nimble thief' who 'has stolen away your one and twentieth year.'[13]

Their father may have been the senior figure in the lives of the Nelson boys, but there can be no doubt that an uncle seemed the most dramatic. Captain Maurice Suckling was by no means the first in the family to distinguish himself at sea. In March 1711 his grand-uncle, Captain Galfridus Walpole of the *Lion*, had lost his right arm in a battle with the French in Vado Bay. It brought his active career to an end, but relatives secured him a post as treasurer of Greenwich Hospital. Maurice was a year younger than his sister, Catherine Nelson, but he inherited what glamour her sons saw in their ancestry. Unemployed on half-pay after the Seven Years War ended in 1763, he was striking nonetheless. He could show his nephews uniforms and swords, and tell them stirring tales of faraway places, and – if exhorted – describe the daring scrap he had had with the French in the West Indies back in 1757. Listening to Uncle Maurice gave Horace his first taste for action at sea.

5

The importance of the captain greatly increased in the severe winter of 1767 and 1768. Cold east winds from the Continent bit through the walls of the old rectory, and the snow lay deep in the lanes. Tragedy struck the Nelson household that Christmas. On 26 December 1767 Catherine died, leaving her husband with eight children, the youngest a mere nine months old. Four days later Edmund buried her in the chancel of his church, placing above the grave an armorial stone bearing a Latin inscription and the grief-stricken words 'Let these alone – let no man touch these bones.'

More followed. Catherine's mother, Ann, had been staying near her daughter at Burnham Thorpe, either in the rectory or a cottage in the village, and she, too, was ill. In fact, only six days before Catherine's death she had dated her own will, beseeching the family to bury her in 'as plain a manner' as decency permitted but at Barsham, in the same grave as her husband. She had some £300 in the hands of her youngest son, William, and desired what her funeral left of it to be passed to her daughter, along with her household furniture, plate, china and clothes. There were also some keepsakes for four of her Nelson grandchildren – Maurice, Susanna, Ann and baby Katy. Ann, for example, received 'my old purse containing some gold medals'. The clause dividing her daughter's legacy between the three grand-daughters if Catherine predeceased her was eerily prophetic. Perhaps it was the death of Catherine Nelson that pushed the old woman into the abyss, for barely had the former been laid to rest than the mother died also, at Burnham Thorpe on 5 January 1768, in her seventy-seventh year.[14]

Stricken by these deaths Captain Maurice Suckling arrived at Burnham Thorpe, burdened with the sad duties of burying his only sister and removing the body of his mother back to Barsham. He found the Reverend Edmund heartbroken and fearful for the future of his children. The death of his wife had somehow put a little spare money into his hands, which he invested in South Sea annuities for a usable interest, but as late as 1801 it only amounted to £908. Nevertheless, he intended to educate all the children, boys and girls, and find positions for them. The boys, deemed to be future bread-winners, were a particular worry but members of the family rallied round. John Fowle undertook to place the eldest boy, his godson Maurice, in the Excise Office in London, and Captain Suckling told Edmund that he would provide for one of the others when an oppor-tunity arose.[15]

The job of launching the children in life bore upon Edmund heavily, and even with the aid of nannies and maids he doubted he was equal to it. 'As it has fallen to my lott to take upon me the care and affection of double parent, they [the children] will hereafter excuse where I have fallen short and the task has been too hard,' he wrote. To the end of his days he fretted about his performance, and Christmas 1797 found the old man spending 'many a useless hour at the fire in an easy chair, reflecting on the various events of a long life. It is this day twenty-nine years since your poor mother was laid in the peacefull grave. How I have acquitted myself in the important charge which then fell upon me, posterity must be my judge. In many instances I fear I shall not be acquitted.'[16]

Horace was nine years old when he lost his mother, but he remembered her, and when he did he recalled a line in *Henry V* and said it could be seen in the tears in his eyes. In fact Catherine had so often been confined child-bearing that it is unlikely her son ever got as much attention from her as he wanted. He said that she 'hated the French', a common enough English sentiment of the time. His father, too, became increasingly remote, spending long winter months in Bath to recover his health. The first of the fledglings also flew the nest. After turning fifteen in May 1768, Maurice went to London, where Mr Fowle put him to work as an auditing clerk in the Excise Office, off the Old Jury. Later a Mr Stonehewer facilitated the boy's progress in the office, but for the moment the younger siblings remained at Burnham Thorpe. Their priority, Edmund decided, was schooling. The girls too, for he had no means of supplying them with attractive wedding dowries, and like their brothers they would have to pass through school to paying trades.[17]

Accordingly William and Horace, an inseparable pair, were soon exchanging the isolation of Burnham Thorpe for the rigours of the boarding school.

6

They went to two schools, first to King Edward VI's grammar school in Norwich and then to Sir William Paston's grammar school in North Walsham. We do not know when the boys made their way to Norwich; perhaps in 1768, when Edmund was wrestling with the problems left by his wife's death. But James Harrison correctly places Nelson's attendance at Norwich during the period of Edward Simmons's headship.[18]

Edmund probably decided to send William and Horace to Norwich because he had a sister in the town, with whom they could board.

The boys would have found Aunt Thomasine and her husband, John Goulty, a shoemaker and free cordwainer of Norwich, in their late thirties. In 1768 they had been married eleven years, but only one of their children up till then, William, born in 1763, appears to have survived infancy, and so there was room for nephews in the Goulty household. They lived in the parish of St Andrew, where John also seems to have based his business at 18 London Lane.[19]

After Burnham Thorpe, Norwich must have seemed a veritable metropolis to a small boy. It was then the second largest town in England, and home to thirty thousand people. The dwellings clustering around the cathedral alone swallowed as many inhabitants as Burnham Thorpe, while the coaches and horses clattering to and from the nearby Maid's Head Inn made the main street of the village seem a mere farm track. Never had Horace seen a grander place than Norwich Cathedral, though he was more likely to have been impressed by the skeleton on its macabre memorial to Thomas Gooding than the magnificent vaults and arches.

The bulk of King Edward's occupied buildings that had once been a chapel dedicated to St John the Evangelist, adjacent to the majestic cathedral. There were then probably fewer than a hundred boys in the school. Some were free scholars from the town, but others like the Nelson brothers had been recruited as fee payers from further afield and boarded in lodgings. Horace's teacher was probably Thomas Nichols, the 'usher', or assistant master, who inculcated Latin grammar into the reluctant lower forms. The Reverend Edward Simmons reserved for himself the privilege of harassing the older pupils with equally colourless fare.

At home Horace had read the Bible and perhaps even some Shakespeare, but he probably found the largely incomprehensible curriculum and the long, uncomfortable wooden benches at Norwich less than adequate compensation for his rambles across the fields near Burnham Thorpe. Frustration was at least relieved by admonitions to Christian virtue, an annual production staged for the mayor, and the 'Guild Day' rituals commemorating the inauguration of each new dignitary elevated to that office. On Guild Days the pupils assembled at the school porch to hear one of their fellows speechify in return for a ride to a Guildhall banquet and ball in the mayor's carriage. Nonetheless, boredom and bad behaviour still went hand in hand, surviving the occasional wielding of the rod, and so many windows were broken that Simmons was told to pay for repairs from his own pocket.[20]

Nelson was not long at Norwich, for by 1769 he and his brother transferred to the Paston School in the small market town of North Walsham. A Tudor foundation established close to the market place, which could be reached through a gateway at the rear of the school, the Paston had a new three-storey schoolhouse of red brick and a fresh constitution. The master, the Reverend John Price Jones, was as Welsh as his name suggests though he had formerly been a curate at Yateley in Hampshire. He delivered the inevitable Classics and a little English and Mathematics with the assistance of his good wife (Mrs G. M. Jones), an usher, James North, who managed the lower forms, and a French master known to the boys as 'old Jemmy Moisson'.

By no means all the faces who passed beneath the coat of arms engraved above the school entrance were new ones. A number of the boys were, like the Nelsons, former pupils of Norwich Grammar, including John Ashmul of Worstead, William Booty of Walsingham, Thomas Taylor of Norwich and Richard Ellis of Repps. The surviving names of the other youngsters also demonstrate a huge preponderance of Norfolk lads, among them Paul Johnson of Runcton, Gunton Postle of Hoveton, Nathaniel Gooding Clarke of Attleborough, Thomas Decker of North Walsham, Charles Mann of Norwich, William Earle Bulwer (whom Nelson remembered 'perfectly well' thirty years later), and probably also Horace's relative, Horatio Hammond.[21]

Horace was a fee-paying boarder at the Paston until 1771, when the annual charge of £21 12s. od. covered lodgings, tuition, laundry and an entrance fee. The boys went home for holidays, and the forty-mile pony ride along the leafy lanes between North Walsham and Burnham Thorpe was the subject of one of two stories William used to tell of his brother's schooldays. The Christmas holidays had ended, and in January 1770 the Reverend Nelson saw his boys disappear along the snowy track that passed the rectory gate. The brothers had not gone far before they were halted by the drifts and turned back. William, the elder, was their spokesman, and presented their story to a stern parent, who insisted they try again. 'If the road should be found dangerous, you may return,' he told them. 'Yet remember boys! I leave it to your honour!' On the second attempt William was again ready to retreat, but Horace urged him on. 'Remember, brother,' he cried. 'It was left to our honour!'

William's second story concerned a certain pear tree that flourished in the grounds before the schoolhouse. One night (probably in 1770) the boys lowered Horace from the dormitory window by some knotted sheets, and he rifled the tree, scaling the sheets to return with his plunder. This he distributed among his fellows, reserving not a single pear for himself. 'I only took them because every other boy was afraid!' he explained. Five guineas were offered for information about the theft, but no one betrayed the culprit.[22]

William's stories were probably embellished, but even if they are taken at face value they misrepresent the young Nelson. Looking back upon a misty past in the distorting glare of hindsight, William paid homage to his brother's subsequent reputation for courage and integrity, abstracting what was commendable and suppressing anything that detracted from the desired image. Horatio Nelson may have been a daring child, but he was also a boy much like any other, and it is that broader, and no doubt more colourful and ambiguous, portrait that we have lost. William's depiction of the unshakeably fearless, disinterested and upright boy was part of familiar selective processes that turn real men and women into myths.

Two others who remembered Nelson as a schoolboy were Elizabeth Gaze and Levett Hanson. Elizabeth was a local girl, the third of seven surviving daughters of Robert and Jane Gaze, farmers who had moved to North Walsham after losing their stock in a 'cattle plague'. Born in January 1752, she was literate and eighteen or nineteen when young Nelson saw her working as a nurse at the Paston. Elizabeth's story that Horace went down with measles at the school – set down by one of her great-grandchildren – rings true. The disease ran rife in such establishments and Horace was a weak child, 'much impaired by an aguish complaint' according to his brother. Moreover, the school minutes for 9 August 1770 show that the 'stable chamber' and 'space over the muck bin' were earmarked as quarters for sick children, an entry that suggests several infectious pupils needed isolating. The following January the school governors, all of them members of the local gentry, allowed the Reverend Jones five guineas to maintain the room he had hired for that purpose.[23]

Levett Hanson of Yorkshire was a fellow pupil. Many years later, on 29 September 1802, he wrote to the famous admiral, 'Your Lordship, though in the second class when I was in the first, was five years my junior, or four at least, and at that period of life such a difference in point of age is considerable. I well remember where you sat in the school room. Your station was against the wall, between the parlour door and the chimney. The latter to your right. From 1769 to 1771 we were opposites . . .' Born in December 1754, Hanson was in fact almost four years Horace's senior. His remark about the different classes indicates either that Nelson was already a pupil at the Paston when Hanson arrived from Bury St Edmunds in 1769 or that he was more academically advanced.[24]

Hanson certainly seems to have been a less than conscientious pupil. He reminded Nelson that 'Classic Jones' the headmaster was a 'flogger' of the first water, but perhaps that was merely how he chose to remember it. As an adult Hanson was a flamboyant author and traveller, fair-complexioned, red-haired and round-faced, but school records suggest an unruly boy. Just before Horace left the Paston in 1771 Hanson absconded. On 24 February Jones explained to Hanson's guardian that the boy had been 'out of bounds after dark', and on one occasion had negotiated a hedge to smoke a pipe in the master's garden with another boy. Hanson had also failed to form a Greek verb, and received one or two punitive blows over the shoulders, but Jones protested that 'my natural disposition is rather to mildness than severity, and my punishments are never proportional to a boy's faults'.[25]

There is no evidence that Nelson particularly distinguished himself at school. He was unquestionably intelligent, but his mature letters contain few of the Classical allusions Jones and his staff attempted to instil. Dawson Turner, who studied at North Walsham a dozen years later, testified that stories about Nelson were still going round at the time, and that the name of the future admiral was cut in a pew in the school church. A subsequent pupil, the father of the novelist Henry Rider Haggard, thought he discerned it carved upon a brick in the playground wall at the back of the school.[26]

It was of little consequence, for Horace's schooldays ended abruptly. He was the second of the Nelson children to leave home.

7

In time the Reverend Edmund Nelson would guide all but one of his children into employment. In 1773 eighteen-year-old Susanna, who answered to 'Sukey', was apprenticed to Messrs Watson, milliners of Bath, and in three years became a shop assistant in the same town. William, despite a growing capacity for self-interest, went to Christ College, Cambridge, in 1774, destined for holy orders. Neat and taciturn Ann ('Nancy' or 'Nan') eventually left school in 1775 and embarked upon her apprenticeship in millinery at a 'Lace Warehouse' in Ludgate Street, London. Edmund ('Mun') and Suckling were also apprenticed, the former to Nicholas Havers of Burnham and the latter to Mr Blowers, a linen draper of Beccles, though neither would be particularly successful. Only little Catherine, who everyone called 'Katy', would be rescued from an apprenticeship by a timely legacy. Their father loved his children and worried that he had served them inadequately, but the evidence suggests otherwise. Ann's apprentice-ship alone cost a premium of £105, one of the highest demanded by a London trade, a clear indication that Edmund was stretching his meagre means to find good positions for his offspring.[27]

But, apart from Maurice, Horace left home before any of them, at the tender age of twelve. It happened suddenly.

The winter of 1770–71 was lonely and dark at the rectory, for the reverend had retreated to Bath and the boys spent their Christmas holidays under the charge of the hired help. But perusing the pages of the *Norfolk Chronicle*, Horace read something that enlivened even that timeless place. Britain and Spain were squabbling for possession of the Falkland Islands, and the Admiralty was commissioning addi-tional ships, and calling captains from retirement. One of them was Horace's uncle, Maurice Suckling, who was appointed to a new sixty-four-gun line of battle ship, the *Raisonable*, on 17 November. She was fitting at Chatham, and taking on men, and impulsively Horace asked William to write to their father. He wanted Uncle Maurice to take him to sea.

The Reverend Nelson probably did not blanch at the proposal. He knew that Captain Suckling had offered to take one of the boys, and the navy was by no means a bad option. Indeed, there were few more acceptable alternatives. As a clergyman Edmund had a traditional place among the country gentry, but it was a rank to which his modest income was barely equal, and like many wearing the cloth he mixed uneasily with local landowners, merchants and professional men far wealthier than himself. Money was a particularly serious concern when it came to starting sons in life. The professions were the obvious outlets, but most demanded considerable and enduring investment. Promotion in the army was based upon purchase, and threatened constant embarrassment to families of limited means. The law was a possibility, but the road to the Bar through the inns of court might drain a modest purse, and even an apprenticeship with a good London attorney could cost a hundred pounds. The Church involved the expenses of a university education. The navy, however, was different. A commissioned officer had status and the prospect of making a fortune through prize money. But more immediately, provided a boy had the 'interest' to get aboard a ship as the protégé of some captain, his promotion would depend upon influence and kinship rather than money, and he would receive his education at the king's expense. Edmund would have to pay for Horace's uniforms, equipment and sea chest, but, all things considered, the navy was a respectable and inexpensive way forward. True, the service was a hard one, but then Captain Suckling would be on hand to monitor his nephew's progress.

As William remembered it, Uncle Maurice himself was not so sure. It was common for captains to take fledgling relatives on board their ships, and Suckling had himself gone to sea at thirteen. He had also promised to provide for one of the boys, but perhaps it was William he had had in mind, rather than his fragile younger brother, so readily stricken with the mild marsh fevers of the East Anglian flats. 'What has poor Horace done, who is so weak, that he above all the rest should be sent to rough it out at sea?' Suckling is said to have replied. 'But let him come, and the first time we go into action a cannon ball may knock off his head and provide for him at once.'[28]

Not yet though. The ship was still being prepared and Horace was ordered back to school with his brother for the beginning of the new term. Not until early one gloomy March or April morning in 1771 did their father's servant arrive at the Paston with a summons. The brothers parted painfully, and the school doors closed behind Horace for the last time. He was bound for London and a new life at sea.[29]

Nelson would miss home, for all its grim silences and stunted horizons. He remembered his early associates in Norfolk with great affection, and referred to them often in his letters to William. There was Horace Hammond, 'my old school-fellow', the son of Dr Horace Hammond, who had not only married a cousin of Nelson's mother but stood as one of the boy's godparents. And among those whose kindnesses remained with him were Dr Poyntz, Henry Crowe, Lord Walpole, and Mrs John (Charlotte) Norris, daughter of Edward Townshend, sometime Dean of Norwich, and another of the Suckling–Walpole–Townshend tribe.[30]

But homesickness would have to be cured, for as Horace sat excitedly beside his father, shaken this way and that as the coach sped over rutted roads to London, he could not have known that he would not see Burnham Thorpe again for ten years.

III

CAPTAIN SUCKLING'S NEPHEW

From thence a NELSON, – DUNCAN sprung,
Brave HOOD, and numbers yet unsung;
Let not then a despiteful tongue,
Defame the name of midshipman.
                    'Peter', *The Midshipman*, 1813

1

EIGHTEENTH-CENTURY London was very different from the London of today. No part of it was more than an afternoon's carriage ride from the open country, and while the main roads that stretched from its nucleus like tentacles were built up for miles, the ground between was covered in fields, market gardens and rural villages. But it must have still seemed overwhelmingly stirring to a twelve-year-old from Norfolk, even one familiar with Norwich. Pedestrians of every description thronged the pavements, while carts, coaches, sedan chairs, carriages and wagons plied furiously through the streets. The air was full of the smells of an eccentric sewage system and new sounds, the echo of wood and iron on cobbles, the chimes of huge bells and the incomprehensible cries of street vendors. The Reverend Edmund Nelson might have led his wide-eyed son through myriad interesting sights to the house of William Suckling, apparently then at New North Street in Red Lion Square. Horace knew that Uncle William had been with the customs service as a boy. His station was probably the Customs House off Thames Street, but at home he lived with his wife Elizabeth (née Browne) and their nine-year-old son, also called William. There was little time for Horace to explore, however. After completing his sea outfit, which included navigational instruments and the long, plain single-breasted uniform coats of a midshipman, he was soon careering downriver on the Chatham stage with instructions to find the *Raisonable* and report to Captain Suckling.[1]

In all probability the ship was at Sheerness, for it had slipped down to the mouth of the Medway on 15 March. The *Raisonable* still had only about half of its complement of five hundred men, but was already being licked into shape. On 1 April a man received the customary twelve lashes for fighting. The ship's rigging was being set up, and stores of beef, bread, wood, beer, pork, oatmeal, butter, cheese and water were loading.[2]

When the bewildered Horace finally arrived at the moorings there was no one to meet him or take him aboard. According to the story told by his brother William, Horace wandered forlornly about the quayside until an officer acquainted with Captain Suckling encountered him, and, learning his plight, took him home for refreshments. When Horace did reach the *Raisonable*, it was to the news that his uncle, the captain, had not yet arrived. He stowed his gear and spent that day and several that followed pacing the quarterdeck, lonely and homesick. Even William, still enduring the mercies of 'Classic' Jones, seemed to have been dealt a kinder hand.[3]

It was an uncomfortable introduction to the dark, arduous, cramped and dangerous world of the eighteenth-century warship, but slowly Horace adjusted to its tarry smells, the creaks and groans of wood and rope, the shifting, ceaseless swell beneath him, the shouts and oaths and running feet, and the crowded sights of an arterial waterway. If the *Raisonable* did little but rock at anchor, other vessels glided here and there beneath billowing sails, ships with such names as the *Conquistador*, *Glasgow*, *Cornwall* and *Augusta*. One, a passing yacht, drew a rumbling gun salute, and Horace would have learned that it contained Lord Sandwich himself, recently restored to the head of the board of Admiralty.

While new recruits climbed aboard and volunteers received their 'bounties' from the dockyard clerk of the cheque, Horace tackled the everyday complexities of shipboard life as a 'young gentleman of the quarter-deck' training to be an officer, from mastering sleeping in a hammock and keeping himself in a presentable condition to fathoming the mysteries of navigation and seamanship at the behest of the sailing master, William Clark. He also quickly learned to jump at a word from the superior officers on the quarterdeck: the captain himself, and

Matthew Anderson, St Alban Roy, William Scott and Faithful Adrian Fortescue – lieutenants with the king's commission in their pockets.

There were new friends to be made too, many of them aspirants like himself, including a score of 'captain's servants' and five other midshipmen. It was the last – Thomas Underwood, John Cook, Thomas Pewtress, William Swan and Charles Boyles – who were his immediate associates. Boyles was his favourite and he probably assumed the role of a protective older brother. Five years Horace's senior, he was a lively Norfolk lad whose father, the collector of customs at Wells, was known to the Nelson–Suckling families. In fact, Charles owed his presence on board to one of their Townshend relatives. Horace watched Boyles mature into 'an exceedingly good character', very 'much beloved' by his colleagues. He was capable too: he became a post-captain in 1790, distinguished himself in Calder's action with the French in 1805 and reached flag rank a year later.[4]

The *Raisonable* was supposed to be bound for the Falklands but did not put to sea. The dispute between Britain and Spain subsided when the Spanish restored a British post they had seized on the islands, and the two powers agreed to let the question of sovereignty simmer. *Raisonable* was decommissioned, but Captain Suckling was not returned to the half-pay list. Instead, he was transferred to a larger warship, the seven-year-old, seventy-four-gun *Triumph*, which was anchored at Blackstakes, an anchorage on the River Medway, doing duty as a guardship. On 15 May the captain shifted to his new berth, and among those duly following was his nephew. Horace was discharged from the *Raisonable* on Tuesday 21 May 1771, and the following day rated a captain's servant on the *Triumph*.[5]

As we have seen, the navy was a logical choice for boys of Nelson's means, status and connections, but he was probably tempted by what seemed to him a glamorous profession, one that was also adventurous, prestigious and popular. The life was hard, but those who endured it, whether officers or common seamen, walked ashore with a certain pride and approbation. For in the eighteenth century the Royal Navy was not an occasionally useful but secondary arm: it was the very foundation of the security, independence and prosperity of an island nation living in dangerous times.

Going aboard the *Raisonable* and the *Triumph*, Horace was taking his place in the front line of his country's defences. Britain had been involved in three significant wars since the beginning of the century: the wars of Spanish and Austrian Succession of 1702–13 and 1740–48, and the Seven Years War of 1756–63, which for the British, French and American Indians began in skirmishes along the Ohio River in 1754. France was the principal adversary in each of the conflicts, and remained a major threat to Britain's sovereignty and her greatest rival for overseas empire. Compared with France, Britain was a poor underpopulated country of eight million people and militarily weak. But, luckily, she was also an island power with the sea for her borders and a powerful navy to protect her from invasion and allow a degree of freedom of action.

The Royal Navy both shielded the realm and enabled its politicians to distance themselves from continental wars, ready to profit while more vulnerable European powers with debatable land frontiers were sucked into ruinous conflicts. The British tended to risk their redcoats on the mainland sparingly, to prevent strategic areas, such as the Low Countries across the English Channel, falling under the control of a threatening power; to protect essential sources of supply, such as the naval stores acquired from the Baltic; or perhaps to stem the growth of hostile combinations of power inimical to Britain's interests. Britain had developed a maritime strategy, subsidising heavyweight allies doing their fighting in Europe, and using the navy to destroy Spanish and French sea power, shipping and colonies.

This blue-water strategy had yielded dividends of which most Englishmen were becoming proud, despite war debts. Its potential had been demonstrated in the War of Austrian Succession and the Seven Years War, conflicts which in Europe pivoted upon the competing territorial ambitions of Prussia and Austria in Silesia. During the general conflagrations that ensued, Britain used European allies to divert France and Spain on land while she shredded their sea-going capacity and colonies elsewhere. Britain emerged from the Seven Years War in 1763 as the most powerful of all maritime and colonial powers. She possessed the largest mercantile marine in the world, more than half a million tons of shipping, and the Royal Navy was able to field one hundred and thirty ships of the line with eighty-five thousand men, a force larger than the fleets of Spain and France combined. In the fighting she had stripped her rivals of Canada, Louisiana (east of the Mississippi), Tobago, Dominica, St Vincent, the Grenadines, Florida and Minorca, and eliminated French competition in India.

An impressive roll of victories had stirred British hearts, bringing the names of such new heroes as Robert Clive and James Wolfe to the fore, but everyone knew that the country's achievements were

ultimately predicated on sea power. Even as a young child, Horatio
Nelson must have understood, however imperfectly, that the navy was
not only vital to the country's power and security but also a service
of terrific prestige and popularity. He had probably listened to stories
of Admiral Hawke's famous victory over the French at Quiberon Bay
(1759), won when Horace was little more than a year old, and heard
the lusty strains of the ubiquitous 'Hearts of Oak', celebrating the
battle:

> Come cheer up, my lads, 'tis to glory we steer,
> To add something more to this wonderful year.

The navy was a shield, but it was also a protector and creator of
trade and wealth. Britain was still largely an agricultural country,
dominated by aristocratic landowners, but her growing middle classes
depended upon a thriving overseas trade, and the gathering momentum
of her manufactures, racing towards the 'industrial revolution', was
spearheaded by the export of textiles. The country had won vast overseas possessions, where markets and raw materials were to be had or
strategic areas secured, but it was more interested in customers than
colonies and in building a trade empire. Though some of Britain's
older markets, such as the Levant and the Iberian peninsula, were
declining, Atlantic, West Indian and East Indian trades were creating
a new prosperity, and in 1760 Britain's exports far exceeded the government's national budget.

And it was almost universally understood that naval power was
essential to that rising wealth. Nothing illustrated the acceptance of
that premise more graphically than the navigation laws, which were
at the heart of the country's mercantilist system. Those laws attempted
to bind the mother country and her colonies into an interlocking, self-
sufficient trade system that would shut out commercial rivals and
maintain the foundations of naval power. They stipulated what each
colony might manufacture and export, and from where it might import
other necessaries, and insisted that such trade be carried in ships built
in Britain or her dependencies and predominantly navigated by their
citizens. Similarly, about half the European goods imported into Britain
had to be carried either in the ships of the producing country or in
'British bottoms', and all European goods destined for the British
colonies had to be shipped through Britain and in British vessels. By
protecting ship-building and a pool of experienced seamen, the

maritime laws supported the foundations of naval power and under-
lined the interdependence of war and trade.

With land frontiers and continental rivals to watch, France and
Spain were unable to match the resources Britain willingly channelled
into her might at sea, and when Horace joined the Royal Navy it was
a vast organisation by the standards of the eighteenth century. Indeed,
its most prominent living historian has accounted it 'by far the largest
and most complex of all government services' and 'by a large margin
the largest industrial organization in the western world'. Apart from
the enormous fleet of ships of the line, frigates, sloops, brigs and
tenders, the Admiralty office in Whitehall controlled extensive auxiliary services, including dockyards at home – in Deptford, Woolwich,
Chatham, Sheerness, Portsmouth and Plymouth – and abroad – at
Gibraltar and Minorca in the Mediterranean, Halifax in Canada, and
Antigua and Jamaica in the West Indies.[6]

Nelson had not stepped into a backwater but into a powerful,
vibrant, professional fraternity of the utmost importance to his country,
and a shaper of its destiny. But there was a long road to travel before
he could stamp his own personality and purpose upon it. He had
taken his first steps towards becoming a commissioned king's officer,
but from the beginning 'interest' was an essential prerequisite for
progress. There were no formal entry qualifications for an aspiring
officer, but an influential patron, usually a serving captain, was needed
to take the hopeful aboard, either as a captain's servant or midshipman
or even a master's mate or able seaman. These protégés might be
selected from promising common sailors already on board, but most
were friends or relations of existing naval officers and drawn from
the middling or upper classes.

An early start and rapid promotion were essential if maximum
benefit was to be derived. In theory, to qualify for a lieutenant's
commission 'young gentlemen' had to serve at least six years at sea,
two as a midshipman or master's mate; be twenty or more years old;
and pass an examination of nautical competency. Once a lieutenant,
the officer's object was to be made post-captain as soon as possible,
for that put him on a captains' list from which neither interest nor
wealth could oust him. Moreover, an officer ascended the captains'
list to admiral or flag rank purely by seniority. The snag was that the
process was a protracted one, and only an officer who had been 'made
post' at a reasonably early age could expect to live long enough to
reach the head of the list and achieve his flag. The importance of

interest, therefore, both for entry and a speedy promotion to the captains' list, was paramount.

2

Horatio Nelson relied entirely upon his uncle to clear a way for him, and that support was already working. Young men who were not the sons of naval officers were supposed to enter the service at the age of thirteen or above, but Nelson got in at twelve. Furthermore, by rating Horace's service from 1 January rather than from March or April, when he actually came on board, Captain Suckling had given his nephew two or three months' additional 'sea time' towards the six years he needed to qualify for a lieutenancy. These were, of course, subterfuges, but subterfuges were far from uncommon in the scramble for promotion and position that characterised the life of the young naval officer.[7]

Nelson's patron was still an imposing figure. The captain of the *Triumph* was just turning forty-five and in his prime, apart from having what he called 'gout' in his right hand. His hair was thinning, but he was handsome and slim, and seven years earlier had struck a dramatic pose sitting to the painter Thomas Bardwell at Woodton Hall, near Norwich, the ancestral home of the Sucklings. Captain Suckling's mettle had been shown in battle. As captain of the *Dreadnought* he had joined two consorts in an engagement with seven French ships off St Domingo in the West Indies on 21 October 1757. The battle was indecisive, but Suckling acquitted himself gallantly and his ship suffered the greatest British losses. Perhaps even more important from Horace's point of view, Captain Suckling made friends easily, and many would live to serve his nephew. They included John Rathbone, master's mate of the *Dreadnought*; Captain Peter Parker, who had served with Suckling in the Mediterranean; and Captain John Jervis, who had benefited from Suckling's kindness as a boy aboard the *Gloucester*.[8]

Professionally, Suckling was in a fairly strong position. His name had adorned the captains' list for fifteen years, and he had prospects of becoming an admiral. As it was, he advanced steadily. On 26 June 1771 he received the additional responsibility of superintending naval affairs in the Medway and the Nore. The job was unexciting, but the Medway and the Nore were principal channels for ships passing along the Thames, and Chatham and Sheerness were dockyards of the first importance. Suckling was soon handling a considerable range of duties, including naval discipline and the deployment of marine detachments and fourteen or so ships at a time.[9]

One reason for Suckling's success was the interest at his disposal, for notwithstanding the views of some historians to the contrary, the captain had powerful friends. His great uncles had included Galfridus Walpole, treasurer of Greenwich Hospital and postmaster general; Horatio, Lord Walpole; and the great Sir Robert Walpole himself. Indeed, it was under the auspices of the latter that Maurice had first gone to sea under Captain Thomas Fox. By the time Sir Robert died in 1745 Maurice had become a lieutenant, and further preferment was to be had at the hands of George Townshend (the son of his great aunt, Dorothy, Viscountess Townshend), who was himself a naval officer. In 1748, at the end of the War of Austrian Succession, when ships were being decommissioned and less favoured officers retired on half-pay, Suckling was appointed lieutenant of the *Gloucester*, bound for the West Indies under Townshend. Later, as post-captain of the *Dreadnought*, he was briefly Townshend's flag captain in Jamaica, where the latter was a rear admiral.[10]

Not surprisingly, Suckling's promotion had been sure and steady. A lieutenant before his twentieth birthday, he became a post-captain on 2 December 1755 at the age of twenty-nine. In 1761 his claims to attention had increased with his marriage to Mary, a sister of the second Lord Walpole and sister-in-law to a daughter of the third Duke of Devonshire. Although Suckling's wife had died early in the marriage, his connections to such political powerhouses as the Walpoles, Townshends and Devonshires left him with a residue of useful friends and acquaintances.[11]

Nor was Captain Suckling without property and expectations of more. As his responsibilities in London increased during the 1770s he acquired town houses in the capital – for example, one in Park Street, Mayfair, which he sold in 1776. His principal properties remained in East Anglia, however, at Barsham, Winfarthing, Diss and elsewhere. The captain was also in line to succeed to the Suckling estate of Woodton Hall, a handsome property of three storeys with a wine cellar, built in spacious grounds in 1694. It had descended to Denzil and Hannah Suckling, but their heir, Robert, was what the family ungraciously called a 'lunatic' and there were plans to transfer the estate to Captain Suckling, his cousin.[12]

The trouble was that, for all his success, the captain nursed a worrying void in his life. There was no one close to him to share his

fortunes. Suckling had never known his father, who had died when
he was four, and had grown up adored by his mother and older sister.
His wife, Mary, died in 1764 after three childless years of marriage,
and was buried at Wickmere near Wolterton, leaving only a strand of
her fair hair in a locket of pearls and blue enamel as a memento. Then
came that cold, bleak, tragic winter of 1767–8 when, as we saw in
the previous chapter, Suckling lost his sister and mother almost at a
single stroke in Burnham Thorpe. In less than three years the women
in his life had been taken from him. Although his younger brother,
William, had a family of his own, Maurice had no one. Captain
Suckling's will, written in 1774, proclaimed this vacuum. Among
bequests to his brother and a few others, including some of the
Walpoles who had shown him 'continued friendship', he bestowed
extensive bequests upon the progeny of his dead sister. Each of the
Nelson nieces received £1,000 and the nephews £500.[13]

Captain Suckling was more than happy to forward young Horace
in the service. There was no one to whom he felt a greater duty and
he was constantly alert to opportunities for the boy. He had brought
him, with Boyles and a few others, to the *Triumph* but in truth there
was relatively little to be learned on a semi-stationary guardship. Plenty
of small boat work, assisting ships to moor, running errands and
shifting men and stores to and fro, but no real taste of experience
under sail. The ship remained moored at Sheerness. It was provisioned,
cleaned and refitted. There was a search for a leak, three men got a
dozen lashes each, two of them for striking an officer and the third
for mutinous remarks, and a man fell overboard and drowned. But
this was not going to make his nephew a deep-water seaman.[14]

Then Captain Suckling learned something interesting. A merchantman belonging to the West India magnate Thomas Hibbert, and his
partners Purrier and Horton of London, was bound for Jamaica and
the other islands, and its captain was none other than Suckling's old
shipmate John Rathbone. Rathbone had come to Suckling's *Dreadnought* from the *Sphinx* and been rated master's mate on 3 June 1757.
The two had served in the West Indies together. Now Rathbone offered
to take Horace with him and turn him into a sailor, and when he
navigated the *Mary Ann* out of the Medway on 25 July 1771 the boy
was aboard. Four days later the ship left the Downs, heading west.[15]

Despite his earlier misgivings about Horace's constitutional frailty,
and the boy's obvious susceptibility to the seasickness that would
trouble him throughout life, Captain Suckling must have believed his

nephew had toughened up. Life at sea was harder – much harder – than sitting at moorings. The work was unrelenting, and under the watch system Horace was going to have to combine hard labour with as little as four hours' sleep a day. The merchant service was also a particularly demanding school. Compared to the Royal Navy it was poorly manned, and the sailors often struggled with larger workloads and greater indiscipline. Even more worrying, the West Indies was a notoriously fever-ridden destination. Maurice had been there himself, and as a teenager he had heard Richard Glover's chilling ballad, 'Admiral Hosier's Ghost', which broadcast the fate of Hosier and four thousand of his men, wiped out in the islands by yellow fever, a year after Suckling was born. But for all that, Horace would be out on deep water, knotting and slicing ropes, taming the terrors of climbing aloft on lurching ratlines, and working his way out along the yards, scores of feet above the heaving main deck to bring in or make sail. If nothing else, it would establish once and for all whether young Nelson was cut out for the life he had chosen.[16]

During his period at sea Horace would be kept on the books of the *Triumph*. Officially, he was still aboard. It was another of those subterfuges, designed to preserve the boy's sea time even when he was somewhere else. In addition, he would continue to draw the pay of a captain's servant, about half that of a midshipman. Between 1 July 1771 and 30 June 1772 the sum of £11 8s. 10d. was accordingly paid the missing boy, at least on paper. We do not know what arrangement Suckling had made with Rathbone. It is possible the captain had made it worth Rathbone's while to take the boy, and that he pocketed Horace's wages as compensation.[17]

The *Mary Ann* reached Tobago in the Windward Islands at the end of the year 1771 and then wove her way around tropical islands towards Jamaica. A year after leaving London she returned, reaching Plymouth on 7 July 1772 and Gravesend ten days later. The muster of the *Triumph*, which still stood on guard at Sheerness, records that Nelson was 'discharged' as captain's servant at his own request on 18 July 1772, and re-rated as an ordinary seaman the same day. Obviously the boy rejoined his uncle's ship the day after his return, and the new rating reflected his increased seafaring status.[18]

Horace found the captain in the thick of ceremonial pomp rarely seen in the merchant service. No sooner had Suckling treated the first lord of the Admiralty to 'a most elegant entertainment' aboard the *Triumph* than he was preparing for the visit of Lord Suffolk and three other peers at the end of July. Horace had room to ponder. Unquestionably he had benefited from his spell in the merchant service but there was one unanticipated consequence. As he later recalled, 'if I did not improve in my education, I returned a practical seaman, with a horror of the Royal Navy, and with a saying then constant with the [merchant] seamen, "Aft the most honour, forward the better man!" It was many weeks before I got in the least reconciled to a man-of-war, so deep was the prejudice rooted, and what pains were taken to instil this erroneous principle in a young mind.'[19]

In the minds of many merchant sailors, a good number of whom, like Rathbone himself, had served in the Royal Navy, the king's service was thoroughly unattractive. The officers lived 'aft' and enjoyed the privilege of walking the quarterdeck, cornering the glory and most of the prize money, while the common mariners of the 'forecastle' – the living space they used up front below the old forecastle deck – bore the burnt of the work. It was a service in which merit seldom secured just rewards. A considerable time had to elapse before life on the *Triumph* convinced Horace otherwise.

3

For the next year Horace remained with his uncle on the *Triumph*. He found most of the personnel of the ship unchanged. John Boyle and Robert Shipman, lieutenants of seven and nine years' standing, were still in post, but the kindly first lieutenant, Lambert Brabazon, was replaced soon after Nelson's return by Thomas Tonken, and Second Lieutenant Henry Jackson, an Orford man, by Anthony Perry.[20]

In August or September Horace was re-rated a midshipman, and slung his hammock and possessions in the midshipman's berth below the lower gun deck, either in a space near the aft hatchway known as the cockpit or possibly in the gun room with the gunner.

The nine 'middies' with whom he shared the following year were a mixed bunch. Almost fourteen, Horace was certainly the youngest, although whether he experienced any of the bullying that plagued some midshipmen's messes is doubtful. As the captain's nephew he was plainly destined for promotion, and help was still readily at hand in his friend Boyles, now nineteen years old. There was an even older acquaintance from the *Raisonable* in the mess, James Etheridge, a former acting mate who had been recommended to Suckling by the captain of the *Alderney*.

The rest of Nelson's companions were either fresh-faced hopefuls like himself; deserving and experienced men raised from the ordinary seamen by a benign captain, but without the prospects of the 'young gentlemen'; or older men who simply lacked the ability to get promotion and remained trapped as midshipmen, increasingly humiliated by their advancing years. Among the first of these groups may have been Richard Puddicomb from Topsham, aged twenty-one; James Urmston, an Irishman, and Thomas Bagster, a former able seaman from Cowes, both twenty-four; the Welshman John Morgan, aged twenty-five; and Thomas Manley Hulke of Deal in Kent. Former able seaman Thomas Jaynes probably belonged to the second group, having been promoted in June 1771 to fill a hole left by two departing officers, Hamlin and Baker. But the senior midshipman in the mess may also have been the least able, for Jonathan Ferry of Woodbridge, Suffolk, another ex-able seaman, was forty-nine years old.[21]

As an admiral Nelson spoke up for midshipmen, whom he believed 'a deserving set of young men', and probably his judgement reflected memories of serving in that rank. It was primarily a learning time, a period in which the trainee officer grasped the principles of a difficult and dangerous trade. Unlike the army, the navy not only required its people to steel themselves for battle and destruction, the most brutal of occupations, but also to survive the rigours of the sea itself. Those who would command one of His Majesty's ships needed first to know how to preserve it in uncertain tides, winds, currents and seas; how to manoeuvre among shifting shoals or along threatening shores; and how to build a team capable of confronting a life of constant danger. Study was an essential part of the midshipman's lot. It is not surprising, given the difficulty of the job and the stifling disadvantages of those deficient in 'interest', that most midshipmen never reached commissioned rank. Of the ten aboard the *Triumph* only three Boyles, Hulke and Nelson – ever made lieutenant.

Horace turned out for lessons in seamanship and navigation from the master, Richard Williams, and kept logs of his daily observations, and he put his hand to signalling and supervising watches, but it was the boat work he particularly enjoyed. The Medway and the Thames provided ideal training grounds in navigation, because both were silting up and the depth of water was ever changing. Horace remembered how Captain Suckling allowed him to go 'in the cutter and decked long boat, which was attached to the Commanding Officer's ship at Chatham. Thus, by degrees, I became a good pilot for vessels of that description, from Chatham to the Tower of London, down the Swin, and the North Foreland; and confident of myself among rocks and sands, which has many times since been of great comfort to me.'²²

With the *Triumph* stationed at Chatham, it was the boats that plied back and forth, transporting detachments of marines between the shore and such ships as the *Portland*, shifting provisions, water, fuel and powder, carrying messages and moving prisoners. Suckling had cutters, a longboat, jolly boat, yawl and pinnace at his disposal, and no doubt his ardent apprentice learned to handle them all, but their work could be punishing and at any time one or other might be put out of action. Only a few weeks after Nelson rejoined his uncle's ship, the *Wells* cutter was caught by wind and tide as it headed downriver and grounded on Prince Bridge. It was towed off, but the following day, 9 August, Captain Suckling informed the Admiralty that he needed an additional sailing cutter. Every time he had to change parties of marines at the Nore or Sheerness he had to apply to the naval commissioner at Chatham for the use of his boat. In response the Admiralty offered Suckling the *Goodwill* cutter as a personal tender, but it was not until 18 December that she was fit to be collected from the dock at Sheerness by Lieutenant Tonken. In the meantime, Suckling's resources suffered a further loss in October when the *Greyhound* cutter went to Sheerness for repairs.²³

In some respects Horace's first years afloat seem to have been lonely ones, devoid of the company and care of women, and spent with older men in arduous and testing circumstances. Considering the sensitivity that was always evident in Nelson's character, it would not seem at face value to have been a world he could have enjoyed. And yet apparently the boy thrived, eagerly embracing every new opportunity for adventure and experience, and pressing forward with undiminished enthusiasm. His life had long been fragmented and unsettled, and it was nothing new to a boy who had moved so quickly from Burnham Thorpe, Norwich and North Walsham to be thrown into different companies with strange faces to learn and new modes of life to master.

But the language of the midshipmen's mess was less refined than anything he might have heard at boarding school, and the sustained and difficult labour and occasional brutality required major adjustments. The navy was not the merciless institution of popular folklore and made many enlightened efforts to care for its own. Young Nelson had nothing but good to say of most of his commanders and companions, and like other sailors came to accept the necessity for sharp, physical punishment. It was an ugly spectacle to see men bound to the upraised grating of a hatch and stripped to the waist, grimacing as their backs were cut by the knotted tails of a 'cat' wielded by a boatswain's mate before the assembled company. Between 26 July 1772 and 1 June 1773 there were some twenty-nine such sessions aboard the *Triumph*, punishing offences such as the embezzlement of stores, neglect of duty, quarrelling and drunkenness. Most floggings involved the statutory twelve lashes, but some offenders received more salutary lessons. Yet this was not necessarily considered a harsh regime in eighteenth-century terms, and enjoyed some support among men as well as officers. Every seaman knew that shirkers did more than multiply the already heavy workload of their fellows; they threatened lives. Each ship's company was engaged in a treacherous, dangerous and unforgiving business, and could only survive by working as a cohesive team. The loyalty and application of every member was essential, and most men looked to the captain to protect their crucial fraternity from those who would abuse it.

Like everyone on the *Triumph*, Nelson was forced to watch each flogging, standing straight-faced while the drum rolled and the whip fell. He never questioned the captain's right to flog, but perhaps it was in these early days that he also learned something most good officers already knew: that while men accepted a fair use of the cat, the minority of captains who flogged gratuitously or indiscriminately quickly forfeited respect. And justice was not easily dispensed, even by well-disposed officers. The severest punishment Horace witnessed with the *Triumph* was also the saddest, inflicted upon a twenty-two-year-old able seaman from Blackfriars in London named Edward Smith.

Smith was neither a rogue nor a rebel. Officers acknowledged him to be a 'very sober man, alert and attentive to his duty', but on 31 August 1772 he had been unlucky enough to go ashore in the pinnace the day a new warship was being launched in Chatham dockyard. The party had landed at New Stairs, where James Downie, the coxswain, allowed his men some leave, provided they returned at an appointed time. Smith and his friends drank at the Red Lion but returned promptly, clear evidence that desertion was not on their minds. However, before the pinnace could get away Lieutenant Brabazon appeared at some waterfront steps and shouted Downie over. The two men went to see the *Prince George* being launched, and when they returned to the pinnace Smith and a companion were missing.

The attractions of the taphouse had lured them away, and Smith finally got back to the harbour side after the pinnace had left. Desertion was a serious offence and Smith panicked. Afraid to return to his ship and no doubt befuddled to boot, he attempted to escape, but in due course fell into the hands of an Admiralty marshal who returned him to the *Triumph* for the almost inevitable sequel. At Smith's court martial in January 1773 Lieutenants Tonken and Shipman and the master, Richard Williams, spoke up for him, but the charge of desertion was proven.

The common penalty for such an offence was harsh and brutal, and in February it was visited on Edward Smith. One hundred and fifty lashes were administered, half in a boat alongside the *Triumph* and the remainder beside the *Dunkirk*. No doubt it was intended to serve as an example, but as the fourteen-year-old Horace saw the yellow flag climb the foremast of the *Triumph*, heard the macabre drumbeat that accompanied the prisoner to his fate and glimpsed the bloody, swollen back of a decent seaman, he may well have blanched. This was a man the navy had failed. In time most under Nelson's command would consider him a firm but fair commander, willing to hear the stories of accused men and to consider mitigating circumstances. Perhaps some of those seeds were sown aboard the *Triumph*.[24]

However, after many months about the Thames and the Medway, it was time for Midshipman Nelson to seek other diversions. Moved by a spirit of adventure, he was finding life on the river increasingly bland. On the afternoon of 15 February 1773 there was brief excitement when fire bells were heard ringing in the Chatham dockyard. Captain Suckling replied immediately with a bell and musket fire, and tumbled a party in the boats to fight the blaze. The fire had started in some rotten wood ignited by sparks from a smithy forge and was soon extinguished. Yet such episodes probably left the fourteen-year-old Horace yearning for more permanent excitement. He began to look for an escape.

In May 1773 he found it. Someone told him that a voyage of discovery was being fitted out for the North Pole. It was a dangerous mission, and only picked men were being recruited. No boys were to be allowed aboard. In fact, it sounded just the sort of adventure young Nelson so desperately wanted.

IV

NORTHWARD HO!

From earliest youth, to ev'ry worth allied,
In ev'ry danger prov'd, and peril tried.
Lines Written by an Officer of the Royal Navy, 1805

1

MEN had dreamed of it for at least two centuries. Finding a north-east passage through the polar seas – a short cut to the riches of the East that would spare ships the laborious voyages through the Mediterranean, by the Cape of Good Hope, or westwards around the globe. In Tudor times sailors perished in the Arctic wastes trying to find the passage, but even two centuries later little was known about the area north of eighty degrees. Spitsbergen had been discovered, but only whalers went there. Nevertheless, as the eighteenth century drew to its close, it was inevitable that new attempts would be made to probe the mysteries of the north. It was a period of growing intellectual and scientific enquiry. The month young Horatio Nelson sailed from the Thames in the *Mary Ann*, Captain James Cook returned from his first great voyage of exploration, in which he had observed the transit of Venus in Tahiti, charted much of New Zealand and Australia and brought back innumerable examples of fascinating flora and fauna. A year later, as the fourteen-year-old boy returned to his guard ship, the Yorkshire navigator set out again, poised to bring Antarctica to the attention of the 'civilised' world and to explode the myth of *Terra Australis Incognita*, the great southern continent.

It was probably a Swiss scholar, Samuel Engel, who nudged the hoary old question of the Northeast Passage back into focus. In 1765 he published a book in Lausanne suggesting that ice gathered mainly around land masses, and owed its existence to the fresh water discharged into the seas from rivers. Out in the deeps, he hypothesised, the polar seas might be open and navigable. In 1772 the French explorer Louis-Antoine de Bougainville proposed an expedition to explore the region north of Spitsbergen, but his government declined to back the plan.

The next year the Honourable Daines Barrington, vice president of the Royal Society in London, and Lord Sandwich of the Admiralty, put a similar proposal to George III with greater success. Soon a couple of ships were being fitted out, the *Racehorse* bomb vessel, under Commodore the Honourable Constantine John Phipps, who commanded the expedition, and the *Carcass* bomb, captained by Skeffington Lutwidge. Phipps's final instructions were dated 25 May 1773. They ordered him to pass between Spitsbergen and Greenland, keeping as far out to sea and as close to the meridian as possible, and to attempt to reach the North Pole. But the dangers were recognised, and even if Phipps found a free passage he was told to go no further, but to return before the winter closed in.[1]

To increase his chance of success Phipps was ordered to recruit only 'effective men' for the venture; they should all be volunteers, entitled to bounties of three pounds apiece, and little more than ninety men would be required for each of the two vessels. On the face of it, there seemed little prospect of Midshipman Nelson finding a place.[2]

Yet the arm of Captain Suckling was long. He, like Phipps, was a trusted crony of Lord Sandwich. Moreover, Captain Lutwidge of the *Carcass* knew Suckling well, and had occasionally acted under his orders, for example when cruising against smugglers in 1771. The two officers were on good terms. Years later Horace described Lutwidge as 'that good man', which suggests the benevolence with which he had been received. Be that as it may, the boy used 'every interest' with Captain Lutwidge, 'and as I fancied I was to fill a man's place, I begged I might be his coxswain, which, finding my ardent desire for going with him, Captain L[utwidge] complied with; and has continued the strictest friendship to this moment'.[3]

The upshot was that Nelson was discharged from the *Triumph* on 6 May 1773 and joined the *Carcass* at Sheerness the following day as a midshipman. Lutwidge was committed to the boy, and kept him on on 27 May, when he shed six of his eight six-pounder guns and accordingly scaled his company down to eighty men. Most of the ten discarded were able seamen, who might have been expected to give a better account of themselves than a mere boy. Horace was fourteen – the youngest person with the expedition – and the muster added two years to his age to add credibility to his enrolment. Officially there were only three others of similar age on the *Carcass*: Robert Hughes, an eighteen-year-old midshipman from Greenwich who joined six days after Nelson; Richard Praper, an able seaman from London, also eighteen; and a seventeen-year-old clerk.[4]

When Horace saw the *Carcass* at Sheerness he must have compared it unfavourably to the statelier ships of war on which he had already served. Moored beside the *Success* hulk, she was as old as he was and a stubby affair, some ninety-one and a half feet by twenty-seven and a half feet, with three masts and a powerful hull designed to withstand the recoil of heavy mortars. Bomb vessels had been chosen because they were small enough to handle restricted spaces and strong enough to break through ice, and both the *Racehorse* and the *Carcass* had been reinforced by additional oak sheathing and supports for the bows and hull.

Nelson was one of five midshipmen on the *Carcass*. With him were Hughes; Charles Deane from Newhaven, Sussex, aged twenty-nine; and two Londoners, twenty-year old John Creswell and twenty-four-year-old Edward Rushworth. Deane, Creswell and Rushworth had all been able seamen, and at the end of May another such, John Toms, was promoted to midshipman. Robert Hughes, closest in age to Horace, was probably the young officer whom Lutwidge later characterised as the 'daring shipmate' of Nelson, 'to whom he' became 'attached'. Even less experienced than Nelson, Hughes was on his first ship and owed his place to a considerable manipulation of interest.

Assisting Lutwidge and supervising the midshipmen were three lieutenants. First Lieutenant John Baird had carried a commission for sixteen years and served in numerous ships, and it was not long before the crew began to idolise him for his steadiness, rectitude and equanimity. It was noticed that he never swore, even in a crisis. The junior lieutenants were Joseph Pennington, whose life would be ended in a duel three years later, and George Wickham, who had been promoted only two years before. The master, James Allen, who instructed the midshipmen in navigation, was less inspiring. A portly, pompous individual with a windy disposition, he was nicknamed 'Major Buz'. All in all, however, Lutwidge had chosen his men well.

The *Carcass* was a hard-working but happy ship, and not a single flogging marred the voyage.

Considerable thought went into supplying the expedition. The Admiralty provided special clothing, tools and foodstuffs: ice saws were included as well as portable soup (cakes of meat essence boiled with vegetables and oatmeal) and additional quantities of comestibles, wine, tea and sugar. Dr Charles Irving was shipped aboard with his apparatus for distilling salt from sea water, and two whalemen were assigned to each vessel as pilots. The Board of Longitude, which investigated navigational problems, supplied an astronomer, two Harrison chronometers proof against climatic change and the vicissitudes of ship life, and a new device named Bouguer's log after the mathematician and hydrographer, designed to calculate the speed of a ship and the distance it had travelled. And Sir Joseph Banks, the celebrated botanist who had sailed with Cook, studiously drilled Commodore Phipps about the natural phenomena he was likely to encounter.

Unfortunately, none of these extensive preparations, including discussions with Greenland whalemen, exposed the chimera upon which the expedition was based. There simply *was* no open water at the Pole, and the whalemen knew it. One hundred and fifty miles north of Spitsbergen the pack ice was permanent, and it swept south on the skirts of polar summers. Nevertheless, Phipps, who would later become Lord Mulgrave, was a hardy thirty-year-old northerner, prudent and intelligent as well as enterprising, and willing to pitch into anything he asked of his men, while Lutwidge was much respected by his crews.

Given the impossibility of sailing to the Pole, and the extreme dangers awaiting any who tried to do so, it was fortunate indeed that the expedition had been put in capable hands.

2

On 30 May 1773 the *Carcass* left its moorings at Sheerness and joined the *Racehorse* at the Little Nore. They sailed at three in the afternoon of Thursday 3 June, and headed north, for the most part borne along by fresh or light breezes. Flamborough Head and Scarborough Castle passed by to larboard, and on 10 June the ships anchored in Robin Hood's Bay and Whitby Road. There was water and food to take aboard, and the next day the voyage continued, carving a wake towards the Shetlands, where the ships bought cheap fish from local boats that plied offshore.[5]

It was also near the Shetlands, in about latitude sixty degrees, that on the afternoon of 15 June the two ships temporarily separated in the first of many all-enveloping fogs that were to trouble the expedition. A thick white veil blanketed off everything beyond the length of a ship. On this and subsequent such occasions Phipps fired guns on the half-hour, and sometimes used volleys of musketry, drums, bells, horns and trumpets to penetrate the murk. The *Carcass* replied, but Lutwidge was secure in the knowledge that if he lost the *Racehorse* he still had written instructions from Phipps detailing places of rendezvous.

As the ships continued, everyone had their own preoccupations. Phipps was scientifically inclined. He tested the chronometers, his 'watch machines', comparing the one on the *Carcass* with his own, as well as with his independent calculations, and he studied the variation and dip of the compass. Amid daily decisions about course and speed, he also amused himself with Pierre Bouguer's log, recorded the changing temperature of the water, and decided that the Irving distilling equipment answered his requirements. Another on board the *Racehorse*, eighteen-year-old Midshipman Philippe d'Auvergne, one of the youngest members of the expedition, was set to prove himself an accomplished artist, while on the *Carcass* Nelson himself enjoyed the curiosities of new seas as only young men of his age can, noting the eerily light nights; the sun seven degrees above the horizon at midnight as they approached the Arctic circle; the first whale, seen off the northeast quarter of the *Carcass* on 20 June; and the seals which occasionally peered and plunged around the vessels to remind him of the north Norfolk coast.[6]

Less comforting was the increasingly inclement weather, the swiftly falling temperatures, persistent fogs, rain that froze as it fell, snow and variable winds. On 18 June Lutwidge issued the Admiralty's special clothing, and Horace found himself with six 'fearnought' jackets, two milled caps, two pairs of 'fearnought' trousers, four pairs of milled stockings, a strong pair of boots, a dozen pairs of milled mittens, two cotton shirts and a couple of handkerchiefs. How much use a rather small fourteen-year-old could make of these must be left to the imagination, but during the voyage both Nelson and Hughes also obtained 'slop clothes' from John Parry, the purser, for which they were charged 1s. 8d.[7]

As the ships pressed northwards through the Greenland Sea the signs of approaching land raised expectations. A redpoll alighted upon the *Carcass* on 27 June, and shortly before midnight the following day the west coast of Spitsbergen was sighted eighteen or twenty leagues to the east. The sea birds which had been shadowing the ships since they had passed the Shetlands suddenly abandoned them to head for land. On 29 June Horace was able to study the bleak shores of Prince Charles Island to starboard as the ships ran northwards offshore. Benefiting from the North Atlantic drift, the craggy coastline was in its short spring and summer, and the sun was surprisingly warm, but it was inhospitable and barren all the same. Huge sharp-pointed mountains of black, bare rock, their crests wreathed in cloud and snow and their valleys hidden beneath glaciers, slipped by. Fantastic sculptures, labyrinthine gullies and the pinnacles of distant ice castles fed the eye, captured for us in sketches made at the time. Thomas Floyd, a nineteen-year-old midshipman on the *Racehorse*, thought it 'a most desolate appearance indeed'.[8]

On the evening of the 30th as the ships steered northwards between Spitsbergen and Greenland they encountered a whaler, one of several British, Dutch and Danish whalers and sealers they had seen on their travels. This one had mortifying news.

The ice was close by.

According to what the master of the whaler told Phipps, it closed so quickly that three ships had recently been 'crushed to pieces'. In the following few days other whalemen they encountered 'sang the same song'. The number of whalers lost to the ice varied with each shuddering tale, but some put it as high as seven, and it was said that only the people of the British *Springfield* had been saved. More directly, notwithstanding the scientific theories, the whalemen insisted that the North Pole could not be reached, and that Phipps's expedition was foolhardy.[9]

Although the whalemen reported ice to the westward, the weather itself was disarming. The sun remained warm and nothing could be seen from the tops of the *Racehorse* and the *Carcass*. For a few days all seemed well, and some reassured themselves with hopes that the whalemen might have been scaremongering. The pathfinders passed to the north of Prince Charles Island to reach the mainland, where, on the evening of 4 July, Phipps and Lutwidge made a landfall in a small bay south of Magdalena Hook. The boats watered, Lutwidge noted the bleakness of the place and Phipps prepared to take bearings until an enveloping mist drove them back aboard and the ships stood out to sea firing signal guns. The next day the fog was almost impenetrable, and the *Racehorse* and *Carcass* groped their way forward like blind men on a precipice. It was then, as their senses stretched to the limit, that the ice came upon them.

Just after noon, somewhere northwest of Dane's Gat, an island at the northwestern extremity of Spitsbergen, an almost imperceptible but sinister sound was heard on board the ships: the sound of surf beating upon a shore where no shore should be. Phipps determined to proceed slowly north-northeast, convinced that if he lay too his ships would not be 'ready and manageable' enough to handle a sudden 'emergency'. Blocks of ice, some three or four feet square, began floating past as if harbingers of danger. Every officer now knew the ice pack was near, but how near? On the *Racehorse*, which led the way and faced the greater danger, Phipps reckoned it was a quarter of a mile away, but most thought it less than half that, within the length of a single cable.

It was a time for steady nerves. The ships had shortened sail, but on both, all hands were on deck, ready to haul up whenever necessary. As the signal guns rumbled like muffled thunder, eyes focused intently on the shifting fog ahead. Phipps thought he saw 'something' on the bow, a spectral whiteness, but he was not sure. Then, suddenly, just before two o'clock, the fog lifted, and there – dead ahead, at a distance of no more than four hundred and forty yards – a solid wall of ice rose from the sea, its hollows grey and black in the snowy white mass and the high surf lashing wildly at its foot. Instantly, the men fell to their business, and Phipps declared that he 'never saw a ship worked more briskly, or with less noise and confusion' than the *Racehorse* as it responded to that threat of imminent disaster. The helm was thrown to starboard, and Phipps tacked westwards, but he realised that he could not weather the ice that way and put the ship about, raising all sail east. It was not before time. Marvelling at their escape, Midshipman Floyd wrote, 'Had the fog lasted but two minutes more, we must inevitably have been in the ice, and in all probability would have been cut to pieces.'[10]

During the night the fog descended again, sometimes masking the ships from one another at a range of a half pistol shot, but Horace and his friends could hear the ice grinding and cracking and the surf driving against it. The sixth of July brought an improvement, however, and allowed the ships to range along the ice pack for several days, searching for a way through. Minds had to be concentrated, because the navigation was fiendishly tricky amid drifting bergs big enough to damage ship timbers and near an ice pack that could close, trap and crush with fearful speed. On one occasion Phipps summoned the pilots of the *Carcass* to the *Racehorse* for a conference, and their boat was barely able to return, so quickly did the ice mass around them.

For days the ships tacked to and fro, using ice poles to stave off bergs and ice anchors thrown from each bow. The small boats were constantly out, hauling the ships this way and that. Nelson was probably employed on the boats of the *Carcass*, the longboat, launch and cutter. As the ship did not answer her helm efficiently, she was forever being towed to the *Racehorse* or away from looming obstacles. But try as they might, neither ship could entirely avoid colliding with chunks of ice, and the succession of severe shocks they received proved the worth of the additional strengths that had been built into the tough little vessels before sailing.

Never did the Northeast Passage seem a greater illusion, for there was simply no way through that frozen wilderness. From the masthead of the *Carcass* it appeared that an 'immense mass of ice extended northeast as far as they could see'. Progress was impossible, the crews were wet, exhausted and cold, despite the issue of extra spirits, and the numbing, bone-chilling fog returned. On the nights of the 9th and 10th Horace and his companions fought the ice without eyes, lost the *Racehorse* twice, and 'steered a hundred different courses to follow the channels'.[11]

The next day Phipps abandoned the theory that the ice was thinner in deep water, and stood east to discover whether he could find an opening nearer Spitsbergen. But that too proved unavailing, for the shallow coastal seas were iced solid. Whatever faith the commodore had ever had in the Arctic waterway must have been ebbing fast, but he was not a man to retreat prematurely. He decided he would rest his men before trying again.

3

On 13 July the ships put into Smeerenberg Sound, at the extreme northwest of Spitsbergen, a mile from where a bare and lonely rock known as Cloven Cliff broke above the ice-grey sea. Several Dutch whalers were sheltering in the intersecting passages that wove around the islands that formed the sound, and the remains of an old whaling station were still to be seen ashore. Stark it was, but the place had a rare beauty. The mountains, when not enveloped in cloud, were sometimes dark and sometimes veined in 'red, white and yellow', while on their southern and western slopes they supported precarious colonies of brown lichen or brilliant green moss. The glaciers shone sapphire-blue in the sun, or flashed like prisms, 'exceeding in luster the richest gems in the world, [and] disposed in shapes wonderful to behold'. Looking at them, a diarist on the *Carcass* mused that 'a stranger may fancy a thousand different shapes of trees, castles, churches, ruins, ships, whales, monsters and all the various forms that fill the universe'.[12]

By his own account Horace was the coxswain of Lutwidge's gig, and it was probably he who steered the captain to an island where Phipps had set up some observation points on the morning of 15 July. Most likely he also accompanied watering parties, but on the 18th the ships quit the sound and renewed their reconnaissance of the ice pack, cruising along it eastwards for several days. On 25 July they reached Moffen Island, a low, flat, round piece of stone and sand, with a frozen pond at its centre, and the two-year-old grave of a Dutch sailor. Captain Lutwidge sent the master, James Allen, ashore with ten men.

There, for the first time, they encountered polar bears, although what exactly happened is open to dispute. Allen's log merely records that they 'saw three white bears, one of which we shot, but it got off', but the diarist of the *Carcass*, who disliked 'Major Buz', turned the incident to the master's disadvantage. According to him, two of the three bears were shot and killed, although not before one of the wounded animals had pursued its tormentors. Allen fell behind his more agile companions. His hair 'stood on end', he dropped his gun, fell headlong into a goose nest, and 'filled his breeches' before the rest of the crew rescued him, but once the bear had been downed the master recovered his spirit and stabbed the unfortunate creature in the belly. This account was published anonymously before the end of the year, but it is doubtful that Allen himself ever saw it. Before its appearance he had been sent to the Falkland Islands and was washed overboard and drowned on the return journey in 1774.[13]

Another sad reflection on the eighteenth-century attitude to wildlife occurred the following day, when one of the boats of the *Carcass* encountered a walrus while exploring drift ice to the northeast. The 'sea horse' measured eleven feet in length and 'made a desperate defence' before it was killed with the aid of a boat's crew from the *Racehorse*. The animal was hauled aboard Lutwidge's ship for inspection, but probably little if any of it was eaten.[14]

With whales, dolphins, and 'fin fish' for company, the ships made another attempt to make their way northeastward on the 27th and 28th, reaching latitude eighty degrees forty-eight minutes north. On 29 July they were at the entrance to the Hinlopen Strait, which passes between Spitsbergen in the southwest and North East Land, and one of the *Racehorse*'s boats was sent to examine an island. Ashore they noted some uprooted fir trees and whale bones scattered about, shot a reindeer and commented upon the presence of Arctic foxes, ermines, snipe, ducks and geese. Returning in the small hours of the 30th, they attacked a walrus found sleeping on the ice. Wounded, the animal plunged into the water, stirring other walruses that were lurking there unseen. If we may believe the accounts of the expedition, the animals attacked the boat 'with great ferocity', and wrested an oar from one of the seamen. Indeed, the craft was in danger of being upset before the walruses were dispersed by the arrival of another boat from the *Carcass*. Some biographers have given young Nelson the dubious credit of having commanded the *Carcass* boat, following a rash statement in the early biography by James Harrison. There is no evidence for the assumption. None of the primary accounts mentions Nelson in connection with the incident, and by Horace's own account he was coxswain of the captain's gig at this time. It was extremely unlikely that the small gig would have been risked in such an encounter, and it was probably the cutter or the longboat, under the command of a more senior officer, that went to the relief of their companions.[15]

In contrast it *would* have been Horace's job to take Captain Lutwidge and the master of the *Racehorse* to visit one of the Seven Islands off the north coast of North East Land, five or six miles north of the ships, on the evening of 30 July. They strode through the driftwood and deer horns on the beach and scaled a modest eminence to find out if there were any passages through the ice to the east and northeast. The mainland was only less spectacular here, with its far mountain slopes gentler than those of Prince Charles Island or north Spitsbergen, but the faces of the cliffs fell sheer to the sea and seemed to have been gouged by the successive strokes of some giant being. Nor did the vista north and east bring any hope, for the sea was 'entirely frozen over, not like the ice we had hitherto coasted, but a flat even surface, as far as the eye could reach, which was undoubtedly ten leagues at least'. The weather was clear but cold, and Horace's gig, if such it was, faced a hard return trip. The ice was closing the narrow watercourses and sometimes the men had to haul the boat from one to the other.[16]

In fact, it was at this time that the ships became locked fast between the Seven Islands and North East Land, about latitude eighty degrees and thirty-seven minutes. They sat motionless, imprisoned at their moorings by the thickening pack ice, the *Racehorse* some two ship lengths in front of the *Carcass*, while all around them stretched a forbidding, low, flat, empty landscape broken by the small mounds of ice being pushed up by the relentless pressure from below. Sometimes the boats struggled along briefly navigable channels, but more often they were dragged over the ice in watering expeditions, when the men dug pits in the snow and waited for them to fill. At other times the best the crews could do was to exercise on the ice, forming lines to play leapfrog.

There were unwelcome visitors, too. About the morning of 1 August a large polar bear approached the ships across the ice, attracted by the smell of cooking, but it fell to musket fire from the *Racehorse*. A more wanton incident occurred four days later. For no better reason than apparent sport, a boat crew under Lieutenant Pennington of the *Carcass* had slaughtered a walrus and burned its body on the ice not far from the ships. Early on 5 August a female bear and two partly grown cubs arrived, attempting to salvage something from the remains. All three were shot dead by men on the *Carcass*, and the skin of the parent was found to measure six feet nine inches from head to tail.

By far the most famous such episode had occurred the previous morning. At the time it was considered a minor incident, and earned far less attention than the other encounters with polar bears; in fact, only one of ten logs or diaries of the expedition refers to it at all, and that only briefly. But legend would magnify the event in literature and art until it became the most famous of all the stories about the young Nelson. In the years that followed the admiral's death the publishers of popular prints eagerly pounced upon it. As early as February 1806 a plate, graphically depicting a confrontation between a boy, armed with a musket and cutlass, and a bear, was issued under the title, 'Youthful Intrepidity/Young Nelson's Attack and Chase After a Bear'. A rival print appeared two years later, and in 1809 Clarke and McArthur's official biography reproduced, and consequently endorsed, the most familiar representation of them all by Richard Westall. And that was how the story was remembered, dramatic but grossly distorted: a diminutive but grim-faced youngster, standing toe to toe with a ferocious polar bear, and wielding the butt of his useless musket in an effort to down the beast. Even today the altercation between Midshipman Nelson and the bear is repeatedly presented as indisputable proof of sterling courage and enterprise.[17]

But what really happened on that 4 August? If the popular perception of the incident was an accurate one, why did Horace himself, always willing to advertise his bravery, make no reference to it, either in the brief memorandum of his services written in about 1796 or in the much longer 'Sketch of My Life' produced three years later? As far as we know, Nelson gave no account of the skirmish, and our knowledge of it depends upon two stories told long afterwards by Captain Lutwidge, one version somewhat different than the other.

The one contemporary allusion to Nelson's brush with the bear occurs in a log written by Master James Allen of the *Carcass*. From it we can deduce that the encounter took place south of the largest of the Seven Islands, where the ships were held by the ice and fanned by light, pleasant breezes. At about six in the morning 'a bear came close to the ship on the ice, but on the people's going towards him he went away'. There seems to have been nothing particularly heroic to record. The bear simply fled at the approach of members of the crew and no more was said about the incident. Neither Nelson nor anyone else was named.[18]

What seems to have been Lutwidge's first account of the incident was published in a sketch of Nelson in 1800. It illuminates the beggarly reference in the Allen log, but remains entirely compatible with it:

As a proof of that cool intrepidity which our young mariner possessed . . . the following anecdote is preserved by an officer [Lutwidge] who was present. In these high northern latitudes the nights are generally clear. During one of them, notwithstanding the extreme bitterness of the cold, young Nelson was missing. Every search that was instantly made in quest of him was in vain, and it was at length imagined he was lost. When lo! As the rays of the rising sun opened the distant horizon, to the great astonishment of his messmates, he was discerned at a considerable distance on the ice, armed with a single musket, in anxious pursuit of an immense bear. The lock of the musket being injured, the piece would not go off, and he had therefore pursued the animal in hopes of tiring him, and being at length able to effect his purpose with the butt end. On his return Captain Lutwidge reprimanded him for leaving the ship without leave, and in a severe tone demanded what motive could possibly induce him to undertake so rash an action. The young hero with great simplicity replied, 'I wished, Sir, to get the skin for my father.'[19]

In this version, Horatio merely pursues the bear, which evidently ran away leaving the boy to return empty-handed. It exaggerated his intrepidity by implying that he pursued the bear alone, but even so Nelson unquestionably emerges from the incident as a youth of uncommon pluck and initiative. It was this version which Nelson's earliest biographers, John Charnock, James Harrison and Francis William Blagdon, substantially reproduced, though Charnock changed the wording but not the meaning of the young midshipman's reply to his captain, and Blagdon added fantasies of his own. His story of the boy slaughtering the bear with a gun butt and dirk exceeds all credibility.

However, the public waited until 1809, four years after the admiral's death, for the most elaborate and famous account of the incident, furnished by Clarke and McArthur, the editors of the *Naval Chronicle* who had published the original version of the story. Revamping the episode for their biography of the naval hero, Clarke and McArthur apparently went back to Admiral Lutwidge for a fuller account of the incident, and he complied, looking, however, through a fading backward lens that flitted in and out of focus. 'Among the gentlemen on the quarter-deck of the *Carcass*, who were not rated midshipmen, there was, besides young Nelson, a daring shipmate of his, to whom he had become attached', ran the new narrative. But even that was wrong, for both Nelson and Hughes – if Hughes it was – *had* been midshipmen in the *Carcass*.

One night, during the middle watch, Lutwidge now said, Nelson and his companion stole off in the clear night, using the haze of an approaching fog to avoid being seen. Armed with a rusty musket, Nelson led the way, crossing 'the frightful chasms in the ice' and making towards a large polar bear he had seen from the ship.

By this time the audacious pair had been missed, and Lutwidge grew concerned lest they got lost in the thickening fog. However, between three and four in the morning the mist began to disperse, and the hunters were seen at a considerable distance from the ship attacking the bear. The signal gun to return was fired, and Nelson's companion urged his leader to obey. However, the other tenaciously pursued his object. His musket flashed in the pan and his ammunition was spent, but he proclaimed, 'Never mind, do but let me get a blow at this devil with the butt-end of my musket, and we shall have him!' If it had not been for a fissure in the ice between Nelson and the bear, the boy would have been in difficulties. As it was, Nelson's companion retreated to the ship and Lutwidge fired a cannon to frighten the bear away. Later the captain reprimanded the fretful youngster. Nelson began 'pouting his lip, as he was wont to do when agitated' and replied, 'Sir, I wished to kill the bear that I might carry its skin to my father.'[20]

The problems of this account are obvious. One might ask how Lutwidge knew what Nelson had said to his companion when confronted by the bear, or whether he would even have remembered it after so long. But the principal weaknesses in the account are its implications that Nelson got close to his prey, that far from retiring the bear was ready to attack its assailant, and that it only fled at the sound of artillery fire from the ship. In short, this version magnified the danger faced by the young hero. And not even this was enough, for Westall's painting, which accompanied Clarke and McArthur's new account, went further still, removing the life-saving chasm in the ice that had divided the combatants and placing them merely inches apart. Such is the thirst for exaggeration.

4

Back in August 1773 there were real problems to face. If the ships could not be freed the alternatives were stark. The men might stay aboard, hoping for a change in conditions, but even if the ships were not crushed by the ice, provisions would run out and all would surely perish at the onset of winter. Alternatively, they could abandon the ships and haul the boats to clear water, but the prospect of surviving a journey in open boats through those climates was hardly strong.

On 3 August, Phipps suppressed such fears and set the men to cutting a passage for the ships, furiously hacking at the ice with axes and saws. It was too thick, twelve feet in places, and a day of strenuous effort yielded little result. Worse, although they worked the ships almost three hundred yards westwards, the ice was moving with the current and carrying them in the opposite direction, east and northeast towards Spitsbergen. Phipps sombrely pondered the possibility that his ships might be drawn inshore and broken on the rocks even before their timbers caved in before the pressure of the ice. Soundings were already indicating that the water below was becoming shallower.

Phipps knew that the short summer season was ending, and whatever decision he made needed to be taken quickly. On 6 August pilots whom Phipps had sent to reconnoitre westwards reported clear water five leagues away. The commodore made up his mind. He would abandon the ships, haul the launches to the open water and try to get to Hakluyt's Headland at the northeastern extremity of Spitsbergen, where they might be lucky enough to encounter Dutch ships leaving the whaling grounds for the winter. At a grim meeting with his officers Phipps gave his orders. The boats would have to be hoisted on the ice, and coverings fitted above the gunnels of the launches to combat wet and cold. Some provisions had to be boiled for storage in the boats and each man was to fill a canvas bag with twenty-five to thirty pounds of bread. No inessentials were permitted and the only clothes allowed were those the men stood up in.

Feverish activity ensued as the crews of the ships readied themselves for what was transparently a desperate measure. On the *Racehorse*, Midshipman Floyd put on two shirts, two waistcoats, two pairs of breeches, four pairs of stockings, boots, and a woollen cap beneath his hat, and packed a comb, razor, pocket book, pistol and precious journal, along with the musket and cartouche box allowed each man. Aboard the *Carcass* the youngest member of the expedition was at similar work, but even at this pass, Horace was awake to every opportunity. 'When the boats were fitted out to quit the two ships blocked up in the ice,' he recalled, 'I exerted myself to have command of a four-oared cutter . . . which was given me, with twelve men; and I prided myself in fancying I could navigate her better than any other boat in the ship.'[21]

The hauling started on 7 August. Fifty men from each ship were harnessed in long lines to their launches, which they heaved westwards over the jagged field of ice, one line competing lustily with the other. Phipps himself sweated with the *Racehorse*'s men, while Lutwidge remained aboard his ship, attempting to move the vessels forward as best he could, just in case the conditions swung in their favour. Horace might have struggled in the *Carcass* line, but it is unlikely. Physically, he was the weakest member of the crew, hardly suited to exhausting man-hauling, and as we have seen he had been given a special responsibility for the ship's cutter. The master, James Allen, recorded that the *Carcass* line consisted of the second and third lieutenants, two master's mates (Joshua Mulock and James Gee Burges), four midshipmen and forty-two men, and it seems highly probable that young Nelson was the missing midshipman employed elsewhere.[22]

Six hard hours and a mile later the men returned to the ships to eat and rest, but they were back with the launches early the following morning, sucking a thick fog into their lungs with every cruel breath. But then their luck changed. Aboard the ships, some four miles behind the launches, movements in the ice were detected. 'Rending and cracking with a tremendous noise', it changed direction with the current and started moving the ships westwards, towards the launches and open water. Once again, the deliverance seemed Heaven sent. 'Every officer and every idler on board laboured now for life,' wrote one diarist. Sails were spread, and anchors, poles, axes and saws joined the battle to push the ships through the shattering ice pack. Soon those men out ahead, straining with the launches, abandoned their task and streamed back to the ships, overwhelmed by their sudden reprieve. 'It is impossible to conceive the joy which, like wildfire, spread throughout the ship at this news,' Floyd wrote.[23]

In a day or two the vessels had bulldozed their way through the ice, overtaken and reclaimed their launches and got underway, liberating themselves with relatively little damage. They made Smeerenberg harbour on 11 August, where they sat recuperating with four Dutch whalers. During his few days there, Horace took his cutter out to make soundings but found time to admire the huge three hundred-foot-high glacier at Fair Haven, shining 'light green' in the sunlight, and sparkling with the water cascading down its face.[24]

On 19 August the ships put to sea again but the general situation had not improved. A barrier of ice extended through more than twenty degrees of longitude in the latitude of about eighty degrees north, and there was no way through it. Finally, on the 22nd, with the season rapidly closing, Phipps admitted defeat and headed for home.

Considering their privations the ships were still in respectable shape, although the *Carcass* was indisputably the less manageable of the two vessels, and the men of the *Racehorse* cursed her 'dull sailing'. Lutwidge had occasionally to lower his boats to help her manoeuvre, and Nelson may have been in charge of the cutter when it helped tow the *Carcass* clear of its consort on 24 August. The boy may have assumed the worst of the voyage was over as the polar seas heaved astern, but he was roughly awakened by a tempest that enclosed them on the evening of 10 September, some twenty leagues from the coast of Norway in latitude fifty-seven degrees and thirty eight minutes. Indeed, it was as savage a storm as Horace had ever endured.

The winds strengthened after the ships passed the Shetland Islands and entered the North Sea on the last leg of their journey home. For a while they briskly blew the vessels forward, but 8 September was a gloomier day and the winds less dependable. When the storm broke two days later it was ferocious, sluicing the cleared decks and ripping at the ropes that secured the small boats. 'It blew as hard almost as we thought it well could,' remarked Floyd from the sea-tossed *Racehorse*, and the waves 'tumbled in upon us exceedingly', rising so high that the *Carcass* was blotted from sight. The people on both ships feared the other had gone to the bottom. The main deck of the *Carcass* continually rolled beneath sheets of water, and when the storm slackened in the earlier part of the 11th and the battered ships struggled to repair their wounds they were still separated.[25]

The respite was brief, however. Late that same day a sudden clap of thunder heralded a fresh attack, and by midnight 'the sea [was] making a free passage' over the *Carcass*. Provisions, casks lashed to the deck, spars and booms were taken over the side, and the launch was scuttled and shoved overboard to relieve the ship. Men laboured to take in sail aloft, tie themselves down or keep their feet on careering decks awash with sea water. The carpenter Abraham Purcell, who was trying to secure hatches and stores, was swept both out of and into the ship by different waves, and a mate and a foretopman also went overboard. The gale eased at ten o'clock on 12 September, and the sails were reset, but it had been a close thing. The *Carcass* was 'almost waterlogged from the weight of water on her decks'.[26]

Meanwhile, the *Racehorse* too had survived the latest onslaught, though 'everybody agreed that they had never been but once in so great a tempest'. Two guns were jettisoned, three boats lost and the ship was thrown upon its side several times. When the seas subsided and the winds fell on the 13th the sailors of both ships, weary and wasted from constant battle, looked for a haven.[27]

For Midshipman Nelson, the man in the making, some of the sights that now opened before him must have been welcome reminders of the boy he had been not so very long ago. To starboard of the *Carcass* the beautiful Norfolk coast slid by. Cromer lighthouse blinked in the distance on 18 September, and the next day the ship put into Yarmouth. They remained a few days waiting for a suitable wind, repairing the

ship and replenishing stores, and acquaintances of Nelson may have
been among the several visitors who travelled from Norwich to come
aboard.

There was still no word of Phipps. Lutwidge had orders to proceed
to the Nore in the event of a separation, but he feared that Phipps
had drowned and wrote to the Admiralty notifying them of his return.
On the 23rd the *Carcass* was compelled to resume its voyage without
any further news of the commodore, but three days later her crew
were greatly relieved to find the *Racehorse* in Harwich harbour. The
adventure was now thoroughly over, and another week took Lutwidge
to Deptford, where he moored his ship alongside a sheer-hulk and left
her for a complete overhaul.

The expedition had not reached the North Pole. It did not even
convince every party that the Northeast Passage was mythical or at
least unnavigable, but it had been a creditable performance nevertheless, and reflected favourably upon all concerned. The camaraderie,
forged in peril, was warm and infectious, and when the ships were
paid off on 14 October First Lieutenant John Baird was almost mobbed
by the men who even wanted to strip off their shirts to lay them at
Baird's feet so that his shoes should not be dirtied as he withdrew to
his coach. Sadly, talented though he was, Baird had little 'interest' in
the service and never reached that elusive captain's list. Nor did
Horace's friend, Robert Hughes, who transferred to the *Dublin*. He
sailed on six other ships before passing his examination for lieutenant
in 1780, but evidently died the same year, just after his commission
was confirmed.[28]

Horatio Nelson had been greatly enriched by the experience, and
imbibed lessons in seamanship, resourcefulness and resolution. He had
grown in confidence, ability and enthusiasm for new challenges. After
all, he had filled a man's place, asked no favours, and won the respect
of picked men. Nelson took away not only the continuing goodwill
of Phipps and Lutwidge, but also one of the silver pocket watches
inscribed with the words, 'for strict attention to duty with H.M.S.
Racehorse. North Pole Expedition 1772.' Every time he looked at the
watch it told him more than the time. It told him he had met a difficult
job head-on and shaped up.[29]

On 14 October he received £8. 2s. 2d. in wages, after various deductions totalling 10s. 4d., and the next day rejoined the old *Triumph*
moored at Blackstakes. Captain Suckling still commanded, and immediately put his nephew's name back on the ship's books with the rating

of captain's servant. The ship moved to Chatham on 20 October, but now Horace left her for good. On 26 October he was discharged to the *Seahorse*, bound with new shipmates for new climes, and the long voyage around the Cape of Good Hope to the East Indies.[30]

Once again, it seems, Captain Suckling had found just the right situation to further his nephew's progress in the service.

V

EAST INDIES ADVENTURE

Blake and Rooke, and Vernon near him
  Crown'd with glory's laurel wreath,
Chase despairing thoughts, and cheer him
  On to victory or death.
Like a giant from his slumber,
  Swift he starts, with freshen'd soul;
'Yes – among that sainted number
  Nelson shall his name enrol!'
H. L. Torre, *Nelson's Vision*

1

ONE thing is certain. For all its rigours, the Arctic voyage had left Horace's appetite for adventure unscathed. Stimulated by his personal success on the polar expedition, his eyes sparkled when his uncle told him about the two ships fitting out for the East Indies.

The twenty-four-gun *Seahorse* was one of them, a primitive frigate launched in 1748, with a lower deck 112 feet long and a beam or width of thirty-two. Her captain was George Farmer. Farmer's progress in the service had been steady despite misadventures. A lieutenant the year after Nelson was born, he had stepped up to commander in 1768 and taken the *Swift* sloop to the South Atlantic the following year. The assignment was not a particularly fortunate one, for in 1770 he was wrecked upon the Patagonian coast. Farmer struggled ashore with his crew, and within a month was rescued by another sloop, but in the ensuing June it was he who surrendered Port Egmont in the Falkland Islands to the Spanish and prompted the crisis that gave

Captain Suckling the *Raisonable*. Still, back in England Farmer was exonerated and promoted to post-captain in January 1771, while not yet forty. He was appointed first to the *Launceston* and then to the *Seahorse*.

Farmer was another of Captain Suckling's friends. Indeed, he had been a midshipman on Suckling's *Dreadnought* in the West Indies and owed him favours. Moreover, although Farmer's roots were in Northamptonshire and Ireland, he had spent several years in the impress service in Norfolk, recruiting for the navy, and living at Facolneston, near Wymondham. It was not until the August and September of 1773, when the *Seahorse* was being prepared, that he moved to Sussex. Most probably Farmer and Suckling, both naval officers based in East Anglia, had seen much of each other over the years.[1]

The *Seahorse* gave Farmer means of patronage, with places available to family and such useful friends as Captain Suckling. His son, George William Farmer, was entered on the ship's books as captain's servant. However, though George was seventeen and entirely capable of sailing, he remained at home when the *Seahorse* left England, leaving the books to provide him with an entirely fictional career as a midshipman and able seaman. It was fraud, if fraud of a type common to the service. Someone, perhaps Farmer or officers who authenticated his books, collected the wages the absentee was supposed to be earning, while young George gained years of valuable sea time without ever quitting terra firma. As for Nelson, Captain Farmer was quite willing to oblige Suckling and take him aboard, and the youth was accordingly rated midshipman of the *Seahorse* on 27 October 1773. He was fifteen, but the muster made it eighteen, compounding the misstatements about his age in the books of the *Carcass*.[2]

Since there was no knowing how long a ship might remain on a station as remote as the Far East, Captain Suckling searched for another reliable officer who might share with Farmer the job of looking after his nephew. Supervising affairs in the Medway and the Nore had given Suckling new contacts through the office of the Navy Board, the department responsible for governing dockyards, building and maintaining ships and appointing warrant officers such as masters, pursers and surgeons. It was to one of these contacts, Samuel Bentham, the naval architect and brother of the philosopher Jeremy Bentham, that the captain now turned. Thus, on 28 October, Bentham addressed a short letter to a certain Mr Kee. He understood that Kee was agent for

Thomas Surridge, who had just been appointed master of the *Seahorse*, and asked him to draw his client's notice to young Horatio Nelson, destined to join that ship at Spithead. 'The master is a necessary man for a young lad to be introduced to,' opined Bentham. It was, it transpired, a fortunate choice, for Surridge was a protector and role model of outstanding ability.[3]

Both were needed because the *Seahorse* was not the happiest ship.

Nelson was good at winning friends among peers and seniors alike. He recalled many with affection in later years, and if he encountered meanness of spirit or incompetence in his travels, he seems to have thought them best buried with the past. He spoke well of his chosen profession, for all its faults. Reading the piece of autobiography he produced in 1799, one is struck by a service abundantly supplied with capable, responsible, and well-meaning officers. The original tapestry, it has to be said, was of a richer weave.

His fellow 'young gentlemen' presented the usual variety. Most of the midshipmen who worked with him on the *Seahorse* were older than he was. There was James Gardiner, William Sullivan of Greenwich, Richard James and Henry Darracott, both from Plymouth, the West Indian Charles Burt, and George Hicks of Norwich, all entered on the books as eighteen or nineteen years of age. James, Burt and Darracott would eventually become lieutenants, but none reached 'post' rank. Richard Lodington of Plymouth, another fellow midshipman, was considerably older at twenty-six.

Thomas Troubridge and Thomas Hoare were also mustered as eighteen-year-old recruits and became special friends. Troubridge was the son of Richard Troubridge of London, and exchanged stories of the merchant service with Horace. Originally rated an able seaman, he replaced Gardiner as a midshipman when the latter quit the ship in March 1774, and remained in the *Seahorse* until 1780, long after Horace had been invalided home. We will encounter him often in these pages. Thomas Hoare, who later took the surname Bertie, served as master's mate and able seaman before succeeding Horace as midshipman on 14 March 1776. He would eventually get his commission in 1778 and die a full admiral in 1825.[4]

Horace discovered other kindred spirits on the *Seahorse*'s consort, the fifty-gun *Salisbury*, captained by George Robinson Walters. She flew the broad pendant of Commodore Edward Hughes, an able officer who was being sent to command the small naval squadron in the East Indies. Commodore Hughes 'always' showed Nelson 'the greatest kindness', but the youth developed a remarkable rapport with one of his inferior officers, Charles Pole. A Devon lad, Pole was the great grandson of a baronet and one of the rare graduates of the Portsmouth Naval Academy.[5]

Nelson was fifteen when he stepped on board the *Seahorse* for the first time, and approaching eighteen when malaria forced him home. He spent impressionable years on the ship and it is surprising that biographers have had so little to say about them. Horace enjoyed his East Indian service and often but vainly contemplated a happy return to those waters. He learned a great deal about managing and navigating ships there, enjoyed a feast of new experiences, made valuable friendships and saw hostile action for the first time. However, it was also a time of shadows, closed by serious illness and marred by disturbing social relationships on board. In Captain Farmer, Nelson had his first inadequate commander and met some of the dangers of weak leadership.[6]

2

The *Salisbury* and *Seahorse* were bound upon a protracted service. The East Indies was the furthest station maintained by the Royal Navy and those assigned to it could expect to be parted from homes and families for a long period. As usual when sustained hardship was anticipated, the Admiralty made special provision. Once again portable soup was supplied, ready for twice-weekly servings with peas on the haul across the Indian Ocean, and Irving's equipment for distilling salt water reappeared, this time reinforced by Osbridge's machine for sweetening water. While the ships waited for fair sailing weather – the longboat of the *Seahorse* was overturned by rough water in Spithead harbour, losing boat hooks, oars and spars – the men were also treated to two months' pay in advance, distributed by naval commissioner James Gambier on the afternoon of 6 November. Horace found, no doubt ruefully, that his pay totalled £4 11s. 6d., but that deductions for the Chatham Chest and Greenwich Hospital, both in aid of sick, injured or aged seamen, left just £2 5s. od. for himself.[7]

Finally, on the morning of 19 November 1773, the ships put to sea, using small boats to help tow them out of harbour. There was an uncertain start. When Captain Farmer fired a thirteen-gun salute in honour of the commodore's broad pendant, the wads were blown out of two of the cannons and carried away the *Seahorse*'s lower fore studding sails. Nevertheless, they were soon underway and making an uneventful voyage towards the Cape of Good Hope.

At Funchal road in Madeira there was a major provisioning stop early in December. Two hundred and nine gallons of the *Seahorse*'s beer were found to have gone 'calm, sour and stinking', but they were able to replenish with water, wine and a few provisions before sailing on 11 December. Captain Farmer had kept his people in excellent health. 'I think it worthy [of] remarking that the ship's company has been remarkably healthy since we sailed,' Surridge wrote in his log for 13 January, 'and this day when we crossed the Equator there was but three men on the sick list with slight complaints.'[8]

Mr Surridge, the ship's master, to whom Nelson had been referred before sailing, was ubiquitous on board. There was only one lieutenant, James Francis Edward Drummond, so Surridge commanded a watch, in addition to handling and navigating the ship and instructing the 'young gentlemen' in the mysteries of mathematics and setting a course. He was, as Horace quickly discerned, no common man. A master was a warrant officer, appointed by the Navy Board rather than the Admiralty, and though his position was an important one and he took station with the lieutenants he lacked their status, for they and their superiors held the king's commission from the Admiralty. Masters were often from the lower middling classes, with clerking or shopkeeping backgrounds, normally short of the social connections of the commissioned officers but possessing the rudiments of education. Occasionally men of remarkable talent emerged from the ranks of the masters. The most famous was the explorer James Cook, whose people were hardy hill farmers, but Thomas Surridge, the mentor of Nelson, almost deserves mentioning in the same breath. Like Cook, Surridge used sheer ability to switch to the commissioned officer ladder, and remarkably he not only made lieutenant but eventually became a vice admiral in 1819.

He was still young when he fashioned Nelson into a fully-fledged seaman. Born about 1747, Thomas Surridge was an Irishman from Passage, near Waterford. He had joined the navy in December 1769, enlisting as able seaman and yeoman of the powder room on the *Tweed* frigate at Spithead. Richard Surridge, a sixty-two-year-old clerk aboard the *Tweed*, and said to have been from 'Donmore' in Galway, was probably his father or uncle. No doubt it was to reward the elder Surridge's loyalty that Captain George Collier advanced the boy to midshipman and master's mate. James Irving was master of the *Tweed*, and it was from him that Thomas learned the basics of navigation, but Collier himself may have been an influence, for he was an exceptional naval officer, skilled in languages and interested in astronomy, surveying and writing. Young Surridge followed Collier to the *Levant* and *Rainbow*, and also sailed under Captains Samuel Thompson, Richard Collins and Richard Onslow. His appointment to the *Seahorse* followed ten months as master of the *Achilles*.[9]

Surridge taught Nelson navigation and seamanship, and there were few better able to do so. The lessons stuck. Fifteen years later the pupil advised Commodore William Cornwallis, who had been appointed to the East Indies, that Mr Surridge 'was a very clever man, and we constantly took the lunar observations'. Nelson suggested Cornwallis consult Surridge's log, and had 'no doubt' that it would be found the 'best of any in the Navy Office'. Obviously Surridge impressed the pliable young man, but the respect was mutual. Years later Surridge remembered Nelson as 'a boy with a florid countenance, rather stout [strong] and athletic', and fired by 'ardent ambition'. He was a good scholar and during his spell on the *Seahorse* got a thorough grounding in all necessary nautical skills and arts.[10]

With Surridge at his elbow Horace and the other juniors learned how to make lunar observations against a fixed star, using a quadrant or sextant, and then to turn them into Greenwich time through a process of spherical trigonometry. A comparison of the result with local time, ascertained from routine observations, gave an estimate of the ship's longitude. Each day the readings were carefully entered into the logs, often in Surridge's own sloping hand, with illuminating remarks that testified to the pride he took in the work. 'The observation this day,' he wrote on 17 January 1774, 'is seventeen miles to the southward of the reckoning, and as we have not had an opportunity of trying the current, I suppose it must set strong to the south ward.' The master also had his students testing Foxon's hydrometer, a new navigational device the Admiralty wanted to evaluate, but they found it gave very different results from those produced by orthodox practices. It measured sixteen miles short over a trial of 193 miles towards the Cape.[11]

It was as the ship forged southwards from Madeira with young Nelson garnering wisdom from Mr Surridge that the first difficulties occurred.

Some one hundred and thirty men and boys made their homes on the *Seahorse*, less than half the number manning the *Salisbury*, but necessarily shoulder to shoulder all the same. Many of the men slung their hammocks in cramped, uncomfortable spaces only big enough to accommodate them when one watch was up and about, and they messed eight to twelve at a table. There was little or no privacy. Yet these men lived with each other month after month, and sometimes year upon year, working as a team. Indeed, their lives depended upon it, for neither the sea nor the enemy forgave easily. Every man depended upon the others, and a failing in one became a failing in all. Whether one of the top men out on a yard to reef a sail in ferocious conditions, with nothing but a foot rope between him and eternity; a member of a gun crew with an allotted part in the complicated manhandling and firing of huge pieces of artillery amidst the carnage of battle; or one of a gang laboriously extricating the heavy and obdurate anchor cable from the bitts, each had to synchronise movement and work with precision. There were no facilities for rehabilitating slackers or malcontents, or for providing them with time out on a working man-of-war. If the efficiency and safety of the ship, and all aboard her, were to be preserved it was necessary for men and boys to shape up fast.

Those who threatened the equilibrium of a crew, impairing its efficiency or damaging its cohesion, were far from popular. Antisocial activities such as quarrelling or theft damaged fragile relationships, and a man too drunk, lazy or inattentive to do his duty merely increased the heavy burdens on his fellows, who had to make good the deficiency. Most men accepted that a degree of disciplinary violence was necessary to the wellbeing of the crew as a whole and expected a good captain to provide it. As long as it was justly administered and measured in its severity, they regarded it as an inevitable if bloody deterrent to undesirable and dangerous behaviour.

Captains enjoined loyalty at all times. They regularly had the Articles of War read to the ship's company, reminding them of the penalties of disaffection, as well as a portion of an act of parliament for the encouragement of seamen in the Royal Navy. The endless gun salutes commemorating the king's birthday, his accession and coronation, and such notable events in royal history as the foiling of the Gunpowder Plot, the restoration of Charles II and the landing of William of Orange, also emphasised the connection between obedience, duty and patriotism. Equally, all captains flogged substantial offenders.

During his twenty-nine months with the *Seahorse* Horace saw eighty-eight floggings on board, but most of them (87.5 per cent) consisted of the token twelve lashes. On one occasion a mere six lashes were administered, which suggests that mitigating circumstances were weighed, and rather more often severe offences earned twenty-four lashes. The majority of floggings concerned a minority of difficult men. Forty-eight (54.5 per cent) were inflicted on just ten individuals, such men as the marine Thomas Harrington, an incorrigible thief and shirker, who received 204 lashes in twelve floggings, and a seaman named John Clark, who ran up a total of seventy-two lashes covering drunkenness, theft and neglect of duty. Among other offences punished by flogging were disobedience, fighting, and being absent without leave.[12]

There is no evidence that the official violence on board the *Seahorse* raised any eyebrows, but unfortunately an undercurrent of bullying was developing. The trouble was Lieutenant Drummond. His commission was two years old but he had a weak grasp of the responsibilities of command. Drink betrayed him first. One day he came to relieve Surridge on watch, 'reeling about the deck' in an inebriated condition. When the master refused to surrender the watch, Drummond tottered back to his cot and could not be roused hours later. Nelson, who would never be a heavy drinker and was rarely intoxicated, may have learned that duty and drink made poor shipmates on this voyage in the *Seahorse*. Even when Drummond took his watches, he was sometimes semiconscious, and slumped on the arms chest swaddled in his boat cloak, oblivious of whatever danger might threaten the ship. At other times he was livelier, but to no advantage. On one occasion he sent his servant to bring a bottle to the quarterdeck, and distributed drink to the inferior officers, including the 'young gentlemen' unfortunate enough to be assigned to his watch. Then, calling for a fiddler to strike up a tune, he commanded his company to dance. A mate, John Murray, seized the lieutenant by the coat to warn him that the commodore might hear the ruckus from the *Salisbury*, and eventually dismissed the servant to avoid further damage.[13]

No less disturbing were rumours of gratuitous brutality. Farmer himself may have set the pattern, for according to Murray the captain once urged him to 'beat the scoundrels all round' in order to get the topsails hoisted faster. If so, it was an appalling example to set before the likes of Drummond. One day a seaman reported to the sick bay complaining of bleeding in an ear. Though the surgeon, John Bullen, could find nothing amiss upon examination, he was perturbed to hear that Drummond had beaten the sailor about the head with the end of a rope.

The lieutenant's litany of misdemeanours expanded to include insubordination. Somehow he had an entirely mistaken view that when officer of the watch he had the right to issue every order given on board. The captain directly ordered a ladder to be 'shipped up' during Drummond's watch one day, but the lieutenant had it brought down again because the order had not been given through him. Shortly thereafter Farmer tramped up from his cabin and ascertained what had happened. He exchanged words with Drummond but failed to impose authority.

Almost inevitably the breach widened. The ships reached Table Bay at Cape Town on 3 March 1774. They had survived some punishing weather, and the *Seahorse* needed a new mizzen mast as well as supplies. Working into the bay to join five Dutch and French East Indiamen sheltering there, Farmer lost his longboat, which was swept under the *Seahorse*'s stern as she was turning her bow into the teeth of a strong gale. Capsizing with the loss of two men, the boat's fate reaffirmed the old lesson that at sea, even entering a haven, danger and death were never far away. But instead of reinforcing the importance of cooperation, the stay at the Cape merely drove the captain and his first lieutenant further apart.

Words between the two grew so heated that Farmer threatened to report Drummond to Commodore Hughes. The lieutenant declared 'he did not care a pin who he complained to' for 'he [Drummond] was first lieutenant of the ship and would be so'. Unwisely Farmer faltered and dropped the matter, and when he spoke to Hughes it was only to request the services of a second lieutenant. At the back of Farmer's mind was Drummond's inability to perform satisfactorily, but he did not say so, and when the commodore inspected the *Seahorse* the case the captain made for additional help was simply a general one. Hughes was amenable, nonetheless. He promoted an able seaman, Samuel Abson, to the post of second lieutenant of the *Seahorse* on 6 January 1774. Abson seems to have been an adequate officer because he got command of the *Swallow* in February 1776, but his career was cut short when he drowned two years later.[14]

Allowing his threat against Drummond to lapse, Farmer hoped his difficulties would go away, or maybe that Drummond would mature in time. But he merely advertised his own weakness and encouraged waywardness. There was more trouble ahead.

3

The long passage across the Indian Ocean began on 23 March, when the ships left Table Bay. They took what was known as the 'outward' course, proceeding eastwards to the islands of Amsterdam and St Paul before turning north towards India, rather than by way of Madagascar. For a boy the trip had many fascinations. Horace saw the great guns exercised regularly, and men fish for sharks, and on 5 April he was rated able seaman and sent to watch from the foretop. The reason for this is not clear, but the weather had got squally and gusty again, and there was much to be done aloft. Visibility was often poor, and the day before Nelson got his fresh rating the ships had lost sight of each other in gales and had to use signal fires and guns to keep in touch. Conceivably Farmer decided new eyes were needed above.

Horace, it seems, belonged to what was called the larboard watch, kept originally by Mr Surridge and perhaps now also by Lieutenant Abson. If so he was fortunate, for the starboard watch was in the hands of Lieutenant Drummond, and on that steamy leg between the Cape and Madras it sank into greater disrepute.

The bullying climaxed with a disgraceful attack upon a seaman, Thomas Muckle. He was supposed to have been in the tops with the 'young gentlemen' but for some reason went missing. A fuming Drummond sent the boatswain's mates to find the absentee and haul him onto the quarterdeck, where he was evidently beaten with the end of a rope. Exactly what happened depends on the version preferred, but the chastised Muckle hurried up the main shrouds, either fleeing in fear of his life or merely returning to duty. According to one account he was encouraged to climb by blows aimed at his toes. However, before completing his ascent the unhappy miscreant was summoned back down. If we may believe the testimony of Bullen, the surgeon, Muckle was then struck in the face until he fell to the deck, where Drummond kicked him once or twice as he lay helpless. Though sent up to the top again, and told to climb in silence, the sailor reported to the sick bay the next day. His shoulders were bruised, his face swollen, one eye was inflamed and he complained of a pain in his side.

The best relationships between captains and crews were partnerships. In return for the loyalty and industry of the men, the good captain offered protection. As far as he was able, he ensured the crew got fair treatment, and he was prepared to intervene with superiors and naval authorities to secure the payment of wages or prize money owed, or to assist the injured get necessary compensation. Many captains took these obligations extremely seriously and amassed considerable followings among their men, followings that went with them from ship to ship. But conversely, captains who disappointed their men attracted little support and found their standing and authority undermined.

While crews accepted a measure of corporal punishment, they quickly turned against officers who perpetrated or condoned gratuitous brutality. We cannot say how Farmer stood with his men, but he had failed to protect at least one of them from an incompetent lieutenant. It seems that the captain learned of Drummond's excesses and summoned him, Surridge and probably Abson into his cabin to declare that he would not suffer an officer to strike the men.

It was not the issue that finally prompted him to act decisively, however. That occurred on the evening of 19 April, some time in Drummond's dogwatch between the hours of four and six in the afternoon. The quarterdeck was crowded with inferior officers, while others, including Lodington, one of Nelson's companions, were working on a damaged main mast. Farmer wanted the fore-topgallant sail set to catch more wind and ordered Murray, the mate, to see to it. Drummond, still labouring under the misapprehension that all orders had to pass through himself, protested in public, and the captain and lieutenant went head to head before an astonished audience. Farmer said he would order Drummond below, to which the irate lieutenant replied that the quarterdeck belonged to the king, not Farmer, and as he carried the king's commission none but His Majesty could tell him to leave it. In effect he was denying the captain's right to command. Turning to the embarrassed spectators Farmer could only appeal, 'Gentlemen, is this to be borne?'

But he could no longer prevaricate and reported the incident to Commodore Hughes. There was a swift response from that capable officer. On the evening of 25 April Drummond was arrested and suspended from duty. When the ships eventually reached Madras he was court-martialled on board the *Salisbury* on 30 May. For some reason a charge of inhumanity was deemed unproven; perhaps the court thought that one or two incidents did not warrant a conviction, or that Farmer himself had set a bad example to an inexperienced lieutenant. Anyway, indictments for drunkenness and disobedience were carried and Drummond was dismissed the service – the first officer Nelson saw disgraced in that way.

Unfortunately, Drummond was not an isolated case. A replacement, promoted on 5 June, was sent to the *Seahorse*, but Thomas Henery was little improvement. The same patterns of misbehaviour began to reappear and it is difficult not to believe that Farmer was somehow to blame.

For Horace Nelson, able seaman and sentinel, the gossip about Drummond was merely one facet of a diverse learning experience. He continued to stand by the master's side when the observations were made each day at noon, profiting from Surridge's endless curiosity. As the *Seahorse* bowled northwards under the influence of the southeast trade winds, the master scrupulously pondered the interplay of wind and current. 'This day the current had set the ship nine miles to the Northwest of the reckoning,' he wrote on 6 May, 'and the weather, which before was cloudy with frequent squalls, became serene with very smooth water; and, as the wind continues steady, I suppose we must have advanced into the southwest monsoon.' The next day the ship seemed to be as much as sixteen miles northwest of the reckoning, and Surridge concluded that the current was pushing them westwards of Ceylon, when they were purposing to pass east of it to Madras. He therefore hauled the ship up to get around Ceylon, and put into Madras road on 16 May. We know that young Nelson absorbed these lessons well. Fourteen years later he warned Cornwallis that the Indian Ocean currents in April to June could confound reckonings so much that ships fancying themselves east or north of Ceylon could actually be around about the Maldives, to the southwest, or even on the Malabar coast of India.[15]

Horace found Madras hot, wet and throbbing. It was one of the three principal outposts of the East India Company, the legendary fraternity that still controlled Britain's rich eastern trade in Indian cottons, muslins, tea and oriental spices. The company was mired in debts and peculation, propped up by loans and bedevilled by internal unrest in the subcontinent, but to youngsters such as Nelson, raised on romanticised tales of Clive's victories, it represented fabled wealth and excitement. Certainly sweltering Madras was busy. Ships were plentiful. The *Northumberland* was still there, flying the flag of Rear Admiral Sir Robert Harland, who was waiting to hand the East Indies squadron over to Hughes before heading for England with some of his ships. Others came and went, exchanging salutes as they did so, naval vessels such as the *Buckingham*, *Warwick* and *Dolphin*, and British, Dutch and French Indiamen. Boats rushed here and there shipping supplies or transporting officers to and from meetings with the commodore, and guns from Fort St George, a garrison of the East India Company, and the garden of the Nabob of Arcot added to the constant thunder that heralded the exits and entrances.

The navy had disciplinary matters to resolve. Drummond's career disintegrated in the cabin of the _Salisbury_, while on 3 June the ferocious punishment reserved for serious cases of desertion was meted out to three men of the same ship. To a sinister drumbeat the prisoners were 'flogged around the fleet', rowed from ship to ship to receive twenty-five lashes alongside each. Nelson remembered poor Smith of the _Triumph_, but the two hundred strokes each of these men received exceeded any punishment he had seen.

Before the end of the year Horace met another hazard of the tropical service, disease. Harland left for home on 20 July, and after the _Salisbury_ and the _Seahorse_ had been refitted and provisioned, Hughes took them back to sea with the _Dolphin_. They sailed north to Kedgeree in the Hooghly River in September. There was little of interest there – a few houses, a small sandy bay, and a trio of merchantmen riding at anchor – and sickness increased the discomfort. Two men on the _Seahorse_ died and twenty-three had to be carried ashore to a hospital. On this occasion all the invalids appear to have been retrieved before the ship left for the return journey to Madras on 16 January 1775, but these were climes and conditions to which Europeans were little accustomed and death by disease was a continuing concern.

For the moment Nelson seemed immune. As his teens advanced the frailty of his earliest years diminished, and away from the marshy, damp atmosphere of the Norfolk coast his frame and constitution toughened. With Surridge to turn to in difficulty, and Troubridge and Hoare to share boyish foolishness, these years were good ones for Nelson, if not for British India.

4

The subcontinent was in chaos. The old Moghul empire based on Delhi had collapsed and everywhere resurgent Hindu powers fought over the bones. Bloodshed, murder and intrigue were rife. To protect their trade amidst such turmoil, the East India Company's 'presidencies' at Bombay, Madras and Calcutta were reluctantly drawn into expensive entanglements with various Indian princes, and took direct control of Bengal and part of the Coromandel coast. Particularly worrying to the British were the Mahrattas, who controlled a huge swath of northern and central India, and Haidar Ali, the ruler of Mysore on the Malabar coast south of Goa. The Mahrattas had already expelled the Portuguese from Bassein and the island of Salsette near Bombay, and seemed destined to clash with the troublesome British.

This delicate situation, as well as the possibility of a return of the French humbled by Clive less than twenty years before, kept a small squadron of the Royal Navy on station. It had various duties to fulfil. Hughes himself sailed from Kedgeree to escort transports to Calcutta and to confer with Warren Hastings, the crown's new governor general in Bengal. The *Seahorse* was careened at Kedgeree, heeled over against a frame so that the bottom could be scrubbed clean of barnacles, seaweed and infestation, and then also left, bound on East India Company business. For Horace, who had spent more than four years in a peacetime navy, the assignment brought a new experience – his first taste of battle.

Eighty-nine boxes of company rupees were lowered into the dark hold of the *Seahorse* before Farmer returned to Madras for orders. There the *Seahorse* was instructed to ship the treasure to Bombay on the west coast, and to offer support to its governor and council. There had been talk of a Portuguese expedition leaving Goa to recapture Bassein and Salsette from the Mahrattas. If anything frightened the East India Company more than Hindu princes, it was European rivals, and to pre-empt any Portuguese action the British had seized the disputed areas themselves. Naturally, the Mahrattas were furious and retaliation was expected. The company clamoured for naval protection.[16]

Consequently, the *Seahorse* made its first appearance on the west coast of India, putting into Anjenga road on 15 February 1775, just in time to witness a three hour partial eclipse of the moon. Moving northwards along the coast, they reached latitude nine degrees forty-six minutes, near the southern fringes of the coastal state of Mysore, ruled by Haidar Ali. It was Sunday 19 February, calm but hazy. Captain Farmer's log tells the story of Nelson's first ever skirmish:

At 5 AM weighed and made sail. At 7 saw two sail standing towards us, which we imagined to be Bombay [Company?] cruisers. At 1/2 past 7 they hauled their wind to the southward, and stood after the *Dodley* [a 'country ship in company' since the previous evening] and hoisted Hadir Aly's colours.

We immediately tacked, and stood after them. At 8 fired several shot to bring one of them to, thinking her to be a Marratta. At 9 one of the [enemy] ketches sent her boat on board us, and told us they belonged to Hadir Aly, but as the [other] ketch did not bring to, nor shorten sail, and several other vessels [were] heaving in sight, which we imagined to be [enemy] consorts, we kept firing round and grape shot at her until noon. Broke 6 panes [of] glass in chase. At 1/2 past noon the ketch brought to, and struck her colours. We hoisted out the cutter, and sent her with an officer on board, who found her to be one of Hadir Aly's armed cruisers. At 1/2 past 2 PM hoisted the cutter in and made sail. Upon examining the shot racks, and the grape shot which were hung under the quarter deck, we found that we fired at the above vessel fifty-seven round shot, nine pounders; fifteen grape shot, nine pounders; two double-headed hammered shot, nine pounders; twenty-five round shot, three pounders; and two grape shot, three pounders.[17]

Lively as the exchange was, it merely punctuated Farmer's important mission north and he reached Bombay almost a month later on 16 March. The news had improved. It appeared that the Mahrattas had no plans to recover Bassein and Salsette by force, and that they were about to conclude an armistice with the East India Company. Indeed, the supreme council of the company had sent a plenipotentiary to the Mahratta capital, Poona, and it was expected that Salsette would be yielded without violence. This is, in fact, what happened. By playing one faction among the Mahrattas against the other, the company secured Salsette in 1776 by the treaty of Purandhar.[18]

At Bombay, Horace saw an astonishingly spacious and beautiful haven, with a lighthouse, fort, dry dock and church, but the combined efforts of the navy and the company kept him busy. The rupees were unloaded and two detachments of the company's troops with an artillery train embarked for Surat road, further north. However, while Farmer was effectively an arm of the company, he maintained the privileges and status of the Royal Navy. When a company ketch flew the broad pendant of a commodore in Surat road, Farmer decided that a prerogative of his commander-in-chief had been breached. He fired a swivel gun at the vessel and sent one of his officers on board to remove the offending object.

Now for the first time in his life Nelson experienced the prolonged frustrations of one of the least popular but most common duties of the naval officer. Convoy work. Waiting for merchantmen to gather, shepherding them from one place to another, keeping them together,

moving forward stragglers and cruising ahead or on the flanks to intercept enemies was nearly always calculated to raise the blood pressure.
It was often a distraction from the more exciting and profitable work
of chasing prizes. On this occasion there were compensations, for these
were new seas and scenes to Nelson. The *Seahorse* proceeded northwest across the Arabian Sea to Muscat, and then with the *Betsy Galley*
through the Strait of Hormuz and along the Persian Gulf to Bushire.
On 24 May they ran into Bushire road to clean, refit and provision.
The local sheik was entertained aboard as well as the head of the
English trade factory at Bussorah, who had been driven from his town
by a war between the Turks and the Persians.

If we may believe Nelson's account, during this time he was much
in the foretop, from where he was well positioned to spot potential
dangers. On the voyage to Bushire, for example, a large area of
discoloured water was seen in the path of the ship off 'Cape Verdeston'
on 22 May. It was taken to be shallows, and while the *Seahorse* shortened sail a cutter went ahead to investigate, only to discover that the
focus of their interest was an immense shoal of fish spawn. Coming
back from Bushire to Bombay, life in the foretop largely consisted of
keeping convoys under surveillance in the generally hazy weather.

It was important work, for the convoy was typically unmanageable. The *Seahorse* sailed from Bushire on 16 July with a party
consisting of the *Eagle*, an armed snow belonging to the East India
Company; the aforementioned *Betsy Galley* and another 'country' ship,
the *Fatty Eloy*; the *Betsy* schooner; and two ketches, the *Euphrates*
and the *Tigris*. Making along the coast, the ships soon got separated
and when the *Seahorse* reached Muscat on 30 July only the *Euphrates*
was still in company. Fortunately, some of the others had already made
the harbour, and the balance came in shortly afterwards. The journey
was resumed on 6 August, with the ketches replaced by a ship named
the *Indian Queen*. The *Fatty Eloy* proved herself to be a sluggish
sailor, and acted as a drag on the convoy, and after satisfying himself
that the ships were in no particular danger, Farmer urged them to
make more sail and forged on ahead. He reached Bombay with only
the *Betsy Galley* in company on 15 August and the remainder of his
charges strung out behind.

The voyage from Bushire to Bombay had given Able Seaman Nelson
his first full taste of the fretful drudgery of convoy duty, though the
foretop protected him from the petty annoyances that worried his
seniors below. Not all the frustrations related to the everyday vexations

of sailing a ship of war and herding merchantmen, for fresh personnel problems were surfacing under Farmer's troubled command.

On 28 July the captain had received a written complaint from the gunner, George Middleton, charging Lieutenant Thomas Henery with various offences, including tyrannical behaviour. Henery responded sharply. Although others stood ready to support the gunner's stories, he said Middleton was 'a lying good for nothing'. When the *Seahorse* returned to Madras in September and found the *Salisbury* anchored there, Farmer brought Middleton's complaint to the attention of Commodore Hughes. On the 15th Hughes suspended Henery from duty, but for the moment there were not enough post-captains to form a court. The matter had to be left to fester.[19]

5

Horace probably didn't like Henery. He was a foolish, blustering fellow, always threatening to have people flogged around the fleet for trivial offences that no court martial would ever have taken seriously. In particular he enjoyed baiting the 'young gentlemen'. Some or all of the midshipmen were quartered in the gun room in the bowels of the ship, and shared Gunner Middleton's distaste for the lieutenant. Apparently Henery suspected that both were plotting his downfall, and declared the midshipmen 'a parcel of puppies, and he would send one half of them [to be flogged] round the fleet, and not two Captain Farmers should save them'.

But with Henery suspended, and Surridge and Abson again sharing watches, life on the *Seahorse* improved for the midshipmen. The ship itself, enduring the longest voyage Nelson had made so far, was no less in need of attention. The tropics were hard on wooden sailing ships, and encrusted worm-ravaged hulls, rotting masts, frayed weathered ropes, rat-gnawed casks and canvas, stinking beer, vermin-ridden bread and men drained by debilitating climes were all too evident to Commodore Hughes. Now, in his second year on the station, he also knew the great monsoon was on its way and ships and crews needed to be in shape. After taking a detachment of East India Company soldiers to Pandarty road, Farmer accordingly found himself under the command of Captain Benjamin Marlow of the *Coventry*. On 14 October the two ships were ordered to Trincomalee on the eastern coast of Ceylon for wood, water and supplies. They were then to rejoin Hughes on the

Malabar coast, preparatory to wintering in Bombay and going into dry dock.

Nelson got his first sight of Trincomalee as the *Seahorse* was towed into harbour on 22 October. Farmer welcomed the Dutch governor aboard, and amidst compliments and clinking wineglasses secured permission for a wood detail to camp ashore and cut timber. Two petty officers led the shore party and threw up a tent as a base. The job was done, but four of the detail deserted and a marine was drowned during the boat journeys to and from the ship.

On some of the nine days the two ships stayed at Trincomalee, Horatio Nelson also went ashore, enjoying a brief period of leisure with his friends. At the behest of the ever mindful Surridge, Farmer restored the youth to his former rank of midshipman on 31 October and he was again freely fraternising with other petty officers of the quarterdeck. In later life Nelson recalled that at the age of seventeen he was induced to play at a gaming table and actually won £300, which in those days was a large sum of money for a naval petty officer. However, he suddenly realised that, had he lost rather than won such an amount, he could never have paid the debt. It was a sobering thought. Horace had been brought up to pay his way and vowed he would never gamble again. The story may have grown in the telling but probably referred to some incident that occurred in Madras, Trincomalee or Bombay.[20]

Reprovisioning complete, Marlow led the two ships to the Malabar coast in November and found Commodore Hughes at Anjenga. The *Seahorse* was then sent north, taking one convoy from Tellicherry to Goa and picking up another there for Bombay, where Hughes was concentrating his squadron for the winter. The finer days of these final voyages of the year may have given Midshipman Nelson his first opportunity to tack a ship, as if he was a master or lieutenant. Surridge had found the boy obedient and conscientious, ever eager to learn and serve, and no doubt prevailed upon the senior officers occasionally to allow him to tack the *Seahorse*. Tacking was a particularly tricky method of changing a ship's direction by turning its bow through the wind, but Horace performed the task with efficiency and authority, while Surridge stood by approvingly, knowing he had turned this boy into a capable sea officer.[21]

The *Seahorse* eventually arrived at Bombay on 19 December and remained for several months. On 19 February Nelson witnessed a formidable ritual aboard the ship. The captains of the squadron were piped aboard and swallowed by Farmer's cabin. While red-coated marines stood sentinel outside the door, inside Commodore Hughes presided over a court consisting of Marlow of the *Coventry*, Walters of the *Salisbury*, John Clerke of the *Dolphin* and James Pigott of the *Swallow*. Lieutenant Henery was marched in, surrendered his sword and seated himself to listen to a succession of witnesses to charges of drunkenness, disobedience, profaning the sabbath and tyrannical conduct. There was enough to show that the accused had neither judgement nor popularity, but the court did not feel he merited a conviction. Surridge and Abson both cleared Henery of malpractice.

Henery was more of a fool than a rogue. He damned and threatened freely. Lodington was menaced with four hours at the masthead, a common punishment for erring midshipmen, and young Troubridge was driven from the carpenter's store room with the threat that he would be flogged around the fleet for leaving the deck without permission. The carpenter's servant, though innocent of any wrongdoing, also endured a tirade, in which Henery threatened to flog him because his master had planned to take him ashore without asking the permission of an officer. Henery particularly picked on Midshipman William Sullivan, subjecting him not only to the usual threats about flogging through the fleet, but to habitual name-calling, such as 'Coolie' and 'Puppy'.

Henery's inability to sympathise with the 'young gentlemen' was recollected by one of them, Master's Mate Joseph Keeling, then about twenty-one years old:

I was going on board the *Salisbury* once to answer a signal, and one of the boat's crew was very insolent to me and refused to row. On my coming on board I acquainted the lieutenant of it, and he told me I certainly must have made too free with the men or else they never would have used you so, and told me to go away. I recollect another time between decks two men were fighting. I went to part them, and one of them struck me. I immediately went aft and made a complaint to the lieutenant, who gave me no satisfaction at all.[22]

It was this acerbic, unhelpful personality, rather than serious misconduct, that seemed to have rebounded upon Henery. George Middleton, the gunner, brooded over what he considered to be an unjustified rebuke during the firing of a salute. The lieutenant complained that the powder was being brought up from the magazine too slowly. 'God bless me, sir,' puffed the hapless gunner. 'I make what haste ever I can.' 'God damn me, sir,' replied Henery, 'make more haste, or else I'll haste you elsewhere!'

Whether the lieutenant's bluster turned into actual physical abuse was another matter. It was said that Henery had ordered excessive floggings in November 1774, when the ship was at Kedgeree and the captain absent in nearby Calcutta. One marine was reported to have been flogged, and his regimental clothes, fiddle and sea chest thrown overboard. And the lieutenant was supposed to have regularly employed a rattan 'to forward the people to their duty'. But neither this, nor some testimony relating to intoxication, weighed sufficiently with the court, hence his acquittal.

A sensible man would have treasured the reprieve, internalised its lessons and set about rehabilitating his reputation, but Henery was consumed with resentment. He racked his brains to find mud to fling at Farmer, furious that the captain had allowed the complaint to go forward. Thus, two days after Henery's court martial, Hughes and his officers reassembled on the *Seahorse* to consider charges the first lieutenant had proffered against his own captain.

They were flimsy indeed, but Henery hit the bull's-eye when he accused Farmer of keeping his son and a slave boy on the books when neither was present. This sin was of a type so widely practised in the navy that most officers turned a blind eye towards it. Many, if not most, had committed such frauds themselves, or at least benefited from them. The purser, Alexander Ligerwood, and Surridge were placed in the embarrassing position of owning that they had authenticated false books, but the captain's guilt was felt worthy of no more than a mild reprimand.

Henery's other attack drew attention to indigo, piece-goods and bales of cloth that Farmer had taken aboard at Surat and Anjenga. The implication was that the captain was making money out of illicit freight, but it collapsed when Commodore Hughes revealed that the goods had been embarked upon his, not Farmer's, orders. Without too much trouble the court dismissed the charges as 'dictated by a spirit of malice and litigiousness' and honourably acquitted the defendant.[23]

The sight of a captain and first lieutenant exchanging courts martial was an uncommon one, and Horace may have pondered its lessons in leadership. In some mysterious way the captain had failed to meld his senior officers into a team and suffered the consequences. Though his record had been exonerated, the bad blood aboard the *Seahorse*

raised questions about his powers of command. As for Henery, he can
only have been an object of derision among the 'young gentlemen'.
He had acted badly and compounded his errors by a misguided prosecution of his captain. Juniors who turned upon superiors without
good cause seldom did themselves a favour. In this case Thomas Henery
survived to become a commander the following year – probably
because in the East Indies there were few alternatives to fill available
posts – but it is doubtful that his early death deprived the navy of an
outstanding officer.

Had Horace remained in the East Indies it is likely that promotion
would have been a speedy prospect for him too, for he had acquired
all the basic skills of handling and navigating ships, and boasted a good
mind and a thorough devotion to his profession. On paper at least he
was near qualifying for lieutenant. He was approaching his eighteenth
birthday, but the ship's books had advanced his years by three and
now had him over twenty, the official minimum age for a lieutenant's
commission. Moreover, he was close to completing the six years of sea
service that were also needed, and there was little doubt about his
ability to pass the obligatory oral examination. The tantalising prize
of a first commission from the king seemed to be just around the corner.

But then, about the time Henery and Farmer were locked in combat
by court martial, he was struck down by a stealthier foe. It was almost
certainly malaria.

In the autobiography Nelson wrote twenty-three years later he
simply described it as a life-threatening illness, and Surridge remembered it as a disorder 'which nearly baffled the power of medicine'.
The midshipman was wasted, his frame reduced almost to the skeleton
and for a while he lost the use of his limbs. For years after his eventual recovery he suffered recurrent febrile attacks. Little was known
about malaria in Nelson's day, except of course for its devastating
onset. The work of Ross, Manson and Bignami, establishing the role
of the female mosquito in human malaria, was still a hundred or more
years away and the prevailing eighteenth-century opinion attributed
the disease to insanitation and fetid air.[24]

Nelson's enemy was most probably *Plasmodium vivax*, the
commonest form of malaria in India. Though a 'benign' form and
rarely deadly, if untreated it is prone to recur for several years and
the acute attack can be extremely debilitating. The weakness of
Nelson's limbs may simply have reflected his emaciated condition, or
been an indication of additional complications.

He was seen by the surgeon of the *Seahorse*, David Dalzell, and probably by others too. Captain Clerke of the *Dolphin*, Lieutenant Mather Fortescue of the *Coventry* and Marine Lieutenant Evan Evans of the *Seahorse* were also sick, and we know they were all examined by the surgeons of the naval hospital in Bombay as well as by doctors employed by the East India Company. Given the severity of Midshipman Nelson's illness, it is to be presumed that he received no less attention.[25]

Commodore Hughes certainly gave the youth every consideration. On 14 March 1776 he discharged Nelson from the *Seahorse*. The *Dolphin* was bound for England. Though about the same age, armament and dimensions as the *Seahorse*, she was worn out by her eastern service. Even though she had been dry docked in Bombay and the bottom rendered more or less watertight, many of her timbers were much decayed. Captain James Pigott, who was switched to the *Dolphin* and ordered to take her home, subsequently reported that 'in bad weather [the ship] complains much in her upper works, her sides and decks being very leaky, notwithstanding she has been twice caulked since she came out of Bombay Dock'. With the ship went some four-teen serious invalids, including Clerke, Fortescue, Evans and Nelson. A return to England was considered essential to their recovery.

Nevertheless, Nelson would lose neither sea time nor pay, for Hughes had him rated midshipman on the *Dolphin* from 15 March and thereby protected his employment until the ship was paid off in England. Horace always spoke of Hughes with gratitude, and no less affectionately did he remember Pigott, the newly promoted post-captain who took him home. Pigott's 'kindness at that time saved my life', he said.[26]

The *Dolphin* slipped from Bombay on 23 March, victualled for a six-month voyage. Her lieutenant was John Jervis, her master Richard Ogilvie and the surgeon and surgeon's mate, who tended Horace in his sickness, were respectively Joseph Davis and Bernard Penrose. Of the three other midshipmen – Peter Templeman, Frederick Ross and William Scott – the last, a lad from Ashford, was officially of Nelson's age. That Horace's duties aboard the *Dolphin* were negligible or light is obvious, but over the six-month voyage his health improved, and when he got home he was fit enough to take an immediate position with another ship.

He must have missed the companions with whom he had shared the past two and a half years. He would meet Troubridge again and the two would stand together in brilliant victories and a humiliating defeat.

Thomas Surridge would also flourish. In fact, he sailed for home within months of Nelson, passed his examination for lieutenant in England on 10 September 1777, and had his commission confirmed on 9 June 1779 by an appointment to the *Isis*. He could easily have remained a lieutenant, and served on several ships in that capacity, but the outbreak of the wars with revolutionary France created more opportunities. Surridge was appointed commander of the *Goelan* sloop, went to the West Indies, where he transferred to the *Alligator*, and in 1794 made the key rank of post-captain. In 1804 he commanded his largest ship, the sixty-four-gun *Trident*, but in retirement with his wife, Mary, he continued to rise in the service, achieving flag rank in 1812 and becoming vice admiral of the blue squadron on 12 August 1819. As if satisfied, he died towards the end of the same year in Chichester, Sussex, at the age of seventy-two, the last surviving mentor of the young Nelson.[27]

The homeward run of the *Dolphin* was uneventful. She put into Anjenga roads on 2 April 1776 and then sliced through squally seas and variable weather towards the coast of Africa, which was sighted on 11 May. Ten days later she entered Simon's Bay, in False Bay at the Cape of Good Hope, controlled by the Dutch. Apart from the three-gabled hospital to the right of the anchorage, the simple settlement consisted of a jetty, magazines, stables, workshops and a few houses, one using a flag to proclaim its status as a command post. Nevertheless, it was a safe haven and a French frigate, a number of Dutch merchantmen and the *Prince of Wales*, a British Indiaman, enlivened it during the month the *Dolphin* remained moored. Whether or not Nelson was hospitalised on shore for any time is unknown, but on 20 June his journey continued, and the next day the *Dolphin* rounded the Cape on large swells.[28]

There was little for Pigott to record in his log. Routine discipline had to be maintained and there were fourteen floggings between Bombay and Spithead. A man fell overboard in the North Atlantic, but the boats were able to save him, and in July and August Pigott's sick list fluctuated between eight and thirteen. It does not appear that Nelson was ever numbered among these invalids, who were most probably the ratings transferred from the hospital in Bombay. When the ship anchored at Spithead on 30 August, eleven of the 145 men on the books were listed as invalids.[29]

During that long sea voyage on a leaking ship Nelson slowly regained his strength, but there were occasions, no doubt, when the darkest fears gathered around his cot as he hovered between sickness and recovery, perhaps even death and life. According to what he told a friend long afterwards, while walking in the grounds of Downton Castle in Hertfordshire, his determination to survive and distinguish himself rallied in the deepest depths of despair. 'I felt impressed with an idea that I should never rise in my profession,' Nelson is supposed to have said. 'My mind was staggered with a view of the difficulties I had to surmount and the little "interest" I possessed. I could discover no means of reaching the object of my ambition. After a long and gloomy reverie, in which I almost wished myself overboard, a sudden glow of patriotism was kindled within me, and presented my king and country as my patron. My mind exulted in the idea. "Well then," I exclaimed, "I *will* be a hero, and confiding in Providence, I will brave every danger."'[30]

Although the ascribed words cannot have been accurately remembered, the gist of them may be true. There must have been useless, depressing days on the *Dolphin* and Nelson's nature was somewhat volatile. Yet in one sense the Downton Castle anecdote rings false. However bleakly he construed his prospects, Nelson knew that he had more than a 'little' interest – much more. In fact, the career of Maurice Suckling had progressed considerably in the years that Horace had been away, and news from home must have alerted him to it.

Young Nelson was probably less aware that his uncle's success had a black lining, for, though barely middle aged, Captain Suckling was ill. This was probably why in 1775 he applied to the Admiralty for shore-based positions in Newfoundland or Jamaica. By the beginning of 1777 he was 'in much bodily pain' for days at a time, and there were fears for his life.[31]

But as if to compensate for physical infirmity some juicy professional plums had fallen into Suckling's lap. On 12 April 1775 Lord Sandwich, the first lord of the Admiralty, appointed him to succeed Sir Hugh Palliser as comptroller of the Navy Board, one of the most important positions in the service. It put him at the head of the Navy Office, and responsible for dockyards, ships and such warrant officers as masters, pursers, surgeons and boatswains. The recruitment of dockyard workers themselves was largely in the hands of the dockyard officials, and as the senior board the Admiralty could always impose candidates for warrants upon the Navy Office, but the comptroller was still a man of prestige and patronage. He wielded enough sway over posts and dockyard contracts to reward those befriending him, and made a powerful ally.[32]

Not only that, but such was Sandwich's faith in Suckling that on 18 May 1776 he was returned Member of Parliament for Portsmouth. Portsmouth was a corporation borough that confined the franchise to the few members of the civic government. However, the navy's influence in the town was immense, and the corporation usually returned a nominee of the Admiralty as their Member. The incumbent, therefore, was almost always a parliamentary placeman, approved by the current administration and ready to do its bidding. Captain Suckling never took his place in the House of Commons, but his 'election' increased his influence and his ability to serve expectant protégés.

The consequences of Suckling's triumphal march were not long in coming. His oldest Nelson nephew, Maurice, was offered a position as purser of the *Swift*, but opted instead for a clerkship in the Navy Office, where from November 1775 he busied himself among bills and accounts. Both jobs were within the remit of the Navy Board, but Midshipman Horace looked to the Admiralty for his promotion and was a more difficult problem. Even so, while the boy was sailing eastern seas his uncle was recommending him to Lord Sandwich, and within weeks of reaching England, Nelson reaped the benefit.[33]

After notifying the Admiralty of his arrival with dispatches from Commodore Hughes, Pigott took the ailing *Dolphin* to Woolwich. On 18 September she was lashed alongside a sheer-hulk in the dockyard, terminally ill, and on the 24th Nelson and the rest of her complement were paid off. Receiving net wages to the value of £9 17s. 4d., Horace may have pondered anew his good fortune in winning that skirmish at the gaming table.[34]

Only two days later he received an order from Sir James Douglas, the port admiral of Portsmouth. It appointed him acting lieutenant of the sixty-four-gun *Worcester*, preparing to sail for Gibraltar.[35]

VI

LIEUTENANT NELSON

Nelson, who, when cheering out of port in spirit grew
To make one purpose with the wind and tide.
                Hilaire Belloc, *Ballade of Unsuccessful Men*

1

IN 1776 Portsmouth knew the name of Captain Maurice Suckling. The town's dockyard, with its sprawling complex of slips, storehouses, jetties, yards, mast houses and ordnance depot, and the chain of formidable fortifications that protected it, underwrote the economy of the entire community. Directly or indirectly it supported artisans, labourers and suppliers of every description, from brewers and bakers to block and instrument makers. The port pulsed with the energy that radiated from its ships. Smoky taphouses heaved with seafarers, carts and wagons choked the streets leading to the dockyard and ebullient hordes of workers streamed through its gate each morning to be mustered by their officers. Although established in his office in London, Captain Suckling's writ ran far in Portsmouth. He clearly had the ear and confidence of the first lord of the Admiralty, and as comptroller of the Navy Board was ultimately responsible for the dockyard. In 1776 he became the borough's sitting Member of Parliament.

It was not surprising that many were willing to serve Captain Suckling, either to repay past kindnesses or to bank goodwill in expectation of future favours. The captain was able to trade on that influence to help his nephew. Thus it was that young Horatio Nelson was summoned to serve on the *Worcester*, a locally built 'third rate' ship of the line. The captain of the *Worcester* was Mark Robinson, whose association with the comptroller of the Navy Board dated back at least as far as the latter's command in the Medway.[1]

Robinson's private journal hints at the hand the comptroller had in Nelson's promotion to the *Worcester*. The youth arrived on board on 8 October 1776 with letters of introduction from his uncle, and Captain Robinson wrote to Suckling to notify him the following day. He rated the youngster fourth lieutenant on his ship's books from the first of the month, and apparently advanced him money. On 1 February 1777, for example, Robinson gave Nelson four guineas for an unstated purpose, and on 29 September following – long after Horace had actually left the *Worcester* – Robinson noted, 'Received of Maurice Suckling, Esq., what I paid Mr Dalrymple for Mr Nelson – £1 14s. 6d.' It would seem proof at least that Robinson accounted to the comptroller in matters concerning the young lieutenant.[2]

Robinson also took Nelson under his wing. The day after Horace arrived in Portsmouth the ship moved to a mooring in the Solent at nearby Spithead, but Robinson found time to introduce the protégé to Sir James Douglas. On 10 October he invited the acting lieutenant to dine at his table on the *Worcester* with the mayor of Portsmouth, Philip Varlo, and on two separate days before finally weighing anchor for Gibraltar Robinson went ashore to dine as a guest of Varlo with Nelson by his side. In Portsmouth the nephew of Captain Suckling might have been merely an acting lieutenant but he appeared to have a privileged air.

2

Lieutenants were the most junior of sea officers carrying the king's commission, but that commission made them 'gentlemen' whatever their birth, and solicited respect and status, on shore as well as at sea. A lieutenant might be entrusted with the command of a small vessel, such as a schooner, but most were deputies to captains, acting under their orders and supporting them in the management of a ship. Often they commanded the watches, the shifts into which a crew was divided, and effectively ran the ship during the period of their watch. Some were also assigned additional responsibilities, such as exercising the men in small arms or commanding a section of the gun deck during action. The rank was an essential step towards the captains' list, and the talk of every lieutenants' mess was who was or was not likely to be made 'post'. They knew that many lieutenants, even good ones, never achieved that ambition.

As acting lieutenant Nelson was entitled to sling his cot and stow his chest in one of the small cabins in the 'wardrobe', which the lieutenants shared with the master, Kenneth Mackenzie, and the surgeon, George Hair. The weather the *Worcester* experienced on its voyage was atrocious, but despite his youth Nelson shouldered a fair share of duties. Robinson, whose own son had just qualified as a lieutenant, was encouraging, and entrusted Horace with the command of a watch. He assured the lad that 'he felt as easy when I was upon deck, as any officer in the ship'.[3]

Robinson probably recognised Nelson's exceptional ability, and the senior lieutenants, David Shuckforth, John Robson and George Dunn, may have been jobbing officers with little to mark them out. Shuckforth had been commissioned for twenty-three years and Robson for eighteen; neither they nor Dunn made 'post', although Shuckforth was retired as a commander in 1796. By contrast, Captain Robinson was an entirely respectable hero for Nelson. He had stories of the gallant Admiral Hawke, under whom he had been a young officer, and there was a steel core beneath his amiable disposition. Robinson would wear wounds as badges of bravery. Later he participated in two fleet actions against the French and lost a leg. Nelson always remembered him kindly, and spoke of 'Admiral Robinson, my old captain, with a wooden leg'.[4]

The *Worcester* was ordered to take dispatches and a convoy to the British base of Gibraltar, but was two hundred men short of her complement of five hundred. Some men were borrowed from His Majesty's ships *Barfleur*, *Royal Oak* and *Egmont*, but Robinson had to loose a couple of press gangs on the waterfront on 30 and 31 October. They brought in five men the first night. The problem did not seem to affect morale and discipline adversely, however. There were seven floggings before the ship sailed and rather more on the voyage itself, but considering the pedestrian duties and dirty weather inflicted upon the ship, it was not an unusual number.[5]

Nelson recalled it as a voyage of dogged duty rather than excitement. Urged on by an impatient Admiralty, Robinson mustered his convoy and sailed on Tuesday 3 December. Three days out two of the convoy collided with the *Worcester* off Portland, apparently because of the lubberly seamanship of one of their helmsmen. One ship ran upon the *Worcester*'s hawse (the space between her bow and where her anchor had lodged on the bottom), and entangled its foremast with her jib. The offending vessel was no sooner cut clear than she fell alongside the *Worcester* and damaged the foreyard. Still, Robinson's carpenters soon got their ship to rights, and the convoy put into Falmouth the next day to pick up a further detachment of merchantmen. Having done so they headed out into the Atlantic, fifty sail in all.

Horace already knew about convoy work but this voyage was unusually difficult. The outward journey was merely a matter of hard, dull and routine work. The ragged armada was ushered forward, shedding detachments at Oporto, Lisbon and Cadiz, and passing the capes of St Vincent and Trafalgar, where Nelson would eventually win glorious victories. On 9 January 1777 the *Worcester* anchored in the Bay of Gibraltar, near His Majesty's ship *Levant* and eight Dutch and Spanish warships.

The next day Nelson went ashore with a letter Robinson wanted to be mailed to Josiah Hardy, the British consul at Cadiz. This was his first opportunity to study the famous gateway to the Mediterranean. To see the 'apes' (actually macaque monkeys) scurrying about the rock, or smell the fetid streets of a town humming with men of many hues, where soldiers and sailors jostled with babbling bartering traders; to walk quietly among the prickly pears and pink geraniums of Europa Point; or gaze upon gun-studded ramparts or the brilliant blue waters of the Mediterranean, which he now saw for the first time. Horace was hoping to meet his old messmate, Charles Boyles, who was stationed at Gibraltar, and carried a letter and parcel to deliver to him. Unfortunately, Boyles was nowhere to be found, and after the *Zephyr* sloop arrived on the 24th Nelson entrusted his mail to one of its officers.[6]

It was not until 14 February that the winds permitted the *Worcester* to start the return leg of the voyage. With her went Lieutenant Henry Charles Bridges of the *Zephyr*, who had developed an eye problem, and a less willing passenger, the supercargo of an American prize taken by the *Levant*, with a box of papers from the same unfortunate vessel.

Off Cadiz the next day they endured the most perilous part of their journey. A number of ships had followed the *Worcester* from Gibraltar, but Robinson expected other homeward-bound merchantmen to join him at Cadiz. He had arranged with Consul Hardy that any ships waiting for convoy there should be ready to join the moment the *Worcester* appeared. But when the ship arrived on the morning of the 15th and Robinson raised a signal to his fore-topgallant and fired a gun, nothing happened. The waiting merchantmen sat snugly in the bay refusing to budge. For six hours the *Worcester* lay off the port, slowly being enveloped by a savage gale at west-southwest. Robinson reduced sail, but his main yard was destroyed in the slings, and it took an hour to bring the broken spar down, clew up the main-topsail and unbend the mainsail.

For a while the ship was in a situation every seaman dreaded – crippled, with a hard squall driving it towards the shore. Indeed, a Spanish brig in a similar predicament was pounded to pieces against the rocks. Finding it impossible to work out to sea on either tack, Robinson signalled his convoy to follow him into the bay, and a local fishing boat eventually piloted them to a safe haven among the ships already secured there.

An embarrassed British consul redeemed himself by prompting the Spaniards to live up to their well-earned reputation for hospitality, and the courteous hosts provided the *Worcester* with various necessities, including timber for a new yard. Some of the convoy, loaded with perishables, were unable to wait and sailed on as soon as the weather improved, but the *Worcester* had thirty-two ships in company, eleven of them from Cadiz, when she put to sea again on 3 March. There were more reluctant passengers for Robinson to embark too, including four army deserters for delivery to Portsmouth.[7]

For almost two weeks strong north winds and rain scourged the stubborn ships as they furrowed towards the English Channel. Robinson's charges were repeatedly appealing for help, to supply a new bowsprit here or a mizzen mast there, or even a surgeon to splint a broken arm, but as the voyage drew to its close they became more unmanageable and aloof. Their masters knew that the Royal Navy often impressed seamen from homeward-bound merchant ships, and all but four of the convoy slunk away to Falmouth or other places on their own hock. It was six o'clock in the evening of 2 April that the *Worcester* itself anchored in Spithead.

Nelson had written to his brother William from the Gulf of Cadiz, informing him of his intention to travel to London at the first opportunity. With more than six years of sea time under his belt, and a spell as acting lieutenant to boot, he wanted to confront the final hurdles that divided him from the king's commission, hurdles anticipated, and sometimes feared, by every midshipman. He would present himself for examination to a board of three post-captains.

3

At Portsmouth Captain Robinson took to his room, his rheumatism inflamed by the inclement rigours of his latest service, while his acting lieutenant climbed inside a coach bound for London, armed with the journals of his voyages and certificates of service from their various commanders. His destination was the Navy Office, then occupying an open space within the angle of Seething Lane and Crutched Friars. Lieutenants' commissions were issued at the Admiralty, but the drudge of examining candidates was delegated to the Navy Board, partly because the ships' books used to corroborate claims of service were stored in the junior office.

Nelson had prepared himself for the examination as best he could, but there were hidden problems in his candidacy. He had been eighteen on his last birthday, and a commissioned officer was supposed to be at least twenty. Although the books of recent ships had falsified his age, then and throughout life he looked younger than he was, and there was a possibility that some officious inquisitor might probe the matter. Then there were the necessary six years of sea time on His Majesty's ships. Again, officially Nelson had been in the navy for slightly more than six years, but a year of the time he was supposed to have been with the *Triumph* had actually been spent in the merchant service. The examiners were entitled to see his sea journals, so Horace discreetly left behind any he had kept on the *Triumph*.

As for the substance of the examination, it would be a limited exercise. There would be no questions about naval warfare, nothing about strategy, tactics, combat training or leadership. Professional education in the navy had not yet got that far. The examiners would simply be interested in Nelson's ability to handle a ship and in establishing that he was eligible for a commission.

Still, there was no telling how punitive the interrogation might be, for it depended upon the particular post-captains drafted into service. Lieutenants' examinations were sometimes perfunctory indeed, especially if 'interest' was at work. Two of the three who tested James Anthony Gardner were 'particular' friends of the candidate's family, and only 'a few questions' were needed to persuade them that 'we need not ask you any more'. On the other hand, there were midshipmen in the service who had sailed into middle age because of their inability to pass the examination.[8]

Horace appeared expectantly at the Navy Office in his best uniform

on Wednesday 9 April 1777. After a nervous interlude he was shown
into a room, 'somewhat alarmed' according to the story later told by
his brother William. And well might he be. The three men sitting
resplendent across the table were Captains John Campbell and
Abraham North, both strangers, and the comptroller of the Navy
Board – Captain Maurice Suckling himself.

In an effort to deny the nepotism in Nelson's unusually swift promotion, William later gave an attractive but fictitious account of what
followed. He said that the comptroller kept his relationship to the
candidate to himself. Only after the youth had answered the questions
with increasing confidence and mastery, and exhibited his journals and
certificates, did Captain Suckling rise to introduce his nephew. His
fellow captains expressed their surprise that the comptroller had not
mentioned the fact before. 'No,' replied Suckling righteously, 'I did
not wish the younker to be favoured. I felt convinced that he would
pass a good examination, and you see, gentlemen, that I have not been
disappointed.'[9]

There can be little doubt that Nelson knew his business, and would
have passed a fair examination, but William's story is nonsense. Even
if Campbell and North had not been told about the relationship
between Suckling and his nephew, the clues to it were plain in the
documents the boy offered for inspection. As his passing certificate
records, Nelson presented journals he had kept on the *Carcass*,
Seahorse, *Dolphin* and *Worcester*, as well as 'certificates from Captains
Suckling, Lutwidge, Farmer, Pigott, and Robinson, of his diligence,
&c. He can splice, knot, reef a sail, &c. and is qualified to do the
duty of an able seaman and midshipman.' Given the modes of officer
entry, it must have seemed highly probable that a candidate who began
his career with Suckling was related in some way.

The comptroller put his name to a definite subterfuge, however,
when he initialled Nelson's passing certificate, which attested that the
candidate 'appears to be more than twenty years of age'. Suckling
hardly rated this deception as unusual. In fact, his own former captain,
Thomas Fox, had done him exactly the same favour when he had
stood for lieutenant more than thirty years before.[10]

Passing was one thing; getting a post to confirm the rank another.
But Suckling had not allowed Lord Sandwich to forget Nelson, and
recommended him again while he was out in the *Worcester*. On 10
April, the day after Horatio passed his examination, he was accordingly appointed lieutenant to the *Lowestoffe*, a frigate fitting at

Sheerness for the Jamaica station under Captain William Locker. Nelson was delighted, and not only on account of the employment itself. The American War of Independence was fully joined, and Jamaica held at least some promise of action and prize money. Eagerly he wrote to Captain Robinson, seeking his discharge from the *Worcester* (duly sent with best wishes), and even got the Admiralty to pay him a lieutenant's rate for his acting service on that ship, including an allowance for a servant.[11]

Still excited five days later, Horace rushed a letter to William, then at Christ's College, Cambridge, preparing for his Bachelor of Arts:

I passed my degree as Master of Arts on the 9th instant (that is, passed the Lieutenant's examination) and received my commission on the following day, for a fine frigate of 32 guns. So I am now left in [the] world to shift for myself, which I hope I shall do, so as to bring credit to myself and friends. Am sorry there is no possibility this time of [us] seeing each other, but I hope that [a] time will come in a few years when we will spend some merry hours together.[12]

4

William may have been far away, but other members of the family were in London to help Horatio celebrate his elevation to the ranks of officers and gentlemen. We have no information about where he stayed, but two uncles lived in the city. Captain Suckling had succeeded to a house in the parish of St George's, Hanover Square, previously the property of his former admiral, the Honourable George Townshend, and his brother William, the collector of customs, was in Red Lion Square, not far from Gray's Inn.[13]

Some of the Nelsons were also in London to congratulate him, including his father, who arrived on 11 April. Horace's brother, Maurice, newly ensconced with his uncle at the Navy Office, still resided in the city, as now did their sixteen-year-old sister Ann. After finishing school at the age of fourteen Ann had been apprenticed to Alice Lilly, a citizen of London and member of the Goldsmiths' Company, on 5 April 1775. She was entitled to board, lodging and tuition for the seven years of her apprenticeship, and was registered with the Chamberlain's Court. Once fully-fledged at twenty-one, she would command all the economic privileges that went with being a member of the Goldsmiths' Company and a 'freeman' of the town – provided she had the means to establish herself in business.[14]

Nelson had not seen Ann for more than six years, and, though he was proud of his sister now taking on the world, he must have recognised her vulnerability so far from home. Fortunately, her mistress seemed to be a responsible woman. In her forties, Alice Lilly, the daughter of a Wiltshire yeoman, had completed her apprenticeship and become a 'freeman' in 1754. Though a member of the Goldsmiths' she was in fact a milliner by trade and had simply enrolled with the liveried company to obtain its benefits. Seven apprentices in millinery had successfully passed through her hands before Ann's arrival. Some of the girls were relatives for whom Miss Lilly waived the premium, while others were the daughters of gentry, clergymen and merchants who paid considerable sums. When Ann joined Alice, she was established in a Capital Lace Warehouse at 9 Ludgate Street with Mary Lilly, a niece or cousin who had been her former apprentice. There, in a large terraced four-storey building with its upper floors lit by trios of plain, regular windows and a balustraded roof, Ann boarded with the other remaining apprentice, Sophia Vassmer, the daughter of a gentleman who was already two years into her training.[15]

Given Horatio's commitment to the family it is probable that he made at least one visit to Ludgate Street to cast a protective eye over his young sister. Legend has besmirched Ann's reputation. She is supposed to have been seduced in London, given birth to an illegitimate son and forced to return home in disgrace. These stories of skeletons in the cupboard and a lost Nelson nephew, though repeated by several biographers, appear to be entirely misguided. It is true that Ann eventually forsook her apprenticeship, and with it the prospect of becoming a 'citizen' of London, but her motives were altogether more prosaic. On 5 February 1777 she and her fellow apprentice had been turned over to another mistress with their full consent. Mary Ann Jackson, a spinster of Ludgate Street and citizen and wheelwright of London, who acquired the Lilly business, was no more a wheelwright than Alice had been a goldsmith, and undertook to complete Ann's training in millinery. It is possible that the transfer unsettled Ann and contributed to a decision to abandon her trade, but two legacies were the real root of it. One from Captain Suckling, worth £1,000, was paid in 1779, the same year that the nineteen-year-old Ann quit London and returned to Norfolk to care for her aged father.[16]

Whatever domestic considerations may have engaged Lieutenant Horatio Nelson in 1777, he was increasingly independent and self-assured, willing to express and act upon his opinions. Those qualities, and a desire to commemorate his achievement, induced him to sit for his first portrait. He chose the artist John Francis Rigaud, a native of Turin of about thirty-five who had worked in Italy before coming to England in 1771. An associate of the Royal Academy, Rigaud was reputed to be a competent portrait painter though he also depicted historical scenes and tackled wall, staircase and ceiling work. Nelson probably sat to him in his studio in Great Titchfield Street. William Locker, his new captain, commissioned Rigaud to paint a group portrait of his family about this time, and may have recommended the artist to Nelson.

Because Captain William Locker later acquired the Rigaud portrait, biographers have assumed that it was he who actually commissioned it. There seems to have been no reason why Locker should have paid for a portrait of a lieutenant he hardly knew at the time, and the truth seems to have been that Nelson commissioned the likeness himself, through his prize agent and banker, William Paynter. Locker, who returned to England earlier than Nelson and spent more time in London, supervised its completion, and ultimately received it as a present from his young friend.

The portrait was still unfinished when Nelson left for sea. Upon his return four years later, damaged by fresh onslaughts of disease, he admitted that it would no longer 'be the least like' him. He authorised Locker to tell the artist to 'add beauty' to it, and even managed a fresh sitting. As it has come down to us, then, Rigaud's portrait reflects the twenty-two-year-old captain of 1781 rather than the fresh lieutenant of 1777. But an X-ray of the painting, made a few years ago, peers into the original we have lost – a chubby-faced Nelson in a pigtail and lieutenant's uniform, a hat under his arm, standing proudly at the beginning of his career as a commissioned officer of the king.[17]

5

Nelson joined the *Lowestoffe* at Sheerness. She was a thirty-two-gun frigate, launched in 1761, and ideal for prize-taking out of Jamaica. The possibility of action seemed good. Ever since the end of the Seven Years War in 1763 the quarrel between Britain and her American colonies had been growing. As far as the crown was concerned it was a matter of suppressing a treasonable trade that had developed between the colonies and the French West Indies during the war, a trade that contravened the navigation laws; of compelling the colonies to make a contribution to the cost of their own defence; and of enforcing what the king regarded as his prerogative to impose colonial taxes and duties.

But many Americans thought differently. They said the navigation laws, which regulated trade between the mother country and its possessions, were restrictive, and the standing army the British had stationed on the western frontier a potential threat to the liberties of the people. More particularly, they insisted that the colonial assemblies had the right to confirm or veto all taxes, a privilege that enabled the people to arrest any tyrannical tendencies of government. As the quarrel intensified both sides lost the will to compromise, and fighting broke out in 1775. The bloodiest battle of the revolutionary war was fought at Bunker Hill outside Boston, and on 2 July 1776 the Continental Congress approved a resolution that the 'United Colonies' ought to be 'free and independent'. Two days later the birth of the United States of America was officially proclaimed.

Everywhere in Britain and America people were divided about the war. In America many stood neutral, and rather fewer remained loyal to the crown, although perhaps half supported independence. In Britain there were Whigs who saw the colonial struggle as a reflection of their own concern for the traditional rights of the people – those much vaunted liberties Englishmen professed to enjoy as subjects of a monarchy whose powers were checked by the rights of Parliament. Others complained about the expense of yet another conflict so soon after the last, and groaned under an oppressive tax burden. And for some, including Horatio Nelson, this battle between English-speaking peoples seemed a little unnatural. Peace might have settled uncomfortably upon Europe for the time being, but for most Englishmen France was the traditional enemy.

Still, the war had begun and action was certain. The American navy was small, and Britain commanded the coasts as well as the cities of New York and Philadelphia. As Lieutenant Nelson prepared to cross the Atlantic, he expected no large naval battles to greet him, but there would be prizes for the taking. American merchantmen were fair game, and the West Indian waters teemed with enemy privateers. In those days the value of such captures, once condemned as legitimate seizures in the vice-admiralty courts, was distributed among the captors as incentives to duty, and Nelson, no less than every other naval officer, looked forward to supplementing his modest salary through prize money.

Locker was under orders to bring his company up to 220 men before proceeding to the Nore, but manning remained a problem, partly because thirty men went down sick before sailing. As his first lieutenant was on leave Captain Locker ordered Nelson to lead a party to a 'rendezvous' near the Tower of London to get more men. A rendezvous was a recruiting station, usually a tavern, where volunteers were enlisted and press gangs were based under the supervision of a regulating captain. From this particular rendezvous, gangs sallied out to round up sailors about Tower Hill.

With Nelson went another officer, a young Londoner named Joseph Bromwich. Born in about 1754, Bromwich was older than Nelson but little if any 'interest' smoothed his path. He had volunteered to join the *Lowestoffe* as an able seaman in March 1777, but Captain Locker had been impressed and re-rated him midshipman on 8 May. Though inferior in rank to Nelson, Bromwich's extra years were reassuring to Nelson on what was perhaps his first outing at the head of an impress party. It was fortunate that Bromwich was there. Nelson was still suffering from the after-effects of the illness that had brought him from the East Indies, and was troubled by severe pains in the chest and occasional febrile onslaughts that left him weak and drained. One cold night, while searching for recruits about the Tower, his legs gave way and Bromwich carried him back to the rendezvous on his back.[18]

Nelson's health, in fact, was now seriously fractured, and a major impediment to someone with his prodigious capacity for work. In that sense Jamaica was not, perhaps, the place to go. The most important of Britain's possessions in the West Indies, and for more than a century the command centre of her imperial ambitions in that region, Jamaica was aesthetically impressive. Kingston, on the south shore of the island, flourished as a focus for commerce, its large, sheltered harbour hidden from outsiders by a firm spit of land that stretched several miles westwards and terminated in the fortified town of Port Royal, once the haunt of legendary privateers and buccaneers. Yet despite the undeniable beauty of the island, where shining strips of white sand separated green forests from turquoise seas, there was an uncomfortable chill to the sunlight. Within, the prosperous sugar plantations were maintained by slave labour, and forever threatened by rebellion; and without, beyond the blue horizons bastions of Britain's imperial rivals, Spain and France, could be found in all directions. Every European war made Jamaica a target. More lethal still, and apposite to Nelson's physical condition, the area was pestilential. Diseases such as yellow fever and malaria could sweep the unacclimatised with fierce, uncontrollable power.

Nelson knew Jamaica and knew what it could do. Sobering the natural optimism of youth and his hunger for adventure and action were dark fears for what it held in store for his weakened body. His chest pained him on the outward voyage, surviving the attentions of John Cunningham, the ship's surgeon, and Joshua Doberry, the servant to which his new rank entitled him. There was a naval cemetery near Port Royal named Green Bay, and during his years on the island Horace would come to regard it as a ravenous beast, waiting with open jaws to devour him.

6

The *Lowestoffe* got into Spithead with no greater loss than a yawl, submerged in a heavy squall outside Margate as it was being towed behind. Accompanied by the *Grasshopper* sloop under William Truscott, she sailed again on 16 May 1777, heading into the setting sun with a bevy of merchantmen. Locker was ordered to load wine and other necessities at Madeira, before continuing to Barbados and the Leeward Islands.[19]

The Atlantic crossing was mundane. Occasionally the escorts had to lay to or fire guns to keep the merchant ships together, and Lieutenant Nelson carefully entered these and other daily aggravations in his log. 'At 4 PM [26 June] committed the body of the deceased [Edward Clark, a seaman] to the deep,' he wrote. 'At 1/2 past 5 the *Betsey* hailed us and informed us of some of her people being mutinous. Immediately hove to, hoist[ed] the boat out and sent her on board. At 7 the boat returned with 2 men, having left one [of our own] in their room.' A seaman and a marine of the *Lowestoffe* were also lost overboard during the voyage. Surprisingly, in those days few sailors could swim, and by the time a frigate could be brought to and a boat lowered the chances of rescue were slim. Other than that, the seizure of a schooner on 1 July was the only relief from routine. She seemed to be American property, so Locker brought her into Carlisle Bay, Barbados, two days later, but she established her innocence and had to be released. From Barbados the *Grasshopper* proceeded with part of the convoy to St Vincent, while the *Lowestoffe* pressed on with the rest to Port Royal by way of Antigua. Though the seas were 'infested by rebel privateers' Captain Locker brought all his charges safely to their destination on 19 July.[20]

During the voyage Nelson occupied a frugal larboard (left-hand side) cabin on the lower deck between the surgeon and purser, across from the quarters of the first lieutenant and master on the starboard side. But his warmest relationship was with the men who occupied the grander cabin on the deck above, a friendship unusual in its closeness and durability. It developed between a middle-aged man and a youth twenty-seven years his junior, who was barely a man. Nelson liked most of his captains, but Locker was special: he became his best friend and professional confidant, always there as if he had been close blood kin, and always strong.

Nelson's biographers have noticed the friendship without ever explaining it. The captain's increasing reliance on a green eighteen-year-old when a senior lieutenant shipped aboard seems to have struck no one as unusual, nor has any previous attempt been made to identify the officers of the *Lowestoffe*. In fact the first lieutenant was Charles Sandys. Sandys was a commissioned officer of four years' standing, but he was incompetent nonetheless and worse. He was a drunkard to boot. To a colleague who knew Sandys in later years he was 'one of those vulgar, drunken dolts who bring discredit on the naval service'. As usual, Nelson was generous, but retrospectively admitted that Sandys had exhibited the same weakness aboard the *Lowestoffe*. 'The little man, Sandys, is a good-natured laughing creature,' he wrote to Locker in 1784, 'but no more of an officer as a captain *than he was as a lieutenant.*' The next year he added that 'little Charles Sandys is *as usual – likes a cup of grog as well as ever* . . . What a pity he should have that failing. There is not a better heart in the world.'[21]

The captain of a man-of-war bore the loneliness of command more keenly than most. Isolated on the ocean, his responsibilities were always heavy and sometimes awesome. It was he who was ultimately responsible for the discharge of the ship's duty, and for the safe return of his vessel and her people to port. Faced with the exigencies of the service, even a good captain needed colleagues to share that burden. Sandys was Locker's senior lieutenant, in age, rank and experience, but we can see why the captain considered him to be unreliable. Nelson, by comparison, was responsible, conscientious and eager, and like Locker he loved the profession. It was consequently to him, and the master Arthur Hill, that the captain learned to turn.

Nelson always reacted positively to praise and to those who trusted him. It lifted him, and intensified his effort. He had already acquired the habit of actively cultivating friendships with people he admired, and during the voyage innumerable conversations on the quarterdeck or at the captain's dining table told Horace that William Locker was another kindred spirit.

Locker was born in February 1731, the second of nine children of John and Elizabeth Locker, parents not unlike Nelson's own. John Locker, a clerk with the Leathersellers' Company, was 'highly esteemed in the literary world for his knowledge in polite literature and remarkable for his skill in the modern Greek language'. His wife was the daughter of a Norfolk parson, the rector of Wood Norton and Swanton. William Locker had been educated at the Merchant Taylors' school, and joined the navy in 1746, enlisting as a captain's servant at the age of fifteen under a relative, Captain Charles Wyndham. He served in both the West and the East Indies, and was a favourite of Edward Hawke, arguably the most distinguished admiral of the eighteenth century.[22]

When Nelson met Locker, the captain did not have the obvious appearance of a warrior. He was well read and knowledgeable like his father, and a hearty looking, round-faced man, his receding hair greying at the temples. The limp gave him away though, and often led social conversation to the story that always inspired Nelson the most. Back in 1756, during the Seven Years War, Hawke had appointed the young Locker lieutenant of the twenty-gun *Experiment* under Captain John Strachan. In June 1757 Strachan engaged a French privateer, the *Telemaque*, off Alicante. She had twenty-six guns and three times the men, but after a desperate struggle the British boarded and captured her, and Locker had never fully recovered from the splinter he received in a leg that day.

Many years later, after Nelson's victory at the Nile had turned him into an international hero, he wrote to his old captain recalling that story. 'You, my old friend,' he said, 'after twenty-seven years' acquaintance know that nothing can alter my attachment and gratitude to you. I have been your scholar. It is you who taught me to board a Frenchman, by your conduct when in the *Experiment*. It is you who always told [me] "Lay a Frenchman close, and you will beat him", and my only merit in my profession is being a good scholar. Our friendship will never end but with my life.' Imagine the feelings of the ageing officer, reading that tribute from the greatest admiral of the time. But then Locker would have remembered that Nelson had rarely hidden his emotions. If he loved people, be they men or women, he had always said so. It was part of the magic that bound them to him.[23]

Whether Locker gave Nelson some of his first lessons in naval tactics must remain a matter of conjecture. In time Nelson unquestionably learned that ship for ship the Royal Navy had its Spanish and French adversaries beaten; the close-quarter tactics of his great battles reflected his confidence in the superiority of British seamanship and gunnery as well as his own fiery temperament. Although his marked prejudices against the French in particular sometimes led him to attribute the navy's success to a fancied superiority of the Anglo-Saxon stock, his more thoughtful utterances betrayed greater understanding. Our knowledge of that process of education in Nelson is far from complete, but it seems to have started with William Locker.

Locker's stories, for example, extended to Hawke's great victory in Quiberon Bay in 1759, in which he had served aboard the *Sapphire*. Locker had later been a flag lieutenant to Hawke in the *Royal George*, and it is likely that some of the famous admiral's precepts passed vicariously to Nelson through Locker. Hawke, whose coat of arms enshrined the motto 'Strike', had a genuine taste for battle Nelson would have appreciated. His emphasis on close-range action and readiness to depart from the written fighting instructions to achieve a result presaged Nelson's career. As a captain, for instance, Hawke left the hallowed 'line of battle' formation to capture a Spanish capital ship in 1744. Later, raised to flag rank, he tried to marry the strength of the 'line' to the 'general chase', which allowed ships to break formation in order to pursue a flying enemy, a feature of his most famous victory over the French at Quiberon Bay.[24]

At the time Locker knew Nelson he probably talked even more about his young wife, Lucy (nineteen years the captain's junior and the daughter of Admiral William Parry), and of the three sons and two daughters she had borne him. A William Parry among the captain's servants on the *Lowestoffe* was probably a brother or nephew of Lucy Locker. The captain's concern for his family increased soon after the ship's arrival in Jamaica, because he suddenly fell ill and had to retire to rooms ashore. After his ship's hull had been sheathed in copper in the dockyard she was ready to sail, but the captain remained incapacitated and it was Sandys who took the *Lowestoffe* for her first cruise on 8 August. Back in his bed Locker feared the worst during black, lonely reveries, and worried about what would become of Lucy and her children. Searching for a colleague to handle his affairs and do his best for the family, he wrote to the eighteen-year-old stripling who was second lieutenant of his frigate. The reply, when it came, was full of the spontaneous but sincere generosity for which Nelson would become known:

Lowestoffe, at sea, August 12th, 1777.

My most worthy friend,

I am exceedingly obliged to you for the good opinion you entertain of me, and will do my utmost that you may have no occasion to change it. I hope God Almighty will be pleased to spare your life, for your own sake, and that of your family, but should any thing happen to you (which I sincerely pray God may not) you may be assured that nothing shall be wanting on my part for the taking care of your effects, and delivering safe to Mrs Locker such of them as may be thought proper not to be disposed of. You mentioned the word 'consolation' in your letter. I shall have a very great one, when I think I have served faithfully the best of friends, and the most amiable of women.

All the services I can render to your family, you may be assured shall be done, and shall never end but with my life, and may God Almighty of his great goodness keep, bless, and preserve you and your family, is the most fervent prayer

Of your faithful servant,

Horatio Nelson

P.S. Though this letter is not couched in the best manner be assured it comes from one entirely devoted to your service.

H.N.[25]

This letter, the outspoken testimony of a young man willing to accept the grimmer burdens of his friendship for an ageing captain looking into the abyss, illustrates the characteristics that had and would continue to endear him to a succession of superiors. Reading it we can understand why William Locker would fight for him through years of obscurity, and take pride in living to know that he had nurtured the country's greatest national hero.

7

While Locker recovered in Jamaica, the *Lowestoffe* was out at the beginning of the hurricane season, looking for prizes. They chased numerous sails but had no luck until eleven in the morning of 21 August when a strange vessel was seen in the northwest quarter. Sandys ordered a tender, the *Gayton*, commanded by a midshipman, to give chase and in four hours it returned with a Charleston sloop laden with rice. A crew of nine was put aboard the capture to sail it to Port Royal, where Locker's prize agent, the Kingston merchant Hercules Ross, began the process of condemnation in the vice-admiralty court. Two more prizes were taken towards the middle of September. Between Cape Maisi in Cuba and Cape à Foux in French Haiti a ship they had pursued to windward turned out to be the Charleston sloop *Mary Angelic*, bound for St Nicolas Mole in Haiti with rice and timber. Two days later Sandys took the *Burford*, a North Carolinian schooner with a cargo of pitch, tar and other stores. It was with some self-congratulation, therefore, that the *Lowestoffe* returned to Port Royal on 30 September to report to her recuperating captain.[26]

Locker himself commanded when the frigate returned to her patrol on Guy Fawkes day. One of the prizes taken on the previous cruise had been fitted as a new tender, christened the *Little Lucy* in honour of Locker's infant daughter, and sailed fifteen days earlier. Locker soon came up with her to discover that she had engaged an American privateer and lost three men killed and wounded. It was not long before the *Lowestoffe* herself was in action, perhaps with the same privateer. In 1799 Nelson boasted that the incident 'presaged my character' by demonstrating 'that difficulties and dangers do but increase my desire of attempting them'. Accepting his account the public agreed, and the episode became another of Nelson's canonical feats of courage, inspiring one of the stirring paintings by Richard Westall which were engraved and published after the admiral's death.

At six in the morning of 20 November, when the *Lowestoffe* was haunting the Windward Passage off Cape Maisi, lookouts reported two sails to the northward. The frigate gave chase and after four hours brought one of the strangers to by firing a cannon and ten double-shotted swivel guns at her. She was the *Resolution* brig, an American privateer on her way from St Nicolas Mole to North Carolina, but she carried a mere eight guns, ten swivels and twenty men and made little resistance. Her consort, a schooner laden with powder for the American colonies, escaped, and it is possible that Master John Meredith of the *Resolution* diverted the British ship to allow her to get clear.

In the afternoon, as the prize was brought close by, a fierce storm engulfed both ships, punishing them with rain, bruising gales and heavy seas. Locker ordered Sandys to board and secure the prize, but the first lieutenant flunked the job. Our sources conflict. Nelson's own, written in 1799, said that the first lieutenant tried to reach the prize but was driven back by the furious waves, but Bromwich, who gave an account even later, maintained that Sandys never left the frigate, but merely went below to rummage for his hanger. Whatever the case, Captain Locker is said to have appeared on deck in consternation. 'Have I no officer in the ship who can board the prize?' he called.

The ship's boat was being jostled alongside, but as the master stepped forward to board it young Nelson stopped him. 'It is my turn now,' he said according to his own story, 'and if I [too] come back it is yours.' In the meantime the privateer was shipping a great deal of water, and Bromwich said that after Nelson's boat had ploughed through huge waves it was swept onto the deck of the prize and carried 'out again with the scud'. Nevertheless, he got on board. The log of the *Lowestoffe* recorded that at seven in the evening Locker fired a swivel to signal the prize to come under his stern, but made no reference to Nelson's exploit.

The weather remained so foul that the prize separated, and Locker feared her lost. On the 22nd he backed the topsails of his frigate to wait for her, and both vessels eventually made Port Royal on 24 November. Whatever the prize was worth, Locker and Nelson gained some valuable information from her. The Americans reported that the French at St Nicolas Mole were predicting that their country would soon enter the war in aid of the rebellious colonies, and that a fleet and thousands of soldiers would arrive via Cape François on the north coast of Haiti. Indeed, the French forts at St Nicolas Mole were already well garrisoned, and British ships had been ordered out of the harbour.[27]

The *Lowestoffe*'s next cruise, which began on 9 December, took her back through the Windward Passage to the northern coasts of Hispaniola and Cuba and the island-studded seas of the Bahamas. She returned to Port Royal on the last day of January 1778 without any prizes, but Lieutenant Nelson had gained in experience. On this occasion Locker had given him command of the *Little Lucy*. In his usual style, Horatio later bragged that 'even a frigate was not sufficiently active for my mind' so he pressed for the tender, in which 'I made myself a complete pilot for all the passages through the islands situated on the north side of Hispaniola.' This suggests that Locker took the American intelligence seriously, and was on the watch for the French fleet as well as further prizes.

When the *Lowestoffe* returned to Jamaica, Nelson obtained Locker's permission to cruise independently, and he made two voyages from Port Royal in the *Little Lucy*. During the first in February he took a prize off the island of West Caicos after a chase of eight hours, apparently the *Abigail* sloop of Boston, laden with molasses and dry goods. The second cruise occupied much of March and April. In the Bahama Straits on 25 March he captured the *Swan* sloop, master Daniel Smith, en route from St Nicolas Mole to Nantucket with molasses, but nothing else came his way before he returned to port on 19 April. If relatively unprofitable, these voyages were significant as the first that Nelson made as an independent commander.[28]

But his training with William Locker was reaching its end. They put to sea for their last cruise together on 5 May. For fifty days the *Lowestoffe* and *Little Lucy* searched for prizes, particularly two notorious privateers with the striking names of *Rattlesnake* and *Thunderbolt*. Locker worked industriously but with conspicuous bad luck, pursuing sails here and there only to discover them to be French, Spanish or British. On 10 May Nelson ran the *Little Lucy* alongside a longboat heading for Jamaica. It was filled with the crew of a British ship captured by an American privateer, but of the privateer itself there was nothing to be seen.

Another disappointment occurred near West Caicos. On the afternoon of 24 May two strange vessels were seen and chased in the southeast quarter. Shots were exchanged, but it was not until the next morning that the British came up with the fugitives. One of them was the *Inconstant*, a French frigate, and the other a schooner. Britain and France were at peace, but the French sympathised with the Americans, and Locker decided to examine the schooner in case it belonged to the rebel colonies. Accordingly Lieutenant Nelson advanced in the *Little Lucy*, but he was greeted by small-arms fire from the frigate and Locker signalled him back. Anticipating a fight, no doubt with relish, Nelson sent a boat to the *Lowestoffe* to know whether Locker wanted his men back on board but the captain kept calm. As he expected, the French decided that national honour had been satisfied. Unfortunately, to the chagrin of the British, when Sandys boarded the schooner he found it, too, was French.[29]

On 23 June the *Lowestoffe* was back at Port Royal. Nelson never sailed with Locker again but had learned much from him. Overall, the captain had been an ideal commander, inherently gentle but professional and bold when necessary, and firm and just with his men. Twenty-four had been flogged aboard the frigate during the period Nelson was with her, some several times, but it was not a large number for a ship of its size. More significantly, small-scale as the exploits of the *Lowestoffe* were, they provided Nelson with his first real experience of war and command. His only previous action had been an isolated skirmish off India. It was in the West Indies that Nelson learned to cruise in a combat zone. Though there had been no serious fighting, chasing suspicious ships, taking prizes and gathering intelligence were very much the stock in trade of wartime frigate patrols. In the *Little Lucy* Nelson had also tasted the full responsibility of command, without any superior to guide him.

It was the friendship of Captain Locker himself, however, that constituted Nelson's greatest benefit. Hitherto, he had looked exclusively to his uncle to protect and create opportunities for him, but now he felt as secure in Locker's patronage as if the man had been his own flesh and blood. Locker was not so prominent in the service as Suckling, but he was a respected and popular officer, and his name was capable of opening doors. In him Lieutenant Nelson had found an enduring aid.

8

One person to whom we can be sure Captain Locker spoke about Nelson was the new commander-in-chief at Jamaica, Rear Admiral Sir Peter Parker. Parker had replaced Admiral Clark Gayton, and Nelson had probably met him for the first time upon returning to Port Royal on 1 March after his first independent cruise with the *Little Lucy*.

Nelson would have seen a portly gentleman of fifty-one. A lady diarist later thought Parker 'the oddest figure in the world', but though his active career had not been exceptionally distinguished, he made friends and prospered. A captain since 1747, Sir Peter had served throughout the Seven Years War and been rescued from a Portsmouth guard ship by the outbreak of the rebellion in the American colonies. The experience had been checkered. As commodore Parker had badly bungled an attack on Charleston, losing his breeches (when a magazine exploded), a frigate and heavy casualties. Regaining dignity and credibility under Howe further north, Parker successfully invaded Rhode Island. Newly promoted a rear admiral, he had then come to

Jamaica as commander-in-chief, accompanied by a kind but mothering wife, Lady Margaret, formerly Nugent.[30]

It was usual to greet a new commander-in-chief with a measure of trepidation, but Nelson was relieved to find Sir Peter already well disposed towards him. In fact, exceedingly so. The immature lieutenant was regularly whisked to the house the Parkers had taken in Kingston, where he listened to stories of the old days, when Sir Peter and Captain Suckling had served together in the Mediterranean. Parker and Suckling had both participated in an engagement off Toulon in 1744, though as junior officers of different ships. Furthermore, the Parkers told Horatio that Suckling had recently approached them on his behalf. The comptroller had given them a letter to deliver to Lieutenant Nelson, and 'recommended me in the strongest manner to Sir Peter Parker, who has promised me he will make me the first captain'.[31]

Parker was as good as his word. Sir John Knox Laughton, one of Nelson's earlier biographers, saw Sir Peter's patronage as entirely self-serving, and the charge has too often been repeated. It is doubtful if an active flag officer needed to ingratiate himself with the comptroller of the Navy Board, and we should remind ourselves that most of the favours Parker bestowed upon Nelson occurred *after* Suckling's death. Rather, the Parkers acted out of a genuine friendship for Captain Suckling, and quickly developed their own bonds with a likeable youngster. They called him 'a son'. Almost a decade later, when Horatio became a battle hero, Lady Parker gushingly assured him that 'your mother could not have heard of your deeds with more affection'. Nelson acknowledged as much himself. 'I am sensible as ever,' he wrote to her, 'that I owe my present position in life to your and good Sir Peter's partiality for me, and friendly remembrance of Maurice Suckling.'[32]

Tangible proof of the Parkers' goodwill followed quickly, for nepotism came easily to such a practised hand as Sir Peter. The muster of the fifty-gun *Bristol*, Sir Peter's flagship, was peppered with the names of Parkers and Nugents, all earmarked for advancement. Indeed, it was the promotion of one of them – Lieutenant Charles Nugent – to the post of commander on 1 July 1778 that created the first opening for young Nelson. On the same day the books of the flagship rated Horatio third lieutenant in Nugent's stead. His first cruise in the new ship began on 4 July and lasted for thirty-three days.[33]

This was an important step, for although Nelson remained a lieutenant, everyone knew that a flag lieutenancy under the immediate eye of a commander-in-chief was a special privilege. Such admirals gathered their favourites around them, and when vacancies for promotion occurred they headed the queue.

Nelson's next target was the position of commander, a halfway step to the most crucial rank of all, that of post-captain. Once Horatio became a post-captain he would be eligible to command a ship of the 'sixth rate' or above, carrying twenty or more guns, and take the lion's share of any prize money. Better still, he would inexorably ascend the captains' list through a process of seniority, and if he lived long enough become an admiral. To be made 'post' was the dream of every ambitious lieutenant, but many never realised it and died lieutenants. Many others who did become post-captains achieved their ranks too late in life to complete the long march to flag rank. Lieutenant John Larmour, 'sea-daddy' of the famous Lord Cochrane and 'a most deserving officer' in his own right, waited more than sixteen years to be made post. Even the gifted Philip Beaver, reckoned by the poet Wordsworth among the most intelligent men of his time, remained a lieutenant for a score or so years. Neither got any further.[34]

Nelson had seen too many embittered lieutenants to be complacent about reaching post rank, but Sir Peter's words and the transfer to the flagship were massively reassuring. The *Bristol* was full of officers up for promotion, including the commander-in-chief's son, Midshipman Christopher Parker, named for a grandfather who had also been an admiral. The ship's captain, Toby Caulfield, also had his protégés aboard, and three or four namesakes graced his immediate retinue. Nevertheless, Sir Peter promoted rapidly, creating a quick turnover of faces in the lieutenants' wardroom, and Nelson's progress accelerated.

When Nelson joined the *Bristol* he was third to Lieutenants Robert Deans and James Douglas, while the fourth was Acting Lieutenant George Dundas, formerly an able seaman and master's mate of the *Lowestoffe* and an officer Horatio considered agreeable. After the ship completed a short excursion in August, Sir Peter took his flag ashore and ordered the *Bristol* to join a squadron under Captain Joseph Deane of the sixty-four-gun *Ruby*. Supported also by the *Niger* and *Lowestoffe* frigates and the *Badger* and *Porcupine* sloops, Deane stood off Cape François hoping to intercept traffic between the rebellious American colonies and the French islands. On 4 September, just before sailing, Deans and Douglas were promoted out of the *Bristol*, and Nelson found himself moved up to first and senior lieutenant. To

support him John Packenham and James Macnamara were appointed
second and third lieutenants respectively. The latter, transferred from
the *Niger*, was twice Nelson's age but formed an excellent relationship with his youthful superior.[35]

Under Parker's patronage, Nelson's career filled its sails in more
respects than one. For the rest of the year he made some prize money
from profitable cruises. In July, France had finally declared war on
Britain, encouraged by the American victory at Saratoga to believe
that the time had come to settle old scores. Thus, Captain Deane's
squadron occupied the busy shipping area around Haiti in search of
both French and American prizes.

There followed a brief but exciting period in which the British ships
snapped up victims like Humboldt current squid in a nocturnal feeding
frenzy. When the squadron returned to Port Royal on 20 October it
had fourteen prizes to its credit, nine of them French ships, brigs and
snows, and five American brigs and schooners. The *Bristol* had played
its part in the harvest, taking a French sloop on 28 September, two
French ships and an American schooner two days later, and a final
prize on 6 October. Describing the last of these captures, the log
reflected the pace and character of the operation. The *Bristol*, it said,
was 'still in chase. Hoisted [out] the boats and sent them manned and
armed after two schooners to windward. Saw one of the schooners
fire at the boats. Fired a gun and made signal for the boats to return.
Brought to a schooner from Virginia loaded with tobacco [and] bound
to Cape François. Sent an officer and eight men on board of her.'

The voyage gave Nelson a little of the action he craved and, he
estimated, £400 in prize money. After replenishing water and victuals,
refitting, and bringing their crews back to strength in Jamaica, the
same ships left to return to their station on 8 November. In eager
anticipation the men of the *Bristol* were exercised at their great guns,
and fired volleys of musketry from the poop, forecastle and fighting
tops. At least another seven prizes were taken before the end of the
year. The *Bristol*'s tender captured a French schooner on 16 November,
and in the first days of the following month Caulfield overtook a
Frenchman bound for Cape François and 'a rebel ship' that had fired
upon the *Badger*.[36]

To cap these successes, Nelson returned to Port Royal on 20
December to be discharged from the *Bristol*. Sir Peter had promised
to make him a commander as soon as a ship became available and
he had kept his word. On 8 December 1778, while Horatio was still

at sea, he had been commissioned master and commander of the *Badger* sloop. After eight years in the service, he had a ship of his own.

But there was a bittersweet poignancy in this latest promotion, for shortly after Nelson had returned from the first spell of prize-taking on the *Bristol* in October a letter arrived for him from England. The handwriting on the envelope was his father's. Inside Horatio found a letter dated the previous July. It told him that Captain Maurice Suckling was dead.

9

Nelson was a commander, only a short step from becoming a post-captain, but the man to whom he owed almost everything – who had managed his career, planned every move and cleared away every obstacle – was gone. All Horatio's professional life, Uncle Maurice had been there to guide, advise and protect. Now, suddenly, the world seemed a lonelier, less friendly place.

It had happened on 14 July 1778 about two weeks after Nelson's official enrolment on the *Bristol*. Captain Suckling had been ill for a long time. He attended his last meeting at the Navy Board on 4 March and died in London at the age of fifty-two. He was taken home to be buried near his parents in their beloved Barsham.

Horatio had known about his uncle's illness. Suckling had mentioned its persistence in a letter he had written in the spring, but the admiring nephew had entertained hopes of a recovery, and the sudden loss of his 'dear good uncle' fell 'very heavy' upon him. It stirred deep insecurities. Nelson knew his swift and seamless promotion had been due to his uncle. To the end Captain Suckling had served him. He had asked Sir Peter Parker to intervene, and reminded Lord Sandwich that the youth was his nephew and that any assistance given him would be counted a personal favour. Horatio's future, which seemed so bright, suddenly clouded over.[37]

For the past two years Nelson had cultivated the habit of writing letters. Most were informal, confiding in William and other members of the family, and such close friends as Captain Locker, whose 'goodness' continued to be 'more than ever I expected'. The relationship with Captain Suckling appears to have been less casual, however. Horatio still addressed his uncle as 'Dear Sir'. But for all that Uncle Maurice had been his principal counsellor.[38]

The man was gone, but his legacies remained and still propelled Horatio forward. The captain's will, completed four years before, bequeathed £1,000 upon every Nelson niece and £500 upon each of the boys. Apparently Suckling also wanted Horatio to have his sword, for William Suckling gave it to him when the young officer next visited London in 1781. The heirloom was rumoured to have once belonged to Captain Suckling's great uncle, the naval hero Galfridus Walpole. If so, it fittingly passed to the youngest member of the family to seek his fortune upon the sea.[39]

Somewhere in his sea chest Nelson already had other valuable mementos of his uncle's stewardship. There was a volume on navigation the captain had given him, and six sheets of paper in his uncle's hand, providing advice on all aspects of managing a ship. They prescribed respect for superiors and dwelt upon simple but effective means of keeping a ship 'in very high order'. Captain Suckling had always paid attention to detail, and his advice ranged from the stowing of hammocks to the raising of sails ('always be particular in working . . . sails together, for nothing is so lubberly as to hoist one sail after another'); from fixing days for washing clothes and decks to stipulating that provisions be issued at five in the morning and four in the afternoon; and from safeguarding the keys of storerooms to basic security in the magazine. As Horatio prepared to command his first ship and read those notes, he may have drawn consolation from knowing that his uncle was still at his elbow, guiding his hand.[40]

Two legacies of Captain Suckling were especially important. One was the residue of goodwill he had left behind, goodwill such as Parker's that could still be tapped. The other was a tradition of service. Suckling had taught Horatio that duty came before financial self-interest, and that in the end it would bring its own reward. It was an optimistic philosophy perhaps, but one calculated to stimulate effort. Eight years later Nelson wistfully recalled this greatest of all his uncle's legacies. 'I feel myself to my country his heir,' he wrote. 'And it [England] shall, I am bold to say, never lack the want of his counsel. I feel he gave it to me as a legacy, and had I been near him when he was removed, he would have said, "My boy, I leave you to my country. Serve her well, and she'll never desert, but will ultimately reward you."'[41]

VII

THE FIRST COMMANDS

Who, if he rise to station of command,
Rises by open means; and there will stand
On honourable terms, or else retire,
And in himself possess his own desire.
William Wordsworth,
The Character of the Happy Warrior

1

THE *Badger* was not much of a craft, it was true. A captured American merchantman, she had needed extensive renovation after being purchased by the navy in 1776, and even when Horatio Nelson was piped aboard at Port Royal on the first day of 1779 her condition suggested imminent condemnation. Sir Peter Parker reckoned she had a few months left, enough to provide Nelson with a command until something better turned up. The *Badger* was a puny vessel, a brig with two square-rigged masts and a feeble armament of a dozen four-pounder cannons and a couple of half pound calibre swivels. That being the case, she had no business taking on serious warships, but could run errands and root out small enemy privateers.[1]

Nelson's commission named him master and commander. The rank of commander entitled its holder to captain a brig or a sloop, vessels deemed too small to justify the appointment of both a post-captain and a master or navigating officer. The functions of these dignitaries were therefore combined in the rank of commander, which was considered equivalent to that of a major in the army.

Ninety men formed the complement of the *Badger*, with one

lieutenant, Osborne Edwards. Nelson inherited the crew from her previous commander, Michael John Everitt, but he brought Francis Forster, a surgeon's mate, from the *Bristol* and promoted him to surgeon, and looked around for more petty officers. In March Locker sent two from the *Lowestoffe*. Of these George Cruger made a respectable midshipman but Edward Capper turned into a drunkard. 'I wish I could give [him] a good character,' Nelson said, regretting that he would have to press a better master's mate from some unfortunate merchantman.[2]

The command of a ship, even one as inconsiderable as the *Badger*, conferred elements of patronage. Nelson had the right to take four captain's servants on board, but so far from home he had no relatives to slot into the vacant positions. Nelson picked out four likely ratings for the honour – William Sylvan, Frank Lepee, William Orswood and John Smith. Lepee, an eighteen-year-old Londoner, had joined the *Lowestoffe* as a boatswain's servant in 1777, and would follow Nelson for sixteen years.[3]

Nelson was troubled with deserters during the six months he commanded the *Badger*. Whenever the ship was moored in a port, malcontents seized opportunities to run. Twenty-one in all did so, two-thirds of them members of the *Badger*'s crew, and the rest 'supernumeraries' being given passage or awaiting distribution to other ships. The defectors even included a midshipman, Henry Lee, who fled at Rattan (Roatan) Island in March. It was not a good record, especially for a brig looking for prizes, and suggests the inexperience of her captain. On the other hand, Nelson apparently preserved reasonable order. A few men followed him to other commands, including the purser John Tyson and the assistant master John Wilson. Only one was punished – Thomas Rochester, a pressed man from Brentwood in Essex, earning the dubious distinction of being the first man ever flogged on Nelson's orders when he received two dozen lashes for drunkenness and disobedience.[4]

Sometimes men were disturbed by any change of captain, as the history of that excellent ship the *Ruby* demonstrated. After the death of her popular commander Joseph Deane in 1780 there was widespread disaffection. As Nelson wrote, 'Of that noble ship's crew, three hundred took boats and are gone off. Every method has been used to bring them back, which I hope will prove successful.'[5]

Possibly the departure of the *Badger*'s previous captain unsettled some of her men and increased the difficulties of the young successor.

Nelson hardly cut an imposing figure. He was surprisingly adolescent, barely months beyond the age of majority and had something of a schoolboy about him. A mop of sandy brown hair fell about a thin, sensitive, almost effeminate face with alert blue eyes, a wandering nose and sensuous mouth, until drawn into a ribbon or queue behind. His height was no more than average for the time, perhaps five feet six inches, and he was slim with a waist about thirty-two inches and no more than thirty-eight across the chest. Clothes sometimes hung on him casually. Contemporaries later spoke of Nelson as 'small' and 'slight', 'not a tall man', or 'about the middle height, thin, and somewhat inelegantly formed' with 'few words and plain manners'. It is easy to excuse sun-burnished tars aboard the *Badger* looking incredulously at each another as this apparently insignificant and whimsical little creature with a Norfolk drawl hopped aboard. As yet his lust for distinction and genius only flickered freely within, out of sight.[6]

There is no evidence that Nelson himself had misgivings. His instructions directed him westwards to the British settlements clinging like limpets to the Mosquito coast of Spanish Honduras and Nicaragua, scratching a living from logging, farming and fishing for green turtles. There were several of them – St George's Key near Belize and Black River, Rattan Island and Omoa in the Gulf of Honduras – all of them surviving at the sufferance of Spain and in fear of the depredations of American privateers and French naval forces. They were even more afraid that Spain would also pitch into the war against Britain. Now that France had allied herself with the American colonies, Britain was fighting on both sides of the Atlantic and was dangerously stretched. There was a reasonable chance that Spain would also attack her, and try to regain control of Gibraltar, which Britain had acquired in 1704. If Spain declared war, the British settlements in Honduras and Nicaragua would become easy targets, and as they struggled to improve their defences they cultivated good relations with the local Mosquito Indians. Nelson was charged with communicating with the British settlements and bringing an Indian leader named King George to Jamaica for talks with the governor, Major General John Dalling.

The *Badger* sailed on 25 January 1779, and five days later made the mouth of the Black River in Honduras. Nelson had a letter from Dalling for the settlers, but there was a reef across the estuary and he fired a gun for a pilot. Unfortunately, the weather was blustery and the water broke so menacingly across the reef that no one dared risk coming out to him. The next day he slipped a few miles further east towards Cape Camaron, anchored off what he called 'Prinaw Creek', and dispatched a boat upstream to reach the Black River settlement that way. Then, continuing along the coast as far as Cape Gracias a Dios, he sent more of the governor's messages ashore before returning to Black River and finally getting the *Badger* to its moorings. King George and two of his attendants duly arrived on board. George was the leader of the Sandy Bay 'samboes', a mixed Indian–black community descended from the survivors of a slaver shipwrecked upon the coast a hundred or so years before. These blacks, as well as Indian warriors throughout the region, were being courted by the British as potential military auxiliaries in case a war broke out with Spain.

Nelson visited Rattan Island, where the guns were hoisted out and the ship careened, and St George's Key before setting sail for Jamaica in March. By his own story the trip was a success. He 'gained so much the affections of the [Mosquito coast] settlers that they unanimously voted me their thanks, and expressed their regret on my leaving them, entrusting to me to describe to Sir Peter Parker and Sir John Dalling their situation should a war with Spain break out'.[7]

On 2 April the *Badger* reached Port Royal, where ten of His Majesty's ships, including the old *Lowestoffe*, were gathered. Although desertions increased in port, he had reasons to believe the efficiency of his crew had benefited from the cruise. No prizes had been taken, but the men had sharpened their skills in exercises with the guns and the pursuit of half a dozen suspicious sails. Nelson's first mission in command of a ship of war might have lacked incident, but it was nothing of which to be ashamed.

2

On reaching Port Royal, he was sorry to find Captain Locker ill and talking about returning home. The thought of losing another close friend worried Nelson, though he believed Locker would recover in England. As a favour to his old captain, on 21 April Nelson entered his eldest son, William Locker junior, on the books of the *Badger* as a captain's servant, re-rating Frank Lepee as an able seaman to make room. A pay book lists Locker's son as 'prest', but both that and his very presence were fictitious. In fact the boy was not on the ship at all. He was not even in the West Indies. Nor had he reached his eleventh birthday, the minimum age at which a son of a naval officer might enter the service. Less than ten years old, William Locker was too young to serve legitimately on any warship. He was still at home with his mother, but if he ever chose a naval career the bogus sea time he had accumulated on the *Badger* would ease his promotion.[8]

The next day Nelson sailed again, submerging his sadness about Captain Locker in a hunt for privateers.

He enquired of every ship he 'spoke' and chased all doubtful sails in vain, but on the clear afternoon of the 28th his luck seemed to change. The *Badger* pursued a ship for an hour before halting it with a warning shot. She was the *La Prudente* sloop of eighty tons, on her way from Cape François to New Orleans with dry goods, sugar, coffee and other French produce. Though she mounted no artillery, a few muskets, pistols and cutlasses, as well as powder and shot, were taken from her. Her master, Pedro Guinard, protested that the ship was Spanish, but most on board were French and Nelson searched her for two days. The ship's papers, eventually discovered hidden inside a shoe, were recently dated and suggested that *La Prudente* belonged to three Frenchmen who were naturalised Spaniards residing in New Orleans. Nelson was sure of his prize but her status was ambiguous. Was she French, and therefore fair game, or the property of Spaniards, with whom Britain was not yet at war? In the event, Nelson's prize agent in Jamaica, Hercules Ross, failed to get her condemned in the vice-admiralty court. More unfortunately, Nelson had to hold the sixteen prisoners, including a master, two of the owners and a black servant, on board the *Badger* for a week before landing them at Port Antonio. In the intervening time some of his crew became infected with what he was told was the plague.[9]

Nor was there compensation elsewhere. On the afternoon of 30 April Nelson encountered an enemy privateer off the northeast coast of Jamaica and pursued it for the rest of the day, discharging futile rounds of shot and grape. The next morning the wind dropped and the *Badger* lay becalmed under lifeless sails while her target propelled itself to safety under oars. Six days later another promising 'chase' escaped in dark, cloudy weather leaving Nelson cursing his lack of a night glass.[10]

Potentially more damaging to a young commander was a disagreement with the master of a British merchantman in Port Antonio in May. Still short of seamen, Nelson sent a boat around the traders anchored in the port, looking for likely men to press into service, and his officer brought five hands from the *Amity Hall*. Reconsidering,

Nelson regretted the action. He had left the merchantman with enough seamen to function, but worried that his conduct might appear high-handed and planned to return the pressed men. But when the master of the *Amity Hall* stormed aboard in 'a most impertinent manner, and with very abusive language told me he should take [me to] the law', Nelson saw red. Growing what he modestly termed 'warm', he returned two of the five sailors, added one of the less useful of his own men and declared he would keep the rest. The master appeared mollified. At least he apologised to Nelson on his next visit to the *Badger* on 13 May, but a bad account of the affair was already circulating in Kingston.[11]

For the first time Nelson felt his public reputation endangered. The captain of a man-of-war was accountable not only to professional superiors but also to the mercantile community and society at large. He wrote to Locker in search of help and reassurance, but it was a sad letter, written after he had learned that his 'sea-daddy' had at last been given leave to return to England. For some time Locker had been afflicted with a violent scorbutic disorder that pained his back and loins and he went home in May. Personally impoverished as he felt, Horatio knew that Jamaica was no place for a sick man:

I see you are quite settled about going home [he wrote], which in all proba-bility may happen before you can hear from me again, but I shall always write to you in England. I hope you will have a good passage, and find Mrs Locker and all your family in good health. I hope you will soon recover when you get home. The friendship you have shown me I shall never forget, and though I lose my best friend by your going, I would not have you stay a day in this country. I am very sorry indeed Captain [Joseph] Deane [of the *Ruby*] is ill. I beg you will give [him] my best wishes for his speedy recovery.[12]

Behind him Captain Locker left his young admirer with a certifi-cate of good behaviour covering service on the *Lowestoffe*, a prayer book signed by the two of them, now in the Royal Naval Museum, a treasure chest of memories and the comforting knowledge that he had a professional ally at home. But the ailing captain did not return home to the happiness he anticipated. He recovered his health, but his young wife, of whom he had never stopped speaking, died in child-birth the following year and was buried in the village of Addington, Kent, where the couple had married ten years before.

Back in Jamaica, Nelson witnessed a misfortune of a different kind.

At Port Antonio on 23 May 1779 he picked up a small convoy for Bluefields on the Mosquito coast. Preferring to search for a privateer haunting the region, he discharged the ships at Montego Bay to make a fruitless cruise, and was back in the same place at the end of the month.

At three-thirty on the afternoon of 1 June five ships entered the bay and moored near the *Badger*. Four were London merchantmen and the other was their escort, the twenty-gun *Glasgow* under Captain Thomas Lloyd. About two hours later an alarm was raised on the *Glasgow*. The ship was on fire. A purser's steward, Richard Brace, had been stealing rum from the after hold and dropped a light into the cask. Soon the flames were out of control and smoke was billowing from the quarterdeck hatchway on the starboard side of the ship, creating what Nelson described as 'a most shocking sight'.

A terrifying scenario loomed, for Lloyd's was no ordinary cargo. He had been shipping gunpowder to Jamaica, and if it exploded the *Glasgow*, the other ships sharing the anchorage, and the warehouses and magazines were all threatened with violent destruction. There could have been a panic, but Lloyd kept his head and for part of the time directed operations from the unsafe station of a boom. The court martial, held on the *Bristol* at Port Royal the following month, recognised his efforts to save the ship. Sir Peter Parker happily reported the captain's acquittal, declaring that he had behaved 'remarkably' and been 'well seconded by his officers and crew'. Only the miserable steward was held culpable, and he was lucky to get no more than one hundred lashes for conduct leading to such calamitous consequences.

Nelson learned of the disaster from Lieutenant Richard Oakley of the *Glasgow*. Oakley was out in a boat pressing sailors when the fire broke out, but seeing the smoke and confusion on board he returned at once. Calling alongside the *Badger*, Oakley demanded as many buckets as could be found, and collecting the first dozen pulled strenuously back to the *Glasgow*. Nelson had his boats manned, commandeered two more from nearby merchantmen and with the rest of the buckets hurried after Oakley to help.

Nelson's official biographers, Clarke and McArthur, gave their hero the full credit for evacuating the *Glasgow*. In their version Nelson finds the *Glasgow*'s men abandoning the burning ship by jumping into the sea, but turns them back, insisting that the powder first be thrown overboard and all guns be pointed upwards. This story, designed purely to inflate Nelson's reputation, was a libel on the officers and men of the unfortunate ship, and erased Lloyd and Oakley from the rescue completely. Nelson himself never made so extravagant an assertion. Though characteristically effusive about his contribution, he allowed that 'it was owing to my exertions, joined to his [Lloyd's], that the whole crew were rescued from the flames'. Inasmuch as he provided many of the boats needed to evacuate the one hundred and sixty men there was some justification for this claim.

In reality, Lloyd's men were desperately fighting the flames before Nelson arrived. Hammocks soaked in water were thrown into the after hold to dampen the fire, and attempts were made to contain it beneath the lower deck before the suffocating smoke and heat between decks drove the men back. Oakley and the gunner both claimed the honour of prompting the removal of the powder, and Lloyd later said that he gave orders that none should leave the ship until every cask had been thrown overboard. Oakley, the gunner and a dozen men broke open the magazine door, and by six o'clock barrels and munitions were being handed up the fore hatchway. Last to be cleared were the filled cartridges. If a major explosion had been averted, however, the ship itself was doomed. At about seven the flames were breaking through the quarterdeck, licking up the mizzen and main rigging and running forward, and the order to abandon ship had to be given.

Nelson's contemporary statement, hitherto unused by biographers, was given to the court martial in Port Royal and completely destroys the Clarke and McArthur fable:

On the first of June between five and six in the evening I saw the alarm of fire on board the *Glasgow*. Immediately ordered all assistance from the *Badger*, which was immediately sent. I went alongside and saw the ship in a blaze, about one quarter of an hour after the first alarm. After seven o'clock the flames broke through the quarter deck and ascended the main and mizzen rigging, when the boats were ordered by Captain Lloyd to the bows of the ship to receive the men. They were carried from thence on board the *Badger*. Several of the men were much burned, particularly the master [Thomas Cobby] who died the next day. When I went first alongside I heard Captain Lloyd encouraging the men in getting the powder out of the magazine and to throw the powder out of the arm chest on the quarter-deck. Likewise to lay down the guns to prevent their doing any damage to the shipping or the town. The ship was lined entirely from the bowsprit to the quarter [deck] with men drawing water to extinguish the fire with expedition and good order.

On the decks of the *Badger* officers and men of the *Glasgow* huddled in disbelief, but although some had been burned most were safe. The master of a merchant ship then came aboard to protest at the danger to his ship, and it was decided to haul the burning carcass out to sea. Nelson and Lloyd cut the bower anchor cables securing the dying ship, got a hawser aboard her and at about eight-thirty turned her loose before a wind from the land. She drifted away, the flames patterning the dark water and consuming her to the waterline, until about midnight when the ruined shell exploded and then sunk swiftly.

The master of the *Glasgow* died of his injuries at seven the following morning, and nine days later another seaman also died, although whether in consequence of the fire is unknown. Unfortunately, the rainy season broke the day after the tragedy, and sickness spread among the refugees squatting on the open decks of the little *Badger*, unable to find shelter below. Horatio shed his burden as quickly as he could. Some sailors were left at Montego Bay when he put to sea on 2 June, and six days later another seventy were transferred to the *Achilles* victualler at St Ann's harbour, where Nelson also disembarked over twenty muskets, eighteen cartouche boxes, fifty-two four-pound shot, half a barrel of powder, a dozen boarding pikes and a number of match paper cartridges and powder horns. The remaining passengers were discharged at Port Royal, which Nelson reached with a convoy on 19 June.

Nelson usually felt for unfortunate officers, and wrote a week after the event that Captain Lloyd was still 'very melancholy indeed', while poor Oakley, 'a very good young man', had lost everything but the clothes he stood in. Though exonerated by court martial and re-employed, Lloyd never prospered. Eventually he retired to Carmarthen in Wales, but Nelson never forgot him, nor failed to express his greatest respect for the unfortunate officer. A little more than four years before his own death off Cape Trafalgar, he wrote to Lloyd that 'my heart is always warm to you, and your friendship will be the pleasure of my life, let the world either smile or frown upon me'.[13]

It was a melancholy end to Nelson's first official command. On 13 June, in the voyage from St Ann's to Port Royal, he chased a brig that refused to respond to warning shots. A hundred round and grape shot were fired before the quarry submitted, but investigation merely revealed her to be a Jamaican privateer.

However, exciting news awaited Nelson in port: Sir Peter Parker had a frigate for him to command and was promoting him post-captain.

On 20 June, Nelson consigned the *Badger* to the capable hands of his good friend Cuthbert Collingwood, thrilled to have gained that life-changing foothold on the bottom of the captains' list. He was still only twenty-one years old, with plenty of time to travel the long road to flag rank.

Before his death Captain Suckling had predicted that the Reverend Edmund Nelson would live to see his son an admiral and now it looked as if the prophecy might be fulfilled.

3

Officers hungry for promotion and prize money used to toast the Jamaica station with the words, 'A sickly season and a bloody war!'[14] Promotion came quickly out there. Partly it was the remoteness, which compelled commanders-in-chief to fill vacancies from available officers, rather than to wait for Admiralty appointments. And partly it was the speed at which such vacancies occurred. Disease took more men than battle and the turnover of officers and men was ferocious. The Jamaica station offered fine opportunities to take prizes and to step into dead men's shoes – if you survived.

Certainly Nelson was making progress. In 1779 Captain Everitt, formerly commander of the *Badger*, was killed in action. A chain of promotions followed, as gaps were filled, and on 11 June Nelson succeeded Christopher Parker to the captaincy of the *Hinchinbroke*, a French prize that had been converted into a nine-pounder, twenty-eight-gun frigate. The *Hinchinbroke* leaked like an old bucket, and had only been brought into service to meet the increasing demands upon the Jamaica station, but it put Nelson on the captains' list. The problem was that the ship was still at sea on a trip to Florida, and her new captain had to kick his heels in Jamaica until her return.

In one of his news-packed letters to Locker, Nelson admitted that he was 'never well in port', but on this occasion his disappointment was the greater because Captain Deane wanted him to accompany the *Ruby* to their old cruising grounds off Haiti. Instead, Horatio had to content himself sharing the captains' mess in Jamaica, cultivating new friends as if they were exotic plants.[15]

Deane, Collingwood and Cornwallis were particularly close companions during this time. Collingwood, a round-faced Tynesider who had known Nelson since 1773, was ten years older but inferior in rank. He seemed to step into every post Nelson vacated and followed him to the *Lowestoffe*, *Badger* and *Hinchinbroke*. Captain William Cornwallis of the *Lion*, a ruddy-complexioned, quiet and self-effacing officer, was five years older than Collingwood, but Horatio also enjoyed his company. 'I hope I have made a friend of him,' he told Locker. The remark, though casually made, reveals much about young Nelson's character. He was a taciturn, sober man, but there was nothing stony or stiff about him. Far from one of life's unemotional passers-by, falling indifferently in and out of acquaintanceships at the drop of a hat, he actively sought like spirits, and invested time and effort into making them friends. To them he was fiercely loyal and compassionate, rejoicing in their successes and commiserating over tribulations. In time his circle widened, as he infected one colleague after another. We have already seen him standing by Captain Locker, and here in Jamaica he forged lifelong friendships with Deane, Collingwood and Cornwallis.[16]

To Nelson's relief his enforced spell ashore was not devoid of incident. A large French fleet from Toulon was already among the West Indian islands, under the command of the Comte d'Estaing. In June it seized St Thomas and Grenada, two British islands in the Lesser Antilles. And then, amid rumours of the approach of this overwhelming force, came the news that Spain, too, had finally declared war on a harassed Britain, hoping to regain Gibraltar in any peace negotiations. It was not unexpected but serious all the same. Suddenly the dangers from occasional American corsairs seemed small indeed, for the seas were full of powerful enemies.

At the beginning of August 1779 the *Gayton*, a Jamaican privateer, came into port with a tender. Its company had seen some of d'Estaing's ships on 29 July, eight ships of the line, several frigates and many transports, and they were close by, off the northeast coast of Hispaniola, within striking distance of Jamaica. Some Spaniards, as ignorant as the *Gayton* of the deteriorating relations between their respective countries, told the captain of the privateer that d'Estaing's full force was larger still, and consisted of twelve line of battleships, as many frigates and a hundred or so transports. They were going to embark twelve thousand soldiers at St Nicolas Mole, guarding the Windward Passage, and then fall upon Jamaica itself.

For a few days the island was in turmoil, as every scrap of news seemed to confirm the ominous tidings. His Majesty's ships *Charon* and *Pomona* reported seeing eighteen large ships at Port au Prince on 4 August, evidently preparing to join d'Estaing, and on the 17th a neutral Dutch vessel put into Jamaica from Hispaniola. It brought word that d'Estaing's fleet had reached Cape François on the north coast of Haiti, and twenty-six ships of the line, up to a dozen frigates and twenty-two thousand troops were massing for the invasion of Jamaica. There was a panic. Without waiting for the approval of the island's assembly, on 7 August the governor, Major General John Dalling, declared martial law from the King's House in Spanish Town and summoned a considerable proportion of the militia into service. Blacks were mustered to complete unfinished fortifications, and batteries and redoubts were thrown up along a thirty-mile front from six miles to windward of Kingston to the old harbour. Letters for help went from Dalling and Parker to Sir Henry Clinton commanding the British troops on the American mainland, and to Vice Admiral John Byron. They explained that a full-blown attack was 'daily expected'.[17]

For more than a century Jamaica had stubbornly represented Britain in the Caribbean, defying the powers of imperial Spain and France, but now the island seemed doomed to fall before overwhelming forces. The tension, tightened by the heat and humidity of the hurricane season, lasted for weeks. At the dead of night on 24 August, Kingston was jolted from sleep by the sound of gunfire, and the militia spilled out 'with wonderful alacrity', evidently determined to resist the enemy as if they were not most indifferently armed. But it was a false alarm. This time the invaders proved to be no more than a convoy of London merchantmen, being escorted in by His Majesty's ship the *Pallas*.[18]

Nelson was flattered with a key command in the defences. Admiral Parker had all his ships except the *Hinchinbroke* and four sloops, and disposed them to command the approaches to Kingston. A boom was placed between Gun and Pekin Keys to divert attackers into the channel between Gun Key and Fort Charles, situated at Port Royal on a spit of land that curled around the harbour. A redoubtable seventeenth-century fortress dominating the harbour mouth with a hundred guns in double tiers, Fort Charles would be the focus of any battle for Kingston. Despite his youth, Nelson was put in charge of it with five hundred soldiers. Supporting him were the *Salisbury*, *Charon*, *Lion* and *Janus*, anchored about a cable's length apart in a line across the harbour entrance, from the point at Port Royal to what was called the western middle ground. If the French overwhelmed them, the ships had instructions to fall back to the *Bristol* and *Ruby* in the narrows off Fort Augusta, which was also defended by a boom. Five more men-of-war, including the *Lowestoffe*, were stationed at various points of danger and four fire ships had been prepared.[19]

Yet, for all this, Nelson could see the defences were flawed. There were simply not enough men. Jamaica had only two regiments of regulars, the 60th (Royal American) Regiment and the 79th (Liverpool Blues), of which only the first was acclimatised to the tropics. For the rest reliance had to be placed in a discontented militia consisting of a few whites, many blacks and a large number of mere conscripts. Furthermore, the entire 6,800 troops available were widely scattered to cover different points. Five thousand were 'between the ferry and Kingston', another thousand at Fort Augusta, five hundred at Fort Charles and three hundred at the Apostles Battery. The guns at Forts Charles and Augusta were principally served by privateersmen, who were to be summoned by an alarm system, but the other batteries were largely manned by untrained blacks drummed up from the plantations by Hercules Ross. It did not inspire Nelson with confidence. 'I think you must not be surprised to hear of my learning to speak French,' he told Locker dryly on 12 August.[20]

Seventeen days after Nelson's pessimistic prediction, the *Punch* tender arrived with new intelligence. She had spoke a vessel that had been at Cape François only hours before, and learned that d'Estaing had sailed on 17 August with a hundred and twenty warships and transports and thousands of soldiers. The master of the *Punch* reconnoitred Cape François and St Nicolas Mole himself, and confirmed that the French fleet had gone, leaving nothing larger than a frigate behind. Wherever d'Estaing was heading it was obviously not Jamaica, and the imminence of the hurricane season seemed to preclude any later descent upon the island being made. Everyone breathed easily again, martial law was lifted and ships were allowed to come and go as before.[21]

Nelson was proud of the confidence that had been placed in him and would boast that his was 'the most important post in the whole island', but the appearance of the *Hinchinbroke* soon restored him to his proper element. The first of September was a clear day. Captain Nelson went on board the frigate and solemnly listened while his commission was read to the assembled ship's company. Then he prepared his new command for sea.

4

Again Nelson inherited the men, but this time he had a small band of followers – the first in his career – to accompany him. Among them were the four captain's servants (if we include the absent William Locker), Forster the surgeon, Frank Lepee and petty officers such as Cruger, Tyson and Thomas Gore.

The books of the *Hinchinbroke* also suggest that Nelson was not going to be above the minor financial abuses so commonly practised by captains of the day. His new frigate had a complement of two hundred men, twice that of the tiny *Badger*, and entitled him to another four captain's servants, although he was in no better position to exploit the privilege. He filled three of the vacancies with seamen – William Fry, James Hatton and John Notes – and invented the fourth incumbent. 'Horace Nelson' never existed and was presumably borne on the books purely to earn the captain the full allowance paid for servants.[22]

Nelson encountered a few problems acquiring a stable team of officers for the *Hinchinbroke*. John Walker was master and Robert Huggins the purser, but during the eight months of his command Nelson had no fewer than three first lieutenants, one succeeding another. Notably, all three – Arthur St Leger, Charles Cunningham and George Harrison – were merely acting lieutenants still waiting to take their examinations. Of them Cunningham, whose scant, two-month stint began in November, may have been the ablest. Hailing from Eye in Suffolk, he was actually two years older than his captain and had experience of both the naval and merchant services. Harrison, who followed him, had been the second lieutenant of the *Hinchinbroke*, and Joseph Bullen, a former protégé of Captain Cornwallis, joined the ship to replace him as the junior commissioned officer on board. Bullen became one of the most steadfast of all Nelson's followers. Born in April 1761, the son of the rector of Kennett in Cambridgeshire, he had gone to sea as a thirteen-year-old midshipman in Cornwallis's *Pallas*, and followed his captain to four more ships before transferring to the *Hinchinbroke*.[23]

Bullen was the only one of Nelson's lieutenants to hold a full commission, dated two years earlier. The use of so many unqualified officers reflected the shortages on the Jamaica station and the necessity for constant promotions, but hardly helped maintain good order aboard the ships. Nevertheless, Nelson did rather better on the *Hinchingbroke* than the *Badger*. He felt it necessary to flog nine of his men, but there were only ten desertions, one from the hospital in Port Royal.[24]

Nelson enjoyed reading his new orders, which dispatched him to join the *Niger* (Captain Robert Lambert) and the *Penelope* (Captain

James Jones) in patrolling the Lesser Antilles to the southeast. Here, close to the fabled main, there were opportunities to profit from the new war with Spain. Spanish wars had always been popular in the Royal Navy, because treasure was still shipped from the rich American mines to Spain and fortunes in prize money had occasionally fallen to fortunate officers. Nelson was by no means a slave to lucre, but he was a man of sorely measurable means with a career ahead, and far from blind to the advantages of money. The potentially rich pickings were probably at the forefront of his mind when he sailed from Port Royal on 5 October 1779.[25]

Improving the efficiency of his crew on the way, he reached the *Niger* and *Penelope* off the Dutch island of Curaçao on the 28th, and two days later experienced his first contested action as a commander. At about midnight of 30 October the squadron spotted four sails to the northeast and gave chase. One quickly surrendered, but the *Niger* and *Hitchinbroke* had difficulty with the second. About three-thirty, after exchanging broadsides with the *Niger* and resisting for an hour, she hauled down her colours. By daylight the other two fugitives had also been taken by the *Penelope*. They were American vessels, two fourteen-gun ships, the *Conference* and the *Rachel and Betsy*, and a brig and a snow, the *Penelope* and *Adrianne*, both unarmed, all four owned by Daniel Ross and Company, manned by a total of sixty-eight men, and bound for Curaçao with sugar and coffee. The Americans had been hopelessly outgunned and outnumbered, but they had fought gamely. Nelson's frigate received several shot, her pinnace was broken and some of her rigging cut. But her captain was richer in more than experience. His promotion to post-captain had increased his share of prize money, and he estimated that the captures would net him £800.[26]

On 6 November the *Hinchinbroke* and the *Niger* also seized a sloop, but somewhere east of Jamaica Nelson separated from his consort. The end of the month found his frigate being punished by a powerful head sea. Her fore-topgallant yard, main topmast and main top were sheared away, with much standing and running rigging. The men cleared the wreckage and fashioned repairs, but Nelson put into Port Antonio for help. There he was asked to escort a merchantman to Port Royal, and gathering others along the way reached his destination on 12 December.

Back in harbour, the *Hinchinbroke* was refitted and reprovisioned, ten men were pressed to make good desertions and Horatio punctuated the seasonal festivities with letters to his much-missed 'sea-daddy'. Locker learned that his rum, stored on the *Lowestoffe*, was still safe, and that Nelson was sending him some shaddock fruits as a gift; in the meantime he received a chronicle of the ravages of life on the Jamaica station.[27]

'Poor Hill', the former master of the *Lowestoffe*, had died of a fever at Rattan, and 'your old coxswain' had perished in action. Sadder still, Horatio had just attended the funeral of one the most respected of their colleagues. 'I am now going to tell you what you and many others will be very sorry to hear,' he wrote. 'The death of that worthy, good man, Captain Joseph Deane [of the *Ruby*]. He died on the 12th of January, and was buried next day at Green Bay amidst the tears of his officers and ship's company and his many friends.' Nelson, most likely, was among those friends overcome by emotion. He never hid affection from close comrades and was usually tearful at meetings and partings. He would always find deathbed scenes unbearable.

The end of Deane seems to have broken up the captains' 'mess'. Horatio, who shared lodgings with Cornwallis, was sure that he would soon be returning to England himself. He was ill again and his doctors were advising him to leave Jamaica. He even applied to the captain and first mate of the *Rover*, an American ship brought in as a prize, for a particular bottle of medicine. His '*old* complaint in my breast' was to blame, he informed Locker. 'It is turned out to be the gout there,' and he had been twice 'given over' to 'that cursed disorder' in the past eight months. Gout was a diagnosis eighteenth-century physicians conveniently ascribed to almost any unidentifiable pain, but Nelson was probably actually experiencing recurrent attacks of the malaria he had contracted in the East Indies.[28]

Before going home, however, he anticipated performing one more service and Sir Peter was trying to find him a better ship. The admiral offered Nelson a Spanish prize he was converting into a thirty-six-gun frigate, but the captain opted to wait for a purpose-built warship to become available.

Just what that final service would be was rapidly becoming clear and providing the gossip for the island. Excitement and speculation were rife, but few, perhaps none, realised that what began as an adventure of dazzling imperial vision was to disintegrate into a hideous nightmare of broken dreams and death.

VIII

IN THE WAKE OF THE BUCCANEERS

To him, as to the burning levin,
Short, bright, resistless course was given,
Where'er his Country's foes were found
Was heard the fated thunder's sound.
Till burst the bolt on yonder shore,
Rolled, blazed, destroy'd – and was no more.

Sir Walter Scott, *Marmion*

1

MAJOR General John Dalling was almost fifty and had been a soldier for most of his life. He regaled listeners with colourful memories of the Jacobite rebellion and service in North America under Amherst and Wolfe, but he had also spent many years in Jamaica, where he rose from the humble command of Fort Charles to become governor and commander-in-chief of the island in 1777. Dalling was a man it was possible to underestimate. He suffered from an old war wound, cursed a stubborn gout and looked homely, plump and amiable. Entertaining in some style at the King's House in Spanish Town, a few miles northwest of Kingston, he looked suitably tailored to a life of sedentary administration. But the truth was that Dalling had a vestigial thirst for military glory and was thoroughly fed up with Jamaica. He constantly feuded with the assembly, which was not only corrupt but eager to appropriate powers claimed by the royal governor. Now that Spain had entered the war, joining France and the American colonies, Dalling saw a way out – a means of winning that coveted military reputation with plunder and an honourable retirement to boot.

The immediate threat to Jamaica had passed, and in Dalling's opinion it was time to go on the offensive. At home the colonial secretary, Lord George Germain, agreed. Spain was now a hostile power, a potential threat not only to Britain's West Indian possessions but also to her forces struggling to subdue the rebellious colonies in North America. In fact, Spaniards were soon proving a nuisance on the Mississippi and in Honduras, where they fell upon the British settlement of St George's Key. But if Britain launched her own attacks, the Spanish would be employed defending their own colonies and prevented from interfering elsewhere.

Dalling's ideas raced forward after a small force he sent to the Bay of Honduras in October 1779 successfully stormed Omoa, defeating a superior Spanish garrison and harvesting plunder reckoned at several million dollars. Although Jamaica was soon torn by an unseemly squabble over the spoils, the raid whetted appetites for further adventures. Treasure, patriotism, security, glory . . . Soon Dalling was turning an expectant eye towards Nicaragua, a Spanish province in Central America, and fashioning a plan to recruit volunteers and Indians on the Mosquito coast for a foray up the San Juan River to Lake Nicaragua, where they could seize the town of Granada and blaze an outlet to the Pacific.

Over his shoulders, as Dalling traced the course of the San Juan River in Thomas Jefferys's *West Indian Atlas* of 1775, stood the ghosts of far greater forebears. Sir Francis Drake, that tireless but chivalrous and pious plunderer of all things Spanish, had always wanted to stunt his enemy's European ambitions by severing the flow of her silver from the New World. He had taught the English to ally themselves with Indians and escaped blacks familiar with the terrain of the main and islands, and had once planned to ascend the San Juan himself, but never achieved it. A century later a colonial conflict of astonishing ferocity had made the West Indies the refuge of pirates and buccaneers as well as the cockpit of Europe. Whether or not a formal state of war existed at home, the various colonies loosed ragged forces upon each other as if they were spurred roosters, some of them bloodying and butchering with little compassion. Between 1665 and 1670 no fewer than three armies of irregulars successfully ascended the San Juan to sack Granada, the first led by the privateer Henry Morgan. Two were launched with the support of Sir Thomas Modyford, the governor of Jamaica, whose purposes were not dissimilar to those which motivated Dalling.

Memories of the privateers and buccaneers, and their historic role in the defence of Jamaica, still lingered in Dalling's time, but there were more immediate, and therefore more potent, inspirations. Jefferys's *Atlas*, for instance. It portrayed the San Juan River as an ill-defended waterway across the isthmus of Panama. There were two Spanish forts, neither of any strength. The one near Lake Nicaragua contained only a hundred men, many conscripted criminals. The lake was navigable to flat-bottomed boats, and though the river contained 'several rapid falls', its secrets were known to the Indians.[1]

Also bewitching Dalling were the opinions of James Lawrie, the superintendent general of the British settlements on the Mosquito coast, which Nelson had recently visited in the *Badger*. Lawrie assured Dalling that he could raise thousands of volunteers, including blacks and Indians, and furnish sufficient small boats for an expedition up the San Juan River. Soon Dalling was concocting a plan of majestic proportions. A force would ascend the San Juan, capturing a castle the Spanish had established on it to check the incursions of buccaneers, and reach Lake Nicaragua. By erecting one or more vessels on the lake and capturing the city of Granada at its upper end they could command the entire region, receiving supplies and reinforcements from Jamaica either by the San Juan or the Bluefields and Matina rivers to the north and south of it.

Dalling's plans went far beyond temporary conquest. From Lake Nicaragua, the British could open a way to the Pacific, seizing the towns of Leon and Realejo, and stationing a naval squadron on the western coast of the isthmus. In short, the expedition would cut Spanish America in two, severing South America from the northern provinces such as Mexico. More, controlling such a strategic portion of Central America, with a Pacific squadron to raid Spain's vulnerable but rich west coast, Britain might also foment rebellion in the Spanish possessions, destabilising and perhaps invading Nicaragua, Honduras, Guatemala, Yucatan – maybe even Mexico and Florida. Their silver and resources could be commandeered and the regions thrown open to British commerce and exploitation. This, then, was no hit-and-run raid but a bid to control Central America and dismember Spain's overseas empire. If it was successful, Dalling thought, Britain could offer homes in Central America to Loyalists displaced from the rebellious colonies further north, and even send an expedition to establish a permanent British foothold on the Pacific coast of North America.

It was a vast dream but Dalling was convinced that it could be realised. He turned a deaf ear to those in the Jamaican assembly who wanted nothing to do with an idea that would strip them of men and resources in such dangerous times. The French fleet under d'Estaing had sailed for Georgia, they said, but who knew when it might return? Even Sir Peter Parker doubted the wisdom of Dalling's plan.

But the governor was a stubborn, almost ineducable, man, as he was showing in a battle he was having with Parker over prize money. When the island's attorney general declined to prosecute the admiral, Dalling dismissed him from his post; and far from heeding the Admiralty's orders to reinstate the discomfited dignitary, Dalling proceeded to remove four junior judges he also deemed unsympathetic to his cause. The governor was not a man to be swayed easily, and with the Nicaraguan bit firmly between his teeth he knew no restraint. 'Give me but the direction of a force, and that of no great extent, and I'll be answerable to give you the domination of Spain in this part of the world,' he wrote to the British colonial secretary on 4 February 1780. A few days later he was telling him, 'My ideas are every day strengthened as to the feasibility with which blows of the greatest consequence may be struck with little probability of detriment on our side, nay almost with certain impunity.'[2]

Shortly, others were catching the bug. Empire, silver and fame beckoned them. 'Enthusiasm was never carried to greater height than by those who had promised to themselves the glory of shaking Spain to her foundation,' said Benjamin Moseley, surgeon general of Jamaica. 'The colours of England were, in their imagination, already even on the walls of Lima.' One of the expedition's backers was Nelson's prize agent, the Kingston merchant Hercules Ross, who acquired the right to supply it with provisions and handle any plunder taken.[3]

The excitement overruled a serious assessment of the difficulties of the enterprise, or of the amount of support it would command among the white settlers, blacks and Indians of the Mosquito coast. It had long been known that the Indians had little love for the Spaniards, and even in Morgan's day they were reported to have been 'driven to rebellion by cruelty, and there is no reconciling them'. But Lawrie's claims that he could 'arm some thousands upon the coast' and 'bring in the Wooliva and Valientas, almost as numerous as the Moskito men, and good pilots into [for] the Spanish country', were to be brutally ill-founded. In fact, Lawrie, the superintendent-general of the Mosquito coast, would not even supply the quantity of small light craft that were needed to ascend such a difficult river as the San Juan.[4]

Not only that, but although Dalling planned to launch his expedition in January, 'when the fine weather will permit of operations', he underestimated the medical problems involved. He hoped that before the rainy season began in the spring the troops would have fought their way up the San Juan and reached the higher altitudes around Lake Nicaragua, where the air was reckoned cooler and wholesome. Indeed, he argued the campaign might actually invigorate soldiers who were falling sick in Jamaica. When he was later accused of denuding the island of valuable troops, Dalling declared that those dispatched to Nicaragua were 'only of the convalescent kind, the greatest part of whom would perish here, when from the salubrity of the sea air they will probably recover and be useful there'. In this last protestation Dalling was being disingenuous, because the troops shipped to Nicaragua were not convalescents and had been mustered as fit. Nevertheless, the governor did pinpoint the importance of getting the expeditionary force out of the swamps of the Lower San Juan and up to Lake Nicaragua before the rains came. 'Our operations must commence sometime in January,' he told the commander of the expedition, Captain John Polson of the 60th Regiment, 'and consequently dispatch is indispensably necessary.'[5]

Unfortunately his timing too proved to be fatally optimistic.

2

Dalling needed naval support to escort his troopships, first to the Mosquito shore, where Lawrie's detachments and boats were to be collected, and then to the mouth of the San Juan. Once the soldiers were disembarked the navy's job was merely to protect the estuary, guard the expedition's back and keep the supply line open. Sir Peter Parker was not sanguine about the chances of success but Nelson was available and ideal for the job. He was desperate for action, and after his voyage on the *Badger* knew the Mosquito coast as well as any captain on the station. Horatio willingly accepted the assignment, though he shared his admiral's doubts. 'How it will turn out, God knows!' he wrote to Captain Locker.[6]

Nelson watched the expedition assemble in Kingston and Port Royal. Once the San Juan was in British hands, the governor planned to push regular reinforcements up the river, and had more professional soldiers coming from England. But the bridgehead would have to be established by Polson. At Polson's disposal were about three to four hundred regulars of the 60th and 79th regiments; a Loyal Irish Corps raised by Dalling; about sixty sailors; and some two hundred Jamaican volunteers under Major James MacDonald, a detachment that included sixty or seventy Irish, a few foreigners and seamen, and blacks, Indians and mulattoes. Of these the 79th, just shipped from England, was unacclimatised. Nonetheless, the force was provisioned for six months and Polson, 'a steady and good officer' as well as an experienced one, was given the local rank of colonel.[7]

As a post-captain, Nelson was actually the highest ranking officer on the expedition, but though he demanded and received full control of the flotilla and its naval and civilian personnel, his authority was confined to the sea. Polson was named overall commander-in-chief, and it was expected that Nelson would have little to do once he had disembarked the army at the mouth of the San Juan. Few reckoned with Nelson's unusual spirit, however. Colonel Polson was to marvel at the energy and enterprise of the ridiculously young man sent to ferry his expedition around. 'A light-haired boy came to me in a little frigate,' he recalled later. At the time he seemed of little consequence, but 'in two or three days he displayed himself, and afterwards . . . directed all the operations.'[8]

After annoying delays Nelson led the expedition to sea at six in the morning of 3 February 1780, the *Hinchinbroke* and several transports – the *Penelope*, four brigs and sloops and a tender named the *Royal George*. Stowed away were the pieces of a shallow-draft vessel intended for service on Lake Nicaragua. The convoy slipped southwest across the Caribbean, towards Providence, a small island held by the British east of the Mosquito coast. It was a peaceful voyage, although Nelson had to punish a marine and a seaman with twelve lashes each for neglect and insolence.

Providence was not the most accessible place. It was surrounded by a rugged, treacherous reef that only admitted ships to the harbour through a narrow, winding passage. On 10 February Nelson brought his squadron offshore and sent a cutter to pick up a pilot for the Mosquito coast and San Juan. As he knew, the coast of Nicaragua was tricky, spotted with small islands, shoals and protecting reefs, and the San Juan itself was dangerous and, in the words of Jefferys's *Atlas*, 'full of cataracts'. Yet here, right at the beginning of the adventure, the support promised by Lawrie failed. A guide, Richard Hanna, came out to join the ships. He claimed to have been up the San Juan as far as the Spanish fort, but he proved to be what one of Lawrie's local rivals described as 'worthless'.[9]

Nelson was now bound for Cape Gracias a Dios, where Lawrie's detachments of volunteers, blacks and Indians were supposed to rendezvous. Unfortunately, in the early evening of the 11th the *Penelope* ran aground on the reef around Providence. Her master signalled distress and tried to lighten the ship by throwing all but three of his guns overboard. Nelson brought up the smaller vessels to help and sent a lieutenant and boat's crew to supervise the unloading of powder and stores. However, the job of refloating the *Penelope* looked as if it was going to be a long one so Horatio sent word ahead to Cape Gracias a Dios, urging Lawrie to use the delay to prepare his forces for a swift embarkation. By 13 February he was fretting so much about the time being lost that he decided to go on, leaving the *Penelope* to catch up when she could, though his convoy had no sooner departed than the ship slipped off the reef into deep water. Luckily she was relatively unscathed and quickly crowded on sail to catch up with the others, but two valuable days had been lost.[10]

The next day Polson and Nelson met a greater disappointment at Cape Gracias a Dios. Polson was looking forward to picking up forty men of the 79th Regiment who had already been sent to this coast, as well as Lawrie's volunteers. To encourage the volunteers he had some blank commissions to offer those who would serve as officers. But when they reached the rendezvous no forces were there to meet them. No regulars, no militia, no blacks, no Indians, no boats and no Lawrie. No one except an officer to report that the superintendent-general of the coast had not yet arrived. Lawrie was still gathering forces on the Black River to the northwest.

Nothing at all appeared to have been done about mustering the local Indians and Sandy Bay 'samboes' under their ambitiously named leaders King George and Julius Caesar. These peoples inhabited scattered small villages of thatched houses, hunting, fishing, gathering and practising a slash and burn horticulture, and rallying them would be a time-consuming business. But there was no alternative and Polson hurried a message to a local Indian leader named Isaac, Duke of York. Isaac was invited for talks and entreated to use his influence with King George, as well as with the chieftain of Pearl Key Lagoon, Admiral Dick Richards, who was believed to control most of the Indians south of the cape. Somehow Polson also got word to General Tempest, reportedly the principal Indian leader to the west. To all of these important people Polson sent gifts, hoping to counteract any adverse impressions that might have retarded their willingness to come forward.[11]

The process bit yet more time out of their fraying schedule, but Polson could not proceed without the only allies who knew the country and who could supply the shallow-draft canoes they needed to ascend the San Juan. Nelson occupied his men filling water casks and cleaning and repairing the ships, but he disembarked the soldiers. There was no point in leaving them on the packed transports. So far their health had held up. About thirty men were sick, but the only two who had died on the passage had been feverish before the voyage had started. Eagerly, the troops now climbed into the boats to be ferried ashore, and scrambled through grass and mangroves to reach a low-level but marshy area known as Wank's Savannah. It was damp and mosquito-ridden and one day a fierce northwesterly blew down most of the tents, but the weather was generally kind and, though a precautionary 'hospital' was established, the soldiers remained in reasonable health and spirits.[12]

Polson and Nelson were also talking to their pilot, Hanna. He assured them that the San Juan was navigable to vessels of up to four feet in draft. They therefore unloaded the pieces of the shallow-draft vessel Dalling had provided for Lake Nicaragua, and had the carpenters put it together. Named the *Lord Germain*, it was taken in tow by the *Hinchinbroke*.

In the meantime Indians and blacks began to arrive. From 22 February they dribbled in, many of them ready for war. The recruits included Admiral Dick Richards and General Tempest, who said that he was too old to campaign himself but was contributing his brother and followers to the campaign. Using interpreters, Polson tried to dispel a rumour that the British only wanted to enslave them in Jamaica, and oiled his blandishments with presents and a promise of shares in the plunder. Fresh misunderstandings were already developing. The Indians later insisted that Polson had said they could keep any black slaves they captured from the Spaniards, something the colonel steadfastly denied. Nevertheless, for the time being, Polson's diplomacy had secured a few native allies.

On 22 February Lawrie himself arrived. Nelson and Polson must have shaken their heads in frustration, for the forces he brought were scant. He said he had two hundred or so men, including the missing detachment of the 79th, and thirteen Black River craft, but even these modest reinforcements had been scattered in the recent gale. In fact, four of the boats had been wrecked and some of the regulars lost with them. Those regulars who did arrive were in 'a most deplorable condition', according to the expedition's surgeon general, Dr Thomas Dancer, and riddled with dropsy, fevers and dysentery.[13]

Disappointed at the turnout, Polson saw no point in lingering any longer, and hoped to pick up additional Indians and boats on his journey southwards towards the San Juan. Five or six days were consumed re-embarking the troops, and at one-thirty in the afternoon of 7 March Nelson fired a gun to signal the squadron to sail. The following day they passed Sandy Bay, and Lawrie was landed with presents to rally the blacks there while Polson continued along the coast to Tebuppy to speak to a prestigious Indian leader known as the Governor. After a few difficulties caused by incompetent pilots, the expedition reached its destination late at night, and on 9 March yet another round of negotiations with the natives began.

A white man named Cairns, who lived with the Indians, came aboard the ships to explain that it was absolutely necessary for Polson to speak to them directly. By this time the commander-in-chief was becoming increasingly dependent on Nelson, and flattering him by using his name as a camp password. Ever willing to share the burdens of command, Nelson offered to accompany Polson, and that afternoon the two officers went ashore to meet the Governor and some of his headmen at Cairns's house. The Indians wanted presents before committing warriors to the expedition, but as Polson had given Lawrie his remaining store of gifts, he had to wait at Tebuppy for the superintendent-general to come up. Two more days elapsed, but on 12 March Lawrie arrived and the Governor informed. Once the gifts had been distributed the following day, however, the Indians scattered for provisions, and it was not until 16 March that they reassembled for departure. Nelson and Polson were fuming, sure that Lawrie had entirely misled Dalling about the readiness of the Indians to join the campaign.

The journey to the San Juan resumed on 17 March. It was a bizarre sight, and History has seldom spoken of the strange composition of the first fleet commanded by its greatest admiral. Nelson led the way south in a dilapidated frigate, followed by seven transports and tenders, some shallow Black River craft and a flotilla of dugout pangas, pitpans, dories and canoes manned by Indian and black warriors. The Mosquito Indians were a ferocious sight. Almost naked, some of their lithe, bronzed bodies were tattooed or painted, their ears, noses and lips pierced for ornaments, and the arms they had received from the British supplemented by bows and arrows, spears and perhaps blowguns. Some of their weapons may well have been tipped with poison.

As the ships passed along the low, flat coastline Nelson was also being taxed by his local pilots, whose inefficiency reached a nadir at seven in the morning of the 18th when the ships ran upon 'a hidden reef'. Horatio signalled them to anchor and successfully refloated every vessel, but part of the *Hinchinbroke*'s false keel and copper sheathing had been ripped off. Complicating matters, one of Nelson's carpenters had fallen out of a boat and drowned at Tebuppy, and repairs had to proceed short-handed. But, undeterred, Nelson brought the force to Pearl Key Lagoon, where several small islets guarded a large lagoon rich in shellfish and turtles, and Admiral Dick Richards and the last Indian contingent were to meet them.

For Nelson every step of the wretched voyage had brought its own frustrations and Pearl Key Lagoon ran to form. On the 20th, while Lawrie was mustering the Admiral's men, the masters of the transports brought Nelson the unwelcome news that they had only two days' worth of fresh water left. There was no water at Pearl Key, so the next day Nelson left Lawrie to complete his business ashore while he sailed on to Monkey Point. Again he found himself misled. Despite assurances that the ships could water at Monkey Point, the landing parties returned empty handed, and Nelson had to ration his remaining supplies. He crowded on all sail for the mouth of the San Juan on 22 March, and the ships, with some of the Black River and Indian craft, finally reached their destination in two days. Here there was water, here the troops and military stores were to be put ashore and here Nelson's greatest responsibilities came to an end.

The vexations of the Mosquito coast were over but they had cost the expedition dear. It had left Jamaica late in the first place, and now a whole month had been wasted waiting for people and boats and negotiating with Indians and blacks, work that was supposed to have been done already. The results themselves were also disappointing, for nothing like Lawrie's paper army of auxiliaries ever appeared. According to Robert Hodgson, admittedly a prejudiced opponent of Lawrie, only 12 whites, 60 black slaves and 220 'Mosquito Men' eventually joined the campaign. Nelson himself complained that the few men General Tempest supplied soon defected. Weeks of effort had eventually given Polson a number of black and Indian allies, who would prove themselves adept scouts and boatmen, but they were far too few for the job in hand.

The rains, which everyone had thought it essential to avoid, were looming ominously, and the time left for the British to ascend the San

Juan, capture its fort and reach the healthier climes of Lake Nicaragua was very short indeed.

3

Apart from sitting at anchor in the mouth of the San Juan, guarding the supply line, Captain Nelson's job was done. The men had reached the river in reasonable shape and the rest was now up to Polson.

The difficulties of the army soon became obvious, however. The San Juan estuary was uninviting. Its harbour, where Nelson drew up the ships, seemed 'very fine', but it was graced by no more than a shabby collection of deserted wooden shanties collectively known as Greytown, and accessed a drab low-lying shoreline covered in grass, scrub and mangrove swamp. Beyond, through a strong current of shallow, muddy water spilling into the sea, the river had to be entered by tricky channels threading between sandy islands and shoals. Polson sent his chief engineer to erect a battery and rough defences at a suitable place for a base. Lieutenant Edward Marcus Despard of the 79th was one of the strengths of the expedition. A delicately featured, slim Irishman in his late twenties, he discharged this and all other duties with exceptional ability and determination.[1]

On 26 March, Polson began the onerous job of landing men, provisions and stores. For two days the *Chichito*, supplied by Lawrie, the *Royal George* and *Lord Germain*, and the Black River and Indian boats ploughed back and forth to one of the islands in the mouth of the river. They were too few for the work and inevitably made their trips overloaded. Some capsized, stores were lost or damaged and one man drowned.

Nelson decided to intervene. He was already chafing at the thought of remaining on his frigate while the serious action moved upriver, and knew Polson's problems would only increase. The published atlas said that the river had many 'cataracts', but little else was known about it, and even its length was uncertain. A hundred miles of difficult water were thought to connect the estuary to Lake Nicaragua. At the moment it was still the dry season, and the water would be broken into runs or narrow channels, but that would make the transportation of heavy stores and siege guns a hazardous toil. The enemy fortifications were also mysterious. According to Lawrie, San Carlos, the fort at the entrance to Lake Nicaragua, was garrisoned by only a handful of men with about twenty-five pieces of artillery, but then

Lawrie had revealed himself a dismal prophet. Another castle, Fort San Juan, was some thirty miles below the lake. A stone structure erected the previous century to halt privateers and buccaneers, it was likely to be a formidable obstacle. Bearing all this in mind, Nelson concluded that Polson needed all the help he could get. He put the *Hinchinbroke*'s cutter and pinnace at the colonel's disposal, with thirty-four seamen and thirteen marines, and offered to command them himself. Furthermore, he would conduct the entire convoy upstream. Gratefully, Polson accepted.

Invigorated, but still with insufficient boats to move the whole of his force at once, Polson split the men and stores into two divisions. Nelson would take the first and largest, including Polson and most of the regulars, as the advance, while Major MacDonald would bring the second division upstream as soon as boats became available. Some of Polson's boats would be sent back at the first opportunity, and Lawrie was expected to arrive with others from Pearl Key Lagoon.

As the first division was poised to begin its journey, Polson received a new inducement. A boat arrived from Jamaica with a letter from Dalling, dated 17 March, eleven days earlier. It informed Polson that reinforcements of three hundred regulars and as many volunteers were being shipped from Kingston under the command of Lieutenant Colonel Stephen Kemble of the 60th (Royal American) Regiment. A forty-year-old, Kemble had earlier applied to command the expedition, but only after Polson and Nelson had been appointed. Now he would be assuming overall command, Dalling said. If anything was calculated to galvanise Polson into greater action, it was the knowledge that he had to capture San Juan fort before Kemble appeared and got the credit for the operation.[15]

The morning the letter arrived the first division of Polson's force headed upriver. A little above its mouth, Nelson found the San Juan perhaps half a mile wide, sliding between low grass-covered banks and around sandy shoals and islands. Caymans basked along some of its muddy margins and manatees browsed peacefully on the plants they found in the adjoining creeks. The water was shallow, and every mile upstream was hard won, with the Indians and blacks proving their worth as boatmen at every twist and turn. Nelson had repeatedly to order the men to stow their oars and plunge into the water to help haul and push the vessels on when they grounded. The heavier boats, such as the *Lord Germain* and the *Chichito*, were constantly beaching in the rear, and Nelson's solution was to move the cutter, pinnace and Indian boats forward so that they could be unloaded and sent back to relieve the burdens of the larger craft lagging behind. In three days the men fought the river in heat, humidity and mosquitoes, making barely six miles a day. On 31 March the soldiers were allowed a day of rest in one of their nightly encampments on shore, but for Nelson's men the battle with the boats continued.

Once Nelson got past the mouth of the Colorado River on 1 April he found deeper water and mended his pace. The jungle closed in on lofty banks, looking black and threatening beneath huge trees that shot up to reach the light and wove their crowns into an unbroken canopy. The persistent heat and humidity gave the forest a high metabolism, and many of its creatures completed their life-cycles quickly, generating a swift turnover and astonishing diversity. Large butterflies, moths and dragonflies flitted in the still moist air, and iridescent hummingbirds hovered busily before brilliant flowers. But for Nelson and his men there were rapids, falls, currents and countercurrents to absorb their attention, and the extremes between the exhausting daytime heat on the river and the falling temperatures that enveloped the makeshift camps at night to endure.

Working arduously side by side, Nelson and the Indians developed a considerable mutual respect. On his part, Horatio was impressed by the durability of the natives, and their skill in weaving the boats around grassy islands and through tumbling rapids. On theirs, the Indians saw a young man of no great strength or size struggling with them in the van without any of the common European arrogance. In this relationship Nelson trod surely in the footsteps of Drake.

An unconfirmed story published by the biographer James Harrison after the admiral's death relates to the Indians' regard for Nelson. Its provenance is unknown, but perhaps it came from members of Nelson's family, who supplied Harrison with some of his information. The story tells how Nelson was accustomed to slinging his hammock between trees in the overnight camps. On one such occasion he was rudely awakened from sleep by a lizard that crawled across his face. Jumping up in alarm, Nelson cast off his blanket, only to see a venomous snake, probably a coral snake or pit viper, fall from its folds and slide into the undergrowth. The watching Indians were astonished. They believed that people possessed individual guardian spirits, and convinced themselves that Nelson's must be potent indeed to have protected him from the snake. Their confidence in the young officer consequently increased.[16]

Whether this incident happened or not – the ethnographic data at least is reliable – it is certain that the Indians liked Nelson. They would shortly desert the expedition, and among several grievances count their unsatisfactory relations with the British officers. Polson had warned his men of the dangers of alienating valuable auxiliaries. The blacks, he said, had 'to be treated with the utmost humanity', and the Indians were not to be deprived of 'their private plunder' in case 'a general defection' proved 'fatal to the enterprise'. Indeed, 'the necessity of keeping such people in good humour' was so 'obvious' that 'inconsistencies and even absurdities' had to be tolerated. In an effort to preserve interracial harmony Polson had ordered his men to avoid fraternising with the Indians, but however well intentioned the order it may have simply suggested an aloof contempt. Certainly the Indians later complained of 'Polson's severity' but admitted themselves 'very fond of Captain Nelson' and a number of other leaders.[17]

Setting off before daylight the boats were now moving ten miles a day and the Spaniards were not far ahead. Polson ordered his men to make as little noise as possible, even in camp, and kept his boats closer together. On 5 April the British passed an island with the ruins of an old Spanish fortification on it, and the next day they camped at the foot of rapids which the Indians said were only six miles below an enemy lookout post. Polson forbade any more fires to be kindled, and, rather than blundering forward to disturb the Spaniards, he detached Lieutenant (Acting Captain) James Mounsey of the 79th, Despard and some thirty men to go ahead with the Indian 'spies' to reconnoitre.

While waiting for Mounsey, Polson learned that he could at least ascend the rapids without alerting the Spaniards, and on 8 April ordered the men to march up the north bank of the river to the top of the rapids while the Indians took complete charge of the boats. Nelson went with the soldiers on this occasion, hiking through a forest humming with insects and alive with movement. Wild pigs rooted in the wooded glades, ducks and pigeons started noisily and large lizards scuttled for cover. In the green treetops brilliant parrots flitted and squawked, while monkeys clambered about, some discernible only by the distant crashing of branches and others setting up furious vocal battles that rang through miles of dark forest. At the head of the rapids Nelson and Polson were not only reunited with the triumphant Indian boatmen, but also met Mounsey's party.

The Spanish lookout post was on an island ahead, about seventy-five yards from the north bank of the river. Only three sentries were seen on night duty, but they appeared to be regular soldiers and alert. Later the British discovered that the river was fordable near the upper end of the island, but at the time no one knew it. Some of Mounsey's Indians had stolen forward to test the depth of the water but withdrew when it began to lap about their waists only a short distance from the river's edge.

Nonetheless, Despard had a plan. To prevent the Spaniards carrying news of the approaching British upriver to Fort San Juan it was imperative to seal off the lookout post before making an attack. On the south side of the island the water looked deep enough for light boats to steal by in the night. Despard suggested sending a force around the post that way, cutting off the Spanish retreat and making a surprise attack on the island from behind at daylight. Another party could offer covering fire from the north bank of the river. Nelson immediately offered to command the boats and make the main attack, while Mounsey was entrusted with the land party. That night Nelson led his small force forward. He had two boats from the *Hinchinbroke*, two Indian pitpans, forty soldiers (including Despard) and some Indians and sailors. Ahead lay the first hand-to-hand action of his life.

As usual, it was the Indians who went ahead, sneaking past the island in the darkness without being seen. Nelson had more trouble. One of his boats grounded and had to be left behind, and as dawn broke on 9 April the others were still below the lookout post. Nelson continued to row forward, hoping the poor light might still shield him as he passed, but he was spotted. The island of Bartola was five or six miles below Fort San Juan and about a quarter of a mile wide and twice as long. Manned by fifteen Spanish regulars, it had a semicircular battery mounting four swivel guns, all pointing downstream. As soon as they saw the British boats pulling fast towards them, the Spaniards fell to those guns and opened fire.[18]

Mounsey's men opened their covering fire but shot still spattered around Nelson's boats. One man was hit in the abdomen and was fortunate that the ball spent itself working through his cartouche box; another had three of his fingers shattered. As the keel of Nelson's boat drove ashore, Horatio jumped out, sword in hand. According to his official biographers his feet sank so deeply into the mud that he left his shoes behind and stormed the redoubt in his stockings. Shoeless or not, he won a speedy victory. After a token resistance the defenders ran to their boats and fled, straight into the hands of the waiting Indians, and all but one were rounded up as captives. The only fatality suffered by either side was one of Mounsey's soldiers, bitten beneath his left eye by a snake hanging from a tree as he marched through the forest. The wretched fellow's body swelled up, his skin turned a deep yellow and the injured eye 'entirely dissolved'. Within hours he was dead.[19]

From the prisoners Nelson learned that Fort San Juan was only five or so miles upstream. When Polson arrived, and decided to make Bartola a base for the final advance, Horatio offered to make a personal reconnaissance of the fort ahead. After dark the same day he set off in a pitpan with Despard and one of the prisoners. It was dangerous work, paddling several miles against a strong current in an unknown river strewn with snags and shoals, while around them gathered an eerie blackness intensified inshore by looming trees. But on the morning of 10 April they suddenly passed around a sharp right-hand bend to see the fort straight before them.

4

It stood on the summit of a steep green hill, situated on a spur of land jutting from the south bank of the river, and appeared to measure about sixty-five by thirty-one yards. A hundred feet below the fort the water frothed white and wild, and the newly whitewashed walls themselves were strong, four feet thick and fourteen feet high. There were regular bastions at each corner and a flag flew above a fifty-foot keep. A small barrack and a picket linked the northwestern and south-eastern bastions and an imperfect ditch enclosed the whole. Using a glass, Nelson noticed the detached redoubts too, some on an eminence that commanded the south of the fort, and another near a few huts on the river at the foot of the hill. The garrison drew its water there, for it had no well. Round about the hill the timber had been cleared to give the fort a field of vision, but the place looked calm against the brooding jungle beyond. To all appearances there was no sign of alarm.

Yet Don Juan d'Ayssa, the commandant of El Castillo de la Immaculada Concepción, to give it its full name, knew about the British from the refugee who had tumbled in from Bartola. He had no illusions about holding his post against a determined attack. He had some twenty cannons, twelve swivels and a mortar, but only 149 armed defenders, near half of them regulars and the rest a mixed collection that included seventeen boatmen. The eighty-six other souls in the place included artificers, a chaplain, women, children, slaves and three malefactors. It was far from a formidable list, and hearing of the British advance d'Ayssa herded his cattle into the fort, stored as much water as possible and packed his wife and two messengers into a canoe to summon help from Granada.[20]

Back at Bartola, Lawrie had arrived in camp at last, telling Polson that MacDonald was now fighting his way upstream with the second division of the troops. Polson sent word back, urging them forward, and upon hearing from Nelson continued his own advance. He proceeded cautiously, sending Captain Richard Bulkeley of the 79th ahead with an advance to enfilade the Spanish garrison and secure a ridge that commanded the fort from the west and south. While Bulkeley's men slogged through the jungle, where one was attacked by a disoriented jaguar, Nelson's boats slowly proceeded upstream and Polson's men marched on the adjacent banks.

The eleventh of April found them making camp a few miles below the fort, hidden from it by a bend of the river. Nelson landed the stores and four four-pounders. By nightfall Bulkeley, whose force was strengthened, had seized the ridge, discovering abandoned Spanish outworks, and taken a position on the river above the castle. D'Ayssa had managed to rush one more boat up the river, but was now effectively sealed off. A sixty-man relief force and supplies from Granada failed to reach the fort. Impatient, Nelson suggested the fortifications be stormed. In hindsight some merit can be seen in the proposal, but in truth it was reckless. An assault party would have had to advance against enemy fire up a bare hill, cross a ten-foot-wide ditch and climb seventeen feet to the rampart without scaling ladders or a breach having been knocked in the walls. Polson opted for the obvious alternative. To the south and west the commanding ridge was not more than three hundred yards from the castle, and effective batteries placed on its summit would soon compel the Spaniards to surrender.[21]

Guns would have to be hauled up the ridge and a supply route cut. A rough back trail was eventually hacked through the jungle southwest of the landing place. Most of it was out of sight of the garrison, winding along and within the skirt of the forest and then north, either to a British base in the woods southwest of the fort or ascending the reverse slope of the ridge that overlooked the castle. The most laborious work was done at night. Late on 12 April Nelson and his seamen dragged one of the four-pounders across the open space from the river to the ridge, bullied it up the slope and prepared a platform. By daylight the weapon was grinning devilishly upon the enemy fortress from the south-southwest. It began firing at first light with what Polson described as 'great success'. Nelson pointed the guns himself, but perhaps with less than the precision of a practised siege artillerist. Experienced siege men knew that fortifications were best weakened at the base, so that the masonry above crumbled to form an incline into the breach. Nelson seems to have fired high. Indeed, one of his first shots brought down the Spanish flagstaff and colours.[22]

There was more difficulty bringing the other guns to bear. All three were brought up by Polson's men the same morning, but at first they were badly positioned and discharged to 'little effect'. The next day one was given to Nelson, while Despard shifted the other two further along the ridge to the west of the fort. Nelson situated his new piece between his first gun and Despard's, and the bombardment at last began to tell. By now Polson was beside himself with admiration for a young naval officer who exceeded his duty to share every tribulation. The boy who had gratuitously negotiated with Indians, led the boats upriver, stormed a lookout post and reconnoitred the fort was now erecting and fighting batteries. 'I want words to express the obligations I owe that gentleman,' Polson wrote to Dalling in his official dispatch. 'He was the first on every service, whether by day or by night. There was scarcely a gun fired but was pointed by him or Lieutenant Despard . . .'[23]

For a while Nelson and Despard did well and brought down the merlon on the keep but on the fourth day of firing their shot ran out. Only two hundred and fifty of three hundred and fifty four-pound shot supposed to have been packed in the boats could be found. Nelson, who would enjoy a reputation for detailed planning, may have learned expensive lessons from what was swiftly becoming a fiasco. Polson had arrived to attack a fort without scaling ladders or enough shot and the British guns fell silent. As urgent messages raced downstream to summon more ammunition the attackers wasted five days worrying the garrison with small-arms fire. They wormed into positions under the hill and near the river to prevent thirsty Spaniards from scrambling down to refill water casks, and started a mine from a distance of forty yards. The idea was to undermine and blow the fort wall with explosives, but the tunnel ran into rock and got no more than seventeen yards. In reply the Spaniards fired briskly with cannons and muskets, much of it directed against an advanced British breastwork, but there were few casualties on either side. During the entire siege no more than fifteen Britons were hit by hostile fire. One of the wounded was a man from the *Hinchinbroke* who got drunk and ran down the ridge towards the fort in pursuit of a pig.[24]

On 21 April the ammunition from MacDonald's division arrived. Polson, whose men were busy making scaling ladders, was relieved – but not for long. Instead of the two hundred four-pound shot expected, only fifty-three were counted; the rest had been lost, either shipped by mistake up branching creeks, or gone to the bottom of the river in accidents with the boats. Nelson and Despard did what they could. They pummelled the fort again, knocking down a sentry box at one of the angles, but ran out of shot in two days. MacDonald's men had also brought a couple of short-range twelve-pound carronades but only forty shot to serve them. To achieve even the most futile of bombardments nine-pounder balls had to be loaded. First, the carronades threw their shot short. Then, when the powder charge was increased to improve range, they lost velocity and one gun was blown off its carriage.

Outright incompetence had turned the siege into a farce and already much darker clouds were gathering. On the 19th the shortfall in provisions compelled Polson to cut rations, and the following night the weather finally broke. The rains, dreaded from the beginning, had come.[25]

5

The rain poured down all that night and the next day, and for much of almost every day after that. The river was turned into a raging flood, and the camp of crude shelters was transformed into a sea of misery and mud. At night horrific flashes of lightning stabbed through the black sky. In the words of Benjamin Moseley, the surgeon-general of Jamaica, whose deputy was on the ground, the 'horrid tempests of lightning and thunder' constituted 'a magnificent scene of terror unknown but in the tropic world'.[26]

And the men – fatigued, tormented night and day by mosquitoes, sodden, and stinted on food and medicine by the slow and uncertain communications on the river – suddenly fell sick. The Indians began to die first, but on the 24th or after the soldiers also started 'falling down in great numbers', seized by a crippling distemper.[27]

Matters were soon serious. According to Dancer, the physician with the expedition, men initially went down with tertian fevers, suffering 'cold, hot and sweating fits' every other day. Many patients then slid into 'quotidian' fever, daily attacks during which the cold fits diminished but the others became more violent and exhausting. Dancer was soon alert to warning signs. In some the stricken boils about the body or pustules at the lips and nostrils 'generally indicated a crisis or solution of the fever', but other patients displayed 'a universal yellowness' that generally indicated the end was close. In mature cases a bloody flux and 'obstructions of the viscera, particularly of the spleen' developed, and occasionally disorientation and derangement.[28]

Bogged down in a mosquito-ridden river valley and the marshy estuary at the mouth of the San Juan, the expedition was probably being scourged by malignant tertian malaria and dysentery, and perhaps also typhoid fever caused by the ingestion of food and water contaminated by the human sewage upstream. Horatio Nelson was among the first to be struck down. He had not been well in Jamaica and was arguably weakened by subsequent misfortunes. Years later he told the Duke of Clarence that he had drunk from a spring in which branches of the manchineel tree had been thrown. Manchineel contained toxic substances, and was used by the Indians to tip arrows, but whether Nelson drank enough to occasion the 'severe and lasting injury' he claimed may be doubted. More likely the campaign through jungle, marsh and water had taken its toll.[29]

For a while he struggled on, but release came suddenly. On 28 April, as Polson prepared to summon the Spaniards to surrender, more news and letters came into the camp. For Polson the most material revelation was that Kemble's reinforcements had arrived at the mouth of the river from Jamaica. Kemble had two hundred regulars and two hundred and fifty volunteers, additional stores and two howitzers, which Dalling pronounced 'by far the best kind of artillery' for siege work. He also had instructions to supersede Polson in command, fortify the harbour and river of San Juan, and forward Dalling's plans to control Lake Nicaragua, and capture Granada, Leon and Realejo. There was also a letter for Captain Nelson from Sir Peter Parker. He was to hand the *Hinchinbroke* to Captain Cuthbert Collingwood and immediately return to Jamaica on the sixteen-gun *Victor*, which had accompanied Kemble's troops. Captain Bonovier Glover of the forty-four-gun frigate *Janus* had died, and Nelson was to take command. When Sir Peter had promised to find Nelson a better ship he meant it, and Horatio's new commission was backdated to 22 March 1780.[30]

At twelve noon on 28 April, Nelson set off downriver, lying pale and feeble in the bottom of an Indian boat and attended by John Tyson, his former purser from the *Badger*. He left his men to follow in the pinnace, and carried with him a letter from Polson to Kemble. Acknowledging the confusion upriver and the 'flux' ravaging the Indians and troops, Polson's epistle was entirely frank about the crucial role Nelson and his seamen had played in the siege:

Captain Nelson's going off directly puts it out of my power to be full on any subject, but I shall write you tomorrow by his pinnace, which he leaves for that purpose. I want words to express the praise due to Captain Nelson for the many services he did the army in coming here, and the great assistance he gave me in carrying on the siege. Hardly a gun [was fired] but was laid by him or Lieutenant Despard, and I shall miss him and his good men more than double their number of any others.[31]

But Polson wrote too early to transmit the really important news. On the afternoon of the day following Nelson's departure the Spaniards surrendered their fort. Polson searched for a British flag to raise over the keep but found only one. It flew quite fittingly, though its master was gone . . . Nelson's 'jack'.[32]

The British found El Castillo de la Immaculada Concepcion in a wretched condition, disease-ridden, fetid and pervaded by an 'unsupportable' stench from badly located privies. There were no proper sick quarters and the health of both the British and their Spanish prisoners deteriorated. When Kemble finally reached the fort on 15 May he was shocked. The soldiers were 'in a most deplorable state' and 'everything' was 'in the greatest confusion. No part of our works destroyed, nor any preparations for defence.' It was only 'with difficulty' that it was possible to find 'one subaltern . . . to mount the castle guard'. As men fell sick they lay helplessly, some with legs swollen to 'an enormous size' and discharging water. Those who rallied relapsed after the slightest exertions, and the burdens on the dwindling numbers of fit or partly fit men became insuperable. The Indians and blacks, afraid of the sickness, were also disgruntled. They had been restrained from hunting, denied access to the fort and deprived of what they deemed to be legitimate plunder, especially the Spanish slaves. Muttering angrily, they simply defected.[33]

As Horatio descended the San Juan, he passed supplies and men moving up. Some, noticing the shocking state of the young captain, got their first intimation of what lay ahead. But the river mouth proved to be no relief. Nelson found a pestilential fort being erected at Greytown, Kemble organising his troops ashore and several transports riding in the harbour with His Majesty's warships the *Hinchinbroke*, *Victor*, *Resource* and *Ulysses*. The old *Hinchinbroke* was opening at the seams, and a few desertions and a couple of floggings had been logged since Nelson had left. Much worse, disease was appearing in the ship.[34]

First Lieutenant George Harrison had died first, on 24 April. He was not an old man. Harrison had come to the *Hinchinbroke* from the *Lowestoffe*, and served as a master's mate and able seaman the previous year before passing for lieutenant. Only three months before, on 14 January, he had moved up to first lieutenant, and during Nelson's absence the ship had been his to command. So briefly an officer and gentleman, he was now buried ashore, far from home. He had learned the hard way that in the islands promotion – and death – came quick. Harrison's place was taken by Joseph Bullen, and Peter Burns, an experienced officer, was borrowed from the *Resource* to support him.

Three days after Harrison's death William Clark, a mariner of the *Hinchinbroke*, died. Then, on 30 April, the last day of Nelson's command, two more seamen, William Robertson and John Mockler, also died. Mockler was a boatswain from Waterford. He was twenty-nine years old.

Collingwood was there to take command of Nelson's frigate but the contagion gathered strength despite all his considerable efforts. Selections from the ship's log tell their own sad story:

1 May: John Stockbridge departed this life.
2 May: James Huggins, surgeon's mate, departed this life.
3 May: Peter Bird, seaman, died.
4 May: James Dunn and Edward Eustace died. The number of sick increasing daily.
5 May: John Petson died.
6 May: Sent a party ashore to erect tents on the beach for the sick.
8 May: Peter Greveson departed this life. Sent forty sick to the tent.
9 May: Ninety men sick.
10 May: Michael Burchel and James Boyle died.
14 May: John Leonard departed this life.
16 May: Robert Needham, Thomas Ray and William Green departed this life.

17 May: John Alexander died. Eighty-six men exceedingly ill with
fevers, fluxes and scorbutic ulcers, and the number daily
increasing.

18 May: John Williamson, seaman, died . . .

And so it went on: the young and old, brave and weak, efficient
and incompetent. Hosier's expedition had been wiped out in these
waters, and Vernon's, and now it was happening again. By the end of
the year one hundred and seventy of the two hundred on Collingwood's
muster had died, and 'scarcely any of those who had been attacked
by the distemper have recovered so as to be able to serve again'. The
story was a similar one aboard the other ships at San Juan. On eight
or nine transports barely twenty men were fit for duty early in July;
the rest were sick or dead.[35]

Nelson missed the worst. He gave verbal reports to Kemble, Captain
Patrick Fothringham, now the senior naval officer at San Juan, and
Collingwood, and transferred to the *Victor* (Captain Samuel Hood
Walker) for his passage to Jamaica, sailing on 2 May.

But he remained long enough to hear of the capture of the fort
from two Indians who arrived at the river mouth grumbling about
the sickness and lack of plunder. Horatio's frail hand managed to write
two letters, one to Polson expressing satisfaction that the job had been
done before the arrival of Kemble, and the other to Dalling. From the
governor he received a most gratifying reply. 'Thanks to you, my
friend, for your kind congratulations. To you, without compliment,
do I attribute in a great measure the cause.'[36]

6

On 17 May the *Victor* arrived at Port Royal, and an emaciated Nelson
was carried ashore in a cot and taken to the lodging house of Cuba
Cornwallis, a black woman who had taken her surname from the
captain who had given her her freedom. She was popular among people
of every colour, and a competent nurse, and it was she, rather than
John Tyson the servant, who slowly put Horatio Nelson back on his
feet. The *Janus*, his new command, was moored at the wharf preparing
for sea, but for some time Nelson fought for life and thought of home.
His illness set into a pattern of remission and resurgence, and there
were days when he felt able to make shaky excursions out of doors.[37]

He met Dalling a few times and told him about the expedition, pointing out Polson's chronic need of boats, boatmen, provisions, ordnance stores and an artillery officer. He liked the colonel and defended him, but dwelt on Lawrie's broken promises and explained how the delays had exhausted the campaigning season so that the rains caught them in the swampy river valley rather than the airier uplands. To his English agent he expressed some annoyance that whatever prize money accrued from the capture of the public property in Fort San Juan would probably be shared with Kemble's detachment as well as the crews of the *Resource*, *Victor* and *Ulysses*, none of which had played any part in the victory.[38]

But in reality there was no victory. Dalling persevered with his dream for some time, recklessly preparing more men for the pestilential reaches of the San Juan, and planning the annexation of Nicaragua and the establishment of naval squadrons on both sides of the isthmus. Praising Nelson to the colonial secretary, he recommended the captain be given command of the Pacific squadron. The other, he opined, might not suit a constitution that was 'rather too delicate'.[39]

Slowly, however, the plan fell apart. The soldiers Dalling got from England were too sick to send to the San Juan, while those already there under Kemble lost all interest in their duty and dropped like flies. Ragged, some without shoes and stockings, living in filth, and savaged by malaria, liver problems and dysentery, they reached new depths of demoralisation and despair. Some died raving. Others, with shivering shrivelled frames, yellowing skins and haunted faces, were too weak to bury their comrades and had to lay them out for scavengers by the riverside, waiting and wondering who would die next.

On the ships so many corpses were seen floating in the sea that men stopped eating fish. As one witness wrote from the harbour, 'The *Venus*'s complement is very short. The men are almost all sick . . . The *Horatio* has lost several men, and has now only two able to do duty. The *Julia* has one only, and the *Penelope* two . . . I am told the soldiers die here very fast. Poor Gascoigne is dead, as is Mr Fead of the artillery, lately arrived . . . Captain Fothrington [Fothringham] told me . . . he had 70 men sick. Capt. Collingwood only five able to do duty . . . Sickness and dependency prevail here. All is a lifeless disagreeable stillness, and in some of the transports there are hardly men to bury the dead. All the surgeons are sick and neither officers or soldiers get proper attendance.'[40]

Few survived, though the precise toll has never been ascertained.

In November, Robert Hodgson, Lawrie's predecessor as superintendent general of the Mosquito settlements, estimated that only some 130 men of the 1,500 to 1,800 whites sent to Nicaragua as soldiers, volunteers and auxiliaries then remained. This may not have been much of an exaggeration, for one of the officers testified that 176 of 290 men of the Loyal Irish Corps were dead by 21 September. More than a thousand sailors were also dead, most of disease, but a few drowned when two store ships foundered in a hurricane in October. Even most of the wretched Spanish prisoners perished before they could be returned to their people in Cuba. Such losses, amounting to more than two thousand five hundred men, made the San Juan expedition the costliest British disaster of the entire war.[41]

And ultimately it was for nothing. Kemble had not the stomach to press on to Lake Nicaragua, only thirty miles above the fort, and as the force at San Juan reeled under the terrific mortality the plan to hold it was abandoned. The British evacuated the fort before the end of the year and it was reoccupied by the Spaniards.

Recriminations flew – against Lawrie for the delays on the Mosquito coast, against Polson for not storming the fort at the first onset as Nelson had suggested, and perhaps most of all against Dalling. The planters of Jamaica petitioned for his recall, complaining that he had bled the island's defences dry and damaged its economy. Almost as if he had not supported the venture, Lord George Germain upbraided the governor, telling him that he could only:

lament exceedingly the dreadful havoc Death has made among the troops . . . especially as from the entire failure of the expedition no public benefit has been derived from the loss of so many brave men. Indeed, from the moment I heard no considerable body of the Mosquito Indians had been collected to go with the troops, or employed in making eruptions into the country, and that the few which had accompanied them were disgruntled, and suffered to depart, I ceased to flatter myself that any thing important would be effected, for you must remember the commencement of this undertaking was directed to be by desultory enterprises of adventurers, joining themselves to the natives, and stirring them up to make incursions into the Spanish settlements, and when by these means an opening was made . . . then to throw in a body of troops to overturn the Spanish government and support the inhabitants and adventurers in forming a new state in the centre of the country. The first object therefore certainly was to secure the hearty and general concurrence of the Mosquito Men, and it was unfortunate that more pains were not taken to effect it before any troops were sent down.[42]

Dalling survived an investigation by the council and assembly of Jamaica, but the government called him home, where stories of the terrible losses in the isthmus had shocked the public. Of all the officers engaged in the service, only two seem to have emerged with public credit – Nelson and Despard. Coincidentally, ironies are attached to both cases.

The publication of Polson's dispatches brought Nelson to the attention of British readers for the first time, and his undeniably spirited performance raised his stock among naval officers, merchants and public officials in the West Indian islands. It gave Horatio some of the recognition and attention he craved. That, for him, was the principal gain. Proud of his part in the expedition, in England Nelson had Rigaud complete his portrait by painting Fort San Juan into the background to commemorate his one public achievement. And in 1799, when he was a much bigger hero, he dwelt upon the enterprise in a bragging review of his services. 'Major Polson, who commanded,' he said, 'will tell you of my exertions: how I quitted my ship, carried troops in boats one hundred miles up a river, which none but Spaniards since the time of the buccaneers had ever ascended. It will then be told how I boarded, if I may be allowed the expression, an outpost of the enemy, situated on an island in the river; that I made batteries, and afterwards fought them, and was a principal cause of our success.'[43]

Dalling had wanted to deliver a serious blow to the Spanish empire, but lost two thousand five hundred men achieving nothing. It seems ironic that a quarter of a century later it was the most talented of his officers who irreparably damaged Spain's ability to defend that empire by destroying her navy off Cape Trafalgar, and for only a fraction of the loss suffered in Nicaragua.

Yet an even stranger fate awaited Lieutenant Despard, the other hero of the San Juan debacle. Unlike Nelson he remained in the West Indies, and added to his laurels by defeating a Spanish force that invaded the Black River settlement in 1782. He became Superintendent of British Affairs in Honduras two years later, after Britain negotiated the acquisition of Belize in return for surrendering the Mosquito settlements to Spain. Unfortunately, Despard's career was then stymied. Intrigues led to his recall, but although cleared of misconduct he was not reappointed. The embittered Irishman slipped into London's tavern world, finding other friends and other causes. He associated with Irish patriots and English radicals, and familiarised himself with the inequalities and injustices of British society. In the 1790s he joined the London Corresponding Society, a largely working-class organisation seeking, among other things, universal manhood suffrage, but his sentiments were actually closer to the revolutionary republicanism of Tom Paine and his adherents. In 1802 Despard was involved in a desperate plot to assassinate the king, seize the Tower of London, the Bank of England and the Houses of Parliament, and to inaugurate a new political order. He was taken and arraigned for high treason.

It was embarrassing for a man who was then the foremost national hero to be asked to speak for a traitor, but Nelson did it. He had not seen Despard since the day he left San Juan castle, and it seemed strange to behold him now, a shabbily dressed, ageing revolutionary in the dock of the Newington Sessions House, fighting hopelessly for his life before the Grand Jury of Surrey and a judge notorious for his severity. Under cross-examination Nelson tried to save him:

We went on the Spanish Main together. We slept many nights together in our clothes upon the ground. We have measured the height of the enemy's wall together. In all that period of time no man could have shown more zealous attachment to his sovereign and his country than Colonel Despard did. I formed the highest opinion of him at that time, as a man and an officer, seeing him so willing in the service of his sovereign. Having lost sight of him for the last twenty years, if I had been asked my opinion of him, I should certainly have said, 'If he is alive, he is certainly one of the brightest ornaments of the British army.'[44]

But it was useless, and Nelson could do no more than try to secure a pension for the wife of a condemned man. Despard died on the scaffold, accepting his fate as bravely and as defiantly as he had once honoured a different flag in the green hell of Nicaragua.

IX

FIGHTING BACK

You need not be sorrowful. Have I not often told you who
was almost as little, as pale, as suffering as you, and yet
potent as a giant and brave as a lion?

Charlotte Brontë, *Shirley*

1

IT was not often that Horatio Nelson was less than passionate about
active service, but the late spring and early summer of 1780 found
him exhausted and thinking about home. Even the careful ministrations of Cuba Cornwallis and the powerful frigate waiting for him in
the harbour at Port Royal could not rekindle the fire the sickness had
drained out of him. It was not until 25 May that he visited the *Janus*
and had the commission authorising him to take command read to
the crew. Even then he was too ill to give it serious attention.[1]

It was part of the business of every good captain to build up a reliable following, which he might take from ship to ship. A kind of
unwritten contract bonded officer and followers. The latter provided
a bedrock of support and facilitated the captain's purposes; on his
part, he looked after their welfare and intervened when necessary to
secure their pay or other entitlements. The captain, in effect, represented his men in circles from which they were socially excluded.
Hitherto, Nelson had not been able to recruit a ship's company from
scratch, and inherited reasonably full complements with his ships, but
in a short while he too, even as he lay sick, had the makings of a
following growing around him.

We can see it in his transfer to the *Victor* on 1 May, when he quit the *Hinchinbroke* to return to Jamaica. Seventeen men from his frigate went with him, all hoping to find a place aboard the *Janus*, their captain's new ship. The seventeen were Nelson's six personal servants (seven if we include the absent Locker), several petty officers (Tyson, a servant, Gore, a boatswain's mate, Boyet, a thirty-four-year-old Norwegian coxswain, Cruger, a master's mate, and Hayward, a midshipman), and six able seamen, Lepee, McAfee, Wilson, Bradley, Bamfield and Irwin. At least nine of these had been on the *Badger*, but by no means all found berths aboard the *Janus*.

Nelson's new frigate had a paper complement of two hundred and eighty, entitling the captain to twelve servants, roughly four to every hundred men. Unfortunately, the death of the previous captain left his protégés bereft of a protector, and Horatio evidently lacked the heart to disrate them. He was able to rate Locker, Sylvan, Lepee and Irwin as captain's servants on the *Janus*, but renewed the postings of four of the existing servants and added three or four newcomers to make up his quota. It seems that some of his old captain's servants either became incapacitated or found more promising openings on other ships. But Gore, Boyet, Hayward, McAfee, Wilson and Bamfield all got places on the *Janus*, and two other veterans of the *Hinchinbroke*, able seaman Bartholomew Lyas and Thomas Lawson, also caught up with their old captain and joined up.[2]

During his three months in command the *Janus* remained in harbour, where the temptations to seamen to desert and misbehave were constant. Forty-eight men 'ran' (in the vernacular of the navy) and six were flogged. The usual punishment was twelve lashes, but a man convicted of mutiny and drunkenness received three dozen. Two men guilty of insolence received different sentences, one man getting twelve strokes, twice as many as his partner. This suggests that Nelson was concerned with degrees of guilt, and believed that one offender had misled the other. How far Horatio supervised these events it is difficult to say, however. Much, if not most, of the day-to-day work on the *Janus* must have fallen upon the lieutenants (George Hope Stephens, James Crosby Haswell and Charles Pusick Codrington) and the master (James Fenwick). Given his condition, the officer Nelson probably saw most often was Thomas Jameson the surgeon.

However brief Horatio's conversations with the officers of the *Janus* may have been, they cannot have failed to provide news of one of his mentors. Thomas Surridge, the old master of the *Seahorse*, had been lieutenant on the *Janus* as late as January, but had fallen ill and gone home. Nelson would have missed the reunion. He was sick himself, and, after an attempt at his duties on the *Janus*, relapsed in June. This time the Parkers took him to their own house, 'Admiral Penn', near Kingston, to convalesce. Horatio was not happy there, the dreary drumming of the rain upon the windows and the lack of attention combining with the infuriating feebleness of his body and lack of spirits. 'Oh, Mr Ross,' he wrote to his agent the day after his arrival, 'what would I give to be at Port Royal. Lady P[arker] not here, and the servants letting me lay as if a log, and take no notice.'[3]

Some days he managed to rise to a quaky normality, his malarial fever appearing to recede, only to return and resume its regular pattern of attacks every other or every third day. At times he lay with his head throbbing and his stomach retching, feeling cold enough to shiver, while on other occasions it seemed as if he was burning up and his body sweated profusely. One of his physicians was probably Moseley, the surgeon general, whose *Treatise on Tropical Diseases* Nelson would one day enlarge with observations of the San Juan expedition. But he was not a good patient. Sir Peter and Lady Parker often sat by his bedside, a tribute to their regard, and Mrs Yates the housekeeper administered to his needs, but Horatio often did not take his medication. The Parkers discovered their most powerful weapon in getting Captain Nelson to do so was their youngest daughter, a mere child who invariably got her way with the guest.[4]

Despite the persuasive little girl, by 15 August it was obvious that Horatio would not be taking the *Janus* to sea. He was officially discharged to the sick quarters and Lieutenant Manley Dixon assumed acting command. Fifteen days later Nelson was no better and applied to Sir Peter for permission to sail for England. His health had deteriorated, with the attacks now occurring daily, and the hospital at Port Royal certified that he was also suffering from 'bilious vomitings, nervous headaches, visceral obstructions, and many other bodily infirmities'. He was 'being reduced quite to a skeleton'.[5]

Sir Peter feared for his life. He granted Nelson permission to leave Jamaica 'with my very sincere wishes for your speedy recovery', but privately confided to the Admiralty that the patient was 'so emaciated, and in so bad a state of health that I doubt whether he will live to get home'. 'I wish much for his recovery,' he added. 'His abilities in his profession would be a loss to the service.'[6]

2

Privately Nelson had often shared Sir Peter's pessimism and felt himself destined for nothing better than a place in Green Bay, the sad little naval cemetery near Port Royal where his friend Captain Deane and so many other men, good and bad, had been laid to rest. His predicament was not a new one, however. He remembered being shipped home from India, and surviving. The thought of leaving these pestilential climes and going home put new life into him.

Glory was one thing guaranteed to spur him on, to recharge his spirit and help keep him alive. It mattered to him more than money. Like most naval officers, Nelson enjoyed the thought of building a fortune on prize money. The Duke of Clarence, who later became one of his friends, would hugely exaggerate when he claimed that Nelson 'never [had] a thought' for prize money. Nelson was not rich enough to entertain such indifference, for money was essential to anyone wishing to cut a credible figure in 'gentle' society. Never more so than in generations experiencing a revolution in taste and pursuing increasingly extravagant lifestyles. For Captain Nelson the prospects of maintaining his own establishment, marrying well and supporting a family and social standing may have been distant, at least for the moment, but money underpinned all those natural ambitions.[7]

But for all that, wealth seldom excited him. He said so, and those who knew him said so. 'Riches are not his first object,' wrote his admiring father. 'Corsica in the prize way produces nothing but *honour*, [but this is] far above the consideration of wealth,' Nelson would write from the Mediterranean years later. 'Not that I dislike riches; quite the contrary, but [I] would not sacrifice a good name to obtain them.' Indeed, he was inclined to regard the pursuit of money as a dirty business, and to contrast 'justice' and 'honour' on the one hand with 'power, money and rascality' on the other.[8]

Nelson's emphasis upon 'honour' reflected a desire to be known for integrity, principle, public service and doing right, whether he actually realised these aspirations or not. But he wanted more than simple honour. He craved that transcendent form called 'glory', the exalted honour that linked service to the state with martial achievement, exhibited extreme physical courage and brought fame and applause. Thus, Nelson was apt to console himself with the thought that, while money might elude him, the bigger prize of immense acclaim would not. 'Had I attended to the service of my country less than I have I might have made some [money] too,' he once famously wrote. 'However, I trust my name will stand on record when the money makers will be forgot.'[9]

Horatio's glory-mongering seems stranger now than it would have done then. Britain's roll of victories had grown during the century, and included Blenheim, Quebec and Quiberon Bay. She had wrested control of Canada and India from the French, extended her claims to empire into the South Seas and expanded her wealth and international trade. A rising national pride and confidence rode on the back of military and naval endeavour, and pointed the road to immortality. As the historian Linda Colley has written, Nelson 'only practised to a remarkable degree what the cult of heroic individualism fostered very broadly among the class he aspired to'.[10]

Nelson had known that cult all his life. He had met those same ideals of patriotism, honour and martial heroism in the Classics drummed into him at school, and greatly admired Benjamin West's famous painting, *The Death of Wolfe*, depicting the hero dying at the moment of victory. Even more, he had been influenced by his role models, Captain Suckling and William Locker, and by the patriotic plays of Shakespeare, with their frequent allusions to national triumphs over Gallic rivals. Nelson was particularly fond of the stirring close to *King John*, with its proud boast:

> This England never did, nor never shall,
> Lie at the proud foot of a conqueror . . .
> Come the three corners of the world in arms,
> And we shall shock them. Nought shall make us rue,
> If England to itself do rest but true.

Most lovingly of all did Nelson misquote the words Shakespeare gave his hero Henry V before the battle of Agincourt:

> By Jove, I am not covetous for gold,
> Nor care I who doth feed upon my cost . . .
> But if it be a sin to covet honour,
> I am the most offending soul alive.

As several of Nelson's biographers have remarked, the admiral made a significant substitution in his version of the speech. In 1801, for example, he wrote, 'I feel myself . . . as anxious [now] to get a medal or a step in the peerage as if I never had got either, for "if it be a sin to covet *glory*, I am the most offending soul alive".[11]

Why Nelson needed this public acclaim no one can now say. Psychologists might probe his childhood, and ponder the mark those lonely Norfolk years made upon a boy who lost his mother before he was ten and whose father spent long months from home; perhaps also the transition into adolescence and manhood spent at sea in a man's world of hard work and danger. It is entirely possible that Horatio's lifelong need for attention and affection was in some way rooted in that turbulent and deficient upbringing, but while these speculations must trouble the novelist, historians are unable to enlarge upon them. What we do know is that from an early age Nelson fought for every scrap of glory he could get, and fiercely resented any denial of his just deserts.

Back in 1780, while fighting for life against a diseased body, Nelson found his deep-seated drive for recognition a powerful weapon of survival, and acknowledged its importance in one of the most revealing of all his early letters. It was addressed to Hercules Ross, who had so often put his house, carriages and purse at Nelson's disposal in those difficult days in Jamaica. On 1 September, as the enfeebled captain stirred himself for the passage home, he talked about riding to Ross's house. 'Now assured I return to England, hope revives within me,' he confessed. 'I shall recover, and my dream of glory be fulfilled. Nelson will yet be an admiral. It is the climate that has destroyed my health and crushed my spirits. Home, and dear friends, will restore me.'[12]

3

Captain William Cornwallis took Nelson home in the *Lion*. Horatio was entered on the ship's books from 16 August, the day after his discharge from the *Janus*. He was a supernumerary, entered for victuals only, and took with him only two or three followers, including Frank Lepee and William Irwin as servants. Nelson was not the only invalid aboard. Thirty others were brought from the hospital on 2 September, but Nelson probably received the most attention. He already knew some of the ship's officers, including the third lieutenant Joseph Bullen, formerly of the *Hinchinbroke*, the surgeon, James Melling, who had signed his sick certificate, and Cornwallis himself. The captain of the *Lion* was the son of an earl and belonged to a distinguished military family, but a modest man compared to Nelson, yet they nonetheless gelled. In fact Nelson credited the senior man's 'care and attention' with saving his life.[13]

The *Lion* left Jamaica at four-thirty on the morning of 4 September. There was convoy work to be done and for several days other contingents joined up. From his ship Nelson saw a sea studded with white sails, some 127 merchantmen shepherded by warships he knew – the *Magnificent, Niger, Thunderer, Sultan, Elizabeth, Conqueror, Bristol, Sterling Castle, Berwick, Hector, Trident* and *Ruby*, all controlled by Rear Admiral Joshua Rowley from the *Grafton*. They went west before steering east, by way of the Grand Caymans and the Strait of Florida, but on 24 September Cornwallis parted with the convoy and pushed northwards into the cold Atlantic. At the end of October, east of Newfoundland, Nelson would have been interested in the warship that stood towards them masquerading under French colours. She turned out to be the old *Raisonable*, now under Sir Digby Dent, and the eighteen days she accompanied the *Lion* on the homeward leg must have reawakened memories in Horatio of his first lonely days at sea. Other than that there was little of interest, though Nelson witnessed a novel penalty when Cornwallis had an incorrigible thief 'punished by all the boys in the ship' and compelled to wear an onerous collar.

The ship reached Spithead on 25 November, finding the *Diligent* flying the flag of Admiral Sir Thomas Pye and other ships, some of them from among the escorts that had left Jamaica with the *Lion*. Nelson and his servants were discharged the same day, and the captain made his way to London, where he temporarily lodged at the home of Sir Peter Parker. He also made an inevitable visit to Captain Locker's rooms at Gray's Inn before taking a coach out of town in search of that 'most precious jewel', his health. Like many sick people, he was beginning to appreciate what the fit take for granted.[14]

In Nelson's day health meant one place above all others: the town of Bath, close to the border of Wiltshire and Somerset, the last word in resorts for ailing men and women of fashion. It was an eighteenth-century health farm with a clientele that included almost every layer of the 'gentler' classes, from royalty to parsons. Horatio had known about it most of his life. His father regularly wintered there, and his sister Susanna had served her apprenticeship at Watson's, a local milliners, before working as a shop assistant in the town until she married in 1780. Almost everyone had heard of the famous but mythical healing properties of Bath's thermal spring waters, and Nelson believed the stories implicitly. Accordingly, the *Bath Journal* of 22

January 1781 proclaimed his arrival in the town in its customary roll
call of visiting dignitaries.

The town had numerous attractions. It was packed with apothe-
caries and physicians, a few of them respectable, but many peddling
cure-all cordials and pills to the sick, old and lame. The waters, they
said, relieved everything from gout and jaundice to deafness and
infertility, whether imbibed in the Pump Room or taken immersed to
the neck in one of the five baths. The streets were full of puffing sedan
chairmen, hauling patients to and from the baths. Once there, admission fees included the loan of linen waistcoats, shorts or smocks, all
yellowed by the sulphur in the water, and towels. That winter of 1781
Nelson must have shivered as he padded barefoot over the cold stone
passages that led from the dressing rooms to the steaming open-
air ponds in which he was supposed to wallow to the musical
accompaniment of bathside bands.

It was certainty a novelty for one who had spent years at sea, and
in addition to the bathing there was the chance of making useful
contacts among the well-to-do who gathered in the town. They sat
and talked in coffee houses and tea rooms, danced in their best finery
in the new assembly rooms, and turned the town into a maelstrom of
gossip, spiced not only by local newspapers but also the London dailies
that arrived in Bath within hours of publication. Aesthetes patronised
the circulating library, the bookshops and a floundering philosophical
society, or watched Sarah Siddons perform at the Theatre Royal on
Orchard Street. More frivolous souls defied the gambling laws and
entertained themselves with such games of chance as Evens and Odds,
a forbidden form of roulette. Nor was sexual titillation very far away
in Bath. The streets were haunted by prostitutes, some mere children
of fourteen or fifteen, and though attendants at the popular Cross
Bath were supposed to preserve propriety the place was said to be
'more famed for pleasure than cures'. In it were 'performed all the
wanton dalliances imaginable; celebrated beauties, panting breasts,
and curious shapes, almost exposed to public view; languishing eyes,
darting killing glances, tempting amorous postures, attended by soft
music, enough to provoke a vestal to forbidden pleasure, captivate a
saint, and charm a Jove'. In some Bath circles a man of modest sexual
appetite was considered an 'unfashioned fellow of no life or spirit'.[15]

Horatio boarded in the house of an apothecary, Joseph Spry, at no.
2 Pierrepont Street. It was a mid-terrace property with attic windows
in the pitched roof and a basement for the servants, but Nelson

probably occupied the ground floor to the left of the front door because his legs were still extremely weak. A physician and a surgeon attended him, the former Dr Francis Woodward, a man of almost sixty, who practised from no. 8 Gay Street. Yet notwithstanding their services, Nelson told Locker that he was 'so ill' that he 'was obliged to be carried to and from bed with the most excruciating tortures'. He was 'physicked' thrice a day with pills and cordials, drank the waters at the Pump Room near the abbey as often, and in the evenings, when the crowds had dispersed, bathed, probably either in the Cross or the King's Bath. 'Worst of all,' he said, he abstained from drinking wine with his meals. Nelson was generally a rebellious patient, but on this occasion he was eager to command a ship again. While scrutinising the Navy Lists to gauge his standing among post-captains, this time he stuck to his regime.[16]

For a while Horatio remained debilitated, 'scarcely able to hold my pen', but gradually felt himself 'a new man'. On 15 February he was able to declare that 'my health, thank God, is very near perfectly restored, and I have the perfect use of all my limbs, except my left arm, which I can hardly tell what is the matter with it. From the shoulder to my fingers' ends are as if half dead, but the surgeon and doctors give me hopes it will all go off.' His ailment was probably polyneuritis, a legacy of the illnesses that had floored him in Nicaragua. The immediate cause was the degeneration of the nerve fibres in the small nerves, and recovery was slow because of the need to grow replacement nerve fibres.[17]

During this extensive rehabilitation Locker was his favourite correspondent. He sent Nelson news from London, and acted as a kind of referee for him. Whenever Horatio met sea officers he introduced the name of Locker as a talking point, and was forever passing their compliments back to his old mentor. In short, he was using Locker to introduce himself to professional colleagues, and to gain credibility by the relationship. Locker would have wished it no differently, and though many years Nelson's senior was unrelentingly enthusiastic about their friendship. He happily referred old comrades to his young protégé. One such was Captain James Kirke, under whom Locker had gone to the West Indies when himself a youngster in 1747. Kirke and his sick wife arrived in Bath at the end of February 1781 with Locker's advice to call upon Captain Nelson at an early opportunity. The Kirkes took different lodgings, but Nelson recommended his own doctor and surgeon, and was sure the bathing would be of 'infinite service' to Mrs Kirke. Sadly, her condition proved incurable: 'I am very sorry for her, poor woman,' wrote Nelson, 'it must be a most lamentable situation to remain in her state for the number of years she may live.'[18]

Locker also handled Nelson's affairs in London, visiting Rigaud's studio to supervise further work on the portrait which Horatio wanted altering so that it depicted a captain rather than a teenage lieutenant. The likeness was one of three portraits of individuals that Locker appears to have been overseeing, one of them of their mutual friend Captain Charles Pole. 'When you get the pictures, I must be in the middle,' Nelson wrote, 'for God knows, without good supporters, I shall fall to the ground!'[19]

Locker had not put his own health problems behind him and Nelson tried to persuade the captain to join him. 'I wish you had come to Bath when your sons went to school, instead of being cooped up in Gray's Inn without seeing any body,' he said. 'I am sure yours is a Bath case, and therefore you ought to come for a month or six weeks.' There was a vacancy in Kirke's lodgings, but Locker went instead to an older friend, Captain Robert Kingsmill of Sidmonton Place, near Newbury, Berkshire. Indeed, Kingsmill extended the invitation to Nelson. A little weak but feeling better, Horatio took the London stage on the morning of Monday 15 March, travelling as far as Newbury with the Kirkes. There he enjoyed a brief reunion with Locker and found Kingsmill a remarkably agreeable companion, before proceeding to London to stay with his uncle, William Suckling.[20]

Suckling had acquired a country house in what was then the village of Kentish Town, an agreeable rural area waiting to be swallowed by the rapacious metropolis and reached by a short coach ride from the city. The house was a regular-fronted two-storey residence on the west side of Kentish Town Road, adjacent to the Castle Tavern and Tea Gardens and sporting a view from the rear towards the famed beauty spot of Primrose Hill. The extensive grounds, both front and back, were ornamented with shrubs and 'extraordinary box trees' that later generations decided were planted by Nelson himself.[21]

It was Uncle William who led Horatio's campaign for employment. Nelson was a post-captain, and would ascend the captains' list by seniority as a matter of course, but he had no wish to remain on 'half-pay' without a command, and used his surviving interest to get a ship. There was less of it now, after the comptroller's death, and William Suckling was the best patron at Nelson's disposal. He lacked the standing of his brother, Maurice, but was still deputy collector at the Customs House on the river and had a few useful friends.

The most powerful of these was Charles Jenkinson, the secretary for war, who may have become acquainted with Suckling when he was Lord of the Treasury. Suckling wrote to him at least once, and perhaps twice. Accordingly, on 12 February 1781 Jenkinson tackled Lord Sandwich, first lord of the Admiralty, on behalf of the 'nephew of the late comptroller', a young man, he understood, of 'very good character'. Sandwich hesitated, but on 6 May Nelson personally appeared before him at the Admiralty, and the first lord promised to employ him at an early opportunity. With that, for the time being, Horatio had to be satisfied.[22]

During his short stay in London Nelson returned to Rigaud, and had him complete his portrait and add the castle of San Juan to the background. There were also friends to look up, including his brother Maurice and Locker, and new physicians to find. He placed himself in the care of Robert Adair, the surgeon general to the army. In May a relapse cost him a temporary loss of the use of his left arm and part of his left leg, but Adair assured him that a few weeks' rest would repair the damage. In the meantime his account with Robert Winch, apothecary, for ointments, vial drops and decoctions ran to nearly £9 in two months.[23]

Nelson's resources were modest, and his pay was slow in coming. As captain of the *Janus* he had been too ill to keep adequate records, and although he petitioned the Victualling Board to pass his deficient accounts, a portion of his wages would be withheld for four years. But moving here and there about town demanded a new wardrobe, and Nelson presented himself to one Richard Shepherd, a gentleman's outfitter. To judge from his purchases his taste was entirely suited to a sober parson's son. Though he chose 'silver Tishua' and 'striped satin' waistcoats, he preferred black outer garments, and ordered a 'super fine cloth coat lined with silk' and Florentine breeches, the four items costing him £6 12s. 0d. He also had an existing pair of silk breeches dyed black. Three years later we find him at the same store, replenishing his civilian attire with another black cloth silk-lined coat, a black silk waistcoat and breeches, and a sleeved flannel under-waist-coat for £7 5s. 0d. There were other necessities, and buried among his accounts are payments for such items as stockings, shirts and lace and for the dressing of his hair. Nor, as he prepared for his next ship in 1781, did Nelson forget the requirements of his servant – probably

Frank Lepee, whom he had retained. Domestic staff were essential tokens of gentrification, and their deficiencies an almost indispensable subject of polite conversation. Nelson paid Shepherd £2 7s. od. to mend his servant's coat and breeches and supply him with a new suit of 'thickset materials'.[24]

Adair was right about getting Nelson on his feet, for in May he felt fit enough to brush the cobwebs off an old promise. 'Now you will say, "Why do[es] not he come into Norfolk?"' he wrote to his brother William on 7 May. Some time in the late spring or early summer of 1781, after ten long years away, Captain Nelson returned to the quiet county of his childhood. William, he discovered, had just been awarded his Master of Arts and was on the verge of being ordained a priest, while his sister Susanna and her new husband, Thomas Bolton, a worthy merchant in corn, malt and coal, were established at Wells. Horatio's younger brothers, Edmund and Suckling, were both apprentices, 'Mun' to one Nicholas Havers of Burnham and Suckling to a linen draper, Mr Blowers of Beccles.[25]

Much as he loved Burnham and thought of it as his home, Horatio found it a lonely, provincial place, far from the affairs that had now become his life and the news he longed to hear. Almost indecently he hurried back to London, and the letter he had been awaiting from the Admiralty. On 15 August 1781 he was appointed captain of the frigate *Albemarle*, fitting out at Woolwich.

4

Nelson was on the ship the same day, and watching it being caulked, repaired and readied for coppering in the dock. His commission was read to the assembled company. *Albemarle* was a prize taken from the French and converted into a twenty-eight-gun, nine-pounder ship, among the weakest class of frigates, but her new captain was proud of her and brought friends aboard. Captain Locker thought the ship deficient, as she indeed proved to be. She had the lines of a ponderous store ship rather than a fast frigate, and would serve her purposes ill. But Nelson's less practised eye saw no imperfections in his new command. After taking his brother Maurice aboard on 23 August he declared himself 'perfectly satisfied' with the *Albemarle*, and fancied her far superior to the *Enterprize* being fitted alongside. Though he acknowledged that the space between the *Albemarle*'s decks was low, 'she has a bold entrance and clean run'.[26]

The Admiralty allowed him to choose some officers, and the ship was short of its complement, so Horatio commanded his first substantial powers of patronage. It seemed sensible to offer opportunities to the people at home, strengthening his position in the local community and tapping the existing support of family and friends. His appointment was announced in the *Norfolk Chronicle* and his brother William was soon offering one man the position of master's mate, with a volunteer's bounty of £5 and an additional £2 for every recruit he could raise in Wells and ship to Woolwich. Eventually, some twenty lower-deck volunteers answered Nelson's call, and a few officers also applied. John Oliver, 'a very good man', was provisionally rated a quartermaster, and Valentine Boyles, whose father collected the customs duties at Wells and regularly joined William for cards, apparently sought a lieutenancy. Horatio liked the Boyles family, especially his old shipmate Charles ('I wish much to meet him'), but on this occasion was unable to oblige; perhaps at that time his lieutenants had already been appointed.[27]

For key officers he turned or bowed to naval colleagues. His two lieutenants were 'very genteel young men'. First Lieutenant Martin Hinton was about Nelson's age and had gone to sea in 1771 with Captain James Ayscough of the *Swan*. He had completed his six years of sea time as an able seaman and midshipman on that ship and the *Leviathan*, serving also under Captains Dewey, Tatty and Tathwell. When Nelson met Hinton in 1784, he was a lieutenant of two years' standing. Horatio's second lieutenant, William Osborne, was the son of Admiral Sir Charles Hardy's secretary. Hardy had been dead a year, but Nelson probably wanted to please one of the late admiral's friends, since he also took Charles Hardy junior as a captain's servant and midshipman. Less fortunate than Hinton and Osborne was Horatio's old friend Joseph Bromwich of the *Lowestoffe*. Despite his qualities as an officer, Bromwich had slipped and slid on the promotion ladder. He had remained in the *Lowestoffe* after Christopher Parker succeeded Locker in command, and followed his new captain to the *Diamond* in 1780, rising to the position of acting lieutenant. But then his diligently acquired knowledge of the Bahama keys proved to be his undoing, for he was asked to surrender his acting lieutenancy in order to pilot Sir John Hamilton's *Hector* home. Bromwich arrived in England in June 1781, just in time to sign up with his old messmate on the *Albemarle*. He had lost sea time, however, and Nelson was obliged to ship him aboard as master's mate, though he backdated

Bromwich's appointment to 24 June to strengthen his claim to any acting lieutenancy that might arise.[28]

On the whole, Nelson was pleased with his efforts. He had a good carpenter, Samuel Innes, transferred from the *Hound*, and thought his master, a Londoner named Donald Trail, 'exceeding good'. The surgeon (James Armstrong), purser, boatswain (Joseph Pike) and lieutenant of marines (Charles Stuart) pleased him, while the other marines were 'likewise old standers'. Cordially Nelson concluded, 'I have an exceeding good ship's company. Not a man or officer in her I would wish to change.'[29]

The empty spaces among the hands were not filled without difficulty, and the muster bore considerably fewer names than the official complement of two hundred. The ship was only shifted to the Nore on 14 October with the aid of forty retired seamen from Greenwich Hospital and twenty-five yachtsmen sent by the Navy Board. At the Nore recruits being held for him on the *Greenwich* and *Conquistadore* and seamen from a recently decommissioned ship replaced the temporary labour, but Nelson remained ready to profit by every opportunity to improve his manpower.[30]

A tender hailed the *Albemarle* with news that some homeward-bound East Indiamen were on their way upriver. It was a chance to press men, but Nelson was warned that the crews on the Indiamen were bragging that the navy would not be allowed on board. He had already prepared himself for such an encounter by enquiring of the local admiral what force he could legitimately use to press men from merchant ships, as well as what inducements were at his disposal. 'Leave of absence they will want,' he remarked. Armed with the reply Nelson resolved to halt the Indiamen, but on 28 October he found himself boxed in by them and lost an anchor extricating his ship. Struggling clear, he caught up with the four leading vessels, but they refused to heave to until Nelson fired twenty-six nine-pounders at their masts and rigging. He anchored close to the *Haswell*, the leading ship, and tried to send a boat across, but her master truculently refused to accept any boarders. It was midnight, so Nelson gave the master until daylight to think it over, and sense prevailed. When the *Albermarle* ran alongside the *Haswell* at five in the morning his men boarded without difficulty and recruits were obtained.[31]

A more satisfying outcome attended Horatio's efforts to dissuade his brother William from enlisting on the *Albemarle* as a naval chaplain. After chewing over the unexpected suggestion with Uncle William

Suckling, Horatio warned his brother that 'he thinks as I do that fifty pounds where you are is much more than equal to what you can get at sea'. Although Nelson feared his brother's obstinacy ('In that, I know you will please yourself,' he wrote), he gently weaned him off the idea for the time being. 'I hope you have lost all ideas of going to sea,' Horatio said in December, 'for the more I see of chaplains of men [of] war the more I dread seeing my brother in such a disagreeable station of life.' Parson Nelson took the hint and deferred his naval service for three more years.[32]

In the meantime Nelson's health had improved, but fears of a relapse continued to overshadow his new command. There were still days when he was confined to bed, and he dreaded being posted to an exacting climate. The East Indies station was his preferred destination, and it was with some mortification that he heard that he was being sent to the North Sea, as if 'to try my constitution'. When they came the instructions were dated 23 October and confirmed those forebodings. Taking the *Argo* and *Enterprize* under his command, Nelson was to collect the homeward-bound merchantmen of the Russia Company at Elsinore in Denmark and bring them to England. Their cargoes of tar, hemp and timber were essential for Britain's naval dockyards, but it was dull and cold work. Nelson consoled himself with the thought that the Dutch, with whom Britain had just gone to war, might intervene and give him some action, but the greater indications were that the *Albemarle* would be a cold and unstimulating command.[33]

X

'THE POOR *ALBEMARLE*'

> Each change of atmosphere disdaining
> With scarce the wreck of health remaining
> Never of toil or wound complaining
> Serv'd brave, immortal Nelson
> Anon, *Nelson and Collingwood*, 1805

1

NELSON'S command of the *Albemarle* spanned the last two years of the American War of Independence. It had developed from a colonial revolt into an international conflict, as first France and then Spain had opportunely attacked Britain, taking advantage of the deployment of her naval and military forces across the Atlantic. Almost twenty years before, Britain had triumphantly emerged from the Seven Years War as the most powerful sea power, with major gains in North America, the West Indies and India, but by 1781 she was visibly paling. Though Canada had remained firm, despite its French tradition, the American colonies looked irretrievably lost. A mere ten or eleven days before Nelson sailed for the Baltic, Lord Cornwallis surrendered a second British army to the rebel forces at Yorktown. At the same time Britain was isolated in Europe. She was not only threatened by a combination of the next two largest naval powers, France and Spain, but had alienated much of the rest of the Continent. In attempts to prevent the Baltic powers from shipping essential naval supplies of timber, hemp, tar, canvas and iron to her enemies, Britain had insisted upon the right to seize neutral ships carrying contraband items. In 1780 Russia, Sweden and Denmark-Norway formed the League of

Armed Neutrality to resist British pretensions, and in 1781 Britain attacked the Netherlands in an effort to pre-empt them reinforcing the opposition. Yet the British people were war and tax weary, and as Lord North's government tottered beneath an avalanche of criticism, it was apparent that a new administration would have to wash its hands of America in order to settle its more threatening differences in Europe.

To command a man-of-war during those final years of the conflict undeniably offered opportunities, but the glory and prize money that interested Captain Nelson continued to slip through his fingers. Biographers have generally drawn a veil over what was plainly a frustrating period, and yet the cruises of 'the poor *Albemarle*' were not devoid of interest. Horatio recovered his health, advanced in experience and confidence and widened those all-important contacts to include senior admirals and royalty. He also enjoyed, or suffered, the pangs of first love.

But if Horatio had been asked for words to describe his first voyage in the *Albermarle*, he might have chosen 'cold', 'dull' and 'drudgery'. It began at twelve noon on 31 October 1781, when one of Nelson's nine-pounders signalled his departure from the Downs with the *Argo* (Captain John Butchart) and *Enterprize* (John Willett Payne). Four days across the North Sea, through the Skagerrak and into the Baltic Sound, brought the trio to Elsinore (Helsingor). Nelson found fifty British merchantmen waiting for him, and heard that twice as many were on their way, so he endured a few more weeks 'almost . . . froze', trying to gather as many charges as possible. Showing increasing confidence, young Nelson upbraided a Danish midshipman who came on board to enquire the purpose and strength of his forces. Sensitive to national honour, and incensed that a mere midshipman had been sent to speak to him, Nelson curtly informed the unfortunate Dane that he was at liberty to count the *Albemarle*'s guns as he went down her side, and to assure his superiors that they would be well served if ever the need arose. Eventually Nelson sent a boat to the castle of Cronenberg, and it was decided that a fifteen-gun salute on the part of both parties would satisfy pride all round.[1]

On 19 November the *Sampson* arrived and her captain, William Dickson, assumed overall command as the senior officer. Nelson gave him a list of fifty-nine sail ready to receive orders, but warned that another fifty sitting in the roadstead wanted to 'run' for home and chance the enemy rather than wait for the convoy to be completed.

The rebellious skippers complained that some of the Baltic merchantmen would not arrive before Christmas and there was a danger of being iced in. Although their orders required them to wait for the whole of the merchant fleet to assemble, Nelson convinced Dickson that they should leave with the ships they had rather than wait indefinitely for stragglers. But they were anticipated by the master of the twelve-gun Hull merchantman *Crow Isle*, who cajoled sixty or more of the merchantmen into a sudden departure by promising to act as their escort. The winds were unfavourable, but on 7 December the rebels put to sea, ignoring a warning gun fired by the *Sampson*.

The next day Dickson and Nelson followed with their convoy, and soon three warships, the *Albemarle*, *Sampson* and *Argo*, and two hundred and sixty merchantmen were spread across a vast expanse of sea. They were vulnerable, but no enemy ships seemed to be about and apart from bad weather the voyage proceeded quietly. Early on the 13th Nelson pursued a suspicious cutter approaching the convoy but failed to run it down. It was, he fumed, 'Fall the pirate', who had recently harassed the Scottish coast under French colours. Most of the time was spent more tediously, shepherding the undisciplined merchantmen forward. 'Very few of the ships paid the least attention to any signals that were made for the better conducting them safe home,' he complained.[2]

The convoy soon fragmented. Forty-five separated on the 11th, and off the Dogger Bank Captain Payne, who had joined with the *Enterprize*, led another detachment away towards the northeastern ports. The *Argo* ran into the Humber with a few of the ships, while the *Albemarle* and *Sampson* reached Yarmouth with most of the others on 17 December. Nelson was now bound for the Downs with those ships for the Thames, Portsmouth and Plymouth, but as one year turned into another the weather was fitfully appalling. His frigate was penned in Yarmouth for almost two weeks by fresh southerly gales.

2

Captain Nelson spent an unusual Christmas 1781 fretting at his inability to get to sea. There were advantages in being close to home, and his brother William was among several who visited him at Yarmouth, but enforced idleness encouraged dissatisfaction in the crew. Already undermanned, the ship lost more men through desertions and discharges in Elsinore and Yarmouth, including some petty officers.

A midshipman deserted at Yarmouth, while an excellent master's mate recommended by Captain Locker asked for his discharge so that he might join a ship bound for America with Admiral George Rodney. Another midshipman, George Mitchell, also left after difficulties with bills. Nelson had placed the boy with other midshipmen and master's mates in Bromwich's mess. Every member of the mess was expected to contribute to its upkeep, but Mitchell soon declared that he was incapable of keeping pace and insisted upon leaving the ship. Nelson was not unsympathetic; indeed, he was advancing money to another youngster (probably John Wood of Yarmouth, a captain's servant) 'whose friends are Norfolk people who had not made an allowance for their son'. But he was annoyed to learn that the impecunious 'middy' was going around claiming that Nelson had told him that at least £30 a year were needed to maintain a place aboard the *Albemarle*. 'What in the name of God could it be to me whether a midshipman in my ship had not a farthing or fifty pounds a year?' he stormed to Locker.[3]

With the *Argo*, *Sampson* and *Preston* (Captain Patrick Leslie) Nelson finally got the convoy free of Yarmouth on New Year's Eve, and made a difficult run into the Downs, which he entered on the night of 1 January 1782 with up to forty merchantmen and naval store ships in company. The commanding officer in the Downs, Baronet Sir Richard Hughes, rear admiral of the blue squadron, detailed the *Argo* and *Preston* to chaperone the ships bound for the western ports, but kept Nelson awaiting the Admiralty's pleasure. Unfortunately, the weather deteriorated and the *Albemarle* was imprisoned again. For a month the gales drove his ship 'from one end of the Downs to the other' and strewed the coast with wrecks. Off Yarmouth alone thirteen sail were on shore in the middle of January. Ravaged by the raw winds, Nelson fell so sick that he believed the doctor saved his life, and realised that Captain Locker's misgivings about the *Albemarle* had been justified.[4]

The ship embroiled Nelson in a short-tempered exchange with his superior officer. Sir Richard Hughes was in his fifties and came from a naval family. Both his father and grandfather had been commissioners of the navy at Portsmouth, and though Hughes himself had served in all the principal theatres of naval operations his services had been routine rather than distinguished and administrative rather than active. For many years he commanded guard ships at Plymouth and Portsmouth, and prior to his appointment to the Downs had served as naval commissioner at Halifax in Nova Scotia. A sightless eye suggested a little colour to his career, perhaps, but Hughes had sustained the injury at the table, not in battle. In his twenties he had accidentally pierced an eyeball with a dining fork.[5]

Scholars have missed Nelson's brief falling out with Hughes in 1782. It was insignificant in itself, but generated bad blood between the two men that affected subsequent and more notable altercations. The pitiable state of the *Albemarle* was the root of the problem. As Locker had foreseen, she sailed 'exceedingly crank'. The *Albemarle* was no purpose-built warship: she was a merchantman, captured a couple of years before and converted for naval use. Before Nelson assumed command a report had noted her poor sailing and steering qualities, and on the voyage from Elsinore her new captain was forced to acknowledge that the masts were too long, and took a topgallant down to give the ship more stability in violent weather. The tempestuous journey from Yarmouth to the Downs confirmed that the frigate was dangerously top-heavy, and upon arrival Nelson applied for fifteen tons of iron ballast so that he could create additional buoyancy by packing the keelson at the bottom of the ship. Soon afterwards he wrote to Hughes again, this time in search of an anchor and cable to replace one ripped from the *Albemarle* by a gale that swept the Downs on 9 January.[6]

Nelson had inconvenienced Hughes from the beginning. When his convoy had first been spotted beating towards the Downs in foul weather, Hughes doubted that the ships were English, and dithered over whether to risk sending out help. In the event, wind and tide precluded the attempt, but Hughes started complaining about the need for convoys to identify themselves more clearly. Now, writing from his flagship, the *Dromedary*, Hughes replied artlessly to Nelson's request for an anchor and cable. The demand for both had been so great, he said, that few were left, and he had to issue them sparingly. Nelson was instructed to use his 'utmost endeavors to sweep [recover] the end of the cable that you parted in the last gale of wind', a task Hughes supposed easy since the position of the sunken anchor had been marked by a buoy and the weather had moderated. 'It is at least necessary that you should make every possible effort to perform this service,' Hughes went on, 'as I cannot direct you to be supplied with any anchor or cable from hence.'[7]

Hughes did Nelson less than justice, as the logs of the *Albemarle* demonstrate. The weather remained poor for a day or two after the frigate lost its anchor, but as soon as it moderated on 11 January

Nelson had indeed searched for the missing equipment, if without success. Nothing irritated him more than to be undervalued or presumed negligent.

To some officers, Hughes's letter would have prompted little more than suppressed annoyance, but Horatio Nelson was always a deeply sensitive man, badly scorched by slights, however small. Moreover, intelligent and capable, he was increasingly confident and outspoken, proud not only of his independence of mind but also the fearlessness with which he expressed it. Strength and authority had begun to ooze from his assertions. When his brother reported local animosity to an officer of Nelson's acquaintance, he rose powerfully to his defence. 'Whatever may be the opinion of the Wells people respecting Captain [Alan] Gardner's behaviour . . .,' he wrote, 'I will answer he was *right*. There is not a better officer, or more of a gentleman this day in the service.' With all the assurance and ideals of intemperate youth, Nelson was already viewing himself a champion of the true purposes and interests of the service, and reacted badly to criticism.[8]

Hughes touched a raw spot and Nelson dashed off a short but fierce reply the same day. He resented the suggestion that he would request a new anchor lightly as a slur on his professionalism. 'I am very sorry you should have so bad an opinion of my conduct as to suppose that every effort had not and would not be made to sweep the anchor,' he told Hughes on 12 January. 'I knew if the weather was moderate we could get it with ease, but at the same time I thought it my duty to demand another anchor and cable that no accident might happen to His Majesty's ship [in the meantime] through my neglect.' The cable on his anchor was, in any case, 'so very bad that I must request you will be pleased to order another for us.' In other words, if a mishap befell the *Albemarle* for the want of an anchor, it would be on Hughes's head.[9]

Nelson got his ballast and his anchor and cable, but Hughes neither apologised for nor referred to the perceived insult. He had not intended to offend Nelson, or to charge him with incompetence, and should have said so. He was probably embarrassed and angered by Nelson's rebuke, and tried to hurry the incident by, but he had created a lasting bad impression in the younger officer's mind.

However, for the time being Hughes was banished from Nelson's thoughts by a new round of storms that lashed the Downs anchorage. A Dutch ship ran upon the treacherous Goodwin Sands on 21 January, and at eight in the morning of the 26th a savage squall descended

from the north. The *Kite*, captained by Wilfred Collingwood, brother
of the Cuthbert Collingwood whom Nelson had known in the West
Indies, was driven against another ship and damaged her gunwale and
mainmast gaff. Even worse befell the *Albemarle*. An East India store
ship, the *Brilliant*, ran upon the *Albemarle*'s hawse and swung the two
ships together with a grinding crash. The damage, done in a mere five
minutes, ran the length of Nelson's frigate, from bowsprit, bow, bump-
kins and larboard cathead at the head to the quarter gallery on the
stern. Two holes were stoved into the larboard hull, and her sheet, or
supplementary, anchor was torn away with fathoms of cable. Aloft
the ship lost her foremast head, fore topsail, topgallant yards, main
yard, mizzen gaff and spanker boom, and much of the wreckage
crashed down to hang precariously over the side, dangerously destabilising a ship that was already top-heavy.

Never had the *Albemarle* been in greater danger. 'What a change!'
Nelson noted, 'but yet we ought to be thankful we did not founder.'
Fortunately, as the swell rose and the wind freshened, he had taken
precautions against being capsized. Axemen stood by, ready to hack
away the mainmast if needs be. According to an account Nelson gave
the Admiralty, his ship 'laid so much down on her broadside that there
was much fear she would be overset, although the yards and topgallant masts were struck'. But his axemen leapt forward to clear the
wreckage, and the carpenter, Samuel Innes, turned in a bravura
performance. Working like a fury he single-handedly put replacement
jury masts in place within twenty-four hours.[10]

Clarke and McArthur, Nelson's official biographers, published a
dramatic account of this incident in 1809. According to them the
captain was ashore when the storm struck:

Captain Nelson immediately ran to the beach, and with his wonted contempt
of danger, when any duty called for his exertions, employed every method he
could devise to return on board, fearing lest the *Albemarle* might drive on the
Goodwin Sands; but the dreadful surf and increasing violence of the gale,
made even the skilful mariners of Deal regard the attempt as utterly impracticable. At length some of the most intrepid offered to make the trial for fifteen
guineas; this produced a competition, and Nelson, to the astonishment of all
beholders, was long seen struggling with a raging and mountainous surf, in
which the boat was continually immerged. After much difficulty he got on
board his ship, which lost her bowsprit and foremast.[11]

Like many of the stories of Clarke and McArthur, this is less than the truth. The admiring biographers misdated the incident, rolled two stories into one and magnified the sum. It is true that Nelson went ashore at Deal, for we have a letter he wrote there to his brother William. But it was dated 25 January, the day before the storm, and we can be fairly sure that Nelson did not stay overnight because he specifically said that he had but 'half an hour on dry land'. Nelson returned to the ship, therefore, *before* and not *during* the storm of the following morning. No doubt the water was pretty choppy on the 25th too, under what the ship's log called 'fresh breezes', but somehow his journey was confused with the subsequent storm and transformed into the dramatic wild boat ride described after his death.[12]

When Nelson's new orders arrived they sent him to Portsmouth with seven East Indiamen, but the collision with the *Brilliant* ended his hopes of taking them out to the Indian Ocean. Instead, on 12 February he had to dock his frigate in Portsmouth for repairs, lashing it to the *Launceston* hulk. The delay irritated, and it may have been at this time that Nelson unsuccessfully applied to the Admiralty for a larger frigate. However, perhaps it also had its uses. The men had been 'very uneasy' over arrears of pay, and Nelson had urged the naval commissioner at Chatham to solve the problem. He understood that the loyalty and respect of the men depended upon his willingness to advocate their just grievances, and the days at Portsmouth may have helped to satisfactorily wind the matter up.[13]

In addition there were other distractions.

3

Portsmouth, more than anywhere else, was the home of the British fleet, with its battery of slips and jetties, dockyard, marine barracks, naval college and hospital flanked on both sides by powerful fortifications. Nearby was Spithead, where the principal shield of the realm, the Channel fleet, was accustomed to anchor between the mainland and the Isle of Wight, while St Helens acted as a forward base for any ships waiting for a wind to sail. Ashore, in a maze of dirty, ill-lit streets, taphouses, shops and lodging houses offered services of every kind. During the two months that Nelson spent in the town there was much to see and report to Captain Locker, still his greatest professional confidant. He missed Boyles by one day, but found other good friends to dine with and worry and write about, among them

Captain Robinson, Major General Dalling, who came from Jamaica on the *Ranger*, and Charles Pole, for whom he was developing an almost brotherly affection. Nelson was able to inform Locker both of Pole's departure ('I wish he was safe back. I think he runs great risk of going to Cadiz') and his return as the captor of an enemy frigate ('I am exceedingly happy at his success'), and marvelled that 'no man in the world' was 'so modest in his account of it' as Pole himself. And amidst the comings and goings of ships and squadrons, Nelson extended his acquaintances, attempting to assess the worth of each. Sarcastically he decided that Sir Richard Bickerton, who headed a force for the East Indies, was 'a *great* man' who seemed 'to carry it pretty high with his captains,' but in Vice Admiral Samuel Barrington there was a kindred soul. 'He is in very good spirits,' Nelson told Locker. 'He gets amongst all the youngsters here, and leaves out the old boys.'[14]

Believing he was about to be posted abroad, Nelson also thought of home. The previous November his first nieces, twin girls Jemima and Katherine, were born to his eldest sister, Susanna. In February Susanna decided to go to Ostend, where her husband was transferring his trading business, and Nelson persuaded William to release some family money in aid of their venture. As for William himself, he was bidding for a living at Newton, and Nelson wrote to him on 8 February:

I wish I could congratulate you upon a rectory instead of a vicarage. It is rather awkward wishing the poor man [present incumbent] dead, but we all rise by deaths. I got my rank by a shot killing a post-captain, and I most sincerely hope I shall, when I go, go out of [the] world the same way. Then we go all in the line of our profession, a parson praying, a captain fighting. I suppose you are returned from Hilborough before this, and taken Miss Ellen and the living. As Miss Bec takes so much notice of my respects to her, tell her I think myself honoured by being in her favour. Love to Mrs Bolton [Susanna] and Mun [his brother Edmund], not forgetting little Kate [his youngest sister].[15]

At least for the time being William appeared to harbour no further ideas of going to sea.

One story that seems to belong to this period is somewhat removed from the no doubt scrupulously upright dalliances of the clerical brother, for it suggests that Horatio himself was not inexperienced with women. He was now twenty-three and had spent most of his life in the company of men and boys, but he had mixed with women at the houses of colleagues and friends, women such as Lady Parker, and apparently respected them and enjoyed their company. He had also seen, both on board ship and about seedy waterfront taverns and lodging houses, women of the loosest kind in most of the ports he had known.

The naval service, which took men far from their homes for long periods of time, naturally generated interest in women. Nelson had seen boatloads of them, many prostitutes and some devoid of the refinements he associated with the sex, rowed out to the ships, where they were allowed gross fraternisation with the ratings while they were in port.

Officers could be more discreet. Some even took wives and sweethearts to sea with them, and the distinctions between the married and unmarried were not always clear. Others took advantage of ports, where commissioned officers at least could usually arrange some leave and access services of most kinds. Prostitutes interested in the wealthier clients used side boxes in pleasure gardens, theatres and opera houses to make contacts. Some even advertised. John Harris's *List of Covent Garden Ladies*, for example, gave regular updates of the names, addresses and characteristics of such paramours in London. Among the women bluntly offering their favours in its pages were several touting specifically for naval officers, who at least promised few long-term encumbrances. Thus, the 'port' of Miss Devonshire of Queen Ann Street was 'said to be well guarded by a light brown chevaux-de-freize', but 'once' entered offered 'very good riding'. Moreover, she was 'ever ready for an engagement, cares not how soon she comes to close quarters, and loves to fight yard arm and yard arm, and be briskly boarded'.[16]

There were Miss Devonshires in all large ports, and Nelson knew officers who boasted of the mistresses awaiting them in different havens. On twenty-two occasions between 1750 and 1800 the commissioners issuing pensions to the widows of commissioned officers were confronted with applications from two women seeking the same pension. The ease with which temporary sexual partners were found was illustrated by Prince William Henry, the third son of King George III, and shortly a naval officer of Nelson's acquaintance. The prince was every bit as licentious as his older brothers, and happy to regale them with his amorous adventures in port. 'I was on shore there but once,' he said of Yarmouth when a newly promoted lieutenant, 'and had no opportunity of getting hold of a girl. My next excursion was in Yorkshire, where I was going on horseback from Burlington [Bridlington] Bay to Hull and intended to lay two in a bed that night.' If the shore leave of this officer was consumed in romps and loose living, he was far from alone in such diversions.[17]

Of a more sober cast and the son of a clergyman, Horatio Nelson was less focused on sexual gratification, but it is unreasonable to suppose that a young man of his age had not experimented amid so much opportunity and temptation. Indeed, since we know that he later kept two mistresses after his marriage, we should not be surprised to consider the possibility of other liaisons before. There is one little-known and obscure piece of evidence that suggests that Nelson was no virgin when he found himself beached in Portsmouth early in 1782.

Curiously enough, it is to be found in a tract on the subject of dentistry, published in 1797. Since its purpose was to instruct rather than titillate, and it appeared in Nelson's lifetime though before he became famous, the pamphlet is entitled to some credit. Proudly outlining several of his techniques for treating teeth, the Chevalier Bartholomew Ruspini, at one time dentist to the Prince of Wales, recalled that 'some years since' he 'accidentally' met 'Captain Nelson of the Royal Navy' in Portsmouth. The captain complained of a 'fleshy excrescence' on his gums that pained him whenever he shaved. 'He applied to one of the surgeons of the hospital [at Portsmouth], who assured him the case was *venereal*, and had prepared him to go through a mercurial course. I gave my opinion of the complaint, and the surgeon, upon a consultation having no objection to its being extir- pated, I removed it with a bisto[u]ry, and the cure was completed in a few days without any other application than the tincture. I saw this gentleman [Nelson] two years afterwards, when his perfect state of health confirmed my prognostic, and convinced the hospital surgeon of his mistake.'[18]

This information is revealing. The diagnosis that his complaint was venereal proved to be incorrect, but that the captain thought it plausible and prepared himself to undergo treatment on that basis is evidence that by that time he had already had sexual relations. Our difficulty lies in dating the incident. Ruspini says that he met Nelson in Portsmouth, and saw him again two years later. An examination of the occasions on which Nelson visited the town would suggest that the first meeting occurred between February and April 1782, and the second in April 1784. If this deduction is correct, Horatio Nelson was not entirely an inexperienced lover when he left for Canada in the *Albemarle*.

4

Painful teeth or otherwise, Nelson worried more about his wider health. In March he received the instructions for which he had been waiting, but they were not to his liking. He was ordered to Cork to pick up a convoy bound for Quebec. In Ireland he would place himself under the command of Captain Thomas Pringle of the *Daedalus*, no stranger to the Canadian run.

Nelson shuddered at the 'damned voyage'. He did not rate Pringle, and surmised that the man's main motive for going to Canada was the money he could make out of shipping specie. 'See what it is to be a Scotchman,' Nelson grumbled. 'I hope their times are over.' Even worse, he knew how the winter had already scourged his frail constitution, and dreaded spending the spring in a damp and cold country. Listening to his complaints, friends suggested he apply to the Admiralty for another ship. There was a new first lord at the Admiralty, Augustus Keppel, and it just happened that he was brother-in-law to Nelson's doctor, Mr Adair. Adair, to whom Nelson made a flying visit in March, was hoping to put the captain to rights before sailing. Friends pressed Nelson to use Adair to persuade the Admiralty 'that in such a country' as Canada he would be 'laid up' sick, but in the end Nelson declined to complain. It seemed improper to grumble to one First Lord about the orders of another and he held his peace. Captain Locker did speak up but failed to get Nelson's orders changed.[19]

Fully repaired, the *Albemarle* sailed from Spithead on 7 April 1782, and braving bad weather made Cork on the 17th. There the men had fun helping to haul His Majesty's ship *Jason* off a shoal at the entrance to the harbour, and for some reason Nelson's second lieutenant, Osborne, switched to the *Preston*. Nelson was not displeased because it enabled him to promote Bromwich acting lieutenant on the 24th. The preferment increased Bromwich's claim to any prize money, but Horatio thought he did 'his duty exceedingly well' and dearly wanted to get his commission confirmed; in return he received unswerving loyalty.[20]

On 26 April the Atlantic voyage began. The *Daedalus* and *Albemarle* ushered thirty-five more or less disobedient merchantmen through gales and fogs. One passage from Nelson's log is enough to indicate the tenor of the month's travail:

At 1 PM [10 May 1782] bore down to the *Jane*. Fired a shot at her for her to make more sail. At midnight dark and cloudy. Convoy in company. At 3 AM up topgallant masts and yards. At 6 made the signal for the *Jane* to make more sail, which she paid no attention to. Brought to, spoke her, and ordered she would set her fore topgallant sails, stay sails and studding sails. She [master, William Henderson] answered she had no main topmast or middle stay sails. After much delay she set fore topgallant sail and fore topmast studding sail. At noon three sail in company.

Ships being damaged and lagging . . . one man falling overboard from the *Albemarle* and drowning . . . murky North Atlantic rain and fog. One problem succeeded another, and the convoy split as it approached Canada. On 27 May Nelson anchored in St John's, Newfoundland, 'a disagreeable place', and assembled up to half a dozen merchantmen, while the *Daedalus* groped its way into nearby Capelin Bay with most of the others. Reuniting with his senior officer, and reinforced by the *Leocadia* and *Aeolus*, Nelson eventually helped push the convoy up the St Lawrence through more thick weather until he reached the Isle of Bic, below Quebec, on the evening of 1 July. There, where a naval squadron under James Worth of the *Assistance* was stationed, he conceived his mission complete and relinquished both his charges and letters and packets he had brought for Quebec.[21]

Like most naval officers, Nelson disliked convoy work, but it had not been as bad a trip as he feared. He realised that he had misjudged Captain Pringle, whom he would soon pronounce 'my particular friend, and a man of great honour'. Furthermore, contrary to his expectations, his health had actually improved, and now there suddenly loomed an opportunity for prize-taking – something not to be squandered in these final years of the war. Coming from Newfoundland, Nelson had discovered that American privateers were active in the Gulf of St Lawrence, and he persuaded Worth to allow him to return downriver to hunt for them before proceeding to Quebec. On 4 July the *Albemarle* was on its way back to the open sea in search of the enemy.[22]

However, in his eagerness for action Nelson neglected a fundamental foundation for any success at sea: an adequate supply of victuals. The master's log of the *Albemarle* shows that though the ship took on wood and water several times after reaching Canada – at St John's, Capelin Bay and in the St Lawrence – she failed to replenish food supplies reduced by the Atlantic voyage. Nelson was sailing towards an enemy coast with a serious shortage of fresh food. It was a mistake for which he would pay, but from which he would also learn an important lesson.

5

He was away for two months but for the most part without luck. 'In the end our cruise has been an unsuccessful one,' he told Locker on 19 October. 'We have taken, seen and destroyed more enemies than is seldom done in the same space of time, but not one arrived in port.' Even this was an exaggeration, for the ship's logs show that few prizes were taken, and those inconsiderable ones at that. Compared with the fruits of that cruise in the old *Bristol* back in '78 this was an exceedingly lean harvest.[23]

On 6 July Nelson came up with the *Pandora* off Cape Rozier, bent upon the same errand. Captain John Inglis was sick, and complaining about the Canadian climate, but at least his cruise would net him a Salem privateer. Nelson was not so fortunate. On 11 July he found what might have been an enemy privateer, but it was too close inshore to be captured, and the following month other promising 'chases' were lost in the all too frequent fogs. Nelson's first successes occurred on 11 and 12 July, when he recaptured two British vessels taken by the Americans, the last a schooner from Madeira taken only the previous day by the enemy privateer *Lively*.[24]

Operating in Boston Bay, Captain Nelson found little to whet his appetite. True, there were prizes to be had, but they promised meagre amounts of prize money, and one gets the impression that Nelson thought the work dirty. These were not privateers but small fishing schooners, each manned by about half a dozen men eking an uncertain living by working the offshore banks. Some British officers would have happily destroyed the trade, and did so. Three-quarters of the Chatham fishing fleet were lost by the last year of the war. But the captain of the *Albemarle* showed no such zeal. Several times during the cruise he 'spoke' enemy fishing vessels – that is, he exchanged words with their masters without boarding, and then allowed them on their way, and at least once, on 24 August, he 'left off' a 'chase' after discovering that it was merely a fishing schooner. In fact, Nelson's exploits off the American coast in July and August were marked by acts of generosity on both sides that are pleasing to record.

Nelson's first real prize was a fishing boat from Cape Cod, which fell into his hands on 13 July. The master, Richard Rich, and his five companions were taken aboard the *Albemarle* to act as pilots, while Nelson threw a tow rope onto the vessel itself, intending to use her as a tender. Though the prisoners had little choice but to cooperate, they forged a reasonable relationship with the British captain, and when he took a Plymouth fishing boat off Cape Sable on 9 August Nelson not only discharged his 'pilots' but also returned their ship.

An almost daily catalogue of escapades followed. Early in August Nelson spent several days chasing a square rigger he took to be a French warship. He got close enough to force the 'chase' to jettison small boats and spars but lost her on the 5th. On the 9th and 10th Nelson captured fishing boats from Plymouth and Marblehead, while the 12th saw him overtake an American prize of His Majesty's ship *Charlestown*. It was leaking and he destroyed it and shifted the prize crew to his own frigate. The next day a Cape Cod fishing schooner with six men was captured, and on the 14th the *Albemarle* drove another ship ashore near Cape Cod and dismasted it. On the 15th a Plymouth fishing boat fell into the bag, but Nelson merely used her to receive his remaining prisoners and spare his thinning provisions. A Boston fishing boat taken the following day was less fortunate. Nelson suspected it was spying for French warships sheltering in Boston harbour, and destroyed the vessel after removing her four-man crew. There were one or two more prizes, the last on 29 August when a shallop was boarded inshore from the *Albemarle*'s pinnace.[25]

The most attractive incident occurred on 18 August, when the *Albemarle* spotted a schooner inshore and sent a tender after it. To Nelson's surprise, the vessel made no attempt to escape but turned towards the British frigate. It was the *Harmony*, of Plymouth, Massachusetts, owned by Thomas Davis and commanded by Nathaniel Carver. In some way Davis and Carver were connected with the prize Nelson had taken in July and then released after her master had served him as a pilot. The Americans had been overwhelmed by Nelson's generosity in restoring the prize, and when the *Albemarle* reappeared Davis sent Carver out with a strange but remarkable offering.

The 'pilots' had noticed the lack of fresh provisions aboard the British frigate, as well as the first signs of scurvy, a disease feared by all sailors. In gratitude for the return of his ship, Davis sent Nelson animals, fresh vegetables and a copy of the current Boston newspaper. Captain Nelson was greatly moved. He sent the provisions to his sick, pressed an unwelcome payment upon his benefactors and also a gift equal in value to their own. It was a written testimonial that Carver's ship had been captured and returned 'on account of his good services', and that he deserved well of British officers. In effect, it gave the *Harmony* immunity from the British cruisers, and enabled her to fish the banks unmolested for the duration of the war. Davis was so proud of his certificate that he had it framed and exhibited in his home for many years.[26]

It had been an unsuccessful cruise, but Horatio made a notable escape on 14 August, when he hovered outside Boston harbour. At about three in the afternoon five ships were seen coming out, but fog reduced visibility and Nelson had to close in for a better look. An hour later brought him near enough to see four ships of the line and a frigate. They were French, part of a force under the Marquis de Vaudreuil, which had been driven from the West Indies by the British under Admiral Rodney and was holing up in Boston. Every one of the oncoming enemy ships was superior in strength to the *Albemarle*. At four-thirty one of the big ships of the line fired a signal gun, and the squadron turned towards the lone British frigate. It was then that Nelson realised the mistake he had made. He had closed upon an enemy force he could not fight.

Coming towards him the five French warships were ultimately bound for Piscataway to bring some mast ships back to Boston. The ships of the line were seventy-four- or eighty-gunners, and their frigate was the thirty-two-gun *Iris*. Any one was capable of crushing the little *Albemarle*, a mere twenty-eight-gun frigate. Nelson did the only thing he could; he wore his ship and fled.

What happened next is uncertain. According to the logs of the *Albemarle*, Nelson simply outstripped his pursuers. The captain's log, for instance, states that 'at 7 the ships in chase had dropped much [behind]', and Master Trail's more detailed account as well as Hinton's log carry the same story. It appears that a chase of about two-and-a-half hours left the enemy far astern, and the *Albemarle* out of immediate danger. This is much as we would have expected, for if frigates could not outfight ships of the line they were generally able to outsail them.

However, when recounting the incident for Captain Locker two months later Nelson resorted to fantasy. The French, he said, 'gave us a pretty dance for between *nine or ten hours*, but we beat all except the frigate, and though we brought to for her, after we were out of sight of the line-of-battleships, she tacked and stood from us. Our escape I think wonderful: they were upon the clearing up of a fog *within shot of us* and chased us the whole time about one point from the wind. The frigate, I fancy, had not forgot the dressing [drubbing] Captain [Elliot] Salter had given the *Amazon* for daring to leave the line-of-battle ships.' In this account, therefore, Nelson outsailed the ships of the line in a prolonged chase and then offered battle to the frigate, which mercifully opted for discretion rather than valour. Though an improved version of the incident, even this was a mere halfway house.

For in the 'Sketch of My Life', written for the *Naval Chronicle* in 1799, Nelson claimed to be 'chased by *three* French ships-of-the-line and the *Iris* frigate. As they *all* beat me in sailing very much, I had no chance left but running them amongst the shoals of St George's bank. This alarmed the line-of-battle ships, and they quitted the pursuit; but the frigate continued, and at sun-set was little more than gun-shot distant, when the line-of-battle ships being out of sight, I ordered the main topsail to be laid to the mast, when the frigate tacked, and stood to rejoin her consorts.'

Obviously the details were cloudier in 1799 than seventeen years earlier, but Nelson seems to have embroidered his escapade for public consumption. His claim to have shaken off the ships of the line by running his frigate between dangerous shoals has no counterpart in the contemporary evidence, not even in the exaggerated story sent to Locker. However, it echoes the then forgotten achievements of Elliot Salter, to which Nelson had alluded in the letter to Locker. Salter's exploit had occurred about the same place and time – off Cape Henry on 29 and 30 July 1782, a mere fortnight before the chase involving Nelson. Salter's frigate, the *Santa Margaretta*, had been reconnoitring Vaudreuil's ships before two enemy frigates, the *Amazon* and *Iris*, chased him away. Boldly deciding to fight, Salter squared up to the superior *Amazon* and defeated and took her before the sluggish *Iris* saw fit to intervene. The *Iris* then retreated towards her reassuring ships of the line, but the following day the impudent Salter was pursued by the entire French squadron. He had to relinquish his prize and only escaped by running the *Santa Margaretta* into the tricky shoals off the Delaware.

Though writers have accepted Nelson's final and heroic version of the pursuit of the *Albemarle*, the kernel of truth it contained was probably deliberately inflated to exalt the captain's prowess. Nelson was becoming increasingly besotted with public attention and learned to be his own publicity agent. He never invented incidents, but was prone to magnify his achievements, sometimes (as here) to the point of grossly misrepresenting the facts. Nevertheless, even unvarnished, the escape off Cape Cod was fortunate and dramatic enough, and Horatio justly regarded it as compensation for the barren returns of his prize taking.[27]

A more formidable enemy than the French was scurvy. That scourge of long-haul sailing was caused by a lack of vitamin C and a reliance on salted provisions rather than fresh fruit and vegetables. Debilitating and painful, it was usually heralded by swelling gums, falling teeth and excruciatingly painful joints. In Nelson's time nothing was known about vitamins, but it was well understood that scurvy was caused by the poor diet and sensible commanders did what they could to supply fresh food and issue lemon or orange juice as antiscorbutics. As an admiral Nelson was remarkable for his ability to maintain healthy crews, and this early scurvy outbreak aboard the *Albemarle* was due entirely to inexperience and carelessness. He was so intent on finding those suspicious sails he had seen between Newfoundland and Quebec that he neglected to provision properly. By the end of August, notwithstanding the generosity of the *Harmony*'s people, the rations on the *Albemarle* were stretched paper-thin. Twenty-eight supernumeraries and prisoners or British prize crews picked up during her operations had helped to deplete the provisions. The men were soon 'knocked up with the scurvy' and early in September one died. Nelson ran for Quebec.[28]

His need to get the sick ashore arguably put the ship at risk in the St Lawrence. Above the Isle of Bic, Nelson rashly navigated the difficult north traverse in light winds on 15 September. The gales that opened the day promised an easy passage, but by ten in the morning the wind had dropped and the ship found itself becalmed and sliding steadily with the current towards threatening shallows. Francis Roillet, a local pilot picked up at Bic, was 'frightened out of his senses' according to Bromwich's story. But Nelson would not be deterred. He lowered a pinnace and had the men row forward with a kedge anchor to drop it into the water ahead. Then, to the 'astonishment' of the pilot, he wound the anchor on the capstan and painfully drew his ship out of danger.[29]

On 18 September he anchored in Quebec and discharged twenty-five of his men to the local hospital. The cruise had been gruelling, but the sequel bore an entirely different character. For the first time Horatio fell in love.

6

Mary Simpson was twenty-three years old and an exceptional beauty. 'If Mary was not the most beautiful girl in Quebec, she was at any rate the most handsome she [I] had ever beheld,' recalled one who knew her. Nor was this all reflective romanticism. Mary featured in a celebration of the local belles published in the *Quebec Gazette* only months after Nelson's visit:

> Sure you will rather listen to my call
> Since [of] beauty and Quebec's fair nymphs I sing;
> Henceforth Diana in Miss S—ps—n see,
> As noble and majestic is her air,
> Nor can fair Venus, W—lc—s, vie with thee,
> Nor all thy heavenly charms with thee compare.[30]

Mary was a North American by birth, and a war baby, born as New France was being overthrown. Her father was a Scot, Alexander Simpson, known in the Scottish way as Sandy. Apparently he had come to America with his first cousin, James Thompson, both part of the 78th Regiment of Foot (Simon Fraser's Highlanders) raised in Scotland in 1757. The two friends saw action in some of the decisive engagements of the Seven Years War, at Louisbourg in 1758, Quebec the following year and Montreal in 1760. Simpson became provost marshal under the celebrated Wolfe, but remained in the colonies after his regiment was disbanded in 1763, and somewhere along the way married and started a family.[31]

The Simpsons settled in Quebec, where Alexander is said to have resided at Bandon Lodge, the first house outside the narrow archway of St Louis Gate, opposite the parliament building. The Simpsons were hospitable, kind and accomplished people, and Alexander was known as 'a loving husband, a tender and affectionate father, a good master and a faithful friend'. But when Nelson met them they had fallen upon hard times. Mary, or some of her acquaintances, must have told Horatio of the series of misfortunes that had recently reduced the family's prospects. It began early in 1781 when Mary's mother, Sarah, fell dangerously ill of an overgrown fistula. It was a painful and difficult condition in the eighteenth century, but Sarah was still middle aged and strong and survived two 'desperate' operations. The burdens of nursing the sick woman and maintaining the home presumably bore heavily upon Mary.[32]

Unfortunately, another disaster waited in the wings. The day Sarah attempted to leave her room and venture downstairs her husband suffered a sudden apoplectic stroke. He died the following afternoon, 27 March 1781, a man in his prime without even a will made out. The funeral two days later was well attended, attracting most of the worthies of the town, who respected Alexander as a merchant and a man. Sarah applied for an administration of the estate, and gamely resolved to carry on the family business, trading from their house as her husband had done. Given her situation, she placed a courageous advertisement in the local newspaper declaring that she would 'esteem herself under great obligations to her friends for the continuance of their custom and favour'.[33]

But it was a very hard road, as James Thompson, now an overseer of military works and fortifications in Quebec, testified. 'Her [Sarah's] condition is really deplorable,' he wrote. 'The reflection on the loss of a dutiful husband is not the only difficulty she has to labour under, though in her present weakly condition is alone more than she is able to bear. But her large concern in trade will fall heavy on her without the assistance the head of her family naturally afforded.' Thompson himself had recently boarded with the Simpsons after losing his first wife. They had endured his never-ending stream of business callers with unfailing cheerfulness, but in December 1780, at the age of forty-seven, and shortly before Sarah fell ill, Thompson married a Miss Frances Cooper and moved into the old bishop's palace. Thompson's removal had reduced the drudgery of housekeeping, but also cost the household a pair of hands, hands that were now needed.[34]

Miss Mary Simpson may have been a beauty when she met Nelson, but her life had already been seared by tragedy, and she had borne responsibilities of the gravest kind. Yet her gaiety, amiability and sense of humour remained, and she was rated a girl of accomplishments. Mary had been educated at the school of a Mr Tanswell, mastered French, and wrote in a competent if scrawling hand, and she was by no means the stereotypical narrow provincial. Though Captain Nelson only knew her in the few short weeks between 18 September and

14 October 1782 he was thoroughly enchanted. In those few soft days of fair weather, sharpened by the occasional fresh breeze and splashes of rain, Mary seemed a vision more glorious than the woods turning to flame in the maturing Canadian autumn. She made him feel better in every way. 'Health, that greatest of blessings, is what I never truly enjoyed till I saw *Fair* Canada,' he wrote to his father. 'The change it has wrought I am convinced is truly wonderful.'[35]

We can only speculate how they met. One link was Alexander Davison. During his stay in Quebec, Nelson consorted with the officers of His Majesty's ships *Daedalus*, *Hussar*, *Astrea*, *Canceaux*, *Cockatrice* and *Drake*, but the most enduring new friend was a thirty-three-year-old Anglo-Scottish shipowner named Alexander Davison. Davison and his younger brother George were importers and suppliers familiar with all the local merchants and accustomed to offering hospitality to naval officers. As a member of the Quebec Legislative Council, Alexander also knew his way around administration. Nelson liked the man and became a regular guest. The captain expected to be posted back home and learned that Davison too was bound for England. He had just sold the premises of 'Messrs Davison and Lees' on Notre Dame Street in the Lower Town and was merely awaiting the transfer of money before shipping to London, where Horatio promised to visit.

Although Nelson had matters to deal with aboard his frigate, including the punishment of deserters and a tippling steward, and filling the gaps left by the sick, he attended social events ashore, and it was possibly through Davison that he met Mary. After all, as notable and personable members of the mercantile community the Davison and Simpson families were well known to each other.

Another link might have been Freemason's Hall, later known as the Chien d'Or, a small hostelry near the top of Mountain Hill in the more fashionable Upper Town. It had once been used for Loyalist balls, attended among others by Mary's father, but it was widely frequented by officers of the armed services, partly because of its location opposite the government quarters. Mary may also have visited the place because she was related to the Prentice family who ran it. Old Miles Prentice had been provost marshal of Quebec before clearing out for New York under a cloud, leaving his beleaguered wife to maintain the hostelry with the help of two British nieces, the 'Mesdemoiselles Prentice'. The older of the girls was the previously mentioned Frances Cooper, who became Mrs James Thompson in 1780. Mary looked upon Thompson as something of a benevolent uncle and may have visited him or his in-laws at Freemason's Hall.

Possibly even then Captain Horatio Nelson had a rival for Miss Mary's attentions. Robert Mathews was a captain in the 8th Regiment of Foot as well as military secretary to the Governor of Canada, Frederick Haldimand. The two met and Mathews liked Nelson, as most people did. Mathews was considerably the older (he had been an ensign in 1761), but he was no wealthier and actually junior in rank, a military captain being inferior to the naval post-captain. Nevertheless, in America, where he had been serving his king for several years, he was known to be an efficient officer of good character. At the time of his death the year before Waterloo it would be said that 'a man of more universal and active benevolence of mind, and greater urbanity of manners never existed'.[36]

Mathews had time on his side, but Horatio's suit came to a head when he had to leave. Suddenly he faced a future without the girl with whom he was besotted. On 12 October he wrote to Haldimand, requesting a pilot for the trip downstream, and reclaimed as many of his men from the hospital as possible. The ship shifted its berth to Point Levi on the morning of the 13th and the next day to St Patrick's Hole. Nelson spent part of the 14th winding up his affairs in the town, mailing pay books to London and taking leave of friends, and it was not until seven-thirty in the morning of 15 October that the *Albemarle* weighed anchor and headed for the open sea.

Somewhere in this bald chronology there had been a difficult parting with Mary. Whether she knew the extent of his passion is questionable, but she certainly liked Horatio, and a quarter of a century later remembered him with affection. Davison also saw his companion away, and returned to preparing his own trip to England, sure that he at least would meet Nelson again in London.[37]

Those farewells probably took place on 14 October, a cloudy day of rain and growing gales, but the following morning Davison was taking a stroll along the beach when he saw a boat pulling towards the shore with the slight but familiar figure of Captain Nelson sitting anxiously inside. Hurrying to the landing place, Davison met Nelson as he alighted, and they walked 'up' to Davison's house together. Horatio explained that he had become 'violently attached' to Miss Simpson and could not leave Quebec without her. He had decided to see her, propose, and lay 'myself and my fortunes' at her feet.

Davison was a bachelor and a career man to boot. He was appalled and told Horatio that his course was rash indeed. No doubt he pointed out that neither party then had the means for a successful union. Nelson was still a junior captain without a fortune and bound for who knew where. Mary was desperately needed at home, where she was helping her mother keep a precarious business afloat. Davison told Nelson that if he persisted 'utter ruin . . . must inevitably follow'.

'Then *let* it follow!' stormed Nelson impetuously. 'For I am resolved to do it.'

'And I also positively declare that you shall *not*,' proclaimed Davison, resuming his argument with such force that Nelson eventually returned grumpily to his ship. He sailed the same day and Mary left his life forever.[38]

Mathews persisted, however. Reportedly Mary rejected his first proposal of marriage on the grounds that he held too junior a rank, but their relationship continued to flourish. Mathews went to England, where he was appointed to the Horse Guards, Mary followed, and they married at St George's Church, Hanover Square, in London, on 22 November 1798. Mary was described in the record as a resident of Clapham in Surrey. It was a hugely successful marriage, for the two were devoted. He said his 'dearest Mary' was 'amiable as ever, and every day renders herself more dear to me' and she spoke of him as 'my warm-hearted Mathews'. About the end of 1799 they had a son, Frederick, who became a captain of the 21st Royal North British Fusiliers before retiring through ill health. Age did not diminish their natural generosity. In 1803 they used their influence with Lord Chatham to get George Thompson, a son of James, in an academy at Woolwich, paying for the boy's passage from Canada, taking him into their home, and putting him through additional schooling. 'Mrs Mathews is really [truly] a very amiable lady,' George wrote home.[39]

The family remained in London, and Mathews became a lieutenant colonel of the 53rd Regiment, inspector of army clothing, the non-resident lieutenant governor of Antigua, and in October 1801 major of Chelsea Hospital. There is no record that Robert and Mary met Nelson in London, but both remembered him with affection and admiration. We know that the admiral's funeral put them 'in very low spirits'. Young George Thompson would watch the sombre procession from a Charing Cross window, but Mary owned that 'such a scene would be too much for my feelings', for she mourned not only 'an irreparable national loss' but also 'a friend of my early life'. Neither Mathews, 'who was also well acquainted with him', nor she 'had fortitude enough to witness the melancholy sight – the most awful and dismal that ever caused the British heart to ache or tears to flow . . .'.[40]

Those memories survived many years. Robert Mathews died in his apartments in Chelsea Hospital in 1814, bequeathing some two thousand pounds to provide an annuity for his 'beloved wife', among a small number of other bequests. Mary herself spent her later years at 57 Sloane Street in a five-storey terraced house overlooking Cadogan Square, a site now occupied by the Danish Embassy. There she continued to receive such British and Canadian friends as General William Twiss, Sir Alexander and Lady Bryce and the Duke of Kent, and to correspond with James Thompson until his death in 1830. Mary lived to see at least two grandsons, the 'horrors' of the cholera and the Reform Bill, and died in her house of 'gout of the stomach' on 26 October 1840 at the venerable age of eighty.[41]

When Nelson met Mary Simpson he was reaching an age and disposition to marry, and though he studiously avoided mentioning her in his letters home, the theme of feminine attraction would repeat itself over the next few years. In 1782 it was perhaps fortunate that he was kept busy after leaving Quebec. At the Isle of Bic 'old Worth' dashed his hopes of returning to England by detailing the *Albemarle* and *Pandora* to convoy twenty-three transports to New York, one of the American cities still in British hands. 'A very pretty job at this late season of the year,' complained Nelson, still worried about his health, 'for our sails are at this moment frozen to the yards.' However, he sailed dutifully on 19 October, with his first fleeting vision of marriage and lasting romance slipping gently by with the green skirts of the great St Lawrence.[42]

7

On 11 November Horatio Nelson was taking the *Albemarle* through a tricky channel winding through sandbars and leading towards the large anchorage at New York. The navy was here in force. In addition to the fleet of Rear Admiral Robert Digby, commander-in-chief of the station to which Nelson had been consigned, there were twelve sail of the line under Rear Admiral Samuel, Lord Hood. Hood had come from the West Indies in pursuit of Vaudreuil, who was still skulking in Boston, and was planning to return shortly. It was believed that Vaudreuil would embark soldiers at Boston and sail for the West

Indies to threaten Jamaica or other British possessions, and Hood hoped to intercept him.

Nelson met Hood when he reported to Digby aboard his flagship anchored off Sandy Hook. He saw a thin, Punch-like figure, with a pointed chin and hooked nose, but had no doubt he was speaking to a commander of the first order. He did not see, at this stage, that Digby and Hood were on poor terms. Their difficulties seem to have begun with prize money, but a 'paper war' was accumulating other bones of contention. Digby resented Hood's efforts to gather ships for the West Indies voyage at his expense, and Hood blamed Digby for interfering in the internal affairs of the force he had brought from the Leeward Islands. Unaware of the dissension, Nelson soon became embroiled.[43]

On 13 November the *Albemarle* put into New York, passing Staten Island where Hood's huge *Barfleur* lay at anchor with his fleet, and to a berth in the East River. When Horatio visited the admiral he found an unusual midshipman on the flagship – no less a person than Prince William Henry, the third son of the king, establishing a tradition of naval royalty. He had joined the service three years before as a stocky thirteen-year-old. Urged to obedience by his father and chaperoned by tutors, William Henry had acquired the makings of a naval officer; he had seen more action than Nelson and participated in Rodney's victory over the Spaniards at Cape St Vincent in 1780. However, the royal midshipman was not personally prepossessing. He was aggressive, boorish and bawdy, and the fair hair, blue eyes and round, red blubbery face pierced by a babyish mouth belied the elements of a severe disciplinarian.

Nevertheless, Nelson, a confirmed royalist, probably took to him at once. The prince himself was perhaps less enamoured with Nelson, undistinguished as he then was by appearance or deed. In an account he gave Clarke and McArthur many years later he remembered thinking Horatio 'the merest boy of a captain he ever saw, a long stiff Hessian tail hair hanging lank – hanging on his shoulders without powder'. Somehow, the admiral's biographers expanded this into an amusing word portrait of Nelson as a young officer:

I was then a midshipman on board the *Barfleur* [the prince is quoted], lying in the narrows off Staten Island, and had the watch on deck, when Captain Nelson of the *Albemarle* came in his barge alongside, who appeared to be the merest boy of a captain I ever beheld, and his dress was worthy of attention.

He had on a full-laced uniform. His lank unpowdered hair was tied in a stiff Hessian tail of an extraordinary length. The old-fashioned flaps of his waistcoat added to the general quaintness of his figure, and produced an appearance which particularly attracted my notice, for I had never seen any thing like it before, nor could I imagine who he was, nor what he came about. My doubts were, however, removed when Lord Hood introduced me to him. There was something irresistibly pleasing in his address and conversation, and an enthusiasm when speaking on professional subjects that showed he was no common being . . . I found him warmly attached to my father, and singularly humane . . .[44]

As interesting as meeting the future King William IV may have been, it was Hood that Nelson had come to see. He pressed the admiral to take him to the West Indies, where Horatio supposed there were still hopes of meeting the French in a major battle, and discovered that Hood had known his uncle, Maurice Suckling, and was disposed to be of service. Possibly, Hood had met Suckling in Portsmouth, where both men had cut significant figures. Hood's father-in-law, Edward Linzee, had been nine times mayor of Portsmouth, and held that office when Suckling was the borough's Member of Parliament. In fact the Linzees, a prominent local family, probably had a hand in choosing Suckling for the position. Admiral Hood himself had served Portsmouth, as naval commissioner and the governor of its naval academy. However they arose, Hood's feelings for Suckling were warm ones, and he invited Nelson to dine with him the following day, giving him a letter, promising his goodwill and hinting that the command of a ship of the line might be in the offing.

Hood's knowledge of Nelson was scant, but he saw he knew something of the Caribbean and was short of frigates, so he spoke to Digby about transferring the *Albemarle* from the North American to the West Indian fleet. The switch was made, though not without difficulty. Digby was tired of Hood poaching resources, and when the *Albemarle* tried to join Hood's ships on 16 November the senior admiral intervened and sent Nelson ashore. Nelson, ignorant of the sour exchanges between the admirals, protested to Hood, who persuaded the disgruntled Digby to give way. Thus, Horatio got his wish. The *Albemarle* joined Hood's squadron at Sandy Hook on 20 November, carrying one hundred and fifty boxes of essence of spruce, from which beer could be made, as a peace offering from Digby. Well might the young captain be pleased, for Nelson not only anticipated the active service he craved but fancied he had also found a new patron and protector.[45]

If Nelson courted Hood, he was himself a most generous friend and provider. While in New York he was much in the company of Captain William Peacock, a former comrade of Locker's, and Acting Lieutenant Pilford. Peacock had been a commissioned officer for six years and a post-captain for two, and was widely admired on the station, even by Digby himself, who had just shifted him from the *Carysfort* to a spanking new prize, the *L'Aigle* frigate. Horatio followed Peacock around the ship, listening to a proud exposition of its virtues, but was horrified when his companion was suddenly 'seized with a fit of apoplexy'. A doctor was summoned and efforts made to revive the stricken officer by bleeding. Peacock temporarily recovered, but it appeared that this had not been his first attack. 'I wish he may have health,' Nelson told Locker, 'or I am sorry to say, life to enjoy her [*L'Aigle*] . . . He is very much beloved by everybody here, and I think, from my little personal acquaintance, he is a very genteel man.' But, shortly after Nelson left New York, Peacock died, on 13 December 1782.[46]

As for Lieutenant Pilford, he had been a young captain's servant on the *Lowestoffe*, but had since outstripped Nelson in height and strength. 'He is a charming character,' Nelson told Locker, 'beloved by his captain, and all [of] his acquaintance . . . He has the same gentle disposition and modesty as when a youngster. You must remember the little fellow well.' Horatio wanted to help him, but the possibility of finding him a place on *L'Aigle* foundered with poor Peacock's illness.[47]

Nelson himself was bound for the West Indies. He was glory-hunting, at least according to Bromwich, who recalled the first time Nelson met Hood and Digby off Sandy Hook. 'You are come on a fine station for making prize money,' Digby encouragingly told the young man with the long Hessian tail. 'Yes sir,' Nelson allegedly replied, 'but the West Indies is the station for *honour*!' There are reasons for believing that Bromwich's memory did not fail him. Prince William Henry also noted that Nelson's priorities lay in glory rather than money, and that he longed to command a ship of the line. And Nelson himself complained disapprovingly of the New York station to Locker. 'Money is the great object here,' he said disapprovingly. 'Nothing else is attended to.' Above all things, the captain of the *Albemarle* still wanted an opportunity to distinguish himself before the war came to an end. He had still never seen a fleet action, and if there was to be a final clash of arms he desperately wanted to be in it.[48]

No one seemed more likely to supply that battle than Lord Hood. The son of a clergyman, like Nelson himself, he was almost sixty but at the peak of his powers. Some thought him England's ablest admiral, and he was certainly incisive, passionate, outspoken, supremely confident and dedicated to the service, all qualities designed to bowl over an impressionable young captain burning for battle. Hood talked as if he knew what he was doing, and spared no admiral who failed to meet his standards. 'His pen was acid and constantly to hand', it was justly said of him. Rodney was a child who needed a minder, Thomas Graves a mere ignoramus and Sir Charles Douglas as fit to be an admiral as Hood an archbishop. Stinging as this sort of criticism was, it invested Hood with a superficial authority and increased his inspirational power.[49]

Nelson learned a great deal from Hood. Several of the admiral's operations presaged much that made Nelson famous. At St Kitts in January 1782, for example, Hood prepared to attack a superior French fleet anchored in the Basseterre roadstead by concentrating his ships upon part of the enemy line, a plan similar to that Nelson executed so brilliantly in Aboukir Bay sixteen years later. And during the same campaign Hood used meetings with his officers to inculcate his ideas and intentions and reduce his dependence on inefficient signalling systems, just as Nelson would do.

Most significantly of all, Hood's aggression and belief in total victory suggested the same striving for perfection in the naval art that would distinguish Nelson. He had been Rodney's second-in-command in the battle of the Saintes near Dominica in April 1782, when the British broke with tradition, abandoned the customary line-ahead formation, and passed through the French line of battle to double on the enemy ships and inflict a sharp defeat. Although the battle was remembered for Rodney's cutting of the French line, that manoeuvre had apparently been more accidental than premeditated, and the engagement was at least as notable for the views of Hood. For Hood the victory, however famous, was not enough. He was furious that Rodney's failure to pursue the defeated and disoriented French fleet yielded only five prizes. Even the two additional sail of the line Hood added to the bag six days later did not console him. He wanted a decisive victory, and no half measures would do. His reaction to Rodney's 'Come, we have done very handsomely' attitude was an exact precedent of Nelson's criticism of Admiral Hotham in 1795. Had Rodney signalled a general chase, raged Hood, 'I am confident that we should have had twenty sail of the enemy's ships of the line before dark. Instead of that he pursued only under his topsails . . . the greatest part of the afternoon, though the flying enemy had all the sail set their shattered state would allow. Had I . . . had the honour of commanding His Majesty's noble fleet on the 12th, I may . . . say the flag of England should now have graced the sterns of upwards of twenty sail of the enemy's sail-of-the-line.'[50]

Here, Hood certainly showed himself a true predecessor of Nelson, but there was another side to the fierce old admiral that his young pupil saw less readily. Hood was often impervious to advice, bullied juniors, created corrosive relationships with equals and refused to be controlled by superiors. Though ever ready to direct, his leadership skills were otherwise primitive in comparison to Nelson's. Furthermore, for all his bombast, he sometimes lacked initiative, and by 1782 had suffered one of two major catastrophes that would mar his career. As commander of the British rear at the battle of the Chesapeake the previous year, his rigid adherence to the line of battle and failure to act upon a signal for closer action had contributed to a strategic defeat of the British fleet. A very costly one too, since it led to the surrender of the Earl of Cornwallis's army at Yorktown, and ultimately – to some extent – to the loss of the American colonies.

Nevertheless, to the captain of the *Albemarle* Hood was an awesome figure. Nelson harnessed himself to the admiral's star in the belief that he, if any, would take him into battle and forward him in the service. He could not know that in this war there were to be no more great naval battles.

8

A dozen line of battleships with the *Albemarle* and two other frigates sailing pluckily on their flanks left New York on 22 November. Hood made the West Indies early the following month, and was reassured by news that the French from Boston had not slipped by him and joined their Spanish allies in Havana. He had an opportunity to intercept Vaudreuil's ships as they came south, but where should he wait for them?

People who had served on the Jamaica station told Hood that the French usually approached the West Indies from the north by way of the east end of Hispaniola, rather than by the Caicos and Windward Passages further west. Nelson, for one, informed the admiral that he 'does not remember to have seen a ship of any burthen coming to Hispaniola by that [Caicos] passage'. Hood believed him, partly because navigating the western passages from the north needed exceptional skill in the calculation of longitude. Consequently, he scattered some of his smaller vessels about in case the French did something surprising, but stationed the English battle fleet further east, near Cape Samana on the northeastern shore of Hispaniola, a little windward of Monte Christi.[51]

Nelson was with the main force, acting as Hood's 'repeater', watching for signals from the flagship and repeating them to one ship or another. Usually the orders concerned chasing unfamiliar sails, but occasionally the *Albemarle* investigated herself and stopped Danes, Russians, Flemings and Prussians. Captain Nelson filled his log with such entries as 'Admiral made our signal to chase', 'out cutter', 'fired a shot and brought her to', and 'found her to be a neutral'. There were two prizes, however. The first was the *Atlantic*, an American lumber brig from Salem, taken on 7 January 1783 off Monte Christi. Nelson put a six-man prize crew aboard to take her to Jamaica, and brought her own complement, eleven men under Samuel Grant the master, on to his frigate.

The second prize was more important, but effectively sailed into the British fleet and offered itself to Nelson's frigate. She was the *Queen of France*, manned by Auguste Paris and fifty-four men, and carrying up to three hundred French soldiers and a large quantity of masts and naval stores. What was more, she was from Vaudreuil's fleet. The mast ship had parted company with the rest of the French fleet during gales and snowstorms up north, and consummated her misfortune by losing her main topmast in a squall off Hispaniola. Running pretty helplessly before the wind, she had finally mistaken Hood's fleet for Vaudreuil's, and at one o'clock in the morning of 25 January unwarily passed through the British ships to come under the stern of the *Albemarle*. Nelson happily snapped her up.

He mused with mortification that though the ship would fetch a lot of money in Jamaica, where masts were in short supply, the proceeds would have to be shared with the fleet, according to custom. The most significant yield, however, was information. Hood's surmise that Vaudreuil would steer for the eastern, rather than the western, passages was right, but he was missing him all the same. Six days before, a report had placed the French off Puerto Rico, even further east, and Hood had begun beating in that direction against wind and current.

Now the prisoners of the mast ship confirmed that the enemy fleet was bound for the Mona Passage between Hispaniola and Puerto Rico, and, realising that he had 'a small chance indeed of meeting the enemy', Hood crowded on all sail.[52]

But the battle was not to be; Vaudreuil reached the passage first, slipped through towards the Spanish havens on the Venezuelan coast and sat out the rest of the war in Puerto Cabello. Hood had screened the British islands from the hostile force but muffed the chance to destroy it.

In lieu of a battle, Captain Nelson had to content himself with scouting and prize taking. On the morning of 29 January 1783 he drove a sloop ashore under an enemy battery near Cape Donna Maria, but six days later the British fleet put back into Port Royal. Nelson renewed old friendships about the town, but was eager to get back to sea. One delay occurred on 6 February when he ran his frigate aground in the harbour and lost more than a day getting her afloat, disembarking and re-embarking iron ballast and ten of his guns in the process. He eventually cleared Port Royal on the 16th, accompanied by the fourteen-gun brig sloop *Drake*, under Captain Charles Dixon.

Hood wanted him to find the missing French fleet, which was reportedly about Curaçao, but for some time Nelson searched the islands in vain. 'Where they are God knows!' he confessed to Locker. Yet he was far from dispirited and sailed in good heart. More than anything else he felt valued by an admiral he had begun to idolise, with all that that augured for his future. Hood could become a powerful patron, far more so than the genial Locker. He was an admiral, and a good one, but also the confidant of some of the most powerful men in the realm. The king himself relied upon Hood's counsel and had made him a baronet. The Grenvilles, than whom few were bigger in politics, were family friends, and by the marriage of his brother Hood had secured a connection to the Pitts. In fact the admiral's rise was due in no small part to his ability to secure and manipulate interest.[53]

Nelson was sure he had Hood's good opinion. He 'treats me as if I was his son', he wrote; he seemed to be ready to 'give me anything I can ask of him'. Prince William Henry, who was often at Hood's side, told Nelson that he had heard the admiral say that no officer in the fleet knew more about fleet tactics than the captain of the *Albemarle*. This is our first indication that Nelson had given any serious thought to fleet tactics, and Nelson himself was surprised. 'I cannot make use of expressions strong enough to describe what I felt,' he told Locker with transparent pride. He had reason to be satisfied, for he had been without a permanent patron in high places for four years, and Hood looked like filling the vacuum.

Eager to vindicate Hood's regard, Nelson thought he had found his opportunity when some news reached him in the southeastern Bahamas early in March. He had been cruising rather unsuccessfully off Monte Christi. On 4 March he sent the *Drake* to examine the anchorage at Cape François, but nothing more interesting than a corvette was found there. Early on the 6th, however, three sails were seen to the north-east, and the *Albemarle* and *Drake* cleared for action. The newcomers proved to be the *Resistance*, an old fifth-rate warship of forty-four guns under Captain James King, and two prizes, one of them a French twenty-eight-gun frigate named *La Coquette*, now commanded by King's first lieutenant, James Trevenen, and the other a sloop. When King's boat bumped alongside the *Albemarle* and he climbed aboard he bore more than interesting news.

A little to the northwest were the Turks Islands. They were rela-tively insignificant little possessions of the crown, inhabited only by a few fishermen, but they stood sentinel over the approaches to the Windward Passage that led to Jamaica and thus enjoyed a certain strategic importance. Two days earlier the *Resistance* had discovered that the islands had been seized by the French. Two enemy frigates drove the *Resistance* away, but Captain King concluded that the inva-sion force came from Cape François in Haiti and amounted to about 150 regulars and three warships.

Early in the afternoon Nelson summoned Dixon of the *Drake* aboard to hear King's story, and within three hours had decided to expel the French. His reasoning was sound. Grand Turk, the principal island, was unfortified, and it was unlikely that the French had had the time to make many improvements. Then, too, Nelson's force was reinforced at about noon by the arrival of the twenty-eight-gun frigate, *Tartar*, under Captain William George Fairfax. Including their prizes, therefore, the British had a fifth-rate warship, three frigates, a brig sloop and a sloop at their disposal. Nelson decided to chance it, and led his flotilla towards Grand Turk.

At about four to five in the afternoon of Friday 7 March the ships entered the bay at the eastern end of Grand Turk and anchored on a bank within half a cable's length of the beach. Scanning the shore Nelson picked up the blue-coated soldiers hurrying to their positions, muskets in hand, but tried to avert blooshed. A boat flying a flag of

truce put out from the *Albemarle* with Captain Dixon sitting in the
stern with a summons to the French garrison to surrender. The demand
was rejected, and Nelson was further mortified to find his scant assault
force depleted by the defection of the *Tartar*. The frigate had twice
attempted to anchor on the bank and twice found herself swept away,
losing an anchor in the process. Finally, Fairfax simply sailed away.
Nelson fumed but wrote a restrained report, merely presuming that
the ignoble officer must have had 'good reasons' for failing to rejoin
the squadron and support the attack.

During the night the British amused themselves lobbing shots at the
French campfires, but the principal attack began at about five in the
morning. The weather was fresh and blustery, with considerable rain,
but Nelson judged that it would not hinder his operation. At six he
raised the signal for a general cannonade, and the ships trained their
broadsides on the landing places and swept away the immediate opposition. All seemed to be going well, and Nelson's second signal launched
his landing parties. A total of 167 marines and seamen from the
Albemarle, *Drake* and *Resistance* pulled furiously for the beach and
landed with little difficulty under the direction of Captain Dixon. To
add to Nelson's optimism, reinforcements fortuitously arrived in the
shape of a fourteen-gun brig, the *Admiral Barrington*, under Lieutenant
Charles Cunningham.

However, as Dixon's men trudged towards the French defences, it
became clear that they had bitten off more than could be comfortably
chewed. Dixon rattled off a request for a diversion. Accordingly, at
about eleven Cunningham and Lieutenant Hinton of the *Albemarle*
took the *Admiral Barrington* and *Drake* a little northward to anchor
as close to the town as they could. They had orders to bombard the
French until Dixon raised a blue-and-white flag to signify his men
were in position. In an hour or so the two ships were firing, but the
French gunners replied from a hastily constructed three gun battery
that included at least one big eighteen-pounder. Nor were they mean
marksmen. During an hour's exchange their shots smashed into the
ships' hulls, cut up rigging and disabled the *Drake*'s gaff. The master
and several men of the *Drake* were wounded, as were seven aboard
the *Admiral Barrington*. Both ships had their cables cut by the French
fire and were obliged to retire.

Ashore the British fared no better. Dixon's heroes found the French
solidly entrenched behind seveal field pieces and a couple of naval
cannons, and judged the attack too dangerous. Nelson called it off

and re-embarked the men. He summoned King aboard the *Albemarle* for a further consultation, but they agreed that nothing more was to be done.

Nelson was criticised for the affair, then and later. Lieutenant Trevenen complained that the 'ridiculous expedition' had been 'undertaken by a young man merely from the hope of seeing his name in the papers, ill depicted at first, carried on without a plan afterwards, attempted to be carried into execution rashly, because without intelligence, and hastily abandoned at last for the same reason that it ought not have been undertaken at all'. It is possible to sympathise with this to some extent, but it has been uncritically reproduced. It owed much to hindsight. Unfortunately, military operations are not precise sciences, and failures are as often the result of unforeseen circumstances or mere misfortune as of incompetence. Risks can be minimised, but seldom eliminated. Nelson may have failed to gauge obvious strengths in his opponents, but even if this was true Trevenen's was a harsh judgement. After all, Nelson barely committed his forces. He learned about the French occupation, tested its defences, found them stronger than expected and withdrew his men before they suffered serious casualties. In short, he did his duty.

The truth was that Trevenen's complaint was motivated less by professional dissent than pecuniary loss. What really grieved the lieutenant about the Turks' Island affair was that it delayed his return to Jamaica with two prizes. That delay allowed the impending news of peace to interfere with the legal proceedings and cost the captors several thousands in prize money. But that was simple bad luck. Hood made no public criticism of Nelson. He forwarded the captain's dispatch to the Admiralty without comment, and the relationship between the two men was unimpaired. This last raises a doubt about Prince William Henry's subsequent claim that Hood verbally reprimanded Nelson. Nelson was a man who brooded over criticism, but he remained steadfastly loyal to Hood, cheerful and positive. In fact a month later he was urging his admiral to retain the services of the *Albemarle* during the peace. 'If you remain in this country it will be truly grievous to me to be sent to England,' he said.[54]

A few days after leaving Grand Turk, Nelson overhauled a French ship sailing under a flag of truce, and learned that she carried a copy of the preliminary articles of peace agreed in Europe. Nonetheless, until there was an official ceasefire he had to maintain a war footing. At last, on 29 March, he tracked the missing French fleet to Puerto

Cabello on the luxuriant Venezuelan coast, and counted eleven sail of the line, two frigates, an armed auxiliary and several merchantmen at anchor. Then he enjoyed a late supper, making some of the last captures of the war about the Lesser Antilles and the Main.

An eight-man Spanish schooner was taken on 25 March, and two days later another, which six of Nelson's men crewed to Jamaica. The 28th was a busier day. Nelson chased one vessel aground beneath Cape Blanco, and took two more near Puerto Cabello. One was a schooner, which Nelson used to receive his prisoners, but the other was altogether stranger: a royal launch crowded with French and Spanish dignitaries and scientists on a pleasure cruise. The master, who went by the remarkable name of Waken Lanatera, had mistaken the French-built *Albemarle* for a friend and obligingly come alongside, just as the mast ship had done two months before.

Horatio brought the thirty-three occupants of the launch aboard his ship and found that they included three officers of the French army. He entertained his prisoners in some style for several days before discharging them ashore, allowing the officers one of his captured schooners, and placing most of the other guests on a Dutch sloop arrested on 2 April. The brief interlude seems to have entertained all parties. Nelson relished the terror Hood's name seemed to inspire, while one of the prisoners was so taken with the English captain that the following year he invited him to his home in Paris. What was more, it was only then that Nelson realised he had been holding no less a personage than Maximilian Joseph, Comte de Deux Ponts, then a French general travelling incognito but later to become the King of Bavaria.

After the launch Nelson took the *Alexandrine*, a French brig on its way from Nantes to Puerto Cabello. Sending the ship to Jamaica, he put the prisoners aboard a Spanish schooner seized the following day and ordered a course back to Port Royal. Since peace was imminent (the treaty had been signed in Paris and ratified in England) it was doubtful that the prizes would be condemned, and the *Albemarle* was leaking badly. But at least Nelson had ended his war on an active note.[55]

9

Admiral Hood was not in the best of moods. The order to suspend hostilities had reached Jamaica on 29 March and put an end to his plans to destroy Vaudreuil's fleet. The war was over, and the thirteen American colonies had won their independence, though the former French colonies in Canada remained with the British crown. Overall France, Spain and Holland, which had opportunely entered the war, gained little, more or less satisfying themselves with the restoration of the old *status quo*.

Nelson, too, wrung little satisfaction from his predicament. He had been ordered home with the next convoy and spent most of April in port. At the root of his troubles was insecurity, a fear of slipping from the notice of Hood. He wrote to the admiral promising to call and pay his respects when they were both in England, and thanking him for 'the many favours' bestowed. But he had one last service to perform. On the 26th he was at sea again with orders to take dispatches to St Augustine in Florida before sailing to Spithead. First, however, he was bound for Havana, where the Spanish governor, Don Luis de Unzaga, was celebrating the peace by opening the city to Prince William Henry. Hood wanted Nelson to chaperone the royal personage.[56]

The *Albemarle* reached Havana on 9 May, in time to join the *Diamond* as part of the prince's retinue. Twenty-one British guns proclaimed William Henry's appearance, and amid considerable pomp the prince and his officers went ashore. His Royal Highness was no easy burden, and Hood had swamped him with attendants, including Nelson and Captain William Merrick, two of the admiral's favourites.[57]

Despite the prince's lewd conversation, coarseness, boisterous bullying and compulsive interest in women, Nelson managed to like him. In Jamaica William Henry had been much feted, as shallow, obsequious sycophants swept aside personal shortcomings and jostled for royal attention. Nelson was quieter and more discreet, but no less aware of the advantages that might accrue from the prince's friendship. He was also a genuine 'Church and King' man and flattered that William Henry obviously enjoyed his company. More commendably, Nelson actually detected admirable traits beneath the prince's bluster. Here, for example, was a member of the royal family who intended to learn his trade and work his passage. He was dedicated to the service and showed little truck with the appointment of unqualified favourites. 'He is a seaman, which you could hardly suppose,' Nelson told Locker, and 'says he is determined every person shall serve his time before they shall be provided for, as he is obliged to serve his.' These were sentiments hardly to be expected from a young man in William Henry's position, and certainly foundations for growth.[58]

But first, to see that William Henry didn't disgrace himself. There were two days of nonsense – troop reviews, tours of the dockyard and castle, and one marathon evening embracing the opera, supper at the governor's house, and a late-night ball with what even Hood heard contained a 'brilliant show of ladies'. The particular Spanish beauty who attracted the prince was sixteen-year-old Donna Maria Solano, one of two daughters of Admiral Don Solano, with whom the visitors were lodged. According to the prince's earliest biographer, whose sources seem to have been generally reliable, it was Nelson who noticed the jealousies being aroused by the drooling William Henry, and who ushered him out of harm's way. Whatever, decorum was preserved, and the prince was treated to a magnificent display when he left on the morning of 11 May. As the Spanish launches towed the *Albemarle* out of harbour, and the prince followed in the first of a procession of naval barges heading seawards to the rumble of another furious salute from the frigate, Nelson may have sighed with relief. One day the prince would cross his path again.[59]

In the meantime, Nelson sailed for St Augustine, sent a boat ashore with the dispatches, and sailed for home on 19 May. The *Albemarle* reached Spithead on 25 June and anchored in Portsmouth harbour the following day. Nelson wrote first of all to Captain Locker, for whom he had brought a present of rum. 'My dear friend,' said he, 'after all my tossing about into various climes, here at last am I arrived, safe and sound.'[60]

XI

LOVE IN ST-OMER

A wonderful man, he loved a woman well
Thomas Hardy, *The Dynasts*

1

NELSON found a room at no. 3 Salisbury Street, a small thoroughfare linking the River Thames with the Strand. It was a convenient situation. Walking along it southwards, between the large, plain but impressive three- and four-storey houses, Nelson could pass through an arch and down a flight of steps to reach wharves where boatmen plied a shuttle service here and there; in the opposite direction lay the city itself, beneath the imposing dome of St Paul's Cathedral. Nelson lodged in the third house from the Strand on the northeastern side of the street, and paid rent over a six-month period to one Thomas Hudson. He could not have known it, but this temporary home was little more than a stone's throw from the site upon which his most famous statue would one day gaze imperiously from its column above the capital.[1]

After such a prolonged absence visits were the order of the day. On 11 July, Lord Hood took him to St James's Palace and introduced him to an 'attentive' sovereign, while another invitation summoned him to Windsor, where Prince William Henry wished to see him before leaving for a sojourn on the Continent. Horatio knew that royal connections could do his interest no harm, but he had little real talent for sycophancy. The day he met the king he was glad to take refuge in the quarters of the Davison brothers, at the Chapel Stair Case in Lincoln's Inn Fields, off Chancery Lane. Alexander was at home, and after dinner Nelson threw off his walking coat, accepted the dressing gown proffered by his host and spent a pleasant evening in conversation, talking about Mary Simpson and Quebec.[2]

Horatio believed he was making necessary progress socially, but the summer heat and stench of London increased the attraction of trips out of town. Pringle had asked him to Edinburgh, and of course there was Burnham Thorpe. Predictably, his peregrinations were delayed by an illness that confined him to his room for fourteen wretched July days, an 'invalid' but under the watchful eye of 'an exceeding good surgeon' who spoke confidently about 'a perfect cure'. Nelson's sentence was relieved by caring visitors, including his Uncle William, hotfoot from Kentish Town and a gout-afflicted wife; his brother Maurice; his sister Susanna, with her husband Thomas Bolton, another sister, and gifts of a hare and brace of game birds; and a messenger Captain Locker had sent from his home at Malling near Maidstone.[3]

A few official matters also temporarily tied him to the capital. On 3 July a commissioner had boarded the *Albemarle* to pay off the men and close the command, but he still felt himself their protector. They had made a good company and most of the officers, as well as a high proportion of the ratings, had stayed with him throughout his command. There had been problems, of course. During his two years with the ship Nelson had posted forty-seven men as 'run', including his own cook (William Halloway), a corporal of marines and Alexander St Clair, a midshipman who decamped at Yarmouth on Christmas Day 1781. The high number of deserters and would-be deserters was substantially due to the amount of time the *Albemarle* was penned in port by bad weather. Ports provided many opportunities to desert, and were always a temptation to disgruntled seamen. On 13 November 1781, for example, seven men had jumped in a cutter at Elsinore and pulled strenuously for the shore. The long weeks in Portsmouth allowed another thirteen to 'run' early the following year, and when Nelson reached Capelin Bay in Canada in June two men defected in a launch, another trio bolted in the cutter, and two, not to be outdone, leaped overboard to swim ashore.

The *Albemarle* had also had its share of floggings. There had been about fifty of them, involving some 14 per cent of the men who served on the frigate at one time or another during Nelson's command. Given the two-year period it was probably considered fair discipline. The severest punishment Nelson inflicted, thirty-six lashes, was reserved for deserters or exceptionally mutinous seamen such as Evan Griffiths, though a few men received lighter sentences more than once. These recidivists included George Marr, a thief, John Cooper, a disobedient seaman who attempted to desert, and a purser's steward named Robert Bostock, who got drunk too often. As usual, Nelson attempted to discriminate between degrees of guilt. Thus Charles O'Neal and John Hughes were flogged for theft one February, but Hughes took twice as many strokes of the cat as O'Neal.[4]

In general, however, Nelson won the respect of most of the men, and characterised them with almost paternal affection as 'my good fellows'. Indeed, the whole crew told him that if he got another ship they would 'enter for her immediately'. Most had served him well, and though the voyage was over, still expected him to defend them in the world of officers and gentlemen beyond their ken. And he tried to fulfil those expectations, troubling the Admiralty with requests for an early payment of all wages owed his men for services during the war. Horatio particularly cursed his inability to do much for Trail, the master, and Acting Lieutenant Bromwich. 'If I had interest with the comptroller,' he said of the former, 'I would wish to get him to be superintendent of some of the ships in ordinary. He is the best master I ever saw since I went to sea.' Bromwich was also 'an attentive good officer' and after returning with the *Albemarle* passed his examination for lieutenant on 7 August. But Nelson suspected that talent would not be enough, and that Bromwich's unfortunate loss of sea time as an acting lieutenant in 1781 would militate against his commission being confirmed. He lobbied the Admiralty. 'Depend upon it, my Lord,' he addressed the first lord, 'I should not have interested myself so much about this gentleman did I not know him to be a brave and good officer, having been with me for several years.' Unfortunately, it was to no avail. Nelson's request was endorsed, 'without remedy with others under similar embarrassments', and Bromwich had to wait more than ten years for his commission.[5]

Nelson's own cause progressed unevenly. His pay as captain of the *Albemarle* did not reach Paynter, his prize agent and banker, till the last day of the year, and like most unemployed officers on half-pay he was short of money. Eventually he was driven to making an unsuccessful application for full pay covering the period between his quitting the *Janus* and arriving in England on the *Lion*. As for prize money, he ruefully concluded that his campaigns had not enriched him. 'I have closed the war without a fortune,' he told Hercules Ross, 'but I trust (and from the attention that has been paid to me believe) that there is not a speck in my character. True honour, I hope, predominates in my mind far above riches.'[6]

Recovering his health late in July, Horatio spent two days with his uncle in Kentish Town, tried and failed to visit Ross, who divided his time between London and Scotland ('the innumerable favours I have received from you, be assured, I shall never forget', Nelson wrote to him), and in late August joined his brother Maurice on the Lynn diligence heading for Norfolk. His father was in Bath, attended by Ann, while Susanna and her husband had transferred their business to Ostend. With them was Horatio's brother, Edmund, who was working for the Boltons. Yet something of a family reunion still took place, and Horatio grounded himself more thoroughly in family affairs. William was about to receive the rectory of Little Brandon from a relative, John Berney, and reckoned it worth £150 a year, and other brothers and sisters were spending the legacies left them by Captain Suckling. Fifteen-year-old Katy was spared an apprenticeship on account of her money, while Suckling was squandering his, along with sums incautiously advanced by William, in running a general store at Witton. Suckling was difficult to blame, Horatio thought. He was amiable and contented, and good company, but far too interested in greyhounds and coursing to make much of himself.[7]

Early in October Horatio was back in London, but not looking for a ship. He had decided that peace offered a rare opportunity to visit Britain's nearest neighbour and greatest rival, and to master the French language. Many times in the West Indies he had felt his want of French, even in the hailing of prizes and interrogation of prisoners. French, thought Nelson, was an essential mark of the good naval officer, and it was high time he learned it. Lille might be a good place. Accordingly, on 8 October he asked the Admiralty for six months' leave.[8]

2

He even had a travelling companion. Captain James Macnamara, who had just returned from Jamaica, had shared the lieutenants' mess with Nelson aboard the *Bristol* and many another West Indian memory. 'Mac', as Nelson called him, was an older but junior officer, of about forty-six years. He had been a lieutenant since June 1761, when Horatio was an infant under three, but, lacking 'interest' and displaying too independent a mind, he had been overtaken by more favoured officers, including Nelson. Sir Peter Parker had marked his worth though, and made him a commander in 1779 and post-captain in February 1781, when he was appointed to the *Hound* sloop. More experienced than Nelson, Mac had even been to France before and was probably the least incompetent of the two when it came to the language. He was an ideal partner for the enterprise.[9]

Nelson loved the company of friends, and squeezed in a visit to the Parkers in Essex before starting his journey with Mac outside 3 Salisbury Street on Tuesday 21 October. Their way led them to Malling, where they dined with Locker and stayed overnight, and the next day to Canterbury. Sandys lived there, and they called upon him hoping for a bed, but as he was not home the duo continued to Dover to spend the night. At seven on the morning of 23 October the two captains caught the packet boat, and a fresh northwesterly wind had them in Calais in three and a half hours. There they breakfasted where newly arrived Britons always breakfasted. Nelson informed Locker that Monsieur Grandsire's house just within the city gate had been depicted by Hogarth in *The Gate of Calais*. They marvelled at what seemed to them the bizarre manners, houses and food, but overall Nelson's opinion of the French was every bit as sceptical as Hogarth's had been thirty-five years before.

At this point the two captains disagreed. Mac was all for going straight to St-Omer, where a considerable English community could give them support, but Nelson decided to 'fix' at Montreuil, sixty miles along the coast road to Paris. The younger man, in whom obstinacy was becoming a trait, unfortunately prevailed, and they caught the coach. As Nelson reported it:

They told us we travelled *en poste*, but I am sure we did not get on more than four miles an hour. I was highly diverted with looking what a curious figure the postillions in their jack boots, and their rats of horses, made together. Their chaises have no springs, and the roads [are] generally paved like London streets. Therefore, you will naturally suppose we were pretty well shook together by the time we had travelled two posts and a half, which is fifteen miles, to Marquise. Here we [were] shown into an inn – they called it – I should have called it a pigsty. We were shown into a room with two straw beds, and, with great difficulty, they mustered up clean sheets, and gave us two pigeons for supper, upon a dirty cloth, and wooden-handled knives. O what a transition from happy England! But we laughed at the repast, and went to bed with the determination that nothing should ruffle our tempers.[10]

The next day's journey began at daylight, and the travellers were able to take breakfast in Boulogne and reach Montreuil the same evening. Nelson's estimation of France rose as he jogged along, peering out at the countryside. It was, he confessed, 'the finest country my eyes ever beheld', with flourishing fields, 'stately' woods, splendid trees skirting the roads as if they were avenues, and game 'in the greatest abundance: partridges, pheasant, woodcocks, snipes, hare, &c. &c., as cheap as you can possibly imagine'. Nonetheless, he added shrewdly, 'amidst such plenty they are poor indeed'.[11]

At Montreuil, which Nelson found situated on a hill in a fine plain, they camped at the inn with 'the same jolly landlord' described by Laurence Sterne in his A Sentimental Journey Through France and Italy (1768). There was no sign, however, of what Sterne had regarded as the most interesting feature of the inn when he had passed that way twenty years before – the bold and versatile Janatone. 'There is one thing . . . in it very handsome, and that is the inn-keeper's daughter,' Sterne had written in another account, Tristram Shandy. 'She has been eighteen months at Amiens, and six at Paris, in going through her classes; so knits, and sews, and dances, and does the little coquetries very well.' In the absence of Janatone, Nelson was left to admire the resources of the country and shudder at the divisions between rich and poor. 'Here we wished much to have fixed,' he told Locker, 'but neither good lodgings, or [language] masters could be had here, for there are no middling class of people. Sixty noblemen's families lived in the town, who owned the vast plain round it, and the rest very poor indeed.' This was a country only half a dozen years from a revolution.[12]

On Saturday 25 October Nelson and his companion proceeded to Abbeville, a large fortified town on the Somme. Momentarily, Nelson wondered whether this might be a good place to 'fix' but 'unluckily for us', Horatio told Locker, 'two Englishmen, one of whom called himself "Lord Kingsland" (I can hardly suppose it to be him) and a Mr Bullock, decamped at three o'clock that afternoon in debt to every shopkeeper in the place . . . We found the town in an uproar.' After being hoodwinked by a couple of English sharks, the locals were not disposed to offer the new arrivals an enthusiastic welcome, and to make matters worse Nelson could not a find a single tutor who 'could speak a word of English'. At last Horatio confessed that Mac had been right all along, and without further ado they ought to take the north road to St-Omer, where numerous English families had gathered after the peace to take advantage of the cheap living and warmer weather. And so on Tuesday 28 October, the friends reached St-Omer after what they estimated had been a round trip of 150 miles.

Nelson was pleasantly surprised by St-Omer. 'Instead of a dirty, nasty town, which I had always heard it represented [to be],' he wrote to Locker, he found 'a large city, well paved, good streets, and well lighted.' It had powerful fortifications and housed a large garrison, but there was a cathedral and a considerable number of English were to be encountered about the streets. This, Nelson admitted, was the place to 'fix' and a few days after his arrival he confidently purchased a copy of Chambaud's *Grammar of the French Tongue* and proudly inscribed it with the date of 1 November. His campaign to conquer the language had officially begun.[13]

They found rooms at the house of Madame Bertine Lamoury, as Nelson explained to Locker. 'We lodge in a pleasant French family, and have our dinners sent from a *traiteur's* [caterer]. There are two very agreeable young ladies, daughters, who honour us with their company pretty often. One always makes our breakfast, and the other our tea, and play a game at cards in an evening. There, I must learn French if 'tis only for the pleasure of talking to them, for they do not speak a word of English.' The husband, Jacques Lamoury, was a master potter in his sixties, who had accumulated several properties in the town, one a fine old house at 136 rue de Dunkerque, and another three in nearby rue Hendricq. The English officers obviously found equitable accommodation in whichever Lamoury used as his personal home, for they were diverted by the eligible daughters, twenty-eight-year-old Marie-Alexis-Hennette Isabelle and Marie-Françoise Bertine, who was two years younger. Neither was married, although the following year both attached themselves to older men, the one to a captain of dragoons and the other to a pharmacist. Given their attentions, Nelson found no space in his letters for the fifth member of the Lamoury family, a younger brother named Omer.[14]

From Madame Lamoury's the friends explored the town and soon ran into a number of fellow countrymen and women. Some were even naval officers. There were dinners with Captain William Young, but Nelson studiously avoided two other captains, Alexander Ball and James Keith Shepard, who, he observed with distaste, had adopted the French practice of wearing epaulettes upon their uniformed shoulders. 'They wear fine epaulettes,' Horatio informed Locker, 'for which I think them great coxcombs. They have not visited me, and I shall not, be assured, court their acquaintance.' The distrust was mutual. Many years later Ball would recall it for the poet Coleridge, and ascribe the coolness to uncertainty about which officer owed the first visit.[15]

As Nelson struggled indifferently with the French language he realised that it was only by mixing with French, rather than English people, that he would improve, but some of the many invitations he received still proved irresistible. Visits to two or three English families began as welcome breaks from toil. Among his new friends he found Henry Massingberd, a brother of a shipmate on the *Lowestoffe*, to be 'very polite' and his lady, Elizabeth, 'a very complete gentlewoman'. Another household made an even stronger claim upon his time, as Horatio hinted in a letter scribbled to his brother on Monday 10 November. 'Today I dine with an English clergyman, a Mr Andrews, who has two very beautiful young ladies, daughters. I must take care of my heart, I assure you.'[16]

3

Visiting the Andrews household, Nelson saw a family very much like his own. Like Edmund Nelson, the Reverend Robert Andrews had married into a more distinguished lineage than that from which he came. In 1783 he was about fifty years old, evidently a Londoner by birth, and a graduate of Christ Church, Oxford. After obtaining his Master of Arts the year Horatio was born he was inducted into the adjacent vicarages of Wartling and Hooe in Sussex, just across the Straits of Dover from the Artois coast and nearby St-Omer. However, for the most part he seems to have been one of a common breed of absentee clergyman who paid curates to perform their clerical duties while residing elsewhere. It was this arrangement, no doubt, which allowed him to visit St-Omer. He was probably the 'English gentleman' of the same name who took a three-year lease on 4 rue Wissocq in 1776. It was a well-furnished house, for which notary M. Delamer received the substantial rent of 1,440 livres, but war intervened. Now, with peace between Britain and France restored, the good reverend returned with his large family.[17]

When Andrews married Sarah Hawkins, probably in London, on 25 April 1758, he attached himself to a prestigious brood. For Sarah was one of six surviving children of Sir Caesar Hawkins and his wife Sarah Coxe. Sir Caesar was in his seventies in 1783, but he had enjoyed a most eminent career as a surgeon at St George's Hospital, and attended both George II and the current monarch in his professional capacity. He was a baronet and owned a manor in Kelston, Somerset. The Hawkins family was full of divines, surgeons and physicians, and possessed considerable means, and Sarah, to judge from her sisters, may have brought a dowry of £4,000 to her marriage.[18]

Chatting amiably to Andrews and his wife, Horatio quickly learned that the family also had naval connections. Sir Caesar had some influence with Admiral Lord Howe, and it was through him that young George Andrews, the eldest of the reverend's four sons, got a place in the navy. The boy was eighteen and had been in the service since March 1778 when he had joined the *Greyhound*. Eighteen months had raised him to midshipman, and in 1780 he had joined Captain James Ferguson on the *Terrible*. Like Nelson he had served in America and the West Indies during the late war, but unlike him had seen fleet action under Rodney and Hood. Unfortunately, his principal protector and uncle, Captain John Nott of the *Centaur*, had been fatally shot in the chest during a scrap with the French in 1781, and since July of that year, when his term as able seaman of the *Carcass* had ended, George had been unemployed. Nelson probably met George in St-Omer. Certainly he responded to his friendless predicament with his normal generosity, promising that as soon as he got another ship he would find a place in it for the young man.[19]

But it was neither George nor passing pleasantries with his parents that particularly drew Nelson to the Andrews household. Among the bevy of youngsters there were three budding daughters. One, Charlotte, was only sixteen, but two older sisters were of marriageable age. In describing the visits he and Mac made to the 'very large' Andrews family, Nelson spoke gingerly to Captain Locker of the 'two very agreeable daughters, grown up, about twenty years of age, who play and sing to us whenever we go', and again intimated that his 'heart' was endangered. One of the girls in particular, young Elizabeth Andrews, aged about twenty-one, was beginning to captivate him. He knew she was not rich, and gathered that her fortune was only some £1,000 or so, but she was well connected, and in any case Horatio's heart cared little for money. She was kind, accomplished and attentive, and he found her invading his thoughts. Just as Quebec had grown upon him during his infatuation with Mary, so now he admitted that St-Omer 'increases much upon me, and I am as happy as I can be separated from my native country'.[20]

However, at about the beginning of the last week of November a

letter from Uncle William Suckling pushed even Elizabeth to the back
of Nelson's mind. It was dated 20 November and notified Horatio of
the sudden death of his sister, Ann, and the extreme grief of his father.
Ann's life had been tragically short – she had just reached her twenty-
third birthday – but with £2,000 invested in 3 per cent consols to her
name her future had not been without prospect. Since leaving London
she had attended her ageing father, dividing her time between Burnham
Thorpe and Bath. The two places were a contrast. Ann's native village
was rural and lonely, and scarcely attractive to a woman of her age,
class and intelligence, even one as modest, neat and taciturn as Ann
is said to have been. But the winters in Bath put gaiety into her life,
and opened the door to a world of theatre, balls, and exciting, like-
minded society. Sadly, that very liberation was Ann's undoing. She left
a ballroom one cold November evening and caught a severe chill. Her
constitution, like that of other Nelsons, was delicate, and pneumonia
set in.

On 2 November, as she lay ill at her lodgings in New King Street,
'being weak in body but of sound [and] disposing mind, memory and
understanding', Ann made a will before a surgeon and a lawyer. She
had a special regard for her naval brother, and received occasional
letters from him, though none has survived. Now she named him a
joint executor of her will with her father, despite the fact that he was
far away and older brothers lived close at hand. Her money was to
remain in government stocks to supply an annuity to her father for
the term of his natural life, and when he died it was to be divided
between Horatio and Ann's sisters and younger brothers. Catherine,
the baby of the family, received the largest portion, and, if the Reverend
Nelson died before she was twenty-one, Horatio was to invest her
legacy in government stocks until she came of age. Ann left a modest
collection of possessions, including a locket with a design in hair and
mother of pearl, and they all went to her father. She died at her lodg
ings on 15 November 1783, and was buried out of town, in the simple
little church of St Swithun in Bathford, with her father and youngest
sister among the mourners. The old man plunged into a grief so great
and enduring that one suspects that Ann had been his favourite
daughter.[21]

Uncle William Suckling's account of the reverend's suffering
distracted Nelson for several days, keeping him to his room and away
from the elegant ball attended by Mac on the evening of 25 November.
Horatio not only mourned his 'dear' sister, but worried for his father's

life and for the consequent threat to the youngest sister, 'Kate', the only sibling left in the parental nest. He contemplated leaving for England, and on 4 December told his brother William that 'my surprise and grief upon the occasion are, you will suppose, more to be felt than described. What is to become of poor Kate? Although I am very fond of Mrs Bolton [Susanna], yet I own I should not like to see Kate fixed in a Wells society. For God's sake write what you have heard of our father.' If he died, 'I shall immediately come to England, and most probably fix in some place that might be most for poor Kitty's advantage. My small income shall always be at her service, and she shall never want a protector and a sincere friend while I exist.'[22]

No sooner did his worries about home subside than Miss Bess Andrews returned to haunt him. No doubt she was sympathetic to his plight, and as the cold, dark weather blended with the wine, lights and conviviality of his first French Christmas, his infatuation with her grew. Some primitive verse, into which he lapsed, aptly summed up the situation: 'and when a lady's in the case, all other things they must give place'. Among matters giving 'place' was an unexpected invitation from Maximilian Joseph, Comte de Deux Ponts, whom he had captured and entertained off Puerto Cabello earlier in the year. Somehow the count heard about Nelson's travels, and offered him hospitality in Paris. Horatio was flabbergasted to learn that his prisoner had been 'a prince of the Empire, a general of the French army, knight of the grand order of St Louis, and was second in command at the capture of Yorktown'. Furthermore, he was in line to become Elector of Bavaria, and as King Maximilian I of Bavaria would one day be counted an ally of Napoleon. Nevertheless, interesting as the invitation was, Nelson decided to defer visiting Paris until the spring. His head was still full of Elizabeth.[23]

On the morning of Thursday 4 December, before leaving his lodgings in his finest clothes, Nelson broached an idea to his brother. 'My heart is quite secured against the French beauties,' he allowed. 'I almost wish I could say as much for an English young lady, the daughter of a clergyman, with whom I am just going to dine and spend the day. She has such accomplishments that had I a million of money, I am sure I should at this moment make her an offer of them. My income at present is by far too small to think of marriage, and she has no fortune.'

That idea only deepened, especially when the impulsive young captain realised that he could not remain in St-Omer indefinitely and might soon be parting from Elizabeth. He was afraid the bad weather would destroy his health, and considered consulting a good London physician, and he also wanted to remind the Board of Admiralty of his existence and to steal a visit to his father in Bath. But there was no snow in St-Omer, the frost gave way at the turn of the year, and on 3 January Horatio was still hurrying out to share tea and an evening with 'the most accomplished woman my eyes ever beheld'.[24]

At twenty-five Horatio might have married with sobriety, but it was still a big step for him to contemplate. He was a post-captain and a gentleman, but had no money and needed to pursue his career to accumulate reserves. Not only his own future, but also those of the less advantaged members of his family – in fact most of them – to some extent looked towards that career. A marriage was not, of course, necessarily a handicap to a career. In fact, in a society in which advancement depended so much upon 'interest', a 'good marriage' was an obvious way of uniting the finances and connections of one family to another. And in that sense, Bess was hardly a bad catch. True, she had little money of her own, but like him, she had useful connections. Money or not, Elizabeth was a 'gentlewoman', from the professional classes and socially a suitable partner for a captain in the navy.

Yet without money Nelson felt himself a weak suitor. He had neither property nor fortune, nor even, at the moment, a satisfactory income, and it was to be doubted whether he could support a wife let alone raise a family. Wrestling with the problem, Nelson thought the unthinkable. He might be able to wheedle an allowance from Uncle William, who had always supported him, but if not . . . Just as he had been prepared to 'ruin' himself for Mary Simpson, so now he wondered whether some career change might place more regular sums in his hands. Suppose he abandoned that 'dream of glory' and settled for a more sedentary, shore-based or civilian appointment? Momentarily his entire naval career hung in the balance, as he hinted to his 'dear uncle' on 14 January 1784:

The critical moment of my life is now arrived, that either I am to be happy or miserable – it depends solely on you.

You may possibly think I am going to ask too much. I have led myself up with hopes you will not – till this trying moment. There is a lady I have seen, of a good family and connections, but with a small fortune, £1000 I understand. The whole of my income does not exceed £130 per annum. Now I must come to the point. Will you, if I should marry, allow me yearly £100 until my income is increased to that sum, either by employment, or in any other way? . . .

If you will not give me the above sum, will you exert yourself with either Lord North or Mr Jenkinson to get me a guard-ship or some employment in a public office, where the attendance of the principal [incumbent] is not necessary, and of which they must have such numbers to dispose of [in government]? In the [East] India Service, I understand, if it remains under the directors, their marine force is to be under the command of a captain in the Royal Navy. That is a station I should like.

You must excuse the freedom with which this letter is dictated. Not to have been plain and explicit in my distress had been cruel to myself. If nothing can be done for me, I know what I have to trust to. Life is not worth preserving without happiness, and I care not where I may linger out a miserable existence. I am prepared to hear your refusal, and have fixed my resolution if that should happen, but in every situation I shall be a well-wisher to you and your family, and pray they or you may never know the pangs which at this instant tear my heart.[25]

Nelson wanted to marry Elizabeth, but the problem was *how*. In the event the embarrassment was short-lived. His uncle immediately complied with his request, Horatio proposed to Elizabeth and she refused him point-blank. Suddenly, life became prosaic again, and France, to which he had been warming, was restored to its prominent place in his pantheon of bigotries. Leaving Mac in St-Omer, he hurried back to London. 'I return to many charming women,' he told his brother, 'but no charming woman will return with me. I want to be proficient in the language, which is my only reason for [my] returning [to France]. I hate their country and their manners.'[26]

But his disappointment soon evaporated and Horatio never allowed it to destroy his friendship for the Andrews family. He took George aboard his next ship, as he had promised. As for Elizabeth, we are left to wonder how much she felt for Nelson, or whether she ever regretted rejecting the first suit he had ever made. Certainly, he cannot have been the only young man she refused, and whose hopes she dashed, for despite her attractiveness she remained single until she was in her forties, an uncommonly late age. Then, in 1804, Bess married the Reverend Richard Farror at Walcott, Somerset, and after his early death chose a final husband in Roger Warne, a lieutenant colonel in the East India Company's private regiment. Warne was four years or so Nelson's senior, and had been at the taking of Tipu of Mysore's capital, Seringapatam, in 1799. She probably met him in the east, where she seems to have spent some time, and he gave her a diamond ring, which she bequeathed to him before her death. Warne's will suggests a religious and compassionate man, but their marriage was childless, and Elizabeth's life was tainted with misfortune. Three of her brothers died young. Henry and Hugh, both army officers, died of disease in San Domingo in the West Indies during the 1790s, while George's promising career was destroyed by accident, sickness and alcohol.

Elizabeth herself spent her final years with her husband in Bath, at 3 St James's Square. In 1836 she willed most of her possessions to her 'dearest husband', and left remembrances to nephews, nieces, cousins, sisters and other relations and friends, including her 'faithful affectionate friend and servant', Elizabeth Kirby. She died at her home, perhaps of cholera. Curiously it was the afternoon of 21 October 1837, the thirty-second anniversary of Nelson's own death at the battle of Trafalgar.[27]

4

On Saturday 17 January Nelson arrived back in London, still suffering from a severe cold contracted during the midwinter journey from St-Omer. Some financial and professional matters delayed him in the capital, and in the course of dealing with them he ran 'the ring of pleasure' in a city he had come to realise contained 'so many charms'. What these pleasures were he did not say, but the pursuits of the day were well known. Taverns, clubs and coffee houses; walks along the Mall or between the tree-lined avenues of St James's Park, where milk could be had fresh from the cow; theatres in the Haymarket or Drury Lane; sampling the orchestras and supping in the kiosks at Vauxhall; exploring the huge glass-chandeliered rotunda at Ranelagh; and eyeing the fashionable but painted and feathered ladies gossiping in the Pantheon dome on Oxford Street. Certainly he dined with such friends as Ross, Kingsmill and Hood, and it was probably Nelson's visits to the latter that drew him towards the political arena.[28]

Nelson 'danced attendance' at St James's Palace on 19 January, most probably under Hood's auspices, and politics increasingly permeated his correspondence. The previous month the government had fallen, an unholy coalition between two old enemies, Lord North, a king's man, and the Whig leader Charles James Fox, a critic of the crown, under the nominal leadership of the Duke of Portland. As the extreme political wings in Parliament floundered, the way opened for any weighty politician capable of winning both the support of the king and sufficient Members of Parliament to form a government. William Pitt was young, but enjoyed the confidence of some of North's old followers as well as Whigs, and although a mild reformer he was a friend of the king. His Majesty invited him to become the first lord of the Treasury, the then prime minister, but for a while his position remained shaky and a general election was in the offing.

The Portland administration had tainted itself as self-seeking and factious. In particular, its ill-starred attempts to reform the corrupt and inefficient East India Company by bringing it under greater state control only suggested a grubby attempt to increase the extent of government patronage. People were increasingly suspicious of the misuse of patronage. The king and his government, it was widely claimed, used their powers of patronage to reward supporters and silence opposition. It thereby became a means to undermine the English constitution, in which power was supposed to be shared and balanced between king, lords and people.

These criticisms of the Portland–Fox–North coalition sat especially badly with Fox, a Whig and therefore ostensibly a defender of the rights of the people against the encroaching power of the king and his government. Fox had not only looked hypocritical and corrupt, opposing excessive government patronage out of office and extending it when in power, but he also appeared decidedly unpatriotic. His coalition had been willing to accept what many believed to be humiliating peace terms during the negotiations that had ended the American War of Independence and the associated conflicts with France, Spain and Holland. More, Fox had reinforced the impression by his obvious sympathy for the rebellious colonists and his sharp criticism of Britain's military and naval commanders.

Pitt, by contrast, was unsullied. He presented himself as an independent patriot, free of faction and self-interest, and neither a Whig nor an outright king's man. He said he would weigh policies purely according to their value to the country. The king, who hated Fox, supported Pitt, as did Hood, who eventually partnered Sir Cecil Wray in an attempt to oust the Whig leader from his own constituency of Westminster.[29]

These simple ideals of independence, patriotism, selfless service and public good over private gain, appealed to young Nelson, particularly as filtered through Hood and his entourage. Hood spoke of unity, an end to 'party' and the need for independent men to pack the Commons. 'I shall ever most carefully and studiously steer clear, as far as I am able, of all suspicion of being a *party* man . . . whether for or against a minister,' he declared. He supported Pitt by principle as well as blood. Nelson uncritically reproduced these ideas. He wanted to 'unkennel' Fox 'and all that party', and prayed for an election, 'that the people may have an opportunity of sending men that will support *their* interests, and get rid of a turbulent faction who are striving to ruin their country'.[30]

When Nelson reported that 'Lord Hood's friends are canvassing' he should have included himself among them, for he spoke fully and frankly for the admiral at every opportunity. Not even parson William was spared. Nelson hoped 'sincerely' that William would vote for Pitt's man, and pressed upon him a revised opinion of their old benefactors, the Walpoles. Only two years before Nelson had spoken with 'regret' at missing 'Mr Walpole' when the *Albemarle* anchored in Yarmouth, and promised to purchase 'best' wines for him in far-off countries. And only the previous year Lord Walpole had assisted Nelson's father to equip the church at Burnham Thorpe with a new oak pulpit. But now parson William learned that the Walpoles were 'the merest set of ciphers that ever existed – in public affairs I mean. Mr Pitt, depend upon it, will stand against all opposition. An honest man must always in time get the better of a villain.' Indeed, influenced by the toadies around Hood, Nelson even considered standing for Parliament himself and joining the army of placemen at Pitt's back. But he could not find a seat. 'I have done with politics,' he told his brother on 31 January. 'Let who will get in, I shall be left out.'[31]

It was just as well, for he had no talent for such a duplicitous trade, and once his cold had benefited from the ministrations of Doctor Richard Warren he found better entertainment, first in calling upon Lord Howe at the Admiralty to advertise his availability, and then at the end of January in taking the coach for Bath. He probably stood mournfully beside poor Ann's grave, but was cheered to see his father in an unusually robust condition and up till ten and after each evening. As for young Kate, she was learning to ride. 'She is a charming young woman,' Horatio confessed, 'and possesses a great share of sense.' They decided they would all spend the following Christmas in Norfolk, for Nelson had no expectation of getting a ship. He talked about

returning to France for the summer before buying a horse and riding
to Burnham.[32]

In March, Nelson was back in London. He surrendered his room
at Salisbury Street and moved to a short passage nearby, between the
Strand and St Martin-in-the-Fields. These new lodgings, at the residence of Thomas Harrison at 3 Lancaster Court, next to the Roasting
House, were only temporary, and Horatio directed his mail to his
uncle in Kentish Town.[33]

By whatever means, on the 18th he received important news. His
visit to the Admiralty had yielded dividends, despite the lowly position he occupied on the captains' list and the limited number of ships
being commissioned in peacetime. He was appointed to the *Boreas*,
another twenty-eight-gun nine-pounder frigate, already manned and
fitting for sea at Woolwich. She had been built in Hull nine years
before and was destined for an ignominious end as a Sheerness slop
ship, but in 1784 she came as a blessing, rescuing Nelson from an
impecunious existence on half-pay. The duties were likely to be dull.
As they dribbled in, his orders directed him first to Spithead and then
to Plymouth, where he would embark a detachment of marines and
proceed to the Leeward Islands in the West Indies.[34]

But at least he would be employed.

5

Captain Nelson reacted tartly to William's suggestion that some
'interest' had got him the appointment. 'You ask by what *interest* did
I get a ship?' he answered. 'I answer, having served with credit was
my recommendation. So Lord Howe, first lord of the Admiralty, told
me. Anything in reason that I can ask, I am sure of obtaining from
his justice.'[35]

In fact, Hood had almost certainly been his referee. Such is the
inference of Howe's words to Hood in July 1787, when Nelson was
judged a disappointment. 'I am sorry Capt. Nelson, whom *we* wished
well to, has been so wanting in his endeavours,' remarked the first
lord regretfully. Moreover, Hood's influence is indicated by the return
Nelson made on the favour. He found places on the *Boreas* for several
of Hood's friends. The admiral was embroiled in politics, with more
than the usual number of supporters to reward, and a supply of naval
appointments was useful. A few months after being appointed to the
frigate 'my dear Nelson' received a letter from Hood soliciting a place

for George Goodchild, 'the adopted son of my friend, Sir Cecil Wray',
one of his political partners. For some reason Goodchild did not, in
the end, join the 'young gentlemen' of the *Boreas*, but others preferred
by Hood did. There are grounds for believing at least three of the
ship's youngsters, the thirteen-year-old Honourable Courtenay Boyle,
John Talbot and William Tatham, were Hood protégés, and there were
probably more.[36]

Nelson was still unwell. A few days after receiving word of his
appointment he went down with his old malarial fevers, sickening like
clockwork every other day. He did not manage to assume command
of the *Boreas* from his predecessor, Thomas Wells, until 24 March.

There was much to occupy the ailing young captain, some of it
trivial but necessary. He had his cabin and table to furnish, and spent
£10 on dishes, plates, cutlery, glasses, decanters and a tureen alone.
Turning to the big issues, he found the ship being well victualled and
most of the required one hundred and eighty men in their places,
although some were so unfit that Nelson sent them to hospital. Both
lieutenants were already appointed. James Wallis, the first lieutenant,
had held a commission for five years, but Nelson's second was young
Digby Dent from Hampshire, an untried son of Admiral Sir Digby
Dent. On paper Dent had as much naval experience as his captain,
for his father had put him on the books of the *Dolphin* when he was
only six years old and transferred him from ship to ship as he moved
commands. How much of this sea time was real was anybody's guess,
but in 1780 Dent junior went to the *Hannibal* under another captain.
He passed his lieutenant's examination the following year, but his
commission was not confirmed until he reached the stipulated
minimum age of twenty and joined the *Boreas*. Despite the racing start
Dent did not prosper, and sixteen more years would give him nothing
more impressive to command than a cutter.[37]

Nelson often saw the best in people, but his master, James Jameson,
left something to be desired. An experienced, middle-aged, gout-ridden
Scot, he was reasonably efficient but prone to drinking, and four years
before had been dismissed from the *Camilla* for drunkenness and
neglect of duty. However, neither his post nor those of the other
warrant officers were in Nelson's gift, and it was only among the
lower ranks that the captain made room for protégés of his own. He
asked Locker and other friends whether he could serve them, but
requests soon flooded in right and left, swamping his official entitle-
ment to two master's mates, four midshipmen and eight captain's

servants – the traditional ratings into which young gentlemen were slotted. His two master's mates were really lieutenants in waiting. Henry Power, an Irishman from Youghal, County Cork, was three and a half years older than Nelson, and had been acting lieutenant on previous ships. He spent only six months of 1784 with Nelson. The other master's mate was the unfortunate Joseph Bromwich, late of the *Albermarle*, who was still trying to get his lieutenant's commission confirmed.[38]

The other young officers pressed upon him had to be rated midshipmen, captain's servants, able seamen or even surgeon's servants. Nelson justified their excessive number by describing his ship as a 'nursery' for good officers, but more than anything else he was satisfying friends and potential patrons, old and new. The dependants of 'Lord Howe, Lord Gower, Lord Hood, Sir Peter Parker, Sir John Jervis, Earl Cork, Lord Courtenay Hood, William Cornwallis, Captain Pole and [Captain] Douglas' mixed aboard the *Boreas* with favourites of his own.[39]

Among those Horatio personally added to the haul were old *Albemarle* adherents, Bromwich and Charles Hardy, new acquaintances such as George Andrews, Elizabeth's brother, who caught up with the ship in the West Indies, and a cousin, Maurice William Suckling. Suckling had spent a few months on the *Monkey* cutter the previous year, tossing about the North Sea, but now got a rating as surgeon's servant at the age of fourteen.

If the quarterdeck of the *Boreas* resembled a boys' academy that is what, in effect, it partly was. Several of the pupils were relatively inexperienced, and some graduates of other establishments. Robert Parkinson, a twenty-one-year-old volunteer from London, had come from the *Polyphemus*. Sixteen-year-old Thomas Stansbury of Holmer, Hereford, sometime able seaman, had been in the *Atlas* and *Speedy*. For William Nowell, who remained with Nelson only five months, and Edmund Bishop, who came from the *Concorde*, the *Boreas* was their fifth ship.[40]

Although many months had passed since the *Albemarle* had been paid off, Nelson also received a few requests from old lower-deck ratings wishing to serve with him again. Some found a berth aboard, including Frank Lepee, who shipped as able seaman. Once it became known that the *Boreas* was bound for the Leeward Islands, rather than the East Indies or Jamaica, the frigate was also 'lumbered' with passengers. To his chagrin Horatio discovered that Lady Jane Hughes and her family were among them. She was the wife of Rear Admiral Sir Richard Hughes, who commanded in the Leeward Islands – the same man with whom Nelson had acrimoniously fenced in Portsmouth two years before.

Lady Hughes joined the ship at St Helens on the Isle of Wight on about 17 April, with her daughter Rose Mary, her son Richard, a servant and three other boys intent on joining Sir Richard or his retinue. At first Horatio viewed Lady Hughes an 'inconvenience and expense' as well as 'a fine talkative lady', but there was an even more unwelcome guest. Leaving a curate to manage his affairs at Little Brandon, Parson William Nelson finally decided to fulfil his ambition to go to sea, despite the advice and wishes of his brother. William was not known for his ability to tolerate hardship, and Horatio doubted he would enjoy the navy. But the man persisted, and for the sake of family accord Nelson relented, hoping his brother would sample life as a naval chaplain and hurry back to England within a few months. Among other things, he worried about his father and his sister Kate living at Burnham Thorpe without William close by, especially if they had to winter in 'that lonesome place'.[41]

Nelson visited Locker, promising to look into the state of some land he had in Dominica, and then sailed for the Nore on 11 April. A pilot ran the frigate aground in water so shallow that men were able to wade all around her at low tide, but Nelson got her to an anchorage near the Nore light at six in the evening. More trouble awaited him in the Downs, which he reached in two days after delays caused by gales and snow. On 14 April he fell into a dispute with the master of a Dutch East Indiaman. The master refused to release sixteen Britons from his service, insisting they owed him money. Nelson felt a responsibility for distressed nationals and doubted the master's story. He blockaded the recalcitrant ship, preventing boats coming from or going to her, and refusing to allow her to move until the men and their chests of belongings were liberated. The master complained to the Admiralty, and the board thought their man was acting too strongly. Nelson was ordered to remove his restraints, but to obtain a statement of any belongings still being withheld from the British seamen to facilitate a more diplomatic protest. But the captain of the *Boreas* had already got the desired result, and he triumphantly reported to superiors that the matter had been 'amicably' settled.[42]

No doubt Nelson was glad to get away from the Downs on the 15th, and reach Portsmouth by way of Spithead and St Helens. There another adventure awaited him on 20 April, as he was riding about the town. He narrated his hair-raising escape to Locker the following day:

And yesterday . . . I was riding a blackguard horse that ran away with me at Common, carried me round all the works into Portsmouth, by the London gates, through the town out at the gate that leads to Common, where there was a wagon in the road – which is so very narrow that a horse could barely pass. To save my legs, and perhaps my life, I was obliged to throw myself from the horse, which I did with great agility, but unluckily upon hard stones, which has hurt my back and my leg, but done no other mischief. It was a thousand to one that I had not been killed. To crown all, a young girl was riding with me. Her horse ran away with mine, but most fortunately a gallant young man seized her horse's bridle a moment before I dismounted, and saved her from the destruction which she could not have avoided.[43]

We are left to ponder the identity of the 'young girl' in Nelson's company on the occasion, but the most likely candidate was Rose Mary Hughes, the daughter of Lady Hughes, who had joined the *Boreas* three days before. 'Rosy' was then searching for a suitor, but if Nelson was gallant enough to show her the town, he remained solidly unattracted. 'God help the poor man,' he wrote more than a year later when he heard that Rosy had at last ensnared a major of the 67th Regiment of Foot. 'Has he taken leave of his senses? Oh, what a taste! The mother will be in a few years the handsomest of the two.'[44]

Rosy was a poor substitute for Mary Simpson and Bess Andrews, but after quitting Portsmouth and picking up a detachment of marines at Plymouth, the *Boreas* slipped elegantly out of the sound on 21 May. Soon she was dipping through the deep and rolling swells of the Atlantic, bound for new islands, new exploits and new romances.

XII

HURRICANE HARBOUR

Thither shall youthful heroes climb,
The Nelsons of an aftertime,
And round that sacred altar swear
Such glory and such graves to share.
                    John Wilson Croker, *Songs of Trafalgar*

1

ANTIGUA, the largest of the British Leeward Islands, sweltered in latitude seventeen degrees. A mere 108 square miles, it was set in bright blue Caribbean seas that swept over coral reefs onto pale sandy beaches, penetrated secluded coves or lashed themselves into a milky foam against craggy promontories. The island's central valleys were dotted with sugar plantations maintained by thirty-five thousand black and mulatto slaves, a system of which Nelson was largely ignorant and wholly uncritical. The countryside was sprinkled with cane-producing windmills, but the only significant extended settlement was St John's in the northwest, a town of eighteen hundred houses and huts with spacious but unpaved streets sprouting scrub and prickly pear.

In August 1784, however, His Majesty's frigate *Boreas* lay in English Harbour on the south coast, a couple of interlocking anchorages hidden from the sea and sheltered by green, lofty hills. There, in a broiling sun trap, even the winters were warm. In the summers, secured from the northeast trades that gave relief elsewhere, the air became uncomfortably hot and the water itself stagnant and fetid. There was only one spring and storage tanks were needed to conserve fresh water.

English Harbour was nevertheless naturally strong. Ships entered through a thin strait flanked by Fort Berkeley and the Horse-shoe battery and steered a few points to larboard to pass northwards through the outer anchorage and into a second channel, graced by a small sixty-year-old dockyard on the left. Once inside the inner anchorage, another turn to larboard enabled them to be warped into a secure berth. More than a haven difficult for enemies to breach, English Harbour was also a bolt hole safe from the cyclones that stormed over these seas between August and October. That, more than anything else, was why Captain Nelson was shut in the place, waiting for the hurricanes to blow themselves out.

A peacetime commission was a dull blessing at any time, but English Harbour had few attractions. The dockyard consisted of little more than a few wooden warehouses and workshops, with a 'neat' house for the naval commander of the station made from a storehouse near the wharf. At the head of the three-quarter-mile harbour, situated furthest north in the inner anchorage, was a hospital and powder magazine, while across the narrows from the dockyard rose Mount Prospect with a house flying a flag upon its summit. Positioned to escape the worst of the dockyard clamour and to gain the cooler air above, the residence was named 'Windsor' and housed John Moutray, the resident dockyard commissioner, and his wife Mary.[1]

Nelson spent much of his time on board the *Boreas*. His cabin occupied the full width of the aftermost part of the upper deck, with gun ports at the sides, and a row of stern windows through which the brilliant tropical light could relieve the gloom. The quarters were divided into a day cabin, a dining area to which Nelson's servants brought food from the ship's galley and a place where his cot was slung from the beams. A gallery at the stern supplied a convenience. On the voyage out chivalry had probably banished Captain Nelson to one of the officers' cabins in the gun room below, while Lady Hughes and her daughter used his own quarters, but now the suite was again at his disposal. Frugally furnished and dimly lit, it provided sanctuary, with a red-coated marine standing guard outside his door with a musket and bayonet. Thus protected, Nelson read, reflected and wrote between his duties on deck and the occasional business ashore.

2

The outward passage had not been as bad as Nelson had feared.

True, his quarterdeck had been crowded, but although Lady Hughes was 'an eternal clack' time had shown her a 'very pleasant good' person, while the many young gentlemen darting here and there had become 'my dear good children'. Captain Nelson loved young people, and saw himself in their thirst for adventure. He fussed over them like a proud father, daily haunting the schoolroom to monitor their progress, and ensuring they learned every kind of task. 'All the young-sters, I hope, learnt and did the[ir] duty, from rigging the topgallant mast to stowing the ballast; they never were confined to any partic-ular part of the service,' he recalled. 'The trouble of breeding up offi-cers properly I need not state, and it is only by their turning out good men that a captain is repaid.'[2]

At noon, when the boys assembled on deck to calculate the ship's position with the master, they also found Nelson there with his quad-rant; and when the *Boreas* crossed the line in June, they no sooner enjoyed the spectacle of seeing King Neptune in the traditional seamen's ceremonies, than they were bled and given 'purgative medicines' on the orders of a captain mindful of the health of those who had never seen the tropics before. In the opinion of First Lieutenant James Wallis the youngsters benefited from these ministrations to a 'wonderful' degree.[3]

Lady Hughes was also impressed by Nelson's 'attention' to the boys and his patience with those still learning their trade. He 'never rebuked' those intimidated by the fearful climbs aloft, she noticed. 'Well, sir,' he told one reluctant apprentice, 'I am going a race to the mast-head, and beg I may meet you there.' As she recalled it, 'No denial could be given to such a wish, and the poor little fellow instantly began his march. His lordship [Nelson] never took the least notice with what alacrity it was done, but when he met [the boy] in the top instantly began speaking in the most cheerful manner, and saying how much a person was to be pitied that could fancy there was any danger, or even any thing disagreeable in the attempt. After this excellent example, I have seen the timid youth lead another, and rehearse his captain's words.' According to Lady Hughes, the boys responded to their captain with adulation and vied with each other for his approval.[4]

On 2 June, the day after the *Boreas* reached Funchal in Madeira, Lady Hughes and her daughter accompanied Nelson, his brother and senior officers ashore to visit the Portuguese governor. As the boat pulled from the ship it fired a salute for her ladyship but it was not this she remembered but the entourage of ten young gentlemen in the captain's train. It resembled a school outing, with excited juveniles outnumbering their supervisors. 'I make it a rule to introduce them to all the good company I can,' Nelson explained, 'as they have few to look up to besides myself during the time they are at sea.' He understood that though the boys were receiving lessons in mathematics, navigation and seamanship from the master, their formal education contained little about fighting and commanding a ship. For that they had to rely upon role models, and Nelson was determined to be the best he could. At Funchal his budding Nelsons not only learned something about international niceties, but also the fraternity of all seafarers, because Nelson supplied emergency rations to a Danish frigate.[5]

Yet even on this first voyage there were indications that Nelson's partnership with the *Boreas* might frustrate more than excite. The captain did not enthuse about the ship in his usual fashion, and a few hard cases were beginning to emerge among the crew. In Plymouth one of the seamen, Thomas Johnston, had grumbled when his wife and the other women on board were ordered off the ship just before sailing. Standing between decks near the fore hatchway, where he could be heard by men loading water and beer into the hold, Johnston declared that 'if his wife was not permitted to go out in the ship, that no woman should go out in her'. Ordinary ratings were not allowed to take wives and sweethearts to sea, although officers sometimes did, and female passengers were not uncommon. Evidently Johnston took exception to the Hughes women and the wife of Daniel Letsome Peers, the purser, being given passage. His words sounded subversive and Bromwich reported them to Lieutenant Wallis. Nelson called Johnston onto the quarterdeck to warn him 'what the consequences would be if he continued to make use of improper expressions', but left it at that. Unfortunately, Johnston did not improve. Indeed, he took pride in his incorrigibility. 'I am reckoned one of the worst men in the ship,' he later bragged, claiming that if his fellows had been 'as bad' the *Boreas* 'would never have got . . . to Barbados or Antigua'.[6]

A truculent marine named John Nairns was also becoming troublesome. Though generally attentive to duty he was 'frequently drunk' and threatening to hit one officer or another. Off Madeira, Nairns earned one of the three floggings seen on the outward voyage by receiving a dozen strokes for abusing his sergeant, John Cochran, but he remained unreformed. At Barbados he struck a petty officer and was lucky that the victim chose not to make an issue of it.[7]

Nelson, too, was unusually contentious throughout his spell in the Leeward Islands. As a rising officer he had generally endeared himself to superiors and peers, and had few bad words for any of them. But during this command he was forever standing upon his dignity, and reacting powerfully and sometimes tactlessly to fancied affronts or anything that smacked of slackness of duty. Although many have admired his conduct and seen courage and principle in it, a few historians have admitted the strain of arrogant intemperance and self-righteous pedantry that developed. Out in these islands Nelson tended to be irritable, uncompromising and severe with his men. He was, of course, still in his twenties, and might be excused the confidence and follies of youth, but professional frustration, sexual tension and indifferent health may also have influenced his behaviour.

An early example of this punctilio had occurred at Funchal. Nelson's time there had been pleasant enough. He embarked some wine to soften up the governor of Dominica, with whom he intended to broach the matter of lands Captain Locker had inherited there, saluted the king's birthday, fraternised with the captain of the *Resource* and sent his brother ashore to preach in an English trade factory. But he took umbrage when Charles Murray, the English consul, neglected to return a visit Nelson had made, and grumpily declined to have further dealings with the man. The quarrel, he admitted to Locker, was rooted in nothing more than 'a little etiquette about visiting', but there would be similar occasions in the next few years. Salutes were another raw spot. Any failure to fire the correct number of guns to acknowledge his flag he deemed a national insult. There must have been diplomatic ways of correcting such oversights but Horatio was not always good at finding them. The governor of the Dutch island of St Eustatius received one protest, and in December 1784 Nelson even fired two nine-pounders at the British fort at Barbados for neglecting to salute a national French schooner leaving port.[8]

However, leaving Funchal on 8 June the *Boreas* had reached Carlisle Bay, Barbados, in the Windward Islands eighteen days later. Here things had looked up. Rear Admiral Sir Richard Hughes, commander-in-chief in the Leeward Islands, was there in the *Adamant*, along with a number of other captains. It was with 'no small degree of satisfaction' that Nelson discovered he stood next to Hughes in seniority, and was consequently second-in-command of the station. As such he had the privilege of presiding over the courts martial in Carlisle Bay. Moreover, the admiral seemed to bear him no grudges for their previous difficulty. Hughes came aboard the *Boreas* the day she arrived, reclaiming his family and the dispatches Nelson had brought from the Admiralty. Lady Hughes gave Horatio an excellent 'character', and Sir Richard was relentlessly amiable, regretting only that Nelson did not have the opportunity to 'partake of family fare' at his table more often. On his perambulations ashore the admiral dutifully introduced Horatio to all the eminent islanders.[9]

Nelson had left Barbados on 20 July with orders to 'lay up' for the hurricane season in English Harbour. He sailed northwards by way of Martinique and Dominica. Dominica was merely a wood and water stop, but at the French island of Martinique Horatio was at his most insistent. He berated the governor for not greeting His Britannic Majesty's ship with colours above the citadel, and only when national dishonour had been expunged by an exchange of fifteen-gun salutes between frigate and fort did fraternisation commence. The governor visited the *Boreas*, and Captain Nelson went ashore, each greeted by salutes of eleven guns. Nelson arrived accompanied by as many young gentlemen as could tumble into his boat, and enquired after some British seamen in the town jail. He also discovered that the French officer who had been inattentive to his ship's colours when he arrived had likewise been incarcerated, and upon reflection allowed his inherent generosity to prevail. Horatio gallantly pleaded for the offender's release. All things put to rights, the *Boreas* eventually sailed into English Harbour on 28 July.[10]

The Leeward Islands squadron divided for the hurricane season. At the island of Grenada was stationed Nelson's old friend Cuthbert Collingwood, with his forty-four-gun frigate the *Mediator* and two sloops, the *Rattler* and the *Experiment*, the first under the younger Collingwood brother, Wilfred. The rest of the ships were with the *Boreas* at English Harbour – the *Adamant* (Captain William Kelly), flying the flag of Sir Richard Hughes; the *Latona* frigate under Captain Charles Sandys; the *Unicorn*, *Zebra*, *Fury* and *Falcon*, all sloops and brigs, respectively commanded by Charles Stirling, Edward Pakenham, William Smith and Velters Cornelius Berkeley; and the *Berbice* tender of William Lucas. It was a contemptible flotilla compared to some of the fleets Nelson had known, but he had authority within it and organised both the captains' mess and any necessary courts martial. Briefly, before the tedium wore him down, there was a little satisfaction.

3

But time hung heavily, and Captain Nelson lingered on in the heat
and mosquitoes of English Harbour. He tried to keep the men busy.
They refitted and repainted the ship and in spare moments danced,
sang and juggled with the captain's blessing. The young gentlemen
entertained the company by performing simple plays but the place
seemed oppressive. One man was lost overboard and a few died of
fever. His brother William, his appetite for the life of a naval chaplain thoroughly sated, fell sick and was packed off home in the *Fury*
at the end of September. Among those who stayed tempers began to
fray.

The first day of August put both Johnston and Nairns before courts
martial. Lieutenant Dent had stopped Johnston's grog ration on
account of his bad behaviour and he became surly and insubordinate.
According to young Stansbury 'he said that while his grog was stopped
he would stop the ship's duty'. Dent ordered him confined below, but
Johnston replied that 'he'd be damned if he would not open the
captain's eyes', and continued to complain as he pulled on stockings
to receive the irons about his ankles.[11]

Johnston was tried a week later on board the *Unicorn*. Captain
Stirling presided because the defendant had called Nelson as a witness.
In fact, even at this pass, Johnston appeared to regard his captain as
a protector. He attempted to put an innocent construction upon his
remarks, advertised the years he had spent in the navy without punishment and appealed to Nelson for 'a character'. Horatio was not unsympathetic, and had no personal issue with the prisoner, but he had to
support the authority of his junior officers. Nevertheless, he did what
he could. He had only known of Johnston's seditious remarks 'from
complaint' and acknowledged his strengths. 'I never had any complaint
against him except for his making use of improper words, and had I
not received these complaints I should have esteemed him one of the
best men that I ever sailed with.' Bromwich, who had been troubled
by Johnston, had to admit that he had only seen the man drunk once,
when they all celebrated crossing the line. But the court decided that
Lieutenant Dent's charges were partly proven and sentenced Johnston
to two hundred lashes around the squadron. It did not cure him, for
he received three subsequent but routine floggings aboard the *Boreas*
in as many years for drunkenness, threatening a boatswain, disobedience and neglect of duty.

The same Sunday Johnston ran foul of Dent, Nairns also got into trouble. Nelson was told that the marine had just returned from shore after being absent without leave, and brought him to the quarterdeck to explain himself. Horatio was offering Nairns a means of mitigating his offence, but the fellow merely became abusive and got a dozen lashes in return. After receiving his punishment Nairns went below to clean up and was soon quarrelling with Sergeant Cochran, who wanted him to join a guard being formed to welcome Admiral Hughes aboard the ship. Exasperated, Cochran said there would be consequences if Nairns did not turn out. 'They may flog and be buggered, for I don't care,' retorted the bloodied marine. 'They never shall make a good soldier of me. See what kind of satisfaction I gave them! Bugger my eyes if I would cry out if they would flog me to death!' The chagrined sergeant complained to his superior, Lieutenant Theophilus Lane, who formally demanded a court martial.

Again, Nelson was called to testify and his evidence is worth quoting because it tells us something about his attitude to punishment:

Q: You have heard the charge read?

A: Yes.

Q: Have not repeated complaints been made to you of the prisoner's ill behaviour?

A: Yes.

Q: What has in general been the cause of these complaints?

A: Drunkenness, striking his officers, neglecting his duty, using improper words such as, 'I might flog and be buggered, for that I should get no good out of him', and going on shore without leave.

Q: Was the prisoner punished in consequence of these complaints?

A: Sometimes he was, and sometimes not. He was punished so frequently and reprimanded so often to no purpose. He was past my power of *reclaiming* him.

Q: Did any instances of the prisoner's misbehaviour fall immediately within your knowledge?

A: Yes, drunkenness and contempt for me.

Q: Did you punish him for that contempt?

A: Complaint was made to me for his going on shore without leave by the first lieutenant. I sent for the prisoner on the quarter-deck to hear his reasons for going out of the ship. His actions were so contemptuous that I was obliged to order him to [be flogged at] the gangway.

Q: Do you recollect the punishment you inflicted on him at that time?

A: A dozen lashes.

Q: Do you recollect how many times you have punished him since he has been under your command?

A: Twice at the gangway.

Q: You say you had complaints lodged against the prisoner for striking his officer. Was he punished for that?

A: The day after we left Madeira to the best of my recollection a complaint was made to me that the prisoner had struck or attempted to strike the corporal, and I punished him for mutiny.[12]

Nelson, it seems, gave his men opportunities to explain their actions, and punished to reclaim – at least in theory, but he regarded Nairns as irredeemable. The court agreed. Nairns received two hundred and fifty lashes through the fleet, was 'drummed on shore' and dishonourably discharged from his corps.

Difficulties were not confined to the ranks, for tensions were also stretching in the airless gun room, where the lieutenants, officers of marines and the senior warrant officers shared cramped accommodation. Wallis, the snuff-taking first lieutenant, was a conscientious officer, up spryly at seven each morning, and a fine seaman. But he was abrasive and haughty. He had 'strange whims', someone said long afterwards, and though a man of 'many good qualities' occasionally 'appeared half mad'. Although second-in-command aboard the *Boreas*, he began feuding with the supersensitive Lane about who had the greater authority over the marine detachment. A court martial confirmed the supremacy of Wallis, but Nelson regretted the divisions sown among his officers. Dent, for example, had supported the first lieutenant, but Thomas Graham, the surgeon, had seconded Lane.[13]

Nelson helped where he could. Despite his own privileged rise, he sympathised with junior officers tripping over a treacherous career ladder and greatly valued loyalty. It was the unfortunate Bromwich who most concerned him, and he appealed for his promotion to both Sir Richard and Lady Hughes. Bromwich's preferment, he said, was 'the only favour' he presumed 'to ask'. As a result of such overtures, on 20 December Bromwich was appointed acting lieutenant of the flagship, and fourteen months later acting commander of a government brig, but even these advantages failed to get his lieutenancy confirmed. As late as 1790 he was having to drop back down to master's mate. Bromwich became a lieutenant ten years after passing his examination but never received the opportunities he deserved.

Though out of sight Nelson continued to fight for him, but with only modest success.[14]

Nelson's own dissatisfaction with the Leeward Islands manifested itself in almost constant irritability. On more tiresome days the silence of his cabin was broken by the scratching of his pen as he wrote to Locker, Kingsmill and almost everyone else he knew, though not 'a single creature in England' seemed to reply. To Cornwallis he sent a cask of haddock by way of the *Zebra* sloop and confessed a nostalgia for Jamaica, regretting that no ship was available for him to send 'poor Cuba [Cornwallis]' some of the provisions perennially in short supply in Port Royal.[15]

His letter writing partly reflected loneliness, the want of satisfying associates in Antigua and his own frustration. He castigated his fellow creatures mercilessly. Hughes, who usually eased his gout ashore, was 'tolerable' though entirely uninspiring; he 'bows and scrapes too much for me', Nelson thought. Lady Hughes's incessant chatter he had grown to 'detest' while the flag captain, Kelly, was 'an ignorant self-sufficient man'. Sandys of the *Latona* had once been Horatio's superior on the old *Lowestoffe*, but now stood nearly four years his junior on the captains' list. Nelson recognised the good in him, and liked him as a man, but Sandys failed wretchedly as an officer and went through 'a regular course of claret every day'. As for the other captains of the squadron, they were – bar two – mere 'ignoramuses'.[16]

The exceptions were the Collingwood boys. Wilfred, slightly the younger man, had only been promoted commander the year before and was not dissimilar to Nelson, for his flimsy constitution belied a sharp and strong mind. Cuthbert was ten years Nelson's senior, and in some ways a contrast. Where Nelson hungered for attention, Collingwood regarded fame as a transitory and futile possession. Its 'trumpet makes a good noise,' he once said, 'but the notes do not dwell long on the ear'. Where Nelson was impatient and opportunist, Collingwood was steady and solid as a rock. And where Nelson was quiet but endearing, Collingwood suffered from a somewhat dour and dull disposition. Yet overriding such discrepancies were common attributes. Both were men of the modest middle classes and had gone to sea at twelve; both enjoyed reading and wrote reasonable letters; both were conservative politically; and, more than anything else, both were basically decent men sharing a powerful sense of public duty. Horatio felt a deepening friendship for 'my dear Coll', and grieved that the hurricane months had shut him in Grenada, rather than Antigua. 'What

an amiable good man he is!' he told Captain Locker. 'All the rest
are geese!'[17]

If Nelson had few good words for his colleagues, he had even fewer
for the islanders themselves. 'I detest this country,' he wrote; English
Harbour was an 'infernal hole', and the island a 'vile place'. Its people,
he came to believe, were disaffected and selfish, and in blacker
moments he thought them 'trash'. Perhaps he was thinking about the
plantation managers who cheated their absentee landlords, drank the
newly fashionable claret and dallied with mulatto mistresses,
discarding any inconvenient offspring. This was far from a measured
opinion, however. A midshipman who arrived at English Harbour a
couple of years later told a very different story. The island 'society'
was 'excellent', he recalled, 'particularly' in Antigua, where 'I . . .
experienced all that hospitality could give. They were men of education, and had seen a good deal of life.' At about the same time another
observer thought the British women possessed 'refined sense' and made
'good wives, excellent parents, worthy friends, free from affectation,
and blessed [with] every amiable quality'.[18]

Sometimes Nelson rode the twelve miles to St John's, on the north
coast, where balls and dances occasionally enlivened the impressive
stone-built courthouse, whist, cribbage and all-fours were played at
Smith's tavern, and ladies protected their complexions by walking
masked along the streets. At English Harbour he rarely dined ashore,
but received a few invitations, some to the home of Samuel Eliot, both
of whose eligible daughters were being pursued by naval officers. But
there was one house to which he found himself returning with an
increasing frequency, and where his troubles, real or imaginary, diminished. It was Windsor, high up on the hill above the dockyard, where
breezes kept the heat at bay. There lived John Moutray, the elderly
naval commissioner of Barbados and the Leeward Islands, and his
fascinating young wife.

4

They were hospitable from the first. When the *Boreas* was being
repainted in the latter half of October Nelson even stayed a week
there. As he informed Cornwallis, Windsor was always 'open to me,
with a bedchamber, during my broil at this place'. A road skirting the
harbour linked Windsor to the dockyard, but Nelson used a boat to
cross the narrows between the two.[19]

John Moutray was the seventh laird of Roxobie, Fifeshire, and was sixty-two. He had become a lieutenant in 1744, commander of the *Thetis* thirteen years later, and post-captain of a forty-gun hospital ship three months after Nelson was born. His career had not only been long, it had also been undistinguished. Periods of unemployment punctuated his service record, and though the American war had provided a succession of commands – including the *Warwick*, *Britannia* and *Ramilles* – he had blighted his prospects taking a convoy to Madeira in August 1780. There had been a Franco-Spanish attack, and though Moutray saved his warships he lost all but ten or eleven of the sixty-six or so merchantmen under his care. Moutray was lucky to have survived the ensuing clamour. Still, he got his career back on track, took the *Vengeance* to relieve Gibraltar in 1782 and made a voyage to Ireland.

Moutray shared Nelson's distaste for his present posting. Indeed, he had asked the Admiralty to excuse him tropical appointments. His health, he said, had been ruined by scurvy, gout, and 'a bilious complaint' picked up in the West Indies, and any 'return' to a 'warm climate' was 'hazardous'. Unfortunately, someone at the Admiralty had a wicked sense of humour. The captain was retired from active service, given a civil appointment with the Navy Board in July 1783 and shipped out to supervise the sleepy dockyard in Antigua.[20]

Moutray's misfortunes may have made Nelson better able to bear his own, though the commissioner was compensated with an annual salary of £500. It was the wife, rather than the husband, who attracted Nelson to Windsor, however. Mary Moutray was thirty-three or thirty-four years old and hailed from the Scottish Border. Only months before meeting Nelson she had lost her father, Thomas Pemble, a naval officer of some education. Pemble had entered the service as surgeon's servant of the *Lowestoffe*, and taken seven years to pass for lieutenant in February 1744. He joined the *Tryal* sloop, but spent Christmas Eve of 1745 marrying eighteen-year-old Catherine Selby at Belford in Northumberland. Two daughters, Catherine and Mary, grew to maturity. In June 1765 Pemble became commander of the *Hazard* sloop, but there his active career ended and he was never promoted post-captain. Two years before Horatio first puffed up the hill above English Harbour, Commander Pemble had asked to be transferred from Whitehaven to a vacancy in the Newcastle impress service, nearer his roots. Perhaps he sensed his life was closing. The switch was made, but Pemble died on 17 May

1784, and his wife, though only fifty-seven or so, also died within the year.[21]

Doubtless because of their father, both the Pemble girls married naval officers. Catherine took a relative, Captain Gerard Selby, and was widowed in 1779. On 2 September 1771, when Mary was about twenty-one, she stood before members of her family in Berwick-on-Tweed to marry John Moutray, a man nearly thirty years her senior. They moved to London, where the intelligent and immensely personable young woman mixed easily in genteel society. Relatives of the Marquess of Lothian and the Duke of Richmond would one day speak for her, and in 1773 Admiral Hood acted as godfather to her son James. To the end of her life Mary attracted. The novelist Maria Edgeworth, who lived close by during Mary's later years in Ireland, was impressed by her positive attitude and 'usual amiable temper and good sense', and so charmed by her wit and spontaneity that she described her as 'our Irish Madame de Sévigné'. Looking at her in 1784, Nelson beheld the mother of engaging eleven-year-old twins, James and Kate, and a woman of considerable personality and beauty. Mrs Moutray was slender, with a high, open forehead, straight nose, delicate face and light hair and eyes. Before long she had captivated both Collingwood and Nelson, the one a fellow Northumbrian two or three years her senior and the other seven or eight years her junior.[22]

Collingwood weakened first, for it was he who had brought out the Moutrays with their servants and baggage in the *Mediator* the previous year. In the course of the long passage between Portsmouth and Antigua, Mary had penetrated the captain's natural northern reserve and dissipated his annoyance at the inconvenience of carrying passengers. Thereafter, especially in May 1784 when the *Mediator* was being overhauled in English Harbour, Collingwood became what Mary called 'a beloved brother in our house' and enjoyed rare moments of domesticity. He would correspond with Mary until his death, remembering how she had allowed him 'to frizzle your head for a ball dress at Antigua'.[23]

The Nelsons too, Horatio and William, soon attended her, though she must have marvelled at the contrasts between the thin and taciturn naval officer and his garrulous, robust and grasping brother. Mary chided the parson about his friendship for an heiress he knew, Dorothea Scrivener, and soothed the distraught Horatio. As early as 24 September she had the captain writing that 'was it not for Mrs Moutray, who is *very very* good to me, I should almost hang myself at this infernal hole'. Later he movingly spoke of the times he had shared with 'a treasure of a woman' on the hill, where the close leaves and profuse branches of a beloved tamarind tree had screened them from the burning sun as they surveyed the magnificent blue harbour below. It was a place, he said, 'where I spent more happy days than in any one spot in the world.'[24]

Nelson was probably motivated by psychological dependency more than lust. Throughout his life he needed attention, and to feel valued and important. He resented indifference or neglect, but soared mightily upon recognition and praise, a drive that influenced both his professional and private relations. It drove him to become a public hero, made him susceptible to the grossest flatteries and deepened his vulnerability to women. Their interest and attentions, however innocent, encouraged his sense of self-importance, and assuaged his insecurities. At any time he would have been vulnerable to Mary, but at this time, in friendless Antigua, his isolation made her devastating. Mary became a lifeline. Where several others learned to avoid him, burned by his fiery interpretation of duty, she liked him, talked to him about his life and opinions, and proved that he mattered. In an ocean of indifference and some hostility she was an island of consideration, and he was drawn irresistibly back to her.

Commissioner Moutray was by no means ignorant of the goings-on between his wife and the two naval officers, and like many an elderly man thus placed sensed his own insecurity. Compared with Collingwood and Nelson, Moutray lacked talent, prospect and youth. He must have understood the attractions they possessed for someone of his wife's age, attractions that he had lost long before. After all, all three belonged to the same generation and he could have been their father. But whatever flirting that went on remained within bounds, and Commissioner Moutray seems to have kept his suspicions to himself.

Perhaps the most attractive story of the strange situation at Windsor tells how Collingwood and Nelson painted each other's portraits under Mary's approving eye. Nelson was suffering from one his fevers and had lost much of his hair. Turning to the less than expert services of the local perruquier, he secured an ill-fitting wig that occasioned much merriment among associates. 'I must draw you, Nelson – in that wig!' Collingwood declared one day, and with evident heavy-handedness eventually produced a miniature profile. It was a primitive composition, but at least preserved some of its subject's obvious physical characteristics. Surveying the unflattering result with good-humoured dissatisfaction, Nelson replied, 'And now, Collingwood, in revenge I will draw you in that queue of yours!' Taking watercolours and a small piece of paper the captain of the *Boreas* proved himself a rather more proficient amateur, and supplied a pleasing monochrome portrait – his only known sortie into art, but one that suggested undeveloped skills. Mary kept both pictures, but at the end of her life searched for a safe haven and gave them to Sarah Collingwood, the admiral's daughter. These remarkable mementos of English Harbour may still be seen in the National Maritime Museum at Greenwich.[25]

When the hurricane season of 1784 was finally spent the ships prepared for sea. Sir Richard planned to take the squadron to Barbados, where bread might be had, and then to direct the captains to their different stations. Before leaving Antigua he hosted a 'grand dinner' on the last day of October, though Nelson thought it a great nuisance. The Moutrays made it bearable, but Nelson's hunger for activity probably raised his spirits when he sailed with the squadron the following day.[26]

5

Out at sea Hughes exercised his ships in 'different manoeuvres and evolutions' before reaching Barbados on 6 November and reuniting with the *Mediator* and *Rattler*. The admiral lodged at Constitution Hill, and amidst preparations for a personal inspection of his station issued orders for the men-of-war under his command. Nelson was to patrol the northern islands with Wilfred Collingwood's *Rattler*, and to call at the island of St John in the Virgins to see whether it offered wood, water and shelter.[27]

While the *Boreas* was being fitted out an altercation between two of Nelson's young officers resulted in a pistol ball cutting through the stomach of George Andrews and lodging in his back. Nelson was distressed by the tragic dispute between two of his 'children'. Andrews had joined the ship late, arriving from England in the *Unicorn* in July, but he had been making good progress. Perhaps he created tensions among youths who had already bonded or formed some kind of pecking order. Whatever the case, without telling any superiors four of them went ashore and Andrews and Thomas Stansbury exchanged shots. Close to death, Andrews was confined to a hospital bed in Barbados while Stansbury and his second, William Oliver, were confined in the *Boreas*, dismally reflecting on how their own lives now also hung by a thread. Fortunately Andrews returned to duty in April, and Stansbury and Oliver were transferred to other ships to preserve harmony.[28]

It was while he was in Barbados that Nelson also first turned his mind to one of the most vexing questions of the day, the navigation laws. They had been the props of the mercantilist system since the seventeenth century, and endeavoured to create economic self-sufficiency within the empire by regulating trade between Britain and its overseas dependencies and shutting out rivals. Foreign trade was excluded from the colonies, and the empire bound into an interdependent network, with each territory producing only specifically enumerated goods to be purchased by the others. In that way competition could be reduced and markets ensured. Moreover, the navigation laws recognised the mutual dependence of trade and naval power. The navy protected Britain, her colonies and their trade, but equally relied upon that trade for the prosperity to maintain itself. The navigation laws went further, decreeing that all trade commodities be carried in ships built in Britain or her dependencies (in 'British bottoms' rather than 'foreign bottoms'), and predominantly manned by their citizens. Thus the acts encouraged two of the crucial foundations of naval power, a thriving shipbuilding industry and the maintenance of a pool of experienced seamen. Given the fundamental way in which the acts linked trade and the wellbeing of the navy, it was perhaps natural that patriotic sea officers would be fiercely protective of them.

Acts of 1660 and 1696 enjoined naval officers to enforce the navigation acts, but the job was difficult and the American War of Independence introduced a new problem. Before the war the American colonies had enjoyed a profitable trade with the British West Indian islands, a legal trade protected by the navigation laws. The islands particularly relied upon the mainland colonies for inexpensive lumber and food, and in their turn supplied sugar and rum. But the rebellion threatened to end that traffic, for it made the Americans foreigners and liable to exclusion. In London the matter became clear. The navigation laws now excluded American merchants from the British islands, which now needed to turn for their timber and grain to the developing colonies of Nova Scotia and the Canadas. It was the duty of the navy to expel or seize any American vessels engaging in contraband trade.

But the West Indian communities saw it differently. Recovering from the disruption and expense of the American war, and plagued by a succession of appalling harvests, they were only interested in restoring prosperity. The essential goods supplied by the Americans were not readily available elsewhere, since the Canadian colonies, even fortified by an influx of American Loyalists, were sparsely populated and economically underdeveloped. Moreover, the established bonds between former trade partners could not be easily broken. Not all of the American traders who continued to fraternise with the British West Indian islands after the war were the out-and-out 'rebels' described by Nelson and his associates. Some, whose livelihoods depended upon maintaining commercial links with the British possessions, had sympathised with the crown during the revolution, or at least broken away with less than wholehearted enthusiasm. When the war ended they wanted to resume a relationship of patently mutual benefit. Some resented the way politics had intruded upon, and threatened, their economic security and peace.

The British government was not entirely unaware of these sentiments or the difficulties of a strict enforcement of the navigation laws. In 1784 a commission considered restoring relationships between the former American colonies and the islands, but the hard line was reaffirmed. That intransigence did nothing to endear the mandarins of Whitehall to the islanders. In fact, it stimulated disaffection, and in 1789 the Jamaican assembly denied that Parliament was 'competent to destroy' or 'partially to mutilate private properties'. Ultimately, it also failed. Jamaica unilaterally authorised a free trade with the United States, and in 1787 Britain had to declare Jamaica, Dominica, Grenada and New Providence to be free ports open to necessities from Spanish vessels, although even then there was no relaxation of the laws in respect to American commerce.[29]

Nelson and the Collingwoods saw few complications. Wise leaders understand that those who would rule effectively need to protect the interests of the governed in order to gain their consent, and are aware of the considerations and compromises that are needed to secure loyalty and affection. But junior naval officers were not required to be statesmen; theirs was simply to obey political masters. Nelson imposed the navigation laws without distinction, as if a square peg could always be sledge-hammered into a round hole, and without understanding. As far as he and the Collingwoods were concerned, any trade with the Americans was treasonable and beyond contempt. The Americans were rebels, guilty of an ungrateful uprising against the British crown, and had disqualified themselves from the benefits of the intercolonial trade. In fact, lacking abler direction, Nelson and the Collingwoods exhibited the same dogmatism, inflexibility and aggression that had contributed to their country's loss of the American colonies, and their language often reflected the strength of their ill-considered opinions. When Wilfred Collingwood of the *Rattler* came upon an American ship at the British island of St Kitts in the spring of 1784 he reportedly called the master 'a damned Yankee rascal', and swore, 'by God, you shall not lie in this bay!'[30]

In Barbados the issue began to crackle ominously. Nelson had a sharp eye for the enforcement of the navigation laws, partly because it relieved the tedium of his commission, but overwhelmingly from a sense of duty. In Antigua he had seen foreigners unloading their cargoes, and on the voyage to Barbados boarded a Boston vessel and apparently told its master that he had no business sailing for the British island of St Kitts. At Barbados officers familiar with the station fuelled Nelson's concern by telling him that while an illicit American trade was flourishing, no orders to check it had been received. Admiral Hughes, it seemed, believed the matter best left to civil governors and revenue officers.

Too often Nelson's attack on the navigation laws and his looming dispute with the admiral about Commissioner Moutray's distinguishing pendant have been seen in isolation. It is as though a young and principled officer, perhaps an overzealous one, almost single-handedly inspired a revolt against his commander-in-chief and the civil authorities. The Collingwoods, though his coadjutors, are generally represented to be followers rather than instigators. It is certainly true that Nelson became the most outspoken and least compromising of the rebel captains, but the papers of Cuthbert Collingwood show him to have been a full partner in the affair. On both issues of the navigation laws and Moutray's pendant he independently reached the same conclusions as Nelson, and acted firmly if occasionally more tactfully. Indeed, it was Collingwood, not Nelson, who first stirred the controversy about the navigation laws. In August he had alerted Sir Richard to the illicit trade being conducted at Grenada.[31]

When the admiral's new orders came, dispersing the ships about the islands, Nelson had food for thought. He was to reconnoitre the Virgin Islands for useful anchorages and patrol St Kitts, Nevis and Montserrat, but there was nothing about contraband trade. With Collingwood beside him Nelson confronted Sir Richard about the

matter on 10 November. The admiral, an inherently benign old-fashioned gentleman, explained that he had neither orders nor acts of
Parliament from England regarding the navigation laws. Nelson, by
his own account, said that if such was the case it was 'very odd'
because he understood that every captain was equipped with copies
of the Admiralty statutes as a matter of course. Producing his own,
he read the significant passages to the admiral. The next day the two
captains were back with a copy of the appropriate Navigation Act
itself. Sir Richard wavered, and on 12 November amended his orders.
His officers were now instructed to enforce the navigation laws during
the course of their other duties. Nelson needed no more encouragement. When Hughes left on the 16th to tour his station, Nelson became
the senior officer in Barbados, and several American merchantmen
entering Carlisle Bay the following day were summarily ordered out.[32]

On 21 November the *Boreas* weighed anchor and sailed for the
Virgins, reaching St John four days later. Scraping the stern of his frigate
over a coral reef, he managed to chart the anchorage on the east coast
of the island, sounding the finger-like coves in what is now the Hurricane
Hole of Coral Bay. Then he returned to Barbados, where there were
more American vessels to be turned away. Throughout these perambulations, the image of Mrs Moutray continued to interrupt the new
campaign in Nelson's mind. He could not free it of her, and used English
Harbour both to and from his voyage to the Virgins – on 22–23
November and 3–5 December. 'You may be certain I never passed
English Harbour without a call,' he confided to his brother.[33]

The close of the year saw Nelson flitting back and forth. First he
returned to Carlisle Bay, where he visited the hospital and learned that
young Andrews would be ready for duty in about a month. Then he
anchored in English Harbour on Christmas Eve to share seasonal cheer
with the Moutrays. And on the third day of 1785 he was on the other
side of Antigua, in the roadstead at St John's, where he briefly conferred
with Collingwood before setting out to patrol the other islands. What
Collingwood told him made Nelson realise that the enforcement of
the navigation laws was going to be no simple matter. The two coadjutors had seized a lion by the tail.[34]

6

Both the Collingwood boys had been assiduously searching for foreign
interlopers since leaving Barbados. Wilfred, for example, had found

American ships trading at St Kitts with the apparent collusion of the island's customs officials. It seemed to Nelson that as soon as the navy was out of sight, the illicit traders sneaked back, shielded by many individuals who were charged with suppressing them. Cuthbert Collingwood of the *Mediator* related a whole saga about his experiences at Antigua the previous month.

All sorts of irregularities were afoot, Collingwood said. The *Fair American* was cleared by the customs in St John's, though it was reported to Collingwood that the ship was owned in Philadelphia. Another vessel, the *Royal Midshipman*, was also fully accredited ashore, yet a naval officer who boarded her said the crew were American sailors, a clear breach of the navigation laws. Collingwood was convinced that customs and other officials, as well as merchants, were shielding the contraband trade once it got to anchor, and his best chance of keeping the foreigners out was by stopping them entering port in the first place.[35]

But in pursuing this tactic Collingwood had caused a furore in St John's. He stopped an American sloop, the *Liberty*, entering port. Her master said he needed to repair a mast, but Collingwood supposed him to be merely feigning distress to gain unlawful entry. Once in port, the master would either supply false registration papers to effect British ownership, be furnished with such papers by colluding islanders or contrive a sham trade by selling his cargo to pay for supposed repairs. Collingwood therefore ordered the *Liberty* alongside his *Mediator*, where an inspection seemed to confirm the captain's suspicions, and the sloop was turned away.

Soon angry merchants were complaining to the governor of the Leeward Islands, Thomas Shirley, that the *Mediator* was blockading St John's. If Collingwood regarded the officials and traders as a nest of rebels conspiring to frustrate the navigation laws, they had as little use for him. When the captain defended his conduct, Shirley submitted his justifications to Messrs Burton and Byam, respectively a king's counsel and the attorney-general for Grenada, and received an unequivocally hostile response. Rowland Burton was also the speaker of the island assembly and hand in glove with Shirley, who would help him to become chief justice of Antigua in 1786, while Ashton Warner Byam belonged to one of the most influential families in the islands. They agreed that His Majesty's customs, not naval officers, were responsible for determining the legal standing of vessels in port, and their investigations in the case of the *Royal Midshipman* were to be preferred to the 'mere hearsay' promulgated by Collingwood. Samuel Martin, the collector of customs in St John's, was 'zealous' and 'vigilant'. Certainly, the navy was charged with apprehending illicit traders outside of the jurisdiction of ports, but the legal wiseacres pointed out that a law of 1764 allowed foreign ships to remain in or about British possessions for forty-eight hours after receiving notice to leave, and that nothing could interfere with the time-honoured right of ships in distress to seek a haven. Collingwood's actions were 'repugnant to this established benign usage of nations'.[36]

Governor Shirley was caught between two fires, with the islanders on one side and the navy apparently on the other. Yet everyone admitted that some irregularities were occurring. Even the collector of customs conceded that the *Liberty*'s register was out of order, her master was an American and that had it not been for her alleged distress she would have been 'inadmissible'. Consequently, the governor looked for a way of investigating the claims of American ships without alienating either the customs or the navy. He addressed Collingwood, who appeared to be the eye of the storm, 'hinting . . . in a friendly manner' that injured ships should always be allowed shelter, and notifying his superior, Admiral Hughes, of the 'disquiet and dissatisfaction' among the merchants. Somewhat testily he asked Hughes what instructions the government had sent relating to the navigation laws, and why the admiral had not conferred with him about how they might be implemented without antagonising the people.[37]

This kicked the complacent Hughes into action. He decided to revise his order of 12 November, the one Nelson and Collingwood had previously pressed upon him. The superseding instruction was dated 30 December 1784. It said that if foreign ships attempted to enter British ports, naval captains and commanders should intercept them and assess any alleged damage, as Collingwood had done. But the final decision to admit would rest with the governor of Antigua or his representatives in the other islands, the presidents of their local councils. The naval officers were merely required to submit their reports and hold the foreign ship pending a decision by the aforementioned civil authorities.[38]

The revised order reached Nelson at St Kitts, where the locals were growing alarmed. On 7 January the council at Basseterre complained that the actions of the Collingwoods portended 'great distress' to the islanders, and resolved to petition Shirley and Hughes for 'such relief as may be in their power to grant'. The next day the council decided to petition the home government to allow the import of foodstuffs and the use of small American vessels to export indigenous produce. But Nelson and his allies were in no mood to relent. He had been patrolling the northern islands warning away foreign ships. In January Nelson interrupted the *Fanny* of Connecticut unloading illicit cargo on one of the islands and firmly ordered her out, and at St Kitts he came across the sloop *Rattler* and listened to Commander Wilfred Collingwood's stories of similar transgressions. When the captain of the *Boreas* read Hughes's revised order and learned that such cases were to be referred to the civil authorities, he exploded.[39]

Hughes, following Shirley's suggestions, had sought a middle way, but to Nelson it was a simple abrogation of the responsibilities the navigation laws had placed upon the navy. It was worse than that, for Hughes's orders placed the final decision with those least equipped to take it – the civil authorities Nelson believed to be colluding with the illegal traders. From everything he had learned the customs officials encouraged these misdemeanours, supplementing their own incomes by the fees they charged to supply false registers to interlopers and facilitating their transactions. Nor did he trust the governor of Antigua, who, he recalled had once forwarded a petition of the assembly for a relaxation of the navigation laws to Lord Sydney, the British secretary of state. In Nelson's eyes Shirley was suspect. He might have been corrupted, or at least deceived and turned into an instrument of the illegal trade lobby.

Technically, Nelson was obliged to obey his superior officer. If he doubted the wisdom or legality of the admiral's orders, he might voice his reservations and if necessary refer them to the Admiralty for a definitive opinion, but it was his duty to abide by the received instructions in the meantime. But he chose confrontation instead. On 9 January he wrote a lecturing and subversive reply to his commander-in-chief, declaring that he would be no party to the revised procedure. American merchants were inventing all sorts of pretexts to enter British ports and swearing their innocence 'through a nine-inch plank', and public officials were collaborating with or ignoring the practice. 'The governor may be imposed on by false declarations,' raged the young captain. 'We, who are on the spot, cannot.' Nelson left Hughes in no doubt that neither Shirley nor his representatives in the islands could be trusted, and that he held their legal advice to be worthless:

Whilst I have the honour to command an English man-of-war, I never shall allow myself to be subservient to the will of any governor, nor cooperate with him in doing illegal acts. Presidents of Council I feel myself superior to. They shall make proper application to *me* for whatever they want to come by water. If I rightly understand your order of 29 [30] December, it is founded upon an opinion of the king's attorney-general [Byam], viz. 'That it is legal for governors or their representatives to admit foreigners into the ports of their government if they think fit.' How the king's attorney-general conceives he has a right to give an illegal opinion, which I assert the above is, he must answer for. I *know* the Navigation Law.[40]

This riposte was a bombshell to Hughes, and amounted to an outright refusal to obey his order of 30 December. Professionally Nelson was skating on very thin ice, but Sir Richard's own position was little less unenviable. For though this immature firebrand was challenging his authority, his legal interpretation of the matter might conceivably be correct. After all, Nelson spoke confidently as well as loudly. If so, the commander-in-chief, rather than the captain, might be called to account.

A stronger admiral would have reduced Nelson to obedience, if necessary by court martial, but Hughes was not only unsure of himself but also a basically genial soul who knew the value of keeping his head down. More than that, he quickly realised that dissatisfaction with the new orders went beyond one man. On 13 January the elder Collingwood joined the protest. In a long letter to Hughes he railed at a confederacy of American merchants, West Indian landowners looking for ways to escape debts, and 'those in office [who] taste the sweets of exorbitant fees, and forget their trust or betray it'. Unlike Nelson, the captain of the *Mediator* stopped short of refusing to obey the revised instructions, but he forcefully argued that the enforcement of the navigation laws lay solely with the navy, and that captains were responsible to their admirals, not governors. No longer able to dismiss Nelson as a lone voice, Sir Richard stopped stirring the pot.[41]

Horatio was also sensing his vulnerability, but had no intention of yielding. Pouring his heart out to Locker, he said that Hughes had 'not that opinion of his own sense that he ought to have' and had allowed himself to be manipulated by Shirley and vested interests. But Nelson, 'for one', would not be intimidated. Groping towards some political justification of the navigation laws, he ventured that if the American trade was allowed, the colony of Nova Scotia would be cut out and the political complexion of the West Indian islands become treasonable. 'The residents of these islands are American by connexion and by interest, and are inimical to Great Britain.' Some tortuous logic allowed him to believe that the loyalty of the islands could be improved by bludgeoning them into accepting trading conditions for the benefit of Nova Scotia rather than themselves. Yet his moral courage was undeniable. 'I have not had a foot in any house since I have been on the station,' he said with his usual exaggeration, 'and all for doing my duty by being true to the interests of Great Britain.'[42]

By the end of January 1785 Captain Nelson was engaged in recriminatory correspondence with both his commander-in-chief and the governor of the Leeward Islands, and felt his isolation keenly. He leaned upon Collingwood, whose opinions buttressed his own, and the consoling warmth of Mrs Moutray. But black clouds were gathering even in that quarter, and when he returned to English Harbour on 5 February a second storm broke.

7

The admiral's revised order about the navigation laws was not the only unwelcome news that had overtaken Nelson at St Kitts.

Included in the very same package was another order of Sir Richard's, dated 29 December. It informed the captains that Commissioner Moutray had an 'especial commission' from the Admiralty authorising him 'to superintend and carry on the business' of English Harbour 'in the absence of a flag or senior officer', and to fly the broad distinguishing pendant of an active commodore proclaiming his authority over the other captains. In accordance with the practice established by his predecessors, Rodney and Pigot, Hughes required all officers to accept Moutray's orders when he himself was not in the port.[43]

The pendant cut Nelson to the quick. As far as he was concerned he – not Moutray – was second to the admiral. He was the senior serving captain 'in commission', and presided over courts martial, the accepted privilege of a second-in-command. Moutray's appointment as dockyard commissioner, on the other hand, was merely a civil one, made by the Navy Board rather than the Admiralty, and conferred no authority over active officers. In Nelson's view Hughes had blundered again. By elevating Moutray he confused civil with active appointments, and effectively demoted Nelson whenever he entered English Harbour.

Hughes was thoughtless, not malevolent: he had intended to serve Moutray rather than slight Nelson. In fact, previous admirals on the station had empowered naval commissioners without provoking complaints, and Hughes remembered that when he had himself been a naval commissioner at Halifax, Nova Scotia, in 1778, his instructions had explicitly authorised him to act as commander-in-chief when no 'flag' or 'senior' officers were present. Hughes, therefore, assumed that he was acting entirely within naval custom. He never asked to see Moutray's supposed 'especial commission', nor stopped to ponder the technicalities. For example, in Halifax Hughes had been both an active sea officer 'in commission' and a dockyard commissioner. Moutray, on the other hand, liked to wear his old naval uniform, but offered no proof that he held a commission as an active officer from the Admiralty.[44]

Sir Richard's misfortune was to command two bright young officers whose grasp of naval procedure and maritime law far exceeded his own. Nelson and Collingwood responded to the admiral's announcement about Moutray in the same breath as they protested his injunctions on the navigation laws. Their letters were double-barrelled blasts at Hughes's authority. Collingwood's protest was the most conciliatory. Though admitting Moutray's pendant 'quite an affliction', he assured the commander-in-chief that he had no wish 'to appear petulant and contentious' and suggested a way out of the difficulty. Moutray could not act as a commodore because he was not a serving officer; very well, then Collingwood would temporarily make him one by entering him as a supernumerary on the books of the *Mediator* every time the ship entered English Harbour. In that way, Collingwood felt he could obey the commissioner's orders without creating an irregularity.[45]

Nelson, however, rejected Moutray's authority outright. 'I beg leave to say that whenever he [Moutray] is in commission as commodore or captain I must obey him,' he wrote to Hughes on 9 January. 'It is my duty, and I shall have great pleasure in serving under him. Till then, as a [dockyard] commissioner, I never will obey any order of his. I should lower the rank of the service, and be unworthy to have a command in it.' Notwithstanding Hughes's order, he would continue to regard himself as the station's second-in-command: 'all officers . . . who are junior to me must obey my orders.' His letter was deeply offensive to Hughes, for it did more than decline to obey. First, it dismissed and clearly disbelieved the commander-in-chief's statement that Moutray had a special commission from the Admiralty; and second, by declaring that he could only comply with Hughes's orders by acting unworthily he was accusing the admiral himself of being unworthy.[46]

Perhaps Sir Richard hoped the problem would go away, but it didn't. No one did anything about the pendant dispute, in written word or deed . . . until the *Boreas* put back into English Harbour on 5 February 1785.

Sure enough, there was Moutray's pendant, flying from the *Latona* as if the commissioner was a commodore with authority over the squadron. Nelson was in a quandary, partly because he saw a showdown coming and partly because of his friendship for the Moutrays, man and wife. He must have worried about Mary, and what would happen if an open quarrel developed between himself and her husband?

The next day aggrieved messages flew back and forth. Nelson drafted one to Sandys of the *Latona*, upbraiding him for not paying the respects due to the senior captain arriving in port. In other words, poor Sandys must repudiate the pretended authority of Moutray and publicly acknowledge Nelson's supremacy.

Another of the messages Nelson received from the commissioner himself, upset at the *Boreas*'s failure to salute his pendant. Moutray was obviously still ignorant of Nelson's opinions. Styling himself a 'commander-in-chief' he referred to Hughes's instructions and required Nelson to place himself under orders. Nelson was ready with his answer. Enclosing a copy of his vitriolic letter to Hughes, he assured Moutray of his 'personal esteem' but stated unequivocally that he could accept no orders from him until he was placed in commission.[47]

Like Hughes, the wounded commissioner suffered with dignity. He shammed amicability, inviting Captain Nelson to dinner as usual, and allowing Mary to steer the conversation to safe ground with her exceptional dexterity. We must suppose that Nelson tried to explain, but he certainly held his ground and on the morning of the 7th called the captain of the *Latona* to account. Sandys had continued to act as Moutray's flag captain, and flew signals on his behalf. When he called for the naval commanders to send details of their ships to the commissioner, Nelson peremptorily ordered him to the *Boreas*.[48]

It was an uncomfortable moment for the junior captain. He was several years older than Nelson and had been his superior on the *Lowestoffe*, but ever since he had been falling behind and winning little respect from colleagues. Then in hot pursuit of one of the Eliot sisters, he was often ashore and even more often drunk and incapable. Nelson liked but pitied him. 'Little Sandys, poor fellow, between Bacchus and Venus, is scarcely ever thoroughly in his senses,' he said. 'I am very sorry for him, for his heart is good, but he is not fit to command a man-of-war . . . such men hurt the service more than it is in the power of ten good ones to bring back.' Sandys was no stranger to Nelson's forgiving nature, but knew he was in trouble as he warily climbed aboard the *Boreas* to the customary shrill of pipes.[49]

Inside the captain's cabin Nelson came directly to the point. 'Have you any order from Sir Richard Hughes to wear a broad pendant?' he asked.

'No,' replied the embarrassed Sandys.

'For what reason do you then wear it in the presence of a senior officer?' Nelson continued sternly.

'I hoisted it by order of Commissioner Moutray,' Sandys blurted out.

'Have you seen by what authority Commissioner Moutray was empowered to give you orders?' Nelson asked.

'No,' admitted the other miserably.

'Sir,' said Nelson grimly, 'you have acted wrong to obey any man who you do not know is authorised to command you.'

Sandys had no retreat. 'I feel I have acted wrong,' he confessed, 'but being a young [junior] captain did not think it proper to interfere in this matter, as there were you and other older [senior] officers upon this station.'

Nelson did not order the wretched fellow to haul the pendant down and Sandys sailed the next day. The *Boreas* followed shortly afterwards, heading for Barbados to collect Andrews from hospital. In reporting to Hughes Nelson referred to Moutray's pendant but simply declared 'he did not think [it] proper to pay the least attention' to it.[50]

Nelson seldom saw himself as he appeared to others. Only recently he had written of a fellow captain, 'I do not like him at all. He is a self-conceited young man.' That, in truth, was how Hughes was now seeing Nelson: someone stuffed with opinions, constantly questioning or refusing orders, and, most terrifying of all, entirely capable of exposing incompetence in a commander-in-chief. All Hughes wanted to do was to survive his tour of duty with the minimum aggravation. Now Moutray was also complaining to him. He had raised the distinguishing pendant 'in consequence of your several orders to me', wailed the commissioner, but Captain Nelson had refused to recognise it.[51]

Reluctantly, Sir Richard tackled the firebrand again. On 14 February, when both were in Barbados, the admiral sent Nelson a letter. In it he repeated his claim that Moutray had a 'special commission' from the Admiralty, and said his authority to act as commodore was 'comformable to the example of two late commanders-in-chief, my predecessors of high rank employed upon this station'. Hughes was plainly angry. 'Why you should . . . judge that it was not your duty to pay any attention to that distinguishing pendant, or to receive any orders from Commodore Moutray, I cannot possibly conceive . . .'[52]

The water was beginning to boil around Captain Nelson and his reply was more conciliatory. He wrote a vindication of his conduct for the Admiralty, and begged Hughes to do him the justice of forwarding it. Hughes probably had not wanted the issue to reach their lordships back home, but now Nelson left him no choice. In his official report he made light of Nelson's objections. It was true, for example, that the captain of the *Boreas* had presided over courts martial, but only when Hughes himself was on the station; Moutray's acting powers became applicable solely when the admiral was away. However, Hughes let slip one interesting admission. Moutray, he said, had told him that he had 'the same additional powers as had been vested in the hands of his predecessor, Commissioner [John] Laforey, namely with an especial commission from the Board of Admiralty, authorising and requiring him in the absence of a flag or senior officer to superintend and carry on the duty of the port . . . and . . . to take under his command such of His Majesty's ships or vessels of war as might occasionally arrive'. Thus, it appears, Hughes himself had never actually seen Moutray's supposed commission, but depended only upon precedent and hearsay.[53]

The affair of the pendant had unsettled more people than it was worth. Moutray felt rejected and bleated to Hughes, while Hughes, who had taken Moutray at his word, felt vulnerable and challenged. Nelson and Collingwood rejected the story about the special commission and thought their status was being undermined. And in between was the hapless Sandys, ducking and diving to avoid brickbats from both sides. It had become a tragicomedy and an entirely unnecessary one. For the truth was that Moutray really *did* have a commission from the Admiralty.

It was dated 25 July 1783 and designated Moutray 'commander-in-chief, in the absence of a flag officer or senior captain, of such of His Majesty's ships and vessels as shall, at any time, be at Barbadoes or the Leeward Islands'. He was empowered to expedite the dispatch of ships making use of the dockyard; 'to oblige their commanders' to return to their sea-going duties as soon as possible; and to request details of ships using the dockyard, just as Moutray had attempted to do through the luckless Sandys. He was even authorised to keep naval commanders afloat and prevent them dallying ashore if he thought it would restore their ships to service more speedily. If Moutray had produced this commission much, if not all, of the heat about the pendant would have dispersed. The whole storm had been brewed by poor communications in a climate of pride and distrust.[54]

Nelson was beginning to appreciate the danger of being branded unreliable and insubordinate, but the Admiralty's view when it came – that he should have submitted his doubts about Moutray's status to the admiral, rather than taken unilateral action – was not expressed forcefully. To the board, far away and ignorant of the wider difficulties between Nelson and his commander-in-chief, the issue seemed trivial. And in the event it disappeared as quickly as it had blown in, for while Nelson was still in Carlisle Bay in Barbados he received a letter in a small, neat hand that sloped forward in a way he knew well.

What Mary wrote shocked him. The Moutrays were going home.

8

The commissioner's health had not, as he expected, borne up well in the West Indian climate, but that was not the reason for his return. Now that the war was over, the lords of the Admiralty had decided to scale down the dockyard at Antigua and withdraw its naval commissioner. Moutray's post was struck down by the economic benefits of the peace.

Collingwood had been expecting it, dolefully. 'I shall miss them grievously,' he told his sister. 'She [Mrs Moutray] is quite a delight, and makes many an hour cheerful that without her would be dead weight.'[55]

Nelson was devastated. His behaviour towards the commissioner now seemed irrelevant and churlish, a spiteful act against a sick old man near the end of his career. Worse still, Horatio suddenly contemplated the emptiness that Mary would leave behind. As he told William a few days later,

I am not to have much comfort. My dear, sweet friend is going home. I am really an April day, happy on her account, but truly grieved were I only to consider myself. Her equal I never saw in any country or in any situation. She always talks of you, and hopes (if she comes within your reach) you will not fail visiting her. If my dear Kate goes to Bath next winter, she will be known to her, for my dear friend has promised to make herself known. What an acquisition to any female to be acquainted with. What an example to take pattern from! [Commissioner] Moutray has been very ill. It would have been necessary he should have quitted this country had he not been recalled.

The sense of impending loss did not blind Nelson to the other gossip on the Leeward Islands station.

Come [he told William] I must carry you to our love scenes. Captain Sandys has asked Miss Eliot – *refused*. Captain Sterling [Stirling] was attentive to Miss Elizabeth Eliot, but never having asked the question, Captain Berkeley is, I hear, to be the happy man. Captain Kelly is attached to a lady at Nevis, so he says. I don't much think it. He is not steady enough for that passion to hold long. All the Eliot family spent their Christmas at Constitution Hill – came up in *Latona*. The *Boreas*, you guessed right, [was] at English Harbour. Rosy [Hughes] has had no offers. I fancy she seems hurt at it. Poor girl! You should have offered; I have not gallantry enough. A niece of Governor Parry's [of Barbados] is come out. She goes to Nevis in the *Boreas*. They trust any young lady with me, being an old-fashioned fellow.[56]

Mary Moutray looked forward to England but promised to write to Nelson and Collingwood, and started packing the family possessions. Nelson sailed north again towards her, and on 26 February anchored in English Harbour for a precious thirteen days. Collingwood joined them on 7 March for a final rendezvous, and three days later the *Boreas* slipped out of harbour after a difficult parting. 'My sweet amiable friend sails the 20th for England,' wrote her captain. 'I took my leave of her with a heavy heart three days ago. What a *treasure* of a woman. God bless her.'[57]

Collingwood remained about the island for a dozen more days and saw Mary again. When she gave him a purse, which she had made as a 'trifle' keepsake, the stern sea captain was moved to verse:

Your net shall be my care, my dear,
For length of time to come,
While I am faint and scorching here,
And you rejoice at home.
To you belongs the wondrous art
To shed around your pleasure;
New worth to best of things impart,
And make of trifles – treasure!⁵⁸

For some time Nelson's own heartaches remained, mixing promiscuously with other troubles. He called at Dominica on Locker's business, but found the house Admiral Parry had bequeathed him levelled and the soil round about unprofitable, and the problem of the navigation laws refused to go away. With Mary gone, everything irritated him. The people in the islands were 'a sad set', he concluded. 'Yesterday, being St Patrick's day, the Irish colours with thirteen stripes in them was hoisted all over the town [St Kitts]. I was engaged to dine with the President, but sent an excuse, as he suffered those colours to fly. I mention it only to show the principle of these vagabonds.'⁵⁹

Returning to English Harbour was the hardest of all. At seven in the morning of 26 April the ship anchored below Windsor once again. Sometime during the day, in moderate weather punctuated by an occasional stiff breeze, he climbed the hill for the last time and reflected mournfully about the empty house. It was silent in the sunlight, but in Horatio's mind still echoed with the ghostly laughter of the woman he had loved and lost. 'This country appears now intolerable, my dear friend being absent,' he told William. 'It is barren indeed. Not all the Rosys can give a spark of joy to me. English Harbour I hate the sight of, and Windsor I detest. I went once up the hill to look at the spot where I spent more happy days than in any one spot in the world. Even the trees drooped their heads, and the tamarind tree died. All was melancholy. The road is covered with thistles. Let them grow. I shall never pull one of them up. By this time I hope she is safe in old England. Heaven's choicest blessing[s] go with her. We go on here but sadly.'⁶⁰

He consoled himself by anticipating her letters, anxious at the time that passed without them. Actually, Mary was beset with troubles of her own. In June 1785 the Moutrays went to Bath, where John hoped to recover his health. He applied for light work with the Navy Board or in one of the outposts, but did not get well, and he still worried about the relationship between his wife and the two captains across the Atlantic. When Mary wrote to them, he (or someone) broke the wafers sealing both letters before they were posted. 'They are welcome to read mine,' Nelson observed to Collingwood. 'It was all goodness, like the dear writer.'[61]

John Moutray died at Bath on 22 November. By the terms of her marriage settlement, signed at Berwick two days before her wedding, Mary had a pension of £150 per annum on Roxobie and four other properties in Scotland, willed by her husband to their children. She also inherited the use of furniture, plate and linen for the period of her life. But with two youngsters to bring up, the future looked bleak, and she petitioned the Admiralty for an allowance. It was refused, and Mary's second letter to Horatio was 'full of affliction and woe' and talked about retiring to France, where the cost of living was cheaper. 'What has this poor dear soul undergone in one twelve months,' Nelson sighed. 'Lost father, mother, husband and part of her fortune, and left with two children.'[62]

Mary was supported by a generally positive outlook, however, and lived a long life. Her son James entered the navy, won the praise of Hood and Nelson, and died of a fever at the age of twenty-one. In October 1805 the surviving heir, his sister Catherine, sold the Scottish properties to William and John Adam (of the famous architect family) for about £9,000. Kate, as everyone called her, then married Thomas de Lacey, the archdeacon of Meath, in Sussex in 1806, although when she died some ten years later she appears to have been childless. Mary outlived them all. Her last decades were spent in Ireland, where she died in her ninety-first year in 1841.[63]

It is surprising that Mary, who was widowed in her mid-thirties, never remarried, and we are left to ponder what might have happened if Commissioner Moutray had died nine months earlier, in Antigua rather than Bath. The impression Mary had made on Nelson and Collingwood endured. A decade later Nelson leaped to her defence over 'a scandalous report', protesting that no more 'amiable woman or a better character exists on earth'. But his last letter to 'my dear Mrs Moutray', written in 1803, was a polite but terse nine-line affair. She had approached him in support of Lieutenant Edmund Wallis of the *Victory*, but while he agreed to be useful he squashed immediate prospects of promotion. His reply, neither offering nor soliciting personal news, suggests that the flame kindled in English Harbour had at last been extinguished.[64]

Not so with Cuthbert Collingwood, who corresponded warmly with Mary until his death in 1808. She asked for his portrait and keepsakes; he, though happily married with a family of his own, forever concerned himself in her affairs. Cruising off Toulon shortly before his death the ageing admiral wrote to her, 'I wish you had one of those fairy telescopes that can look into the hearts and souls of people a thousand leagues off. Then might you see how much you possess my mind, and how sincere an interest I take in whatever relates to your happiness, and that of your dear Kate.'[65]

One finds it impossible to disagree with writer Tom Pocock who voiced the opinion that if Mary had lost her husband in Antigua she might have married one of her naval admirers, but that person would probably have been Cuthbert Collingwood.

XIII

OLD OFFICERS AND YOUNG GENTLEMEN

'He was a thorn in our flesh,' came the reply –
'The most bird-witted, unaccountable,
Odd little runt that ever I did spy.'

Robert Graves, *1805*

1

MAJOR General Sir Thomas Shirley, captain general and governor-in-chief of His Majesty's Leeward Caribee Islands, was fifty-six and at the stage of life when an honourable and rewarding retirement looked attractive.

He had come to the islands from England, but colonial service was in his blood. Boston born, he was the son of Lieutenant General William Shirley, the governor of Massachusetts and commander-in-chief in North America at the outbreak of the Seven Years War. Both Thomas's older brothers had died defending Britain's North American empire, one with Braddock's ill-fated army, slaughtered by Indians and French on the Monongahela River in 1775, the other during a march from Oswego. Sir Thomas himself had been in the army since 1745, fought at Louisbourg, Minorca and Belle Isle, and commanded a regiment in Portugal. He had served as lieutenant governor of Dominica.

Since May 1781 Shirley had governed the Leeward Islands, and to him had fallen the task of protecting Antigua, Montserrat, St Kitts and Nevis during the last dangerous years of the American war. In February 1782 he had made a creditable though not uncriticised defence of Brimstone Hill against superior and ultimately overpowering French forces invading St Kitts. Both Nevis and St Kitts had fallen, but they were restored to Britain by the Peace of Paris, and Shirley resumed his stewardship from within the impressive walls of Clarke's Hill, his residence in St John's. Sir Thomas had enemies but he was widely respected in the islands, where he was known to be 'a mild and humane governor', but he was hoping to write a handsome finale to his full career. His wife had been dead some years, but he had a young son, William Warden, and before he withdrew to England he wanted to ennoble his posterity by petitioning the crown for the restoration of a family baronetcy extinct since 1705.[1]

Retirement would bring relief, for it had not taken Shirley long to discover that peace was sometimes little less turbulent than war. He was an astute man. In one of his earliest letters as governor, for example, he had drawn attention to the ecological consequences of deforestation, which he realised exposed and dehumidified the soil – a remarkably modern view. Unlike Horatio Nelson, the governor respected the islanders, and knew them to be fundamentally loyal to the crown. 'I have always met with a very cheerful concurrence on the part of this island to the requisitions I have occasionally made to them for the good of His Majesty's service and the protection of the colony,' he wrote. The local press was squarely loyal in sentiment, and fussed over royalty, and during the war the islanders had invested large sums in defence. Antigua alone had spent £88,000. Though their merchants had occasionally indulged in treasonable trade with foreigners, their motives had been commercial rather than political. After all, they needed Britain. Unlike the mainland American colonies, which were relatively secure from traditional European enemies after the conquest of New France, the islands were vulnerable to Spanish and French forces. They looked to the British crown for protection.[2]

But loyalty, Shirley knew, was not written in stone. If the rebellion in America had taught him anything it was that the empire could only thrive with the consent of the governed, and that was what was beginning to worry him about the navigation laws. Some of the island traders were doing well. With a monopoly of the British sugar market their exports were picking up nicely, though the rum trade, which depended more upon American outlets, was faltering. But there was a widespread perception that the crown's strict enforcement of the navigation laws spelled ruin.[3]

The truth was that Antigua was still impoverished. The war had disrupted trade, and forced the colonists to spend heavily on fortifications, improvements to the ports and the maintenance of extraordinary numbers of British troops. The embarrassments had coincided with a run of wretched harvests that year after year returned less than cost. In 1779–80 the distress was such that the crown granted a loan of £20,000, but though that money had to be repaid, the economy got no stronger. The sugar harvest of 1783 was only a tenth of what it had once been, and Antigua's debt to Britain stood at £38,000. In July the assembly begged the king to consider their many disbursements and seven years of drought,

the severity of which cannot be more justly described than by a detail of the disappointments and misery it has produced. Our crops have been destroyed, our labours and industry frustrated, our debts accumulated by a deprivation of the only means to reduce them. Families, falling from ease and affluence into penury and want, have been obliged to abandon the estates of their ancestors. Our lands, which when blessed with rains were fruitful and abounding, are become sterile, and debarred thereby of our usual resources, our expences in the cultivation of our plantations have continually increased. Such has been, and such still is, our situation, and this too at a time when the calls upon us for the defence of our country, and for the accommodation of your Majesty's garrison, required more than usual supplies. And at this unfortunate period, when your Majesty's faithful subjects thought the measure of their woes complete, they saw their metropolis [St John's] a second time in flames, and the most valuable parts of it, which had before escaped a similar conflagration, were now laid in ashes.[4]

Nor were these merely the words of paranoid planters. 'This country is poor, most of the landholders being impoverished from a series of bad crops previous to the last three years,' reported one visitor. 'In fact the greater part of the estates in this island are in trust or under mortgage to the merchants of London, Liverpool and Bristol.'[5]

Similar problems beset most of the other British West Indian islands, and just when the fractured American trade was beginning to return and relieve their battered economies, the issue of the navigation laws swept ominously in from the sea. Everywhere people worried that the exclusion of essential American supplies would dry up provisions, fuel inflation and blight recovery. There were riots in Barbados and St Kitts, noisy complaints in the press, inflammatory handbills and an increasing number of anti-British voices in the local assemblies. Petitions were prepared in the islands while in England in 1785 the

Society of West India Merchants and Planters lobbied Parliament for a committee of enquiry. Antigua begged the crown to rescind its debt, and in 1783 petitioned that 'foreign bottoms' be allowed to deliver provisions at moments of crisis.[6]

Appointed by the crown, Sir Thomas Shirley was ultimately responsible to the king for the enforcement of the navigation laws in the Leeward Islands, but his salary was voted by the Antiguan assembly, and his friends and the members of his advisory council belonged to the controlling planting class that expected him to articulate its grievances. At first Shirley doubted the navigation laws would do the islands much damage, and he had been unwise enough to say so in one of his dispatches home, but as his appreciation of the local predicament deepened he edged towards a compromise.

In February 1784 he forwarded a petition of the St Kitts assembly to ministers. It prayed that their ports be declared free and open to all. Shirley thought the measure 'beneficial', and pointed out that the island was well favoured; properly supported it might capture trade from the rival Dutch colony of St Eustatius with its open ports. At any rate, it merited 'the benignity and attention' of government 'in a very high degree' because of its 'strong and steady attachment . . . to His Majesty's service in many instances previous to, and during, its subjection to the arms of France' during the war. Like the other islands it was, he later added, groaning under 'a very heavy load of debt'. On 30 July Shirley even suggested that American vessels of a small tonnage be allowed into the islands, all of which 'depend very much on America for almost all kinds of trade . . .'[7]

Unfortunately, the temper and inclinations of the British government were tracing a different path. In 1783, during the dying days of Lord Shelburne's administration, Pitt indeed proposed a bill removing the restrictions upon commercial intercourse between the new American republic and the West Indies, but the government fell and the bill with it. Fears then spread that any relaxation of the navigation laws would ravage the British carrying trade and its 'nursery of seamen'. Lord Sheffield, a Member of Parliament, used a wealth of argument, statistics and a silver pen to rally the country behind the navigation laws in his famous tract, *Observations on the Commerce of the United States*, published in 1783. Sheffield was sure that the growth of Canada and Nova Scotia would meet the requirements of the West Indian islands, while the mother country herself would simultaneously benefit from a direct American trade. There was no need to threaten the country's naval resources by a hasty repeal of the navigation laws. In Antigua, therefore, Shirley found that whatever inclination to temporise had existed in Britain was evaporating. Few in London were interested in his plan for concessions.

Shirley had not given up hope, however. He received Lord Sydney's insistence on the full implementation of the navigation laws in January 1785, and warned that 'there is a great reason to apprehend that these islands will feel many inconveniences from the want of a regular supply of corn . . . and of some species of lumber, which last, for a time at least, our own colonies in North America [Canada] will not be able to furnish'. He asked for more directions.[8]

It was amidst this exchange that Governor Shirley first heard of the young, boyish looking captain of His Majesty's frigate *Boreas*. Horatio Nelson, bent upon a zealous self-righteous enforcement of the navigation laws, contemptuous of the islanders, whom he regarded as corrupt, self-seeking rebels, and beyond the control of his admiral, was unlikely to make a constructive contribution to the problem. A clash with him was almost inevitable.

It gathered quickly, beginning with Collingwood's interception of the American ship the *Liberty* trying to reach St John's in December 1784. Collingwood claimed the vessel was attempting to enter under the pretext of distress to unload its illegal cargo, and in return was accused by the islanders of blockading their port. Shirley had tried to establish an acceptable routine for handling such matters, and it was on his prompting that Admiral Hughes had revised his instructions to captains at the end of the month. As we have seen, those orders required foreign ships to be intercepted by the navy, and held in abeyance while their credentials, as well as the British captain's report, were submitted to the governor or his representatives. Ultimately, therefore, it was the governor who decided upon the propriety of the ship proceeding.

In January 1785 Nelson refused to obey the revised order, declaring that it was for the navy alone to determine whether foreign ships be allowed into British ports. The civil authorities, and by implication, Governor Shirley himself, could not be trusted. Nelson made a candid response to Hughes on 9 January, but for some time Shirley remained ignorant of the disagreement. Naturally he presumed that Hughes commanded his own officers. It was not until mid-January, when the governor wrote directly and innocently to Captain Nelson, begging 'leave' to suggest the 'surest mode' of putting Hughes's order into practice, that he himself came directly under fire.

Far from anticipating outrage, Shirley believed he was successfully marrying authority ashore and afloat. He had accepted that the claims of incoming foreign ships needed investigation, and that naval officers were qualified above all others to assess any alleged damage. Every foreign master seeking admission to a port would have to submit a report from the intercepting naval commander. Though the governor or his representative would be the final arbiter, Shirley promised Nelson that 'if it shall be very manifest that there is not a necessity for such vessels coming into port to repair . . . you would send them about their business'. It was through 'our joint endeavours' that the navigation laws could best be implemented.[9]

In fact, the day Shirley wrote his personal letter to Nelson, seeking to induct him into the new procedure, he also addressed the presidents of the councils in Nevis, St Kitts and Montserrat asking their cooperation. The Americans were now foreigners, he reminded those authorities, and enclosing copies of his letter to Captain Nelson urged them to 'aid him as much as lies in your power to carry the several acts of parliament relative to trade with foreigners into execution'. Shirley did not approve of the navigation laws, but his government had ordered him to enforce them and it was a matter of creating a uniform approach. There is no reason to doubt his integrity, though he underestimated the extent to which merchants and officials alike were prepared to shirk their duty and evade the legislation.[10]

Nelson, on the other hand, had the poorest possible opinion of the civil authorities. Most recently he had sent Wilfred Collingwood's *Rattler* to Sandy Point at St Kitts, where four American merchantmen were found on 14 January. Investigating, Collingwood uncovered a catalogue of irregularities, evasions and illegalities. The law only admitted ships that were British built and owned, and piloted by a British master and crew. But the American master of one of the ships claimed to be British purely on account of having served in British merchantmen during the war. Another of the four ships was the *Nancy*, owned by Seth Doane of New London. She had been to St Kitts, where she was turned into a 'British bottom' by purchase. Her cargo was sold to the Basdens, merchants of the island, and after an alleged sale the ship itself was re-registered at the customs house as a British vessel.

All four vessels, in one or more particulars, smashed holes through the navigation laws, and Wilfred Collingwood confronted Henry Bennett, the collector of customs at Sandy Point, demanding to know why they had been given registers authorising them to trade. Bennett was slippery. He did not defend all the illegal practices of which Collingwood complained, but was clearly at loggerheads over some important issues. The law required owners and masters to be British subjects, but Bennett was willing to accept the mere swearing of an oath of allegiance in lieu. He also had a liberal interpretation of what constituted a 'British bottom'. According to him, only American ships built *after* 1783, when the independence of the United States was formally recognised by Britain, were 'foreign bottoms'; those built during the War of Independence itself, between 1776 and 1783, could be accepted as British because at that time the colonists were simply rebellious subjects of the crown.

Wilfred Collingwood was not a man to be put upon, especially by Bennett and a bunch of crown lawyers and customs officials. He replied crisply. During the war any American vessel captured by the navy was deemed legitimate prize. They were obviously regarded as foreign ships. In time it was Collingwood's opinion, rather than Bennett's, that would be regarded as the definitive interpretation of the law, and it was the experiences of both Collingwood brothers that coloured Nelson's reaction to Shirley's overtures.[11]

Searching further afield for allies, Nelson rushed papers relating to the *Rattler's* debacle direct to the Admiralty, without even submitting them to his commander-in-chief. The affair convinced him that the civil authorities were rotten to the core and hand-in-glove with the illegal traders. He had already thrown out Hughes's revised order, and now he just as summarily dismissed Shirley's plea for 'joint endeavours' by the navy and the governors and presidents of council.

At the end of January Nelson rocked Governor Shirley back on his heels with a furious missive from St Kitt's. Cuthbert Collingwood, who until then had been the focus of the navy's campaign, had responded to Shirley's suggestions without enthusiasm, but at least obediently. Certainly, there was no indication that he would eschew the procedures outlined. But Nelson completely denied the right of civil authorities to intervene in the process, and charged them with negligence if not corruption. The navigation laws were directed to the officers of the navy, 'well knowing that those whose profession is the sea must be the best judges of the accidents which may happen upon that element', and their duty was to report solely to a superior professional officer. Nelson declined to hold himself accountable to any civil official, though if one of an appropriate rank enquired he would receive 'such information as is proper he should know'. Only if no warship was present should the presidents of council and customs officers handle the business. 'Thus,' said Nelson, in almost a mock parody of the governor's letter, 'by *our joint endeavours* will illegal trade be suppressed.'[12]

Nelson hoped that when the civil authorities did act, they would 'do their duty' and exclude foreign commerce, but he made no bones about what he thought of the customs officers who registered ineligible ships as legitimate traders. In his final sentences Nelson went so far as to suggest that Shirley himself might want commitment. He was giving the governor this information, he said, so 'that you may, *if you think fit*, take methods to hinder' illegal acts; as for himself, the captain was transmitting accounts of the fraudulent trade to the home government.[13]

This letter was a blow to the face of Governor Shirley. It told him that his procedures were going to be ignored, whether backed by the admiral or not, and that neither he nor any other civilian was to be trusted. Nelson's statement that he was sending his findings direct to London sounded very much like a threat. Suddenly all Shirley's plans to steer between the contending parties were scuttled. The governor was also 'hurt and insulted' by Nelson's letter, as he lost no time in explaining. He told Nelson that he had never intended to slight the navy, and took great exception to the 'insinuation that you thought either I connived at the malpractices of others, or was negligent of my own duty'. As for the captain reporting to government, that too was unsettling. 'If I am at all concerned, or mentioned, in such accounts,' Shirley demanded, 'I make no doubt but you will have candour enough to inform me of it.'[14]

Nelson's belligerence was often founded on impulse rather than reflection, and on this occasion, as on others, he tried to take a short step backwards. Realising that he had been excessively abrupt, he tried to mollify the governor and explain himself more tactfully. He disapproved of the idea of allowing the masters of the American ships ashore, he said, because experience had taught him they 'uniformly' wheedled what they wanted from customs people. However, he intended no personal offence to Shirley, for whom he held 'great respect'.[15]

But the damage was done. Shirley complained to Hughes, in whom he still held misplaced faith, and on 1 March wrote again to the captain himself. 'I must . . . observe to you, sir,' he told Nelson, 'that old respectable officers of high rank, long service and of a certain [time of] life are very jealous of being dictated to in their duty by young

gentlemen, whose service and experience do not entitle them to it.'
Indeed, the governor had himself reported transgressions of the navigation laws to ministers in London. 'It will appear, I believe,' he said
sarcastically, 'that Captain Nelson has not been the only alert, active,
patriotic servant of the Crown upon this occasion.'[16]

Nelson was never good at taking criticism and abandoned his brief
attempt at reconciliation upon reading Shirley's letter. He resigned
himself to having made yet another enemy. He would hold no 'further
correspondence' with 'your Excellency', he wrote to the governor, but
'General Shirley and Sir Richard Hughes will understand the ideas of
each other, I doubt not, and the distinction of old and young [will]
be obliterated'. It was as well that Shirley remained unaware of
Nelson's low estimation of Hughes, or he would have seen the venom
of this last barb from the captain of the *Boreas*.[17]

Sir Thomas smarted at being sabotaged and bypassed by an upstart.
Had he been privy to the letters Nelson was sending home, not only
to the lords of the Admiralty but also to Lord Sydney, the home secretary, he would have regarded them as inflammatory and more calculated to excite the government's prejudices than to illuminate. Still,
there was nothing he could do. He had failed to rein Nelson in and
could only remain a disapproving bystander to whatever followed.
What was more, the governor was decisively outflanked.

For in the spring he learned that Whitehall had fully endorsed the
actions of Messrs Nelson and Collingwood, and expected Shirley to
support them. In fact, Lord Sydney had already been primed by alarming
rumours of the falsification of ship registers in the West Indian islands,
and on 8 January he had written to the various governors calling upon
them to investigate. The charges were denied, but Sydney was convinced
the navigation laws were being flouted, and, when the correspondence
about the *Mediator*'s dispute at St John's in December reached him,
weighed in manfully. On 9 April Sydney wrote forcefully to Governor
Shirley. He upheld Collingwood's stand without reservation and flatly
ordered the governor to give the navy every support. Later still, Shirley
was instructed to defend Nelson against the suits of outraged merchants
at public expense.[18]

Shirley had insight, but he was no crusader and had no intention
of rocking the boat within sight of retirement and the baronetcy his
sights were set upon. Shelving his doubts, the old officer toed the line
obediently, and handed the palm of victory to the impudent young
gentleman commanding the *Boreas*.

2

Captain Nelson may have been a growing pup of twenty-six, but he had conjured almighty allies and wielded moral outrage like a cutlass.

He was no saint, of course, and even indulged in a level of corruption himself. The illicit perks of his trade were not unused. For example, even as he lambasted crooked officials he wilfully carried his absent brother William on the books of the *Boreas*, garnering unearned wages as a naval chaplain. William had actually left the ship before the end of September 1784, but the musters had him at his post until 4 October 1786, except for two months of alleged absence in 1785. 'You will accumulate a fortune if you proceed this way,' Nelson wrote to the beneficiary. 'You shall give me a horse, however.' The essential difference between the minor fraud practised by Nelson, and the grosser malpractices of the West Indian officials, was not purely one of extent. For by Nelson's lights the latter were putting private gain before duty and the common good. They were subverting policies designed, however inadequately, to protect Britain and its empire. Horatio was often wrong-headed and intemperate, but to his credit he never put financial profit before public duty. The existence of William's name on the musters of the *Boreas* did not, as far as the captain knew, inhibit the service.[19]

That sense of moral rectitude urgently drove young Nelson forward, imparting purpose, importance and sanctimoniousness. He was a champion of the people, beset by grubby profiteers and powerful protectors, and he would neither be corrupted nor swayed by argument or threat. The impetuosity and ingenuity of his attack swept Sir Thomas Shirley aside, but even more did it defeat Admiral Hughes.

Sir Richard's position was more humiliating than Shirley's. He might have been a middle-aged baronet, knight of the realm, and what was more to the point a rear admiral and commander-in-chief, but he had lost control of cleverer juniors. He had seen his orders discarded and the official command structure ignored. It was usual for captains to send their reports and supporting papers to their commanding officers, who used their discretion to judge what needed to be forwarded to the Admiralty. In its turn the Admiralty would communicate, if necessary, with other government departments or with ministers. But from February 1785 Nelson began forwarding material about the navigation laws directly to London, and furnishing Hughes with copies. It was not only discourteous to the admiral, but also rather insulting,

since it implied that he could not be trusted to handle matters satisfactorily. It confirmed both his irrelevance and unworthiness.

Even more embarrassing were Sir Richard's meetings with island
officials and merchants, meetings that absorbed much of the time of
a commander-in-chief. The admiral was uncommonly civil on such
occasions, pleasing of address and immensely likeable at the dinner
table or in the ballroom, but when people complained to him about
the doings of Nelson and the Collingwoods he had no remedy. He
was demeaned by his impotence, a somewhat pathetic figure, a
commander-in-chief unable to command. He could only prevaricate
unconvincingly and duck out of the way as fast as possible. He should
either have backed Nelson or suspended him, but he shrank from both
alternatives. They involved confrontation, and Sir Richard was not
good at confrontations. Nor was he willing to stick his neck out on
an uncertain issue. It was not until 10 May that the Admiralty sent
Hughes a copy of the latest act of Parliament on the subject of the
navigation laws.

The truth was that the significance of these laws had completely
eluded him, and they did not appear in his correspondence with the
Admiralty until May 1785. His indifference and indecision left a
vacuum for Nelson and the Collingwoods to fill. While he kept out
of the way in Barbados or made a social round of the islands with
his chattering wife and man-hunting daughter, they wrenched policy
from his grasp and turned the navigation laws into the burning issue
of the day. Nelson lost all respect for his superior. Hughes was, he
told Locker, 'a fiddler; therefore, as his time is taken up tuning that
instrument, you will consequently expect the squadron is cursedly out
of tune'.[20]

By February 1785 Nelson had effectively taken control of the naval
affairs of the Leeward Islands from both the governor and the admiral,
and squared up for a straight fight with the illegal traders. His course
was a bold one, for the final position of the British government was
still unclear at that time, and most of the squadron continued to
languish behind Admiral Hughes. The majority of the planters,
merchants, lawyers and civil servants were also against him, and his
only important support had come from the Collingwoods, officers
even more junior than himself. Yet Nelson did not hesitate. Indeed,
he raised the stakes to meet the challenge head-on.

3

The offensive 'young gentleman' of the *Boreas* was ever more incensed by the corruption and deception being uncovered.

April saw Wilfred Collingwood back at St Kitts, where some of the grossest frauds were practised. He apprehended a ship named *The Friends* there. Ostensibly she was registered in Cork, Ireland, in 1779, but Collingwood found that the ship was really the newly built *Polly* of Boston, and that her register and the articles signed by her crew were forgeries.[21]

Yet for a while Nelson's attack on such abuses brought him little but travail. His admiral was usually conspicuous by his absence, while customs officers often refused to cooperate, declaring that they were not answerable to naval officers for their conduct. Merchants and planters signified their disapproval by shutting Nelson out of polite society. Every ill-natured report about him was eagerly circulated.

On 19 March he intercepted an American brig threatening to enter Basseterre road in St Kitts, and was informed by her master that the ship was sinking and needed to dock. Nelson suspected it was a ruse to get into the protective clutches of the customs officials, and ordered the ship to anchor offshore, forbidding it to communicate with the shore. Nelson's carpenter, with an officer and men, boarded the brig to look for damage. She was in a poor state, so Nelson's men helped at the pumps throughout the night, and the next morning the brig was moved into a safe anchorage. To his chagrin, Nelson soon heard that, from one end of the island to the other, he was being charged with cruelty, and that it was being said he had tried to send the brig back to sea in a sinking condition. Nelson felt marked by the stain upon his humanity, and made the first of several reports to the home secretary, explaining that the 'character of an officer is his greatest treasure. To lower that is to wound him irreparably.' Inside he enclosed a copy of General Dalling's flattering tribute to him, written in 1780 in a letter to Lord George Germain.[22]

At first Nelson's policy was to warn foreign ships away, but it was abundantly clear that more stringent measures were needed. Ships turned away came back as soon as the coast was clear, and some officials abetted their evasions. The degree of official obstruction encountered by Nelson and his allies varied. As the government's pressure to enforce the navigation laws increased, more of its servants toed the line. In St John's, Antigua, for example, where the governor's

influence was gradually applied, the collector of customs was concerned to establish his integrity. Though differences in the interpretation of the law remained, he assured Collingwood of the *Mediator*
that it was his 'wish to give every information that can in any shape
prove the attention paid at this office to the laws of trade'. But in
some of the other islands the opposition was stubborn, and Nelson
found officials who were significantly indifferent to the unloading of
illegal cargoes.[23]

As the spring advanced and the contraband trade continued, Nelson
judged it time to act more decisively. Warnings were going unheeded.
So, without consulting Hughes, he issued an ultimatum: any vessels
found trading in breach of the navigation laws after 1 May 1785
would be seized and confiscated as legitimate prize. The traders were
threatened with the entire loss of ships and cargoes.

In customs houses and shipping offices throughout the islands the
deadline provoked amusement. It was absurd, people said. No captain
would dare to seize merchant ships for fear of incurring crippling
damages in lawsuits. They risked ruin in the courts. Surely, Nelson's
law would die at birth.

Almost immediately – on 2 May, the day after the deadline expired
– the ultimatum was tested. Nelson discovered the schooner *Eclipse*
hovering inshore near St Kitts. She was under English colours, but
tried to flee when the *Boreas* appeared, and Nelson brought her master
and mate aboard. He questioned them separately to prevent the two
squaring their stories, and discovered that the schooner was really
the *Amity* of Philadelphia and that the master, like the ship, was
masquerading under an alias. Two registers were found on the vessel,
and her crew was American to a man. The following day Nelson sent
her into the local vice-admiralty court for trial. It was the first seizure
since the war and created a sensation in St Kitts.[24]

But Nelson had not finished. He heard that four heavily laden
American brigs, the *Fairview*, *George and Jane*, *Hercules* and *Nancy
Pleasants*, had slipped into the roadstead at Nevis to trade under what
were called 'island colours' – a white flag bearing a red cross. Horatio
picked up a crown lawyer at St Kitts and sent his boats to investigate. All four vessels were arrested on 19–20 May. Marines were put
aboard to secure the prizes, which were turned over to the vice-
admiralty court of Nevis at the earliest opportunity. Nelson might
have felt on stronger ground in Nevis, for he was on unusually good
terms with the president of the council, John Richardson Herbert.

Herbert admitted that Nelson was a threat to his commercial enterprises, but he recognised a man of principle in the little captain and rather liked him.

Nelson would need whatever goodwill he could get. He had backed his words with actions, and shaken the mercantile community, and five ships were awaiting unprecedented trials. But they had yet to be condemned, and if Nelson failed his campaign would be in ruins, and possibly his reputation and fortune also. The encounters that lay ahead would be decisive, but they would not be fought on the familiar if restless sea that was Nelson's element. Instead, enterprising lawyers would fence across the floors of sultry island courtrooms.

4

The days that followed were difficult and dangerous for the captain of the *Boreas*. At St Kitts, where the trial of the *Eclipse* was imminent, the signs were bad. The defendants were hiring the best counsel in the islands, while Nelson's natural allies wavered. Admiral Hughes arrived at Nevis on 23 May, but did not associate too closely with his besieged subordinate. He neither condemned nor supported Horatio's conduct, but warned him that if he persisted he could get into a scrape. The crown's advocate, Abraham Charles Adye, who was presenting Nelson's case, also began to get cold feet. A member of the island council that advised Governor Shirley, he knew the damage a strict enforcement of the navigation laws might cause, and in January had helped compose a petition praying for a relaxation of the acts. But although Adye did his duty and argued Nelson's case despite personal misgivings, he warned that the seizures might be declared unlawful because Nelson had not been deputed to act by the customs. Evidently defence lawyers were citing an act of 1765 to contend that ships could only be seized at sea with the authorisation of the commissioner of customs. Nelson had not acted at the behest of the customs service, which he considered corrupt, and had independently taken the prizes on behalf of the king and the navy. Things therefore looked black.[25]

The trial took place on 23 May and Nelson attended personally. He could see that Adye was faltering and intervened to speak for himself. Though young and certainly no orator, and pitted against experienced lawyers, Horatio emerged victorious in a bruising contest. The judge dismissed the claim that the navy lacked the right of seize and the vessel was condemned.

Even Hughes suddenly seemed to catch Nelson's spirit. He started speaking up for his officers and two days after Nelson's victory forwarded Wilfred Collingwood's complaints about *The Friends* to the Admiralty. Hughes now spoke strongly of the use of phoney registers, the attempts of masters to hide the nationalities of their crews and the way some foreign traders were depositing their goods on the Dutch island of St Eustatius so that British merchants could collect.[26]

However inspiring, this had been merely a preliminary skirmish, and Nelson's attention was then focused on the four brigs coming to trial on Nevis. It promised to be a far uglier contest, with the defending masters filing suit against Nelson for personal damages. They alleged that he had imprisoned them on their ships, preventing them contacting the shore, and had them assaulted and intimidated. According to one account, the masters had been forced into false depositions with one of Nelson's officers standing over them with a drawn sword. All of which, the writs stated, warranted compensation of £4,000.

It was a sum utterly beyond Nelson's reach. While rumour had it that subscriptions were being opened in the islands to support the prosecution, Nelson had barely the means for his defence. After the verdict against the *Eclipse*, Adye, who again prosecuted the ships, was a new man. 'In justice to him,' Nelson wrote, 'I must say that by night as by day his advice has always been ready, and that too without fee or reward.' But while Adye believed he could condemn the ships, he cautioned Nelson about the writs for personal damages and urged him to avoid being arrested. For seven or more weeks Horatio kept his ship, like an animal secure in its burrow, resisting every inducement to go ashore, as well as at least one undignified but unsuccessful attempt to remove him from the frigate by force. In between competing for the attentions of Mrs Peers, the purser's wife, Lieutenants Wallis and Dent and Dr Graham stood steadfastly behind their captain. 'The marshals had frequently come on board to arrest him,' recalled Wallis, 'but by fair words I was always able to elude their vigilance.'[27]

Help also came from more unlikely quarters. Despite Nelson's tendency to see corruption and disaffection around every corner, 'my good friend' Adye was not the only eminent islander to come to his support. Mixing with the Adyes he also met their neighbours, the Georges. More important, the hugely influential John Richardson Herbert, president of the Nevis council, whose pretty niece was attracting Nelson's attention, offered to stand bail at £10,000 if Nelson was arrested, while the island's attorney general, John Stanley, a neighbour of the Herberts, tried to stop the suit against the captain. Like Adye, Stanley was a member of the council of St Kitts and a party to its protests against the navigation laws, but he scrupulously adhered to the letter of the law. He asked Judge John Ward of the vice-admiralty court to go aboard the *Boreas* and examine the prisoners from the four prizes, who were being detained there. Ward found them unanimous that there had been no ill usage. Indeed, the detainees 'were never more contented or better treated than they were on board the *Boreas*', and Ward formed the opinion that the charges of assault and false imprisonment had originated with malignant merchants rather than seamen.[28]

Nevertheless, public opinion still ran against Nelson. 'The admiral was in Nevis roads the whole time of my persecution,' Nelson later reported, but neither he nor crown lawyers were able to protect him from insults. When the case went to court on 8 June the judge gave Nelson protection so that he could attend. The merchants had promised to indemnify the local marshal for any losses he suffered in arresting Nelson as he came ashore, but the judge threatened the marshal with imprisonment if he interfered and the captain was able to enter the courtroom unmolested.[29]

Supported by 'an honest lawyer' Nelson won a second victory at Nevis. After a two-day battle all four ships were condemned. Though the masters' suit for personal damages remained, his conduct with regard to the seizure of ships had been vindicated.[30]

First St Kitts and now Nevis. Nelson's successes raised the morale of his brother officers. The rejuvenated Hughes was still in the offing as the Nevis court deliberated, while both the *Mediator* and the *Rattler*, commanded by the indefatigable Collingwoods, had arrived to give support.

It was the Collingwoods who took the same battle to Antigua, which immediately followed suit. Early in July Cuthbert Collingwood sent three ships into St John's, where the collector of customs quickly declared them contraband traders. Two at least had illegal registers. In October another foreign ship was sent into St John's by the *Rattler*.[31]

From so bleak a beginning, the campaign had gone from success to success, and the relationship between Nelson and his commander-in-chief began to thaw. On 19 June Hughes was able to give the *Boreas* an assignment to her captain's liking. A French frigate, *L'Iris* of thirty-two guns, appeared off Nevis, cruising close enough to draw warning shots from the forts before putting out to sea. France and England were now at peace, but acutely suspicious of one another nonetheless. Hughes asked Nelson to investigate, and the next day he tracked the French frigate to St Eustatius. The governor hosted a dinner ashore, shared by Nelson and the French captain, and Horatio courteously offered to escort *L'Iris* around the British islands if it was so desired. As he anticipated, the French had no wish to attract such close attention, and protested their ship was bound for Martinique.[32]

As for Nelson, he was again destined to spend the hurricane season in English Harbour, but this time without the compensation of Mrs Moutray's company. He arrived on 10 August in a lighter mood than might have been expected. His successes, and those of Collingwood, had fused with Lord Sydney's voluble support to create a more cooperative environment in Antigua. The officials, at least, were falling over themselves to prove their loyalty to the crown, now that they knew it wholeheartedly supported the enforcement of the navigation laws. Hughes was beginning to portray his deviant captains as heroes, and the doors of Shirley and other public officials graciously opened. Nelson felt a new spirit abroad and cooperated accordingly. In July he had sent a brigantine into Nevis, forwarding her papers to the local customs officers with his observation that he suspected the register to be false. The officials examined the documents and exonerated the ship, and Nelson happily allowed her to proceed.[33]

There was still far to go, however, as the unfortunate elder Collingwood was even then discovering. While Antigua, Nevis and St Kitts – all in the Leeward Islands within the remit of Shirley's authority – had been brought into line, the Windward Islands were another matter. Collingwood induced the authorities in Grenada to seize the *Speedwell* in October, and before the end of the year had sent three more ships for trial there, but the outcomes were as yet unclear. But the hardest nut to crack was undoubtedly Barbados, where the people were blaming the shutting out of American ships for the high cost of grain and the miseries of the poor, especially the blacks. A petition seeking the admission of American maize during times when harvests failed was afoot, and Governor David Parry was unwilling to exert himself against powerful island cliques. Nothing exemplified the growing conflict between the navy and the Barbadian court than the case of the *Dolphin*.[34]

Collingwood seized the ship in July, soon after Nelson's victory in Nevis, and innocently sent her into Barbados for adjudication. To proceed with the case the king's advocate in Barbados, Attorney General Charles Brandford, demanded extraordinary advance fees from Collingwood, and when it finally got to court in October it was thrown out. Despite the decisions in the other courts, Judge Nathaniel Weeks ruled against the navy's right to seize, and the *Dolphin* was not only released but also given a new register. It was a terrific blow to Cuthbert Collingwood. He was now personally liable for fees, expenses and court costs, and had to tout around to raise a bond to cover them pending an appeal.

The navy was furious. Even Hughes, a traditional English gentleman, pronounced the decision 'shameful' and the judge 'a good-for-nothing dirty fellow'. He urged the Admiralty to support Collingwood. Nelson too was appalled, and wrote to Uncle William Suckling, a lifelong employee of the Customs House in London, asking him to secure the opinion of their solicitor.[35]

Barbados was a shock but failed to check growing optimism. While sheltering in English Harbour Nelson received an exhilarating piece of news. Back in June, when a lawsuit for personal damages had been filed against Nelson in Nevis, the crown lawyers had suggested he petition the king for assistance through Lord Sydney, the home secretary. As the suit remained, even after the condemnation of the ships in question, Nelson had done so, and on 4 August Sydney replied. 'His Majesty has been pleased to direct that the Law Officers of the Crown should defend the suit upon this occasion,' Nelson eventually read. If his defence still failed, Sydney indicated that an appeal against the judgement would be favourably considered. The same day the home secretary fired off a brief letter to Governor Shirley. Nelson's reports had been received by government, and 'from the character' he bore there was no reason to doubt their accuracy; consequently, the law officers of the crown should defend him at public expense. There could no longer be any doubt that Nelson enjoyed the government's full confidence, and that it was the duty of the king's servants to support him. Equally, there was little likelihood of the suit for personal damages now being pressed against him with any success.[36]

Captain Nelson, the scourge of the islands, had been vindicated – by some of the courts and now by the king. Notwithstanding the setback in Barbados, the navy hungered to return to its hunt for contraband traders, its predatory instincts fully aroused. 'My dear boy,' Nelson wrote to Collingwood, 'I want some prize money!' Nor would the *Mediator* miss out on the excitement, for in October Hughes authorised Collingwood to cruise entirely for the purpose of enforcing the navigation laws.[37]

The *Boreas* herself got to sea on 17 October. There was another reason why Nelson was pleased to see the hurricanes blow themselves out. At Nevis he had met an interesting young lady and he longed to return.

5

He steered straight for St Kitts and Nevis, where the ship ran aground on the point and had to be hauled off by her stern. It was the fourth time the *Boreas* had been ashore since leaving England, so Nelson or the master, Jameson, might have been less than attentive to the business of navigation. However, the damage was repaired and for several months Nelson patrolled the northern islands in search of suspicious merchantmen, occasionally retreating to Antigua or Barbados for supplies and maintenance.[38]

On 21 October he arrested the *Active* brig off Nevis. Her colours were British but she was illegally manned and American built. This new seizure, heralding the return of the most feared of the naval captains to these waters, threw the islands into what Nelson termed 'a violent ferment'. The merchants and their coadjutors had used the respite given them by the hurricane season to arm themselves with a formidable new weapon from London: the opinion of Judge William Scott, later Lord Stowell. An advocate for the Admiralty, Scott was already well into a career as the foremost authority on English prize law.

It says much for the disturbance Nelson had caused that interested islanders had written to England for the advice of Scott. Nevertheless, they found his views largely satisfactory, for they raised serious doubts about the right of the navy to seize in support of the navigation laws. Scott maintained that acts of 1662 had reserved such powers to customs officers and those authorised by either a warrant from the Treasury or by a special commission from the king under Great or Privy Seal.

If anyone thought that such legal jargon would silence Nelson, they were mistaken. Scott's interpretation denied the navy the right to intervene and turned them into powerless observers of flagrant illegalities. Horatio pored over his copies of the various acts in his cabin, sometimes beneath a flickering light in the quieter hours after dark, and steadily picked holes in his opponents' case. As he told his Uncle William to whom he turned for an opinion of his own:

I am clearly of opinion that we [naval officers] *do* hold our commissions eventually under the Great Seal, for the Admiralty is only a Patent place during pleasure; and that the act seems to think so. Read the next clause, 'an indemnification for all officers of the customs, or any officer or officers, person or persons authorised to put in execution the act for increasing shipping and navigation, their deputies,' &c. What occasion could there be to indemnify the officers enjoined to put the navigation act in force if the power had been taken away by the preceding clause? It appears to me that the parliament was afraid it might be wrong construed, [and] therefore included them by name in a subsequent clause. Well done, Lawyer Nelson!³⁹

He was soon framing complicated arguments about the circumstances in which naval officers could or could not seize transgressors, but in November appealed again to Lord Sydney. 'A doubt is now started (and I may probably be persecuted in this country upon it),' he explained, 'that if the Custom House give leave to a foreigner to trade, I have no right to hinder him, but must look on as an idle spectator.'⁴⁰

Nelson's points went home and the *Active* was condemned.

Next came the forty-ton sloop *Sally*, owned and navigated by Seth Warner of Connecticut and stopped at Nevis on 23 January 1786. Here, Nelson discovered, was outright deception. The original *Sally* had been an older vessel, registered by Governor Shirley in 1784 after she entered St John's in an unseaworthy condition. At that time it was sworn that the ship was a former American prize eligible for registration. The owner himself claimed to be a subject of the British island of Dominica, and although no proof supported any of these protestations, the ship got her register permitting her to trade. But then something strange happened. The ship returned to the United States, where a new vessel was built to the specifications of the old and took her name. Being foreign-built, the new vessel had no right to trade with the British islands, but she did so, claiming to be the old *Sally* and flaunting her register and documentation.

The case incriminated the customs officers in Antigua, especially since Seth Warner excused his deception by claiming that he had actually been persuaded to apply for a British register. Nelson suspected that the officials were registering foreign vessels purely to coin in the registration fees.

In Antigua attempts to clean up the customs had already begun to bite. Even before Nelson got involved, the home secretary had been complaining about registration scandals, and on 2 June 1785 repeated his calls for an investigation, telling Shirley that the business was 'carried to a pitch' and culprits had to be named and punished. Spurred on, Shirley was making progress, and revealed that registers were being hawked from one trader to another in the West Indies. He promised that any official involved in fraud would be 'immediately' dismissed. Under the inquisitorial glare of government, the courts in Antigua strove to show integrity and efficiency. Captain John Holloway, who dealt with them the next year, was 'fully persuaded' that the law officers of Antigua, unlike those on some other islands, were 'zealously attached to His Majesty's government'.[41]

Nelson's new evidence, therefore, hurt a bureaucracy struggling to clean up its image. In its defence the collector of customs asserted that Seth Warner had originally represented himself to be a Loyalist who wanted to move to Dominica where he had once lived. A clerk in the customs department had claimed to be acquainted with Warner, and supported his story. However, the customs office admitted that after the *Sally* got her register suspicions had grown and the clerk was dismissed for 'nefarious practices', but there was never enough information to prosecute Warner. Notwithstanding this, he was prohibited from trading in Antigua again.[42]

Nelson refused to be appeased, and forwarded the register to Lord Sydney together with a further diatribe against the frauds of customs officials. He accused them of granting registers to whomsoever they pleased, fattening themselves on registration fees, and of obstructing his efforts to bring interlopers to account. So rife was the corruption that he advised 'exemplary punishments', and the recall of all existing ships' registers for replacement with a new form of certification.

In some respects Nelson derived enormous satisfaction from leading the charge against illicit trade. In these dull times it was a substitute for naval glory, and a means of satiating his need for attention. Even without a war he could be the sword of the people, cutting a swath through corruption and selfishness. 'I shall stand acquitted before your Lordship and my country of any interested [partisan] views in thus representing these malpractices,' he informed Sydney with pride, 'for I have no interest to obtain any place, nor do I ever expect any but what rises from a faithful discharge of my duty.'[43]

6

Paradoxically, in the drawn-out struggle over the navigation laws the praise Nelson craved so desperately sometimes fell upon those who had been less than enthusiastic about his activities. There were few rewards to be had from this squalid slugging match, but Sir Thomas Shirley and Sir Richard Hughes, the 'old officers' once affronted by a young gentleman, were in for their shares.

Sir Thomas was quick to realise that Whitehall was more interested in enforcing the navigation laws and purifying their administration than listening to a parade of their shortcomings. Sydney had supported Collingwood and Nelson, and demanded reform. Under the shadow of the home secretary, Shirley put his quarrel with the captain of the *Boreas* behind him. Now that the little fellow and his allies were being praised by government, Shirley supported them to the hilt. He assured Sydney that he often met Collingwood and was at one with him, while he would certainly enquire closely into Nelson's allegations of corruption. What was more, he took credit for their captures, proudly telling the minister on 23 July 1785 that 'there have been lately several seizures at the different islands under my government!' Nelson bore no grudges. In August 1786 he even took Shirley's son William as a protégé aboard his frigate.[44]

Sir Richard Hughes earned even more from Nelson's achievements. As commander-in-chief of the station he was due a share of the prize money his wayward captains were earning. He got £97 for the *Fairview*, taken at Nevis, compared with the £388 distributed between Nelson and his ship's company. The admiral's professional credit also rose at home. The Treasury, the senior ministry, was pleased with the seizures and impressed by the information Nelson had forwarded about the *Rattler*'s early difficulties with the customs at St Kitts. In August 1785 the Treasury informed the Admiralty that whatever a ship's register said, proof of a vessel being foreign-built or manned by foreigners was sufficient to warrant condemnation, and revenue officers would be made answerable to the enquiries of naval captains; any corrupt officials would be punished. Furthermore, in a passage the Admiralty sent appreciatively to Hughes, the secretary of the Treasury declared that 'the commander-in-chief of the Leeward Islands and officers under him have shown a very commendable zeal in endeavouring to put a stop to the illicit practices which were carrying on in the islands'.[45]

In England ministers assumed that Nelson had acted with the support, rather than the indifference, of the commander-in-chief, and Hughes found himself praised on account of a subordinate he had left to the wolves. When he saw the Treasury paragraph Nelson, who had driven the lauded campaign, felt cheated of credit. 'The captains Collingwood were the only officers with myself who ever attempted to hinder the illicit trade with America,' he complained, 'and I stood singly with respect to seizing, for the other officers were [at first] fearful of being brought into scrapes.' To Locker he admitted that he felt 'much hurt that after the loss of health and risk of fortune, another should be thanked for what I did *against* his orders'.[46]

Not surprisingly, the praise from Whitehall and shares in prize money completely reconciled Sir Richard Hughes to his estranged second-in-command. He was 'highly pleased' with the captain's conduct, and to Nelson's astonishment the two became 'good friends'. When the *Boreas* put into Barbados, where the admiral occupied rooms, Nelson called for dinner. Horatio always had his doubts about Hughes. The man lacked professional judgement and resolution, as well as a certain social propriety. While his wife, Lady Hughes, and their daughter (now ensnaring Major John Browne of the 67th Regiment into marriage) were residing in Antigua, the admiral was paying rather too obvious attention to a certain Miss Daniels in Barbados. But once the animosity between Hughes and Nelson had melted, the captain discovered his superior a man of much personal charm. His 'politeness and attention to me is great,' he wrote in March 1786, grudgingly confessing that he liked Hughes after all. And the next month he was able to report with even greater certainty that, 'I have been upon the best terms with the admiral, and declare I think could ever remain so . . . He is always remarkably kind and civil to every one.' It seemed that Nelson's fortunes, after suffering so many tribulations, were coming full circle.[47]

In a sense it was a triumph for the junior captains, although one that must be seen in context. The strict enforcement of the navigation laws was hardly the noble cause Collingwood and Nelson supposed, and their victories were of very doubtful utility. Even in St Kitts and Nevis, where the courts had supported the navy, the 'rigid execution' of the laws was blamed for inflation 'at a time when our situation could ill bear any additional burthens, and when we had cause rather to expect the fostering assistance of the parent state'.

Then again, in 1786 the complaints of Nelson and the Collingwoods prompted the Admiralty to declare unequivocally that American ships built during the rebellion and found engaging in trade were as liable to seizure as those launched after the peace of 1783. They were equally deemed to be foreign vessels. At home the government thought it was protecting native shipbuilding by insisting that trade moved in 'British bottoms', but merchants in St Kitts knew that their coastal trade went in American 'droghers' built since 1776 and subsequently purchased by islanders. Wood decayed quickly in the West Indies, vessels had to be replaced regularly and the closest supply of 'droghers' remained the United States. The Admiralty's new regulations outlawed the 'droghers' at a stroke. Sugar piled up in creeks and bays, unable to be moved to the ports, and British merchantmen sat idle, waiting to ship it to England. In the spring of 1786 the islanders asked Governor Shirley to suspend the new regulations, at least until the harvest was cleared and the matter could be reconsidered.[48]

Ultimately the navigation laws, serving neither Britain nor the West Indian islands, could not be defended. For a while the government persisted, passing an act to tighten the registration of ships in 1786, and renewing orders to naval and civil officers to stamp out illegal trade. But the islands needed the foreign trade, and hopes that the Canadian colonies would supply their wants proved delusive. As late as 1790 Nova Scotia was importing large amounts of American grain, foodstuffs and timber, the very products it was supposed to be supplying the British West Indies. Nor were the contrary arguments of Shirley and others entirely ignored. When the Navigation Act was renewed it contained a clause allowing governors the discretion to permit imports from foreign 'islands' in cases of acute public distress. They jumped upon it. In the Leeward Islands, Sir Thomas was besieged with applications for a relaxation of the navigation laws, and by July 1787 was having to grant general indulgences permitting merchants to import goods from America and foreign islands in the West Indies. The same year the British governments declared partially free ports throughout their possessions in the Caribbean.[49]

However, if Nelson's cause was doomed to eventual retreat, he had triumphed in the short term, and his campaign had encapsulated the man's weaknesses and strengths. It showed him hasty, myopic, arrogant, disobedient and contentious, but it also betokened leadership and tremendous moral and physical courage. He had refused to be overawed, intimidated or swerved from a matter of principle; his willingness to lead where others hesitated in the face of danger had seized the initiative from superiors, and inspired followers; and he had persevered, making light of difficulties, until a victory had been won. He had engaged propertied merchants, artful lawyers and shifty officials in the strange ill-lit labyrinthine world of imperial and prize law, and emerged victorious into the sunlight. It is not surprising that the reputation that spread through the islands was that of a young man worthy of weighing in any reckoning.

7

Among the few who had admired Nelson in the darker days was the president of the council of Nevis, Mr John Richardson Herbert. Herbert was an unlikely benefactor. He was one of the richest merchants in the colony and related by marriage to the governor of Barbados. It was a niece Herbert shared with Governor Parry – Miss Parry Herbert – who may, in fact, have been the means of bringing Nelson and the president together. In the spring of 1785 Nelson transported Miss Parry from Barbados to Nevis, and probably for the first time walked between the globe-topped stone pillars that welcomed visitors to the Herbert mansion, Montpelier. Soon, it seems, Nelson found himself being observed rather closely at the dinner table, and shortly afterwards an intrigued female guest at Montpelier was penning her impressions to a friend:

We have at last seen the little captain of the *Boreas*, of whom so much has been said. He came up just before dinner, much heated, and was very silent, yet seemed according to the old adage to think the more. He declined drinking any wine, but after dinner, when the president as usual gave the three following toasts, the king, the queen and royal family, and Lord Hood, this strange man regularly filled his glass, and observed that those were always bumper toasts with him, which having drank, he uniformly passed the bottle and relapsed into his former taciturnity. It was impossible during this visit for any of us to make out his real character. There was such a reserve and sternness in his behaviour, with occasional sallies, though very transient, of a superior mind. Being placed by him, I endeavoured to rouse his attention by showing him all the civilities in my power, but I drew out little more than 'yes' and 'no'. If you, Fanny, had been there, we think you would have made something of him, for you have been in the habit of attending to these odd sort of people.[50]

The recipient was yet another of Herbert's nieces, a twenty-four-year-old widow named Mrs Frances Nisbet. A little later, early in May, she met Nelson herself, apparently for the first time, and they talked of a mutual acquaintance who had been in Nevis some years before. Writing to his brother William on the 12th of the month, almost as an afterthought, Nelson recounted how he had 'just come from Nevis, where I have been visiting Miss Parry Herbert and a young widow [Frances Nisbet], the two latter known to Charles Boyles [who commanded the *Barbados* on the station in 1784]. Great inquiries after him by the damsels in that island.'[51]

That 'young widow' would become Nelson's wife.

XIV

DEAREST FANNY

Nelson for ever – any time
Am I his to command in prose or rhyme!
Give me of Nelson only a touch,
And I save it, be it little or much:
Here's one our Captain gives, and so
Down at the word, by George, shall it go!
Robert Browning, *Nationality in Drinks*

1

NELSON saw much of Nevis in the months after he met Fanny. The capture of the American ships in May, the trial in June and the contingent controversy kept him on the island for much of the spring and summer of 1785. After Nelson's victory in the local vice-admiralty court he spent some time as a guest in Herbert's house, Montpelier. The trips away were brief and increasingly to be regretted. Sometimes the *Boreas* crossed the shallow two-mile strip to St Kitts to search for more foreign traders, but Nevis kept drawing him back with intensifying power.

The island itself was not unattractive. Merely six miles by eight, it was the tip of a submerged and dormant volcano, rising from the sea to some three and a half thousand feet and a peak so often wreathed in white clouds that distant voyagers were reminded of the snow-capped mountains in Europe. What settlements there were hugged the lower reaches. Sugar plantations were cut into the green slopes, a collection of picturesque, red-roofed houses formed the capital, Charlestown, on the west coast, and a little to the south, where an imposing three-storey stone house provided accommodation, the afflicted eased rheumatic limbs in famous thermal springs. In all fewer than ten thousand people lived on the island, 1,500 of them whites and the rest coloured slaves. Montpelier, to which Nelson's feet kept taking him, was one of the largest of the plantation houses, but it was Mrs Frances Nisbet who attracted him.

Everyone called her Fanny. She was baptised Frances Herbert Woolward in St George's Church, Nevis, in May 1761, and belonged by birth to the colonial elite of the islands. Her mother, Mary Herbert, was one of three sisters of John Richardson Herbert. The Herberts were descended from a younger son of the fourth Earl of Pembroke, and Mary and John's uncle had himself been president of the council until his death in 1768. William Woolward, Fanny's father, had been a senior judge on Nevis, and a partner in the firm of Herbert, Morton and Woolward. She grew up close to plenty, and owned a black man-servant named Cato. Given these circumstances Fanny might have expected a comfortable and privileged life.[1]

It was not to be so. Fanny was little more than a child when she lost her mother, but she was old enough to witness the sufferings of her sick father, who reportedly died of tetanus in February 1779 before she was eighteen. Woolward was only fifty-three. He left £100 to his brother, Thomas, and the rest of his property to his only child, but most of the assets seem to have been devoured by creditors. Orphaned three years short of her majority, Fanny commemorated her lost parents by placing a tablet in the local church of St John's, but only months after her father's death she married, on 28 June 1779. The groom, Josiah Nisbet, MD, was a physician, qualified in Edinburgh in 1768, and approaching his thirty-second birthday.

Whether Fanny went hastily into marriage to fill the vacuum left by the loss of her family will never be known, but she was loyal to her husband and the match was a fair one on the face of it. The Nisbets were a Scottish family. Josiah's father was Walter Nisbet (a junior grandson of the fourth Earl of Moray), who had migrated to Nevis, established the estate of Mount Pleasant and connected himself to a prestigious local family through his marriage to Mary Webbe in 1743. He had died a member of the island council in 1765, leaving his eldest boy, Walter, to inherit Mount Pleasant and four other children to share his legacy. Josiah may not have been wealthy, but he had received £1,000 from his father, practised as a doctor, and was probably a man of some means.

Unfortunately, Fanny's marriage had been brief. The couple had gone to England, where they lived in Cathedral Close, Salisbury, where property may have been inherited from the Webbes. Perhaps Nisbet hoped to get well, for he was seriously ill soon after reaching England and died on 5 October 1781, supposedly insane. Certainly, he made no provision for his wife and young Josiah, her seventeen-month-old son, and many of their possessions, including Fanny's beloved harpsichord, were auctioned. For the second time in her short life she found herself testifying to her love for the lost. A pathetic plaque recording the regard an 'affectionate widow' held for a dead husband was placed in the church of Stratford-sub-Castle.[2]

Widowed at twenty and in a strange land, Fanny's position was hardly enviable. Her husband's money had disappeared, along with, it seems, some £2,000 promised by her uncle, John Richardson Herbert, on her marriage. But though a fragile and understated little creature, Fanny possessed unexpected reserves of resilience, courage and discipline, and she was not entirely alone. A few old Nevis friends were at hand, and for a while Fanny appears to have acted as a guardian to three offspring of the Nevis planter John Pinney. Indeed, when John Pinney returned to England in 1783 and Fanny presented his children to him he did not recognise them. 'Good God! Don't you know them?' exclaimed Fanny. 'They are your children!' Pinney's wife was so surprised she set her headdress alight on a nearby candle.[3]

Eventually, Fanny returned to Nevis, where her uncle opened his home to her, and when Nelson used to call she was sharing the house with the widowed president, his ailing, unmarried sister, various other nieces, the infant Josiah and a babbling stream of guests. Herbert had lost his wife and was on poor terms with his only child, Martha, who was about to marry into the same Hamilton family that spawned the famous American federalist. It was, therefore, upon Mrs Nisbet that the old man bestowed the most affection.

Providentially, therefore, Fanny had become, at least to outward appearances, the belle of the island – young, reasonably pretty, single and what was more an heir of the richest and most powerful man in Nevis. President Herbert had lost track of how much he owned. Jointly with Magnus Morton, a brother-in-law, he held a lease to the large estate of upper Gingerland, and many houses on the island were mortgaged to him. He had slaves and livestock in abundance, exported five hundred casks of sugar a year, and was described by Governor Shirley as the 'senior councillor' of Nevis and 'a gentleman of the first fortune in this country'. Nelson not only recognised 'a man who must have his own way in everything' but also one who was 'very rich and very proud'.[4]

Captain Nelson and President Herbert should not have been friends. In his attack upon trade abuses the former was tilting dangerously at the planting class Herbert exemplified. Yet the two men liked each other, and Herbert did not object when Nelson began spending more time with his niece. He offered to stand bail for Nelson if he was arrested on account of irate merchants, and spoke well of him to important island officials. There is an attractive but entirely uncorroborated story that it was five-year-old Josiah who first forged the bond between Fanny Nisbet and Horatio Nelson. The captain certainly loved children. One he played with remembered in adult life that Nelson 'was kind in the extreme, and we all loved him'. We are told that on one occasion President Herbert emerged from his dressing room at Montpelier to find Nelson under a table playing with his niece's child.[5]

Truthfully, however, no one can say exactly what drew Herbert or Fanny to the embattled young captain of the *Boreas*. Fanny herself was capable of attracting him, lonely, frustrated and far from home as he was. She was a woman of some accomplishments. She painted with watercolours and produced fine embroidery, to judge from relics carefully preserved by the family. More impressive, she spoke excellent French and served her uncle as an interpreter when diplomats visited Nevis, a skill that mystified Horatio to the end of his days. Her penmanship in her own tongue was comparable to Nelson's, though less vigorous and informed, and narrow in scope, extending little beyond the doings in her social circle.

People thought Fanny pleasant looking rather than beautiful. To Prince William Henry she seemed 'pretty and sensible', while Midshipman Hotham of the *Solebay*, who saw her test Nelson's limited social skills by joining him in the minuet on Nevis, remembered her as 'pretty and attractive, and a general favourite'. A less gallant midshipman, while admitting that Fanny had 'some beauty, and a freshness of countenance not common in that climate', considered her intellect unremarkable. Fanny's portraits suggest a slim, delicate and dainty woman, but Sir Gilbert Elliot, who met her a dozen years after she met Horatio, thought her 'a buxom widow, and *just* the *sort* of wife he would like. She is a much better one than . . . Lord Malmsbury will be able to make for some time.' Beyond question the Nevis belle was kind, well-intentioned, courteous and steadfastly loyal, though perhaps she lacked the sparkle that had been so attractive in Mrs Moutray.[6]

Nonetheless, before the end of June 1785 Nelson had decided to ask for her hand in marriage. In an oblique reference to the Shakespearean hero of *Much Ado About Nothing*, he told his brother on the 28th, 'Do not be surprised to hear I am a Benedict, for if at all, it will be before a month. Do not tell.'[7]

2

Before returning to Antigua to sit out hurricanes in August, Nelson had proposed and been accepted, at least provisionally. The couple needed Herbert's blessing, and Horatio put his intentions in a letter to him and left it in Nevis. He waited anxiously for a reply.

On 19 August, when the first of his gossipy letters to Fanny was produced, he was still waiting, but trusted her uncle would not stand in their way. 'Most sincerely do I love you,' he pledged somewhat stiffly, 'and I trust that my affection is not only founded upon the principle of reason but also upon the basis of mutual attachment. Indeed, my charming Fanny, did [I] possess a million [pounds] my greatest pride and pleasure would be to share it with you; and, as I am, to live in a cottage with you I should esteem superior to living in a place with any other I have yet met with.'

Despite his temper ('I possess not the art of concealing it') and situation, which he confessed told against him, he felt sufficiently secure in her affections to unload a farrago of news, chatter ('Kelly I could and would tell you a long history of was I sure this would come safe to your hands'), and trivial tales ('Captain Acres' and 'your shoe friend, Captain S., a gentleman well versed in the business of carrying off young ladies', had conspired to help an unidentified 'Miss' to elope from Antigua). Among good news was word from his brother William that the death of their uncle Robert Rolfe had given him the living of Hilborough, worth £700 a year, and that a long letter from Mrs Moutray had arrived. 'A more amiable woman can hardly exist,' Nelson told Fanny. 'I wish you knew her. Your minds and manners are so congenial that you must have pleasure in the acquaintance.'[8]

When it came the awaited letter from Herbert was 'deferring' on the main question, but promised a discussion when they met and left Nelson's expectations undiminished. He was painfully conscious of his comparative poverty, though he turned it into a virtue, since 'the world knows I am superior to pecuniary considerations in both my public and private life, as in both instances I might have been rich'. He convinced himself he would not be penalised for putting duty before money, and that the president would respect the wishes of his niece. Some explanation for the delay in communications from Nevis was also afforded by news that Fanny's aunt had died after a long illness. He consoled her with the thought that her aunt was released from pain, and that 'religion' should 'convince you that her conduct in this world was such as will ensure everlasting happiness in that which is to come'.[9]

The hurricanes gone, Nelson hurried to Nevis for a reunion with Fanny and that man-to-man talk with Herbert. As he later recounted the conversation, Nelson 'told him [Herbert] I am as poor as Job, but he tells me he likes me, and I am descended from a good family, which his pride likes. But he also says, "Nelson, I am proud, and I must live like myself. Therefore, I can't do much in my lifetime. When I die she [Fanny] shall have twenty thousand pounds; and if my daughter dies before me, she shall possess the major part of my property. I intend going to England in 1787, and remaining there my life. Therefore, if you two can live happily together till that event takes place, you have my consent."'[10]

In other words, Fanny could expect much in due course, but little short-term financial aid, although Horatio understood Herbert to say he would allow her an interim annuity of two or three hundred pounds, with something for her child. The discussion had secured a blessing, but left the immediate situation difficult, and Nelson turned to his own uncle, William Suckling of Kentish Town, to whom he had successfully unburdened his passion for Bess Andrews.

In another tremulous letter he allowed that Uncle William 'will smile . . . and say, "This Horatio is for ever in love!"' But he needed money, and solicited either a lump sum of £1,000 or an annual allowance of £100, promising to do his utmost to redeem the debt by being of eventual service to Suckling's family. 'Don't disappoint me,' he entreated, 'or my heart will break; trust to my honour to do a good turn for some other person if it is in my power.' He coupled his plea with a highly inaccurate account of Fanny's career, and an affirmation of the love he bore her. 'Her personal accomplishments you will suppose *I think* equal to any person's I ever saw, but, without vanity, her mental accomplishments are superior to most people's of either sex; and we shall come together as two persons most sincerely attached to each other from friendship.'[11]

Nelson's finances were precarious. During times of peace he had no assurance that his command of the *Boreas* would be succeeded by another appointment. He had earned a little prize money from the American seizures, but it was hardly excessive – the *Fairview* yielded him less than £200 – and there was still the possibility that some lawsuit would be pressed against him. Furthermore, his income was constantly suffering from the attrition of everyday living, the maintenance of a hospitable table and a compulsive generosity. Surviving notes of his expenses record occasional hand-outs to needy mariners. 'Sailor, 1s.', he wrote, or 'gave a seaman 2s. 6d.', or even 'for a seaman (too much) 3s. 6d.'. A more unlikely example lay in the large assortment of letters from home that periodically accumulated in the post offices of Bridgetown or St John's, letters addressed to the men of the *Boreas* and other ships on the station. Nelson was distressed to find that the costs of postage, payable upon collection, were so high that some of his 'people' were unable to retrieve their mail. He appealed to the postmaster general for cheaper postage, and in the meantime paid for many of the unaffordable letters himself.[12]

Nelson's request reached William Suckling at a bad time. He had his own children to support. William junior was also likely to become a candidate for marriage before long, and to boot he was a lieutenant in the guards, where promotion had to be purchased. There were other offspring too: Benjamin, who was in the church; Horace, who was set to follow; and Elizabeth. Furthermore, Uncle William had lost his first wife, Elizabeth, and was drifting towards remarriage himself. Without troubling Horatio with the news he eventually wedded Mary, the daughter of Thomas Rumsey of Kentish Town, on 26 October 1786.[13]

Unaware of his uncle's uncomfortable deliberations, Horatio fell ever more deeply in love, and the periods when business parted him from Nevis became increasingly tiresome. Towards the end of 1785 he was charged with returning Mrs Parry from Nevis to her husband, the governor of Barbados. A fierce storm overtook the *Boreas* as it struggled eastwards. The mainmast was badly cracked and almost lost, and the sails and rigging torn to pieces. Bringing his battered ship into Antigua in mid-December, Nelson resolved to proceed to Barbados against the advice of dockyard officers. As he explained to Fanny, 'We know that if a person does not perform what he promises, the world

is very apt to say he never did intend to do it. Therefore I will get up
and bring down Mrs Parry [to Barbados] at all risks.'[14]

He did – and was back at Nevis for Christmas, where he spent an
unusually enjoyable festival and discovered delight in such domes-
ticities as trying to teach little Josiah to read. 'I am well, and as merry
as I [could] wish,' he told his brother William on New Year's Day.
'So I must be, you will conclude, sitting by the woman who will be
my wife, and every day am I more than ever convinced of the propriety
of my choice, and I shall be happy with her. You will esteem her for
herself when you know her, for she possesses sense far superior to
half the people of our acquaintance, and her manners are Mrs
Moutray's.'[15]

Unfortunately, the engaging interlude was curtailed by another
voyage to Barbados, which had Nelson opening a long poetic love
letter to Fanny at sea early in the morning of 3 March 1786:

Separated from my dearest what pleasure can I feel? None! Be assured all my
happiness is centred with thee, and where thou art not, there I am not happy.
Every day, hour, and act convinces me of it. With my heart filled with the
purest and most tender affection do I write this, for was it not so, you know
me well enough to be certain that even at this moment I would tell you of it.
I daily thank God who ordained that I should be attached to you. He has I
firmly believe intended it as a blessing to me, and I am well convinced you
will not disappoint His beneficent intentions. Fortune – that is, money – is
the only thing I regret the want of, and that only for the sake of my affectionate Fanny. But the Almighty who brings us together will, I doubt not, take
ample care of us, and prosper all our undertakings. No dangers shall deter
me from pursuing every honourable means of providing handsomely for you
and yours, and again let me repeat that my dear Josiah shall ever be considered by me as one of my own. That Omnipotent Being who sees and knows
what passes in all hearts knows what I have written to be my undisguised
sentiments towards the little fellow.[16]

When Nelson reached Carlisle Bay in Barbados five days later,
he found a letter waiting for him. It was dated 3 January and written
by William Suckling, and it threw Horatio into torment. Though
his uncle did not refuse help, and remained 'very kind', his tone
betrayed a distinct lack of enthusiasm. If necessary his purse would
serve, but Horatio should reflect that as a bachelor he was at least
financially self-supporting. Before marrying he should clarify what

immediate provision Fanny's uncle would make for her and her son.[17]

Nelson was cut to the quick. Instinctively generous himself, he hated playing the supplicant. 'O my dear uncle!' he replied, 'You can't tell what I feel. Indeed, I can hardly write, or know what I am writing. You would pity me did you know what I suffer by that sentence, for although it does not make your act less generous, yet it embitters my happiness. You must know me, and consequently that I am guided by the strictest rules of honour and integrity, and that had I not been more ambitious of fame than money, I should not most probably [have] been under the necessity of making the present application to you.' Worst of all, he was forced back upon Mr Herbert, whom he little knew but wished to please, to establish exactly what he would do. No proud man enjoys badgering another for money.

But on the afternoon of 9 March the deed was done. 'In the course of the morning I have wrote to Mr Herbert,' he told Fanny, 'and have touched in as handsome a manner as I was able about you. *I fear* but hope it will have that effect I wish it. I am going to dine at Pilgrim [the governor's house]. I wish the dinner was over, for I am miserably low spirited.'[18]

Things did not go right for Nelson in Barbados, which became another 'detestable spot'. Worries about Fanny, the merciless sun and yet more debacles with the authorities contributed to ferocious headaches, which were probably stress-induced migraines. Only occasionally was he able to dilute the tension with the felicities of a shopping list supplied by Fanny and her relations, and expeditions in search of 'strings', a riding hat and ribbon, and a red parrot.[19]

3

'Duty,' Captain Nelson wrote to his fiancée at the beginning of May, 'is the great business of a sea officer. All private considerations must give way to it, however painful it is.'[20]

The particular business prolonging his stay in the 'detestable spot' was the most blistering round yet fought in the battle over the navigation laws. Fanny, fearful of further consequences, had begged Nelson to let sleeping dogs lie; and that is what most of the captains in the squadron did. When the *Boreas* nosed into Carlisle Bay, the fine, large, open gulf upon which the Barbadian capital was situated, she found the *Adamant* and the *Latona* riding gently at anchor. Neither seemed to worry about whether the merchantmen dropping in and out of the bay were legitimate or not, but Captain Nelson rested his reputation upon the stand he had made. In his opinion to suffer irregularities was to condone and encourage them.

He knew, though, that Barbados was a special case. The customs and prize-court administrations here were very different from those in St Kitts, Nevis and Antigua, over which Nelson and his allies had already prevailed. They were probably corrupt and certainly obdurate. One naval officer was sure that Judge Nathaniel Weeks of the vice-admiralty court held 'republican principles'. Whether true or not, Barbados was the hardest nut to crack in all the Lesser Antilles.[21]

The Barbadian court had already triumphed over Cuthbert Collingwood, turning loose his prize, the *Dolphin*, and saddling the captain with fearsome costs. Despite the reaffirmation of the navy's rights in other courts, Judge Weeks continued to espouse Scott's dictum that naval officers had no right to seize vessels, unless armed with a 'deputation' from the board of customs. Even mild-mannered Sir Richard Hughes was reduced to indignation, ranting to Lord Sydney about the 'shameful and unjust decision' that had stripped Collingwood of the *Dolphin* and made the navy a toothless watchdog. The Admiralty sympathised, and decided that the quickest way to neutralise the court was to have the English Customs House send out 'deputations' to all naval officers on the station, but by March 1786 those documents had yet to arrive.[22]

Almost as destructive was the behaviour of the island's attorney general, Charles Brandford, who was also king's advocate, responsible for representing the captors in the vice-admiralty court. A political appointment of Lord North, the former chief minister in England, Brandford had demanded extraordinary advisory fees from Collingwood in advance – fees that would have burned a hole in many a captain's purse and deterred him from proceeding with his case. In short, between them the attorney general and judge had immobilised the navy. Nor was the governor of any use. In the Leeward Islands, Shirley had suppressed his private reservations to lean upon wayward officials on behalf of the navigation laws. But Governor David Parry of the Windward Islands openly acknowledged his powerlessness. When he suggested that he might issue naval officers with 'deputations' himself, the court quickly informed him that he had no legal right to exercise such powers, which were the preserve of the customs. 'I have no control over the officers of His Majesty's customs, except the power of reporting their delinquencies,' Parry wailed to Sydney in April 1784. 'I find it very difficult to stimulate them to a proper execution of their duty.'[23]

But now a more formidable figure than Parry, Hughes and Collingwood had entered the contest. Ridiculously young, slight and insignificant in appearance, and far from well, Captain Horatio Nelson of the *Boreas* was nevertheless the acknowledged champion of the navigation laws. His arrival in Carlisle Bay presaged the ultimate clash of wills.

From the beginning Nelson's boats were out, and her officers scrambling aboard more or less unwilling merchant ships to examine their credentials. Most of the masters were allowed to proceed, and a few went on their way with advice about correcting one minor irregularity or another. But on 16 March a brig named the *Jane and Elizabeth* was seized. The ship flew English colours and carried a register purporting to show that she hailed from Dartmouth, England. Her master, John Frazier, claimed to be making a voyage from Nova Scotia to Barbados and Grenada. Unfortunately, Nelson's investigation penetrated the disguise; the *Jane and Elizabeth* was really owned by the Sheaffe family of Portsmouth, New Hampshire, and was engaged in illegal trade.

Two days later Nelson struck again. He had gone ashore leaving Second Lieutenant Dent in command of the *Boreas*. Some of his men had been left in Nevis, including the first lieutenant, who had fallen sick, and the master, 'Jemmy' Jameson, who was relieving his rheumatism in the spa waters. That day the *Brilliant*, a schooner under British colours, attracted Dent's attention and a boat under the ship's gunner and Midshipman William Batty was sent to board her. When Nelson was piped back aboard he examined the schooner's papers, interviewed her master and decided that the ship was foreign built and owned. He put prize crews aboard both ships and sent their own crews ashore.[24]

The merchants rose in fury, complaining that Nelson was blockading the port and acting as a revenue officer. Someone said that aggressive tars from the *Boreas* had physically attacked seamen aboard the impounded ships. Governor Parry dutifully passed the allegations to Rear Admiral Hughes, who was spending most of his time in Barbados, but Nelson briskly defended himself. He had not interrupted 'the *legal* business of the port', he reminded his accusers, nor had anyone been assaulted. In fact, the owner of the *Lovely Lass*, which he had also examined but released after due consideration, publicly admitted in the presence of Brandford and other officials that Nelson had actually done him a service by pointing out that he had an 'improper' register.[25]

Sweeping criticisms aside, Nelson proceeded against his prizes and made several important calls upon Brandford, the king's advocate who had fleeced Collingwood the previous year. He confidently presented him with the papers of the two ships, and at his request lodged them with William Forbes, the king's proctor, who prepared an 'information' in the king's name. For a while all ran smoothly. Perhaps there was something steely about Nelson, or maybe his reputation went before him, but the ludicrous fees levied upon Collingwood the previous year appear to have been postponed in this case. However, when the case went before the vice-admiralty court on 6 April the notorious Judge Weeks declined to proceed upon a technicality. He said the suit could not be made for the king alone as Brandford wished, but had to be the joint venture of the king and captors.

There followed a ridiculous deadlock. Brandford insisted the crown's rights could not be compromised by including Nelson in the suit. The ship had to be condemned to the king, who would then confer the proceeds of its sale to the captors through largesse. 'The judge is wrong – egregiously wrong,' he told Nelson, and refused to amend his presentation, praising the captain for standing 'cool and guarded' in court on 10 April, when Weeks 'told you some whimsical tales not at all applicable to the business in hand'. However, with equal tenacity the judge stood his ground like a boar at bay. He flatly refused to try the suit as it stood. And to complete the farce, counterclaims were made to the *Brilliant*. Shortly after Nelson's men had taken possession, a customs boat had sped from Bridgetown and come alongside. On this flimsy basis the customs service also claimed to have made the seizure. Possibly, the customs officials anticipated that Weeks would disqualify the navy from seizing, and wanted to claim the rights as captors themselves.[26]

In the meantime, Nelson received the sort of abuse he had known in St Kitts and Nevis the previous year. The vice-admiralty court showed no interest in overcoming the deadlock, Governor Parry offered wine and sympathy but spread his hands helplessly, and the captain was threatened with another damaging lawsuit. Someone even challenged him to a duel. By the middle of April almost all the ships of the squadron were in Carlisle Bay, including the flagship and the

Latona, Mediator, Falcon, Rattler and *Unicorn*, but only Nelson was embroiled in the battle.

Parry was a big disappointment. Horatio had enjoyed a good relationship with him, and in 1785 shuttled the governor's family between Barbados and Nevis a number of times. Parry had even extended an open invitation to Nelson to visit his house, Pilgrim. During Nelson's visits the family seemed to like him, and it was natural that on 15 April he should appeal to Parry to break the deadlock in the vice-admiralty court.[27]

Parry floundered helplessly, and worse. For at this point the two men were divided forever by a brutal incident that has escaped the notice of every previous scholar. A man was killed on the waterfront.

4

The evening of Friday 14 April 1786 was mild but dark in Bridgetown, and Horatio Nelson was ashore with one of his officers. He was not without apprehension. Enforcing the navigation laws had not made the men of the *Boreas* popular in the town, and a number of ugly incidents had occurred. Nelson himself had once been waylaid in the streets, and he and his officers were in the habit of carrying pistols with them. That night a number of men were hurrying here and there, but nothing unusual troubled the captain of the *Boreas* until about seven o'clock, when he heard a shot from close by. It came from the marketplace near St Michael's churchyard, only about one hundred yards away.

Rushing to the scene, Nelson and his officer saw several people from adjacent houses gathering about a wounded man being supported by John Scotland, the boatswain of the *Boreas*. Scotland was one of the captain's prime men. He had joined the ship in 1783 and been promoted to boatswain on 14 August of the following year at English Harbour, proving himself among the 'best' Nelson 'ever saw'. In that capacity, Scotland had gone ashore earlier in the day to punish some of the ship's company in hospital; that job done, he had Lieutenant Dent's permission to remain in the town off duty until the evening gun was fired at eight o'clock. As for the injured man, bleeding heavily from his right side, Nelson did not recall seeing him before, but he was James Elliott, a young sailor belonging to the army brig *Fortitude* of Grenada. A single pistol ball had passed between his two lowest ribs, cut through the right lobe of his liver and penetrated the upper stomach.[28]

Nelson asked who had shot him and Scotland admitted that his pistol had 'gone off by accident, and that he had done it'. Nelson ordered the wounded man to be taken to the naval hospital, and, aided by a few onlookers, Scotland carried Elliott away in his arms. Eventually, he found Nelson again. The boatswain was in serious trouble, with none but his captain to help him. He apparently told Nelson that in hospital he had supported Elliott while the surgeon probed and extracted the ball; moreover, he had surrendered his pistols to the hospital steward. He was ready to give himself up to the authorities, but begged Nelson's advice. Horatio said it was 'too late' and sent him back to the *Boreas*, but the following day Elliott died without leaving hospital.

On board Scotland told his story in the presence of Lieutenant Dent. He had been crossing the old churchyard and encountered a number of armed men running about in all directions and shouting out that a press gang was ashore. Passing him, one of the men said, 'That's one of them', and another – looking closer, 'the boatswain of the *Boreas*, by God!' Scotland drew his pistol to warn the mob to keep its distance, and then bolted in the direction of one of the ship's boats some one hundred and fifty yards away. He slipped, pistol in hand, and a man was hit. 'This is his story,' Nelson wrote, 'and I think it most probably to be true. He could have no reason for shooting any person, more especially one whom he never saw before in his life.'

Credible or not, that, at least, is how Nelson represented the whole affair more than four months later, but the depositions taken at the time tell a different story. Only two witnesses were material: James McCormick, a twenty-one-year-old sailor, and John Mitchell, an illiterate sailor of twenty-four who had shared lodgings with the dead man. They did not impress Captain Nelson, who thought them men of 'infamous character, one . . . what is vulgarly called [a] "bully to a house of ill fame", and the other a street vagabond', but that was not the opinion of the civil authorities. They seem to have accepted the depositions at face value, and the story of press-gang violence and wilful murder they contained.

According to McCormick and Mitchell two press gangs from the *Boreas* were raiding the waterfront for recruits that fatal evening, one led by a midshipman, the other by Scotland. The officers clapped pistols to the heads or chests of local sailors, demanding to know whether they belonged to any of the ships in the bay.[29]

Scotland, armed with a brace of pistols, with two marines and several cutlass-carrying sailors at his back, twice stopped McCormick, who protested – with a pistol in his ear – that he belonged to the *Latona*, one of Hughes's squadron. At about the same time another gang consisting of the midshipman and two stalwart tars intercepted three more seamen in St Michael's churchyard – Mitchell, Elliott and one Robert Hall. These last had been warned about the press gang, but with the midshipman's pistol pointing at him, Mitchell stood still. Elliott, unfortunately, ran down an alley and straight into Scotland's party as it was taking the unfortunate McCormick in tow. The boatswain flourished his pistol at Elliott and demanded to know the name of his ship. 'The general's brig,' Elliott replied, catching his breath. Scotland did not believe him, and pronounced him a prisoner, and it was then that Elliott made his fatal mistake. He promised to go quietly, begging not to be dragged away 'like a dog', but as his captors relaxed he suddenly darted away and made a dash for freedom. Scotland raised his pistol, shouting that if Elliott did not stop he would 'drop him'. The fugitive ignored him, and Scotland fired. Elliott staggered into the marketplace and collapsed.

Nelson's story that Scotland took Elliott to hospital received no support at the inquest on 16 April, which merely implied that the truculent boatswain fled after the shooting. According to the statement of the doctor who attended Elliott, a hospital steward reported that 'a gentleman whom he did not know who addressed him as a doctor' asked for assistance to be given a wounded man. Since Scotland was known in the naval hospital, and indeed was said to have been there that very day, this hardly converges with Nelson's claim that Scotland took Elliott to hospital, assisted in the operation to remove the bullet and surrendered his pistols to the steward. At the inquest the doctor did testify that he was personally acquainted with the boatswain of the *Boreas*, who was supposed to have shot Elliott, but failed to mention his presence in hospital. Had Scotland acted as Nelson said, it seems inconceivable that the doctor would not have mentioned it.

Mystification only increased during the following days. When the inquest was finished Governor Parry was called upon to bring the murderer to justice. He heeded protocol, and applied to Rear Admiral Hughes, asking that a boatswain named Scotland, said to belong to the *Boreas*, be surrendered for a civil trial. On 20 April Sir Richard went aboard the frigate, partly on the business of a court martial being held there to try three deserters from the *Rattler*, and spoke with

Nelson about the killing. Later the same day the admiral reported back to Parry that no one 'answering the description' given in the coroner's investigation was known, but if such a person was found aboard any of His Majesty's ships at Barbados Hughes would certainly hand him over.

This, of course, was pure prevarication, at least on the part of Nelson, who knew very well that the offender was his boatswain. The admiral himself might have been an innocent party, because the following day he addressed a letter to the captains of the squadron informing them that 'a man called Scotland, said to belong to one of His Majesty's ships in this bay' was charged with murder. 'It is therefore my particular direction that if there is any person of that name on board the respective ships and vessels under your commands, that you do immediately acquaint me therewith in order that he may be delivered to the civil power to take his trial.'[30]

Yet even this order failed to produce the fugitive and Nelson continued to shield Scotland. Secrets, unfortunately, have a way of slipping out. On the 21st the same Mitchell and McCormick who had deposed to Elliott's last moments got talking to seamen belonging to watering parties from the *Boreas*. Someone blabbed that Scotland was still aboard their frigate, but 'kept himself close in his cabin to prevent his discovery'. Messrs Mitchell and McCormick swore to what they had heard before a justice of the peace, and Parry not only relayed the information to Hughes, but also directed Judge Weeks to issue a warrant for the boatswain's arrest.[31]

Both tactics failed miserably. Hughes probably asked his flag-captain to tackle Horatio about the subject when he went aboard the *Boreas* on the 22nd to participate in a trial of the officers of the *Cyrus*, a government store ship wrecked on the coast a few days before. At any rate, the same day Hughes wrote to Parry saying that no such person as Scotland was on board any naval vessel in Carlisle Bay, nor could the admiral say what had become of him.

On 23 April, Weeks ordered Marshal Thomas Gretton to board the *Boreas* and apprehend the wanted man, but though under marshals Arthur and Jones immediately took the warrant and copies of relevant depositions to the ship they got no more satisfaction. Nelson was suffering from a violent migraine produced by the trial of the previous day and was nowhere to be seen. Lieutenant Dent received the marshals and disappeared with their papers to consult the sick captain. He returned shortly with the report that Nelson had said 'it was very well, and he would send the papers to the admiral'. Scotland's presence on board was neither denied nor admitted, and the marshals were forced to retreat without even recovering their documents.[32]

Nelson certainly did send the sequestrated papers to the admiral, and Hughes responded by telling Parry that a 'report had been made from Capt. Nelson that the said Scotland was not on board her'. Parry did not believe it, but he could only publish a proclamation on 23 April. It called upon justices and officials to cause 'all and any places and place throughout the island' to be scoured for the offender, and cautioned all merchant ships against taking him aboard. A reward of £20 was offered for information about the fugitive, or for his apprehension.

When Parry wrote to Lord Sydney, the home secretary could not believe that Nelson or Hughes would have contrived Scotland's escape, but on that subject Parry had the surer view. Despite the reward, the searches and the warnings to merchant ships Scotland was never seen again in Barbados. Nelson, who later admitted dissuading Scotland from surrendering to the authorities on the day of the shooting, unquestionably facilitated his subsequent escape and reported dishonestly on his whereabouts. His responses to Hughes and the under marshals were transparently obstructive, and he was no more candid in writing to Fanny on the 23rd. The Parrys were relatives and friends of the Herberts, and Horatio's dilemma was to explain his estrangement from them. He claimed to be one of four naval captains who had experienced 'a little difference' with the governor, and that he would never set foot in Pilgrim again unless Parry tendered 'a very handsome apology'. If Fanny ever heard the true story, she never held it against him.[33]

5

Given the entrenched contradictions in our primary sources, the Scotland affair remains puzzling today. None of the essential questions can be answered satisfactorily. How was Elliott really shot? What happened to Scotland? And why did Nelson shield the fugitive? Yet this was the most extreme example of Nelson's willingness to intervene on behalf of distressed followers. It reflects upon both his commitment to his men, and their loyalty to him, and it is worth pursuing in detail.

While the McCormick–Mitchell account of Elliott's death may have been inaccurate, Nelson's own version of the shooting is the least convincing of the two, and vulnerable at every stage. To begin with, Nelson denied that his men were hunting recruits that night. His complement was complete 'to a man or two' and 'dozens [of applicants] were daily refused from merchant ships'. Horatio went so far as to admit that a master and some marines with side arms had been sent ashore on the night of the shooting, but that was to search for a deserter who had swum from the ship. This expedition, Nelson claimed, 'they turned into a press gang'.

But this would seem to have been at best only a half-truth. The muster of the *Boreas* does record that Able Seaman Hugh Robinson fled the ship the day of the shooting, and men were probably sent to search for him. But the muster also contains other telltale facts. We learn, for example, that four men were recruited that same night. Their names were John Jones, Robert Anderson, George Devereaux and George Long, and they were certainly not all volunteers. Anderson deserted five days later, and Devereaux was discharged on 7 May as 'unfit for His Majesty's service through drunkenness'. These entries alone suggest that parties from the *Boreas* were pressing sailors into service the day Elliott was shot.

More than this, the muster contains the name of a fifth man enrolled that night. He was none other than James Elliott, the unfortunate victim who died in hospital without ever setting foot on the ship. Incredibly, on 14 April Elliott was rated on the books of the *Boreas* as no. 361, a captain's servant, and discharged dead the following day. Why Nelson should have officially recorded a dead man as a member of his ship's company is a mystery. It is just possible that he was trying to represent the matter as a purely naval affair, between Scotland, a petty officer and his subordinate, and thereby to remove the shooting from civil jurisdiction to the more lenient and malleable environment of a naval courts martial. Whatever the case, this remarkable entry supports the view that, notwithstanding Nelson's smoke screen, there had been an element of recruitment in the waterfront fracas.[34]

If Nelson's denial of the press gang fails to convince, what about his version of the shooting itself? Scotland's account of his pistol being discharged accidentally as he ran from a mob sounds very implausible. One wonders, for instance, what happened to this mob, and why, if a bystander was hit, it did not gather round in indignation. Yet Nelson, who arrived almost immediately, mentions nothing about an irate or outraged crowd. Equally, if Scotland took Elliott to the hospital, assisted the doctor in treating him and surrendered his pistols to the steward, as Nelson claimed, why did the doctor make no reference to it at the inquest?

Whatever happened, there is no doubt that Nelson protected Scotland. He sent him to the ship instead of surrendering him to the authorities and frustrated attempts to root him out. Eventually, as we shall see, he went further, discharging Scotland from the *Boreas* without declaring him a deserter and fighting for the full payment of his wages.

As one would expect, Scotland's escape is equally wreathed in conjecture. Governor Parry believed that he was aboard Nelson's ship as late as 23 April, when the marshals failed to make an arrest. The muster of the *Boreas* seems to bear him out, since it recorded Scotland as being present at two full musters following the shooting, on 16 and 23 April. Further, against the boatswain's name is the discharge date of 30 April – seven days after the under marshals had attempted to serve their warrant.

Some months later Nelson admitted to Sir Charles Middleton, the comptroller of the Navy Board, that he had discharged Scotland willingly and with the approval of Sir Richard Hughes, something about which the admiral himself was understandably silent. At that time Nelson also gave an account of Scotland's flight that contradicts the signed muster of his ship but strikes a chord with other circumstances. According to Nelson, Scotland remained doing his duties on the *Boreas* until the afternoon of Saturday 15 April, when he was discharged. This makes sense. Elliott's death that day changed the boatswain's prospects. If convicted he stood to hang, and Scotland probably preferred to take his chances running. A flight on or soon after the 15th would also have allowed Nelson truthfully to deny that Scotland was on his ship between the 20th and the 23rd, though in a way that afforded no help to the authorities whatsoever.

Scotland apparently got aboard the *Cyrus* store ship, or at least the carpenter of that vessel later deposed as much. The log book of the *Boreas* records one possible means of transfer in its reference to a delivery of staves made to the *Cyrus* shortly before the store ship sailed for Antigua on 16 April. But Captain Sandys was shipping aboard the *Cyrus* as an invalid, and it is possible that Nelson prevailed upon him to take Scotland aboard. Whatever, the *Cyrus* was unlucky, and ran upon a rock one and a half miles off the northwestern shore of Barbados the day she sailed. She sank in seventy fathoms with some loss of life, and Nelson took a number of the survivors on to his own ship and presided over the court martial that condemned her commander and master for the accident. Scotland made it ashore but was not among those survivors who returned to service. With some comrades he apparently reached a coastal plantation and then slipped away again to work his passage to England.[35]

The affair ended with Parry and Nelson wrestling for Scotland's fate with mutual dissatisfaction. The governor urged the Admiralty and the British home secretary to bring the boatswain to justice and reprobated Nelson's conduct, while at the end of August Nelson made a serious attempt to secure the fugitive a pardon and his pay. In support of these requests he sent the Navy Board three depositions he had caused to be sworn by himself, Jameson, the master, and Balentine, the gunner, of the *Boreas*. Nelson's statements have been given, and those of Jameson and Balentine carry little weight. Neither saw the actual shooting, and their accounts lack the diversity of detail one would expect of spontaneous, undirected statements, and were obviously contrived to reinforce circumstantial points favourable to Scotland. However, they emphasised the hostility naval parties encountered ashore. Some days before the fatal incident Balentine and Scotland were abused by a waterfront crowd, had bottles thrown at them and took refuge in a house. The mob only dispersed after 'expressing the most bitter oaths that if they had catched [sic] this deponent and the said boatswain they would have done for us'. Jameson, who was ashore the day Elliott was killed, took six armed men for security against 'the several bodies of armed men who constantly paraded the streets of Bridgetown'. The master also testified that he was on the spot immediately after the shooting. 'He, this deponent, ordered the said [wounded] man to be carried to the naval hospital, when the said boatswain with the assistance of some others, conveyed him there.'[36]

Nelson spoke with passion for his boatswain. It had all been a tragic accident, whipped up by a hostile Barbadian population. The inquest had reached a decision without consulting anyone from the *Boreas*. 'If the said jury had taken the trouble to enquire of this deponent,' he said, 'or summoned any one of the supposed press gang . . . they would never have been able to state upon their oaths such falsities as would deprive the boatswain of even that pity which the most vile of men deserve.' But his pleas fell unheeded. In August, Scotland visited his agents in London, explaining that he had come home to recover his health, and applying for the wages that had accrued over several years on the *Boreas*. Unfortunately, the Admiralty had put a stop on his pay and a warrant was issued in Bow Street for his arrest. A constable even went to Deptford, where Scotland was supposed to be hiding, but arrested the wrong man. The final upshot is unclear, but the probability is that Scotland neither received his pay nor ever answered for his offence before a court. Had he done so Nelson would surely have been summoned as a witness.

But why did Nelson defend Scotland so disingenuously and determinedly? It is a fair question given the gravity of the charge and the risks attending the obstruction of justice. Captain Nelson's conduct pitted him against the civil authorities in Barbados and created difficulties for Sir Richard Hughes and the Admiralty. More crucially, even today it bears upon his reputation as a law-abiding man of honour.

Loyalty was one dimension. Nelson obviously respected Scotland. He had promoted him, and probably knew that if occasion demanded the man would have fought and died for his country. In deciding whether to surrender or shield Scotland, Nelson also had to weigh his own standing with his men. The company of the *Boreas* worked to an unwritten contract. The men obeyed, and if necessary suffered for their officers, but in return they looked to the captain for protection and help in difficulties. He was their representative in the mysterious, inaccessible and intimidating world of gentrified officialdom above. He knew how to fight for their just rights, and what to do if they got into trouble. Scotland now put that contract on trial. Perhaps no one aboard the frigate but Scotland knew the truth about the shooting, but they all knew that a man with whom they had forged a clannish camaraderie in a dangerous service was facing a hanging offence, and they looked to the captain to arbitrate his fate.

Nor must Nelson's actions be judged outside another essential context. As Dr Rodger has informed us, eighteenth-century naval justice was considered to be more lenient than that exercised in English civil courts. It stipulated, for example, only a tithe of the number of offences for which men could be executed. Naval officers were apt to regard the civil courts as vindictive and unjust, and Nelson's case was not unique. Commodore Keppel had once refused to surrender a marine to the attorney general of Jamaica in the belief that he would not receive a fair trial. Nelson had exactly those same misgivings in 1786. The people of Bridgetown were prejudiced against the navy, and particularly the *Boreas* for her part in stopping illegal trade. The cases of the *Jane and Elizabeth* and *Brilliant* were stirring those embers at the very time Elliott had been shot. In the captain's opinion Scotland would not have been tried fairly in Barbados. The civil authorities had already proved themselves to be corrupt and incompetent in the matter of prize, while in the proceedings against Scotland an inquest had been wound up without any witnesses from the *Boreas* having been called. Reflecting thus darkly, Nelson believed there was no justice to be had in Bridgetown. He could not abandon Scotland to its mercies. Nelson's actions may have been misguided, and were unquestionably duplicitous, but they were not devoid of principle or courage.[37]

One thing is certain: the Elliott affair ended cooperation between Nelson and Parry, and with it any hopes that the governor would unlock the stymied proceedings in the prize courts. As late as October, Parry stormily reminded Nelson of the steps he had been 'compelled' to take 'in support of the dignity of the king's government' and 'the lives, liberties, and properties of His Majesty's subjects' as a result of the activities of the *Boreas*. Nelson was so furious that he forwarded the correspondence to Lord Sydney, affecting 'total' ignorance of the roots of Parry's insinuations and demanding the governor specify his charges.[38]

And against this background Nelson's battle with the Barbadian prize court raged on and reached a dramatic climax.

6

The Elliott–Scotland case smouldered but Nelson's search for illegal traders continued without remission. Among the suspicious vessels he examined was Collingwood's old nemesis, the *Dolphin*, now renamed the *Greyhound*. Horatio would have loved to arrest her, but the vessel was still under judicial appeal and beyond his reach. In fact no more ships were seized at Barbados, and as Nelson's relations with the islanders deteriorated he was ever more impatient to bring the suit against his existing prizes to a conclusion and be gone.[39]

The *Jane and Elizabeth* and *Brilliant* were still in his hands, but the people of Bridgetown were so 'very tumultuous' that Nelson feared an attempt might be made to take them from him by force. He even had the king's mark, a broad arrow, carved into their masts so that they could be identified if stolen. Yet without proper maintenance the vessels themselves were also decaying. Their hulls leaked and their cables rotted, and Nelson talked about unloading their cargoes to save them from shipwreck. Still 'the door of Justice' remained closed. Judge

Weeks obstinately refused to act on the crown suit, and Brandford, the king's advocate prosecuting the case for Nelson, would submit no other. 'Thus circumstanced the vessels will soon require no information to be filed against them,' Nelson complained to Parry on 1 May. 'They will either be driven on shore or out to sea, for their cables are getting very bad.'[40]

But Parry was refusing to see him, and when Brandford waited on the governor Parry would only say that while he thought the judge wrong he had no powers to intervene. Perhaps he spoke the truth, for Nelson heard that when Parry's secretary called upon Weeks to persuade him to give way, the judge declared that he would 'never' yield to the governor, nor to any order but that of the king in council. Finally, on 20 May Brandford informed Nelson that he doubted there was any 'probability' of the ships 'being brought to a speedy trial *here*'. He planned removing the case to England.[41]

By then similar ideas were occurring to the naval officers. In May, Hughes and Nelson had sent three letters across the Atlantic voicing their frustration to the Admiralty, and the law did eventually vindicate their opinion. In August, Admiralty solicitors would rule that Weeks was wrong to refuse to proceed against Nelson's prizes, but back in steaming Barbados such long-winded procedures were of no use whatsoever.[42]

Nelson had a quicker remedy up his sleeve. Very well, he decided: if the Barbadian court refused to deal with his prizes, he would take them to a court that had no such qualms. It was a high-risk strategy, involving the removal of prizes from one jurisdiction to another and a pick-and-choose courts policy of doubtful legality, but Nelson had never been afraid of using his initiative.

Reclaiming the relevant papers from an astonished king's proctor, Nelson had the sails of the *Boreas* set and put to sea on the 21st, taking both of the prizes with him. He sailed for Nevis, the scene of earlier victories over the illegal traders, where his influence with island officials was the strongest. President Herbert, his prospective father-in-law, and the attorney general Stanley were both worried about their health and planning to retire to England, but at the moment they were still at their posts and powerful allies of the little captain. Magnus Morton, Herbert's brother-in-law, and John Ward, who had helped Horatio in the past, were both judges of the vice-admiralty court. They did not fail Nelson at this crucial moment. The ships were condemned on 26 June.

In Bridgetown the administrators were furious. The court had lost its fees for processing the suits, the customs service saw its claim to the *Brilliant* disappearing and Governor Parry was forced into the open about his own ambitions to profit from the sale of the *Jane and Elizabeth*. He insisted that it was a governor's prerogative to share in confiscated prizes, and when the ship was condemned in Nevis he appealed against the distribution of the proceeds. He wanted a traditional third for himself, 'for the sake of his successors'. Equally, perhaps, he and his associates felt a loss of face. Nelson's actions volubly proclaimed the inability of the Barbadian court to perform its duty.[43]

Parry thundered that Nelson had acted in 'direct violation of every existing act and statute in the parliamentary and constitutional annals of Great Britain, for which he will, doubtless, on a future day be made responsible'. Later in the year his agent went to London to pursue 'the general conduct of Captain Nelson' with the home secretary, but the mission may only have prompted more questions about the governor's relationship with officials he affected to be unable to control. The agent was none other than Joseph Keeling, the collector of customs at Barbados.[44]

In England an investigation was mounted. From letters written by Sir Richard Hughes on 10 and 18 May 1786, the Admiralty learned that Nelson had the entire confidence of his commander-in-chief. On 17 July the board asked their proctor, George Gostling, to prepare an opinion of the case, and eleven days later his résumé went for confirmation to senior law officers of the crown, the attorney general, king's advocate and advocate for the Admiralty. All agreed that the Barbadian court had erred in declining to proceed with Brandford's suit, but matters stalled when a memorial arrived from Judge Weeks himself. Dated 8 October, it gave his version of the affair, and the Admiralty delayed announcing their judgement until the new document had been fully considered. Finally, on 5 July 1787, the legal process torpedoed the hopes of Weeks and Parry by reaffirming the initial decision. Though 'willing to believe that the judge [Weeks] acted to the best of his judgement', the law officers concluded, 'we cannot but censure the irregularity of his proceedings . . . Captain Nelson's conduct in carrying the ships away to another jurisdiction was certainly not regular, but under the circumstances in which he stood we do not think that it calls for reprehension.' Dissatisfied, Parry continued to press his case until the end of the year, but without success. The reputation of his administration had been damaged, and its morale may have already been weakening. Brandford had resigned in January 1787, ostensibly because of ill health.[45]

The captain of the *Boreas* had met the most obdurate court in the Lesser Antilles head-on and beaten it on every front.

But the personal cost had been considerable. His relations with Parry were ruined and the months of sliding on thin ice had drained him. He suffered from severe headaches, and the malarial pains that had intermittently troubled his chest for ten years returned. For a time his physician feared that Nelson had consumption, but the diagnosis was revised and the patient consigned to a regimen of ass's or goat's milk and beef tea. He was exhausted. 'My activity of mind is too much for my puny constitution,' Horatio wrote wearily. 'I am worn to a skeleton.'[46]

7

Looking over his accounts Nelson decided that the profiteering in the Barbadian prize court ran scandalously deep. Now that the *Jane and Elizabeth* and *Brilliant* had been condemned he was able to compare the charges for the unsuccessful suit in Barbados with those in Nevis, and he was incensed by the result.

There, on the Barbados account, was Mr Brandford's notorious retaining fee of £26 8s. 0d., as he expected. But the differences in the charges made for similar services in the two courts were the most striking. In Nevis, for example, the charge for drawing up the indictments was £3 6s. 0d.; in Barbados it also amounted to £26 8s. 0d. In Nevis Mr Adye had charged £30 6s. 8d. for travelling from St Kitts, arguing the cases against the two ships in court, and securing condemnation; in Barbados Brandford's fee for attending with 'nothing done' was £33. And Nelson found several entries in the Barbadian account that utterly baffled him. There was the £39 12s. 0d. for consulting Captain Nelson. 'What could they consult with me about!' Horatio raged. 'My only questions were to know when the vessels were likely to be tried, and if I might not carry them away if trial of them was refused.' A further charge concerned appeals, though technically no appeals could have been lodged in Barbados, since the judge had refused to allow the suits into court. Summing it all up, Nelson found that fees for the successful proceedings at Nevis totalled £44 3s. 0d. and those for the unsuccessful suits in Barbados £174 17s. 4d.[47]

Nothing annoyed seamen more than the feeling that quill-pushing bureaucrats were creaming the prize money granted captors to encourage their perilous exertions at sea. As late as 1811 there were no standard rates for fees at the vice-admiralty courts, and the firebrand naval officer and Member of Parliament Lord Cochrane fiercely condemned the rapacity of officials. On one occasion he amused the House of Commons by unfurling a proctor's bill 'long enough to reach from one end of the House to the other'. The result was a commission in 1812 and the consequent establishment of scales of fees. Back in 1787 Nelson similarly fumed at the parasites he believed to be robbing honest sailors and damaging the public service. That February he fired off a complaint to the Admiralty. It was not a thoughtless document, and praised more officials than it condemned, but it accused Brandford and Byam, his counterpart in Grenada, of being unworthy of their offices.[48]

These were transitory times in the evolution of public service. The past, in which individuals accepted the burdens of office and compensated themselves by charging fees, was slipping away too slowly; the future, in which professional civil servants were rewarded by regulated salaries and pensions, was still whimpering in its cradle. Nelson had no doubt where he stood, but his charges went to the Treasury and disappeared in obscure government files.[49]

Some things were changing in the Leeward Islands, however.

There were signs that the campaign against illegal traders was having an effect. On 8 July, while cruising off St Kitts, Nelson seized his last contraband trader, the schooner *Eagle* from Trinidad. She sailed beneath Spanish colours, and was filled with Spanish mules and cattle, but papers on board revealed a remarkable 'transmogrification'. She was an American ship taking advantage of a twenty-year-old loophole in the navigation laws that allowed Spanish colonists to export bullion to the British in return for manufactured goods. Originally the loophole had been considered beneficial to the British islands, enabling them to exchange any unwanted English products for bullion that could be used to import foodstuffs from other British colonies. Gradually the latitude had been extended from bullion to livestock. From what Nelson could make out, American merchants began to use this route as their attempts to trade directly with the British colonies got riskier. The ruse involved discharging part of their merchandise in the Spanish colonies, hiding the rest behind fresh cargoes of livestock and sailing for British ports under Spanish flags and papers. Nelson vowed to stamp out the practice, and this ship was condemned at Nevis on 17 July, but at least it suggested that the navy's enforcement of the navigation laws was achieving some success.

Nelson felt further vindicated when the British government strengthened the navy's powers to deal with clandestine trade. 'I have smoothed the way for those who may come after me,' he wrote. 'The captains of men-of-war are now invested with great additional powers, enough to carry on the business of doing good for the nation without interruption.'[50]

Another change occurred on 1 August 1786, when the *Boreas* fired a final salute to Sir Richard Hughes as he sailed from Nevis for England. Sir Richard Bickerton was supposed to be coming out to succeed him, but in the meantime Nelson was *de facto* commander-in-chief of the station. The rebel had taken charge. When the *Boreas* holed up in English Harbour for his last hurricane season, Nelson occupied the commanding officer's house ashore and received invitations to the table of Sir Thomas Shirley.

The two men had already restored their working relationship, and in July Nelson had performed a mission for Shirley by visiting the Swedish island of St Bartholomew as an ambassador. Nelson admired Scandinavians, whom he considered kin of the English, and the previous year had written to the Swedes to extend his best wishes for their 'new' settlement and 'the ties of friendship between our countries'. He had offered his help, and true to his word ferried the Swedish governor, Baron Rayalin, from St Kitts to St Bartholomew in February 1786. Nelson was therefore an ideal choice for the new assignment. In Antigua there were worries that a new Swedish proclamation would entice enslaved blacks of British islands to St Bartholomew in search of sanctuary. On 13 July Nelson spoke to the governor, and received assurances that his proclamation would not be allowed to act to the detriment of British territories.[51]

Nelson and Shirley buried the hatchet, but Horatio never really trusted him. He had grown cynical during his dealings with West Indian politicos, and learned that 'artful men will never want an artful story, and oaths will not be wanting to confirm any tale'.[52]

With Hughes gone, there were also new burdens, and few caused greater irritation than appointments. At the end of August, Commander Wilfred Collingwood passed him a letter he had received from William Lewis, surgeon of the *Rattler*. Lewis was ill, and charged Nelson with behaving 'no better than a brute' in refusing him permission to seek sick quarters ashore. The evidence suggests that Collingwood, through whom communications between Lewis and Nelson had gone back and forth, was at fault. Lewis said that Nelson refused him a sick ticket; Nelson that neither the necessary report on Lewis's health nor a ticket had been presented him or sought. As soon as he grasped the situation, Horatio implemented the relevant procedures, and Lewis went ashore while Thomas Morgan, surgeon's mate of the *Boreas*, stood in for him. The matter should have ended there, but Lewis's attack on Nelson had been so public and intemperate that he was discharged from his post and the Navy Board refused to appoint him to any other unless he obtained a letter expiating his offence. There followed a grovelling letter from Lewis to Nelson, and the captain declaring, with his deep-seated decency, that honour was satisfied.[53]

Throughout all these tribulations, new and old, Nelson had at least one pleasurable task to pursue, a suit not less diverting but entirely different from any of his tiresome clashes with furtive officials and foreign traders. His quarry was the recipient of the series of gossipy letters he was now addressing to 'my dearest Fanny'.

8

September 1786 found him languishing amid the heat, mosquitoes and monotony of English Harbour, ritually sitting out storms and reporting on the number of French ships about the islands. He felt strength returning. A few months earlier a doctor had said that he had to get out of the islands, but the pains in his lungs had subsided and he concluded that the 'Great Being who has so often raised me from the sick bed has once more restored me, and to that health which I very seldom enjoy'. Still, he had been more than two years on the station and expected to be recalled. Unfinished business demanded attention.[54]

In particular, he looked to a permanent happy union with Fanny. Family and friends approved, as their letters had told him, and Mrs Moutray, in the midst of losing most of her significant others, also sent her blessing. Nelson was surprisingly frank about Mary, and Fanny had become accustomed to reading his impassioned tributes. Mary wished them happiness 'equal to what she enjoyed but *far far* more lasting', but was beset with misfortunes. 'My dearest, I can't express what I feel for her,' Nelson continued, 'and your good heart I am sure will sympathise with mine. What is so truly affecting as a virtuous woman in distress? . . . When you know her you must love her.'[55]

Money remained an obstacle to his own matrimony. Still uncertain about how deeply President Herbert would dip into his pockets to assist them, the couple decided to postpone the marriage until Horatio received his recall to England. Nelson hoped that further employment would then support whatever Suckling and Herbert might supply. He was still corresponding with Lord Hood and hoped to tap his patronage.

But in the meantime he would have to find other ways of satisfying his love for Fanny. In August he wrote to her:

Monday, seven in the evening: As you begin to know something about sailors, have you not often heard that salt water and absence always wash away love? Now I am such a heretic as not to believe that faith, for behold, every morning since my arrival I have had six pails of salt water at day-light poured upon my head, and instead of finding what the seamen say to be true, I perceive the contrary effect. And if it goes on so contrary to the prescription, you must see me before my fixed time. At first I bore absence tolerably, but now it is almost insupportable, and by and by I expect it will be quite so. But patience is a virtue, and I must exercise it upon this occasion, whatever it costs my feelings. I am alone in the commanding officer's house, while my ship is fitting, and from sunset until bedtime I have not a human creature to speak to. You will feel a little for me, I think. I did not use[d] to be over fond of sitting alone. The moment old *Boreas* is habitable in my cabin, I shall fly to it, to avoid mosquitoes and melancholies. Hundreds of the former are now devouring me through all my clothes. You will, however, find I am better, though when you see me I shall be like an Egyptian mummy, for the heat is intolerable. But I walk a mile out at night without fatigue, and all day I am housed. A quart of goat's milk is also taken every day, and I enjoy English sleep, always barring mosquitoes, which all Frank's [Lepee's] care with my net cannot keep out at present. What nonsense I am sending you![56]

Weddings, indeed, were very much on the minds of the Nelson–Suckling brood as 1786 came to an end. There was a veritable stampede to the altar. Uncle William Suckling married in October, while Horatio was visiting Martinique, and a few weeks later, on 9 November, Nelson's brother William finally abandoned the attentions of Cousin 'Miss Ellen' and her fortune of £2,000 to marry Sarah, the daughter of the Reverend Henry Yonge of Great Torrington in Devon. The Reverend Yonge was a cousin to the Lord Bishop of Norwich, and Sarah probably met William in East Anglia. In time she would become 'Norfolk Sally', and her compassion and beauty would contrast with the rotund figure and avaricious nature of her husband. Early the following year, 1787, it was the turn of Horatio's younger siblings. On New Year's Day the feckless Suckling arrived in his finest at St Stephen's, Norwich, to marry Sophia Smith of Bungay, while the next month the baby of the family – Horatio's beloved Kate – became Mrs George Matcham in Bath.[57]

Horatio seemed glad that these things were so, for he regarded marriage as the natural condition. 'So then,' he chided his brother William, 'you are at last become a husband. May every blessing attend you. It is, I have no doubt, the happiest – or otherwise – state, and I believe it is most generally the man's fault if he is not happy.' Somehow, even then, he knew.[58]

XV

THE PRINCE AND THE POST-CAPTAIN

> Admirals all, for England's sake
> Honour be yours and fame!
> And honour, as long as waves shall break
> To Nelson's peerless name!
> Henry Newbolt, *Admirals All*

1

ROSEAU Bay, in Dominica, the largest of the British Windward Islands, Saturday 2 December 1786. Captain Nelson of the frigate *Boreas*, acting commander on the Leeward Islands station, had found what he was looking for, anchored among His Majesty's ships riding serenely off the one significant settlement boasted by this newly acquired territory. For there, fresh from Barbados with the *Amphion*, *Solebay* and *Rattler*, was the twenty-eight-gun frigate *Pegasus* and her unusual captain. Forewarned, Nelson had been waiting for Prince William Henry, the king's sailor son. His task, according to 'secret' instructions inherited from Hughes, was to show the prince around the station, acquaint him with the crown's possessions, and then to return him to Commodore Herbert Sawyer in Halifax, Canada, by 'the second week of May'. Now an irritating spell of 'prince hunting', something Horatio thought 'a bad sort of business', was over and he could discharge his burden.[1]

Within a few hours of her arrival, the guns of the *Boreas* were reverentially saluting the royal personage as he came on board. Nelson had last seen William Henry at Windsor Castle, preparing to visit Hanover. The prince had been a midshipman then, but the uncommonly short period of time since had made him captain of the *Pegasus*. The previous April, a mere ten months after passing for lieutenant, the twenty-year-old had skipped the grade of commander and been made post-captain by Lord Howe at the irresistible suggestion of His Majesty. Then the prince's interest in the daughter of the Portsmouth naval commissioner had intervened. With the approval of the king and Lord Hood, still a leading adviser to all persons royal, the Admiralty had packed William Henry off to Canada, where he had served out of harm's way before coming south to the West Indian islands.

The meeting at Dominica brought together the greater part of a small squadron that effectively became Nelson's first supra-ship command. He had lost Cuthbert Collingwood, who had taken the *Mediator* home the previous summer, and some of the other ships that had served Hughes, but for the six months following the rendezvous at Roseau Bay Nelson headed the frigates *Boreas*, *Pegasus*, *Solebay* and *Maidstone*, and the sloop *Rattler*. It was a small force, but the personnel were far from contemptible. Henry Newcome of the *Maidstone* had been a captain for four years and was destined for distinction fighting the French in the East Indies, while John Holloway of the *Solebay*, a plain-speaking, honest, pious Somerset man, was also a thorough professional. Almost fifteen years older than Nelson and married to a woman of Antigua, he eventually became governor of Newfoundland. The other captain, William Henry, would become King William IV, the sailor king.[2]

Nelson had liked William Henry three years before, and admired his occasional generosity and dedication to the service. Today the Royal Navy has become an almost obligatory part of the education of a prince of the blood, but for this pioneer it was much more. William Henry saw it as a career and something worthy of a life's work. Even at the end he considered himself a naval officer as well as a sovereign. The prince cut a more impressive figure than Nelson remembered, with a manly bearing and fashionable hair that compensated for the remains of puppy fat, but if he looked a naval officer and still showed some virtues, his was a character of peculiar difficulty.

Nelson noticed it straight away. As a junior captain William Henry was under Nelson's command, but had the status to manipulate. He showed the captain of the *Boreas* two sets of instructions, one from Lord Howe of the Admiralty and the other in the hand of Commodore Sawyer of the North American station. The first ordered the prince to return directly to Halifax upon completing his tour of the Leeward Islands, but it was obvious he preferred Sawyer's orders, which allowed him to go where he pleased in the West Indies provided he returned to Canada by the middle of June. Nelson had to explain that, if the orders were inconsistent, Lord Howe's instructions would have to prevail.[3]

Nelson also saw that all was not well aboard the prince's ship, *Pegasus*. William asked Nelson about his officers and he replied that they were entirely to his satisfaction. The prince observed that he wished he could say the same of his own men, 'for although I think mine know their duty, yet . . . they give themselves such airs that he could not bear them. Do you know that they would not go to the ball which Governor Parry gave me at Barbados, which I think a mark of great contempt to me?'

William Henry reserved his principal fire for his first lieutenant, Isaac Schomberg, a man of aristocratic and handsome cast and more than thirty years old. Nelson knew Schomberg to be a good officer and a favourite of Lord Hood. In fact, it was effectively Hood who had put the lieutenant on the *Pegasus* to 'dry nurse' the inexperienced prince, but the task was defeating him. William Henry resented any interference in his management of the ship and bad blood was soon running. While Schomberg remained popular with the junior officers, disenchantment with the captain spread. Midshipman Martin would recall that 'the strictness' with which the prince enforced duty amounted 'almost to torture, so that as growing boys we had scarcely strength for the work he took out of us'.[4]

The next day Nelson got a glimpse of that bad blood for himself. He went aboard the *Pegasus* to find His Highness preparing to receive a party from a French twenty-gunner, *La Favourite*, which arrived to invite the prince to visit Martinique. William had ordered his men into formal dress and was distracted to find them still casually attired. 'Sir,' he snapped to his first lieutenant in Nelson's presence, 'I ordered the ship's company to have their uniform jackets on.'

Schomberg said that he thought the weather too hot. The uniforms were too warm for the West Indies, but if the captain wished it he would see to it directly. Horatio noted that 'the manner [in] which this was spoke made a much greater impression upon me than all [that] happened afterwards, for I plainly saw all was not right'.

A day later these suspicions were confirmed in a conversation with Captain Brown of the *Amphion*, who had come with the *Pegasus*,

Solebay and *Rattler* from Barbados. He warned Nelson that a court martial was threatening and advised him to try to head it off. Nelson understood what Brown meant. If Schomberg demanded a court martial on account of some rupture with the prince, and was acquitted or even merely reprimanded, it would reflect badly upon William Henry. The dignity and honour of the royal family were at stake. After landing this grim bombshell, and predicting that Nelson's time would be 'disagreeable', Brown set about taking the other ships to Antigua. Nelson was left with the unhappy *Pegasus* and the unenviable job of chaperoning the prickly prince around the islands.

2

There were several related problems.

To start with, William Henry was still dissolute, and easily lapsed into a miasma of drinking, gambling, wenching and coarse table talk. His own family fully acknowledged the difficulty. The king and queen were continually bombarding their son with paper broadsides, reproving him for the company he kept, and they lamented that his annual allowance of £3,000 had been blown within six months. His brother also admitted William Henry's 'natural inclination for all kinds of dissipation', while one who spent three months with the prince shortly after his visit to the Leeward Islands breathed a huge sigh of relief when it was over. 'I believe I shall never spend three months in that way again,' he said, 'for such a time of dissipation, etc., etc., I cannot suppose possibly to happen [again].'[5]

At Dominica, Nelson witnessed the prince's boisterous and boorish indecorum at innumerable functions thrown in his honour. Horatio was ill-fitted for such nonsense. Though he wore his full dress uniform ashore and enjoyed attention, he was quiet in company and a modest drinker. Tea was Nelson's daytime drink, and while he occasionally enjoyed a glass of champagne after dinner he seldom touched wine. In all the prince's stupefied revels he never once saw Captain Nelson drunk. Nonetheless, from the beginning Nelson gave William Henry the benefit of any doubts. In a letter to Fanny he owned that the royal guest was driving women from the dinner table, but spoke strongly in his favour:

Our young prince is a gallant man. Some ladies at Dominica seemed very much charmed by him. He is volatile, but always with great good nature.

There were two balls during his stay, and some of the old ladies were mortified that His Royal Highness would not dance with them. But he says he is
determined to enjoy the privilege of all other men, that of asking any lady he
pleases. Mrs Parry dined at table the first day at the Government House, but
afterwards never appeared at dinner, nor were any ladies at Governor [John]
Orde's dinner.[6]

Another major problem was the prince's attitude to command, which
verged upon sadistic bullying. He relied on coercion rather than
example, resorted to the cat-o'-nine-tails with a will and gathered little
love with his flint-filled, stiff-faced autocracy. Nor was William Henry's
violence confined to crews. Later, at English Harbour, a German artist
waited on him with a letter of introduction from the governor of
Dominica. At first all went well, but after some upset the outraged
prince had the German sprawled over a gun and a whip vigorously
applied to his posterior. The man beat an undignified retreat, but
subsequently sued and won several hundred pounds to meet his medical
expenses. Even women could be threatened with rough justice. When
one subsequently spoke with less than the required respect at court,
the prince threatened her with 'a stinging dozen before all the pages
of the back stairs'. This was not a man to endear, nor did he always
care. He was happy to be 'respected and feared'.[7]

Given the talent for leadership that Nelson developed, it may seem
surprising that he failed to temper the prince's deficiencies. Yet such,
sadly, was the case. In fact, far from improving in Nelson's company,
the prince's fitness for command deteriorated. He became increasingly
petty and hypercritical. As Midshipman Martin of the *Pegasus* noted,
'a change took place in the conduct of our royal captain on reaching
the Leeward Islands station . . . it was as discreditable to him as it
was unjust and disgreeable to all on board'.[8]

But there was worse. Despite the problems Nelson detected aboard
the *Pegasus*, and the clear symptoms of incompetent leadership, he
did more than fail to reform the prince; he actually imbibed some of
William's bad practices and sullied his own record.

Consider the following. On the one hand the prince, overbearing,
autocratic and aloof. 'In the navy we must keep the officers at a
distance in order that they may remember the respect due to their
captain,' he said. On the other hand Nelson, whose generosity to and
consideration for brother officers became legendary, a man who built
a career on drawing commitment and affection from subordinates,

and forging teams. Yet as early as 29 December 1786, within a month of dining and talking with the prince, we find Nelson admitting to his brother, 'I begin to be very strict in my ship, and as I get older, probably shall be more so. Whenever I may set off in another ship, I shall be indifferent whether I ever speak to an officer in her but on duty.' This appalling maxim, which Nelson fortunately forsook in time to change history, would have been entirely in place in a letter from Prince William Henry. But in Horatio Nelson it was nothing less than an aberration.[9]

Unfortunately, Nelson even persisted with his new policy when its inevitable consequences began to surface. 'I fancy the king's servants *and the officers of my little squadron* will not be sorry to part with me,' he wrote in February 1787. 'They think I make them do their duty too strictly . . .' It sounded as if the *Boreas* was turning into the *Pegasus*. However, he went on, it hardly mattered for William Henry 'has honoured me as his confidential friend', and Nelson loved him 'as a man and a prince'. These passages are not only sad ones, but carry a thoroughly depressing import. They tell us that when William Henry and Nelson mixed, it was the older and wiser head that fell under the spell of the other.[10]

Neither the first lord of the Admiralty, Earl Howe, nor Hood would be impressed by Nelson's performance in respect of William Henry. They hoped he would mentor the prince and help Schomberg to keep him on an even keel. Instead, Nelson seemed mesmerised by William Henry. 'He has his foibles as well as private men,' he wrote, 'but they are far over-balanced by his virtues. In his professional line he is superior to near two-thirds, I am sure, of the [captains'] list, and in attention to orders, and respect to his superior officers, I know hardly his equal . . .' In time he would assure the board of Admiralty that *Pegasus* was 'one of the first disciplined frigates I have seen.' Nelson was able to suppress the evidence of disaffection on the ship from his mind and present a radically deficient portrait of his royal master.[11]

But why? How can this peculiar myopia be explained in a man whose intellect and professional expertise were so exceptional? The answer seems to lie in Nelson's simple view of patriotism, his susceptibility to flattery and to self-interest.

Nelson was a strong monarchist. To him the monarchy, the Church of England and the nation were almost synonymous. They were interchangeable symbols of the country itself and demanded the loyalty of every patriot. As Nelson said of William Henry, 'as an *individual* I love him [and] as a *prince* I honour and revere him'.[12]

But to be the prince's commanding officer and principal confidant amidst a plethora of pageantry and pomp was also deeply flattering. Wherever William Henry went the elite of the islands obsequiously jostled for his hand, fawning, flattering and eulogising for all they were worth. Nelson tired of the dinners and dances, but he had long been intoxicated with attention. We must remember that only a short time before he had been almost an outcast in the islands, at odds with its premier citizens and in danger of arrest. Those battles were still being fought, and in February 1787 Nelson had opened a new round with complaints about the fees charged by the vice-admiralty courts of Barbados and Grenada.[13]

The prince was changing that. He wholly agreed with Nelson about 'the commerce in these islands' and 'the maritime laws', and writing to his father fully credited the captain with educating him about those subjects. More, he was not only under Nelson's command and a willing subordinate but transparently also his best friend. Anyone seeking access to the royal presence had to deal with Nelson, and suddenly the remaining opposition to the captain of the *Boreas* went underground, hidden beneath an unseemly display of servility to the prince. William Henry was a reinforcement of overwhelming power and multiplied Nelson's importance. He was besieged with invitations and fair words. It might have been reflected glory, but to Nelson it was no less sweet.[14]

Another consideration was Nelson's need of 'interest'. He had relatively little family influence left, and his career prospects were overly dependent upon the uncertain goodwill of Lord Hood. Nelson felt his weakness keenly. Often he cheered himself with the words of his late Uncle Maurice, that the country would always reward good service, but he had seen too many good men neglected to completely believe them. He needed powerful patrons, and would have been less than human not to have seen William Henry as a tool of considerable utility. This was a man destined to command huge influence.

From the beginning Nelson milked his new friend. Ten days after meeting him Nelson told Fanny that the prince 'has made me promise him that he shall be at my wedding, and says he will give you to me'. Two months later he was writing home about his brother Maurice. 'I have never lost sight of his preferment in the line he is in,' he said, 'but my interest is but rising. I have already spoken to His Royal

Highness about him, but it must take time to get on, and the prince has it not in his power to do all he wishes at present.' Yet again, Horatio was simultaneously raising Fanny's worries with William Henry, and finding him 'anxious' to return a 'favour'. Nelson hoped that in due course the prince would pull some powerful strings for him, and occasionally William Henry spoke encouragingly. A decade later, when he was expecting to sit at the head of the board of Admiralty, he reminded Nelson that 'I loved and esteemed you from the beginning as an ornament to the service'. But the dream was illusory; the prince never delivered.[15]

In 1786 and 1787 Nelson found it hard to criticise the wilful and explosive William Henry and to risk his displeasure. The more the prince confided in him or bestowed kindnesses, the less resistance Nelson was capable of offering. He always reacted positively to goodwill, valued loyalty fiercely and made emotional and strong attachments. Now patriotism, self-interest and generosity alike stripped him of objectivity. Rather than antagonise a man notoriously resistant to interference, he allowed the prince to go his way, and found himself being sucked into the wake, towards a world of inept authoritarianism.

3

On 13 December the *Boreas*, *Pegasus* and *Rattler* reached Antigua, where Nelson would be detained for two months, apart from a brief trip to Nevis. The *Pegasus* was in poor shape. Her timbers needed repairing and bolts replacing, while some of her men were sick, and she docked in English Harbour to be readied for her captain's progress through the islands. Since Hughes's departure Nelson had been using the commanding officer's house at the dockyard, but he generously placed it at the prince's disposal and resigned himself to bunking aboard the *Boreas*. William Henry would not hear of it, and for a few weeks the two friends shared the accommodation ashore.[16]

Perhaps it was here that they 'fought over again the principal naval actions in the American war', as the prince later remembered. 'Excepting the naval tuition which I had received on board the *Prince George*, when Rear-Admiral G. [Richard] Keat[e]s was lieutenant of her, and for whom both of us equally entertained a sincere regard, my mind took its first decided naval turn from this familiar intercourse with Nelson.' Lieutenant James Wallis of the *Boreas* also remembered Nelson's interest in fleet tactics during this period, and said he was 'continually forming the [ships into] line [of battle], exercising [the men, and] chasing.' Probably both witnesses exaggerated, looking back more than twenty years. Yet unquestionably Captain Nelson, 'a young man' of 'sound judgement', imparted some things to the prince. 'I received vast pleasure from his instructive conversations about our service in general,' His Royal Highness informed Lord Hood at the time.[17]

Such musings were squeezed between the joyous outpourings of the residents of Antigua, who launched into a glittering round of balls, dinners and ceremonies for the royal visitor. William Henry appeared in full-dress naval uniform and the bigwigs were beside themselves. The assembly and the merchants composed addresses, but John Burke, solicitor general, fumbled through the former almost tongue-tied. Sir Thomas Shirley, who had learned that he was to become a baronet after all, performed no better as the host of a dinner at Clarke's Hill. He 'never cut a worse figure' in Nelson's opinion, and 'was in such a tremor that he could scarce articulate a word'. Towards Christmas there were three consecutive nights of dining and dancing in St John's. Captain Nelson jogged daily across the island on horseback to spend hours watching the prince pursuing Miss Anne Athill ('a beautiful young lady of respectable family', according to one witness) and other finely dressed ladies around tables and ballrooms before crawling back to bed in the early hours of the mornings. The new year stimulated more festivities, and Horatio was dragged to regimental dinners, mulatto balls, dances and cockfights. He confessed himself an unsuitable courtier, hanging on to the prince's coat-tails like a two-legged guard dog, but was wretchedly 'reconciled to the business' and figured that 'if we get well through all this I shall be fit for anything'. In private he scribbled necessarily short and prosaic letters to Fanny, and wished the new commander-in-chief, daily expected in Barbados, would come and take this cup from him.[18]

When the tedium of the social round was relieved, it was in the least desirable way. Relations aboard the *Pegasus* went from bad to worse. William Henry spent much of his time ashore, but his midshipmen were kept on board and the lieutenants had to sign in and out as they came and went as if they were untrustworthy school-boys. More pointedly, the prince eschewed the established naval tradi-tion of inviting lieutenants to dinner, and would have none of them in the house he shared with Nelson ashore. Horatio did nothing to educate his guest in harmony and *esprit de corps*, and was openly

criticised by the officers of the *Pegasus* for encouraging him. 'The lieutenants of the *Pegasus* I saw were displeased with me,' Nelson later
admitted, 'and the officers of the *Boreas* told me they attributed HRH['s]
change of conduct to me.'[19]

One bone of contention aboard the *Pegasus* was a book in which
the prince caused his standing orders to be entered. Some of these
instructions were onerously trivial and a few crass beyond belief. The
men, for example, were prohibited from raising huzzahs as they
performed great labours and from hanging laundry out to dry between
decks, while the barge crews were 'not by any means [to] move their
heads from side to side but [to] look steady' on pain of severe punishment. The prince's habit of publicly reprimanding officers for the
smallest infraction was another source of grief. In January the captain
exchanged words with Schomberg over the lieutenant's failure to collect
sheets from the hospital. The public rebuke was followed by a testy
exchange of letters in which Schomberg excused his conduct by referring to 'the visible change in your Royal Highness's conduct since the
Pegasus arrived in English Harbour'. The prince fulminated against
disobedience and neglect of duty and threatened a court martial, and
Schomberg eventually made a humiliating apology before the junior
officers.[20]

Matters quickly ran to a head. On 22 January the prince accused
Schomberg of sending a boat ashore without his permission, and
entered the incident in the order book, damning him as negligent and
disobedient for all to see. It was a public censure Schomberg felt unable
to ignore. He also concluded that the captain was trying to push him
into a court martial to break him, and the next day, while William
Henry was dining with Nelson ashore, the lieutenant launched a pre-
emptive strike. He addressed a letter to Nelson, the senior officer on
the station, demanding a court martial on the issue of the boat. If he
was acquitted, or simply rebuked, as he no doubt expected, he could
reasonably expect a transfer to another and more equitable berth and
be done with the whole business.[21]

That same evening William Henry was giving Nelson his own
version of the affair as they travelled home. He was furious that
Schomberg should disobey him so soon after being forgiven over the
matter of the sheets, and declared that in future he intended to record
every such transgression in the public order book. Nelson did not
disagree. He did not even seem to construe the incident as the product
of poor leadership, and apparently uncritically accepted the prince's

interpretation. At least, he would write to Locker that William Henry 'had more plague with his officers than enough'. But when a tired Nelson returned home that evening and found Schomberg's letter he realised that new levels of gravity were being reached.[22]

For courts martial tried accusers as well as accused. There were no good witnesses to the altercation over the boat, and the court would have to decide which of the contending principals was to be believed. If Schomberg was convicted, a fine officer would be ruined. If he was acquitted the prince stood to be dishonoured. And there were other implications. If Schomberg got a transfer to another ship by demanding a court martial on so trivial an incident, might it not encourage similar indiscipline from any junior officer who disliked a superior?

As it happened Nelson could delay the ordeal. Even when the *Maidstone* joined him on 14 February he did not have enough captains to form the necessary quorum for a court martial. Pending that, Nelson suspended Schomberg from duty, sparing him further dealings with his captain, and more or less confining him to his cabin. On the face of it Nelson's action was a neutral one, but when he issued a general order five days later, cautioning other officers against resorting to courts martial on any 'frivolous pretence', his criticism of the stricken lieutenant was obvious. Certainly William Henry used Nelson's order to mount another vindictive tirade against Schomberg. Summoning the suspended lieutenant and other officers to his cabin, he read it aloud. 'I told him [Schomberg] in the presence of the officers, I should try him *after* his court-martial for mutiny, that if he was found guilty he should be hung or broke . . . that if a court-martial could not investigate the business for the particularity of the case, I should send the business to the Admiralty, who have it in their power to scratch his name off the list . . .'[23]

For weeks the disgraced lieutenant was confined with 'unwarrantable severity' by the prince, forced to pace his small cabin and the main deck, and to fraternise only with officers willing to risk being ostracised. Lieutenant William Johnstone Hope, whom the prince libelled an instigator of 'mutiny and sedition', was also threatened with a court martial and searched anxiously for an escape to another ship, while the young gentlemen of the *Pegasus*, traduced in the ubiquitous order book for 'shameful inattention and remisseness', particularly disliked their captain. Perhaps it was one of them who broke into the store room one day to steal William Henry's spare cot in a pathetic display of resentment. At any rate, Midshipman Martin found himself excluded from the captain's table after mixing with Schomberg. 'I was rather a green hand,' he recalled, 'unskilled in the sycophancy of the courtier.'[24]

Nelson was tossing on the horns of a dilemma. For some time His Royal Highness would admit of no reconciliation. When Schomberg offered to make amends on 12 February and urged his captain to 'forget and forgive' he was turned down flat. Several months later Commodore Alan Gardner, who commanded the Jamaica station, would find a way to bring the two together to avoid a damaging court martial, but whether or not that was possible earlier it is difficult to say.[25]

Nelson does not appear to have tried. Probably he expected Hughes's official replacement to arrive and relieve him of the burden, and perhaps it was as well that he did not intervene for he had shown himself less than an unprejudiced broker.

4

Nelson was ill and lovesick as well as beleaguered. 'Poor Nelson is over head and ears in love,' Prince William wrote to Hood. 'I frequently laugh at him about it. However, seriously my lord, he is in more need of a nurse than a wife. I do not really think he can live long.'[26]

Amidst the seemingly interminable social engagements and the festering problem of Schomberg, Captain Nelson spoke of Fanny to the prince. 'His Royal Highness often tells me he believes I am married,' he admitted to his fiancée with more temerity than tact, 'for he says he never saw a lover so easy, or say so little of the object he has regard for. When I tell him I certainly am not, he says then he is sure I must have a great esteem for you, and that it is not what is vulgarly – no, I won't make use of than [that] word – commonly called love. He is right, my love is founded on esteem, the only foundation that can make love last.'[27]

Nelson was certainly not well. Three years in the West Indies had damaged him as surely as they had ravaged the timbers of the *Boreas*, and one of his doctors was soon advising a return to England. Nelson occasionally alluded to his health in letters, but he had learned to live with discomfort and was not unduly alarmed. Rather, he set his mind on marriage, a voyage home and a more congenial appointment. He had never liked the Leeward Islands and was desperate to see the back of them.

He reached Nevis at the end of January but it was only a flying visit, and the *Boreas* was soon being steered back for Antigua with John Richardson Herbert on board. Perhaps the prospective father-in-law was winding up business affairs in preparation for his retirement to England, but he was no sooner in sight of shore than he went down with a fever. Captain Nelson cheered himself in the knowledge that the next leg of the prince's progress would incorporate Nevis. Leaving the rotting *Rattler* behind, Nelson sailed from Antigua with the *Boreas*, *Pegasus* and the *Solebay* on 10 February. A few days were wasted on jollification in Montserrat but they reached Nevis on the 15th, where the *Maidstone* was already at anchor. The royal person went ashore two days later to the roar of twenty-one-gun salutes, and enjoyed £800 worth of island hospitality, including such doubtful delights as a hundred-man dinner, horse races and cockfights. At some stage Nelson introduced him to Fanny and she shared a dance with him. In between dancing to the prince's tune himself and fixing his wedding day with his fiancée and her relations, Nelson was more than fully employed.[28]

The prince's relationship with Fanny got off to a shaky start. Inadvertently he created a minor difficulty visiting George Forbes, a friend he had made from a previous tour of duty in the West Indies. Fanny's uncle, back from Antigua, was mortified to find his own, and prior, invitation from Forbes suddenly withdrawn. The prince, it seems, wanted a quiet evening alone with an old friend, free of weary formality. Herbert was deeply wounded, and fancied the prince objected to his presence, brooding about how he might have warranted such disfavour. Nelson, too, felt the sting when he heard of it, but soon satisfied himself that no slight had been intended. The prince, it appeared, had been entirely ignorant of Herbert's invitation, and Forbes alone was responsible for its cancellation. Somehow Nelson smoothed things over, and his wedding plans advanced to the next hurdle.

President Herbert was still infuriatingly reserved about how much money Fanny might expect from him, and when he suggested the betrothed couple should postpone marrying until they were all in England it smacked of prevarication. Whatever happened, Nelson would have no delay. In the end he was sure the president would 'do everything which is handsome' and save his niece from poverty, and he was eager to distinguish his wedding with a royal presence. The prince was due to leave the station in May or June.[29]

Horatio loaded Fanny's pianoforte on board the *Boreas*, where a tuner was set to work, and moved the prince on to St Kitts on 22 February, where Governor William Woodley and other dignitaries paid homage in another exhausting schedule of dinners and balls. William Henry found more entertainment chasing ladies, but in one of his regular epistles to Fanny Nelson described it as an unrelieved 'fag':

Today we dine with the merchants. I wish it over. Tomorrow a large party at Nicholas Town, and on Friday [another] in town here. Saturday, sail for Old Road [also St Kitts]. Sunday, dine on Brimstone Hill. Monday, [with] Mr Georges [chief justice of the Leeward Islands] at Sandy Point, and in the evening the Free Masons give a ball. Tuesday, *please God*, we sail.[30]

The festivities at St Kitts were performed beneath a punishing sun and debilitated both Nelson and the prince, but on 8 March they limped back to Nevis to recuperate before attempting the final leg of the royal tour to Tortola. During that brief respite Nelson was married.

On Sunday 11 March, on a fair day that opened with rain, the finest of the island trooped seven hundred feet up a hill to gather expectantly within the impressive white walls of Montpelier, President Herbert's home three miles from Charlestown. The clerk and rector of Figtree church, William Jones, performed the ceremony. Only one of the groom's relatives was present, Horatio's cousin, Midshipman Maurice Suckling, but some of his officers were there and the ship's company of the *Boreas* sent their best wishes in the form of a silver watch. Mustering his undoubted charm, William Henry gave the bride away as he had promised, and signed as a witness. Fanny put her name to the marriage certificate below Nelson's, and signed 'Frances Herbert Nisbet'. She kept it forever.[31]

Nelson also pronounced himself satisfied at the time. He made a will in the presence of Lieutenant Wallis and Master James, naming his new wife his sole beneficiary and his uncle William Suckling the only executor. Captain Locker learned that he had married 'an amiable woman' and was 'morally certain she will continue to make me a happy man for the rest of my days'.[32]

Others were not so sure. The next day that irrepressible Scot, Captain Thomas Pringle, formerly of the *Daedalus*, was on hand to confess to Lieutenant Wallis that the navy had lost its 'greatest ornament'. He, like many another officer, regarded marriage as a serious impediment to a successful naval career, something that often led men to abandon the sea altogether. Perhaps William Henry agreed, for much as he took pleasure in Nelson's joy he too doubted the outcome. 'He is now in for it,' the prince wrote to Hood a few days later. 'I wish him well and happy, and that he may not repent the step he has taken.'[33]

5

A month later, on 13 April, two gentlemen of St John's delivered a package to Captain Nelson for the attention of Prince William Henry.

They were back in Antigua. Eight days after the marriage the *Boreas* and *Pegasus* had sailed for Tortola, but the further royal entertainment done they returned to Nevis at the end of the month and anchored in English Harbour by 6 April. Nelson expected to be recalled at any moment, and needed to prepare his frigate for an Atlantic voyage. There was little more he felt able to accomplish in the islands and he was impatient to take his bride home. This phase of his career, he thought, was drawing to its close. Then along came Messrs William Wilkinson and Joseph Blake Higgins.

They were merchants, what people in those days called 'men of business', and shrewd and sensible if Nelson was any judge. Both had been associates of William Whitehead, who, with his late partner, Francis Colley, had supplied government establishments throughout the West Indies, including the naval hospital and the dockyard at Antigua. Certainly Wilkinson and Higgins were extraordinarily well versed in public expenditure, and the former had been employed by the Victualling Board and for five years had sat in the Antigua assembly. Now the two had a startling proposal for His Royal Highness. They promised a massive exposure of fraud throughout the islands and the means of ripping it out root and branch. Millions of pounds of public money would be saved.

For those days the figures were stunning. According to Wilkinson and Higgins, £900,000 or so was annually being lost in Antigua, St Lucia and Barbados, while upwards of another million was being siphoned off in Jamaica. Whitehead's company had been at the core of the frauds. When it had been dissolved, Wilkinson and Higgins had purchased the business, with both its stock and debts, and in due course acquired its books and papers. It was from these that they planned to lay bare the whole corrupt operation. Their proposal to William Henry was a simple but attractive one. If he would prompt a full-scale investigation on the lines they suggested, they would ask for no additional reward from government. Their sole remuneration would be a percentage of whatever sums they helped to recover, 15 per cent on the first £100,000 and half that amount on any further sums.

Although the prince made encouraging noises, he had no time for the business at present, but Captain Nelson took a different view. His enquiries revealed that the remarkable proposal followed a history of ill will between Whitehead and Wilkinson and Higgins. Whitehead was filing a suit, and Wilkinson and Higgins were threatening to retaliate by exposing Whitehead. According to John Burke, the solicitor general of Antigua, whom Nelson consulted, Wilkinson and Higgins had even demanded 'hush money' from dockyard officials implicated in the frauds. Nevertheless, in Nelson's opinion all of that merely worked to the government's advantage. If an opportunity to detect corruption had appeared as a result of a falling out, it ought to be seized with enthusiasm. From his own experiences, Nelson was sure that dishonesty and peculation were rife in the islands, and now a way of bringing the perpetrators to justice had come into his hands.[34]

Wilkinson and Higgins drove one charge home with the skill of a Nantucket harpooner. They told William Henry that Whitehead had been the principal prize agent during the last war and that thousands of pounds of prize money due to British sailors remained unpaid. If nothing else, the thought of honest hard-working tars being swindled by shore-bound sharks was guaranteed to elicit Nelson's interest.[35]

The enforcement of the navigation laws had been one arm of Nelson's purification campaign, and despite preoccupations with the prince, his orders to the squadron were still to make illegal traders a prime concern. Collingwood of the *Rattler* had been his busiest weapon. The previous September, Collingwood had taken the *Fanny* brig of North Carolina and the *Maria* ship at Grenada, and in January 1787 he was at Barbados taking possession of the *Dolphin* schooner. The vice-admiralty courts at Grenada and Barbados were both unreconstructed, and history repeated itself. Collingwood was told he had no authority to seize, and in both places he was asked to pay advance fees. The attorney general in Barbados, Brandford, had handled Nelson warily, but his insistence on being paid to press the suit of the *Dolphin* forced Collingwood to release her. In February, Nelson renewed his campaign, this time pouring a fire upon the corrupt prize courts.[36]

When Wilkinson and Higgins came forward with their charges they found a reforming but frustrated naval captain ready to attack on new fronts. He rode to St John's a few times to interview the two merchants, fired demands for documents to the dockyard and greedily pored over the sample materials his informants produced. Backed by pages of item-by-item accounts, with bundles of receipts and vouchers, their indictment appeared truly formidable.[37]

What Wilkinson and Higgins termed 'the English Harbour plunder' originated, they said, with three men – Whitehead, Peter Alsop, the ordnance storekeeper at the dockyard, and James Young, the surgeon at the naval hospital. After 1779, when Anthony Munton became naval storekeeper and clerk of the cheque at English Harbour, the devious trio soon 'initiated [him] into the mysteries of defrauding government'. As examples of the frauds, Wilkinson and Higgins presented Nelson with irrefutable evidence of two types of scam. In one, false musters were concocted for the hospital and certified by Young, so that inflated sums for the subsistence of the sick could be extracted from government. Accounts for one quarter in 1782 showed that Young's share of the proceeds from the phantom patients amounted to £544.[38]

The second type of fraud involved charging government for more than supplies and services had actually cost, and pocketing the differ-ence. Thus, during one quarter of 1781 the government paid £6,878 for articles of ordnance when the real cost, including 'above twelve per cent' commission for Whitehead as agent, amounted to only £5,528. The difference was split fifty-fifty between Whitehead and Alsop. Similarly, in a three-month period of 1782, Anthony Munton paid £12,357 for items that should have cost a total of £9,190. In this instance Whitehead and Munton divided the excess profits with the master shipwright and the master attendant of the dockyard. According to Wilkinson and Higgins, frauds of a like nature perme-ated the whole service, from the hire of black labour to the use of watering vessels.[39]

Nelson noted that there was no effective system for ensuring that goods and services were supplied to government at competitive prices. Contractors were supposed to certify the current market prices of wares on vouchers, but they were suffered to set down the highest rather than the going rate. He discovered that Munton even appeared to be purchasing government supplies from himself, under the ficti-tious name of 'Cornelius Cole'.[40]

Once again Horatio Nelson felt the self-gratifying impulses of the crusader, the champion of government and taxpayer and scourge of the corrupt. In May he scribbled various letters in support of Wilkinson and Higgins – to Sir Charles Middleton, the comptroller of the Navy Board, to Lord Howe at the Admiralty, to the Master General of the Ordnance Board which supplied the armed services with guns and ammunition, and to the king's senior minister, William Pitt. Frauds were notorious, he told Lord Howe, 'but how to detect them has hitherto been a matter not to be accomplished. But a door is opened from which I hope will, if not the means of recovering back large sums of money, at least be the means of preventing frauds in future.'[41]

Sure that he could interest the government in mounting an investigation, Nelson's greatest worry was that the culprits would be forewarned by careless talk in time to disguise their chicanery. He suggested Pitt pass an injunction against the removal of property pending the outcome of any enquiry, and cautioned William Henry against mentioning the matter during his constant fraternisations. 'Silence . . . is [the] best mode to be pursued at present,' he said, for 'although every person is talking of it, yet no person knows for a certainty where the blow will fall.'[42]

Nelson impressed Wilkinson and Higgins, who were disappointed when the captain had temporarily to suspend his investigations after being 'seized with a severe fever peculiar to this climate'. And at home there were those also ready to listen to allegations of fraud. Lord Howe for one determined to examine the business when Nelson came home and could be interviewed. But therein lay a partly submerged reef, for the Admiralty's view of the captain of the *Boreas* was starting to cloud. Until now Lord Howe, encouraged by Hood, had viewed Nelson as a promising new talent but that opinion was being damaged by the latest tidings from the Leeward Islands. The catalyst for those mounting misgivings was Prince William Henry, who seemed to be twisting Nelson around every finger.[43]

6

On 9 March, Philip Stephens, secretary to the board of Admiralty, wrote to Nelson in a clear hand that their lordships were 'much disappointed and dissatisfied at the little attention you have shown to the rules and practice of the service, as well as the directions contained in the 10th and 11th articles of the General Printed Instructions, in having authorised His Royal Highness to disregard the applications of the deputy muster master to be furnished with a perfect muster book'. Evidently, the prince had decided that it was not necessary to supply an up-to-date muster of the *Pegasus*, and Nelson had failed to disabuse him. Horatio later professed to have been guided by other sections of the captains' instructions, but he knew the prince was behaving irregularly, and continued to supply musters for his own ship in the usual way.[44]

A small bore broadside perhaps, but the letter of 9 March was no isolated rebuke; it was merely the opening salvo of what would become a regular bombardment.

The prince did not help. His private letters to Hood indiscreetly aired grievances Nelson had disclosed in confidence. Thus, Hood learned that Nelson had suffered disgraceful 'neglect', and that Lord Sydney had been a stauncher ally in the defence of the navigation laws than Howe. Unfortunately, Hood was thick with Howe, and Nelson's complaints probably circulated and fed a rising ill will. Nor did William Henry do Nelson a favour by reporting that he 'approves entirely of my conduct'. Hood and Howe were not the greatest admirers of the prince's judgement and conduct.[45]

Nelson earned more criticism over a court martial he supervised in Antigua in the spring of 1787. The Admiralty's concern was a minor one, but we are unable to dismiss it hastily because it feeds into a divergent but important consideration of the wider discipline exercised by Captain Nelson during his command of the *Boreas*. As some recent historians have noted, his record was a severe one, and before we examine the minor contemporary charge levied by the Admiralty it is necessary to remark upon the graver concerns of today.

Examining the flogging records of seventy-three ships that served on the Leeward Islands station over a twenty-eight-year period, the American scholar John D. Byrn has estimated that the average percentage of men punished aboard British men-of-war was 9 per cent. Some captains greatly exceeded this, and two ships in the survey had particularly high rates of punishment, the *Rattler*, in which 31 per cent of the men were flogged on the station, and the *Boreas*. Between 1 May 1784 and 31 July 1787, Byrn explained, Nelson flogged 86 of 334 men on board his frigate, 25.7 per cent of the ship's company. Though the statistics are imprecisely known Byrn's figures were fair as far as Nelson was concerned. In my independent analysis of floggings aboard the *Boreas* for the full duration of Nelson's command between 24 January 1784 and 30 November 1787, an almost identical rate of 25.9 per cent was produced.[46]

Relatively few of the floggings were severe. There were about 148 aboard the *Boreas* in all, with the annual rate peaking in 1786. Seventy-six per cent of the floggings involved twelve or less strokes of the cat, with all but one of the remainder consisting of between one and two dozen lashes. The most scourged victim was a captain's servant, William Dixon, who received forty-eight lashes in February 1786 for siphoning Nelson's rum and sharing it with some of his mates. His partner in crime, another captain's servant named John Noley, got two dozen strokes and four men who received the stolen rum between six and twelve each.[47]

This rate of punishment was exceptional for one of Nelson's commands. He had punished relatively few people aboard the *Badger* and *Hinchinbroke*, and the rates aboard the *Albemarle* and later the *Agamemnon* were unremarkable. To some extent the *Boreas* figure may reflect the long, dreary peacetime commission and the excessive amount of time holed up in ports where the temptations to abscond or drink were greater. It is also worth remembering that punishments not only reflected Nelson's discipline, but also those of his officers. Occasionally floggings arose out of disputes between men and the lieutenants and petty officers whose authority Nelson was obliged to uphold. They did not always originate with the captain. Finally, as Byrn has rightly observed, a single unfortunate incident might occasion multiple floggings. Thus, for example, six men were punished for helping themselves to Nelson's rum in February 1786, and the entire crew of a longboat was chastised for sneaking liquor on board the ship the following May.

Having said all that, the sharp rate of punishment aboard the *Boreas* must in a large measure reflect upon her captain. We have noted Nelson's irritability at this time before, and his readiness to engage one official after another in controversy. Nelson was a young and somewhat intemperate man in his twenties, but in the Leeward Islands it seems that his tolerance was additionally eroded by frequent illness, professional frustration and the stresses of the continual battle with authority. He hated Antigua and Barbados, and when Prince William Henry arrived at the end of 1786 he found an acting commander-in-chief increasingly susceptible to the narrow royal vision of formal and overregimented officer relations.

In short, Nelson's discipline was not at its best in the Leeward Islands, but that does not mean that he was customarily unjust. One previously ignored indicator of his sense of justice at this time was his performance in courts martial. During his entire spell in the islands Nelson presided over the naval courts. He supervised twenty-two trials involving twenty-six defendants (one of them tried twice for different offences) and heard evidence over a total of nineteen days. The charges ranged from drunken and disorderly behaviour to wilful disobedience and neglect of duty to desertion and mutiny. Each court consisted of a president and four other captains, chosen according to availability and circumstance, and was served by a judge-advocate whose job it was to read the order for the assembly and the indictment contained in the letter of complaint, administer oaths to witnesses and act as secretary. Each member of the court had a vote and a simple majority decided the verdict. Moreover, the proceedings were governed by articles of war that stipulated mandatory punishments for some offences. As president, therefore, Nelson had to accommodate other opinions and written regulations, but still held considerable sway. His courtroom career deserves our attention.

Nelson first sat as president of a naval court in the cabin of the *Boreas* at Carlisle Bay, Barbados, on 1 July 1784, shortly after arriving on the station, with Cuthbert Collingwood, Thomas Boston, William Hancock Kelly and Edward Pakenham as his captains. They tried William Holland, gunner of the *Champion*, for drunkenness and disobedience. He had, it transpired, refused to come on deck when bade, but the court judged that he had been drunk rather than ill or purposely disobedient, and dismissed him from the service. He thus escaped severe physical punishment. The same day William Wilson, corporal of the *Adamant*, was convicted of a serious case of desertion that could have earned him the death penalty. However, in view of his former good character the court reduced his sentence to five hundred lashes, to be administered over different occasions and throughout the squadron in the usual way. It was a cruel punishment, and the first stage of it had to be suspended when Wilson fainted alongside the *Boreas* after receiving only seventy-two strokes, but within the norms of the day the court believed that it had acted leniently. For the second trial Sotheby of the *Champion* replaced Kelly of the *Adamant* as a member of the court to protect defendants from being judged by their own captains.

The following day Nelson reconvened his court and two deserters from the *Mediator* were convicted. One man received three hundred rather than two hundred lashes because he denied belonging to the ship when apprehended. Of the remaining two men tried by Nelson in Carlisle Bay that July, one was acquitted and the other, Charles Alexander, surgeon of the *Zebra* sloop, escaped with a reprimand. Three of the five charges against Alexander were thrown out, one was only partly proven, and although he was judged to have used 'disrespectful language' ashore it was not only 'in the hour of general riot and revelling' but provoked.[48]

Given its limitations, Nelson's court attempted to deal justly with its defendants, and to explore motive and degrees of guilt. It also searched for any mitigating circumstances that would justify the reduction of sentences. Indeed, the courts over which Nelson presided during his years in the Leeward Islands moderated the sentences of fourteen of the twenty-four convictions returned. Consider the cases of:

Thomas Ray, who twice deserted from the *Unicorn*, and was tried at English Harbour on 18 August 1784. The court was 'very much concerned to find that they are obliged to sentence the prisoner to death', and 'in consideration of his gallant services during the war, and his good behaviour upon many occasions, and the exceeding good character which he bears from officers under whom he has served unanimously recommend him as a fit object for mercy to the commander-in-chief'. The following day Nelson was able to announce that Admiral Hughes had pardoned the defendant.

James Couch, carpenter of the *Adamant*, convicted at English Harbour on 23 August 1784. The court considered 'that the prisoner's disobedience of orders did not proceed from intentional neglect, and therefore do not think that any punishment ought to be inflicted upon him'.

William Sympson, lieutenant of the *Whitby*, tried at Nevis on 14 and 16 June 1785 and found guilty of embezzling oil, paint, canvas, spirits and bread for subsequent sale. The court thought 'the conduct of the prisoner had been very reprehensible, but from the small quantity of the stores sold they do not think that it could be with an intent to injure government'.

Dennis Mahoney, cook on the *Unicorn*, convicted of mutiny at Nevis on 17 June 1785. However, 'in consideration of the said Dennis Mahoney having been wounded in the service of his country and the good character given him by his captain and officers the court only adjudge him to have his warrant taken from him and to receive one hundred lashes' instead of suffering death.

William James, mate of the same ship, tried at English Harbour on 16 August 1785. He had destroyed a boat in the storehouse and used insubordinate language, 'but the court out of lenity, and in consideration of the prisoner's situation do only . . . adjudge him to serve seven [instead of six] years in the Royal Navy before he shall be deemed qualified to pass for a lieutenant'.

John Freebairn, a seaman of the *Rattler*, convicted of desertion at English Harbour, 17 August 1785. But 'in consideration' of his 'good character' the court reduced his sentence from sixty to fifty lashes.

John Hale, carpenter's mate, also of the *Rattler*, tried in Barbados on 20 April 1785. He and his associate, James Humphreys, attempted to desert. 'In consideration of the very good character' given Hale by his captain his sentence was commuted to fifty lashes, but Humphreys was awarded the full three hundred. Punishment had to be suspended after Humphreys had received 121 strokes of the first 150 to be administered.

Whatever difficulties Nelson was experiencing, no one hauled before his courts appears to have received inadequate consideration. His final judgements were dispensed at Antigua on 9 and 10 April 1787 and conformed to the pattern already described. Of the five captains sitting augustly in cabin of the *Solebay*, the oldest was Nelson himself, at twenty-eight. The youngest members were Prince William Henry and Wilfred Collingwood, both aged twenty-two, and Holloway and Newcome made the necessary quorum.

Two seamen of the *Solebay* were convicted of desertion, but neither was heavily punished. Benjamin Williams was commended for his 'long and faithful servitude' in the navy and his 'exceeding good character' and given the comparatively lenient sentence of fifty lashes. Thomas Rickaby suffered twice as many strokes, but his penalty had also been reduced on account of his former good conduct.

John Woodhouse was found guilty of theft, deserting from the *Adamant* and attempting to desert from the *Rattler*. He cannot have expected less than a capital sentence, and duly received it. However, 'the court, as the ship's books of His Majesty's ship *Adamant* have not appeared before them, from motives of humanity, and to show the squadron how cautious they are of taking away the life of a fellow creature, think proper that the sentence of death just passed should not be carried into execution until the pleasure of [their] Lords Commissioners of the Admiralty is known'. The court felt it imperative that Woodhouse's desertion from the *Adamant* be confirmed by reference to the relevant musters, and wanted to provide the Admiralty with an opportunity to stay the execution.

Ironically, it was another act of compassion that drew further official obloquy on Nelson's head. The focus of the controversy was William Clark, a sailor belonging to the *Rattler*. He was an incorrigible deserter who had exhausted the patience and penalties of the authorities. Clark first fled his ship in July 1785, but he was recaptured within weeks, brought before Nelson's court at English Harbour on 17 August and sentenced to five hundred lashes. The prisoner received three hundred and forty strokes in two sessions before being spared further punishment by Admiral Hughes. This clemency did not reform Clark, and in January and June of 1786 his captain flogged him twice for drunkenness and being absent without leave. It was only days after the last punishment that he absconded from a party sent to the dockyard in English Harbour and made his way to St John's hoping to escape on a merchantman. But he was not free for long. Two weeks later the fugitive was taken drunk in the market place, and on 9 April 1787 Nelson and his captains again sat in judgement of him. The man pleaded drink as his only excuse, and a mere handful of witnesses were needed to establish his offence. There could be but one verdict. Nelson sentenced Clark to hang.

At ten-thirty on the morning of 16 April the sound of a gun rolled ominously across the still waters of English Harbour. It was a signal for the boats of the squadron to bring spectators to an execution. A yellow flag flew aboard the *Rattler* to symbolise its grim task, and the miserable prisoner was led from below and carried to the ship's cathead, where he stood while a rope was run through a block at the fore yardarm. While perfect silence was preserved on board the *Rattler* and in the surrounding boats, an officer read the Articles of War, a bag and noose were placed over the prisoner's head, and a death squad stood at the safe end of the rope, braced to haul Clark to the yardarm at the trill of a boatswain's pipe. But that chilling sound never came. At eleven-thirty the execution was halted, and Clark was told that he had been reprieved by the wish of His Royal Highness, Prince William Henry. The boats were dismissed and Clark was extricated from his halter. His luck was boundless, for he was not only alive but free; Nelson gave the man a total discharge and he left the service.[49]

In circumstances such as these it was usual to pardon publicly at the last moment – if, of course, any pardon was intended. Nelson was no doubt relieved that he had avoided executing anyone in the Leeward Islands, and was sure his actions conformed to precedent.

He remembered, for example, that Sir Richard Hughes had pardoned Thomas Ray in exactly the same way two and a half years before.

But the Admiralty did not agree with Nelson's assessment. Their lordships eventually told him that only the king himself could pardon a convicted felon, and if there were grounds for clemency the sentence should have been suspended and the case referred to London for due process. Clark should have remained a prisoner. The fact that William Henry had approved of the pardon, or even suggested it, did not legitimise Nelson's action. Then there was the issue of the prisoner's discharge. By releasing Clark, Nelson had merely compounded the original offence of desertion. Defending his decision, Horatio explained that he had always understood that a man was 'dead in law' once he had been condemned to death, and consequently no longer under the navy's impress. The Admiralty did not find the argument convincing.[50]

On the whole Nelson's management of the court martial proceedings on the Leeward Islands station had been reasonable, and his treatment of Clark compassionate and consistent with practice as he understood it from his predecessor. In the eyes of a jaundiced first lord of the Admiralty, however, the young captain had exceeded his authority with Clark and added one more blot to an increasingly chequered record.

7

At the heart of Howe's disapproval of Nelson was Prince William Henry, whose every act was subjected to an anxious scrutiny. In blaming Nelson, Howe was less than fair. After all, if Nelson – a junior captain – had failed to control the volatile prince so too had the Admiralty. The board had allowed the king to impose upon it, and had promoted a boy to a position that would have tried a man, yet their lordships expected the likes of Schomberg and Nelson to save their bacon.

Almost everything Nelson did intensified the blight. Towards the end of April he was sailing from Antigua to Nevis when bad news overtook him. Wilfred Collingwood was dead. He had been ill for some time. At English Harbour a pestilence had run through the ships and a number of men went to hospital. Nelson became feverish, perhaps his old complaint, and Collingwood, whose constitution was similar, declined so rapidly that a doctor advised him to put to sea. Nelson was preparing to scatter his ships to various destinations, and sent the *Rattler* away early to Grenada. On the evening of the 21st her commander died quietly, according to William Henry of a sudden inflammation of the bowels.

Nelson had left Antigua on 25 April, bent upon preparing Fanny and her uncle for their prospective voyage to England. He was deeply moved by the death of Collingwood, for through all his troubles in the islands he had had no stauncher ally. 'I have lost my friend, you an affectionate brother,' he wrote to Cuthbert. Nelson organised a funeral on the island of St Vincent, and arranged to have personal effects sent home. 'If the tribute of tears are valuable, my friend had them,' he reflected.[51]

From the professional point of view the death of an officer, however regrettable, created a promotion for somebody else, and Nelson had to find an acting commander for the *Rattler*. He rewarded his own first lieutenant, James Wallis; Dent moved from second to first lieutenant of the *Boreas* in turn; and a vacancy opened up below. At this point William Henry intervened again.

For some time relations between Third Lieutenant Hope of the *Pegasus* and his captain had been deplorable. Hope's criticism of the prince for his treatment of Schomberg had reached Nelson through several channels, though the acting commander-in-chief had done nothing useful to reconcile the parties. When Hope heard of the opening on the *Boreas* he saw a way out and applied for a transfer. Nor was William Henry inimical to the idea. One of his friends had advised him to get Hope exchanged, and now the prince asked Nelson to oblige. Accordingly a relieved Hope went to the *Boreas*, though William Henry was spiteful enough to withhold his necessary certificate of good conduct until Nelson personally appealed for it. Hope's transfer left the *Pegasus* a lieutenant short, and Nelson allowed William Henry to elevate one of his own protégés, Stephen George Church, to an acting position. Church would shortly be having his own difficulties serving the prince.[52]

In making these appointments Nelson acted out of plain necessity, and he asked the Admiralty to confirm them. Unfortunately, since he only commanded the station on an acting basis he suspected that his appointments might be revoked, and asked William Henry to support him in the event of resistance. His prophecy came true. Church, probably for no better reason than that he was a choice of the prince, got his lieutenancy confirmed in August, but poor Wallis had to wait seven years for a permanent place on the list of commanders.

As the spring matured Nelson's difficulties with the prince and the Admiralty came to a head. There was the matter of his next destination. William was under orders to return to Commodore Sawyer's squadron at Halifax for the summer, and as late as 15 March Nelson assured the Admiralty that the *Pegasus* would be 'fitted for [her] voyage to the place mentioned in their Lordships' secret orders'. However, the gangrenous plight of Schomberg worried him. That miserable officer had been under confinement since January, waiting for a court martial that never came. Nelson had expected to be superseded by a new station commander, but weeks had turned to months without a sign of his replacement. In the meantime he still lacked a quorum to try Schomberg in the Leeward Islands. Since the dispute had become a personal one between William Henry and his lieutenant, involving the veracity of one or both, the prince could not take his regular place in a court and Nelson was a captain short. He doubted a quorum would be found anywhere in the West Indies or even in Halifax, but felt that something had to be done to end Schomberg's uncertainty.[53]

By May Nelson had an idea that promised to solve several problems at a single stroke. For some time he had been convinced that the rotten state of the *Rattler* necessitated her return to England. He had sent her to English Harbour for preparatory repairs, and informed the Admiralty of his intentions. The prince approved, because the *Rattler* could take his letters home, explaining his conduct to his father, but Nelson was more concerned to pack the prince back to Halifax in compliance with his instructions and release Schomberg from his predicament. He therefore suggested the prince return to Canada by way of Commodore Alan Gardner's squadron in Jamaica, taking the *Rattler* with him to enable a court martial to be formed on that station. The Schomberg affair settled, both ships would be freed to continue, the *Pegasus* to Halifax and the *Rattler* to England. It was another proposal that pleased William Henry, who had been clamouring to detour to Jamaica before returning to Halifax, and he may even have thought up the idea himself.[54]

In his letters to Gardner, Nelson carefully left the question of Schomberg's guilt open, but speculated that neither party had acted dishonourably and that the accused lieutenant might have 'misunderstood' his captain's order about sending boats ashore. Though he realised that diverting the *Pegasus* to Jamaica rather than dispatching her direct to Halifax also breached the Admiralty orders he had inherited from Hughes, he weighed it a minor digression against the opportunity to end Schomberg's dilemma. The prince's further movements Nelson left to Gardner, supplying him with a copy of Howe's instructions and alerting him to the somewhat contradictory orders the prince had received from Commodore Sawyer. In effect, Nelson was passing the buck to a superior, though for the commendable purpose of bringing the dispute aboard the *Pegasus* to a conclusion.[55]

And so in May, while Nelson remained in Nevis preparing his wife for her homeward passage ('it is impossible to move a female in a few hours,' he complained), he ordered William Henry to take the *Pegasus* and *Rattler* to Jamaica. The prince arrived at Nevis on 20 May and sailed the same day. For the last time twenty-one guns roared their salute as the pugnacious prince finally put the station behind them.[56]

Nelson's plan worked because Gardner was an experienced senior officer with a sure hand. He did what every sensible person wanted, putting together a shaky compromise between William and Schomberg and sparing them a damaging court martial.

But little of this was satisfactory in the boardroom of the Admiralty, where the unauthorised redeployment of the *Pegasus* and *Rattler* added to a feeling that the Schomberg affair had been botched. Howe evidently thought Nelson might have done more to prevent the Schomberg affair reaching such a pass, or at least waited for a new commander-in-chief of the Leeward Islands to handle the matter. The first lord also disapproved of the prince's diversion to Jamaica, although confusion about the Admiralty's wishes in that respect were rooted in the board's own contradictory orders. 'I am sorry Capt Nelson, whom we wished well to, has been so much wanting in the endeavours which I think could not have failed of success, if they had been judiciously exerted, to dissuade the prince from the idea of going so prematurely to Jamaica,' Howe confided to Lord Hood. On 17 July the Admiralty secretary, Philip Stephens, wrote to Nelson – after he had returned to England – censuring him for sending two ships to Jamaica.[57]

Thankfully, Nelson's troubled West Indian commission was at an end. Only four days after the departure of the prince a government brig arrived at Nevis with letters from the new commander-in-chief, Commodore William Parker. He and his second, Sir Richard Bickerton, had left Barbados with the *Jupiter* and *Sybil*, and Nelson was ordered to meet them in St John's, Antigua. For the last time Nelson's frigate steered towards the detested hurricane hole. He was there when Parker and Bickerton arrived on 3 June but too sick to see them that day.

Bruised by three years of service, his morale and body were wasted.

Parker lost no time in throwing more mud on Captain Nelson. He was furious that Nelson had sheered two ships from his squadron. Presuming that Nelson had known of his imminent arrival, Parker erroneously concluded that the *Rattler* and the *Pegasus* had been sent to Jamaica in a deliberate effort to keep them out of his hands. In particular he resented losing the opportunity to fill the vacancy caused by the death of Commander Collingwood, an important piece of patronage. Parker told Howe that Nelson had sent the *Pegasus* and *Rattler* to Jamaica purely to reward his own followers, either through the prince's influence with Gardner or by the *Rattler* sailing direct for England. Unjustified as these charges were, Nelson would certainly have wanted the best for Wallis, and found his next task a disagreeable one to perform. When he left Antigua on the morning of 4 June, the welcome orders to sail for England in his pocket, he carried one of the new commander-in-chief's protégés on board as a passenger. Lieutenant John Watheston, Parker wrote to the Admiralty, should be promoted commander of the *Rattler* in Wallis's stead.[58]

Weary, Captain Nelson wanted only to leave. He felt dreadfully ill, and if he was fit for a ship at all he wanted it to be in the British home fleet. He called at Nevis to wish his wife and the Herberts an anxious farewell, and sailed for England from St Eustatius on 7 June. Inside the hold of the *Boreas* were presents for friends, including a sixty-gallon cask of rum for Locker, but one puncheon of spirit served an altogether more macabre purpose. It was there to receive the body of the captain if he should die on the voyage.[59]

The frigate reached Spithead on 4 July 1787 and Captain Nelson was still alive. Somewhere behind President Herbert and Fanny followed in a merchantman named the *Roehampton*.

8

Nelson arrived home amid talk of war. The French were building a powerful naval base at Cherbourg, and by a 1785 treaty with the Dutch had increased their influence across the Narrow Seas. In Parliament the opposition howled at Pitt for sitting a silent spectator to the growing strength of the arch enemy across the Channel.

Fanning the excitement was internal unrest in the Dutch United Provinces, where the *stadtholder*, William V, was defending his power against a reforming but fragile alliance of aristocratic families and populist radicals. The French used their enhanced sway in the United Netherlands to encourage the 'patriots', so the harassed *stadtholder* turned to Prussia and Britain for help, and Prussian soldiers were soon marching across the Dutch frontier to support William and to clear the rebels out. When Horatio Nelson came home the Dutch factions were on the brink of crossing swords, and there was a possibility of the Royal Navy entering the fray.

As it happened, British arms were not needed. The French declined to intervene, the Prussians gained control of Amsterdam and the triumphant *stadtholder*, the head of the Dutch republic, was soon unscrambling the Dutch treaty with France and forming new agreements with Britain and Prussia. Yet for the brief period that the affair hung in the balance, Nelson was itching to see action, battered as he was. Though English rain and cold greeted him on his return from the tropics, adding a cold and a slight fever to other afflictions, his health was improving and he felt capable of handling another command.

Refreshed to be home and pleased to meet such old friends as Pole and Kingsmill, Nelson was still as sick in spirits as body. He believed that his conduct had been entirely conscientious and self-sacrificing. He had championed the navigation laws in a campaign praised by the government, and defended the public purse from profligacy and corruption in the dockyards, surely no unwelcome act to a government striving might and main to reduce the burden of national debt left by the late war. But instead of accolades he received a series of stinging rebukes.

During much of July and August he was kept busy in Portsmouth. Nelson was one of a twelve-captain court occasionally convened on the *Pegase*, but no longer the presiding officer. Four cases of desertion were proved and the offenders flogged around the fleet.[60]

The fire of Nelson's naval masters soon became unmistakable. Hood, whom he looked upon as his patron, flew his flag from the *Triumph* at Portsmouth, and seemed less enthusiastic about seeing him again than Nelson expected. And at the end of August, when the captain returned to Kentish Town and visited the Admiralty, he found the first lord even more saturnine and impenetrable than usual. Nelson raised the matter of the dockyard abuses Wilkinson and Higgins stood ready to expose, and expressed a wish to command a ship of the line, but Howe was interested in retrenchment and had set himself against any but necessary promotions.

The letters from the Admiralty were critical. Throughout July and August he was justifying one matter after another – the *Pegasus* muster book, the Schomberg affair, the sending of the *Pegasus* and the *Rattler* to Jamaica, the pardon given Able Seaman Clark, the commissions of Church and Wallis, and the appointment of a boatswain, Joseph King, to be an assistant to the sailmaker at English Harbour. The Admiralty even threatened to cut the expenses that the redeployment of the *Rattler* had caused them out of Nelson's pay.

He realised that those few months with William Henry had done him considerable harm, and though he continued to court the prince's friendship he found it easier to shrug off the prince's baleful influence once back in England. For the first time he counselled the temperamental prince in the spirit of conciliation. With overdue words that mirrored Nelson's own true instincts for leadership, he urged William Henry to forgive Schomberg and save a useful naval career. It was good that a court martial had been avoided, he wrote to the prince. It would 'ever' have 'hurt' Schomberg:

Resentment I know your Royal Highness never had or I am sure ever will bear anyone. It is a passion incompatible with the character of a man of honour. Schomberg was too hasty certainly in writing his letter, but now you are parted, pardon me my prince, when I presume to recommend that Schomberg may stand in your royal favour as if he had never sailed with you, and that at some future day you will serve him. There only wants this to place your character in the highest point of view. None of us are without failings. Schomberg's was being rather too hasty, but that, put in competition with his being a good officer, will not, I am bold to say, be taken in the scale against him.[61]

It was vintage Nelson, and the prince's reply in December was likewise true to form. 'I must confess myself surprised that you should recommend him after what I have so often said, and in what we do both agree: namely, the never forgiving an officer for disrespect. Rest assured, I never shall, and particularly Schomberg.' As for other matters, they went happily for William Henry. 'In my own ship I go on pretty well,' he chirped. 'I have had two courts-martial, one on the master-at-arms, who was broke and received 100 lashes, and the other on a seaman who received 50 lashes on board his own ship. [Lieutenant] Church is confined. With him I have had some unpleasant work, and I am afraid he is of a sulky disposition.'[62]

Nelson's attempt to reform the prince had been fiercely rebuffed, and though William Henry wrote of his willingness to take 'young Andrews' or another of Horatio's protégés aboard his ship, there were doubts about the extent and utility of the royal favour. When the Reverend William Nelson began scavenging for 'interest', Horatio told him he had no sway with the prince at all.[63]

But of all the shots fired at him that summer and autumn, few hurt Nelson more than the slights to his officers. As his efforts on their behalf failed Nelson was upset both on their account and his own, for his standing as a captain depended upon his ability to protect and promote followers. He failed to persuade the Navy Board to give William Cutts a warrant as a sailmaker, and more strenuous efforts to assist Joseph King, who had fallen upon difficult times, likewise foundered. King, a native of Lisbon, had been 'one of the best' boatswains Nelson had seen, fit no doubt to stand beside the fugitive Scotland, but sunstroke and other afflictions had temporarily disabled him. Nelson had found him indoor work in the Antigua dockyard, but the appointment of such workers was primarily a matter for dockyard officers, not naval captains, and Nelson's good intentions provoked an outcry. It would be many years before Horatio could offer King more secure and suitable employment.[64]

Lieutenant Wallis worried Nelson even more. He had brought the *Rattler* into Spithead only eighteen days after the arrival of the *Boreas*, having executed Nelson's orders to the letter, and it was heartbreaking to tell him that Parker was overturning his appointment as acting commander. Nelson urged the Admiralty to confirm the promotions of Wallis and Church, believing that he had acted within the powers left him by Hughes and that any failure to regularise the appointments would reflect adversely upon his conduct. Through William Henry he even got the Prince of Wales interested in the officers' plight. But Howe was not listening. Church's commission as lieutenant was regularised, probably to avoid offending William Henry, but Wallis was not promoted. He eventually reached the rank of commander six years later, in January 1794.[65]

Nelson was mortified. It seemed that he used his initiative only to be slapped down, and the Admiralty wanted mere dog-like servitude. On 18 July he resentfully told the board 'that in future no consideration will ever induce me to deviate in the smallest degree from my orders'. Whether their lordships detected the hidden barb in this submission was questionable.[66]

Other business helped to occupy his mind when he visited London at the end of August, much of it private. Fanny and her uncle had reached England, and Herbert moved into a fashionable house at 5 Cavendish Square, sporting a first-floor balcony and a front door flanked by ornamental pillars. Nelson probably used it during visits, and Fanny temporarily lived there while her husband cast around for something more permanent.

Nelson had also to get the many presents he had brought home off his hands. The hold of the *Boreas* contained gifts for Locker, Kingsmill, Lord Walpole and the like, but the customs duties imposed by Pitt's money-raking government outmatched the captain's purse. He thus unashamedly resorted to smuggling, one of the brisker trades of the day. Locker was then in Kensington preparing to take charge of the impress service in Exeter. His sixty-gallon cask of rum and half a hogshead of Madeira, Nelson informed him, would be shipped through the London customs house, but the tamarinds and noyau would have to be 'smuggled, for [the] duty . . . is so enormous that no person can afford the expense'. Friends were useful for such services, and later in the year Nelson was shifting some of his imports to the *Scipio* guard ship, under his old commander Captain Lutwidge.[67]

Of the business outstanding from the Leeward Islands the professional issue that most engaged him after his return to England was that of dockyard abuses. He felt honour bound to pursue the charges made by Messrs Wilkinson and Higgins, charges he resolutely believed to be well-founded. Of several bodies originally approached by Nelson the most interested appeared to be the Navy Board, at the head of which sat the reforming Sir Charles Middleton. When interviewed by Middleton in London, Nelson impressed. Sir Charles asked the captain to write to Wilkinson and Higgins and assure them that matters could safely be put in the board's hands, and it was the comptroller who gave the two merchants their first official response by addressing them himself on 14 November. Middleton also loaned Nelson books containing all the instructions the board had sent to the dockyards. From these Nelson deduced that the regulations were indeed being widely flouted. Dockyards were supposed to advertise for the cheapest tenders, but Nelson could remember no notices in the island papers, while although naval bills of exchange were inscribed with the specific rates to be used, local dealers were gaining up to 7 per cent on them during encashment.

Middleton's interest in reform gave Nelson faith. It made him feel that he had done and was doing something valuable, but it could not arrest a growing disaffection. The Admiralty, not the subordinate Navy Board, employed commissioned officers, and Nelson's next orders, issued on 15 August and transmitted through Hood, were not attractive. They assigned him to the impress service in the Nore, and he sailed on the 18th.[68]

On 23 September the ship moved from the Little to the Great Nore, but it was already a day into its job of recruiting men. Her boats, with those of other ships, were out regularly, raiding the waterfront, shifting more or less recalcitrant recruits from place to place and boarding merchantmen. Eleven hundred men were pressed in a single night. It was degrading if not dull work, and for the most part Nelson remained aboard the frigate several miles offshore, brooding over the censures and his failure to obtain a line of battle ship. The men were also restless. Wages had been paid in August, and returning to England after years of service tempted some to desert. The number of floggings aboard the *Boreas* rose. There were none in August and September and fifteen the following month.[69]

Fanny remembered those first difficult months in England for a long time. Her husband was bitter, and spoke about resigning his commission and joining the Russian Navy, as Sir Charles Knowles had done seventeen years before. He also considered working ashore, but could not see how ends could be met. Yet even the campaign against abuses, from which he alone derived satisfaction, stumbled forward on leaden feet. Horatio was constantly applying a whip. Middleton still remained at his post, but the Treasury, to which Nelson had sent additional papers in July, was keeping mum. One day Nelson called unannounced upon George Rose, the secretary of the Treasury. Rose, like Middleton, was impressed by the young man's public spirit, and arranged to see him over breakfast the following day. They talked from six in the morning till nine, and when Nelson left he had a promise that the whole business would be laid before Pitt, the first lord of the Treasury, at an early opportunity.[70]

By the time the *Boreas* returned to Sheerness finally to be paid off on 30 November, Nelson was deeply frustrated. A sensitive man, he was acutely vulnerable to those daily lacerations of the spirit inseparable from life and suffered from occasional depression. Twice in his career he would talk about quitting the service altogether, both times from a sense of neglect. This was the first. According to his biographers, Clarke and McArthur, he confided in the senior officer in the Medway one morning. If true, the conversation was probably with Vice Admiral Richard Edwards, commander-in-chief in the Medway and at the Nore. He was glad his ship was being paid off, and that he was going to be discharged from an 'ungrateful service', Nelson said, and he intended to surrender his commission. Edwards is said to have tried to dissuade Nelson from so drastic a course, and to have alerted the Admiralty. As Clarke and McArthur heard it, Howe responded immediately. He wrote Nelson a generous letter, inviting him to come to London after the *Boreas* was paid off. The first lord still did not have a ship to offer him but he promised to serve him in the future, and presented him to the king at the next levee day.[71]

If Nelson's hopes of getting another command rose, he was to be disappointed. The talk of war subsided, few ships were put in commission and Captain Nelson was left on the 'beach'. The only ranks he joined were those of the unemployed. It was thoroughly disheartening. In the past he had made little money, but believed that if he followed his profession dutifully it would provide him with means and glory enough. Now he was not so sure, though somehow he could not convince himself that justice would not be done. As he told his newly retired 'old friend' Hercules Ross on 6 May 1788:

But in this next, my friend, you have got the start of me. You have given up all the toils and anxieties of business, whilst I must still buffet the waves – in search of what? That thing called *Honour* is now, alas, thought of no more. My integrity cannot be mended [improved upon], I hope; and my fortune, God knows, has grown worse for the service. So much for serving my country. But the Devil, ever willing to tempt the virtuous (pardon this flattery of myself) has made me offer, if any ships should be sent to destroy His Majesty of Morocco's ports, to be there, and I have some reason to think that should any more come of it, my humble services will be accepted. I have invariably laid down and followed close a plan of what ought to be uppermost in the breast of an officer: that it is much better to serve an ungrateful country than to give up his own fame. Posterity will do him justice. A uniform conduct of honour and integrity will seldom fail of bringing a man to the goal of Fame at last.[72]

XVI

BEACHCOMBING

While war shall rage around,
May Nelsons still be found,
To guard our Isle.
  A Lady's Additional Verses to
  'God Save The King', 1803

1

FOR several months Nelson moved from place to place looking for
health, home and work. He had not seen Burnham Thorpe for five
years, and only twice since childhood, but busy visits to London had
kept him abreast of the local news. At the end of August 1787, with
the *Boreas* rocking gently at the Nore, he had lodged at 10 Great
Marlborough Street rather than impose upon convenient relatives, but
there had been reunions with his brother Maurice and the Sucklings
of Kentish Town. Maurice even stayed on board his frigate for a while,
diverting him from the troubles of impressment, and at the end of the
year, with the unhappy ship finally behind him, his thoughts again
returned to Norfolk, the country of his birth.

He anticipated putting 'my little fellow' Josiah, now seven, into
school there. Nelson felt his own lack of a decent formal education,
and recommended midshipmen to master French and dancing among
the more obvious accomplishments essential to a naval officer.
Unfortunately business tied him to the capital over Christmas, and in
January 1788 he dispatched Josiah to Norfolk under the charge of
Frank Lepee, his servant. His brother William, now rector of
Hilborough, was instructed to put the boy in a suitable boarding

school, but he was 'not [to] allow him to do as he pleases' and ensure he received 'the same weekly allowance as the other boys'.[1]

In London Nelson now lodged at 6 Princes Street, Cavendish Square, from where he reclaimed his wife from the nearby home of her uncle. He probably looked up Howe, and certainly ventured into the Navy Office, looking futilely to secure William the illegitimate wages supposedly earned as chaplain of the *Boreas* after the incumbent had, in fact, returned to England. More creditably and typically, he fought for his men, for while his command was over he still saw himself as 'their friend and protector'. He tried to ensure they got their prize money, wrote testimonials and almost invariably answered calls for help. Thus, during the year following the discharge of the *Boreas*, two of its young gentlemen, Talbot and Lock, sought help when they were denied access to the lieutenants' examination on the grounds that they had spent too long rated captain's servants. Nelson supported them, but realised that the excess of apprentice officers on the *Boreas* had created a downside. He had wanted to provide 'a set of young men to make officers [of], without a nursery for whom, I am well assured, our service must suffer', but their number had outstripped the ratings available and some had consequently been stinted of necessary sea time as midshipmen or master's mates.[2]

Among others needing Nelson was the master of the *Boreas*, James Jameson, accused of cruelty by the former steward, Thomas Watts. December 1787 found the captain backing his master without reservation. He was 'by no means of a cruel and oppressive disposition', whereas Watts was 'a bad character' who had been flogged in Dominica for sneaking liquor to the quartermasters. 'I am afraid that if Mr Jameson had confined the steward till I came on board,' Nelson explained, 'I should have punished him at the gangway.' He suggested that in this instance the Admiralty resist any civil prosecution 'for acts committed under martial law', or at least defend the master at public expense.[3]

Nelson's most notable intervention took him into the witness box of the Old Bailey on 17 December. The defendant was an elderly cooper of the *Boreas* named James Carse, charged with murder. Carse had always been a quiet, orderly man of good character, but the last few years had changed him. He became morose, and drew into a world of his own, and spoke to almost no one. Nelson described him as 'melancholy' with the appearance of 'a man' who 'had seen better days'. Those ashore, who had known him years before, thought him much altered upon his return from the West Indies. What little he said was confused and rambling.[4]

Carse had left the *Boreas* with fifty or sixty guineas of accumulated pay in his pockets, heading for his former home in Shadwell. He spent two evenings in a public house babbling about having been robbed on his way from Gravesend. The second of December found him drinking rum and water in the Ship In Distress, a squalid waterfront tavern in Wapping, where he encountered a young prostitute, Mary Mills, who ushered the inebriated sailor to a house she shared with one Sarah Hayes. Carse drank some more, got into bed and shortly rose in a befuddled panic. Apparently convinced a plot to rob him was afoot, he cried, 'I will! I must! I must!' and pulling out a large twopenny clasp knife he made for Hayes as she prepared to smoke her pipe in the chimney corner. Carse backed Hayes against the chimney breast and cut her throat, while Mills fled in her shift for a watchman. 'How I got out, were I to die this moment, I cannot say,' she recalled. Carse was apprehended with little difficulty and hauled to jail. There was no denying the offence, and the prisoner faced public execution, but he declared that he was 'not afraid of getting through it' for he had 'very good friends'.

He was relying upon Nelson, and told how the captain had addressed the ship's company the day it was paid off, assuring all that his interest in their welfare would not end with the command. At the trial Nelson testified in the august presence of Mr Justice Heath, and speculated that some publican might have plied Carse with drink to relieve him of his pay. The cooper was not 'by any means' a habitual drunkard. 'Seamen, I know perfectly, when they come home, the landlords will furnish them with raw liquors. I saw myself thirty or forty men from that ship [*Boreas*] that were as mad as if they were at Bedlam, and did not know what they did.' Nor was Carse violent, but 'the quietest, soberest man that I ever saw in my life', if one increasingly melancholic and reserved.

William Garrow, the defence counsel, asked Nelson if Carse was 'likely to commit a deliberate foul murder?'.

'I should as soon suspect myself,' came the reply, 'because I am hasty; he is not.'

Nelson even posited an explanation of the cooper's strange behaviour: a brain-damaging fever induced by sunstroke. 'At the island of Antigua, I think it was, he was struck with the sun, after which time he appeared melancholy. I have been affected with it [myself]. I have been out of my senses. It hurts the brain.' He had hospitalised Carse and would have sent him home had the ship itself not been recalled. The cooper was said to have been cured, but Nelson doubted it, and speculated that the fever might have returned under the influence of drink. The testimony was decisive. Carse was convicted but referred for further consideration rather than sentenced to the gallows. He was eventually pardoned, but the discharge was conditional upon his being taken on another ship and in the meantime he went to Newgate prison. There the unfortunate fellow languished until April 1795, but at least he lived.

While Horatio wound up naval affairs, Fanny coughed her way through a cold, wintry Christmas wreathed in London smoke. The couple abandoned the idea of keeping a house in the city, and in January 1788 Nelson bundled his wife onto a coach for Bath. There he established her in relative comfort before proceeding to Plymouth at the invitation of William Henry, who was holding outrageous court in the town. Nelson confessed himself 'sorry' that the prince remained bitter towards Schomberg, but still found much to admire. The old *Pegasus* appeared in good order, while William Henry not only remained independent of mind ('the great folks above now see he will not be a cipher') but also 'respected by all. Those who knew him formerly say he is a most altered young man, and those who were prejudiced against him acknowledge their error.'[5]

On 24 January he was back in Bath to share its fabled recuperative processes with Fanny. In March they were fit enough for an extended foray into the milder West Country, taking the coach to Bristol to stay at Redlands with the Tobins, some of Fanny's in-laws. The Tobins had made their fortune in Nevis, and for Fanny there was also a delightful reunion with their mutual friends the Pinneys, who had settled in Bristol four years before. Then the couple proceeded to Exmouth by way of Plymouth, with Horatio feeling his strength returning. 'As usual my health is got up again, after the doctors telling me they could do nothing for me,' he told Hercules Ross. 'Dame Nature never has failed curing me.'[6]

Older concerns still lapped around, however, rolling from the Caribbean on the warm westerly currents. Some appeals were still pending against the sentences condemning American ships he had taken, and suits for damages could not be ruled out. Nelson referred these disturbing correspondents to the Admiralty, trusting the Treasury would defend him, but he took greater pains when letters from Messrs

Wilkinson and Higgins reached him, asking what progress he was making on the issue of the West Indian frauds. By threatening to expose rampant corruption, Wilkinson and Higgins had ruined themselves in the islands, where every trader's hand was now against them. Even John Burke, the solicitor general of Antigua, in whom Nelson had inadvertently confided, was obstructing the investigation and encouraging creditors to drive the informants to the wall. Receiving nothing from London but a letter from the Navy Board, the whistle-blowers were desperate to know that Nelson was still behind them. New frauds were emerging all the time, they wrote to him in January: 'The amount is immense beyond even our expectations . . . Would to God we had you now here, with fit powers to complete the good work you have begun!'[7]

Apart from his interest in rooting out corruption, Nelson felt responsible for Wilkinson and Higgins, for more than any one else he had encouraged them. He felt honour-bound to back them, even if it transpired that people he had respected, such as Dr Young of the hospital in Antigua, were implicated in the frauds. It was obvious from their letters that Wilkinson and Higgins presumed he had approached the Sick and Hurt and Victualling boards, though in fact Nelson's overtures had been to the Admiralty, Navy, Ordnance and Treasury boards. Perhaps he felt remiss, although he had been far from idle. The Admiralty had waived their interest in favour of the Navy Board, where Middleton was still showing interest, while the Treasury, Nelson thought, had been kicked into action by his visit to Rose. Nevertheless, from the Ordnance Board the captain had heard nothing. They had mislaid the letter he had written from Antigua, and did not take the matter up until Wilkinson and Higgins themselves wrote to them in January 1788.[8]

Nelson sent his collaborators an inspiring reply. He had not forgotten them, nor lost his determination to expose malpractices. His 'interest' was 'very small' but he relied upon his known 'integrity and public spirit' to gain his points, and believed the boards he had canvassed would respond. Nelson suggested Wilkinson and Higgins write to the Sick and Hurt Board, which managed the naval hospitals and supplied surgeons and medical supplies to the fleet, and promised to follow the matter up personally when he reached London. If appropriate, he would also try to interest the Victualling Board in Wilkinson and Higgins's proposals.[9]

Letters from the two merchants were already stirring the Sick and

Hurt, Victualling and Ordnance boards, however, and Nelson became their referee. He understood the frustration they felt as their futures lingered in piles of papers in dusty government offices, and wrote to London again, characterising the informants as 'men of strong natural parts', and recommending that their allegations be heard.[10]

In May the Nelsons returned to London and were installed in one of Herbert's rooms. Nelson tackled the fraud issue again, haunting Middleton at the Navy Office, but his own cause, the search for a ship, was buried by the complete inaccessibility of Lord Howe. William Henry had said that Howe was persecuting Nelson because of his friendship for the prince, and Horatio was beginning to believe it. He was also reflecting upon his dwindling finances. His new London agents and bankers, Marsh and Creed, paid him £250 for his service in the *Boreas*, but something more permanent was needed to support a wife, a stepson and continuing expenses. His half-pay amounted to a mere 8s. a day, hardly enough to cover the costs of board, lodgings and travel. He asked the Admiralty to recompense him for trips made in Antigua to investigate the frauds, and appealed for an additional allowance covering the period he had acted as commander-in-chief in the Leeward Islands. In June desperation drove him to the only straw of 'interest' that still stood in a stony and barren field – the prince himself, now rather more satisfactorily assigned to the squadron at Spithead. First he begged William Henry to buttonhole Herbert and urge him to serve his niece more substantially, only to find the rich uncle unmovable. Then, swallowing his pride, Horatio tried, and failed, to use the prince to get Fanny appointed to the household of the Princess Royal.[11]

Talking their doubtful situation over with his wife, Nelson considered removing to France, where fallen aristocrats and middling folk alike might still eke out a shabby gentility. With Fanny's help he might even acquire that elusive facility with the French tongue. But first, he realised, it was necessary to introduce his wife to the people in Norfolk. It was time to take Fanny home.[12]

2

It was not something everyone anticipated with pleasure. The Reverend Edmund Nelson was now in his sixty-seventh year, and his retiring disposition, ill health and want of money had given him a preference for seclusion.

According to Nelson's first significant biographer the reverend suffered from 'paralytic and asthmatic' conditions and was sometimes speechless early in the mornings. Indeed, he 'had actually been given over by the physicians almost forty years prior to his decease [in 1801]'. The verdict was not unanimous, since another contemporary maintained that Edmund took long walks before dinner, occasionally accompanied by his naval son. The old man did not fool himself though. He knew his 'every power' was 'in decay' and that he was 'very unfitt for society' and 'not likely to revive by practice'.[13]

Retirement was also decreed by the old man's purse. In addition to his modest gleanings as a parson, Edmund had three small annuities: one from his late wife invested in South Seas speculations; another the legacy of their daughter Ann; and a third the return on £700 his son William had invested as a condition of succeeding to the patronage of Hilborough in 1785. Nevertheless, he was apt to reach into his pockets for deserving causes, and had joined Lord Walpole in supplying the church at Burnham Thorpe with a new pulpit. More, he maintained the parsonage and a small staff, including Peter Black ('poor, forlorn, tho' as wise as ever'), the Browns and Kents, and a maid or two, and intermittently supported two feckless sons, Maurice and Suckling. To economise, the ageing minister had largely abandoned his visits to Bath and London, 'where every man pays by the inch and must shorten his own train'. An inherently gentle man who worried about sick and struggling parishioners, he disdained the 'dogs, guns, great dinners, claret and champagne' set, regarded the hunting fraternity as 'the class licensed to destroy', politics as a 'noisy nonsense' and writers as mealy-mouth self-promoters driven by 'pride and ambition' rather than 'a desire to inform others'. He was happy writing to his family and a few friends in solitude, or enjoying a 'chat' with visitors and members of the flock.

Fanny had written to the old gentleman when Nelson was at the Nore, but the prospect of welcoming a 'lady' to his cold, cheerless parsonage filled Edmund with dread. 'I am not now anxious to see them,' he wrote to Kate. 'Him for a day or two I should be glad of, but to introduce a stranger to an infirm and whimsical old man, who can neither eat nor drink, nor talk, nor see, is as well let alone.' Consequently Captain Nelson received a letter from his father, beseeching him to trail Fanny round the other relations before risking Burnham Thorpe.[14]

Accordingly, in July and August 1788 Nelson and his bride were in Norfolk, moving from one set of relatives to the next. They were all new to Fanny, but Horatio also met a brother-in-law and nephews and nieces previously known to him only through letters and word of mouth. Back from Ostend the Boltons were found at Thorpe, just east of Norwich, breeding a tribe sufficient to infatuate any naval uncle. Horatio's love of children enabled him to fuss over the six-year-old twins Jemima-Susanna and Catherine, and the latest additions, Thomas and George. Elizabeth and Anne would follow in 1789 and 1791. Nelson had met Thomas Bolton before. In 1780 he and William had also signed their sister's marriage settlement, casting a protective eye over her fortune of £2,000, but it had become clear that Susanna had made a good match. Six years older than Nelson, Bolton was a distinguished looking fellow of a respectable family. The elder brother had inherited the family home, another had become a rector and one of two sisters was a musician. Thomas himself was prospering as a merchant, and like Horatio had become a patron of the family, employing Edmund Nelson junior, who occupied rooms in the Bolton house and shared their ownership of a trading vessel.[15]

Nearby at Barton Hall, on the wild, flat wetlands known as the Broads, Nelson introduced his wife to his youngest sibling, Kate, a dainty, slim and sparkling young lady with a shock of wavy hair. Horatio had always been protective of Kate, especially after sister Ann's death, but he was not disappointed when he met her new husband, George Matcham, a handsome, enterprising, well-spoken man with a firm, open face. George was in his mid-thirties, but his insatiable wanderlust had given him experiences beyond those of most men. He had followed his father into the East India Company and been their man in Baroche, in India, before his discharge in 1783. Coming home overland, George accomplished a remarkable horseback ride from Baghdad to Pera in Turkey with Arab guides, storing the details for an account he would publish when he reached England. Among many bizarre people with whom he was acquainted was the unfortunate emperor of Austria, Joseph II, the very exemplification of enlightened despotism.[16]

Further east Nelson took Fanny to the small village of Hilborough, where her son was spending his holidays. There also she met Nelson's surviving grandmother, and the family of the Reverend William Nelson. William had succeeded to the rectory upon the death of his uncle, Robert Rolfe, and was cutting a larger figure in local affairs. We find him, for example, preaching at St George's, Tombland, in Norwich, seeking support for charity schools. Perhaps an infant daughter was increasing his interest in the young. Born on 20 September 1787, Charlotte Mary Nelson would grow into by far the most striking of the family, if we may judge from a portrait Isaac Pocock later painted of a slim, dark-haired beauty. Her brother, Horatio, would arrive in October 1788 in time for the uncle whose name he took to stand as godparent.[17]

The captain and his wife may also have called upon Nelson's youngest brother at North Elmham. Suckling also had a bride, the daughter of Theodore Smith of Bungay, and had used his legacy from Captain Suckling and a donation from Uncle William Suckling to open a grocery store in the village.

These travels were punctuated by sudden errands. Nelson went ahead to Burnham to prepare his father for Fanny's appearance, and found the reverend (as he said himself) in respectable health, 'happy, and as usual replete with the most affectionate love and good wishes towards his friends'. And twice the captain was drawn to London, first to rescue Maurice from a 'galling chain' of debt he had accumulated, and then to see a new first lord of the Admiralty. Howe was gone, replaced by Pitt's brother, the Earl of Chatham, and Hood was a member of the board, but Nelson made no progress. Even Hood held out no hope for a ship.[18]

Fanny was probably relieved for she was tired of wandering without the luxury of organising a home. She craved permanence, whether in France or England mattered not, and waited in Norfolk until her husband returned. Then at last Nelson took her along the quiet country lanes that led to Burnham Thorpe and a crumbling old parson with long white hair falling about a lugubrious face. From the beginning the creaking philospher and the petite belle from the islands liked each other. As she remembered it, the rector's 'joy at seeing this best and most affectionate of sons was so great that he told us that we had given him new life . . . this good old man seemed to suffer much at the thought of our leaving him, saying his age and infirmities were increasing, and that he could not last long, which made us give up entirely our former plan.' Nelson abandoned his vision of a French retreat and opted to remain in Burnham Thorpe.[19]

The reverend never regretted the decision, for Horatio was dutiful, reliable and ready to share the burdens of caring for the wider family, and Fanny proved an enduring friend. Towards the end of 1790 the rector moved out of the parsonage to give the newly-weds more room, and with the aid of a housekeeper, respectable furnishings and the caddy of tea he considered an essential element of civilisation, comfortably established himself in a cottage in Burnham Ulph, where he also preached. He rode to Burnham Thorpe fairly regularly, but when at home received almost daily visits from Horatio, particularly during spells of bad weather. 'My good, very good son,' the old man wrote gratefully. 'He is in the superlative, believe me.' Nor was this testimony mere parental loyalty, for Edmund was no sparing critic of undeserving children, and outsiders echoed his sentiments. Indeed, it was Nelson's 'filial duty to his infirm father' that particularly recommended him to the local landowner, Sir Mordaunt Martin of Westgate Hall in Burnham Westgate. The rector valued the utility of an able son's watchful eye, and perhaps more so his company, which he described as 'not the least' of his 'many blessings' and a 'felicity' he could scarcely bear to be without. Horatio's brief absences he thought 'an age'.[20]

Nelson had put a roof over Fanny's head but his lingering hopes of employment were crushed at the end of the year. In October 1788 he grovelled to one of the few friends left in a position to help. William Cornwallis, he heard, was to sail to the East Indies as commodore. Nelson had enjoyed his time in the east, and would have been happy to return, so he wrote obsequiously that he had long wanted to serve under Cornwallis. But either every ship was spoken for or Cornwallis had more valuable friends. More chastening still, early the next year Nelson's application for the command of a guard ship was rejected in a single sentence by the Admiralty.[21]

He retired from the service wounded, grieving for the loss of a career he had loved and in which he still burned to succeed. 'Not being a man of fortune is a crime which I cannot get over, and therefore none of the great care about me,' he sulked. 'I am now commencing farmer. Not a very large one, you will conceive, but enough for amusement. Shoot I cannot. Therefore, I have not taken out a licence. But notwithstanding the neglect I have met with, I am happy, and now I see the propriety of not having built my hopes [entirely] on such sandy foundations as the friendships of the great.'[22]

3

Grudgingly, Horatio Nelson took his place among those loosely known as the 'gentle' classes. They were not all members of the titled aristocracy refurbishing and landscaping their country seats to advertise their elite staus, among the substantial landowners who badged themselves 'gents' or 'esquires', or from the thrusting commercial middle classes whose assets were of a more liquid kind. But for all that they formed a recognisable elite socially superior to the small owner-occupiers, tenant farmers and shopkeepers, and a world apart from the 'common' people who made up the bulk of the working population. Typically they were men and women of some education, status, wealth and power, and mixed at dinners, balls, concerts, fairs and sporting meets. They supported the church and constitution, exercised local patronage, dispensed a little philanthropy and served as parish officers or justices of the peace. They intermarried, strengthening their interest if they could, often entailed their homes and almost always maintained servants.

Nelson, of course, was a man of more modest means and reserved manners than most such gentlefolk. He was a professional man and lacked the land and rents to avoid a regular attendance to a livelihood. As readers of Jane Austen will know, professions such as the clergy, law and armed services became sanctuaries for many a younger son displaced from the ancestral home by the law of primogeniture, and compelled to make his way in the world. Some such refugees were more successful than others, but nearly all of them clung to their rank in society. Even members of the church, perhaps the least remunerative of the professions, were not above throwing themselves into the social round, and a famous agricultural commentator knew parsons who 'spent the morning in scampering after hounds', the 'evening' dedicated 'to the bottle', and Sundays reeling into the pulpit.[23]

A naval captain capable of placing sons in midshipmen's berths was a welcome addition to any locality. And so, when a new county map of Norfolk delineated the residences of the socially significant, the humble parsonage of 'Capt. Nelson' found itself earmarked among the grander piles of Hill, Humphreys, Townshend and Coke.[24]

That first winter back in Norfolk was abysmally cold, the coldest some remembered. Nelson was attacked by rheumatism and moved little beyond the bedchamber much of the time, while Fanny hardly dared stir from beneath her stout moreen bed sheets. When the weather improved and her mobility increased, the new wife examined the neighbours, but satisfying friends were few and far between the village rustics, and she missed her pianoforte and the social evenings it had allowed her. Nevertheless, her affection for her father-in-law increased, and she gamely tackled his infirmities. Fanny was an old-fashioned wife; she might not have been a full partner in Nelson's mission to achieve, but she fully lived up to her belief in submissive loyalty and duty.

On his part Horatio attacked the garden, where his father and old Peter Black had been raising a ha-ha, preparing beds for roses, lilacs and hyacinths, and creating a pond by digging a trench from the River Burn. He began cultivating the rough glebe land, and managing a few sheep which he turned out to graze on the salt marshes and bottom lands in the spring.[25]

Nelson started married life with very little money. His net half-pay only came to about £106 a year, and the couple had an annuity of £100 from William Suckling. Fanny may have received a similar stipend from her uncle, but there is no proof that it was ever paid, and on the whole Herbert had been a huge disappointment. This was a frugal income, barely enough to sustain the status of a 'gentleman'. The wages Nelson had earned on the *Boreas* were still being paid into his account with Marsh and Creed, but most of it probably offset advances he had already received and spent. The only fresh windfalls he could expect – barring the promised legacy from his father-in-law – were occasional payments of prize money, but appeals against the condemnation of some of his American prizes dragged on uncertainly, and proceedings against two ships convicted in Nevis in 1785 were still pending four years later. Horatio therefore dipped into his savings. He and William sold £833 worth of government stocks in November 1788, and Horatio probably applied his share to setting up house in the parsonage. He also had a financial share in Bolton's house at Thorpe, although it realised only £300 when it was sold in 1792, which, reinvested, yielded a mere £15 a year in interest. His eighth share in a ticket for Pitt's new national lottery won him nothing at all. These resources promised a threadbare future and barely covered the couple's costs of living. By 1793 Nelson's annual balances with Marsh and Creed had slipped into the red.[26]

Horatio and his father both suffered for their generosity to others. The rector farmed his glebe land and received a modest income as a minister, but incurred considerable expenses. In 1796–7 his land taxes amounted to £18 16s. 9d. per annum, all but 8s. 9d. of it on account of the glebe which was assessed at an annual value of £92, and the rest due on a small property leased from a Mr Elliott. The years 1791 to 1793 also saw substantial repairs being made to the church in Burnham Thorpe. Windows, pews and a roof had to be replaced and the south aisle dismantled, and it would be surprising if the rector did not make small contributions to the costs. Most distressing of all to Edmund Nelson and his son was the seemingly endless need to bail out impecunious relatives.[27]

Nelson's eldest brother, Maurice, seemed perennially in want. 'There was a day when he might have catched a gleam of sunshine [but] it is now clouded,' said his father. Exiled in London, Maurice was still a clerk at the Navy Board, occupying the position of what we would today call a civil servant, and he rarely got to Norfolk. None of the family knew his business very well, and though he cohabited with a few women during his lifetime, neither his father nor brothers could say for certain whether he was ever legally married. One of these liaisons, 'Sukey', is only known to us by a series of letters Maurice wrote to her in 1793 and 1794, after he had quit the Navy Board to become assistant commissary to Lord Moira's forces and been sent to the West Country and the south coast. Sukey's very identity is mysterious. Maurice addressed his letters to 'Mrs Nelson' of 8 Rathbone Place, Oxford Street, London. She was probably named Susanna, for which 'Sukey' was a recognised short form, and apparently had two children, possibly by a previous paramour, John Andrews, one of Maurice Nelson's colleagues in the Navy Office.[28]

The youngest brother was even more troublesome. Suckling cheerfully failed at almost everything he did. His life at North Elmham soon withered. At first he had shouldered his communal responsibilities, and in February 1787 joined other parishioners in a plan to prosecute felons, but he soon forsook their meetings. His marriage, about which none of the Nelsons spoke, ended, and his grocery business failed, consuming what he had inherited from Captain Suckling. Still in his twenties, Suckling was soon back at Burnham Thorpe sponging on Horatio and their father. They provided him with private tuition, and in 1791 packed him off to Christ's College, Cambridge, to study for holy orders. This got him out of their way from October to June of each year, but though early reports suggested he was buckling down to work, Edmund doubted that his youngest would ever amount to much. At best he might 'pass . . . amongst a crowd of undistinguished preachers, and gain some respect . . . from his quiet disposition, his liking to a little conviviality, and his passion for greyhounds and coursing'.[29]

If relations tried Horatio's meagre resources, nothing emphasised his relative poverty more than the company he was now obliged to keep. Drinking at the Plough (licensed in the village to John Hubbard), he might have seemed the local hero, but with the Hilborough, Wells or Norwich sets he was embarrassed by his indigency. Even the Boltons and Matchams had more money at their disposal. Elsewhere some of the people with whom he had to cut a respectable figure were grander still. The Martins of Westgate Hall in Burnham Westgate made agreeable companions. Sir Mordaunt Martin, the fourth baronet, was eighteen years Nelson's senior, and coincidentally an absentee marshal of the vice-admiralty court in Jamaica, though his job was actually performed by deputies. His wife was a local girl, the daughter of the Reverend William Smith of Burnham Westgate. At the Hall in Burnham Thorpe lived another clergyman, the Reverend Mr Crowe, whose engaging brood inspired much of the local gossip. But the large landowners who came within Nelson's ken were Ann, Lady Camelford, who owned scattered properties about the village; the mighty Thomas Coke, who reigned to the east in Holkham; and Lord and Lady Walpole of Wolterton Hall, near Norwich. Horatio may have counted a prince of the realm a close friend, but disabled by penury he was uncertain about his standing with such folk.

Lord Walpole was Nelson's godfather, but it was not until 1790 that the captain and his lady were invited to stay at Wolterton. Wolterton Hall was a splendid mansion, its elaborate coat of arms proudly embossed on the gable above the front entrance, and the Nelsons worried whether Fanny's wardrobe was equal to a prolonged trial. However, the Walpoles proved to be gratifyingly down-to-earth, and the visit was so successful that it became an annual event to relieve the gloom of approaching winter. Despite that, when the third Earl of Orford, the head of the Walpole clan, died the Nelsons were not invited to the funeral. Horatio felt slighted, even though the succeeding earl, the famous writer Horace Walpole, apologised for the oversight and explained that the arrangements had not been in his hands.[30]

At Wolterton, Lady Walpole introduced Nelson to the greatest landowner in the county, Thomas William Coke, then a parliamentary member for Norfolk and later to become Earl of Leicester. He was one of the great agricultural improvers, and his famous estate lay only a mile east of Burnham Thorpe. Holkham was a huge chunk of countryside, with crops, woodlands strategically placed to break the chilling easterlies, pastures, a lake, ornamental grounds designed by Lancelot 'Capability' Brown and an impressive obelisk. At its heart stood the palatial hall.

Coke visited the parsonage in 1791, and in later years greatly admired Nelson and sent gifts of game to his father. Nelson reciprocated when he could. He would find places for Coke's protégés aboard his next ship, and must certainly have visited so important a neighbour, reaching his ornate mansion through the estate's west gate. But it is doubtful if he was overawed: Nelson was seldom impressed by wealth alone, which he often attributed to unworthy actions, and in Coke's case had other reservations. The Nelsons had never supported the Cokes politically. In the general election of 1768 Reverend Edmund Nelson had cast his two votes in favour of candidates de Grey and Woodhouse rather than for Wenman Coke, Thomas's nephew. As far as Captain Nelson was concerned, Thomas Coke was a Whig grandee and an associate of Fox and his cronies, whom he stigmatised as corrupt and unpatriotic. Given these views, Nelson steered clear of talking politics at Holkham, but when Coke organised a huge party on 5 November 1788 to celebrate the centenary of William of Orange's landing in England, a benchmark of Whiggism, the captain abruptly declined to attend.[31]

Nelson occasionally extended his acquaintances at social events, though he was by no means a gadabout. He visited the Lynn feast, and on 6 October 1792 was hobnobbing at the Aylsham assembly. There he talked to Lady Durrant, who looked 'quite the old woman' without 'her front teeth', though 'Miss Durrant' ('a very fine tall young woman'), 'Mr Church the clergyman', and 'Miss Caroline Aufrere and Miss Emily . . . who are grown extraordinary fine ladies' probably attracted more of his attention. He even made a stab at entering sporting circles, and suppressing doubts about his marksmanship reluctantly paid forty-three shillings for his first shooting licence in September 1788 and acquired a pointer. He shot on his own glebe land, as well as further afield at Fakenham and elsewhere, but only one bag, a partridge, was remembered, and he was notorious for carrying his gun at full cock and blasting from the hip as soon as birds broke cover. Hare coursing was another common Norfolk pursuit, but Nelson did not care for it. He 'seldom escaped a wet jacket and a violent cold' on such expeditions, and admitted that 'even the ride to the Smee is longer than any pleasure I find in the sport will compensate for'.[32]

At other times he entertained visitors at home, serving tea in the parsonage and occasionally dinner. In school holidays the house was filled with Josiah's noise ('Josiah came home yesterday just in time to be shut up'), and other members of the family were frequent boarders, including Nelson's brothers and Horace Suckling, the son of his Uncle William, who arrived in between his terms at Cambridge. Space and money limited Nelson's hospitality, and in April 1792 we find him warning his brother William that, with one of his two or three rooms undergoing repair, he 'could only offer you the tent bed through our room'. But the visits were essential to keeping up with the local gossip the Nelsons enjoyed. Thus, in one of the letters Horatio used to send his sister Kate after she left Barton Hall in 1791, he eagerly reported that Miss Crowe had danced pleasurably with Lieutenant Robert Suckling of the Royal Artillery at the Norwich sessions ball. His information was good. Lieutenant Suckling and his brother Maurice, both old West Indian friends and the last once his midshipman, had stayed at the parsonage a few days, while Robert Crowe had called for tea one day with the obvious intention of learning about the lieutenant's prospects. Horatio happily encouraged the match with the information that Lieutenant Suckling stood to inherit £1,500 a year.[33]

Blessings are usually mixed, and one advantage of Nelson's return to Norfolk was his reconnection to a family to which he had become almost a stranger. Apart from the precious, irreplaceable years it gave him with an ageing but beloved parent, Nelson reoccupied the hub of an enlarged family circle. Of its new members Thomas Bolton dealt with him the most. Bolton was strategically placed near Norwich, and although Nelson often visited the town, he relied upon his brother-in-law to handle his business there when he remained isolated in Burnham Thorpe. Bolton was on hand for specialist shopping and attentive to Horatio's meticulous instructions. He supplied bottles of port, 'a cake' for 'Master [Josiah] Nesbitt', loose coverings for the parsonage furniture ('a handsome, rich blue, but not dark'), Norfolk turkeys and sausage meat for Captain Locker to use as Christmas presents, 'a good old Gloucester cheese', and in 1792 a horse to replace Nelson's black mare. It had to be 'sound in every respect', Nelson said, at least fourteen hands, and not a 'starter' with any 'vicious tricks'. Riding was essential in rural Norfolk, and Nelson stabled his animals at the parsonage and consigned their welfare to Peter Black.[34]

Sadly, family obligations involved exits as well as entrances, and bereavements were commoner then than now, especially with the high rate of infant mortality. As Nelson said, commiserating with Kate after one such loss, there were 'so many complaints which the poor little things are subject to' it was surprising that so many survived to maturity. Two deaths in 1789 struck the family particularly hard. On 4 July Horatio lost his remaining grandmother, Mary Bland, who died at her house in Hilborough at the venerable age of ninety-one. Her will, which the Reverend Edmund had witnessed in 1769, made provision for her three daughters (Horatio's paternal aunts), with the principal beneficiary being the older and still unmarried Mary, who received first claim upon her mother's house and property.[35]

Even closer to Horatio was his younger brother, Edmund. 'Mun' had been in business with his brother-in-law, Thomas Bolton, but was wasted by consumption. At the age of twenty-seven he returned to his birthplace to die. Fanny, Horatio and the rector did what they could at the parsonage, but although the patient ate well he declined rapidly and slipped into occasional delirium. 'Dame' Smith was brought in from the village as a regular nurse, but the end came thirteen days before Christmas. 'Poor fellow,' Nelson wrote to Bolton, 'thank God he went off perfectly in his senses, which for the last week were more collected than at any other period since his being here. He sent for my father on the day before his death to ask where he was to be buried, and on my father telling him somewhere near where he [himself] should one day be laid he answered he hoped so, and then told my father two or three things which he wished you to do, and which he had omitted to tell you.'

Nelson organised the funeral for 15 December. A hearse was brought from Fakenham, and Mr Crowe, who met it at the church, was rewarded with a scarf, hatband and gloves, while the six veteran parishioners who carried the plain oak coffin each received a crown and a handkerchief. Edmund was lowered seven feet into a grave within the communion rails of the village church. There appears to have been no will, but Mun's property went to his father, who insisted upon meeting the expenses of the funeral, and the Boltons, as he had wished. Horatio sadly noted the usual creditors. Among the 'demands' coming in were some from their brother Maurice of which Nelson was 'ashamed'.[36]

It is not surprising that as the Reverend Edmund Nelson cast fading eyes over his surviving children he fixed upon Horatio as the rock upon which their hopes would most likely rest.

4

There may have been compensations but working the land and shackled to the small world of Burnham Thorpe remained deeply

demoralising to Horatio Nelson. His 'dream of glory' remained unful-
filled, far, far away in this quiet corner of agriculture and parochial
gossip. He had turned thirty with nothing but a purposeless life before
him, and little to stimulate his tremendous energy and talent.
Sometimes he affected to revel in rural retreat, but the truth was that
he resented it and longed for a new command.

A child of his own might have filled the void, but as the years
passed it became obvious that Fanny was not going to conceive. Nelson
must have been disappointed, for he regarded children as the natural
consummation of love and marriage and probably felt incomplete.
Josiah's presence must have suggested that the infertility was his, rather
than Fanny's, though this was not in fact the case. It is impossible to
say how their relationship was affected, but in the long run a child
might have saved their marriage.

For one as widely travelled as Nelson, who had explored the fringes
of international history, Burnham Thorpe was excruciatingly dull. He
rambled in the woods with his wife, revisiting the haunts of his bird-
nesting childhood, and listened amiably to the village small talk with
a distant look in his eyes. Sometimes a remark touching one of his
prejudices would elicit fiercely expressed opinions, but for much of
the time disinterest and a natural reserve left the roomier reaches of
his mind unlit. Most of the chatter washed over his head. 'Our news
here is but little,' he told his brother William in February 1792. 'Mr
Christian of Brancaster is presented to the living of Workington, called
£700 a year. The Martins in the same state of uncertainty as when
you were here. Dr Poyntz [the parson of North Creake] told me a
long story a little time past about walnut trees and red filberts, but
really, I can hardly tell you what he said.'[37]

There were some lifelines. He spent long dark evenings reading and
writing beneath wavering candlelight, poring over naval charts, rediscovering the Americas through William Dampier's published *Voyages*,
and corresponding with favourite sea officers. He devoured what news
penetrated from the outside world, running up bills for papers with
those for wine and groceries. The *Norfolk Chronicle*, published in
Norwich every Saturday, was compulsive reading. Most of all he
hungered for employment.

Frankly, his naval career had hitherto been more routine than distinguished, and his experience as a fighting seaman particularly narrow.
Nelson had served with ability in the Central American jungle and
led a campaign against illegal traders in the West Indies, but those

achievements hardly made him a master of naval warfare. True, he had captured or destroyed thirty-odd ships as a commander, but the number was not a remarkable one, and at best his adversaries had been armed merchantmen or privateers. He had never been in a fleet action, nor ever fought a regular warship, not even a naval brig or sloop. Not only that, but there is little evidence that at this time he had any extensive or original views about fighting at sea. Later, long after he had become famous, friends alluded to the embryonic admiral they professed to have seen in those early days, but such reminiscences had probably gained from hindsight.

We search Nelson's contemporary correspondence in vain for discussions of or allusions to the great questions that exercised the conscientious late eighteenth-century admiral. There is nothing about that formidable naval defence, the line of battle, and the difficulty of breaking or doubling it to achieve a significant victory; no references to naval theorists such as Paul l'Hoste and John Clerk, or to the limitations the signal books imposed upon developing flexible fleet tactics. Nor, for that matter, do we find any clearly stated recognition of the means by which the Royal Navy was increasingly achieving ship-for-ship battle superiority over opponents of similar strength. That superiority rested upon the exceptional gunnery and seamanship of many British crews, but Nelson's letters show none of the preoccupation with rates of fire that would distinguish Cochrane and Broke. That he had learned much from Locker and Hood is not to be doubted, and he had exercised his crews in the manner of the time, but for the most part his views remained dormant, submerged beneath the business of the moment.[38]

Nelson's career had hardly flourished, but close observers would have seen outstanding qualities in him, primitive indications of a future leader. Most notably, even the young Nelson possessed the personality to surpass. He was more than brave, conscientious and competent, the hallmarks of every good officer. He was driven. This is a quality every teacher recognises as decisive. The *need* to achieve matters as much, if not more, than mere ability, because it galvanises and focuses that ability towards specific goals. It imbues ability with terrific energy and purpose. Nelson brimmed with it. He desperately wanted the admiration, applause and affection of fellow creatures, and his thirst for it sharpened his aggression, energy and enterprise. It alerted him to opportunities complacent officers missed, and drove him further than others cared or thought to go. In 1780, for example, it led him not only to convoy Polson's troops to the San Juan River but also to usurp the role of the army and lead the expedition upstream to bombard the Spanish castle.

Nelson's zeal was also marked by a self-confident political courage that was perhaps even rarer. Rightly or wrongly, he held firm views about what the navy ought to be doing, and a readiness to discard and disobey orders he considered to be misconceived or inappropriate. In the way he had wrenched policy from the hands of his commander-in-chief and civil officials in the West Indies he had fearlessly, indeed almost recklessly, endangered his career in pursuit of a principle. No one who had witnessed those acts of a man in his twenties could have doubted that a force was in the making.

Compare Nelson for a moment with his estimable colleague, Captain Cuthbert Collingwood. Collingwood was the more experienced seaman. His crews were equal, if not superior, at their guns, and Collingwood's courage and public spirit were unquestionable. He was every bit as intelligent and articulate as the younger man. Yet Nelson consistently outperformed Collingwood. The dour northerner was no hungry fighter. Money for its own sake he deemed an ignoble aim, and the foolish clamour of human beings a transient illusion. To him 'contentment' was 'wealth' and a satisfaction that he had done his duty was enough to allow him happiness at home. Nelson's drive for distinction, therefore, gave him an important advantage over Collingwood. His opportunism, initiative and eagerness to take personal responsibility for actions unlicensed by others made him the leader and Collingwood the follower. We have already seen the younger man seizing control of their campaign to enforce the navigation laws in the West Indies, and in 1797 we will encounter an even more dramatic illustration of the differences between them. In the famous battle of Cape St Vincent, Nelson would pursue an independent and significant course of action that Collingwood may not have seen and, if he did, certainly hesitated to follow.[39]

Regrettably, Nelson's talents had not yet found a satisfactory stage, and in the eyes of some superior officers they had been dimmed by his inability to control Prince William Henry. Not all the criticisms thrown at him on that score were justified, but some exposed the vulnerable underbelly of Nelson's hunt for fame. It gave early notice of his susceptibility to anyone or anything that fed his insatiable ego. Good friends noticed it, even those who loved him anyway. 'He liked fame,' recalled Collingwood, 'and was open to flattery, so that people sometimes got about him who were unworthy of him.' William Henry had flattered Nelson by his friendship, and subverted his judgement in the process. There would be more and graver examples ahead.[40]

Doubts about Nelson seem to have damaged his standing at the Admiralty, though at that time there were more senior captains than ships in commission and few excuses were needed to leave a junior officer unemployed. Nevertheless, even in the relatively supine years of peace the name of the little officer from Norfolk had a habit of forcing its way forward. His campaign against fraud, the threat of civil suits over his actions against illegal traders and applications for a ship kept Nelson before the organs of government during this barren period.

The fraud issue was beginning to bubble, and not before time for its unfortunate instigators, Wilkinson and Higgins. January 1789 brought Nelson the sad news that the West Indian merchant Wilkinson had been jailed in Antigua the previous September. Despite being elected a member of the assembly for St John's, his threats to expose frauds had brought enemies upon his back. On 4 June 1788 a report of both houses of the assembly of Antigua, establishing that William Whitehead – the arch conspirator at the heart of the abuses reported by Wilkinson and Higgins – had in one instance defrauded the public of £1,213, was passed by fifteen votes to two. The offender was compelled to refund his ill-gotten profits. But the island's solicitor general, one of the dissenting voters, stimulated Wilkinson's creditors to counterattack. The luckless merchant was thrown into prison. The situation of Messrs Wilkinson and Higgins grew increasingly invidious. While Wilkinson languished in jail, their resources evaporated and Higgins hoarded their cache of incriminating papers in his house in St John's, jumping at shadows in fear of the building being burgled or burned down. Nelson was furious. In his view Wilkinson and Higgins were performing a public service, and if they suffered now he could not, as their ally, hold himself blameless.[41]

Hidden away in the Norfolk countryside and devoid of powerful friends in government, Nelson felt his weakness but flailed about with considerable spirit and effect. He had not relaxed his grip. In October he had written to the Sick and Hurt and Victualling boards, and two months later dispatched more papers to the Ordnance Board. Now he renewed his fire, trusting that 'the good work begun under my auspices' would be completed and the frauds investigated.[42]

Suddenly the cumbersome machinery of the state groaned into

action. In January 1789 the Ordnance Board assured Nelson that they had fully embraced the proposals of Wilkinson and Higgins, and were writing to them 'by the next packet'. Its head, the Duke of Richmond, had sometime enjoyed a reputation as a reformer, and was keen on reducing the ordnance budget, so there were hopes for progress on that front. The Victualling Board also promised an investigation. Eventually they posted statements of their entire dealings with the West Indian islands to Wilkinson and Higgins. In June the board seemed eager to act before any misappropriated funds could be dispersed, and summoned Nelson to London for an opinion. Unlike most of the other boards, they even paid his expenses. Most weighty of all, perhaps, was the Navy Board. In February, Sir Charles Middleton called Wilkinson and Higgins to London, accepting their proposal to expose abuses for a percentage of the sums saved, and in May he framed a preliminary charge against Whitehead and Anthony Munton, the naval storekeeper at English Harbour, for frauds committed in 1782. For a while it seemed that wholesale corruption was about to be exposed.[43]

The assault did not proceed smoothly, however. Although the Navy and Sick and Hurt boards undertook to cover the cost of Wilkinson and Higgins's passages to England and their legal expenses, the finances of both men were exhausted. The latter argued for an on-the-spot trial in Antigua, where records were to hand, and also for a broad-based enquiry, rather than board-by-board investigations. By the end of 1789 some officials in London were tiring of what they considered to be prevarication, and predicted it would all 'end in smoke'. Nelson urged them to stand firm, and though the issue is unclear it seems that some satisfaction was eventually achieved. Wilkinson later congratulated himself upon having been 'serviceable' to various 'departments' of the Admiralty, while long afterwards George Rose, then secretary to the Treasury, admitted that several frauds were detected through the instrumentality of Wilkinson, Higgins and Nelson, and their perpetrators punished. One of these was evidently Munton, the naval storekeeper, who was fined and imprisoned.[44]

If all this happened, it was due in no small measure to Nelson. William Henry, to whom Wilkinson and Higgins had originally directed their proposals, had done nothing to investigate the charges of abuse, and it had been left to Nelson to spearhead the attack. He had done so creditably, carefully sifting the documentation, directing the allegations to the appropriate boards, and arguing Wilkinson and Higgins's cause in letter and person. Despite his own reduced circumstances, he had stood behind the two merchants in moments of despair, and spent his own money in postage, travel and lodgings. Indeed, he neither asked nor expected any material reward for his efforts, and as far as we know was only reimbursed for the one trip he made to London for the Victualling Board in the summer of 1789. Though Nelson's biographers have shown little interest in this sortie against Old Corruption, it testified to his tenacity in pursuit of a principle and adds to his stature.[45]

Sadly, whistle-blowers court reprisals, and Wilkinson ruined what was left of his life. Though released from prison in Antigua by the Insolvency Act of 1790, he was pursued by a single creditor and suffered another eighteen months' incarceration in Virginia. Soon afterwards he showed up in London, where he was committed to the King's Bench, a debtors' prison for gentlemen. He was still there in 1798, counting nearly nine years in one jail or another. At that time he made another appeal to Nelson, then something of a national hero. 'It is with sorrow I inform you that I have not the smallest power of being useful to you,' Nelson replied, reflecting upon an episode that now belonged to his past. 'I was probably in a great measure the cause of your exertions to detect bad men who were cheating our country, and I hope the desire of preventing bad men from fattening on the plunder of my country is still uppermost in my mind.' But he believed his interest minimal, and could only refer the unhappy supplicant to Sir Andrew Hamond, the current comptroller of the Navy Board as well as 'a good man'. It did no good, and the *Gentleman's Magazine* recorded the miserable finale for 24 August 1798. '[Died] at his apartments in the King's Bench prison, William Wilkinson, esq., of Antigua. He was one of those whose debt exceeded the limitations of the late insolvent act.' Even though he had outlived his greatest adversary, Whitehead, who had died in England seven years before, Wilkinson's end illustrated the crippling penalties of eighteenth-century debt.[46]

It was a fate that could so easily have plucked Nelson from his rural retreat and lodged him behind a powerful prison door. In 1790 he had to seek Admiralty protection as the last rumbling aftershocks of his other West Indian campaign against the contraband traders again threatened him with ruinous lawsuits. Nelson had heard the distant thunder. There had been stories of an impending pamphlet that would accuse him of branding the planters disaffected smugglers, but it was not until 20 March that the counterattack came to the door.

On that day the captain received a letter from solicitors acting for James and William Sheafe of Portsmouth, New Hampshire, owners of the *Jane and Elizabeth*, the American brig Nelson had seized in Barbados four years before. Nelson was invited to admit he had been 'hasty' and to negotiate damages; otherwise the solicitors demanded to know the attorney to whom he wanted their writ delivered. Whatever amount Nelson was being sued for, it was beyond his means. Into his third year of unemployment, his resources were evaporating, and he had just returned from a trip to London in which he had even begged the Admiralty to pay him for the time he had commanded a garrison in Port Royal more than ten years earlier. Now thoroughly alarmed, Horatio sent the letter to the Admiralty, seeking an assurance that he would not be left to the wolves. It was with relief that he learned that his case had been referred to the Treasury with a recommendation that he be defended from prosecution.[47]

But he did not breathe easily for long. About a month later, on 26 April, Nelson returned to the parsonage after a trip to a nearby fair, pleased with a small horse that he had purchased. Fanny greeted him with an anxious face. A man from London had called during his absence and served the aforementioned writ. Nelson examined the document. It was dated that very day, and gave notice that an action for damages would commence against him in a month's time. The *Jane and Elizabeth* and its cargo of timber and fish were valued at £5,000, but Nelson was also held liable for inconveniences and such expenses as the wages of the crew and the cost of returning them to their homes. Although no overall sum was mentioned, Nelson stood to be arrested and imprisoned for debt.[48]

Still unsure that a definite decision to defend him had been made, Horatio immediately scribbled another letter to the Admiralty and in the meantime concocted a desperate plan to escape to France. If he was arrested and imprisoned it would be all the harder to organise his defence, so he decided to quit the country first, leaving Fanny to pack essentials and follow in the safe keeping of his brother Maurice. Fortunately, Nelson's friends were alerted by anxious letters and rallied around. William Henry, now the Duke of Clarence, stood on hand, while Captain Pole appealed to the Prince of Wales, who declared his support for Nelson 'in the highest terms'. More instrumentally, Captain Pringle marched into the Treasury building to confront secretary Rose. The reply was reassuring and unequivocal: Nelson was reckoned a good officer and could rely upon a publicly-funded defence. The news

reached Horatio on 4 May and the flight to France was duly abandoned.[49]

The matter never destablised him again, but it left him shaken. Even
a public defence could fail, and incarcerate and ruin him. 'I see a
person may do their duty too well,' he sighed. It was his reputation
that most worried him. 'The character of an officer is his greatest
treasure,' he observed. 'To lower that is to wound him irreparably.'[50]

5

The career of Horatio Nelson was always something of a roller coaster
ride, weaving exhilarating heights and depressing lows, and the summer
of 1790 ran true to form. No sooner had his morale been mended by
the forthright intervention of the government over the issue of the
lawsuit than it was crushed by new evidence of Admiralty animosity.
His hopes for employment were raised and destroyed within months.

The spark of optimism was struck far away, in an obscure and
rocky inlet in the coast of Vancouver Island. The previous year two
Spanish ships had arrived in Nootka Sound to claim this corner of
the Pacific Northwest for their king. A pair of British trading ships
found bartering with the local Indians were seized, their crews carried
off to a Mexican jail, and the formal pretensions of the Spanish governments duly presented in London. Pitt was not impressed. He demanded
the release of His Britannic Majesty's subjects and countered with
territorial claims of his own. Sabres rattled ominously.

When Nelson read about the affair he scented war, and with it a
ship. Leaving Fanny at Swaffham in Norfolk, where she had decided
to settle if her husband was employed, he hurried to London, depositing
his belongings with his uncle in Kentish Town. At last, after many
years a beached whale, he was optimistic. The navy began pressing
sailors, and on 8 May Nelson found the Admiralty in a 'bustle' and
the waiting room thronged with aspiring captains looking for ships.
As Chatham was unable to see him, Nelson sat down to declare on
paper that he was 'ready to undertake such employment as their lordships shall judge most proper'. At some stage he was led to believe
that though the first ships were already spoken for he would soon be
employed, but then Hood delivered a thunderbolt. Gone were the days
when Hood had acted the willing patron. When Nelson asked for his
recommendation the reply was so crushing that he later admitted it
could 'never be effaced from my memory'. Hood flatly refused support,

and declared that the king had a poor opinion of Nelson. The captain was flattered. The king rarely approved of the friends of his sons, and Nelson could only suppose that his friendship with William Henry had created offence. Deeply wounded, he returned to Norfolk. 'My not being appointed to a ship is so very mortifying that I cannot find words to express what I feel on the occasion,' he wrote from the depressing silence of the parsonage.[51]

Now Nelson was sure there were members of the Admiralty who had it in for him. In July, Hood wrote to explain that his patronage was 'of no use to anyone' while so many unemployed captains were lobbying Chatham, but that he would certainly try to get him a ship if war broke out. Yet only a month earlier the board had appointed Collingwood, a junior captain, to the command of the *Mermaid* frigate.[52]

Back in Kentish Town Uncle William Suckling had a large enough family of his own to protect. William junior was now an army officer, Benjamin a rector and Horace a student, while a daughter, Eliza, and a grandson, William Benjamin, still enlivened the house. But Suckling had a special affection for his naval nephew and sympathised with his predicament. He tried to reach Lord Chatham through Lord Hawkesbury, but with no apparent effect. About the same time Nelson himself was writing to anyone he thought capable of applying pressure. In September he wrote over the head of the Admiralty secretary to the first lord himself. He addressed barren appeals to the Duke of Clarence, now captain of a ship of the line. 'Dear Nelson . . . by God there is no man I should so soon go out of my way to serve as yourself,' shouted the prince, but despite the flattering sentiments in his miserably written letters he achieved little for Nelson. The only other straw of encouragement came from Lord Mulgrave, who as Commodore Phipps had led the young Nelson to the Arctic. He was now a commissioner for the affairs of India, and said it would give him the 'greatest pleasure' to help Nelson get a ship.[53]

By then time was running out. On 28 October Spain agreed to a humiliating convention recognising Britain's prior claim to the Pacific Northwest, and the need for ships and captains eased. Nelson's ambition was dashed again, and he was disappointed in friends he had loved and respected. As an officer he had always responded when worthy subordinates called for his help; others, he reflected bitterly, seemed less constant. 'I certainly cannot look on Lord Hood as my friend,' he complained, and as for Cornwallis, who had gone to the

East Indies without him, 'I may now tell you that if Kingsmill had gone to India, I was to have been his captain, and the senior one sent out.'[54]

Events the following spring deepened his emptiness. A dispute with Russia had Pitt mobilising the fleet once again, and Hood himself was to command twenty-nine sail of the line. Several of Nelson's friends were earmarked for ships, and March and April saw Horatio again trudging around London. He left a message at Hood's door but received no answer. The Duke of Clarence, he was relieved to find, still welcomed him and spoke as loudly as usual, this time about commanding a division in a fleet bound for the Mediterranean. Briefly Nelson fooled himself into believing his luck might change. He did not underestimate the difficulties of campaigning in the Baltic ('narrow seas and no friendly ports are bad things'), but judged that neither Pitt nor Catherine the Great, whom he compared to England's own Elizabeth I, would back down. As it happened, it was the British Parliament that blinked and refused to support its first minister. Nelson made another sad journey home.[55]

There seemed no way forward, and Nelson's next trip to London more than a year later was to a large extent less self-serving. Again, he was answering calls of distress. In March 1791 we find him writing to the Navy Board in an effort to clear the name of a seaman of the *Albemarle* unjustly listed as a deserter. The next year he received a letter from Donald Trail, the former master of the same ship, asking Nelson to testify to his character. Trail was in a serious mess. He had voluntarily surrendered to answer charges of brutality and murder relating to his command of the convict ship *Neptune*, and was incarcerated in Newgate awaiting trial at the Old Bailey before the High Court of Admiralty. Trips to London always gave Horatio the opportunity of 'bowing to the high and mighty potentates', as his father put it, but it was primarily to help Trail that the captain arrived 'in town' in June 1792.[56]

Waiting for Trail's case, Nelson sat through the trial of Captain John Kimber on 8 and 9 June. Kimber, a Bristol slaver, was indicted for appalling acts of cruelty said to have been committed upon a slave girl during a second leg of the infamous triangular run from Africa to Grenada in the West Indies. Broadcast by the emancipator William Wilberforce, the affair attracted considerable public interest, and Nelson found himself sitting beside such illustrious observers as the Duke of Clarence, Lord Sheffield and Admiral Barrington, most of them friends of the accused. Kimber was acquitted, but Nelson took exception to one published account that alleged Clarence had tried to influence the result by 'gestures' and 'improper conduct'.[57]

Trail and his boatswain, William Ellerington, were tried in three hours on Friday 9 June. The *Neptune* had left England in February 1790 with five hundred convicts bound for the penal colony in Australia's Botany Bay, and returned by way of China. Nelson regarded Trail as an exceptional master, but had never seen him command a ship and listened to some very disturbing charges. One seaman was supposed to have died after being strapped to a longboat and then flogged and kicked. Evidence was given that another who died had suffered beatings involving fists, feet and a rope, and was left in irons on an exposed deck for days and nights in violent winds. A third alleged victim was John Joseph, a Portuguese cook guilty of some minor misdemeanour. According to the prosecution he was punched by the boatswain and hit with a rope and some wood before being bound to the rigging and flogged. After receiving punishment Joseph was reported to have been kicked as he lay unable to walk, and put in irons for several hours. A quartermaster testified that he 'went to Joseph that night and found him very ill and crying in his cot', and that though he eventually resumed his duties he was 'never . . . well afterwards' but 'got worse and worse'. A cabin boy who saw him dying in a Macao hospital said the cook 'thought he was going to a better world' but asked that his family be told that he had been murdered. The cat Trail used for floggings, said one witness familiar with naval discipline, was 'too severe for anybody but a sodomite'.[58]

But Nelson was relieved to see the prosecution collapse. It appeared that most of the stories originated with crewmen who had deserted in China and had been refused their wages. They were now trying to justify their actions and regain their pay by proving 'bad usage and want of victuals'. Nor were the allegations consistent. They said Trail had allowed female convicts to be used by the crew, and also that he had antagonised the men by refusing to allow them among the women. After hearing the case against Trail the justices, Sir James Marriott and Sir William Henry Ashurst, dismissed the prosecution as malicious. It does not appear that Nelson and the other defence witnesses were even called upon to testify.

While he was in London Nelson probably called at Lord Hood's house in Wimpole Street to leave his respects, but the admiral was not to be found and Horatio made no ground in his fight for employment. There seemed so little to do, with such slight prospect, that he spent only a few days in the capital before boarding a coach for Norfolk. To get a ship, it seemed, he first needed a war.

6

According to 'the very best authority' a young Whig joining His Majesty's ship *Agamemnon* in 1793 was treated by his commander to a piece of heartfelt advice. 'There are three things, young gentleman, which you are constantly to bear in mind,' Captain Nelson reputedly said. 'First, you must always implicitly obey orders, without attempting to form an opinion of your own respecting their propriety; secondly, you must consider every man as your enemy who speaks ill of your king; and thirdly, you must hate a Frenchman as you do the devil.'[59]

This famous if unverifiable quotation offered at least two principles upon which Nelson generally founded his conduct: his uncomplicated love of king and country. If, for an unthinking obedience, we substituted a reverence for the supreme deity, as envisaged by the Church of England, we would have what the captain regarded as a sacrosanct trinity: God, king and country.

Like most Britons in the eighteenth century he directly linked the three. The law was rooted in God's commandments, and the Almighty, Nelson believed, had ordained the institution of monarchy and the unequal nature of society, which, he presumed, had developed naturally in accordance with divine wishes. Providing the monarch was a good pastor who protected his people, there could be no reservations about serving him, for God, king and country advanced together beneath supernatural providence. Faithful service to them would make a just claim for assistance and ultimate reward in the hereafter. As Nelson told the Society for the Promotion of Christian Knowledge, which regularly supplied him with bibles and prayer books for his ships, he was sure 'that good to our King and country may have arisen from the seamen and marines having been taught to respect the established religion'.[60]

Piety, indeed, was never far from this preacher's son. Every one of his cabins was furnished with a bible, and a bulky edition of The Book of Common Prayer he took aboard the *Albemarle* can still be seen in the Nelson Museum in Monmouth. 'When I lay me down to sleep I recommend myself to the care of Almighty God,' he wrote in a private journal of 1793. 'When I awake I give myself up to His direction. Amidst all the evils that threaten me, I will look up to Him for help, and question not but He will either avert them or turn them to my advantage. Though I know neither the time nor the manner of my death, I am not at all solicitous about it because I am sure that He knows them both, and that He will not fail to support and comfort me under them.'[61]

In Nelson's mind the essential relationships between a man and his god, a flock and its pastor, a subject and his ruler and a seaman and his captain were similar. They involved accepted differences in power and position, with benign superiors dispensing aid and protection in recognition of loyalty and service. Nelson was an eighteenth-century paternalist, politically as well as spiritually. He accepted the hierarchical nature of society, and supposed that the deference and obedience of inferiors would bond them to superior but caring patrons. Upward social mobility was entirely acceptable if it was achievable, but those locked into their station were also entitled to consideration. The system, as we have seen, was demonstrated on board his ships. He expected men to obey, and punished to reclaim or deter transgressors, but in turn offered protection. The instances of Scotland, Carse and Trail confirm how seriously he took that obligation. Those vertical social relationships, in which men of all levels reciprocated commitment, were keynotes of Nelson's view of the world.

Rather naively, Nelson often assumed that his values leavened British society in general, and it is true that the gist of his conservatism was very widely diffused at the time. As one historian has written, 'the widespread manifestations of popular conservatism were the result of deep-rooted prejudices and widely-held opinions in favour of the existing constitution in church and state. The desire to preserve traditional institutions and established values was not restricted to the propertied elite, but was shared by a majority of the middling and lower orders.'[62]

Perhaps it was the intensity, rather than the nature, of Nelson's beliefs that marked him out, especially with regard to paternalism. Later, in the midst of increasing industrialisation and class conflict, writers such as William Cobbett harked back nostalgically to a supposed pre-industrial golden age dominated by such benign paternalism, but in reality its existence had always been questionable. There had never been a land of lost content. Of course, it was necessary for the ruling classes to appease the masses below by some attention to their needs, but naked self-interest was all too evident. Landowners enclosed the open fields, sweeping away the customary rights of villagers to glean and graze, and driving them into the ranks of the landless wage labourers. Capitalist clothiers laid off their outworkers, spinners and weavers harnessed to punishing cottage industries, whenever markets contracted. Grimy women toiled along dark, subterranean tunnels in mines, hauling coal on their backs, while raw-faced puddlers shortened their lives stirring molten iron in the searing heat of new reverberatory furnaces. In none of these cases did paternalism offer much protection, but Nelson believed in it and generally tried to live accordingly.

In the later eighteenth century the British people were predominantly conservative, but naval officers who spent their lives in the king's service were even more universally so. Their pride was the English constitution, a mature constitution which, it was said, secured the nation the most liberal governments in Europe and the blessings of a limited rather than an absolute monarchy. Nelson agreed entirely with Collingwood that 'miseries ... would undoubtedly be the consequence of any attempt to disturb the present most excellent constitution'. In theory, it was a balanced constitution, dividing power between the crown, the House of Lords and people (the latter represented by the House of Commons), and preventing the concentration of authority that always bred tyranny. It created stability, adjusting the interests of one group to another, protected Britons from slavery and conserved their basic freedoms and rights. So, at least, thought Nelson. He inflexibly upheld the principle of monarchy and accepted the pretensions of the aristocracy. But his ideal sovereign, the head of the Church and figurehead of the nation, was not only a benevolent but a constitutional monarch, governing wisely and honourably in return for the fealty of his subjects, but also accountable to the Lords and Commons in Parliament.[63]

Nelson distrusted anyone who tinkered with the constitution, including the Whigs, who affected to be the people's defenders against a potentially tyrannous crown. They stood ready to attack any unwarranted royal imposition that would tilt the balance of the constitution against the people, but their obsessive suspicion of the crown struck Nelson as unpatriotic, and their attacks on the king's government during the American war almost treasonable. Nelson viewed the Whigs as self-serving and devoid of principle, critics of government corruption out of office and willing beneficiaries of it in. His disdain showed in his refusal to join their celebration of the centenary of the 'glorious revolution' of 1688, one of the sacred milestones in Whig history.

There was little egalitarian or democratic about Nelson. He had no interest in reforming an increasingly outmoded and inequitable representative system, and little understanding of the political dimensions of economical reform, which for him was simply a practical matter of saving public money. He regarded the constitution as fundamentally sound. However, Nelson was by no means insensitive to injustices and hardships suffered by the people, but attributed them to the inadequacies of members of the ruling classes or public servants rather than to any systemic failure. For such delinquents Nelson had some very hard words. He eventually came to the conclusion that the Prince of Wales was a criminal spendthrift who deserved to be punished for the burdens his profligacy imposed upon the poor, and that both the Tories forming around Pitt and the Whigs were mere competitors for the spoils of public office. 'The changes and politics of ministers and men are so various that I am brought to believe all are alike,' he wrote. 'The ins and outs are the same, let them change places.'[64]

We do not think of Nelson as a radical in any sense, but although his thought remained intrinsically conservative in nature, his belief in the wellbeing of the underprivileged could have eventually made him a Tory radical. In fact, in his inherent conservatism, belief in monarchy, distrust of the emerging political factions and conviction that only independent Members of Parliament could work any good, he approached the philosophy of the Burdettite radicals of the early nineteenth century.

The shortcomings of rulers struck Nelson as betrayals of the necessary bonds between masters and servants. So long as the people were loyal, their betters were obliged to protect them, and the miseries of the poor were symptoms of a shameful dereliction of duty. They damaged Nelson's illusion of the paternal society. We will remember his powerful reaction to the gross disparities between the rich and poor when he visited pre-revolutionary France. During his years of unemployment in Norfolk he also witnessed the struggles of the English farm labourers at first hand. In 1794, when his finances had recovered, Nelson began to demonstrate his personal commitment to the needy of Burnham Thorpe with Christmas donations. 'Accept our best new year's gift [in return],' his father wrote, acknowledging a gift of £200. 'Good wishes, the poor man's all!' Earlier, on 10 December 1792, Nelson had put the plight of the poor before the Duke of Clarence:

That the poor labourer should have been seduced by promises and hopes of better times, your Royal Highness will not wonder at when I assure you they are really in want of everything to make life comfortable. Part of their wants, perhaps, were unavoidable from the dearness of every article of life; but *much has arose from the neglect of the country gentlemen* in not making their farmers raise their wages in some small proportion as the prices [of] necessaries increased. The enclosed paper will give your Royal Highness an idea of their situation . . . I have been careful that no country gentleman should have it in his power to say [that] I had pointed out the wants of the poor greater than they really are. Their wages have been raised within these three weeks, pretty generally, one shilling a week; had it been done some time past they would not have been discontented, for *a want of loyalty is not amongst their faults*; and many of their superiors in many instances might have imitated their conduct with advantage.[65]

In an enclosure Nelson itemised the annual income and outgoings of a labourer in full employment in Norfolk with a wife and three children. Shoes (including 'mending') cost £2 3s. 0d.; clothes (two shirts, a pair of breeches and a jacket, and 'woman's and children's clothes') £1 19s. 0d.; rent £2 0s. 0d.; soap and candles, 12s. 10d.; and coal £1 19s. 0d. When deducted from what could be earned in the fields, these expenses left the family with only £14 7s. 2d. to feed five people throughout the year. 'Not quite two pence a day for each person,' Nelson noted, 'and to think nothing but water, for beer our poor labourers never taste, unless they are tempted, which is too often the case, to go to the Alehouse.' Nelson's appeal not only illustrated his belief that the poor were being betrayed by the ruling classes, but also the conditions in the agricultural counties of eastern England that were shortly to prompt the controversial Speenhamland system of poor relief.

However, while the welfare of the people was certainly the business of those in power, Nelson regarded disloyalty or rebellion against the monarch or the state as treasonable. That did not mean that people suffering legitimate grievances should not protest. Like most eighteenth-century men and women Nelson distinguished between protest and treason. Riots were commonplace, but as the historian Roy Porter has said, 'Protesters' aims were usually concrete, defensive and limited: they wanted bread at old prices, the restoration of long-standing wage-rates, the clearing of rights of way. Their appeal was to a traditional order, to be restored by society's traditional leaders.' Such protesters called upon their rulers to govern responsibly, in accordance with their duty to inferiors, but not for the overthrow of governments or constitutions.[66]

The clearest examples of Nelson's thinking in this respect are, of course, naval. In 1797, when dangerous mutinies ran through the British fleets, he immediately differentiated between one set of mutineers and another. Those at Spithead, who demanded improved pay, food and medical facilities, he deemed essentially loyal. Though they struck, they proclaimed their willingness to put to sea to protect convoys or to meet the enemy at any time. In Nelson's view the Spithead mutineers were justly demanding their right to protection and consideration, and he extolled their action as 'the most manly thing I ever heard of', one which did 'the British sailor infinite honour'. Not so the mutineers at the Nore, who conducted themselves with an extreme insolence and appeared to be influenced with republicanism. In Nelson's opinion they were 'scoundrels' who deserved to be blown out of the water or hanged.[67]

Similarly, he disliked the radical political movements that emerged in Britain during the 1790s because he considered them the monstrous offspring of growing republicanism across the Channel. The strand of protest that took its lead from Tom Paine's *The Rights of Man* and *The Age of Reason* was particularly dangerous in his view. Paine's attacks upon the monarchy, aristocracy and church, his espousal of atheism, 'natural rights', equality and the sovereignty of the people, and his suggestions for the redistribution of wealth and republicanism were anathema to everything Nelson considered necessary to an ordered, moral and disciplined society. Even the most restrained of Paine's followers, such as the humble artisans of the London Corresponding Society, who spread the cause of annual parliaments and universal manhood suffrage, were in Nelson's eyes the irresponsible assailants of a constitution that was basically sound.[68]

In Nelson's mind king and country were one, and his extreme patriotism is shown, as much as anything, by his strong suspicion of most things French, an opinion he had expressed as early as his trip to St-Omer in 1783. Today it seems xenophobic, and the term has tripped easily off biographers' tongues, but Nelson was far from an undiscriminating hater of foreigners. In 1787 he had spoken about joining the Russian navy, and expressed a positive admiration for the Danes and Swedes. The French were, for him, a special case, and to understand his prejudices we have to place them firmly in their eighteenth-century context.

At that time such prejudices would have seemed unremarkable and even commonplace. For Nelson's was not a complacent generation brought up on decades of late twentieth-century security. In fact half of the forty-eight years of Nelson's lifetime, from 1758 to 1805 inclusive, saw Britain at war, and all but two of those years of conflict involved France. France was more than a rival for commercial and overseas power: she was a formidable threat to Britain's sovereign survival. With a population of twenty-five million, two and a half times that of mainland Britain, France possessed a far greater army and immense continental influence. Indeed, she was the most dreaded land power in Europe, her most effective rivals merely rambling, ill-coordinated, mid-continental empires with calcified forces. True, her navy was second to Britain's, with between only 76 and 115 operational ships of the line in 1793, but France was even capable of neutralising that disadvantage through diplomacy. Thus in the closing years of the American revolutionary war, she had drawn Spain, the third largest naval power, into an anti-British alliance, and encouraged most of the rest of Europe to go as far as resisting Britain's crucial naval blockades. The so-called 'league of armed neutrality' included the other major continental navies of Russia, Holland, Sweden and Denmark, and Britain was temporarily isolated and surrounded by hostile or unfriendly powers. Across the Atlantic, on the rebellious Atlantic seaboard, the French navy had used a temporary superiority over the Royal Navy to force a British army to surrender at Yorktown in 1782.

Nelson's generation grew up under the shadow of France. Overseas, British naval power had got the better of the French in Canada and India, but in Europe the great continental power still seemed a giant and hungry ogre only a bound away, separated from England by a thin strip of water that Bonaparte dismissed as a contemptible ditch. Only the Royal Navy stood in its way. There seemed no worthier ambition, and no more useful patriotic service, than to topple France and disperse the cloud it had thrown over Albion for good.

Horatio Nelson spoke endlessly of England. An act of union had bound England and Wales to Scotland at the beginning of the century, but Nelson seldom referred to 'Britain'. His England embraced the whole island, but it was an island of free-born men and women, protected by an advanced constitution, ruled by a relatively benign monarch and shielded by its navy from the despots of Europe. Nelson's concept may have been basic, but it was neither singular nor eccentric, and most of his countrymen would have recognised it. The closing years of the eighteenth century tested every shibboleth, but Nelson's beliefs only intensified as the political landscape of Europe was torn apart by revolution.

7

On the morning of 14 July 1789 the Continent changed forever when a ragged Parisian crowd made a murderous assault on the Bastille. They were afraid that their king, Louis XVI, was gathering soldiers to halt the process of constitutional reform.

The 'French Revolution' was in fact the sum of successive waves of revolution, unwittingly unleashed by an insolvent king scratching around for additional resources. In 1788 the clerics and nobles had defended their ancient exemptions from taxation, and forced Louis to convene the long-defunct Estates General. The election of the commoners to the third estate the following year brought a battery of civil servants, lawyers and merchants of the rising bourgeois into government, all imbued with classical liberalism and eager to attack the inequitable tax system and the aristocratic monopoly on the higher offices of state. Behind them railed the voices of a poor battered by rents, low wages, unemployment, inflation, famine and manorial dues. No sooner was the third estate elected than it was refashioning government into a National Assembly, increasing the power of its own and dismantling the *ancien régime*. A declaration of rights vested sovereignty in the people rather than the king, and declared men free and equal before the law.

Following the story in the *Norfolk Chronicle*, Nelson was initially neither surprised nor alarmed, for he had seen the destitution in the French countryside and had never been blind to burdens that oppressed the poor, at home or abroad. He was willing to urge reform within a constitutionally acceptable framework, and like many, perhaps most, educated Britons saw little to concern himself in the early stages of the French Revolution. After all, for a few years it seemed that France was simply shifting from continental absolutism towards the British model of a limited monarchy accountable to the people. If it improved the lot of the people in the process, that was all to the good.[69]

But then the revolution across the Channel lurched ferociously to the left, leaving the vaunted English constitution in its wake. The French king gave ground, humiliated and debased. On a wet, cold October day in 1789 he was brought with his family from Versailles to Paris with the mob running before him to announce the arrival of 'the baker, the baker's wife and the baker's boy'. Violence increased and the Catholic church had its lands confiscated and its links with the pope savaged. In 1791 a constitutional monarchy based on a taxpayer suffrage was established, but the Jacobin republicans, who overthrew their moderate opponents, fanned hatred against the king, aristocracy and Church.

It was the outbreak of European war in 1792 that sealed the fate of king and nobles. The crowned heads of Europe, some of them related to Louis, were the principal threats to the revolution in France. On 20 April the French Legislative Assembly, which had been elected under the new constitution, pre-empted foreign intervention by declaring war on Austria and Prussia. War was useful to the revolutionaries at that time. It helped unite a divided people behind them, as wars generally do, and legitimised the elimination of aristocrats and royalists who could now be portrayed as dangers to the realm from within.

In August the French monarchy collapsed in violence. A Jacobin mob stormed the royal residence in Paris, butchering the Swiss Guards and smashing the place to pieces. The next month the jails were rifled for royalists and nobles and a thousand or so were slaughtered outright. On 22 September the republic was proclaimed and four months later the king was guillotined before a baying crowd. A year later three thousand five hundred heads rolled in a single month. Perhaps up to forty thousand French people were massacred in the Terror.

Infused with the popular English ideal of a stable society based on a partnership of Church, aristocracy and people, Nelson shared the general shock at news of the Gallic excesses. They only strengthened his own beliefs. The republicans had merely unleashed alien, destructive and violent forces that were not delivering any of the essentials of good government. Instead of order there was chaos, and in place of freedom and security of person and property there developed a vindictive repression and wholesale plunder, torture and murder. Against this background the virtues of the English constitution shone brighter still. 'All this part of the world who have seen republican principles hate and detest the name,' Nelson would write from the Mediterranean in 1796. 'God forbid England should be so miserable. She would be poor indeed. The dominion of modern republicanism is so cruel to the very poor as well as to the rich that England never, I hope, will submit to such slavery. Our liberty is, I hope, too firmly fixed to be moved but with our lives. Every village through which the French retreat takes arms against them, and [they] even kill those who are sick, and this is in a country where the will of the monarch constitutes the law.'[70]

Nelson had always disliked the French, but it was the revolutionary

wars that turned his prejudice into a corrosive hatred. He began them
by doubting the wisdom of intervention, though from a personal point
of view he was grateful for the employment. Convinced that the revolution would destroy itself, he actually believed his country's 'wisest'
course was to stand back and watch it happen. But the appalling atroc-
ities the republicans visited upon their own dissidents – anti-centralists,
anti-Jacobins and monarchists – sharpened Nelson's hostility. He
witnessed the fates of the defeated Royalists of Toulon in 1793, and
in 1795 and 1796 saw the devastation Bonaparte's pillaging hordes
created in Italy. French imperialism was not invariably destructive. It
introduced some benign reforms and adopted anti-denominational
rather than anti-religious policies, but nowhere was its capacity for
plunder more obvious than in Italy, where French armies lived off the
land and a sum of fifty-three million livres was levied on the occupied territories before the end of July 1796. Nelson's determination
to spare Britain similar ruin increased his ferocity. 'To serve my king,
and to destroy the French I consider as the great order[s] of all, from
which little ones spring,' he wrote in 1799. 'And if one of these little
ones militate against it . . . I go back to obey the great order and
object, to *down, down* with the damned French villains. Excuse my
warmth, but my blood boils at the name of a Frenchman. I hate them
all – Royalists and Republicans.'[71]

Nelson's extremism was stimulated by fears, not so much from any
regard for French arms, for which he cared little, but from the more
invidious infiltration of their political principles. For the wars that
broke out were not in the end just dynastic and national disagreements,
territorial squabbles and commercial and imperial competitions,
although they were in part all five. They were also ideological conflicts
fought for minds. Monarchism, Christianity and self-determination
were, in Nelson's view, pitted against republicanism, atheism and imperialism. 'It is their infernal principles I dread, not their prowess,' he
remarked. He knew that those ideas, cloaked in the language of liberty,
popular sovereignty and natural rights appealed to every suppressed
group. They were capable of slicing through ancient orthodoxies as a
hot knife through butter, and of infecting and destabilising England
without a single French soldier landing on her soil.[72]

The war of ideas intensified the conflict and forged the minds of
generations, even in Britain, which eventually escaped direct invasion. There the earlier stages of the French Revolution were favourably
received, but opinion soon veered. The first flickers of political

radicalism were stifled by vigorous government repression, and more effectively flattened by the mass loyalism that followed the outbreak of war with France in 1793. As the years passed French excesses eroded the enthusiasm of some of the most liberal Englishmen, even though the momentum of the republicans waned after 1795. The radical poet Wordsworth, one of many inspired by the birth-throes of the revolution, dismally pronounced it a failure. Coleridge gave up on it after the French invaded neutral Switzerland in 1798 and the utopian Southey was turned into a Tory.

If minds as razor keen as these, predisposed to welcome reform, were bent in the white heat of revolutionary conflict, it is not surprising that Nelson, who had damned republicanism from the beginning and seen it face to face, felt vindicated. It was the Whig rhetorician Edmund Burke who perhaps came to speak most clearly for his later opinions. Once the scourge of the king's 'friends' and an architect of economical reform, the author of *Reflections on the Revolution in France* and champion of tradition wrote in a private letter that 'our all, body and soul, is at stake. We must be the victims of Jacobins, or what is worse, we must be Jacobins, if this whole is not levelled with the ground.'[73]

8

The winter of 1792 descended upon Burnham early. A heavy fall of snow had come and gone by the middle of December, but even in that deadened land Horatio Nelson felt the pulse of life quickening.

Towards the end of the year he had stayed for a second time with the Walpoles at Wolterton, and uncomfortably noted that the activities of the new corresponding society in nearby Norwich promoted 'principles certainly inimical to our present constitution, both in Church and State'. The Dissenters, whose struggles with the disabling Test and Corporation Acts had put them among the foremost critics of government, particularly annoyed him, and he wished someone would arrest their outspoken champion, Joseph Priestley. Nelson greatly applauded the Lord Lieutenant of Norfolk when he summoned magistrates to meet him in December with the intention of stripping the licences from any publicans who offered their premises for radical meetings.[74]

The war in Europe exercised Nelson's mind much more urgently. Things looked grimmer towards the end of 1792, when the Prussian and Russian armies were surprisingly overthrown and the French overran part of the Rhineland, invaded the Austrian Netherlands and opened the

Scheldt. The old enemy, wracked as it might be with social schism and administrative chaos, had reached the shores of the North Sea. In December Pitt called out the militia, and the dockyards began to hum. On the 29th the French batteries at Brest fired on a British sloop of war.

Nelson's friends were unsure about what would happen. Never had France seemed more burdened with problems of her own, and Clarence doubted that Britain would go to war. Even Collingwood, who had written from the northeast, seemed resigned to more months on the beach. 'My regard for you, my dear Nelson, my respect and veneration for your character I hope and believe will never lessen,' he said. 'God knows when we may meet again, unless some chance should draw us again to the sea-shore.'[75]

However, after so many humdrum years Horatio Nelson was wasting no opportunities. In December he wrote again to the Admiralty. The dispiriting reply was little more than an acknowledgement that his letter had been received, but during the first days of the new year Nelson made a freezing journey to London and presented himself to Lord Chatham on 6 January. The next day he scrawled a hurried note to Fanny:

Post nubila Phoebus: Your son will explain the motto – after clouds comes sunshine. The Admiralty so smile upon me that really I am as much surprised as when they frowned. Lord Chatham yesterday made many apologies for not having given me a ship before this time, but that if I chose to take a 64-gun ship to begin with, I should be appointed to one as soon as she was ready; and that I should as soon as in his power be removed into a 74. Lord Hood has sent for me to nominate the first lieutenant . . . Everything looks war. One of our ships looking into Brest has been fired into. The shot is now at the Admiralty.[76]

He rushed jubilantly back to Burnham, where he learned within a few weeks that he was being appointed to the *Agamemnon*, a sixty-four-gun ship of the line fitting at Chatham. His commission was dated 30 January 1793.

Two days later France declared war on Britain, Spain and the Dutch United Provinces, and on 4 February Nelson left Norfolk 'in Health and Great Spirits'.[77]

BOOK TWO

'TO GLORY WE STEER', 1793–7

XVII

CAPTAIN OF THE *AGAMEMNON*

When Peace disturb'd recalls him to his post
He issues forth, like Mars, himself an host,
Undaunted braves the peril of the seas,
Preferring Glory to his private ease.
        S.H., *Of the Late Lord Nelson*, 1805

1

No one knew how long the war would last, but as one power after another entered the lists against France there were reasons for believing they would make short work of it. Pitt himself was complacent. He did not want to involve Britain in the Austro-Prussian campaign to restore the French monarchy, and contented himself with limited war aims. His country's security was paramount, so a few battalions of soldiers were sent to Holland to clear the French from the Austrian Netherlands. Beyond that the fighting in Europe could be left to the allies, fortified by British subsidies, while the country searched overseas for juicy French colonies to purloin. Little was prepared. The army was under strength and poorly led, and a year of conflict had to pass before the home secretary, Henry Dundas, was turned into a war minister.

The navy at least was in respectable shape, and as the mainstay of the realm was fully mobilised. Ships were put into commission, and the dockyards buzzed with noise and industry. The streets of Chatham, Portsmouth and Plymouth were choked with cartloads of provisions, horny-handed artificers and excited seamen. Across the country sea chests were packed and tearful farewells made as officers and men returned to service. Some were bound for the Caribbean with Rear Admiral Alan Gardner, more for the Mediterranean under Lord Hood, and others would man the crucial Channel fleet with 'Black Dick' Howe. There were too few seamen. Bounties never attracted enough volunteers, and incoming merchantmen had to be embargoed and stripped of suitable hands, while the impress service worked at full stretch. On 10 February 1793 a warrant authorising Captain Horatio Nelson of His Majesty's ship *Agamemnon* to press seamen into service was signed at the Admiralty.[1]

The *Agamemnon* was special to Nelson, the most favoured of all his ships. Because she brought long, barren years to an end and took him through many and distinguished services, he identified with her. So did her men, who proudly called themselves *Agamemnons* for the rest of their lives.

As a sixty-four-gunner, armed with a dozen nine-pounders and fifty-two eighteen- and twenty-four-pounders, the *Agamemnon* was actually one of the weakest ships of the line. In fact sixty-fours were gradually being dropped from the line of battle altogether. Yet though she pitched against head seas and her helm responded indifferently, the ship handled easily and could make ten knots before the wind. Captain Nelson found her at Prince's Bridge, Chatham, on 7 February and formally took command in the presence of his first lieutenant and master. He thought she was magnificent. Launched at Buckler's Hard in Hampshire almost a dozen years earlier, the *Agamemnon* was built of solid English oak, and measured one hundred and sixty feet in length by forty-four and a half in breadth. Her figurehead depicted the King of Mycenae for whom she had been named, and gazed grimly ahead, armoured, helmeted and brandishing a sword.[2]

Manning her was Nelson's first objective. For the first time Horatio had to raise a crew from scratch. He distributed posters, directed recruiting officers to forward men to ports between Newcastle and Great Yarmouth, and circulated friends in East Anglia. Many locals answered the call, including Joseph Levrington, John Chadd, J. G. Anniss and Christopher Cook from Wells and the Burnhams, and eventually almost a quarter of the ship's company hailed from Norfolk and Suffolk. Other men were recruited in Kent and Essex while the *Agamemnon* was at Chatham, and Nelson was fortunate that the trusty Captain Locker commanded a ship in the Thames, the *Sandwich*. Locker used it to house London recruits for the *Agamemnon*, and even helped prepare Nelson's ship for sea during her captain's absences.

Every month saw a steady increase in the ship's company. With late entrants picked up at Spithead, she eventually came to within about sixty men of her official complement of five hundred before she was ready to sail in May. The majority appear to have been volunteers, in receipt of the king's bounty, though numbers of pressed men were also aboard.

Nelson was now a credible patron, and the gentry wanted positions as trainee officers for their sons. The class of the *Agamemnon* included relatives of Nelson and protégés of Norfolk notables. Maurice William Suckling, who had been to the East Indies since quitting the *Boreas*, was rated master's mate, while the captain's servants included Nelson's thirteen-year-old stepson, Josiah, urged to sea by Fanny, and sixteen-year-old William Bolton, a son of the Reverend William Bolton of Hollesley in Suffolk, brother of Thomas. The Walpoles proffered a twenty one year old volunteer, Midshipman Samuel Gamble from King's Lynn, while Coke of Holkham rewarded two friends by getting places for their boys. Both sons of Norfolk parsons, they made the finest material. John Weatherhead was about twenty and the son of Thomas Weatherhead of Sedgeford, while thirteen-year-old William Hoste was the son of Dixon Hoste of Tittleshall.[3]

So many eligible young men competed for places among the petty officers that Suckling, Gamble and Weatherhead had to be rated able seamen until they could be raised to midshipmen. Another aspirant, Thomas Bourdon Fellows, possibly a relation of the ship's purser, was twenty-two years old and claimed to have served on seven ships in the past thirteen years, but also had to enter as able seaman before he could be more suitably rated master's mate. Less experienced protégés took refuge among the score of captain's servants to which Nelson was entitled. Bolton, Nisbet and Hoste began as captain's servants, but elbowroom remained, and Nelson filled his allocation with charity boys from the Marine Society. At least twenty joined him on 19 and 20 February, aged between thirteen and nineteen years, many of them undersized for their age but each thoroughly scrubbed and equipped with a sea outfit.[4]

Good officers were needed to train the recruits into an efficient team and Nelson turned to tried and tested followers from his past. Martin Hinton, formerly of the *Albermarle* and known to be 'a good sailor', became first lieutenant, and Joseph Bullen of the *Hinchinbroke* his second. Since his previous spell under Nelson, Bullen had returned to his old patron, Captain Cornwallis, and commanded half a gun

deck on the *Prince George* during the battle of the Saintes, but the
Agamemnon rescued him from half-pay. Nelson got George Andrews
of the *Boreas* for his third lieutenant, though the fourth and fifth
commissions went to Wenman Allison and Thomas Edmonds, men he
knew but with whom he had never worked. Allison had gone to sea
as a captain's servant on the *Suffolk* in May 1778, a protégé of Captain
Adam Duncan, the future hero of Camperdown. Duncan had just been
promoted vice admiral of the blue squadron in 1793, and either he,
or Captain John Vashon, another of Allison's patrons, may have
pressed Nelson to take the young man. Allison came to the
Agamemnon from half-pay, but there was no reason to expect a novice
because he had been a lieutenant for three years. Nelson's new master
was John Wilson, possibly the same man who had served him on the
old *Badger*.[5]

Further down other familiar faces came to rejoin their old
commander. They included Frank Lepee, now rated coxswain; Richard
Pryke, a thirty-five-year-old Colchester man rated master's mate; and
the boatswain and sailmaker of the *Boreas*, Joseph King. King had
spent twenty-one of his thirty-five years in the service, and with the
help of the Duke of Clarence got a special discharge from the *Valiant*
to return to his old captain. When the existing boatswain, Alexander
Moffat, fell ill in Gibraltar later that year, Nelson was able to restore
King to his old office.[6]

After the spiritless years ashore everything Nelson saw magnified
his excitement. The *Agamemnon* was 'the finest 64 in the service' and
a 'remarkably' good sailer, and her officers appeared to know their
duties. He spoke with most of them, including the purser Thomas
Fellows. Pursers had a bad name on warships. They made up their
salaries by conserving the stores entrusted to them, for which they
had paid a bond in advance, and were notorious for their stringency
in meeting the men's needs. Nelson assured Fellows that supplies would
be used carefully, but he would not 'suffer any poor fellow to be less-
ened of his due'.[7]

In March Nelson learned that he was to sail to the Mediterranean
with his old patron, Lord Hood, but first he must hurry to Spithead
for a preliminary cruise in the Channel. He hopped happily between
London and Chatham, setting interminable arrangements in train.
Charts, teacups, wineglasses, shirts, towels and a fine new quadrant
made by Richard Hornby made their way to his cabin at the rear of
the quarterdeck. Nelson spent £50 on as many dozen bottles of port,

sherry and claret, a third of them for consumption in the officers' wardroom, and purchased bread, butter, beef, pork, mutton, tea, coffee and rum for his table. In Spain he would top up with ninety-six chickens and twelve turkeys. Various delicacies, along with personal belongings from the parsonage, were shipped through Wells by his father, taking months to dribble in for sorting. The hams and bacon had chafed while rocking in a wagon and Nelson's bureau arrived without its key. Nevertheless, he contrived a degree of comfort in his new quarters, with a cheery coal-fired brazier to drive away the cold and damp.[8]

The *Agamemnon* slowly readied for sea. Hoys bumped alongside with iron and shingle to furnish ballast for the hold. Sacks of bread, flour, raisins and biscuit were hauled aboard, along with casks of beef, pork, peas, oatmeal, sugar, cheese, butter, water, beer, wine and spirits. The masts, yards and rigging were set up, and men scrubbed the timbers and applied fresh paint. Nor were the educational and spiritual needs of the company ignored. In March Nelson's appeal to the Society for the Promotion of Christian Knowledge produced 150 psalters and 125 copies of *The Christian Soldier*, or *The Seaman's Monitor*. It took Nelson longer to get a satisfactory schoolmaster for the boys, for twenty-four-year-old Thomas Withers of the *Victory* did not join him until May. Withers, it transpired, was one of the most remarkable men on board. The son of a yeoman of North Walsham, where Nelson had gone to school, he was trusting and transparent but intelligent. The nephew of a naval purser, Withers had been a nautical scholar of Christ's Hospital and a merchant seaman in the Indian Ocean. Nelson was so impressed that he re-rated him midshipman within five months and was repaid by unflinchingly loyal service.[9]

March brought Fanny and Josiah to London, where they lodged with the Sucklings in Kentish Town. The new year had brought much joy to Horatio, but not to his wife. Her uncle John Richardson Herbert had died in Nevis on 18 January, increasing her isolation on a wintry, wet island far from the place of her birth, and his will, upon which the Nelsons had placed hopes, was a disappointment. Herbert's property was entailed on his daughter, Martha Hamilton, with the right of reversion upon her death to Fanny's cousin, the younger Magnus Morton. The £20,000 once promised Fanny had shrunk to £4,000, and that could be withheld for up to six years on the payment of 5 per cent interest. Josiah would receive a further

£500 on his twenty-first birthday, and in the meantime receive the interest for his maintenance and education. The annual yield from the whole package barely made up for the loss of the one or two hundred pounds the couple had previously been receiving from their uncles' annuities.[10]

The Nelsons had expected Herbert's will to secure their immediate future and erase the humiliating spectre of a propertyless gentleman and his lady utterly incapable of returning the hospitality of the likes of Coke, Walpole and Martin. It had done neither, and one can only assume that Fanny sold a £100 investment in 3 per cent consols for £76 because of their shortage of ready cash. If the war was going to be merely the brief spat many predicted, Horatio could anticipate more needy years on half-pay. Only the possibility of quick prize money suggested a long-term solution.[11]

Fanny worried more about bidding farewell to her husband and son, and confronting a lonely, quiet and cold existence in Norfolk than anything else. On 4 April Nelson took Josiah on board the *Agamemnon* at Sheerness, where she had a new berth. The boy had missed the guns being hoisted aboard, but he was in time to see the powder hoy come alongside and the most dangerous part of the ship's cargo being loaded. Josiah's 'high glee' at getting under sail would soon disintegrate into seasickness when the ship weighed anchor for the Great Nore, but his stepfather was in good spirits after the brief trip down the Medway. 'We appear to sail very fast,' he marvelled. 'We went, coming out, nearly as fast without any sail as the *Robust* [of seventy-four guns] did under her topsails.' Recruits were coming in handsomely and officers and men were forming a productive partnership, 'the greatest comfort a captain can have'.[12]

Fanny wanted to see her husband before sailing. Their own partnership had not been blessed with children, and she was sterile, but her husband had been affectionate and kind and she loved him deeply. She always would. Nelson supposed the *Agamemnon* would stop for a while at Portsmouth, and Fanny arranged to stay with the Matchams, who had just taken Shepherd Spring, a house at Ringwood, Hampshire, not far from Portsmouth. Horatio's letters to her were dutiful, but lacked the impassioned urgency of those he would later write to Lady Hamilton, and his sentiments expressed almost indifference as to whether he saw Fanny or not. Rather, he was absorbed by his command. He talked about escaping to Ringwood if he could, or of Fanny renewing her acquaintanceship with the Palmers at the George inn at Portsmouth. On 28 April, Nelson brought a convoy to Spithead, just outside the town. 'If you and my sister [Kitty] wish to come [to Portsmouth], [I] shall be glad to see you,' he wrote to Fanny, 'but do as you like.'[13]

Two days later the *Agamemnon* sailed on a short prize hunt. With the swell beneath his feet and the old enemy before him Nelson was alive again. The second day out he found four French merchantmen in La Hague roads, and at seven in the evening almost ran them 'on shore' beneath two forts that guarded a harbour near Pointe de Barfleur. Shallows and threatening rocks on one side of the anchorage deterred him from pressing the attack, and after counting four small warships in Cherbourg he reluctantly returned to Spithead on the fifth. During the cruise he had shared his cabin with his brother Maurice, who had been trapped aboard by the bad weather while visiting at Spithead, and apparently also young, wide-eyed William Hoste. While Josiah was conquering his seasickness, Hoste – watched protectively by Weatherhead, the older of the two – felt 'very well and very comfortable' and found Nelson the perfect hero. 'I like my situation very much,' he told his father in one of his entertaining letters. 'Captain Nelson treats me as he said he would, and as a proof I have lived with him ever since I have been on board.'[14]

In May the *Agamemnon* was ready for her voyage to the Mediterranean, and there were final moments ashore and partings to manage. Suckling passed his examination for lieutenant, while Hoste spent an interesting day about the quayside at Spithead with Weatherhead and his brother, the latter attached to the *Edgar*. They watched some treasure being unloaded and carted to Portsmouth, accompanied by a band and a regiment of horse.[15]

After surviving rather more perils, including the overturning of her coach, Fanny reached Ringwood. It was apparently on the 'fine' morning of 10 May that she bade farewell to her husband at Portsmouth. Neither of them expected the separation to be a long one, but they would not meet again for four years; when he returned to her he would be rich in honour but ruined in body and spirit, a half-sighted, one-armed creature with a stomach hernia. Fanny never really understood the fires burning within her husband, but she knew every bit as much about duty as he, and steadfastly took his place as the supporter and comforter of his old father.[16]

Her letters, whether written from Ringwood, Hilborough or new lodgings at Swaffham, did not always reach him in the Mediterranean, and sometimes he missed her. Horatio wrote a few times most months, and even managed the occasional sentimentality. 'How I long to have a letter from you' was the message of 4 August. 'Next to being with you, it is the greatest pleasure I can receive. I shall rejoice to be with you again. Indeed, I look back as to the happiest period of my life the being united to such a good woman, and as I cannot show here my affection to you, I do it doubly to Josiah, who deserves it as well on his own account as on yours, for he is a real good boy, and most affectionately loves me. He tells me he intends to write you all the news.'[17]

2

On 11 May the *Agamemnon* sailed from St Helen's as part of a division commanded by Vice Admiral William Hotham from the *Britannia*. Three seventy-fours – the *Colossus* (Captain Charles Pole), the *Courageux* (Captain William Waldegrave) and the *Fortitude* (Captain William Young) – and two frigates (one of them the old *Lowestoffe*) made up the rest of the squadron, but Nelson felt that it was wasted cruising west of Guernsey where no enemies were to be found. 'Indeed,' he complained, 'I believe we are sent out for no other purpose than to amuse the people of England by having a fleet to sea.' They remained doing 'worse than nothing' until Lord Hood joined them off the Lizard on 25 May.[18]

For two weeks the combined squadrons stood off the Scillies in fog, rain and cold trying what remained of Nelson's patience. 'What the fleet is doing here, I can't guess,' he grumbled from his place in the rear of the force, 'not having seen a single Frenchman.' Regular 'naval evolutions' barely relieved the frustration, but on the 7th they fell in with a large convoy of British merchantmen plodding home from the West Indies. This, Nelson thankfully concluded, must have been the reason for Admiral Hood's interest in such a 'very barren' spot, and he looked forward to greater activity. Sure enough, once the merchantmen had passed, the fleet sailed for Gibraltar, eleven ships of the line and attendant frigates bowling elegantly into the Atlantic.[19]

Nelson's thirst for action remained unquenched, though Pole captured 'a poor miserable National brig', but at least the captain of the *Agamemnon* renewed his friendship with Lord Hood. It was the first time they had met since Hood had crushed Nelson's hopes for employment three years before, but now the tension was brushed aside.

The admiral was 'very civil', Fanny learned, and 'I dare say we shall be good friends again'.[20]

Hood needed good officers for the job he had been given. At the outbreak of war Britain had not a single ship of the line in the Mediterranean. Now the admiral was expected to establish naval superiority, if not complete supremacy, in that quarter by destroying the French fleet or bottling it in Toulon. While stifling enemy trade and supplies, he had to protect British commerce and the country's important communications with India and the East Indies, and assist the allied powers to resist French aggression. One such power, Sardinia, had already lost Villefranche and Nice.

Unfortunately, Hood got little support from home. His government was not expecting a long war, for while France had won some military victories she was still internally divided and ringed by predatory powers eager to stove in her boundaries and restore her monarchy. The coalition against her grew as one state after another – Austria, Prussia, Britain, Holland, Spain, Portugal, Sardinia and Naples – entered the fight. Against this background Pitt's war effort remained minimalist. He was content to contribute money and advice, but as long as the Low Countries were kept free of the enemy, he saw no reason to deploy British troops on the Continent. Certainly not in the Mediterranean. Instead, he planned to use the navy and most of his army to advantage overseas. While France was enmeshed in the European quagmire, Britain would ravage her seagoing trade and strip her of rich Caribbean islands. By recycling the pillage to finance allied armies, Britain could make her great rival pay towards her own defeat.

Time would prove that the British had greatly misjudged the situation. Pitt and his advisers underestimated French endurance and overrated the utility of the allies. The war was not a quick, lusty clash of arms. It intensified, and went on and on. Pitt's finances, which had begun to erode the national debt, were premised on a short war and fell into disarray. Instead of imposing emergency taxation to create a war chest, he relied upon uncertain spoils from the enemy and ruinous loans. Even more disastrous, Britain's colonial and commercial strategy did not spare her casualties. Indeed, it cost her the flower of the British army. Between 1793 and 1796 eighty thousand troops were killed or disabled by diseases in the West Indies without having landed one significant blow upon the French.

Hood, therefore, had few soldiers to help him regain the

Mediterranean, and no base east of Gibraltar. He was expected to rely heavily upon the allies, particularly Austria and Spain. Unfortunately, Austria was bogged down in continental campaigns, and Spain's great days as an imperial power, when she had tantalised the world with riches hewn from the New World, were spent. True, Spain had tried to reverse the decay of her fleet, and massively increased the numbers of her capital ships and frigates from the mid-century. With seventy-six ships of the line in 1790, Spain had the third largest navy in the world, boasting such impressive battle units as the *Santissima Trinidad*, the biggest warship afloat. But her fleets were chronically under-manned, and had yet to shrug off the unfortunate habit of carrying too great a proportion of soldiers to seamen. Moreover, like the French, the Spanish spent too much time languishing in port, recruiting hands for voyages at short notice. Without enough trained seamen or sea-going experience, even brave and patriotic Spanish crews tended to be undisciplined and incompetent.

It did not take Nelson long to gauge the worth of the Spanish navy. To ease the watering situation at Gibraltar, Hood ordered Captain George Elphinstone to take six ships of the line, including the *Agamemnon*, into Cadiz. They reached the Spanish port in uncomfortable heat on 16 June. Nelson's ship was in good shape, and he was able to wander around the dockyards, the arsenal on Isla de León, and the fortifications of Cortadura. He and the other captains sampled lavish Spanish hospitality dining with their admiral aboard the huge *Concepción*. The 'Dons', Nelson observed, had 'very fine ships' but they were 'shockingly manned' and unlikely to be of 'much use'. In fact, 'I am certain if our six barges' crews . . . had got on board one of their first rates they would have taken her.'

One spectacle Nelson and his fellow captains beheld at Cadiz filled them with revulsion. They were invited to a 'bull feast' in which ten animals were driven one by one into an amphitheatre to be baited, tortured and slaughtered before a blood-lusting, baying crowd of twelve thousand people. 'We had what is called a "fine" feast', Nelson wrote home, 'for five horses were killed and two men very much hurt. Had they been killed it would have been quite complete. We felt for the bulls and horses, and I own it would not have displeased me to have had some of the Dons tossed by the enraged animal[s]. How women can even sit, much more applaud, such sights is astonishing. It even turned us sick, and we could hardly sit it out. The dead, mangled horses with their entrails tore out [and] the bulls covered with blood was too much. However, we have seen one [bull feast] and agree that nothing shall tempt us to see another.'[21]

On 24 June Hood reassembled his fleet at Gibraltar, bringing together Elphinstone's squadron, his own and a detachment of ships that had been sent in advance. Captain Nelson shopped for a cask of sherry for Locker, and exchanged warm greetings with old friends on the streets and quays of the great stronghold. The captain of the *Britannia* was John Holloway of Leeward Islands fame, while Skeffington Lutwidge, who had commanded the *Carcass*, was now at the head of the *Terrible*. No doubt opinions of the Spanish navy passed freely during these conversations, and the worst of them were vindicated when the fleet proceeded through into the Mediterranean.

Nelson used Sunday 7 July to distribute his psalters and monitors to the crew, but towards the end of the day his attention was drawn to a large number of sails spotted off the Spanish port of Alicante. In case they were French ships from Toulon, Hood had his nineteen ships of the line in battle formation the next morning, but the newcomers proved to be part of the Spanish fleet bound for Cartagena. Nelson watched their allies wasting four fumbling hours trying to form a line of battle, and marvelled even more to hear that a mere sixty days at sea had reduced their ships to such a poor state that they had been forced to run for port. This seemed 'ridiculous' to the British, said Nelson, 'for from the circumstance of [us] having been longer than that time at sea do we attribute our getting healthy. It has stamped with me the extent of their nautical abilities. Long may they remain in their present state.'[22]

Impatient for action, Nelson may not have known that he had learned the decisive lesson of the outward voyage. Instinctively he understood that though the Spaniards and British were presently allies they were not naturally so, and might one day meet in battle. For that eventuality he was astutely priming himself, measuring the strengths and weaknesses of the Spanish fleet and finding it wanting. It was information he would supplement in the years ahead and tap for his first great battle.

If the Spanish failed to impress Nelson, the French navy held no greater terrors for him. Even word that the French were installing forges in their ships so that they could fire red-hot shot did not diminish his ardour to fight them. He merely observed that 'we must take care to get so close that the shot may go through both sides, when it will not matter whether they are hot or cold.' Hood appreciated Nelson's offensive spirit. His fleet advanced upon Toulon and Marseilles in three divisions, one headed by his own *Victory* (Captain John Knight) and the others by the *Colossus* and *Agamemnon*. The admiral declared the French coast to be under close blockade. Nelson, sanguine about the efficiency of economic warfare, hoped that starvation might drive 'these red hot gentlemen' out to offer battle. He was a terrier straining on a leash, desperate to distinguish himself and reluctant to tolerate anything protracted or sluggish.[23]

Late on 15 July, after days crossing seas empty of French sail, the men of the *Agamemnon* heard distant firing to leeward. It came from the direction in which the *Leda* and the *Illustrious* had pursued strange sails, and everyone expected prizes in which the fleet would share. However, the next day their comrades brought in only a French corvette. They admitted that three enemy frigates had been engaged the night before but had escaped. How was it possible, Nelson grumbled? The weather had been fair, the night moonlit and clear and the British the more practised seamen. If he ever made a fortune, he complained to Fanny, it would not be through gentlemen like the captains of the *Leda* and *Illustrious*. Somewhere, in the frustration of such moments, Nelson realised that one of the most important tasks of the admiral was to instil spirit and enterprise into his captains, and to encourage them to achieve with or without immediate supervision.

Indeed, Nelson was already showing what could be done in the way of leadership on his own ship. His people were learning what was expected of them, and more or less working as a single body. William Hoste, who Nelson increasingly recognised as an unusually appreciative, bright boy, felt that moulding. His bubbling letters suggest a happy ship. 'I like the sea very much indeed', his father learned. 'Captain Nelson is very well and is uncommon kind to me. I have the pleasure to inform you that Mr Weatherhead is made mate. I like him very much. We have a schoolmaster [Withers] on board. He is a very clever man.' Nelson, said the boy, was 'acknowledged to be one of the first captains in the service, and is universally beloved by his men and officers'. Most men liked Nelson because he liked them; even youngsters who could do little for him understood his interest in them. 'In his navigation, you will find him equally forward,' Nelson wrote to the Reverend Dixon Hoste of his son. 'He highly deserves every thing I can do to make him happy . . . I love him; therefore shall say no more on that subject.' When Hood offered Nelson the command of a seventy-four – the type of ship he had always wanted, the type that played the major part in fleet actions – he surprised the admiral by turning it down. 'I cannot give up my officers,' he told Fanny.[24]

Conquering calms and inconstant winds, the British battleships finally closed the road into Toulon on 19 July. Hood sent in a flag of truce, ostensibly to negotiate an exchange of prisoners but in reality to spy. Sixteen French ships of the line were discovered in the outer road ready for service, and another five fitting in the harbour. Nelson supposed that once the French had put all of their ships into commission and tilted the odds in their favour, professional pride if not starvation would prompt them to test the British blockade. But though Hood's ships braved fierce gales for several days, suffering and scattering, no such movement occurred.

Both Toulon and nearby Marseilles were, in fact, gripped by civil strife. In some parts of France the forces of counterrevolution were on the move, prompted by the extremism of the National Convention in Paris. Supporters of the crown and Church had risen in rebellion in Vendée in the west, while in Marseilles and Toulon coalitions of royalists and moderate republicans overthrew their Jacobin opponents. The Toulon fleet was divided and paralysed. Its admiral, Jean-Honoré, Comte Trogoff de Kerlessy, struggled to keep it free of the local factions, but waited in vain for instructions from his government.

The situation revealed itself to the British gradually. After probing towards Nice in August, Hood detailed the *Agamemnon*, *Robust*, *Romulus* and *Colossus* to maintain the watch in the Toulon area while he took the fleet to Genoa, a neutral port from which the enemy were securing supplies. No doubt Nelson enjoyed the greater freedom it gave him. Privately he complained that Hood had 'done nothing but look into Toulon', and relished the liberty to enforce the blockade in his own way.

However, he was increasingly conscious of the difficulties created by neutral shipping. The Mediterranean was full of small, neutral states trying to continue their business with the war raging around them. The British allowed their ships to pass in and out of Toulon and Marseilles as long as they did not transport French freight or 'contraband' items deemed of value to the French war effort. In practice, distinguishing between what was and was not legitimate commerce was largely beyond officers on the spot. On 16 August, Nelson seized the *Madonna di Bisson*, a snow sailing from Marseilles to Smyrna under Ragusan colours. Among her cargoes were clothes, sugar and linen that Nelson believed to be French property, but though he sent the ship to the prize court in Leghorn he doubted that she would be condemned.

The afternoon of 18 August saw Nelson in action again, pursuing two armed ships east of Toulon into the harbour of Cavalière. A French shore battery opened fire to defend them, but the ships themselves raised neutral Genoese colours. Nelson's suspicions remained, however, and after exchanging some shots with the French he withdrew out of range to watch what happened next. In the morning he decided to use bluff. Intercepting a Genoese brig, he sent it into the harbour with a message for the masters of the fugitive vessels. If they were truly Genoese they should come out, or face being attacked and burned at anchor. The French certainly thought the British capable of landing in force, and while some locals fled up the hillside six hundred militia marched into the settlement to resist any assault. In the event Nelson's message alone did the trick. The two armed ships, with five or six others using the harbour, came out for examination. Nelson was sure they were 'loaded' with French property, but their neutral papers seemed in order and he let them go.[25]

Apart from pursuing ships back and forth, Captain Nelson gathered intelligence, and everything he discovered increased his animosity to the revolution. Though the people were starving, the squabbles of the political factions in Marseilles and Toulon sowed terror and murder. At the moment the more conservative republicans and monarchists had the upper hand, but the blade of the guillotine rose and fell all the same, dispatching radical opponents with a cruel and vengeful finality. The jails heaved with radical activists. Nelson was told that the people were tired of the dogma-ridden Jacobins, and that Provence might even declare itself a separate republic under the protection of Britain.

On 20 August, Hood was back and Nelson had someone else to blame for a lack of progress. Nelson vacillated between his instincts and sense. Much as he admired Hood, he thought the fleet 'inactive' and convinced himself that Marseilles was so short of provisions and politically divided that it would prove an easy conquest if only the British had the courage to attack. 'We have attempted nothing,' he said, yet 'Marseilles must fall if we attack it.' But at the same time he knew that even if the town was captured it could not be held without larger numbers of troops than Hood could muster.[26]

The admiral himself pursued a surer strategy by opening negotiations with representatives of both Marseilles and Toulon. After earlier military disasters the National Convention was striking back hard, introducing mass conscription to hurl ragged but fervent troops against reactionary invaders and internal insurrectionists alike. As food ran low in Marseilles and Toulon, and the avenging forces of the convention threatened to enclose them, the ports turned in desperation to Hood, suggesting the British take them under their protection. Hood's luck was remarkable. Though Louis XVII was an imprisoned child, the admiral demanded the authorities declare for the monarchy, as defined in the reformed constitution of 1791, and surrender the dockyards, ships and forts at Toulon into British keeping. Nelson impatiently watched the boats hurrying to and from the *Victory*, but on 26 August he was summoned on board the flagship himself. He could scarcely have imagined better fortune. At a single stroke and with hardly a shot fired Toulon, the second greatest French naval base – indeed the whole of France's sea power in the Mediterranean – was about to be enclosed within the British fist.

However, to garrison the forts at Toulon, Hood desperately needed soldiers. As the *Agamemnon* was one of the fastest ships in the fleet, Nelson was ordered to carry dispatches to Sardinia and Naples. The allies were told that Toulon was expected to fall. Had he '5,000 or 6,000 troops' with him, the war would soon be over, Hood wrote confidently to Sir William Hamilton, Britain's man in Naples.[27]

Nelson hurried away, sailing deeper into the Mediterranean than he had ever been before, but he was lumbered with the job of escorting a Sardinian frigate to Oneglia and Sardinia and on his way also seized a vessel carrying corn from Genoa to Marseilles. A prize crew was put aboard, though it would take almost a year for the vessel to be condemned in Gibraltar. On the last day of the month Nelson was still at sea when he encountered the *Tartar* under Captain Thomas Fremantle, carrying Lord Hugh Seymour Conway with dispatches for England. They gave Horatio the latest news from the fleet.

Marseilles had fallen to the national French army, and the party that had treated with Hood crushed. Royalist refugees had streamed into Toulon, strengthening the moderates there and edging them closer to the British. Hood offered Toulon protection provided he was given control of the military and naval installations. Soon the town had declared for the monarchical form of government outlined in the French constitution of 1791 and agreed to let Hood in. The day the *Tartar* left thousands of marines and seamen were being landed to secure the dockyard and forts, and the French fleet had been commandeered. A Spanish fleet had also arrived to support the British admiral, but his need of soldiers to man fortifications had intensified. Conway said that he had written a personal letter to Hamilton urging him to 'hasten the Neapolitans' and gave it to Nelson to deliver.[28]

Britannia's triumph exceeded anything Nelson had imagined. Never had he supposed that the French Mediterranean fleet would be so bloodlessly and effortlessly overthrown. True, the way Hood put it the French ships were being held in trust, awaiting a restoration of the monarchy, but if the Jacobin army now massing to attack Toulon forced Hood out the British still had it in their power to destroy the port and its fleet before retiring. As Captain Nelson strolled his quarterdeck he even wondered whether Toulon might become a bridgehead for an invasion of 'that unhappy distracted country' in support of royalist rebels and an honourable peace? At the very least news of its fall into British hands had to inspire the allied powers to greater efforts. Nelson was personally bound for Sardinia and Naples, both of them already smarting from the threats of the French navy. Sardinia, which then governed the island of Sardinia, as well as Piedmont, Lombardy and a stretch of the riviera, had lost Nice, Villefranche, Monaco and Menton to the French, but now stood to regain ground.[29]

On the last day of August, Nelson landed Hood's dispatches for John Trevor, the British minister to Sardinia, at Oneglia. He and his Sardinian consort then headed east and south, around Corsica, where French republican garrisons held the natives in subjection, and towards the Tyrrhenian Sea. Off Bastia, on the northeast coast of Corsica, Nelson sent a message to anti-French partisans ashore, telling them of the fall of Toulon. Then, on 8 September, after parting with the Sardinian frigate, he captured a Ragusan brig of ten guns on its way from Smyrna to Marseilles with French cotton. Nelson had not been having much luck with prizes. 'All we get is honour and salt beef,' he said, reflecting on the nineteen weeks or so his people had survived without fresh meat and vegetables. This prize seemed about to change things. He detached Lieutenant Andrews to take her into the neutral port of Leghorn for adjudication, and calculated she might make £10,000 if condemned and sold. But money was destined to elude Nelson: the ship was acquitted and released.[30]

He was not going to be rich, but there was that mission to the Kingdom of the Two Sicilies at Naples to complete. The city and its court were among the most fabled in Europe, and there he was to deliver a packet to His Britannic Majesty's Envoy Extraordinary and Minister Plenipotentiary, Sir William Hamilton.

3

Nelson was tired and weather-worn when he saw Naples, but he was impressed from the very beginning.

The bay of Naples was wide, open and awesome, the deep blue of the sea, spotted with fishing boats, contrasting with the green and yellow of the hills above with their olive groves and fields of wheat. The city, a loud, brassy, indulgent metropolis only a little smaller than Paris, seemed from the sea to be dominated by the Castel St Elmo, and it was flanked a few miles to the right by Mount Posillipo, and to the left by the towering twin peaks of Vesuvius. Even then the rugged heights of the volcano coursed with burning lava, and it spat red fire and black ash into an eerily illuminated sky. On either side the extremities of the bay disintegrated into beautiful craggy islands, Ischia and Procida in the north and Capri to the south. Arriving on 10 September, Nelson thought the volcanic exhibition 'grand'. The next day he wrote to Fanny that 'we are now in sight of Mount Vesuvius which shows a fine light to us in Naples Bay, where we are laying to for the night . . . We were in the bay all night becalmed and nothing could be finer than the views of Mount Vesuvius.'[31]

The *Agamemnon* anchored close to four Neapolitan ships, the *Guiscardo* ship of the line and three frigates. Soon an officer from one of the frigates came alongside. He offered the Neapolitan admiral's compliments, granted permission to remain in the bay, and most remarkably passed an invitation to Captain Nelson to come aboard and meet the King of Naples himself, who was present. Ordering out his barge, Nelson clambered into it to the shrill of pipes and was rowed out for the first of many meetings with the famous Ferdinand IV. He was a Bourbon, Nelson knew, the brother of Charles, King of Spain. Maria Carolina, his queen, was the daughter of Marie Theresa (late Empress of Austria), and the sister of the present emperor, Leopold II, and also of the unfortunate Queen of France, Marie Antoinette, who then lay incarcerated in a French prison awaiting execution. The Neapolitan royal family was related through blood to two of Britain's allies, and had its own reasons to hate the republicans.

Horatio did not find His Majesty physically prepossessing.

Ferdinand was a coarse, powerfully-built man, ugly and pig-eyed, with the grossest manners. He was ignorant, bullying and buffoonish, a man who knew little of the affairs of state, but much about gambling, billiards, ogling women and gratuitously butchering huge quantities of wildlife. In any one of the king's hunts hundreds of animals might be slain, deer, pigs, wolves, and even his own dogs – the more the merrier, for Ferdinand wallowed in the butchery and boasted of the thousands of creatures he had done to death. His abuse effortlessly extended to people, whether chasing servants with the contents of his chamber pot or forcing coachmen to swallow live frogs. Yet none of this boorish brutality deterred the clergy and the Neapolitan mob, the *lazzaroni*, from supporting him. The king's rule was corrupt, ineffi-cient and did little to improve the condition of his subjects, but at least he mixed with them, talking to them in a language they under-stood, and developing a rough-hewn camaraderie.

Though Ferdinand ruled the Kingdom of the Two Sicilies, the largest of the Italian states, embracing Sicily and the southern half of the peninsula, he was not its prime policy maker. That was largely in the hands of his far abler and forceful queen, Maria Carolina, and the principal minister, John Acton. Guaranteed a place in the councils of state by her marriage settlement, it was Maria Carolina who steadily extricated Naples from the orbit of Spain and strengthened its links with Austria. She cemented the relationship by marrying off two Neapolitan princesses to the Austrian crown prince and his younger brother, the Grand Duke of Tuscany. Incapacitated by one of her frequent pregnancies, the queen was temporarily out of circulation when Nelson arrived, but even Ferdinand appreciated the significance of his visit.

In Naples the antics of the French had aroused fear and horror, but the Kingdom was wide open to Jacobin aggression, and not all its subjects were ignorant of the desperate need for political reform. For some time the country had shrunk from outright hostilities with France, but it had prevaricated about recognising the new republic in 1792. That December a French squadron had arrived in the bay and intim-idated the Kingdom, and it was not until 12 July 1793, when the war appeared to be tilting against the Jacobins, that the king finally committed himself to an alliance with Britain. He undertook to supply six thousand soldiers and a dozen ships if required. In short, Naples was throwing in with what seemed to be the stronger side, and became largely dependent upon the Royal Navy for its security. Only British ships could prevent another French squadron from menacing their capital. Nelson, therefore, was an important visitor.[32]

Speaking through interpreters, Nelson quickly learned that the capture of Toulon had been known in Naples for five days, although their information made the feat a joint accomplishment of British and Spanish arms. Standing firmly for national honour, Nelson quickly disabused the king of his misconception, and Ferdinand amicably agreed that the credit belonged to Hood alone, 'and that the Spaniard had "*Trompe Trompe*"'. Well might Ferdinand rejoice, for the list of captured French ships flourished by Nelson virtually assured the temporary security of his country. Dwarfed by the burlesque figure of the sovereign, the little captain then pressed his advantage with a request for troops. It should have been made through Britain's man in Naples, but the king had no reason to refuse. The news of the occupation of Toulon had warmed his heart, and Naples had already contracted to supply the men in their treaty during the summer. Without committing himself on the spot, Ferdinand waxed positive. No one admired Hood more than he, the king said, and the British 'were the saviours of Italy and of his kingdom in particular'. When Nelson left he was not only elated by the warmth of his royal reception, but satisfied that the current was running in his favour.[33]

The captain then directed his barge ashore, where for the first time he saw that jumble of narrow, bustling alleys and colourful street life that characterised central Naples. The houses rose large and gloomy, storey upon storey, as if striving for light, peering down into narrow, paved streets and innumerable little courtyards, where ragged urchins ran wild and townspeople scattered before the footmen running ahead of the carriages of the wealthy. This was a lax resort of lethargic nobles, idling while their estates were worked by small leaseholders; of assignations between married ladies and their *cicisbei*; and of the famous but dishevelled *lazzaroni*, scratching a living on the streets where they could. Sometime in the afternoon Nelson reached his destination – the Palazzo Sessa, a white, three-storey residence on the hill beneath the Castel St Elmo, overlooking the bay. This, leased from the Marchese di Sessa, was the residence of His Britannic Majesty's Envoy Extraordinary and Minister Plenipotentiary to the court of the Kingdom of the Two Sicilies.

There, in an office on the lower floor, Captain Nelson was received by an old, stick-thin, frail, stooped man, his deep-set eyes glinting beneath craggy brows and his nose curved like a beak, as if he was some emaciated bird of prey. But when he spoke it was fluently and to the point, and Nelson felt that here was a man who could show him how business was done in this exotic place. As Sir William Hamilton himself once said, though sixty-three, he had spent many years hobbling in and out of scrapes.[34]

Hamilton read Hood's letter of 25 August and Conway's, and listened patiently as Nelson spoke. He knew there would be no difficulty in meeting the admiral's wishes. The English were riding on the crest of a wave in Naples. The mob had ripped the arms of the French republic from outside the house of its representative and destroyed them, while the king had just concluded his treaty with Britain and feted her every visiting officer. Hamilton was having few difficulties getting what he wanted. The previous month Ferdinand had agreed that the Neapolitan navy might be put at the disposal of Lord Hood, provided the security of his kingdom was not compromised. 'I will answer for this court's readiness to supply your lordship whatever you may stand in need of,' Hamilton wrote to the British admiral. Indeed, the very day Nelson arrived in the bay Hamilton was taking steps to provide soldiers for Hood. 'I think it highly probable that Lord Hood may have occasion for the six thousand Neapolitan troops stipulated in the late convention to garrison Toulon,' Sir William told his political masters in England. 'They have been ordered to hold themselves in readiness to embark at a moment's warning.'[35]

Although Nelson liked to attribute the speedy reinforcements to his own entreaties, we can see that Hamilton had already prepared the ground. Sir William had put everything in hand. All the captain did was fire the starting gun.

Sir William escorted Nelson straight to the leading minister of the country at his office in the Segretario, opposite the royal palace, probably taking him along the mole and past the stark walls of the Castel d'Ouvo that grimly guarded the foreshore. Nelson was pleasantly surprised to find that Sir John Francis Edward Acton, though born in France fifty-seven years before, was of English ancestry and by profession a naval man. He was decidedly pro-English, and enjoyed the confidence and patronage of the queen. Acton had served in the navies of France and Tuscany before coming to Naples in 1779 to organise the Kingdom's fleet as minister of marine. His reforms were by no means universally applauded, but he expanded the country's fleet, and advanced in stature, becoming in addition minister of war and minister of finance. In all but name he was the prime minister, and played a key role in breaking the influence of Spain upon the Kingdom of the Two Sicilies and developing a British orientation.

Acton was pressed by business but received Nelson cordially and read the letters he had brought. They agreed to meet again at nine that evening. When the captain arrived, shepherded again by Hamilton, Acton was able to inform him that Hood's request for troops would be 'immediately' granted. However, he worried that if the soldiers were sent at once, before their provisions could be assembled, they would 'be a trouble to Lord Hood instead of a service'. Perhaps the reinforcements should wait until they could be fully victualled. Before Nelson could reply Hamilton had his answer. Two thousand men sent now would be of more use than six thousand in two weeks. Sir John thereupon declared that two thousand soldiers would sail in the space of three or four days, and the rest would follow as soon as possible.

That night Nelson returned to his ship exhilarated. In one day the king, Hamilton and Acton had successively received and complimented him, and Hood's every wish had been met. Never had he felt more valued or more instrumental. Hamilton, who rushed a cutter to Hood with the news, would give Nelson his due for the result. The captain, he said a few days later, 'has been very useful to me in urging the necessity of immediately sending off the succours for your lordship'.[36]

The next few days raced from one high to another. On the 12th Nelson and Hamilton were invited to dine with Acton, and the guests took their seats after receiving the welcome tidings that the king had ordered Hood's troops to be prepared that same day. After dinner, Nelson suggested to Hamilton that a personal letter from the king to Hood would be appreciated. Immediately Sir William put it to Acton, and before the night was out Nelson heard that the boon would be granted. Sir John had another surprise for them the following day. Nelson and Sir William were to dine that evening with the king at Portici. Easily flattered, Nelson proudly recorded in a detailed journal he had begun to keep that Ferdinand was 'attentive' and complimentary at dinner. The king said he would personally visit the *Agamemnon* the coming Sunday, and that afterwards Nelson would dine with him again at his royal palace at Caserta, north of Naples.

Constantly in demand, Nelson bunked ashore with the Hamiltons at the Palazzo Sessa, bringing his young stepson with him to trouble Lady Hamilton. It was an extraordinary residence, in which Sir William's remarkable collection of art, antiquities and curiosities followed Nelson up every staircase and through every room, all of them capable of inducing the host to expound with an enthusiasm that quite defeated a naval captain. The upper apartments, where Nelson stayed, commanded fine views. A room on the southwest corner of the house was circular, and its balconied window offering a vast panorama over the bay was reflected in a wall of mirrors opposite to create the illusion that its occupants were entirely surrounded by water.[37]

Sir William Hamilton, whose destiny would inextricably entwine with Nelson's, was an unusual man. The backgrounds of the two could not have been more different. Sir William was a Scottish aristocrat to his toes, a grandson of the third Duke of Hamilton and the sixth Earl of Abercorn. His father, Lord Archibald Hamilton, had been a lord of the Admiralty, the governor of Greenwich Hospital and a governor of Jamaica; his mother a favourite of the Prince of Wales; and Sir William himself had been equerry to George III. To Nelson it seemed that there were few members of the British upper crust with whom his host was unacquainted.

Sir William had served in the army, an experience he seems to have regretted, and been a Member of Parliament. He had waited on the court of Naples for nearly thirty years, with efficiency if not enthusiasm. Sometimes he longed for a more prestigious diplomatic post in Vienna, but he was by no means unsuited to the lazy life of a backwater like Naples. For above all Sir William was a connoisseur and antiquary. A virtuoso of the violin, member of the Society of Arts, man of science and avid collector of art and antiquities, he knew that nowhere offered more opportunities for study than Naples. Here he enjoyed an immense amount of leisure time, with the remains of the Classical world he admired so much on his doorstep. There were the ash-covered ruins of Pompeii and Herculaneum to explore, as well as the volcano itself. Many people feared Vesuvius, but not Sir William. He confessed himself 'much pleased' whenever it spat out its 'vast' columns of ash or punctuated the air with noisy flashes of 'lightning'. Occasionally when the shocks rattled his villa below, the ageing philosopher would hike up the mountain and spend nights within range of its fury, merely to observe its dazzling manifestations at first hand. In quieter moments he visited the crater, sampling the cinders and lava, or made pilgrimages to Etna and Stromboli to inform his pioneer publications in vulcanology. Sir William's first wife, Catherine Barlow, had been an heiress; her remains now lay in her native Wales awaiting a final reunion with a beloved husband. She had often urged him to embrace religion but never successfully, for at heart Hamilton responded to logic and reason rather than faith. He remained stubbornly philosophical and secular.

It was Catherine who in a great measure had given Sir William the resources to amass his magnificent collections, treasuries of antiquities that would one day be a foundation for the British Museum. He was forever collecting and selling. By 1771 Hamilton had more than eight thousand vases, terracottas, ancient glasses, bronze, ivory and gold pieces, and antique gems and coins. A sumptuous description of only part of this remarkable hoard, published in 1766 and 1767, extended to four volumes, and gave impetus to the neo-Classical movement already then underway. He had no sooner sold one collection than he began another, and by 1798 he owned more than two hundred paintings and drawings by old masters such as Rembrandt, Titian, Rubens, Velasquez and Van Dyck.

Though Hamilton had little intrinsic interest in politics, his conversation was informed, direct and populated with a dazzling range of friends and acquaintances. Nelson listened to anecdotes of luminaries as varied as the Emperor Joseph II of Austria, Tsar Paul of Russia, Goethe and Voltaire. Hamilton had served under the victor of Culloden in the Netherlands, and met the loser drinking himself into decline and death in Rome. He had entertained the infant Mozart. He mused in one breath about Banks, Reynolds and Wedgwood, and in another detailed the antics of his pet monkey, Jack, which peered at ladies in closets and learned to use a magnifying glass. Nelson presented as a rather serious young man, but we can imagine the suggestion of one of his uncommon but charming smiles.

Then, at some stage, Sir William introduced Nelson to a person of whom he was extrovertly proud – Emma, the new Lady Hamilton.

Nelson said little about her at the time, but she was helpful to his boys. Hoste was packed off with tickets to the King's Museum and the ruins of Herculaneum, while Fanny read that 'Lady Hamilton has been wonderfully kind and good to Josiah'. The Hamiltons must have told Nelson something of her bizarre past, because the captain added, 'She is a young woman of amiable manners and who does honour to the station to which she is raised.' Nevertheless, nothing in this simple testimony betrayed that its writer had met the great love of his life.[38]

More than fifty books have been written about Emma Hamilton and they vary greatly in the portrait they present of her. Few people have been so damned and so sainted. Her powerful compound of

strengths and weaknesses led contemporaries to extol or detract vigorously. That potent cocktail should not be forgotten, for we will shed
little light on Emma simply to reproduce the prejudices of one side or
another. Traducers considered her low-born, and therefore coarse,
vulgar and graceless; she spent much of her life in Naples, imbibing
its liberality, and was consequently indecorous; she was beautiful,
forward and infectious, and therefore a magnet for the jealous and
envious. Above all, perhaps, she was something of an outsider. Her
experiences transcended classes and kingdoms, and though she was
raised to that threatened order of aristocracy she never quite fitted
into it. Emma wore her faults on her sleeves. Talented rather than
intelligent, ridiculously theatrical, tempestuous, vain, attention-seeking
and ruthless in pursuit, she was a spendthrift and trivial socialite. But
she was also warm-hearted, humane, generous, loyal, energetic and
brave. We will never understand her blistering impact on a succession
of individuals, be they painters, diplomats or naval officers, if we do
not realise that first and foremost she was a most remarkable woman.

Her beauty would have struck Nelson immediately. Emma was tall,
strong and almost Amazonian – too much so for some men's tastes –
but she also sported a voluptuous figure no clothes could disguise.
Her form may have been at its best that first time Nelson saw her,
for it expanded disastrously in the following years, when it seemed to
grow by the day. Classically moulded, her commanding and expressive countenance was lit by lively blue eyes and surmounted by an
immense chestnut mane. Some men spoke of her as 'one of the most
beautiful creatures' they had ever seen, though not everyone agreed.
Certainly she entranced painters, who had made her a leading model
of the time. Chief among them was the fashionable English artist
George Romney, for whom Emma was 'superior to all womankind'
and worthy of the dozens of canvasses he devoted to her. In Italy such
was the scramble for her services that as many as half a dozen or
more sculptors and artists might be working on her likeness at any
one time.[39]

Most of all Emma loved to perform, to move and inspire. Confident
in her looks and powers, she danced with 'a volupte, a grace which
would set on fire the coldest and most insensible man', sang like 'an
angel', and created 'a new source of pleasure to mankind' with her
famous 'attitudes'. The attitudes were costumed poses, most of them
drawn from Classical mythology, the sort painters used but now
endowed with movement and expression. Emma successfully plied

them before fashionable gatherings in Naples and London, but no one left a better description than Goethe, who sat through a performance in Caserta in 1787. Dressed in a Greek outfit, Emma:

lets down her hair, and with a few shawls gives so much variety to her poses, gestures, expressions, etc., that the spectator can hardly believe his eyes. He sees what thousands of artists would have liked to express, realised before him in movements and surprising transformations – standing, kneeling, sitting, reclining, serious, sad, playful, ecstatic, contrite, alluring, threatening, anxious – one pose follows another without a break. She knows how to arrange the folds of her veil to match each mood, and has a hundred ways of turning it into a head-dress . . . This much is certain: as a performance it's like nothing you ever saw before in your life.[40]

Her public thought the attitudes extraordinary, and men found them sexually charged, with Emma's flimsy draperies and short male tunics revealing in art what would have been indecent in society. The applause only fired Emma's 'passion for admiration' and made her work the harder. In fact, in her own way she was as much a perfectionist as Horatio Nelson, but whereas he hungered for the perfect naval victory she needed the ultimate public performance. 'I sung after that one with a tambourin in the character of a young girl with a raire-shew [raree-show], the pretist [prettiest] thing you ever heard,' she told a former lover in 1787. 'I left the people at Sorrento with their heads turned. I left some dying, some crying, and some in despair.' Emma, like Nelson, was bent upon conquest.[41]

Sir William doted on a young wife thirty-three years his junior, and proudly exhibited her talents. He stage-managed the attitudes, control-ling the lighting, and finding the inspiration for many of her poses in the vases and sculptures of his vast collection and the pages of a well-stocked library. If he felt threatened he managed to hide it. Emma's ability to captivate and her appetite for attention made her a formi-dable figure in any social gathering, in which she was a tireless hunter of the hearts of men and women alike, wooing them with generosity, warmth and endless attention. Sir Gilbert Elliot, who knew her well, said she had the 'easy' manners 'of a barmaid, [was] excessively good humoured and wishing to please and [to] be admired by all ages and sorts of persons that come in her way'. Significantly he noticed that 'with men her language and conversation are exaggerations of anything I ever heard'. But her ageing husband seemed only proud of her powers.

'She makes me happy and is loved and esteemed by all,' he wrote to a kinsman in Toulon. 'Come and see, and my life for it, she will *gain* you!'[42]

Nelson, of course, was susceptible to being gained by anyone who fed his own huge ego, let alone one as overwhelming as Emma Hamilton. From the beginning he liked her, and since it was his nature to return goodwill extravagantly, whatever the station of its bearer, he had no time for those who whispered malignantly about Lady Hamilton's background.

Still, that background was important and underpinned her behaviour. Always there was an insecurity in Emma, a need to prove herself worthy of the great station she had reached. And always there was another lurking in corners of her mind – that former lover whose work of rehabilitation she desperately wanted to consummate, and for whom she still nursed a suppressed jealousy and half-hidden need to please. Hers had been an eccentric rags-to-riches Pygmalion past that constantly leaked out. The fine gowns of the diplomat's lady could not disguise the down-to-earth manner and Liverpudlian accent that made precious English women with cut-glass voices shake their heads. Nor did they, or their wearer's infectious influence, match the care-worn, homely, round-faced, retiring person usually found behind Emma, sitting quietly in the corners of rooms away from the more splendid company. A shadowy companion with the look of an elderly retainer recruited from the plain hard labour of another world, Mrs Cadogan, as she called herself, was actually Emma's mother. She was, wrote one observer with scarcely veiled contempt, 'what one might expect'.[43]

Nevertheless, the Hamiltons were not reluctant to admit Emma's lowly origins, and viewed her progress with a degree of pride. Nelson learned something of Lady Hamilton's story during his first days in Naples. She had been born on 26 April 1765 in Neston parish on the Wirral peninsula in Cheshire. Her father was an illiterate Ness blacksmith, Henry Lyon, and to her dying day Emma's letters betrayed her lack of formal education. Like many a girl of that class she entered domestic service, but there her life took a wholly individual turn and began to read like modern romantic fiction. Somehow the young woman found her way to London, and after a number of domestic situations ended up in the home of a noted 'madame' in Arlington Street. At her tender age she was probably being groomed for prostitution, but in 1781, when she was sixteen, she was whisked to Uppark on the South Downs, the house of Sir Harry Featherstonhaugh, an intemperate young baronet, and in the spring of 1782 gave birth to a child.

From red-blooded Sir Harry, Emma passed to the Honourable Charles Greville, second son of the Earl of Warwick. It was Greville who put the girl on an upward course. He established Emma and her mother in his house in Edgware Row in London, undertook to protect and educate her, and to introduce her by and by into society. She unquestionably loved him deeply, but when Greville decided he wanted to marry an heiress and found Emma suddenly inconvenient, he palmed her off on his widower uncle, Sir William Hamilton. Tricked into going to Naples in 1786, she ultimately accepted her fate, though for long afterwards the bitterness and sense of betrayal was wont to slip from her pen. Sir William was middle-aged, but he was kind, and she eventually learned to love him. Moreover, she prospered in Naples, attacking the deficiencies of her education, gaining a rudimentary command of French and Italian, mastering the art of entertaining, and winning considerable acclaim for her social accomplishments. She married Hamilton in 1791 and was accepted at the Neapolitan court, where her growing friendship with the queen was fast making her a political force in the Kingdom. We still await a full assessment of her role in Italian politics, but the journey from Neston to the Neapolitan palaces was certainly the stuff of legend.

Her future was to be no less erratic. Since Emma and Fanny eventually competed for Nelson's love and grew to hate each other, it is usual to compare them. They are depicted as fire and ice, with Emma vibrant, burning and passionate, and Fanny cold, controlled and correct. Emma wordly, ambitious, adventurous and extrovert, Fanny domestic, retiring and dull. Emma the exotic beauty, Fanny the plain sparrow. And most of all, Emma, who understood, nurtured and shared Nelson's genius, and Fanny who stifled it with a blanket.

They were very different women, of course, but Fanny has suffered more from the exercise than she deserves. Until recently many Nelson biographers, concerned to defend their hero at all costs, enhanced the image of a loyal but cold and suffocating wife. What she did, particularly in caring for Nelson's father during long years the captain spent at sea, has seldom been truly reckoned, and no one who reads her letters can doubt the passionate love she bore him or her pride in his achievements. Unlike Emma, there was nothing flamboyant or overstated about Fanny, but she had considerable charm and impressed people. 'I am more pleased with her if possible than ever,' wrote Captain Thomas Masterman Hardy after breakfasting with her in 1802. 'She certainly is one of the best women in the world.' She was also a woman of silent strengths, and though ultimately defeated by Emma survived a sad old age with considerable dignity. The victor, on the other hand, self-destructed within a few years of her lover's death.[44]

None of those shadows were there in 1793, when Nelson first set eyes on Emma Hamilton. She debuts modestly in his letters and journals for 14 September, and while Horatio happily added the Hamiltons to his list of regular correspondents it was to Sir William that he usually wrote. On their part they often spoke of 'you and your good boy' after Nelson's departure, but there was no hint of the notorious triangle that would eventually develop.[45]

The fourteenth of September 1794 was another memorable day for Nelson, however. Leaving the *Agamemnon* preparing for the king's visit, he accompanied Sir William to Acton's for dinner. Among the dignitaries at the table were a Spanish naval captain and the Spanish ambassador, but Nelson eagerly recorded that he and Sir William were held behind when the others had gone, and personally shown around the first minister's 'most magnificent house'. That evening a contented Nelson retired to the Palazzo Sessa, where Emma received some 'princess' who doubled as first lady of the chamber to the queen. The princess promised to visit Nelson's ship the following Monday, and flattered the captain with the queen's good wishes.[46]

The next day was Sunday, and Sir William and Nelson were on board the *Agamemnon* at nine in the morning awaiting the visit from the king. Hamilton received a fifteen-gun salute as he arrived. Unfortunately, the swell was too great for Ferdinand to attend, but he asked the pair to dine with him again and Nelson found himself 'placed' at the king's 'right hand, before our ambassador and all the nobles present'. His Majesty promised to visit the *Agamemnon* the next day, but also told Nelson that the first two thousand men for Hood would be marched into town at dawn and he was welcome to review them. Consequently, Nelson and Hamilton pitched up early on 16 September and jostled their way to the front of a thin part of the large crowd that had gathered to watch as Ferdinand pompously led three battalions of the garrison of Capua through the town. When the king saw Nelson and Hamilton he halted the march and 'dressed' his men before parading them before the important observers.[47]

Back on board the *Agamemnon* Nelson entertained the Hamiltons and other English expatriates to a ten o'clock breakfast, an event one suspects that was largely of Emma's making. The captain duly found himself shaking hands and bowing to the Bishop of Winchester, Mrs Henrietta North, Lord and Lady Plymouth, Lord Grandison and Lady Gertrude Villiers. But the pleasure of the king's company was again and finally foregone. At noon, just before the breakfast guests were departing in readiness for His Majesty, a message from Sir John Acton arrived. A French frigate with an English prize and two French merchantmen had been seen off the southern tip of Sardinia on the 12th. They had been repairing topmasts at the time, and there was a chance that Nelson might catch them if he hurried. With seven Neapolitan ships and a Spanish frigate in the harbour, he did not hesitate. Though Nelson's ship had not finished provisioning and some of her casks were still ashore, he felt on trial. 'I considered that the city of Naples looked what an English man of war would do, [and] I ordered my barge to be manned, sent the ladies on shore, and in two hours my ship was under sail . . .'[48]

There was something special about Naples. Goethe had spoken of it as a 'paradise' in which 'everyone lives in a state of intoxicated self-forgetfulness'. As the city faded behind the wake of the *Agamemnon*, Nelson too tasted that heady draught. It is not difficult to understand why. Naples had given Nelson everything he craved in abundance. Here he had met exciting new friends, who had thrown their house open to him and attended his every need. Here he had met a prime minister and king who had feted and flattered him, and granted his every wish. Here, too, he had been treated with immense reverence, and placed above all others. Thousands of men had been instantly mobilised at his command. Within hours of Nelson's departure from Naples two thousand soldiers, two seventy-fours, four frigates and corvettes and a transport were on their way to Toulon. Nelson lapped up his new status like a thirsty dog. Never had he been treated like this before, and as Naples receded he was in a state of warm euphoria.[49]

In a journal clearly written with posterity in mind, Nelson confided, 'I believe we carry with us the good wishes of Naples, and of Sir William and Lady Hamilton in particular, which I esteem more than all the rest. Farewell Naples! May those who were kind to me be repaid ten-fold. If I am successful, I return. If otherwise, [I] go to Toulon.'[50]

4

Nelson's plan to return to Naples went awry, however, and the French frigate eluded him. He was left with a mysterious incident that took place in the night of 18 September. Nelson was summoned from his cot with the news that two ships seemed to be converging upon the *Agamemnon* from different directions. It was dark, but Nelson suspected the sinister shapes materialising from the gloom might be Algerian pirates mistaking the British warship for a fat merchantman. Two days before he had heard that two such raiders had plundered a ship in the area, and receiving no replies to his signals he fired a fusillade of round and grape and closed in. By the time the British were able to board the two vessels, which turned out to be a ship and a galley, they had been abandoned. Both were armed with ten guns and swivels, and many small arms were found aboard, but the prize court in Leghorn later considered them harmless Genoese traders. Nelson rued that he did not even get salvage money.[51]

Soon he was at Leghorn himself, collecting the various prize crews he had sent there and replenishing his ship's supplies. His men were worn out by the relentless service, and three died in a week. 'I am going into Leghorn absolutely to save my poor fellows,' Nelson wrote.[52]

Leghorn belonged to the Grand Duchy of Tuscany, one of the small neutral powers that complicated war and displomacy in the Mediterranean. When the *Agamemnon* arrived on 25 September, John Udny, the British consul, came aboard to inform Captain Nelson about local sensibilities. Things could be better, Udny said. Apart from the disappointments in the prize courts, the British had annoyed the governor by trying to ship oxen to Hood's fleet in Toulon. A forty-gun French frigate, *L'Imperieuse*, was also in the harbour, full of die-hard republicans. Like many of the French ships at that time it was in a state of turmoil, and the captain was being deposed by his men. Looking at her through his telescope Nelson judged the frigate easy prey, but his hands were tied. This was a neutral port, open to belligerents of both sides so long as they observed a truce. Nelson kept the Frenchman under constant surveillance, ready to follow her the moment she ran for the open sea, but days passed without the frigate stirring. Finally Nelson blinked first. He was needed in Toulon and had to sail at the end of the month.[53]

Along the way he took two more prizes, both carrying supplies to the French garrisons in Corsica. One was a Genoese bark with hides and fruit and the other a Frenchman laden with wine. Nelson also saw the Neapolitan reinforcements at sea. When he reached Toulon on 5 October the first two contingents from Naples had already arrived, and the last, with provisions and thirty-two pieces of artillery, was due to sail. As the *Agamemnon* slipped among the other British ships in the outer roads Nelson realised how badly those reinforcements were needed, for affairs at Toulon had taken a turn for the worse.

Hood's position was serious. A superior French army investing the town had gained command of the surrounding heights. Its artillery, including pieces served by an ambitious young officer named Napoleon Bonaparte, were throwing shot and shells at the allied forts and across the harbour. Hood had fifteen miles of vulnerable defences to man, and was putting together a polyglot force of 12,500 Britons, Spaniards, Neapolitans, Sardinians and Piedmontese, but the redcoats were few and many of the others proved almost useless. The Spaniards, who were holding important positions, appeared to confuse their right and left shoulders in drill, and were apt to 'run away, officers and men together'. Yet Hood's ships sat as oblivious to the descending shells as if they were anchored in Spithead, and the admiral remained optimistic. He still hoped for major reinforcements, his men were conducting brilliant sorties against the encircling forces and there were hopes that the besiegers would quarrel among themselves. When Nelson went on board the *Victory* on 6 October it was difficult not to catch some of the old admiral's enthusiasm. 'He is so good an officer that every body must respect him,' Nelson told his wife.[54]

He was a hard taskmaster though, with steely words for those such as the captain of the *Iris* who tried to excuse failure. Nelson's performance at Naples pleased Hood, however, and he asked the captain what he could do for him. Typically, Nelson's thoughts were for his followers and Hood promised to serve the *Agamemnon*'s officers. Bullen and Suckling were taken aboard the flagship and promised promotion. Bullen became a commander before the end of November, while Suckling received his commission as a lieutenant the following March, and got the command of the small *St Croix* to boot. In August 1794, Hood took Fellows, another of Nelson's young gentlemen, into the *Victory*.

Hood also had further orders for Nelson, and the *Agamemnon* left the fleet on the evening of 9 October. He was bound for Cagliari in

Sardinia, where he was to join the squadron of Commodore Robert
Linzee of the *Alcide*. Linzee's squadron had just failed to uproot the
French garrisons in Corsica, and the island remained a good hunting
ground for prizes as numerous small ships slipped back and forth with
enemy supplies. Skirting the eastern coast of Corsica on the 16th the
Agamemnon intercepted a French tartan, *L'Aimable*, on its way from
Bastia to Toulon with sixty-five sick soldiers. He entrusted the prize
to the British *Colossus*, which was making for Leghorn, and spent the
next day trying to flush a French privateer from the nearby island of
Capraia, a possession of neutral Genoa. Landing one of his officers,
Nelson got the permission of the local governor to move against the
elusive Frenchman, and sent Hinton in with two rowing boats loaded
with armed men. The privateer was nowhere to be seen, but on the
18th Hinton brought out a Genoese vessel from Bastia, laden with
French wheat.[55]

Then, having sent the prize to Cagliari with a skeleton crew, Nelson
sailed into his first real sea fight.

5

Two o'clock in the morning, 22 October 1793, off Monte Santo on
the east coast of Sardinia. The *Agamemnon* was steering south on its
passage to Cagliari when five sails were seen ahead, standing across
their path to the northwest. No one could make them out, either from
the quarterdeck or the fighting tops, but Nelson supposed the ships
to be Neapolitan or Sardinian. But they were certainly large ships,
possibly even sail of the line . . . in the darkness it was possible to
take one of them for the *Duquesne*, an eighty-gun French ship known
to be at large.

About thirty minutes passed before the distant ships spotted the
Agamemnon approaching. Nelson watched as signal rockets flew
above the strangers, and then they tacked across the wind and stood
away to the eastwards, in the direction of the open sea. The ships
were some three miles away on the windward bow and Nelson turned
to pursue.

The *Agamemnon* may have been a ship of the line, but under sail
she sped like a frigate and by four Nelson had come within hailing
distance of the nearest of the ships. She was plainly a big frigate, but
Nelson was puzzled by her shyness and uncertain of her nationality
so he withheld his fire. The men waited anxiously at their stations as

the captain had the stranger hailed in French. There was no answer. Instead the frigate made more sail. Nelson opened his lower gun ports, and fired an eighteen-pound shot ahead of her as a signal to come to, but this merely prompted the frigate to run for it. She fired more rockets to signal her consorts to windward and crammed on all sail.

Nelson now ordered all his sails to be set, and chased the enemy ship, trying to keep her within two compass points on the bow to prevent her from gaining any advantages of the wind. At the same time he kept an eye on the other ships which were coming after him on his windward quarter, and wondered what part they might play if there was a serious battle. The frigate had a start on him, and in a fresh breeze the pace reached six or so knots, but by daylight the *Agamemnon* had got within gunshot again. By five they were at half gun range. The French, who had been signalling to each other all night, now raised their colours in defiance. It was an accepted custom of war that a ship never fired under a false or masked flag, and every officer on Nelson's quarterdeck knew that there would now be a fight. Puffs of smoke from the frigate's stern guns opened the exchange.

Now Nelson got a smart, and perhaps surprising, lesson in battle tactics. The enemy ship was the *Melpomene* of forty guns, 'one of the finest [frigates] ever built in France', according to Hood, and she was exceptionally well handled by Captain Gay, an officer with a reputation for intrepidity. Gay resorted to 'yawing', periodically bringing his ship's head round to allow her broadside guns to bear instead of relying solely upon her small stern battery. The tactic posed a considerable threat to the *Agamemnon*, because it exposed the pursuing British ship's vulnerable bows to terrific discharges while Nelson was confined to the use of his few forward bow-chaser guns. As Midshipman Hoste noted, 'our situation was rather unfavourable, as our shot did not at all times hit her'. The *Agamemnon* was saved from severe damage and casualties by the French custom of firing high to tear away masts, yards, sails and rigging. Her main topmast was 'shot to pieces', and her mainmast, mizzenmast and fore yard seriously damaged, but only one man was killed and six wounded, apparently from wreckage crashing down from above.[56]

Despite the frigate's attempts to cripple Nelson's advance, he gradually worked close enough to get in broadsides of his own, and the British gunners fearlessly wreaked their revenge, blasting at the *Melpomene*'s hull, throwing wooden splinters about and cutting men

down. Nelson greatly exaggerated when he claimed to have reduced
the frigate to a 'shattered' if not a sinking condition, but even young
Hoste, who had no superiors to appease, told his father that 'our last
broadside did her infinite damage'.

While firing was continuing Nelson anxiously swept the other enemy
ships on his weather quarter with a telescope, and thought he could
pick out a ship of the line, two frigates and a brig. Though poor sailers
compared with the *Melpomene*, they were coming up fast, and Nelson
doubted whether he could finish the frigate off before they entered
the fight. At about seven he summoned his officers and asked them
whether they agreed that the biggest vessel on the weather quarter
was a line of battle ship. They thought so, though erroneously. In fact,
she was the forty-gun frigate *La Minerve* (Captain Zacharie Allemand),
armed with twenty-six eighteens and fourteen nines, while her consorts
were two frigates and a fine corvette, the thirty-six-gun *La Fortunée*,
Le Mignonne of thirty-two guns and the twenty-gun *La Flèche*. The
Agamemnon was more than a match for any one of her antagonists,
but together they considerably outgunned and outnumbered the British
ship, and their manpower was far greater. Nelson's company had been
reduced by the crews he had put on prizes, and only three hundred
and fifty men now stood at their quarters. There were probably more
on the *Melpomene* alone.[57]

As Nelson weighed his chances in a battle with an entire enemy
squadron, his troubles multiplied. At about eight or nine the wind fell
away. With her masts and sails injured, the *Agamemnon* was sluggish
in the calm and open to attack from the undamaged ships of the
French squadron as they responded to the urgent signals of the stricken
Melpomene. Gradually the wounded enemy frigate hauled up towards
her sister ships, which were soon lowering boats to send her reinforcements and aid. On her part, the head of the bruised *Agamemnon*
paid round to the southward, leaving the enemy ships within a league
to the northeast with their sails set. Suddenly, after only about fifteen
minutes of stillness, the breeze returned and the sails began to fill. It
was time for both sides to assess their situation and decide whether
or not to renew the engagement.

At this moment Nelson's inexperience came to the surface. With
none of his usual decisiveness, he summoned his officers to the quarterdeck for their second consultation. Apparently they still believed
they were up against at least one ship of the line, the forty-gun *La
Minerve*, an 'enormous frigate', looking grotesquely large in the poor

light. 'Do you think we can, by hauling our wind to the northeast after the frigate, close with her before she joins her consorts?' asked the captain.

'No, it is impossible' was the general opinion.

'From what you see of the state of our ship, is she fit to go into action with such a superior force which is against us, without some small refit, and refreshments for our people?' Nelson wanted to know.

'She certainly is not,' the officers replied. Or, at least, that is what Nelson said they said.

He glanced at the Frenchmen, now bearing away northwest by west, and turned to the master. 'Mr Wilson, wear the ship, and lay her head to the westward. Let some of the best men be employed refitting the rigging, and the carpenters getting crows and capstan bars to prevent our wounded spars from coming down, and to get the wine for the people and some bread, for it might be half-an-hour before we were again in action.' He had decided to pause for breath – and then to fight again if he had to, even against five opponents.

But neither side wanted to renew the contest. Nelson was so short-handed that it took him till noon to get his rigging, masts and yards in a condition to proceed, and the French made no attempt to interfere. Accordingly, the combatants withdrew. With the carpenters slaving to plug the shot holes, the *Agamemnon* limped into Cagliari on 24 October. Commodore Linzee was Hood's brother-in-law. He was there with the *Alcide* and four other ships, but seemed totally uninterested in Nelson's plight and refused to loan carpenters, sail makers and tools to help repair the battered ship, despite the fact that he planned to take his squadron to sea in the morning. Nelson was ready on time, but his people had had to work all night mending sails, replacing top and topgallant masts, splicing rigging, fixing holes and fishing the mainmast.

Nelson was probably stung by Linzee's reception, and perhaps worried that he would be blamed for failing to secure an inferior vessel. He made a careful note of the advice his officers had given during the fight, as if he expected to be called to account, and put the best gloss on the action he could. But if Hood made no complaint, nor did he look as if he had the time to acknowledge Nelson's adventure, and Horatio prepared his own account for the newspapers. Never before had he resorted to such blatant self-publicity, but he would soon use the method again, also in the belief that he was being undersold in the official dispatches. Nelson's version, which went through his brother Maurice to the London papers, totted the opposition up to 170 guns and 1,600 men, as if he had fought all five enemy ships simultaneously, and *The Times* published a brief but laudatory summation on 13 December. However, it was enough to do the trick. According to those back home this one brief clipping brought him 'very great credit'. Alerted to the power of the press, Nelson thoughtfully stored the information away. He hoped Hood would report any successes of the *Agamemnon* in his dispatches, and that they would appear in the *London Gazette* in the usual way, but if not the news-hungry press seemed happy to publish independent accounts from the Mediterranean.[58]

In the months that followed Nelson was also gratified to find that his sea fight had been more decisive than at first appeared. Indeed, it led to the capture of the entire French squadron. His opponents had been sailing steadily under top- and foresails from Tunis to Nice when they encountered Nelson, but the *Agamemnon* inflicted considerable damage upon the *Melpomene*. In January the following year a French deserter claimed that she lost twenty-four men killed and fifty wounded, and was 'so much damaged as to be laid up dismantled in St Fiorenzo. She would have struck long before we parted but for the gunner who opposed it, and the colours were [about to be] ordered to be struck by general consent' when the ships were becalmed and she was re-inforced. The skirmish deflected the French squadron to Corsica, where the *Melpomene* could be repaired. When the British captured the island in 1794 all five ships consequently fell into their hands.[59]

As he reckoned the pros and cons of his first naval engagement Nelson must also have realised that if the enemy had been more enter-prising they might have defeated the *Agamemnon*. Indeed, it was relief rather than disappointment that dominated his first reflections. As he wrote in his journal after the action closed, 'How thankful ought I to be, and I hope am, for the mercies of Almighty God manifested to me this day.'[60]

6

Linzee led his ships out of Cagliari at seven in the morning of 26 October. There were four sail of the line – the flagship *Alcide*, and the *Berwick*, *Illustrious* and *Agamemnon* – and two frigates. The squadron sailed south, following sealed orders Nelson had brought from Hood, and five days later anchored in the Bay of Tunis on the Barbary coast.

Tunis was a place quite unlike any Nelson had yet seen in the Mediterranean. It was nominally part of the Ottoman empire, but was known – and feared – as a city state thriving on the fruits of piracy. Even the French found it convenient to pay the bey of Tunis protection money. When Linzee sailed in he saw a Spanish squadron and two French warships, the eighty-gun *Duquesne* and a corvette, sitting smugly at anchor, as well as a large number of French merchantmen sheltering further up near a fort. Tunis was supposed to be a neutral port, open to ships of every nation, but Nelson expected a fight. With his instinct for finding the hottest spot he anchored the *Agamemnon* between the two French warships, planning to use both his broadsides to engage them simultaneously if firing began.

After a few days Linzee began 'a damned palaver' with the bey in his green-domed palace. Nelson, of course, thought it even more frustrating than Hood's inaction before Toulon earlier in the year, and wanted a speedy and decisive resolution of the matter. The bey, he reasoned, was not going to agree to any attack being made upon the French, but presented with a *fait accompli* he might be reconciled by a cut of £50,000 in spoils. Besides, there was another reason for acting quickly: prize money. Fearful of being seized, the French merchantmen were feverishly unloading their precious cargoes, worth some £300,000. If the convoy was stripped bare, it might scarcely be worth the taking, while in the last extremity the enemy warships could always evade capture by declaring for the French royalists. Nelson had no difficulty advising Linzee's council of war that they should seize the convoy forthwith, and then negotiate with the bey from a position of strength. In unguarded comments to Fanny and the Duke of Clarence he was even more bullish, and suggested knocking the bey's forts down 'about his ears' if he objected. Fortunately, Commodore Linzee understood that admirals had to be statesmen as well as fighters, and did not care for such heavy-handedness. The principles of neutrality could not be dishonoured with impunity, and the bey was entirely capable of retaliating against British commerce. Moreover, Linzee had Hood's express instructions to avoid giving offence. 'My spirits are low indeed,' a rebuffed Nelson confided in his journal. 'Had I been commodore most likely I should have been broke by this time, for certainly I should have taken every Frenchman here without negotiating . . . I believe that the people of England will never blame an officer for taking a French line-of-battle ship.'[61]

Nelson's thinking, in this instance, was influenced by financial considerations as well as his customary pugnacity. Those dozens of French merchantmen up the bay represented an enormous amount of prize money. Linzee, Nelson later admitted, 'lost my fortune'. The commodore was not oblivious to either the political or the pecuniary advantages of seizing the French ships, but tried diplomacy instead. He asked the bey's permission to attack the French ships, and was refused. In fact, the bey was neither as mercenary nor as foolish as the British supposed, and declined to be bribed or persuaded. Linzee offered him one of the smaller French merchantmen, and described the French as enemies of all mankind, unworthy of neutral protection, but the bey politely pointed out that the English had also once executed their king, and that it was not for him to intervene in disputes between Christian powers. He would be grateful if the British respected the neutrality of his port.[62]

Stumped, Linzee sent a frigate to Hood for more instructions and got rid of Nelson on a ten-day cruise. The *Agamemnon*'s sortie was fruitless, and Nelson was merely buffeted by wind, rain and thunderstorms, but he was glad to escape the humiliating tedium of Tunis. The sight of that big French eighty-gunner sitting ripe for the taking was more than he could stand. It was a large battle unit to let loose in the Mediterranean, and impudent, too. Every morning and evening her men sang the 'Marseillaise' with an English flag draped contemptuously over the roundhouse. When Nelson returned to Tunis on 26 November he found the stalemate intact, though the French had hauled their ships up against the shore to make them more difficult to attack. Fortunately, relief was at hand.[63]

On the 29th the *Nemesis* frigate came in from Hood, and Nelson was summoned to Linzee's flagship. The admiral endorsed Linzee's policy of negotiation, but had some 'very handsome' words for Nelson as well as independent work for him to do. Indeed, he was to command a small squadron – his first since that unofficial command in the Leeward Islands many years before. It was a heartwarming compliment, because there were senior captains in the fleet who would have enjoyed a detached command, however modest in scale.[64]

Nelson's orders, dated 15 November, were satisfying. Hood had been worrying about the French garrisons in Corsica. They had refused to declare for the royalists, and when Linzee's squadron had tried to subdue them by force in October he had taken a beating and lost fifty men killed and wounded. The only alternative was to blockade their strongholds, starve them of supplies and force them to surrender.

Ashore Corsican partisans were trying to liberate their island from the French, but only a comprehensive naval campaign could effectively shrivel the enemy positions. For this work Nelson was given the *Lowestoffe* frigate at Tunis and several ships already stationed in the waters between Corsica and Genoa, the *Mermaid*, *Tartar* and *Topaze* frigates and the *Scout* brig. Nelson's instructions also mentioned the French squadron he had fought the previous month. It was believed to be at St Fiorenzo in Corsica, but if victuals ran low it might make a run for the mainland, and Nelson was to keep a lookout. Hood cautioned Nelson to give as little offence to neutrals as possible, but clearly reposed confidence in his judgement. With the orders came one of the admiral's 'my dear Nelson' letters, wishing him good fortune. Liberated from Linzee's uninspiring leadership, Nelson perked up at once. 'Thank God, Lord Hood . . . has taken me from under his command,' he said.[65]

Arriving on his station, Nelson found that his force effectively amounted to two or three frigates, the *Lowestoffe*, *Meleager* and *Leda*, and a twenty-four-gun sloop, the *Amphitrite*. Though little known, their commanders were Nelson's first captains, and seemed to have liked him. Charles Tyler of the *Meleager*, a slight, handsome, hawk-faced officer who limped from a wound taken in the American war, would grace two of Nelson's great victories and carry a lock of his admiral's hair into retirement. On his ship were two lieutenants Nelson also learned to admire. One, Walter Serecold, would distinguish himself at Nelson's side in Corsica, and the other was the celebrated Thomas Masterman Hardy. The captain of the *Leda* was George Campbell, who would later sign himself Nelson's 'very much obliged and faithful friend' in days before his life soured and turned him to suicide. Anthony Hunt commanded the *Amphitrite*, and William Wolseley the old *Lowestoffe*. Two years older than Nelson though junior in rank, Wolseley was another who had been tried and tested in battle, and carried inside him a bullet received during an attack on Trincomalee ten years before. He and Nelson formed a good friendship during their brief service together, and even agreed to pool prize money. It seems that Nelson benefited most from the arrangement; he only salvaged a deserted French gunboat that December, whereas the *Lowestoffe* sent six neutrals into Leghorn, all suspected of shipping French supplies. Nonetheless, Wolseley reaped a reward of a different kind when the following spring Nelson persuaded Hood to transfer him to a better frigate, the *Imperieuse*. 'I hope we may soon meet again,' Wolseley wrote to his benefactor, 'and that I shall have the pleasure of shaking you by the hand.'[66]

Nelson's ships cruised off St Fiorenzo, where the French kept the greater part of their Corsican troops, and as far southwest as Calvi, punished by December gales. Fortunately Tuscany had now thrown in its lot with the allies and Leghorn was a secure base at their backs. The captains intercepted some supplies running to or from Corsica and kept the French frigate squadron holed up in St Fiorenzo, but Nelson was occasionally diverted to other duties. In December, Hood ordered the *Agamemnon* to patrol the Italian riviera, and towards the end of the year Nelson was given the job of escorting a mutinous ship, the *Arethusa*, to Porto Ferraio in Elba, where she was to be temporarily decommissioned.[67]

Although the year drew to its close with the Jacobins counterattacking on different fronts, Nelson clung to his belief that the war would not last. As long as Hood held the French fleet in his fist, Britain's command of the Mediterranean was unchallenged and hardly warranted the maintenance of a large fleet. Some of the captains began talking of going home, and Nelson flirted with the possibility of going out to the West Indies as second-in-command to the Duke of Clarence. There were also times when he thought of the world he had left behind and the people who loved and waited for him, but active service remained in his soul.[68]

The first letter from Fanny had reached him in Tunis at the end of November, brought from the fleet by the *Nemesis*. It reminded the captain of sleepy, silent Norfolk, where the harvest was in, the barren fields were being swept by cruel east winds and the salt marshes were spotted with redshanks, gulls and oystercatchers. There, he knew, were two people who yearned for his return. The Reverend Edmund Nelson confessed that though he loved silence and solitude he felt a superfluity of both when his favourite son was away. He and Fanny comforted each other when they were together. Fanny had taken apartments at Swaffham during the summer, trying to maintain a semblance of normal existence with the help of one or other of the Thurlow girls of Burnham as her maids. Her music amused her, but she had little society and even the annual visit to the Walpoles seemed empty without her husband. The first of many lonely Christmases followed, and then she began thinking of following the reverend to Bath in the spring . . . if Horatio did not come home.[69]

7

Seventeen hundred and ninety-three had been a momentous year, but its dying gasps had one more dramatic twist of fate for the war in the Mediterranean. British naval supremacy was suddenly overthrown. In the last days of the year Toulon fell, and with it all immediate prospects of ending the naval war east of Gibraltar.

It was a huge blow and a serious blot on Hood's record. He had been starved of satisfactory reinforcements to the last, and wretchedly served by the allies, but he had also stubbornly refused to listen to the advice of his military men and failed to make adequate preparations for a withdrawal. When the besieging Jacobins drove in important outposts on the night of 17 December the old admiral finally knew the moment had come. It was his duty to destroy the dockyards, arsenal and enemy warships before pulling out his forces, but the job was botched. Thirteen ships of the line were taken out or destroyed, but eighteen were abandoned to the republicans. Eighteen capital ships were left to challenge the British Mediterranean fleet and to threaten her allies. For Hood, the man who had criticised Rodney for failing to consummate a victory, Hood the completist, Hood who had inspired Nelson with his perfectionism, it was a terrific oversight, and one that would cast a long and dark shadow.

Hood was showing serious weaknesses in leadership. The British military men were fed up with him, and dissatisfaction was spreading to some of the naval officers. 'He has had the ingenuity of making nine out of ten in this squadron his avowed enemy by his overbearing and tyrannical conduct,' wrote Fremantle of the *Tartar*. The admiral was accused of favouritism, and was said to have treated one of his senior subordinates, Rear Admiral Sir Hyde Parker, with 'acrimony and vile humour'.[70]

When the allies abandoned Toulon the dire plight of the local French royalists and any townspeople suspected of sympathising with them created fearful scenes at the waterfront. Some were taken off by the retreating forces, while others, wailing and weeping, stampeded for what boats there were, terrified of being sacrificed to a brutal enemy, and leaving homes, property, friends and families behind. Those who escaped were lucky. Behind they left chaos, as the rabble ran bawling about the streets like bulls, smashing into shops and houses, looting and murdering. 'The mob rose,' Nelson heard from refugees who reached Leghorn. 'Death called forth all its myrmidons, who destroyed the miserable inhabitants in the shape of swords, pistols, fire and water. Thousands are said to be lost . . . Fathers are here without families, and families without fathers, the pictures of horror and despair.' When the republicans marched in, their ferocity was unbridled. Hundreds of people were executed. The mob bound loving couples back to back and tossed them into the harbour to jeer at as they drowned. 'Each teller,' said Nelson, 'makes the scene more horrible.'[71]

Nelson heard the news at Leghorn. He had realised that Toulon was difficult to hold without sufficient soldiers to command the surrounding heights, but expected the allies to cling to the harbour, at least until the French fleet and arsenal were destroyed, a feat he believed to be the work of no more than 'an hour'. Nelson blamed Hood's subordinates for the failure to burn the enemy ships, rather than the admiral himself, whom he still judged 'the best officer I ever saw'. He was relieved to hear that his patron was safe in Hyères Bay outside Toulon and notified the Admiralty. Furthermore, with typical consideration he also wrote to Lady Hood to say that her husband was safe. 'She must be very uneasy,' he remarked. No other officer in the fleet seems to have imagined the anxieties the black tidings from the Mediterranean would cause Lady Hood, and she was deeply moved by Nelson's letter and kept it to show her husband. 'Lady Hood speaks much of you,' Fanny told Nelson a year later. 'Will never forget the letter you wrote her.'[72]

What most distressed Nelson was the stream of refugees that reached Leghorn, old and young, sick and well, all ruined and destitute with their own harrowing stories to tell. To Nelson it was a stark demonstration of the corrosive effects of revolution. However unfeeling Britain's rulers might be, it seemed to him, they had never in his lifetime sunk to this. Instead of protection 'the poor inhabitants' of Toulon were subjected to the tyranny of a crazed mob, oppressed, pillaged and murdered. It had happened in Paris and other places, as Nelson had read in the papers, but this he saw at first hand. It brought home to Nelson the humanitarian and moral dimensions of constitutional conflict as nothing had done before, and fed his growing hatred for the new republic.[73]

He found himself the senior British officer at Leghorn when the first boatloads of refugees from Toulon arrived. Late in December two bulging brigs arrived filled with two hundred or so miserable passengers, some women and children, and about half wounded British servicemen. The next day it was *La Billette* corvette with another seventy French men and women. When Nelson tried to send them ashore old John Udny, the British consul, explained that the governor had refused the refugees permission to land. The fall of Toulon had sent a shock wave through the Mediterranean because it portended a major shift of power. Tuscany, which had only recently gone into the allied camp, was beginning to reconsider the propriety of its decision. Udny was ailing and ready to take to his bed, but no doubt encouraged by Nelson he managed to persuade the governor to compromise. The British and some of the sick and wounded from the first two transports were allowed to occupy buildings outside Leghorn on a temporary basis, but the rest and the passengers on the corvette were left on the ships in a 'wretched state'. Udny could only suggest that Nelson authorise him to hire a ship to house them in better quarters offshore while the politicians thrashed out a solution.[74]

Nelson was not on the best of terms with Governor Franco Seratti. The governor did not like the way Nelson talked to him man to man, rather than through Udny, and Hood had even felt it necessary to order an apology. Besides, Nelson could scarcely contain his contempt for a man he believed to be 'frightened to pieces' by the Jacobin successes. Perhaps wisely the refugee issue went to Hood and Lord Hervey, Britain's man in Florence, who arrived in Leghorn to discuss the problem at the beginning of the New Year. After some difficulties the Grand Duke of Tuscany consented to give the French refugees temporary asylum on Elba, and four thousand of them were soon landing there 'in want of every necessary of life', many of them sick or injured survivors of days at sea without access to a surgeon.[75]

The fall of Toulon did more than displace a dejected stream of humanity. It cost Britain a naval supremacy in the Mediterranean that would not be regained within five war-torn years.

XVIII

CORSICA

He leads: we hear our Seaman's call
In the roll of battles won;
For he is Britain's Admiral
Till the setting of her sun.
George Meredith, *Trafalgar Day*

1

'CORSICA is a wonderful fine island,' Nelson wrote to Fanny from his cabin in the *Agamemnon* on 13 February 1794. Certainly it was wild, its granite masses towering above a beautiful blue sea and some of its peaks snow-capped even in the most sweltering summers. It was a land of mountains with deep, ragged gorges, of marshy coastal plains, narrow, rocky harbours, and hills covered in timber and thorny maquis thicket. It was a land where a hardy peasantry fished for coral or cultivated olives, fruit and cereals while their sheep, goats and cattle foraged in the scrub. It was also, as every informed Briton then knew, a tortured island, ruled for centuries by foreigners, and torn by brave but bloody struggles for independence.[1]

Britons of that time went into Corsica the way the Philhellenes later went into Greece, stuffed with romantic ideals about freedom and self-determination, but most of them emerged bruised and disillusioned. Nelson was no exception. In 1794 he regarded the unruly and proud Corsicans as 'brave' and 'free' spirits, led by a great champion. Even in England Pasquale de Paoli was a symbol of patriotic fortitude. He had spent forty of his seventy years trying to liberate his homeland, first from the Genoese and then, after their claim to the island was

sold, from the French. A man of considerable ability and huge determination, Paoli had created a regular army, established a semblance
of order and democracy, founded a university and defeated the
Genoese, but in 1769 he was driven out by the French and began
years of exile. The British applauded him, giving him a pension and
admitting him to select circles, but after the French Revolution he
returned to Corsica, lured by possibilities of the island achieving a
more autonomous relationship within a new liberal France. He was
installed as governor in 1791, but soon saw his people sliding into a
fresh revolt, disaffected by a raft of issues that included sovereignty,
religion, land ownership, taxation, language and access to public
offices. Now, aged but unbroken, Paoli was a rebel again, with a price
on his head and an army of partisans. Nelson was moved by the
loyalty he inspired. 'This is pure affection,' he wrote. 'Paoli has nothing
to give them, no honours to bestow. It is the tribute of a generous
people to a chief who had sacrificed everything for their benefit. I
hope he will live to see the Corsicans truly free.'[2]

Paoli's forces may have been durable and sure-footed mountain
fighters, but they were undisciplined and ill-equipped, and resembled
nothing so much as a savage *banditti*, armed with fowling pieces and
clad in woollen jackets, waistcoats, breeches, buff leather gaiters and
dirty old ill-fitting French uniforms. They outnumbered the several
thousand French troops who held Corsica with the aid of some native
sympathisers, but were unequal to expelling them. The French
controlled the strategic northern peninsula of Cape Corse, and their
garrisons in St Fiorenzo, Bastia and Calvi were strongly entrenched
and impregnable to irregular forces. Paoli turned to the British for
help.

Nelson was not by nature an interventionist. He had begun the war
believing that French republicanism would burn itself out if left alone,
but the oppression of people generally disturbed him and he understood the importance of defending important liberties. He also knew
that Corsica was important to Britain – increasingly so. As long as
the French had bases in Corsica, its ports were havens for hostile
warships and privateers. British shipping in the eastern Mediterranean
was unsafe, and the Italian states, whether allied or neutral, were
exposed to attack. Hood's expulsion from Toulon had now increased
the island's significance tenfold. The Royal Navy needed a new base
in the Mediterranean. Naples was too far from the French coast, which
the British needed to watch or blockade, while Genoa was unfriendly.

Tuscany had suitable ports at Leghorn and Porto Ferraio in Elba but was wavering in its allegiance to the allies. The obvious alternative was Corsica. It had to be taken.

No one knew that more than Lord Hood. He was sceptical of the amount of support Paoli could provide a British task force, and was still smarting from the hiding Linzee's squadron had taken at St Fiorenzo the previous year, a defeat some blamed upon the inadequacies of the partisans. However, the admiral's needs had multiplied. He needed a base, and he needed a victory to restore morale among the allies and silence critics at home. On 4 January he put Captain Edward Cooke and an engineer on Corsica to investigate the feasibility of an invasion. Their report was encouraging. Despite their strength, the enemy garrisons seemed conquerable. Small boats were still shifting supplies along the coast from one French stronghold to another, but Nelson's blockade had reduced provisions and sickness was said to be spreading among the defenders. Enemy morale was believed to be low. Hood decided to go ahead.[3]

A more distinguished party stepped upon Corsican soil on 14 January. One of the trio was Sir Gilbert Elliot, an urbane diplomat soon to rule the island as Britain's viceroy, and with him were two senior army officers, Lieutenant Colonel John Moore (later the hero and victim of Corunna) and Major George Frederick Koehler. They were charged with preparing the ground for an invasion. Elliot ascertained that Paoli was willing to swap one set of masters for another and allow Corsica to become a British protectorate in return for the expulsion of the French, while the army officers studied the military situation. They were told that the French had 2,600 men on the island (actually an understatement), and concluded that though Calvi would be a hard nut to crack there was 'every reason to hope for success'. At about the same time Nelson was landing Lieutenant Andrews, where he spent three days practising his French upon the partisans, assuring Paoli that Hood would help him and looking for suitable places to disembark men and stores.[4]

For Hood the liberation of Corsica was imperative, but the job had to be done quickly. Now that a residue of the French fleet was at large and the Jacobins were counterattacking on land, the British fleet had to be stretched thin to meet its many obligations east of Gibraltar. Hood could not tie forces up in Corsica indefinitely.

At Hyères, Hood gathered his forces. Sixty sail of warships and transports were needed, but men were scarce. The fleet was so under strength that Hood applied for help to Malta and Naples, while hundreds of British soldiers from the 11th, 25th, 30th and 69th regiments were serving as auxiliary marines on the ships. Altogether, even reinforced by the 50th and 51st regiments from Gibraltar at the end of 1793, the British had no more than three thousand of their soldiers cooperating with the fleet. A few French royalists joined them, but after the repossession of Toulon there was a reluctance to rely on foreign soldiers.

While Hood fought with logistics, the invasion of Corsica suddenly thrust Captain Nelson to the forefront of the Mediterranean campaign. His blockade of the island, previously simply precautionary, became an operation of the first importance, paving the way for the British landings by gathering intelligence, encouraging the partisans and reducing the resources of the French garrisons. In recognition Hood increased the size of Nelson's command. During January four frigates, the *Juno*, *Romulus*, *L'Aigle* and *Tartar*, the twenty-four-gun *La Billette* and the *Fortune* gunboat joined his squadron, though Hood was soon having to recall the *Lowestoffe*. By trying to ensure that no more than one ship at a time reprovisioned at Leghorn, Nelson tightened his vigil, focusing his efforts on clearing the coasts of enemy gunboats and starving St Fiorenzo and Calvi of supplies.[5]

It was gruelling, wintry work. On 8 January the first of six days of gales, lashing rain and awesome seas savaged the ships. 'Such a series of bad weather I never experienced,' observed a sodden Nelson. But while his ships were driven a little to leeward they kept their order and station. Indeed, the Corsican campaign was turning *Agamemnon* into the finest battleship in the Mediterranean, honing its seamanship and gunnery to perfection in daily and difficult encounters. When Hood's fleet eventually joined him towards the end of the month Nelson's men demonstrated their worth in another burst of blustering gales. On the 27th, when even such a seasoned blockader as the *Leda* parted company under signals of distress, Nelson noted in his journal the 'appearance' of a storm. 'Made the ship as snug as possible,' he wrote. 'All night it blew such a gale as is very seldom felt. Neither canvas [n]or rope could stand it. All our sails blew in pieces. Made a great deal of water. A most amazing heavy sea. The ship under bare poles.' When the tempest peaked it drove every ship in the fleet off the station bar two – a frigate and the *Agamemnon*. Nelson fell back to Leghorn for brief repairs, but must have been satisfied that the watch had been maintained in such difficult circumstances.[6]

Day in, day out Nelson's ships stuck to their task, fair weather or foul, though they had their reverses. On the morning of 12 January two of the French warships, the *Melpomene* and *Le Mignonne*, broke out of St Fiorenzo and fought their way southwest into Calvi, exchanging shots with the *Leda* and *Meleager* as they did so. The French had only succeeded in shifting strength from one port to another but Nelson was disappointed. 'I had so closely blockaded Calvi that they must have surrendered to me at discretion,' he complained. 'Not a vessel before got in for the six weeks I have been stationed here. This supply will keep them a week or two longer.' Nelson exaggerated the effect of his blockade but not entirely, and Hood informed superiors that 'repeated information' testified that provisions in Corsica were in short supply.[7]

Also weighing on Nelson's mind were disturbing rumours that the eighty-gun *Duquesne* and a dozen small warships and twelve thousand men were planning to dash from Nice to relieve the beleaguered Corsican garrisons. Fortunately, his squadron only had to brush with the interfering French forces from Nice once. On 17 January, Nelson sent the *Leda* and *Amphitrite* in chase of a French warship and galley trying to get into Calvi with flour and other supplies. The wind dropped, and the galley's sweeps pulled her inshore and out of gunshot, but as the breeze improved the British worked so close to the warship, *L'Armée de Italie* of eighteen guns and swivels, that her crew set her on fire and jumped over the side. The British lowered boats, threw hawsers onto the stricken craft and towed it into deeper water, but the fire could not be extinguished and she was run upon a reef to burn.[8]

Reluctant to confine his attention to shipping, Nelson also began to launch amphibious raids upon French positions ashore. A tip-off that four hundred sacks of flour were stored at the only mill situated near St Fiorenzo led him to the first of these operations on 21 January. Nelson arrived offshore the previous evening with the *Lowestoffe* and the *Meleager* frigates in company and the *Fortune* gunboat. During the night the ships were in danger of being wrecked upon the rocky coast by large seas, but at six in the morning one hundred and twenty seamen and sailors were rowed to a landing place under the cover of the gunboat. A sputtering opposition was dispersed, and up to a thousand French regulars rushed by sea and land from St Fiorenzo and Bastia arrived too late. Nelson's raiders had burned the watermill, thrown the flour into the sea and gone. In addition the British also intercepted a pair of tartans trying to ship provisions, and two days later destroyed a third vessel.⁹

Nelson's operations were small-scale but significant, fine-tuning the skills of the British crews, withering the resources of the French and gathering intelligence for Hood. When the task force itself arrived on 25 January it was immediately scattered by the gales and blown towards Elba, and not until 7 February did fourteen hundred British soldiers begin splashing ashore in Mortella Bay at St Fiorenzo. The landings, supervised by Linzee, were clumsily made, according to Nelson. 'Expedition ought to be the universal word and deed,' he grumbled. Nevertheless, a mixed force of soldiers and sailors were soon pulling guns into place to attack the forts at St Fiorenzo while the fleet occupied the bay.¹⁰

The arrival of the fleet with large numbers of senior officers threatened Nelson's independence, but Hood had been impressed by his services and immediately transferred his small squadron to Bastia. When St Fiorenzo fell Hood intended to advance upon Bastia, a much stronger position, and once again Nelson would prime the assault with a preliminary blockade.

Thrilled to be free of moribund superiors, the captain of the *Agamemnon* happily embraced his new duties. As the pulse of his life quickened with renewed purpose the last lingering charms of domesticity slipped gently into the background. The campaign generated the excitement he loved and put him at the epicentre of the naval war in the Mediterranean, opening a way to martial glory. 'We are still in the busy scene of war,' he told his uncle, 'a situation in which I own I feel pleasure, more especially as all my actions have given great satisfaction to my commander-in-chief.'¹¹

2

On the eastern coast of Corsica, at the foot of the mountainous Cape Corse peninsula jutting confidently northwards into the sea, was Bastia. It was a large town in those days, the largest in the island, containing more than eight thousand citizens, and until recently had been the Corsican capital. Nevertheless, when Nelson first gave Bastia his close attention it was unusually well stocked with corn, animals and the coal needed to heat shot because it was close to supplies in Italy. Even with British cruisers on the prowl, it was comparatively easy for small boats to run to Bastia from the neutral islands of Elba and Capraia.

Moreover, Bastia was formidably fortified. A high wall skirted the sea, punctured with twenty or more embrasures bristling with guns. Inside the harbour, behind a fine mole, nestled *La Flêche*, the corvette from the squadron Nelson had engaged off Sardinia, but now stripped of her cannons to strengthen the batteries ashore. The entrance to the harbour was relatively narrow, passing between a lighthouse at the end of the mole on the right and an ancient citadel with its keep on the left, the latter mounting a formidable array of artillery. As Captain Nelson's glass swept above the lines of white houses to the low hills between the rear of the town and the mountains towering grandly behind, he also picked out four stone forts – Monte Sorrato, Lacroix, Gaetano and Straforelle, small, clumsily constructed, but for all that of considerable strength. Above those he counted three more works, perched precariously on the heights. Closer to the sea front, the approach to the town in the north was guarded by an appreciable redoubt, Camp de Cabanelle, while south of Bastia, close to malarial swamps stood a command post, Camp St Michel, supported by new batteries. If these fortifications were resolutely defended they would not be overcome without difficulty. Nelson consoled himself with a notion that only about four hundred regulars and sixteen hundred irregulars manned the town's defences, and that provisions and supplies were daily being eroded by his blockade.[12]

In addition to the garrison at Bastia the French had small forces spotted about the area, especially at Rogliano, commanding Cape Corse. It seemed obvious to Captain Nelson that if the local peasantry could be convinced that the balance of power had changed and their former French masters were impotent, it would be possible to isolate the smaller enemy detachments and compel them to withdraw. In addition to his war on supplies, therefore, he encouraged resistance against the French at every point. He loosed the frigates *Lowestoffe*, *Tartar*, *L'Aigle*, *Romulus* and *Dido*, and *Tysiphone* sloop and the *Fox* cutter upon the enemy supply lines, while the *Agamemnon* concentrated upon lightning raids on outlying enemy posts, shredding the fringes of French control and encouraging the peasantry. These attacks attract little comment today, but it was the experience of numerous small successes that made the *Agamemnon* a crack force. The constant manipulation of the ship about a treacherous coastline, the lowering and raising of boats, the sallies ashore, the trust and reliance that developed in the company as each man learned his part, the solidarity forged in shared dangers, and the facility with which guns and sails were handled, all

1. Captain Horatio Nelson, aged twenty-two, painted by John Francis Rigaud in 1781. He stood proudly in the full-dress uniform of a post-captain, with Fort San Juan in the background, commemorating his most notable achievement thus far.

2. Rear Admiral Sir Horatio Nelson, K.B., 1797. This pencil-and-ink drawing made by Henry Edridge in London has the appearance of being the foundation for a new commemorative portrait that was never painted. Nelson wore the undress uniform of a rear admiral, and the gold medal and red ribbon of Bath, awarded him for the victory off Cape St. Vincent, featured in the background. Note the ribbons tying the slashed sleeve over his injured arm.

3. The Reverend Edmund Nelson (1722–1802), Nelson's father, painted by Sir William Beechey two years before the reverend's death.

4. Catherine Nelson (1725–67), Nelson's mother, painted by John Theodore Heins (then based in Norwich). She died leaving her husband five sons and three daughters.

ANNE SUCKLING.
Ob. 1768.

5. Ann Suckling (1691–1768), Nelson's maternal grandmother. It was through her that the Nelsons inherited their principal social influence. The daughter of Sir Charles Turner and Mary Walpole, Ann was the niece of the first Baron Walpole and Sir Robert Walpole. She outlived her daughter, Catherine, by ten days, and died at Burnham Thorpe.

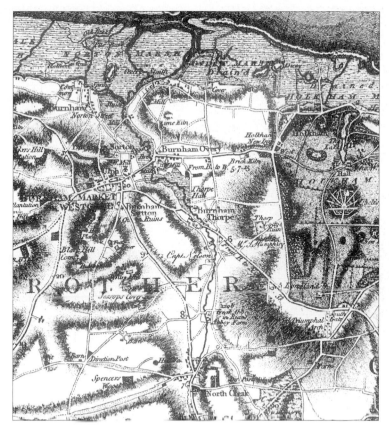

6. Nelson's Norfolk, from Faden's map, surveyed during the years Nelson resided at Burnham Thorpe rectory as an unemployed captain. It shows the exact location of the rectory and its gatehouse, south of Burnham Thorpe.

7. The rectory at Burnham Thorpe, Nelson's birthplace, was demolished in about 1804. A neighbour reputedly made this wash and sketch from memory in 1806, though it may have been based upon an oil miniature of 1760.

8. Norwich Grammar School, to the left of the chapel, attended by William and Horatio Nelson about 1768.

9. The Sir William Paston Grammar School, North Walsham. The main entrance appears to have been elaborated since Nelson's day, several windows bricked up, and an annexe built on the left-hand side, but the school retains much of its eighteenth-century character. Photograph taken by the author in 2002.

10. Captain Maurice Suckling (1728–78), Nelson's uncle and patron, portrayed at Woodton Hall, Norfolk, in 1764 by Thomas Bardwell, the son of one of the Suckling family servants.

11. Skeffington Lutwidge, who took the fifteen-year-old Nelson aboard the *Carcass* in 1773. He died an admiral in 1814.

12. The *Racehorse* and the *Carcass* trapped in the pack ice off North East Land, Spitsbergen, on 31 July 1773. The men are exercising by playing leap-frog on the ice. The engraving was made from a watercolour by John Cleverley, based upon a drawing done on the spot by a midshipman of the *Racehorse*.

13. Captain George Farmer (1732–79), under whom Nelson served in the East Indies aboard the *Seahorse*. Painted by Charles Grignion.

14. Vice Admiral Sir Edward Hughes (died 1794), painted by Joshua Reynolds. As a commodore he commanded the East India squadron to which Nelson belonged in 1773–76.

15. Sir Charles Morice Pole (1757–1811), from a painting by James Northcote. As one of the 'young gentlemen' of the *Salisbury*, the flagship of Commodore Hughes, he formed a lifelong friendship with Nelson in the East Indies.

16. Captain William Locker (1731–1800), Nelson's 'sea-daddy', portrayed with his wife, Lucy, and their children by Rigaud about 1779. Their eldest daughter (on her mother's left), the 'Little Lucy' for whom Nelson's first independent command was named, died a nun in Bruges. Left is the oldest boy, William, whom Nelson illicitly entered on the books of the *Badger* and *Hinchinbroke*.

17. Admiral Sir Peter Parker, Bt. (1721–1811), an engraving of the 1799 portrait by Lemuel Abbott. A friend of Captain Suckling, Parker guided Nelson's early career in the West Indies.

18. Captain Cuthbert Collingwood (1748–1810), portrayed by his friend, Horatio Nelson. Probably done in Windsor, English Harbour, Antigua, in 1785, this only known example of Nelson's artwork was kept by Mary Moutray and eventually passed to Collingwood's daughter.

19. Mary Moutray (c.1750–1841), sketched by John Downman three years before her amiability, lively conversation and attentiveness fascinated Nelson in English Harbour.

20. English Harbour, by Walter Tremenheere. The view is from the west shore of the inner anchorage, looking southeast across the dockyard. The house on the summit of the hill on the eastern side of the narrows, identified by a flag, may have been Windsor or another property later built on the same side.

21. William IV (1765–1837), formerly Prince William, Duke of Clarence, who cast a unique shadow over Nelson's service in the Leeward Islands.

22. Frances, Lady Nelson (1761–1831), sketched by Daniel Orme about 1798.

23. The house of William Suckling (10), Nelson's uncle, in Kentish Town, drawn by James Frederick King, whose father owned the Castle Tavern to the right. The property was a favourite resort of Nelson and his wife, and tradition credited the captain with planting some of the shrubs and box trees in the garden.

24. The Hon. Courtenay Boyle (1770–1844). The son of the 7th Earl of Cork, he apparently joined Nelson's *Boreas* at the behest of Admiral Hood. Later Boyle became a trusted frigate captain under Nelson in the Mediterranean (1803–1805) and rose to flag rank. This portrait was painted about 1810.

25. George Andrews (1765–1810), the brother of Elizabeth Andrews, and another of the 'young gentle-men' of the *Boreas*. Subsequently, Andrews served with distinction on Nelson's *Agamemnon* and rose to the rank of post-captain, but his career disintegrated amid ill-health, drink and bad luck. This portrait of a post-captain is thought to show Andrews before the darkness enveloped him.

26. Samuel, Viscount Hood (1724–1816), an irascible commander-in-chief, who gave Nelson crucial opportunities in the Mediterranean and moulded many of his ideas. Nelson complained that he was inadequately noticed in the admiral's public dispatches, but generally saw only the best of Hood's professional side. The portrait was painted by Reynolds.

27. Sir John Jervis, later Earl St. Vincent (1735–1823), an effective fleet commander who restored Nelson's morale in 1795–96. Although he could be merciless on mutineers or the incompetent, Jervis indulged Nelson and many other industrious officers. An engraving of a portrait by T. Stuart, painted about five years before Jervis took Nelson under his command.

28. Sir Gilbert Elliot, Earl of Minto (1751–1814), viceroy of Corsica and governor-general of India, painted by G. Chinnery. A close associate and confidant of Nelson in the Mediterranean, he witnessed his part in the battle of Cape St. Vincent and wrote that 'Commodore Nelson [was] a hero beyond Homer's. It is impossible to give . . . a notion of his exploits.'

29. General Charles Stuart (1753–1801), by George Romney. A son of the Earl of Bute, Stuart joined the army in 1768 and rose to become a brilliant but difficult officer. Though he maintained good relations with Nelson during the siege of Calvi in 1794, he feuded with Hood, and drove Elliot to report that working with him was like being 'locked up with a madman in a cell'.

30. Francis Drake (1764–1821), engraved from a portrait by William Beechey. As the British minister-plenipotentiary in Genoa, and representative to the Austrian allies on the Italian Riviera, Drake formed a remarkably close partnership with Nelson in 1795–96. His confidence in Nelson was unbounded, and he urged the allied governments to supply him with ships, troops and small boats to facilitate amphibious assaults on French positions ashore.

31. John Trevor, 3rd Viscount Hampden (1749–1824), by Thomas Lawrence. The son of the first viscount, Trevor was a career diplomat at the court of Sardinia-Piedmont in Turin, and served as minister-plenipotentiary from 1789. Supporting Nelson's Riviera operations of 1795–96, he developed a great admiration for the 'worthy and excellent officer', urging his superiors to promote him, and regretting that he was not commander-in-chief of the British fleet.

32. Thomas Francis Fremantle (1765–1819), painted by Domenico Pellegrini in 1800, one of Nelson's ablest colleagues and subordinates. Fremantle did not always agree with Nelson. Unlike Nelson, he was a critic of Hood and an admirer of Admiral Hyde Parker, but the two co-operated brilliantly in many of the major actions between 1794 and 1797 and became close friends.

33. Thomas Troubridge (1758–1807), from a portrait by Beechey. An outstanding no-holds-barred sea fighter, Troubridge became a great favourite of Sir John Jervis, who thought him 'capable of commanding the fleet of England'. His partnership with Nelson, which led to the ill-fated Tenerife operation of 1797, dissolved in jealousies several years later. Troubridge served on the board of the Admiralty and became a rear admiral but was drowned off Madagascar.

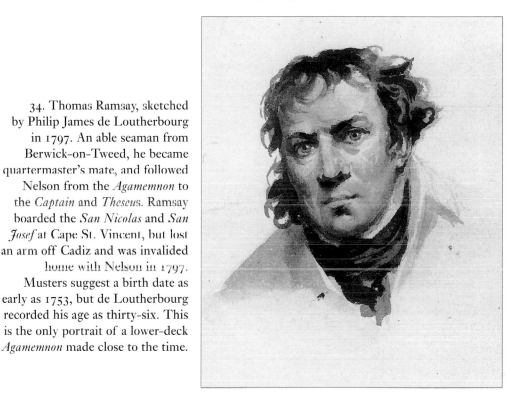

34. Thomas Ramsay, sketched by Philip James de Loutherbourg in 1797. An able seaman from Berwick-on-Tweed, he became quartermaster's mate, and followed Nelson from the *Agamemnon* to the *Captain* and *Theseus*. Ramsay boarded the *San Nicolas* and *San Josef* at Cape St. Vincent, but lost an arm off Cadiz and was invalided home with Nelson in 1797.

Musters suggest a birth date as early as 1753, but de Loutherbourg recorded his age as thirty-six. This is the only portrait of a lower-deck *Agamemnon* made close to the time.

35. Captain Sir William Hoste, Bt. (1780–1828), painted by Charles Taylor. The most successful 'young gentleman' of the *Agamemnon*, *Captain* and *Theseus*, Hoste became a renowned frigate captain. Six years after his mentor's death he successfully led a British squadron into battle against a superior enemy off Lissa flying the signal, 'Remember Nelson'.

36. The battle of Cape St. Vincent, 1797, painted by Nicholas Pocock about 1809. It shows Nelson's *Captain* (left) running upon the *San Nicolas* (centre), with the *San Josef* behind (right). The evidence divides as to whether the *San Nicolas* had lost her mizzen topmast, as shown here, or the *San Josef,* but the artist— a professional seaman—was said to have used a sketch made by Nelson's flag-captain, and may have produced a reliable reconstruction.

37. One of the better interpretations of the boarding of the *San Nicolas,* showing Nelson's party using the cathead of the *Captain* and Berry's in the distance, reaching the enemy poop by means of the bowsprit.

accrued skill, resolution and know-how that no French ship could achieve sitting in port.[13]

Nelson's new campaign opened at the small port of Centuri. He had heard that a Genoese vessel seized by the *Lowestoffe* in January, but subsequently lost in the gales, had fallen into the hands of the French at Centuri. Several wine vessels were also hiding in the port, ready to sail for St Fiorenzo. On 5 February the *Agamemnon*, *Lowestoffe* (Captain William Wolseley), *L'Aigle* (Captain Samuel Hood) and *Romulus* (Captain John Sutton) blocked the entrance of Centuri, and a party of marines went ashore. The French were scattered, and four polacres destroyed in the harbour, but Nelson ordered that no inhabitants of the town were to be plundered or molested. This was a war of liberation, not conquest, and the support of the people was needed if Britain was ever to rule Corsica.

Next was Rogliano at the extremity of Cape Corse, an important town because of its ability to monitor the movement of ships around the north of the island. The French had installed a small garrison in an old castle and raised national colours, but on the morning of 8 February the *Agamemnon* and the *Tartar* anchored off the mole head and trained their broadsides upon the town. Here Nelson was united for the first time in battle with Thomas Francis Fremantle of the *Tartar*, destined to become one of his most famous captains and already displaying exceptional ability. Two days earlier the *Tartar* and the *Fox* had driven a vessel aground near Bastia, but had been prevented from taking possession by heavy fire from ashore; now Fremantle was with his commanding officer, eager to inflict another blow. Drums beat the men to their quarters and a flag of truce went ashore. Nelson urged the French commandant to declare for the monarchy, but the reply was defiant and at ten-thirty the captain personally led his boats towards the mole. Making almost no resistance, the French fled to adjacent hilltops, from which they glared banefully while Nelson secured the town and with his own hand struck the enemy colours. A liberty tree the French had planted in the middle of the town was cut down, a storehouse destroyed and eight vessels and five hundred tons of wine found at the mole set on fire. Three other ships, one of them intercepted on its way in, were removed as prizes.

The French soon marched back into Rogliano, but its capture sent a ripple of excitement through the Cape Corse peninsula. Alert to the propaganda value of his coup, Nelson wrote of it to Paoli, while on 18 February a group of Corsicans soliciting muskets and ammunition admitted to the captain that they had only swung over 'since the day you took Maginaggio [Rogliano]'. Of course, Nelson was not entirely green. 'They may be good friends if it is their interest to be so,' he told Hood, 'but I am rather inclined to believe they will always cry, 'Long live the conqueror!' He knew that in wars of this kind a belief in victory was essential, and his raids were suggesting that the French could neither defend themselves nor their supporters.[14]

The *Agamemnon*'s next foray took her eastwards to the island of Capraia, a possession of the neutral state of Genoa but one habitually used by French privateers and supply vessels. On 12 February 'Mr Andrews' (now Horatio's first choice for dangerous excursions) explored the craggy coves and inlets with a boat and gunboat. Inside one inlet was a French dispatch boat, with many of its men, including a few soldiers, secreted ashore with levelled muskets. They opened fire as the British approached, wounding one of Andrews's men. Hearing the shooting, Nelson put forty redcoats into a pinnace and the *Fox* cutter and personally led them inshore, aided among others by young Midshipman Hoste. The British forced their way into the cove against a splatter of musketry, replying with grape and small-arms fire of their own. Unable to outflank the French boat, which was buttressed between steep, rocky shores, Nelson made a head-on attack and captured it by boarding. The action lasted six hours and cost Nelson as many men wounded, but the prize, he discovered, could sail 'like the wind' and seemed likely to fetch a reasonable sum in Leghorn. On this occasion Lord Hood was less impressed. Such raids, he warned Nelson, violated neutral territory.[15]

The next day Nelson intercepted a Genoese ship taking corn to Corsica, and then, after embarking supplies at Leghorn and communicating with the fleet, he arrived off L'Avisena, five miles north of Bastia, on 19 February. Paoli had reported a Ragusan ship unloading at the town, and Nelson and Fremantle were there to investigate. Again Nelson headed the shore party, supported this time by Lieutenant Andrews and Captain Clark of the 69th Regiment. Only about sixty soldiers were needed to seize the town, but the Ragusan had gone. Nelson therefore marched his men two miles south to the small town of Miomo, where they drove a weak French detachment from a tower and raised English colours over it. Once more local inhabitants crowded around excitedly, showing Nelson Paoli's portrait as proof of their loyalty to the partisans. 'All the people up to the walls of Bastia had declared for us,' Nelson was told by one peasant, 'and that from our landing the French were prevented from coming with their gun boats and troops and burning all the revolted [rebelling] villages.' It was a mood that needed more than example to grow, and two days later Nelson landed four hundred muskets with ammunition for the Cape Corse partisans.[16]

Watching his company develop their skills and confidence made Nelson increasingly keen to broadcast its exploits, and of course to advertise his own prowess. He was beginning to understand that one way of spreading recognition was to maintain an active correspondence, apprising important parties of his work and spreading his interpretation of events. In this case the recipient was John Udny, the British consul at Leghorn. After reading of the latest successes of the *Agamemnon*, Udny wrote that Nelson was 'the most active of His Majesty's commanders in these seas where none are idle'.[17]

But the pace of the wider campaign was quickening. The night Nelson took Miomo, he saw a fiery glow to the west, blazing red in the clear night sky over St Fiorenzo, some twelve miles away across the narrow neck of the Cape Corse peninsula. He had a good idea what it was. The French frigates *La Fortunée* and *La Minerve* had been trapped in St Fiorenzo ever since their skirmish with *Agamemnon* the previous October, and now they were most likely on fire. That meant Hood had taken the town. In fact, the port had fallen the day before Nelson captured Miomo, but rather than surrender the French survivors had fallen back across the isthmus towards Bastia. One of the captured warships, *La Fortunée*, was destroyed, the other taken into British service. As Nelson saw those distant flames over St Fiorenzo, he knew that Bastia would be next.

The expectation was evident in a letter Nelson wrote to Hood the same day, in which he assessed the defences of Bastia and suggested that a thousand soldiers would be needed to take the town, besides seamen and Corsican partisans. Soon afterwards he received official word of the fall of St Fiorenzo, and sailed for Bastia, determined to find places suitable for landing men and to frustrate the enemy's preparations to meet the inevitable attack.[18]

The twenty-third of February found the *Agamemnon*, *Romulus* and *Tartar* testing Bastia's fortifications. They closed in on a new battery of six guns that the French were feverishly throwing up a mile south of the town, close to a command post. The ships found their range with their third shot, drove the French artillerists from their posts and damaged the battery, but without enough soldiers to land Nelson was

unable to finish the job. Instead he moved north, leading his diminutive force in line-ahead formation past the formidable frontal defences
of the town. As he did so the captain ordered his main topsail to be
backed to reduce the *Agamemnon*'s speed and opened fire. For an
hour and a half the ships and shore batteries hammered at each other,
filling the air with black smoke. Nelson claimed that his ships hit two
vessels at the mole, knocked down some houses and part of the mole
wall, caused an explosion about the southeastern battery, and set
fascines on fire. He also heard that considerable panic had ensued and
that several defenders had been killed.

At the same time Nelson's squadron was unequal to a protracted
duel with the shore batteries and all three ships were damaged before
they broke off the fight. The *Tartar*'s mainsail was ripped and part of
a cabin smashed in, while the *Romulus* had her mainsail set on fire
by red-hot shot and took a beating about the bowsprit and quarter
gallery. Indeed, Captain John Sutton had had enough. The next day
Fremantle found him ranting about the damage to the *Romulus* and
insisting on returning to port for repairs. Sutton's readiness to quit
disappointed Nelson, but he let him go. As he explained to Fremantle,
he would rather not have an officer who wanted to be somewhere
else.

Nothing Nelson saw suggested that any time should be wasted
making a general assault on Bastia, especially as the garrison was daily
strengthening its fortifications. The influx of the soldiers expelled from
St Fiorenzo was both a boon and an embarrassment to Bastia. On the
one hand it increased the numbers of the defenders to some five thousand men, most from the 26th and 52nd regiments of the French line,
battalions of the Bouches du Rhône and the departmental regiment
of Aveyron, and detachments of Corsican volunteers. On the other
hand the refugees exacerbated supply problems. Nelson's blockade had
reduced the French in St Fiorenzo to about a month's provisions. Their
defeat had cost them lives, including a company of regulars almost
wiped out, but equally artillery, ammunition and food, abandoned to
the British in the precipitate flight. The retreating soldiers, packing
into Bastia, created temporary confusion and ultimately decisive
shortages of food and ammunition.

Nelson felt that an attack ought to be made quickly, before the
French could regroup and strengthen their defences. Over the next
three days he renewed his efforts to disrupt enemy preparations. He
found them building a new half-moon battery near a lagoon south of

the town, hoping to prevent the British landing there, and sent its gunners scurrying from the works with a few well-directed shots. Nelson's confidence was tip-top. 'I wish the troops were here,' he told Hood. 'I am sure in its present state it [Bastia] will soon fall.' He drew the admiral's attention to a landing place three miles north of the town. To Udny he even recklessly admitted 'if I had five hundred troops, by laying my ship and frigate for two hours against the works, I am certain of taking it.'[19]

On the 23rd, the day Nelson fought the batteries, the first British soldiers had appeared on the summit of the hills to the rear of Bastia after a smart hike from St Fiorenzo. Lieutenant General David Dundas, their commanding officer, had even watched Nelson's engagement, though he believed 'many' of the captain's 'shots struck the land'. On his part Nelson did not miss the soldiers on the hills, and smelling a battle thought them 'the grandest thing I ever saw.'[20]

But several days passed without any sign of action. The soldiers disappeared from the hills, leaving them strangely silent. For a while Horatio reassured himself that all would be well. 'Seamen think they [the army] never mean to get forward,' he told Fanny, 'but I dare say they act on a surer principle.'[21]

Unfortunately, his confidence melted. On 3 March Nelson was astonished to learn from Hood that after reconnoitring the town with his officers General Dundas had had enough. Without substantial reinforcements he considered any attack on Bastia a ridiculous folly. Far from mounting an assault, Dundas and his advance had already turned back to St Fiorenzo.

3

Nelson was dumbfounded.

'What the general could have seen to have made a retreat necessary I cannot conceive,' he complained. 'The enemy's force is 1,000 regulars and 1,000 or 1,500 irregulars.' Nelson had assumed the army would march from St Fiorenzo and assault Bastia from the heights while the navy blockaded it at sea, and he had also picked out a place on the waterfront where men and guns could be landed to form auxiliary batteries. In his head he was still pursuing his idea of storming the town himself, with the *Agamemnon*, some frigates and five hundred or a thousand soldiers. The sea wall could be battered down, its guns silenced and troops landed to rush the town. As for the forts on the heights above, they would hold out longer of course, but their position was truly hopeless. They would be completely – overwhelmingly – isolated. The interior was held by thousands of fierce partisans. St Fiorenzo and the road to it were in the hands of the British, and the Royal Navy controlled the harbour and all approaches to the island. Deprived of every supply, the small garrisons in the hill forts could have no reason to hold out or bombard the town once it fell into British hands. Their capitulation was inevitable. From what Nelson had heard about the state of morale in Bastia, he convinced himself that there would be no great resistance from the French.[22]

Hood's letters shed little light on the mystery as far as Nelson was concerned. The admiral merely told him that General Dundas was 'palsied' and had 'made up his mind to walk off'. These terse, uninformative phrases scarcely touched the explosive situation underneath. For at Toulon and St Fiorenzo, beyond Nelson's ken, relations between the army and navy had been steadily disintegrating.[23]

For one thing General Dundas, who commanded the British armed forces assisting the fleet, was a ditherer. A tall, thin and crabbed Scot whose mannerisms were the amusement of the rank and file, Dundas had abilities but just what they were was becoming increasingly mysterious. Most observers credited the success at St Fiorenzo to the general's subordinates, Moore and Koehler, who had selected the site for the crucial British battery; to Captain Edward Cooke of the Royal Navy and a detachment of seamen whose 'extraordinary exertion' got the guns in place; and to the common redcoats who finally stormed the Convention redoubt. Even Moore, an army man if ever there was one, berated his superior's vacillation. Dundas, he said, was terrified of hauling up the bigger guns and unable to decide how to use the lighter ones. However, it was less indecision than the general's ingrained pessimism that constituted the greatest handicap to a man of his uncomfortable calling. As Sir Gilbert Elliot, a mere civilian, said, he was 'always ready to throw up the game instead of playing for it', and twice almost abandoned the enterprise. Back home his namesake, the new minister for war, grew so tired of the general's negativity that he delivered a metaphorical boot to the seat of his breeches by bluntly complaining that 'you only state a difficulty, and say nothing of the means of removing it'.[24]

The most regrettable sequel of the combined operations at St Fiorenzo was a corrosive jealousy between the army and navy. The remarkable success of Cooke's seamen, who had hauled guns three miles over precipices and up steep mountain heights to accomplish what the army had declared to be 'impossible', was one source of resentment. Another was the way the sailors had swept into the captured port and seized choice pieces of plunder. But leadership was the root of the problem. Some sea officers were dissatisfied with 'the old rascally general', but Lord Hood was by far the bigger fly in the ointment. For all his strengths Hood had serious professional failings, of which arrogance and a wilful disregard for the opinions of others were notable. Those shortcomings never did more damage than in Corsica, where they inflicted a compound fracture of interservice relations.[25]

Determined to have his way, Hood repeatedly slighted the army officers, especially Dundas, who considered himself to be on an equal footing. Difficulties had begun in Toulon, where the general and other army officers had entreated Hood to prepare to evacuate the town only to be contemptuously ignored. The result was the last-minute bungled attempt to burn the French fleet and the loss of Britain's naval supremacy in the Mediterranean. In Corsica the admiral's presumptions intensified. Without consulting Dundas, Hood sent Moore and Koehler, the general's own officers, to meet the partisans in January and personally received their report, something he later claimed proved that he was recognised as the supreme officer. During the siege of St Fiorenzo the admiral behaved as if he was the overall commander-in-chief, rather than the joint leader of a combined operation, and it was he who accepted the captured French colours. Immediately after the port's fall he was pressing the forces towards Bastia without any regard for Dundas's opinion.

It was not just redcoats who felt the animosity Hood was breeding. Elliot, a firm admirer of the formidable admiral, watched with growing alarm, while Captain Fremantle considered that 'the presumptuousness and overbearing conduct of Lord Hood to Dundas and all the army has been such as not to be borne with by any corps whatsoever, particularly from the army who are independent of us'. The spirit of cooperation and joint endeavour so essential to combined operations waned, and several aggrieved and underappreciated army officers found themselves resisting the admiral not only because they felt he was mistaken but also from an instinct to preserve the independence and dignity of their profession.[26]

It was in this context that Dundas led a party in pursuit of the flying French and found himself looking upon Bastia from the mountain heights of the Colle de Teghime behind the town on 23 February.

The general's officers agreed that the ideal place for a battery was the ridge where a village named Cardo stood, commanding the four stone hill forts guarding the rear of Bastia. Moore, who was present, did not expect an easy victory. He worried about getting guns and supplies along the difficult road from St Fiorenzo and estimated that the town was defended by about four thousand men, a quarter of them Corsicans allied to the French, but he did not foresee a withdrawal. However, when the French made a sortie, expelled Dundas's Corsicans from Cardo and began to dig themselves in there, the British made no attempt to intervene. Worse, to the surprise of 'everybody', the general ordered the force back to St Fiorenzo without making any effort to resecure what he deemed to be crucial ground.[27]

Back at base Dundas told Hood that he thought Bastia 'out of [the] reach of any attempt that we can at present undertake', and that he would need another two thousand men to launch an attack. Within a few days he was accumulating a formidable collection of pretexts for inaction. The weather was bad; the communication lines were difficult; the enemy had too many men; and the partisans were not holding the summit of the heights. He pointed out that an enemy sortie of 25 February seized the very ground from which Dundas and his staff had reconnoitred Bastia two days before, driving off the partisans and placing guns on a nearby height. They had also burned Cardo. In effect Dundas was admitting his failure to secure significant positions, but his argument was that the French were getting hold of the heights above the town and making an assault impossible. Without more men no more than a naval blockade of Bastia was feasible.[28]

Although the capture of St Fiorenzo gave Hood a base for his fleet, he could not tie up forces reducing Bastia and Calvi for long, and was also conscious of the need to wind up operations before the ferocious summer heat attacked his forces. He could scarcely contain his anger at Dundas's procrastination, and a flurry of testy letters flew back and forth. On 2 March, Hood wrote that he was 'extremely concerned to find that you have given up all thought of reducing Corsica until you are reinforced by additional troops from Europe, because I do not see there is a prospect of any coming'. High-handedly he asked Dundas to return those members of the 11th, 25th, 30th and 69th regiments who had formerly served with the fleet as temporary marines, and demanded that any lost through sickness be replaced by men from other contingents of the army. At this further erosion of his forces, Dundas protested his inability both to supply the men and defend

St Fiorenzo. He went further. He expressed his opposition to attacking Bastia in blunter terms than ever. 'I consider the siege of Bastia, with our present means and force, to be a most visionary and rash attempt, such as no officer could be justified in undertaking,' he fulminated. The battle lines between the two commanders were solidifying. It had become personal, with neither man willing to think or yield.[29]

Momentarily Hood was deflated by Dundas's opinion, backed as it was by the authority of at least one personal reconnaissance of the target. He began to reflect upon the unpleasant prospect of a costly, drawn-out blockade pinning down men and ships while allied powers screamed lustily for help elsewhere. 'Poor Paoli,' said Hood, was 'distressed beyond measure by our inactivity, which I cannot cure because the more I urge a contrary conduct the more he [Dundas] is determined to lay upon his oars, by which our difficulties will daily increase.' Then, after an abortive attempt to reconnoitre Bastia for himself, Hood got a letter from his man on the spot. Horatio Nelson had been blockading Corsica for more than three months, and no naval officer knew more about Bastia. Even more important, amidst counsels of despair Nelson alone talked the sort of language that Hood wanted to hear.[30]

At the beginning of March, Nelson's squadron, cruising all hours off Bastia, was reinforced by the *Romney* of fifty guns, captained by the able William Paget. In late February the *Leda* intercepted a Danish ship leaving the port, and learned from her that fear was spreading in Bastia, bread was scarce, merchants were preparing to flee and some residents were burying their valuables in the earth. The picture seemed to be confirmed by a Ragusan brig taken by the *Agamemnon* and *Tartar* in March and the talk of every local Nelson could find, as well as the activities revealed through his telescope. When he wrote to Hood on the 5th the tone remained decidedly upbeat. Nelson confirmed Dundas's report that the enemy was at work on the ridges above the hill forts and noted the strengthening of other defences, but dwelt upon the panic in the town itself, where the citizens dreaded being exposed to Paoli's wild partisans and spoke about burning *La Flèche* at anchor. 'I learn that the enemy are in the greatest apprehension of our landing near the town, which in my opinion would fall on the first vigorous attack,' he said.[31]

Words like these were a tonic to Admiral Hood, and sent the blood coursing through his veins. He decided to sidestep Dundas, and on 7 March called upon two lieutenant colonels, Moore of the 51st and

William Anne Villettes of the 69th Regiment, for independent opinions of the propriety of an attack. Though Moore disagreed with Dundas, he felt as if he was being asked to betray a superior officer, and to the admiral's annoyance declined to report. Instead he told Dundas what had happened. The general was 'warm and irritated to the highest degree' and snorted to Moore that Hood 'never reasoned himself nor would he listen to reason from others'.[32]

Well might Dundas boil, for Hood was moving decisively to neutralise him. In two letters the admiral arrogantly informed Dundas that 'however visionary and rash an attempt to reduce Bastia may be in your opinion, to me it appears very much the reverse and to be a perfectly right measure'. Far from needing Dundas's blessing, he would make the attack 'at my own risk', and what was more he would use the soldiers as he saw fit. 'I do not hesitate to say that your power most undoubtedly ceased after the evacuation of Toulon, when the troops as well as ships were at my disposal,' he wrote. Dundas read in horror that he had only been consulted in Corsica at all as a mere 'courtesy'.[33]

Dundas was being treated as if he was in charge of a detachment of marines rather than a field army, or worse 'a mere passenger'. Storming to his officers, he won their support and then resigned his command, sailing almost immediately for Civita Vecchia on 11 March. His parting shot to Hood mentioned his indifferent health and demanded to see any written authority that put the soldiers under the admiral's command. Justifying himself to the home secretary (soon to become the minister of war), Dundas comprehensively catalogued his difficulties: the number of the enemy (at least fourteen hundred regulars, a civilian militia and the crew of La Flêche); the inclement mountainous weather; the problem of bringing artillery from St Fiorenzo; and shortages of camp equipment, medical supplies, men, carriages and guns. In such circumstances, opined the general, a direct attack on Bastia was 'visionary and hazardous in the highest degree, and most likely to be attended with loss and disgrace'. He had made some good points, though his unrelieved pessimism failed to consider a single problem of a caged enemy. Elliot observed that Dundas's resignation was regrettable but 'necessary' for the service to go 'forward'.[34]

The departure of the doubting general failed to ease difficulties because the resentment he and Hood had generated lived on. Even moderate, sensible men were taking sides. Elliot the diplomat was leaning towards the navy, convinced that sea officers were a 'manly' breed, 'full of life and action' and entirely preferable to the 'high lounge and still life' in the army camps. Moore, on the other hand, grew to detest Hood, who was 'illiberal to a degree' and whose 'actions in the Mediterranean have been unwise . . . He is so false and so unmanageable that it is impossible for any general to carry on service with him.' Not surprisingly, Brigadier General Abraham D'Aubant of the engineers was no blank sheet when he temporarily succeeded to the command Dundas had vacated. His mind had already been poisoned by the feud between the service chiefs.[35]

More, professionally speaking D'Aubant was much poorer material than his predecessor. Moore found him 'much averse' to attacking Bastia without ever having seen the town, and thought he should be 'broke' for it. 'It is difficult to speak more nonsense than he does with more gravity and decorum of matter,' thought Moore. In fact the lieutenant colonel's opinion of his new superior was so poor that he began to question the wisdom of moving against Bastia. His former opinion, in favour of an assault, began to quake. With D'Aubant in charge Moore was sure it would be botched.[36]

Wrapped in his blockade, Nelson hardly knew that the task force was disintegrating behind him at St Fiorenzo. He appealed to Hood for shallow vessels to help him fire on fortifications ashore and stop supplies edging along the coast, and busily stationed them as each arrived, *La Billette*, the *Fortune, Swallow, Scout, Fox, Vanneau, Rose, Petit Bonbon, Jean Bart, Vigilant* and the *St Croix*, which was now commanded by an old *Agamemnon*, Lieutenant Suckling. Nelson's confidence remained unshaken. His temperament was to make light of his own difficulties and fix upon those of the French. Indeed, in his impatience for action he overeagerly seized upon every indication of the enemy's weakness. He was told, for example, that Bastia was so close to panic that Lacombe St Michel, a one-time artillery officer the French National Convention had sent to defend the town, was threatening to blow himself up in the citadel rather than yield to the public clamour for surrender. This, however, dangerously caricatured the strength of resistance.[37]

But Nelson was right about the eventual futility of the French predicament, and about himself and his men. There would be no stinting on the part of the captain of the *Agamemnon*. It was not in his nature, and he felt duty bound, in part to the Corsican struggle for independence. As he promised Paoli, 'nothing shall be wanting on my part to assist your brave Corsicans'. As for his ship's company he believed them capable of most things naval. He had sharpened them in success after success until they were as keen as bayonet points. 'My seamen are now what British seamen ought to be,' he told his wife. 'To you I may say it – almost invincible! They really mind shot no more than peas!'[38]

4

There were many differences between warfare on land and sea, and Nelson never fully grasped them. The finer arts of siege work, the interplay of infantry and cavalry, the rapid fluidity of movement ashore and to some extent the importance of ground were apt to confound him. Intelligence was crucial to all armed services, but never more so than in operations on land, where the true state and scale of an opposing force could easily be masked behind terrain or buildings. In Corsica Nelson's information about Bastia proved seriously deficient and courted disaster. For a while, supposing the enemy on the point of collapse, he talked about launching a frontal attack upon the town, using ships to bombard the defences before storming them with a few hundred soldiers. Fortunately, as he saw the enemy improving their positions, he abandoned the idea early in March. An alternative plan began to evolve.

Even Nelson the optimist understood that his experience of military affairs left much to be desired, and he requested the services of Lieutenants John Duncan of the Royal Artillery and Augustus de Butts of the Royal Engineers to help him examine a landing site he had found north of Bastia. A battery erected close by would not be ideal, Nelson realised. It would be incapable of troubling the hill forts, and was no substitute for batteries the army might have established above the rear of the town, but if it could be positioned high enough and defended it might play with effect upon the citadel, town and Cabanelle outpost. At least Nelson thought it worthy of investigation.

In the midst of such industry Horatio read the latest letter from Hood, dated the 16th, and worried. There was a new despondency in his admiral. Hood promised to react immediately upon a favourable report from Duncan and de Butts, but hinted that if the troops declined to cooperate the enemy would have to be reduced by blockade and starvation. On 18 March Nelson scratched an inspiring rejoinder. He had taken de Butts and Duncan to the proposed landing site that morning, and they had agreed that a battery might reasonably be established within a mile of it. Bastia was 'certainly not a place of strength'. Given good weather, it could eventually be reduced by blockade, of course. Though a boat had recently got some corn into the port it was reputedly short of bread. But a formal siege was desirable to drive the business on. Nelson supposed the enemy to consist of no more than one thousand regulars and fifteen hundred auxiliaries (he underestimated the defenders by over two thousand) and encouraged the attempt. Using words that would weigh with an admiral interested in retrieving a damaged reputation, Nelson added that 'it would be a national disgrace to give it up without a trial'.[39]

The same day Nelson received another message from Hood. The captain was needed at St Fiorenzo to set his opinion against the army's. Leaving his blockade in the capable hands of Captain Paget of the *Romney*, he hurried to the admiral's assistance.[40]

Nelson's suspicion that Hood had taken several steps backward was right. Unquestionably it was Elliot who had warned the admiral that his claim to hold the supreme command was breeding 'a great jealousy and quickness to suspect and to resist' among the army officers, and that now a new general was in place appeasement should be the order of the day. Hood took the point and dropped his pretensions. He even visited D'Aubant to assure the general that he alone exercised overall authority over the troops. Though their country was committed to ridding Corsica of the French and every delay enabled the enemy to strengthen Bastia, the decision to deploy the army would rest solely with D'Aubant.[41]

With Hood's fresh approach came the job of persuading, rather than ordering, the army to attack Bastia, and it was that task that undermined the admiral's confidence. He summoned a council of war in which the seniors of both services could thrash the matter out, and recalled Nelson from Bastia to help him prepare for it, but privately he was losing heart. Some of D'Aubant's senior officers, including Moore and Lieutenant Colonel David Douglas Wemyss of the 18th (Royal Irish) Regiment, had favoured an assault, but opinion was now swinging the other way. On 17 March, Moore and Koehler had gone back to the heights above Bastia only to return with long faces. They reckoned the delays had enabled the French to occupy the tactical ground above the hill forts on which Moore had originally wanted to establish batteries. Now it and nearby sites were occupied by four small interconnected camps or redoubts, the principal of which could only be attacked head-on along a narrow ridge. Moore and Koehler consequently threw up their hands. There was no alternative to a sluggish victory by naval blockade.[42]

Nelson found Hood and Sir Gilbert wilting when he led Duncan and de Butts into the great cabin of the *Victory* as it rocked gently in Mortella Bay on 19 March. The trio soon got to work, describing their site at the north end of the town and declaring 'in the strongest and clearest terms that Bastia and its citadel may be taken from that quarter and that the other outposts must fall also'. Nelson told Hood that if eight hundred soldiers and four hundred seamen were landed to establish and fight batteries they could take the town, and repeated his opinion that any failure to make the attempt would be 'a national disgrace'.[43]

Backed by Duncan and de Butts, Nelson convinced the sea officers and Elliot that his attack was feasible and worth trying, and changed the complexion of the next morning's council of war. Nelson, as a junior captain, was excluded, but there was a formidable gathering of shoulder bullion and scarlet and blue uniforms. In the middle of the blue coats sat the severe, hook-nosed features and spare frame of Admiral Hood, flanked by Admirals Hotham and Goodall and Commodore Linzee. On his part D'Aubant fielded nine senior officers. As an attempt to find a consensus, the summit failed abjectly. D'Aubant had already shown himself impervious to argument, and merely dug his heels in further, while Hood was now as intransigent the other way. According to Moore the admiral entered 'little further into the subject than to say "Take Bastia" just as he would say to a captain "Go to sea!" He conceives they are both to be done with equal facility.'[44]

Not that Moore himself showed greater impartiality. Having previously condemned D'Aubant for opposing an attack on Bastia without personally reconnoitring the heights, he now proceeded to ridicule the opinions of Nelson, de Butts and Duncan without ever having inspected the ground they proposed to occupy. In the meeting Duncan was at hand to defend his view, but Moore and Koehler dismissed it as 'impossible to think of' and 'perfectly absurd'. The two officers credited the navy with little capability, and apparently embraced an extraordinary idea that Nelson's position north of Bastia could not be supplied. Moreover, they were overwhelmed by fears of an enemy counterattack. The trouble was that neither Moore nor Koehler had much of an alternative, and so they threw in with D'Aubant and said that nothing could be done.

A simple question was put to each member of the council of war: 'Is it expedient, in a military point of view, to attempt the reduction of Bastia with the force of the present fleet and army?'

A dispiriting queue of army officers gave the proposal the thumbs down. Major Koehler, deputy quartermaster general of the army, led off with, 'In the present circumstances, all things considered, it is not.' Some of the other army men were more equivocal, but all declared the attempt would be hazardous and unlikely to succeed, including Lieutenant Colonels Moore, Wemyss and Villettes. The dismal conclusion was – in Nelson's phrase – 'the impossibility of taking Bastia, even if all the force was united'.

Then came the navy men. 'Taking in every circumstance, and considering the great assistance the fleet can afford, I think an attempt ought to be made,' said Commodore Linzee. The admirals followed suit and the meeting was deadlocked.

While the army sat on its hands, Hood radiated a new resolution. The council over, he swept aside the military objections and declared that if the army declined to participate the navy would go ahead without them. Soon he had alerted those soldiers who had been serving as auxiliary marines – almost half of D'Aubant's command – to prepare for service, and informed two of their officers, Villettes of the 69th and Major Robert Brereton of the 30th, that they would probably head the landing party. The admiral also wrote to D'Aubant, telling him that he was sorry the army had decided against action, but he intended to attack according to the Duncan–de Butts–Nelson plan. He asked for Lieutenants John and Alexander Duncan of the Royal Artillery, some artillerymen, and de Butts, and for the use of guns and stores.[45]

Then came another bombshell. D'Aubant flatly refused to allow his guns and stores to be used. Hood was flabbergasted. The navy, with that part of the army it controlled, was embarking upon a task the army had declared beyond the combined abilities of both services, and now essential stores and guns were also to be denied. Instead of wishing his imperilled comrades well, and supplying what he could, D'Aubant proposed to sit idly by at St Fiorenzo denying them the means to fight. The darkest thoughts must have rumbled through the fleet, but one thing was plain. Sir Gilbert's policy of appeasement had failed, and the feud between the services was degenerating into a black farce.

5

'Why you should deny me every possible assistance in your power to give towards my effecting a most important object, I am at a loss to account for,' Hood wrote to D'Aubant in growing disbelief.[46]

It was true that the general's resources were limited. The army had arrived in Corsica with a field train of only nine guns, and only four howitzers and three mortars were imported thereafter. However, D'Aubant descended into outright obstructionism. He had captured additional guns at St Fiorenzo, and must have known that there was no immediate need for any of them. After all, the French garrisons in Corsica were isolated and surrounded, while the island itself was covered by the might of the British fleet in Mortella Bay. Gradually, as Hood clamoured for guns, entrenching tools, artillerists, sandbags, even kettles, a pattern took shape. D'Aubant's practice was to refuse, then to reflect and relent a little, and finally to raise more difficulties. 'You told me in one of your letters that you had granted all the mortars,' raged a frustrated Hood, 'and I am now informed you have changed your mind. This is highly prejudicial to the king's service . . .'[47]

The case of the 12th Regiment of Light Dragoons stationed in Civita Vecchia typified the duel. Hood and Elliot tried to have them shipped to Corsica to give D'Aubant the men he said he needed to attack Bastia. First the general agreed, but after speaking to his adjutant general and reconsidering orders that told him the light dragoons could only be deployed as a mounted force he began saying they should be sent to Flanders instead.

At the end of March, Elliot was still shuttling helplessly between the ships and the army headquarters ashore in search of an elusive reconciliation. D'Aubant seemed to weaken when Sir Gilbert suggested that the 12th Light Dragoons, the fleet marines and perhaps Sardinian or Neapolitan troops might be added to the general's forces. But on board the *Victory*, Hood had had enough imponderables. *If* they could get additional troops D'Aubant *might* agree . . . but time was slipping away. The admiral declared 'his mind was made up', the army men were merely prevaricating, and 'he would not be made a fool or a tool of by them'. Maybe he was right. The next time Elliot saw D'Aubant the general was singing a different song, and declaring 'he was determined not to entangle himself with any cooperation'. Even the long-suffering Sir Gilbert began to bubble angrily. Appalled at the 'want of spirit' in the army he muttered about cowardice and treason.[48]

In the end Hood wrung few more than his minimum needs from D'Aubant. The army spared him twenty-five artillerists, but kept more than a hundred uselessly sitting at St Fiorenzo. That meant that seamen would have to man the siege guns at Bastia. At the same time Hood and Nelson applied to Naples for the mortars, cannons, fuses, entrenching tools, ammunition, timber and stores they could not get from St Fiorenzo.[49]

Back at sea Horatio was mystified by the dispute. He knew little if anything of Hood's mismanagement, and had always been good at interservice relations himself. All he saw was an admiral standing tall against younger faint hearts. 'Upwards of seventy, he possesses the mind of forty years of age,' Nelson said. 'He has not a thought separated from honour and glory.' As for D'Aubant, his conduct was reprehensible. 'What are we come to that 1,500 or 2,000 British troops . . . are not thought able to attack 1,000 French?' he told Fanny. The same outrage marked his report to Sir William Hamilton. What would 'the immortal Wolfe' have made of it, he railed?[50]

Yet historians have been wrong to picture this as simply a tragic quarrel between soldiers and sailors. Certainly the navy united behind Nelson's plan to besiege Bastia, but far from being all 'peaceable gentle-folks' (as Elliot sarcastically labelled them) the officers of the army were themselves at loggerheads. Until 17 March, Moore theoretically favoured an assault and was contemptuous of his own generals. It was after reconnoitring Bastia again that he finally changed his mind. The Moore–Koehler report of 18 March then swung army opinion against Hood in the decisive council of war, but unity only lasted until the ground was inspected again. After the meeting Lieutenant Colonel Wemyss and Major Smith twice reconnoitred Bastia from the heights, and completely rejected Moore's opinion. They were so 'thoroughly convinced that Bastia may be attacked successfully from the mountain' that Wemyss offered to do the job with four hundred men. Moreover, unlike Moore, Wemyss saw something in the Nelson–Duncan–de Butts plan. He agreed 'entirely' with Lieutenant Duncan about the security of the ground he had chosen, and accepted 'the practicability of annoying the enemy from thence'. Though Moore dismissed Wemyss's views with a favourite reproof ('absurd') they plunged the army into unhappy disagreement. Its leader, D'Aubant, stubbornly opposed an attack for reasons no one could divine, while two lieutenant colonels argued diametrically opposite opinions. Others squirmed all ways. Koehler wavered, 'very fluctuating and equivocal',

while the adjutant general, Sir James St Clair Erskine, was one moment
so violently opposed to fighting that it seemed 'as if he had an interest
that way', and the next muttering incomprehensibly about a plan of
his own to advance from the south. The force was all over the place.[51]

Although the mutual malevolence of senior army and navy men
and interservice jealousies were involved, the dispute was as much
rooted in the different abilities, perspectives and personalities of the
officers themselves. Consider for a moment the conflicting positions
of Moore and Nelson, both fine warriors in some ways. They, more
than D'Aubant and Hood, represented the true poles of the argument.
It was Moore who briefly bonded his colleagues behind a report, and
it was Nelson who conceived and most ardently championed the alternative approach ultimately adopted by the navy. Neither opinion was
entirely right or wrong. Their differences sprang to a large extent from
contrasting leadership styles and temperaments, each with strengths
and failings.

From the purely military standpoint, Moore's evaluation of the
enemy defences was professional. The best way of directly attacking
Bastia lay through the hill forts, for once captured they could be used
to command the rear of the town and trap it in a crossfire. But Moore
showed himself to be an overcautious soldier, prone to exaggerating
his own problems rather than exploiting the enemy's. Indeed, he seldom
seems to have put himself in the French camp, but remained paralysed
by imaginary fears of ferocious resistance at every stage of an attack.
If the redcoats attacked the hill forts he saw them being punished
heavily as they advanced over the rough ground, and suffering progres-
sive attrition as they battled from one post to another. Although the
enemy was simultaneously defending the citadel, harbour, town and
ten or so redoubts, camps and forts Moore believed they would concentrate forbidding forces to meet his attack.

The same thinking powered his reaction to the Nelson plan. Its
supporters saw a use in pinning French forces to different places. Thus,
when D'Aubant refused to attack the heights, Hood turned to Paoli's
two thousand Corsicans and asked one half to support Nelson north
of the town and the other to worry the hill forts to prevent the French
from moving men from place to place. But Moore could only see the
dangers of dividing his own men. He worried that troops landed by
the fleet would be overpowered in a savage counterattack, and took
little account of the navy's ability to supply or assist them. In the event
the French showed none of the spirit Moore ascribed. Not a single

sortie was ever launched against the British lines. In short, while Moore's caution was never going to squander men or ammunition, it risked losing opportunities and creating a demoralising inaction. In Corsica it kept men and guns idling in camp with a vulnerable enemy only twelve miles away.[52]

In the other corner, across from the robust redcoat, stood the slight, blue-coated figure of Horatio Nelson, captain of the *Agamemnon*. He worked to a different beat, forever on the move, prowling for opportunities and victories. No enemy could show him a weakness that would be missed. His letters rang with the problems of the French, with their irresolution, fears and shortages, and they also exuded a heart-raising confidence – perhaps overconfidence. For though Nelson's policy avoided despair and defeatism, it too was flawed. It risked overextending men and inviting a drubbing, and if Moore overrated his opponents Nelson underestimated them. The French commander, St Michel, spoke highly of his soldiers: 'Their enthusiasm is such that even the wounded are eager to leave hospital to join in the battle,' he wrote. Civilians, including women and children, would help to repair broken fortifications and batteries. Nelson expected that the French would quickly succumb to a two-fisted attack. 'We shall, in time, accomplish the taking [of] Bastia, I have no doubt, in the way we proposed to assault it, by bombardment and cannonading, joined to a close blockade of the harbour.' But he would be surprised by his enemy's endurance.[53]

The differences between Moore and Nelson were now to be tested. As Nelson had requested, he was rewarded with the responsibility of leading the land attack, alongside Lieutenant Colonel Villettes, who headed the seven hundred soldiers Hood had raised. Nelson liked and respected Villettes as an easy-mannered gentleman and 'a most excellent officer', considering him the ablest soldier in the army. From a French émigré family, he had lived for forty years and served in the army for almost twenty of them, two as a lieutenant colonel. Apparently he enjoyed his profession, for he had abandoned a career in the law to follow it, and at Toulon won the praise of superiors. When the task force sailed from St Fiorenzo on 25 March it was at least well officered. Nelson bundled Captain Paget and Lieutenant Alexander Duncan off to Naples for the necessary military supplies, and tightened the blockade of Bastia. The *Tartar* and the *Scout* brig were anchored on the flanks of the town, guard boats sealed the harbour mouth by rowing back and forth, and the *Fox* and a few gunboats threw occasional shots at the defences. Corsican volunteers climbed aboard the *Agamemnon* to replace temporarily men earmarked to work with the troops ashore.[54]

The talking was done and it was time to fight, but on the eve of the attack Nelson received important new intelligence. It was bad news. The number of troops waiting for him in Bastia was far greater than anyone had supposed – four thousand, perhaps more. Nelson now knew he was attacking not only well-placed positions, but also superior numbers of soldiers. When the flagship *Victory* appeared in the offing on 2 April with the first of the larger ships assigned to the blockade, Nelson deliberately kept the new information to himself. Even at this hour, when Hood had staked his reputation and forces on Nelson's judgement, he feared the attack might still be called off.[55]

For Moore the tidings would have justified his caution. He doubted that the army and navy together could take Bastia, and prophesied disaster. 'Without more good luck than can be expected some misfortune will happen,' he said.[56]

Nelson thought otherwise, and that nothing could be gained without being ventured. 'I feel for the honour of my country,' he said, 'and had rather be beat than not make the attack. If we do not try we never can be successful. I own I have no fears for the final issue: it will be conquest . . .'[57]

6

An impressive amount of sail lay off Bastia on 3 April. Six ships of the line, one of them the *Agamemnon*, two frigates and a brig formed a threatening display, but at the masthead of the *Victory*, Hood's impressive flagship, flew a flag of truce. A boat pulled out with a last offer to spare the town. Perhaps the admiral was willing to give the garrison passage to France, or accept a declaration in favour of the monarchy. It hardly mattered, for the appeal went unheeded and before the day was out another flag was running up. It was red, and everybody knew it meant the contest had begun.[58]

The larger British ships strung out in a huge crescent to the south, beyond the enemy guns, while the *Scout* brig and some gunboats and launches edged forward to close the harbour and entertain the enemy batteries and gunboats. The greatest threat to the inshore blockade (managed by a big, good-humoured Canadian named Captain Benjamin Hallowell) was the nearby island of Capraia, where French ships were accustomed to shelter. Even before the British net closed around Bastia a few panic-stricken merchants shot out and made for Capraia. Hood sent Captain Wolseley in the *Imperieuse* to watch the island, ready to intercept any more vessels that tried to run to or from Corsica.[59]

Hood controlled the entire operation from the *Victory*, but the landing party was entrusted to Nelson and Villettes and the *Agamemnon* was generally found hovering maternally offshore near their camp. As a post-captain Nelson outranked Villettes, a military lieutenant colonel, but in a striking contrast to recent interservice relations the two men stuck to their own spheres of influence and became close comrades in arms. In fact, the only demarcation disputes occurred among the naval officers serving ashore. Verbally Hood had authorised Nelson to command all the seamen cooperating with Villettes, but the captain's written instructions were clumsily worded. They gave Nelson charge of the seamen 'attached to the batteries', as if sailors otherwise employed thereabouts were not his responsibility. There was some difficulty, therefore, when Anthony Hunt, a junior captain, appeared. Hunt had served under Nelson before, and Horatio conceded him 'a most exceedingly good young man', but he was also one of the admiral's favourites and his purpose was unclear. Hood assured Nelson that Hunt had no distinct authority, and was entirely subject to Nelson's direction, but the unnecessary confusion would have unfortunate results.[60]

Villettes and Nelson went ashore on the 3rd, preparing for an embarkation of men, ordnance and stores during the hours of darkness. In the early hours of the following morning boatload after boatload of redcoats made for the shingle beach three miles north of Bastia and near the tower of Miomo Nelson had captured less than two months before. There were 853 soldiers of the 11th, 25th, 30th and 60th regiments and the Royal Artillery, as well as 218 marines, 112 chasseurs and 250 seamen. The total force amounted to 1,500 and though the work was going to be dangerous there was considerable cheer. Even fourteen-year-old William Hoste had volunteered to accompany Nelson ashore, but the captain kept him aboard the *Agamemnon* with the rest of his young gentlemen.[61]

But there was no restraining the old admiral whose attack it was. Hood rose every day before dawn and inspired the whole force. He had himself rowed ashore in his barge, oblivious of the enemy shells splashing around, and no sooner were his feet on land than he scrambled up the hill like a mountain sheep to inspect the site selected for the batteries. Fourteen hundred armed Corsicans were there to pay homage to their liberator, and Hood pronounced himself satisfied. He believed that Bastia would surrender within ten days of a bombardment being opened, while Elliot, who accompanied him, reported 'the men . . . in the highest spirits, and the officers . . . very confident of success, which is rendered the more probable both by the destitute conditions and the ill disposition and temper of the garrison, as well as the inhabitants'. From the beginning everyone understood that success rested not simply upon one operation, but upon the simultaneous application of naval and military power to the moral and physical capabilities of the defenders.[62]

The attack was made upon the northern flank of the town, and the force sweated to reach a position for their batteries, some 2,300 yards from the citadel. Not far ahead the enemy held the tower of Toga, defending the northern approach to the town, and Villettes posted pickets and raised a wooden abattis to guard against any sudden counterattack. The British had tents to the rear of their batteries but no beds or fires. However, despite the dire predictions of some army men back at St Fiorenzo, there were no French sorties. It was a good sign, Nelson thought. Maybe the French were already resigned to defeat. Maybe they felt the risks of counterattacking were just not worth the effort.

Enemy inaction helped, but the job of building the batteries was famously hard labour. Some of the guns were more than nine feet long and weighed three tons, and their small, solid wheels were utterly unsuited to moving on land. With them had to be hauled many tons of powder as well as shot and shell, all landed from the *Agamemnon* and other ships and dragged over broken ground up to the batteries. Daily Nelson's sailors struggled, slashing their way through scrub and maquis, bridging ravines and blazing crude tracks if there were none. Following the example of Cooke's men at St Fiorenzo, they made sledges for the guns and hauled them over the uneven ground by slinging huge straps around rocks and using them as pulleys. By one means or another the tars were soon 'dragging guns up such heights as are scarcely creditable [credible]' with enormous willpower. Their goal was a rocky crag 1,000 yards from the nearest enemy redoubt (Cabanelle), 1,800 from a twenty-four-pound battery at the north end of the town and 2,300 from the citadel. There Nelson's men stacked sandbags and casks and packed them with earth to make redoubts, laid gun platforms and mounted an elaborate battery consisting of four mortars, a howitzer, two carronades, a field piece and eight naval cannon, including five twenty-four pounders. On 9 April the French had seen enough, and fired the first shots from mortars and cannons. Drums beat an alarm in the British camp and some tents were torn up in a long bombardment, but not a man was hurt.[63]

On 11 April, Nelson and Villettes were ready to reply. Again Hood summoned the garrison, but this time his messenger was insulted, and Lacombe St Michel, who commanded in Bastia, brazenly replied that 'he had hot shot for our ships, and bayonets for our troops, [and] that when two-thirds of his troops were killed he should then trust to the generosity of the English'. The British were not surprised. St Michel was not a man to be easily cowed, and served a particularly unforgiving government that knew how to deal with failures. Indeed, one argument for supporting the blockade of Bastia with a formal siege was to create additional pretexts for an honourable surrender. But that time had not yet come. Hood's red flag rose ominously to his main topgallant mast and English colours were raised over Nelson's tent, while his men punched the air and gave three rousing cheers. At nine-thirty the British batteries roared, and shot and shells began to hurtle upwards and then to shelve down towards the French positions. The Corsican allies were difficult to manage, but many were crack shots, and they squirmed between boulders to snipe at enemy officers.[64]

The French bit back, however, and that afternoon the British suffered their first serious reverse. As the frigate *Proselyte* engaged the tower of Toga, which sat on the shore about seven hundred yards from Nelson's battery, she was hit by red-hot shot. Thick smoke billowed out of her hatchways, and as boats from the fleet rallied round her crew scurried over the side while the ship crackled into flames. She burned to the water's edge, but two of her officers chose to fight with Nelson on shore rather than quit the contest. One was Captain Walter Scrocold, the last man off the doomed frigate, and the other Nelson's old protégé Commander Joseph Bullen, who had been serving aboard the *Proselyte* as a temporary volunteer. Though badly burned Bullen reported to Nelson's batteries for duty.[65]

Inevitably the landing party was soon suffering casualties of its own, and Nelson and Villettes reported twenty-six between 4 and 25 April. The captain of the *Agamemnon* himself was usually found where the fight was hottest and had two remarkable escapes. On 12 April a select gathering ascended a rocky ridge dividing two branches of a stream that united and fell into the sea south of Toga. The men were Lieutenant Colonel Villettes and Captain Nelson, the leaders of the British assault force, Captain John Clark of the 69th Regiment, normally assigned to the *Agamemnon* but now acting as brigade major ashore, Lieutenant John Duncan and a leader of the Corsican partisans. They were there to see whether the ridge would support another battery, for its summit was five hundred yards nearer the town and commanded the Camp de Cabanelle to the southeast. For a while the men discussed the problems of hauling and siting their guns, oblivious to a persistent fire of musketry, round and grape spitting at them from behind the wall of the Cabanelle a few hundred yards or so away. Their reconnaissance completed, they were about to retire when a cannon shot ploughed straight into them. Clark was glancing over Nelson's right shoulder towards the Cabanelle when the ball wrenched off his right arm and part of his side. Though fearfully mutilated he survived, but the Corsican chief was killed outright. Nelson himself was untouched.[66]

A week later Horatio sustained the first of many wounds he would receive in the line of duty. Again he was in the van. On the 13th he had begun to build two new advanced batteries, consisting of five cannons and two or three mortars situated close to the seaside where they could fire upon the Toga tower at close range. After days of heaving guns, ammunition and materiel into place, the seamen opened fire at daylight on the 21st, battering the tower and Cabanelle and raining missiles upon another battery the French had established near the government house. The town battery was soon knocked out of action and its gunners had to be flogged by their officers to be kept at their posts.[67]

During the establishment of his new seaside batteries Nelson customarily walked from the main camp to inspect the work, taking a circuitous but safe route sheltered from enemy fire. But on the 19th he and Captain Fremantle, who occasionally served on shore, took a short cut. A shot from the Toga tower whined by, thumped into a nearby rock and flung stone and earth with the force of a bursting grenade. Nelson rose shakily to his feet to find that he had nothing more than an unpleasant cut in his back, while the captain of the *Tartar* was showered with dirt. Brushing himself down, Fremantle waggishly vowed he would never take the short cut again.[68]

7

In normal times the French relieved their garrison at Bastia regularly, every fortnight in the formidably hot summer months. But there was no relief from the British ships and boats hugging the harbour, or from Villettes and Nelson's guns as they hammered day and night, the shells tracing fiery arcs when they flew through the hours of darkness. Military positions were the main targets, but much fell indiscriminately upon civilian buildings. Hood expected the town to stand only ten or so days of bombardment, but he was wrong. Ten days passed, then twenty and then thirty, but still the French held out and the monotonous thud of the guns and the shriek of shot and shells went on. At the beginning of May the defenders remained defiant, and swore they would 'give bomb for bomb'. Like his admiral, Nelson marvelled at their dogged resistance.[69]

It was not that the seamen and artillerists manning the British batteries were not scoring hits, though some of the foreign equipment was proving to be poor stuff. 'The Neapolitan mortars [are] not worth a farthing,' growled Fremantle. 'They crack. The shells don't fit them, [though they] were very pretty in the nights to see the shells flying.' But 'great damage' was being inflicted on the northern part of the town, where even stone houses were being reduced to rubble or having their roofs smashed in. The Cabanelle camp was quickly silenced, and the town batteries twice demolished, though the French worked desperately to repair fractured barricades and restore guns to action. Reports intimated a rising toll of dead and wounded. A surgeon who got out of the town on the 23rd said that several had been slain and most of nearly three hundred hospital patients were battle casualties. A boat loaded with fifty-four sick and wounded, including the former captain of the frigate La Fortunée, tried to flee Bastia on 12 May and was captured by the Agamemnon. Its occupants put the casualties at five hundred and fifty, and gave a 'dismal' account of the 'distresses' in the town. At the end of the siege the figure had climbed to some 743, most of them dead, a higher casualty rate than Calvi would suffer in the months ahead.[70]

The bombardment multiplied the misery of the defenders and probably weakened their morale. They failed to counterattack, and apparently dreaded an overwhelming general assault, something that suggests that they thought themselves greatly outnumbered. The French were also low on food and gunpowder, and rested their hopes on small

boats bringing supplies and reinforcements from Capraia. The inhabitants of Bastia had probably been short of provisions when the siege
began, stinted by Nelson's ships over recent months, but now Hood's
tight blockade almost closed the port. The admiral knew the important role the blockade would play. 'All we have to do is to keep
succours out of Bastia,' he said. At the end of April a formidable
number of ships and boats were still before the port. The *Victory*,
Princess Royal, *Fortitude*, *Agamemnon* and *Illustrious* ships of the
line, the fifty-gun *Romney*, the frigates the *Tartar* and *Meleager*, the
Gorgon store ship under Nelson's old comrade James Wallis, the *Scout*
brig and a flotilla of gunboats all busied themselves offshore. Elliot
believed that their work was 'the chief means' of British success.[71]

By the last week of April the contest had become a grim battle of
wills, but both sides were reviewing their situations. Among the French
despondency was growing. Little food was getting through, the dispiriting fire continued and the British were closing the range with new
advanced batteries. On the dark night of 25 April two figures in disguise
crept like criminals to a felucca in the harbour and fled the doomed
town. They were Lacombe St Michel and his military commander. They
got away, but to no advantage to the besieged. In France, St Michel
excused his flight by saying he wanted to prevent a relief expedition
risking the trip from Toulon when Bastia was so close to surrender;
the town, in other words, had to be abandoned. Back in the forlorn
town his deserted soldiers, especially those crouched in squalid redoubts
and behind shot-splintered walls, hoped he was bringing flour and
gunpowder but when nothing came drew their own conclusions.[72]

While the defenders faced each dawn with diminished hope, Nelson
had also realised that his attack had not lived up to expectations,
and that Bastia was a tougher nut to crack than he had anticipated.
He had banked on the bombardment and blockade inducing the
garrison to surrender, but the French were showing remarkable
steadiness under fire. Their obduracy invited the British to storm, but
that prospect seemed some way off. Nelson's guns were too distant
to make a breach in the citadel, and while the nearest enemy strong-
point, the Cabanelle, was being battered and broken it was powerfully manned. Eight hundred men defended the camp, enough to deter
Villettes from launching a premature assault. On 26 April, Nelson
was almost as deflated as his French opponents, and had begun to
talk about the futile bombardment and need for reinforcements as if
his name was D'Aubant.[73]

It was increasingly obvious that while Nelson's attack was a useful supplementary or diversionary operation, it fell short of substituting for the proper assault that ought to have been made from the heights behind the town. The new redoubts the French had thrown up below the mountain crest, occupying places the British troops ought to have secured after the fall of St Fiorenzo, were far from ideal for bombarding the citadel. Only one of them, the Guaduola redoubt near Cardo, was as close to the citadel as any of Nelson's batteries, though British guns established there would have gained something from elevation. But they certainly commanded the indifferently manned hill forts immediately below, and in British hands those posts, positioned just above the town itself, would have outflanked Bastia and soon foreclosed any resistance.

As Hood, Nelson and Villettes fretted at their slow progress they were increasingly intrigued by the possibility that even at this stage a successful attack might be made upon the upper posts. According to enemy deserters and the Corsican partisans who stole about to snipe at French sentries, they were weakly garrisoned. It appeared that the four stone hill forts had been bled of men to create the same number of advanced redoubts further up. All eight forts or redoubts were connected, but only Guaduola was thought to house as many as two hundred men. Admiral Hood and Elliot pondered the subject again in the *Victory*, and wondered whether the French on the heights might have grown complacent. Hitherto, the British had concentrated their attack solely upon the town below, and even in Bastia it was now known that most of the redcoats were refusing to advance. Perhaps a sudden fog-shrouded assault might yet catch the upper posts off guard.[74]

Sir Gilbert was a genial, worldly man, but the testier tone his letters adopted in April betrayed a dwindling patience with General D'Aubant. He had long since addressed a 'secret and confidential' letter to the minister of war seeking the general's immediate recall. 'We are at this moment entirely ignorant whether he proposes to stir or not,' carped Sir Gilbert, 'and I am internally convinced that nothing will move him but the fear . . . of Lord Hood's separate success.' At home the recipient, Henry Dundas, thought Hood part of the problem. He hurried out a new military commander with orders to repair the damage between the services, but was careful to ensure that his instructions clearly made him independent of the imperial admiral.[75]

While the wheels of the administration turned slowly, in Corsica the final appeals were being made to General D'Aubant. On 18 April, Hood and Elliot jointly invited the general to attack the heights. Now, however, the gulf between the commanders was wider than ever. Hood had been commandeering any army supplies he could find in the ships without a by-your-leave, and the appeal itself was laced with acid sarcasm:

If you had happened, in the course of the last fortnight, to have visited the ground or observed the operations of His Majesty's troops at this place, which is within four hours' walk of your headquarters, whatever your first opinion may have been concerning this expedition or whatever it may still be of its ultimate success, you would have had an opportunity of satisfying yourself beyond a doubt that the enemy may be effectually annoyed . . .[76]

Neither this, nor the statement that D'Aubant would be held to blame for 'the evils' that flowed from a delay in the capture of Bastia, moved the general. He was as unyielding as the rocky Corsican heights. Whatever their differences his officers also rallied behind him in a meeting of 22 April, and reaffirmed the judgement that 'with the whole of our force we were unequal to the taking of Bastia'. On 1 May Hood tried again, and for the last time. Even 'a show of an intention' to attack the upper posts might distract the French, he suggested. The general's reply was as specious as it was final. When Hood read that 'a mere show' of attacking would only 'lessen the respect in which the enemy should ever be kept to hold [off] a British force', he must have realised that there could be no meeting of minds.[77]

With the enemy in sight Captain Nelson was rarely depressed for long. His warrior spirit was soon returning, and he searched for new and more effective sites for his artillery. At the end of April he established batteries upon the ridge above Cabanelle, where poor Clark had been hit, shifting two eighteen-pound carronades and twelve- and nine-pound cannons up horrific gradients. 'The work of getting up guns to this battery was a work of the greatest difficulty, and which never in my opinion would have been accomplished by any other than British seamen,' Nelson said proudly. Manned by Lieutenant Andrews and five sailors, and protected by soldiers and Corsican skirmishers, the fresh pieces opened fire on May Day. No sooner had they spoken than Nelson had his men dragging a big twenty-four and a howitzer to another part of the ridge. By 8 May three cannons, two carronades and a howitzer were barking from above the Cabanelle. Stationed only a mile from the citadel, their fire also gained from the greater elevation and was soon 'sorely' mutilating the French defences.[78]

On 15 May the British captured a boat attempting to bring gunpowder from Capraia to Bastia, and on board was a brother of Jean-Baptiste Galeazzini, the mayor of the besieged town. As Hood interrogated the prisoner aboard the *Victory* it became obvious that the citizens of Bastia lived in dread of their town being sacked by wild and uncontrollable partisans. To rule out a massacre the mayor's brother offered to act as an intermediary, and to send the town his disheartening news that their gunpowder was no longer coming. Suddenly events began to move quickly.

On the 19th someone excitedly drew Nelson's attention to a flag of truce ascending the *Victory*, and during the dying afternoon boats began flitting between the fleet and town. Something was afoot, but with the guns silent and waiting, Nelson, Villettes and their sweat-stained followers could only sit tense and expectant.

Then suddenly enemy officers were striding out of the Cabanelle to shake hands with the besiegers. After forty-five days it was over. Despite self-doubts and the forebodings of 'Fiorenzo wiseheads' Bastia had fallen.[79]

XIX

A LONG AND HAZARDOUS SERVICE

Nelson, by valour led to deathless fame,
All toils surmounted, and all foes o'ercome,
Braved every danger, calm and undismay'd,
Whilst some new triumph marked each step he made.
                        Georgiana, Duchess of Devonshire

1

ON 24 May a tired but excited Captain Nelson made an entry in his journal. 'At daylight this morning the most glorious sight an Englishman, and which I believe none but an Englishman, could experience was to be seen. Four thousand five hundred men laying down their arms to less than 1,000 English [British] soldiers. Our loss of men in taking this town containing upwards of 14,000 inhabitants, and [which] fully inhabited would contain 25,000, was the smallest possible to be conceived.'[1]

It was a magnification, of course, though perhaps an excusable one, for the capture of Bastia was a triumph plucked from professional pessimism. After the formal capitulation on the 22nd, Nelson saw his foes yield their outposts and then the citadel, and watched thousands of French soldiers and their Corsican auxiliaries tramp grimly to the mole head to ground their muskets and board the transports waiting to ship them home. He had transmitted the heartfelt thanks of Admiral Hood to all the men who had served ashore.

The British had fired twenty thousand round shot and shells during the siege, and expended a thousand barrels of powder, but in terms of manpower it had been an inexpensive conquest. Only sixty men had been killed or wounded. The casualties included seven from the *Agamemnon*, one of them Lieutenant Andrews, who retired to Leghorn to heal his wounds. By comparison the enemy had suffered 743 casualties, as noted most of them dead, and yielded four thousand five hundred prisoners, a figure that presumably included the wounded. Nearly eighty artillery pieces, substantial supplies, and *La Flêche* corvette as well as the town itself, the largest in Corsica, also graced the triumph.[2]

There were those in the army who felt discomfited by a victory that confounded their predictions of a more protracted or bloody struggle. A competent soldier, Lieutenant Colonel Moore, was reduced to joining an incompetent one, General D'Aubant, in sneering from the sidelines. At times they had implied that the capture of Bastia was beyond the present means of the combined services, and increasingly they exonerated their inaction by disparaging Nelson's bombardment and insisting that it added nothing to the naval blockade but a waste of ammunition. Their remarks about the siege have sometimes been accepted as objective statements; but in one sense Moore and D'Aubant's professional reputations rested more easily with a failure of the siege than its successful outcome.

It was true, of course, that the bombardment ran down munitions, though we can imagine Nelson scoffing that those who did not fight always conserved ammunition. The end of the siege left reserves of powder particularly low. The fleet was in need of twelve hundred barrels, while at the arsenal at Gibraltar, which had sent six hundred barrels of powder to Hood, the reserves were uncomfortably low. It was also true that the siege was an inadequate substitute for the attack that should have been made from the heights, and made for heavier work than Nelson expected. But to argue, as some historians have done, that the bombardment added nothing to the situation is merely to imbibe Moore's wilful negativity. The dearth of food, produced solely by the blockade, seems to have been the most immediate cause of the town's surrender, but there is nothing surprising about that. In many, if not most, sieges that end in a negotiated surrender the lack of food and water are key issues, as they had been in Nelson's previous military operation in Nicaragua, but that hardly entitles other contributions to be dismissed. Evidence from inside Bastia suggests considerable structural damage, heavy and rising casualties and a serious shortage of gunpowder produced by the firing. In fact, both St Michel's flight from the town and its final surrender were partly justified by the lack of powder. It is reasonable to presume that the total package, including the strain of living under fire and fears of the town being stormed by ferocious Corsicans, influenced the result. Calvi's fall, no less than Bastia's, would be precipitated by the exhaustion of food and ammunition.[3]

Early in May, after a period of doubt, the confidence of the Hood–Nelson party had increased. The new advanced batteries had opened fire, and the French suddenly looked shaky. With a victory looming, D'Aubant looked for a way out. On 13 May reinforcements arrived from Gibraltar. There were only six hundred of them, and they probably made a smaller difference to the comparative sizes of the opposing forces than the casualties wrought by Nelson's siege guns had done, but they gave the general a means of saving face. On the 14th two of D'Aubant's officers went to the *Victory* with an offer to collaborate. A week before Hood would have jumped at the opportunity, but now he eyed the ambassadors with scarcely veiled contempt. As far as he was concerned, they were merely cutting themselves in for a piece of credit at the end of a hard-won fight. Scathingly he told the officers that their general 'need not give himself that trouble'.[4]

Hood had not wholly mistaken his man, and when the surrender of Bastia was finally agreed D'Aubant descended like a vulture upon the spoils, appearing in force upon the heights above the town on 21 May. It was his duty, of course, to occupy the abandoned redoubts and forts, but in an extraordinary dispatch to the home secretary he had the gall to suggest that the news of his advance might have hastened the French surrender. The general had now abandoned all consistency. He asked Dundas to believe that his advance, after the enemy had agreed to capitulate, was helping to end the siege, when he had spent two months vociferously refusing to move on the grounds that such an advance was pointless. Hood gave the general no relief. The day D'Aubant's warriors marched over the heights the admiral told him Bastia would have fallen 'long since' if the troops had acted properly, and warned that he now intended to attack Calvi, the last French stronghold in Corsica.[5]

There were lessons for everyone, including Nelson. As he inspected the town from the inside, he marvelled at a strength he had earlier denied. It should have told him something about the need to base military decisions upon the best intelligence, but he was naturally exhilarated by his success and for the moment voiced rather the opposite conclusion. Whatever some historians have said about the capture of

Bastia, the naval officers of the day, as well as many in the army, regarded it as a victory dragged from the teeth of pessimism. It certainly reinforced Nelson's impressions of the capabilities of his seamen. As for the enemy, they had shown no spirit whatsoever, he mused. 'I always was of opinion, have ever acted up to it, and never have had reason to alter it, that one Englishman was equal to three Frenchmen.' It was a favourite boast, but fortunately Nelson's tendency to loose egotistical talk was not always a true indication of his deeper reflections or actual conduct.[6]

In the case of Bastia he had made mistakes, but it is difficult to deny him considerable credit. He had urged the attack, and whether blockading or besieging he had been its most energetic instrument. None reading the letters and journals of the day can doubt his strenuous commitment. Yet, remarkably, the man who profited as much as any from his labour paid it the most meagre public tribute. Admiral Hood was surely aware of Nelson's need for recognition, as well as the sacrifices he had made to earn it, but the admiral's public dispatch of 24 May damned his leading subordinate with faint praise and credited some of his achievements to another officer.

In stating that Nelson 'had the command and directions of the seamen in landing the guns, mortars, and stores', Hood made it sound as if he had merely conducted a routine disembarkation. Nelson complained that it put him 'in the rear' of the action instead of its van, but there was worse. 'Captain Hunt,' said the admiral, 'was on shore in the command of the batteries from the hour the troops landed to the surrender of the town.' As worded, this was more than an astonishing remark; it was an untruth. Hunt, Nelson grumbled, 'scarcely ever saw' a battery, nor did he render 'any service during the siege. If any person ever says he did, then I submit to the character of a story-teller.' Others agreed. Some were 'thunderstruck' by Hood's dispatch, and Captain Serocold even talked about publishing a correction. Others would have seen it as another example of the admiral's favouritism; Captain Fremantle, for example, had long concluded that Hood judged actions by the man, rather than a man by his actions.[7]

Hunt was also sent home with the admiral's dispatches, a privilege that offered him further opportunities to press his claims and the right, so he said, to a gratuity reserved for those who brought news of important territorial acquisitions. Nelson understood that Hood possessed some personal reason for pushing Hunt forward, but he was understandably hurt that it had been done at his expense. The attack was 'almost a child of my own', he wrote. 'The whole operations of the siege were carried on through Lord Hood's letters to me. I was the mover of it. I was the cause of its success.' More than 'a little vexed' with his admiral, Nelson, however, resolved not to quarrel. He had too much to lose, for Hood had already promised that Nelson would enjoy further opportunities for distinction at Calvi. Bottling his resentment, he consoled himself with the belief that Sir Gilbert Elliot, 'a stranger and a landsman', would report more accurately and 'do me that credit which a friend and brother officer' had denied.[8]

In the meantime he wrote to the families of the four *Agamemnons* who had died in the fight, and prepared the rest of the company for the next siege. This time it appeared that the army would play its full part. As Bastia fell a new military commander-in-chief arrived to replace the smouldering D'Aubant. Lieutenant General the Honourable Charles Stuart was slim and handsome, a ball of energy, and a soldier to the soles of his boots. He had been twice briefed, once by his government and again by Sir Gilbert, and gave every indication of wanting a better relationship between the two services. Announcing his regret at missing the siege, Stuart generously acknowledged that the victory was 'alone due to Lord Hood', and spoke about a new and cordial partnership.[9]

It was not going to be plain sailing, however. Stuart might have started off on the right foot but Hood was soon antagonising him, and like many brilliant military men Stuart himself was temperamental, stubborn and unbalanced. Even the level-tempered Elliot eventually found him impossible. 'Of all the vain, haughty, absurd and wrongheaded men I ever had the ill-fortune to meet with, he is the *facile princeps*,' Sir Gilbert would complain. Dealing with him was like being 'locked up with a madman in a cell'. Fortunately, though Nelson occasionally ran afoul of Stuart's prickly disposition, he saw the gold underneath and admired and liked the general.[10]

Before the campaign against Calvi got underway, some urgent naval business intervened. The French fleet gave Vice Admiral Hotham's squadron the slip outside Toulon and escaped into the Mediterranean. No one knew where it was going, but the probability was that the French were engaged in a last, desperate effort to save Corsica. Hood put to sea with all available ships on 7 June, the day after the news reached him in Bastia. The *Agamemnon* was already loaded with men and materiel for Calvi, but Nelson quickly shed her excess to catch up with the departing fleet, fancying that at last he was on the eve of a fleet action. 'I pray God we may meet this [enemy] fleet,' he wrote. Hood was also dead set on a decisive result, and 'was in hopes to have taken or destroyed them . . . which I certainly should have done had not the wind failed me' and enabled the French to slink into Golfe Jouan, west of Nice. When the British came up on 10 June the enemy ships were anchored close inshore in a strong defensive position, protected by banks and shore batteries. Hood considered whether he might double the enemy line by using the shallows to interpose some of his ships between the land and the French fleet – much as Nelson's 'band of brothers' would do at the Nile four years later – but the manoeuvre seemed impracticable. Hood withdrew like a hungry tiger driven from a kill. Even reinforced by Hotham's division, he could only appoint guard ships to keep the French under observation, and return to Corsica to cover the siege of Calvi.[11]

Nelson was sent back to Bastia early to complete his task, and on 12 June embarked the soldiers and stores for the next campaign. He knew the capture of Calvi would be a hazardous enterprise and accepted the personal risks it promised. At Bastia he had been lucky, but this time he was sailing towards his first major injury.

2

The fleet of victuallers, transports and store ships swallowed 1,450 officers and men and left for Mortella Bay at St Fiorenzo under Nelson's careful stewardship. Stuart went as far as St Fiorenzo overland, and Nelson was also sorry to leave Villettes behind. The lieutenant colonel remained in Bastia as acting governor, installed in a house always open to his naval friend. Nelson, said Villettes, had 'a very good right' to call it his own, and would always find board and a 'tolerable dinner' within its walls. Still, the captain was relieved to be serving under a new military commander-in-chief who believed in making life unsafe for the enemy. During the delay Stuart had inspected Calvi and was impatient to begin, and Nelson agreed. He was supposed to wait for Hood but to Stuart's delight quickly got underway, and with the *Dolphin* and the *Lutine* was soon shepherding the army toward France's last foothold on Corsica.[12]

The position of Calvi was majestic and intimidating. To the west jutted the rugged Cape Revellata, while north and east the town confronted a large but shallow bay. Towards the sea Calvi's defences were formidable, with large granite walls and a powerful citadel making any frontal attack difficult in the extreme. When Stuart and Nelson arrived the small harbour was also guarded by a gunboat and the *Melpomene* and *Le Mignonne*, the last surviving frigates from the squadron that had skirmished with Nelson the previous year. More substantially, the town was backed against steep, jagged peaks, deemed to be almost inaccessible, supported by a string of back-door forts and batteries that swept around the town to the west and southwest and covered the land approaches from the rear.

The most northerly of these rearguard fortifications was Fort San Francesco, where three eighteen- or twenty-four-pounders glinted ominously from a rock that the sea battered endlessly below. The most important was Fort Mozzello further south. Perhaps six hundred and fifty yards west of Calvi, Fort Mozzello was a pentagon, with strong stone-casemated faces mounting ten guns (variously described as eights, eighteens and twenty-fours) enclosing a central four-gun cavalier and bombproof that commanded views of both land and sea. To its right, a little north, the Mozzello was supported by an old tower with a howitzer and the Fountain battery, a fascine work of six eighteens sitting on the shoulder of a hill. On a steep rock to the left of Fort Mozzello, and about 2,200 yards to the southwest of Calvi, stood Fort Mollinochesco, its eighteen-pounder and four or five smaller guns watching protectively over the town's communications with the interior.

In terms of manpower Calvi was much weaker than Bastia. It quartered a battalion of light infantry, several companies of Provençal grenadiers, and the crews of a pair of frigates, in all about twelve hundred defenders. Far more than their counterparts in Bastia, they started the siege short of ammunition and food, and they had few gunners. Nevertheless, their morale remained good, and the natural defences of their mountain fastness led some to consider it almost impregnable.[13]

The *Lowestoffe*, *L'Aigle* and other ships were hovering off Calvi harbour when the task force arrived, but Nelson's ships passed on in search of a landing place. Three or four miles to the southwest they came upon Port Agro on 17 June. It was a forbidding sight, sharp-featured and dangerous to shipping, but there was no ready alternative. The 'port' was nothing more than the stubby, narrow outfall of a ravine that cut steeply through impressive cliffs rising almost sheer from the sea. There was no anchorage for ships, and sunken rocks rose black and menacing from the deeps offshore. With the summer winds blowing and a powerful swell rushing upon the reefs and bluffs, it was a treacherous landfall. Nelson had to keep his ships far out so his boats – longboats loaded with soldiers, artillery and equipment, towed by rowing boats – struggled for a mile to reach the inhospitable entrance to Port Agro. In miserable weather they passed inside, weaving between sharp volcanic rocks of red and yellow for another three hundred yards or so before grinding into the shallows. Supervised by Captain Cooke, one of the heroes of St Fiorenzo, the men stepped onto a rocky beach hemmed in by crags and slogged up a gruelling, boulder-strewn incline that led to a plateau a few hundred feet above. It was a grim place to land more than sixteen hundred men, but all the redcoats were ashore early in the morning of 19 June, along with bulky guns, tent equipment and stores manhandled through a heavy surf.[14]

Stuart and Nelson had made a brave decision. Instead of attacking Calvi from the waterfront, and confronting its powerful frontal defences, they were coming from behind, landing at Port Agro and hauling their guns across the mountains to attack the rear of the town. The move completely wrong-footed the French, who regarded the route as impracticable. In a council of war on 23 March an engineer told their commander, Major General Raphaël Casabianca, that guns could not be dragged over such ground, and so completely was he believed that not even a corporal's guard stood watch at Port Agro.

Despite the mountains speed was important to the task force. If the mistakes of Bastia were not to be repeated, the British had to advance rapidly before the French could fully prepare or secure strategic ground. Shifting the guns, ammunition and stores was a terrific toil, and fell originally to the seamen. About two hundred and fifty followed the redcoats ashore, almost half from the *Agamemnon*, and another fifty under Captains Serocold and Hallowell joined five days later. Nelson ordered his men to throw up a makeshift camp on the beach, and set them to heaving the artillery, ammunition and stores up the ravine and two more torturous miles to the Madonna, a hilltop shrine among the La Macarona rocks just southwest of the town's perimeter defences. As if to punish their heresy the heavens opened during the first night, and the men struggled over slippery rocks with thunder crashing above and lightning stabbing through a black sky. 'Dragging cannon up steep mountains and carrying shot and shells has been our constant employment,' Nelson scribbled to Fanny.[15]

In his journal Nelson implied that this was wholly the work of his sailors, but such was not the case. The gradients sometimes ran at forty-five degrees, and almost immediately progress became insufferably slow. Hudson Lowe, destined for fame as Napoleon's jailer but at the time a young army officer, gleefully reported Nelson's difficulties. 'A party of the navy were [was] employed in endeavouring to raise one of the 26-pounders up the hill,' he wrote in his diary. 'They began in the morning, and by the exertions of 150 men with the assistance of double blocks, pulleys, etc., the cannon was brought the greatest way up in about twelve hours, but the carriage or truck in which it was laid having broke[n], they were obliged to leave the cannon on the road.'[16]

Stuart looked on disapprovingly. The next day he suggested Nelson dispense with his pulleys and use three hundred soldiers and two hundred sailors to man-haul. 'The navy opposed the attempt at first, upon the principle that the aid of mechanisms was necessary,' said Lowe, 'but the event showed the general's superior judgement.' Setting a hundred men to each of four ropes attached to the pieces, Nelson was able to bring three guns to the batteries by the same afternoon.

Even with soldiers to help, the sinew-stretching work was painful, and went on day after day and night after night. One by one huge twenty-sixes and twenty-fours, eighteen-pounders, mortars and howitzers scaled heights up to one thousand feet to arrive at the Madonna, the new base camp, together with mounting platforms, ammunition, casks of powder and other stores. By 13 July, Nelson reckoned their labour equal to that of dragging a twenty-six-pound gun, with all its accountrements, 'upwards of eighty miles', seventeen of them up 'a very steep mountain'. Nine days later he proudly declared that twenty-five pieces had been mounted, all but three of them manned by sailors.[17]

In his letters Stuart praised 'the efforts of Capt. Nelson' and his men, but privately he grumbled that the soldiers were 'working like slaves' with the guns instead of establishing proper guard posts. His darker suspicions, primed by subordinates who filled his head with pernicious opinions of Hood, seemed to be confirmed by the frequent absence of ships offshore. Stuart felt like an old conquistador, landed upon a hostile coast with his boats burning behind him. The weather had not improved, and within a day or two of the troops being disembarked most of the ships had cut their cables and ran out to sea to avoid being wrecked upon the coast. Eventually they regrouped, but the supply line they provided was constantly endangered. The *Fox* cutter brought additional British and French royalist troops, raising Stuart's force to two thousand men, and the *Agamemnon*, *L'Aigle*, *Lowestoffe*, *Lutine* and *Fortune* remained more or less in the offing trying to maintain supplies, but the general's complaints about inadequate naval support grew louder.[18]

The small number of men with Nelson, the wavering communications and the missing admiral all fed Stuart's disaffection. When Hood did appear offshore to land stores and ordnance, he immediately interfered with the conduct of the siege by urging Stuart to send the French a summons to surrender. Stuart refused, 'for deprived of his [Hood's] cooperation hitherto and finding that it is not his intention to do more than hover off this coast, I am really at a loss to know what he means by joining me in sending a summons which would only discover to the people of Calvi intentions which cannot be kept too secret . . .'. In Stuart's opinion, 'difficulty upon difficulty here increase by Ld. H[ood] withdrawing almost every assistance from us', and he went so far as to warn that the admiral's interference, the product of 'personal vanity', could 'occasion the loss of many brave men'.[19]

Stuart was very much a land animal and there was a good deal he did not understand about the sea, despite the efforts of Nelson and Elliot to educate and conciliate him. No less than the general was Hood irritated by the damage the bad weather was doing to his communications, but his ships could not invariably maintain their positions on a dangerous lee shore. Moreover, for Hood the siege of Calvi was only one of several responsibilities demanding his attention, and he did not have large numbers of men to spare for the military operation. A year of sickness, injuries and battle casualties had wasted the strength of the Mediterranean fleet and Hood was applying to Malta and Naples for a thousand men to keep it going. 'Nothing can equal the distress of the ships on this station,' Captain Fremantle told his brother. Canvas and ropes were in short supply, and 'few' of the seventy-fours 'have more than 400 men. I . . . have but 160 on board [my frigate] instead of 200.'[20]

Another interservice crisis was looming, and only a week after landing at Calvi General Stuart was threatening to quit.

3

Nelson believed that such an act would be a disaster. As he watched Stuart bounding from rock to rock like a goat, oblivious of enemy fire, and examining one position after another, he had nothing but admiration. 'No man in the expedition has undergone the fatigue of the general,' he wrote. He was 'an extraordinary good judge of ground', and spared no personal effort, though he was wretchedly served by his officers and in danger of wearing himself to breaking point. So tireless was Stuart that he had to be begged to retire at night.[21]

Nelson's task was even more difficult than biographers have admitted. The military situation demanded extraordinary exertions and the thorny relationship between the services required the utmost tact. We rarely think of the forthright, opinionated and volatile Nelson as a diplomat. Reading intemperate personal letters, we are apt to forget that he was capable of more measured judgements in the line of duty, and that he reacted positively to goodwill and good work, and had a natural sympathy that enabled him to pacify and condole. The younger Hotham, who knew Nelson in Corsica, was not a great admirer. Nelson, he said, had nothing of 'the manner of a gentleman' in either appearance or behaviour, but he could bring people together. He was, Hotham admitted, 'perhaps, more generally beloved by all ranks of people under him than any other officer in the service, for he had in a great degree the valuable but rare quality of conciliating the most opposite tempers and forwarding the public service with unanimity amongst men not of themselves disposed to accord'.[22]

Never was that quality needed more than now. The old interservice animosities that Stuart had been sent to quench were resurfacing, threatening to pull the campaign apart, and Nelson was the only senior officer trying to keep the parties together. Moore was certainly no help. Infused with what Hood called the 'St Fiorenzo leaven' he intensely disliked the admiral, whom he considered 'a mean fellow' stinting the expedition to pamper his own vanity. It was shortly after mixing with Moore that Stuart began faithfully reproducing this opinion. Nelson wished Moore '100 leagues off' and undoubtedly attributed to him the malicious 'endeavours to poison the mind of a good man'.[23]

Whatever the origins of Stuart's bile, freely revealed to the new British Viceroy of Corsica, it specifically exempted Captain Nelson, who had 'certainly exerted himself'. Nelson swam warily between two larger and more voracious fishes, trying to reconcile them as they snapped at each other. In the early days of the siege Hood had been ready to share Nelson's opinion of Stuart. 'General Stuart, most fortunately, is not only a very able officer,' wrote the admiral, 'but [also

a] most amiable man, but he is without real assistance – such a miserable staff I believe no general ever had upon service. Happily, he has
great abilities and judgement, with a will of his own.' These words
almost parodied Nelson's, but the affair of Hood's summons began
openly dividing the senior commanders. Stuart regarded the summons
as premature, and Nelson backed him and tried to bridge the rift.
Hood reluctantly accepted Nelson's arguments, though he was careful
to wash his hands of the consequences ('if things do not go altogether
right no blame shall lay at my door') and would later accuse the
general of unnecessarily prolonging the siege.[24]

After the summons issue Nelson's job got trickier, but he pressed
Hood to satisfy as many of Stuart's endless demands as he could. 'It
was necessary to come to the point whether the siege should be persevered in or given up,' he told Hood. 'If the former, he [Stuart] must
be supplied with the means, which were more troops, more seamen
to work, and more ammunition.' Hood did not consider his support
tardy, and was not always hospitable to plain-speaking, but he took
the point. The Victory itself supplied 5,115 cartridges and 8,000 gun
wads as well as guns, stores and men. In the afternoon of 6 July,
Hood also responded immediately to a request for two more eighteen-
pounders, supplying them the same night, along with Lieutenant James
Moutray and forty seamen to man them. The guns were mounted by
daylight. Unfortunately, sickness and injury undermined every step,
and by the 20th of the month Nelson's shore party had lost more than
one hundred men. Once again Stuart reinforced the sailors with
soldiers, but Nelson persuaded Hood to strip the Victory and the
offing frigates of every spare man and to land another three hundred
sailors for service ashore.[25]

Juggling such irascible spirits as Hood and Stuart, Nelson inevitably
sustained some hits himself. After 27 July, Hood more or less remained
off the port, and Stuart grew suspicious of his daily communications
with Nelson. He warned the captain against speaking too freely about
sensitive information aboard the Victory. On the other side, Hood got
short with Nelson's tiresome requests. 'What can you mean for
applying to me for empty casks when there are a number on shore
. . . and the Nancy transport is full of them?' ranted the fiery admiral.
Nelson was volcanic himself, but to his credit battened down his feelings and worked for the common good. It seemed to succeed and
somehow Nelson kept the respect of both parties. 'I am very confident all you do will be well done,' Hood later told him.[26]

Throughout the siege Nelson and Stuart were rarely far apart. They slept in the same redoubt, reconnoitred together, shared the enemy fire and confronted the same emergencies. On 27 June, for example, they were both on hand during unusually fierce fighting on their left flank, where a party of Corsicans were first driven from a dangerously exposed outpost and then recaptured it with a courageous rally. Nelson directed a couple of guns against an enemy gunboat that threatened to intervene, and Stuart deployed a corps of light infantry, but both officers were cheered by the spirit shown by their Corsican allies. The skirmish cost the partisans one of their military commanders, shot through the heart.[27]

Nelson and Stuart also recognised the worth of each other, and if they never became friends in the way Nelson and Villettes became friends, at least they worked relatively harmoniously and productively as colleagues. Ultimately the general would commend 'the assistance and cooperation of Captain Nelson' and 'the exertions of the navy'. Given the prevailing climate between the services, a tempest waiting to break, that itself was a small miracle.[28]

4

Calvi was France's last stronghold in Corsica. It was surrounded and beyond outside help. Though a few boats fled the harbour by keeping to the shoreline east or west, British battleships and gunboats waited at sea and pounced upon more than a dozen craft during June and July. The French defenders of Calvi were without hope of succour, but determined to make an honourable resistance. They occupied a formidable defensive position, deployed more than a hundred guns and displayed substantial courage.[29]

Unfortunately, Stuart and Nelson came from behind, over heights they had thought proof against the passage of artillery, and began fighting their way through the ring of posts that covered the town to the west and southwest. The two British commanders formed an agreeable partnership. Stuart was the commander-in-chief, but in deciding where batteries needed to be established or when and if enemy positions should be stormed he conferred with Nelson and other officers, and the seamen ably seconded him. It was they who for the most part brought the guns and supplies up to the huge grey crags of La Macarona, usually at night, and it was they who generally erected and manned the batteries. Stuart also allocated a professional army artillerist to each gun, and Nelson found them impervious to advice. 'They don't seem to mind me,' he complained when they insisted on using two wads in the bore instead of one, but he deferred to their expertise when it came to pointing the pieces.[30]

Despite occasional shortages of men and spells of bad weather, Nelson had established two batteries by the end of June. One, known as the hill battery, stood 1,500 yards southwest of Fort Mozzello and a thousand northwest of Fort Mollinochesco, menacing both. The other was erected near the point of Cape Revellata and entrusted to a shadow from Nelson's past. James Moutray was the son of Mary, Horatio's old flame in Antigua. The 'very fine young man' was not quite twenty-one years old, but Nelson thought he saw the mother in his 'amiable disposition'. Moutray had succeeded Courtenay Boyle as second lieutenant of the Speedy sloop, and got a transfer to the Victory after only a year, falling under the protective wing of Lord Hood. Apparently Hood was the youngster's godfather, but he also respected the boy's professional abilities and described him as a 'most amiable and gallant officer'. He sent him to command the shore battery without any misgivings.[31]

A third battery was established on 3 July, this one by Stuart's French royalists, who also manned it. It was the only battery that was not the work of the seamen, and opened fire on Fort Mollinochesco at daylight the next morning. The royalist barrage dismantled the principal enemy gun, muzzling the French fire, but its other purpose was to cover the men who were to establish the fourth and most important of all the British batteries, one designed directly to target Fort Mozzello, the keystone of the enemy defences.

Raising the crucial new work proved complicated. According to Stuart's plan, the first attempt was made on the evening of 4 July. Most of the serviceable British guns, supported by Corsican muskets, opened up on Mollinochesco to convey the impression that it was to be the focus of the fresh attack. Apparently the deception worked, and some French artillerists in the Fountain battery or the Mozzello even pummelled Mollinochesco themselves, convinced that it was being occupied by the British.

While gunfire shattered the night on all sides, Stuart's working parties prepared to advance towards the Mozzello with the stuffed casks and sandbags needed to build the foundations of the new battery, and Nelson and his men stood ready to follow with the guns themselvs, four hulking twenty-sixes and two twenty-fours. The plan soon misfired. By ten-thirty Stuart was storming back and forth, damning his engineer for failing to appear. Soon afterwards hundreds of sappers and seamen surged forward to establish the battery, but Stuart called them back. It was too late, he had decided; if those men were caught in the open at daylight without their guns mounted, they would be cut to ribbons by French fire.

Try again! The plan ran more smoothly on the evening of the 6th. With silent but 'excessive labour' the pioneers and sailors threw up the advanced battery about seven hundred and fifty yards from the Mozzello, but it took longer than Nelson expected and daylight found him with only one gun in place. For a while there was a deathly stillness, as if the enemy gunners were paralysed in astonishment at the sight of a British battery suddenly materialising in the early light, but then a fusillade of grape, shot and shell was thrown at the feverish workers. A mate of a transport ship fell in agony, with holes ripped through both thighs. Two crowns in his pocket had been driven through one of his legs and into the other. A seaman of the *Agamemnon* also went down, and three soldiers of the guard. Captain Serocold, 'a gallant good officer, and as able a seaman as ever went to sea' according to Nelson, was hit behind the ear by grape shot as he cheered on the men hauling the last cannon into position. His friend, Captain Hallowell, a burly thirty-three-year-old whose 'indefatigable zeal, activity and ability' was served by the frame and face of a pugilist, helped carry the injured officer from the field. In a small valley with a gentle stream Serocold found a brief, merciful sanctuary from the noise of battle before he died.[32]

Still in the thick of the fire, Nelson finished the battery and turned it upon their molesters. Roaring like a wounded lion, it simultaneously engaged the Mozzello, the Fountain battery and Fort San Francesco, and soon began to dowse their fire. This battery, manned by seamen, was Stuart's principal weapon, especially after the French abandoned and burned Fort Mollinochesco on the 7th and allowed the redundant royalist battery to be dismantled. Nelson and Hallowell took alternate twenty-four-hour shifts supervising the advanced guns. They found that Stuart had chosen his ground well, close enough to inflict terrific damage on the French defences but to some extent shielded by Fort Mozzello from the San Francesco battery and the town bastion of Calvi.

Nevertheless, the new British battery was so obviously a danger that it drew exceptional fire. On its first day it 'was hit almost every time' the Mozzello fired, and even when Nelson's guns silenced or demolished French batteries during the day, the defenders spent the nights in frantic efforts to renew them for the mornings. An unremitting and murderous thirteen-day slogging match ensued, during which thirty people were slain or injured at the advanced British battery and five of its guns dismounted. "Tis wonderful!' Nelson remarked.[33]

Fortunately, with one gun after another being disabled, Nelson was still able to bring replacements from the fleet. Stuart's advance was giving the British control of more ground, and between Cape Revellata and Calvi Nelson found a little cove that he could protect by gunboats and Moutray's battery. By using it for landings, Nelson was able to eliminate much of the three-mile, back-bruising journey between Port Agro and the batteries, though the weather continued to sap vitality. During the day the men worked beneath a ferocious glare Corsicans called 'the Lion sun', but Nelson's battery maintained its fire. It had to rely upon more eighteen-pounders as the heavier guns were disabled, but continued to maul the French positions.[34]

The delicate figure of the captain of the *Agamemnon* seemed inexhaustible, and while many comrades sickened he seemed to exult in the combat, and was invariably at the front, ever at hand in emergencies, ever decisive and confident. Sometimes commanders need to stand at a distance in order to coordinate or oversee an action, but Nelson was never one to enjoy leaving subordinates to execute his orders at the sharp end. For good or ill, he usually stood foursquare with his men, sharing their dangers and toils, and at Calvi he routinely braved the fierce enemy fire that ravaged the British works. Once again Nelson came within seconds, or inches, of destruction. On the second day of fire an enemy shell screamed into the centre of the advanced battery and burst among a hundred people gathered around the captain and General Stuart. The magazine went up, but miraculously not a man was seriously hurt.

Then, at seven in the morning of 12 July, it happened.

A shot, probably nothing more than a chance blind discharge from the town or San Francesco batteries, smashed into a sandbag in the merlon of Nelson's battery and spattered the vicinity with stones and sand. According to one of the soldiers, Nelson and some of his companions saw it coming and threw themselves face down. If so it was too late. Nelson's face was covered with blood. When Michael Jefferson, the new surgeon's mate of the *Agamemnon*, who was on shore, cleaned the wound he found lacerations and part of the right eyebrow blown away. In considerable pain, and unable to see with his right eye, Nelson let Hallowell take charge for the day, but after that he was back, his eye bandaged, looking like a stereotypical sea rover of less than honest intent.

In those days no diagnostic instruments for optical problems existed, and the ophthalmoscope was still half a century away. Consequently, there is much uncertainty about the nature of Nelson's injury. He spoke of the eye as being 'cut down', but referred to the surrounding skin rather than the eyeball, which was hit but not perforated. The immediate loss of vision and pain experienced has been variously attributed to a detached retina; swelling and watering caused by the concussion; and a vitreous haemorrhage or temporary bleeding within the cavity of the eyeball behind the lens and iris. Whatever the case, though camp talk predicted that Nelson would lose his sight, his initial pain eased and there were signs of visual improvement. 'The surgeons flatter I shall not entirely lose the sight,' he told Elliot five days after suffering his injury, 'which I believe for I can clearly distinguish light from dark. It confined me, thank God, only one day.'[35]

Certainly he talked bravely. He did not enter the injury in the ship's logs, or even put himself on the official list of wounded. 'I got a little hurt this morning,' he wrote to Hood, but it was 'not much, as you may judge by my writing.' A few days later his Uncle William was told that Nelson felt lucky to have a head on his shoulders. It was not until 1 August that he broached the subject to Fanny, from whom he had hidden the injury to his back at Bastia. Yet even then she only learned that Horatio had suffered 'a very slight scratch towards my right eye which has not been the smallest inconvenience'.[36]

But others knew their Nelson, including Lord Hood. Writing of the wound to Elliot, the admiral admitted, 'He speaks lightly of it, but I wish he may not lose the sight of an eye.' Rightly, Hood suspected that Nelson was minimising what was, in fact, a major injury.[37]

5

Putting fears for his sight behind him, Nelson returned to his guns and soon brought the siege to its climax.

As early as 9 July his battery had got the better of the gunners in the Mozzello and the Fountain battery, and systematically disabled their pieces. By the end of the day only Fort San Francesco, sitting behind the Mozzello at a difficult angle on Nelson's left, and the town were replying. The town's projectiles were lobbed blind at the British, over the crippled Mozzello and Fountain batteries, and most missed their mark while a few burst harmlessly in the air soon after leaving the muzzles of their guns. That night Nelson also mounted a ten-inch howitzer near his battery. Its job was to fire every three minutes during the hours of darkness to deter the French from repairing their broken defences.

With what Hood called 'rapid firing' Nelson's guns soon had the town ablaze in one place for three hours, but they concentrated most fire upon the Mozzello, shooting away sandbags, splintering stone and battering breaches in the walls. Hudson Lowe watched the formidable fort 'crumbling into pieces from the effect of our shot, and the enemy so dismayed as not to return our fire'.[38]

It was time to storm the Mozzello and Stuart planned a tripartite attack from Nelson's advanced battery. While the seamen gathered guns and scaling ladders made on the *Agamemnon*, their captain accompanied Stuart to ground a mere three hundred yards from the Mozzello. Stuart explained that if Nelson built a new battery there it would cover the troops storming the breach. On the dark night of 18–19 July large bodies of men moved purposefully about the British positions. At dusk Lieutenant Colonel Wemyss went first, with a detachment of Royal Irish and two field pieces hauled by seamen under Lieutenant Edmonds of the *Agamemnon*. Striking grimly to the left they bloodlessly occupied the Fountain battery, which they found abandoned. Then Edmonds quickly trained his guns on Fort San Francesco and fired a salvo to a furious huzzah from the Royal Irish. Splitting the darkness those shots and cries signalled the main advance.

Nelson was ready for it. About the time Wemyss's movement began the captain's party had also set off for the site of the new battery Stuart wanted, pulling two twenty-six pounders and a mortar. With the aid of Lieutenant Colonel Patrick Wauchope of the 50th Regiment they worked furiously in the dark and had the guns mounted by one-thirty in the morning. As Moore's grenadiers flowed forward towards the Mozzello, Nelson unleashed a savage point-blank covering fire upon the fort. Soon the redcoats were upon their enemies, battering down the remaining French palisades with the stocks of muskets and pouring through the breach to clamber lustily over the fractured stones and sandbags behind flashing bayonets. There was little opposition, and a party of seamen advancing with the grenadiers helped clear it away with a pair of field guns. A brief flourish of French pikes, the flash of a hand grenade, and the enemy buckled, running away so fast that Major Brereton's Light Corps, circling round to the right to cut off their retreat, could not get to the rear in time. Nelson's battery had so comprehensively destroyed the Mozzello that it fell with little loss to either side. Two gallant Frenchmen who stood in the breach were hacked down and two others overtaken in flight, while the British casualties amounted to thirteen. The fort itself was found to be 'an absolute heap of ruins'.[39]

By far the greater British losses were suffered the next day, when the Royal Irish detachment under Wemyss came under heavy enemy fire as it sheltered in the old Fountain battery and lost eighteen killed and wounded. However, the basic military position could no longer be reversed. The French abandoned Fort San Francesco at daylight, leaving the British in sole possession of all the enemy's significant defences to the west and southwest of the town. Its imminent surrender seemed assured.

The French were not through yet, however. The garrison in Calvi was badly short of provisions and powder, their casualty list was growing, and they had been beaten back to the limits of the town, which itself now faced punishment. But a dogged spirit survived, and when Stuart offered terms the day after the Mozzello fell he was simply reminded of Calvi's motto: 'Civitas Calvi Semper Fidelis'. Stuart immediately started regrouping his guns for another onslaught. For several days the artillery of both sides fell silent, as if the antagonists had been exhausted by the struggle, but Nelson's men were hard at work nonetheless. They helped to tow thirty-two pieces of artillery to new positions and to establish several batteries at distances of from 560 to 900 yards from the town.

Amid these labours, Nelson still arbitrated between unfriendly commanders-in-chief. Stuart never seemed satisfied, and fired a series of terse 'my dear sir!' notes to Nelson demanding more guns, more powder and shot and more men. Horatio passed them on, and Hood grumpily did his best. He complained that while powder was to be had from allies, shot was in short supply, and hinted that Stuart was asking for far more than he needed. Hood even suspected that Stuart was actually courting a refusal so that he could blame the navy if the siege was criticised at home. Nelson's regard for Stuart never sank so low, but he confessed that while the army's requests kept coming the materiel piling up behind the captured Fort Mozzello strikingly reminded him of Woolwich arsenal.[40]

By 28 July, Stuart had the guns to his satisfaction, but with relatively little powder and shot he decided to reopen negotiations with the French before resorting to further violence. General Casabianca, the governor and commander of the town, was ready to agree that if no supplies reached him within twenty-five days he would surrender. That seemed an awful long time to Stuart, who estimated that his ammunition would only survive seven more days of firing, and he went aboard the *Victory* to see Hood. The old admiral was sick but listened with Admiral Hotham at his side. They offered their ideas as suggestions, rather than orders, but made it clear that anything more than a ten-day truce should be ruled out and that Hood favoured a three-day bombardment of the town to bring the French to terms.

Stuart grasped the intermediate position and told Casabianca that he would hold his fire if the French agreed to surrender within eleven days, by 10 August. These terms might have been accepted but for an unfortunate event that occurred on 29 July. While some of the British frigates were away collecting munitions for the siege, four French supply boats slipped into Calvi during the night, the first to get through in two months. They were essential to the besieged town, where food supplies had failed and inhabitants were eating mules, horses, donkeys and – by later report – cats and rats. Eggs were selling for thirty sous apiece. Nelson put little stock in truces, but as the cheers of the embattled garrison carried through the darkness he knew the fight would have to continue. Stiffened by the reinforcements, Casabianca firmly rejected Stuart's new terms.[41]

Stuart loosed his artillery on the defences again, savaging civilian and military positions alike. The British opened fire at five o'clock on 30 July and the garrison immediately replied, but it was a one-sided duel. Some of the defenders were driven from their ordnance, three or four of their guns were dismounted before dark and the French fire languished. During the night five fires blazed in the town. For two more days the seamen pounded the helpless town, and young Hoste believed that had the battering continued 'not one house would have had a stone standing'.[42]

As at Bastia, there was no shortage of grit in the defence and noncombatants showed inspiring courage and fortitude. Women as well as men went forward under fire to supply the soldiers or repair broken fortifications. A dying boy, his chest opened by the fragment of a shell, bade his mother not to weep because his life had been given for the nation. But the British fire told terrifyingly. Every house was damaged or reduced to rubble or cinders, and part of the 'palace' crumbled, crushing sheltering refugees beneath the falling masonry. Fever and Nelson's guns combined to destroy the garrison. Only ten of eighty gunners reportedly remained in action; the rest were dead, wounded or sick. A mere two hundred and sixty effective men remained to defend three major breaches that Stuart was battering through their walls, and among them divisions were appearing. Casabianca blamed the Provençal grenadiers for allowing the Mozello to fall, while one of their commanders replied that Casabianca had spent part of the siege hiding in a cellar.

Hood had been right about the effect of another sharp, short bombardment, and on 1 August a white flag flew over Calvi. Stuart's terms were accepted and the town offered to surrender on the tenth. The siege was over and with it, for the moment, French rule in Corsica.

6

Captain Nelson peered into a mirror on the *Agamemnon*. His right eye remained painful at times, and he could see that its pupil was abnormally dilated. When he covered his left eye to leave the right unsupported, he also had to accept the unwelcome fact that for all useful purposes it was blind.

Though Nelson was grateful that his 'beauty' had not been greatly impaired, and tried to shrug away the worst prognosis ('never mind, I can see very well with the other') the prospect of a full recovery seemed to be receding. John Harness, the fleet physician, and the available surgeons were not optimistic, and on 18 August Horatio decided to tell Fanny more about his injuries:

. . . as it is all past, I may tell you that on the 10th [12th] of July last a shot having struck our battery, the splinters of stones from it struck me most severely in the face and breast. Although the blow was so severe as to occasion a great flow of blood from my head, yet I most fortunately escaped by only having my right eye nearly deprived of its sight. It was cut down, but is as far recovered as to be able to distinguish light from darkness, but as to all purpose of use it is gone. However, the blemish is nothing – not to be perceived unless told. The pupil is nearly the size of the blue part, I don't know the name. At Bastia I got a sharp cut in the back.[43]

Legend depicts Nelson with a ridiculous black eyepatch, as if hiding an empty socket, but his many portraits and the few descriptions suggest that time more or less restored the appearance of the injured organ. Only the fine pastel made by Johann Schmidt of Dresden in 1800 depicts the slightly clouded aspect it presented to more intent observers. Nelson's 'beauty' survived, but his vision was irreparably damaged. Within a year the eye had begun to cause him occasional pain again and its sight had relapsed towards total darkness. It is possible that damage to the nerve was causing optic atrophy, or that secondary glaucoma was developing with a corneal oedema.[44]

The Corsican campaign had left a permanent mark upon him, but Nelson still viewed it with mixed feelings. Calvi had surrendered as promised. At ten o'clock on 10 August its haggard defenders had marched out to hand over their arms: 300 French, 247 Corsican auxiliaries and 300 seamen. In the hospital another 313 sick and wounded were found, while for one reason or another four hundred civilians, one of them reputedly the prettiest woman in Calvi, also marched out to be shipped to France with the defeated troops. One hundred and six artillery pieces, more than eight thousand shot and shells, two frigates, two merchantmen, a gunboat and several small craft became undisputed spoils of war. Nelson got great satisfaction from sending Lieutenant Moutray to take possession of the *Melpomene* and *Le Mignonne* frigates because they were the survivors of the squadron he had fought off Sardinia ten months before.

Neither side had suffered heavy casualties, judged by the warfare of the time. Stuart reported his losses as thirty killed and sixty-one wounded, including those sustained by partisan and French royalist allies, while Nelson heard that, despite the severe damage to the town and works of Calvi, the French had only sustained eighty killed and wounded in the fighting.[45]

Nelson had not entirely approved of the handling of the siege. Nine days between 1 and 10 August had been spent waiting for the French to surrender, as they had agreed to do if no further assistance reached them. Nelson had wanted to bombard the bastion or destroy it with explosives to speed up the result. 'I had rather take a place by our own fire and efforts than by the enemy being starved and sickly,' he lamented. There was more glory in a conquest by arms.[46]

Hood held similar views, but was spiteful enough to air them to government. The admiral was ill and irritable, and inflamed by Stuart's refusal to involve him in the final negotiations for a capitulation.

Furthermore, he had been talking to a French engineer who visited the *Victory* the day after Calvi surrendered, and was sure that Stuart could have battered the enemy into a speedier submission. The French were starving and sickening, and they only had two days of powder left, having lost sixty barrels in an explosion of their magazine. Nor were the fortifications in the town casemated, so that their occupants had little shelter from enemy artillery. Weighing it all up, Hood's flag captain scoffed 'that our *marine* ideas of the distressed, defenceless, deplorable situation of the town and inhabitants of Calvi were well founded'. Another day's firing was all that was needed, but 'the humane generosity of the British general is [now] extolled by the bearer of every party-coloured [French] cockade'.[47]

Stuart, of course, had not been privy to this information when he had agreed his truce on 1 August. He was worried about his own shortages of powder and shot, and was foggy about his enemy's resources. In using hindsight to wound Stuart the admiral had been less than fair, but he had a point when he complained that those final days of the war in Corsica had been expensive. An enemy older and deadlier than the French guns, one Nelson knew only too well, had begun to damage the British forces. Disease. Men crowded in flimsy tents and unsanitary camps, and working to their physical limits in violent extremes of weather close to the malarial margins of the sea, became targets for several predatory diseases. 'Every hour our troops and seamen [are] falling ill and dying,' Nelson wrote the day Calvi surrendered. 'On that day not 400 soldiers were fit for duty.' He exaggerated, but not wildly. 'Considerably more than two-thirds of our number are in hospital; men and officers tumble down daily in the most melancholy manner,' said Moore. The sailors, perhaps more inured to hardship in foreign climes, fared better than the soldiers, and Nelson had divided his men into two shifts so that only half were at the batteries at any one time. Yet by 5 August thirty had been invalided to the *Agamemnon* and seventy more were ill. Many of Nelson's friends and officers were down with fever. Lieutenant Colonel Wemyss, with whom he had formed good relations ('God bless you,' Wemyss had written to him) asked for a ship to take him away. Hallowell, Suckling, Moutray, Hoste and Bolton were all sick.[48]

Nelson's own health wavered but held. Apart from his injured eye, his old feverishness had returned. 'This is my ague day,' he told Hood at the end of July. 'I hope this active scene will keep off the fit. It has shook me a good deal, but I have been used to them, and don't mind them much.' Somehow he kept going. As he marvelled to the Duke of Clarence on a day when a thousand men looked like phantoms, 'I am here the reed amongst the oak. All the disorders have attacked me, but I have not strength for them to fasten upon. I bow before the storm, whilst the sturdy oak is laid low.'[49]

When Calvi fell, Hood had hastened back to Mortella Bay, signalling again, as far as Stuart was concerned, his latent indifference to the state of the task force. Nelson's job had delayed his departure. Transports were needed for victors and vanquished and guns and stores had to be retrieved and returned to the ships. Horatio felt indebted to the agent for transports, Lieutenant Richard Sainthill. 'Your readiness at all times to expedite the king's service I shall always bear my testimony of,' he told him.[50]

On board the *Agamemnon* the battle to save sick sailors and marines had also continued, not always successfully. 'Departed this life John Murfey, seaman,' ran a typical log book entry. 'Received on board six bullocks, six baskets of onions, seven boxes of lemons for the sick . . . Received thirty-five sick men on board.' Fresh meat, vegetables and fruit helped combat dietary disorders such as scurvy, but life-threatening fevers needed more. By the end of October, Nelson reckoned some fifty *Agamemnons* had been lost.[51]

Nevertheless, after many tribulations the Corsican campaign had at last been a success and Nelson was proud of his part in it. The victory owed much to Hood's determination and Stuart's extraordinary leadership at Calvi, but probably no officer counted for more in the liberation of Corsica than the captain of the *Agamemnon*. He had been there at the beginning, blockading the hostile ports in winter storms, and he was there at the end after a monumental labour, commanding the guns that fired fourteen thousand projectiles to silence Calvi. He had refused to be beaten by towns others had thought impregnable, and spared nothing in their capture. Some had criticised his judgement, understandably so to a point, but others had seen his achievements as inspirational, no less understandably. To such as young William Hoste, Nelson's operations suggested that the navy could occasionally transcend its traditional role and reduce major strongholds ashore. He would remember those lessons and draw strength from them twenty years later when he captured the great mountain fortresses of Cattaro and Ragusa in the Adriatic.

Nelson was a sailor, but his only naval engagement so far, the fight with the French frigate, had been a mediocre stand-off, and his most newsworthy activities had been ashore in Nicaragua and Corsica, working more as 'a besieging general' than an admiral. Yet however unorthodox, he wanted his achievements to be recognised. Privately there was some congratulation. When Admiral Phipps Cosby got home and met Fanny at a ball in Bath he told her that 'no man in the Mediterranean had done what you [Nelson] had'. Sir William Hamilton wrote agreeably to the man himself, 'I do not believe that ever man or ship went through so long or so hazardous a service as you both have done.' But these opinions remained within the private domain, for the public dispatches again glossed over Nelson's services.[52]

Hood, who had done Nelson such an injustice in his Bastia dispatch, forwarded two copies of the captain's Calvi journal to government but left Stuart to make the full report. His own résumé referred vaguely to the captain's 'unremitting zeal and exertion'. Stuart acknowledged that the sailors under Nelson and Hallowell had 'greatly contributed to the success of these movements' but wrote them out of much of the action. Reading the accounts of the night of 18 July in Stuart's dispatch and Nelson's journal one can only conclude that both men were perpetuating prevalent interservice jealousies. Nelson barely mentioned the soldiers who helped him build the new battery outside Fort Mozzello, and Stuart credited the same achievement to three army officers without making any reference to the seamen whatsoever.[53]

Nelson had left Stuart on good terms and suspected that the general's dispatch had been influenced as much by his dislike of Hood as a natural wish to serve the army. He still felt hugely cheated. As Lord Radstock, who knew Nelson at this time, testified, his 'perpetual thirst' for glory was 'ever raging within', and he was bitter that the names of so many nonentities seemed preferred to his. 'Others have been praised who, at the time, were actually in bed, far from the scene of action,' he grumbled. Then, as optimism reasserted itself, he would redouble his efforts. 'Never mind,' he told his sister, Susanna, 'I'll have a *Gazette* of my own [one day].' One of the most lasting lessons Nelson took from Corsica was the necessity for self-publicity. In the future he would prepare accounts of his own for the press.[54]

In the meantime he could at least use his improved leverage with Hood to help his followers. 'I shall be very glad to attend to your wishes in favour of your surgeon's mate immediately,' the admiral told him, 'and if you will send Mr Fellows on board the *Victory* I will promote him as soon as I can.' Five days later Hood promoted Lieutenant Hinton of the *Agamemnon* to the flagship.[55]

Unfortunately, it was not in Nelson's power to help another who had attracted his attention. Lieutenant James Moutray of the *Victory*, Mary's only son, fell sick in Calvi and never recovered. The youth had endeared himself to many officers, including the admiral, who described Moutray as 'universally lamented'. But only one chose to record the fact for the public. A modest plaque could long be seen in the church of St Fiorenzo, a prosaic but sincere tribute from a senior professional to a junior. It read:

Sacred to the memory of Lieutenant James Moutray, R.N., who, serving on shore at the siege of Calvi, there caught a fever of which he died, sincerely lamented, on August 19th, 1794, aged 21 years. This stone is erected by an affectionate friend, who well knew his worth as an officer and his accomplished manners as a gentleman.[56]

The author placed his initials at the end. They were 'H.N'.

XX

TWO MEETINGS WITH
FRENCH GENTRY

Awake my muse, assist my lyre,
My feeble untun'd tongue inspire
To sing of glorious deed.
How gallant Hotham did defeat
The French, and made them to retreat
With nimble-footed speed.
                Richard Lovat, armourer's mate

1

THE fleet felt neglected by the powers at home. It was short of sails, masts, cordage and men, and none of its ships had seen harder service than the *Agamemnon*. Instead of sailing to Gibraltar to refit as planned, she limped towards Leghorn, the nearest suitable port, where she anchored on 30 August, a day ahead of Hood's *Victory*. Perhaps a dozen men had been killed and wounded in the winning of Corsica, and a few had deserted, but sickness and fatigue had taken the greatest toll of her men. There had been more sad tasks to perform than usual: men to be buried at sea, and their clothes and possessions sold, shared or secured as circumstances demanded. One hundred and fifty of the crew were sick.[1]

Recovery was slow. Ten days later the fleet physician reported the company much debilitated, and as late as 10 October seventy-seven men were still on the sick list. Again Hood pressed Nelson to leave the broken *Agamemnon* and transfer to a seventy-four-gun ship. Everyone knew that the seventy-four was the line of battle ship par excellence, the ultimate blend of power, speed and manoeuvrability, but Nelson clung to his beloved sixty-four. 'I could not bring myself to part with a ship's company with whom I have gone through such a series of hard service,' he wrote.[2]

Some of the men seemed beyond repair, but most slowly returned to duty and Nelson was able to take Josiah and Hoste to Pisa, where the supposedly medicinal waters and the sights seemed to aid convalescence. The *Agamemnon* herself was in such poor shape that Nelson expected to be ordered to sail her to England, perhaps with Lord Hood. The admiral had wanted to go home for a while. Ill and barely able to write, he was still feuding with General Stuart and mired in controversy. Nelson remained unwilling to admit flaws in his hero, and attributed the army's jealousy to the success at Bastia. Soldiers 'hate us sailors', he told Fanny. 'We are too active for them. We accomplish our business sooner than they like.' Stuart, he was sure, had 'deeply imbibed this diabolical leaven'. Irrespective, the upshot was that Hood requested and was granted leave, and Nelson encouraged Fanny with talk about a homecoming and finding 'some snug cottage' that would free them from the parsonage. His ambition, in reality, was merely to refit his ship and rest in England, and then to return with his rejuvenated admiral to the Mediterranean. Liberating Corsica had been intoxicating. At last he was at the forefront of military and naval endeavour, winning golden opinions, exalting his station, and – as he saw it – doing something valuable. He wanted more of it. As he shortly said to his wife, 'not an hour this war will I, if possible, be out of active service'.[3]

No ship deserved a respite more than Nelson's leaking sixty-four, but despite the seizure of Corsica the war in the Mediterranean was not going well. French power was growing. Shrugging off the attacks of the hostile coalition in northern and eastern Europe, the republicans went onto the offensive, marching into Spain and squaring up to the Austrians and the smaller powers to the east. Their eyes rested hungrily upon the Italian states and they resented the loss of Corsica, but as long as the British fleet commanded the sea both were difficult to reach. The French fleet was still divided between Toulon and Golfe Jouan, but more ships were being fitted out and its capacity increased. As naval rivalry in the Mediterranean intensified, the consequence of the failure of Hood and Hotham to destroy their opponents in 1793 and 1794 became increasingly evident. In these circumstances every capital ship counted and any plans to withdraw the *Agamemnon* were quickly shelved.

On 18 September, Hood's most enterprising captain received fresh orders. He was to proceed to the republic of Genoa and deliver a letter to Francis Drake, the British minister plenipotentiary.[4]

This was an important mission. Genoa was a small power, uncomfortably located between France to the west and the other Italian states to the east, politically neutral but economically bound to the former by trade. It was rumoured that members of the Genoese government were in the pay of the French; certainly, the state had loaned money to their powerful neighbour and expected due returns. Relations between Britain and Genoa had accordingly been less harmonious, and the previous year Hood had become so incensed at the small republic's failure to prevent French attacks upon British shipping in their territorial waters that he had sent a squadron into the Ligurian Sea. Sweeping aside the niceties of neutrality it had seized a French frigate in Genoa and subjected the port to a spasmodic blockade.

A year on, there were grounds for believing that the Genoese might now be more sensible of the need for better relations with the British and their allies. The war had marched closer. French armies were moving eastwards along the riviera into Genoese territory, and it was thought that General Bonaparte ('represented to be a man of uncommon capacity and courage, and of a very bold and enterprising spirit') planned to quarter them in Savona for the winter before loosing them against Genoa and northern Italy the following spring. On the other hand, Britain and her allies, Austria and Sardinia-Piedmont, were poised to interpose themselves between Genoa and the Gallic horde, and an Austrian army was soon advancing to occupy Savona before the French arrived.[5]

It was time for Britain and Genoa to repair bridges, and Nelson seemed the right man for the job. He had demonstrated some diplomatic talent in Naples and Corsica, and had not been tainted by the previous difficulties with Genoa. Accordingly he was sent ahead of Hood to help restore amicable relations. On 19 September the *Agamemnon* entered Genoa after a short voyage, exchanging generous salutes with the batteries before anchoring near the mole. Nelson noticed two French privateers and some British merchantmen in the harbour, evidence of Genoa's effort to steer between powerful belligerents, and thought the 'magnificent' palaces and buildings comparable to Naples, but briskly buckled down to business. The British consul, Joseph Brame, said that Drake was daily expected from Milan, but in the meantime arranged for Nelson to meet the doge at the Piazza San

Lorenzo on the evening of the 20th. Horatio duly presented himself in full-dress uniform, and was gratified to see the doge advance from a throng in the middle of an opulent room to greet him. The two exchanged pleasantries, but Nelson sensed that while the Genoese understood that the British fleet and Austrian army might protect them they were deeply afraid of provoking the French. The doge munificently received Nelson's assurances that the Royal Navy would respect Genoa's neutrality, but declined to enter allied plans to defend Italy.[6]

To the good, Nelson had broken some ice, and Hood and Drake, who arrived on the 23rd and 24th respectively, got no further. Hood sent notes ashore, offering to use the fleet against the republic's enemies, only to receive the reply that Genoa had none, and the day Drake reached the city it learned that the French had taken possession of their forts at Vado Bay forty miles to the southwest. The Genoese were too frightened to step one way or the other, and Drake decided that only a successful Austrian counteroffensive would drive the French back.[7]

The Genoa mission was the last important service Nelson performed for Hood, as the admiral was bound for England – never to return, as it transpired. On 30 September the *Agamemnon* was sent to Golfe Jouan, where the new acting commander-in-chief, Vice Admiral Hotham, was directing a blockade from his three-decked *Britannia*. Disappointed to be leaving his old patron, Nelson dutifully obeyed, seizing a brig from beneath enemy batteries near Cape Martin on 1 October before joining Hotham's force the following day. He saw Hood again, when the *Victory* came up on the 11th, and then the admiral sailed for Gibraltar.

Nelson and Hood made a good parting. Nothing had diminished Nelson's regard for Hood as an admiral, not even his failure to destroy the Toulon fleet in 1793 and the damage he had done interservice relations in Corsica. 'He is the greatest sea officer I ever knew,' wrote Nelson, 'and what can be said against him I cannot conceive.' Hood's public dispatches had never done justice to Nelson, but privately he knew that he had stumbled upon an officer of exceptional ability, and owed much of his victory in Corsica to him. He had learned to respect his opinions, and loved to read them in retirement. As he wrote to Nelson more than a year later, 'I flatter myself with the pleasure of a letter from you by every mail, and I entreat you to write as often as you can.'[8]

2

Nelson hoped Hood would return, but in the meantime he was stuck with Hotham. A rotund, pot-bellied man of fifty-nine, William Hotham was the third son of a baronet and a convivial, generous, warm-hearted man. He meant well, for which he was popular, but manifestly lacked the ability of Hood. At home disturbing reports of deteriorating discipline rippled into the boardroom of the Admiralty, and Hotham was ordered to 're-establish . . . strict subordination and obedience' in the Mediterranean fleet. Out on station there were doubts whether the new commander-in-chief was up to it. 'Admiral Hotham is a gentlemanlike man, and would, I am persuaded, do his duty in a day of battle,' remarked the new viceroy of Corsica. 'But he is past the time of life for action. His soul has got down to his belly, and never mounts higher now, and in all business he is a piece of perfectly inert formality.'[9]

Nelson had no illusions about Hotham, who had not been 'intended by nature for a commander-in-chief, which requires a man of more active turn of mind'. To be sure, the man was beset by unusually intractable problems. 'Admiral Hotham has had much to contend with,' Nelson admitted. 'A fleet half-manned, and in every respect inferior to the enemy; Italy calling him to her defence; our newly-acquired kingdom [Corsica] calling might and main; our reinforcements and convoy hourly expected; and all to be done without a force or any means adequate to it.' Much of this was beyond the admiral's control. Unable to refit adequately, the ships were breaking up, and were so short of naval stores that sails and cordage that had been condemned were having to be recycled.[10]

Unfortunately, Hotham's numerous professional shortcomings also sprung readily to mind. It had been Hotham who had allowed a dozen French sail to run from Toulon to Golfe Jouan in 1794. 'The opportunity was lost by admirals of fighting them, and it is a thousand to one if we ever have so fair an opportunity [again],' Nelson complained. Equally telling by Nelson's lights was Hotham's lenient handling of a mutiny on the *Windsor Castle*. Upon enquiry the complaints of the men had been found to be frivolous, and Nelson believed the admiral had done nothing to deter similar insubordination. 'I am satisfied it would have been better to have burned the ship and all the villains in her,' he said fiercely.[11]

As far as Nelson was concerned, Hotham's command lacked energy. The admiral's ships of the line were in such a poor way that he dreaded the damage a battle or storm might bring, and preferred to conserve them in St Fiorenzo or Leghorn rather than risk them at sea in all weathers. Although his frigates watched the enemy the 'blockade' was a farce. Impudent coasters plied to and from the French relatively unchecked, and British merchantmen were left open to the attacks of enemy privateers and naval squadrons. With his bases far to the east, it was impossible for Hotham to keep the enemy battle forces at Golfe Jouan and Toulon under proper surveillance.[12]

Nelson's doubts about Hotham were soon confirmed. On 3 November he returned to Golfe Jouan from Leghorn, where he had picked up stores and mail, and found that the French had slipped through the net once more, putting to sea after the British scouts had been driven eastwards by gales. Hotham sent the tireless *Agamemnon* to find them while he withdrew with his battle fleet to St Fiorenzo, and after two days Nelson saw the missing squadron back in Toulon, reunited with the rest of the enemy Mediterranean fleet. Another chance to attack the French piecemeal had been lost, and the French fleet now numbered twenty-two warships, a force comparable to its British counterpart. 'I see plainly they will keep us in hot water the whole winter,' Nelson scribbled in one of his regular letters to the Duke of Clarence.[13]

With such a force at their disposal the French could make sorties against British merchantmen, or transport soldiers to Italy or Corsica. Corsica was indeed a sore point for Nelson, especially when he heard rumours that the French were boasting that their New Year's dinner would be eaten on the island. He had lost the sight of an eye liberating the island, as well as Lieutenant Moutray and other good men, and he fancied that British suzerainty was proving beneficial, and that 'the inhabitants [would] grow rich, and, I hope, happy under our mild government'. On his visits to the island he occasionally walked into the countryside with a stick and noticed changes that pleased him: wheat fields where there had once been scrub, and the increased security of the ordinary people. Even though Hotham had united his force at St Fiorenzo, Nelson worried that the French might force a landing on Corsica through Ajaccio, and advised Elliot, the viceroy, to station enough men in the port 'to keep the gates shut for a few days' until relief forces could be mobilised. Italy Nelson conceived to be in even greater danger.[14]

The captain of the *Agamemnon* may have been concerned for the safety of his country's allies and possessions, but it was not from a conviction that the French fleet, even with the advantage of numbers, could maintain any extended superiority at sea. Rather the danger arose from their ability to use weather and circumstance to produce a local, short-lived superiority that might nevertheless be decisive. Nelson made no mistakes about the respective fighting qualities of the competing navies. If the French were 'mad enough' to tackle the British fleet, he said, the result would entirely vindicate the bullish expectations of an English public accustomed to naval victories.[15]

Nelson was influenced by that tradition of victory, but still regretted that in this naval arms race the numbers were beginning to swing in favour of the French. For although an outnumbered British fleet would, he felt sure, defeat the French it would not achieve the victory Nelson wanted. He aspired to achieve something altogether overwhelming and decisive: in fact, the most an admiral or general could achieve under arms, the total destruction or irreversible overthrow of an enemy force. Like Hood he worked towards annihilation. Showing contempt for a lauded naval victory of Lord Howe, won in the Atlantic on 'The Glorious First of June' in 1794, Nelson wrote to his brother, 'If we *only* make a Lord Howe victory, take a part [of the fleet] and retire into port, Italy is lost!'[16]

The implication was plain. In Nelson's opinion nothing short of the total, the perfect, victory dreamed of by Lord Hood would do in the Mediterranean. The trouble was that Hotham, devoid of the means and disposition, seemed unlikely to supply it. Nelson himself was soon temporarily mothballed. After reporting to the admiral at St Fiorenzo, Nelson was sent to Leghorn to refit and load fresh water and supplies. He arrived on 13 November, and while the weary *Agamemnon* underwent essential repairs indignantly suffered a period of frustrating inaction.

3

The sustained excitement of the Corsica campaign and its aftermath was gone, and in its place there endured the dull tedium of Leghorn, a town of two commodious harbours, walled forts and straight streets. Without momentum Nelson lapsed into his familiar irritable despondency. Sometimes he was left the senior officer in Leghorn, and found himself ordering 'surveys' of ships and stores, but he still felt neglected and grumbled about being 'tired' and 'kicked about'.[17]

A pause was, he realised, necessary. Without her wounded masts the ship looked 'little better than a wreck' in the dockyard, and it took the best part of two months to replace them and overhaul the hull, rigging and sails. The men also needed a respite. About fifty men had died since the siege of Calvi, and seventy were still sick, some seriously. Frank Lepee, Nelson's servant of many years and the owner of a set of china much admired by Fanny for its beauty, was sinking beneath epilepsy and mental illness. Eventually he became so 'deranged' that Fanny suggested a place be found for him in Greenwich Hospital, of which Captain Locker was now governor. Instead, Nelson first entrusted him to the naval surgeon at Leghorn and then in posts aboard the *Zealous* and *Diadem*, but his sense of responsibility for the man remained, and in 1798 he willed Lepee a legacy of £50. Eventually Nelson found another servant as durable as Frank, the ever-loyal Tom Allen, who had left the land in Sculthorpe, Norfolk, to go to sea as a youth.[18]

Necessary for ship and men as the recess may have been, Nelson was worried that the French would leave Toulon and offer battle to Hotham while the *Agamemnon* was unfit for sea. He still doubted the wisdom of the war, and thought Britain's allies incompetent, fickle and undeserving of support. He suspected that they would merely drain Britain of resources. 'Had we left the continent to themselves, we should have done well, and at half the expense,' he sighed. As far as he was concerned Britain could do worse than make a peace on fair terms and leave the continentals to squabble among themselves. The general trend of the war had become dispiriting, but Nelson's competitive spirit was always aroused by the prospect of battle, and at least a crisis seemed to be looming. Using timber from Genoa and Leghorn, the French had seven new ships of the line almost completed in Toulon. When launched they would raise the number of capital ships in the French Mediterranean fleet to twenty-two, enough to create serious mischief. And it was afoot. At Marseilles and Toulon more than a hundred transports were being fitted out, and thousands of soldiers mobilised. But whither were they bound? Italy? Corsica? Perhaps Spain? Nelson did not know, but he was sure they would be at sea soon and every week the *Agamemnon* spent in Leghorn seemed an agony.[19]

While new opportunities remained remote, old occurrences still caused concern. Nelson's damaged eye still pained him and its residual vision had dissolved into a general darkness. As the gravity of the loss became obvious he measured it against the tardy recognition of his

Corsican achievements, almost passed over by both Hood and Stuart. 'I have got upon a subject near my heart, which is full when I think of the treatment I have received,' the aggrieved captain told his uncle. 'Every man who had any considerable share in the reduction [of Corsica] has got some place or other – I, only I, am without reward.' To Fanny he wrote the same day, 'Had I been done justice . . . I believe the king would not have thought any honour too great for me.'[20]

Even the prize money generated by the sale of public French property and ships in Corsica was threatened by innumerable 'ridiculous' applications. Looking after themselves, Nelson and Villettes, who had commanded the land forces at Bastia, contended that their claims were superior to those of the naval captains who blockaded the port. No doubt Nelson was trying to distinguish between those who did 'hard fag' and others whose duties were routine, but he also resented the many unworthy attempts to dip into the proceeds. In addition to the eight ships regularly involved in the blockade of Bastia, others which 'accidentally assisted for one moment and were gone the next' were at the trough. As the proceedings dragged on over one to two years and then three, Nelson concluded that Corsica had impaired his pocket as well as his health. Some three hundred pounds' worth of expenses had never been refunded, and Nelson felt so stinted that he made an unsuccessful application to the secretary for war for an allowance covering his period of service with the army.[21]

He relied upon Lord Hood to put matters right. The admiral had misrepresented Nelson's part in the Corsican campaign but at least felt guilty about it, and armed with medical certificates relating to Nelson's injury he had gone home promising to raise the whole affair with the authorities. Hood reached England by the end of November 1794, and 'took the earliest opportunity of explaining' to Lord Chatham at the Admiralty 'the very illiberal conduct of General Stuart'. He handed over the testimonials, and even tackled the Speaker of the House of Commons on the subject. While the Hoods made the inevitable pilgrimage to Bath, where his lordship gave 'ten thousand thanks' for Nelson's informative letters from the fleet and happily entertained 'your good little woman', Chatham approached the king. But for some reason the suit stalled, perhaps because of the appointment of a new board of Admiralty with Earl Spencer at its head.[22]

Hood did not fail Nelson at this point, however. He again pitched into the fray, beseeching Spencer to grant Nelson a pension for the loss of his eye. The new first lord demurred. The only precedents he knew for such pensions compensated the loss of a limb, and he doubted Nelson's injury could be considered an equivalent, but he promised to assist the captain when a 'proper opportunity' presented itself. Out in the Mediterranean, Nelson learned about the machinations, but, thinking of the numerous influential applications falling upon the new first lord of the Admiralty, he did not expect that 'proper opportunity' would arrive soon. He eventually fixed his hopes upon the next general promotion. Now high in the list of post-captains, he stood a chance of being elevated to the rank of rear admiral, but surprisingly shrank from getting a 'flag' at the moment. There were too many admirals in the Mediterranean, and such a promotion would probably send him home, unemployed and surplus to requirements. At this stage he rather hoped to be made colonel of the marines, a sinecure sometimes available to senior captains. As colonel of marines Nelson would receive an additional stipend without threatening his chances of employment.[23]

Passing through this slough, Nelson sampled the diversions of Leghorn, a substantial town sandwiched between the bay and irregular mountain peaks. He strolled along its broad main street between weathered frescos, or explored the church with the painted ceiling in its spacious square. He visited the lodgings of fellow officers at Coulson's or the Lion Rouge, or dined with them at Curry's. And somewhere, perhaps at the Teatro dagli Armeni opera house, he met Adelaide Correglia.[24]

4

We owe our introduction to Adelaide to Captain Thomas Francis Fremantle, a Hampstead man by birth and the son of a Buckinghamshire squire, sponsored by, among others, the Marquis of Buckinghamshire. Like so many naval officers, Fremantle had gone to sea too early, and though seven years younger than Horatio Nelson he had packed more into his life than most men twice his age. He had survived shipwreck, imprisonment, unemployment and battle, and earned the plaudits of many superiors. Nelson had seen him command the *Tartar* off Corsica and though he probably thought Fremantle's discipline too severe, he knew him to be a top-class professional. Baby-faced, soft-featured, short and shading towards the portly, he nonetheless made agreeable company and was dependable and considerate to fellow officers. His conversation, like Nelson's, reflected considerable reading, and ninety works of history, literature, languages and nautical procedure accompanied his travels. But in addition Fremantle was particularly sensuous, and his insatiable appetite for women features in a singular diary in which Fremantle exposes for us the colourful underbelly of life in the Mediterranean fleet.

Fremantle's short but startlingly frank entries recorded his perpetual search for prostitutes, or 'dollies' as he usually called them. Thus, we read 'as before, found Nina, who is the prettiest little woman in Leghorn' in 1794; 'called on an uncommon[ly] pretty dolly whom I christen Mrs Hill', and 'sleep with Mrs Hill' in 1795; and 'called to see a Venetian dolly – ravenous bitch!' in 1796. When polite society came calling, Fremantle frequently bundled his dollies out of the way. 'Nelson, Harneck, Anna dined with me,' he wrote on 27 December 1796. 'Carried Dolly on shore at one o'clock.' Fremantle's diary has now been lost and is known to us only from excerpts published half a century ago, but we owe to those our first as well as our clearest glimpses of Adelaide Correglia.[25]

Nelson had been eighteen months at sea when he evidently struck up with her in Leghorn towards the end of 1794. The relationship begins inconsequentially in Fremantle's pages. 'Dined at Nelson's and his dolly,' he wrote on Wednesday 3 December 1794. The use of the phrase 'Nelson's and his dolly' suggests that the captain of the *Agamemnon* was already established in a property ashore and sharing it with his paramour. A letter Nelson wrote to Thomas Pollard the following February appears to confirm this conclusion. In it Nelson notified Pollard, an English merchant who acted as his Leghorn prize agent, that his 'female friend' should be paid ten echus as well as the rent for her house.[26]

There are so few facts about Adelaide that any speculation as to her identity and relationship to Nelson is perilous. Her name, age, appearance, occupation and circumstances remain mysterious. She appears to have been a Ligurian, for her mother still lived in Genoa, and one supposes that she had the petite, dark-haired and dark-eyed looks prevalent in that region. At least that impression is encouraged by one who knew her, Captain George Cockburn, who wrote to Nelson of 'your little Adelaide' in 1797. Apparently she was or had been married: both Nelson and John Udny, the British consul at Leghorn who also knew her, addressed Adelaide as 'Signora' rather than 'Signorina'. It is possible to guess, but again with more than a little uncertainty, that Adelaide had left Genoa to live with her husband in

Leghorn and was widowed or separated soon after. There are no references whatsoever to children.[27]

At the end of 1794 Horatio Nelson was thirty-six, but he looked younger, and despite his quiet, introverted manner quite capable of attracting women. It was in December that he succumbed to Fanny's requests for a likeness and sat to an unknown Leghorn miniaturist for his second official portrait. Compared to the magnificent Rigaud canvas the result was modest, painted in oils upon a tiny card, and Nelson and Josiah were not the only ones who thought the likeness a bad one. But most people disagreed, and saw much in the portrait that was true – the slim figure, contemplative features, sensitive, mobile mouth, long nose and physical fragility. Most notably, although the miniaturist included the small scars above Nelson's right eye and below his left, and shaded the grey into his long hair, he successfully captured the almost perennial youthfulness of the sitter's appearance. He suggested the body and face of an innocent midshipman rather than an experienced, war-hardened post-captain. Certainly Fanny loved the portrait, and within two years was wearing it proudly around her neck. She continued to wear it long after suffering her husband's final and irreparable betrayal, and treasured it to her dying day. It was perhaps ironic that even as Nelson sat for that priceless memento he was living with a mistress of whom Fanny never knew.[28]

If the portrait shows a not unattractive man, it is likely that Nelson's relationship with Adelaide Correglia arose out of prostitution rather than a fortuitous attachment. There are grounds for believing that she was, in fact, a superior call girl serving officers and gentlemen, and that the consul, John Udny, facilitated the introduction. Like most ports, Leghorn had its prostitutes. Anchoring ships were beset with boats loaded with musicians and sweetly singing women, and ashore 'dollies' could be found for secret liaisons, among them ladies who regarded the officer class as their clientele. According to Fremantle, Captains Wells and Rowley 'had doleys [sic] to dinner with them daily'. The more select women used the theatre or opera house and other sophisticated places to meet their customers, and Udny may have acted as a procurer. To all appearances a homely old English gentleman down to the harpsichord, his services to countrymen far from home seem to have gone beyond the realms of postmaster, prize agent, victualler and consul. 'Called on old Udney,' Fremantle entered in his diary in December 1794. 'Went to the opera with him. He introduced me to a very handsome Greek woman.' Certainly Udny knew Adelaide, and almost certainly she offered casual sexual services, so it is entirely possible that some similar episode marked the beginning of her more enduring relationship with Nelson.[29]

Adelaide was discreet, though she went aboard the *Agamemnon* when invited and met Nelson's friends. Her poor English inhibited her in such gatherings, for her native tongue was Italian and Nelson wrote and possibly spoke to her in bad French. He had secured a French master for his stepson and William Hoste, and conveniently benefited from the lessons himself. The likelihood is that most of the papers that passed between the pair were destroyed in 1797, when Nelson burned sensitive documents before launching a dangerous attack upon Teneriffe, and only one survives today. It is undated and written in painful French deficient both in syntax and grammar. 'My dear Adelaide,' he wrote, 'I am setting out to sea this very moment. A Neapolitan ship is sailing with me to Livorno [Leghorn]. Believe me always to be your dear friend, Horatio Nelson. Be a great success.'[30]

This, like most other pieces of evidence about Adelaide, scarcely lifts the veil of secrecy surrounding her. She kept a home for Nelson in Leghorn for perhaps eighteen months or more, and was on hand to help him entertain, but always mysteriously. 'Dined with Nelson and Dolly,' Fremantle wrote on 27 September 1795, just after both host and mistress had returned from Vado Bay. 'Very bad dinner indeed.' But the next day he was back and wrote, 'Dined at Nelson's. Went to see at the theatre a man who was blind play upon a flute well enough.' On such occasions we can imagine Adelaide hovering in the background while the English officers talked a language she barely understood, fondly returning the occasional remark and filling the wineglasses.[31]

She no doubt consoled Nelson during his depression, and diverted him from the wearisome duties of an inactive command. For much of the time the captain of the *Agamemnon* had nothing more stimulating to attend than courts martial in Leghorn roads or St Fiorenzo. His ship was ready for sea in December, but Hotham put into Leghorn at about the same time and had the whole fleet lingering there for ten days.[32]

Then and afterwards Nelson's close associates met and accepted Adelaide, and through him paid their respects to her. 'Make my compliments to la belle Adelaide,' Admiral Jervis wrote to him in July 1796. But they never spoke of her back home, not even young Josiah, who was doubtless misled about Adelaide's function but was unquestionably aware of her existence. Many naval officers serving far afield had relationships with local women, but they learned to remain silent about them on home ground, screening one world from the other.[33]

Nelson would enjoy a far more notorious mistress in time, but Adelaide was the one about whom Fanny never knew.

5

He told Fanny he loved her, collecting 'many little things' for her on his travels, and she had no reason to believe otherwise. 'Indeed, my dear Fanny,' he wrote, 'my love, regard and esteem for you cannot, I think, be exceeded by any man whatever.'[34]

Yet she was undeniably lonely, deprived of her 'dearest husband' and child, and living in what was still something of a foreign land. He was always talking about coming home but never did. In the autumn of 1794 his plan to return with Hood raised her hopes. After toasting his second birthday away from home at Kentish Town, she wrote, 'I . . . look every day for one telling me you are coming.' The news that he was, after all, to remain at sea devastated her. 'My disappointment in not seeing you and my child as soon as you gave me some hope that I should is very great,' she admitted. 'The thoughts of soon seeing my affectionate husband had made me quite well, but still I flatter myself it will not be very long before you will come home. This winter will be another anxious one. What did I not suffer in my mind the last?'[35]

It was unfair on both of them, imprisoned as they were in situations beyond their control. Nelson tried to reassure his wife that the war could not last long, and that if there was peace in the spring 'we must look out for some little cottage' where he would 'return to the plough with redoubled glee', but he was hardly telling the truth. Even Fanny, reading newspapers and talking to her few friends, doubted the war was reaching its end, though she and her father-in-law encouraged each other to think that Nelson might in some way soon return to the suffocating domesticity he hated. They both needed him, and wanted him to enliven their small, quiet world, barely comprehending the fire that fed his soul. While he thirsted for glory, they worried that the battle he longed for might cheat them of a beloved husband and son. 'I hope the French will not get out so as to give you an opportunity of engaging them,' Fanny wrote to him. 'Could I hope for this, I should endeavour to make myself easy. My mind and poor heart are always on the rack.' So too wrote the good reverend, eager to spend his last days with his favourite human being. 'Let others hear a little of the roaring cannon,' he urged. 'I trust the fatigue of life is over with you. In days of peace you will enjoy your cottage.'[36]

Month after month, year after year, those hopes were crushed, and Fanny's grass-widowhood continued. At the beginning of December 1794, Hood wrote to Nelson that he expected to return to the Mediterranean in the spring, and that the *Agamemnon* was due for recall. Nelson formed the idea of taking some leave in England, and then transferring his company to a seventy-four and going out again with Hood in the spring. The plan, attractive because it combined seeing his wife with a return to duty under his hero, was shipwrecked by the growth of French naval power in the Mediterranean and British delays in reinforcing Hotham's fleet. In those circumstances the acting commander-in-chief clung to every ship he had. Nelson was genuinely disappointed but tried to console. The war might not last long. Perhaps this year, or the next. And at least remaining in the Mediterranean would furnish more money for the Norfolk cottage he wanted. 'Much as I shall regret being so long parted from you,' he told Fanny, 'still we must look beyond the present day, and two or three months may make the difference of every comfort or otherwise in our income.'[37]

For Nelson, depressing as the lull in the fighting had become, the Mediterranean was still a fascinating honey pot that might at any time produce a life-changing opportunity. Battles at sea were rare at any time, but now the competing fleets seemed to be bracing themselves for just such an encounter. If it happened Nelson wanted to be there. As he explained to Drake, the 'object' of a sea officer was 'to embrace the happy moment which now and then offers – it may be this day, not for a month, and perhaps never'. If Hood resumed command of the fleet, as everyone expected, that tantalising prospect would brighten, but whether he came or not it possessed Nelson night and day, and kept him at his post.[38]

Like many sailors' wives Fanny was lonely, but she was also root-less. After Nelson's departure she had considered living at Swaffham in Norfolk, where the Nelsons had relatives and associates and the social amenities boasted assembly rooms, but she felt cold, sick and isolated there, and her father-in-law invited her to winter with him in Bath. The summer and autumn of 1794 were spent at Shepherd's Spring in Ringwood with the Matchams, but Kate was pregnant and ill and left for London so Fanny gratefully accepted an invitation to

Kentish Town. She liked the Sucklings, especially Miss Elizabeth, then pursuing Captain Henry Wigley of the Scots Greys (Nelson would send her a diamond ring for their wedding in November 1796), and stayed with them until November, when she removed to Bath with Nelson's father. Some references to occasional sallies further afield, for example to Plymouth in 1794 and Lyme Regis two years later, may reflect attempts to repair broken health. Fanny appears to have been a rather frail individual, commonly troubled by aches and anxieties.

The Reverend Edmund Nelson had left his parsonage in the hands of a younger son, the newly ordained and habitually 'reclaimed' Suckling, who acted as curate and worked the glebe land. With his daughter-in-law and such domestics as the Thurlow girls of Burnham, he eventually rented a terraced house at 17 New King Street in Bath. Considering how apprehensive Edmund had once been at the thought of meeting Fanny, the strange pair formed an exceptionally close friend-ship, each supporting the other 'in mutuall comfort', and sharing their ambitions for the return of 'our precious treasure'. At first Edmund stood as the guardian. 'If you can put yourself under my protection, a poor substitute [for Horatio], all shall be done that can be. Don't . . . consider the expense; it can, it shall be made easy,' he wrote to her. But as he grew older and weaker he became more dependent upon his daughter-in-law. He was still able to ride, once falling from a pony near his church in 1793, but tired easily and recoiled from travelling afar, where 'bad roads, dirty inns and insolent post boys' seemed the order of the day. Bath became Edmund's favourite 'place of warmth, ease and quietude'. He could make gentle pilgrimages to Ann's grave, bathe in the waters and linger at home, where Fanny fulfilled his need to 'chat' and supplied his 'news-reading eyes' by reading aloud to him from the newspapers. The bonds the two forged in those years were never broken, and held strong during the difficult years ahead. 'Mrs Nelson,' admitted the old man, 'truly supplies a kind and watchful child over the infirmities and whimsies of age.'[39]

As for Fanny, in between 'cheerful' visits to the theatre, concerts and friends, and occasional rides into the countryside, she too tended to remain indoors. Her father-in-law absorbed some of her energies, and she explored a new pianoforte, but was in a continual 'hurry and fret' about her husband, imparting her 'little news' to him in modestly penned letters she barely felt capable of writing. They told of the doings of her relatives, such as the Hamiltons, Herberts and Mortons, and of chance meetings with mutual acquaintances. Sir Thomas Shirley had visited, effusive about the captain he had once decried; a Miss Hawkins had said that two of the Andrews girls, one of them probably Elizabeth, as well as a younger brother had gone to the East Indies; and the Scriveners had fallen on hard times, the wife dead and the husband odder than ever. The Hoods were attentive to Fanny in Bath, and invited her to join them on Christmas Day, but she found the admiral a rather dour companion. 'Of all the silent men, surely he is the most so,' she wrote to her husband, but 'I was determined to make him smile.'[40]

Fanny perked up most when officers from the Mediterranean brought news of her missing men. Josiah, Hood told her, was 'one of the finest colts he ever saw', but she continued to mother him, and reminded Horatio that the boy had to clean his teeth up and down, and not across. John Harness, formerly the fleet's physician, brought her stories of Nelson in Corsica. He 'spoke so handsomely of you, and did tell me many little things which to bystanders might be thought trifling, but to me highly gratifying. I have heard of your breakfast on the fig tree. My son – they all say I shall not know him.'[41]

Of the many services Fanny did Nelson in the years he was away, the most essential was the care of his father, but she proved a valuable aid in other ways. She was affable and able enough to converse with the useful, including Sir Andrew Hamond, the comptroller of the Navy Board, and the Hoods, and gently to fight her husband's corner. She also handled everyday naval and family business on his behalf, drawing upon Nelson's London agent, Marsh and Creed of 23 Norfolk Street in the Strand, for money. She wrote letters for her husband, and saw to the gifts he was forever sending to friends and relations. The captain remained as generous as ever, even when far from home. It was Fanny who sent sugar, tea and wine to Nelson's aged Aunt Mary at Hilborough, and the rector who distributed his son's largesse in Burnham Thorpe. Like the good patron he was, Nelson felt an obligation to the poor of his parish, and customarily sent £200 each Christmas to provide warm clothing for the needy. 'Accept our best new year's gift [in return],' Edmund replied at the beginning of 1795, 'good wishes, the poor man's all!'[42]

In many respects Fanny made a good wife, and she shared some of her husband's characteristics. She was a regular churchgoer, and no respecter of those who would subvert the hallowed British constitution. Believing the treasonable stories in the newspapers, she was sure that the reformer John Horne Tooke and the leaders of the London

Corresponding Society then being tried for their lives by an alarmed government were 'a wickeder set' of men than ever existed. And like Horatio, Fanny was never a slave to money ('the love of wealth ruins many'), could mix with the grand without envying them, and if she was less self-righteous than her husband she was no less dutiful. To the end Fanny played the loyal daughter-in-law, mother and wife. She never failed her 'father', the ailing rector. She never failed Josiah. And as far as she was able, she never failed Nelson. Fanny delighted in pleasing her husband. When he cautioned her against travelling by coach she replied, 'No stage coach, I give you my honour, do I travel in, [nor] do anything in your absence that I thought would give you an opportunity to say that you wished it had been otherwise. No, not for the world.'[43]

The one thing she could not share with Horatio was his passion for fame. Fanny would have been content to live in her cottage, married to a retired rear admiral, and building a sedate social world around them, but she never felt his fierce need to achieve. Nor in the early years did it seem to matter.

6

For a naval officer the alignment of time, place and circumstance that made the 'happy moment' was always elusive. At the beginning of 1795 Nelson had been in the navy for twenty-four years without seeing a fleet action, but now that was about to change.

The first cruises of 1795 portended nothing so remarkable. Still more than a hundred men short of a full complement, the *Agamemnon* sailed with Hotham's fleet on 21 December, but the voyage was a thumping 'series of storms and heavy seas' and deposited Nelson in St Fiorenzo on 9 January. The weariness of Leghorn was renewed in what Nelson declared a 'damned place . . . where nothing is to be had for love or money', and relieved only on the 15th when the seventy-four-gun *Berwick* rolled over and lost her masts. For eight days Nelson sat in the great cabin of the *St George* as part of a court trying her officers. He felt sorry for the 'poor young man' who commanded her, but Captain William Smith and two of his officers were held accountable for the disaster and dismissed.[44]

The fleet sailed on 7 February and forged through 'a perfect hurricane' to reach Leghorn on the 24th. It was 'a very bad cruise', Nelson concluded. Many of the ships were damaged and sickness was returning. '*Agamemnon* wants almost a new ship's company,' he said. 'I have just sent 40 to the hospital and I have 100 on board without strength or spirits. Indeed, we are equal to an English 50-gun ship, nor is myself [free] from complaints. I have been so low by a flux and fever this last cruise that I sometimes thought I should hardly get over it. I am now on shore by leave from the admiral to see if I can get up again.'[45]

Then, on 8 March, came the news the British were waiting for. The French were at sea with fifteen sail of the line and several smaller warships. Hotham's look-out sloop, the *Moselle*, hovering off Leghorn, also saw the fleet in the northwest, steering south. It seemed as if the French were heading for Corsica.

The British were right. The enemy ships under Rear Admiral Pierre Martin included the hundred and twenty-gun *Sans-Culotte* and three eighty-gunners and carried seven thousand French troops and a siege train for the invasion of Corsica. So sanguine were some of success that the mayor and municipality of Bastia were carried as passengers, ready to resume their civic duties as soon as the French regained control. The French had heard that Hotham's fleet had been incapacitated by the storms and reduced to ten or so fit capital ships. Hastily they filled their ships with troops, and prepared another eighteen thousand men to follow in one hundred and thirty transports as soon as Admiral Martin had cleared the British away and established a bridgehead on Corsica. At sea, Martin soon had a crumb of success. He intercepted and captured the rehabilitated British ship of the line *Berwick*, as it struggled towards Hotham from St Fiorenzo. Despite this and his apparent superiority, Martin was not eager to meet the British fleet and probably hoped to sneak to Corsica while Hotham was refitting in Leghorn. If so, that hope was quickly crushed. After a furious bustle, the British got to sea at daylight on the 9th, steering for Corsica with fourteen ships of the line.[46]

The fate of Corsica hung in the balance as the British fleet forged ahead. Admiral Hotham flew his flag from the *Britannia* of one hundred and ten guns, with John Holloway, Nelson's old associate, as his captain. One of Hotham's ships was the Neapolitan seventy-four *Tancredi*, which had joined on 1 March under Captain Francesco Caraccioli. Sir William Hamilton regarded Caraccioli as 'surely the best officer in the Neapolitan navy', a man who had 'distinguished himself as a gallant officer and a good seaman' on 'many occasions', but scattered also through the fleet were many who would one day become Nelson's 'band of brothers', among them Thomas Foley, flag captain of the *St George*, Fremantle and Hallowell in the *Inconstant* and *Lowestoffe* frigates, and Ralph Miller on the little *Paulette*. This, the first fleet action in the Mediterranean, was to be a lesson to more than one captain of the Nelson 'school'.[47]

Throughout the first day the hostile French fleet remained beyond the horizon, visible only to Hotham's lookouts, but towards noon of the 10th the *Moselle* signalled. The French were in the northwest, standing back towards Toulon. It appeared that far from seeking battle they were scurrying home at the first sign of trouble. On board the *Agamemnon*, Nelson saw Hotham's signal for a general chase climb the mast of the flagship at noon, releasing his ships to pursue the enemy as best they could. The wind was light, and notoriously fickle in these parts, but the *Agamemnon* was swift and Nelson fully expected to engage the enemy. It was the chance he had been waiting for, and after giving the necessary orders he retired to his cabin to scratch a note to Fanny. It prepared her for the worst and oozed with his determination to fight, but was written in a clear, composed, well-formed hand as if death was a million miles away:

The lives of all are in the hands of Him who knows best whether to preserve it or no, and to His will do I resign myself. My character and good name is in my own keeping. Life with disgrace is dreadful. A glorious death is to be envied, and if anything happens to me, recollect death is a debt we must all pay, and whether now or in a few years hence can be but of little consequence.[48]

Back on deck, he discovered it was not to be that day. The French had caught a wind, leaving the British behind, and the chase was called off after five and a half hours. Nor could they get close to the enemy the next day, though the French appeared to have continued westwards throughout the night. But there was almost an engagement on the 12th, when daylight revealed the British becalmed some ten miles east of the enemy fleet and dangerously dispersed. The French had the advantage of a southerly breeze, and Hotham's ships were divided into two groups, the one nearest the enemy consisting of only six ships, including the *Agamemnon*, all wide open to attack. Nelson's ship was still undermanned, but he wrote to Vice Admiral Samuel Cranston Goodall on the *Princess Royal*, the senior officer with the smaller British division, congratulating him on being 'so near' the enemy and promising support, but soliciting a reinforcement of fifty or more men if they could be supplied.[49]

The French had a tremendous opportunity to steer between the two divisions of the British fleet and turn upon the smaller one, and for a while looked intent on doing so. Considering that they had to defeat the British fleet to achieve their objective, the subjugation of Corsica, they were unlikely to be presented with a better opportunity. Nelson saw the French making 'a very easy sail' towards them, but his sharp eye noticed something else too. 'They did not appear to me to act like officers who knew anything of their profession,' he wrote. 'At noon they began to form a line on the larboard tack which they never accomplished. At two P.M. they bore down in a line ahead, nearly before the wind, but not more than nine sail formed.'[50]

In short, Nelson was measuring the French fleet and finding it wanting. He was absolutely right. Despite unsteady government finances, France had invested large sums in her navy since the Seven Years War, and won a significant victory on the Chesapeake in 1782, when the Royal Navy was repulsed and a British army forced to surrender. But stubborn problems remained, including shortages of skilled manpower, uncertain supplies of naval stores and a tendency to adopt defensive and defective tactics. Furthermore, to these long-standing weaknesses the revolution brought new strains. The view that legitimate political sovereignty was vested in the popular will, rather than executive authority, eroded respect for the navy both without and within. Revolutionary governments failed to protect the service from abuse by local communes and Jacobin clubs, and politi-cised sailors challenged their officers and reduced ships to chaos. By 1792 most of the established officers of the French navy had quit the troubled service in despair, abandoning its upper ranks to swarms of relatively unskilled upstarts. Rear Admiral Martin was forty-three when he sailed to meet Hotham, but two years before he had been a mere lieutenant, and partly owed his elevation to his ardent Jacobinism. The National Convention, which governed France between 1792 and 1795, had tried to restore order in the fleet, but difficulties were compounded by the policy of keeping ships in port. Cooped up, barely putting out before running back again, the French were incapable of developing disciplined, well-knit and practised crews. The professional seamen among them were denied the hands-on experience they needed to create efficient teamwork, and the amateurs swept in to make up numbers had no means of learning a new trade. If French fleets sailed, even with a sufficiency of ships, they lacked the basic human resources to fight the British on equal terms. No one doubted that men of the highest calibre could be found in those fleets, but as a whole the personnel lacked skills, experience, discipline and confidence.[51]

Now those problems showed. About three miles from Goodall's division, the French abandoned the attack; their ships hauled their wind on the larboard tack, threw away their advantage and retired. Though Hotham united his ships in battle order later in the day, the wind continued to abort action, and darkness found both fleets off Genoa, standing to the southward under a fresh breeze.

On 13 March, Nelson's first 'happy moment' finally occurred.

As the first light filtered over the water, the French were seen about four leagues to windward in the southwest, their sails full in a brisk breeze. Again, with the wind in their favour, they might have attacked, but betrayed no such inclination. Their only interest, it seemed, was flight, and once more the British admiral signalled a general chase. Undermanned as she was, the *Agamemnon* was soon nimbly outperforming its larger consorts, and cutting through the squally weather after the retreating fleet. At seven or eight o'clock something happened. Two of the big French eighty-gunners, the *Ça Ira* and *La Victoire*, collided. The main and fore topmasts of the *Ça Ira* cracked, and plunged down, hanging with a trail of wood, rope and canvas over her leeward side, and acting as a drag upon the ship. Though men threw themselves into clearing the wreckage, Captain Louis-Marie Coudé found his ship lagging behind and heeling over so much that most of his lower-deck guns on one side were unable to bear.

The *Ça Ira* was a huge opponent, the biggest two-decker in the world, and 'large enough to take *Agamemnon* in her hold'. On board her quota of the troops embarked for the reconquest of Corsica had raised her manpower to at least one thousand and sixty men, three times that of the *Agamemnon*, which had only 344 hands at their quarters, including Nelson himself. In terms of fire power the *Ça Ira* was the equal of a three-decker, its eighty-four guns including a formidable lower-deck armament of French thirty-six-pounders. Against that Nelson's ship could dispose only sixty-four guns, the largest of them mere twenty-four-pounders. Moreover, when the larger French pound is also taken into the balance (a Gallic thirty-six was equal to thirty-nine English pounds), the *Ça Ira*'s advantage in weight of metal fired over the *Agamemnon* was something like two to one. It was a terrific superiority, and it was compounded by the French ship's use of red-hot shot and the close proximity of other powerful antagonists, including the gigantic hundred and twenty-gun *Sans-Culotte* and the seventy-four-gun *Jean Bart*.[52]

At nine-fifteen the British frigate *Inconstant* of thirty-six guns headed the chase and came close enough to the *Ça Ira* to open fire on her, like an impudent coyote yapping at the heels of a buffalo. The *Inconstant* was not a happy ship. Captain Fremantle had been accused of cruelty and had had to suppress a mutiny; five of its ring-leaders were still awaiting trial. Now, however, the ship acquitted herself magnificently in a duel with a massively superior opponent. Under normal circumstances a frigate would not have tangled with any ship of the line, let alone a monster like the *Ça Ira*. But Fremantle realised that the wreckage pulling the French ship over to leeward was immobilising her starboard broadside, and though her men were frantically clearing the debris away he had a brief opportunity to attack. Fremantle knew he could not fight the *Ça Ira* for long, but if he damaged and delayed her he could buy time for British ships of the line to come up.

Fremantle was a man of Nelson's stamp. He too chafed at Hotham's supine leadership and longed for chances to show his mettle, and he did not lead the British chase by accident. As soon as he had seen the collision among the enemy ships he had cleared for action and thrown his livestock overboard to remove every impediment to his gun crews. The little *Inconstant* passed under the crippled lee of the French giant and fired a broadside into her, then tacked and fired another. The *Ça Ira*'s upper-deck guns and some of the lower tier managed an indifferent reply, cutting up the frigate's rigging and sails, but, as the French ship's wreckage fell away and she righted, her murderous broadside swung into position. Nevertheless, with remarkable courage Fremantle went in for a third attack, and fired another broadside. But now the *Inconstant* was mauled by a withering discharge from the *Ça Ira*, as well as a broadside from the French frigate the *Vestale* as she moved in to throw a tow hawser to her injured consort. With a serious hole through the *Inconstant*'s hull, 'between wind and water', and seventeen of his men killed and wounded, Fremantle finally had to forgo the unequal contest.[53]

His fight had not been in vain, for as the *Inconstant* retired she was passed to windward by the leading British ship of the line, the *Agamemnon*. It was about ten-fifteen, and from his quarterdeck Nelson could see that he was to windward of the oncoming British fleet and far in advance. The nearest consort was the *Captain*, a seventy-four under Samuel Reeve, but she was still too far away to help. Ahead, however, the lumbering *Ça Ira* had not only cleared away some of her wreckage and restored most of her guns to order, but was being supported. The *Sans-Culotte* and *Jean Bart* fast approached 'about gun-shot distance on her weather bow', while the *Vestale* was taking her in tow. It may have been at this point that Nelson called for an opinion from Andrews, now first lieutenant in the place of the promoted Hinton. Should he attack? We cannot be sure, but Nelson later wrote that 'if the conduct of the *Agamemnon* . . . on the 13th was by any means the cause of our success on the 14th . . . [then] Lieutenant Andrews has a principal share in the merit, for a more proper opinion was never given by an officer than the one he gave me on the 13th, in a situation of great difficulty'.[54]

Nelson made his decision. Size, range, weight of metal and manpower were heavily against him, but speed and skill were something else, and he knew the capabilities of the *Agamemnon* and her crew. Grimly the sixty-four closed upon its big antagonist. Aboard her Nelson's 'poor brave fellows' had been summoned to action stations by a stirring drum tattoo, and gone about their routine with effortless precision. Decks were cleared, seven unfortunate bawling bullocks were pitched into the sea to prevent them plunging about the ship in terror, galley fires were extinguished and water thrown over vulnerable inflammables. Every man stood silently to his own dreadful calling: the surgeon and his mates waiting for the mutilated casualties, the uniformed marines ready to pick off officers or snipers from the enemy decks and fighting tops, and the sweaty sailors in trousers and kerchiefs, some scrambling aloft like monkeys but most standing expectantly by their guns. Each man was schooled in his part. Gun captains stood ready to train the cannons, prick open the cartridges beneath the touchholes, and release the firing locks with their lanyards, while their crews took their allotted positions. Some waited to sponge bores or ram down cartridges, wadding and shot, while others with strong limbs and backs braced themselves at the blocks and tackle, poised to haul the heavy pieces in and out of their ports or raise or depress them with chunky wooden quoins. Juniors stood nervously by, ready to feed shot and cartridges to the guns.[55]

Most of the lieutenants were supervising the gun crews, but Andrews was beside Nelson on the quarterdeck with the master, John Wilson, and some of Nelson's favourite midshipmen, who scurried about as aides, determined not to let their captain down. A fortnight later Nelson wrote of Hoste, 'what a good young man – I love him dearly, and both him and Josiah are as brave fellows as ever walked'. They had obviously discharged their duties with credit.[56]

The *Agamemnon* was within range of the *Ça Ira* by ten-twenty, but Nelson reserved his fire. He wanted to get within point-blank range of the Frenchman's stern before raking her from one end to the other, but the enemy had better gunners than he suspected. Though the *Ça Ira* could only bring its stern chasers to bear on the advancing ship, it made every shot count. Blasts of smoke and flame and the thunder of guns from the crippled Frenchman opened the contest, blowing holes through the *Agamemnon*'s sails, and splintering masts, spars and rigging aloft. Nelson must have been relieved. As they so often did, the French were firing high, hoping to damage his mobility, but this was not the most effective way to fight. If the *Agamemnon* lost her masts she would be paralysed and cut to pieces by the French ships, but most of the enemy shot screamed into thin air to splash harmlessly astern.

Chillingly silent, the *Agamemnon* crept closer without deigning to reply, her guns peering menacingly from her ports and their crews listening for the command. Nelson was still not as close as he wanted, but after twenty-five minutes under the *Ça Ira*'s guns he had had enough. He ordered Mr Wilson to put the helm a-starboard and the driver and after sails to be braced up and shivered. This made the bow of the ship fall off, and swung her broadside towards the towering stern of the *Ça Ira*. The guns roared along the whole of the *Agamemnon*'s side, recoiling savagely against their tackle, and sending ball after ball into the enemy ship. It was no amateur broadside, but a performance no other ship in the Mediterranean could have surpassed. These gunners had practised again and again, at sea and ashore, and fired tens of thousands of shot and shells in Corsica only the year before. The rate and accuracy of their fire were awesome, and they discharged their guns double-shotted, loading two round shot instead of one to increase the power of each broadside. It was a practice that sacrificed range and accuracy for velocity, but at this distance it did not matter; gunners like these did not miss. They directed a full broadside straight into the *Ça Ira*'s most vulnerable target – her stern and quarter – smashing through the after cabins, throwing wood and glass everywhere, and ploughing along the decks with terrific force, hurling guns off carriages, filling the air with hideous flying splinters and butchering men.

After the first broadside, Nelson ordered the after sails to be braced up and the helm put a-port so that the *Agamemnon* recovered its sailing position. Then he went after the *Ça Ira* again, and as he closed he repeated his earlier manoeuvre, sending another broadside into the French stern and quarter. The seamanship and gunnery of the British ship now told with devastating effect. The *Ça Ira*, her mobility crippled by the loss of her topmasts, was also fettered by the towing frigate, which kept her head forward. Not only that but unknown to Nelson she was 'miserably manned in point of seamen'. Only about fifty of her crew were able seamen, a few more 'ordinary seafaring people', and the mass of her enormous complement raw conscripts and soldiers. The officers were little better, if Elliot, who later entertained them at his table, is to be believed. He excepted the captain as 'an intelligent fellow', but thought his juniors 'such ragamuffins as have seldom been seen out of France'. Lady Elliot was so repelled by their appearance and manners that she sat silent for two hours, nursing an opinion that the ship's second officer could have passed for Bluebeard. During the battle the men of the *Ça Ira* fought bravely, but without discipline, order or skill.[57]

For two hours it went on. Held fast by her frigate, the *Ça Ira* was unable to turn to train her formidable broadside upon the diminutive assailant hammering volley after volley into her stern and quarters, and skipping about 'with as much exactness as if she had been turning in to Spithead'. Only a few stern guns could reply, and their futile fire was wide of the mark. Slowly the French ship was turned into 'a perfect wreck'. Her sails were shredded and her mizzen topmast, mizzen topsail and cross jackyards shot away. As parts of her wooden walls imploded, her decks were bloodied by dead, wounded and dying men.[58]

Remarkably, though for part of the time the *Sans-Culotte* and *Jean Bart* were at no great distance, on the *Agamemnon*'s starboard bow, they made no attempt to aid their stricken colleague, as if mesmerised by the savaging she was taking from such an undersized antagonist. But at about one in the afternoon the towing frigate hove in her stays and turned, bringing the broken *Ça Ira* around with her. Now prey and predator approached each other on opposite tacks, and for the first time those fearsome French broadside guns were brought to bear. The two ships passed each other 'within half pistol-shot', exchanging a furious fire as they did so.[59]

This was the most desperate moment of the fight as far as Nelson was concerned. This, if ever, was the time when the *Agamemnon* risked taking a terrible beating, but the flawed French tactic of firing high saved her. Though the British ship's sails and rigging were slashed to ribbons, most of the French shot flew right over the *Agamemnon*. Hardly anything hit her hull. As Nelson told his brother, 'That Being who has ever in a most wonderful manner protected me during the many dangers I have encountered this war [is] still shielding me and my brave ship's company. I cannot account for what I saw. Whole broadsides within half-pistol shot [range] missing my little ship, whilst ours was in the fullest effect.'[60]

After the ships had passed one another, Nelson fired his after guns and then hove in stays to turn her round, his 'poor brave fellows' serving their pieces so well that they were able to recharge and maintain an almost continuous fire. But now the *Sans-Culotte* and several other French ships had wore, and were under the *Agamemnon*'s lee bow, standing with their topgallant sails billowing to pass to leeward. Nelson had done the best he could, but he had no choice other than to leave off action. His struggle was being seen from the British fleet, and at one-fifteen Hotham signalled Nelson to disengage. The *Agamemnon* hauled off, and stood for her consorts, and the final shots – fired by the *Sans-Culotte* – failed to reach her. The French did not chase the retreating battleship. Instead they gathered in their wounded eighty-gunner and continued their retreat.

It had been a remarkable fight. Nelson lost only seven men wounded (three fatally), while the *Ça Ira* reportedly suffered losses of 110 men. The French ship was so badly damaged that she could not replace her missing topmasts, and remained crippled the following day, thus setting up the final round of the action. Her adversary, the *Agamemnon*, rejoined Hotham's line of battle, and her men worked into the night to complete their repairs as the fleets continued westwards. Nelson was proud of his performance, but decried the failure of the other British ships of the line to support him. 'What has happened,' he trilled to Fanny, 'perhaps may never happen to anyone again – that only one ship-of-the-line out of fourteen should get into action with the French fleet, and for so long a time as $2^1/_2$ hours, and with such a ship as the *Ça Ira*, but had I been supported, I should certainly have brought the *Sans-Culotte* to battle, a most glorious prospect!' This was not entirely true, however. The log of the *Captain* records that she, too, engaged, exchanging shots with an unspecified enemy ship of the line and a frigate for the thirty minutes before one o'clock.[61]

The consummation of the intrepidity of Fremantle and Nelson occurred the following day when the battle resumed, though the French had misplaced two of their ships, one the *Sans-Culotte*, their only three-decker, which accidentally separated from her companions and found sanctuary in Genoa. Daybreak of 14 March saw the rest of the fleets seven or so leagues further southwest, making the best of light winds, haze and drizzling rain. The wretched *Ça Ira* had been unable to restore its topmasts, and was being towed by a seventy-four, the *Censeur*, captained by Jean-Félix Benoît. She, like the *Ça Ira*, was carrying part of the army destined for Corsica and was overmanned, with 921 or perhaps even a thousand men aboard. Both ships were, however, in serious trouble. They had fallen astern and to leeward of the rest of their fleet, which was struggling in light winds on the larboard tack some one and a half miles to the southwest. About three and a half miles away were the British, and when Hotham picked up a northerly breeze that put him to windward and in a good position to attack, he made for the isolated ships. The British admiral was strongly placed. At least he could cut off and capture the two Frenchmen, and he might even provoke their countrymen into offering battle to save them.

Despite the failing wind the British bore down in a rough line of battle, steering between the French divisions, and just after seven the leading seventy-fours, the *Bedford* (Captain Davidge Gould) and the *Captain* (Captain Samuel Reeve), opened fire on the *Ça Ira* and *Censeur* with their starboard broadsides. The risks Fremantle and Nelson had taken engaging the *Ça Ira* the previous day were now demonstrated, as the guns of the two cornered Frenchmen cruelly mauled the approaching ships. In very little time the *Bedford* and *Captain* were disabled and knocked out of the battle. But behind them came the rest of the British fleet, led by three seventy-fours, the *Illustrious* (Captain Thomas Lenox Frederick), *Courageux* (Captain Augustus Montgomery) and *Princess Royal* (Captain J. C. Purvis and Vice Admiral Goodall). The weaker *Agamemnon* followed, and Nelson was close enough to mark again the French habit of firing aloft. The battered *Captain* lay 'like a log on the water, all her sails and rigging shot away'.[62]

With the leading ships out of the fight, the *Illustrious*, *Courageux*, *Princess Royal* and *Agamemnon* headed the British line, but while their starboard guns bore upon the *Ça Ira* and *Censeur* their attention was also drawn to larboard. The French main body had picked up a wind, turned to rescue their comrades, and begun advancing towards the British on the opposite tack with the powerful *Duquesne* at their head. It was then that a 'false manoeuvre' on the part of the French cost them dearly. Admiral Martin, who had transferred to *La Minerve*, one of his frigates, had signalled the attack even though his line was reduced to eleven capital ships, but the captain of the *Duquesne* misunderstood his superior's intention. Instead of steering north and to leeward of Hotham's fleet, interposing the French line between their besieged stragglers and the enemy, the *Duquesne* led Martin's ships to windward, firing from their larboard batteries at the masts of the British van from about eight o'clock. Hotham's front ships were therefore able to engage the enemy on both sides, simultaneously firing at close range upon the *Ça Ira* and *Censeur* to starboard and over a greater distance to larboard as the main French line came within range. Powder smoke soon wreathed a thunderous cannonade heard miles away in Genoa, with some belligerents firing almost blindly through the stinking, man-made fog. The *Courageux* was firing on the *Ça Ira* for fifteen minutes after she had struck, and had to be told to stop by Goodall on the *Princess Royal*.[63]

The battle was particularly fierce to leeward of the British line, where the trapped French ships fought with astonishing determination. The sails, rigging and yards of the *Illustrious* were riddled with shot, she lost her fore topmast, and her mainmast fell, carrying the mizzen mast with it and crashing hard upon the poop deck, fracturing its stout wooden beams. Though ninety of his men were killed and wounded and the debris had dismantled many guns, Captain Frederick kept firing until the end of the fight. Behind her the *Courageux* was similarly served. Her main and mizzen masts were toppled, her fore topmast severely damaged and she suffered forty-eight casualties; eventually she had to be taken in tow by Fremantle's *Inconstant*. It was fortunate for the British van that the French line to larboard posed no serious challenge. It sheered off to windward, exchanging only a few broadsides with the *Illustrious* and *Courageux*, and more distantly with the *Princess Royal*, *Agamemnon* and other ships, before hightailing it from the conflict and abandoning its embattled colleagues to their fates. Two more French ships, the *Victoire* and the *Timoleon*, had been damaged in the brief cannonade, and Martin judged his force too weak to challenge Hotham again.

Nelson joined the attack on the *Ça Ira* and *Censeur*, and both surrendered a little after eleven o'clock after more than three hours of punishment. The *Ça Ira* lay like a stricken whale, strewn with ropes and wreckage, her masts down and guns silenced, while the mainmast of the brave *Censeur* had also been felled. The *Illustrious* and *Courageux* had done the greatest damage, but their boats had been shot to pieces and Goodall hailed Nelson to ask him to take possession of the prizes and raise the English colours. It was not unfitting. Lieutenant Andrews, who led a party over water littered with the remains of the conflict, was 'as gallant an officer as ever stepped', while the *Agamemnon*, by its action the previous day, had been the key instrument of the victory.

Aboard the French ships Andrews found horrific devastation. Guns and wreckage were tossed about the decks and hundreds of men killed and wounded. Of some two thousand men on the French vessels, perhaps as many as eight hundred were killed and wounded – the four hundred or four hundred and fifty casualties of the *Ça Ira* having been sustained over the two days of battle. Other 'officers' later described the aspect to the naval historian, Edward Pelham Brenton:

The holds were filled with dead or dying men, who, as they fell at their quarters, were tumbled headlong down without any regard to their condition, and four days after the action dead bodies were [being] dragged out from the cable tiers and the wings. It was found, on enquiry, that not only were the people made drunk, but the ferocious republican officers stood behind them, and with drawn swords or pistols compelled them to fight.[64]

The *Agamemnon* herself emerged from the second day of fighting 'very much cut up', but she had no difficulty towing the *Censeur* away in triumph. Another seven men had been wounded, one of them the master, but overall the ship had not suffered extensive casualties, and several British ships, including the *Captain*, *Bedford*, *Illustrious*, *Courageux* and perhaps the *Princess Royal*, paid a higher 'butcher's bill'.[65]

Nelson paid tribute to the resistance of the *Ça Ira* and *Censeur*, but thought the rest of the French fleet, which continued its flight westwards, behaved 'most shamefully'. Considering they had orders to invade Corsica, the French had performed lamentably.[66]

The British celebrated a victory, and both Houses of Parliament voted their thanks, but actually Hotham had achieved relatively little.

The battle did not even directly save Corsica, since the French had aborted their mission at the very sight of the British fleet, without exchanging a single shot. The most that can strategically be said for the action off Genoa is that it prompted the French National Convention to abandon temporarily their invasion project. True, the British had taken two capital ships, but they gave Hotham no lasting advantage. Before fighting Hotham the French fleet had captured the British *Berwick*, and four days after the battle of 14 March Frederick's dismasted *Illustrious* was driven ashore and lost. In short both sides had lost two ships, and it is impossible to disagree with Elliot when he pessimistically remarked 'The French can hardly be said to have lost by their cruise.'[67]

7

Yet from Nelson's point of view the battle off Genoa was significant, perhaps more so than has generally been admitted. It was the first fleet action in which he played a crucial part, and in some respects his first naval victory, more impressive than the indecisive action with the French frigates nearly eighteen months earlier. He also profited from the experience. In fact, it arguably effected his purpose and ideas profoundly.

To begin it is necessary to consider the famous account of the battle he sent to Fanny later that March, when Hotham's fleet was once again languishing in port:

we are idle and lay in port when we ought to be at sea [he complained]. In short I wish to be an admiral and in command of the English [British] fleet. I should very soon either do much or be ruined. My disposition can't bear tame and slow measures. Sure I am [that] had I commanded our fleet on the 14th that either the *whole* French fleet would have graced my triumph, or I should have been in a confounded scrape. I went on board Hotham so soon as our firing grew slack in the van, and the *Ça Ira* and *Censeur* struck, to propose to him [Hotham] leaving our two crippled ships, the two prizes, and four frigates to themselves, and to pursue the enemy. But he is much cooler than myself and said, 'We must be contented. We have done very well.' But had we taken ten sail [of the] line and allowed the eleventh to have escaped if possible to have been got at, I could never call it well done. Goodall backed me. I got him to write to the admiral, but it would not do. We should have had such a day as I believe the annals of England never produced, but it can't be helped.[68]

Although this much-published passage has been accepted at face value, it was less than a candid account of what happened. As we have seen, Nelson was prone to exaggerating his achievements, even to misrepresent them. His picture of the fiery zealot storming to Hotham in the closing stage of the battle and demanding a hot pursuit, laced with its implication of flag-rank incompetence, does not really fit the circumstances in which the fleet found itself at midday on 14 March. Hotham himself alluded to the 'want of wind' as the reason for the escape of so many French ships, and Captain Tyler of the *Diadem* agreed. 'Nothing but its falling calm saved at least 7 or 8 being captured,' he wrote to his wife. The captain's log of the *Diadem*, among others, made several references to the wind in its account of the action. It was so slight that the British ships kept drifting out of their stations, and Tyler had to drop a jolly boat and hawser to help keep the *Diadem*'s head forward and her broadside towards the enemy. About noon, as the battle ended, light airs and calm were noted. Nelson chose to forget the wind in the letter to Fanny, but had been thoroughly aware of its importance. A few days before he had told his uncle that 'had the breeze continued so as to have allowed us to close with the enemy . . . we should have destroyed their whole fleet'. And Sir William Hamilton heard the same: 'Had the breeze only continued we should have given a decisive and destructive blow to the French fleet.'[69]

Nelson's attempt to persuade Hotham to pursue the French, therefore, probably did not happen on 14 March, after the battle; it would have been thoroughly inapplicable.

It was probably on the 15th that Nelson confronted Hotham, angry at the admiral's decision to fall back to port instead of returning to the chase, for it was on that day that he wrote to Goodall asking for a fresh supply of shot. 'The enemy are fled and we are not running after them,' he complained. He trusted that Hotham would 'get rid' of the prizes and 'lame ducks' at once and press on westwards, if for no other reason than to protect an expected British convoy.[70]

Laying aside the strict accuracy of Nelson's letter, its significance still beams brightly from its pages. This was as clear a statement of his concept of total victory as he ever made, and one remarkably similar to that penned by Hood after Rodney's battle of 1782. On both occasions the criticism was that a defeated fleet had been allowed to escape. Nor was Nelson unaware that Hood would have shared his opinion. 'I wish from my heart Lord Hood was arrived,' he told Fanny. 'We make but a bad hand of managing our fleet.'[71]

This meeting with French gentry, as Nelson put it, confirmed his view that the republican navy was grossly deficient in fighting qualities. The *Ça Ira* and *Censeur* had fought bravely, but the French fleet as a whole had been defeatist, running rather than fighting, and using all its 'endeavours . . . to avoid an action'. Its discipline, by all that could be learned from prisoners, had been deplorable, something bewailed by the French admiral, who reported that 'for the most part' officers were 'neither seconded by experience nor by sufficient capacity'. In seamanship and gunnery the enemy fleet had been transparently incompetent. The French ships had struggled to form line, collided with each other and separated. Their biggest ship, the *Sans-Culotte*, had disappeared in the night of the 13th and missed the next day's battle completely. Their gunfire was far from accurate, and at times seemed to have been discharged 'at random', but when it was on target it was directed at masts and sails. It was a defensive fire, designed to cripple mobility and facilitate escape, rather than the destructive hull-smashing fire that destroyed ships and won battles. Ship for ship and gun for gun such forces were no match for their British counterparts, whose seamanship had been shaped by years at sea, and whose gunnery, both in the rates and focus of their fire, had reached levels of fearful efficiency.[72]

That being the case new opportunities were unfolding, and Nelson saw them plainly. It was time to bring decision to naval combat, to reach for the complete victory using more aggressive tactics. The old line-ahead formation, which had fleets of comparable power firing distant broadsides at each other, was powerful defensively. However, once respect for an enemy's ability declined, once men with Nelson's confidence in battle superiority rose to the fore, its rigidity could be abandoned for more adventurous close-quarter tactics capable of delivering more impressive results.

The battle off Genoa may have been a scrappy Mediterranean victory, but it played its part in the making of Britain's most famous admiral. Watching the rival fleets joust for two days vividly exposed the gulf between the two, and alerted Nelson to the prize that awaited an admiral willing to exploit it. And more than ever, he wanted to be that admiral. 'I almost wish myself at the head of this fleet,' Nelson confided to Hamilton. 'Don't accuse me of presumption. It is only from an anxious desire to serve our country.'[73]

8

Nelson's part in the battle found only a modest place in Hotham's public dispatch, but he was not dissatisfied. Earl Spencer, the new first lord of the Admiralty, had promised to serve Nelson when a 'proper opportunity' occurred, and he hoped that the fresh victory might be the encouragement needed.

Most of all he wanted another crack at the French, but the prevailing lethargy of Hotham's command returned. The enemy fleet retired to Hyères and Toulon, while Hotham's ships were soon 'idling' again between St Fiorenzo and Leghorn. Now a full admiral, Hotham was approaching sixty and the shaky hand of some of his letters betrayed a precarious state of health. He sometimes cruised off Minorca but seemed incapable of great exertion, and Nelson's log brimmed with the dull minutiae of tacking and wearing ship as required. Even employed thus, he managed to impress his divisional commander, Vice Admiral Goodall of the *Princess Royal*, who formed a 'high opinion' of Nelson's 'bravery and activity'. When the British consul at Genoa asked Hotham to send a squadron to aid the Austrian army on the Italian riviera, it was Goodall who recommended the captain of the *Agamemnon* for the job.[74]

Nelson chafed at his commander-in-chief's 'doing nothing' policy but also blamed the Admiralty, whose new board he reckoned worse than the last. Many of Hotham's ships were worn out, but neither replacements nor reinforcements appeared. His adversary, Vice Admiral Martin, was increasing his forces. Two line of battle ships were being built in Toulon, and six arrived from Brest, giving the French twenty capital ships to Hotham's fourteen. The British were unequal to their many commitments. Merchantmen could not be provided with escorts, though the enemy fleet was almost able to sail at will and the seas swarmed with privateers, and safe passage could not even be guaranteed important convoys bringing military and naval supplies from Gibraltar to St Fiorenzo. Plans to support the Austrians on the riviera stalled.[75]

The British were outnumberd, but the battle near Genoa had confirmed Nelson's belief that they could beat the larger enemy fleet, a belief that was only vindicated by every skirmish. In June 1795 the *Dido* and *Lowestoffe* garnered fresh laurels for the Royal Navy by defeating two superior French frigates in a classic encounter off Minorca, an event Nelson rated 'the handsomest thing this war'. In

Nelson's opinion Hotham's fourteen ships of the line, including two Neapolitan men-of-war, were 'sufficient at any time to fight twenty French ships . . . However much our armies may have failed, yet our seamen are as superior to the French as ever during this war. We have never once failed, neither in single [ship] action[s] nor in a fleet.'[76]

All that was needed, Nelson felt, was a leader. 'Truly sorry am I that Lord Hood does not command us,' Nelson informed his Uncle William. 'He is a great officer, and were he here we should not now be skulking.' The fleet would be watching Toulon and not cruising fruitlessly off Minorca. Then sad news reached the Mediterranean. Hood had been quarrelling again, and deeply upset the first lord of the Admiralty, and he was not coming back. Nelson was thunderstruck. 'Oh miserable board of Admiralty!' he cried. 'They have forced the first officer in our service away from his command.'[77]

The consolation was that reinforcements under Rear Admiral Robert Man of the *Victory* reached the fleet in June. Among them Nelson was delighted to find one of his boyhood friends from the *Seahorse*, Thomas Troubridge, now a post-captain and a truly masculine figure, with a strong frame and ruggedly handsome features set beneath prominent brows. Nelson liked Troubridge. With a ready intelligence, cultivated perhaps by an education at St Paul's School, Troubridge had graduated from Mr Surridge's classes in seamanship to serve on the flagship of Sir Richard Hughes in the East Indies, where he had participated in several skirmishes with the French fleet. His luck had varied since. Re-employed on the outbreak of war like Nelson, his frigate the *Castor* was captured by the French in the Atlantic and he witnessed the battle of 'The Glorious First of June' as a prisoner aboard one of the enemy men-of-war. Liberated by Howe's victory, he had been appointed to the *Culloden* seventy-four, but had to suppress a mutiny to bring her out to the Mediterranean. There the two friends resumed their old intimacy, masters of their profession and united in a determination to defeat the French.[78]

Nelson shared his disappointment about Hood with Troubridge, but the reinforcements raised his spirits. Before, when the British had been outnumbered, he had known they were capable of trouncing Martin's fleet, but now the issue of a battle would be 'certain'. More important still, it increased the possibility of the Royal Navy winning the 'complete victory' he wanted. As he would famously say many years later, only numbers could annihilate.[79]

Nelson only needed another rendezvous with the French to be made happy. 'God send us a good and speedy meeting!' he said.[80]

It came upon him suddenly and dangerously.

9

In the evening of 4 July the *Agamemnon* was towed out of St Fiorenzo and got under sail, making northwards towards Genoa with the frigates *Ariadne* and *Meleager*, the *Moselle* sloop and *Mutine* cutter.

It was a relief. The previous day Nelson had been sitting in the *Princess Royal* as part of a court reaffirming the right of the navy to command all soldiers serving aboard their ships, including Lieutenant Gerald FitzGerald of the 11th Regiment of Foot, who had brooked such authority on the *Diadem*. The new task was far more appetising. The Austrian army was attempting to halt the French advance along the riviera and needed naval support. After many delays Nelson was on his way with a small force and orders to join the *Inconstant* and *Southampton* in Genoa, and to deploy the entire squadron to the detriment of the French. With alternative and senior officers at hand, Hotham honoured Nelson by the command, although the suggestion was Goodall's. The acting commander-in-chief was not a gifted man, and wanted to be relieved of the awesome responsibility of ruling the Mediterranean, but he did his duty insofar as he could comprehend it. He knew Nelson to be the right man.[81]

On this occasion Captain Nelson never reached Genoa.

For two days he sailed along, detaching his ships to investigate such craft as appeared. On the 6th Captain Robert Plampin of the *Ariadne* spoke to the master of a Swedish brig a dozen leagues off Cape di Noli and heard that the French fleet was out again and had been seen the previous day. The information was no sooner relayed to Nelson than at about noon a cry from the masthead of the *Ariadne* drew Plampin's attention to several large ships west-by-north. Nelson signalled a chase, but the *Ariadne* was soon reporting fifteen sail, and both sides gingerly probed for information. Two strange frigates hung in the offing, reconnoitring the British ships, while Nelson's lookouts quickly realised that this was no merchant convoy before them, but the main French battle fleet. It was, in fact, Vice Admiral Martin with seventeen sail of the line and six frigates.

Early the next morning four large ships pushed towards the British ships under Spanish colours, but Nelson was not deceived. Calling in his cruisers, he ordered them to save themselves, and turned back towards St Fiorenzo to warn Hotham. A furious twenty-four-hour chase ensued. 'We fear much for poor Nelson, who has led them the dance there,' wrote Udny when the news reached Leghorn, and there were indeed some dangerous moments. Captain Charles Brisbane only escaped an enemy frigate by running the *Moselle* between Cape Corse and a small island, and Nelson himself did well enough until the wind failed on the morning of the 8th, not far from St Fiorenzo. The French fleet had the better of the available breeze, and for a while Nelson cleared his ship for what would have been a hopeless defence, but the wind as quickly revived and enabled the *Agamemnon* to flee through shallows towards St Fiorenzo. Nelson fired signal guns to alert Hotham, but the French ships quickly scurried away as the British ships frenziedly prepared for sea. They were 'neither seamen nor officers' snorted Nelson in disgust.[82]

Hotham had been taken by surprise, but got his full force out that night, twenty-three sail of the line that made what Nelson described as 'as fine a fleet as ever graced the seas'. Martin had disappeared westwards, and Hotham went after him, flying his flag from the hundred-gun *Britannia*. Among his ships were the three-decked *Victory* and *Princess Royal*, bearing the flags of Man and Goodall, but the two-decked seventy-fours were the mainstay of the fleet and included the *Courageux* and *Culloden*, captained by Nelson's friends Hallowell and Troubridge. Though sixty-fours were seen as rather weak for the line of battle, Nelson excitedly took his place determined that the *Agamemnon* would be among the foremost.[83]

The French were tracked to south of the Hyères islands on 12 July. At daylight on the following morning they were seen in an irregular line four leagues or so to leeward in the southeast, steering northwards towards the land about Fréjus Bay on the larboard tack. Acting smartly the British might have cut them off, but Hotham was moving away from the shore on the opposite tack and lost considerable time reforming his fleet in battle order on the larboard line of bearing. The *Princess Royal* had to signal the *Agamemnon* to take its proper station no less than four times. It was not until eight o'clock that Hotham decided that the enemy was intent only on escape, and signalled a general chase, freeing his captains to pursue as each was able. A later signal, ordering captains to engage the enemy ships as they came up with them, increased the measure of independence allowed, but although the British ships plunged after the retiring Frenchmen under all possible sail it was too late.

Many officers in the fleet seethed at the admiral's sluggishness, so volubly that Elliot reflected 'in other times it might very possibly have come to a shooting bout'. Vice Admiral Sir Hyde Parker of the *St George* later claimed that most if not all of the French ships might have been taken if Hotham had gone about immediately. For two hours Hotham had persisted on the opposite tack, sailing away from the French, and the final signal for a general chase was not made until four hours after the enemy had first been spotted. During that time, Parker raged, the distance between the fleets had grown to five leagues, and it had become impossible to cut them off from the land. Other captains added to this chorus, and the charge got back to officers who had not been present, including Captain Collingwood and Admiral Hood, muddying Hotham's reputation.[84]

In the event only a few of the British ships came up with the hindmost French vessels. Fickle winds retarded their advance, and it was noon before the *Victory* (Captain John Knight), *Captain* (Captain Reeve), *Agamemnon*, *Cumberland* (Captain Bartholomew Samuel Rowley), *Defence* (Captain Thomas Wells) and *Culloden* (Captain Troubridge) – what a lieutenant of the first of these called the six 'fastest and best managed' ships – got within gun shot, leaving their fellows wallowing behind. They cheered each other into action, first the *Victory* and *Culloden* and then their consorts, and for a while they were head to head with the enemy rear, their bows to the northwards, enveloped in the thick gunsmoke of mutual fire. The winds played the British false, however, fading as the brief but furious cannonade intensified and then turning into a calm. It was impossible for the ships to close, and Nelson, who had been engaging the enemy centre and rear, complained that another ten minutes would have put him alongside an eighty-gun flagship. The highlight of the action came at about two o'clock when the French *Alcide*, a seventy-four battered by the *Victory*, *Culloden* and *Cumberland*, struck its colours, but accidentally took fire in her foretop and shortly detonated with a terrifying explosion. The British boats saved about three hundred men but another four hundred were lost.

The wind shifted, enabling the French to retreat into Fréjus Bay where it was dangerous for the British to follow. Nevertheless, at about three-thirty the *Cumberland* and *Agamemnon* were coming up with the hindmost once again, one the former British *Berwick*, when the signal to discontinue action was flown from the *Britannia*, eight miles astern. Hotham's ship sailed badly, and may have fallen so far behind that the admiral had lost his ability to read the battle. In his view his foremost vessels 'had approached so near to the shore that I judged it proper to call them off by signal'. But others took a different view. Goodall is said to have kicked his hat about the deck in rage, and some of his men supposedly went even further, heatedly declaring that they would no longer serve under Hotham. Nelson was equally critical. 'The risk might have been great,' he told Fanny, 'but so was the object.' His brother William got a damning account of the 'miserable' engagement: 'To say how much we wanted Lord Hood at that time is to say, "Will you have *all* the French fleet or no action?" For the scrambling *distant* fire was a farce. But if one [enemy ship] fell by such a fire, what might not have been expected had our whole fleet engaged!'[85]

One French ship, the frigate *Alceste*, had made a desperate attempt to get a hawser to the injured *Alcide* before she surrendered, advancing under heavy British fire until the attempt was palpably forlorn. The captain's courage astonished British opponents, but the French performance as a whole had not been impressive. Hotham's fleet suffered little loss, a mere thirty-eight men killed and wounded and some structural damage aloft, and Nelson's unflattering opinion of the republican navy was reinforced. Only one man on the *Agamemnon* had been badly wounded, and though a few French shots had struck the ship below the waterline most had damaged sails and rigging. 'Thus,' he told the Duke of Clarence, 'has ended our second meeting with these gentry . . . the French admiral, I am certain, is not a wise man or an officer. He was undetermined whether to fight or run away. However, I must do him the justice to say he took the wisest step at last [running away]. Indeed, I believe this [the British] Mediterranean fleet is as fine a one as ever graced the ocean . . . The enemy will have still twenty-one sail at sea in a month, but I don't believe they can ever beat us in their present undisciplined state.' Others shared these conclusions around the mess tables. 'The enemy were very badly manoeuvred, and fired without doing any execution of consequence for two hours,' recalled the *Victory* lieutenant.[86]

More diplomatic than in days gone by, Nelson confined his reservations to private letters and remained on excellent terms with Hotham. After returning to St Fiorenzo he was dispatched once again to the riviera, sailing on 15 July with the *Ariadne* and *Meleager* frigates, the *Tarleton* brig and the *Resolution* cutter under his command. He also had the authority of a new rank, possibly an echo of the promises made by Lord Hood or maybe an acknowledgement of his part in the battle of 13 and 14 March. Whatever the case, newspapers sent by his father informed him that a general promotion of 6 June had raised him to Colonel of Marines of the Chatham Division with its welcome increment in salary.[87]

It was belated perhaps, but at least it preserved his chances of remaining on the station, where the French were still at large and there were battles to be fought. It also imparted some sense of progression. Nelson's health was troubling him and he confessed to Sir Gilbert Elliot that 'my exertions have been beyond my strength. I have a complaint in my breast which will probably bear me down.' The ship's surgeon, Mr Reynolds, prescribed rest, but his promotion and the independent command fed his vanity, and put him back at the forefront of the military struggle in the Mediterranean. He had found the one active theatre left within Hotham's command.[88]

10

Since the Corsican invasion Nelson had felt more frustrated than fulfilled, but his education had benefited. The foundations of his future successes were nearly all in place.

He had been an apt pupil, intelligent, diligent and determined, driven by his own dreams of distinction and honour and a strong personality. His progress also reflected the work of many minds – of Captain Suckling, who had preached the gospel of duty; of Mr Surridge, who had taught him to handle and navigate a ship; and of William Locker, who had given him his first major lessons in command and filled his head with the glorious deeds of Hawke.

Perhaps most of all Nelson's progress reflected his ultimate role model, Lord Hood, the very epitome of duty, determination and daring. Hood shared Nelson's energy, aggression and self-confidence, and the two men, one a greying sea dog nearing the end of his active life, the other a zealot who commanded the future, had probably often talked about the complete victory they both wanted, and how it might be won. It is easy to believe that in Nelson's tactics at the battle of the Nile there were distant echoes of what his old mentor had tried to do at St Kitts and Golfe Jouan. Nelson was outspoken in his admiration for Hood, 'the best officer, take him altogether, that England has to boast of. Lord Howe certainly is a great officer in the management of a fleet, but that is all. Lord Hood is equally great in all situations that an admiral can be placed in.' Nelson's homage was most obvious in his criticisms of Hotham. Whenever he censured Hotham, he insisted that Hood would have acted differently – in other words, as he himself would have acted. The professional views of Hood and Nelson were therefore interchangeable, distinct from Hotham's and as one.[89]

Today it is impossible to endorse Nelson's exalted opinion of Hood, at least in every respect. Undoubtedly the admiral possessed professional courage and resolution, but we have seen how his refusal to heed advice had contributed to the disaster at Toulon and almost derailed (perhaps we should say shipwrecked) the invasion of Corsica. Even Nelson, something of a Hood protégé, had suffered from his blatant favouritism and failure to appreciate talent. According to Fremantle, one of Hood's most aggrieved captains, 'most of us are tired of serving under him'. Surprisingly, Nelson remained unusually blind to his mentor's failings.[90]

Nevertheless, Nelson had seen the British fleet reach a state of professional perfection under Hood, and learned essential lessons about the importance of discipline, training and health. Rather than 'loitering' in port or at sea, Hood had schooled the ships in manoeuvres and battle procedures. The *Agamemnon* herself was a crack unit. For gales and seas, he said, his men cared nothing. Sometimes waves and winds rolled the ship violently, smashed her stern galleries, sprung masts, ripped sails from their yards, damaged the rudder or streamed her decks with water, but the company handled her beautifully, and she was at the head of every general chase. Her gunnery, seasoned on sea and land, could probably not be bettered. Even 'worn out' Nelson doubted there was a two-decker in the world that could have captured the *Agamemnon*. 'I am sure this ship's company feel themselves equal to go alongside any seventy-four out of France,' he said. 'Every man has seen so many shot fired that they are very superior to those who have not been in action.'[91]

Health was another legacy of Hood's command, an important one since sick crews and efficiency did not make good partners. Of course, there would always be sick lists, especially in the Mediterranean where arduous work in feverish climates and disease-ridden ports was inseparable from life. The *Agamemnon* suffered brutally during her Corsican campaigns of 1794. But away from the specific damage of particularly demanding assignments, the fleet had made gains under Hood. Scurvy was practically eliminated from the fleet, partly no doubt through the aegis of the fleet physician, Dr John Harness, who came to the Mediterranean from Haslar Hospital in Portsmouth. The admiral made little use of salted provisions, and shipped live oxen and other livestock on his ships, while efforts were constantly made to procure lemons, onions and oranges as curatives. 'No fleet ever was in better order to meet an enemy than I conceive ours to be at this moment,' Nelson wrote soon after Hood's departure. 'We are remarkably healthy.' Scurvy, he later added, was 'not known'. In fact, before 1796, when Gilbert Blane persuaded the Admiralty regularly to issue lemon juice to the fleets, Nelson and other Mediterranean captains had been schooled in the maintenance of basic health.[9]

Much that Nelson brought from his experiences with Hood was allowed greater expression under his successor, Admiral Hotham. Most significantly, it was during Hotham's command that Nelson had finally come gun to gun with the French fleet and judged its worth. The vast superiority of the Royal Navy's combat skills, he almost instinctively realised, could best be turned to account in close-quarter engagements, and that meant greater tactical flexibility and a readiness to modify or discard the traditional line of battle.

The power of the line-ahead formation, which protected vulnerable bows and sterns and presented discouraging broadside batteries right and left, was obvious. To approach such a line head on, or even at an angle, offering the weakly defended bow or quarter to those formidable rows of guns, invited terrific risks. The safety of the line, and the potential disaster courting any who departed from it, was written into the printed Admiralty fighting instructions, but a consequence had been the distant sterile exchanges between fleets facing one another in roughly parallel lines, each afraid of abandoning the standard defensive formation.

Nelson understood the importance of the line, but appeared to have relatively little reverence for it in his early years, placing more emphasis upon the need for individual captains to use their initiative to get to close quarters. He was by no means alone in his desire for greater tactical flexibility, but rather part of a tradition that had been growing for half a century.

Some admirals had long elaborated the standing Admiralty instructions to erode the tyranny of the line. Hawke used a 'general chase' to release ships to pursue flying enemies in the preliminaries to his defeat of the French at Quiberon Bay in 1759, a victory immortalised in the patriotic song 'Hearts of Oak', which Nelson had known since childhood. In 1780 Admiral Sir Charles Henry Knowles opined that while the line was useful as a way to approach an enemy fleet, it was advisable for ships to pursue their opponents as they saw fit once engaged. Two years later the battle of the Saintes appeared to demonstrate the potential of aggressive tactics when an accidental rupture of the French line enabled some of Rodney's captains to slip through, double the enemy's ships and catch them in a destructive crossfire. A Scottish laird, John Clerk of Eldin, advocated exactly such manoeuvres in his *Essay on Naval Tactics*, published in 1790.

Perhaps the most inventive assault upon an enemy fleet, however, was that made by Lord Howe in 1794. He planned to attack from windward, pierce the French line and finish the engagement in the lee of the enemy fleet. Theoretically, this would have given him the advantage of the wind in the opening phase of the battle, and enabled him to attack when he chose. Passing through the enemy line, the British ships would also have been able to rake the French sterns and bows with their broadsides, and once under their opponents' lee they would have been well positioned to cut off the retreat of any disabled enemies. A badly crippled ship unable to work to windward had to fall to leeward before the wind. Howe's plan was complicated, but at 'The Glorious First of June' some of his ships managed to cut the enemy line and produce a modest victory. Howe had also contributed to more sophisticated tactics by issuing an improved signal book in 1790.[93]

In his willingness to shed the line, therefore, Nelson was in keeping with the changing perceptions of enterprising forebears. There were a growing number of precedents for new and aggressive tactics. But those battles under Hotham had arguably been even more formative, for they confirmed Nelson in his opinion that a tremendous gulf was opening up between the French and British fleets. Its implications were not lost upon him. The defence offered by the line was no longer imperative, and captains were justified in taking risks to get to close quarters.

Professionally, Nelson had grown in his year with Hotham and become an admiral in the making, but a commander-in-chief needed more than a grasp of the naval tactics. A grasp of the broader strategical situation and the elements of interstate diplomacy were essential. Nelson had seldom been required to think through the ramifications of policy, and sometimes gushed intemperate opinions about what should or should not be done, with little regard for their political consequences. However, when Nelson returned to his duties off the riviera in the summer of 1795, he entered a vortex where the ambitions of enemies, allies and neutrals crunched head-on. The captain not only acted as a commodore, developing his leadership skills at the head of a squadron, but he also entered the murky waters of Mediterranean diplomacy, filling the one obvious vacuum in his professional education.

XXI

DRIFTING TO LEEWARD

As Nelson's calm eternal face went by,
Gazing beyond all perishable fears
To some imperial end above the waste of years.
Alfred Noyes, *The Phantom Fleet*

1

WRITING to the Honourable John Trevor, the British minister plenipotentiary in the Kingdom of Sardinia-Piedmont at Turin, Horatio Nelson admitted wearily that 'We English have to regret that we cannot always decide the fate of empires on the sea.'[1]

Never did he feel the truth of that assertion more than during his operations off the riviera coast in 1795 and 1796. Despite all his customary energy and will he watched Britain's position in the Mediterranean disintegrate, her allies humbled and the triumphal *tour de force* of her foes gather spectacular pace. Try as he might, Nelson found himself largely a tool of damage limitation. It was a dispiriting, disempowering business, akin to being the commander of a crippled ship driven to inexorable destruction by wind and tide. During the eighteen months Nelson cruised off the riviera the old fleet phrase 'drifting to leeward' reasonably described his country's position east of Gibraltar.

There were many reasons for the deterioration. While the British wasted tens of thousands of redcoats in largely fruitless West Indian forays they had no significant military force for the Mediterranean. They relied on allies – allies who proved to be ropes of sand.

Prussia made peace with France in 1795, then Holland, and then

Spain. Even before the Franco-Spanish alliance of August 1796, diminishing tension between the two countries allowed the French to transfer soldiers from their western frontier to Italy. Off the riviera, where the war continued, Nelson found the remnants of the once mighty allied coalition frail and fractious. The Austrians were afraid the Sardinian king would strike a separate bargain with the French, and try to regain his lost possessions of Nice and Savoy at the expense of Austria. On their part the Sardinians resented the overall command of the allied armies being given to a sixty-three-year-old Austrian general, Joseph Nikolaus, Baron De Vins, an officer notoriously unpopular with the Piedmontese. Further east the score of Italian states were incapable of uniting against French invaders. The republic of Genoa, supposedly a neutral buffer between the French and Italy, was economically bound to its powerful western neighbour as well as afraid of her, and it was rife with Jacobin sentiment. The other Italian states were enfeebled by mutual suspicions, internal revolt and irresolute leadership, and to Nelson it seemed that only the Neapolitan Kingdom of the Two Sicilies showed any spirit whatsoever.

With little support from home, and irresolute and fragmented allies at his elbow, Nelson felt a crumbling breakwater against the eastward tide of French imperialism. These new soldiers of the French republic were the fodder of mass conscription, many of them mere ill-provisioned boys, but they fought with a new spirit and in a new style. The time-honoured lines of the traditional armies that faced them were repeatedly weakened by musket fire or artillery before being pulverised by loose but powerful columns of infantry. Rediscovering the military secrets of the ancient Mongols, the French often moved swiftly and flexibly, without the encumbrance of ponderous baggage and supply trains. If they had no artillery, they did without, and food was pillaged from the ground they marched over. What they lacked in discipline they requited by numbers, a reckless courage and the experience of battle after battle. Even 'half-naked' they 'determined to conquer or die'. Reluctantly, Nelson acknowledged the new vibrancy of the French armies. When it came to war they were as unorthodox as he was, and as enthused by revolutionary fervour as he was by a growing hatred of it. On land these alien warriors were 'like our seamen; they never stop, and know not the word halt'. The contrast with the Austrian whitecoats opposing them became inescapable. As a British army officer with the Austrians wrote, the emperor's forces were paralysed by 'indecision, indifference and indolence'.[2]

What was more, from among Lazare Carnot's new breed of young and vigorous generals, the French had found a leader of unusual ruthlessness, ambition and enterprise. He would face Nelson for the first time here, on the riviera coast, but his towering figure would throw a giant shadow over the remainder of the admiral's life. His name was Napoleon Bonaparte.

2

The evening of 17 July 1795 found Nelson in Genoa, making a careful note of the four French frigates and corvettes that sat invulnerable at their moorings. Unable to do anything about them in a neutral port, Nelson talked to Francis Drake, the British minister plenipotentiary who had been appointed to liaise with the Austrian army and had also just arrived. Six years younger than Nelson, and like him the son of a parson, Drake shared the captain's appetite for business and soon briefed him on the military situation.[3]

In June the Austrians and Sardinians had thrown the advancing French 'Army of Italy' under General François-Christophe Kellermann, the hero of Valmy, back across the Apennines, but now the opposing forces were stalemated near the coast at Albenga. Thirty thousand French had dug into the St Esprit mountains with Nice to their rear, while the Austrians under De Vins were quartered at Vado Bay near Savona with their advanced posts a few miles further west, near Loano. For the moment both sides glowered at one another, unable to move forward. But the ability of the French to advance or even to hold their existing positions depended upon supplies. With the Sardinians at Ormea and Garessio threatening the enemy's land communications, most of their provisions had to be brought in by sea. If Nelson could stifle them and drain the French of strength, he might be able to force them to retreat or at least weaken their lines and expose them to Austrian attack. The Austrian general was grumbling about the lack of naval support, and not without some justification. Even as Drake was briefing Nelson in Genoa a score of feluccas were landing provisions for the French at Oneglia and rescuing them from a regimen of a quarter of a ration a day.[4]

Stopping such supplies would not be easy, however – if possible at all. For one thing many of the sea-borne supplies were sneaked along the coasts at night, in light-draught vessels capable of exploiting the treacherous shallows inshore, where larger ships could not go. For another, the trade was largely in the hands of Genoese, Italian and Algerian neutrals who had endless ruses to protect their livelihoods. False flags and forged papers were used to disguise the ownership of freight, and any legitimate property seized by mistake could involve the hapless captors in damaging lawsuits. Nelson had been ordered to avoid offending the neutral states whenever possible, but as the French had now penetrated the republic of Genoa itself it was possible for Genoese merchants to supply them without leaving their own territorial waters. It was a diplomatic minefield. To help his allies Nelson had to stop those provisions, but in doing so he risked financial penalties and the full weight of diplomatic disapproval.

Back in the reassuring surroundings of his cabin on the *Agamemnon*, Nelson was mortified to find that Hotham's instructions were also peculiarly obstructive, ordering him to abide by a misconceived Admiralty circular. It demanded that inventories of the cargoes of impounded neutrals be sent to London, where any decision to prosecute would be taken. This long-winded and preposterous injunction would not only have congested the processes of seizure and trial, but also have destroyed the bulk of the disputed cargoes, which consisted of perishable foodstuffs. Spoiled goods could not be restored, even if the Admiralty deemed them unlawful prize, and the captors would inevitably become liable for their value. Neither Nelson nor any of his captains could be expected to labour under such an imposition.[5]

Nelson liked Hotham but not his inertia and want of 'political courage'. The admiral was 'alarmed at everything, and dreads doing wrong, which makes him err twenty times in a month'. He 'must get a new head', wrote Nelson. 'No man's heart is better, but that will not do without the other.' So, encouraged by Drake and Trevor, Nelson decided to overturn the Admiralty's instructions himself, presenting Hotham with a *fait accompli*.[6]

With typical self-confidence, Nelson waived his instructions and resolved to seize all vessels, whether neutral or not, found transporting supplies to the enemy, either in France or territories occupied by the French. Captures would be brought into Vado Bay for Nelson's inspection. Neutral ships would be released, but any suspect cargoes would be taken to Leghorn, their perishables sold and the proceeds held by an agent pending the outcome of the legal process. As for Genoese merchants shipping goods to areas of their republic occupied by the French, but for the specific use of the native populations, they would be required to show passports from De Vins, Drake and the secretary of state in Genoa, who went under the exhausting name of Felice Giacinto Gianelli Castiglione.

Nelson's dictum would not endear him to neutrals, whether they were shipping contraband or not, but he intended to back it all the way. In July he ordered Cockburn to be 'particularly vigilant' in examining vessels sailing under Genoese colours, as he suspected that many of them were transporting money from France. The Genoese government acquiesced reluctantly. Mindful of the rights of neutrals to trade with whomsoever they pleased, it stopped short of positively approving Nelson's plans. There was even the shadow of a challenge to them in August, when Castiglione attempted to send a national war galley to escort a convoy of provisions to the Genoese garrison at San Remo. But when Nelson made it clear that he was still prepared to intercept the convoy, seizing any merchant ships without the necessary passes, Castiglione retreated and agreed to ensure the supplies were solely discharged to Genoese officials who would keep them out of the hands of the French.[7]

A procedure decided, Nelson and his associates sent to Hotham, who found himself beseeched by Trevor and Drake to back 'the temporary resolution which that spirited officer [Nelson] had taken upon him', and publicly affirm the new policy. Hotham was sick and waiting to go home. There were times when his hands shook so desperately he could hardly hold a pen. But to give him his due the admiral agreed without the slightest prevarication, and even reiterated Nelson's orders to the fleet captains under his own authority.[8]

That train set on its way, Nelson took Drake to Vado to confer with the Austrian commander-in-chief in his camp at the bottom of the bay. When they arrived after a voyage of calms on 20 July, Nelson was distinctly unimpressed by the anchorage. There was a fort on a commanding promontory, which the *Agamemnon* saluted with seventeen guns, but the bay itself was merely a bend in the coastline; 'if it had not been called a bay, I should not have named it one,' Nelson said. However, the next day Nelson and Drake locked themselves in long, earnest discussions with Baron De Vins and Britain's men from Turin, John Trevor and Thomas Jackson, who had themselves just arrived. The general had been thrown into an ill humour by the arrival of the Genoese victuallers in Oneglia four days before, and did not look like a conqueror. He was old and diseased, but spoke confidently. Starved of provisions the enemy would be driven back to Nice. The Austrian army might winter in Provence, and Nelson's ships anchor in Villefranche. In fact, so important did De Vins consider the work at sea that he was already commissioning Sardinian privateers to attack the enemy coasters. Captain Nelson assured the Austrians of his full support and established a system by which the army could signal any of his ships offshore, but no doubt he also explained the difficulties of chasing small provision ships through coastal shallows. At this point Trevor had a powerful contribution to make. Foreseeing the problem, he had already applied to Admiral Hotham for the assistance of a flotilla of small boats from Naples. Though Trevor did not know it, his request was then going before the Neapolitan government; the response was positive, and in August two galliots and eight feluccas were being fitted out to serve under Nelson's command.[9]

Applying the strategy, even after Hotham's approval of Nelson's plans, was more complicated. Nelson's force increased to thirteen or so ships, and he dispersed them widely, some cruising between La Spezia in the east and Oneglia in the west, and others doing escort or dispatch duty. Nelson commanded from Vado Bay, and relied a great deal on information from Genoa, where Drake and Joseph Brame, the local British consul, had spies watching French ships like hawks, and noting when cargoes were loaded in the harbour and vessels prepared for sea. Nevertheless, as the British cruisers began to strike there was an immediate howl of protest. When Nelson returned to Genoa to drop Drake and Trevor, an angry, hooting crowd gathered on the waterfront. Neither that, nor the bewildering shades of complicity that emerged as cases went to court, intimidated the captain of the *Agamemnon*, who stood his ground. He held his captains accountable for their conduct, but understood they had to make decisions quickly, and when in doubt preferred to seize rather than risk supplies reaching the enemy. It was 'better', he said, that the British 'should pay for twenty cargoes [taken wrongly] and finish the war, than the war be continued into another campaign'.[10]

The legal cases were certainly thorny. What was the status of a ship owned by a Swiss national domiciled in Marseilles? Or of the French ship *L'Africaine* with doubtful papers that claimed she had been sold to an Algerian? Or of a Dutch-built brig using the cover of a Danish consul but evidently owned by the French? Outright dishonesty, as well as confusion, was endemic. Take the case of the *Belvedere* polacre, seized by the *Meleager* as it ran for the shelter of batteries near Alassio on 21 July. The quarry landed up to forty bags of money and threw a packet of papers overboard before Captain George Cockburn's boats got alongside, but a search of the ship unearthed considerable wealth, including a chest of silver, some gold and a quantity of loose and set diamonds and other jewels. The *Belvedere* was unquestionably French and the crew staged a brief resistance, but her master filed an entirely false if ultimately unsuccessful claim that she had been taken within a neutral harbour, and was therefore under diplomatic protection and exempt from capture.[11]

Despite every precaution the neutral shipowners in Genoa clamoured vociferously against Nelson's campaign, but, forewarned by Drake, Admiral Hotham stood firm, insisting that all seizures would be fairly investigated by the prize courts. Nelson himself knew he had a real war with the French to win. Though he painfully explained himself to the Genoese, he would not be swayed. As he truthfully observed, 'it almost appears a trial between us, who will first be tired, they of complaining, or me of answering them. However, my mind is fixed.'[12]

3

After landing Drake and Trevor at Genoa, Nelson went to Leghorn for wood, oxen, lemons and onions. He took Adelaide aboard, too. Her voyage began gently on 28 July, when Nelson quit Leghorn with the *Inconstant* and *Ariadne* to hit a dead calm that kept them off the port for a day. It probably ended when the *Agamemnon* returned to Leghorn for provisions on 24 September. One wonders what Adelaide made of life at sea, and her voyage to and from Vado. She must have learned to recognise the chilling drum roll that accompanied the fourteen floggings administered on her lover's ship during that period, and at Vado seen boats leaving on forays against the French. Most probably she saw the dead and wounded return from a bloody skirmish near Oneglia at the end of August.

On 8 August, a week after reaching Vado, Nelson contemplated establishing Adelaide ashore at Savona. It was not unknown for selected officers to board on land, and the purser of the *Agamemnon*, Mr Fellows, treated the house of one local dignitary as if it was an inn. Fellows had good reasons to be ashore, for he was in constant communication with Giovanni Firpo, an acting vice consul at Savona, regarding the supply of provisions and local services. Among the purser's requests for cabbages, meat, fish, salt, water, lemons and onions for Nelson's ship, we find one for six pairs of women's silk hose, probably on Adelaide's account. Nelson also alerted Firpo to his interest in a good sitting room and bedchamber ashore, and told him to look out for 'two cool good rooms'.[13]

But in the end Adelaide seems to have remained on board, where Captain Fremantle of the *Inconstant* found them later in the month. As he wrote in his diary on 21 August: 'A convoy arrived [at Vado] from Genoa. Dined with Nelson. Dolly aboard, who has a sort of abscess in her side. He makes himself ridiculous with that woman.' Nelson may have flirted outrageously with his mistress, but the war against French sea-borne trade was his principal concern, and there were times when Adelaide had to be put ashore. Five days after the dinner with Fremantle the captain sailed to raid Alassio. Adelaide had gone overland to Genoa to visit her mother, and Nelson sent a letter after her through Brame. On 28 August she rejoined him at Vado, and Brame returned Nelson's letter. 'As you have found the Signora Correglia,' he wrote, 'I return the letter for her.' The day the couple reunited they again entertained Captain Fremantle, who dutifully noted the fact in his diary: 'Dined with Nelson and his Dolly.'[14]

We know nothing else about Adelaide's excursion to Vado, and she next appears in Fremantle's diary on Sunday 27 September, three days after Nelson's return to Leghorn. 'Dined with Nelson and Dolly,' wrote Fremantle, 'Very bad dinner indeed.' Afterwards the couple probably communicated through the interconsular packets that passed by land between Udny and Brame, both of whom knew Adelaide. On 5 March 1796, for example, Brame wrote to Nelson to acknowledge a letter he had sent with two enclosures. Both would be carefully delivered, he assured the captain, but he added that 'the letters from Livorno [Leghorn] are not arrived . . .'[15]

Adelaide may have soothed Nelson's physical infirmities through the warm summer nights, but they could not relieve the pressures that came with the riviera command. The status of the small Genoese harbours behind the enemy lines was increasingly causing him concern. Technically, these havens were open to all on the understanding that no acts of war would be committed within their limits, but all along the Genoese coast they were sheltering enemy supply ships. The French were systematically abusing the system, occupying weakly garrisoned Genoese ports and turning them into French havens. Alassio and Oneglia, in the rear of the French lines, particularly worried Nelson. They were Genoese towns, and supposedly neutral. But while the flag of Genoa still flew from the castle in the centre of Alassio it was controlled by the French soldiery, who debarred the British from entering and offered the harbour as a bolt hole for their coasters.

Nelson's response was typically decisive. If neutral ports became belligerent ports the laws of neutrality would be suspended. On 12 August nine boats of the *Agamemnon* rowed towards Alassio, where they paused beyond the blue horizon until darkness allowed them to move in. With muffled oars they slid silently into the harbour under the command of Lieutenants Andrews and Spicer, and at about one in the morning eight vessels at anchor were successfully boarded. Unfortunately, the town soon rang with alarm and as the prizes were being towed out Andrews and Spicer came under fire. Four French gunboats sallied out to recover the prizes, and all but one had to be relinquished; only the timely arrival of the *Mutine* cutter enabled the British to withdraw with their remaining trophy, which they found laden with black pepper and wine.[16]

Not to be thwarted, Nelson was back with a larger force on the 26th, on the lookout for an enemy convoy, and this time he attacked in full daylight. Captain Fremantle was directed to take the *Inconstant* and *Tartar* (Captain Charles Elphinstone) to the town of Languelia on the west side of the bay, while Nelson raided Alassio with the *Agamemnon*, three frigates (the *Meleager*, *Southampton* and *Ariadne*) and the *Speedy* brig. Sitting comfortably beneath the shore batteries at Alassio were six coasters, some if not all Genoese but full of supplies for the French. They were guarded by a French national warship, *La Resolve*, a rakish black polacre of ten long guns, four swivels and eighty-seven men, as well as two galleys armed with five guns or swivels apiece. Nelson wanted to minimise the offence his attack would cause Genoa. Both Cockburn, whose *Meleager* led the line into Alassio, and Fremantle were told in writing to avoid firing upon the inhabitants. Fremantle, for instance, was instructed 'not to fire on the battery or town [of Languelia] unless fired upon or by signal to engage from me'.[17]

At ten in the morning Nelson's ships sailed audaciously into Alassio, anchoring with their guns flanking the batteries and beach with springs on their cables for easy manoeuvring. From the *Agamemnon*, Nelson could see the Genoese colours above the castle, but a French flag was also draped over a wall and he had no doubt who really controlled the port. Messages went forward, charging that the French had made the area 'an enemy coast'. Nelson demanded the surrender of *La Resolve* and warned the Genoese commandant not to interfere. Soon a party under Andrews had effortlessly boarded the polacre, cut her cable and brought her out with 'spirited and officer-like conduct'.[18]

Then, as the British boats made for the coasters, Plampin's *Ariadne* grounded while trying to turn. Nelson had to redirect his men to assist her by lodging the frigate's best bower anchor in deeper water so that she could be hauled towards it by turns of the capstan. The delay enabled the supply ships to retreat further inshore, to unload some of their cargoes and to orchestrate resistance. About two thousand French soldiers, both horse and foot, were soon crowding the beach on either side of the fort, some solemnly stood beneath their colours ready to withstand attack. The delay had been expensive, but Nelson always defended good officers and reported that Captain Plampin's difficulty arose solely from his 'great zeal . . . to do much'.[19]

After the *Ariadne* had been refloated, French musket balls greeted the return of the British boats, but Nelson swept the beach with artillery fire and drove the bluecoats back. By three o'clock one of the supply ships had been wrecked upon the shore, where enemy cavalry quickly surrounded it, and the rest boarded and brought out. The only British casualty was little William Hoste, who fell down the cable scuttle of one of the prizes and broke a leg. Fremantle, Nelson learned, had been equally successful at Languelia, where a large French gunboat, *La Republique* of six guns and fifty men, had been found protecting two merchantmen. Showing less than his commander's independence, Fremantle thought it necessary to signal Nelson for permission to cut them out, but once he had the go-ahead he mounted a flawless operation and scooped up the three prizes without suffering a single casualty.[20]

Though Nelson had committed hostilities in a neutral port, the Genoese government was also on weak ground because it had allowed the French to reserve Alassio for their own use. Genoa complained to London but did nothing stronger, while in the Mediterranean Nelson's stock rose in British circles. Hotham commended his services, and Udny wrote approvingly to Drake: 'I rejoice to hear of Captain Nelson's successful operation . . . He is the most indefatigable man I know.'[21]

Active certainly. The day after the attack on Alassio the British drove another French gunboat ashore and would have landed to burn it had a detachment of enemy cavalry not sped up. The triumphs and disappointments of the everyday work of Nelson's cruisers are well illustrated by a single passage from the log of Captain Charles Brisbane's *Moselle* for the evening of 27 August:

Saw the *Southampton*'s boats board a tartan and ship at anchor in a small bay to the westward of Genoa. Several muskets were fired from the shore on the boats. At 7 or 8 [o'clock] guns were fired from the *Southampton* [Captain William Shield] for to cover [h]is boats. About 9 PM the boats brought out the tartan and ship. Sent a[n] officer and eleven men on board the ship and one petty officer and one man on board the tartan, which we took in tow . . . Parted company with the *Southampton*. The prizes proved to be Genoese. At 4 AM the officer on board the tartan informed us that the tartan had sprung a leak and that the water was up to the fore and main hatches. Hauled the tartan alongside to pump her out, she having no pumps on board. She went down and was lost before we had time to put a pump on board her.[22]

Not until the night of 29 August did the riviera squadron take a hit. That evening fifty-four men from the *Southampton*, *Ariadne* and *Agamemnon* scrambled into the two galleys captured at Alassio and pulled out of Vado Bay, steering for Oneglia to cut out a supply ship. The moon was full and the weather warm, and the boats reached their destination without much difficulty, but instead of the reported merchantman they found three large and mysterious lateen-rigged vessels lashed together. Lieutenants Andrews and Spicer ordered a warning shot to be fired in front of the strangers and raised English colours, but there was neither reply nor any flag of identification; only an eerie silence. Andrews put his galley under the quarters of one of the ships to investigate, but a vicious burst of fire suddenly illuminated the blackened ship, riddling the British boat with bullets at close range. Calling for boarders, Andrews flung himself upon the enemy vessel and climbed to the deck, where his party impetuously drove their adversaries overboard with cutlasses and pikes. Cutting the prize free, the British then tried to engage the other two vessels but their ammunition ran out and they were badly outnumbered. They had to retreat with what they had. The prize turned out to be Turkish, but its consorts got safely into Genoa.

An Austrian boat brought the first casualties back to Vado, where Nelson was greatly upset at the loss of seventeen 'poor brave fellows' dead or wounded, 'the best men in my ship'. To fight without colours, as the Turks had done, was barbaric 'piracy', and Nelson appealed to Genoa to withdraw its protection from the surviving Turkish ships so that he could take them out. The protest was unsuccessful and Nelson was left to mourn his dead. Three quarterdeck officers of the

Agamemnon were wounded, Midshipmen Gamble and William D. Williams, and Thomas Withers, then a mate, who underwent a painful operation to have a musket ball removed from his foot. Poor Williams was less lucky. A Plymouth man of twenty-seven, he had risen by merit, serving as able seaman and quartermaster on his way to the rank of midshipman. Now it was over. He lingered until the morning of 1 September and was buried at Vado. Saddened but resigned to the fortunes of war, Nelson wrote to Fanny that 'they who play at bowls must expect rubbers'.[23]

4

Fortunately, there were few such tragedies and Nelson's confidence increased. Every success raised the *Agamemnon*'s efficiency and reputation, and brought music to her captain's ears. Comments such as Sir William Hamilton's 'your activity and constancy is [are] known all over Europe' were by no means insincere but had the effect of feeding a growing ego. Nelson's letters bristled with self-congratulation, some of it understandable and much of it delusory. He exaggerated when he told his brother that his professional opinions had invariably been sound, while his claim to have been 'pointed out as having been this war one hundred and twelve times engaged against the French, and always successful to a certain degree' neglected to add that only he had done the counting. Others received similar self-advertisements. Uncle William was informed there was 'no person so active as myself', and Drake that the allies were 'fortunate in having an officer of this character' on their side. Nelson even persuaded himself that in Genoa he was 'beloved and respected by both Senate and lower order[s]', that the Austrians 'knew my name perfectly', and that throughout Italy there was 'not a kingdom or state where my name will be forgot – this is my gazette!'.[24]

Braggadocio is hardly endearing, but in Nelson's case it at least reflected a genuine professional pride and a readiness to back each boast. For a while Nelson hoped to exalt his stock by sharing in a fast-paced, successful campaign against the French, while they were still dispirited by their retreat from Vado in the summer. As usual, Nelson emphasised the moment, and the need to press an advantage before the enemy had time to reform. He fancied that Nice might fall 'without a blow' if De Vins pushed forward. Yet the summer temperatures had barely peaked before despondency began to set in. Illness did not help. Nelson still had a 'complaint' in his chest, the remaining vision in his damaged right eye was disappearing and long letters written and read were causing him great pain in the left. 'I am almost blind,' he wrote in August. Two days later he was 'very ill' – 'alive, and that's all'. His physical condition was momentarily so serious that the diplomats and soldiers around him began to worry.[25]

Nelson's growing apprehensions were also rooted in the apparent neglect of Admiral Hotham, whose appreciation fell short of permanent reward or sufficient help. The captain deeply resented Hotham's failure to authorise him to fly a distinguishing pendant as an acting commodore in charge of a squadron. Even Captain Frederick, a junior officer, had received such a pendant when entrusted with a squadron. Nelson's new friends sympathised and worked for his promotion through the foreign secretary, William Wyndham, Lord Grenville. 'The admiral best knows how much Captain Nelson's abilities, gallantry, good conduct and zeal for the king's service render him worthy of this distinction,' wrote Drake, while Trevor chorused, 'It is hardly possible to do justice to the zeal and intelligence of this excellent officer.' Unfortunately, that distinguishing pendant Nelson craved did not come.[26]

Even more important, Nelson wanted the admiral to bring the fleet to Vado Bay to inspire the allies, as De Vins and Drake urgently requested. Drake agitated for a conference between De Vins and Hotham 'without loss of time', but two letters Nelson fired to Hotham on 14 and 16 August produced no movement, even though the admiral was actually passing Vado on his way from Corsica to Leghorn. Nelson went out to the flagship to entreat Hotham to spare a few hours, but 'nothing could turn him' from his original course. Not only that but the admiral's other observations were far from encouraging. Informing Nelson of the Admiralty's wish that the fleet be kept together, he warned that some of Nelson's frigates would have to be withdrawn. Hotham did promise to shield the riviera from the Toulon fleet, but given the fact that the French were old hands at giving him the slip and his fleet sat far away in Leghorn 'as idle as is possible to conceive', it was not a guarantee that instilled confidence. De Vins was 'hurt' at Hotham's indifference, and so was Nelson. He agreed with Jackson, Trevor's deputy in Turin, that if the Austrians were looking for an excuse to delay their offensive, Hotham had given them one.[27]

The ardour of Baron De Vins himself was more crucial still, but as Nelson beat up and down the coast with his cruisers, he realised that, for all the rhetoric, the geriatric Austrian commander-in-chief either had little appetite for the war or was the puppet of a supine court. Drake realised this before the end of August, when De Vins failed to seize an opportunity to occupy Savona and secure defensible winter quarters on the coast. De Vins, Drake predicted, 'must now . . . remain encamped [outside] during the whole of the winter, and a great part of his troop must be employed in guarding a range of bleak mountains where the cold is even now intense'. The next month Sardinia-Piedmont joined the attack, implying that the general's inaction related to restraining orders from his emperor, something Vienna strongly denied. In reply, apologists for De Vins pointed accusing fingers at Sardinia-Piedmont. De Vins could not advance until the hesitant Sardinians and Piedmontese moved against the French post of Ormea, which threatened the Austrian right. Both allies smelled fear and treachery. The Sardinians suspected the Austrians had no intention of suffering losses to regain Nice, a territory Sardinia had lost; De Vins worried that Sardinia-Piedmont was going to make a separate peace with France and leave him in the lurch. Amid raging recriminations, the campaign atrophied.[28]

Something that gnawed at Nelson was the fear that De Vins fully intended to sit where he was and 'lay the blame of the miscarriage of the enterprise against Nice . . . to the non-cooperation of the British fleet and the Sardinian army'. Nor was he entirely deceiving himself. Writing to the emperor, De Vins was complimentary about Nelson: 'He speaks with great gratitude and satisfaction of Captain Nelson's readiness on all occasions to assist him,' said the British representative to the Viennese court. But at the beginning of September the general was also complaining that so many provisions were reaching the French by sea that the plan to starve them into retreat would have to be abandoned.[29]

Putting his anxieties behind him, Nelson determined that no one was going to make him a scapegoat. If the war had become bogged down, it would have to be reinvigorated. As the summer passed he came up with a plan.

5

That September two men, very different in some ways and alike in others, grumbled discontentedly about the war on the Italian riviera. History has linked their names, but here for the first time they stood in direct competition, one a sick but vainglorious naval officer and the other an excitable, ruthless, supremely ambitious Corsican in the service of France, now called from unemployment to the Bureau Topographique in Paris. At the age of twenty-six, a short but lean man of boundless energy and great intelligence, Napoleon Bonaparte was at the heart of the military planning of his adopted country.

Bonaparte was thoroughly dissatisfied with the lacklustre performance of the Army of Italy, and clamoured for more enterprise and aggression. Vado should be retaken, he said, and the French front reinforced, while further inland, on the borders of Sardinia-Piedmont and Genoa, Ceva should be occupied and a wedge driven between the Austrian forces and their Sardinian and Piedmontese allies. A new French general, Barthelemy Louis Joseph Scherer, was soon in command of the Army of Italy with orders to invigorate the war along the lines Bonaparte suggested.[30]

Captain Horatio Nelson of His Britannic Majesty's ship *Agamemnon* had less power to stimulate reluctant allies, even as an acting commodore, but he also urged a determined offensive. His idea had been hatched with Drake and Trevor during their voyage from Vado to Genoa in July, and by August it was being openly espoused. Drawing upon his propensity for land operations, Nelson suggested amphibious operations. The military balance, he thought, might be tilted in the allied favour if his ships landed soldiers in the rear of the French army and cut its communications.

But though De Vins led his political masters to believe that he was ready to embrace any practicable proposition from Nelson, he acted otherwise in the field. Drake used 'every argument' he could think of to recommend the plan to the Austrian commander-in-chief, but found him 'very lukewarm'. He promised to consider it 'in so cold a manner' that Drake was left in no doubt of his disinterest, and when De Vins suggested that three thousand soldiers from Corsica be used instead of Austrians his prevarication became glaringly transparent.[31]

Early in September, Nelson examined the coast behind the French lines as far as Nice. He noticed that the road along which the French were marching to the front and hauling many of their supplies was vulnerable to naval attack, because the mountainous interior frequently forced it to twist alongside the sea. Grasping the strategic significance of the road, Nelson was back in Vado Bay on the 12th, urging De Vins to give him five thousand men, some field pieces, and a few days' provisions for a descent upon San Remo. San Remo was a Genoese town, but the French had occupied it during their advance and now it straggled the enemy communication line. It not only commanded the road, which was full of mules braying under provisions for the French army, but also possessed a haven for ships, one used by the tiny coasters that sneaked supplies along the shore from Nice. By seizing and occupying San Remo, Nelson contended, the allies could rupture the enemy supply system by sea and land. The captain had no doubt the job could be done, for the French had only a pair of beach camps and few cannon in the town. Once installed, an allied force could be supplied by Nelson's ships, or taken off by them if the enemy massed to counterattack.[32]

But De Vins disagreed. Captain Nelson impressed him, but he had no wish to be drawn into anything risky or premature and the captain went back to Genoa to commiserate with Drake. They both decided the Austrians had no real interest in the war, and were simply posturing to get their hands on the subsidies the British government were offering allies. However, on 17 September they jointly addressed De Vins. If the general thought San Remo an unsuitable target, they offered to find transports to attack any place he preferred. De Vins wavered, and after his men successfully stormed a French outpost in the St Esprit mountains during ten furious hours on the 19th, his blood ran uncommonly fast. He talked about landing troops between Nice and the Var, and rallying five thousand peasants to his standard. He even said he would lead the sortie himself.[33]

For a moment it looked as if Nelson had made progress on one front, but now he needed transport ships to shift the strike force westwards. And to get those he needed the support of Admiral Hotham.

The day after the Austrian attack on the 19th, Nelson submitted his request for transports to Hotham, but it ran counter to the admiral's inclinations. In fact, Nelson's squadron was already being pared down. Early in September, Hotham had withdrawn all of Nelson's frigates bar the twenty-four-gun *Ariadne*, supported by the *Moselle* sloop, on the presumption that the impending arrival of a light-draught flotilla from Naples would fulfil his needs. Besieged by different claims upon his force, Hotham decided to redeploy his frigates elsewhere. Enemy privateers, dislodged from the riviera by Nelson's ships, were haunting the approaches to Corsica, turning the Genoese island of Capraia into 'a den of pirates', and almost bringing unguarded British commerce to a stop. 'No stores, or provisions and money get safe to Corsica,' Consul Udny complained in Leghorn.[34]

Nor, in truth, had Nelson and Drake laid the ground for their request well. Indeed, disillusioned by the sluggish De Vins, Drake had already advised the foreign secretary that it might be 'advisable to lessen the number of ships now cooperating with the Austrian army in order to employ them in protecting our own trade, since it is apparent that nothing further is to be expected . . . during this campaign'. If Drake had now shot himself in the foot, so too had Nelson. Only three days before writing for the transports Nelson had sent his admiral a quite different letter, suggesting that whatever might be done for De Vins was likely to be pointless. The general was unreliable, and would find one excuse or another for inactivity. Ill, tired and depressed, Nelson had spoken carelessly but the mistake might have been costly. How could Hotham take De Vins's new request for transports seriously after receiving such a damning assessment from his man on the spot?[35]

Not surprisingly, his answer was in the negative. Because of 'arrangements brought to me by the last messenger from England' Hotham was unable to supply the transports, and 'the very extensive plan proposed by the general must for the present be suspended'. Even worse, from Nelson's point of view, the reductions in the naval squadron continued. The *Ariadne* was recalled for a 'secret service' and the *Meleager*, which Nelson had hoped would have been returned to him, was sent for caulking. In the ensuing weeks Nelson received occasional reinforcements, but it was abundantly clear that the riviera squadron was a low priority.[36]

Nelson was outflanked on all sides. De Vins could not act without ships Hotham would not supply, and neither seemed interested. After the general's sudden conversion to an offensive, he relapsed into his usual torpor. Drake was 'decidedly of opinion that this project has been brought forward for no other purpose but that of amusing us for a few weeks'. Nelson got no further with Hotham. In October he suggested that the *Dromedary* and *Dolphin* store ships be used for his amphibious operations, but when the admiral submitted the idea to his senior officers it was dismissed as 'a wild scheme'. So little value did Hotham attach to the riviera squadron that on 10 October he temporarily withdrew it completely. Instead of working with the allies, Nelson would reconnoitre the French fleet in Toulon. In the meantime Hotham's main fleet remained immobile in Leghorn, 'in readiness'.[37]

Nelson took a few prizes off Toulon – three in one day towards the end of October – but they offered little to sugar the pill. One of the prizes was laden with powder and gun carriages, but Nelson felt so sorry for the master–owner of another that he returned it after removing the cargo. 'It was his all, and he was a poor man,' Nelson wrote. There were also plenty of French fishing vessels to be had, but 'of course' Nelson left them alone. He was pleased to return to Vado, even though he knew he had become the token representative in an increasingly futile naval campaign.[38]

6

Winter approached; bitter northerly winds came, with fierce ground frosts, but still the armies watched each other. Nelson concluded they wanted 'to see who can stand the cold longest', but Trevor's opinion was the surer when he told Nelson that the French, rather than the Austrians, would force a battle, and that when they did 'no very vigorous resistance' would be made. That was how it happened. Partly due to pressure from Bonaparte, while the Austrians slept the Army of Italy prepared for an assault.[39]

Gradually, De Vins was exhausting British patience. In October, Drake toured the entire Austrian front line and concluded that there was 'nothing more to hope from General De Vins'. He was, Nelson believed, 'afraid of an attack by sea and land', and after some French gunboats cheekily slunk into Vado Bay during Nelson's absence and fired on the Austrian positions, the baron became obsessed about his left flank. He kept insisting that a British ship be permanently stationed at Pietra, a few miles from Vado, where the Austrian line met the sea. Unfortunately the ground there was a quicksand, in which no anchor could hold, and the winds were treacherous. Two of Nelson's ships were almost lost trying to satisfy De Vins, one the *Moselle*, which was driven to within a cable's length of the shore by a heavy southwestern swell on 2 November and deprived of an anchor. Five more days found Nelson explaining the dangers to his ships to generals who knew nothing of seamanship. He would keep ships at Vado Bay, but agreed a system of gun signals by which they might be summoned to Pietra in emergencies, trusting that 'the general will remember the fable of the boy and the wolf, and not call us too often'.[40]

In grumbling about his allies, Nelson was more than conscious that the navy had not done all he had wished. Through no fault of its own, Nelson's squadron had failed to halt the enemy's sea-borne supplies. For a while he had enjoyed some success, stationing two or three ships outside Genoa and others off Alassio to shut down the contraband shipping between the two, and driving many French privateers off the riviera. In August and September the *Inconstant, Tartar* and *Moselle* bottled four French warships in Genoa for a month and more, costing their government considerable sums for provisions and wages.[41]

But this was a record that could not be maintained. Hotham's economies began to bite just as the autumn gales and their dark, wild, rain-filled nights created conditions in which grain convoys could scuttle swiftly along the coast unseen. True, a pair of galliots and eight or so feluccas arrived from Naples, but they barely stirred from the Savona mole and in the little action they saw were 'totally useless' to Nelson. During the summer, autumn and winter of 1795 Nelson's squadron rounded up or destroyed about thirty-five vessels of all descriptions, but some were released by the courts and scores more got through to the enemy. In late September a fierce northeasterly and driving rain blew the guard ships from Genoa, and a convoy of Greek victuallers escaped to Alassio with enough food to last the French army till Christmas. This disaster alone killed Austrian ambitions to starve the enemy into retreat, but it was followed by another – on the evening of 29 September – when a second convoy bolted for Villefranche. The *Southampton* and *Moselle* had been active off the coast, and taken two wheat ships a few days before, but they fell in with the convoy in the midst of a pitch-black tempest and were unable to stop it. Two of the merchantmen were turned back to Genoa, but the others, and the escorting French frigate *Vestale*, which suffered considerable damage and twenty casualties, got away. The *Southampton* limped back to Genoa with her mizzen mast gone, her main and fore rigging cut up, and her topsail halyards and other equipment damaged. Soon she had to sail to Corsica for repairs.[42]

The ease with which ships clinging to the coastal shallows could slip by the British crusiers further out was personally brought home to Nelson in the small hours of 3 November, when the distant beam of the Villefranche lighthouse indicated that the *Agamemnon* was between San Remo and Nice. Lieutenant Spicer roused Nelson from his hammock at three in the morning, and told him that the watch had seen a substantial vessel standing offshore ahead. When Nelson reached the quarterdeck it was still unidentifiable but clearly visible in the moonlight. Suddenly the vessel wore and made sail, trying to cross the bows of the British ship in an obvious effort to get to safer waters inshore. Nelson had a bow gun fired, but when the ship sailed silently on he called for a volley of musketry and a salvo from his main deck guns. After much of the stranger's 'furniture' had been shot away she surrendered, and was boarded by a party under Spicer. The prize was Genoese, but her master had no pass and admitted he was shipping supplies to the French.

It soon became clear that the vessel was only one of many, and at daylight Nelson saw the rest of the convoy running along the land under Genoese and Greek colours. Sailing inshore at night without lights they had almost reached their destinations before being discovered, and now scuttled for the safety of Alassio, Languelia and other supposedly neutral ports. Nelson was unable to impede them, and almost lost the one prize he had taken. At noon the wind dropped, and a French war galley was rowed out of Alassio to try to recapture the prize as it lay becalmed some way astern of the *Agamemnon*. Nelson's boats hurried reinforcements to his prize crew, and their fire forced the galley to retire, but towards evening a second attempt to retake the prize, by two Alassio gunboats, also had to be beaten off. Nelson eventually took his prize in tow and got underway for Vado, but it was no matter for celebration. Yet another convoy had successfully run the blockade and something like one hundred supply ships were sheltering snugly beneath the batteries in Alassio.[43]

The trouble was that Nelson needed at least a dozen frigates, sloops and brigs, and perhaps as many cutters, to stop the coastal trade, and they were simply not available. There was an opportunity to strike the supply ships en masse in Alassio Bay, and again Nelson appealed to Hotham. With three ships of the line and eight to ten frigates he could attack Alassio, as he had done before, and capture the victuallers wholesale. But instead of a green light, Nelson received the news that Hotham had struck his flag on 1 November and gone home, handing the fleet over to Vice Admiral Sir Hyde Parker as a caretaker commander-in-chief.

Few in the fleet were sorry to see Hotham go, but there was less agreement about his replacement. Nelson did not rate Parker, and would have preferred Admiral Goodall. Goodall liked Nelson, and had recommended him for the riviera command in the first place. He had expected to succeed Hotham on an acting basis, and refused to serve under Parker. Writing a generous farewell to Nelson, and no doubt to others in his confidence, Goodall quit the fleet. Nelson realised that he would have got far more from Goodall than Parker, but he renewed his request for reinforcements and received a half-hearted response. On 8 November the new acting commander-in-chief sent the *Dido* and *Meleager* to the riviera with two cutters, but they arrived too late.[44]

The climax of the campaign had come and gone before they appeared.

7

Nelson had only four ships to meet that crisis – his own *Agamemnon*, the *Flora* frigate under Captain Robert Middleton, and the *Moselle* sloop and *Speedy* brig. Though based at Vado they also attempted to cruise off Cape di Noli near Pietra to instil confidence in the allied army but none was there when the French finally made a powerful onslaught on the Austrian front at Loano. The weather was appalling, and a snowstorm postponed the French attack for a week. When it came on 23 November the *Flora*, *Moselle* and *Speedy* had been blown away by dangerous gales, the first two back towards Leghorn and the last towards Corsica, while the *Agamemnon* herself had been drawn to Genoa by a sudden emergency in that quarter.

Nelson had responded to a summons sent by Drake on 12 November. He was needed 'to overawe the crew of *La Brune*, which is become extremely riotous', and to deal with a threat to De Vins's rear. The *Agamemnon* found Genoa gripped by growing Jacobin sentiment. Drake's house was having to be protected by a state guard, and when he and Nelson dined with the Sardinian minister on the 16th a carriage pointedly returned the captain to his boat at the lanthorn battery before dark. The Austrian chargé d'affaires and their local military commanders, as well as the Sardinian minister, were alarmed by the activities of the French frigate *La Brune* at the Genoa mole. It appeared that on 10 November *La Brune* and a number of privateers had embarked three hundred men and carried them nine miles west to Voltri, where an Austrian command post situated twenty miles behind De Vins's lines was seized with its corn supply and £10,000 worth of Genoese livres belonging to the Austrian commissary. The French were quickly expelled by an allied counterattack from Savona, and lost their commander among others captured, but remained unchastened. Indeed, back in Genoa they plundered a Sardinian salt magazine within the town limits and raised seven hundred adventurers for another foray. Rumour had it that they intended joining a party from the French army at Bocchetta and attacking the road between Genoa and De Vins's army at Vado, inciting Jacobin elements within the peasantry to turn out in their support.[45]

Nelson was sceptical, but accepted that the French were flagrantly breaching neutrality by recruiting in Genoa, and that the ultimate possibilities were frightening. The small Austrian garrisons at St Pierre d'Arena and Voltri, near Genoa, were obviously threatened, and if the French got control of the Bocchetta pass between the town and the main Austrian lines they could cut off De Vins's principal supply route and road of retreat. The Austrian and Sardinian ministers were making formal protests to the Genoese, but something more concrete was needed and they begged Nelson to act.

Bringing the *Agamemnon* into harbour, Nelson swiftly terrified *La Brune* and her associated privateers and transports into warping their way into the inner mole and removing their guns and powder. The officers of the enemy frigate were so frightened that their ship would be cut out that they buried it in the middle of a dozen merchantmen. To make doubly sure that none of the hostile vessels left port, on 18 November Nelson laid the *Agamemnon* between the two mole heads, ready to intercept anything trying to leave. It was a partial blockade, and risked offending Genoa, but now that the French had overstepped the mark and abused neutrality hand over fist, Nelson felt justified in a stronger approach.

His position was uncomfortable, notwithstanding. There were reports that French ships of the line might break out of Toulon and come to Genoa, where the *Agamemnon* stood to be trapped alone. Moreover, tied down here Nelson was unable to keep the promise he had given De Vins to keep the French gunboats off the Austrian flank at Pietra. As he later informed Parker, he regretted not being 'able to divide the *Agamemnon*' and cover both points of danger. Almost inevitably, it was while Nelson was at Genoa, and his other ships blown from their stations, that the French general hurled his men against the Austrian front line. At the forefront of the assault were six future Napoleonic generals, including André Massena, Charles-Pierre-François Augereau and Louis-Gabriel Suchet.[46]

The Austrians were superior in numbers and entrenched in a line of strong posts but they broke like reeds. Nelson's purser, who was with their army, found himself running beside soldiers who had thrown down their weapons, and female camp followers fleeing with their skirts in their hands. Old De Vins was ill. His head was swollen and he could hardly speak, and no sooner had the French attacked than he handed his command to a deputy and fled in the dead of night in a sedan chair. It hardly encouraged his wavering soldiers, who without a reserve line to rally behind were soon streaming back towards Genoa, along the very road that Nelson was keeping open. Those who tried to stand in pockets were soon outflanked and forced to withdraw. Vado fell on the 26th and Savona three days later, so quickly that two of Nelson's watering parties were surprised and captured on the 29th. Lieutenant Noble, Midshipmen Withers and Newman, and eleven seamen and marines fell into the hands of the French.[47]

The captain of the *Agamemnon* was mortified that none of his ships had been there when it mattered, and that eighteen enemy gunboats were allowed to worry the left flank of the Austrian army unscathed. But he exonerated himself with a report that the rout of De Vins had begun on the right flank, away from the coast, and the knowledge that he had preserved a line of retreat that saved up to ten thousand fleeing Austrians from capture or death, including De Vins himself. For had the French forces he had shut in Genoa succeeded in establishing themselves in the rear of the Austrian army, and closed the Bocchetta pass, the battle of Loano might have been a far more desperate affair. As it was the allies lost more than three thousand men, tens of cannons and 'magazines of every description'. The allied armies eventually regrouped at Acqui, Ceva and Mondovi, but for a while even Genoa was threatened and Nelson had to warn British ships that not a single port on the riviera was safe to enter.[48]

Bonaparte was angry with Scherer for failing to exploit his advantage, and particularly for not marching upon Ceva to divide the Austrians from Sardinia-Piedmont and force the latter to accept terms. For Nelson it was a sad but not unexpected end to the campaign. As he sailed back to Leghorn early in December, Nelson was convinced that Britain's allies were useless and the war as a whole futile. There was plenty of blame, and insofar as it touched himself Nelson reacted powerfully. The Austrians had been complaining about the inadequacy of British naval support for some time, and General Olivier Remigius, Count Wallis, who succeeded De Vins, was using the absence of Nelson's ships as an excuse for the defeat at Loano. At Leghorn, Nelson suffered the indignity of seeing an aid to Wallis arrive with a file of accusations. He rebutted them immediately, and Drake and Trevor thundered in his defence at every opportunity. Even in Vienna the charges were not taken seriously, for the army was notorious for its lethargy, but Nelson felt himself impugned when he had done his best with inadequate tools.[49]

Nelson acidly remarked that the Austrians had fought so badly that the whole of the British fleet could not have saved them, but in one respect he did sympathise with their plight. They had, after all, fought a campaign on the coast to benefit from the aid of a fleet that had never once appeared. Hotham and Parker had stripped Nelson's force to the bone, and left it utterly unequal to its duties, no matter how well led or how busy. Even after the Austrian defeat Nelson remained acutely embarrassed, for Vado and Genoa had become unsafe ports, and ships were needed to loiter in the offing, warning British traders and men-of-war not to enter. Nothing Nelson had said had moved his admirals, and he felt bitterly disappointed and hoped the neglect might be exposed in some enquiry. He felt so ill-used that he began appealing directly to the Admiralty, over Parker's greying head. 'My squadron has been so reduced by the admiral and storms of wind,' he complained, 'that I had not ships to make the attempt and drive those gun boats away.' Those who had shared his frustrations understood. 'I would to God *you* had been our commander-in-chief!' Trevor told him.[50]

Actually, no one would have been less interested in an enquiry than the British government. As Peter Jupp, the biographer of Lord Grenville, the foreign secretary, has shown, the administration had regarded the riviera campaign as an unwelcome distraction, and had urged Austria and Sardinia-Piedmont to drive through Savoy to the north rather than fritter their resources repelling the French advance along the coast. The campaign on the riviera, however poorly prosecuted by the Austrians and their allies, was their priority rather than Britain's.

We can sense Nelson's depression in the revival of longings for home. When things were going well Nelson preferred active service, enlivened by the prospects of action and achievement. In June Fanny had urged him to quit, but he had palmed her off with excuses, explaining that it was discourteous to rush home so soon after the king had recognised his services in a promotion. However, by Christmas, the springs had fallen from his heels, and he was weary and disillusioned. He had failed to get his distinguishing pendant – even a direct petition to the Admiralty producing a refusal – and he felt he had been abandoned on the riviera. Nelson began talking about relinquishing his naval career again, and taking a seat in Parliament.

In September, Lord Walpole and Coke of Holkham suggested he fill a vacancy for the seat of Ipswich. Nelson was tempted, though he hated political factions and insisted upon being regarded as an independent candidate, at liberty to judge every matter on a non-partisan basis. He was prepared to serve in 'the real Whig interest' with the Duke of Portland's moderates, who understood the extent of French aggression and supported Pitt, but would have nothing to do with the Foxite Whigs. As patriots they might have been equally complicated and naive, but Nelson saw them as 'vile dogs' who excused and condoned the enemy's excesses. The other problem about standing for Parliament was financial, 'for although I have so often seen the French shot, yet truly I have seen little of their money'. Money was needed to buy support during electioneering, and to maintain a London establishment, a respectable table and a place in society. The plan fell through, and the Ipswich seat went to Sir Andrew Hamond, comptroller of the Navy Board.[51]

England still attracted him, so bleak did he construe his future with the fleet. A new commander-in-chief had come at last, the long-awaited successor to Lord Hood and a man to be reckoned with – Admiral Sir John Jervis, renowned, almost feared, throughout the service for strong opinions and an iron discipline. He arrived at St Fiorenzo on 30 November to 'the great joy of some and sorrow of others'. Nelson may have remembered his one meeting with Jervis in the Treasury in London; Sir John certainly did, and recalled that their mutual acquaintance, Captain Locker, armed with a cane sporting an eyeglass in its head, had eagerly made the introductions. Locker had also spoken to Jervis before the admiral left England, and almost certainly reminded him of the merits of the captain of the *Agamemnon*. But in any case the new commander-in-chief was disposed to befriend Nelson. He had begun his career under Commodore George Townshend, a distant relative of Nelson's, and gratefully remembered the kindness shown him by the ship's first lieutenant, none other than Maurice Suckling, Horatio's venerable uncle, whom Jervis honoured as an 'excellent' man.[52]

Despite this Nelson seems almost not to have cared, and was resigned to taking his ship home for an overdue refit. All he immediately asked of Jervis was justice. On 21 December he wrote to the new commander-in-chief to report the *Agamemnon* 'as fit for sea as a rotten ship can be', and to beg that if Jervis was minded to reply to the charges made by the Austrians he trusted he would be given an opportunity to explain his conduct first.[53]

At home the Reverend Edmund Nelson sensed the mood of his son as he read the latest of the regular epistles that reached him from the Mediterranean. On the fourth day of a new year the old man pulled out some paper to reply:

God has blessed me so infinitely, even beyond hope, by length of days to see my posterity in possession of what is more durable than riches or honours, a good name. A virtuous disposition, moral conduct, and pure religion must be the supporters of public fame, and they will fight in its defence against its known foes – envy, calumny and dirty slander.[54]

8

It was Sir John Jervis who made the crucial difference.

Sir John had earned his knighthood the hard way, taking a French seventy-four towards the end of the American war. He was a hard man who feared little. His discipline was sometimes savage, his rule somewhat tyrannical, and his broadsides blistering, whether delivered with the cannon or the pen. Outspoken, arrogant and acerbic, Jervis was a man of many and strong prejudices, intolerant of anything that smelt of indolence or inefficiency.

He was brutally frank with officers who did not measure up. Take James of the *Raven*, seeking promotion, for example: 'I cannot help expressing my astonishment at your presumption in thinking of the rank of post-captain, which you have no possible claim to, Captain Waller who has ten times your merit, knowledge and ability having been named by me to the Admiralty as the person I desire might be distinguished.'[55]

Or Bowen of the *Transfer*: 'Sir, I give you credit for the best intentions, but the history of your loss of men by a miserable Swede does no credit to your judgement. I am, sir . . .'[56]

Or Captain Aylmer, who had succeeded Miller in command of a warship: 'Sir, Had Captain Miller continued in the command . . . the defects which the carpenter . . . has most disgracefully given . . . had never been heard of . . .'[57]

Historians have made much of Jervis, understandably but not always fairly. The old admiral himself was suspicious of the myths that encrusted him like barnacles, and occasionally protested. When one admirer dared to describe the captains of the Mediterranean as his 'school', the old sea dog reportedly scoffed, 'No, that is too much.

They would have been as great anywhere. It was *with* such men that I formed a school!' Perhaps he recognised that much had already been done with those men, and in truth a good deal has been written of Jervis in ignorance of the achievements of Lord Hood. Nelson famously said that 'of all the fleets I ever saw, I never saw one in point of officers and men equal to Sir John Jervis's', but few admit Nelson had applied similar words to the same fleet before Jervis ever reached the Mediterranean.[58]

In fact Jervis was much like Hood. Both were self-confident, domineering, straight-talking, dogmatic even when wrong-headed, and utterly devoted to the service. Like Hood, Jervis had his fleet practising manoeuvres and improving their skills, and relished battle. Like him he knew the needs of the common sailors, and tried to keep them healthy. In one respect Jervis was a more impressive admiral than Hood, however. He was better at identifying talented officers, rewarding them by word and deed, and maintaining their effort and morale. He rescued both Fremantle and Nelson from a deep disillusionment that had brought them to the brink of quitting the Mediterranean. 'You can have no conception how much the fleet are improved in every respect . . .,' Fremantle told his brother after Jervis took command. 'Before every man went his own way, and all was confusion.'[59]

To Nelson the great contrast was not between Jervis and Hood, but between Jervis and his immediate predecessors, Hotham and Parker. Under the new commander-in-chief there would be no malingering in St Fiorenzo or Leghorn. Immediately he tightened the cordon around Toulon, detailing an inshore squadron under Troubridge to shut the port down, and his fleet kept to the sea in all weathers, completing much of their caulking and repairs as they sailed. The gains from Sir John's vigour were not without cost, and years later that brilliant maverick Lord Cochrane flagellated Jervis in and out of Parliament for running down the health of seamen and keeping them afloat in crazy, unserviceable ships. When the old admiral eventually became first lord of the Admiralty, he aroused even greater controversy by ill-timed reforms. He meant well, but brought with him the baggage of an experienced and unreconstructed Whig warrior, obsessed with economical reform, to his administration of the navy. His determination to slay such dragons as extravagance, waste, corruption and inefficiency commended him to the taxpayer, but less to the fleets suffering from dangerous economies and disrepair.[60]

A just assessment of Jervis must await a dispassionate and thorough biographer, but one achievement certainly redounds to his credit. It was Jervis more than anyone else who restored Nelson's faith and fighting spirit in 1796. Reading Jervis's letters through those years, some of them written on elegant letter-headed notepaper, one often gets a softer impression of an admiral whose toughness earned him the sobriquet 'Old Oak'. He was ruthless with backsliders and muti-neers, but embraced effective officers with an almost fatherly affec-tion. He approached them with little of the abrasive aloofness that had marked Hood, and often showed astonishing generosity, kind-ness, sympathy and good humour. Those officers repaid him with their loyalty, none more so than Nelson. The captain of the *Agamemnon* had never felt more valued than under Jervis, and his confidence and achievements flowered.

The first of Jervis's letters to reach Nelson found him disconsolate, embittered and peevish, rather like a slighted prima donna. He was still unwell, visibly according to Lady Elliot, and felt besmirched by the allied generals and abandoned by superiors. The failure of his campaign, the Austrian accusations, the disinterest of his commanders-in-chief, the platitudinous replies from the Admiralty and the with-holding of the distinguishing pendant had all soured him.[61]

Jervis changed all that. In January he demonstrated his regard by offering Nelson the command of a larger ship, suggesting that the *Zealous* would probably suit him more than the larger *St George* because it was a seventy-four more suited to active duties. The *Agamemnon* was due for recall, and by offering a transfer Jervis was clearly signalling his wish to retain Nelson's services. Nelson found the admiral's letter 'most flattering' but refused to be cheered. He wrote to his brother William that he was 'sorry' to note Jervis's interest because in his 'present mind' he was determined to return to England with the *Agamemnon*.[62]

After refitting and reprovisioning at Leghorn, Nelson joined the fleet at St Fiorenzo on 19 January. His men scrambled to the rigging and thronged the bulwark to cheer the new commander-in-chief's flag flying above the *Victory*, and Nelson went aboard to report. He had spent hours with Hood in the cabin of the great three-decker, but the man who greeted him now could not have looked less like the cadav-erous Irish peer. Jervis had turned sixty. His toadlike figure consisted of a stocky body and expanding paunch propped up on thick, tree-trunk legs. The face was formidable. Sir John's jaw was set, his thin mouth firm, and the eyes flanking the sharp nose big and determined. Yet the severity of that formidable mien could quickly evaporate. Young Betsy Wynne, who once visited him with a bevy of ladies, found 'nothing stiff or formal about him', and was amused when the old admiral 'desired we should pay the tribute' due by every female 'entering his cabin, which was to kiss him'. On such occasions a warm geniality crackling within Jervis broke his crusty exterior, and the craggy features flickered benignly. Nelson probably saw that look now.[63]

From every quarter Jervis was receiving golden opinions of Captain Nelson. John Trevor, for example, considered 'that worthy and excellent officer' not only deserving of promotion ('I hope soon to call [him] by another title') but also 'a more active and cordial cooperation between His Majesty's fleet and the allies'. The admiral knew that his own success depended upon encouraging such spirits. When the two met, he asked Nelson a few questions about the riviera campaign, liked the answers, and directly invited him to stay with the fleet. It was a request to warm the heart of any ambitious officer, but Nelson demurred. He needed a rest, he explained, and would go home with the *Agamemnon*. That said, as a senior captain Nelson was close to receiving his flag, and he added that in such a case he would be privileged to return to Sir John's fleet as a rear admiral. Nelson was still set on seeing England, but Jervis had already moved him. The next day he wrote to Fanny that if he was promoted before his ship was recalled, 'my fair character makes me stand forward to remain abroad'. The pessimism was lifting.[64]

Within twenty-four hours came more tangible evidence of Jervis's faith. Far from listening to Genoese and Austrian complaints, the admiral sent Nelson back to the Gulf of Genoa. As he would reassure Trevor, he knew Nelson's 'zeal, activity and enterprise' could not 'be surpassed', and regretted his present inability 'to give him the command of a squadron equal to his merit'. Nonetheless, even the renewal of the riviera command, with all its burdens, had some captains in the fleet grumbling about the plums that constantly went Nelson's way, and the captain of the *Agamemnon* felt obliged to return 'a pretty strong answer'. On 22 January he left for his station, rounding up two prize corn ships en route. He found two frigates already off the coast, the *Meleager* and *Blanche* under Captains Cockburn and Sawyer, and directed them to patrol, keeping a weather eye open at the same time for any French attempt to ship troops to Italy. They made five prizes in as many weeks, one a French tartan with one hundred and fifty soldiers taken by the *Blanche* on 13 February.[65]

By then Nelson had met Jervis again, when he escorted a merchant-man from Genoa to Leghorn. Again the *Agamemnons* cheered their commander-in-chief, and again Jervis welcomed Nelson aboard the flagship. Sir John was bound for Toulon to tighten his grip on the main French battle fleet and ordered Nelson to go in advance. They also discussed the possibility of the French offering battle in terms that convinced Nelson he had found another kindred spirit, very different from Hotham or Parker. Almost ecstatically he wrote to Fanny that if the French got out 'they will now lose the *whole* of them [their ships], for we have a man of business at our head'.[66]

In Toulon, Nelson found thirteen sail of the line and five frigates ready for sea, and word had it that sailors were being recruited and Marseilles full of transports for soldiers. It all augured action, an amphibious descent somewhere, perhaps in Italy or Corsica, and that meant the possibility of another battle at sea. When Sir John brought the fleet up on 23 February, Nelson made his report and abandoned all resistance to the commander-in-chief's solicitations. 'You must have a larger ship,' Jervis said, 'for we cannot spare you either as admiral or captain.' Nelson always found praise, real or pretended, irresistible. With acute disappointment Fanny read that her dream of the country cottage was fading again. Jervis 'seems at present to consider me as an assistant more than a subordinate,' Nelson informed her. He talked about staying at sea.[67]

Jervis rejuvenated Nelson by addressing every one of his concerns. In April he began reinforcing the riviera squadron with the *Diadem* sixty-four and *Peterel* sloop, and Nelson was given to understand that transports for troops would be sought if amphibious operations appeared necessary. For the first time Nelson felt the work appreci-ated. 'We may rely on every support and effectual assistance' from the commander-in-chief, he told Drake. 'We have only to propose, and if possible it will be done.' On 15 April, Jervis did what Hotham had been implored but declined to do: he brought the fleet to Vado, and cruised off the coast for several days. Several months before the diver-sion would have been of great utility, but the French, not the Austrians, now controlled the bay, and Jervis and Nelson were forced to watch an enemy grain convoy pass mischievously by them, impregnable in the shallows. Still, it symbolised a new vitality. The Austrians, who had advanced as far as Voltri, received a much-needed fillip, and

Nelson used the visit to spread rumours that the British intended to land five thousand soldiers to attack the communications of the French army. His hope that the French would weaken their front by sending detachments to the coast was overambitious, but Nelson assured Jervis that 'the opportune appearance of the squadron had created a good deal of sensation amongst the French in Genoa'.[68]

Equally telling, Jervis tackled the corrosive issue of Nelson's promotion. 'No words can express the sense I entertain of every part of your conduct,' he told his irritable subordinate. 'A distinguishing pendant you shall most certainly wear, and now I am in possession of your further wishes, I will write to Lord Spencer upon the subject of them. In short, there is nothing within my grasp that I shall not be proud to confer on you.' Thus, on 8 April, Nelson proudly raised a swallow-tailed, red, broad pendant on the main topmast of the *Agamemnon* to the cheers of the ship's company. It advertised his status as an acting commodore with ships to command, and gave him an additional ten shillings a day in pay and larger shares in prize money. Strictly, a commodore was a temporal post rather than a permanent rank, a title conveyed upon a senior captain commanding a squadron of ships. Nelson's pendant could be hauled down if his squadron or responsibilities were withdrawn, and he also had to wait until 11 August for Spencer to confirm his advancement. Nevertheless, at last he felt reassured that he was making progress in his profession.[69]

Nelson returned to his station with a new authority and new blood.

9

Back in Genoa towards the middle of April, Nelson found others also disposed to turn over new leaves. Even the republic's secretary of state, upon whom Nelson called with Consul Brame, seemed superficially amenable on the issues of neutral trade. He admitted that merchants who shipped goods to or for the French had to accept the risks, and congratulated Nelson upon his broad pendant. De Vins was gone, and was 'as little mentioned' in diplomatic circles 'as if he were no longer in the land of the living', while his successor, Jean-Pierre de Beaulieu, decorated with the Grand Cross of the Order of Marie Theresa, flattered Nelson. As Brame noted, 'The commodore had some communication with General Beaulieu by means of Mr Peirson [of the *Agamemnon*]. Many thanks and compliments passed. The general said

he should acquaint the emperor [of Austria] of the commodore's meritorious conduct and zeal.'[70]

Underneath though, the war was still going badly. Emerging from
a winter of uncommon severity the coast was under even tighter enemy
control, with Vado and Savona still in French hands. France regarded
the German theatre as her prime concern, but the Army of Italy still
numbered sixty-three thousand effectives with two units in reserve.
Some of the 'neutral' coastal towns it had occupied the previous year,
including Alassio, had since been strengthened against naval attack,
and the inshore shipping that had defeated Nelson in the last campaign
was still brazenly plying back and forth. Worse, with Austria the only
major continental adversary remaining, France was poised to deliver
a knock-out punch. Three massive strikes were in the making, from
the Sambre and Meuse, the Rhine and Moselle, and Nice. Bonaparte
was personally in command of the latter and southern thrust, which
was preparing to roll up opposition on the riviera before turning north
through the plains of Lombardy and crossing the Alps into the Tyrol
towards Vienna.

The old triumvirate Nelson had formed with Drake and Trevor was
reconstituted, but most of the remedies they had unsuccessfully applied
in 1795 were just as uncertain as before. Alarmed at the naval build-
up in Toulon, Nelson wrote to Naples as early as 11 March recommending the king equip a flotilla of small warships and light craft to
patrol the coast in case the French tried to land in Italy. As usual, the
Neapolitans reacted with alacrity, and at one time two twenty-gun
xebecs and a score of galliots, gunboats and feluccas were being fitted
for action, carrying a total of sixty guns and seventeen hundred and
forty men. Within weeks moves were afoot to redirect the force to the
riviera to help the Austrians block French advances through the
republic of Genoa, but without Savona and Vado there was no suit
able base for the flotilla. Drake and Nelson failed to cajole the
Austrians into retaking Vado, but in the end it hardly mattered. Though
supposedly at Nelson's disposal, the Neapolitan flotilla had still not
arrived by 17 May. As an interim measure, Trevor tried to substitute
a fleet of lightly armed feluccas and thirty-six-pounder gunboats
manned by a thousand Sardinians, but though the king of Sardinia
approved of the proposal it foundered amid disagreements about who
would pay and victual the crews. The issue was still in the air when
Sardinia suddenly dropped out of the war in May and changed the
military situation.[71]

In March and April, Drake, now generally based in Milan, was no more successful in reviving the plan to mount amphibious diversionary raids behind French lines. His faith in Nelson remained boundless, and for several weeks he pressed the idea of giving him a fleet of gunboats and two or three thousand British marines, Corsican troops or Neapolitans to enable him to strike unpredictably at such places as Stefano, Finale and San Remo. But the British, Austrian and Neapolitan governments pleaded their lack of resources. Jervis judged his fleet unable to supply the gunboats and doubted that Elliot, viceroy of Corsica, could spare the men. In Naples, Acton, the most influential minister, was even more dismissive. 'Mr Drake's plan of operation in having three thousand men wandering about on that extended coast from Perpignan to Voltri' would not 'answer' his 'desires and expectations. As to the landing for taking the rear of the enemy, I cannot see how on that coast without magazines, and no ports to keep the transports, the men could be adventured.' In other words, if the plan had been viable in 1795, when the Austrians commanded relevant ports, it was no longer.[72]

The truth was that the war was different now, and afforded Nelson far fewer opportunities to intervene. Beaulieu, a veteran of the Seven Years War, was seventy-four years old, and if (as Nelson said) he still possessed 'the fire of youth', he could not be drawn into a westward push along the seashore to wrestle with the frustrations that had defeated De Vins. By the end of March the French had seized Voltri and advanced to within five or six miles of Genoa itself, partly to frighten the Italian republic into granting substantial loans. Their allied opponents seemed scattered and vulnerable. The nearest Austrian army, consisting of twelve thousand men, was at Acqui, thirty-five miles inland from Genoa, while twenty thousand Piedmontese were strung out to the southwest watching the mountain passes in an effort to prevent enemy incursions into Lombardy.[73]

On 8 April 1796, Horatio Nelson was in Genoa, sending Beaulieu assurances that he could rely upon British support for any Austrian counterattack. Beaulieu was planning to move upon Voltri, and returned an encouraging reply two days later. Without delay Nelson hurried ashore at five in the evening, collected Consul Brame as an interpreter, and visited the quarters of the Austrian chargé d'affaires, Count Giovanni Girola. There he learned that the Austrians were attacking Voltri at daylight the following day, 11 April, and Beaulieu wanted Nelson to cover his seaward left flank. The commodore had four ships at the mole, the *Agamemnon* and *Diadem* sail of the line, the last under Captain George Henry Towry, and the *Meleager* and *Blanche* frigates. He gave orders for them to prepare as unobtrusively as possible, and led them quietly to sea after dark.[74]

They stole along the coast towards Voltri, their sails filled with a moderate breeze, and the lights of the Austrian army winking in the darkness to starboard. Nelson planned to anchor the *Agamemnon* and *Meleager* within half gun shot of the Austrian flank before daylight, and to position the *Diadem* and *Blanche* ahead between Voltri and Savona, ready to train their guns on the road to batter the French as they retreated. It was useless, however. Instead of moving at daylight on the 11th as scheduled, the Austrians went forward early, in the previous evening, converging upon Voltri in two columns while a third attacked Savona. There was little resistance at Voltri, where ten thousand Austrians took three hundred French prisoners and some magazines, but because the columns were poorly coordinated four thousand enemy soldiers escaped towards Savona. Nelson was unable to punish the refugees. The premature land attack meant that most of the enemy soldiers had escaped before the ships could close in on the road. Nelson's broadsides pounded a few flying detachments of French off Arenzano, and his boats went as far inshore as they dared, but for the most part the horses had bolted. Later that day, in the few hours Beaulieu was allowed to savour victory, he courteously acknowledged 'his great obligations to Captain Nelson' for bringing his ships so close. But the commodore himself dashed off disappointed reports to Drake and Trevor asking them to impress upon their allies 'the absolute necessity of punctuality in joint attacks'.[75]

Little was actually gained by the offensive, which stalled as suddenly as it had begun. The next day Bonaparte brought up reinforcements, and taking personal charge of the French operations went into action like a tightly coiled spring. He threw back the third Austrian column threatening Savona, denuding it of nearly a thousand men and all of its artillery, and stopped Beaulieu in his tracks. Realising that the Austrian forces on the coast could not support their allies, Bonaparte turned north to attack the Piedmontese under General Louis, Baron Colli. It took him only two weeks to smash a wedge between the allied armies, knock Sardinia-Piedmont out of the war, and spill his half-starved, ill-clad, lethal horde through the Apennine passes towards Lombardy. Bonaparte forced the Adda River at Lodi on 10 May, clearing the Austrians out of the way, and entered Milan a few days later, turning it into a satellite of France and stripping it of what was needed to re-equip his army. Then, while the victors marched upon Mantua, where thousands of Austrian soldiers were holed up, Beaulieu's humbled warriors fell back to the Tyrol and the Veneto. British diplomats were dismayed by Bonaparte's blistering speed and aggression. 'If he was not a Jacobin, I should call [him] a fine fellow for his enterprize and abilities,' sighed Trevor.[76]

These operations took Bonaparte away from the coast, where his right had been menaced by Nelson's hungry battleships. Much of the time the commodore was reduced to listening to cannons rumbling in distant mountains, and trying to make sense of garbled accounts of battles that came from Genoa or Leghorn. The war was coursing inland, beyond his direct interference, and all he could do was to fall upon enemy supplies wherever he saw them, relying on Drake and Brame to protect him from the inevitable cascade of Genoese complaints about the violation of their neutrality.

Victory was not something he could expect, but at least his efforts were appreciated in the fleet. Throughout that difficult spring Admiral Jervis's faith in him never wavered. 'I cannot possibly be without you in the Gulf of Genoa,' wrote the commander-in-chief. He meant it, and told the secretary of the Admiralty of 'the satisfaction I feel in having an officer of such zeal and local knowledge on the important station he occupies'.[77]

10

The issue of Genoese neutrality grew thornier with every French success. Almost all the Italian republic's coasts and harbours were occupied by the French, and in Genoa the government struggled to retain some freedom of action against increasingly strident Jacobin voices. Nelson could do no other than regard the coast as hostile. His statement to Jervis that 'to pretend . . . that although our enemies took possession . . . [of] . . . the republic of Genoa that we are not by every means in our power to attack them both at sea and ashore will [not] bear reasoning upon', had the determined admiral nodding fiercely in agreement.[78]

Nevertheless, without the base at Vado it was harder than ever to damage the French supply line. Nelson stationed ships between Nice and Alassio, hoping to intercept supplies going east or west, but the coast was full of neutral and French sails, and he was compelled to admit that his squadron had 'not taken one of two or three hundred [vessels] of different sizes which have passed them'.[79]

Skill and temerity did produce some victories, however. In the supposedly neutral harbours Nelson preferred to provoke the French into firing the first shots to furnish grounds for self-defence. The morning of 25 April saw him approaching Loano in search of an enemy convoy he had heard about in nearby Finale. Only four of the transports remained when he arrived under a drizzling rain, supported by the *Diadem*, *Meleager* and *Peterel*. Between one and two in the afternoon five boats were assembled at the *Peterel*, an eighteen-gun sloop commanded by Charles Stuart. Lieutenants Suckling, Noble and Compton of the *Agamemnon* each took responsibility for a boat, along with Culverhouse of the *Meleager* and an officer of the *Diadem*. As they approached the harbour the French opened fire with artillery and musketry, effectively breaching the neutrality of their Genoese hosts, and Nelson brought his ships in to provide cover. Most of the French missiles howled overhead, but in a lively half-hour the *Agamemnon* was hit and the largest of the French batteries demolished with a score of its attendants killed and wounded. By three-thirty the boats had towed out their prizes, an eight-gun bombard with provisions and ordnance, a ketch laden with powder and sixteen hundred muskets, and two galleys with provisions. Three Britons were wounded, one of them Lieutenant Noble. Young James Noble's commission had been confirmed the previous month, and Nelson spoke of him as 'a most gallant and worthy officer', but he was singularly unlucky. Since joining the ship on 5 October he had been captured by the French and exchanged, and now he fell, hit in the throat by a musket ball. Fortunately, his windpipe was unscathed and the ball was extracted, although not before Noble had almost been strangled by a coxswain who sought to staunch the flow of blood by tightening a black silk stock around his neck.[80]

The success was welcome, because malignant tongues in Genoa were sapping allied morale with stories of French siege equipment getting past the British ships, and in reporting it Nelson did not ignore his own cause at home. Perhaps remembering that his rank of commodore had still to be confirmed, he again resorted to addressing the board of Admiralty as well as his admiral. In the past the practice had served him well, and it did now. Spencer positively encouraged the correspondence, begging Nelson not to 'make any apologies for writing, as it is very satisfactory to hear from you when we can in any way'. As Nelson's missives continued the first lord expressed his appreciation of direct news from the Mediterranean, and asked for more of it.[81]

Nelson revisited Loano on the evening of 7 May, attacking after dusk with all but the *Diadem* of his former contingent. This time he failed. In three-quarters of an hour a red-hot shot fired by the French hissed into the starboard bow of the *Blanche*, where it smouldered ominously. The wind also fell, exposing the ships to a dangerous fusillade, and the wounded *Blanche* was cut up about the hull, masts and spars. Nelson prudently abandoned his attempt to extricate a gunboat and three brigs from the harbour, but recovered his injured frigate after one and a half hours of action. Rebuffed, he tried Finale the same night. This time the operation was performed so stealthily that a brace of vessels were brought out without an alarm having been raised, but daylight proved the vessels to be legitimate Genoese traders and Nelson ordered their release.

Red-hot shot, shoals, vagaries of the wind, enemy guns, collision . . . the risks attending these expeditions were numerous and unpredictable, but whether they involved dangerous battery-baiting descents by the ships or bruising muscle-stretching pulls through darkness in small boats, they built skills and experience. Nelson turned the two galleys taken at Loano into gunboats, and used them to scout ahead. He tended to keep the ships themselves out of sight of land during the day, and to close on picked targets after nightfall, using the intelligence gained by his galleys. Careful planning reduced the inseparable risks. When the boats made their predatory nocturnal incursions they were often tethered in a line, one painter fast to another, to prevent them separating in the darkness, and their oars were muffled.[82]

A believer in nothing ventured nothing gained, Nelson scored his most significant success near Oneglia on 31 May. That day he had been pursuing ships breaking for Genoa, and arrived at Torre del l'Arma, a neutral haven protected by a castle over which the colours of the Italian republic still flew. But the ships beneath its guns were French, and one showed a national flag. Again, Nelson approached quietly but steadily and provoked his nervous opponents to fire, giving him the pretext to attack.

About mid-afternoon Cockburn, whose abilities were 'conspicuous on every occasion', led in with the thirty-two-gun *Meleager*. The *Agamemnon* and *Speedy* sloop (Captain Thomas Elphinstone) followed, while the *Diadem*, *Blanche* and *Peterel* remained in the offing to leeward, near enough to send their boats in support. The *Meleager* anchored opposite the principal battery, but as Cockburn prepared to return enemy fire he was astonished to see Nelson trying to interpose the *Agamemnon* between the frigate and the guns, as if to draw the greater danger upon himself. There was insufficient water for the manoeuvre and the *Agamemnon* ran aground, a sitting duck. Concerned, Cockburn had himself rowed to the stranded flagship to offer Nelson his help. The old *Agamemnon* had a new first lieutenant, a stereotypical dashing blade named Edward Berry, but it was Nelson who provided Cockburn with the defining memory of the attack. The commodore was found sitting calmly at his cabin table, writing letters while his ship lay grounded beneath a dangerous shore battery.

This time the attack went smoothly, even when the Genoese battery joined the enemy ships in firing upon the British. Nelson replied to the neutrals with words rather than shot. Reserving his fire, he sent a message to the governor of the port, demanding to know why a Genoese tower was bombarding his ships. The French had fired first and broken the laws of neutrality, and it was the duty of the port to deal with the aggressors. It worked. The Genoese commandant apologised, his fire ceased, and Nelson did nothing to endanger the flimsy truce; even when French muskets were thrust from the windows of houses, he suffered the spotted volleys to remain unanswered rather than risk damage to the town.

In the meantime a party led by Lieutenant Spicer boarded the national ketch *Le Génie* of three eighteen-pounders and four swivels, and in a brief trade of cutlass blows and pistol shots drove her sixty crewmen over the side. The gunboat *Le Numéro Douze* with one gun and four swivels, and four transports were also taken. After cutting the ships' cables their defenders jumped into the water to struggle ashore, leaving the British to carry hawsers to the prizes to tow them out of harbour.

On this occasion the effort was entirely rewarded, even at the loss of a man killed and three wounded. *Le Génie* was purchased into the navy, renamed the *Venom*, and in July complemented Nelson's scouts in the hands of the worthy Lieutenant Noble. Of the greatest moment, the captured convoy was full of war materiel for the siege of Mantua, including provisions, books and papers as well as guns, ammunition and ordnance stores that amounted to about a quarter of Bonaparte's siege train. Among the documents were inventories of the French army, details of other convoys and a collection of military treatises and histories intended for the general. After leafing through Vauban's discourse on siege work and the lives of such illustrious predecessors as Hannibal and Prince Eugene of Savoy, Nelson observed, 'If Buona Parti is ignorant, the Directory it would appear wish to instruct him. Pray God he may remain ignorant.'[83]

Three days later the *Blanche*'s launch captured a French ship with 152 Austrian prisoners of war on board. Their captors had sold them to the Spaniards for use as mercenaries, and upon being liberated most voluntarily enrolled in British service.

Nelson's stroke at Oneglia probably fortified Mantua's stubborn resistance, and Bonaparte temporarily raised the siege at the end of July. Stalled, he turned south through Tuscany at the orders of the French Directory, the new government in Paris. The Royal Navy could do little to stop him. The commander-in-chief told Drake that 'even if the line-of-battle ships were placed from headland to headland' supplies would continue to reach the French by sea, and Nelson was equally pessimistic. His ships were wearing out, the *Agamemnon* and *Meleager* were 'like two tubs floating on the water', and the allies collapsing like cards. 'I very much believe that England, who commenced the war with all Europe for her allies, will finish it by having nearly all Europe for her enemies,' he told Elliot.[84]

By the middle of May, Nelson was questioning the utility of Britain's presence on the riviera, and told Jervis not to 'hesitate one moment in directing my pendant to be struck' if he saw no advantage in protracting the command. 'Do you really think we are of any use here?' he asked Drake. The minister had been one of Nelson's greatest admirers since the day they first met, but he too was moving on, having been succeeded as His Majesty's representative to the Austrian military headquarters. Of one thing he was sure. 'I shall always be proud of acknowledging the assistance which I have on so many occasions received from your abilities,' he told Nelson, 'and of doing justice . . . to the zeal, the great ability and the prudence and skill which you have shown in so conspicuous a manner.'[85]

11

Nelson's body was protesting again. He was waking in his cot at night, 'as if a girth was buckled taut over my breast' and he had 'to get it loose'. The surgeon's report augured badly, but Nelson believed the spa waters of Pisa might revive him, and Jervis granted him the necessary leave. The significant fact was that poor health and professional disappointments did not enhance the lure of home, as they had done at the end of 1795. This time there was no mental retreat to Fanny and that quiet Norfolk cottage. Sir John's support had made the difference.[86]

The two men were friends as well as colleagues, and Nelson's letters grew more familiar, mulling over the old admiral's problems and encouraging his efforts. Amidst communications stuffed with business are revealing clues. Jervis thanked Nelson for the books he had loaned him ('a fund of amusement'), asked him to find some 'elegant' rich velvet in Genoa for a robe in which Lady Jervis could attend the queen, and made whimsical asides concerning the younger man's known interest in women. 'The [Leghorn] factory will find themselves very happy under your protection,' he promised, we sense with a smile, 'and all our fine country-women, pent up in Italy, will fly into your embraces.' This was not the stiff, flint-faced autocrat portrayed in many books.[87]

The resuscitation of Nelson's morale was complete. 'I cannot bear the thoughts of leaving your command,' Nelson wrote to Sir John early in June. 'You have placed an unbounded confidence in me, and I own I feel that no exertion of mine has been for a moment wanting to merit so great an honour.' The *Agamemnon* was still bound for home. She was unseaworthy and small and the most expendable of Jervis's ships of the line, fit only for convoy duty to England and an overhaul. Nelson no longer wanted to go with her. He urged his commander-in-chief to find him 'any thing' that would keep him in the Mediterranean.[88]

Obligingly Jervis cast around. He assured Nelson that he was determined to get him promoted commodore, and if an expected general promotion gave him a flag there would still be a place for him in the Mediterranean fleet. In the meantime a new ship had to be found. On 22 May, Jervis instructed Nelson to exchange ships with Captain Sutton of the *Egmont*, who was willing to go home. Briefly the matter tottered on a knife edge. Nelson found the *Egmont* in St Fiorenzo, but Sutton had changed his mind and for several unsettling days it looked as if Nelson would be stuck with his homeward-bound sixty-four. Eventually Captain John Samuel Smith came to the rescue, agreeing to yield his seventy-four-gun *Captain* and return to England for his health. Nelson was delighted and tactlessly told his wife that he did 'not feel much regret at not being in England'. After three years of separation Fanny must have read those words with great pain.[89]

He was staying, but 11 June was still a day of some sadness. Nelson had loved the *Agamemnon*. He had met her as an insignificant post-captain, fresh from half-pay, and turned her into the most efficient fighting machine on the Mediterranean. Her officers and men worked with frightening precision in a perfect union of commander, crew and craft. Together they had ridden fearful seas, survived disease and shot, fired thousands of rounds at the enemy and won accolades on all sides. For many on board these had been the times they would remember above all others. Some were proudly calling themselves 'old *Agamemnons*' forty years later.

The most fervent of the *Agamemnons* followed their leader into the *Captain*, but the old warhorse herself went on to new adventures with new commanders. She would endure the humiliation of mutiny, steer to glory off Cape Trafalgar, and end her life in 1809 at the bottom of the estuary of the River Plate. But when Nelson surrendered the ship to Captain Smith that June day in 1796 her finest hour was past.

Jervis, though, was relieved that Nelson was staying in the Mediterranean, for he counted him the best senior officer in the fleet. As he wrote to Lord Spencer, 'I beg I may have no more admirals [sent me], unless they are firm men. Your lordship will readily comprehend that persons holding high situations in a fleet who see everything with a jaundiced eye are a perfect nuisance. Fortunately for me, Commodore Nelson and several of the captains of line-of-battle ships and frigates under my command . . . will work to anything.'[90]

XXII

FROM FLAG CAPTAIN TO SHIP-BOY

'And, Sir, the secret of his victories?'
'By his unservicelike, forsaken ways, Sir,
He made the whole fleet love him, damn his eyes!'
Robert Graves, *1805*

1

SAMUEL Taylor Coleridge never met Nelson but knew a great deal about him. For some time he served as secretary to Alexander Ball, one of Nelson's greatest captains, and the two spoke much of Nelson during long and lovingly recollected discussions. 'Lord Nelson was an admiral every inch of him,' recalled Coleridge. 'He looked at every thing, not merely in its possible relations to the naval service in general, but in its immediate bearings on his own squadron; to his officers, his men, to the particular ships themselves, his affections were as strong and ardent as those of a lover. Hence, though his temper was constitutionally irritable and uneven, yet never was a commander so enthusiastically loved by men of all ranks, from the captain of the fleet to the youngest ship-boy.'[1]

As early as 1793, William Hoste had presaged Coleridge's remarks by telling his family that Nelson was universally beloved by the officers and men of the *Agamemnon*, and there are grounds for believing that it was not a gross exaggeration. When Nelson transferred to the *Captain* in June 1796 no fewer than 118 men, with five women and two children belonging to soldiers serving with the marines, went with him, almost a third of the old ship's company. This despite the fact that the *Agamemnon* was due to sail for England, and many aboard her must have longed to see the green shores of home. But the men who followed Nelson into his new ship reflected an elite cadre he had carefully nurtured aboard the old sixty-four, and formed a dependable core on the *Captain*, filling important positions and helping to fashion the new company in the image of the old. There was much work to do with the fresh command. Smith had removed thirty of the *Captain*'s best men, and though the rest were sufficient in number they were 'not active' as a whole and a few were downright lubberly. Within two days in June two had tumbled from aloft, one making a spectacular descent into the sea from a topsail yard. It was the leavening of old *Agamemnons* that would transform their performance.[2]

Before we leave Nelson's favourite ship, it is worth examining the unusual community over which he had presided for three years and four months to see what it can tell us about his leadership. Sadly, no diaries or journals other than Nelson's take us beyond the bare operational details recorded in the daily logs of the *Agamemnon*, and most of the letters written from the ship have been lost. None of the well-written letters sent home by two of her young gentlemen, Bolton and Weatherhead, for example, have survived. Those written by Nelson and Hoste can be deployed, and the little we can glean from them and other sources suggests that in general a healthy chemistry brought the company together. It was industrious, efficient, ready if necessary to pay the ultimate forfeit, but also a relatively caring community, marked by fellow feeling and a happy camaraderie. There appear to have been few bullying lieutenants or sour, aged midshipmen, most of the men respected their officers and the captain exercised a strong but paternal control over his 'poor brave fellows'.

The spirit a good and active captain could create aboard a warship during the French wars was best described by Captain Frederick Marryat, the novelist haunted by his years as a midshipman on the *Imperieuse* under the command of Lord Cochrane. A cantankerous subordinate, Cochrane was idolised by his young gentlemen, much as Nelson before him. As Marryat recalled in later life:

The cruises of the *Imperieuse* were periods of continual excitement, from the hour in which she hove up her anchor till she dropped it again in port. The day that passed without a shot being fired in anger was with us a blank day. The boats were hardly secured on the booms than they were cast loose and out again. The yard and stay tackles were for ever hoisting up and lowering down. The expedition with which parties were formed for service; the rapidity of the frigate's movements, night and day; the hasty sleep, snatched at all hours; the waking up at the report of the guns, which seemed the only keynote to the hearts of those on board; the beautiful precision of our fire, obtained by constant practise; the coolness and courage of our captain, innoculating the whole of the ship's company; the suddenness of our attacks; the gathering after the combat; the killed lamented; the wounded almost envied; the powder so burnt into our faces that years could not remove it; the proved character of every man and officer on board; the implicit trust and the adoration we felt for our commander; the ludicrous situations which would occur even in the extremest danger and create mirth when death was staring you in the face; the hair-breadth escapes; and the indifference to life shown by all. When memory sweeps along those years of excitement, even now my pulse beats more quickly with the reminiscence.[3]

Perhaps Marryat exaggerated, remembering warmer days when he was an impressionable youth, but almost every one of his words would have held good for the *Agamemnon*. Her spirit could infect the occasional passenger. According to a story later told by a member of Nelson's family, one of the most noteworthy of these was Cardinal Henry, Duke of York, the younger brother of Charles Edward Stuart, the Young Pretender. Somehow the seventy-year-old man got into difficulties, and at Nelson's invitation spent some time in the ship until he could be returned to Austrian protection. Nelson is said to have reduced him to tears with the loan of £100. Restored to his station and equanimity shortly afterwards, the grateful recipient soon found the *Agamemnon* at Genoa, and excitedly went aboard. He repaid Nelson's loan, presented him with a sword and dirk and ran about the ship 'shaking hands with all the crew'.[4]

The men of the lower deck of the *Agamemnon* are the least knowable to historians, for they left no written records, and while the musters preserve scant details, including some ages and places of origin, they capture next to nothing of the personalities themselves. Most of the men, no doubt, conformed in many respects to the stereotypical British sailor, with his seafaring slang, distinctive trousers, shirts, short jackets and hats, and pride in all things seamanly. But over the years the *Agamemnon* created a more cosmopolitan blend by recruiting men of different nationalities, including Italians, Corsicans and Austrians who spoke little English. Nelson still managed to weave them into the fabric and maintain a first-rate ship.

There were floggings, of course, about one hundred and twenty over the entire period of Nelson's command. Just before leaving for the *Captain*, Nelson had to flog 'all the pinnace's crew for bringing liquor on board'. Judging from the number of oars shipped by most pinnaces, eight men may have suffered on that single occasion. Nevertheless, the punishment rate as a whole was probably no more than average, considering the size of the ship, the duration of the command and the turnover of men, and most of the floggings were light. About three-quarters amounted to the token dozen lashes or less, with desertion and one case of sodomy earning four offenders the severest sentences of thirty-six strokes. A number of men also 'ran' successfully, some forty up to November 1794, and Nelson took the common precaution of issuing standing orders that no boat could go ashore without permission.[5]

Punishments such as these, as has been said, were not necessarily divisive or destructive. The usual offences, such as drunkenness, disobedience, neglect of duty, theft and fighting, were a threat to the welfare of the entire ship, and the victims were normally ordinary seamen and marines who needed the protection of a firm captain. Every ship had its more or less cowed malcontents, troubling companies like a grumbling appendicitis, and the *Agamemnon* had her share. One seaman, Thomas Kelly, was apt to drink and fight and got four floggings, while Joseph Turner suffered three times for drunkenness, quarrelling and theft. Most of the men of the *Agamemnon* seem to have felt secure in their captain, however, accepted his discipline and found him approachable and sympathetic in times of difficulty.

2

The liveliest but most vulnerable members of the ship's company were the boys, who perhaps made up around 8 per cent of the total personnel. Some were volunteers, seeking employment or adventure, and others dependants of officers of every rank, originally rated servants but in actuality learning their various trades. A number may even have been formally apprenticed to masters, gunners or shipwrights. But whatever their condition and destination every youngster passed through adolescence in a difficult and dangerous world, divorced from the best female company, and raised among men who had seen life at its rawest. None were more in need of protection than the Marine Society boys. On 6 February 1793 Nelson had written to the society requesting 'twenty lads' for his ship at Chatham, and promising that 'the greatest care shall be taken of them'. Later that month contingents set out for the *Agamemnon* from the Marine Society head-quarters at Bishopsgate, each boy carrying his sea outfit, including clothes, bedding, a comb and a needle and thread.[6]

In 1793 the Marine Society had been in existence for thirty-seven years. It had been founded by the illustrious philanthropist Jonas Hanway, who is said to have introduced the umbrella to the streets of London, and its purpose was to rescue pauper boys for service at sea, either with the navy or in merchantmen. Unfortunately, life afloat was not always conducive to reclamation. Once beyond the society's compass some boys fell into the hands of unsatisfactory guardians or brutal taskmasters. Naval captains might appoint schoolmasters to their ships, but few teachers were the fonts of wisdom or museums of virtue expected today. They were presumbaly men of some educa-tion, but reminiscences of the period suggest that too many were drunken, downtrodden and discontented. Thirty years before Nelson got his Marine Society recruits one critic doubted that such boys were well served at sea, where the skills of 'blasphemy, chewing tobacco and gaming . . . drinking and talking bawdy' were so easily acquired.[7]

The prospects of rescued boys naturally depended upon their own inclinations and talents, the availability of decent guardians and sheer luck, but the most fortunate became 'ordinary' or 'able' seamen, or learned skills with carpenters, sailmakers, armourers, cooks and coopers that could eventually be transferred ashore. Nelson's Marine Society boys have been ignored by historians, but they reveal an inter-esting fusion of self-interest and paternalism. On the one hand captains found it useful to top up their crews with such boys, and the week Nelson received his gang more than sixty other youngsters set out for the king's service on different ships. Nelson filled up his personal allowance of twenty servants with his lads. Despite being labelled servants, few if any were employed as attendants, and their true duties were those of trainee seamen. No matter, Nelson received their wages, paid the boys a proportion and used the balance to improve his own salary. It was an accepted perk in the navy, and when the Admiralty abolished servants in 1794 and paid all boys directly, the captains were compensated for their financial loss. But Nelson married this pecuniary advantage to an act of charity, and genuinely believed he was giving unfortunate boys chances to change their lives. He valued the work of the Marine Society. As an admiral he made regular subscriptions and donations to its funds, and his appointment of

Withers to the *Agamemnon* was due to his desire to equip the ship with a good schoolmaster.[8]

There is some confusion about the number of Marine Society boys Nelson took aboard. Two listings survive – the society's own register of boys sent and the ship's muster of those received – but they are not a complete fit. At least twenty turned up, rather pathetic little chaps if the register is to be believed. Four were thirteen years old, but the average age was fifteen and the average height four feet eight inches, rather small even for those times. Though the Marine Society tried to inculcate the three Rs into their charges, more than half of these boys were functionally illiterate. Only six of the seventeen who sailed to the Mediterranean could both read and write, and two more read only. Six had previous experience of sea work, although it had probably been gained on the society's training ship in the Thames, where boys were 'employed drawing and knotting yarns, making yarn points [and] exercising guns'. They were all endangered youngsters from broken or extinguished homes, arriving with suppressed histories of neglect, abuse, violence and sometimes crime, and were charged with turning over new leaves.[9]

A few examples illustrate the whole:

James Moody, thirteen, measuring four feet four inches in height, illiterate. A 'destitute' orphan, but previously employed in rope-making.

Thomas Amery, thirteen, four feet five inches, literate. Mother a servant at 29 Barbican. Formerly an errand boy.

George Goldring, thirteen, four feet two inches, illiterate. Mother a weaver living two doors from the Fox and Hounds, Hare Street, Bethnal Green. Had 'wound quills'.

John Heney, sixteen, five feet three inches, illiterate. 'Destitute' but formerly a 'plasterer'.

Thomas Cursons or Couzens, sixteen, four feet six inches, could read but not write, sent by the Philanthropic Society. Had been to sea.

Thomas Bates, eighteen, five feet one inch, illiterate. His next of kin was a sister at the Snuff Mills, Hackney. Previously a bricklayer.

John Alderson, nineteen, five feet three inches, illiterate. His mother was Ann Duff of 11 Low Court, Strand. Some sea experience.

To discover how these troubled boys fared under Nelson's command, and whether the Marine Society's hopes for them were fulfilled, we have to turn to the muster and log books of the *Agamemnon*, deficient in sociological detail though they are. Three of the twenty never settled down, and were discharged at their own request within three weeks, but the rest stuck it out and sailed; one rated a master's servant, another a lieutenant's servant and the rest captain's servants. In reality, all were learning the trade of seafaring.

Given their backgrounds, it is not surprising that some of the boys got into trouble during the four years they served under Nelson, and although the captain had an eye to any exonerating circumstances, he allowed the penalties of the service to fall upon proven offenders. Four received floggings, and two of those remained incorrigible, and deserted the ship. Walter Holmes may have been the youngest person Nelson flogged on the *Agamemnon*. The son of a Smithfield smith, able to read but not write, he seems to have fallen under the influence of a habitually drunken and idle fellow named Wilmott, and both were punished for theft on 28 May 1793. The boy received a dozen lashes, though he may not have reached his fourteenth birthday and was less than five feet tall. Nor was he reformed, for on 2 July 1794 he took the opportunity presented by the siege of Calvi to desert.

Two other boys, Richard Firbee and Charles Waters, were punished for attempted desertion on 30 October 1794. Ironically, it was Firbee, at seventeen or eighteen the older of the two, who received the lighter sentence of a dozen lashes. Possibly he had known Waters before their seafaring days. An ex-butcher, his father was a sawyer at a Houndsditch chandler's shop, while Waters and his brother had worked as braziers in the same area. Waters, unlike Firbee, was illiterate, but seems to have been the commanding personality because he received thirty-six lashes, a hard tariff on a fifteen- or sixteen-year-old boy, even if a conventional one for what was deemed to be a serious offence. Like Holmes, Waters, a lieutenant's servant, remained disgruntled, and successfully jumped ship in Genoa in July 1795. Whatever the future held for a malcontented, inadequate youth, far from home in a strange land, his old accomplice Firbee never reoffended. Nor did James Martin, another Marine Society boy who had to be disciplined, though his misdemeanour had been an even more unfortunate one. The son of a Blackfriars nurse, Martin was about seventeen when he attracted the attentions of two Maltese seamen on board the ship. He was judged to have been a willing participant in the resultant 'execrable . . . act', and shared the punishment, receiving three dozen strokes of the lash on 10 May 1795. Fortunately, the youth managed to put the episode behind him and was promoted to 'ordinary seaman' the next year.[10]

Sad as these digressions from prescribed morality or practice were, most of the Marine Society boys buckled down to a steady life afloat, and despite hard service, battle, accident and disease, the deserters, Holmes and Waters, were the only ones to be lost in the four-year sojourn of the *Agamemnon*. Indeed, perhaps it is remarkable that so many of these graduates from the school of hard knocks created no appreciable problems. Fourteen returned in the ship to England with Captain Smith and were paid off at Chatham in September 1796. Four of them were rated 'boys, second class', a new designation introduced by the Admiralty in 1794 to describe seamen in training between the ages of fifteen and seventeen, but ten, including the aforementioned Firbee and Martin, had advanced to the status of 'ordinary seaman'. All appear to have transferred immediately to new ships, the *Montagu*, *York* and *Sandwich*.[11]

The picture that emerges from these records is occasionally stark, but not in its finality unsatisfying. It appears that for all their disadvantages and difficulties, most of the Marine Society boys used their opportunities to build new careers for themselves at sea. No studies of the fortunes of such boys on other ships appear to have been made, but as far as the *Agamemnon* was concerned the Society would seem to have been a moderate success.

3

The practised hands, no less than boys, looked to the captain to mediate their needs and perplexities in a world that frequently baffled them. The seaman of the day was often portrayed as a simple soul. 'Excluded by the employment which they have chosen from all society but people of similar dispositions,' wrote an observing surgeon, 'the deficiencies of education are not felt, and information on general affairs is seldom courted. Their pride consists in being reputed a thorough bred seaman, and they look upon all landmen as beings of inferior order. This is marked in a singular manner by applying the language of seamanship to every transaction of life, and sometimes with pedantic ostentation. Having little intercourse with the world, they are easily defrauded, and dupes to the deceitful, wherever they go; their money is lavished with the most thoughtless profusion; fine clothes for his girl, a silver watch and silver buckles for himself, are often the sole return for years of labour and hardship.'[12]

Nelson realised that many of his men were far more complex, but

he was ready to assist them over everyday hurdles, great and small.
He witnessed a legal document for John Brock, who granted a power
of attorney to his wife to enable her to receive his money in England,
and for others he kept an eye open for suitable promotions and a
watch over their prize dues. It was also his custom to address a
company when leaving a command, and to assure the men in his
Norfolk drawl that his concern for them would continue and that he
would be ever ready to answer their calls for assistance. Examples of
his willingness to fulfil those obligations in earlier times will be remembered, and the men of the *Agamemnon* and *Captain* likewise benefited.[13]

Thus Robert Robinson, a boatswain of the *Captain* who later ran
upon hard times, reminded Nelson that he had once told him he
'should write if occasion required'. Even so humble a servant as Andrea
Peri Romano, who had shaved and dressed Nelson when he stayed
with a Mr North in Bastia in 1796, felt able to send an appeal. Many
sailors remembered Nelson's helping hand. A sailmaker of the *Captain*,
fighting to escape imprisonment for debt, received written testimony
that Nelson knew 'this person very well' and considered him 'a worthy
good man'. The Colletts – William, a gunner, and his son Isaac, a
young gentleman of the *Agamemnon* – left testimony to their captain's
kindness, as did John Wilkinson, a Cumberland man, born in 1762.
He served his apprenticeship in Irish colliers and shipped aboard
traders and transports before being drafted into the *Agamemnon*.
Nelson was impressed with his handling of the wheel during the
Channel cruise of 1793, made him a boatswain's mate and eventually
got him promoted to the *Ganges*. When Wilkinson's career subsequently stumbled, he wrote to his old benefactor, hoping he had not
been 'forgotten', and was rewarded with an appointment as
boatswain's mate of a sloop. As a frail Greenwich pensioner he still
recalled Nelson with a mixture of gratitude and awe:

It is truly gratifying to hear him speak of Nelson [wrote the interviewer]. 'He
was a daring man, sir,' said he. 'There was nothing he would not do if it came
into his head. We could always tell of a morning, when he came on deck,
whether we should have anything to do. When he came up with his iron-
bound hat on and his roast-beef coat, we knew he was up to something, and
it used to be a sort of warning to us to get ready.' The old man's face will
kindle as he speaks, and you see that he feels what he is talking of.[14]

The seamen who followed Nelson into the *Captain* were his most dedicated followers, and nearly all of them were young and vigorous. They included the twenty-four-year-old able seaman Tom Allen, a Sculthorpe ploughman with an almost incomprehensible Norfolk dialect; the Fearney boys of Newcastle, William twenty-four and James a year younger; Francis Cook, aged twenty-six, from Sudbury in Suffolk; Thomas Ramsay of Berwick, a sturdy man of middling height, but in his thirties or early forties; a twenty-six-year-old Lincolnshire man named John Sykes; Joseph King, a twenty-nine-year-old boatswain; and at least one American, a twenty-four-year-old able seaman, William Hayward.

Most were uncomplicated men, loyal, conscientious, valorous and fiercely protective of a commander they had come to rely upon for their employment, welfare and self-respect. King, for example, had been with Nelson in the *Boreas*, and would soon owe to him an appointment as boatswain in the Gibraltar dockyard. Despite the social gulf between the two, one an officer and gentleman of the quarter-deck and the other a petty officer of the lower deck, they became remarkably close. King worshipped Nelson, and acknowledged the many favours done him. When he heard that his old commander had been injured at Tenerife, he wrote from Gibraltar, recalling 'that dreadful moment' when he thought that he had lost 'my best of friends'. A few months later, blessed with a daughter on Christmas Day 1797, the admiring boatswain named her Mary Nelson King. The admiral was touched by the tribute, and as late as 1804 we find him gratuitously sending King one hundred Spanish dollars as a 'present from me'.[15]

Stereotypical sailors apart, Nelson's self-elected guard were by no means all primitive beings. Of sixteen men acknowledging their receipt of prize money in one account, only five were illiterate and unable to sign their names in full. John Lovell, a small, powerful *Agamemnon* from London, was the son of a modest merchant skipper and had benefited from a little schooling. King wrote a fair letter. John Sykes was even more accomplished. He joined the *Agamemnon* in 1793, and devotedly served Nelson as able seaman, ship's corporal, gunner's mate and coxswain. Hailing from humble agricultural folk of Kirton, Lincolnshire, he had lost his father, though a step-parent, Thomas Huddlestone, earned a living as a fishmonger on the riverside in Lincoln. John's brother, Robinson Sykes, was also in the navy, and as far as can be told John himself took to the life. He had raw courage, for which Nelson referred to him as his 'brave Lincoln friend', yet he could write a fair letter, and exhibited unusual sensitivity. Ralph Miller, soon to become Nelson's flag captain, thought Sykes good commissioned officer material. 'His manners and conduct are so entirely above his situation,' he wrote, 'that Nature certainly intended him for a gentleman.'[16]

No fewer than sixty-five of those who followed Nelson into the *Captain* were soldiers of the 69th (South Lincolnshire) Regiment who had been acting as marines aboard the *Agamemnon*. These, too, thought Nelson a good provider and protector. Prompted by his friend Villettes, the lieutenant colonel of the regiment, he had intervened to secure them fair shares of prize money.[17]

Most notable of the six officers of the 69th who transferred was Lieutenant Charles Bradshaw Peirson, a handsome twenty-two-year old Londoner who had become one of Nelson's most dependable supporters. When Nelson first saw Peirson during the sieges in Corsica two years before he was wearing a Neapolitan uniform, for he had somehow got from Britain to Italy and won the patronage of Sir William Hamilton. It was Hamilton who recommended Peirson to Hood and his entourage, and he proved a useful aide-de-camp to Villettes before getting an ensign's commission in the 50th Regiment of British Foot the following September. A man eager to be the first with good news, Nelson assured Hamilton of his own 'sincere regard and esteem' for Peirson, whose 'propriety . . . in every situation' had won the praise of superiors.[18]

In March 1795 Peirson advanced to a lieutenancy in the 69th and it was in that capacity that he served on the *Agamemnon*. Despite his obvious military and diplomatic talents, facilitated by a rare command of the Italian language, Peirson's prospects in a force as elitist as the army were doubtful, and there was an insecure restlessness about him. Josiah, Nelson's stepson, thought him the mercantile type. Nevertheless, Nelson's affection and support for his 'poor soldier-officer' were rewarded with an extreme loyalty. Though a redcoat, Peirson 'always' found Nelson 'my friend and protector', and was so 'distressed' at the thought of being left behind in the *Agamemnon* that he implored the commodore to specifically request his transfer. Peirson wanted 'much to go with me', Nelson wrote Jervis, 'if it be possible, pray sir, indulge me'.[19]

Twenty-two of the seamen who joined Peirson in that transfer had also, in fact, been soldiers by profession. Some of them were Austrian soldiers from De Vins's army, captured by the French and liberated by the *Blanche*, one of the commodore's frigates. Now they happily served as landmen, the rating given to inexperienced sailors, enriching the *Captain* with linguistic skills and specialist knowledge of use to a squadron still cooperating with the allied armies of Europe.

4

Nelson regarded the commissioned officers of the *Agamemnon* as the best in the fleet, and 'much in the habit of doing handsome things'. The admiration was mutual, and all but one lieutenant stayed with him when he went to the *Captain* in June 1796. The exception was Lieutenant Suckling. A family death had left only 'the lunatic' between him and the Suckling estate of Woodton, and he intended to return to England, marry, and claim his inheritance. But the decision to leave the fleet would cost him a part in the battle of Cape St Vincent, for which he later said he almost hanged himself, and an almost certain elevation to the post of commander, and it disrupted his professional progress. He eventually returned to active service and commanded the small *Neptune* in the North Sea until 1801, but never rose above lieutenant.[20]

The other lieutenants remained with Nelson – Berry, Spicer, Noble, Summers and Compton, acting out of solid self-interest as well as simple affection and admiration for their commander. For no captain in the fleet fought more tenaciously for the promotion of his officers than Nelson. He had gained the goodwill of several commanders-in-chief, from Hood to Jervis, and successfully traded upon it by seeking rewards for fellow officers. 'I will not forget Capt. Cockburne [Cockburn], nor any other person you are interested in,' replied Jervis on one occasion. On another he responded, 'I have written in such strong terms to the Admiralty in praise of your first, second and third lieutenants that I think . . . one [Berry] at least will be made a captain immediately, and I think Spicer and Noble cannot be long without it.' Additionally, Nelson's own enterprise created opportunities for his lieutenants to distinguish themselves, and when they did he praised lavishly, pressing their claims to promotion in dispatches and verbal reports. Ultimately several, including Andrews, received 'hero promotions' for conduct in the face of the enemy.[21]

Nelson's success in creating promotions had one disadvantage: the high turnover of lieutenants on the *Agamemnon*. As one officer after another was promoted out of the ship, the captain was constantly searching for new talent to replace the old, and having to begin the process of nurturing and training again. When he was with the fleet, Nelson routinely sat on boards examining prospective lieutenants, and got a view of the upcoming crop, but he was still occasionally obliged to sail short-handed.

But he gained satisfaction from helping good officers and benefiting from the loyalty and effort such favours engendered. Five lieutenants had originally sailed with Nelson to the Mediterranean – Martin Hinton, Joseph Bullen, George Andrews, Wenman Allison and Thomas Edmonds. After his success in Naples, Nelson had persuaded Hood to promote the senior lieutenants to the flagship, Bullen in 1793 and Hinton the following year, and from there both stepped briskly to the rank of commander, the first almost immediately. Neither officer fared particularly well beyond Nelson's ken, however. Invalided home from Corsica, Bullen made the all-important step to post captain in 1796 and did good service in the Mediterranean and Ireland, but ultimately had to settle for a command in the Sea Fencibles. Nevertheless, he lived until July 1857, long enough to climb the lists of captains and flag officers by seniority and become a full admiral in 1841. By contrast Hinton never even reached the post-captains' list and died a commander in the Sea Fencibles in October 1814.[22]

Nelson was proud of his achievements for Bullen and Hinton, but made heavier work of nudging the career of Andrews forward, despite the lieutenant's distinguished services aboard the *Agamemnon*. There was little help at home. Andrews had lost his early patrons, Hugh Pigot and John Nott, and felt adrift in the service. He had met Hood during the 'Dutch armament' of 1789, and used the good offices of both Nelson and Sir Gilbert Elliot to renew the connection in 1794, but even that lever was lost when the admiral sailed to England the same year. Hood's departure also disempowered Nelson, who had less sway with Admiral Hotham, and he resorted to string-pulling in England. While the Andrews family lobbied Earl Spencer, Nelson tried to find Andrews a position in the Channel fleet, but when its commander, Earl Howe, replied with 'a jumble of nonsense', he concluded that the 'great men' had 'neither gratitude nor regard'.[23]

There was an upside to the delay in Andrews's progress, however. It had only been with considerable difficulty that the vacancies left by Bullen and Hinton had been filled. Andrews, Allison and Edmonds had moved up to fill the senior positions on the *Agamemnon*, but juniors proved stubbornly hard to find. After using three temporary stand-ins from the *Victory*, Nelson had eventually replaced Bullen in October 1793 by the newly commissioned William Lucas, and the following August Hinton's place was taken by another raw lieutenant, nineteen-year-old Edward Cheetham. The son of a Derbyshire squire and a favourite of Hood, Cheetham had joined the service at eleven and served aboard the admiral's ship, the *Duke*. Unfortunately, neither of these replacements remained with Nelson as long as a year. Lucas was transferred to another ship after only five months, while Cheetham was wounded in the battle off Hyères in July 1795 and invalided home. The young man fortunately recovered and his career rebounded; he would be buried an admiral in 1862, having fought in the spectacular victory over Algiers in 1816.[24]

Given these problems, Nelson relied upon First Lieutenant Andrews for what stability there was on his quarterdeck between August 1794 and November the following year. Indeed, though Nelson fought for Andrews's promotion selflessly he anticipated that it would precipitate a crisis on the *Agamemnon*. For if Andrews left the ship, it would more than create a gap in the commissioned ranks; it would open a path for the next officer in line to become the senior lieutenant, and Nelson doubted that he could work with him. Wenman Allison was a good-hearted young man when sober, but he was descending into alcoholism, and became 'mad' when drunk. Worse, he was infecting a junior officer, Lieutenant Suckling, who had come back to his old ship to replace Lucas. Normally 'a very attentive, good officer', Suckling became 'rather troublesome' under the influence of Allison. Nelson remembered his days on the *Seahorse* and hated inebriation in officers. He should have disciplined Allison, but was sorry for him, and allowed matters to reach an alarming pass. So bad, in fact, that by May 1795 Nelson had decided that if Andrews left he would rather quit the ship himself than suffer Allison as its second officer. In this mood he wrote an unusually bleak and revealing letter to Fanny:

I am tired of *Agamemnon*. Allison is so much given to liquor and then behaves so ill that I have enough to do to refrain from bringing him to a court martial. I have ever heartily repented taking him. I ought to have known enough of him before. He only, with one other [Suckling], will be the cause of my leaving the ship . . . I think Andrews will go into the *Victory*, and sooner than have Allison first lieutenant I would quit the ship and go home by land. However, he does not know my intentions, or anyone else. He will soon be broke [dismissed the service] when left to himself.[25]

The crisis was solved providentially. Allison went down sick, and a 'survey' of his health, conducted at St Fiorenzo on 1 July, pronounced the climate injurious to a recovery. Three days later he was sent home 'much impaired'. As soon as he reached London the ravaged officer was confined to his bed at 1 King Street in St James's Square, from where he tried to secure half-pay and leave of absence covering his period of incapacity. But there would be no return to duty. Allison made his way to Bedford, and died there on 17 October 1795, mourned by a surviving sister, Phylis.[26]

On the *Agamemnon*, the departure of Lieutenant Allison cleared the shadows from the promotion of the much abler Andrews. To Nelson's delight Andrews was posted commander in November, an acknowledgement of his meritorious services, particularly against the *Ça Ira*. However, he too found the upward ladder a slippery one, and it was not the beginning of the bright career Nelson had wanted. Poor Andrews remained dogged by ill health and bad luck. Too sick to take up his new command, he failed to recuperate in Pisa and was forced to leave, enfeebled, for England at the end of 1795. A year passed and he was still recovering in Bath, but Nelson had attested to his services in writing and got him to post-captain in April 1796. That was the summit of Andrews's career; beyond lay a long, degrading slide downhill. There was no ship, and the new captain began drinking heavily on half-pay, amid bouts of illness and disability. In 1801 Andrews visited the Admiralty, then headed by Jervis himself, and was offered the choice of commanding a hulk or waiting for a frigate, but he got neither. A few years later he was to be seen in a restless retirement in Tiverton in Devon, using a cane to support a knee crippled with rheumatism, and looking for light duties. Captain Andrews was put in charge of the impress service in Dublin in 1806, but another injury the following year damaged his left leg and sent him home for good. The closing years were sad and final. Penury . . . appeals for outstanding prize money, which agent McArthur charitably paid charge-free . . . a humiliating but unsuccessful petition for relief . . . an early death at the age of forty-three in July 1810 . . . a wife, Anne, in search of a naval pension . . . and an only son dying of consumption at thirty-one. Andrews was yet another light, tended into flame by an unusual commander, only to be extinguished by neglect and misfortune.[27]

In 1795 the promotion of Andrews was the last of four quarter-deck losses suffered by the *Agamemnon* that year. In April, Edmonds, another of the original lieutenants, had been discharged sick. Allison and Cheetham had followed in July, and Andrews was promoted in November. But after a stormy passage, Nelson suddenly hit clear water as an exceptionally able set of recruits plugged the gaps. The newcomers were Peter Spicer, James Summers, James Noble, Henry Compton and Edward Berry – the veritable quintet that followed Nelson into the *Captain*.

Spicer, who replaced Edmonds at St Fiorenzo on 18 April 1795, came particularly well recommended. A native of Saltash in Cornwall, he had officially joined the navy as an able seaman in March 1777, though in truth he was only eleven years old and a protégé of his captain, John Robinson of the *Queen*. Despite this early act of patronage and a life at sea – he remained unmarried – Peter moved forward slowly, rising by merit rather than influence. Seven ships later he got his commission in 1794, and served under Nelson's closest friends and allies. At one time or other he was with Jervis on the *Foudroyant*, Locker on the *Cambridge* at Plymouth, Pole on the *Colossus*, and in Hood's *Victory*. Nelson also remembered that Spicer had commanded a gunboat during the Corsican campaign, a perfect training for inshore work.[28]

James Summers also climbed aboard at St Fiorenzo, but not until the following July. Nelson knew less about Summers, and his commission was only a provisional one, but he came with the blessing of Captain Locker. For many worrying months the Admiralty dithered about confirming the boy's commission, but Nelson lobbied for him and eventually got it ratified in September 1796.

Perhaps an even happier discovery was the excellent James Noble. This son of an American Loyalist had been forced to flee to England as a boy, and enlisted in the navy in 1787. He had been on board the *Bedford* when it had taken its historic beating from the *Ça Ira* and *Censeur* in the battle off Genoa in 1795. The following October, Noble was transferred to the *Agamemnon* from Hotham's *Britannia*, initially as an acting lieutenant. William Hoste for one recognised Noble and was glad to see him, for it had been he (then a midshipman) who had first shown the Hostes the sights of Portsmouth back in 1793. Soon Hoste was describing Noble as 'a very good young man' who had 'behaved very well to me the short time he was on board', and Nelson was no less pleased, admiring the new lieutenant's irrepressible enthusiasm to be among the first in every service. Noble, we have seen, was captured in 1795 but exchanged, and it was Nelson who paid for his board and lodging in Genoa during the period he waited, beached, for the ship to collect him. Long afterwards Noble remembered many acts of kindness Nelson had done him, and like King the boatswain named one of his children for the commodore. He wrote of his gratitude in a letter, expressing 'the honour I have been so fortunate as to have had of having served under the immediate command of your lordship, and the obligations I am under to your lordship for the rank I now hold in the service'.[29]

The next year, in 1796, the *Agamemnon* added two more solid lieutenants to its complement, Henry Compton, one of Noble's old shipmates from the *Britannia*, and Edward Berry, who came from England on the *Comet* to join Nelson as first lieutenant in May. Compton had been seven years in the service, beginning his naval career as an able seaman on the *Cumberland* in 1789. Attracting the attention of Sir John Jervis, he passed from the flagship *Victory* to the *Agamemnon* in March as a newly commissioned lieutenant, and followed Nelson devotedly for three years.[30]

Of all the lieutenants of the *Agamemnon* one was destined to achieve a legendary status: Edward Berry, later one of Nelson's greatest fighting captains. The twenty-eight-year-old Berry was of merchant stock, but his family knew Lord Mulgrave, at one time first lord of the Admiralty, and it was through him that the boy had entered the king's service. In 1779 he volunteered for the *Burford*, bound for the East Indies, but it took him fifteen years to get a commission. He came to Nelson from England, where he had met Fanny, who was duly impressed. He certainly looked a hero. Slim, fair-haired, blue-eyed and dashing, he was as nervy as a cat preparing to pounce. 'He seems a gentleman and an officer from appearances,' Nelson told his wife within days of meeting his new first lieutenant. 'I have no doubt but I shall like him.' From the beginning the commodore treated his new subordinate with marked generosity. When Berry helped capture a prize in September, Nelson begged Jervis to make him an acting flag captain of the *Captain* to give him a greater share of the spoils. If Jervis declined the request, he wrote, 'I must endeavour to show my sense of his gallantry and good conduct in other ways.'[31]

Most of Nelson's lieutenants also liked their captain. Of the thirteen principal commissioned officers who served him on the *Agamemnon*, at least nine owed him crucial promotions. Berry would make the most use of his advantages, however. He had sailed with Jervis on the *Boyne*, and the admiral vouched for his 'talents, great courage, and laudable ambition'. And so it turned out. In years ahead, after Nelson had seen him to post-captain, Berry's nose for action became proverbial in the fleet. If there was going to be a battle, people said, there you were sure to find Berry. His very presence seemed to promise powder smoke. True to form, he arrived just in time for the battle of Trafalgar in 1805, commanding – of all ships – the old *Agamemnon* herself. 'Here comes Berry!' Nelson is said to have exclaimed at his approach. '*Now* we shall have a fight!'[32]

5

Berry, Spicer, Noble, Compton and Summers all flourished under Nelson's leadership and played key roles in refashioning the new ship's company.

Below them the young gentlemen of the *Agamemnon* quarterdeck had also benefited from his patronage. Nelson always interested himself in them, partly because something of the boy still lingered inside him, and partly, one suspects, because they substituted for the children he had never had.

The 'class' of the *Agamemnon* were a varied lot, in ability, interest and ambition. Some were hell-bent for promotion, impatient to get their commissions before the war ended. Whereas the eyes of the lieutenants were set upon the post of commander and the rank of post-captain, the midshipmen and master's mates had the lieutenant's commission in their sights. With the king's commission in their pockets they became, if they were not already, officers and gentlemen, and their names were entered on lists of the permanent dependants of the crown. The most successful, such as Weatherhead, Hoste or Bolton, carried the hopes of gentrified families with them, but they rubbed shoulders with others Nelson had raised from the common ranks from time to time. One such was poor William D. Williams, who died of his wounds at Vado in 1795. A number were older men, who had few chances of reaching that treasured lieutenancy. When they joined the ship as able seamen in 1793 twenty-seven-year-old David Lindsey was a pressed man from Dunbartonshire, and Ralph Woodman of Morpeth was thirty-two, while Thomas Lund enlisted as able seaman in 1796 at the age of thirty-five. They were all rated midshipmen by Nelson, but none made lieutenant. John Wood of Sunderland was luckier. He enlisted with Nelson as able seaman at the age of thirty-three in 1793, became midshipman and master's mate, passed his examination, and in July 1796 got an acting position as lieutenant of the *Blonde*.[33]

Nelson fussed over the youngsters like a benign uncle, and praised when they applied themselves. William Bolton, a studious youth who thought nothing of reading late into the night, went beyond his duties to compile a neatly-written manual for junior officers, complete with loving illustrations of knots, ropes and sails and notes on etiquette and propriety. Josiah Nisbet, Nelson's stepson, had the most obvious claim upon his attention. Josiah benefited from Fanny's constant concern and sprouted into a strong, healthy boy as tall as his captain. Occasionally something engaged his interest, such as the epaulettes Nelson had to fit to his uniform in 1795, but though he wrote to his mother two 'Dear Mamma' letters in 1793, he was not a natural correspondent ('Josiah begins to threaten you with a letter, and Time may produce it'), and he rarely shone about his general business. 'You seem to think Josiah is a master of languages,' Nelson disabused Fanny. 'I must say he is the same exactly as when an infant, and likes apples and port wine, but it will be difficult to make him speak French, much more Italian. However, I hope his heart is good, and that is the principal.' 'Hope' was the telling word. Josiah's manners and conversation were boorish, something Nelson never liked even in a man. Although he knew Josiah would 'never be troubled with the graces', he tried to convince himself that he was 'a good officer' and had 'many good points about him'.[34]

Youngest of the aspiring gentlemen of the *Agamemnon* was probably Isaac Charles Smith Collett (the son of Nelson's gunner), who may have been a tender thirteen years when he joined the ship in November 1794. However, the most universally beloved were Hoste and Weatherhead. Like Josiah, Hoste advanced from captain's servant to midshipman, and Nelson could not avoid comparing him to Josiah's disadvantage. Hoste excelled at his work, loved it dearly and was grateful for every favour bestowed. No reverse seemed to crush his love of life, nor sour his inclination to see the best in those around him. 'In his navigation you will find him equally forward,' Nelson wrote to the boy's father. 'He highly deserves anything I can do to make him happy. Do not spoil him by giving him too much money. He has all that he wishes – sometimes more. I *love* him, therefore shall say no more on that subject.'[35]

Hoste's uncomplaining and irrepressible optimism, as well as his infatuation for the ship, leap from the vivid snapshots of life aboard that he put into his letters home. They reveal a community very different from the archetypal picture of the harsh man-of-war. Even breaking a leg in a cable scuttle of the prize at Alassio in 1795 barely dented the fifteen-year-old's verve. As his brother learned:

in a few days [I] shall be as hearty as ever . . . I comfort myself with singing 'My Dearest Peg' all weathers, and I assure you . . . if I were to go on board of any ship in the British navy I could not be more happy, nor could I have more care taken of me, since this accident, than has happened on board the *Agamemnon*. Directly I was brought on board, I was carried down into Mr [Lieutenant Maurice William] Suckling's cabin, where I have remained ever since. Mr Suckling has behaved to me like a father. He has been with me all the while, except when his duty called him away. To add to my misfortunes, my good friend Mr [John] Weatherhead is away. He was sent in a prize to St Fiorenzo. I had a letter from him the other day. He was very well, and desires [me to send] his compliments to my father, &c. As worthy a young man as ever lived. I got up yesterday for the first time, and I think if you were to see poor Billy Shanks [himself] hopping about with two crutches you would split your sides with laughter. Captain Nelson is very well. He often comes down to see me, and tells me to get everything I want from him.[36]

The families of the Weatherheads, Hostes and Sucklings were acquainted, and the boys compared the local news that reached them in letters from home. They also rallied around Midshipman Hoste during a series of trials. The spring after his accident in the cable scuttle he went down with fever. At the earliest convenience Nelson sent the boy ashore to convalesce with the Pollards in Leghorn at his own expense. There, in a homely cottage where Mrs Pollard, 'a very pleasant woman' and 'good doctor', reproduced the comforts of her old Sussex home and William enjoyed the care of the inestimable Miss Wood, every officer of the ship came calling at one time or another. 'The civilities I received . . . are such as I shall never be able to return, but I do every thing in my power to oblige them you may be sure,' William wrote. But back on board, the boy suffered his last disaster – a fracture of the other leg. Weatherhead, who had 'nearly made himself ill in attending me' during previous misfortunes, speedily returned to the task with an astonishing 'goodness of heart' that soon had William back on his feet. 'I have strongly recommended . . . him not to break any more limbs,' Nelson observed wryly.[37]

From the uniform consideration dispensed by Nelson, William never suspected that difficulties were simmering between the captain and his father. Unbeknown to Nelson, the Reverend Dixon Hoste was strapped for money. Financial difficulties had cost him a patrimony, and it was Coke who rescued him with the living of Tittleshall and a residence at Godwick House. Consequently, it was Nelson rather than the reverend who effectively financed the boy's naval career. He started by improving the allowances William's rating as a captain's servant permitted, relying upon the boy's father to reimburse him according to their arrangement, and even after the youngster's wages increased with rank the captain continued to cover occasional extraordinary expenses. Months turned into years, but the Reverend Hoste sent Nelson little or no money, despite a reluctant but direct protest. Nelson shielded young William from the truth, declining to embitter his happy progress, but privately confessed to Fanny that he was 'very angry'.[38]

Most, if not all, of the young *Agamemnons* of the quarterdeck experienced their commander's benevolence. Midshipman Bolton was kindly warned about the dangers of putting loose talk into his letters home, and also received generous amounts of money. And Midshipman Charles David Williams, the son of a police magistrate, who had been captured with five men on a voyage from Leghorn to Toulon at the end of 1793, was loaned money to re-equip himself after his release. Nelson was their role model and guardian, and it is not surprising that eleven of them followed him into the *Captain* in June 1796.[39]

Under Nelson the lieutenants, midshipmen and master's mates had innumerable opportunities to shine, and he invariably advertised their merits, seeking their promotions as a suitable return upon his own valuable services. Before long commanders-in-chief who felt obliged to him were repeating his assessments in their dispatches. Thus, in September 1796 Jervis drew the Admiralty's attention to Cockburn, Spicer, Berry and Noble, who 'expose their persons on all occasions with that cool deliberate courage which forms so prominent a feature in the[ir] commodore's character, and I beg leave to recommend them to their lordship's favour and protection'. Jervis's influence with the board of Admiralty was considerable, but Spencer's actions also reflected a direct sense of obligation to Nelson himself. In October 1796, for example, they made Berry a commander, ostensibly because

of the capture of Porto Ferraio, but in truth – as Jervis told Nelson
– 'more from a desire to gratify you than on account of his merit'.[40]

6

Nelson's leadership was largely based upon personal affection, professional admiration and self-interest, and conformed to the eighteenth-
century ideal of paternalism, with its tradition of service and reward.
Those who follow the *Agamemnons* who served with Nelson until the
summer of 1797, when their patron eventually left the Mediterranean,
will see that no fewer than sixteen lieutenants and young gentlemen
benefited from significant promotions during that time. Three
(Andrews, Bullen and Berry) made post-captain; four others (Hinton,
Spicer, Noble and Nisbet) were promoted commander; and eight
(Suckling, Fellows, Summers, Wood, Bolton, Weatherhead, Charles D.
Williams and Withers) got their lieutenants' commissions, with a ninth
(Hoste) in the offing.

Perhaps it is also significant that although most of those promoted
were fine officers, deserving of further advance, their careers seem to
have been so dependent upon Nelson that they stagnated without him.
The disappointing fates of Bullen, Hinton and Andrews have already
been noted. Spicer, Noble and Compton also failed to maximise their
potential. With Nelson's help they all became commanders, Spicer and
Noble in 1797 and Compton two years later. The first two also
progressed to the rank of post-captain in 1802, but vegetated thereafter, Noble with the Sea Fencibles in Sussex, and Spicer with the Sea
Fencibles and impress services. Spicer finished his war in 1816 with
a humiliating 'out-pension' from Greenwich Hospital, and died in
October 1830. Noble survived longer and received his flag in 1837,
but his career after leaving Nelson's command was still a marked anti-
climax. Compton died a 'retired captain' in 1847, having accepted
redundancy as a condition of reaching 'post' rank.[41]

Of the commissioned officers and aspirants of the *Agamemnon*,
only Berry and Hoste scaled enviable heights, earning knighthoods
and places in the naval pantheon of the day. Three of Hoste's old ship
and schoolmates also eventually became post-captains: Bolton, who
enjoyed several commands and died a knight of the realm in 1830;
Withers, the ex-schoolmaster; and Josiah Nisbet. But Weatherhead
died young; Fellows wasted away with the Belfast impress service, and
he died a 'retired commander' in 1833; Suckling gave up the navy;

and Collett, Williams and Eager never rose above the rank of lieutenant.[42]

So much for the future, but from the quarterdecks, cockpits and wardrooms of the *Agamemnon* and *Captain* those far-distant clouds were hardly visible. With the resilience, optimism and belief in life eternal that distinguish youth, the protégés still spoke of worlds to conquer in the secure knowledge that Nelson would be their aid and mentor. They loved him for it, and when they began returning to England in 1797 said so loudly and publicly. Fanny found Berry 'one of the most grateful creatures I ever met', and saw a man named Brown who had travelled from Bristol to Bath to tell her about the 'great kindnesses' he owed her husband. In London, Nelson's brother Maurice listened to Spicer and Noble speaking 'in raptures' about their commander and venerating him 'as their father', while Lieutenant Peirson had no sooner put a foot on English soil than he was 'very desirous of being with you again'.[43]

As life paled for many of them, the memories of Nelson's command grew ever more poignant, achieving the status of golden interludes in long and uncertain careers. Sometimes they wrote to him, seeking help or to return to his service. Three such letters, from Andrews in Tiverton, Spicer in Saltash and Noble in Bishop Teignton, reached Nelson shortly before his death. And forty years after that Bullen was still thinking of the late 'friend' about whom 'any thing . . . must ever be dear to me'.[44]

Growing up, learning and working aboard the *Agamemnon* and *Captain* may have been habitually gruelling and dangerous, but for many it was neither a barren nor loveless experience, but rather a rich personal heritage.

7

The *Captain* of seventy-four guns was the ship of the line Nelson had always wanted, the ideal compromise between speed, manoeuvrability and punching power. Fourteen years old, she carried an armament of nine-, eighteen- and thirty-two-pounder guns, and the names of 450 men graced her books. The team of officers Nelson had brought from the *Agamemenon* joined newcomers, some already with the *Captain* and others acquired elsewhere. Philip Thomas was master, Thomas Eshelby surgeon and William Williams purser, while Lieutenant John Davies transferred from the *Lively* in August. A commodore was almost always burdened with diplomatic correspondence, and Nelson now had a secretary, John Philip Castang. The ranks of his junior officers were also reinforced. A nineteen-year-old Scot, George Kippin, was already attached to the *Captain*, but Frederick Ruckhart was brought from the *Vanneau* in October and James Francis Goddench and Thomas Knight, with some old *Agamemnons*, were promoted from the lower deck.

As a commodore Nelson deployed a squadron of ships, and at different times commanded many of the captains of the Mediterranean fleet. They were a rich crop, perhaps as good as Britain had ever produced, and shared an *esprit de corps* which even such a preoccupied, love-sick teenage observer as Betsy Wynne could feel. In the Mediterranean with her family, she thought the captains of Jervis's fleet 'good honest creatures' who were 'very kind' and bound in the common cause. 'They live like brothers together,' she wrote, 'and give all they have.'[45]

Nelson had fought to be a commodore, but not every captain made the transition from commanding a single ship to managing a squadron or a fleet successfully. There were some truly disastrous failures – and among officers with first-rate abilities. Rodney had been a weak flag officer, alienating superiors and equals with an unpleasant blend of arrogance, spite and untrustworthiness, but his achievement was rivalled by the even more remarkable Lord Cochrane, who eventually rose to become Rear Admiral of England. Cochrane's brilliant successes were those of a single-ship commander, a creative but restless loner resentful of control or indifference. He inspired immense regard, and sometimes hero-worship, among the crews of the ships he personally commanded, but proved to be unusually inept in charge of a squadron. This weak leadership only surfaced during his command of the Chilean navy between 1818 and 1823. Working with a cabal of favourites, by no means all of them good choices, and indignant at any resistance to his ideas, which he attributed to malice or corruption, he sowed fierce divisions throughout his forces. Estranged, accused and sometimes persecuted, some officers were almost driven to become the enemies Cochrane had imagined them. It was a spectacular failure to build cohesion and team spirit.[46]

Few captains felt undervalued in Nelson's command. True, he was by nature a quiet, introspective man, apt to fall into long silences at the dinner table, but he was approachable and easy-mannered, praised openly and earnestly, and on occasion had a most pleasing smile. One of his attributes, by no means common among men, was inherent sympathy. He was a good listener with an instinct to help, and favours great and small came naturally to him. And since willing horses receive the greatest burdens, diverse problems constantly rapped upon his door. Here we find him shopping for artificial flowers needed by a fellow captain; there, sympathetically aiding and abetting the intrigues of a certain Mrs Wilby, who was distressed that her husband might discover that she had been receiving letters from another man. More often he was approached about promotion, prize money, wages or interpersonal difficulties. People are usually drawn to those who seem to care about them, and Nelson became a resort for the troubled, even among the iron stalwarts of the Mediterranean fleet. In April 1794, for instance, the manly Fremantle, tired of some 'hectoring' colleague behaving 'like a bully of a bawdy house', turned to Nelson. 'Write to Nelson in consequence,' he entered in his diary. 'He condoles with me, and offers to take day and day about with the *Agamemnon*. Very civil, but decline.'[47]

A more substantial beneficiary was Ralph Willett Miller, who became one of the ablest captains in the fleet. Another American Loyalist, Miller had left his native New England as a boy and joined the Royal Navy in 1778. Nelson had known him since the beginning of the French war, and noticed the combination of personal piety and professional initiative not unlike his own. When Miller returned from escapades it was his custom to thank God and to pray for his beloved Ann and their two daughters. He was widely admired for his skill and ingenuity. In 1793 Miller 'very much distinguished himself on many occasions on shore, particularly in burning the ships at Toulon', and the following year he risked his life in gallant but unsuccessful attempts to destroy the enemy squadron in Golfe Jouan with fireships. Nelson considered Miller to be 'a most exceeding good officer and worthy man', and Sir Gilbert Elliot could not praise him too highly. Miller, he said, was 'a very sensitive character, who I ever venture to assure you is more jealous of his honour than desirous even of advancement. He is really one of the best and most distinguished officers in the fleet, and he is also remarkable for more accomplishment and more taste for other pursuits not merely professional than the greatest number of post-captains.' Others agreed that Miller was 'an officer of infinite resource'.[48]

Commodore Nelson was also struck by Miller's protective but firm control of his men. Hoste, who later served under him, said that anyone who felt 'uncomfortable under his command . . . must be miserable indeed under that of any other', and small incidents spoke volumes about his careful stewardship. After a respected oarsman had been killed off Cadiz in 1797, Miller 'had two 18 pound shot tied to the body, and when ready to bury it, I made the crew lay their oars across, and each, by my example, uttering an emphatic "God bless him", we committed his remains to the deep. Few have prayers equally sincere said over them . . .' Men watching this touching tribute of a captain to one of their comrades had no doubts about how deeply they were valued.[49]

Unfortunately, the beginning of 1796 found Miller greatly dissatis-fied with his situation. Despite his services, he had twice seen junior officers promoted over his head, and it was rumoured that an expected promotion to post-captain had not been confirmed by the Admiralty. Miller felt trapped in the unhappy command of the *Mignonne* frigate, and unburdened his thoughts to both Elliot and Nelson. In August, Nelson's own rank of commodore was confirmed. It entitled him to name a flag captain to manage his ship and leave him free to direct a squadron, and he immediately named Miller for the post, supposing the latter 'would be glad to leave his present command'. As it happened, Miller had already got another post, as captain of the frigate *Unite*, but he readily abandoned it to join his benefactor, fully aware that he owed the appointment to the commodore's 'kindness in asking for me from a situation that was intolerable'.[50]

In choosing Miller, Nelson knew he had secured the right officer to establish the regime he wanted aboard the *Captain*, but he also illustrated his aptitude for understanding the problems of other offi-cers and searching for solutions. John Gourly may also have bene-fited. At one time he had been a temporary lieutenant on the *Agamemnon*, and later he commanded the *Vanneau* brig and served with her under Nelson's command in 1796. Gourly was generally a safe officer, but the *Vanneau* struck a rock off Porto Ferraio in October 1796 and sank. Nelson was there when it happened, and his boats tried and failed to haul the stricken brig to safety. There was an inevitable court martial.

That occurred on board the *Barfleur* in Mortella Bay, St Fiorenzo, on 29 October, and Nelson was a member of the court under the pres-idency of Admiral William Waldegrave. The details of the affair need not detain us, except for the small one relevant to our theme. According to the regulations of the time, the senior captain of a fleet took

precedence over the other captains forming a court, and served immediately beneath any admirals present. Nothing was said about
commodores. They were not full-blown flag officers like the admirals,
but superior in rank to any captain, including the senior captain. In
compliance with the strict wording of the regulations, Nelson, although
a commodore, had been deferring to Jervis's flag captain, Robert
Calder, and taking his place with the ordinary captains, but when the
case of Gourly was brought forward he protested. Nelson submitted
a memorial to the court asserting the right of commodores to take
precedence over senior captains. There was no resentment at his intervention, Nelson's claim was willingly admitted, and he duly took his
place before Calder. Pride and punctilio were both important considerations for Nelson, but his decision to mount the challenge at the
beginning of Gourly's trial rather than, say, before the preceding case
of a surgeon's mate indicted for mutinous behaviour, may not have
been accidental. The likelihood is that Nelson wanted a bigger voice
in the proceedings, and used his influence on behalf of the accused.
Gourly would probably have been acquitted anyway, but it was typical
of Nelson to defend good men.[51]

Nevertheless, there was one case that shook even his loyalty to the
core. It concerned a particularly zealous captain of his own squadron,
a man for whom he had considerable professional respect: Charles
Sawyer of the frigate *Blanche*. In September 1796, Sawyer's immediate superior, Captain Cockburn, brought Nelson a disturbing report
with several supporting papers. The commodore was astonished, torn
between his revulsion for the alleged offences and sympathy for a man
obviously ruined. 'How melancholy!' he told Jervis in reporting his
suspension of Sawyer from duty and the arrest of his officers.
'Indignation and sorrow are so mixed in my mind that I know not
which predominates!'[52]

Sawyer was the son of a respected admiral who had begun his career
alongside Jervis, serving under Commodore Townsend and Lieutenant
Maurice Suckling. The son was now about thirty years old and had
been in the navy for near twenty of them, becoming a post-captain in
1794. There was every chance he would eventually receive his flag as
an admiral. Captain Sawyer was also an educated man, and Nelson
had lent him books, as was his wont. Unfortunately, in between reading
he was using his rank to indulge in regular acts of homosexuality,
some of them with minors. Two midshipmen were occasionally
summoned to Sawyer's cabin in the *Blanche*. One, a seventeen-year-

old, later testified that the quartermaster of the *Blanche* sent him to the captain's quarters, where Sawyer 'hauled me down in his cot and put my hand on his privates. When I got up he made me promise that I would not tell any one of it.' At Leghorn the captain even tried to make the boy share a hotel room with him. A black seaman also complained that 'the captain had frigged him, and he had frigged the captain', while Sawyer's coxswain was not only seen in the captain's cot several times, but openly condemned his commander as a 'man-fucking bugger'.[53]

As stories spread the captain became an object of derision, contempt and loathing in the ship, and authority was undermined. The first lieutenant and others attempted to lay charges before Nelson, but as applications for courts martial went through a ship's captain, Sawyer was able to block them. Furthermore, he tried to silence his accusers by threatening countercharges of his own, and warning them that their careers would be damaged 'unless . . . matters can be accommodated'. Throughout the high summer of 1796 Sawyer hung on, prevaricating and threatening whistle-blowers in turn, but the miserable matter simply grew too notorious to hide. After trying to turn a blind eye to the situation, Cockburn finally drew the subject to Nelson's attention, and it went to the naval courts.

Sawyer considered running, but then decided to stick it out in an effort to save his pay and prize money. He tried to discredit the witnesses by laying countercharges against six of them, as he had threatened, but when his case went before a court at St Fiorenzo on 18 October he was convicted and dismissed the service. Nelson was no doubt glad to be elsewhere.[54]

Sawyer's career was finished, and he had made himself a pariah, but Nelson took no pleasure in his fall. Reviewing the charges, Nelson had interviewed Sawyer 'fully', hoping to hear a denial, but none came. Perhaps no one but Nelson would have shown any further charity to the dishonoured captain, but Nelson seems to have written to him after his dismissal, and it was to the commodore that the friendless man turned for help in winding up his naval affairs. Sawyer's letter is worth quoting in full:

I cannot sufficiently thank you for your kind sentiments towards me, which notwithstanding all my misfortunes, I trust I am not altogether undeserving. I am obliged to you for the money for the Hermitage, which I hope you will find good. Herewith, I send you a letter which I had written to you principally on the subject of prize money. Any information you can give me that way I shall be very much obliged to you for. I am sorry to be troublesome to you, but as I have now no boat at command, nor cannot by any means procure one, may I request you will have the goodness to send by one of yours any information you can give me relative to prize money. Believe me, sir, your very obedient servant, C. Sawyer. Captain Preston will return your [copy of] Josephus [probably *Antiquities of the Jews*], for which I return you many thanks.[55]

Sawyer got his prize money.

George Cockburn of the *Meleager* proved a more satisfying beneficiary of Nelson's friendship. The future would grant Cockburn fame of a kind. He captured Washington in the War of 1812, burned the presidential mansion, and became the jailer of Napoleon, but here in 1796 we have him in his mid-twenties, at the beginning of a long and successful career. Although the teenage diarist Betsy Wynne thought Cockburn sprightly, fine and fashionable, and a colleague reported his 'splendid and inexhaustible talents', one gains the impression of an able, dependable and utterly impeccable but stiff Scot, dour and distant. Few people got close to him, and he cannot have been an easy colleague.[56]

Yet Nelson discovered something of a kindred spirit in him, a daring man strong on duty. 'We so exactly think alike on points of service that if your mind tells you it is right, there can hardly be a doubt but I must approve,' Nelson wrote to the junior officer. Accordingly, he pushed Cockburn forward, encouraging his every success. He persuaded Jervis to give him a bigger frigate, prompting his transfer to *La Minerve*, a French prize, put glowing tributes to him in dispatches, and in 1797 quietly ordered a commemoration sword to be made for him in England. It was a small gesture, but typical of Nelson. The sword, which Maurice Nelson thought 'very handsome', was a personal gift, honouring Cockburn's capture of a Spanish frigate while serving under Nelson's command. It was both a personal 'thank you' and an unsolicited and spontaneous tribute from a friend and professional to a colleague. We can imagine Cockburn's feelings on receiving such tangible testimony of his commodore's regard, gratuitously and unexpectedly bestowed. The recipient was not good at expressing intimate emotions, but responded to this and many other favours with a rare attachment to Nelson. 'Next to my own father, I know of *none* whose company I so much wish to be in, or who I have such real reasons to respect,' he told his chief. Half a century later, unconsciously speaking for many, he wistfully recalled Nelson's 'never failing kindness of heart'.[57]

XXIII

COMMODORE NELSON

You – with fidelity the Land –
Shall own the splendours of his High Command –
To him shall be her grateful praises given;
To him – her champion – sent down from heaven!
Ode to the Memory of . . . Lord Viscount Nelson, 1806

1

ON 20 May 1796 Commodore Nelson sat over a desk in Leghorn writing a letter to Sir William Hamilton, one of the closest of his correspondents. Disturbing rumours were abroad and Nelson had been listening to them. Anyway he thought he detected the drift of French intentions towards Italy. 'Although the French Directory tell the Grand Duke they will respect the neutrality [of Tuscany] . . . I have great reason to believe they only wish to lull the Grand Duke, and then to take possession of Leghorn and to treat Tuscany as an enemy. I wish I may be mistaken.'[1]

Essentially he was not. In the summer of 1796, Bonaparte's *tour de force* gathered terrifying momentum. His army marched north of Genoa and into Italy, spreading consternation and terror before it. The French stormed through Tuscany, frightened the papal states into submission, and stripped them of arts, provisions and money at bayonet point. Then they turned towards Leghorn. Bonaparte decided that if the Austrians made another attempt to relieve Mantua, the British might seize Leghorn to annoy his flank, so he moved first.

Everyone had stories of the French invasion of Italy. The Wynnes of Lincolnshire estate, with four charming daughters, learned about it in Florence. 'Nothing can be compared to the alarm in which Papa and Mama were set on their hearing that the French were at Bologna,' wrote seventeen-year-old Betsy. They fled to Leghorn, where Fremantle of the *Inconstant* was evacuating the British community, arriving on 24 June after an all-night coach ride. The British consulate was in 'a most terrible bustle and noise – all packing up and getting on board the ships. We hardly had time to get a little breakfast, they hurried us so terribly to quit the place.' Consul John Udny had much to save. After twenty-three years out of England, he had a carriage, horses, furniture, porcelain, plate and paintings as well as liveried servants divided between Leghorn and a rented house in Pisa, and the procession of his goods trundling to the mole only managed to clear the essentials. All the British round and about were on the move. When Udny's carriage reached Pisa to collect a fellow diplomat and his confined lady, it was seized by refugees trying to reach Leghorn. Lady Elliot, wife of the viceroy of Corsica, was also in town after fleeing Lucca with four of her children. Desperate to reach her husband, she got a place on a departing store ship just as Bonaparte's soldiers streamed into the suburbs, and took the news into Bastia on the 26th.[2]

The Leghornese were alarmed and angry at the French boots crunching contemptuously over Tuscan neutrality, but some inhabitants had personal reasons to fear the incursion. The governor, Francesco Spannochi, was a Neapolitan and noted Anglophile, with service in the Royal Navy and the friendship of Captain Collingwood to his credit. He faced a difficult task defending his country's sovereignty and keeping the French and British apart. For Signora Adelaide Correglia the appearance of the French portended the end of her relationship with a British commodore and the maintenance he provided.

Adelaide was then renting accommodation in the spa resort of Bagno di Pisa, a three-day coach ride north of Leghorn, in the house of 'Carlo Tarbato' – possibly Carlo Lorenzo Turbati, the Pisan lawyer, or one of his family. It was probably not the house for which Nelson had been paying upwards of a year. More likely that was in Leghorn itself, closer to the heart of naval business, but Bagno di Pisa was replete with accommodation to let, much of it in single rooms equipped with a bath, bed and fireplace sufficient for convalescent summers spent drinking and immersing in rejuvenating waters. Late in 1795 Adelaide had been having trouble with what Fremantle had described as 'a sort of abscess in her side', and she was still receiving maintenance from Nelson. Thus, on 15 June 1796, Thomas Pollard, the commodore's agent, paid £20 to 'Adelaide as p[er] order'. This, with whatever else she earned, had probably permitted her to take temporary lodgings in Bagno di Pisa for the purpose of regaining her health.[3]

A fortnight before the French invaded Leghorn, Adelaide had a visitor. The *Inconstant* frigate was moored in Leghorn roads for a refit, and the incorrigible Captain Fremantle was again at large, looking for sex. 'Can't find Madalina,' he scribbled in his diary on 15 June. But the next day he had more success at Bagno di Pisa. 'Went to Pisa baths,' he wrote. 'Called on Adelaide, who was quite recovered and looked well.' Nine days later, within twenty-four hours of definite news of the French advance reaching Leghorn, Adelaide was in Fremantle's frigate. Although Adelaide was Nelson's lover, and Fremantle his friend, it is difficult not to suspect that the meeting was a 'professional' one. At any rate, she seems to have retired quickly upon the arrival of the Wynnes and Mrs Pollard. 'Adelaide came off in the evening,' wrote Fremantle.[1]

Whether two-timing or not, these meetings were brought to an abrupt end when Fremantle was suddenly recalled to duty. If Adelaide made her way back to Pisa on the 26th she would have found the road full of Bonaparte's soldiers marching south.

2

Sent back to his station on 18 June, Nelson was in Genoa when he heard of the thrust at Leghorn, wrestling with different facets of the enemy's successes. He was trying to establish packet services between Leghorn, Corsica and Spain, halt Genoa's slide into hostility, and deal with more neutral complaints about his ships. The republic's coast had become a hostile shore, with only the city of Genoa itself a safe haven for British vessels, and that seethed with Jacobin influence, fanned by a new and bellicose representative of the French Directory, Monsieur Guillaume-Charles Faypoult, the minister plenipotentiary.

Nelson met this fresh round of neutral complaints without the benefit of a strong defender on the spot. Drake had gone to Vienna, and only the British consul, Joseph Brame, manned this threatened outpost. No one had much time for Brame. Nelson thought him 'a poor creature, and more of a Genoese than an Englishman', and Sir John Jervis, who had been responsible for his appointment in the first place, said he was dishonest and confused. The admiral suspected Brame of corruptly inflating the prices of provisions supplied to the

British fleet to benefit some accomplice, and growled that the consul was 'in a state of imbecility during his best days' and 'upon his death-bed would take money from Swede, Dane or the devil'.[5]

Poor Brame, whose wavering scrawl presaged imminent physical collapse, was not the best man to rescue Nelson from the accusations of neutrals. He also knew that French influence in Genoa was increasing while his own wilted, and counselled moderation in all of Britain's dealings with the Italian republic. Perhaps it was his fear of annoying the Genoese that led him to meet their complaints so meekly. When Castiglione, the Genoese secretary of state, sent him three notes dated between 28 May and 16 June and in sum charging Nelson's people with seizing neutral property, attacking ships in Genoese havens, and ill-treating some of their crews, he had not mounted a fierce rebuttal. Instead, he had promised an investigation and forwarded the complaints to the British foreign secretary. Nelson was furious. He was stung by what he denounced as exaggerations and lies, and even more so that Brame should see fit to send them home without first giving him the opportunity to reply.

Nelson's visit to Genoa was therefore unusually stormy. He berated Brame for his weak response to Castiglione's complaints, and refused to be appeased by the consul's excuses. Brame miserably insisted that Genoa would have sent their allegations to London anyway, and he had not consulted Nelson because he thought he had sailed for England. As he worked out his anger, Nelson framed answers to the charges, and countered with some of his own, submitting verbal and written protests that British ships were being fired upon the length and breadth of the Genoese coast.[6]

Then, in the midst of the paper war, Nelson heard the feared news that Bonaparte had marched upon Leghorn.

Among others, Fremantle raised the alarm. Still in Leghorn when word of the impending invasion of Tuscany arrived from Florence, he immediately sent the *Blanche* to Jervis with the news, and appealed to any ship on the riviera to come to his aid. It was obvious that he would have to organise an evacuation, and Nelson sailed from Genoa with Cockburn's *Meleager* for company on 24 June.[7]

The calms and fickle winds typical of those seas were against the *Captain* and *Meleager* as they drove towards Leghorn, and it was the morning of 27 June that they finally made the northern road. Upon his arrival, Nelson saw crowds of ships quitting the mole, more than forty sail in all, and heard the roar of guns. Fremantle had been magnificent. With typical efficiency he had held out till the last minute, securing a place on a ship for every Briton and most of their belongings. According to Udny the operation filled three days and nights and nothing but furniture and bad debts were left behind.

It had been touch and go. As the French penetrated the outskirts of the town Governor Spannochi made a bold stand. While the British were loading their ships at the mole, he doubled his guards to prevent interference as long as he could. But the French cavalry soon spilled into the town and seized the batteries on the mole, and wild shots began flying at the departing *Inconstant*. Ten or twelve enemy privateers swarmed after the British convoy, and one of the ships was actually being towed into captivity as Nelson arrived. The commodore instantly signalled to the *Meleager* to hold the rest of the privateers at bay, and then to support the *Inconstant* in chaperoning the convoy to Corsica, while the *Captain* remained. Before long the last white sails of the fleeing ships dipped over the blue horizon, and Bonaparte was left to vent his fury on Spannochi. Pointedly establishing his headquarters in Udny's abandoned house, the little Corsican defamed the governor as a pro-British rogue and 'macaroni eater', who had allowed Fremantle to impound two French ships and attempted to stir the people to resist Bonaparte's soldiers. He arrested Spannochi, imperiously demanded the Grand Duke of Tuscany punish him and shipped him unceremoniously to Florence under guard.[8]

The British evacuees sailing southwestwards towards St Fiorenzo made the best of their situation, transforming the decks of the ships into occasional ballrooms, and young Betsy Wynne fell deeply in love with Fremantle. The captain was less forthcoming, though he did allow that Betsy was 'a very good humoured sensible dolly, not particularly handsome but a little healthy thing'.[9]

While romance blossomed on the *Inconstant*, Nelson buckled down to blockading Leghorn. He warned unsuspecting British merchantmen that the port was no longer safe, and shut in the enemy privateers and other vessels, save only the local fishing craft which he permitted to go freely about their daily business. Some of the fishermen, such as Giovanni Nere, were sources of information and got his messages in and out of the town as they plied innocently back and forth. Ashore the few remaining threads of neutrality were stretched to their limits. Bonaparte ordered his men to avoid unnecessary confrontations with the Tuscans, and concentrated his soldiers in two forts rather than quartering them with the inhabitants. Nevertheless, he subordinated the Tuscan troops to his control and exercised a firm grip on the town. When he ordered the people to illuminate their houses in celebration they did so, and the streets echoed to the tramping of squads of French soldiery in search of arms and spoils. Bonaparte sequestrated remaining British property, sealed up warehouses and declared that anyone hiding it or treating with the enemy warships would be shot. Still, Nelson's messengers managed to pass warily about the town and perhaps rapped urgently upon Adelaide's door.

With a rudimentary control established, Bonaparte rushed inland with his cavalry on 29 June, alarmed by a report that the Austrians were again massing for the relief of Mantua. Behind in Leghorn he left General Claude-Henri Belgrand, Comte de Vaubois with the 75th demi-brigade, a company of artillery and a squadron of hussars, amounting in all to more than two thousand men, with orders to prepare the means of withstanding a forty-day siege in case the British or Tuscans counterattacked. The next day, the last in June, Nelson also left, satisfied that for the moment no more could be done. His destination was St Fiorenzo, where the squalid streets between the bay and the heights now bustled with refugees from Leghorn. There were important implications to be discussed with the viceroy, Sir Gilbert Elliot.[10]

The loss of Leghorn was a blow to the British. The submission of the papal territories and Tuscany to France had closed their ports to British ships and turned the Italian peninsula between Naples and Genoa into enemy territory. Leghorn in particular had provided the Royal Navy with shelter, dockyard facilities, a prize court and supplies, but these favours were now reserved for the French, and the port had become a dangerous launching pad for the invasion of Corsica. The inconveniences Elliot could handle. Mail for England would have to go through Barcelona rather than Italy. Treasury bills could be cashed in Genoa instead of Leghorn, and provisions purchased there or from Naples and the Barbary ports. But that close proximity of French power cast chilling shadows over Corsica, and if Corsica fell Britain would lose its only Mediterranean base east of Gibraltar.[11]

The truth was that Bonaparte was teaching Jervis, Nelson and Elliot the limits of sea power. Leghorn was only part of a process that would also cost them Genoa, Corsica and the Mediterranean itself. Like Alexander of Macedon before him, Bonaparte would conquer the sea from the land.

3

Nelson soon had formal orders to blockade Leghorn and help Sir Gilbert Elliot to defend Corsica. The *Meleager* and *Blanche* frigates were at his disposal, together with such smaller vessels as the *L'Eclair* sloop, the six-gun *Vanneau* brig and the *Rose* cutter of ten guns.

Sir John was as supportive as circumstances permitted. In switching Cockburn from the *Meleager* to the larger *La Minerve*, he wrote to Nelson, 'I will not keep him four and twenty hours to make the exchange, knowing how much you rely on his arm.' Nelson likewise found a sturdy crutch in Elliot. The sophisticated diplomat, fluent in ideas and strong in his support of the navy, was a reassuring and sympathetic ear, especially now that Drake was in Vienna. Whereas many a naval officer went to Nelson for comfort and counsel, the commodore himself turned to Sir Gilbert, 'a treasure' he had grown to love. Both the viceroy and his lady reciprocated. Sir Gilbert had a huge affection for Nelson, while Lady Elliot declared herself a 'great admirer'. It was Elliot who found a solution to one of the commodore's problems, the loss of the prize-court facility in Leghorn. He incorporated Corsican privateers in the commodore's forces. Though Nelson had to concede them a share in any prize money, he gained access to the courts in Corsica and the speedy resolution of cases.[12]

His resources remained barely adequate, however. He had to communicate with Genoa, where information, provisions and specie could be obtained, with Elliot in Bastia, and with Jervis and the fleet off Toulon, as well as arrange for the safe passage of merchantmen, suppliers and packets east and west. Moreover, there would be no half-measures with this blockade. In the commodore's opinion such a blockade as 'the one we had of Genoa' back in 1793 would be 'of little consequence', and Jervis concurred. Nothing must get in or out of Leghorn without Nelson's permission. As before, fishermen would pass to and fro, but no one else. Nelson imagined the port falling dead, its commerce stilled, and the furious Tuscans turning upon their French guests and expelling them from the town. Relying much upon his reputation, he confidently publicised the blockade throughout the region. 'It will be credited, if my character is known,' he said, 'that this blockade will be attended to with a degree of vigour unexampled in the present war.'[13]

Nelson instituted the blockade on 6 July, but almost immediately received a call for help from Elliot. On his last visit to Corsica, Nelson had spoken to Elliot about the danger of another possession of Tuscany falling to the enemy. The island of Elba was part way between Leghorn and Corsica, and in French hands could be used to threaten Corsica or interrupt British communications with Italy. At the end of June, Trevor had suggested Nelson seize Elba as a precaution, risking whatever offence its occupation might cause Tuscany to ensure the safety of Corsica, and now Elliot agreed.[14]

On 1 July, Elliot sent Major John Duncan of the Royal Artillery with letters to the governor of Elba, Baron Giorgio Knesevich, suggesting a temporary British occupation to protect the island from the French. The baron was by no means sure that a British garrison would improve his security. His political masters had been cowed by Bonaparte, and the governor of Leghorn had already been dismissed for assisting the British. Furthermore, inviting the British into Elba might simply provoke French reprisals against Tuscan possessions on the mainland. Given Bonaparte's current weakness at sea, the French threat to Elba was not, in the baron's view, imminent, and he wanted no bold moves. Rather he would sit tight and await instructions from his government. However, in replying to Elliot he admitted that if the French landed in Elba in overwhelming force, he expected he would have to follow the example of Leghorn and submit rather than fight them.[15]

Elliot was in no mood to risk a French takeover of Elba, and after reading Knesevich's replies and hearing from Duncan on 6 July he mobilised his troops. Five hundred and thirty men of the 18th (Royal Irish), 100th and 51st regiments, Dillon's regiment, and the Royal Artillery were immediately embarked. Duncan, who commanded, was supplied with a summons to present to the garrison at Porto Ferraio, and told to take military control of the place, leaving the governor to command the civil administration. Nominally, the island would remain subject to the Grand Duke of Tuscany. Several ships were speedily assembled for the expedition. The ubiquitous Fremantle commanded the naval force, which consisted of his own *Inconstant*, the *Flora* frigate (Captain Robert Middleton), the *Vanneau* (Lieutenant Gourly) and the *Rose* (Lieutenant William Walker), supported by a Corsican privateer and four transports. To play safe, Elliot sent for Nelson at Leghorn looking for his aid.

As one of the original movers of the business, Nelson responded immediately, leaving Sawyer to blockade Leghorn with the *Blanche*, the *Sardine* sloop under Edward Killwick and three gunboats. Rushing to Elba with the *Peterel* he arrived off the capital, Porto Ferraio, late on 8 July, just as Fremantle's flotilla was working in from the west. Nelson took overall command, and the next day increased his force with the *Southampton* under Captain James Macnamara, which was by chance already anchored off the port.[16]

Porto Ferraio was a formidably striking place, with enveloping green hills and a large citadel crowning the high cliffs above the town, its guns dominating both land and sea. The commodious anchorage below was enclosed on three sides by the town and a long jetty. Porto Ferraio was so powerful that Duncan later said that with five hundred men he could have defended it against 'the whole of Buonoparte's army', and the Tuscans had a hundred pieces of artillery, four hundred regular soldiers and an armed militia. There was no possibility of surprising the place, and after a party of British officers had been rowed around to assess possible landing places frowns began to appear on faces. Nelson held a council of war aboard the *Captain*, and mooted the alternatives. In their dispatches the senior army and navy officers spoke of the 'cordiality' that existed between the services, and Duncan saluted the commodore's 'enterprising and spirited conduct'. But according to Fremantle's private diary old divisions reared their ugly heads. 'The soldiers [were] very undetermined and very jealous of us,' he wrote, and doubted whether the castle could be taken. A 'long consultation' ensued 'about landing the troops', and 'Nelson and I offer[ed] to take the town with the ships [alone]'.[17]

A repetition of Bastia, with the army left looking on, was unthinkable, but Nelson managed to prevail, no doubt invoking his friendship with Duncan, an old Corsican comrade in arms. In two and a half hours the same evening the soldiers were disembarked with a field piece in a bay two miles west of Porto Ferraio. Using four more guns, landed under the cover of armed launches and small warships, they quickly occupied defensible ground, and lay under arms all night. Daylight of 10 July found Duncan moving forward with an advanced guard of the 18th Regiment, taking possession of some windmills four hundred yards from the town, and sealing it off from the landward side. Elliot's summons was then handed in at the nearest gate. It insisted upon a British occupation of the fortifications and overall control, but promised that in all other respects matters would continue as before. The governor's civil authority would be respected, and as soon as the danger to Corsica had been averted, the redcoats would withdraw.

Knesevich was given two hours to reply but needed persuading.

After conferring with his officers and advisers, he agreed to allow the British into the town, but not the castle, and a clash of arms looked inevitable. Nelson and Fremantle went ashore to reassure civilians that they and their property were safe, while Berry menaced the castle by placing the *Captain*'s guns within half a pistol-shot range of the grand bastion. British resolution finally did the trick. At eight o'clock in the morning Duncan's soldiers took possession of the town gates, where they were received by the governor and his principal men, and then marched into 'the Grand Parade'. Another couple of hours gave them control of the fortifications. Nelson's ships anchored in the harbour, and the commodore exchanged a salute with the citadel, firing gun for gun. A garrison of 725 men was eventually installed.

It looked as if Tuscany was being dismembered by the rival powers, with the British purloining Elba to counterbalance the French occupation of Leghorn, but Nelson declared the two actions of a very different character. The people of Elba had been spared the miseries of 'the unfortunate Leghornese', and under British protection would enjoy 'an increase to their happiness'. There was no sequestration of Tuscan property. The only spoils, shared equally between the army and navy, were a French privateer, its English prize and several other vessels belonging to the enemy. Nor did the populace appear dissatisfied. The streets of Porto Ferraio remained 'quiet', and when Miss Betsy Wynne, still enjoying life close to the 'excellent' captain of the *Inconstant*, accompanied a party ashore soon after the occupation, it was received 'with the greatest demonstration of joy'.[18]

4

Jervis was delighted, and promised to recommend Berry's promotion, but the seizure of Elba really did no more than ameliorate Elliot's difficulties. On the mainland to the north and east French influence spread like a black flame. The Royal Navy still held the seas, but one by one the neutral sanctuaries that had provisioned and sheltered its ships were closing, and in August the allied coalition suffered another serious blow, the worst yet. France and Spain signed a defensive and offensive treaty, making it merely a matter of time before the Spaniards declared war on Britain, their former ally. The implications were serious, for despite its decline Spain was still the third greatest naval power in the world, and the combined Franco-Spanish fleet in the Mediterranean far outnumbered the ships of Sir John Jervis.[19]

To Elliot, ruling a small island in an increasingly dangerous sea, the prospects were exceedingly cloudy, but there was a little solace to be had from Nelson's refusal to be intimidated. Indeed, the weather-worn little commodore seemed to relish grappling with the 'Dons'. To some extent he had learned to discount numbers when it came to fighting at sea. In the Mediterranean the variable winds made it difficult for big fleets to manoeuvre as an entity, and it was likely that only a portion of any large enemy force would be effective at a given time. Besides, Nelson did not rate the French and Spanish fleets very highly. He told Jackson, Trevor's deputy, that with twenty-five sail Jervis could beat forty French opponents, 'by taking those advantages which their [our] superior skill and management of the ships would not fail to afford'.[20]

For some time Nelson had been praying the French would break out of Toulon and give Jervis an opportunity to thrash them, and his only fear was that, stuck out in the Gulf of Genoa, he would miss the battle. He begged Sir John to recall him the moment action loomed. 'I have only to hope,' he wrote on 3 July, 'that when it is reduced to a certainty that Mr Martin [the French admiral] means to give you a meeting, that I may be called upon to assist that ceremony.' Early the following month Nelson showed that he was capable of disobeying orders to get a crack at the French. A Spanish fleet of ten ships of the line was supposed to have sailed from Cadiz on 1 August and linked up with a French squadron to enter the Mediterranean. Expecting a battle at last, Jervis called in his ships of the line, including the *Captain*. However, believing that only Nelson could handle affairs in the Gulf of Genoa at such a critical time, he ordered the commodore to remain on that station, and to temporarily transfer his pendant to a frigate during the *Captain*'s absence. Nelson could no more have flown to the moon than allow his ship to leave him behind with a battle brewing. Discarding the admiral's orders, he took the *Captain* to Toulon himself.[21]

That scare eased, and Nelson was soon back with his squadron, though just as willing to profit from the Franco-Spanish alliance. His powerful sense of loyalty told him that Spain was acting dishonourably in changing sides, and deserved punishment. Late in August, with Britain and Spain still officially at peace, Nelson tried to persuade his superiors to loose him upon a Spanish warship that had gone into the Tiber to collect the tribute Bonaparte had wrung from the papal states. He argued that any ship carrying French property, whether belonging to a belligerent power or not, was liable to seizure, and though Jervis agreed Nelson never got to make the raid. A month later, only weeks before the Spanish war actually began, Nelson restrained himself again when he turned a Spanish frigate away from Leghorn. He desperately wanted to capture the ship, but had to accept that as far as either he or the Spanish captain knew their two nations were still at peace.[22]

Nelson remained Nelson, undaunted, undismayed, but there was no doubt that his cause was sinking. The alliance of Spain and France made a direct attack on Britain feasible, and the Royal Navy would need to regroup nearer home, withdrawing forces from the Mediterranean and elsewhere if necessary. In any case, with allies and neutrals being knocked out of the war right and left, there seemed little more than trade to fight for east of the Strait of Gibraltar. In the line of duty Nelson was a fighter first and last, even with allies crumbling around him, but the prevailing tide was surging inexorably in the opposite direction.

5

Nelson now focused his energies on Leghorn, but encouraged by his capture of Porto Ferraio brought a new aggression to the job. If he could expel the French, he could open the port to the British again, weaken the threat to Corsica, and possibly threaten the right flank of the French army as it confronted yet another Austrian attempt to relieve Mantua. Furthermore, the Viennese court was pressing for just such a naval diversion.[23]

Nelson believed a victory essential for morale. Throughout Italy resistance to the French was evaporating, and even the King of Naples, hitherto the surest of Britain's friends, had signed an armistice. However, Bonaparte's violation of Genoa and Tuscany had provoked outrage as well as fear, and it was conceivable that the spirit of resistance might revive. If the new Austrian commander-in-chief, Marshal Count Dagobert-Sigismond de Wurmser, could defeat Bonaparte, and Tuscany be freed . . . In Nelson's limited view of the land struggle, all that was needed to turn the tide against these bedraggled French armies of half-fed boys was unity, resolution and courage.

Several thousand French soldiers still held Leghorn, but the few gunboats they had fitted out had not, as yet, seriously challenged Nelson's blockade. At different times his force included the *Captain* and *Diadem* ships of the line, *La Minerve*, *Blanche* and *Lively* frigates, the *Sardine*, *Peterel*, *L'Eclair*, *Sincere* and *Vanneau* sloops and brigs, and the *Fox* and *Rose* cutters. Two gunboats taken at Oneglia and renamed *Vixen* and *Venom*, and a number of Corsican privateers supplied by Elliot helped Nelson control the shallows while his larger ships occupied the deeper water in the northern road. Small craft were essential to the work of running down enemy ships trying to enter the port, but they were constantly having to be redeployed as packets, and a French privateer taken on 11 August was happily added to the commodore's blockading flotilla.[24]

At first the blockade was unyielding, shutting all ships in or out of Leghorn, but persistent appeals and the advice of Elliot and Jervis induced the commodore to relax his grip. First the vessels of favoured nations – Swedes and Neapolitans ('I have every inclination to befriend every Neapolitan; the good faith of the king of Naples demands and ensures it of us') – and then Venetians, Ragusans and Danes were allowed to leave Leghorn without their cargoes. But nothing was admitted, and by the beginning of September the harbours that once thronged with shipping lay unhealthily silent and still.[25]

The fishermen came and went, of course. Ever since his cruises off Boston years before Nelson had regretted the way wars abused their frugal livelihoods, and on 22 August he notified the governor of Leghorn that he

had given passports to every fisherman to go out as usual with their tartans, and it is with astonishment I find that the poor fishermen, who are obliged to come on board my sovereign's ship to obtain that permission, which not only maintains a number of poor Tuscan families but also supplies the town of Leghorn with fish, are, by your Excellency, as president of the health-office, subjected to a quarantine of ten days, although I have given my word of honour, which till now never was doubted, that I am with my squadron in *libera practica*.[26]

Intelligence as well as humanity was his game, for as many as twenty of these fishing boats gathered under the stern of the *Captain* each morning to secure leave to proceed, bringing with them information and messages from the town. One master (perhaps Giovanni Nere, whose services had already earned a certificate of immunity from Nelson, or maybe an informant named Pensa) became a regular 'reporter'. Nelson paid for spies. They hurried through sunlit courtyards and the labyrinth of shadowy, narrow, interlocking streets, and communicated in whispers to pro-British elements within the town, including old employees of the British consulate. Nelson managed a furtive correspondence with the friendly Neapolitan consul in Leghorn ('I . . . shall endeavour to get a letter to him this evening'), and of course there was Adelaide.[27]

She spoke French as well as Italian, and may now have been consorting as freely with Bonaparte's officers as once she had with their English counterparts, picking up useful tidbits in the process. Probably Adelaide was one source of Nelson's information about what was happening in Leghorn, but scholars who have suggested that she spied for him, exchanging information for money like some eighteenth-century Mata Hari, are probably exaggerating. Nelson did pay spies, but there appears to be no evidence that his donations to Adelaide were made on that account; more likely they represented long-standing maintenance commitments to a mistress.

The impression that Adelaide was something more than an occasional and minor contributor to Nelson's secret service gained strength from a letter the commodore wrote to Elliot on 3 August. 'One *old* lady tells us all she hears,' he said, with a use of italics that suggests his informant was far from undesirable. Almost every biographer since Oliver Warner has supposed that Nelson was referring to Adelaide, but this was probably not the case. Much more likely he alluded to Madame Frances Caffarena of the Strada Balbi in Genoa, the English wife of an Italian merchant. Joseph Caffarena, his wife and two sons supplied provisions to the British fleet. In dealing with Madame Caffarena, who handled much of the correspondence, Nelson found her so politically astute and observant that he asked her to act as an informer, cautioning her – as she said – 'with agreeable pleasantry to take care what I wrote'. The day Nelson wrote his letter to Elliot, Madame Caffarena replied: 'I shall always be happy to obey your commands, and if you can pass over the errors of a female pen, what may come to my knowledge I shall immediately communicate to you with infinite satisfaction. My only fear is getting truth out of the various cross-purposes propagated by the agents of the mushroom republic.'[28]

So Adelaide may have to be acquitted of systematic spying, though Nelson did maintain a complicated communication line to his mistress, and probably benefited from some of her news. 'Signora Adelaide' was still at Bagno di Pisa, where the gossip of creaking crowned heads and tourists had been largely replaced by the political chatter of dislodged Leghornese. It is not clear how Adelaide and Nelson corresponded during the French occupation, but they did. In July, Udny, the former British consul, now banished to Corsica, even directed a letter to the commodore via his mistress's address. Udny knew Adelaide well. 'Remember me to your friend,' he told Nelson. A month later, after moving to Porto Ferraio, Udny wrote to Nelson again, adding that it would 'give me the sincerest satisfaction to obey your commands, or that of your friend, to whom I beg to be remembered'.[29]

Whatever channels Nelson used to reach Adelaide through Leghorn became too dangerous in August, and he began reaching her through Brame, the consul at Genoa, instead. On the 21st Brame wrote to Nelson that 'your message to Signora Adelaide was immediately sent, and any answer I may receive shall go herewith'. The next day he wrote again. 'I this morning received the honour of your kind letter of the 19th instant. The enclosed for Signora Adelaide was immediately sent, and [I] presume Captain Sawyer [of the *Blanche*] will bring the answer. If sent to me shall go herewith.' Early the next month Brame mentioned sending two enclosures to Nelson, but whether these related to Adelaide is unknown. The vehicle for these letters was most probably Adelaide's mother, who lived in Genoa and likely sent correspondence for her daughter back and forth.[30]

The news from these and other sources encouraged Nelson. Pro-British sentiment in Leghorn was strong, he learned. Bonaparte had hoped to raise seven or eight million livres from selling British property in the town, and his agents had combed through the books of the mercantile houses and called in relevant debts. But when Udny's furniture went to auction it found no buyers, and had to be lugged back to his house. Nelson heard that the locals were fed up with the French. Some resented the removal of Spannochi and his foreign minister, Franco Seratti, as well as the alien rule through French stooges, while the poor suffered from the suspension of trade, as Nelson learned directly from the hundreds of destitute people who reached his ships in small boats to partake of what provisions he could spare. So many of the inhabitants were reported to resent the imposition of a French *fête* on 10 August that Nelson believed it would signal an uprising. He told his old friend Collingwood, who had just joined the fleet, that he hoped to prompt the 'starved Leghornese to cut the throats of the French crew', and to Jervis he even ventured a date. 'Almost all Tuscany is in motion,' he said. 'I have no doubt but by the 15th we shall have Leghorn.'[31]

When nothing happened, he blamed the Grand Duke for restraining the people. He also seems to have chided the governor of Leghorn with submitting too tamely to the French, and was gently reminded that the Tuscan troops were outnumbered by the occupying forces, who also commanded the batteries and strong points. Long before then Nelson had decided they needed help.[32]

6

Horatio Nelson always complained impatiently when the seashore divided him from his enemies, and enjoyed landing with men and guns to embark upon adventures conventionally reserved for the army. Anything to discomfort the enemy. The pattern had been woven in the sixteen years between Nicaragua in 1780 and the taking of Porto Ferraio. In the spring of 1796, encouraged by Drake, he bewailed his lack of three thousand soldiers to facilitate such attacks. 'I am vain enough to think I could command on shore as well as some of the generals,' he told Trevor. Now, waiting for the Leghornese to oust the French, he wondered again whether a direct British counterattack might move matters forward.[33]

The starting point for this, his most ambitious military proposal yet, may have been a report from inside the town, apparently by a clerk of the former British trade factory. Nelson had heard that the number of French soldiers in Leghorn had risen to five thousand, but this intelligence painted a different picture. The enemy was down to about eighteen hundred men, and they were billeted in two forts, afraid of an increasingly hostile populace. Their relations with the Tuscan troops were bad, and the latter were being reinforced, both cavalry and infantry having been brought into the town disguised as peasants. An anti-French spirit was abroad and the local militia had been put on alert, ready to act at short notice. Only a signal from the Grand Duke was needed to spark a rising. Nelson was not always good at evaluating intelligence. He sometimes believed what he wanted to hear. When other reports tended to confirm that the occupying French forces had dwindled his warrior spirit rose to its feet.[34]

Elliot became his confederate, lured by the prospect of reducing the threat to Corsica. He felt that if the Austrians gained 'a decided superiority' in Lombardy and drew the strength and attention of the French an attack might be made on Leghorn 'without danger, for the enemy are too few to quit their walls and . . . disturb us, either landing or embarking'. On 5 August, Nelson suggested a thousand regulars from Corsica, stiffened by marines and a party of seamen 'to make a show', could be disembarked with enough artillery to give the French a pretext for quitting with honour. He knew that an orthodox siege was out of the question, but hoped the Tuscans would support him by yielding the town, and that the isolated French garrisons could be induced to withdraw under a brief bombardment. Supposed demoralisation and desertions among the French were also strands in his thinking. 'Our only consideration – is the honour and benefit to our country worth the risk? If it is, and I think so, in God's name let us get to work, and hope for his blessing on our endeavours to liberate a people who have been our sincere friends.' A problem, he thought, might be the command of the operation. Allowing ambition to blunt memories of old squabbles, he suggested that Major Duncan head the army, and that overall command be offered himself, especially as he now held a commission as colonel of marines and was already 'feared or respected in Leghorn'. The suggestion demonstrates, among other things, that despite the problem between the services at Porto Ferraio, Nelson had established a good relationship with Duncan, and was happy working with him. His prediction was that a mere 'twenty-four hours' would 'do the business'.[35]

Elliot was soon preparing his troops, recalling some from Elba to strengthen his regulars. The force he planned to use fell to three thousand British and Corsican regulars and volunteers, in addition to artillery and five hundred marines from the fleet, but it was larger than the inadequate army proposed by Nelson. Moreover, smitten by his own continuing difficulties with army officers in Corsica, Elliot cautioned Nelson against taking overall command of the expedition. It would reopen old wounds and 'blow us all up at once'. Nor was there a need, the viceroy tactfully explained. Major General John Thomas De Burgh of the 66th Foot, who now commanded in Corsica, was not only an experienced 'cool and well-skilled' soldier of 'spirit and courage' but a thorough gentleman. If anything, Elliot underrated De Burgh. The general doubted the accuracy of Nelson's intelligence, but saw advantages in his plan and generously offered to command the soldiers under the supreme command of Nelson. The commodore, he said, 'appears to me to like [to] be the chief.' Fortunately, Elliot did not have to require any such submission, for Nelson accepted the viceroy's reservations with good heart, and readily agreed to a joint navy–army command. As far as the armed services were concerned,

the leaders gave every appearance of wishing a productive relationship.[36]

As the plan for a *coup de main* passed from officer to officer some
raised doubts, and there were gentle hints that Nelson's proverbial
'zeal' for action was apt to outstrip his judgement. Major Duncan,
who had shown a little irresolution at Porto Ferraio, sounded one
cautious note after a ship brought new information from Leghorn on
the 11th. It put the French strength at three thousand regulars, besides
Corsican auxiliaries, and a large number of mounted guns. They had
purloined the ample salted provisions originally amassed for the British
fleet and established a powerful presence in the area. Pro-French
Corsicans, wearing national cockades in their hats, marched about the
streets with drawn swords, while French dragoons daily cantered
through the town gates to patrol the adjacent countryside.
'Commodore Nelson shows his usual spirit in saying it [Leghorn] may
be taken by 1,000 men,' concluded Duncan. 'He must suppose the
French perfect cowards.'[37]

Admiral Jervis did not go so far. He was willing to countenance
the attack, but only in tandem with a successful Austrian campaign
that tied down the French army and prevented the enemy troops in
Leghorn from being reinforced. The British could then foment a Tuscan
uprising, and intrigue, 'poison' and the 'stiletto' would support a sea-
borne attack. However, even Jervis worried about Nelson's enthusiasm
for ill-resourced amphibious operations. 'We have no business with
Vado or Port Especcia [Spezia] until the Austrians enter Piedmont,'
he warned. The admiral cautioned Elliot to steer Nelson from rash
enterprises. 'I am very glad you have a little damped the ardour of
Commodore Nelson respecting the republic of Genoa,' he congratulated the viceroy. 'He is an excellent partisan, but does not sufficiently
weigh consequences.' When Elliot told him he had dissuaded Nelson
from pressing for the overall command of the Leghorn assault, Jervis
agreed. As a naval officer Nelson was 'the best fellow in the world',
but on land 'his zeal does now and then (not often) outrun his
discretion'.[38]

Nelson certainly anticipated further glory. His brother William was
let into 'a secret – that probably the next letter you see from me will
be in the public *Gazette*'. But there were no triumphant dispatches,
and Nelson found himself writing that his expedition had been
'blasted'.[39]

It had been ready to go. Major James Logan of the 51st, sent to

Leghorn to pore over the remaining doubts with the commodore, returned to Bastia on 13 August more or less satisfied that an attack would involve little risk. Nelson assured him that the country folk around Leghorn would support the allies, and thought the prospects of success were good. Accordingly, Elliot had fifteen hundred regulars and a thousand volunteers at Bastia, preparing to embark on the *Rose*, *Vanneau* and four Corsican privateers on the 19th.

Unfortunately the Austrians failed them. Marching south towards Mantua, they suffered successive stinging defeats and retired to the Tyrol, and just as the first rumours of the reverses reached Corsica through Florence, there also came word that six hundred French reinforcements had marched into Leghorn. The viceroy wavered. These bleaker circumstances were hardly going to stimulate the Tuscans to rebel, and Jervis had insisted all along that the expedition must hinge upon Austrian success. The venture was mothballed, awaiting another and more favourable twist in fortune.

By 15 August, Elliot was trying to salvage the expedition by appealing to Austria and Naples to supply three thousand troops. The next day Nelson himself arrived at Bastia to strengthen his determination, and as late as September the indefatigable Drake was still pursuing the idea of using foreign contingents to create a viable force. But by then a *coup de grâce* had been delivered. Before the end of August an order to transfer the 100th Regiment of Foot, some eight hundred regulars, from Corsica to Gibraltar, stripped the viceroy of the men to do the job. On the 25th he told the doubting Major Duncan that the plan had been dropped for good.[40]

Nelson was disappointed. In his dreams he was the liberator of Leghorn. Then he saw himself visiting Civita Vecchia brandishing Elliot's 'manifesto', seizing that Spanish warship loaded with Bonaparte's plunder, and treating the pontiff himself to some 'firm language', even if it meant rowing 'up the Tiber and into Rome' in his barge. His appearance, he expected, might embolden the Italian states. 'Go and thunder at Civita Vecchia,' Admiral Jervis had urged. Both projects were shelved, but in stranger days several years ahead both Leghorn and Rome would, ironically, surrender to Nelson's ships.[41]

In the meantime a serious consequence of leaving Leghorn under enemy occupation quickly emerged, for it was in the town that a new and deadly French plan to invade Corsica by stealth matured. Hotham's battles had taught the French the dangers of confronting the British fleet in open battle, but they had marked the limits of enemy sea power well. Nelson had failed to stop the coastal trade, and ships had continued to use dark nights and bad weather to sneak by his stretched cruisers. Very well, Bonaparte and his advisers decided, Corsica could be invaded piecemeal by small detachments taking their chances in quick voyages. Leghorn was used to muster thousands of soldiers, privateersmen and Corsican émigrés – men dislodged from the island by the British two years before – and to fuse them into an invasion force under General Gentile, who had commanded the French army during the siege of Bastia. There would be no showdown with the British fleet. The invaders would creep out of Leghorn and other ports at night in dribs and drabs, using dead calms to transport men in oared privateers and feluccas to lonely, unguarded places on the wild Corsican coast. Some of these detachments could use the Genoese island of Capraia as a stopover, perhaps changing boats there. Corsica would be reclaimed for France through a gradual process of furtive infiltration and guerrilla warfare.

Some republicans had landed in Corsica in June, scrambling into the interior to hide out and foment discord, but the plan took another two months to get properly underway. Nelson and Elliot got wind of it in August, amongst others from the Caffarenas of Genoa, who saw Gentile and some of his men pass through their town on their way to Leghorn. To hear the adventurers talk of the proposed coup in Corsica 'they think themselves already there,' wrote Madame Caffarena. Unfortunately, there was little Nelson and the viceroy could do. Nelson reported the development to Lord Spencer and recommended extra vigilance all round. Cockburn's forty-gun frigate *La Minerve* ran a French ship ashore and captured it on 8 September, and Elliot hired local *guardas costas* to patrol the Corsican coast, but the French were adept at slipping from one craggy cove to another and running along the shores on moonless nights.[42]

The truth was that Bonaparte, not Nelson and Jervis, controlled this contest. Nelson's plans were constantly unravelling and being overtaken. He had failed to halt the French on the riviera, or to reopen Tuscany and the papal territories to British ships. Then in September he was thrown further backwards, as another crucial source of succour was lost. Genoa finally broke its cosmetic neutrality and Nelson himself was made the unwitting instrument.

7

It had been coming for some time. With the French mastering every neighbour, and occupying the entire Genoese coast bar the city itself, the collapse of the small republic's neutrality seemed inevitable. The Genoese ports sprinkled along the riviera had been turned into enemy strongholds, shut to British ships even in distress, and in the city only a nervous neutrality survived, with internal factions arguing for and against conciliating the invaders. Monsieur Faypoult, the French minister plenipotentiary, seemed to wield ever greater influence in Genoa, and excitable Jacobin mobs quickly gathered in the streets.

Ominous rumblings had been reaching Nelson all summer, and on 6 July Brame had forwarded a petition from worried British merchants in Genoa, recommending the deployment of a naval force. Nelson had written to Elliot for advice, and been warned to tread carefully. He had assured the traders of his readiness to help, but events tumbled too fast, one after another. At the end of August the British consulate advised the merchants to prepare to leave Genoa at a moment's notice, while Madame Caffarena warned that an interdiction on the shipping of provisions to the British was in the offing. She suggested a ship of the line be sent. The British relied on Genoa for fresh meat, biscuit, onions and lemons – commodities essential for the wellbeing of their sailors – and the matter could not be ignored.

To make matters worse, in July the British consul, Joseph Brame, suffered a stroke, and degenerated into what proved to be terminal mental confusion; a few years would see him retire to Pisa, reduced, as Madame Caffarena said, to childhood. Fretting from Vienna, Drake worried about the sensitive documents left about the consul's quarters, exposed to unreliable servants, and suggested Nelson store the papers on board ship. 'What a combination of cross grained circumstances!' sighed Madame Caffarena. 'The want of a minister. The consul's want of health. The want of will. The want of power. I wish the result may be nothing worse than finding myself soon in want of brains to see the repeated insults that mushroom republic causes us!' Nor was her lament undue, because it was just as Britain was stripped of her man on the spot that relations with Genoa reached an impasse.[43]

The diplomatic incident of 11 September 1796 gave Nelson more publicity than he had previously known, and ostensibly caused the breakdown of Britain's fragile peace with Genoa. Since historians have neglected the episode, it is worth unravelling in full.

Horatio Nelson arrived in Genoa on 4 September. He had met *L'Eclair* at sea, and learned from Captain Edward Tyrrell that he had just come from Genoa, where he had been refused permission to load bullocks purchased for the fleet. The embargo Madame Caffarena had predicted was already in place, locking one hundred and seventy British oxen in the port. Nelson had been confirmed in the post of first-class commodore on 11 August, and felt his authority strengthened, but he banked on reason and a leniency he had recently shown at Leghorn, where Genoese ships had been allowed to leave without their cargoes, to count more strongly in his favour. The approach would have satisfied Drake, who advised caution and tact, but it merely opened an unrewarding, almost a humiliating, business.[44]

Nelson memorialised the Genoese senate, and gave the document to James Bird, the stricken consul's son-in-law and temporary interpreter. On the 5th Bird delivered it to Castiglione's own house, but no reply appeared and the next day Nelson collected Bird and personally waited upon the secretary of state. Castiglione uneasily explained that the memorial was with the government and a response was expected shortly. But another empty day passed, and on 8 September Nelson demanded to speak to the newly elected doge. The audience took place at six the same evening. Nelson had Bird read a statement explaining that the shipping of the oxen did not breach Genoese regulations, as had been claimed, and that the animals were effectively being sequestrated. The doge spread his hands. He respected the British, of course, but Genoa was a small, weak country sitting between powerful belligerents, and the interdiction did not rest with him. He was mildly curious that so young a man as Nelson enjoyed such a formidable reputation, and asked the commodore to set his complaint on yet another piece of paper and he would seek an answer. The statement went in promptly the following day, and another on the 10th in which Nelson went so far as to say that if no reply to this note was received he would send expresses to Drake and Jervis. They would withdraw British ships from Genoa and proceed on the assumption that the city had illegally confiscated British property. While impatiently awaiting a response to his ultimatum, Nelson met the British merchants in Brame's office and promised to do what he could. Nevertheless, he warned them that the impending war with Spain might weaken naval cover and necessitate an evacuation of Genoa at any time.[45]

The doge did press the senate, but it would not give way, and speciously justified the embargo by claiming local shortages of meat. The *Captain* secured some wood, sheep and water, even a little fresh beef, but no live oxen, and Nelson concluded that only reprisals against Genoese ships and cargoes might force concessions. Unfortunately, the French army spoke more loudly than His Majesty's ships, a point immediately to be driven home.

During the night of 10 September a soldier and two sailors belonging to the *Captain* jumped ship and made off in a stolen boat. At daylight the *Captain* stood out of the mole, and at about eight-thirty Nelson lowered his barge and pinnace and sent them off under Berry and Noble to hunt the deserters. Drawing a blank about the mole at Genoa, the boats began pulling towards the adjoining haven of St Pierre d'Arena, three hundred yards from the city walls.

A tower and battery, known as 'the lanthorn battery', commanded St Pierre d'Arena, the colours above it pronouncing the port a possession of the republic and a neutral haven open to all ships. But as with so many other supposedly neutral ports, the French had made it their own, hauling four guns to some commanding ground and using the anchorage as a military depot. According to Nelson, that day the beach was strewn with shells, shot, guns, carriages and muskets, and the French flag was flying. A French bombard also happened to be at anchor, laden with guns and ammunition for Bonaparte's army.

What happened next depends upon which version is believed.

Nelson said that his boats went in solely to look for their deserters, and Berry testified that the commodore specifically told him not to board the French bombard unless he was fired upon. The situation changed only after a French battery ashore opened fire. Logs of the British ships support this interpretation. One lieutenant's log from the *Captain* recorded, for instance, that 'the [French] battery at St Pierre d'Arena opened their fire upon our boats, who in return brought out a French bombard'. Likewise, Summers wrote that 'before they [the British boats] reached the shore, the French battery [fired] on them. Immediately they boarded a French ketch'. Nearby, the *L'Eclair* reported that 'at eight the batteries from the shore fired several shot at the *Captain*'s boats as they passed; at half past eight the boats took a French tartan [bombard] in tow; they continued firing from all the batteries; at nine they fired on us'. These and other accounts, like those of Nelson and Berry, offered no doubts that the French fired the first shots.[46]

It was a version that was contested at the time by Genoa's secretary of state, who claimed that statements he saw showed the British went into St Pierre d'Arena for the express purpose of capturing the French ship. The next month the republic's official responses to British complaints, wriggling to evade the charge that they had allowed the French to establish a military presence in the harbour, tied themselves in knots. On the one hand there were few French in St Pierre d'Arena, with four unmounted and unarmed guns on the beach, they said; but on the other, a fire was admittedly directed upon the British boats. However, said the Genoese, the French cannons only opened fire 'subsequent' to the capture of their ship, and the gunners knew nothing of the attack until the dislodged crew of the bombard swam ashore. An independent eyewitness, apparently an English merchant, lends some credibility to this last accusation. Nelson's boats, he said, 'had *begun* to carry her [the bombard] off *when* they were fired upon from the French battery, and immediately after from the Genoese batteries of the Lantern and the mole'.[47]

The truth was probably muddier than either admitted. Nelson had certainly adopted a strong line against Genoese harbours controlled by the French. Indeed, in a 'statement of facts' he gave Genoa to justify his capture of the bombard he candidly stated that wherever the French raised batteries to keep the British out, neutrality effectively ceased to exist. Both he and Elliot worked on the premise that in neutral territory thus occupied it was 'indisputably lawful to take all vessels on that coast, and under the very guns of its forts, which would be prize at sea'.[48]

However, in this instance the harbour was effectively part of the city of Genoa itself, and Nelson had sworn to uphold neutrality there to the utmost extremity. The issue had arisen several times in the previous months. In March, Nelson had complained to Genoa of a French privateer boarding a ship within gunshot of the town batteries, and had been assured that any vessel breaking the neutrality of the port would be fired upon. Equally, the following month Castiglione had accused a British frigate, the *Blanche*, of following a French ship out of the harbour in order to seize it at sea, and in August he charged *L'Eclair* with intimidating a French privateer at the Genoa mole. Nelson, too, had been quick to mollify, and gave his word of honour that his ships would commit no hostile acts within gunshot of Genoa.[49]

Given this history, and the shaky state of British relations with Genoa that September, it is highly improbable that Nelson ordered his boats to attack or even threaten the French bombard in St Pierre d'Arena. British records also leave no doubt that a search was being made for deserters. Nevertheless, Nelson had attacked enemy positions in Genoese ports before, and knew full well that the French normally provided an excuse by nervously firing the first shots as soon as a British force approached. He must have known that there was a good chance of that happening here, and been prepared to capture the bombard.

That morning of 11 September the French shore battery fired on Berry's boats as they rowed into the harbour, and the furious tars attacked and carried the bombard, which turned out to be a valuable military prize. But at this point events began to slip from Nelson's control. The Genoese batteries began bombarding the British boats and ships, first the lanthorn battery and then those at the mole. Even this did not unduly disturb Commodore Nelson, who acted as he had done near Oneglia the previous May. He ordered his men not to retaliate against the Genoese and sent an irate protest ashore, hoping to silence the town's guns.

As the skirmish snowballed, both sides tried to reinforce their combatants. Nelson sent a launch and a cutter to help Berry, and manoeuvred the *Captain* and *L'Eclair* into supporting positions. Three or four French privateers, which rowed from the mole, were quickly driven back under the Genoese batteries by *L'Eclair*'s guns and put out of the fight. Simultaneously the *Captain* also fired some three cannon shots at the French guns in St Pierre d'Arena, and her men expended two hundred musket and pistol balls in defence of the boats. On the other hand she remained under the fire of the guns at the lanthorn and mole without returning a shot. During a period of several hours some fifty shots were flung at Nelson's ship, passing 'over us, under us, and on all sides of us, even to throwing the water upon our decks'. But not one hit. The French later complained that the Genoese not only delayed firing ('we fired more than thirty times before you were disposed to oppose this violation of neutrality') but deliberately missed their targets, and they may have been right.[50]

As firing continued, Nelson scribbled a 'statement of facts' for 'the knowledge of every person in Genoa and its neighbourhood', and enclosed it in a letter to Brame, calling upon him to wait 'immediately' upon the secretary of state. He complained of the existence of the French battery at St Pierre d'Arena and of the Genoese attack upon his ship. Not only that, but sensing matters were getting out of hand he offered Genoa a way out. Lieutenant Compton, who took the messages ashore, was authorised to state verbally that if Genoa ceased its fire, and satisfaction was offered for the insult to His Majesty's flag, Nelson was prepared to place the French prize in their hands. The Genoese might then appease the French by restoring to them the ship Nelson had taken. It was a clear and creditable proposition, recognising the difficult position Genoa occupied between two belligerent powers. Nothing was said of what Nelson meant by satisfaction, but an apology was obviously necessary, with perhaps the lifting of the embargo on British supplies.

Compton's jolly boat dodged the French gunboats that tried to intercept him, and reached the Ponte Reale (Royal Bridge), but a swarm of angry French seamen gathered on the landing. The lieutenant got ashore and rushed off to find Brame, but his four men were ringed by raging adversaries threatening to seize the boat, and a pistol was said to have been fired. With difficulty the Genoese guards eventually intervened, dispersing the crowd with musketry and killing a French sailor before taking the Britons into protective custody and carrying one to hospital. In no great time inflamed Jacobins were rampaging about the town declaring they would murder any English they found, while French privateersmen gathered to board the British merchant ships in the harbour and seize or slaughter their crews. The alarmed authorities advised Brame to stay indoors and placed soldiers on the British ships at the mole. Drawbridges were lowered, sentinels strengthened and gates closed.

While Nelson extricated his vessels and prize from gun range of the batteries, and Brame dispatched the commodore's protests to the secretary of state, the volcanic French minister, Faypoult, fired a furious missive at his hosts. He demanded reparations for the captured bombard, the sequestration of British merchantmen and property, including Nelson's parley boats, and the closure of Genoa and all satellite ports to British ships. Genoa, in short, must now choose between France and Britain. While Faypoult also issued a proclamation urging the French in the city to be calm, he assured them of satisfaction, and his letter to the Genoese government contained implicit threats of civil disorder and armed invasion.

At about one-thirty, with guns still being fired and no response to his earlier message evident, Nelson sent a second boat into Genoa. The commodore challenged the authorities to interview the inhabitants and soldiers of St Pierre d'Arena under oath to learn the truth about the incident, and offered to speak to any Genoese officer sent aboard the *Captain*. Lieutenant Peirson, the Italian-speaking army officer who had attached himself to the commodore's following, proceeded bravely to the Fauxbourg of the River Bisagno with a flag of truce. He was not even allowed into the town, but was kept in a guardroom until he could be sent back to Nelson with the unwelcome news that Genoa would frame official answers to his protests. In the meantime the port was closed to British ships.[51]

The next day found Nelson hovering offshore, plainly shaken by the serious turn events had taken, and scribbling to Drake that his boats had been a mere hundred yards from the lanthorn battery when the French had opened fire. His pacific intent, he insisted, could not have been mistaken by the Genoese. On shore the situation was hopeless as well as fraught. In the afternoon of the 11th and again on the 12th Castiglione notified Brame that the port was closed to his nation and their property confiscated. Nelson had made an unprovoked attack on the French in St Pierre d'Arena, and invented the story of the deserters to cover his real intentions.

Nelson retrieved his last boat, but the first with Compton's party had to be left behind when he sailed from Genoa on 14 September. Brame and Bird tried to pick up the pieces. They took charge of the impounded British boat, which the authorities surrendered to them in due course, and smuggled Compton out of town in disguise, carrying copies of Castiglione's letters to the consul. Astonishingly, the three deserters who had provided the spark for the fracas also gave themselves up to Brame, 'very sorry and penitent', and begged him to intercede on their behalf. But on the central issues the consul made no progress. British property about the town, including four ships trapped at the mole and the embargoed oxen, became hostages to fortune, and the republic's ports were closed to His Britannic Majesty's subjects.[52]

Nelson absolved himself of blame, and put the matter simply: going about his lawful business, his boats had been attacked while under the protection of Genoa, and Genoa had taken the part of the aggressors and committed an act of war. His immediate instinct was to seize Genoese ships, and hold them until the republic gave satisfaction and reopened its ports. His friends rallied around. Elliot was inclined to believe the Russian minister at Genoa, who told him that the Genoese had already decided to break with Britain, and merely needed an excuse. As far as Elliot could see, 'Commodore Nelson behaved with great moderation in refraining from returning the fire from Genoa, and in offering to surrender his prize to the Genoese'. Jervis also

approved of 'every part' of Nelson's conduct, and railed that the existence of the French battery alone justified his capture of the bombard.
For the moment, however, he advised Nelson to temporise with the
Genoese in an effort to extricate British citizens and property. The
only blame Sir John directed to the *Captain* fell upon Lieutenant John
Davies, a recent recruit to the ship from whose watch the deserters
had fled with the stolen boat. The mistake cost Davies a promotion
to the *Victory* the following year.[53]

When the news reached Drake he exonerated Nelson, but understood that Genoa was a frightened pygmy between giants, in acute
danger of being invaded by the French. News of the outbreak of war
between Spain and Britain had also reached Italy in the first days of
September, and further emphasised Albion's growing isolation. It was
obvious in Genoa that Britain would have to review its commitments
in the Mediterranean, and that the Royal Navy might be withdrawn.
Considering all of which, Drake felt that an extreme reaction to the
attack on Nelson would achieve little except the alienation of Britain's
remaining friends in Genoa. He wrote to the republic offering to broker
'an impartial discussion' of the affair, involving parties from all sides,
but his request that British property be first released as a gesture of
good faith condemned the proposal from the start.[54]

Reflecting on the crisis on the *Captain*, Commodore Nelson developed his own and more vigorous scheme to repair the damage. The
blow had undoubtedly been a severe one, costing the navy yet another
major source of succour and supply. It was fortunate for Nelson that
the *Captain* herself had escaped unscathed, and taken aboard necessary supplies of water, beef, onions and lemons before the fight in St
Pierre d'Arena. When the British ship *Sardine* approached the harbour
on 20 September she was fired upon and driven away. But Nelson
was not yet convinced that the matter was irreversible. Underestimating
the impact of more than two years of French successes in that quarter,
he was sure that Genoa would restore its relations with Britain if it
could. If the cost of angering Britain was brought home, the Genoese
might yet atone for their behaviour.[55]

He knew what he would do. Now the British held Elba, the small
Genoese island of Capraia had become the most threatening bridge
between Leghorn and Corsica. Elliot had long worried about the
French privateers and traders that packed its neutral havens, and
suspected the islanders of anti-British sentiment. Until the previous
November it had refused to admit a British consul or agent, although

the French Directory had their man there. Nelson had declined to move against Capraia, especially as Britain's relations with Genoa had been so tense, but now . . .[56]

8

There was no time to refer to the admiral. In a conference in Bastia on 15 September, Elliot authorised the seizure of Capraia and issued orders to his armed forces. Nelson embarked detachments of the 51st Regiment and Corsican volunteers under Major Logan on the *Captain*, *La Minerve*, the *Gorgon* store ship, *Vanneau* brig and *Rose* cutter, and after a slow voyage brought them to their destination on the evening of 17 September.[57]

Capraia's defences were known to be 'very strong', but Elliot and Nelson believed that the Genoese had grown complacent and reduced the number of guns and men in the garrison. However, a plan to disembark on the southwestern part of the island was abandoned after heavy musketry revealed regular defenders strongly posted on the top of a high hill above the landing place. Logan withdrew his boats, and after consulting Nelson probed for an alternative. He eventually ordered his soldiers to land and storm the hill and a tower from the north. The boats pulled inshore. Ahead went rowing boats, manned mainly by sturdy seamen; behind, on towropes, the rest of the boats with the soldiers sitting with their arms. Even here they were greeted by musket fire, and several of the Corsican volunteers panicked as their boats came within enemy range. Some jumped into the sea, and others cut their towropes and rowed furiously out of range, from which safe distance they 'boldly put about' to return an entirely ineffective musketry of their own. Nevertheless, the landings continued and at seven in the evening Nelson himself went ashore in his barge. As a commodore, his business was to command from the ships, but he believed in showing men that he was willing to share their dangers and to set an example in moments of difficulty.[58]

The commodore was back on the *Captain* at eleven for a few hours' rest, but at four-thirty the following morning he accompanied the last of the assault force and several pieces of heavy artillery ashore. The scenes that followed were redolent of old days in Corsica, as Nelson and Spicer directed a party of sailors hauling protesting cannons up a steep gradient to threaten the Genoese garrison. Another key figure in the attack was Lieutenant Peirson, who Nelson had assigned to

Logan with a detachment of troops from the ships and the local rank of foot major. 'I cannot say . . . how much I am obliged to Lt Pearson . . . who is now with me, and has been of the greatest service to me from the commencement of this expedition,' Logan acknowledged.[59]

During the night a French privateer sheltering in the harbour of Capraia made its escape, but four others were trapped, two of them being set on fire by their own crews. Twenty-eight of their men became prisoners of war, although five later managed to escape, steal a boat and reach Leghorn. Some forty-nine merchant ships, including Genoese neutrals and prizes of the French, were also appropriated by the British, and at about six o'clock in the morning Nelson sent a summons to the garrison under a flag of truce. Following the pattern of his success at Porto Ferraio, Nelson linked moderate terms to the threat of overwhelming force. If they surrendered their fortress the garrison would receive every military honour, and a passage to Genoa with their arms and colours. Civil officials would be allowed to govern as before, the safety of private property ensured, and no financial penalties would be imposed. However, the public property of Genoa and the shipping would be inventoried and held pending a satisfactory settlement of outstanding difficulties, and everything French was to be seized as prize.[60]

Resistance was useless. The Genoese commandant, Agostino Aynolo, had only 133 regulars, and when he pleaded for time to consult his government, Nelson said he would withdraw his terms and launch an overwhelming attack. After a flurry of notes, and some going back and forth on the part of Lieutenant Peirson, the colours above the citadel came down at four o'clock and a British flag was raised. Nelson took charge of twenty-two serviceable Genoese guns, 204 muskets, and a quantity of military stores, and installed a small garrison. The task force returned to Bastia on 19 September, and the same day Nelson wrote a dispatch praising both services for their conduct during the operation.

Back off Leghorn, Nelson issued new orders to the captains of the *Diadem*, *Blanche*, *Lively* and *L'Eclair*. All Genoese vessels were to be detained. They were not to be regarded as permanent prizes, but bargaining counters in the dispute with Genoa, and their masters were to remain in charge of, and responsible for, their cargoes. Gradually the seizures came in, beginning it seems with the *Concepción* brig taken on 24 September and a polacre seized by the *Lively*. The unfortunate vessels were taken to Porto Ferraio, where Udny was instructed to act as agent, ensuring 'the good and humane treatment of the crews, who are in no way to be pillaged or evil treated'. The next move was to couple such detainees with the island of Capraia in a bid to release the British property in Genoa and normalise relations with the Italian republic.[61]

The capture of Capraia was a mixed blessing. It severely damaged French plans to infiltrate Corsica from Leghorn because the island was seen as a midway refuge for their boats. The elimination of that base made the French voyages to Corsica more perilous, and enthusiasm for the venture weakened. As far as Genoa was concerned, however, Nelson's latest victory gained him no great advantage. Any impulse the republic felt to conciliate was overridden by fear of the French. On 4 October a note sent to Brame for delivery to London offered to release the British ships in Genoa only after compensation had been paid for the tartan seized in St Pierre d'Arena, and the issue of Capraia and the impounded Genoese vessels had been addressed. Unfortunately, Nelson's stroke did not weaken the Gallic influence in Genoa, but strengthened it. Faypoult, the French minister in Genoa, was furious at the loss of Capraia. He had alerted the Genoese to its vulnerability after the fall of Porto Ferraio, and now fulminated about Genoa's inability to defend her ports, threatening that French soldiers would take over the Italian forts and do the job themselves. Like some monstrous kraken, encircling an unfortunate victim ever more deeply in powerful and sinuous tentacles, revolutionary France bullied Genoa into fortifying her harbours and islands in the Gulf of Spezia to prevent the British from seizing them and thus securing another safe haven for their fleet.[62]

Nor could Nelson's boldness prevail against the wider and relentless political countercurrent. His every effort seemed destined to be overthrown. While he was on the turquoise seas of the Mediterranean, striving to protect Corsica and endeavouring to disable the French juggernaut, in Whitehall the politicians gave up the game.

On 25 September, Sir John Jervis received an ominous packet from the Admiralty. It contained orders to evacuate Corsica and to withdraw from the Mediterranean. The Franco-Spanish alliance had done the key damage. Confronted with what on paper at least was a formidable naval combination, as well as the possibility of the Spaniards using their port of Cadiz to drive a wedge between the British Mediterranean and Channel fleets, the government decided to concentrate its forces nearer home. It made sense, particularly as Britain now had few allies east of Gibraltar and no efficient ones, but after three years of travail it was a bitter draught to swallow.

Jervis wrote to Nelson the same day. For a while Cockburn should continue to blockade Leghorn, but Nelson was to help Elliot evacuate the British from Corsica. Nelson was still at Bastia when he got the news on the 29th. Deep within he was not sorry to relinquish Corsica, for like Drake he had grown thoroughly disillusioned with islanders who seemed to him ungrateful and 'rotten at heart'. But he shuddered for his remaining friends and allies in Italy, and felt personally for Elliot who was left 'very low and distressed' at the destruction of his work.[63]

These new orders put an entirely different complexion upon Nelson's plans for Genoa. It was obvious that Capraia, which he had wanted for leverage, would now have to be surrendered anyway. With the British gone, Elba and Capraia would revert to their original owners. Nelson acted with his usual decision. He embarked upon a final, almost forlorn, effort to bluff Genoa into a compromise before news of the British retreat could spread.

Elliot's terms for the restitution of Capraia were in his pocket, but he was unable to dignify them with his new seventy-four. The *Captain* was due to receive a new foremast at Ajaccio, and Commodore Nelson had switched his broad pendant to the *Diadem* sixty-four on 26 September. He had made satisfactory progress with the crew of the *Captain*, strengthened as it was with old *Agamemnons*. The punishment rate had been moderate: thirty-four floggings, of which eight consisted of more than twelve strokes of the cat. Aboard the *Diadem* he worked with new material, though he took with him a personal servant, James Lenstock, the invaluable Charles Peirson, Lieutenant Noble as a signalling lieutenant, and Midshipman Withers. The *Diadem* also had the distinction of providing Nelson with his first flag captain. He had been entitled to one since becoming an official commodore, and Berry had acted in that capacity on the *Captain*. As commander of the *Diadem*, George Henry Towry served Nelson as flag captain during the mission to Genoa.[64]

Nelson sailed from Bastia on 5 October and made Genoa in three days. There were few chances of success, and even the patient Drake had warned his foreign secretary that French influence had destroyed the prospects of reconciliation. Against Gallic bayonets, Nelson had little to offer. He was authorised to restore Capraia and any detained ships, but only if the republic fulfilled impracticable conditions. British property must be released, Genoa's ports opened to His Majesty's subjects and reparations made for the insult to the British colours. Capraia must remain under British control for as long as any part of Italy remained occupied by the French, and accept a permanent vice consul or agent to protect British interests. They were not terms that could have extricated Genoa from her difficulties, and Admiral Jervis had grown increasingly bellicose and indisposed to compromise. On 7 October, while Nelson struggled to achieve the impossible in Genoa, the admiral was urging Brame to tell the republic that he would 'batter down the mole-head and deface the beautiful city' with his fleet if Britain's terms were refused.[65]

With a distinct sense of *déjà vu* Peirson was rowed into Genoa on 8 October under a flag of truce, bearing news that Nelson was empowered to negotiate and needed permission to land. After an hour in which the lieutenant was kept waiting in his boat an answer arrived in the negative. The Genoese secretary of state said the matter would be pursued in London rather than the Mediterranean. The following day Nelson tried again, but his messenger, Captain Towry, was turned away and had to leave a packet containing the British terms with Brame. On 10 October the *Diadem* sailed away.[66]

It had been a futile exercise from the beginning. Genoa had already drafted an official complaint for their minister, the Marquis of Spinola, to present to the king in London, and published their anti-British interpretation of the dispute in Genoa. The republic was sinking deeper and deeper into French pockets, and even as Nelson waited impatiently off the harbour, her leaders were concluding a humiliating pact with France, granting Bonaparte's army the right to pass through Genoese territory, submitting to a financial levy, and undertaking to keep their ports closed to the British. On the 15th Castiglione dismissed the Elliot–Jervis terms in writing, and a day or two later the wisdom of Genoa's decision was confirmed when news reached the city that Britain was evacuating the Mediterranean. The Genoese had taken their only viable course.[67]

Nelson was incensed beyond words when he learned how his conduct was being represented by the Genoese in London, especially a barb that, as he had seized the French ship after giving his word of honour not to fire in anger within gunshot of Genoa, he had been shown to be faithless. But all his colleagues held him blameless, including Drake and Trevor, who preferred to handle the dispute with tact rather than indignation. Jervis almost boiled over, demanding that

Brame use every organ of publicity to refute the Genoese allegations. In London the commodore also received the unanimous backing of superiors, and Spinola was curtly informed that the king 'entirely' approved of Nelson's conduct 'in all his transactions with the republic of Genoa'. The British government stoutly refused to discuss the affair while British property remained sequestrated, and retaliated with an embargo of their own, seizing all Genoese ships and goods in Britain. The break with the once neutral republic was complete, and southern Europe from Gibraltar to Naples had become a coast of unrelieved hostility.[68]

9

Jervis was stationed with the fleet in Mortella Bay at St Fiorenzo with the awesome job of evacuating Corsica and protecting its retreating soldiers and civilians from French and Spanish interference. The flashpoint, if there was going to be one, was Bastia, the largest of the Corsican strongholds. Jervis ordered the acting commander of the *Captain*, Charles Stuart, to take Sutton's *Egmont* and a few frigates and sloops under his command and begin loading the powder at Bastia. The rumours of unrest were disturbing, and Jervis breathed a sigh of relief when he learned that Commodore Nelson himself had returned from Genoa, and was at Bastia with the *Diadem*. No officer in the navy was as famous in Corsica or more respected. If anyone could evacuate the place without loss it was Nelson.[69]

Bastia was certainly simmering when Nelson arrived before daylight on Friday 14 October. The *Egmont* followed him in before noon, but as yet there was no sign of the *Captain*. A boat dropped the commodore at a wharf in front of Elliot's house, in the north of the town, and he was soon listening to a disturbing tale. News of the British retreat had been spreading like wildfire throughout Corsica, and control was passing to municipal committees. Some of the committees were dominated by Francophiles, but even moderate Corsicans understood the importance of squaring themselves with the incoming regime. Britain's writ melted like frost in sunlight. The road between Bastia and St Fiorenzo was no longer safe, and in Bastia a Committee of Thirty prepared to send deputies to the generals in Leghorn, seeking re-admission to the French republic. Elliot understood their difficulty, and still felt obligations towards them. He agreed to parole any French prisoners being held in Bastia to help the deputies buy influence with their new masters, and generously promised to leave the forts and Corsican artillery in a serviceable condition – provided, of course, that the British were allowed to withdraw without trouble.[70]

Elliot was an idealist who romanticised the Corsicans and he had not reconciled himself to evacuating the Mediterranean. Reporting these events, he would minimise the extent of Corsican disaffection, and claim that stories of threats to the departing British had been 'false and exaggerated'. Despite 'short interludes of uneasiness' he had never heard a 'murmur of resentment' against the British, and the actions of the Committee of Thirty had been 'prudent and honourable' throughout. At the time, though, he seemed less certain. Lady Elliot, whose elegant balls had enlivened the social life of Bastia in their day, had left with her children for Gibraltar, and the viceroy had asked Jervis to cover the evacuation of Bastia with a warship. According to Nelson, Sir Gilbert was in a state of some alarm when he saw him that morning of the 14th. Elliot had a house guard, but it was rumoured that an attempt would be made on his life, and he immediately asked the commodore to store important papers aboard the *Diadem*.[71]

Hurrying on to the quarters of Lieutenant General De Burgh, who commanded the British garrison in the citadel, Nelson sensed the growing unease. It is doubtful if the army was as 'panic-struck' and 'helpless' as the commodore claimed, but the Corsicans had success-fully insisted on sharing guard duties, and De Burgh admitted that as many of them as Britons now manned the citadel, batteries, gates and storehouses. Before long – perhaps that day – he expected to lose control of the citadel, and the prospect of saving guns or provisions seemed negligible. Nevertheless, De Burgh had already made up his mind to take a strong line. He intended to inform the committee that he would use all provisions rightly belonging to his troops, and that any attempt to obstruct his duties would meet with a severe response. Nelson suggested the gates of the citadel be closed against further infil-tration, talked up their chances, and told the general to prepare for a secret evacuation.[72]

Back at Elliot's residence the commodore was mobbed by terrified British merchants and privateer owners, some in tears. Their goods, down to their very wardrobes, had been seized and their ships shut in by a Corsican privateer moored across the mole head. They would be ruined. Nelson called for calm, and promised action, but after dark he played safe by embarking Elliot and his secretary of state, an Anglo-Corsican named Charles-André Pozzo di Borgo.[73]

The chances of the situation drifting out of control had to be closed down, and the next day Nelson ended any speculation about his intentions.

Under a cloudy sky the town saw the imposing, gun-spotted sides of the *Egmont* and *Diadem* ships of the line anchored at the mole head on springs, ready to swing their broadsides in murderous arcs of fire. Boats bristling with men, muskets, pistols and cutlasses headed into the harbour under Captain Towry, ready to tow the imprisoned British merchantmen to safety. The Corsican privateer charged with closing the harbour buzzed with excitement and scores of its armed compatriots clustered on the mole with primed muskets. But Nelson sent Captain Sutton of the *Egmont* ashore with a message to the Committee of Thirty. If the Corsicans interfered with the British operation Nelson would batter the town down about their ears. Sutton pulled out a watch. He gave the Corsicans fifteen minutes to answer before he began firing. Everyone in Corsica knew Nelson was not a man to be trifled with. The privateer held back, and the musketeers at the mole head scattered, some dumping their weapons in flight. Towry proceeded calmly about his business and sixty sail were brought out of Bastia.

That afternoon there was another show of strength. A privateer master or owner asked Nelson to help recover forty hogsheads of tobacco from a locked customs house. Nelson told him to demand access and sent an officer and men as an escort. A few minutes later the grateful owner was back with the keys to the customs house. The Corsican authorities, he said, went 'as white as sheets, and said not a word'. Nelson probably exaggerated his success, but boasted that 'Bastia . . . never was so quiet; not an armed man was found in the streets to the night of our embarkation'.[74]

Though Nelson regarded the army as too 'well-dressed and powdered', De Burgh had earned more respect from Elliot than had his predecessors, Stuart and Moore. He posted a hundred guards to keep the waterfront clear while the seamen loaded the ships and Nelson's own soldiers held Elliot's wharf. As some vessels put out with the first loads, others arrived, transports and men-of-war both. On the 15th it was the repaired *Captain*, to which Nelson and his signalling lieutenant returned with the commodore's broad pendant. Stuart remained aboard as flag captain. The *Southampton* came in the next day, discharged the transports she had convoyed from Mortella Bay, and then left to collect the British garrison on Capraia. Her place at

Bastia was eventually taken by the *Sardine* twenty-four, the *Resolution* cutter and the *Excellent* ship of the line, the last under the command of the hugely reassuring Captain Collingwood.[75]

Night and day the work went on. Men manhandled provisions, equipment, baggage and horses to the boats, rowed them to the ships and hoisted them aboard. The possessions of civilians, diplomats, soldiers and six hundred royalist Corsican and French had to be found a place. According to one 'old *Agamemnon*':

Many novel scenes [were] exhibited in Bastia at this time. Whole families might be seen moving along with their little stock of goods under the protection of British sailors or soldiers, while their enemies could do no more than look on with envy and vexation, and see themselves deprived of their intended plunder . . . It was nothing uncommon to see two or three of our ship's crew marching along with a female under each arm, convoying them safely to the place of embarkation. Here you might see a group of men convoying a lot of furniture, while the family were carrying the lighter articles such as band-boxes, bundles and such-like gear.[76]

Just as Commodore Nelson thought he had everything under control a new shadow loomed. Despite the blockade of Leghorn, a company of French cavalry and several hundred of their Corsican auxiliaries slipped out of the port in bad weather, the advance guard of Bonaparte's invasion by instalments. Under General Casalta they landed at Rogliano on Cape Corse on 18 October, and began marching towards Bastia, gathering volunteers along the way. When he heard about it, Elliot realised that even so small a force as this could fan simmering discontent and disrupt his evacuation. In an audience with the Committee of Thirty he warned that if the French advanced within six miles of the town he would consider destroying the citadel and part of the town. Messengers from the Corsicans in Bastia soon sped urgently northwards, begging Casalta to delay entering the town until the British had left, and delivering a letter from Elliot repeating his threats. The French would not be stayed, however, and tramped resolutely on. These were men inspired by a series of victories over the Austrians and their allies.[77]

At eleven at night on the 19th several shivering representatives of the Bastia committee clambered aboard the *Captain* 'in great terror' to plead with Elliot for 'the last favour they had to request at our hands'. They had not only failed to halt the French but been threatened with retaliation if they allowed the British to leave. Now the committee implored Elliot to evacuate his men immediately, before the French arrived, lest the town be punished. Originally, Nelson had planned to withdraw the troops from the citadel in another two days, but he had already decided to speed up the operation. Though he is represented as having reacted unfavourably to the Corsican request until pressed by Elliot, he had contingency plans for an instant evacuation and agreed to implement them immediately. The Capraia garrison had come in earlier that day, and £200,000 of property and stores had been disembarked.

After days of cloud a heavy gale was whipping up and the night was dark. At midnight De Burgh's men plugged the guns of the citadel with shot and blankets and removed their firing accessories, and marched out through the town towards Elliot's wharf, a couple of field pieces rumbling along behind to deter any attackers. The eyes of the soldiers were fixed upon lights Nelson had hauled to the mastheads of his ships, but no one disputed their passage. 'Every thing was conducted with perfect tranquillity,' reported Elliot, who went ashore to lend Nelson a hand. 'The whole town was as still as if it had not been inhabited, and the "Champ and Mars" was as quiet as it could have been a month before.' At about one in the morning of the 20th, as the redcoats and their allies assembled at the landing place to wait their turn for the boats, three hundred of Casalta's men penetrated the north of the town, spilling into the abandoned citadel and feverishly attempting to restore the crippled artillery. Even at this stage they wanted to bombard Nelson's ships before they could get to sea.[78]

Out in the fading darkness, as dawn broke, Nelson and De Burgh waited on the wharf and saw every man embarked. It was a slow job. Dillon's regiment, composed of French royalists and Germans, was embarked first but congested the boats with baggage, while a powerful wind blowing off the land made return journeys hard going. During the four hours the rearguard, the 51st Regiment, stood waiting on the landing, word of the French arrival reached Nelson, but the embarkation continued calmly and everyone and everything was loaded, including the two field pieces. The last of the fifteen hundred soldiers left the wharf at about six in the morning, and it was only then that Nelson and De Burgh took their places in the last boat. Nelson told Trevor that neither man nor stone scheduled to leave was left behind, and Elliot pronounced the operation 'total and successful', accomplished 'without loss or accident of any kind'. No less exuberant, Jervis reported that although a few bulky casks of flour had been left in the citadel, he judged the evacuation of Corsica 'without the loss of a man, killed or wounded' to be 'the most fortunate event of my service'.[79]

For several hours severe weather delayed sailing, trapping the ships at anchor, and De Burgh's foresight in spiking the citadel's guns proved to be a wise precaution. Happily, at noon conditions moderated, and before the French could bring their cannons to action the British slipped gently away and disappeared in rain and grey cloud. Nelson had brought them to Bastia and now he had taken them away.

Completing a model operation, he reached Porto Ferraio the same day. At first Elba had also been earmarked for evacuation, but at the eleventh hour Britain suddenly bowed to representations from Naples and ordered a stay of execution. For the time being the British would maintain a reduced presence in the area, based on Elba. Reading his new orders from Jervis, dated 17 October, Commodore Nelson took great pleasure in telling Elliot that the troops from Bastia could be disembarked at Porto Ferraio if he wished. Sir Gilbert was delighted, and began dreaming of holding Elba indefinitely as a British outpost, drawing supplies from Naples and rebuilding an Italian front against the French. His faith in British sea power remained unshaken. Nelson's spirits also seem to have risen. He pointed out where a naval arsenal might be established, to replace the one being evacuated at Ajaccio, and envisaged returning to command the station after assisting Jervis to wind up the business of Corsica. Alerting Sir William Hamilton to the good news, Nelson promised to 'endeavour to prove myself the same active officer which the world has said I am'.[80]

The most galling consequence of the government's sudden reversal of orders, as far as Nelson was concerned, was the premature release of Capraia. The accusations levelled against his honour in Genoa and the rebuff of his recent overtures rankled like a severe toothache. On 20 October, as soon as he learned of the new policy, Nelson ordered Collingwood to Capraia with the *Excellent*, *Egmont* and *Southampton* and a detachment of troops under Logan. They were to reinstall the British garrison removed only a few days before. Collingwood found the Genoese powerfully entrenched in their old fortifications, however, and declining to assault the place a second time joined Nelson at Porto Ferraio. His commodore was satisfied that Collingwood had done his best, although he was still too angry with Genoa to allow the issue to rest. In a previously unnoticed letter, Nelson wrote to Brame on

26 October to notify him that Britain was, after all, keeping a force in the Mediterranean. He went on to predict that Jervis would meet and thrash a Spanish fleet then at large in the area, and settle the 'account' with Genoa. The scenario was a misrepresentation of British policy, but it certainly approximated Nelson and Jervis's own preferences.[81]

More immediately, Nelson had to address the task in hand, and took his ships of the line to St Fiorenzo, where the commander-in-chief was removing the last vestiges of British rule. Corsica saw the back of the British at the beginning of November. After demolishing some fortifications, they sailed for Gibraltar in an armada of war and store ships and transports. Nelson went with them, for Jervis needed every capital ship he had. One of his detachments under Admiral Man had unaccountably decamped for England against orders, leaving Sir John woefully under strength at a time when Spain and France were open enemies and a large Spanish fleet under Don Juan de Langara y Huarte was in the Mediterranean. Langara had twenty-six sail of the line, twice as many as Jervis, and was seen off Cape Corse on 20 October, the very day Nelson brought the garrison out of Bastia. If the Spaniards had attacked Jervis's cumbersome convoy lumbering to Gibraltar it would have been difficult to defend, but the admiral's luck held and he reached his destination on 1 December without encountering the enemy.[82]

Jervis and Nelson had evacuated Corsica successfully, but there could be little real triumphalism. Retreat stuck in Nelson's craw. 'We are all preparing for an evacuation of the Mediterranean, a measure which I cannot approve,' he informed his wife in October. 'At home they know not what this fleet is capable of performing, *any and everything*. Much as I shall rejoice to see England in a private view, I lament in sackcloth and ashes our present orders, so dishonourable to the dignity of England, whose fleets are equal to meet the world in arms, and of all fleets I ever saw I never saw one equal in point of officers and men to our present one, and with a commander-in-chief fit to lead them to glory.'[83]

His concern was not for the Corsicans, whom he thought ungrateful, the floundering Austrians, or most of the Italian states, which he reckoned simply gutless. 'Italy has been lost by the fear of its princes,' he said. 'Had they expended half the money to preserve their territories, which they have paid the French for entering them, their countries would have been happy instead of being filled with present misery and diabolical notions of government.' Rather he grieved for the prestige of Britain's arms and for Naples, which had always tried to support him. The troops Naples had sent to Toulon in 1793; the guns and ammunition supplied for the siege of Bastia; the ships that sailed with Hotham in 1795; and the riviera flotillas. None particularly effective contributions, but all made in good heart. Nelson valued loyalty, whether of people to sovereigns, men to officers or officers to men. It implied commitment, obligation and trustworthiness. As Corsica disappeared in the wake of Jervis's convoy Nelson experienced an unsettling sense of shame. His country, he believed, was acting dishonourably, abandoning the most steadfast of friends to its enemies. Even after hearing that Naples had turned an armistice with France into a peace, and it was easier to agree with Drake that Britain had 'nothing more to do here', he remained disturbed by what he was doing. 'I yet hope the Cabinet may . . . change their opinion,' he sighed as late as December. 'It is not all we gain elsewhere which can compensate for our loss of honour.'[84]

The uncertainty about whether he was to leave or remain in the Mediterranean lingered for some time, bedevilling Nelson's personal as well as professional relationships. He asked Brame to send messages to the women. To Madame Caffarena he would write if he had time, and for Adelaide there was a letter – possibly a farewell, but at least accompanied by the hint of future meetings. 'Will you have the goodness to forward the enclosed, and write a line to say I hope soon to see my friend?' he wrote to Brame. 'In doing this you will very much oblige . . .'[85]

As far as anyone can now tell, his feelings for Adelaide did not run particularly deep, and never threatened his commitment to Fanny. It was, it appears, a friendship of convenience, satisfactory and durable and enriched by a working affection. But for Nelson it was always a temporary arrangement, to be dissolved by political circumstance. Adelaide may have thought it more. Her fidelity to Nelson was suspect, but he had maintained her for nearly two years, and whatever he said to her in his last letter it did not suggest finality. The mysterious little Ligurian continued to expect support and waited for his return.

10

Despite more than three years of Hood, Jervis, Nelson and a dozen fine captains Britain had lost her war in the Mediterranean.

The allies had disappointed, of course, but the British had also performed badly. Their sugar island strategy had cost them an army for little gain in the West Indies, and starved the Mediterranean of military resources. Nor was Nelson's beloved navy free from blame. Hood's failure to destroy the Toulon fleet in 1793 had been decisive, but the chances Hotham missed in 1794 and 1795, the failure to protect De Vins in 1795, and Man's inexcusable run home in 1796 had all damaged opportunities. Nelson had been tireless, but his successes had also been interspersed with failures. He had failed to stop the French coastal trade in 1795, failed to prevent enemy gunboats from menacing the Austrians and failed to halt Bonaparte's small-boat invasion of Corsica. As the wars with France would prove time and again, the Royal Navy might command the deeps, but it could not stifle the small traffic that used the shallows, hid behind headlands or in coves, or dashed short distances when shielded by darkness or poor weather.

In this battle between behemoth and leviathan, behemoth had won. The French republicans had recovered their balance, intimidated neutrals and overpowered enemies, leaving Britiain bereft of real support or purpose. If they did not drive the Royal Navy from the Mediterranean, they induced it to leave, and in October 1797 Bonaparte would force Austria to accept a humiliating peace that allowed him to fashion Genoa and Lombardy into satellite republics of France. Nelson's work was entirely undone.

Britain's evacuation of the Mediterranean was a bumbling performance, and in the seven months after October 1796 Nelson had to make three dangerous trips to effect what should have taken one. Shortly after Jervis reached Gibraltar with the first shipment in December, he was mulling over fresh orders. The fleet was to be stationed off Portugal, and the soldiers Jervis had just left in Porto Ferraio would be brought out after all and sent to Lisbon. Someone would have to go back for them.

It was a testing mission now that Franco-Spanish fleets controlled the Mediterranean, for it involved penetrating deep into an enemy sea and plucking an isolated garrison from a place of danger. Transports and about a dozen small warships would have to be shepherded back to Gibraltar without any help from the main British fleet, and no ships of the line could be spared for the expedition, which must depend upon fast and elusive frigates. Weighing these and other considerations, Jervis did not take long to decide who would command. On 10 December, Commodore Nelson was ordered to transfer his broad pendant to *La Minerve* and sail for Elba.

He left five days later on the voyage interrupted by the seesaw battle off the coast of Spain, when he defeated three enemy frigates in the dead of night, only to lose his prizes and a prize crew to Spanish reinforcements the following day.[86]

Otherwise his return to Elba went smoothly, and he captured a French privateer off Sardinia as he went, the *Maria* ketch of six guns and sixty-eight men. Nelson and Cockburn reached Porto Ferraio the day after Christmas, just in time to join Fremantle in escorting the pretty Wynne sisters to a theatre which Lieutenant General De Burgh had done out for a grand seasonal ball. The commodore's entrance was greeted with strains of 'Rule Britannia!' and 'See the Conquering Hero'. Here Nelson was a star and he loved it. In the heady atmosphere three hundred people danced until three in the morning.

The Wynne girls were engaging company, and Nelson, Cockburn and Fremantle were with them again the next evening. Eugenia invariably found the sailors 'kind and good humoured', though Betsy thought Nelson 'very civil and good natured' but too quiet for her taste. As for the commodore, it was Elliot more than anyone else he wanted to see. 'I long to see you,' Nelson once wrote to him, 'for your advice is a treasure.' But Sir Gilbert was in Naples. Nelson contemplated following him there, and renewing his acquaintance with the Hamiltons, to whom he had written of his latest exploits the day after the ball, but finally settled for sending Fremantle of the *Inconstant* to collect the ex-viceroy.[87]

In Elliot's absence Nelson called in ships and stores for removal but suddenly ran into unexpected resistance in the person of Lieutenant General De Burgh. The general protested that he simply had no orders to evacuate his five thousand-man garrison. His last instructions from the Duke of York, the army commander-in-chief, were admittedly obsolete but required him to remain in Corsica or its dependencies as long as possible, and to refer to the viceroy for further authority. These orders had been overtaken by the relinquishment of Corsica, but De Burgh believed that he was still acting within their spirit at Porto Ferraio. Those orders had never been superseded in writing, and he was uncomfortable tearing them up.

Nelson tried in vain to move him. He convinced De Burgh that there was no point in holding Elba. Now that Naples had made peace with the French, the priority was to defend Portugal, Britain's most vulnerable remaining ally, and to cover the approaches to England from the Franco-Spanish fleet. Nelson also pointed out that whatever orders the army did or did not have, his own were perfectly clear, and the naval stores and ordnance would be returned to Gibraltar. If the general refused to leave, Nelson would have to put a few ships at his service, but no more than a couple of frigates and a few sloops. To evacuate Elba now would be dangerous, but to wait longer and risk the enemy fleet putting to sea would be to invite disaster.

Everyone knew General De Burgh to be a gallant gentleman, but he was notoriously 'diffident and doubtful', and procrastinated accordingly. Sometimes he edged towards withdrawing the garrison and urging the French to reciprocate by releasing Leghorn; at other times he fussed about the lack of written orders and hesitated to move at all. Nelson had few documents to ease his plight, and none from the army. Jervis's letter merely referred him to Nelson for details of his 'plan of carrying into execution the last orders I have received touching the troops under your command', and contained no enclosures. Nelson showed the general copies of Jervis's orders from the Admiralty and the secretary for war's instructions for the redistribution of the troops at Gibraltar, but failed to satisfy him. De Burgh asked Nelson to write a letter that might justify evacuation, but finally opted to wait for Sir Gilbert to come from Italy to tell him what to do. Nelson was frustrated by De Burgh's weakness, and suspected that on this issue Elliot would be of little help. On New Year's Day the former viceroy had written from Rome, urging Nelson not to evacuate Porto Ferraio without unequivocal orders to do so. He still dreamed that the Italian states might stand against the French, and was rattling off letters to his old superior, the Duke of Portland, advising him to keep a toehold on Elba.[88]

On 21 January 1797 Elliot arrived at Porto Ferraio and brought matters to a head. In an earnest conference he declined to authorise the evacuation himself, rightly explaining that his position as viceroy had terminated with the withdrawal from Corsica. However, he told De Burgh that if the army commander-in-chief had wanted him to leave Elba, he would surely have said so. What little confidence Nelson had put in the general now evaporated. Though he agreed that the Elba garrison no longer served a purpose, he wrote to Portland that without 'discretionary powers, I can only act from such orders as I have received'. He would wait for further instructions. Elliot happily pronounced the decision 'prudent and proper'.[89]

This 'unfortunate want of unison and punctuality', as Jervis called it, was a farce, but Nelson was powerless to do more. Frustrated though he was, he continued to laud De Burgh in his reports to the Admiralty, and quietly got on with the rest of his job. Conferring with the agent of transports, Lieutenant William Day, he worked out how many ships and stores he would have to leave behind to provide De Burgh with basic services and protection. Fremantle, who had finally married Miss Betsy in Naples, agreed to remain in charge of a skeleton naval force, despite the dangers of being 'caught in a net'. Everyone and everything else would be evacuated as planned.[90]

The work was not entirely onerous, for interspersed with the aggravations were days to remember in the sunset of British rule: convivial evenings, on board *La Minerve* or ashore at the house taken by the Fremantles, with Betsy singing to her own accompaniment on the harpsichord; public dinners organised by the amiable if recalcitrant general. 'If you and Captain Cockburne [sic] come on shore at dinner time tomorrow,' De Burgh wrote to Nelson, 'you will meet some of the emigrant demoiselles at dinner, and some of the prettiest of them.' Wine, women and sun warmed Nelson's last days in Elba.[91]

11

One of Nelson's regular duties as senior sea officer at Porto Ferraio reminded him of long-gone days in the West Indies. He presided over courts martial. He was used to being sucked into courts martial every time he joined the fleet, of course, and during the summer and autumn had been involved in several in or about St Fiorenzo. One, for example, concerned John Clark, boatswain of the *Tartar*, who was tried on the *Princess Royal* for contempt of authority. Linzee presided, but it was Nelson who was delegated to oversee the one hundred and fifty lashes Clark received through the fleet on 24 June. The following December, Nelson sat on another series of trials at Gibraltar, including those of a master's mate and a surgeon's mate charged with theft and drunkenness, and of a seaman hauled up for assault. Saddest of all, from Nelson's point of view, was the case of Edward Tyrrell, the commander of *L'Eclair*. His record already marred by illness and incompetence, he was now dismissed his ship for selling the king's stores.[92]

On those occasions Nelson had been a junior member of courts controlled by Waldegrave, Thompson or Linzee, but at Porto Ferraio it was different. He commanded, sitting by the authority of Sir John Jervis as the chief justice on a bench. Four or more captains would form his court, and his secretary, Mr Castang, supported him as deputy

judge advocate, but it was Nelson more than any other who held the
fates of the unhappy men paraded before him in his hands.[93]

He had headed courts martial before in Antigua, and now, as then,
he tried to be fair within the conventions of the service. In the case
of Lieutenant Robert Pigot of *L'Utile*, heard on board the *Romulus*
on 23 January, Nelson used the inexperience of the accused to reduce
his sentence. Pigot had foolishly cast off a hawser thrown him from
the *Southampton* and made flippant remarks to her captain, and he
was dismissed from his ship but not the service. Three days later, when
three deserters from the *Inconstant* were sentenced on the *Romulus*
to be flogged around the fleet, Nelson gave one of the defendants,
Richard Wright, fifty strokes' remission on account of his former good
behaviour.

Two ships gave Nelson particular problems, the *Speedy* sloop and
the *Dromedary* store ship. John Hoyles, a boatswain of Captain
Elphinstone's *Speedy*, had been drunk and refused to go below when
ordered. In the process he had struck a petty officer, declared he would
be 'ruled by no bugger of a master's mate', and disobeyed a lieutenant.
Nelson wanted to be sure that Hoyles had been in a fit condition to
recognise the officers concerned, and although the defendant was
convicted of contempt a charge of mutiny was dropped. The sailor
was demoted to foretopman.

John Hall and John Maloney of the *Speedy* also appeared before
the court. Maloney, tried with Hoyles on board *La Minerve* on 30
December, was the least fortunate. A recidivist deserter, he had offended
on three previous occasions, once or twice by stealing a launch. The
latest flight had taken place in Naples in November, when he had also
made off with a boat, but the court explored every conceivable innocent explanation of Maloney's behaviour. To satisfy himself that the
prisoner had truly intended to desert, for example, Nelson enquired
whether he had run off with spare clothes. But there was no way out,
and Maloney was sentenced to hang from the foreyard arm.

By far the most exhausting proceedings involved the store ship
Dromedary, a 'rotten' ship rife with insubordination, incompetence
and corruption. It took four separate hearings between 28 December
and 6 January to put the vessel to rights, and no fewer than five
officers were convicted – a boatswain, midshipman, the master George
Casey, Lieutenant Nicholas Meager and the captain himself, Thomas
Harrison. Harrison's case came first. It became obvious that his ship
was a mess and the stores entrusted to his care kept in a poor state.

Requests for them to be issued were sometimes ignored or evaded, the officers inattentive and the captain apt to crawl drunk into his cot. Nelson had few sympathies for inebriated officers, and listened impatiently to Harrison blathering about rheumatism and pains in the head and eyes, probably alcohol-induced migraines. The captain was dismissed the service.

On 3 January it was the turn of the master, Casey, arraigned on charges of insubordination lodged by Lieutenant Meager. Nelson may have had difficulty keeping a straight face during a hearing that verged on the comical. Casey and Meager were at odds, and one night the master had refused to extinguish the light in his cabin while the lieutenant's own remained lit. There was a childish tussle at the master's door, with Meager trying to shove it open to get in to douse the offending light, and Casey as fiercely trying to keep it closed. The court judged that the allegations had been proven 'in part', and passed what it deemed to be a light sentence, dismissing Casey from the king's service. But there was a ridiculous sequel. In retaliation, the dishonoured master immediately indicted Lieutenant Meager for assault, resurrecting an older scuffle of the previous June. Nelson and his captains heard of a scene on the quarterdeck of the *Dromedary* in which the lieutenant had spat in the face of Casey's wife, supposedly because she had been giving him bad language. When the master intervened on his wife's behalf, Meager seized him 'by the nose and pulled it with all his strength'. Even the discredited Captain Harrison appeared before the court to testify that his lieutenant could be 'obstinate and ill tempered', but the prosecution was judged to have been a spiteful one, motivated by revenge, and Meager got away with a reprimand.

If Nelson thought the business of the *Dromedary* had finally been discharged with the case against Meager he was mistaken. When a new acting captain, Bartholomew James, took charge of the ship he discovered that casks of pitch and tar and coils of rope had been smuggled into boats during the dark and windy nights before Christmas, and carried to the *Zephyr* transport. A midshipman and boatswain of the store ship were convicted of embezzlement. The former lost sea time and forfeited pay, and the latter was reduced to the ranks. The master of the *Zephyr* admitted receiving stolen goods, but pleaded for clemency. He was a young man, he said, afraid to incriminate other officers, and besides, he had a large family . . . In all it had been a sad reminder that slack and dishonest leadership on a ship was infectious and undermined its authority, structure and rhythm.[94]

The 'trials' of Nelson, as a pioneer researcher has recently called them, again reveal him in a respectable light for his time and place. He probed intention, investigated alternative explanations, weighed mitigating circumstances and considered the previous records of defendants. Yet he, like other naval officers, believed strongly in punishing established transgressions and drawing clear boundaries between what was and was not acceptable behaviour. There were times when the lives and safety of a ship's company depended upon every man discharging his duty without equivocation.

12

The army was staying, but a number of other important people took leave of the islands with Nelson that January 1797, among them Sir Gilbert Elliot and Pozzo di Borgo, his former secretary of state, both of whom found berths on *La Minerve* with Nelson and Cockburn. General De Burgh was left 'without any instructions whatsoever' and 'in a situation rather unprotected', as he put it.[95]

On the 29th the general and Fremantle, who shouldered the awesome responsibility of protecting Elba in a friendless desert, saw the convoy of warships and transports sail away into the Mediterranean. To avoid enemy squadrons Nelson divided his forces. *La Minerve* and the *Romulus* (Captain George Hope) reached Gibraltar on 9 February, after poking into St Fiorenzo, Toulon and Cartagena along the way. They captured two Spanish feluccas and discovered that their battle fleet was at sea. Macnamara's *Southampton* conducted the store ships *Dolphin* and *Dromedary* south rather than north of Corsica, while the *Dido* and *Sardine* were given the tough job of managing thirteen transports and merchantmen.[96]

The convoy got through safe, and Nelson knew that his commander-in-chief was advancing from the Tagus to cover him west of Gibraltar, but his mission had not been a complete success. In fact it had been botched from the beginning. Jervis had received orders to evacuate Elba but not De Burgh, who lacked the courage to act without them, while Elliot, fired by an agenda of his own, had merely encouraged the general's folly. Two months further on and there were still people isolated in Elba, waiting to be removed. Nelson had spent a lifetime in public service, and probably shrugged resignedly. He had done his best and preserved good relations between the military, naval and political arms in a difficult situation.[97]

His mind, in fact, was beginning to stray from the Mediterranean. Far, far away the shores of his native land and perhaps the face of a long-suffering wife occupied more of his thoughts. The war, he was sure, was ending, and the possibility of a long life on half-pay troubled him. He had wondered how the government might react to a petition for a pension, and at the end of December rallied the support of political friends. Drake, Trevor, Hamilton and Elliot all replied fulsomely to his requests for testimonials. In January he also asked Mrs Pollard to shop for 'such pretty things' as a 'most elegant woman' might like.[98]

Lives are full of turns, however, Nelson's as much as any other. Just as the war in the Mediterranean fizzled to an ignominious conclusion and the commodore contemplated a hiatus in his career, he steered into the dazzling, blood-pumping glory he had longed for since boyhood. He had once said that a sea officer had to wait for the 'happy moment' that might transform his career. His own was about to come.

XXIV

THE HAPPY MOMENT

Nobly, nobly Cape Saint Vincent to the North-west died away;
Sunset ran, one glorious blood-red, reeking into Cadiz Bay;
Bluish mid the burning water, full in face Trafalgar lay;
In the dimmest North-east distance dawn'd Gibraltar grand and gray;
'Here and here did England help me: how can I help England?' – say, . . .

Robert Browning, *Home Thoughts from the Sea*

1

NELSON remained only a day in Gibraltar. The Spanish fleet, he now knew, had left Cartagena and passed through the straits a few days before, heading west. Three of their ships which had detoured to land supplies for their lines at Gibraltar were still at the head of Algeciras Bay, their glasses doubtless trained upon the British newcomers. Nelson wanted to press on to report to Jervis, and to take part in the major battle he was sure lay ahead.

He achieved something at Gibraltar, though. Culverhouse, Hardy and the prize crew of the *Santa Sabina* were prisoners on one of the Spanish men-of-war, and Nelson speedily arranged for their exchange. There was an emotional reunion between Nelson and officers who had sacrificed their freedom to save his. What was more, Culverhouse and Hardy were full of information about the state of the Spanish fleet, which they had observed from within. On 11 February the *Romulus* was still undergoing repairs and the weather was bad, but the commodore ordered Cockburn to get *La Minerve* underway. It was imperative that he reach Jervis. Two of the Spanish ships still in the bay were sail of the line, and they were waiting for Nelson to make a run for it. He took the risk.

As La Minerve worked out of the bay that afternoon, plunging through stubborn eddies, the big Spanish ships made after her, aided by a steady easterly wind. Anxious spectators from the town and garrison of Gibraltar scrambled to high points to witness the grim chase. Once the brazen British frigate got into the strait she caught the breeze and made proudly for the open sea, but one of the pursuers went after her so determinedly that on board La Minerve Sir Gilbert Elliot prepared to pitch his papers overboard rather than allow them to be captured. His aide, Colonel John Drinkwater, nervously asked Nelson if there would be a battle. Maybe, replied the commodore calmly, glancing up at his broad pendant, but 'before the Dons get hold of that bit of bunting I will have a struggle with them, and sooner than give up the frigate I'll run her ashore'.[1]

Cockburn, studying the advancing Spaniard through his glass, reckoned she was gaining on them, but after ordering studding sails to be set to increase speed he joined the other officers filing into the captain's cabin for dinner. They sat down a little after three, but almost immediately started to the cry 'Man overboard!' Lieutenant Hardy was soon being lowered in a jolly boat with some men to look for the missing sailor, Able Seaman William Barnes, but the fellow had drowned, and the rescue party was forced to pull back for the ship empty-handed. But the current was against them, and Hardy was gripped with the realisation that after only a day at liberty he was in danger of being recaptured by the oncoming Spaniard.

The leading enemy ship was still three miles astern, but time was precious. On the quarterdeck of La Minerve Nelson did not hesitate. 'By God, I'll not lose Hardy!' he cried. 'Back the mizzen-topsail.' La Minerve's pace slackened, and Hardy's weary search party redoubled their efforts at the oars and successfully regained their ship. The whole episode had lasted about an hour, but it sealed the bond between Nelson and Hardy. Now both had endangered themselves to protect the other.

As it happened, the advancing Spanish ship profited little from the delay. Apparently the sight of La Minerve backing sail disconcerted her officers. Perhaps they believed that more British ships had appeared in the offing, visible to the frigate but beyond their own horizon. Anyway, the oncoming ship of the line shortened sail and hesitated, waiting for her lagging consort to approach. Using every minute, the

British were able to rescue Hardy and continue their flight, and after dusk lost their pursuers altogether.

Fog as well as night shrouded *La Minerve* as an easterly wind, known as a levanter, took her into large Atlantic swells. Then suddenly, in the early hours of the 12th, large shapes loomed like spectres in the murk about them. Two were fairly close, one on either flank. The British had sailed into a squadron of ships, perhaps even a fleet, but which fleet? As Cockburn and Nelson strained eyes and ears, they realised that the signals were unfamiliar. Mysterious flashes stabbed through the darkness, muffled guns boomed dolefully in the fog, and voices were heard – Spanish voices. Nelson had actually sailed into the main Spanish battle fleet. Lumbered with a valuable convoy for Cadiz, it had been pushed west by the levanter, and was now fighting its way back to the coast. However, at the time nothing seemed certain, and Commodore Nelson speculated that he might have blundered into a detached squadron or a convoy bound for the West Indies. For a while the British frigate could only slip anxiously along, making no sudden moves but gently extricating herself from the ships around her as anonymously as possible. Nelson went to see if Elliot was awake, but the ex-viceroy was sleeping soundly in his cot, worn out by the earlier adventure. Nelson let him alone. In the morning, when Sir Gilbert made his appearance, the Spaniards had gone and the adventure had passed him by as if it had been an illusion.

On the morning of 13 February, Nelson found a very different fleet. It was sheltering under the lee of Cape St Vincent, the Portuguese peninsula jutting out into the Atlantic, and strategically placed between Lisbon and the Strait of Gibraltar. There were fifteen ships of the line under the command of Sir John Jervis, and they were waiting to intercept the very Spanish men-of-war Nelson had seen in the fog.

The features of the craggy British admiral must have cracked into a smile at the sight of Nelson's broad pendant flying above the oncoming frigate. You could send that fellow to the other side of the Mediterranean, but if a battle was afoot he would be there.

2

Jervis knew about the Spaniards. Four days before he had heard that a large fleet had passed the Rock of Gibraltar, and from subsequent reports learned that it had been driven into the Atlantic. He was riding off Cape St Vincent in search of it, determined to give battle.

His fleet was not in the best shape to fight, for it had suffered severely in Gibraltar during furious winter gales. The *Courageux* had broken to pieces on the shores of the Barbary Coast with a loss of four hundred and sixty men, and the *Zealous* was swept onto a reef in Tangier Bay. The poor *Gibraltar* ran twice upon Cabrita Point in Algeciras Bay, and had to go home for repairs. Retreating to the Tagus, which a treaty between Britain and Portugal made available, Jervis had fared no better. The *Bombay Castle* was wrecked upon a sandbank, and the *Culloden*, the wounded *Gibraltar* and the *St George* all took the ground. By the time Nelson returned, Jervis had been reinforced by five sail of the line under Rear Admiral Sir William Parker, but could still deploy only fifteen capital ships.

Yet the old commander-in-chief knew how badly his country needed a victory. Since France and Spain had signed the treaty of San Ildefonso the previous year, Britain was facing a combination of the second and third naval powers. The King of Spain, Charles IV, was said to be a fool and easily manipulated by the French, who set great store in invading England and eliminating the most durable of their foes. In December 1796 France had tried forcibly to enter Britain through the back door by sending an expeditionary force to Ireland, but the discontented Catholic peasantry failed to rise in support, and bad weather drove the French from Bantry Bay before they could even land. Nonetheless, French ambitions remained, and Jervis realised that the Spanish fleet probably figured in any new plans to humble Britain. If the Spaniards got to Brest and reinforced the main French fleet, their united force would constitute a serious threat to England's defences. The fire inside Jervis flickered furiously. Whatever the odds, he would fight the Spaniards and do what damage he could.

He was a man of Nelson's heart and mind. Jervis knew that ship for ship the British were superior to the Spaniards, and that only a close-range engagement could exploit those advantages to the full. In the admiral's book 'nothing' would be 'more unfortuante to the success of His Majesty's arms' than 'a distant cannonade'. He wanted something decisive. When Nelson arrived in the fleet, and brought Hardy and Culverhouse to the *Victory* to report, it must have reinforced the admiral's determination to fight and his belief in the ability to win. Shortly the *Bonne Citoyenne* arrived with intelligence that the Spanish fleet was only twenty miles to the southeast, and, deducing that it was making for Cadiz, Jervis got underway to intercept them.[2]

Leaving Elliot and his suite to transfer to the *Lively* frigate,

Commodore Nelson returned to the *Captain* and ordered Lieutenant
Noble to run his broad pendant to the masthead. The old company
rejoiced to see him, and Nelson was pleased to find that it had been
kept in good shape by his new flag captain, Ralph Willett Miller, who
had assumed command at Gibraltar in December. Indeed, one division of the ship was just completing exercising the great guns as
Nelson's barge came alongside. Her commodore and officers intact,
the ship took its place in a fleet alive with expectation. Jervis bade
his ships keep close order during the night as they stood to the southeast with a southwesterly breeze from starboard and the darkness and
fog thickening about them. Occasionally the distant thud of Spanish
signal guns emerged out of the gloom, and a Portuguese frigate came
up with word that the enemy was fifteen miles to windward. On the
British ships officers hung about their quarterdecks focusing night
glasses over the black water.[3]

The morning of 14 February – St Valentine's Day – was dark and
misty. It found the British several miles southwest of Cape St Vincent,
steering sedately south-southeast, close-hauled on the starboard tack.
The ships of the line described two compact parallel lines, with the
smaller vessels thrown out on the flanks. Hidden in the haze, ahead
and to starboard, sailed the Spanish fleet. For some time the easterly
levanter had forced it out to sea, but after the wind swung round to
the west the admiral, Teniente General (Vice Admiral) Jose de Cordoba
y Ramos, had set a course east-southeast for Cadiz. Unwittingly, as
the Spaniards pressed through patches of haze towards their destination they converged with the predatory British fleet.

It was five-forty before the British began to see them slipping in
and out of the mist several miles ahead. In the van of the British ships,
Captain Thomas Troubridge's *Culloden* signalled strange sails seven
or eight miles to windward, and shortly afterwards they were seen
from Nelson's *Captain* and the muffled report of two signal guns
heard. Before long the *Bonne Citoyenne* sloop was fading into the
mist on a mission of reconnaissance.

Only gradually did the full extent of the enemy fleet appear. At
nine the man at the masthead of Jervis's flagship, the *Victory*, counted
thirty-one sail, twenty of them ships of the line. If true, the Spaniards
outnumbered the British, but even that report actually understated
the enemy's capital ships. As reports from *La Minerve* and *Bonne
Citoyenne* came in the number of enemy ships climbed – eight, twenty,
and (at ten-forty-nine in the morning, when the Spanish fleet was

becoming clearly visible) twenty-five ships of the line. Moreover, it became clear that they included some very big warships indeed, looming 'like Beachy Head in a fog'. Their flagship was the world's only four-decked battleship, the awesome *Santissima Trinidad* of one hundred and thirty or more guns, and she was supported by no fewer than six three-deckers of 112 guns each, every one of them larger than the most powerful of Jervis's ships, the hundred-gun *Victory*. 'By my soul, they are thumpers!' called the signal lieutenant of the *Barfleur*. But for all their apparent power the Spanish ships were in obvious disorder. Crossing ahead of the British line, they had broken into two divisions. The leading but smaller group was to leeward and consisted of two ships of the line and four or more merchantmen, but Cordoba and his main force lagged six or seven miles behind and to windward of the advancing British line. Though their numbers were great they 'looked a complete forest huddled together', and some rode two or three abreast with their broadsides neutralised. The Spanish commander-in-chief was signalling feverishly to get them into line but 'they seemed confusion worse confounded'.[4]

Jervis saw an opportunity and made his most important contribution to the oncoming battle. The Spanish fleet was superior in numbers, and the armed merchantmen in the leeward division made it seem even larger than it really was. Confronted with such a force some admirals might have blanched at combat, but not Jervis. About eleven in the morning signal thirty-one flew from the *Victory*. The fleet was ordered to form a single line of battle ahead or astern of the flagship as each captain found convenient, and to steer a course south-south-west to intercept the main body of the Spanish fleet some four miles away. They were going to attack. The British ships had already been preparing for battle, clearing partitions and furniture for the gun crews and flinging impedimenta overboard, strewing the sea with casks, supplies and struggling livestock. At eleven-twenty they ran up their colours.

Nelson's happy moment had come.

The wind was light but there was no sea, and the fifteen British ships of the line were soon in formation, sliding through the lifting haze under topgallants at a speed of some five knots. The *Captain*'s position was towards the rear of the line, third from the end at number thirteen. Immediately ahead were the ninety-eight-gun *Barfleur* carrying the flag of Vice Admiral William Waldegrave, and the ninety-gun *Namur* captained by James Hawkins Whitshed, while astern came the last two ships of the British line, the *Diadem* sixty-four under the durable Towry and the *Excellent* seventy-four with Cuthbert Collingwood. But as Nelson fell into his place he most envied the ships at the other end of the line, nearest the enemy. Leading the fleet into the fight were the *Culloden* seventy-four under the enterprising Troubridge, Captain Frederick's ninety-gun *Blenheim* and the ninety-eight-gun *Prince George* flying the flag of Admiral Parker.[5]

Jervis was presented with an obvious opportunity to divide the Spanish ships, and steered straight for the gap between the leeward and windward divisions of the enemy fleet. The more they saw, the greater the British grew in confidence. Their adversaries clearly suffered from a gross want of experience and skill. Cordoba's fleet was thousands of hands short, even after the enlistment of a thousand soldiers, and the proportion of practised seamen aboard was distressingly small. The flagship itself was said to have had fewer than eighty skilled sailors in a complement of nine hundred, with the balance consisting of soldiers, landsmen and short-term levies. Such deficiencies showed. The master of the British *Prince George* was unable to discern 'any plan' in the Spanish movements, 'nor did it appear . . . there was sufficient skill or discipline to execute any orders their commander might have given'. When firing began the qualitative difference between the two fleets was confirmed. One British observer felt that Jervis's fire was 'superior in the proportion of five or six to one', while Cordoba himself marvelled at 'the rapidity and accuracy with which the English handle their guns'.[6]

While the British advanced the Spanish leeward division continued to bear away southeasterly. It was, in fact, more important than Jervis supposed, because it included several plodding merchantmen laden with mercury, an essential ingredient for the fusion of the precious metals Spain shipped from the Americas. Cordoba's main force to windward was down to twenty ships of the line, but when the British wedge began to push in front of them, he tried to swing them north-westerly onto the larboard tack. Thus his rear division would pass along the starboard side of the British fleet, steering in the opposite direction, and exchange broadsides with it at a range of a thousand yards or less. Though the Spanish commander-in-chief kept the advantage of the wind, his manoeuvre created immense confusion among his unpractised crews. Three of the Spanish ships, the *Principe d'Asturias*, flying the flag of Teniente General Joaquin Moreno, the *Regla* and the *Oriente*, sheered off towards the leeward division, while the remaining seventeen only completed the turn in ragged groups rather than a respectable line of battle.

Nevertheless, it was entirely satisfactory to Commodore Nelson as he hungrily paced the quarterdeck of the *Captain* towards the rear of the British line. At last the battle was coming his way. Cordoba's windward division was heading towards him on the opposite tack, even though the further it proceeded the more it veered to the northwest and increased the gun range between the opposing fleets.

But the advantage still lay with Troubridge at the head of the British line. He took the *Culloden* into the gap between the two Spanish divisions, double-shotting the guns on both his larboard and starboard sides to fire at both. As soon as the signal to engage went up on the *Victory*, Troubridge opened a disciplined and deadly fire. His starboard guns savaged the Spaniards of the windward division as they passed on their new course, and one by one the other British ships followed suit, spitting fire and shot in succession, their timbers shaking with the thunder, and their decks enveloped in thick black clouds of stinking powder smoke.[7]

The Spaniards replied, but feebly. One of their officers admitted that it was 'impossible . . . to persuade any of the crew to go aloft to repair the injured rigging. Threats and punishment were equally ineffectual . . . The panic-struck wretches, when called upon to go aloft, fell immediately on their knees, and in that posture cried out that they preferred being sacrificed on the spot to performing a duty in the execution of which they considered death as inevitable.' Nevertheless, not every Spanish shot fell harmlessly into the sea. The *Colossus* was reduced to relative impotence when her foresail and fore topsail yards were shot away and her fore topmast mangled.[8]

At about noon it was the turn of the *Captain*, as a large Spanish three-decker approached her on the opposite tack. Nelson's guns blazed at the enemy ships for forty or fifty minutes until the last of them had passed, giving far more than she received. Yet for him it was an insubstantial repast, and he fumed in dismay as the Spanish ships receded in one direction while the rear of the British fleet proceeded doggedly in the other.

At this point Jervis had kept the Spanish fleet divided, but it remained to be seen if he could turn an advantage into a victory. The crucial stage of the battle of Cape St Vincent was only just beginning to unfold.

At about the time Nelson began firing at the rear of the British line, action was subsiding in the van as the last of the Spanish ships passed the *Culloden*. It was now necessary for the British ships to turn in pursuit of the Spaniards, but not until 12.08 did Jervis fly signal eighty, ordering his capital ships to tack in succession as they reached the head of the line. Troubridge did so smartly. Anticipating the signal, he was already putting the *Culloden* about and turning after the retreating Spaniards on the larboard tack as the signal flags ran up on the *Victory*. In due course the *Blenheim*, *Prince George* and *Orion* followed suit, turning in the wake of the *Culloden* as they reached the front of the line, but so sprightly did Troubridge swing towards his prey that a gap of half a mile opened between his and the following ship.

Sir John Jervis, commanding from the quarterdeck of the *Victory* in the centre of the British line, was absorbed by the considerable dangers ahead of him. Cordoba's windward division had been deflected northwesterly onto the larboard tack, but to the British left there still remained the Spanish leeward division, now reinforced and commanded by Admiral Moreno. There was every chance it would beat back to rejoin the main body under Cordoba, either by weathering the head of the British line or even cutting through it. In fact, within a quarter of an hour of Jervis signalling his ships to tack in succession Moreno did lead a spirited assault on the British centre from leeward, trying to break through in front of the *Victory*. For several minutes the Spaniards tried to carve a passage through the tightly bunched British ships, facing a ferocious fire from the *Colossus*, *Irresistible*, *Victory*, *Egmont* and *Goliath* with terrific courage, but finally they were forced to recoil and bear away to southward under a press of sail.[9]

Probably Jervis delayed ordering his van to tack after Cordoba until 12.08 because he anticipated the attack from leeward, or perhaps he was far clearer about what was happening in front of him than behind. The *Victory* was, after all, blanketed in black powder smoke, spurted to starboard in the firing and blown back across the British line by the westerly wind. According to one of the many unsupported stories spawned by this renowned combat Sir John went up to his poop deck to get a clearer view of the action. While there he was spattered by the blood and brains of a man slain at his side by a round shot, but he grimly wiped the gore from his face before resolutely stumping back to the quarterdeck to resume control of the battle.[10]

However, that control was beginning to unravel as the heart of the battle moved northwest towards the rear of the British fleet. Coming a few minutes after noon Jervis's order to his ships to tack at the head of the line did not give them sufficient time to turn, chase and engage the flying Spaniards of the windward division. The rear of the British line was to starboard of Cordoba's flying ships, but its ships were under orders to continue southwest in an orderly queue, away from the Spaniards, until each reached the turning point and could tack in succession to join the pursuit.

Sir John did not miss the problem and tried to speed matters up. At about twelve-fifty, with his leading ships already in pursuit of the enemy, he repeated the signal to tack in succession for those still waiting to turn, but this time directed the movement to begin with the *Britannia* under Vice Admiral Sir Charles Thompson, the sixth ship from the rear. A minute later signal forty-one also ran to the flagship's masthead, instructing the ships to 'take suitable stations and engage as [you] arrive up in succession'. The commander-in-chief was obviously trying to do two things: he was creating a new turning point closer to the rear of his line to get it into action more rapidly, and he was granting ships that had tacked and caught up with the enemy the freedom to choose the best positions to engage.[11]

But even this failed to meet the emergency that was developing. Had Jervis's rear division strictly responded it would still have wasted precious minutes proceeding in the wrong direction before tacking at the new turning place. As it was it did not even do that. For some reason the officers on the *Britannia* missed the commander-in-chief's signal, and failed to tack. The ship merely carried on as before, in obedience to previous instructions, and those behind followed meekly in her wake, completely frustrating Sir John's new intentions.

After so fair a beginning the prospects of victory were dissolving. Continuing southwest, the rearmost British ships of the line opened the expanse of sea behind them to Cordoba's retreating windward division. Nor were the Spaniards blind to their emerging advantage. Noting also that the last British ship of the line – Collingwood's *Excellent* – was lagging, Cordoba saw an opportunity to work around the British rear, or perhaps to slice it between the last two capital ships. If he succeeded he could either rejoin his leeward division or escape to Cadiz with the westerly breeze at his back, leaving Jervis with nothing more than a spirited but indecisive exchange of broadsides to his credit.

Many of Cordoba's ships were still milling in abject confusion, but some responded to the commander-in-chief's signals and began to bear up to close with the British rear. With the Spaniards breaking for freedom, the head of the British line trailing astern and the British rear still obligingly creating sea room for their enemies to the north, Sir John's chances of victory were paling.

But then something unusual happened. Not far from the end of the British line one of the ships began to wear out of formation. Ignoring the admiral's signals to tack in succession, her bow turned to larboard and came round to face in the opposite direction. Soon the ship was underway again, steering to leeward of the oncoming *Diadem* and then swinging once more to larboard and cutting through the British line ahead of the trailing *Excellent*. To the astonishment of many observers the errant warship then struck out boldly for the Spanish fleet.

That ship sailing into history was the seventy-four-gun *Captain* flying the broad pendant of Commodore Horatio Nelson.

3

Nelson had been reading the battle closely, taking the *Captain* a little to windward of the line of battle to get a better view. Through his telescope he swept left and right. To larboard he saw Moreno mounting his ultimately unsuccessful attack on the British centre from leeward, while to starboard Cordoba was trying to bear up against the rear. It flashed through his mind that the two movements, one on either side of the British line, were related.[12]

He could see, too, Troubridge's *Culloden* and the other ships of the British van striving to reach the rear of the Spanish windward division, a force that greatly outnumbered them, but doubted they would come up in time to frustrate Cordoba's manoeuvre. Something had to be done. If Cordoba escaped, or even reunited his divisions to leeward, everything Jervis had done would stand for nought.

Nelson knew that the redundant British rear needed to support their van, and that could not be done trailing uselessly southwest to tack in succession. It was necessary to abandon the line and directly engage Cordoba's division as it struggled to bear up. But breaking the discipline of the line was no light matter. It breached the prevailing fighting instructions, which forbade captains in black and white to quit the line of battle without authorisation. Even more, disobeying the specific orders of a commander-in-chief in the midst of combat flouted the instincts of a service in which discipline was essential to survival. It risked the gravest personal consequences. Failures or disasters were liable to produce scapegoats, and none were more vulnerable than disobedient officers.

It is not surprising that even in the Mediterranean fleet, stuffed with fine captains, few were willing to stick their necks out in the presence of a superior. Close readers of this book will find examples of captains, good captains such as Fremantle and Troubridge, declining to exercise initiative without specific licence. At the battle of Cape St Vincent, even after Nelson's audacious manoeuvre, not one fellow officer in the British rear followed him – not Thompson, Waldegrave, Towry, Whitshed or Collingwood. Indeed, some fifty minutes after Nelson wore to support the embattled van, Jervis had to fly signal eighty-five to encourage the remainder of his rear.

Supreme self-confidence, a willingness to accept responsibility, opportunism and sheer fighting spirit were hallmarks of Nelson, however. He prided himself on what he called 'political courage', and repeatedly acted on it, even in contravention of the orders of superiors. He had disobeyed Hughes in the West Indies, Hotham off the riviera, and even Jervis himself. The previous summer, when Nelson had been blockading Leghorn, Jervis had recalled the *Captain* to the fleet, ordering the commodore to transfer to a smaller ship so that he could remain on the station. Smelling a battle, Nelson had brought the *Captain* into the fleet personally, putting himself in the way of an impending battle but overturning his commander-in-chief's plan to keep him off Leghorn. Later he had also taken Capraia without the specific orders of his superior.

Yet though Nelson's decision to wear out of line was bold, it has to be seen within the context of his close relationship with Admiral Jervis. When it came to fighting the two men beat to the same heart. Both hungered for victory, and if Nelson acted against the strict letter of Jervis's orders he most assuredly remained within their spirit. He explained later that the admiral was 'too much involved in smoke to perceive of facilitating the victory which ensued'. In other words, a commander-in-chief could not be everywhere, and needed like-minded subordinates prepared to exercise initiative in order to achieve the intended result.[13]

Nelson was probably also conversant, as many historians have not been, with Jervis's general ideas about fleet tactics. In about 1796 the admiral had issued a set of 'secret instructions' relating to battle manoeuvres, illustrated by seven diagrams. The circumstances they considered were not, of course, likely to be precisely replicated in a real battle, but at least they primed the admiral's captains for the type of manoeuvres he would want to make. For example, they prepared the captains of leading ships to power through an enemy line to cut off its van, and then to tack in succession to envelop the isolated ships. What is more, this plan also involved an independent manoeuvre on the part of the British rear, which, it was suggested, might break the line and wear its ships directly to enter the battle. If Nelson was familiar with these instructions, he would have known that the admiral was by no means insensible of the value of rearmost ships occasionally wearing out of line to support an embattled van.[14]

Nelson's manoeuvre was, therefore, indubitably the result of insight, courage and initiative, but it was made by an officer who knew Jervis's mind, and had a pretty good idea of what the admiral would have been doing with a fuller knowledge of the battle. It was the perfect union of commander and subordinate: the first inspiring and informing, and the second understanding, interpreting and acting to complete what had been begun.

And so a little before one o'clock on 14 February 1797 Commodore Nelson told Miller to wear out of the line of battle and switch to the larboard tack. Passing to leeward of the *Diadem* they crossed the bows of Collingwood's *Excellent* and made straight for the Spanish fleet. Disregarding the danger of enemy broadsides Nelson struck the rear of their fleet at an oblique angle. Although his targets were among the rearmost of Cordoba's ships, they were also the furthest to leeward, and would have been destined to lead their admiral's attempt to double the end of the British line. No less important, Nelson focused his attack upon the command centre of the Spanish fleet. Crossing the hawses of some of the Spaniards he pitted his seventy-four against the enemy flagship itself, the massive *Santissima Trinidad*.[15]

Watching in amazement from the *Lively* frigate at the rear of the British fleet, Colonel Drinkwater thought the duel a 'preposterous' mismatch. Nelson's 'gigantic' adversary, her vivid yellow sides streaked in black as if to warn of danger, was one of the largest ships afloat. She was planked between the quarterdeck and forecastle to give her an additional gun platform, and carried no fewer than one hundred and thirty cannons firing eight-, eighteen-, twenty-four- and thirty-six-pound Spanish shot. Her double-headed shot for tearing down rigging weighed up to fifty English pounds. 'Such a ship . . . I never saw before,' gasped Collingwood. Not only that but as Nelson opened a heavy fire on the fearsome four-decker he simultaneously engaged two 112-gun three-deckers (apparently the *Salvador del Mundo* and the *Mexicana*) ahead and astern of the flagship, and took occasional fire from two or three other battleships. Captain Miller had drilled the gun crews of the *Captain* daily, attending many of the exercises himself, and the *Santissima Trinidad* was poorly designed and her guns ill served, but Nelson was hopelessly under strength. Fortunately, at about the same time that Nelson manoeuvred into position Troubridge reached the tail end of the Spanish fleet with the *Culloden*, and piled into the fight astern of the *Captain*.[16]

Their attack 'staggered' Cordoba and forced his ships to haul their wind to larboard, abandoning their plan to envelop the British rear. According to Miller 'the whole van of the Spanish fleet' was deflected by the *Captain* and *Culloden*. 'We turned them . . . like two dogs turning a flock of sheep,' he said. Others agreed. 'The highest honours are due to you, my dear friend, and *Culloden*,' Collingwood wrote to Nelson. 'You formed the plan of attack. We were only accessories to the Dons' ruin, for had they got on the other tack they would have been sooner joined, and the business less complete.' In time even *Culloden*'s sterling contribution was forgotten. Had Nelson not joined the assault, remembered a midshipman of the *Britannia*, 'we should probably not have taken a single ship'.[17]

Soon the other leading ships were also reopening fire, the *Blenheim*, *Prince George* and *Orion*, though with diminishing available sea room. Action was occasionally interrupted as one ship or another backed topsails to hold back or filled its sails to move forward again. Nelson battered the hull and rigging of the Spanish flagship, reducing its fire, but his own sails and ropes were being cut to pieces. At about two o'clock, after some forty minutes of carnage, Troubridge nobly interposed his ship between the *Captain* and the Spanish vessels to give the battered seventy-four a temporary respite. For ten minutes Nelson's guns fell silent, while his men furiously spliced and repaired damaged rigging, hauled more shot to the guns and carried broken bodies below. Then the *Captain*'s mizzen topsail filled, she resumed the lead from behind the *Culloden* and reopened her murderous fire. The efficiency of the British guns was telling cruelly, torturing the big Spaniards with shot after shot into the vitals, but physical exhaustion and the sheer durability of the opponents were draining. By two-thirty the sails and rigging of the *Captain* and *Culloden* were wasted and their decks littered with wreckage from aloft. Troubridge hailed Captain Frederick of the *Blenheim*, inviting him forward while *Culloden* completed essential repairs. Eagerly the *Blenheim* slipped inside both the leading ships, briefly shielding them from shot as she took the advanced position.[18]

But the Spaniards were suffering much more grievously. The *Santissima Trinidad* struggled ahead, slugging it out with the *Blenheim*, but the crippled *Salvador del Mundo* and *San Ysidro* both dropped astern, where fresh British warships fell upon them like a pod of hungry grampuses. Nelson's battered *Captain* found herself engaging 'different' foes, the eighty-gun *San Nicolas*, and another of the large three-deckers, the *San Josef* of 112 guns, bearing the flag of a rear admiral, Francisco Winthuysen.[19]

The *Captain* was more heavily armed than historians have realised. In addition to her nine-, eighteen- and thirty-two-pounders she now carried one or two sixty-eight-pound carronades, but both of her new opponents were markedly superior in the weight of metal fired. The smaller of the two, the *San Nicolas*, mounted eighty guns, and apart from eighteen-pounders pitted a battery of Spanish thirty-sixes against Nelson's smaller thirty-twos. Despite her disadvantages, though, the *Captain*'s gunnery skills more than compensated. Young Oliver Davis told his parents that the Spaniards would 'certainly' have sunk the British ship 'if they [had] activated their guns as they might, but the rogues did not know how'. Nelson pummelled the hulls of both adversaries, bringing yards crashing down on the *San Nicolas* and shooting away part of the *San Josef*'s main topmast and mizzen. The three-decker had already taken a drubbing from the *Blenheim*, and was also receiving fire from the *Prince George*, which had run up astern of the *Captain*. Almost blanketed in smoke she fell to windward, behind the *San Nicolas*.[20]

At three or after help came from Collingwood's seventy-four-gun *Excellent*. Signalled into the melee by the commander-in-chief, she passed between the *Salvador del Mundo* and the *San Ysidro* at the rear of the Spanish fleet, mutilating them with brutal broadsides. Both ships, being hammered by more than one opponent, struck their colours, but Collingwood moved on towards Nelson's duel with the *San Nicolas* and *San Josef*. He was probably responding to Jervis's signal number sixty-six, which urged ships forward, but Nelson took it to be an independent act of brotherhood. Instead of taking possession of the prizes, Nelson wrote, Collingwood 'most gallantly pushed up to save his old friend and messmate, who was to appearance in a critical state'.[21]

The *Excellent*'s sails, masts and rigging were already scarred by enemy fire, but her intervention was dramatic. Hauling up his mainsail astern of the *Captain*, Collingwood ran to windward between Nelson's ship and the *San Nicolas*. As he did so, a ruthless rippling broadside from his larboard guns smashed through the Spanish ship at point-blank range. 'You could not put a bodkin between us,' said Collingwood, and some of the shot, he thought, exited the *San Nicolas* on the other side and ploughed into the adjacent *San Josef*. For a moment the *San Nicolas* was silenced by that vicious ship-smashing broadside, while her men desperately slaved to clear wreckage, but after the *Excellent* pressed forward towards the *Santissima Trinidad*, she bravely began to fire again. As the *Captain* luffed across her stern to renew the fight and the *Prince George* worked around towards her bows, the cornered and battered two-decker pluckily fought on.[22]

But Nelson's ship was now little more than a wreck. For more than two hours she had been embroiled in an unequal broadside-for-broadside struggle, engaging five or more of the enemy ships at point-blank range, every one of them more powerfully armed than she was. She had suffered more damage than any other ship in the British fleet, and lay almost incapable of manoeuvre. Her mainmast had three shot holes to what Nelson insisted was its 'heart', her fore topmast had gone over the side, and her jib blown away. Every yard was damaged and every larboard shroud gone, along with all but one of the braces. The stays, rigging and sails were ripped to pieces, and the wheel that controlled the rudder shot away. Several guns were disabled by 'numberless hits', while the rest were low on powder, shot and grape. Nelson's resourceful gunners were having to use nine-pounder shot to make up deficiencies in the larger calibres, and firing seven at a discharge.[23]

Men were also dropping, twenty-five alone on Nelson's blood-spattered quarterdeck. As Nelson and Miller controlled the battle amid shot, grape, bullets and flying debris one man after another was scythed down around them. Major William Morris of the marines was cut down, and one of Miller's young aides. A shot flashed so close to Miller himself that the wind bruised his thigh, while a splinter from a block hit the side of Nelson's abdomen with such force that it bowled him off his feet. Miller, who had come to believe his commodore 'a most noble fellow', caught him before he fell, 'shockingly alarmed at the idea of losing him', but Nelson soon regained his equanimity. He carried on blithely though the wound would worry him for the rest of his life.[24]

Nevertheless, the attrition could not continue. Horribly mauled the *San Nicolas* may have been, but she could still bite, and was firing on both the *Captain* and the *Prince George*. In appalling fire over a mere twenty yards she killed or wounded fifteen to seventeen men on Nelson's ship in a few minutes. On the shambles of his quarterdeck, the commodore realised that the *Captain* was almost spent. She might slink to leeward, out of the battle, but manoeuvring against the wind to fight was entirely another matter. But there was one more alternative.

Nelson ordered Miller to run the wrecked seventy-four upon the *San Nicolas* and called for boarders.

4

The *San Nicolas* could hardly avoid the collision. In recoiling from the *Excellent*'s thunder strokes she had fouled the three-decked *San Josef* on her windward side and was still boxed in. Miller threw the *Captain*'s helm hard over, and the ship lurched towards the imprisoned Spaniard, crunching her bow against the enemy starboard quarter. The British bowsprit pushed over the poop deck of the *San Nicolas* and locked her spritsail yard into the Spanish mizzen shrouds. That bowsprit would become a bridge to the enemy's upper decks.

Nelson's boarders were scurrying up from below and massing at the front of the ship. Rugged tars bristling with sharp boarding pikes, cutlasses, pistols and tomahawks, and grim-faced, redcoated soldiers of the 11th and 69th regiments serving as marines, their muskets primed and bayonets fixed. They were embarking upon a desperate venture. The Royal Navy's advantages in gunnery and seamanship would be of no further use to them once they stormed the enemy ship. This matter would be settled by hot blood and cold steel.

The numbers may have been about equal. Both sides had already suffered heavy casualties. The *San Nicolas* was the larger ship, with a complement well in excess of six hundred, many of them soldiers, but many of her men were down. The *Captain*, on the other hand, was carrying a number of supernumeraries in addition to her ship's company and marines, and many of them were Maltese and ex-Austrian soldiers. Two days before the battle Miller had mustered some six hundred and forty serviceable men.[25]

Looking at those men waiting to go reassured Nelson. At the head of the main party stood Berry who never missed a fight. He had already been made a commander, but scorned to sit idly until a ship became available and chose to remain with Nelson. There was Culverhouse of *La Minerve* and the irrespressible Noble, for whom the seven or eight wounds he had already received in action were evidently not enough. Lieutenant Peirson, back from assorted diplomatic services in Italy, and as ardent as ever, was close at hand to lead the 69th, and Midshipmen Withers and Williams, both schooled in daring adventures on the riviera, commanded parties of tough-looking men. Around the commodore also stood his elite guard of old *Agamemnons*, armed to the teeth. Most of them were young men in their twenties – men such as John Sykes, gunner's mate, Francis Cook, master's mate, John Thompson, quartermaster's mate, and William Fearney, coxswain – but they were willing to fall and die in defence of their leader.

The commodore had no business leading the boarders, and his slight, sensitive figure suggested a man more fitted for poetry than hewing a path through burly soldiers and seamen. Miller stepped forward for the honour, but Nelson had never led from the back and had no intention of allowing a broad pendant to change him. He persuaded Miller to remain behind to manage the ship and its reserves, drew his sword, and climbed to the *Captain*'s anchor cathead, overlooking the ornate stern and quarter galleries of the Spanish ship. As he did so, the main party under Berry swarmed along the bowsprit to drop noisily onto the enemy's poop and quarterdeck or leap into their mizzen chains. Together the parties would converge 'through fire and smoke' upon the Spanish officers and attempt to capture the command centre of the ship.[26]

Jumping across the chasm where the blue water churned far below the *Captain*'s cathead, Nelson's party reached the quarter galleries outside the great Spanish cabin. A soldier of the 69th put his musket butt through the windows and they climbed in. The cabin was empty, but when Nelson reached the doors leading to the quarterdeck he found them locked. Spanish officers on the other side fired pistol shots through the woodwork, but Nelson's men broke down the doors and cleared away the opposition with a spatter of musketry. Then Nelson and his men charged out on deck.

Berry already commanded the poop, and the Spanish officers had regrouped on the quarterdeck where Nelson now caught them between two fires. In any case, the ship's commandant, Brigadier (Commodore)

Don Thomas Geraldino, was mortally wounded and quickly yielded. The Spanish colours came down (in one account by Nelson's own hand) before the commodore and Peirson led a force along the larboard gangway to the forecastle where two or three more Spanish officers were stationed. But they were already prisoners, and as word of the capitulation went below, the remaining guns of the *San Nicolas* finally fell silent. About a score of Spaniards had been cut down in the swift conquest, as well as a few of their assailants, but Nelson had taken a superior vessel.

Miller had lashed the spritsail yard of the *Captain* to the Spanish mizzen chains to prevent his bridge shifting behind the boarders, and more men were soon necessary. For commanding the other side of the *San Nicolas* amidships was the three-decked *San Josef*, flagship of the Spanish rear admiral, with which she was fouled. From the *San Josef*'s elevated poop and the admiral's stern gallery some small-arms fire was directed upon Nelson's boarders below. The redcoats threw their muskets to their shoulders to reply, but Nelson had a remarkable and almost reckless remedy of his own. The *San Josef* had slid around to sit beside the *San Nicolas*, which it dominated in height and power. With hundreds of Spaniards barely battened down on the *San Nicolas*, Nelson decided to lead his boarders over the main deck of the prize and into the *San Josef*. He would make a large prize the stepping stone to a yet greater one.

The *San Josef* was an altogether bigger class of vessel than either the *Captain* or the *San Nicolas*, and to one awestruck observer looked 'large enough to hoist' the British ship on board like an oared boat. The *Captain* was a 'third-rate' warship of seventy-four guns, but the *San Josef* was a 'first-rate', bigger than any vessel in the British fleet, with 112 guns: thirty thirty-six pounders, thirty-two eighteens, thirty-two twelves and eighteen eights, firing in all the equivalent of some 2,214 English pounds – an advantage of perhaps 35 per cent over the weight of metal fired by the *Captain*. The gun deck of the *San Josef* was twenty-four feet longer than the British ship's, her beam eight feet wider and her tonnage burden 50 per cent greater, while her formidable complement amounted to at least 866 men, probably more. Her efficiency, though, was another matter. Later, four of five of her quarterdeck guns were found unused, with their tampions still plugged into the muzzles.[27]

Calling to Miller for reinforcements, Nelson quickly assembled another boarding party, and again put himself at its head. Assisted by

Berry, he flung himself at the side of the *San Josef*, secured a foothold on the main chains, the small platforms on the side of the ship to which the shrouds were attached, and hauled himself upwards on to the enemy deck. His men were soon streaming into the Spanish ship, but there was very little resistance and no loss of life. A Spanish officer looked over the rail of the quarterdeck and said they had surrendered. When Nelson got there and ran forward, sword in hand, the ship's commandant advanced only to drop on one knee and surrender his own. The admiral, he said, was dying. He had lost both legs in the first few minutes of battle and would die that night. Astonished, Nelson asked the officer 'on his honour' if he had indeed surrendered, and was answered in the affirmative. He then shook the miserable commander's hand and ordered him to assemble his officers on the quarterdeck and communicate the capitulation to the crew.[28]

The battle was now assuming an almost surreal quality, with a *tour de force* of successive giant-killing. As the swords of the officers were collected chirpily under the arm of that old *Agamemnon* William Fearney, other loyal followers gathered enthusiastically around the remarkable hero. One, Francis Cook, rushed forward in ecstasy and shook Nelson by the hand. Begging the commodore's pardon, said the excited tar, he wished to congratulate him on the capture of a Spanish first-rate man-of-war.

It was apparently a little before four o'clock. The colours of the *San Josef* were pulled down, the *Prince George* was hailed from the deck of the *Captain* and told to stop firing, and the triumphant ascent of the British flags proclaimed the surrender of both ships. Nelson put one hundred and fifty men aboard his prizes, half under Berry in the *San Josef* and the rest with Spicer in the *San Nicolas*. There were some fifteen hundred prisoners to secure or assist, dozens of them wounded, and Spicer found some fires below the decks of the *San Nicolas* to extinguish, though whether the result of British or Spanish action he could not tell. As Nelson's men went below they found they had turned the prizes into slaughter pens. According to one eyewitness they were 'full of dead bodies, some with their heads off, and others both their legs and arms off, and the rest knocked all to pieces, and their entrails all about, and blood running so thick we could not walk the decks in parts without going over our shoes in human blood, which was a deplorable sight and too shocking to relate'.[29]

The action had not finished, but the defining scenes of the battle of Cape St Vincent had passed. Sir Gilbert Elliot, who watched it all from the frigates, was astounded by what he saw. He congratulated Nelson upon being 'foremost in such a day', and wrote to his wife that Jervis was 'immortalised' and 'Nelson a hero beyond Homer's or any other possible inventions. It is impossible to give you a notion of his exploits in a breath . . .'[30]

5

Ahead of where the *Captain* was entangled with its prizes the great *Santissima Trinidad* was successively or simultaneously engaged by one ship or another. Nelson fancied that he had had 'more action with her than any ship in our fleet', but the *Excellent, Egmont, Blenheim, Namur* and *Orion* had all gone for a piece of the giant flagship. At times she was like a hulking Cape buffalo ringed and torn by lions, desperately lunging away from agile and inflamed adversaries or swinging defiant horns. But her powers were waning. Her topmasts were down, and every other mast and spar damaged; the foremast and mizzen were shattered, and her mainmast, hit some twenty times, hung perilously in place only with the assistance of frayed stays and shrouds. Every sail but the foresail had been torn away, and so little of the rigging and halyards remained that manoeuvres and signals became almost impossible. The ship sagged miserably in the water, listing to leeward with water penetrating two hundred shot holes in her body, and all pumps bar one disabled. For some minutes it looked as if she might capsize. Only six to eight guns were reported service-able, and more than two hundred of her men lay dead or wounded.[31]

She surrendered, showing a white flag and then the English colours above the Spanish, but a remarkable piece of fortune saved the pride of the enemy fleet. Part of Moreno's division had at last got to wind-ward and bore down to fire on the *Britannia*. With the *Captain* and *Colossus* out of action and four prizes to protect, at about five-fifteen Jervis signalled his ships to discontinue the action and concentrate, ignorant of the Spanish flagship's surrender. Remarkably, the British captains on the spot withdrew from the defeated monster. James Saumarez of the *Orion* may have been particularly culpable. He actually saw the Spanish ship strike its colours, but obeyed Jervis's signal without taking possession. Aboard the *Blenheim* it was thought that the enemy flagship raised her colours again when Moreno's counterattack was seen, but Nelson felt that enormous sacrifices had been squandered too readily, and believed the capture of both the *Santissima Trinidad* and the *Soberano* 'only wanted some good fellow to get alongside them'. Even Jervis, who remained tight-lipped in public, appears to have regretted the want of initiative that allowed the flagship to escape.[32]

However, Nelson's own cup was already overflowing. He had been lucky, especially in those dramatic boarding actions. Both the commodore's prizes had suffered heavily in the preceding bombardment, but they still had more than a thousand fit men between them when the battle ended. More than three hundred were found killed and wounded. The casualties on the *San Nicolas* appear to have been particularly high, perhaps as many as two hundred and forty, but the *San Josef* surrendered with less than a hundred of its large crew down. The speed and impetuosity of Nelson's attack, which enabled him to seize strategic points on the enemy ships before they could be reinforced from below, also contributed to his success. Nevertheless, it had been a huge gamble. It was little surprising that Collingwood was beginning to think his friend guided by 'a most angelic spirit' that made him 'equal to all circumstances'.[33]

The British fleet had unquestionably distinguished itself. 'We dashed at them like Griffins spouting fire,' wrote Collingwood. But the greatest honours have to be shared between Jervis and Nelson. Despite the odds, Jervis believed in his team, and committed it to a major battle. To some extent he had also divided his enemy, although both the windward and leeward divisions of the Spanish fleet continued to command the attention of British ships. However, if the engagement off Cape St Vincent was memorable, it was Nelson who made it so. Without him one or two ships of the line might have been captured, and the action, gallant as it was, would have been forgotten. By contrast, those who watched the *Captain* wear out of the British line, take on five or six superior ships in protracted gun duels, and finish by boarding one enemy over another, knew they had witnessed a unique naval spectacle. As a combination of insight, decision and heroism it was unsurpassed in the history of combat at sea.[34]

Nelson's seizure of the two Spanish prizes was seen from the *Victory*, and Jervis recognised the *Captain*'s achievement as much as any man. After the guns ceased, and the British ships formed to protect their prizes, the *Victory* passed the mangled *Captain* and gave her three cheers. Every ship in the fleet followed suit. Horatio Nelson had searched for that applause all his life.[35]

Unable to use his wrecked seventy-four, Nelson got into a boat from *La Minerve* and transferred to his old frigate, receiving the cheers of her company as he came over the side, cheers so loud that they were heard aboard the other frigates. He stayed to see his pendant run up, and at about four-thirty left for the *Victory* without troubling to change his uniform. The commander-in-chief met him on the quarterdeck. Still suffering from his wound, Nelson was 'dirtied and disfigured' and a 'great part of his hat [had been] shot away'. But the admiral embraced him, and instantly gave him leave to hoist his pendant on the *Irresistible*, an undamaged seventy-four captained by George Martin. There was still a possibility of further action, and Nelson was aboard his new ship with Lieutenant Noble by five-fifteen.[36]

Jervis reacted exactly as Nelson expected. An unverified story that may be true tells how Robert Calder, the commander-in-chief's flag captain, complained to Sir John that Nelson's manoeuvre had been a breach of orders. 'It certainly was so,' replied the crusty old veteran, 'and if ever you commit such a breach of orders, I will forgive you also.'[37]

6

There was no more fighting. The Spanish fleet ran for a port with the consolation that, while their men-of-war had taken a thrashing, at least their mercury convoy had escaped. Jervis withdrew to Lagos for repairs and supplies.

The close of conflict had left the *Captain* laying on the water like an exhausted and bloodied whale, with *La Minerve* taking her in tow. The intensity of her struggle can be measured in the munitions she consumed in those brief four hours. One hundred and forty-six barrels, containing between six and seven tons of powder, had been expended. The *Captain* fired 2,531 round shot, 232 anti-personnel grape and case shot, and 151 double-headed hammered shot designed to tear down rigging. Twenty hand grenades had been thrown to clear enemy decks before boarding, and 1,940 musket and pistol balls fired.[38]

Nelson's ship lost eighty killed and wounded, more than a quarter of the three hundred reported for the British fleet as a whole. Among the dead were Midshipman James Francis Goddench, a Portsmouth lad, and two old *Agamemnons*, William Hayward and Midshipman Thomas Lund, who died of his wounds eight days after the battle. Amidst the exultation there was grief for lost comrades and a deepened sense of the fragility and value of life. 'I often . . . think how uncertain a man's life is,' reflected Oliver Davis, whose right arm was broken on the *Captain*. 'I compare it to a flower in the field; in the morning growing and in its full bloom, but before night is cut down and never more seen.'[39]

Nelson's own wound was more than trivial, though the initial swelling of his stomach receded within ten days. The blow appears to have produced an abdominal hernia that gave him occasional pain thereafter. Sometimes coughing temporarily forced part of his intestines into the hernial cavity, causing painful inflammation as big as a fist and difficulty in passing water. Three days after the battle Nelson was too ill to attend the court martial of Benjamin Hallowell, who was acquitted of losing his ship in the winter gales. He included the injury on the official return, remembering how a failure to report a damaged eye in Corsica had eventually rebounded upon him, but he still dismissed his fresh misfortune with a 'they who play at bowls must expect rubbers' and declined to tell Fanny. She learned of it from the casualty list printed in the *London Gazette*, and had to wait until Culverhouse and others returned home from the fleet to get a reassuring account of the wound. More than four years later the Patriotic Fund voted Nelson £500 in compensation for his injury.[40]

The Spaniards lost four ships with 378 carriage guns at the battle of Cape St Vincent, and suffered damage to many others. On board the prizes there were some two hundred and eighty dead and two thousand four hundred prisoners. It was not, admittedly, a huge victory though it was a spectacular and timely one. Cordoba's fleet was still more or less intact, but any participation in France's plans for invading England was indefinitely postponed. The most significant impact of Sir John's battle was on morale. The Spanish navy was damaged in spirit, struck by the humiliation of a significantly superior fleet, and sure as never before that it could not compete with the British in battle. The gloomy defeatism that dogged continental navies was vindicated. Conversely, in the British fleet confidence soared, and captains talked ever more of their ship-for-ship advantages and the possibilities that lay in close-quarter action. As Nelson remarked, 'If our ships are but carried close by the officers, I will answer for a British fleet being always successful.'[41]

At home the news fell upon an anxious public downcast by the poor state of the war and a faltering economy. The government needed a success and reacted with a shower of rewards. Obviously Nelson would be a recipient. The fleet was ringing with quips about a new method of boarding called 'Nelson's Patent Bridge for Boarding First Rates'. His promotion to rear admiral had long been imminent, and now there were rumours that he would be made a baronet as well.

Ordinarily he would have pounced on such honours, but they could never be divorced from economic circumstances. Mindful of his modest fortune, Nelson remembered that even as a captain he had been embarrassed among the Norfolk gentry. A flag and hereditary title, even the meanest, would multiply those discomforts. He would be expected to mix in circles far more affluent than his own, circles dominated by inherited wealth, and to reciprocate hospitality. He would need to meet the accepted standards of a new class, yet his material ambitions had never been extreme, and the proceeds of his prize money were disappointing. His mind was set on a Norfolk cottage. Much as he hungered for status, he was at heart rather a simple man, and did not feel ready to stand among the aristocracy.

The day after the battle Nelson visited the frigate *Lively* and spoke to Colonel Drinkwater, who was accompanying Elliot to England. Nelson stated a preference for the Bath, a privileged order of knighthood with a star and scarlet ribbon, and Drinkwater got the idea that he wanted some visible honour that could be worn and, of course, seen. 'The attainment of public honours' and a desire 'to be distinguished above his fellows were his master passions,' recalled the colonel. The next day Nelson wrote to Elliot, requesting him to use what influence he had in that direction when he reached London. Nelson was less interested in status *per se*, which commonly rested upon inheritance, financial double-dealing or political sycophancy, than in a desire to be known as a self-made man raised by valour and a dedication to public duty. To him medals and ribands were no trivial baubles, but badges of bravery, earned distinctions unavailable to mere men of birth.[42]

In the distant past Nelson had innocently assumed that due credit was usually paid to meritorious officers, but experience had taught him otherwise. He still brooded over those dismissive notices of his service in Corsica, and was determined that this – his finest achievement – would not be buried likewise. Back in 1793, flushed with the excitement of his first naval action, Horatio had sent his brother Maurice an account for the newspapers. Without waiting to see what Sir John Jervis was putting in his official dispatch of the battle, Nelson decided to revive the tactic and prepare his own narrative for the press, though he acknowledged the right of his admiral to send the first account.[43]

As early as 16 February, when Jervis was writing one of the least informative accounts of a victory ever penned by a commander-in-chief, Nelson and Miller were also at work, using the logs of the *Captain* as their foundation. The original may have been Nelson's, or perhaps the work of Castang, the secretary who had followed him to the *Irresistible* with Noble, but it was authenticated by Berry and Miller, who interposed their own considerable claims to attention. With the straightforward story of the battle from the *Captain*'s point of view was a touch of egocentric humour, concocted by Nelson or Miller. Entitled 'Nelson, His Art of Cooking Spaniards', it was delivered as a recipe for 'Olla Podrida' in a style perhaps familiar today. After 'battering and basting' the Spaniards till they were 'well seasoned' ('your fire must never slacken for a moment' till the enemy was 'well stewed and blended together'), a 'hop, skip and jump' was necessary to turn one ship into 'a stepping stone' for another. 'Your Olla Podrida may now be considered as completely dished, and fit to set before His Majesty.'[44]

Nelson considered 'the pruning knife' necessary to fit his account for publication, but copies of 'Remarks Relative to Myself in the *Captain*' were sent to family and friends and one accompanied Winthuysen's sword to the city of Norwich as a gift to his native county. If the commodore had any qualms about self-advertisement he was soon reassured. Jervis's official account of the battle, addressed to the Admiralty secretary on 16 February, did more than marginalise his exploits. It missed him, and all but one other officer, out altogether.[45]

'I would much rather have an action with the enemy than detail one,' the admiral growled. He was thinking of the furore Lord Howe had caused with his formal dispatch about 'The Glorious First of June' in 1794. So much discontent and jealousy had been stirred by Howe's attempt to apportion credit among his captains on that occasion that Sir John decided he would mention none at all, save his own flag officer, Robert Calder, who would bear the wholly unsatisfactory document home. It reached the Admiralty in Whitehall at seven in the morning of 3 March, and made an extraordinary issue of the *London Gazette* the same day.[46]

While the public celebrated their second general naval victory of the war, Nelson's friends were astonished at the way his achievement had been erased from the record. 'I don't like it not being particular enough,' grumbled his brother Maurice, enclosing the offending *Gazette* to Horatio. Culverhouse, returning home to deal with sickness in his family, was still deeply upset about the neglect when he met Fanny in Bath.[47]

Sir John was not entirely negligent, for he did name deserving captains in a *private* letter to Earl Spencer, first lord of the Admiralty. On the same day his public dispatch was completed, a confidential epistle explained that he thought it 'improper to distinguish one [captain] more than another' before the public, but that stars there had been. Among them, he said, Nelson 'took the lead on the larboard [tack] and contributed much to the fortune of the day'. And he reinforced the point by observing that the respective contributions of the ships were reflected in the numbers of their casualties, a criterion that placed the *Captain* before all others.[48]

But none of this would have consoled a man as eager for public praise as Nelson. Reading that beggarly official dispatch, he must have been hugely relieved that his insurance policy was already in full swing. Armed with copies of 'Remarks Relative', friends at home were going on the offensive. He sent copies to the Duke of Clarence and the secretary for war, William Windham. Nelson had met Windham on the polar expedition of 1773, though the latter had abandoned the venture in Norway because of seasickness. Now he was the Member of Parliament for Norwich as well as secretary for war, and owed Nelson a favour for finding one of his protégés a place on a ship. Nelson sent Peirson to him with a letter of introduction begging Windham's patronage, and a copy of the account of the battle. The day Windham received his copy of 'Remarks Relative' he personally delivered it to the king at St James's Palace, and happily forwarded another copy to Earl Spencer. Hood and Locker got their copies through Fanny. The admiral said he would circulate it among useful acquaintances, while Locker took it to the newspapers, assuring 'Horace' that the *Sun* was 'read all over the kingdom'. In fact not only that favourite rag, but also the *True Briton* and the *Star* published the piece on 20 March. 'Nelson's New Art of Cookery' had debuted even earlier, in *The Times* of 13 March.[49]

Nor were these statements isolated blows, for public opinion was simultaneously being moulded by other references to Nelson's prowess. On 2 March, the day before the news of the victory off Cape St Vincent broke in Britain, the papers contained accounts of the commodore's defeat of the Spanish frigates the previous December and of his capture of the *Maria* privateer. And for several weeks thereafter a hungry press, disgruntled at the dearth of detail on Jervis's battle, snapped at every morsel. An admiring family letter of Captain Saumarez was printed, alerting the public to Nelson's capture of the two prizes and remarking that 'his bravery' was 'above all praise', while one or more versions by Captain Miller also found their way into newsprint. Most noteworthy of all was a brief but complete history of the battle written by Colonel John Drinkwater himself.[50]

The commodore's hand has often been seen behind *A Narrative of the Proceedings of the British Fleet . . . in the Late Action with the Spanish Fleet . . . off Cape St Vincent*, published in 1797. Many have worked entirely from Drinkwater's revised edition of 1840, which elaborates Nelson's role and exaggerates the author's connections with a man who had become a national hero since the pamphlet's first appearance in 1797. There is little evidence that Nelson put Drinkwater up to publishing the original account, nor even – as Drinkwater later claimed – that it was produced at the behest of 'friends' of the commodore disappointed at Jervis's dispatch, and that its 'main object' was to 'honour' the hero. Nelson was preparing his own account, as we have seen, and it went round the newspapers. Drinkwater's own distinct and opportunist project was in the making long before the publication of Jervis's dispatch on 3 March.[51]

Drinkwater was on good terms with Nelson, and had reached the fleet as a passenger aboard the commodore's *La Minerve*, though that eventful voyage barely featured in the original edition of the *Narrative*. Switching to the frigate *Lively*, Drinkwater and Elliot had a grandstand view of the ensuing battle from their position in the rear of the fleet, and were immensely inspired both by the conflict and Nelson's part in it. The colonel had a penchant for writing, and would author the standard account of the siege of Gibraltar, and here he had a scoop no journalist could have bettered. Though he claimed he originally wrote his account to entertain freinds, the idea of trading on good fortune and publishing an authoritative eyewitness *Narrative* would have been a wholly natural consequence.

The day after the battle, when Nelson visited the *Lively*, Drinkwater inevitably sought his views of the engagement. Equally inevitably, Nelson was far from unwilling to expand upon the subject. 'I'll tell you how it happened,' he said, and the colonel later claimed that he made some notes in pencil. Drinkwater also enriched his gleanings by conversations with other 'chief actors' and apparently had the narrative written before he reached England, for he dated it off Scilly on 27 February. There can be little doubt that he was encouraged by the appearance of Jervis's threadbare dispatch, which left the public demand for information unsatisfied, and possibly that friends of Nelson urged him to publish. There were several in London in the months that followed the battle, including Elliot, Berry, Peirson, Culverhouse, Spicer and Noble. That said, the impression Drinkwater later gave of an account concocted for no greater purpose than to promote Nelson would seem to rest more upon hindsight, wishful thinking and re-interpretation than strict history.

In the eighteenth century yesterday's news was as doubtful an earner as it is today, and when Drinkwater's pamphlet was published later in the spring it sold badly. Indeed, many copies were pulped. It certainly contributed to Nelson's growing reputation as a public hero, and was the most substantial contemporary account of the battle, but it was far less read than the commodore's own narrative as featured in various newspapers.

Determined to establish his own role, Nelson tended to exaggerate and sometimes overlooked competing captains. His narrative gave the impression that the *Captain* and *Culloden* had fought the Spaniards unsupported for an hour during the crucial phase of the battle, and in one unguarded letter he went so far as to say that no ships but the *Captain*, *Excellent* and *Culloden* had distinguished themselves. Both remarks particularly libelled the *Blenheim*, which suffered sixty-one casualties in the engagement, more than either the *Excellent* or *Culloden*. At least one officer took great exception to 'Remarks Relative'. Rear Admiral Sir William Parker of the *Prince George* angrily informed Nelson that 'positive assertions should be made with good circumspection'. Among other things, he was aggrieved that no mention had been made of the fact that the *Prince George* was also firing upon the *San Nicolas* and the *San Josef* until their surrender. Indeed, in a narrative of his own, called forth by indignation, Parker even claimed that the *San Josef* had actually 'struck to the fire of the *Prince George*', rather than Nelson's boarders – an assertion unsupported by the logs of that ship or any other primary source. Nelson was unimpressed, and replied coldly that he knew 'nothing of the *Prince George* till she was hailed [by us] from the forecastle of the *San Nicolas*'.[52]

Thus the battle of Cape St Vincent, like 'The Glorious First of June', aroused jealousies and disaffection. Jervis had defeated the Spanish fleet, but no more than Howe had he successfully navigated between the sensibilities of men strong on public honour. For the grateful administration the matter was also a tricky one. Sir John became Earl of St Vincent, and received an annuity of £3,000, while all his vice admirals were made baronets, including Thompson who had flunked Jervis's order to tack in succession. In April gold medals with striking blue and white ribands were awarded every captain with the promise that they would be presented at St James's Palace at the earliest opportunity.

Nelson's wishes were respected. He was still no favourite of the king's, but Spencer's admiration for him had grown tremendously over the last two years, and he was receptive to any favour. Nelson became a Knight of Bath, with the right to construct a coat of arms and decorate his breast with a star and scarlet ribbon. In June a dispensation permitted him to wear the order before an official installation by the king, and the new Earl of St Vincent was empowered to make a provisional investiture. The regular general promotion from the captains' list was also announced on 20 February, and on 14 March news reached the fleet that Nelson was now a rear admiral of the blue squadron. Now, at last, that 'dream of glory' he had mentioned nearly two decades before had been fulfilled, and he was entitled to raise a blue flag at the mizzen of his ships. None felt greater satisfaction than an elderly Norfolk parson whose hair now hung snow white about his bony, frail shoulders. The Reverend Edmund Nelson could not help thinking back to his late brother-in-law, Captain Maurice Suckling. For Nelson had been his legacy, as much as anyone's, and he had always told the parson that he would live to see his son an admiral.[53]

7

Several writers, especially in recent years, have attacked Nelson for his blatant self-promotion after the battle of Cape St Vincent, but very few have been interested in the other side of the coin. Readers of this book, however, will not be surprised to learn that Nelson's actions were not entirely self-interested. As usual that paternal protective nature that recognised and rewarded the loyalty of subordinates shone strongly.

One of his first acts the morning after the battle was to visit the battered *Captain* and its exhausted but exhilarated company. He presented Miller with Geraldino's sword, and drawing from his own hand a topaz and diamond ring he placed it on a finger of his flag captain as a symbol of their brotherhood. Miller treasured the ring until his death, when it was bequeathed to his wife and children. The battle had bloodied and bonded the two officers forever. As Miller said, 'those four glorious hours became more than years in affection'.[54]

Both Miller and Berry featured prominently in Nelson's narrative, which they reviewed and revised to their advantage. A commander already, Berry could expect to be 'made post' on account of the exploit, and was extremely moved by Nelson's attention. 'Captain Miller's informed me how honourably you mentioned me,' he wrote. 'I cannot express my gratitude.'[55]

Nelson also spoke for Collingwood on every useful occasion, and the day Miller received the ring he was scribbling lines to his dear 'Coll'. 'My dearest friend,' he wrote warmly. '"A friend in need is a friend indeed" was never more truly verified than by your most noble and gallant conduct yesterday in sparing the *Captain* from further loss, and I beg both as a public officer and a friend, you will accept my most sincere thanks. I have not failed, by letter to the admiral, to represent the eminent services of the *Excellent*.'[56]

Captains such as Collingwood and Miller could defend their own corners, if necessary, but Lieutenants Spicer and Noble were lowlier creatures and more vulnerable. They needed help. A telling, but rarely quoted passage, in one of Jervis's letters to the Admiralty exposes the fight Nelson now made for them. Once more it illustrates his defining particularities. Every captain in the fleet had followers to reward, but none apart from Nelson tried to, or at least succeeded, in pressing those claims upon Jervis after the battle of Cape St Vincent. Nelson, though, would not be denied, and in his effort we again see that vital strut to their loyalty. On 16 February, Jervis told Spencer:

It is with great repugnance I say anything to your Lordship about promotions, knowing how much you must be pressed at home, *but Commodore Nelson being uncommonly anxious to reward Lieutenants Spicer and Noble*, the former now first [lieutenant] of the *Captain*, and the latter most desperately wounded in the belly and shoulder on board *La Minerve*, in her action with the *Sabina*, in addition to a shot he got in his neck on the coast of Genoa, his father an officer in the army, and a brother a midshipman in the navy, having died on service in the West Indies, will, I trust, excuse my naming them to you a second time . . . *I do not presume to call your attention to others.*[57]

In fact, unknown to Nelson, Noble had already been promoted commander for his services aboard *La Minerve*, services that Nelson had also brought to the attention of the Admiralty. Spicer though benefited from his commodore's latest intervention, and was promoted commander on 8 March. Another elevated after the battle was Midshipman Withers, who had led boarders against both of Nelson's prizes. He passed his examination for lieutenant the same month and Jervis confirmed his commission by temporarily promoting him to the captured *Salvador del Mundo* in March. Withers was in London soon afterwards, where he and his mother tried to enlist Nelson's help in securing an appointment in the East Indies. He never returned to Nelson's service, but continued to write to his old commander over the years, and spoke of him during his last days in Norfolk. Like many Nelson had nurtured, the successful and the not so successful, Withers seems to have looked lovingly back upon that period as the highlight of his life, and one that at the time promised a bright future.[58]

As an army lieutenant, Charles Peirson was more difficult for Nelson to usher forward. Army commissions were commonly purchased, but 'interest' was never redundant. Peirson went home with Nelson's personal letters, and from his family home in London did the round of the commodore's more accessible relatives. In March he wrote Nelson an account of the flattering figure the new naval hero was cutting in a fresh stage production. Peirson was armed with a recommendation to the Duke of York, the army commander-in-chief, secured for him by Nelson through the offices of William Windham, and for a while the sun shone on this restless but talented young officer. He was gazetted a captain in the 6th West India Regiment of Foot on 11 July, painted in his scarlet uniform by Daniel Orme, and courted Mary Anne Bolton, the sister of the 'young gentleman' on Nelson's quarterdeck. In about December 1798 they were married.

Peirson wanted to rejoin his old patron in the Mediterranean, but was eventually posted to the West Indies, where he contracted yellow fever. In his last letter to Nelson, written in a shaky hand in 1800, he spoke of his lingering ambition to return to his service:

I have been very ill for three months. I am recovering, but slowly, and [am] not yet out of danger. I am in want of some Mediterranean air. I have cursed my star ever since I was obliged to leave your lordship's immediate command. I have got the rank of captain, for which I must thank you and my patron, Lady H[amilton] . . . I must beg of you to have me put under your lordship's orders, for this is a place of inactivity, which I do not like. I wish to be on a different service, and to be of use to my king and country. I have no hopes of promotion here, and two bad enemies to fight, the climate and illness. Having had the honour of being with your lordship four years and at the beginning of the war, I must beg of you to let me have the honour of finishing the campaign under your orders.[59]

Peirson died not long after, without ever seeing his native land again, leaving a wife and daughter and the memory of moments of unforgettable glory he had shared with a revered chief.

8

Indeed, in that intoxicating spring of 1797 it seemed that all around Sir Horatio Nelson bathed in his reflected glory. He was something of a public hero, and relished its rewards. London, Bath, Norwich and Bristol all voted him the freedom of the city, which he received in ornamental boxes, and the first Nelson memorabilia appeared in the form of ballads, commemoration snuff boxes and engraved prints of Rigaud's portrait. Tributes reached him from many quarters. Enthusiastic letters from Sir Peter and Lady Parker told how they had illuminated their windows for 'Sir John Jervis and the Invincible 15' and regarded Nelson as their own son. The Duke of Clarence, now for the first time feeling himself the lesser partner in their relationship, also penned his congratulations. Basking in 'the praise of every man', Nelson thought his years of struggle vindicated.[60]

Life would never be the same for the parson's son who had become a rear admiral, a war hero and a knight of the realm. Nor would the Nelsons stand on the same footing, although each reacted individually. His brother William, typically, was soon looking for advantage, while Maurice turned his attention towards devising a coat of arms that would reflect Sir Horatio's naval victory. The Reverend Edmund praised God, and on his increasingly rare perambulations about Bath discovered unexpected joy in being accosted by well-wishers at every street corner. 'He is grown young,' said Fanny. 'These blessings in his declining days cheer him.'[61]

Fanny herself has been accused of being the one significant wet blanket, and of suppressing her husband's zest for action with 'leave boarding to captains' letters. She was certainly incapable of the histrionic and hysterical outbursts of enthusiasm that were Lady Hamilton's stock in trade, and proportionately less successful at feeding Horatio's vanity. The notorious 'boarding' letter itself was written on 11 March, soon after she learned of the battle. 'You have done desperate actions enough,' she said. 'Now may I – indeed, I do beg that you never board again. *Leave* it for *captains*.' So strongly did she feel that she repeated the admonition nine days later.[62]

This document has damned Fanny for more than a century. It became the most quotable proof of her utter inability to understand her husband, to comprehend the essence of his spirit, or to share in any meaningful way his search for glory. She was loyal, dutiful and kind, and would have made someone a good wife, but . . . Nelson? Their souls were alien beings.

No one can deny the element of truth in all this, though they hardly justified Nelson's ultimate infidelity. Fanny's was a perfectly understandable response. She had not seen her husband for almost four years and wanted him home. She loved him and feared for his safety. Most recently those fears had been stoked by the secrecy surrounding his mission to Elba, for secrecy nearly always implied danger, and the increasing brevity and infrequency of his letters. Fanny also, as the old reverend warned her, listened to too many scaremongering ladies in Bath. She had hoped that Horatio's promotion to commodore might have delivered her from these anxieties, but it was a dream from which the battle of Cape St Vincent suddenly awoke her. He had even boarded the *San Nicolas* while his flag captain remained behind. But however understandable, Fanny's remarks indicate her underestimation of the passion that drove him forward.

Still, she was by no means indifferent to his reputation and achievements, and proudly passed on the heart-swelling remarks of well wishers. There was nothing dispiriting about Hood's opinion that Nelson's 'glorious share' in the battle would 'immortalise his name in the pages of the history of England', or Lord Walpole's report that 'nothing was yet talked of in London but Nelson'. Or that 'Mrs Pinney declares Mr P. talked in his sleep of you', and Lady Saumarez had come breathless with a letter from her husband that placed Nelson 'above praise'. Even the 'leave it to captains letter' carried several such accolades. Nor did Fanny ever hide her delight at the congratulations that deluged her, the satisfaction she took at being called 'the admiral's wife' and Lady Nelson, and at receiving salutes at public concerts and shows.[63]

Yet Sir Horatio and his wife did dream of different futures. His featured professional advancement and public applause; hers an honourable retirement with war's alarums far behind. The navy divided them, providing Nelson with a full, active and intermittently fulfilling life, and condemning Fanny to a barren loneliness. One senses also that Fanny never really took to England, a cold, damp place far away from the tropical islands of her birth, and her best friendships were with those who reminded her of home. Her closest companion in Bath was Anne, Lady Bickerton, whose life resembled her own. Lady Anne (1769–1850) was the daughter of James Athill, a surgeon of Antigua, and the wife of a naval officer, Sir Richard Bickerton, who she had met in the West Indies and married in 1788. Fanny suffered severely from the cold, and sometimes confined her daily travels to a visit to the post office. There were occasional out-of-town expeditions, to stay with the Sucklings of Kentish Town or the Tobins of Bristol, but the considerable burdens she discharged were also restricting. She had a house to manage, barely satisfactory servants to deploy, scarce resources to stretch, and a sick 'father' to attend. As the years passed, her need for Nelson merely increased.

Fanny's letters seldom flooded with the emotion of a more expressive talent, or with any zest for world affairs, but her unwavering love for her husband rang steadfastly through her pages. She doted over the anecdotes Culverhouse and Berry brought her, and appreciated the many presents Nelson sent, including a chain, Polly the talking parrot, Italian flowers, rice, pearls from Mrs Fremantle and cloth for tailoring. Yet nothing stirred her more than a hint that he would be coming home.

My dearest husband [she began on 10 April], Your letter of March 3rd I received last week, and am glad you have had my letters, [and] that you were kind enough to say [they] give you pleasure. They are full, but truly, of nothing. Your affectionate concern for my want of health has its healing balm. The heartfelt satisfaction at your expression of returning to me 'laughing-back' gives me a pleasure, a something which I am certain none can feel but those who are sincerely attached to a husband. They are fine feelings, but exquisitely painful. I have never shed a tear on my Josiah's account, but when I have known he was not with you.[64]

XXV

WHO WILL NOT FIGHT
FOR DOLLARS?

He brought heroism into the line of duty.
Verily he is a terrible ancestor.
  Joseph Conrad, *The Mirror of the Sea*

1

THERE are times when most people dream of wealth and the better life
it promises. Even the most level-headed of us are susceptible to this
treacherous panacea, the sudden riches that will unlock a luxurious
future, or at least decisively discharge us from everyday toil, discomfort and want. The mere smell of money, the suggestion that some
life-changing treasure trove may be within reach, can bewitch, exciting
wild, extravagant visions, corrupting minds, and beguiling the staid
and the sensible onto difficult and improbable paths. It happened to
Horatio Nelson. For most of his life wealth had been, if not an unim-
portant aspiration, decidedly secondary to his glory hunt, married as
it was to a sense of public duty. Many times he had risked his life in
ventures that offered little financial gain. But in the spring of 1797,
like the Elizabethan privateers of old, he found himself thinking of
Spanish treasure, and the new life it could make for him.

Approaching forty, Nelson was reaching a time when self-made men
begin to feel insecure. Youth, with its long todays and endless tomor-
rows, had passed, and the future now beckoned. Middle age threatened diminishing powers of body and purse. Preparing for retirement
could no longer be postponed to some imaginary date ahead. For
Nelson the realisation that spring and summer were not indefinite

states was sharpened by a conviction that the war and the certainty of employment were coming to an end. Though he might return 'laughing', rich 'in the praises of all mankind', a life on half-pay most probably lay beyond the horizon.[1]

While his means were slender, the demands upon them only grew. His social standing had changed, for he was now a rear admiral, a Knight of Bath and a member of the elite. The idea of playing the local squire, with its opportunities for befriending the community, appealed to him, and at Christmas 1797 he would gift the poor of his native village high-quality blankets with the letter N specially woven into their centres. But it all cost money, and at the moment Rear Admiral Nelson was a knight without any of the inseparable accompaniments of gentrification. He had neither house nor land – in short *property*.[2]

The financial implications of his social elevation were becoming clearer. This was an age when the expectations of the gentry were rising strongly, and houses and gardens were being beautified and estates exploited. It was also an inflationary, tax-ridden age, when every successive reckoning seemed confoundedly inflamed. Fanny knew something about what cutting a respectable figure in society cost. Her house at 17 New King Street in Bath consumed an annual rent of £90, but it was so close to the river that the smell of the sewage drove her from the city during the summers. She liked the houses in Gay Street, which occupied higher ground, but they demanded an additional £70. As for the routine outfit of 'ladies of quality', that was forever changing. 'Such revolutions in our dress since you left me,' she told Horatio. 'Now our waists are lengthened; heads dressed flat at the sides, very high in front and low upon the forehead; short sleeves, some ladies showing their elbows; short petticoats, nay above the ankle with the fashionable; and little or no heels to the shoes. Gloves almost beyond the pocket of anyone, none but the long ones are of use. None less than three shillings a pair. Coloured and white the same price.' Homes, grounds, clothes, horses and carriage, domestics, food, drink and entertainment all drained the modest income.[3]

Property was the greatest bugbear, for in the eighteenth century it alone consummated status and power. It was the essential prerequisite for even modest amounts of political influence. In counties such as Norfolk, land yielding an annual income of £600 or more was needed to stand for Parliament, along with the endorsements of important landowners. Justices of the peace had to command estates worth at least £1,000 a year, and to vote in a county election required a qualification of at least forty shillings freehold. The property owner had a stake in society, something to lose if public affairs were mismanaged, and he incurred considerable taxation. His right to lead, and to dominate the processes of government and administration, was accepted. Indeed, the main reason why Paine's doctrine of universal manhood suffrage was so roundly condemned was its divorce of power from property. Nelson, however, had sprung from the indigent gentry. His previous home, the rectory at Burnham Thorpe, was a patrimony of Lord Walpole, not an independently owned 'seat'. Now Sir Horatio had to change things, and make that decisive, inevitable step towards establishing himself in respectable society. 'We must not be vagabonds any longer,' he told Fanny.[4]

Unfortunately, honours apart, Nelson's account with Marsh and Creed demanded prudence. Fanny had everyone scouring the Norfolk land market for houses for her, but investigations always revealed disturbing snags. Too big, too small, overgrown, no land, a fallen roof – one alternative after another was discarded. Horatio hoped that £2,000 might be spared for the purpose, and while he understood the need for constraints, he realised that his new status demanded something more substantial than they had previously envisaged. 'A cottage, my dear friend, is all I desire, and indeed all that I can afford,' he wrote to one old associate, but his idea of a cottage was turning into a four bedroom house with servants' quarters and outbuildings. Fanny was sensible with money, and more restrained. She even saved on postage by sending her letters to Nelson through the Admiralty, a kindness furnished by Admiral William Young. There could be no trimmings, she insisted. 'We must have nothing to do with more spare bedrooms than one or two,' she explained.[5]

Family matters were additional complications. Though Nelson was not embattled with such encumbrances as deeds of entail, family settlements and dowries, he suffered from being the most fortunate member of a large brood. Financial burdens often fell disproportionately upon him, as relatives looked to him to meet their ambitions and needs as well as his own. To a point he accepted these responsibilities cheerfully, for he was by nature a generous man. His 'only wish to be rich' was in order to serve the 'family', he had told William years before, and it had been no idle brag. 'I know your great liberality, and that it sometimes oversteps itself,' his brother would have to confess. Horatio's purse served numerous kinfolk. Money for ailing Aunt Mary was spent to his entire 'satisfaction', and it was forever necessary to relieve a 'poor father' beset by profligate and insensitive progenies. Then there was the growing, garrulous tribe of small nieces and nephews, a dozen to date, which had their harassed uncle wondering 'where to stop'.[6]

Nelson knew that there were those too eager to exploit him. 'My brother William thinks I have been making a fortune,' Nelson told his father, 'but I have assured him of the contrary.' Maurice had at last got himself out of trouble, and in May 1797 returned to the Navy Office with a salary of £300 per annum; Suckling's new start, however, had not only been shaky but was also now being devoured by drink. After four years at Christ's College, Cambridge, he got his BA in 1795 – but only just. One who remembered him as a student remarked that 'his habits were not those of a man of business', and his two final examiners were divided about whether he had reached the standard necessary for graduation. One thought him 'totally unqualified', but as he had already been ordained a deacon in Norwich it was felt politic to pass him, and he went to Burnham Thorpe to officiate for his father as a curate. He 'will never . . . become respectable,' Horatio concluded. 'If he has again taken to drink, the more he drinks the better. It will the sooner finish his disgrace, and the part we must all bear in it.' But however hard he talked, he ended up paying, if only because of the discomforts he sought to spare his father.[7]

Surveying his finances, Nelson regretfully admitted their inadequacy. Fanny's legacy floundered interminably, with even the interest on it being withheld for reasons that Nelson found impossible to fathom. The £300 a year he had invested in funds yielded a negligible sum, and even pay promised little escape. It was always disbursed late. His pay for the *Agamemnon* totalled £814, and was increased to over £1,400 by compensation paid to captains for giving up their servants' allowances in 1794, but it was not finally paid until the end of 1797. More regularly his rank as colonel of marines had netted him over another £500 a year since June 1795, and he had been drawing the pay of a flag officer from 10 August the following year, when he had become a full commodore. In the eight months to April 1797, Nelson's flag pay amounted to £565, including compensation for servants. Sir Horatio considered himself unfairly deprived of the rate for the several months between his receipt of a broad pendant and official promotion to commodore, and eventually got another £63 on that account in 1799. These sums were considerable, and they would increase as long as he remained employed since he had now been raised from commodore to rear admiral.[8]

On the other hand much was consumed by running costs. He maintained a wife in England and a mistress in Italy, and himself and one or more young gentlemen on his ships. Something as simple as the hospitality of his cabin table burned holes in purses. One list of the stock delivered to his ship on his behalf included 119 birds, among them chickens, ducks, geese and a turkey, in addition to eight sheep and a calf. He provided wines as well as tea, coffee and sugar, and items as diverse as loaves, macaroons, potatoes, hams, barley, spices, fruit, nuts, cabbages, beans and raisins. Occasionally, too, he came upon irresistible furnishings, such as the glass image of Cleopatra that caught his eye in Italy, and remained signally susceptible to hard-luck stories from seamen and friends. Subscriptions to the Navy Society and Marine Widows' Fund entered his accounts.[9]

Prize and head money lubricated his expenses, but amounted to less than many thought. Fellow captains envied Nelson his independent commands, which increased his chances of earning prize money, and he was never inactive. Between 1793 and 1797 he and his cruisers took, destroyed or ran ashore nearly two hundred vessels of all descriptions, some of them detained in disputes with neutral powers. During the first half of 1796 alone his squadron accounted for more than half the prizes taken in the Mediterranean. There were few rich hauls, however, and many captures were released by the courts. 'If I return not poorer than I set out, I shall be perfectly satisfied, but I believe the contrary,' Nelson complained. 'Mine is all honour. So much for the navy!' Including payments made on the seizure of French property in Corsica, Nelson's known share of prize receipts up to the spring of 1797 considerably exceeded £3,000, and more was coming in. It made a very handsome bonus, but was no great fortune for someone without the fundamentals of gentle living in place.[10]

Nelson was interested in money, but it had not been the principal motivation behind his career. While he resented the unjust claims some officers so eagerly pressed for prize money earned by others, he seldom envied deserved winnings and usually rejoiced at the successes of colleagues. 'I long for *poor* Cockburn and Hallowell to enrich themselves,' he once said. People found it easy to trust him. As Jervis once told Elliot, during a discussion of the apportioning of prize money, Nelson 'is a reasonable and disinterested man in money matters, and will come into any proposition you make.'[11]

This was most obvious in the syndicates he founded with the officers and men of other ships. The first, in which the *Agamemnon* agreed to pool prize money with Wolseley's *Lowestoffe*, was made in 1794. Such a deal depended upon each party accounting fairly to the other, and accepting that all would do their best to increase the pot. Typically, while Nelson was happy sharing his winnings with Wolseley ('you will see I have not forgot my friends'), he felt guilty dipping into the money made by partners ('at Fiorenza I shall be a drawback on you – they will not let me share, I dare say'). But the arrangement worked fairly well, and Nelson revived it in the summer of 1795, when the *Agamemnon*, Cockburn's *Meleager* and Plampin's *Ariadne* formed a syndicate. The officers and men of George Hope's *Romulus* voted to enter the arrangement on 18 August, and though they made no prizes themselves, were fully entitled to share in those of their partners.[12]

In the spring of 1797 Sir Horatio Nelson was less complacent about money than ever before. On the one hand his resources had grown and multiplied his balances with Marsh and Creed many fold. At last he was actually earning more than he was spending, and was accumulating money. His balances now hovered between £2,240 and £2,570 in credit, but they would have been annihilated by the purchase of a respectable property with a piece of land. He talked about another £5,000 that might be had as his share in a score of prizes taken by the fleet as a whole, but Fanny preferred to count birds in the hand. She urged him to apply for a crown pension as diplomats did. Nelson dutifully assembled testimonials and lists of his services for the purpose, but the idea of approaching anyone for money remained distasteful. It reminded him of those grovelling letters he had written to Uncle William.

Then against the background of these reveries came exciting news. At the end of February the British fleet was in the Tagus recuperating from its exertions off Cape St Vincent, but it rippled with excitement at word that Spain was expecting the viceroy of Mexico with ships from Havana and Vera Cruz. They contained Spanish-American silver that gossip placed at £6 million. If that convoy was intercepted Spain would receive a severe blow, and the captors would make fortunes beyond their wildest dreams.

2

Sir John Jervis decided to detach a squadron to sweep the approaches to Spain between Portugal and Africa. The mission was laden with prospect. The convoy from Spanish America stirred folk memories of Drake and his Devon lads, but if the Spanish fleet came out to protect it there might also be a serious battle. Furthermore, Jervis heard of another convoy, on its way to Cadiz from the Bay of Biscay, and his detached force was ideally placed to scoop it into the bag.

He gave the job to Nelson, a choice that also titillated. At home Alexander Davison, Nelson's old Canadian friend, was tipped off by Maurice Nelson and wrote to offer his services as prize agent. It was a boon Nelson was unable to confer, for the fleet had its standing agents. The captains with Jervis also sensed battle and loot. As Saumarez of the *Orion*, who was detailed to accompany Nelson, told his brother, 'Be not surprised if, with our desperate commodore, you hear of our taking the whole Spanish fleet should we fall in with them.' The name of Nelson had now become synonymous with decisive action.[13]

Nelson was still in Martin's *Irresistible*, its gaudy 'bright yellow sides' conspicuous as it weighed anchor on 6 March with a mixture of ships of the line, frigates and smaller warships – the *Orion*, *Leander*, *La Minerve*, *Southampton*, *Andromache*, *Romulus*, *Bonne Citoyenne* and *Raven*. The *Caroline* and *Seahorse* joined soon after. His orders were to cruise for fourteen days between Cape St Vincent and Cape Spartel in Tangier, but not a single prize came their way. On 24 March the *Captain* and *Colossus* found them, and Nelson arranged to return to his old ship, sending the *Irresistible* and *Orion* back to the fleet.[14]

On the afternoon of 1 April there was a ceremony that gave Nelson some satisfaction all the same. Jervis arrived with the fleet, steering towards Cadiz, which he intended to blockade. Nelson's barge struck across to the *Ville de Paris*, the commander-in-chief's new flagship, and returned within the hour with a blue bundle. It was Nelson's flag as a rear admiral of the fleet, arrived from England, and he ran it up without delay while the ship shuddered to a salute of seventeen guns.

The commander-in-chief reviewed the situation. His first instinct was to press on to Cadiz, leaving Nelson to continue sweeping with the *Captain*, *Culloden*, *Zealous* and *La Minerve*, but he had no sooner sent the rear admiral on his way than he had second thoughts. Perhaps he worried about dividing his forces before the main Spanish fleet in Cadiz. Anyway, Nelson was recalled to the fleet as it stationed itself outside the enemy stronghold. On 10 April the commander-in-chief gave his most distinguished officer a new job. With the *Captain*, *Orion*, *Zealous*, *Culloden*, *Irresistible*, *Colossus* and *Romulus* he would form 'the inshore squadron' at Cadiz, plugging the port up close while the rest of the battle fleet stood in support further out. In effect, it was Nelson who would be responsible for preventing ships coming out of the port and intercepting the enemy fleet if it offered battle. It was he who officially notified the foreign consuls in Cadiz, as well as the British captains, that the place was officially under blockade.[15]

Many an officer would have wallowed in the privilege, and simply got on with it, but there was nothing inert about Sir Horatio's mind. On the evening of 11 April two old friends sat drinking and talking in the cabin of a British ship of the line riding outside Cadiz. They were men of a similar age and stamp, and had shared adventures on the old *Seahorse*. Admiral Horatio Nelson and Captain Thomas Troubridge were both men of some schooling, had shipped aboard merchant vessels as well as His Majesty's ships, and established reputations as bold, skilful and fiercely patriotic officers. After seeing Troubridge blockade Toulon with an inshore squadron, Jervis was sure he was fit to command the fleets of England. It had also been Nelson and Troubridge who had handled most of the fighting in the battle of Cape St Vincent.

Between these two men – the ruggedly handsome, robust and excitable Troubridge and the light, spindly and reserved Nelson – there was developing a bond of uncommon strength. They both loved action as much as they hated the Jacobins, and were strong-minded but emotional, capable of explosive reactions. Nelson's temperament had an almost feminine quality, with his tearful farewells, constant consideration of friends and brooding sensitivity to slights, but of all his soul mates, the bluff Troubridge was perhaps the closest. That evening, as so often, they struck sparks off one another as they talked.

Soon a remarkable plan was forming. Nothing had been seen of the viceroy of Mexico and his treasure ships, but they were believed to have put into Santa Cruz de Tenerife in the Canaries to avoid the risk of running for Spain in the teeth of British cruisers. More than a century before, in 1657, a naval force under Admiral Robert Blake, Cromwell's famous 'general-at-sea', had successfully attacked a Spanish plate fleet in Santa Cruz. Well then, if Blake could do it, then why not Nelson and Troubridge?

The discussions were far-reaching, and the next day Nelson penned a detailed proposal to Jervis. He had become one of the commander-in-chief's greatest confidants, and Collingwood described him as 'a precious limb from his [Jervis's] body'. It was Nelson, not Jervis's three senior admirals, who got the detached responsibilities. There was never any doubt that Jervis commanded, but when Nelson proposed his lordship always listened. Usually he agreed, and it was sometimes Nelson who shaped the activities of the British Mediterranean fleet.[16]

In his letter of 12 April the rear admiral enthusiastically put his case for an attack on Santa Cruz with a confidence that it would be adopted. At times he found himself telling Jervis what to say to the military minds he must convince to cooperate. 'All the risk and responsibility must rest with you,' he told the commander-in-chief. 'A fair representation should also be made by you of the great national advantages that would arise to our country, and of the ruin that our success would occasion to Spain. Your opinion besides should be stated of the superior advantages a fortnight thus employed would be of to the army, to what [little] they could [otherwise] do in Portugal, and that of the six or seven millions sterling, the army should have one half. If this sum were thrown into circulation into England, what might be done? It would ensure an honourable peace, with innumerable other blessings.' Reading this the uninformed could be forgiven for taking Nelson to be the superior officer.[17]

Six or seven million pounds! It would certainly have dealt a financial blow to Spain, and been appreciated in war weary Britain, but there can be no doubt that the fortune in prize money provided the principal motivation. The war was thought to be flickering to a close, in months if not weeks. The Austrians and French shortly agreed a preliminary peace at Leoben on 18 April, and there was little long-term strategic value to be gained from seizing Santa Cruz at this late stage. In truth Nelson's plan was largely a grab for money.

As Nelson saw it, there were two ways of doing the business. An attempt might be made to cut the ships out of the anchorage, but that operation needed an offshore wind, and when such winds blew they were often squally and uncertain. The other method he reckoned surer. Indeed, it 'could not fail of success, would immortalise the undertakers, ruin Spain, and has every prospect of raising our country to a higher pitch of wealth than she ever yet attained.' Troops might be landed to seize the commanding heights and sever the town's water supply, which passed through wooden troughs outside. Santa Cruz had never been regularly invested, Nelson believed, and had no fortifications comparable with those they had subdued in Corsica. If the sort of generous terms prepared for Porto Ferraio, Leghorn and Capraia were put to the Spaniards, and the rights of civilians protected, there might be no battle at all. The hitch, thought Nelson, was the British army. Soldiers, he believed, 'have not the same boldness in undertaking a political measure that we have', but more troops and artillery than the fleet possessed were needed. He suggested that the garrison at Elba, which was then being evacuated, might serve, or that Jervis might persuade Governor Charles O'Hara to draw upon his garrison at Gibraltar.

This plan neatly dovetailed with a more altruistic proposal Nelson had already laid before his commander-in-chief. For some weeks he had been worrying about De Burgh and Fremantle, still isolated on Porto Ferraio. Final orders had now been given for its withdrawal, but Fremantle's convoy had a long journey to reach Gibraltar, and was open to attack all the way. Since the middle of March, Nelson had been offering to go back with two or three ships of the line, and cover the convoy's retreat. 'My feelings are alive for the safety of our army from Elba,' he told Jervis. Now the extraction of the Elba garrison with its three thousand seven hundred soldiers bore directly upon the new proposal to attack Santa Cruz.[18]

Jervis was also fretting about the Elba convoy. By blockading Cadiz he could keep the Spanish fleet off Fremantle's back, but that still left the field open to the French in Toulon. On 12 April, only two days after entrusting Nelson with the inshore squadron, he therefore accepted his offer to re-enter the Mediterranean. Nelson was given the *Captain*, *Colossus* and *Leander* ships of the line and told to pick up the *Seahorse*, *Caroline*, *Southampton* and *Bonne Citoyenne* during his passage. Both admirals were genuinely concerned for the safety of the Elba convoy, but Nelson at least may also have seen its safe return as a necessary step towards Tenerife. His only reservation about making the trip was the possibility of missing a battle if the Spaniards in Cadiz tried to break the British blockade, but colleagues were sure that if there was going to be a fight Nelson would smell it. As Sutton of the *Egmont* wrote, Nelson had gone to Elba but if there was going to be an action 'he will, according to his custom, cut in just as the Cadiz fleet is coming out!'[19]

Leaving the commander-in-chief to reflect upon his proposal, Nelson made his second foray into a Mediterranean dominated by the enemy. A powerful French squadron was supposed to be lurking off the southern end of Minorca, and Nelson cleared his ships for action upon approaching the area on the 18th, but the sea was empty of hostile sails. The same wind that had swept Nelson eastwards had driven the

French off their station. The next day Sir Horatio's squadron took a Spanish prize, and on the morning of 21 April they ran into Fremantle's convoy near Corsica. Efficiency exemplified, Fremantle had brought everyone from Elba five days before, moving his seventy transports resolutely forward under the watching guns of the *Inconstant* and four or five other small warships. The captain and De Burgh were tremendously relieved to meet Nelson's squadron. As for the admiral, he decided the convoy could not be in 'better hands' and left its management to Fremantle. Nelson dispatched news of the junction to Hamilton and Jervis, and concentrated on providing a shield for the transports.[20]

Betsy Fremantle thought Nelson 'better now than ever I saw him', but behind the tentative but winning smile that lightened his natural reserve the admiral was far from well. He hurt inside, apparently the result of his inflamed hernia, and was contemplating the possibility of going home sick. But he caught up with the Mediterranean news, concluded dolefully from the progress of Bonaparte that 'there seems no prospect of stopping these extraordinary people', and found time to praise where praise was due. This time his cause was the agent of transports, Lieutenant William Day, to whom he paid spontaneous and unsolicited tribute:

I . . . beg leave *again* to recommend Lieut. Day, agent for transports, to your notice [he told Jervis]. I placed my reliance on his judgement (not to leave a ship [at Elba in 1796] more than was necessary) and I am not deceived. A more zealous active officer, as agent for transports, I never met with. General De Burgh also speak[s] of him in the highest terms, and I hope the Transport Board will keep their promise of recommending those officers in their service [for promotion] who eminently distinguish themselves, which I take upon me to say Lieut. Day has not only done at Bastia but [also] at Porto Ferraio. For his conduct at the former place you was so good on my stating his services to recommend him to the Admiralty, [and] I should not do justice to His Majesty's service was I not to urge it again.

The appeal was not made in vain, and through the instrumentality of Jervis, Day became a commander on 27 June following and ultimately a post-captain.[21]

There was one Mediterranean acquaintance Nelson might have been expecting to meet at Porto Ferraio, but who now left his life forever: Signora Adelaide Correglia. A few months later Cockburn wrote to express some regret that Sir Horatio had not, after all, reached Elba, 'though not solely on account of Blue Skin, for [but] I should wish to have heard some news of your little Adelaide and all other Italian friends'. Adelaide, it is true, quit Nelson's story almost as mysteriously as she had entered it.[22]

The previous October, Nelson had sent her a letter and a message via Brame in Genoa, leading her to believe that he would see her again. He was at Porto Ferraio in December and January, though as far as is known he had no contact with his mistress. Probably his payments to her had also finished, and the relationship had run its course. At least as far as Nelson was concerned, but Adelaide may have felt otherwise. In the spring she travelled to Porto Ferraio, where the British still held sway and some of Nelson's agents had temporary homes, apparently looking for him. Nelson had gone, but she contacted Udny, who wrote to the admiral on 11 April: 'Pray write me what you mean to do about your friend, whom I find has been here some time in distress,' he said. 'I return directly tonight to Florence, but have desired Mr John Udny junior to contrive [to] send her to her mother to Genoa, or to Leghorn, as I am setting out directly for Florence and cannot see her.'[23]

If Nelson received Udny's letter, perhaps on his voyage through the Mediterranean, he may have anticipated settling the matter when he reached Porto Ferraio, but he never got there. He intercepted the displaced British community under Fremantle at sea. Thereafter the record of Adelaide's affair with Nelson fell silent, and even friends such as Cockburn were left wondering what had happened to her. Probably Nelson never saw her again.

Did he send her money? Again, no one can say. James Ogle, Udny's prize agent partner who planned visiting Leghorn later in the year, had written to Sir Horatio on 22 March, 'Be so good as to inform me how much money you wish me to pay for you at Leghorn.' On 21 July, Nelson also paid Udny for a bill due to one L. Fenzi. It is possible that either or both remarks may have related to Adelaide, but more probably they alluded to outstanding matters of prize or supply.[24]

More pressing concerns drew Nelson out of the Mediterranean. The Elba convoy, crowded with soldiers, civilians and stores, had to be taken to safety, and from the master of a Danish ship Nelson encountered on 27 April it appeared that the Spanish fleet had orders to quit Cadiz and fight the British. With another battle in the wind, Nelson knew that Jervis needed every capital ship. Hurrying westward, he reached Gibraltar on 19 May. Only one ship in the convoy, loaded with two hundred men of Dillon's regiment, went astray, and it later transpired that it had run upon a neutral shore, where it could be reclaimed. As for the others, some disembarked their passengers and cargoes at Gibraltar while others proceeded to Jervis's fleet. Nelson ordered the *Andromache* to Malaga to rescue some American vessels trapped by French privateers – a gesture of goodwill to the United States – and was himself back off Cadiz on 24 May.[25]

Jervis was ready to meet the thirty-three Spanish ships of the line in Cadiz with only twenty-two, but the last battle had been so demoralising to the 'Dons' that even this advantage did not encourage their new commander-in-chief, the able and popular Teniente General José de Mazzaredo, to stir. In fact, though Nelson sailed into the fleet expecting action, an ambition no doubt amplified by his receipt of the gold medal for the previous victory, he found that enemies of a different kind were the talk of every table. These enemies came from within.[26]

For at home the Royal Navy was in turmoil. That April, with invasion forces still massing across the channel in the Texel, news began to spread across the country that chilled hearts everywhere. The Channel fleet, Albion's shield against her greatest enemy, had mutinied.

3

At Spithead the men refused to put to sea. Instead, they manned the shrouds and cheered. Red flags were run up aboard the striking ships, and delegates were elected to represent the grievances of the seamen. There, and at Plymouth, the protest was both disciplined and restrained, though in due course the mutineers turned unpopular officers out of the ships. The seamen called attention to their beggarly pay, the inequitable division of prize money, poor victuals and deficiencies in the treatment of the sick and wounded. The government acceded to some of the men's demands, and granted a general pardon, but disaffection, once sown, was difficult to contain. A more brutal and unfocused outbreak occurred at the Nore in May, and it spread to the fleet in the North Sea, where most of the ships refused to serve and put back to England.

Nelson had lost none of his notions of mutual obligation on the part of ruled and rulers, and readily understood the distinctions between the men at Spithead and the Nore. The former were fundamentally loyal seamen protesting the failure of government to discharge its duties to them; the latter, in his view, were Jacobin poltroons. As he dared to enlighten an outraged Duke of Clarence, the Spithead 'mutiny' was, in his view, 'the most manly thing I ever heard of, and does the British sailor infinite honour. It is extraordinary that there never was a regulation by authority in short weights and measures, and it reflects on all of us.' Others received similar homilies. To Jervis's flag captain Nelson deplored the way common seamen were sometimes issued inferior rations. 'I take care as far as my power goes that no difference in the issue of provisions is made between the officers and men, which must ever breed discontent,' he said. More pointedly Dixon Hoste learned, 'I am entirely with the [Spithead] seamen in their first complaint. We are a neglected set, and when peace comes are shamefully treated. But for the Nore scoundrels, I should be happy to command a ship against them.' He believed that troublemakers who drew simpler men into difficulties deserved to be hanged.[27]

Jervis was determined to take a strong line and stamped ferociously upon any sign of insubordination. Among the first threats to the equanimity of his fleet were the reinforcements from England, some contaminated with the spirit of revolt. One was the seventy-four-gun *Theseus* from Spithead. Her captain, John Aylmer, was frightened the crew would mutiny and take her into Cadiz, and only days before Nelson rejoined the fleet one of her lieutenants had been tried and acquitted of contempt to a superior. Jervis was not easily assured. As far as he was concerned the ship was 'in a most deplorable state of licentiousness and disorder', and good men were needed to put her to rights. Betsy Fremantle, who agreed, thought the crew of the *Theseus* 'the most tiresome, noisy, mutinous people in the world'.[28]

On 24 May, when Nelson reported to Jervis aboard the *Ville de Paris*, he was invited to exchange the *Captain* for the *Theseus*. In addition to resuming his command of the inshore squadron he would be expected to turn around a rotten ship, and he could take his own team with him to do it. Writing to Miller from the flagship, he requested his 'store room' to be transferred, along with 'such officers as wish to go with me . . . mids Hoste and Bolton . . . and such men as come from *Agamemnon* if they like it.' Even now he thought the old *Agamemnons* his best men.[29]

Forty-seven men, including Captain Miller and the six lieutenants of the *Captain*, shifted with their admiral. The lieutenants included two newly promoted acting officers, Weatherhead and Nisbet. They found five midshipmen on the *Theseus*, all in their forties and incapable of passing the lieutenants' examination. From the *Captain* Nelson was therefore lucky to bring seven midshipmen or master's mates, as well as two surgical staff (Thomas Eshelby and Louis Remonier), a secretary (Castang), a clerk and a schoolmaster. In addition twenty-nine forecastle ratings followed Nelson, some of whom – Cook, Shillingford and William Fearney – were promoted to midshipman, and Sykes to coxswain. The *Theseus* had a complement of six hundred men but all her key posts were put in the hands of proven followers. Furthermore, twenty-eight of the men who transferred were ex-*Agamemnons*, and Nelson's young guard was almost intact.[30]

With a cadre of reliable men about him, Nelson began reforming the wayward ship. Soon after taking charge an inspection revealed that despite her reputation the *Theseus* was in respectable shape. The company was fairly healthy, and used to breakfasting on gruel sweetened with molasses and Monday dinners enriched with peas. No one complained about the food. The ship itself also appeared in a reasonable condition, though Sir Horatio found ropes worn and the shot lockers deficient. But there were lingering signs of discontent. Captain Thomas Oldfield's marines were 'a most excellent' body of men, but among the sailors Nelson noticed some 'very indifferent boys and Dublin men'.[31]

Hoste also believed that the ship was what Sir Horatio might have called reclaimable. In his opinion nothing more than a battle was needed to give 'our brave admiral . . . an opportunity of initiating the *Theseus* crew into his fighting rules, so strictly observed by him in the *Agamemnon* and *Captain*. They are a fine set of men, but have not been in action since they have been in commission.' In the event, the officers rehabilitated the ship without action. On 17 June, Miller read the crew a new act of Parliament promising improved pay and provisions, and to appeasement he added a new regime. Aylmer's stewardship had been harsh, and Miller reduced the number of floggings while maintaining a firm control.[32]

One night a crudely written note was dropped on the quarterdeck of the *Theseus*. 'Long live Sir Robert Calder,' it read. 'Success attend Admiral Nelson. God bless Captain Miller. We thank the admiral for the officers he has placed over us. We are happy and comfortable, and will shed every drop of our blood in fighting the enemies of our country and in supporting the admiral. The Ship's Company.' Once again, with the powerful aid of Captain Miller, Nelson was weaving his magic.[33]

Nelson was viewed as a strong commander, ready to punish genuine transgressions, but just and generally capable of being moved by the misfortunes of simpler men. Two seamen of the *Swiftsure* freshly illustrated this trait. They were in irons, accused of feigning insanity to obtain their discharge. On the reports of a physician and officers Jervis pronounced them guilty, but Nelson disagreed. 'The sight of the two poor men in irons . . . has affected me more than I can express,' he wrote to the commander-in-chief. 'If Mr [Dr] Weir would look at them I should be glad. The youth may, I hope, be saved, as he has intervals of sense. His countenance is most interesting. If any mode can be devised for sending him home, I will with pleasure pay fifty pounds to place him in some proper place for his recovery. The other, I fear, is too old.' Jervis could not be persuaded but Nelson stuck to his guns. 'Depend on it,' he said, 'God Almighty' had 'afflicted them with the most dreadful of all diseases'. In the end the commander-in-chief relented to the extent of shifting the unfortunates to other ships, but he kept them under observation.[34]

Nelson sympathised with the complaints of men neglected or betrayed by those to whom they had rightly looked for protection, but he had no time for the downright treasonable, and supported his commander's uncompromising efforts to prevent them from contaminating the fleet. The risk of going into action, probably against the odds, with fifth columnists in the ranks was not one he felt his companies deserved. He stood foursquare with Jervis in his severe handling of one very troubled ship, the *St George*.

Two men of the *St George* had been condemned to death, apparently for sodomy, but the ship's company refused to allow them to be executed. There was talk of seizing the ship and taking it to Spithead, and officers feared that the malcontents were generating discontent in other companies. Jervis moved rapidly. Four ringleaders were arrested. They were tried on 7 and 8 July and hanged by their own comrades at nine o'clock the following morning – a Sunday. Two boatloads of men from every ship in the fleet were on hand to watch the executions. It was too much for Vice Admiral Sir Charles Thompson, who complained that the Sabbath had been profaned, but Jervis was adamant. He pointed out that few ships were immune to signs of disaffection, and the *Theseus*, *Captain*, *Britannia*, *Diadem* and *Egmont* all contained vulnerable elements. It was necessary to remove the guilty men as soon as possible. Nelson, who had addressed the company of the *Theseus*, thought his men 'a very quiet set', but was not complacent.

Newly restored to the command of the inshore squadron upon his return from the Mediterranean, he ordered boats to witness the miserable fates of the mutineers, and consoled a commander-in-chief smarting under criticism. The hangings were entirely appropriate, he told Jervis's flag captain, and 'had it been Christmas Day, instead of Sunday, I would have executed them. We know not what might have been hatched by a Sunday's grog; *now* your discipline is safe.'[35]

Fortunately, Sir Horatio faced few such incidents. In July he had to endorse Captain Thomas Waller's request for the trial of a boatswain and seaman of the *Emerald* for 'very mutinous and seditious words'. Events overtook the rear admiral, and he had nothing to do with their hearing in August, but would certainly have approved of the execution of the boatswain, who had hinted at seizing the ship and taking it into a foreign port. Legitimate grievances were one thing, treachery another. In a war of survival, Nelson had no doubt that only the ultimate penalty fitted a wilful betrayal of the security of the realm.[36]

4

Among the team that turned the *Theseus* around were valued followers whose welfare Nelson continued to husband. If the war ended and ships were decommissioned, as everyone expected, what would become of those young officers still short of the sea time necessary to try for lieutenant, or to others making those vital but slippery steps from lieutenant to post-captain?

Some of Nelson's old *Agamemnons* were already flying on their own as commanders and captains, and a number had been promoted to continue their journeys in other ships. Thomas Eager from Dingle in Ireland had joined the *Agamemnon* as a twenty-one-year-old able seaman in 1793 and been raised to midshipman. Following Nelson into the *Captain*, he was discharged to the *Belette* in October 1796 and would eventually make lieutenant. Nelson also served Charles David Williams, who had boarded the *San Nicolas*, by finding him a place on the *Ville de Paris* flagship in May 1797, and he too got a commission. Among these young men making their way in the world, many continued to look upon their years with Nelson as formative. Long afterwards Withers reported his progress to his old commander as if his approbation was still necessary.[37]

Compton and Summers were still with Sir Horatio in the early summer of 1797, but he was working assiduously on turning Josiah

Nisbet, Weatherhead, Bolton and Hoste into lieutenants. Jervis promised the young men commissions, but only when they had completed
the necessary six years at sea. That was unfortunate, for neither Nisbet
nor Hoste had reached the mandatory age required for a lieutenancy,
and none it seems possessed sufficient sea time. Nelson decided that
'a little cheating' was required. Ages would have to be falsified and
naval service invented.[38]

Obviously his stepson had special claims upon him. Officially, Josiah
was far too young for a commission – he was merely seventeen and
lieutenants were supposed to be over twenty – and he had only four
years' sea time. Moreover, while he had filled out physically and might
pass for an older boy, Josiah remained diffident and immature, and
had no obvious talent for command. There may already have been
signs of the unreliability that would later worry Nelson. Three years
on a detractor would accuse him of framing 'a story the most infamous and false that ever disgraced the mouth of man'. But back in
1797 Berry, who briefly commanded a sloop before going home in
the spring, wanted to borrow the boy for a spell to broaden his experience, while Nelson talked about persuading old West Indian associates to certify that he had served on their ships. Despite his tender
age, Josiah was confirmed as a lieutenant in May and there is no
doubt that Nelson had prevailed upon Jervis to swallow his principles and favour the boy, and that his record was embellished. Josiah's
'passing certificate' is missing, but from a statement he made in 1817
it seems that Nelson certified that his stepson had served two years
aboard the *Boreas* between 1785 and 1787. In fact, Nisbet was then
with his mother, and rightly so since he was only five, six and seven
years old.[39]

To help the others Nelson loosed his brother Maurice upon the
ships' books stored at the Navy Office in a search for additional sea
time. A certain William Bolton had once served on the *Ardent*, Maurice
discovered, and whether he was Nelson's protégé or not, his service
was commandeered. Thus armed, young Bolton of the *Theseus* passed
his examination for lieutenant in June 1797, and was taken aboard
Jervis's flagship to prove himself a 'steady young man'. He was twenty,
and had received the king's commission at the earliest regular age.[40]

Weatherhead and Hoste were more intractable cases, though Nelson
hoped that their patron, Thomas Coke, might usefully pull some strings
on their behalf. Weatherhead had been rated acting fifth lieutenant
of the *Captain* on 2 April, but technically needed two more years of

service for confirmation. Hoste's problem was different. It turned out that he had been on the books of the *Europa* as a child, but while his service record was fuller, he was more manifestly underage. Nelson resigned himself to leaving the boy with the fleet under the protection and guidance of the commander-in-chief. His efforts for Hoste were particularly public spirited. The Reverend Dixon Hoste had failed to reimburse Nelson the money he had spent upon the boy, but Sir Horatio's patronage never failed. In the end William would repay Nelson in his own way, and become one of the finest frigate captains in naval history.[41]

5

The shield Nelson threw around loyal followers contrasted with the increasing ferocity of the war, for while his Tenerife plan simmered the admiral perpetrated one of the most ruthless acts of his career – the bombardment of Cadiz. Inherently, he was neither an inconsiderate man nor even a warmonger. 'I pray to God to give us a speedy and honourable peace,' he wrote to the Duke of Clarence in June. He felt so ill in any case that he doubted he could 'fag much longer.' However, four years of conflict and the successful savagery of the French armies had also hardened him, and his lifelong distaste for England's Gallic neighbours was turning into hatred. When it came to thwarting their progress, even in a war with their more gentlemanly allies, the Spaniards, he was increasingly open to arguments of expediency. In the words of his favourite playwright, he began to 'disguise fair nature with hard-favour'd rage'.[42]

Back in command of the inshore squadron, Sir Horatio anchored his five ships of the line some four miles out, sometimes with their sterns or heads towards the Spaniards, and sometimes presenting their broadsides. From above the whole formation resembled a drawn bow with the *Theseus* at its centre nearest the harbour mouth. He posted a guard frigate further inshore, ready to warn him of any untoward movement on the part of the Spaniards, and maintained a flotilla of launches and boats to row guard. Supplied by the fleet, and some fitted with guns, these boats gathered for orders or pulled back and forth like water beetles, especially at night when enemy counterattacks were most likely. They exchanged muffled and regularly changing passwords, some recalling such illustrious naval heroes as 'Drake', 'Blake' and 'Anson'. Five miles or so to the rear of the inshore squadron rode the rest of the British fleet, with the big *Ville de Paris* at its head. Admiral Jervis fired a salvo of terse letters to his young rear admiral, sometimes twice a day, and remained in effective control of the blockade throughout.[43]

Nelson virtually closed down the port, although as usual fishermen were given licence to ply their trade within prescribed limits. Others who ventured too far out were snapped up, two apparently by the *Orion*, under Captain Sir James Saumarez. During Nelson's absence in the Mediterranean it had been Saumarez who commanded the inshore squadron at Cadiz, but Sir James bore no resentment at being reduced to second-in-command. Later the two would have their differences, but at this time they exchanged compliments, and Nelson openly lauded his junior's judgement. 'All you do is right,' Nelson told him, 'and can hardly want my sanction.'[44]

From the *Theseus*, Admiral Nelson focused his good eye upon the defences. As his telescope panned downwards from the impressive steeples and domes of Cadiz, and swept over the waterfront houses to the mall behind the long city wall with its parapet bastions, he could see the ladies of the town out walking. Cadiz occupied a spit or peninsula of land that struck northwest, enclosing an inner and outer harbour, both of which had been breached by Drake during his famous raid of 1587. Mazarredo's fleet, with the admiral's flag fluttering defiantly above the *Concepción*, was anchored behind a line drawn on a map between the fortifications of Cadiz, at the end of the spit, and St Mary's on the mainland. With twenty-six sail of the line, the Spaniards outnumbered their British counterparts, but had good reasons to avoid battle. Their ships were in a poor condition and manned by soldiers rather than seamen.[45]

The possibility of storming Cadiz went briefly through British minds. Nelson's action-hungry mind had always driven him towards land operations, of course, and his history was full of direct attacks or ideas and plans for direct attacks on difficult fortifications. San Juan, Marseilles, Tunis, Bastia, Calvi, San Remo, Vado, Leghorn, Porto Ferraio and Capraia . . . they all suggested his clear view that the navy's role went beyond activities at sea. But the plan to attack Cadiz did not originate with its aggressive admiral but in London. It was sent to Jervis in a secret memorandum endorsed by Lord Spencer.

Far from being cautious, the Admiralty apparently favoured a plan to storm Cadiz to destroy or capture the shipping, dockyards and arsenal, and in April Jervis was told 'that under the present circumstances of the war, spirited and vigorous measures, involving some degree of risk, are so far preferable to a system of caution and reserve, as to justify' his serious consideration. The assault was proposed, not ordered, but on the supposition that Jervis might try it he was given a written order to General Stuart, who commanded the British army in Portugal. Stuart was to supply Jervis with the troops and artillery Nelson had withdrawn from Elba, and personally to superintend their use at Cadiz. Furthermore, Jervis was also furnished with an order to O'Hara for a further one thousand soldiers from Gibraltar. Seldom had government seemed so enthusiastic.[46]

On this occasion it seems to have been the admirals on the spot who gave the operation the thumbs down. The commander-in-chief considered attacking St Mary's to gain control of the harbour mouth, while Nelson contemplated an even bolder assault. 'I long to be at them,' he wrote after reading a report that half the guns on the line wall of Cadiz were unmounted. But the place was simply too powerful. According to the British consul at nearby Faro in Portugal, there were four thousands soldiers in Cadiz. Apart from St Mary's, the castle of St Sebastian on the point of the spit and a few mortars near the back of the town and elsewhere, the line wall towards the bay alone bristled with seventy-eight guns. An attack was not feasible. In June, Nelson was commandeering four additional howitzers and field pieces, five hundred shells, 'cases of fixed ammunition', artillery men, 'a devil cart', scaling ladders and a bomb ketch, but the idea of a direct assault on the Spanish fortifications was wilting if not already dead. It is possible that the materiel was then merely being sought for a naval bombardment and the proposed expedition to Tenerife.[47]

Jervis and Nelson probably thought the Admiralty proposal through, and were tempted before eventually discarding it in favour of a less risky naval bombardment. Hitherto, they had banked on their close blockade damaging Spain economically and forcing Mazarredo out to fight. Starved of incoming sea-borne supplies, the Spaniards would have to draw upon their reserves and weaken their ability to threaten Britain's ally, Portugal. More desirable still, the Spanish fleet might be driven to risk battle, either to spare the town or to protect the expected treasure ships. Rumours of the missing treasure ships were still flying about, and Nelson supposed the mercantile community of Cadiz was in a daily lather about them.[48]

Unfortunately, although the blockade was rigorous it manifestly failed to move the enemy fleet, and the British admirals grew more desperate. The contest had begun in a somewhat gentlemanly fashion, with munificence shown on both sides. Jervis ordered Nelson to fore-warn Mazarredo that the British would be firing salutes to honour the king's birthday on 4 June, so that the Spanish ladies might be spared unnecessary alarm. Nelson was also in regular communication with his Iberian opposite numbers. They sent him newspapers and letters, and he gave written testimony in aid of senior Spanish admirals facing enquiries into their conduct off Cape St Vincent. Among many extravagant compliments that Nelson received from ashore were the earnest respects of Don Jacobo Stuart, late captain of the *Santa Sabina*.[49]

Despite the niceties, however, Jervis and Nelson were not content with imprisoning the Spanish fleet. They wanted to destroy it, and Nelson at least was eager to perform before his audience at home and in the Mediterranean. Hoping for a Spanish break-out, he conscientiously monitored every suspicious movement on the part of the trapped fleet. Strange signals, furtive shifts of anchorage and uncommon comings and goings all had Sir Horatio clearing for action. With reinforcements from Jervis raising his force to ten sail of the line, he was sure that his inshore squadron alone could defeat Mazarredo. 'There will be no fighting beyond my squadron,' he wrote. Organising his line of battle, with his own ship naturally at its head, Nelson reassured his superior 'that I will make a vigorous attack upon them the moment their noses are outside the Diamond . . . it will, sir, be my pride to show the world that your praises of my former conduct have not been unworthily bestowed'. When Mazarredo sat still, the British grew angrier. 'What a despicable set of wretches they must be,' Nelson confided to his wife.[50]

There was, in fact, nothing despicable about the Spanish inertia. Their admirals were in no hurry to court certain defeat, especially when peace seemed merely months away, but their inactivity encouraged the British to increase the level of violence. By the beginning of June their commander-in-chief was concluding that more serious action had become necessary, both to spur the lethargic Spaniards and to divert the minds of British sailors from the mutinies in the Channel fleet. It was time to unleash what he called 'hot war'.[51]

Brutality had always been the defining feature of warfare, but the barbaric excesses of the wars of religion in the sixteenth and seventeenth centuries had stimulated something of a reaction. The growth of rationalism and decline of intense religious conflict had encouraged men to think that the difficulties between states were better solved through negotiation than armed struggle. A more humanitarian climate, in which the idea of international law and the influence of the jurists Grotius and Vattel gained ground, tentatively nurtured principles that moderated the impact of conflict in western Europe and increased protection for non-combatants and prisoners of war. But in the new world spawned by the French Revolution, spiced by the resurgence of competing ideologies and desperate struggles for national survival, the powers retreated once again towards savagery. The relatively bloodless warfare of manoeuvre, so prevalent at the turn of the seventeenth and eighteenth centuries, was replaced by terrifying battles of annihilation, battles in which Napoleon and Nelson would demonstrate their genius. Jervis's plan to bombard the town of Cadiz, firing shells directly into civilian quarters rather than the shipping and fortifications, was not entirely wanton. Its purpose was to 'irritate the inhabitants' and 'make them force out their fleet', but it fitted the trend and struck some at least as shameful.[52]

The naval bombardment was intended to inflict psychological as well as physical damage. On 3 June, Nelson was told to leak a warning to the Spaniards that bomb vessels were being prepared to 'lay Cadiz in ashes'. The threat only induced the enemy fleet to hunker down in a securer anchorage, but it was no idle one. On 2 July the *Thunder* bomb, commanded by the redoubtable Gourly and armed with a twelve-and-a-half-inch-calibre mortar and a ten-inch howitzer, arrived from Gibraltar with a detachment of artillery. With her came the *Urchin* gunboat fitted with a twenty-four-pounder and a small howitzer. Without delay a formidable trio got to work on 3 July: John Jackson, master of the *Ville de Paris*, freshly noted for destroying an enemy privateer with one of the gun launches; Lieutenant Charles Baynes, a respected artillery officer, and Captain Miller of the *Theseus*, whose interest in pyrotechnics would ultimately be his undoing. After carefully sounding the water towards Cadiz and assessing the blind spots of relevant Spanish batteries, they pinpointed a suitable station for the bomb vessel. The attack was scheduled for the same evening, and Nelson promised Jervis that Mazarredo would get his fill of fighting if he chose to come out; if he did not it would be 'a warm night at Cadiz'.[53]

Nelson believed in personal leadership. He had learned to live with the risks of mutilation and death, and now performed acts of bravery with almost routine abandon. It was not really his job to endanger himself at the head of an attack, but he grubbed for glory on every occasion and also knew that every time he led from the front he validated his leadership among the men. They knew he was willing to face risks as great as he was asking them to face – even greater, since he took such a prominent position in the uniform of a significant officer. Thus, at about eight o'clock in the evening, Nelson took personal charge of the *Thunder* as it was taken in tow by some of the launches, and slid purposefully through the clear and moonlit night towards the tower of St Sebastian, within 2,500 yards of the city walls. 'I intend, if alive and not tired, to see you tomorrow,' he had time to write to the commander-in-chief.[54]

The advance was uncertain. Miller tried to lead the way in a boat, but the *Thunder* was forever steering off course, and it was about ten before it anchored, supported by the *Goliath* ship of the line, *Terpsichore* frigate, *Fox* cutter and a fleet of launches and barges. The Spaniards were expecting the attack. In fact, the British had advertised it themselves by their futile attempt to goad Mazarredo, and every movement of Nelson's squadron was being hungrily scrutinised. Already the enemy batteries and an intimidating flotilla of Spanish gunboats and barges were firing briskly, but sometime before eleven the undaunted *Thunder* was ready to begin its uncomfortable task. Shells screeched up into the night, and then arched down towards the startled town. Some exploded in midair as their fuses burned prematurely, but others crashed angrily to earth, and the sky above Cadiz soon flickered red where fires had broken out in three places.

After midnight the Spanish gunboats and barges surged forward in a desperate attempt to arrest the bombardment. Their admirals doubted the wisdom of the attack, and apparently tried to call it off, but the order reached the flotilla commander, Don Miguel Irigoyen, too late. This was small-boat work in dangerous waters, and Nelson's own flotilla, consisting of two boats from every ship, was dispersed to protect the *Thunder*. Manned by prime men with pikes, cutlasses, broad axes, pistols, muskets, sledgehammers, handspikes, clamps and ropes – in short, everything necessary for warding off or towing away Spanish vessels or killing and wounding their occupants – it had been assembled beside the *Theseus* and was commanded by Captain Miller.

When he saw the Spanish flotilla advancing through the darkness, Nelson ordered Miller to counterattack, but an unusual unsteadiness troubled the men in the British boats and the admiral grew impatient. Ordering his barge alongside the *Thunder*, Nelson manned it with the ubiquitous Captain Fremantle and eleven of his best men and was soon pulling vigorously towards the oncoming Spaniards. Inspired by the sudden intervention of their leader, some of the British tars raised a cry of 'Follow the admiral!' and made after him.[55]

A fierce, cutlass-clashing boat action was soon in full swing, every bit as impetuous and nerve-testing as the greater struggle off Cape St Vincent. Seeing the angry British moving grimly forward, the Spaniards faltered and the heads of their boats began to turn as if to flee. Miller's ten-man pinnace ploughed into the after oars of a fifty-three-foot Spanish mortar vessel armed with a howitzer and a pair of swivels, but was held off in a nasty exchange of pistol shots and missiles. Miller narrowly escaped injury when one discharged pistol was flung with terrific force across his face. Nelson, in the meantime, attacked another mortar boat further inshore but lost it when Irigoyen ran his large barge, the *San Pablo*, into the starboard side of Nelson's barge and tried to board her. Both sides flung themselves upon each other furiously. The Spaniards had thirty or so men, and outnumbered Nelson and his comrades more than two to one, but a desperate and bloody hand-to-hand melee ensued. Pistols flashed in the dark, and antagonists shouted, cursed and hacked each other down with any weapon to hand. 'It was cut, thrust, fire and no load again – we had no time for that,' one Briton recalled.[56]

John Lovell, one of Nelson's guard, remembered that 'the crew of the [British] barge, hardly waiting for orders, literally scrambled over Nelson, and in a few seconds possessed themselves of Don Miguel Tregoyen [Irigoyen] before Nelson had time to look round him.' But Nelson was himself in the thick of the fight, and two years later boasted that 'it was during' the action 'that perhaps my personal courage was more conspicuous than at any other . . . this was a service hand to hand with swords, in which my coxswain, John Sykes (now no more) saved twice my life'. Certainly Sykes proved his devotion to Nelson with astonishing selflessness that night. Twice he parried blows aimed at the rear admiral, and on one occasion interposed himself in the path of a slashing Spanish sabre. 'We all saw it,' one of his friends recalled. 'We were witnesses to the gallant deed, and we gave in revenge one cheer and one tremendous rally.' Sykes fell with wounds to his head, shoulders and back, and Nelson, it is said, caught him in his arms. 'Sykes,' he is said to have cried, 'I cannot forget this!'[57]

Fremantle was among the others injured, getting 'a good deal cut' about the face as he boarded, and Nelson's party would probably have been shark bait if Miller had not run his boat upon the Spaniard's larboard side, and boarded her in support. Eighteen Spaniards were slain in the debacle, and Irigoyen, downed with at least two wounds, was made a prisoner, along with all of his men who did not swim ashore. The two Spanish boats Nelson and Miller had previously engaged were also captured, the first by a spirited boarding action led by Weatherhead from the *Theseus*'s launch, and the remaining enemy vessels were driven into a creek or under the walls of Cadiz. In British hands the Spaniards also left their dead and 121 prisoners, at least thirty of them fatally wounded. Ninety-one were later handed back to Mazarredo as part of an exchange. It had been a spectacular clash, and spared the *Thunder* to do its work, but the bombardment itself failed. The large mortar was a great disappointment. It threw the shells short and then broke down, and Nelson called off the action towards three in the morning. The results were meagre. A few buildings had been pulverised and some civilians hurt; rumour had it that a house had been demolished with the loss of a child and a woman's arm, and that several priests had been killed in a convent. 'That no harm,' Nelson remarked of the latter, 'they will never be missed.' As a piece of terror the attack had some success, and several women apparently abandoned the town rather than face further fire, but its military value was negligible.[58]

Scholars have followed Nelson in stressing the courage shown in the boat fight, and certainly the admiral, Miller and Weatherhead and their men acted in the finest traditions of the service. Their courage was beyond praise. But that said, the attack was not only savage and futile but also somewhat ineptly conducted. Mention has already been made of the *Thunder*'s shaky advance and her mortar's inefficiency. More alarming was the unsteadiness shown by some of the British seamen under fire. Indeed, many of the boats that were supposed to tow *Thunder* and *Urchin* out of the combat zone after the bombardment ended actually abandoned them and tried to flee precipitately back to the covering fire of the *Goliath* and other ships. Miller rallied some, but resorted to enquiring 'of every boat to what ship she belonged as a security for her behaviour'.[59]

At least Sir Horatio's own losses were small. A launch was sunk by a raking shot from a Spanish gunboat, and had to be salvaged by the *Culloden*, and one man was killed and twenty-seven wounded. Among the latter was another of Nelson's close followers. Thomas Ramsay, a quartermaster's mate, was one of the oldest surviving

Agamemnons, but he had followed his commander into the *Captain* and *Theseus* and boarded the Spanish ships of the line at Cape St Vincent. Here, in another desperate action, his left arm was shattered by a 'ragged [musket] ball', and pieces of bone were still being removed from the wound days afterwards. Within three weeks the injury putrefied and Ramsay's arm had to be amputated above the elbow.[60]

A second bombardment of Cadiz was conducted on the night of 5 July, using the resuscitated *Thunder* (a second howitzer having replaced its defunct mortar), the *Urchin* and the two captured Spanish mortar vessels sinisterly renamed *Terror* and *Strombolo*. This time Miller and his assistants went five and a half miles beyond the British front line to within a mile of the town to find a position from which to attack. It was just south of the lighthouse near St Sebastian and a little west of the peninsula, where the defences were weaker. Nelson controlled the operation from the *Theseus*, and delegated Miller and Captains Richard Bowen and John Waller of the *Terpsichore* and *Emerald* frigates to command the boats towing the bomb and mortar vessels into action. Some stalwart reinforcements joined the attack. 'Johnson, first lieutenant of the *Emerald*, is a man after your own heart,' Jervis told Nelson. 'Put him in a way of taking a gun boat and I will answer he succeeds or loses his life in the attempt.' To increase incentives the commander-in-chief promised that any lieutenant who captured an enemy gunboat would immediately become her captain.[61]

On this occasion the Spaniards were better prepared, and had redistributed their ships and launches. Nor did they repeat their previous mistake, and make any brave but injudicious assaults. Though the Spaniards fired sharply on the attackers, their gunboats made only one half-hearted foray towards the British, and their ships merely manoeuvred themselves into more secure positions. Yet the fresh attack, like the last, revealed unexpected weaknesses in what the British considered to be a crack force. Miller got the *Urchin* and the mortar boats into position, but Bowen, who commanded the bomb, anchored her earlier than Miller planned, increasing the range over which shells would have to be thrown. Furthermore, when Miller was still 450 yards short of his position, and the Spaniards discovered the attack, opening a heavy fire of shot and shell, the indiscipline and cowardice that had marred the previous engagement reappeared. Some of the small boats showed a distressing readiness to cut towropes and scatter which Miller was only partly able to parry with 'great exertions and the strongest language'.[62]

Despite these difficulties Nelson's men were soon blazing away, hurling a total of some eighty-four shells into the town with what Jervis called 'excellent direction'. All but half a dozen appeared to hit the target, producing vast pillars of smoke in the northwestern part of Cadiz. As usual, Sir Horatio found the fighting irresistible and went forward to supervise from the *Thunder*. He was pleased with the bombardment, but annoyed that his small-boat flotilla gave such inadequate cover against enemy gunboats, and Miller was ordered to reform it. Most if not all of the British boats were armed with carronades, but Miller found them 'much dispersed and many at a shameful and completely useless distance'. Again he found himself calling them in.[63]

When the assault force ran out of ammunition and withdrew, the *Thunder*'s masts and hull scarred by enemy hits, Miller and Weatherhead covered the retreat in a pinnace and the *Theseus* launch. Their loss was light, only three men being killed and twenty-one wounded, and Nelson did not seem dissatisfied, but in truth the attack fell far short of its objective. Some damage had been done, but not enough, and far from inducing the Spanish fleet out the attack merely gave it a measure of approbation. National newspapers represented Mazarredo's men as heroes, successfully repulsing spectacular but largely ineffective British assaults.

Never a man to be easily beaten, Nelson still believed a process of attrition might expel the enemy ships, and planned a third attack for the 8th. He hoped to come from the northwest, but unfavourable winds and a strong swell prevented the bomb and mortar vessels from advancing and the attack was called off. By then it was becoming obvious that no provocation was going to succeed. The Spanish ships kept shuffling about, sometimes advancing before anchoring again and at other times digging deeper into 'a nook of the harbour' and filling the approaches with gun launches. They never looked about to fight, but Nelson was out regularly with his guard boats, looking for weaknesses and exchanging occasional fire. One sortie by the Spanish gunboats was repulsed in firing that lasted much of the 9th, and the following day Nelson stood beyond the lighthouse with the *Theseus* and four small vessels hoping to throw some more shells into the town from the south. He drew fire from the entire enemy flotilla, and inflicted losses of sixteen killed and wounded upon the Spaniards in return but without achieving a significant outcome.[64]

The situation had stalemated, and though Sir Horatio found his skirmishes more entertaining than paroling prisoners and arranging exchanges, he was frustrated. 'I hope [the] Ministry will do anything for a peace,' he wrote in June. No doubt it was with some gratification that he learned he was to be diverted from this sterile work, and that the Tenerife expedition, so pregnant with action and prospect, was at last underway.[65]

6

'Who will not fight for dollars?' Nelson had written. It was not much of an exaggeration, and the golden lure of Tenerife was difficult to deny.[66]

Admiral Jervis put duty first. Like Nelson, his greatest desire was to destroy the Spanish fleet, 'for the mines of Peru and Mexico are not to be compared with the glory you and all my companions in arms will derive from an action with the angry Dons'. But Mazarredo was only burrowing deeper, and if Tenerife could be taken without endangering the premier campaign, there was no reason why it should not be considered.[67]

Nelson had continued to encourage. The very day he met Fremantle's convoy off Corsica he had reminded his commander-in-chief of Tenerife. 'What a stroke it would be!' he said. Again Jervis was pressed to approach O'Hara at Gibraltar for troops.[68]

The commander-in-chief investigated, and some of the answers were satisfactory. O'Hara was not interested, perhaps still grieving that Nelson had got the vacant red sash of Bath he had wanted for himself, but Tenerife looked promising. In April, Captain Richard Bowen, a thirty-six-year-old Devonian, took the Terpsichore and Dido frigates to Santa Cruz and found two merchantmen there, the San Jose and Principe Fernando. They were not part of the American treasure flota, but rich nevertheless because they both belonged to the Philippines Company and carried luxury merchandise such as coffee, muslin and pepper. Bowen managed to cut the smaller vessel out, and came away with some £30,000 worth of cargo. The British fleet was soon salivating at the thought of what the larger vessel in Santa Cruz might contain. She was from Manilla, and speculation made her ten times more valuable than Bowen's prize.

The next month two more of Jervis's frigates were off Tenerife, the Lively and La Minerve. Their senior commander, Benjamin Hallowell, pretended he had come to arrange an exchange of prisoners, but furtively looked round. As far as he could make out the Manilla ship was being unloaded at the waterfront of Santa Cruz, but a fourteen-gun French corvette, *La Mutine*, lay exposed in the roadstead. On the 29th the British cut her out. The news thrilled Nelson because Lieutenant Thomas Masterman Hardy, who had distinguished himself under his command in December, was instrumental in capturing the French ship. Sir Horatio urged Jervis to promote him, but the commander-in-chief knew a good man when he saw one, and needed no spur. Hardy became commander of *La Mutine*, the ship he had captured. Nor was Hallowell's raid without its intelligence value. One officer of the *Lively* reported that Santa Cruz could be taken with 'the greatest ease'.[69]

Slowly the Tenerife expedition took shape. On 6 June, Jervis assured Nelson that as soon as his fleet was reinforced he would detach the rear admiral with two ships of the line, a fifty-gunner and three frigates. It was advisable to make preparations. The strike force turned out to embrace the *Theseus*, *Culloden* and *Zealous* seventy-fours, the fifty-gun *Leander*, the frigates *Seahorse*, *Emerald* and *Terpsichore*, the *Fox* cutter and *Terror* mortar launch supervised by Baines of the Royal Artillery.

Nelson's captains were from the cream of the fleet. Miller was there, of course, and Fremantle commanding the *Seahorse*. Bowen of the *Terpsichore*, regarded by Jervis as a rising star as well as 'a child of my own', and Thomas Boulden Thompson of the *Leander* were both familiar with Santa Cruz, while the captain of the *Zealous* was Sir Samuel Hood, a gentle giant and cousin of Nelson's famous mentor. Sir Samuel had served under Nelson off Corsica in 1794, when he was captain of *L'Aigle*, and the rear admiral had already written warmly of him. 'The account you give of my relation and namesake is truly delightful,' replied Admiral Hood. 'He must be a good fellow, by his being so kindly and partially spoken of by you, and I am confident nothing will ever be more pleasant to him than to act upon any service under your orders and immediate eye. This he has repeatedly said to me.' The *Culloden*, of course, belonged to Troubridge, one of the originators of the plan to attack Tenerife. Only recently he had been ill, dangerously ill according to Jervis, but no one was going to keep him from being there.[70]

On 14 July the advanced squadron of eleven sail was signalled back into the main fleet and Nelson received Jervis's orders. He was to demand the surrender of the island of Tenerife, including the cargo of the Manilla ship, and such other cargoes as were not intended for the consumption of the islanders. Government property and the forts had also to be surrendered. Drawing on his Mediterranean experience, Nelson had advised the use of carrot as well as stick, and that was the formula deployed here. The carrot was a guarantee that civilians would be secure in person and property, and their civil and religious rights safeguarded if the island surrendered. The stick threatened that 'a very heavy contribution' would be levied on the inhabitants if they resisted and every species of vessel seized to pay it.[71]

Nelson's orders were to his liking, but perhaps weighing the risks involved he arranged for any prize money due him to be paid to Fanny. Then, when all his squadron but the *Leander* and *Terpsichore* were ready, he sailed on the 15th, sliding southwest over a brilliant blue sea before a good wind.[72]

To Nelson the only deficiency seemed the lack of soldiers. Apparently neither De Burgh nor O'Hara felt able to cooperate, and Nelson had to settle for an extra detachment of marines. He regretted the lack of 'more red coats' to dazzle the enemy, but banked on a sudden surprise stroke 'doing the job . . . the moment the ships come in sight'. After all, he cheered Jervis, 'under General Troubridge ashore and myself afloat, I am confident of success'.[73]

As was his custom, Jervis backed his most energetic officer to the hilt, but his farewell note suggested much less confidence. 'God bless and prosper you,' said the old admiral. 'I am sure you will deserve success. To mortals is not given the power of commanding it.'[74]

XXVI

MORE DARING INTREPIDITY WAS
NEVER SHOWN

Who doomed to go in company with pain,
And fear and bloodshed, miserable train!
Turns his necessity to glorious gain.
    William Wordsworth, *Character of the Happy Warrior*

1

CAPTAIN John Waller of the *Emerald* frigate made an entry in his journal for 17 July 1797. 'At 10 a.m. the admiral made the signal for all captains to consult on the best plans of operation, and [to] gain all the information possible about the town of Santa Cruz.'[1]

Aboard the ships steering southwest across the blue ocean, bent upon a hazardous mission to Tenerife, there were few signs of complacency. The men were being drilled in the use of great and small arms, and weapons were inspected and put into prime order. Admiral Nelson had only one good eye, but it was an eye for detail, and preparations were being made for foreseeable contingencies. Orders were given for the manufacture of additional scaling ladders, of platforms and a sledge for the artillery Troubridge planned to haul ashore, and for a supply of iron musket ramrods to replace the standard but fragile wooden issues. Nelson knew that in a busy exchange of musketry broken ramrods would reduce the rate of fire and risk men's lives.

The attention to detail was revealed in the organisation of the seven hundred and forty seamen chosen to form the landing party. As Miller described it, they were formed into three companies, each with its quota of pikemen, 'a Master at Arms or Ship's Corporal, a Boatswain's mate, and Quarter Master or Gunner's mate, an Armourer with a cold chisel, a hammer, spikes for guns, and a crow, a carpenter with a short broad axe, a heavy mall, and two iron wedges, a Midshipman or mate and a Lieutenant to command it. I gave each company a small red, white or blue flag . . .'[2]

Nor was it just the men and junior officers who had to be conditioned for what lay ahead. Every captain needed to know what was expected of him, and it was to that end that they, now reinforced by Bowen of the *Terpsichore*, were summoned to the *Theseus* on 17 July for the first of several meetings.

The importance of briefing senior officers seems obvious, but it was by no means a universal or even a common practice, even by great leaders. Napoleon, for example, often exercised such a personal command of the battlefield that subordinates were left ignorant of his intentions and overdependent upon his on-the-spot instructions. The disruption of that personal chain of command in the fog of conflict caused serious problems for the egocentric emperor on the field of Waterloo. Indeed, as armies and fleets grew larger, the ability to co-ordinate and control grand forces, sometimes sprawled over miles of front and enmeshed in noise, confusion and smoke, became increasingly central to successful leadership. At sea, where communications were harnessed to inefficient flag-signalling systems, the problem was particularly acute. Although improved, the use of numerical flags keyed to signal books remained cumbersome and imprecise. Even when flags could be seen through the gunsmoke, they were incapable of transmitting complicated instructions quickly and they were easily misinterpreted, as the battle of Cape St Vincent had shown.[3]

Nelson had his own solution to what modern military theorists call problems of 'command and control'. From the beginning he involved his captains in the command process through a series of informal meetings in which strategy and tactics and ways and means were thoroughly aired. As later described by Berry, during these assemblies the admiral's practice was to 'fully develop . . . his own ideas of the different and best modes of attack, and such plans as he proposed to execute upon falling in with the enemy, whatever their position or situation might be, by day or night'. In other words he discussed what might be done in every eventuality. 'There was no possible position in which they [the enemy] could be found that he did not take into his calculation,' and for which he did not suggest 'the most advantageous attack'. Because the captains had been comprehensively briefed, understood Nelson's intentions, and had examined the different ways of achieving them, 'signals became almost unnecessary' and 'much time was saved'. Each captain was theoretically capable of using his own initiative to achieve the corporate end.[4]

There was nothing autocratic about Nelson's process. He valued and liked his captains, and his style of leadership was open, friendly and informal. People felt at ease with him and able to speak in the meetings. Rather than dispensing definitive decisions from above, Nelson set the parameters of debate and encouraged his officers to contribute their own information and ideas. His assemblies were not so much briefings as forums for the exchange of ideas. They were brainstorming seminars. At a time when the only universal formal officer training in the navy was confined to the seamanship tested in examining lieutenants, Nelson's conferences were milestones in the development of professional education.

The council of war recorded by Captain Waller was the first of four summoned over a six-day period. During their deliberations every captain volunteered to lead a division in the attack on Tenerife, leaving Thomas Oldfield of the *Theseus*, and army captain of four years' standing, to command the marines. Unusually, Nelson decided to forgo personal heroics, and agreed to coordinate the attack from the *Theseus*, as befitted an admiral, and Troubridge would command ashore. It was as good a team as the navy of 1797 could field.

In their preliminary discussions, Nelson and his captains had only an imperfect picture of the defences of Santa Cruz de Tenerife. They relied heavily upon the information of a seaman of the *Emerald* and one of Fremantle's servants, both of whom had known the town many years before. In fact, although it was a respectable settlement, with a population of about seven thousand, compared to Bastia, where several thousand troops manned a formidable sea front commanded by powerful hill forts behind, Santa Cruz was not militarily impressive. It had no more than a skeleton garrison of barely four hundred regulars, and was heavily dependent upon an ill-equipped militia of some eight hundred men that needed time to assemble. Fewer than four hundred gunners and about one hundred and ten French sailors marooned by Hardy's capture of *La Mutine* did not raise the armed human resources of Don Antonio Guitierrez, commandant general of the Canaries, to more than seventeen hundred men.

The town and its environs themselves offered little room for manoeuvre, however. A precipitous volcanic rock pushed out of the sea, Tenerife's shoreline was sheer and the water deep offshore, so that landing places and anchorages were difficult to find. Most of the few beaches were black and broken and slippery underfoot and often guarded by a heavy surf. Santa Cruz, which hugged the shore of an open bay on the northeastern coast of the island, was protected to the rear by craggy mountains rising to a central ridge. Its southwestern flank was reputedly difficult to approach, without anchorages or suitable landings, and the only viable attack was from the front or northeast, where the human defences were at their strongest. The six miles of the town's sea wall and front bristled with sixteen fortifications, some of them mere gun platforms but others towers and parapets, the whole defended by eighty-four pieces of artillery. Of these strong points the most impressive was the ancient citadel of San Cristobal, with its bell tower, a massive thirty-foot perimeter wall and corner bastions mounting ten guns. Some of these last commanded the principal landing place – a low, stone, round-headed mole that jutted prominently into the sea not far from the town square.[5]

These defences were far from contemptible, and like all good commanders Nelson knew that his strongest weapon was surprise. A sudden assault, launched against an unwary or startled enemy before they could mobilise, prepare or even think, was a tactic capable of producing astonishing results. The greatest of Nelson's disciples, Lord Cochrane, would definitively demonstrate the point in 1820, when he successfully stormed the Spanish fortresses at Valdivia in southern Chile, deemed the most impregnable in the Pacific, with only a fraction of the force Nelson brought to Santa Cruz.

Nelson's plan was to land Troubridge's force on the northeastern flank of the town, close to a fort known as the Paso Alto. The men would storm the fort, securing it with the heights behind, and thereby allow the ships to anchor in safety below while they turned their attention to the town about a mile away. Taken by surprise and menaced by their own guns at the Paso Alto as well as the ships, the Spaniards in Santa Cruz might be persuaded to surrender.

Some of the British ideas, such as the possibility of taking the Paso Alto quietly as well as quickly and sustaining surprise beyond the initial attack, were long shots, but Nelson understood the importance of speed and shock. Speed could give him key ground or positions before the enemy rallied. Speed forced enemies to act without thinking, and produced panic, confusion and error. And speed exploited defences that were geographically dispersed, denying the time needed to concentrate resources and organise resistance. Nelson emphasised it in his final orders to Troubridge on 20 April. '*The moment you are on shore*,' he wrote to Troubridge, 'I *recommend* you to first attack the [Paso Alto] battery . . .' To allow his executive officer room for individual initiative, he had crossed out the words 'you are directed' and replaced them with the softer word 'recommend'. Once the fort was taken, Troubridge could 'either' storm the town from the flank immediately, or – if he thought best – threaten it and send in a summons. In the last case, Nelson again emphasised the need to deny the Spaniards time to organise or to regain their composure. Only thirty minutes should be allowed for the consideration of terms, and they were not to be negotiable unless 'good cause' required it.[6]

At six o'clock in the late afternoon of Thursday 20 July the northern coast of Tenerife could be seen on a cloudy horizon ten to twelve leagues to the southwest. The squadron hove to and for two days busied itself for the attack. The landing would be launched from the frigates, which were able to work closer inshore. Boats, scaling ladders, equipment and hundreds of men were transferred to them from the ships of the line. Nelson's *Theseus* sent her quota to the *Seahorse*, along with Captain Miller and four of the ship's six lieutenants, Nelson remaining on board with his third and fifth lieutenants. Other men rocked across the choppy sea to the *Terpsichore* and *Emerald*.

It was about four in the afternoon of 21 July, after the admiral's final pre-attack meeting with his captains, that Bowen's *Terpsichore* led the crowded frigates on their journey around the northeastern tip of Tenerife to reach their station some two miles off the fort at the Paso Alto. Bowen was the only captain who knew the island and Troubridge went with him during this final approach. When the frigates got underway, trailing the additional boats they needed to make a landing, Nelson followed with the ships of the line.

The distance was longer than they anticipated, but in the first hour of the 22nd the squadron closed upon its target, helped by a breeze at its back. With lights extinguished, the frigates took their positions, and filled and lowered their boats under cover of complete darkness. Nearly a thousand men gathered about the *Terpsichore* and then pulled hopefully and silently for the shore. The men were short of marines, but Nelson had dressed some of the sailors in red coats with white cross-belts and given them badges for their caps to create the impression of a greater military force. They carried their arms and scaling ladders, and sledgehammers, broad axes, wedges and spikes to batter their way through obstacles or to manipulate and immobilise guns. Linked by towropes to prevent dispersal, the boats struggled onwards through two miles of dark, difficult sea, aiming for a beach to the southwest of the fort.

The ships of the line slipped quietly behind the frigates about three hours later, but with the exception of the light-draught mortar launch, which had advanced to support the landing, there was little likelihood that the squadron's guns would play much of a part at the range involved. Nelson knew that the attack would depend upon those boats Troubridge was leading ashore.

2

Local seamen knew the area to be one of turbulent winds and strong currents, and both were against Troubridge that night. A strong gale funnelled along the Bufadero valley, northeast of the Paso Alto, and out towards the advancing boats, feeding the swell and churning the sea about them. Closer inshore, where the boats were to skirt the beach till they reached the landing place, it was calmer but the current was strong. The assault force should have landed before daylight, but dawn found it still offshore with only the leading boats close to the Paso Alto and all the men weary through heaving at their oars.

Moreover, despite all precautions against discovery the British ships had been seen by vigilant Spanish lookouts. Even as first light showed in the eastern sky lusty alarm bells and three warning cannon shots stirred the sleeping inhabitants of Santa Cruz. The commandant general soon had messengers galloping furiously inland to raise the militia, and soldiers scrambling to their posts. Some manned batteries in the town, while others joined a party of French sailors and began stumbling through the half light along a steep, rocky, bending path that climbed up to the Altura ridge overlooking the town's northeastern flank. The Paso Alto fort itself, though a substantial work with a semi-circular front overlooking the beach, was not as formidable as the British believed. It mounted only eight guns, instead of the twenty-six Nelson had supposed, but as Troubridge's boats approached the battery was being prepared for action.[7]

Troubridge may have seen defenders running to their posts, and certainly heard the alarm from the town. From his boats the shore, gently unveiled by the departing darkness, looked awesome in the new day, its steep-sided, rugged volcanic ridges running seawards to terminate in jagged heights. Weighing his chances, Troubridge made two decisions. The first was to call off the landing. After their gruelling pull the men were turned back.

While the boats reassembled around the frigates, Troubridge, Oldfield and Bowen went aboard the *Theseus* to report to Sir Horatio. We know from a private letter that he was disappointed, and regretted not commanding the amphibious attack himself. Troubridge, he believed, had given up too easily, and he had a point. For though Guitierrez remained calm, his militia were still coming in, his few disposable troops had many assailable points to cover and the citizens were close to panic. Merchants were stripping the custom house of their goods, and the streets thronged with donkeys and people groaning under the weight of salvaged possessions, trunks, mattresses and bags. In the growing heat of a summer day, women herded out of Santa Cruz on foot, fleeing inland to the Laguna. This, if ever, was the moment to attack, but it was a moment that had been allowed to pass.

At its first major test, Nelson's system of drawing captains into his plans and encouraging individual initiative had actually failed. Indeed, in view of Troubridge's seminal role in conceiving the enterprise his need to return 'to consult with me what was best to be done' must have struck Nelson as odd. The culture of command could not be changed overnight, however. Fremantle at Alassio and Collingwood and Saumarez at Cape St Vincent had shown how even fine captains declined to act without the specific approval of a superior officer. Now that rigidity had influenced Troubridge. It was not Nelson's way, but nor was it his practice to reprimand honest service. He received Troubridge sympathetically, commiserated in his obvious disappointment and listened to what he had to propose. The captain of the *Culloden* had been rebuffed, but not beaten. He told Nelson that if a different landing was made, at the mouth of the Barranco de Bufadero just east of the Paso Alto, the men might yet scale the heights above the fort and force it to surrender. At least he was willing to try, even at this stage. That was his second decision.[8]

Nelson consented, and ordered the frigates and the *Fox* cutter further inshore, until they were almost six hundred yards from the beach and within gun range of the enemy fort. After ten in the morning, in the full glare of day, the boats rowed to the shore again. The little opposition to the landing was dispersed with a 'smart fire' and soon Troubridge's men were dragging their boats upon a black, stony beach and toiling up the steep Jurada height in front of them, heaving one or two three pounders over the pathless, fractured ground as they went. It was dreadful work. The wind had dropped, leaving the climbers exposed to the merciless sun as they made their precipitous ascent. The mountain stones twisted this way and that or gave way beneath the exertion of weight, and the hill was 'so perpendicular that it was an impossibility for us to fight or to run away without falling down the rocks right into the sea'. Canteens of water, wine or spirits, which some had slung over their shoulders, were drained or discarded as encumbrances, and when the weary adventurers reached the summit fifteen hundred feet or more up they were dehydrated and exhausted, without water, food or shelter. Though they gamely raised colours, and prepared defensible positions, Miller recalled that 'even on plain ground we could scarcely have moved forward'. Some men fainted, one died, and their leader, Troubridge, still debilitated by a recent illness, became so sick that he seemed likely to follow.[9]

Worse still, their effort was in vain. From the top of the Jurada they could now see that a deep gully divided them from their objective, the Altura height above the Paso Alto. In any case, as they realised before finishing their climb, the Altura had already been occupied. A party of Spaniards and Frenchmen from the town had reached the ridge and fanned along its crest above the fort, muskets in hand, and some of them dropped down to a light battery that supported the Paso Alto from behind a malevolent mountain parapet. There was nothing to be done except exchange a largely ineffectual fire with field guns. Far below in the blue bay rode the ships but they were of no help. The mortar launch fired some shells at the Paso Alto but without obvious success.

Despite terrific exertions, the British were in an impossible position. Men were dropping from heat and exhaustion, and a night on the heights would have killed more than could be spared. Some ventured part way down into the gully to gather grapes or replenish canteens at a rancid pool, enduring a largely ineffective enemy fire, but the Altura height was simply beyond their grasp. Some still had the spirit to fight. 'Bad as we were,' wrote a participant from the *Theseus*, 'we certainly would have [made] a trial of attacking the enemy had the valley not been so unadvantage [disadvantageous] to us.' But the captains understood the Spaniards were posted too powerfully for 'the bravest men'. For the second time, perhaps, Troubridge had made a mistake. He had aborted the first landing, and lost valuable time, and now he had mistaken the configuration of the heights. For the second time he retreated. Trying to mask their intentions the British torturously struggled back to the beach, Captain Oldfield gallantly bringing up the rear with his marines. Two men fell to their deaths in the descent, but by ten that night the survivors were back on board their ships, two or three dying of exhaustion. Early the following morning Nelson withdrew his ships. Miller was visibly dissatisfied, while Troubridge looked 'almost dead with fatigue'.[10]

The vision of wealth and glory that had led them to Tenerife should have faded there. It should have, but it did not.

3

As if to augur a deepening disaster, the weather deteriorated and blustering north easterlies hammered the ships as they stood off Tenerife under close-reefed topsails. The *Culloden* lost her main topsail in dancing, wind-lashed seas. On the morning of the 24th the *Leander* joined them at last, but that proved no blessing. The reinforcement, and Captain Thompson's familiarity with Tenerife, encouraged Nelson to stay when he should have gone. Equally unfortunate, the arrival of the *Leander* revived the suspicions and wariness of their enemies. As one Spanish officer wrote, the *Leander*'s appearance 'convinced me that a vigorous attack was intended. I consequently made every preparation.'[11]

Nelson had never treated the attack lightly. His planning had been careful and detailed, and the officers picked men, the victors of Cape St Vincent. They could have been successful but for adverse weather and irresolution. But they had been repulsed, not defeated. They had lost only a handful of men and no vessel had suffered damage. Perhaps that was the trouble. So much more had been expected.

Many years before, at the Turks' Islands in the West Indies, Nelson had been in this situation and had handled it with admirable circumspection. He had landed his men, found his enemies too strongly entrenched and withdrawn without loss. So far, nothing more had happened at Tenerife. Unfortunately, Nelson was now a national hero and the toast of the fleet. He was a man of whom so much was expected. As Captain Sir James Saumarez had written to his family back in March, 'Be not surprised if, with our *desperate* commodore, you hear of our taking the *whole* Spanish fleet . . .' Nelson had talked confidently of taking Tenerife, and been entrusted with a formidable squadron. Immense expectations had been aroused. To go back now with nothing, with barely a shot fired or received in anger, might have been judicious and scrupulously professional but it would also have been hugely demoralising. The unkind would insinuate that little had been done and Nelson too easily balked. That he had failed to deliver. Nelson's pride and sense of national honour rebelled at the thought. Though the lure of that wealth sitting there in warehouses, ready for the taking, may have bore on some, to Nelson it did not matter any more. He lingered about Tenerife looking for redemption like a hungry wolf around a fold.[12]

The other captains shared his dilemma, and it was they, in that process of democratic command Nelson was fostering, who urged him forward. Late on the 22nd a German inhabitant of Santa Cruz was brought in, and the next day Miller and Fremantle interviewed him aboard the *Seahorse*, using Betsy as an interpreter. Betsy, who spoke French, Italian and German, wrote in her diary that the deserter revealed that the Spaniards had 'no force' in Santa Cruz, and were 'all crying and trembling' at the prospect of being attacked. Miller recorded that the German 'assured' him the town could 'easily' be captured. He (rightly) pointed out that the Spaniards were weak in regulars, and (incorrectly) predicted that the militia would refuse to turn out. He even said that fifty of the regulars in Santa Cruz were Dutch or German, who would come over to the British. Moreover, he had detailed information about the layout of the town and offered himself as a guide. Desperate to salvage something, the captains decided that Fremantle, who had the greatest influence with Nelson, would be their spokesman. The result was a council of war the same day in which the captains recommended storming the town.[13]

Though even the garrulous German, duly enlisted as a pilot, shrank from the idea of a frontal attack on Santa Cruz, Nelson was inclined to try it. With the entire island roused it was a gamble, but the admiral's standing with his men was now more at stake than ever. If he retreated when senior captains felt success still within their grasp, the damage to that glittering reputation might be considerable. He could return now, and make a case for a judicious withdrawal, but in that case no one would know what the outcome of an attack might have been. Some, no doubt, would always have suspected, like the captains, that greater courage might have prevailed, and that Nelson had been defeated by his fears. It was not a reputation he wanted, for himself or his country. He had no gift of hindsight, and that German might be right. But if the town could be taken, it would only be by a desperate and dangerous assault, and there could only be one commander for it.

Nelson approved the attack, though with a sense of deep fore-boding. 'My pride suffered,' he later admitted, 'and although I felt the second attack as a forlorn hope, yet the honour of our country called for the attack, and that I should command it. I never expected to return.'[14]

4

That same sense passed like an icy wind through the squadron's officers as word of the attack spread. Men thought of their parents, wives and children, of the affairs they needed to order, and of home.

Captain Bowen of the *Terpsichore*, who had known Nelson in the Leeward Islands, had made a fortune in prize money and won honour in frigate actions. He talked continually of his native Devon, and the comfortable retirement that he supposed was waiting for him just around the corner. John Gibson of the *Fox* cutter was an older, grey-headed man, but life had been improving for him too. Now, after years as a lieutenant, his ability was being recognised. Elliot was loud in his praises and Jervis regarded Gibson as 'a most meritorious and confidential officer' and promoted him commander. At last Gibson felt able to offer a shred of security to his only daughter back in Hastings.[15]

By contrast, Lieutenant George Thorp of the *Terpsichore* was only nineteen, 'a fine young man' according to Collingwood. In background and character he resembled William Hoste of the *Theseus*. The son of the Reverend Robert Thorp of Gateshead, George had got his commission six months before, and had every expectation of being made 'post'. He loved the service, and the men who worked beside him. 'The *Juno* is a goddess,' he had written at the age of thirteen, 'and all who belong to her are angels.' Now, after a fine record with Captains Hood and Bowen, he drew upon his deepest reserves of courage. The letter he sent his parents bore the character of a will. 'Going to storm Santa Cruz,' wrote the boy. 'As I think there is a chance of my never returning, I leave this directed to you, expressing my gratitude and affection, and the very high sense I have of your care and concern for me, and also to Lady Drake [George's patron] . . . As I never intentionally did wrong, I do not feel afraid, and I think you will have the satisfaction of saying your boy has done his duty . . . My best adieux to you, all I care for in the world.' George feared, but could not have known, that he would be dead within hours.[16]

The plan was to feint towards the Paso Alto, as if to land on the northeastern flank of the town again, and then to strike directly at the centre of the defences, powering through with a packed column of men. They would seize the mole, fight their way into the main square, and regroup for an assault upon the citadel with thirty-foot scaling ladders. Much was against them. Although the feint might wrong-foot the Spaniards to an extent, there was no chance of totally surprising them, and the guns of those frontal defences posed an awful risk. The hope was that by striking swiftly at the mole out of the dark they could create 'panic and confusion' and breach the first defences without suffering too heavily.[17]

At five or five-thirty in the evening of 24 July, amid freshening breezes, Nelson's demonstration to the northeast began. The *Theseus* was too late taking up its position, so Captain Miller's plans for a more elaborate diversion had to be shelved. He had constructed a dummy eighteen-pounder from casks and canvas, and planned to float it towards the Paso Alto to fuel enemy fears that the fort was again to be the focus of an attack. As it was the ships stationed themselves off the Barranco de Bufadero as before, with the frigates closer to the beach, and mounted a simple demonstration. After two hours the mortar launch and frigates opened an earnest but generally unsuccessful fire, managing in the process to score a hit on the ramparts. The Spaniards replied, throwing shots over the ships, and as night blanketed the contest both sides continued to blast away blindly. Frightened of the British landing in force, the Spanish gunners showered the beach with grape shot.

Nelson dined with some of his officers aboard the *Seahorse*. Helping to serve at the table, Betsy Fremantle was reassured by the relaxed and confident table talk, as was intended, and went to bed satisfied that her husband was in no great danger. Throughout the fleet many of the men also appeared in good spirits, trusting the judgement of their officers, but the captains' faces were merely brave ones for none underestimated the uncertainty ahead. As the sun slipped down behind the peaks of Tenerife, and the silence was broken by the occasional bark of guns to starboard, Nelson retired to his cabin on the *Theseus*. At eight, with three hours to go, he scratched a letter he knew might be his last. It was not to Fanny, but to his commander-in-chief, beseeching him to care for his stepson:

. . . this night I, humble as I am, command the whole destined to land under the batteries of the town, and tomorrow my head will probably be crowned with either laurel or cypress. I have only to recommend Josiah Nisbet to you and my country. With every affectionate wish for your health, and every blessing in this world, believe me your faithful, Horatio Nelson. The Duke of Clarence, should I fall in the service of my king and country, will, I am confident, take a lively interest for my son-in-law, on his name being mentioned.[18]

Beneath flickering candles Nelson worked through his papers, sifting out anything that might offend Fanny if his possessions were sent home. All that concerned Adelaide must have gone up in flames that night. Josiah, now a lieutenant of the *Theseus*, was on watch, but at some stage interrupted his stepfather's work, and helped destroy the papers, hardly knowing what most of them were about. Nelson explained that once he had left with his storming party, which included most of the officers, Josiah must 'take care of the ship'.

'The ship, sir, must take care of herself,' said the boy with unusual stubbornness. He wanted to go with his admiral.

'You must not go,' Nelson insisted. 'Supposing your poor mother was to lose us both. What will she do?'

Josiah had not always been a satisfying charge, but this was to be his night and perhaps he sensed it. 'I will go [with you] this night if I never go again,' he said grimly.[19]

Miller saw them as their boat pulled away towards the *Seahorse*, where they were to join Fremantle and the German pilot in the captain's barge. Elsewhere the *Theseus* filled with difficult, last-minute wishes and anxious farewells. William Hoste remained aboard, but his closest friend, John Weatherhead, who had boarded Spanish ships at Cape St Vincent, been in the thick of the Cadiz boat fights and toiled up the Jurada height, was going to Santa Cruz at the head of twenty men in the ship's yawl. Miller paraded the men of the *Theseus* at nine, distributing their last pieces of equipment, 'and said a few words of encouragement to them, caution[ing] against straggling, plundering or injuring any person not found in arms'. Then he allowed them one and a half hours of sleep, and snatched a little himself in his clothes.[20]

Outside, Nelson found the conditions satisfactory. The stars were just visible, but it was not a clear night and the darkness made an ideal cloak for the boats as they pulled for the mole. The vessels rose and fell on a substantial swell and the breeze was stiffening as the ship's bell of the *Theseus* finally signalled the general embarkation at about ten-thirty. The boats of the squadron, filled with seven hundred men, silently assembled about Hood's *Zealous* in six divisions. Nelson and Bowen led the first, Nelson in the *Seahorse*'s barge and Bowen in his gig. The other five divisions were commanded by Troubridge, Hood, Thompson, Miller and Waller, and again, each division roped its boats together to prevent separation and propelled themselves through the water with muffled oars. The men were to preserve complete silence, and show no lights, and in the wake of the ships' boats would come the reserves. They consisted of one hundred and eighty men with Gibson in the *Fox* cutter, seventy or eighty in a small Spanish prize taken the day before, and a handful in the jolly boat of the *Theseus*.

The mole, the focus of the defences of Santa Cruz, lay three miles to the southwest but the boats would have to make a longer journey. They had to pass three or four shore batteries to starboard before even reaching the town, and on Miller's suggestion were ordered to swing wide before making their final swift advance. At eleven they set off, and their comrades on the ships saw them swallowed by the darkness, one by one. For more than two hours the boats pressed on to the rhythmic action of the oars and the sound of wood against water. They were heavily laden and a current increased their travail, but on they went. Behind them the occasional thud and flash marked where the mortar launch continued to hurl shells towards a black, unseen shore, while to the right every spasmodic response from the enemy batteries raised fears that the boats had been seen. Nelson led his men forward, each silent and wrapped in his own world.[21]

5

Their immediate objective was well defended and easily recognisable in a fair light, jutting eighty yards into the sea from the front of the town, and close to the citadel and square. By focusing upon the mole, Nelson no doubt hoped to reduce the chances of his men blundering about in a dark, strange town and becoming dispersed. His plan was to hit the heart of the opposition with the best part of a thousand men. A shock column, reinforcing itself as one division came in behind another, would pile into key defences, overcoming opposition before the Spaniards could pull in the units they had inevitably scattered across a wide front. While his forces were concentrated, theirs would be scattered. Nelson believed that once the mole, citadel and square were taken resistance would crumble, and bargained that the opposi-tion had relatively few first-class defenders.

Adjoining the mole to the north was a small beach upon which the boats might be drawn. Nelson almost got there without being seen. But within about half a gunshot of his destination a form of Hell broke loose. Alarm bells rang, and a furious blast of fire tore at the invaders 'from one end of the town to the other'.[22]

Nelson instantly ordered his division to cast off their towropes and storm the mole, and with outrageous gallantry the men raised a cheer and hurtled forward. They charged into a wall of shot, grape and musketry. The fearful discharge was heard three miles away on the quarterdeck of the *Theseus*, where at about one o'clock in the morning Hoste noted 'one of the heaviest cannonading[s] I ever was witness to . . . likewise a very regular fire of musketry, which continued without intermission for the space of four hours.' He must have shuddered to think that both his best friend and greatest protector were at the epicentre of that thunder stroke.[23]

Perhaps thirty pieces of artillery swept the narrow area through which Nelson made his attack. Seven or eight twenty-four-pounders occupied the sea end of the mole, and at its other extremity a hastily constructed battery guarded the gateway that led to the square. Up to ten guns could be trained from the huge citadel looming at the mole head, and to the northeast were the Rosario and San Pedro batteries, which could rake the beach beside the mole or slash into attacking boats making their final approach. Squatting in buildings or behind every available cover thereabouts were musketeers, ready to deliver a fierce small-arms fire.

Even as Nelson's division dashed into that storm of metal the attack was misfiring. In the darkness most of the other divisions missed the mole completely or were swept past by wind and current towards the rocky, surf-lashed shores beyond. Only one of the five supporting divi-sions – Thompson's – actually joined Nelson's in the attack on the mole.

Under strength and cut down in swaths, they fought their way forward with extreme courage, marking their progress with dead and wounded. Beaching their boats, some flung themselves upon the battery at the end of the mole, and expelling several hundred defenders, spiked all but one or two of the guns. Then the remains of the British force charged the mole head and almost cut their way through. Some of the defenders broke before the fury of the attack and fled to the citadel, but others valiantly held their ground, and Nelson's men simply lacked the reserves to overwhelm them. Now, in these crucial moments, Nelson's failure to secure the thousand or more redcoats he had originally wanted, told. As one Spaniard later admitted, 'if the Nelsons, Bowens or other commanders had united their forces there [at the mole], the result [for us] would have been a disaster'.[24]

In that brave assault nearly all of Nelson's men seemed to be killed or wounded. Fremantle had gone down early, two musket bullets ripping through the flesh of his right arm, near one of the joints. John Weatherhead lay on the guardhouse steps near the beach, his life's blood oozing from a bullet wound in his stomach. Bowen of the *Terpsichore* fell, and young Lieutenant Thorp – he who had written to his family – both dead side by side, surrounded by the bodies of half a dozen of their closest followers cut down by a single blast of canister. Thompson was also hit in the arms, and his lieutenant of marines went down beside him mortally wounded.

Josiah Nisbet had eschewed the safety of the ship to stand with his stepfather that night. They were in the stern of their boat, and when it ran upon the beach beside the mole the men bounded from the front with ferocious war cries. Nelson made his way forward as space cleared, drawing the sword he had inherited from his uncle, Captain Suckling. He reached the middle of the boat and prepared to put one foot over the side. Josiah remembered him suddenly turning his head towards him and away from the flashing of the guns. 'I am shot through the elbow,' he said.[25]

His right arm was now useless, though he had the presence of mind to retrieve his fallen sword with his left hand. With the noise of violence around him, Josiah helped the injured admiral down into the boat and felt his arm. It was a serious wound. A musket ball had shattered the bones above the elbow, and severed the brachial artery. Nelson grew faint at the sight of the blood pumping from his arm, and Josiah covered it with his hat.[26]

6

Among those who blundered past the mole in the darkness were the divisions of Troubridge and Waller. Searching for a landing place through thunderous surf, many of their boats were filled with water 'in an instant' and sunk while the others were staved against the rocks of the Aduana beach, a notoriously difficult place strewn with the

broken timbers of earlier misfortunes. The men lost most of their
equipment, including the scaling ladders they needed to storm the
citadel. They waded ashore in an abrasive wind, soaked to the skin.
The muskets carried by the marines could not be fired because all the
cartridges in their pouches were wet and useless.

There was no retreat, weapons or not, but Troubridge was still
Troubridge. He knew that Nelson was expecting to meet him in the
square, and therefore what he had to do. Sword in hand, he and Waller
collected the bedraggled band and got them into order. They still had
pikes, cutlasses and bayonets, and they were soon clambering over the
line wall and plunging along the dark Calle de la Caleta towards
the northern end of the plaza. The accounts of Troubridge's march
are confused and contradictory, but there appears to have been some
stiff fighting. If one of the Spanish reports is to be believed the steady
nerve of the British got them through, as they scattered the opposition with fierce bayonet charges, killing and wounding several antagonists and taking prisoners. The captives were 'well treated', and
provided Troubridge with something he badly needed – a small but
valuable supply of ammunition.[27]

Perhaps he also got information about where he was; at any rate,
he made the rendezvous with few losses. But Nelson was not there.
Driving his opponents into adjoining streets and alleys, Troubridge
occupied the square and arranged his men in battle formation to wait.
He even sent a sergeant of marines and two Spanish civilians to the
citadel with a summons to surrender, but they never returned. An
anxious hour or so passed in the dark, but still no Nelson. Then
Troubridge somehow got word that another British party had got into
the town, and were holed up in the convent of Santo Domingo a little
to the west. Wearily the men fell in, and Troubridge marched them
from the square, through the black streets and across a narrow bridge
spanning a stream to reach the convent. Muskets occasionally spat at
them from the dark as emboldened Spaniards gathered in the
surrounding streets, and field pieces were being wheeled up to hem
them in. But sometime after four in the morning, perhaps, they reached
the convent. Nelson was not there, but inside Troubridge found the
sodden survivors of two of the other British divisions with their
commanders, Miller and Hood.

Miller had also overshot the mole, even more than Troubridge. His
men had come under fire as they tried to land through the surf and
seven had been hit before the leading boat had beached and filled with

water thirty yards out. Their guns wet and useless, and equipment such as scaling ladders lost, the British had to wade ashore with water up to their chests. Miller and Oldfield gathered as many as possible and relying on pikes and bayonets drove away a picket of sixty Spanish volunteers and stormed the six-gun Concepción battery above them. Then, joined by Hood's men as they came ashore, they fought their way into the town, heading for the citadel. But as they advanced, guns flashed at them through the gloom, ahead and behind, from corners, alleys and windows. With men going down, discipline and morale wavering, and the opposition growing, Miller and Hood turned from the citadel to the main square. They seized a Spanish prisoner and demanded he guide them, but either he dissembled or misunderstood, because he led the bedraggled invaders to the convent of Santo Domingo instead. Still, the British found the place defensible. The ground floor of the convent was secure because it had no windows, and defenders could command the adjacent streets from the upper storey and tower, while directly before the building was 'a sort of broad platform, about ten feet higher than the common street', and useful for forming ranks. Confiscating the arms of about thirty prisoners they had taken, there the British remained, wet, mud-caked and miserable, until sometime before dawn when Troubridge arrived with his men from the plaza and took overall command.[28]

No one knew what had happened to Nelson and Thompson, but as the heavy firing at the waterfront had finished long before, it could only be assumed that they were not coming. The depressing thought that their comrades had been killed began to sink in. Miller, ever the gentleman, worried about Fremantle's young wife. 'Of Mrs Freemantle's situation it was terrible to think,' he wrote. At least seven hundred men should have been at the rendezvous in the square. Some were dead and drowned, others had been driven back by the enemy or the surf, and yet more were scattered about the shoreline with nothing to do but surrender and search for relief. Now Troubridge's survivors, a mere three hundred and forty seamen, marines and pikemen, were isolated in the half-light, far from their ships, and ringed by enemies.[29]

7

Gripping his stepfather's arm above the gushing wound, and then using two silk neckties, one his own, as a tourniquet, seventeen-year-old

Josiah Nisbet managed to stay the greater flow of blood. 'The revolting of the blood was so great that Sir H. said he never could forget it,' remembered Fanny in later years. Five seamen rallied round to help, one the powerful thirty-year-old Londoner John Lovell, one of the admiral's faithful *Agamemnons*. They pushed the boat out on a receding tide, and started the long haul back to the ships in increasingly rough weather.

Spanish guns were still firing hard to larboard, beyond the booming surf, and the boat had to pass eight sets of batteries on its homeward run, most if not all of them blazing blindly into the night. The helmsmen doubted they could make it, and even Nelson, who wanted to be propped up, thought it wise to 'strike out to sea' as they had coming out. But Josiah firmly disagreed. His stepfather needed urgent medical attention. Eventually, Nelson allowed him to take the tiller, and Josiah took the boat through the turbulent sea, the spray tossed here and there by the shrieking shot.[30]

Nearby they heard a great cry and the sounds of men drowning. It was the *Fox* cutter under Commander Gibson, sunk by a single shot below the waterline, and going to the bottom with one hundred and eighty men on board. A few struggling seamen were hauled into Nelson's boat, and two managed to swim back to the *Emerald*. A boat returning with the injured Fremantle also picked up survivors, and a few others managed to keep themselves afloat long enough for the remaining boats with the ships to reach them. Four men of the *Theseus* were in the water so long that they developed pains in their limbs, loins and backs, but they were lucky. Fewer than half the men on the *Fox* survived. Gibson and ninety-six of his fellows were lost at a single stroke.

The flagship was the furthest out, and it was probably a little after three in the morning when her watch heard a voice hailing them out of the night. Josiah's boat came alongside with the wounded admiral, and the men began to lower a chair. Nelson would not hear of it. 'No,' he said, 'I have yet my legs and one arm', and so saying he used a rope and his legs and left arm to struggle up the side unaided. William Hoste was aghast. 'I leave you to judge of my situation, sir,' he wrote home, when he saw 'the man whom I may say has been a second father to me' climbing on to the deck, 'his right arm dangling by his side'. Yet he showed 'a spirit that astonished everyone' and 'told the surgeon to get his instruments ready, for that he knew he must lose his arm, and that the sooner it was off the better'.[31]

He probably went down to the cockpit, a damp, dark place on the orlop deck below the water line, where surgeons normally stationed themselves during an action. There, beneath the shadowy and uncertain light of lamps swinging overhead to the roll of the ship, twenty-eight-year-old Thomas Eshelby examined the wound. Eshelby was a Yorkshireman, and a surgeon of some experience. The company of surgeons in London had authorised him to be a surgeon's mate in 1791 and a surgeon three years later, and he had followed Nelson from the *Captain* to the *Theseus*. Betsy Fremantle thought him 'a sensible young man', but whatever his professional competence, he was certainly short-handed. One surgeon's mate had gone to Santa Cruz and would never return. To help him, therefore, Eshelby turned to Louis Remonier, a twenty-four-year-old French royalist who had worked in Toulon Hospital, and served Nelson on the *Agamemnon*, *Captain* and *Theseus*. Also on hand were two or three seamen to act as assistants, one apparently Tom Allen, the admiral's manservant, and a chaplain gravely preparing for the worst.[32]

Cutting the clothing from Nelson's blood-sodden right arm and cleaning it as best he could, Eshelby found a compound fracture with severe tissue damage and a ruptured artery. Amputation was the commonest operation performed on ships but it caused the most fatalities. Eshelby had to work quickly to prevent the patient bleeding to death or traumatising, and he turned to his formidable array of instruments while the admiral was prepared for his horrific ordeal.

The surgeon needed to reduce the flow of blood to see what he was doing and used a tourniquet to depress the brachial artery. A leather strap was accordingly buckled around the admiral's arm, above the wound, and tightened by means of a screw on the outside that drew its two ends through a compress that closed upon the limb. Ashore this type of amputation was sometimes performed upon patients sitting upright in a chair, but on the *Theseus* Nelson was probably put on his back, with sea chests serving as an operating table beneath him. There was nothing to arrest his pain. Novelists have written that such patients were given spirits and a leather pad to bite upon, but no surgeon's journal of the time records either. Nelson endured the entire operation without an anaesthetic of any kind.

The assistants crouched forward to hold the stricken admiral, one or two firmly pinning his body down and another probably extending the crippled arm taut over the edge of the 'table', holding the limb by the part to be amputated. It was a grisly business, and if the Duke of

Clarence is to be believed one helper fainted and had to be replaced by the chaplain. Eshelby bent over with a sharp incision knife and made a rapid circular cut high above the wound, severing the skin, sinews and muscles of the upper arm to the bone, and allowing residual blood and tissue to fall into a receptacle below or splash freely upon the ship's timbers. Nelson bore the mutilation stoically but he never forgot that first chilling coldness of the knife as it sliced through his flesh. Ever after he insisted that surgical instruments be warmed in water before use.[33]

Then an assistant drew the skin and tissue above the wound as far up the admiral's arm as he could, a procedure that enabled Eshelby to reach the bone deep inside the stump. Before tackling the humerus, the surgeon probably secured the arteries, possibly by relaxing the tourniquet to allow them to be identified by the flow of blood. Peering intently in the gloom, he gently extricated each artery with a pair of forceps and bound them with broad silk ligatures or waxen thread. A fine-toothed handsaw was then applied to the bone itself. Using one hand to steady the shredded arm, Eshelby worked quickly with the saw in the other, skilfully avoiding splintering the bone as he cut through. Once the limb had been amputated, the skin and tissue being held back above the wound were allowed to retract over the severed humerus, leaving the two ligatures attached about two inches up the wound, hanging out. They would help drain the injury of infectious matter, and in several weeks slip out as the arteries below the ligatures rotted away. The operation had lasted about thirty minutes and ended when the edges of Nelson's stump were finally brought together by dry lint and strips of adhesive plaster, and dressed.

Eshelby has since been much criticised for tying the median nerve with an artery in one of Nelson's ligatures, but there are grounds for acquitting the harassed surgeon. Beneath the dim, wavering light of a ship's lantern, it would have been difficult for Eshelby to see the median nerve as he struggled to secure an artery deep within the wound. Moreover, in the late eighteenth century it was not always considered bad practice to include the median nerve with a ligature. Innovative London surgeons were becoming critical of the process, pointing out that ligatures separated more easily from wounds if arteries had been secured independently of the nerve, but their advice was by no means universally accepted elsewhere.[34]

When Nelson was helped to his cot, it seemed that his ordeal had been justified. The patient was given pills of opium and advised to rest. As he closed his eyes, the admiral still knew little of what was happening ashore. No tidings from the town had reached him, and the distant noise of battle continued. Before sleeping, Nelson put a ragged, unpractised left-hand signature to a fine copy of the terms to be offered the Spanish garrison and gave some orders for the disposition of the squadron. Even at this stage he hoped Troubridge might yet be successful and that good news might arrive.

Unfortunately it did not.

8

All the signs were bad ones. As the weather grew squally some of the boats began to return, protesting their inability to land anywhere, and a few found themselves immediately redeployed searching for more survivors of the *Fox*. Firing from the town subsided after a few hours, but the Spanish batteries of the Paso Alto and Torre de San Andres to the northeast continued to exchange shots with the British ships. Indeed, as the morning developed the enemy guns seemed to find their range. They hit the *Culloden*, *Emerald* and the mortar launch and forced the *Theseus* to cut her cable and shift position. It was ominous, for had Troubridge conquered, those Spanish batteries would have been silenced.

In fact, daylight found Troubridge's party still besieged in the convent. From its upper storey the British fired on any opponents intrepid enough to approach too closely, raising cheers as they did so. They replenished some of their military supplies, and had small successes. According to Captain Waller, 'several Spanish officers and near a hundred men came in and laid down their arms'. It encouraged the British to believe that the desertions the German pilot had spoken of might yet take place. Unfortunately, their enemies still commanded the adjacent streets with muskets and field pieces, and time was on their side. Troubridge could not be reinforced, but the Spanish forces were being concentrated and swollen by incoming militia.

The near hopelessness of Troubridge's position was rubbed in whenever he took the offensive. Reflecting upon the ease with which he had stormed the Concepción battery, Miller still thought for a while that fortune might favour them. The captains talked again about making a desperate thrust at the citadel, the command centre of Santa Cruz, but without scaling ladders or adequate ammunition the task looked insuperable. Nonetheless, according to Troubridge's dispatch he marched out on precisely that errand. One of the more fanciful Spanish narratives even speaks of the British making a brave but unsuccessful assault on the citadel, led by a sergeant of marines in shirtsleeves and a frigate captain. The truth seems to be that Troubridge formed his men and probed the investing forces, but quickly realised that he was hemmed in and thought better of the idea. He and Miller led sorties against the enemy field pieces, but the Spaniards wheeled them from one place to another, and after taking casualties the British fell back upon their convent. Finally, Troubridge did the only thing left open to him, and tried to talk his way out.

While his men prepared incendiaries Troubridge sent Oldfield to the citadel, accompanied by two Dominican friars fully able to testify to what was going on in the convent. Oldfield's message was bold and illustrated the sheer lust for plunder that underlay the British operation. Troubridge threatened to burn the town if the royal treasury and property of the Philippines Company were not handed over. It was a bold position, but a preposterous one. Don Antonio Gutierrez de Otero y Santayana was sixty-eight years old, a professional soldier who had grown wise in his country's service, and he recognised a weak hand when he saw one. He had remained calm throughout the entire crisis, even when the British looked about to carry the town, and now rejected the demands outright. The friars were so afraid that they refused to return to the convent; Oldfield was sent back with entirely fictitious but chilling Spanish claims that their forces numbered nine thousand.

That card played and blocked, Troubridge sent Captain Hood to make the best terms he could. They were honourable, so much so that one Spanish officer, sensing his people were on the eve of an historic victory, refused to be bound by them. The British were granted safe passage to their ships with their colours and arms. Both sides agreed to release their prisoners, and Troubridge undertook to withdraw without burning the town or making any further attack upon either Tenerife or any of the Canary Islands. Circumstanced as they were, both sides had a bargain. Troubridge extricated his men from an impossible situation, and Don Antonio saved his town and islands from further damage and claimed the honour of having repulsed the victors of Cape St Vincent. As news of the agreement spread, the outlying Spanish forts, which had been firing sporadically upon Nelson's ships, fell silent.[35]

And so, early on the 25th, the battle-stained rump of Nelson's expeditionary force marched proudly to the mole under their arms and banners, fifes blowing and drums beating. Among the urgent onlookers, the Spaniards observed an old-fashioned courtesy, standing in files with bands playing, but the French sailors jostling beneath their tricolour jeered as the British passed and Troubridge's officers had difficulty preventing their men from retaliating with blows. Troubridge was at the mole when the incident happened, and fired off a furious protest about the 'rascally murderous kill-killing French' to Don Antonio when he heard about it, but there were profuse apologies and equanimity was restored. More; as the war-weary British recovered their prisoners, dead and wounded, and waited to embark, they were served wine, bread and cheese, and their seriously injured received attention at the local hospital. British accounts are unanimous in their praise of the humanity of their Spanish foes. Troubridge reported that Don Antonio 'showed every mark of attention in his power', and reciprocated as much as he could. It was at Troubridge's suggestion, warmly endorsed by Nelson, that the British carried Don Antonio's official sealed dispatches to his country announcing the British defeat.[36]

At about seven in the morning the news of the defeat was brought to the *Theseus* by Captain Waller and a Spanish officer in a boat. Nelson ordered a flag of truce to be raised, and all firing ceased. What boats the British had left were sent to collect the survivors, and other boats were loaned by the Spaniards. The battle of Tenerife was over.

For Midshipman Hoste there was some particularly stinging news. He heard that Lieutenant John Weatherhead had been badly wounded, and was coming out on a Spanish launch. Hoste was almost stupefied with grief. 'This was a stroke which . . . I could hardly stand against,' he wrote. John had been shot on the beach, and found by a Spanish officer, who had torn his own shirt and clothing to wipe away blood and form a tourniquet. The young Briton was a fine man, the Spaniard recalled, and one he was proud to help. While Hoste prepared a berth aboard the *Theseus*, hoping against hope, Weatherhead was brought alongside the ship and hoisted aboard on a cradle. He was in great pain, with a messy hole in his stomach, and violently vomited green and yellow fluids. Eshelby managed to give him a little tea, sago and soup, and dosed him with opium, but there was no hope. At twenty-four one of the brightest of Nelson's protégés was dying.[37]

That day and the next the blood-stained survivors of the attack returned, each with his own story. Some were unhurt. Lieutenant Hawkins brought back his squad of small-arms men, and the only physical discomfort suffered by Summers was a recurrence of a 'gout' in his foot. But many – very many – were not so lucky. Seventy-one men from the *Theseus* were killed or wounded: William Harrison, thirty, his left arm fractured by a musket ball; James Harrison, thirty-two, shot through the gluteus muscles of the buttock and hip and injured in the thigh; John Cowper, twenty-one, his leg broken by a musket ball; Patrick McKinna, twenty-seven, shot in the loins; James McKinna, twenty-nine, hit in both legs; John Clarke, twenty-three, shot three times in the right leg . . .[38]

It would take time for the British to assess the cost of the disaster. Final returns recorded that 158 were killed and missing and 110 wounded, a total of 268. It was not a severe loss for the time, not when the country was in the midst of squandering eighty thousand men in the West Indies. But it was high for the navy, exceeding anything Nelson had suffered before and approaching the three hundred casualties incurred at the battle of Cape St Vincent. The one-sided nature of the conflict was also demonstrated by the losses of the Spanish and French, which amounted to no more than twenty-five killed and up to thirty-eight wounded.[39]

Some have portrayed Nelson's thrust at Tenerife as wild and reckless, and others as a well-planned operation that misfired. It was both and neither. In some respects it illustrated forethought and preparation, but in others it exemplified the underlying weaknesses in Nelson's notions of fighting ashore. His intelligence had been bad, and his men remained vague about local conditions, terrain, and the state of the opposition as well as a prey to rumours. At one time his captains allowed themselves to minimise the likely resistance; at another they believed grossly inflated Spanish statements of the forces gathering around them. The expedition was also undermanned. The thousand extra redcoats Nelson had asked for would very probably have tilted the balance against the Spaniards and given him Santa Cruz. Then there had been tactical errors, particularly the costly loss of surprise. After that a direct assault upon prepared defences was always going to be a difficult gamble – one that perhaps would only have been vindicated by success.

Having said that, hindsight apart, eighteenth-century war was not formulaic, and too often rested capriciously upon changing circumstances and imponderables. Its history is full of gambles that succeeded, and Nelson might have taken the town that night. If the weather had been kinder, or the assault force concentrated instead of scattered, or the Spaniards been less resolute than they were . . . But Fortune was a fickle mistress. She had supported Nelson so often in the past, sometimes in situations of equal or greater difficulty. And now she had deserted him.

9

The next day Nelson was a little better, though still in severe pain. Watched over by Remonier, who would stay up with him for many a night, and sedated with opium he had slept and strengthened himself with tea, soup, sago, lemonade and a tamarind drink. Eshelby gave the butchered stump its daily dressing, and although as yet there was no sign of fever, he would prescribe cinchona over the next few days to help with the pain and reduce temperature. The admiral was also constipated – a product, probably, of the opium – and he was given laxatives such as senna and jalap.

He was well enough to respond to well-wishers and to think of others. 'Our gallant admiral is much obliged for your kind enquiries,' Miller wrote to Captain Thompson. 'He is, as the ladies in the straw say, "as well as can be expected" . . . What a comfort it is to reflect that however great our loss has in other respects been, we have suffered none in honour or our character for humanity. No town was ever so possessed, and so little injury suffered by the inhabitants.' Nelson tried to write a note of his own to Betsy, whose husband was having a miserable time with his injured right arm. In a trembling new hand he could manage five words: 'God bless you and Fremantle.'[40]

He confirmed the terms Troubridge had made with Gutierrez, and sent the commandant general some beer and cheese as a present. Compton went ashore with a carpenter to inspect their surviving boats and found the *Theseus*'s cutter dashed to pieces on a rock and the launch lost to the west of the mole. Troubridge and Hood also went back to Santa Cruz to collect twenty-five of their wounded from the hospital and deliver a note to accompany Nelson's gifts. It offered Don Antonio the admiral's 'sincerest thanks for your kind attention to myself and your humanity to those of our wounded who were in your possession or under your care, as well as your generosity to all that were landed'.[41]

None of these niceties could erase the sorrow and disappointment that gnawed at the British squadron. Troubridge and Hood dined with

Don Antonio that day, but 'at table they hardly raised their eyes', a Spanish observer said. 'One could see that their faces were very sad.' At sunset the flags and pendants on Nelson's ships were at half-mast, and salutes were fired as the bodies of Bowen and Thorp were committed to the deep. Bowen's body had been stripped by some of the islanders, and the sailors had had to dress it in their own clothes to return it to the ship.[42]

On the morning of 27 July, Nelson's squadron finally weighed anchor to leave the scene of its humbling. The admiral faced the job of dictating a brief report to his commander-in-chief. Unlike modern politicians, he sought no scapegoats nor offered excuses. There was no attempt to blame Troubridge for the mistakes of the 22nd, nor criticism of Miller and Fremantle for their plan to storm Santa Cruz. The responsibility had been his, and the gallantry theirs. 'I am under the painful necessity of acquainting you that we have not been able to succeed in our attack,' he said, 'yet it is my duty to state that I believe more daring intrepidity was never shown than by the captains, officers and men you did me the honour to place under my command.' The flawless secretarial hand and the unsteady, pain-laden signature told an even fuller story.[43]

As the ships sailed sadly back to Cadiz, the casualties continued to mount. They told heavily on the small communities that had lived and worked aboard each ship, communities that had bonded in danger and now suffered as families do when losses are close and personal. The muster of the *Theseus* contained almost fifty entries annotated with such words as 'drowned in storming Santa Cruz' or 'killed at Santa Cruz'. There were meagre possessions to sort and distribute. A few of the dead had left wills. Twenty-two-year-old William Marsh, an able seaman from Kent, had bequeathed his goods to a Sarah Cole of Sittingbourne, perhaps a sweetheart. Others had no one waiting for them at home, and their belongings were sold to shipmates, some as mementos of lost comrades.

On 29 July, as they skirted west of Gomera, Lieutenant Weatherhead slipped away, 'seemingly without pain'. He had appeared to improve, sleeping less fitfully and taking some sago, mutton and broth, but the vomiting had returned and he was constipated, his motions few and black. As his stomach swelled with the fatal bullet still inside it the wound turned gangrenous, and anodyne barely relieved the pain. During his last night Weatherhead's pulse faded and his extremities grew cold. He died at about one o'clock in the afternoon. The following day was a Sunday, a fitting day for a final farewell to a parson's boy far from home. At nine in the morning the blue waters nine leagues west of La Palma closed around the body to three volleys of musket fire. A religious service followed, but the burial intensified the gloom about the ship. Nelson promoted Hoste, now seventeen, to act as lieutenant in the place of the dead man, but the boy took no pleasure from it. Weatherhead had been his closest friend from the beginning, and the one with whom he had shared their remarkable adventure over the last four years. When Hoste had been sick or injured it had been Weatherhead, more than anyone else, who had helped him through. Now their partnership was over. 'In losing him I lost a good companion, and a true friend,' wrote Hoste, 'and I believe . . . the nation lost as brave an officer as ever stepped on board a ship. He was the darling of the ship's company, and universally beloved by every person who had the pleasure of his acquaintance.'[44]

Nelson, too, a man of highs and lows, was sinking beneath the weight of the tragedy. On the 27th he had struggled with an unfamiliar pen, scratching his first full letter with the left hand. The strokes which had once confidently sloped to the right, with the occasional flourish, were gone now, replaced by a tortured scrawl, in which letters of all sizes struggled for shape and fell unevenly upright or to one side or the other. His thoughts also ran haphazardly, juxtaposing self-pity and his concern for a stepson left without a protector:

I am become a burthen to my friends and useless to my country [Nelson wrote to his admiral], but by my letter wrote the 24th you will perceive my anxiety for the promotion of my son-in-law, Josiah Nisbet. When I leave your command, I become dead to the world. I go hence, and am no more seen. If, from poor Bowen's loss, you think it proper to oblige me, I rest confident you will do it. The boy is under obligations to me, but he repaid me by bringing me from the mole of Santa Cruz. I hope you will be able to give me a frigate to convey the remains of my carcass to England. God bless you, my dear sir, and believe me, your most obliged and faithful, Horatio Nelson.[45]

Twenty days later, as he approached the fleet, he felt no better. 'A left-handed admiral will never again be considered useful,' he wrote to Sir John. 'Therefore the sooner I get to a very humble cottage the better, and make room for a better man to serve the state.'[46]

XXVII

USELESS TO MY COUNTRY

Yet, yet awhile, the natural tear may flow
Nor cold reflection chide the threatening woe;
Awhile, unchecked, the tide of sorrow swell;
Thou bravest, gentlest spirit! Fare thee well!
George Canning, *Ulm and Trafalgar*

1

THE *Seahorse*, in which Nelson raised his flag to go home, made a wretched voyage. It was a passage of broken men, latterly attended by clouds, squalls and drizzling rain. The main topmast cracked, and one of the fore topmast studding sail booms was wrenched away. Down below the injured and sick being sent home felt every lurch. Betsy Fremantle, who accompanied her maimed husband, may have seemed immature and 'boarding schoolmissish' to some, but she had coped well with the vicissitudes of naval life. That journey home on the *Seahorse* was one of her low points, and recalled a ship filled with the groans of the sick day and night.[1]

The admiral himself was a bad patient. Pain, guilt, professional frustration and fears for the future conspired against him.

The first originated in the remains of his right arm, and was intermittently violent, though Eshelby travelled with him to dress the damaged stump with dry lint and calamine and administer a nightly dose of opium. The ligatures closing his arteries should have come away in about ten days, and one had parted on the last day of July, but the other stubbornly defended its post, remaining a foreign body within the stump and preventing the end from closing. The open wound was still the size of a shilling. The patient complained of 'twitching pains', particularly at night, experienced 'phantom' sensations where his missing hand had been, and suffered bouts of fever. At times his pain was so great that Eshelby was denied access to the ligature. In himself Nelson was regaining colour, but the empty right sleeve, cut and tied with ribbons for the convenience of the surgeon, proclaimed his impairment. 'I find it looks shocking to be without one arm,' Betsy confessed to her diary.[2]

Jervis, now calling himself the Earl of St Vincent, had been a tower of strength. 'Mortals cannot command success,' he had written to a disconsolate rear admiral returning to the fleet. 'You and your companions have certainly deserved it by the greatest degree of heroism and perseverance that ever was exhibited. I grieve for the loss of your arm, the fate of poor Bowen and Gibson, with the other brave men who fell so gallantly.' He would be proud to 'bow to your stump' when Nelson finally got aboard the flagship.[3]

The reunion had taken place on 17 August and had gone well. Summoning what strength he had left, Nelson projected an optimism he did not feel, and Collingwood thought he would overexert himself. In return, the commander-in-chief did everything the wounded hero asked. The *Seahorse* was put at his disposal so that he, Fremantle and a few other seriously sick men could return to England. Some of Nelson's followers were transferred to her, including Eshelby the surgeon, Compton the flag lieutenant, a servant, Tom Allen, and William Sparks, a boy. All but the first were *Agamemnons*, the last of a proud company that was now broken forever. Talking strong, Jervis declared that both Nelson and Fremantle would recover to serve their country, and praised their defeated officers and men in letters to the Admiralty. It was not in the new earl's nature to be swayed by rebuffs.[4]

The gouty old commander-in-chief often showed his human side to Horatio Nelson, and never more so than after the repulse at Santa Cruz. He wrote to Fanny, assuring her that her husband would live and was on his way home, and he attended to Nelson's concerns for Josiah and Hoste. On 16 August, Nisbet was promoted commander of the *Dolphin* hospital ship, and was soon conducting a convoy to Gibraltar. It was his first independent command, and at seventeen he had enjoyed a steeper rise in the profession than Nelson himself. As for Hoste, Jervis promised to watch over the boy. 'I grieved to have left him . . . I pray God to bless my dear William,' Sir Horatio wrote, but the commander-in-chief kept his promise to the letter. A year later he summoned the youth into his cabin, just before William was due to face his examination for lieutenant. The boy was astonished that the old admiral, whose stern face softened with amusement, knew so much about him and welcomed him so kindly. Jervis said that he had heard that Hoste had broken both legs with the *Agamemnon* – words that echoed conversations he had had with Nelson, and inspired Hoste tremendously on the eve of his ordeal. 'I could not help laughing when he laid hold of me and turned me round three or four times, saying I was a smart young fellow,' Hoste wrote home. 'I assure you my heart was so full with gratitude to a person whom I have never seen more than once that I could hardly speak.'[5]

Back in the summer of 1797, Nelson needed such a patron as Jervis, for he felt that his own chances of being re-employed were thin. The first of his new spidery left-handed letters to reach Fanny was dated 5 August. The writer tried to make light of his misfortune as usual. 'I beg neither you or my father will think much of this mishap,' he said. 'My mind has long been made up to such an event.' But unpleasant facts had to be faced. His career was over. 'I shall no longer be considered as useful,' he said. The cottage retreat was 'more necessary than ever'.[6]

2

As the *Seahorse* coursed home, the ruins of the Tenerife disaster went with it. Apart from Nelson, the ship contained a number of its victims. Fremantle kept to his cot, exhausted and depressed, haunted by the thought that his painful right arm, which refused to heal, would turn gangrenous, and that he would have to resign his commission. Among other invalids were Thomas Ramsay, in better health since the left arm injured at Cadiz had been amputated, and John Clarke and John Cooper of the *Theseus*, who had been wounded at Santa Cruz. Ramsay would recover, pass for gunner and appeal for a renewal of Nelson's patronage in 1802.[7]

The dead would remain in the Canaries, however. Nelson was particularly troubled by the fate of Lieutenant Weatherhead, for whom he had developed a great respect and affection. The father would learn of his son's death from the newspapers, and it was a cruel blow, since he had already lost one son in the West Indies three years earlier.

Despite all, the old man hurriedly assured the admiral that he would never forget 'the many and great favours [you] conferred on my poor boy . . . from the moment he entered with you on board the *Agamemnon* to the hour of his fall'. Nelson's reply revealed how the loss of that 'most excellent young man' was affecting him. Whenever he thought of 'that fatal night, I cannot but bring sorrow and his fall before my eyes', he said. 'Dear friend, he fought as he had always done, by my side, and for more than one hundred times with success, but for wise reasons (we are taught to believe) a separation was to take place.'[8]

The memory of Santa Cruz contributed to his depression, for it seemed to close his hitherto consistently successful career on a note of defeat. No sooner had he shot to the zenith at Cape St Vincent than he was plunged into the nadir of Santa Cruz. The contrast is reflected in the first publications devoted to Nelson's exploits that appeared in separate covers. Within months of the issue of Drinkwater's *Narrative of the Proceedings of the British Fleet*, to a considerable extent illustrative of his achievements, there appeared pamphlets of a very different character, pamphlets Nelson probably never saw. They were not written by admiring countrymen, but by Spaniards, and extolled not his successes but his only significant failure. Thus, for example, Antonio Miguel de Los Santos celebrated the 'gloriosa victoria' over 'Baron Horacio Nelson' in one tract of 1797, while the following year Don Jose de Monteverde's *Relación Circunstanciada de la Defensa que hizo la plaza de Santa Cruz de Tenerife*, published in Madrid, became the first ever non-fiction work to carry Nelson's name on its title page.[9]

Of heroics there had been plenty: at Cadiz, where Nelson had failed to achieve his strategic objectives, and at the bloody repulse in Tenerife. But unkind critics could still point to a lack of recent results. The king, for one, a man who had disliked Nelson ever since the captain had chummed up to Prince William Henry in the Leeward Islands. 'I do not wish for empty displays of valour when attended with the loss of many brave men,' was His Royal Highness's considered response to the affair at Santa Cruz. In his gloomier moments, Nelson worried that the swelling, magnificent wave on which he had risen for so long seemed at last to have broken.[10]

Nevertheless, taking a longer view of his career, the admiral being carried home on the *Seahorse* had much of which to speak. By the count he had kept during the present war he had been in action one hundred and twenty times, assisted in the capture of seven ships of the line, six frigates, four corvettes, eleven privateers and taken or destroyed near fifty sail of merchantmen. He might have added the capture of four strongly fortified towns and innumerable small actions. On the strength of these claims, which he enshrined in a memorial of October 1797, he would receive a pension of £1,000 a year.[11]

Nor, the king notwithstanding, did most Britons blame Nelson for what was seen as a gallant defeat in the Canaries. They, and eventually he, would acclaim his successes and courage.

It was the battle off Cape St Vincent, not the hiding at Tenerife, which was remembered. His brothers were preparing a coat of arms to accompany his knighthood, based on an old bookplate used by their father and his motto, 'Faith and Works'. The crest showed the _San Josef_, the shield was supported by a common sailor holding the broad pendant of a commodore and a British lion, both trampling upon the colours of Spain, and the design was elaborated with Spanish doubloons. Soon after getting home the admiral also sat for another commemorative portrait. Just as Rigaud had displayed the victor of the siege on the San Juan many years before, so Henry Edridge would show Nelson as he wanted the world to remember him in 1797 – erect and proud in the undress coat of a rear admiral, his Bath riband and St Vincent medal on his chest, and the famous action against the Spanish fleet raging in the background.[12]

But the first of Lemuel Abbott's portraits of Nelson, which followed soon after, hinted at something less triumphant. There were still the remains of the boy in the sitter, but the mop of untidy hair that had once been sandy brown, though long at the sides and tied with the customary ribbon, was turning to grey. And a severe, almost pained expression had replaced the restrained smile that Rigaud had captured in the younger man.

On the _Seahorse_ it was that darker mood that predominated. If recalled, the past seemed to hold more than the future. Nelson had lived to achieve, and in so doing became alive and fulfilled, but in August of 1797 the glory days appeared to be over. For one thing the war seemed to be finishing. Sir John Jervis was betting £100 that peace was only weeks away, and had already drawn up a plan for a peace-time navy. For another, Nelson was returning to his loved ones a physical ruin, wasted in war, with a sightless right eye, a permanently damaged stomach and a missing right arm. As the admiral struggled to pull on stockings or fasten the buttons of his breeches, as he fumbled with shirts and coats and the stocks about his throat, failed to carve food unaided, or swore at the quill pen that had been cut for a right hand, it was a new war that exercised his spirit. A fight against demons only the sick and disabled know, the fight for dignity and self-respect, and against dependence and disability.

He had never meant it to be so, of course. In his mind he had dreamed of even greater success and the enjoyment of repaying those who had supported him in the years of uncertainty. People such as William Suckling, from whom he had not heard for 'upwards of two years'. He had not reckoned upon returning a broken, pitied suppli- cant. As he wrote again to his uncle, 'I have ever been a trouble to you, and am likely so to continue.' He would strike his flag, hurry to Fanny and find 'a hut to put my mutilated carcass in'.[13]

3

In the immediate aftermath of Santa Cruz, Nelson can be forgiven for despair. There was a substantial psychological adjustment for him to make. But from the perspective of today we can see the great admiral in the Nelson of 1797. It is wrong to invoke the term 'genius' as Mahan so often did, suffused as it is with a sense of supernatural ability. Nelson's achievements, like those of most 'geniuses', were expli- cable, and close readers of this book will easily bring relevant facts to mind.

It is not necessary to regard Nelson as faultless or unique to appre- ciate his abilities. Many of his notable characteristics were widely diffused in the British fleet. The increasing efficiency of the Royal Navy in seamanship, gunnery and teamwork, based partly upon its extended sea keeping, was laying the foundations of a formidable battle supremacy, a supremacy enhanced by the decline and occasional chaos of the navies of France and Spain. A huge gap between the belligerent navies was opening and historic opportunities unfolding. The indecisive line of battle, which had seemed so essential when adversaries were evenly matched, could be compromised, even discarded, by a force vastly superior in combat. More flexible tactics could be employed to bring enemy ships to close quarters, where the best could be gained from that battle superiority. The ultimate prize of total victory began to seem realisable.

Many officers saw it, and Nelson was less a solitary genius than a particularly strong example of a new breed of aggressive naval officers, nurtured in a tradition of victory and increasing professionalism. Both Hood and Jervis cherished and cultivated that tradition, learning to keep their forces at sea in good order and health. Neither doubted the outcome of a battle, even against considerable odds, and both looked for ways of coming to grips with the enemy. Both, for example, explored the idea of concentrating force against part of an enemy line to secure a decisive advantage.[14]

The concept of total victory, so imperative in Nelson, was not confined to him. We have only to remember the widespread disgust at the inadequacy of Hotham's victories in 1795 to realise that Nelson was not alone in seeking a new decisiveness. Or we can look at another occasion, when a British captain advocated an energetic pursuit of French ships in the hope of bringing them to battle. 'Whenever that happens,' wrote the officer, 'I have no doubt of the event, but longer days [in which to prepare] would suit us better, for *whatever is not perfectly decisive will be against us.*' The words sound as if they are Nelson's, but they are not. They were written by Cuthbert Collingwood in 1795.[15]

Yet there was something special about Nelson, and most admirals who knew him saw it. He was more than a professional sea officer, competent in all that went with the job, or even just a patriotic enthusiast, eager to do his best for his country. Hood, Hotham and Jervis selected him for particularly arduous responsibilities, and he helped win battles and honours for all three. His reputation as the star of a fleet distinguished by good captains grew.

He was, people realised, a driven man, intensely focused on his work. Nelson's need for glory and recognition was as strong in 1797 as it had been in his early days. As he told Fanny in August 1796, 'one day or other I will have a large gazette to myself . . . one day or other such an opportunity will be given me. I cannot, if I am in the field of glory, be kept out of sight . . . Whenever there is anything to do, there Providence is sure to direct my steps, and ever credit must be given me in spite of envy.'[16]

In Nelson, patriotism, duty and personal glory united to create an almost messianic zeal. He saw himself as an instrument and champion of his country, and was sure that given an opportunity he would win its acclaim. He never lost sight of that wider, far-off audience, as if it was there, cheering its hero from the sidelines and judging his actions. His defeat of the *Santa Sabina* in 1796, he wrote, was the sort of victory 'I know the English like in a *Gazette*'. After Troubridge's repulse at the Paso Alto in Tenerife he might have thrown up his hands and returned, but the honour of the country had not been upheld; as long as there was a prospect of victory, it had to be redeemed.[17]

The downside of this urgency was the boastfulness and self-advertisement so often encountered in Nelson, the ease with which he succumbed to flattery and flatterers, and tactically a tendency to run his luck hard and underestimate opposition. These pages provide numerous illustrations of these weaknesses, including the deleterious effect Prince William Henry had had upon the young captain's leadership.

Its upside, in professional terms, was his tireless energy, his constant enterprise and opportunism, his need to lead and achieve the ultimate goal, and his refusal to be beaten. He was desperate for distinction, and consistently went beyond the normal bounds of duty to reach it. He was so often in the right place at the right time because he saw what was coming and put himself there.

Another rare quality was his confidence and political courage. Nelson held clear opinions about what the navy's obligations were, and had the courage to discharge those obligations whatever the prevailing opinion or standing orders. His judgements were not always correct. When he overthrew the policies of his superiors in the Leeward Islands in the 1780s it did not rebound to the advantage of the islanders, or possibly even to Britain. Even his unquestioned daring at the battle of Cape St Vincent appears so brilliant largely because it was successful. But in those and other instances he proved himself willing to back his judgement and take whatever personal consequences arose, even if it brought him into conflict with authority.

That combination of professionalism, determination to achieve, missionary zeal, self-confidence, initiative and courage was rare indeed. Any individual, talented and dedicated in his or her field, who strives for perfection – further, to achieve more than anyone had done before – is likely to make a difference.

Nelson's determination to succeed, and to discharge his duty, was revealed in the occasional resolution and ruthlessness that suppressed an inherently sympathetic nature. He was not a man to shirk difficult tasks if he deemed them necessary. At sea he could punish his seamen strongly, as he had done aboard the *Boreas*, though rarely it seems gratuitously, or without looking for mitigating causes. As a combatant he fought his wars vigorously, priding himself on unflinching blockades, and – as at Cadiz – even occasionally extending the conflict to civilians in aid of a specific military end.

His leadership, however, and his ability to win the loyalty of colleagues and subordinates stand out boldly from the record. Among great military and naval commanders, Nelson rates as a fine example of inspirational leadership. Like Alexander of Macedon he almost always led from the front. It was not necessarily a sensible custom, especially in large engagements, where control is best exercised from a clear vantage point, but it invariably raised his stock with the common sailor and gave them an example to follow.

Nelson's leadership was based on more, however. He was a firm commander, as most of his men wanted him to be, professionally admired and personally liked. Not for Nelson a distant, cold autocracy. He stood up for 'poor seamen' who regarded him as their 'friend and protector', and spoke familiarly with them as equals, encouraging them to confide in him. He championed deserving junior officers as did no one else in the Mediterranean fleet. Nelson's relationship with his men was symbiotic. They had an influential and caring champion and he loyal followers. In time, especially on the *Agamemnon* and *Captain*, repeated successes cemented the relationship, for from them also flowed prize money, opportunities for promotion and simple pride in achievement.[18]

There was, in addition, an unusual and infectious attentiveness about Nelson that endeared him to many followers, and the process extended beyond the single ships he commanded. In the Mediterranean, Nelson enjoyed the friendship of most professionals with whom he mixed. A man of strong opinions, he often reacted hastily to events, and incautious, sometimes foolish, remarks are not difficult to find in letters he wrote to family and friends. But reflection and a natural sympathy for others often revealed a surprising diplomacy in his character, and he successfully related to or mediated between difficult parties. In 1798 Elliot thought Nelson 'not less capable of providing for its [the country's] political interests and honour on occasions of great delicacy and embarrassment. In that new capacity I have witnessed a degree of ability, judgement, temper and conciliation.' Politicians such as Hamilton, Elliot, Drake, Trevor, Udny and Jackson, soldiers such as Villettes and De Burgh and members of the merchant community spoke well of him. The massive correspondence generated by the British in the Mediterranean during the period 1793–7, combed assiduously for this book, has much praise and few hard words for Nelson.[19]

Those abilities were most important, perhaps, in binding fellow captains to his purposes. They gave him one solution to the snag in the new kind of battle that was evolving. For with the retreat from the tactics of line ahead came greater confusion, and greater problems of command and control. Nelson knew the importance of detailed planning, but equally that no preconceived plan could entirely encompass the shifting circumstances of battle. Communication and flexibility were essential. By inducting his captains into the process of command, and by imparting his ideas and intentions to them, Nelson unlocked their initiative and reduced dependence upon the signal books. The process may not always have been productive. At Santa Cruz the captains pressed Nelson to make his unwise second attack. But it did send his captains into battle fully aware of what was expected of them. By 1797 he had the germ that would lead to Collingwood's oft-quoted remark before Trafalgar, 'I wish Nelson would stop signalling. We all *know* what we have to do!'[20]

These qualities help explain why he was outstanding and became a successful admiral. In 1797 the foundations of his career as a public hero were also in place. Ability, success and acclamation do not always go together. In the sixteenth century England's first national hero, Sir Francis Drake, understood the importance of broadcasting as well as performing deeds, and planned a series of autobiographical works. Nelson was on the same road. Damned with faint praise under early commanders-in-chief, he sailed into 1797 determined to lay his exploits in print before the public as he saw them. He had learned that heroes sometimes have to make themselves, both on and off the battlefield.

And his appeal, in this respect, was peculiarly potent. For unlike many, whose triumphs were difficult to represent as other than purely personal ones, Nelson always identified his cause with that of the nation. Whether acting rightly or wrongly, he represented his struggle as one for the good of the realm. His honour was his country's honour, and his triumphs the country's triumphs. He succeeded or suffered in 'England's' name, and it was easy for the public to acclaim him their hero.

But of course this benefits from hindsight. At the time of Nelson's homecoming in 1797 most would have cast his ultimate fortune very differently. Many, even those who recognised that he embodied qualities that could have taken him further, might have predicted a respectful retirement. Admiral Nelson, the hero of Cape St Vincent, adorning the functions of local dignitaries, or perhaps even occupying some future seat on the board of Admiralty. Few, probably, would have looked at a middle-aged, disabled war hero without a war and realised that all that had gone before had merely been an apprenticeship, and that Horatio Nelson's great years still lay ahead.

ACKNOWLEDGEMENTS

My interest in Horatio Nelson was kindled in another time – in the immediate post-war world, when the admiral was still generally revered and Trafalgar Day was ritually commemorated on national radio. Boys' literature of all kinds held him up for emulation and I was only nine years old when it first touched me. A few years later I did my first serious reading about Nelson in the long gone S. R. Thomas library of Ainthorpe High and the Central Reference Library in Hull. Later still, I spent much of the sixties passionately collecting and reading books about Nelson, collating detailed bibliographies, and scribbling primitive accounts of aspects of his story. It was in those early years that the idea of writing a major biography of Nelson was born, and it survived my first contacts with the scholars whose books I so enjoyed. Carola Oman and Oliver Warner, at that time the leading interpreters of the admiral's career, overlooked my obvious inexperience, and encouraged me, answering tiresome enquiries and gently pointing me in the right direction.

Discouragement came later, as I imbibed, like most others, the idea that there was nothing else to be said about Nelson. Hundreds of titles had been published about him, and most followed predictable courses, repeating well-known stories and quoting familiar letters. As a university undergraduate I recoiled and turned to new ground, and my doctorate dealt with one of Nelson's naval contemporaries rather than the man himself. However, the expeditions I made to the British Library, Public Record Office and National Maritime Museum in the seventies were an awakening. It was then that I realised the extent of the unused material that existed for a biography of Nelson. Writers were borrowing excessively from previous biographies and histories, and apocryphal stories and statements passed from book to book without any serious attempt having being made to verify them. Moreover, nearly all the biographers drew most, and most commonly all, their primary material from a few long-known printed sources, including nineteenth-century biographies and the classic collections of Nelson letters made by Nicolas, Pettigrew, Morrison and Naish.

These were excellent sources as far as they went. But the sum of all such publications left hundreds of Nelson letters unpublished. Not only that, but some periods and aspects of Nelson's career were only thinly covered by the letters, or not at all, and there were obvious dangers in reconstructing the life of a controversial public figure from his own version of it.

And the archives were brimming with other under- or unused records, including many relevant collections of private papers, logs, musters, court-martial transcripts, legal records, and extensive files of correspondence in the archives of the Admiralty, Colonial, Foreign, War and Home Offices. It seemed to me that a new major biography was needed, one that would transcend the familiar publications, ground Nelson's story in credible primary sources and rest upon a thorough and complete overhaul of all the relevant material. My ambition to write the book was rekindled, but for many years available opportunities and other interests drew me elsewhere. Extensive commitments in American history, focused on the Old Northwest and War of 1812 periods, prevented more than the occasional sortie into Nelsoniana. It was not until the later eighties that I began to rehabilitate my Nelson project along the lines I had devised.

The task has been larger than I anticipated and almost forbidding. At times I felt like one of the figures in Conrad's *Typhoon*, being battered by successive and mountainous seas. No sooner had a hard-won mastery of one set of files been achieved than another rolled threateningly forward. Even now, after several years in the archives, I am sure there are still Nelson nuggets to be quarried. In addition to the major collections, answering many of the troubling enquiries necessitated special searches in far-flung places. It soon became clear that the work would extend to more than a single volume, and I decided to end my first in 1797, when Nelson stood on the brink of international fame and had assumed the appearance that would be remembered, with one sleeve empty and one eye sightless. Here, therefore, I have dealt in full with the part of Nelson's life that has least interested his biographers, his early life and rise to significance. The

campaigns of the Nile, Copenhagen and Trafalgar, as well as the notorious affair with Emma Hamilton, must remain waiting in the wings.

In writing this book I have tried to balance the needs of scholars
and intelligent lay readers; Nelson, after all, always belonged to the
public at large rather than to any narrow elite. The words of a favourite
novelist, L. P. Hartley, have been one guide. 'The past is a foreign
country,' he famously remarked, 'they do things differently there.'
Hartley's wisdom not only warned us that historical men and women
must primarily be judged by the practices, attitudes and values of their
own time and place, and not ours, a truth understood by all good
historians, but suggested the path of the historical biographer. Like
the foreign guide, we must lead readers gently through an alien world.
Footnotes are a particular difficulty in a work of this kind. Some will
have wanted more, while others are quickly intimidated by pages of
apparently meaningless dates and docket numbers, and I have had to
economise. To save space to source quotations and identify the most
useful or unusual of the extensive manuscript materials on which this
book is largely based, I have reduced references to the published documents in Nicolas and Naish. These last are easy to find, as both editors
generally arranged their material in chronological order. On the other
hand, the published transcripts contain errors, sometimes many errors,
and where practicable I have worked from originals. Most of the
manuscript files also employ a rough date order, but additional clarifi-
cation has sometimes been necessary.

Such a project necessarily incurs many debts, and it is pleasing to
record here the names of those who assisted. As usual the staffs of
many institutions extended hospitality and information during my
search for material, and I would like to thank the Archives Nationales
du Quebec; Linda Bankier of the Berwick-upon-Tweed Record Office;
the British Library, London, the British Newspaper Library, Colindale,
London; Roger Bettridge, County Archivist, and the staff of the Centre
for Buckinghamshire Studies, Aylesbury; Jane Smith, the Burrell
Collection, Glasgow; the Central Register Office, Southport,
Merseyside; Claire Bechu of the Centre Historique des Archives
Nationales, Paris; the City Museum and Records Office, Portsmouth;
John C. Dann, Barbara DeWolfe and John C. Harriman who
'welcomed me aboard' at the William L. Clements Library, University
of Michigan, Ann Arbor, and introduced me to the most civilised tradition I have ever met in an archive – the mandatory break for mid-
morning English tea; James R. Sewell, City Archivist at the Corporation

of London Records Office; Dr Jane Cunningham, librarian at the Courtauld Institute of Art; Martine de Boisdeffre, Direction des Archives de France, Paris; Janie C. Morris, librarian in the Rare Book, Manuscript and Special Collections Library, Duke University, Durham, North Carolina; David Beasley, librarian of the Goldsmiths' Company, London; Stephen Freeth, Keeper of Manuscripts at the Guildhall Library, Aldermanbury, London; the John Hay Library, Brown University, Rhode Island; Jennie Rathbun, Reference Assistant in the Houghton Library of the Harvard College Library, Cambridge, Massachusetts; Gayle M. Barkley of the Department of Manuscripts in the Huntington Library, San Marino, California; the Institute of Historical Research, London; Rosemary Reed, the Central Reference Library, Kingston-upon-Hull; H. M. Gilles, Emeritus Professor, and Dr Geoff Gill, Reader, both at the Liverpool School of Tropical Medicine, the University of Liverpool; the London Library; Josh Graml of the Mariner's Museum, Newport News, Virginia, a self-confessed fan of 'Baron Crocodile'; Mrs Pia Crowley of the Mercers' Company, London; Leslie Fields, Associate Curator, Pierpont Morgan Library, New York; Leslie Fields, Associate Curator, the Pierpont Morgan Library, New York; Sandra Burrows of the newspaper division of the National Library of Canada, Ottawa, whose superb assistance has now told in four of my projects; the National Library of Scotland, Edinburgh; the staff of the library of the National Maritime Museum, Greenwich, who suffered my incessant demands for manuscripts with unfailing courtesy and understanding; Sandra McElroy, Assistant Keeper in the Division of Arts and Industry, National Museum of Ireland, Dublin; Ruth Kenny, Erika Ingham and Helen Trompeteler of the National Portrait Gallery, London; Sighle Bhreathnach-Lynch, Curator of Irish Art, the National Gallery of Art, Dublin; the National Register of Archives, London; Andrew Helme and his staff who extended such able assistance during my visits to the Nelson Museum in Monmouth, Gwent; the Newberry Library, Chicago, Illinois; Loraine Barutti of the Department of Manuscripts, New York Historical Society, New York; the staff of the Norfolk Heritage Centre, Norwich, particularly Dianne Yeadon for her invaluable help in tracing Nelson connections in Norfolk; Faith Carpenter, the curator and designer of the Norfolk Nelson Museum, Great Yarmouth, who specially opened to allow me access to the collection; the County Archivist and staff of the Norfolk Record Office, Norwich; the Northumberland Record Office, Newcastle-upon-Tyne; Karen Wright of the Paston College,

North Walsham, Norfolk; Professors Roberta Ferrari and Mario Curreli of the University of Pisa; the Public Record Office, Kew; Dr Karen Schoenewaldt, registrar at the Rosenbach Museum and Library, Philadelphia; Jonathan Spain of the Royal Commission on Historical Manuscripts, London; Mr N. K. D. Ward, Headmaster, Royal Hospital School, Holbrook; the Royal Naval Museum, Portsmouth; the John Rylands Library, Manchester; Sarah Davis, the Shropshire Records and Research Centre, Shrewsbury; Lisa Dowdeswell, the Society of Authors; Dr Peter Beal of Sotheby's, London; the University Library of Michigan, Ann Arbor; Chris Petter, Special Collections librarian at the University of Victoria, British Columbia; the university libraries of Hull, Lancaster and Warwick; Lieutenant Commander C. W. (Dick) Whittington, then of HMS *Victory*; the Wellcome Library for the History and Understanding of Medicine, London; and the Westminster Archives Centre, London.

Among individuals who have offered help, material and suggestions at different times I should notice several fellow members of the Nelson Society, including Ray and Ann Evans, David Shannon, Derek Hayes, Louis Hodgkin, Victor Sharman, Clive Richards, and Jim Woolward. In Britain I would also like to thank authors Carola Oman, Oliver Warner, Professor Christopher Lloyd, Professor Michael Lewis, Leonard W. Cowie, Tom Pocock, Surgeon Vice Admiral Sir James Watt, Sir Ludovic Kennedy, Brian Vale, and Dr J. C. G. Binfield of Sheffield University, who not only reviewed my early explorations into the naval and political history of Nelson's day but also first taught me the difference between a dissertation and a book. Many other individuals made contributions, including Derek Barlow, Stephen Brockman, and Lily Lambert McCarthy, whose collection of Nelsoniana now graces the Royal Naval Museum at Portsmouth, and who eight years ago urged me to write 'the *Nelson* of the decade'. Peter and Dorothy Lowe first took me around the north Norfolk coast and Burnham Thorpe, and their son Julian generously gave of his time in Norwich. For one whose extra-English qualifications are ineffective beyond court shorthand and the rudiments of Swedish, I am greatly indebted to Dr Harold Smyth, Dr Antonelle Bernabo, Isabel Rubio Gomez and Stewart Platts for help with translations. Numerous friends rallied around in North America, including Helen Hornbeck Tanner, Doug Clanin and Art and Shirley Wolfe. The enthusiasm and expertise of Guy St Denis of London, Ontario, proved of great value in clarifying certain episodes of Nelson's career.

Attempts have been made to locate copyright owners. In addition to acknowledgements made elsewhere, I must thank the Society of Authors as the literary representatives of the estate of Alfred Noyes; PFD, on behalf of the Estate of Hilaire Belloc, for use of the 'Ballade of Unsuccessful Men'; and Carcanet Press Ltd for permission to quote from '1805' from the *Complete Poems* of Robert Graves.

All authors need, but rarely get, sympathetic editors and publishers. I had the good fortune to meet Will Sulkin of Jonathan Cape and Pimlico. His vision and understanding have been exceptional, and it was his faith in the project that ultimately turned it into a reality. Throughout long years of toil his support has never wavered. I have also benefited from the valuable observations of Jörg Hensgen and Richard Collins, who read the entire manuscript, and from the assistance of Rosalind Porter. Once again it has been a pleasure to work with Jack Macrae of Henry Holt and Company, New York, who safely piloted two of my previous projects into port. The maps were drawn by Malcolm Ward.

Finally, my debts to two individuals are incalculable. Without the unfailing support and enthusiasm of my partner, Terri Egginton, who has lived cheerfully with the spirit of Nelson, and the advice of my brother, Philip Sugden, whose knowledge of some aspects of the eighteenth century is second to none, the book would have been impossible to complete.

Serious biographical and historical research is a punishing business, especially when the subject is an internationally public figure about whom a mass of documentation survives. In Nelson's case the mythological dimension is another complication, and it is unreasonable to believe that there will ever be one standard view of the man, no matter how dispassionately the evidence is weighed. The views of scholars will vary according to the information they read and the interests, dispositions and purposes of the student. Since writing about Nelson is rather like wading in deep water, I have tried to avoid being sent one way or another by preconceived notions of what I wanted to find. Instead I have tried to keep an open mind, allowing conclusions to form and evolve in the light of the growing body of material, whether fashionable or not. I hope readers are served that way. But while the opinions expressed are my own, they rest upon findings uncovered only with the help and encouragement of many who have made this a rewarding social as well as an intellectual journey.

John Sugden
Cumbria, 2003

NOTES AND CITATIONS

Introduction (pp. 1–13)

1. John Barrow, *Auto-Biographical Memoir*, p. 285.
2. Wedgwood to Tyler, 6/12/1805, in William Henry Wyndham-Quin, *Sir Charles Tyler*, p. 154.
3. Lamb to Hazlitt, 10/11/1805, E. V. Lucas, ed., *Letters of Charles Lamb*, 1, p. 409; Juliet Barker, *Wordsworth*, pp. 337–8.
4. Barbara E. Rooke, ed., *The Friend*, 2, p. 365; Robert Southey, *Life of Nelson*, p. 337.
5. Details of Nelson monuments are scattered throughout the pages of *ND*, but convenient accounts are given by John Knox Laughton, *Nelson Memorial*, pp. 319–23; Rodney Mace, *Tragalgar Square*; Alison Yarrington, *Commemoration of the Hero*, and 'Nelson the Citizen Hero'; Flora Fraser, 'If You Seek His Monument'; and Leo Marriott, *What's Left of Nelson*, pp. 125–37.
6. Matthew H. Barker ('The Old Sailor'), *Life of Nelson*, p. 4; James Harrison, *Life*, 1, p. viii; Fanny Nelson to McArthur, 28/2/1807, Monmouth MSS, E678.
7. Nelson's sketch, sent to McArthur in October 1799 and published in volume 3 of *The Naval Chronicle* (1800), was reprinted in *D&L*, 1, p. 1. It is now with other McArthur papers in the Rosenbach Museum and Library, Philadelphia. The same denial of nepotism was evident in the first biographical notice of Nelson, which appeared in 1798, apparently based upon information from the family. 'That he has risen to his present eminence without the cooperation of powerful friends is perfectly unnecessary to remark' (*Public Characters*, p. 8) ungratefully erases several senior officers from Nelson's early career. See also James Stanier Clarke and John McArthur, *Life and Services*, 1, advertisement, and 2, p. 381. John McArthur, the senior of the authors of *The Life of Admiral Lord Nelson*, had written signal books for Admirals Robert Digby and Lord Hood, and later served as secretary and prize-agent to Hood, Man and Parker in the Mediterranean, in which last capacities he became associated with Nelson.
8. For the biographer see Warren R. Dawson, *Thomas Joseph Pettigrew*.
9. Joseph Allen, *Life of Lord Viscount Nelson*, pp. v–vi.
10. Mark Storey, *Robert Southey*, p. 219.
11. Southey, *Life of Nelson*, p. 43; Carola Oman in *ND*, 7 (2001), pp. 327–32; and David Eastwood, 'Patriotism Personified'. These issues may become clearer with the completion of the work of Marianne Czisnik. See her 'Nelson and the Nile'.
12. The influence of Nelson upon some of these commanders is well known. For Perry see

David C. Skaggs and Gerald T. Althoff, *A Signal Victory*, p. 115, while Cochrane's indebtedness is described in his *Autobiography*, 1, pp. 88–9, and John Sugden, 'Lord Cochrane', pp. 145–6, 308–10. Cochrane modelled his only fleet encounter off Brazil in 1823 upon Nelson's tactics at Trafalgar: ch. 5 of Brian Vale, *Independence or Death!*

13. Material on this period can be found in William D. Puleston, *Mahan*; William E. Livezey, *Mahan on Sea Power*; C. G. Reynolds, *Command of the Sea*; and Paul M. Kennedy, *Rise and Fall of British Naval Mastery*.

14. Mahan to Laughton, 14/8/1895, in Andrew Lambert, ed., *Letters and Papers of Professor Sir John Knox Laughton*, p. 111, and Andrew Lambert, *Foundations of Naval History*. Laughton added some documents to the published stock in his edition of *The Letters and Despatches of Horatio, Viscount Nelson*, and among many secondary contributions produced two short biographies, *Nelson* and *The Nelson Memorial*.

15. For an overview of the film industry's handling of Nelson, reflecting changing popular taste, see John Sugden, 'Nelson and the Film Industry'.

16. A revised but abridged edition of *Nelson*, published in 1967, embodied further new material. Carola Oman (1897–1978), a pioneer of historical biography, described some of her early literary and scholarly advantages in *An Oxford Childhood*. An overdue entry in the *New Dictionary of National Biography* is scheduled.

17. Nelson to Churchey, 20/10/1802, *MM*, 28 (1942), p. 319.

18. The latest biography, Edgar Vincent's *Nelson, Love and Fame* (2003), which appeared as the present work was being prepared for the press, though not without considerable merits exemplifies the excessive reliance upon familiar published sources, most of which are now more than one and a half centuries old. Though few lives of Nelson advanced the subject academically, a number were well written and informed introductions. Personal favourites are Clennell Wilkinson's *Nelson*; Russell Grenfell's *Horatio Nelson*; and Oliver Warner's *Portrait of Lord Nelson*. No comprehensive review of the literature of Nelson has been published, but some four hundred book-length accounts, fact and fiction, have been published in different languages. There are original works in Danish, French, Spanish, German, Italian, Russian, Japanese, Chinese and Thai (the last by a grandson of the King of Siam). The number of pamphlets, booklets, articles and ephemera runs to many thousands. Annotated lists of some items were provided by Laughton, *Nelson Memorial*; Charles J. Britton, *New Chronicles*; Oliver Warner, *Lord Nelson*; and Leonard W. Cowie, *Lord Nelson*.

19. *The New York Times*, 25/10/1998. Coleman appreciated the dangers of judging people by the standards of times other than their own, and made an attempt at even-handedness, but the search for mud to throw remains transparent. The approach is far from new: see, for example, George A. Edinger and E. J. C. Neep, *Horatio Nelson*.

20. For the history and scope of Nelson's papers see K. F. Lindsay-MacDougall, 'Nelson Manuscripts', and P. K. Crimmin, 'Letters and Documents'. Miss Lindsay-MacDougall was the conscientious workhorse behind G. P. B. Naish's *Nelson's Letters to His Wife*, to date the most important supplement to Nicholas Harris Nicolas, ed., *The Dispatches and Letters of Vice Admiral Lord Viscount Nelson*. The 1805 Club has published several discussions of Nelson papers in their yearbook, *TC*, and the lots recently sold at Sotheby's are described in *Nelson, the Alexander Davison Collection*. A fresh collection of hitherto unpublished Nelson letters in being prepared by Colin White.

21. Louis J. Jennings, ed., *Correspondence and Diaries*, 2, pp. 233–4. The authenticity of this famous anecdote has been questioned. On the authority of Henry Graves, who knew Wellington, Robert Rawlinson claimed that the Duke once said that he had only met Nelson on one occasion, as they passed on a staircase in Downing Street: *Notes and Queries*, 2nd series, 9 (1860), p. 141. The provenance of the more famous version seems stronger. Oliver Warner, 'Admiral Page's Comments', p. 377, establishes 12 September 1805 as the only date on which this meeting could have occurred.

I Prologue: Duel at Midnight (pp. 14–27)

1. Jervis's instructions, 10/12/1796, Add. MSS 34938.
2. Jervis to Hamilton, 10/12/1796, in Edward P. Brenton, *John, Earl of St Vincent*, 1, p. 278; Jervis to Elliot, 10/12/1796, NMM: ELL/141.
3. *La Minerve* muster book, ADM 36/13135.
4. Basic sources for the voyage are the log books of *La Minerve* (ADM 51/1204 and 52/3223, and NMM: ADM/L/M292) and *Blanche* (ADM 51/1168 and NMM: ADM/L/B97). The dates of events in ships' logs are sometimes at variance with calendar dates, because the daily entries ran from noon to noon. Usually the entries are sufficiently detailed to allow the correct calendar dates to be determined, and throughout this book I have given these when possible.
5. Thomas Cochrane [and George Butler Earp], *Autobiography*, 1, p. 88.
6. The *Santa Sabina* was armed with twenty-eight eighteens and twelve eights, giving her a hitting power of 600 Spanish pounds, equal to about 608 English pounds. The armament of *La Minerve* is uncertain. She was a captured French prize, and, according to the contemporary historian William James (*Naval History*, 1, pp. 54, 291, 365), who is usually particular about such things, she still possessed her French armament of twenty-eight eighteens, twelve eights and two thirty-six pound carronades. If so, she carried forty-two guns with a combined discharge of 672 French pounds equal to over 725 English pounds, and had a 20 per cent advantage over her opponent in firepower. However, it is possible that the British had rearmed *La Minerve* with their own guns in Portsmouth in 1795. Peter Goodwin, *Nelson's Ships*, p. 141, has her armament as twenty-eight eighteen-pounders, twelve nine-pounders and two eighteen-pound carronades. The total weight of metal would have been 648 English pounds, a more marginal advantage over the *Santa Sabina*. For details of British ships I have generally relied upon J. J. Colledge, *Ships of the Royal Navy*, and D. Lyon, *Sailing Navy List*.
7. The entry in the captain's log of *La Minerve*, evidently written by Nelson himself, says that he hailed the Spanish frigate but received no answer. Later he gave a more colourful version (Nelson to William, 13/1/1797, Add. MSS 34988), stating that Stuart replied, 'This is a Spanish frigate, and you may begin as soon as you please' By this account Nelson called upon his adversary to surrender several times during the engagement, only to receive the reply, 'No, sir, not whilst I have the means of fighting left.'
8. Account from Cartagena enclosed in ADM 1/396: no. 5.
9. John C. Dann, ed., *Nagle Journal*, pp. 206–7; Augusto Conte y Lacave, *Ataque de Cadiz*, p. 36. The dispatches for the battle are Nelson to Jervis, 20/12/1796 (two letters) and Preston to Nelson, 20/12/1796, filed in ADM 1/395. For an account possibly derived partly from Cockburn see Edward P. Brenton, *Naval History*, 1, p 338.
10. Pitcairn Jones, 'Sea Officers' Lists, 1660–1815', PRO and NMM, and David Syrett and R. L. DiNardo, *Commissioned Sea Officers*, give basic details of officers. For Culverhouse see also his statement of 18/4/1797 in HCA 32/845 and Richard Vesey Hamilton and John Knox Laughton, eds, *Above and Under Hatches*, pp. 66, 84. The standard work on Hardy is A. M. Broadley and R. G. Bartelot, *Nelson's Hardy*, John Gore's *Nelson's Hardy and His Wife* largely concerning itself with the latter.
11. Nelson to his father, 1/1/1797, Monmouth MSS, E599.
12. The quotation is from Act IV, scene iii. See also Colin White, 'Nelson and Shakespeare'.
13. Dann, *Nagle Journal*, p. 207; Nelson to Marino, 24/12/1796, and Nelson to Jervis, 29/12/1796, both in Monmouth MSS, E988.
14. Nelson to Jervis, 24/12/1796, *D&L*, 2, p. 317.
15. Nelson to Spencer, 4/1/1797, 28/3/1797, Add. MSS 75795, 75808. The former letter is erroneously dated 1796 and filed accordingly.

16. Culverhouse to Nelson, 23/3/1797, Add. MSS 34905; Jervis to Spencer, 2/3/1797, Add. MSS 75912; Jervis to Nepean, 13/7/1797, ADM 1/396; William O'Byrne, *Naval Biographical Dictionary*, pp. 384–5.

II The Small World of Burnham Thorpe (pp. 31–47)

1. The best source of information for the Nelson family is Reverend Edmund Nelson's manuscript, 'A Family Historicall Register', which appears to have been finished in 1789. A MS copy can be found in NMM: NWD/34, but the whole appears in Ron C. Fiske, *Notices of Nelson*, pp. 5–9. See also *D&L*, 1, pp. 17–18, and several useful secondary works: Thomas Foley [actually Florence Horatia Suckling], *Nelson Centenary*; Thomas Nelson, *Genealogical History of the Nelson Family*; and M. Eyre Matcham, *Nelsons of Burnham Thorpe*.

2. James Harrison, *Life*, 1, p. 11.

3. See also Frank and Jean Pond, 'The Rolfe Tombs', and George A. Goulty, 'Lord Nelson and the Goulty Connection'.

4. Esther Hallam Moorhouse, *Nelson in England*, pp. 7–8; Ben Burgess, 'Who First Painted the Parsonage?'; Faculty Book, Norfolk Record Office, Norwich, DN/FCB/1, p. 588.

5. Nelson to William, 29/3/1784, Add. MSS 34988; Matcham, *Nelsons of Burnham Thorpe*, p. 27; census returns, 1801, Norfolk Heritage Centre, Norwich; *The Poll for the Knights of the Shire for the County of Norfolk*, p. 203.

6. Parish registers, Burnham Thorpe, Norfolk Record Office. Stories that Nelson was born at Barsham or in his grandmother's cottage at Burnham Thorpe (*Notes and Queries*, 11th series, 1 [1910], pp. 483–4, and 2 [1910], pp. 36, 91) are poorly supported. In his auto-biographical sketch (see introduction, above, n. 7) Nelson categorically says he was born in the parsonage. This sketch, like another autobiographical fragment written about 1796 (NMM: STW/2, published in *NLTHW*, p. 52) and a biographical memoir by Nelson's brother, William, in February 1799 (NMM: PHB/15), has little about Horatio's first years.

7. Matcham, *Nelsons of Burnham Thorpe*, p. 118. Sir Mordaunt Martin, who died in September 1815 at the age of seventy-five, remained a lifelong associate of Nelson.

8. William Faden, *Map of Norfolk*, surveyed in 1790–94, marks Burnham Thorpe as the seat of 'Capt. Nelson'. See also Francis Blomefield and Charles Parkin, *Topographical History of the County of Norfolk*, vol. 7; Samuel Lewis, *Topographical Dictionary*, vol. 1; and Michael Stammers, 'The Hand-Maiden and Victim of Agriculture'.

9. This story seems to have first been published in *NC*, 3 (1800), p. 195. Several later stories on the theme of Nelson getting lost illustrate the potency of these local legends. See, for example, Hilda Gamlin, *Nelson's Friendships*, 2, p. 278, and the 'Nurse' Blackett story alluded to in my text. The earliest example of Horatio's use of 'Horace' appears in the Burnham Thorpe marriage register for 13 March 1769, when the child signed 'Horace Nelson' as a witness to the union of Thomas Massingham and Elizabeth Spurgeon. His signature was corrected to 'Horatio', possibly by his father. The boy made no such mistake attesting to the marriage of Peter Dennis and Hannah Pinner on 13 November 1769. On each occasion an additional witness was required, and Nelson was respectively joined by Robert Jacomb and Ann Scott. The latter, like the newlyweds, signed with a mark.

10. Oliver Warner, *Portrait of Lord Nelson*, found that villagers still spoke of Nurse Blackett in the mid-twentieth century, but wrongly inferred that the memory depended upon unbroken 'local lore' (p. 9). In fact the stories came from her grandson's wife, Mrs 'Valiant' High of North Creake, as published in Francis J. Cross, *The Birthplace of Nelson*, pp. 8, 10, 12, and James Hooper, *Nelson's Homeland*, pp. 46–51. Mrs High said that she often heard her father-in-law (James High, the son of John and Mary Blackett High) talk about Nelson.

I have not discovered Mary's birth date. At the time of her marriage to John 'Hie' on 13 February 1783, a ceremony conducted at Burnham Thorpe by Nelson's brother, the Reverend William Nelson, she was described as a member of the parish of Burnham Norton. However, she makes her last appearance in census records in 1851, when, living in Brancaster, she was described as Mary High, a 'pauper' from Burnham Thorpe, aged ninety-six. Mary died at Brancaster on 7 August 1852, and her death certificate gives her age as ninety-eight. I deduce the year of her birth from these records, but have been unable to find a baptism at Burnham Thorpe or Burnham Norton. See the parish records in the Norfolk Record Office; the Brancaster census, 1851, Norfolk Heritage Centre; and the death certificate, 9/8/1852, General Register Office, London.

The other specific Nelson anecdote told by Mrs 'Valiant' High, though repeated by some biographers, is also probably erroneous. By Mrs High's account, Miss Blackett married a man named High, and their son was nicknamed 'Valiant' after Captain Nelson commended his 'right valiant fight' during a scuffle at Burnham Thorpe in 1793. Subsequently the name 'Valiant' passed from this son to his, the husband of the informant. Unfortunately, parish registers show that Mary (Blackett) and John 'Hie' had two boys, John (born on 12 January 1784) and James (born 2 March 1789). It was the latter to whom Mrs High alluded, but he was barely four years old at the time of the alleged street brawl!

Having said all this, there are some convincing details in Mrs High's interviews. After her husband's death, the former Miss Blackett lived with the family of the said son, James, then landlord of the Jolly Sailors inn in Brancaster. According to Mrs 'Valiant' High the old 'nurse' became confused in her last years, but remained devoted to Lord Nelson. A few days before her death, she rose from her bed, dressed and packed sheets and blankets in a bundle. 'His Lordship has come home,' she said upon being discovered, 'and he sent for me to stay at the rectory.' The old lady was persuaded to return to her bed and died soon afterwards. This anecdote, which the informant may have witnessed first-hand, suggests that Mary Blackett High may have worked as a domestic at the rectory at some time, probably during the period 1788 to 1793, when Nelson made his home there. James Hooper (p. 25) records that the last local believed to have known Nelson personally was Mrs Ann Melton, who died at Docking, Norfolk, on 9 August 1879 at the reputed age of 101.

11. Harrison, *Life*, pp. 8–9.
12. Matcham, *Nelsons of Burnham Thorpe*, pp. 46, 50. A silhouette of Edmund Nelson, done by Charles Rosenberg about 1800 or 1801, forms a frontispiece to this volume. For reproductions of two other portraits, the best by William Beechey, see Hilda Gamlin, *Nelson's Friendships*, 1, pp. 164, 303.
13. Matcham, *Nelsons of Burnham Thorpe*, pp. 26, 39, 55, 81.
14. Will of Ann Suckling, 10/12/1767, PRO: PROB 11/936, no. 80.
15. James S. Clarke and J. McArthur, *Life and Services*, 1, p. 14; William to Nelson, 3/5/1802, 19/10/1802, Alfred Morrison, *Hamilton and Nelson Papers*, 2, pp. 188, 199.
16. Matcham, *Nelsons of Burnham Thorpe*, pp. 18, 134.
17. Nelson to Elliot, 8/10/1803, *D&L*, 5, p. 237; Nelson to Allott, 14/5/1804, *D&L*, 6, p. 18.
18. In the 1840s Captain George Manby, inventor of the life preserver, claimed to have been a schoolfellow of Nelson at Downham Market in Norfolk (*United Service Journal* [1841], pt 1, p. 560; Thomas Joseph Pettigrew, *Memoirs*, 1, pp. 2–3). But the Nelsons were clear about the education of Horatio and William (Fiske, *Notices of Nelson*, p. 7; Nelson memorandum, NMM: STW/2; Nelson's 'Sketch of My Life', 1799, *D&L*, 1, p. 1), and by the time Manby (born November 1765) went to his school Nelson was at North Walsham, or perhaps even with his first ship. Manby's claim was clearly bogus. He was

frank about the shock he felt at Nelson's death and his admiration for the admiral in his unpublished recollections (Add. MSS 29893), but made no claim to have been at school with him at that time. 'It was Nelson I had fixed upon as my model' he said. He and the admiral had been born 'in the same district of that county, West Norfolk'. In later life Manby became obsessed with Nelson, turning part of his house into a Nelson museum, and it was apparently then that his story about being a schoolfellow was created. See the judicious discussion by Bob Brister, Ronald Cansdale and Jim Hargreaves in *ND*, 7 (2001–2), pp. 559–60, 632–4, and Kenneth Walthew, *From Rock and Tempest*.

19. Goulty, 'Lord Nelson and the Goulty Connection'. Foley, *Nelson Centenary*, p. 15, suggests that Nelson stayed with a maternal great aunt, Sarah Henley, but the Goultys are far more likely candidates.

20. Details of Norwich school are supplied by H. W. Saunders, *History of Norwich Grammar School*, and Richard Harries, Paul Cattermole and Peter Mackintosh, *History of Norwich School*.

21. C. R. Forder, *Paston Grammar School*; Nelson to Bulwer, 7/5/1801, Bulwer papers, Norfolk Record Office, MF/RO/334/1, 3; Nelson to William, 14/4/1777, Add. MSS 34988.

22. Clarke and McArthur, *Life and Services*, 1, pp. 15–16.

23. W. Loads, 'Reminiscences of a Pastonian of 1864'. Loads was a great-grandson of Mrs Crosswell, formerly 'Miss Gaze', and could 'just recollect . . . a very old lady wearing a "cross-over"'. Although one would ordinarily dismiss such a late tradition, the story is borne out by the school records (Forder, *Paston Grammar School*, p. 91) and the parish registers of North Walsham, copies of which are filed in the Norfolk Record Office. These last establish the existence of the Gaze family in North Walsham. Elizabeth married John Crosswell on 14 September 1773 and bore him ten children between 1773 and 1795. See also Clarke and McArthur, *Life and Services*, 1, p. 16.

24. Hanson to Nelson, 29/9/1802, 'Nelsoniana', Norfolk Record Office, MC20/48; Ron C. Fiske, 'Nelson, Levett Hanson, and the Order of St Joachim'.

25. Forder, *Paston Grammar School*, pp. 86–7.

26. Pettigrew, *Memoirs*, 1, p. 3; Haggard to *The Times*, 16/2/1895, *ND*, 8 (2003), p. 125; letter of Ella D. Maddison Green, 5/11/1897, Paston School papers, Norfolk Record Office, MC20/27.

27. Edmund Nelson briefly details the fortunes of his children in his 'Family Historicall Register'. For Ann's apprenticeship see the Goldsmiths' Company Apprentice Book 8, Goldsmiths' Hall, London, p. 268.

28. Clarke and McArthur, *Life and Services*, 1, pp. 13–15. I attempted to locate the reference to Suckling's appointment to the *Raisonable* in the *Norfolk Chronicle* but the relevant issues are missing both in Norwich and London.

29. Several family statements, including Nelson's, have him joining the *Raisonable* on 1 January 1771. 'Horace Nelson' of Wells was indeed rated midshipman on the books of the ship from 1 January, but he was not marked as actually present until the musters of March/April 1771 (muster, ADM 36/7669, and pay book, ADM 33/676). That Nelson returned to the Paston school after the Christmas holidays and left about March or April also seems clear from the accounts of William Nelson and Levett Hanson given above. Further evidence comes from James Harrison, *Life*, 1, p. 12, who stated that Nelson joined the *Raisonable* at Sheerness. This would place the event after 15 March, when the vessel moved from Chatham to Sheerness (*Raisonable* log, ADM 51/763).

30. Nelson to William, 20/2/1777, 14/4/1777, Add. MSS 34988; Nelson to Crowe, *D&L*, 4, p. 447; and Nelson to his father, 28/5/1779, Foley, *Nelson Centenary*, p. 19.

III Captain Suckling's Nephew (pp. 48–62)

1. W. S. Lewis et al., eds., *Walpole's Correspondence*, 24, pp. 178, 209; Nelson to Collingwood, 28/9/1785, *D&L*, 1, p. 143.
2. Logs of the *Raisonable*, ADM 51/763 and ADM 52/1937.
3. The stories gained from different informants by James Harrison, *Life*, 1, p. 12, and James S. Clarke and John McArthur, *Life and Services*, 1, p. 16, are broadly compatible, although the former authority has Nelson joining his ship at Sheerness and the latter at Chatham.
4. *Raisonable* muster, ADM 36/7669; *Raisonable* pay book, ADM 33/676; Nelson to William, 20/2/1777, Add. MSS 34988; *D&L*, 1, pp. 46, 49, 56. Boyles later transferred to Sir Thomas Rich's frigate, *Enterprize*, serving as midshipman and master's mate in the Mediterranean. He lived to return to the *Raisonable* as her captain. Boyles died on 9 November 1816, leaving a widow, Mary, née Hawker. See 'Biographical Memoir of the Late Charles Boyles'.
5. *Triumph* muster, ADM 36/7688; Nicholas Tracy, 'Falklands Island Crisis of 1770'.
6. N. A. M. Rodger, *Wooden World*, p. 29. This is the finest general account of the eighteenth-century navy, but for naval administration see Daniel A. Baugh, *British Naval Administration*, an exceptionally comprehensive and well-written monograph. Michael Lewis, *A Social History of the Navy*, though sometimes inaccurate, offered insights into many previously neglected themes. Brian Lavery's *Nelson's Navy* is a comprehensive introduction to the navy at the time of the French revolutionary and Napoleonic wars.
7. In addition to the above see N. A. M. Rodger, 'Lieutenants' Sea-Time and Age'.
8. Suckling to Stephens, 24/11/1771, 1/12/1771, ADM 1/2481; Thomas Foley, *Nelson Centenary*, pp. 9, 11; *NC*, 14 (1805), p. 265; and David Syrett, 'Nelson's Uncle'.
9. Suckling to Stephens, 27/6/1771, ADM 1/2481.
10. For Townshend see *DNB*, 19, pp. 1048–50.
11. Suckling (4 May 1726–17 July 1778) became a lieutenant on 8 March 1745, a commander on 3 January 1754 and a post-captain on 2 December 1755. For his 'passing certificate' see ADM 6/86, p. 101.
12. Ron C. Fiske, *Notices of Nelson*, pp. 28–9; Ron C. Fiske, 'A New View of Woodton Hall, Norfolk'; and (for Suckling's London house) Suckling to Sharpe, 29/5/1776, in BL: A. M. Broadley, 'Nelsoniana', 1, facing p. 6.
13. Will of Maurice Suckling, 3/8/1774, PRO: PROB 11/1044, no. 302.
14. *Triumph* logs, ADM 51/1015 and ADM 52/2052, and NMM: ADM/L/T268.
15. Fiske, *Notices of Nelson*, p. 7; Nelson memorandum, c. 1796, NMM: STW/2; *D&L*, 1, p. 2; Clarke and McArthur, *Life and Services*, 1, p. 17; *Dreadnought* muster, ADM 36/1409. Neither Nelson nor his father, who refer to the trip on the merchantman, name the ship concerned, but she can be identified from *New Lloyds List*, 26, 30/7/1771, 31/12/1771; *Lloyds List*, 10 and 21/7/1772; and the *Public Advertiser*, 30/12/1771. A search through the shipping news in the newspapers at Colindale and in the Burney collection at the British Library failed to reveal additional information. Few papers carried extensive port news, and some that did, such as the *Public Ledger* and the *Morning Chronicle*, are now missing strategic issues. The *Public Advertiser*, which is reasonably complete, yielded only one reference to the *Mary Ann*. Two maiden daughters of John Rathbone were later said to have run a boarding school in Kensington: *Notes and Queries*, 4th series, 10 (1872), p. 269.
16. Nelson's seasickness: Nelson to Davison, 13/1/1804, *D&L*, 5, p. 370.
17. *Triumph* pay book, ADM 33/696.
18. *Triumph* muster, ADM 36/7689–7690.
19. *Kentish Gazette*, 21/7/1772, 1/8/1772; *D&L*, 1, p. 2.

20. *Triumph* muster, ADM 36/7689–90; *D&L*, 6, p. 381.

21. In addition to the musters see Richards to Suckling, 5/12/1770, ADM 1/2481. The succeeding quotation about midshipmen is from Nelson to Churchey, 20/10/1802, *MM*, 28 (1942), p. 319.

22. *D&L*, 1, p. 2.

23. Suckling to Stephens, 9 and 18/8/1772, and 14, 15, 18/10/1772, ADM 1/2482; *Triumph* logs, ADM 51/1015 and ADM 52/2052.

24. Court martial of Edward Smith, 14/1/1773, ADM 1/5306.

IV Northward Ho! (pp. 63–81)

1. The best secondary account of the Phipps expedition is Ann Savours, '"A Very Interesting Point in Geography"'.

2. Phipps, *A Voyage Towards the North* Pole, p. 11; Lutwidge to Stephens, 3/1/1774, ADM 1/2053.

3. *D&L*, 1, p. 2; Suckling to Stephens, 11, 28/7/1771, ADM 1/2481; Lutwidge to Stephens, 28/7/1771, ADM 1/2053.

4. *Triumph* pay book, ADM 33/696; *Carcass* muster, ADM 36/7567; *Carcass* log, ADM 51/167.

5. My reconstruction of the voyage rests upon a fresh examination of all the primary sources. For the *Racehorse* these include Phipps, *Voyage Towards the North Pole*, and the manuscript upon which it was based in BL: King's 224; the ship's logs, ADM 51/757 and ADM 52/1416; and Thomas Floyd's narrative published by Albert H. Markham, ed., *Northward*. The view from the *Carcass* comes from the captain's log, ADM 51/167; Lutwidge's journal, ADM 55/12, which replicates the material in the captain's log; two logs of the master, James Allen, ADM 52/1639[7] and ADM 52/1639[8]; and the anonymous diary published as *Journal of a Voyage Undertaken*. Interesting views and charts of the expedition, some if not all produced by Philippe d'Auvergne, can be found in the William L. Clements Library, the University of Michigan, Ann Arbor.

6. For d'Auvergne see 'Biographical Memoir of Philippe d'Auvergne'; G. R. Balleine, *The Tragedy of Philippe d'Auvergne*; and Ann Savours, 'The Younger Cleverley and the Arctic, 1773–74'.

7. The issue of slops: *Carcass* pay book, ADM 33/509.

8. Markham, *Northward*, p. 125.

9. *Journal of a Voyage Undertaken*, p. 35; Markham, *Northward*, pp. 126–7, 130, 141.

10. BL: King's 224, pp. 27–8; Markham, *Northward*, pp. 133–5.

11. *Journal of a Voyage Undertaken*, p. 42.

12. *Journal of a Voyage Undertaken*, pp. 44–6.

13. *Journal of a Voyage Undertaken*, pp. 60–2; master's log of the *Carcass*, ADM 52/1639 [7].

14. *Journal of a Voyage Undertaken*, pp. 62–3.

15. Phipps, *Voyage Towards the North Pole*, pp. 59, 173, and BL: King's 224, pp. 41–2, have the incident occurring on 30 July, as the *Racehorse* boat was returning from reconnoitring the island, but Floyd, who was in the party, says it happened on the outward journey on the 29th (Markham, *Northward*, pp. 181–4). The master's log of the *Racehorse* for 30/7/1773 (ADM 52/1416) mentions the boat returning at 4.00 a.m. on 30 July, but none of the *Carcass* logs refers to the incident. See also James Harrison, *Life*, 1, p. 2.

16. *Carcass* log, 31/7/1773, ADM 51/167.

17. The first plate, by Edward Orme and dated 20/2/1806, was published in Francis William Blagdon, *Orme's Graphic History*, facing p. 7. In 1808 another engraving by W. H. Worthington, after a painting by W. Bromley, was published.

18. James Allen's log, 4/8/1773, ADM 52/1639[7].
19. 'Biographical Memoir of the Right Honourable Lord Nelson', p. 161.
20. James S. Clarke and John McArthur, *Life and Services*, 1, pp. 1, 21–2. Lutwidge was presumably satisfied with this final account because he was privy to the proofs of the book: see the 1809 edition, *The Life of Admiral Lord Nelson*, 1, p. 8 in the list of subscribers.
21. *D&L*, 1, p. 3.
22. The master's logs of the *Carcass* state that the ship's second and third lieutenants commanded the hauling lines, but the anonymous diarist from the same vessel (*Journal of a Voyage Undertaken*) has First Lieutenant Baird at the head of the enterprise. Several details in this account, while colourful, are at variance to the picture presented by the ships' logs. Charts of the voyage are also contradictory at this point. Thus d'Auvergne's chart has the course turning first southeast and then west on 7 and 8 August, while the 'Plan of the North East Lands and Seven Islands' shows the ships proceeding northeast before turning west (William L. Clements Library).
23. *Journal of a Voyage Undertaken*, pp. 81–3; Markham, *Northward*, p. 203.
24. Phipps, *Voyage Towards the North Pole*, p. 72.
25. Markham, *Northward*, p. 221.
26. *Journal of a Voyage Undertaken*, pp. 93–4; *Carcass* log, 12/9/1773, ADM 51/167.
27. Markham, *Northward*, pp. 223–8.
28. Hughes's passing certificate, 2/3/1780, ADM 107/8. He was confirmed as a lieutenant fifteen days later.
29. The watch is now in the National Maritime Museum, Greenwich.
30. Nelson's deductions were: 1s. 8d. for slops, 5s. 9d. to the Chatham Chest (a naval charity founded in Elizabethan times), and 2s. 11d. to the hospital (*Carcass* pay book, ADM 33/309).

V East Indies Adventure (pp. 82–106)

1. Farmer to Stephens, 31/8/1773, 12/9/1773, ADM 1/1789; John Charnock, *Biographical Memoirs*, pp. 16–21; *DNB*, 6, pp. 1074–5. For details of individual ships see David Lyon, *Sailing Navy List*.
2. *Triumph* pay book, ADM 33/696; *Seahorse* pay book, ADM 34/749; court martial of George Farmer, 21/2/1776, ADM 1/5307. The extent of such frauds in aid of sea time is difficult to gauge. Michael Lewis, *Social History of the Navy*, exaggerated their prevalence, but N. A. M. Rodger, 'Lieutenants' Sea-Time and Age', may have defended the navy too strongly. Certainly he erred (p. 271) in denying that Lord Cochrane had gained fictitious sea time before joining his uncle's ship, the *Hind*: John Sugden, 'Lord Cochrane', pp. 37–8; Brian Vale, *Cochrane, the Unhappy Hero*, forthcoming.
3. Bentham to Kee, 28/10/1773, *Notes and Queries*, 4th series, 10 (1872), p. 269.
4. For the personnel see *Seahorse* pay book, ADM 34/749, and James S. Clarke and John McArthur, *Life and Services*, 1. p. 22.
5. *D&L*, 1, p. 3. On Pole see *NC*, 21 (1809), pp. 265–95.
6. Details of the voyage of the *Seahorse* depend primarily upon the logs of Farmer (ADM 51/883), Surridge (ADM 52/1991) and the lieutenants (NMM: ADM/L/S222–23). For Nelson's positive memories of the period see his letters to William, 28/1/1782, 19/3/1784, Add. MSS 34988.
7. Hughes to Stephens, 2/11/1773, ADM 1/164; Farmer to Stephens, 14/10/1773, ADM 1/1789; *Seahorse* pay book, ADM 34/749.
8. Captain's log, 5/12/1774, ADM 51/883, and master's log, 13/1/1774, ADM 52/1991.
9. Muster of the *Tweed*, ADM 36/7523; Surridge's passing certificate, 10/9/1777, ADM

107/7; *Steel's Navy Lists*; Pitcairn-Jones, 'Sea Officers' Lists, 1660–1815', PRO. We are indebted to Admiral S. W. Roskill for suggesting the importance of Surridge in his introduction to Russell Grenfell, *Horatio Nelson*.

10. Nelson to Cornwallis, 13/10/1788, Hist. MSS Commission, *Various Collections*, 6, p. 341; Clarke and McArthur, *Life and Services*, 1, p. 23.

11. Master's log, 17/1/1774, ADM 52/1991; Farmer report, 12/3/1774, ADM 1/164.

12. Floggings were entered in ships' logs, although often haphazardly.

13. Court martial of Drummond, 30/5/1774, ADM 1/5306.

14. The pay book records changes in personnel, but see also Hughes to Stephens, 12/3/1774, ADM 1/164.

15. Master's log, 6/5/1774, ADM 52/1991.

16. Hughes to Stephens, 1/4/1775, 2/7/1775, ADM 1/164.

17. Captain's log, 19–20/2/1775, ADM 51/883.

18. Hughes to Stephens, 11/10/1775, 22/3/1775, ADM 1/164.

19. Court martial of Henery, 19/2/1776, ADM 1/5307.

20. *Seahorse* pay book, ADM 34/749; Clarke and McArthur, *Life and Services*, 1, pp. 22–3; Cornelia Knight, *Autobiography*, 2, p. 286.

21. Clarke and McArthur, *Life and Services*, 1, 23.

22. Court martial of Henery, 19/2/1776, ADM 1/5307. For Keeling, as for Sullivan, the *Seahorse* was a first ship. He was rated master's mate, but was described in the court-martial record as midshipman.

23. Court martial of Farmer, 21/2/1776, ADM 1/5307.

24. Clarke and McArthur, *Life and Services*, 1, pp. 22–3; Ron C. Fiske, *Notices of Nelson*, p. 7; *D&L*, 1, pp. 3–4; Christopher Lloyd and J. L. S. Coulter, *Medicine and the Navy*, pp. 329–47.

25. James Bond and William Tennant of the East India Company and William Perry, Claud Lernoult, Jos. Davies and James Anderson of the Navy signed sick certificates for Clerke, Fortescue and Evans in February and March 1776, enclosed in Hughes to Stephens, 22/3/1776, ADM 1/164.

26. Pigott and Randall to Stephens, 30/8/1776, ADM 1/2303; *Dolphin* muster, ADM 36/7583; *Dolphin* pay book, ADM 33/635; *D&L*, 1, pp. 3–4. Pigott was a lieutenant in 1771, a post-captain in 1776 and a full admiral in 1810. He died in 1822.

27. Correspondence in ADM 1/2490; *Gentleman's Magazine* (1819), ii, p. 570. Nelson's connections put him on fast-track promotion, and he soon overtook Surridge in rank. Indeed, in 1780 Nelson and Surridge almost shared a ship again, the former as captain and the latter as lieutenant. Surridge was appointed third lieutenant of the *Janus* frigate, then on the Jamaica station, on 24 October 1779. Unfortunately he went down with an 'obstinate intermittent [fever] and dysenteric complaints' and was hospitalised at Port Royal before being discharged from the ship on 17 January so that he could recover at home (*Janus* muster, ADM 36/8720; certificate by Deans, Macnamara and Collingwood, 12/1/1780, enclosed in Parker to Stephens, 7/4/1780, ADM 1/242). A few months later Nelson was appointed captain of the *Janus*, but he too was invalided to England. It would have been an outstanding partnership. Surridge remained an admirer of Nelson, and attended his funeral in 1806. He left a widow, Mary, who died aged 89 at Ashling House, near Hambledon, Hampshire, on 15 March 1841: *Nautical Magazine*, 10 (1841), p. 287.

28. Logs of the *Dolphin*, ADM 51/259 and ADM 52/1701[2]; O. Pryce-Lewis, 'Horatio Nelson and Simon's Bay'; *ND*, 2 (1985), pp. 35–7.

29. Pigott return, 30/8/1776, enclosed in Pigott to Stephens, 30/8/1776, ADM 1/2303.

30. Clarke and McArthur, *Life and Services*, 1, p. 23. The story was told by R. W. Spencer.

31. Suckling to Sandwich, 28/1/1777, NMM: SAN/F/10; John E. Talbott, *Pen and Ink Sailor*, p. 25.

32. For the comptroller and his influence see Daniel A. Baugh, *British Naval Administration*, pp. 32–48; J. H. Broomfield, 'Lord Sandwich at the Admiralty Board'; and R. J. B. Knight, 'Sandwich, Middleton, and Dockyard Appointments'.

33. NMM: SAN/3, pp. 39, 53; J. M. Collinge, *Navy Board Officials*, p. 125.

34. *Dolphin* pay book, ADM 33/635.

35. *D&L*, I, p. 4.

VI Lieutenant Nelson (pp. 107–32)

1. Suckling to Stephens, 2/9/1771, ADM 1/2481.

2. *D&L*, I, p. 4; muster of the *Worcester*, ADM 36/8677.

3. *D&L*, I, p. 4.

4. Nelson to Fanny Nelson, 18/1/1794, Monmouth MSS, E806.

5. Robinson to Stephens, 24/10/1776, 7 and 12/12/1776, 2/4/1777, ADM 1/2390; *Worcester* logs, ADM 51/1085 and ADM 52/2095.

6. Nelson to William, 20/2/1777, Add. MSS 34988.

7. Porten to Stephens, 3/4/1777, WO 1/683.

8. Brian Lavery, *Nelson's Navy*, p. 93.

9. James S. Clarke and John McArthur, *Life and Services*, I, p. 25.

10. Nelson's passing certificate, 9/4/1777, ADM 107/6.

11. Patronage book, NMM: SAN/3, p. 39; *D&L*, I, p. 4; Nelson to Stephens, 11/4/1777, ADM 1/2222.

12. Nelson to William, 14/4/1777, Add. MSS 34988

13. Thomas Foley, *Nelson Centenary*, p. 16; will of Maurice Suckling, 3/8/1774, PRO: PROB 11/1044, no. 302.

14. Edmund Nelson mentioned the apprenticeship in his account of the family without actually identifying it: Ron C. Fiske, *Notices of Nelson*, p. 7. I was unable to find any references to Ann in the city of London freedom papers in the Corporation Record Office or the records of livery companies at the Guildhall Library, probably because she did not complete her apprenticeship. Her placement was finally traced through the apprentice lists in PRO: IR 1/28, and Apprentice Book 8, p. 268, Goldsmiths' Company, London. See two articles by John Sugden, 'Tragic or Tainted? The Mystery of Ann Nelson' and 'New Light on Ann Nelson'. Thanks are due to David Beasley of the Goldsmiths' Company.

15. Apprentice Books 7 and 8, Goldsmiths' Company. Alice Lilly served her apprenticeship with Ann Jacquin in 1746–54. Alice's premises were identified from London trades directories, 1769–76, especially *Kent's Directory*, 1769, p. 110, and 1776, p. 112, though the proprietors are listed as A. and M. Lilly. The latter was probably Mary Lilly, a niece or cousin apprenticed to Alice in 1757. Information on London trades and Ludgate Street comes from R. Campbell, *London Tradesman*, and Peter Jackson, ed., *John Tallis's London Street Views*, pp. 52, 293–4.

16. Will of Maurice Suckling, 3/8/1774, PRO: PROB 11/1044, no. 302. I have not identified the second legacy Ann received, but it was *not* from John Norris, who left £500 to Ann's sister, Susanna (Norris will, 26/1/1770, PRO: PROB/11/1031: no. 229).

The story that the noted antiquary Dr William Robinson (1777–1848) was the illegitimate son of Ann Nelson and William Robinson of Tottenham (1737–1811) appears to have originated in the twentieth century with his daughter, Agnes Laetitia FitzPatrick (1820–1912), and first published in 1904. See Jessie Nelson Ward to FitzPatrick, 11/2/1902 and 3/11/1903, Madden papers, City Museum and Records Office, Portsmouth; 'J.W.B.', 'Nelson's Sister Anne', *Notes and Queries*, 10th series, 1 (1904), p. 170; *Notes and Queries*, 9th series, 12 (1903), p. 428. The claim has no dependable foundation. Though Dr Robinson was illegitimate, and his belated baptismal entry of 10 November 1789 describes his parents as William Robinson 'and Anne', the mother's surname is omitted (registers of St Luke's Old Street, Guildhall Library, Aldermanbury, London). Moreover, neither the older nor younger William Robinson appears to have ever claimed a relationship with Ann Nelson (will of William Robinson, 3/8/1808, PRO: PROB 11/1518: no. 39; *Gentleman's Magazine*, 1848, ii, p. 211; Aleck Abrahams and John Ardagh, *William Robinson*; and documents in Alfred Morrison, *Hamilton and Nelson Papers*, 2, pp. 312, 332, 335, 336). Mrs FitzPatrick had a portrait that she says John Opie had painted of Ann Nelson: not only does the painting apparently fail to identify its subject as Ann or anybody else, but she was not in London at the same time as Opie. Opie arrived in London from his native Cornwall in 1783, three or four years after Ann had left. For a full discussion see Sugden, 'Tragic or Tainted? The Mystery of Ann Nelson', pp. 50–4.

17. Richard Walker, *Nelson Portraits*, p. 194; Nelson to Locker, 15 and 21/2/1781, *D&L*, 1, pp. 38, 39.

18. *Lowestoffe* muster, ADM 36/10047; Locker to Stephens, 2, 28 and 29/4/1777, ADM 1/2054; Nelson to Locker, 27/9/1786, *D&L*, 1, p. 197; Joseph Bromwich, passing certificate, 7/8/1783, ADM 107/9; and Clarke and McArthur, *Life and Services*, 1, p. 25.

19. Admiralty orders to Locker, 10/5/1777, ADM 2/102.

20. *Lowestoffe* log, ADM 51/4247; Locker to Stephens, 5/7/1777, ADM 1/2054; Gayton to Stephens, 24/7/1777, ADM 1/240, pt 3. Nelson's log is filed with that of the other lieutenant in NMM: ADM/L/L220. It covers the period 10 April 1777 to 1 July 1778, but was copied from the master's log.

21. Richard Vesey Hamilton, ed., *Sir Thomas Byam Martin*, 1, pp. 124–5; Nelson to Locker, 24/9/1784, 16/3/1785, *D&L*, 1, pp. 110, 127.

22. John Charnock, *Biographical Memoirs*, p. 27; Patricia Richardson, 'Captain William Locker'; and Victor Sharman, 'Nelson's "Sea-Daddy"'. Charnock knew Locker personally.

23. Nelson to Locker, 9/2/1799, *D&L*, 3, p. 260.

24. Brian Tunstall and Nicholas Tracy, *Naval Warfare*, pp. 98–9, 105, 115–16; Nicholas Tracy, *Nelson's Battles*, pp. 66–70. Locker's admiration for Hawke led him to name his third son for the admiral.

25. Nelson to Locker, 12/8/1777, *D&L*, 1, p. 23.

26. In addition to the captain's log see the list of prizes, 1775 to 26/2/1778, ADM 1/240, pt 3.

27. Sources for the capture of the privateer are the ship's log for 20–21/11/1777; list of prizes up to 26/2/1778, ADM 1/240, pt 3; *D&L*, 1, p. 5; and Bromwich's account in Clarke and McArthur, *Life and Services*, 1, pp. 27–8.

28. Nelson to Locker, 9/2/1778, *D&L*, 1, p. 24, names the prize taken early in February as the *Abigail*, but the official list of captures (ADM 1/240, pt 3) credits the *Lowestoffe* with only six in the period up to 26 February: the four already mentioned, the *Phoenix* of South Carolina, laden with rice, and an unnamed Boston sloop with a cargo of molasses and dry goods. I have assumed the latter must have been Nelson's *Abigail*. For the *Swan* see list of prizes, 3/3/1778 to 21/6/1778, ADM 1/241.

29. In addition to the captain's log see Clarke and McArthur, *Life and Services*, 1, p. 29.

30. Anne Fremantle, ed., *Wynne Diaries* (1935–40), 2, p. 91.

31. Nelson to his father, 24/10/1778, Add. MSS 34988; Thomas Foley, *Nelson Centenary*, pp. 9, 18.

32. Lady Parker to Nelson, 15/3/1797, 29/10/1798, Add. MSS 34905, and *D&L*, 3, p. 83; Nelson to Parker, 21/5/1801, *D&L*, 4, p. 377. Later in life the positions of Sir Peter Parker and Nelson were reversed, and the latter reciprocated the early favours he had

received. Acknowledging Nelson's generosity, Sir Peter trusted that his son, Lieutenant Peter Parker, would 'be ever mindful of your goodness to him and unparalleled friendship to me' (Parker to Nelson, 4/2/1804, NMM: CRK/10).

33. *Bristol* muster, ADM 36/8118. Joshua Doberry, Nelson's servant on the *Lowestoffe*, followed him into the *Bristol* and *Badger*. Nelson's certificate of service on the *Bristol*, issued by Caulfield on 20 December 1778, misdates his arrival on the flagship by a month: Nelson's log, NMM: ADM/L/B175A.

34. Cochrane to Chatham, 9/1/1795, ADM 1/1620; W. H. Smyth, *Captain Philip Beaver*.

35. Nelson to Locker, 31/8/1778, *D&L*, 1, p. 24. Two masters, Abraham Rose and Thomas Harvey, served on the *Bristol* during Nelson's occupancy, and the surgeon was Archibald Bruce.

36. *Bristol* log, ADM 51/137; Parker to Deane, 2/9/1778, Parker to Stephens, 9 and 24/10/1778 and 19/11/1778, all in ADM 1/241; list of prizes, 1778, ADM 1/241; Nelson to his father, 24/10/1778, Add. MSS 34988. Nelson's log differs slightly from his captain's. He notes the 'rebel [American] ship' on 3 December 1778.

37. Nelson to his father, 24/10/1778, Add. MSS 34988; appointment book, NMM: SAN/3, p. 33.

38. Nelson to Locker, 31/8/1778, *D&L*, 1, p. 24.

39. Suckling's will, 3/8/1774, PRO: PROB 11/1044, no. 302, disproves William Nelson's story in Clarke and McArthur, *Life and Services*, 1, p. 40.

40. Clarke and McArthur, *Life of Admiral Lord Nelson*, 1, appendix 2, p. 366. The Suckling notes were deleted from the 1840 edition of this work.

41. Nelson to William Suckling, 5/7/1786, *D&L*, 1, p. 186.

VII The First Commands (pp. 133–48)

1. Parker to Stephens, 12/1/1779, ADM 1/241.
2. *Badger* muster, ADM 36/9883; Nelson to Locker, 30/4/1779, *D&L*, 1, p. 25.
3. The *Badger* muster records Lepee's age as eighteen in 1779, but when he was enrolled on the *Boreas* in 1784 his age was given as twenty-one (*Boreas* muster, ADM 36/10525). See also the pay book of the *Lowestoffe*, ADM 34/137.
4. For the voyages of the *Badger* see her logs, ADM 51/78 and ADM 52/1591. The lieutenants' log (NMM: ADM/L/B5) was also signed by Nelson, though his post was that of commander.
5. Nelson to Locker, 23/1/1780, *D&L*, 1, p. 32.
6. *Public Characters*, p. 8. Contemporary descriptions of Nelson's appearance are scanty and imprecise. An informed debate between Colin White and Lesley Edwards, drawing on examinations of surviving uniforms and locks of Nelson's hair, can be found in ND, 4 (1992), pp. 93, 157, 197, and ND, 6 (1999), pp. 492–5. See also ND, 2 (1985), pp. 33–5; ND, 7 (2000), p. 130; Otto Erich Deutsch, *Admiral Nelson and Joseph Haydn*, pp. 70, 98; and Richard Walker, *Nelson Portraits*, p. 257.
7. In addition to the logs and muster see *D&L*, 1, p. 6.
8. For the young William Locker I have additionally consulted the *Badger* pay book (ADM 34/137) and am indebted to Victor Sharman, who informs me that the boy eventually opted for an army career and became a lieutenant in the 8th Regiment of Light Dragoons.
9. Nelson to Locker, 30/4/1779, *D&L*, 1, p. 25; list of prizes taken on the Jamaica station, ADM 1/241; E. Arnot Robertson, *Spanish Town Papers*, pp. 41–3.
10. Nelson to Locker, 3, 13/5/1779, *D&L*, 1, pp. 26, 27, seem to refer to this incident. Writing to his father on 28 May 1779 (Add. MSS 34988) Nelson also mentioned his failure to capture a privateer, but the logs also record a futile chase of 18 May and the letter may have been related to this later episode.

11. Nelson to Locker, 13/5/1779, *D&L*, 1, p. 27.

12. Nelson to Locker, 13/5/1779, *D&L*, 1, 27.

13. The logs of the *Badger* are identical on the destruction of the *Glasgow*. See in addition the *Badger* muster: Nelson's accounts in *D&L*, 1, pp. 6, 29; Parker to Stephens, 14/6/1779 and 26/7/1779, ADM 1/241; *D&L*, 7, p. 423; James S. Clarke and John McArthur, *Life and Services*, 1, p. 43; Nelson to Lloyd, 24/4/1801, in Thomas Pettigrew, *Memoirs*, 1, p. 10; and especially the minutes of Lloyd's court martial, 24 July 1779, ADM 1/5311. This was probably Nelson's first experience of courts martial. The court consisted of Captains Joseph Deane, William Waldegrave, Toby Caulfield, William Cornwallis and Christopher Atkins, with Charles Hamilton serving as Deputy Judge Advocate.

14. Tom Pocock, *Young Nelson in the Americas*, p. 25.

15. Nelson to Locker, 28/7/1779, *D&L*, 1, p. 30.

16. Nelson to Locker, 23/1/1780, *D&L*, 1, p. 32. Collingwood said that he first met Nelson in 1773. He would then have been serving on the *Lenox* ship of the line in the Thames and Medway, when Nelson, of course, was with the *Triumph* and *Carcass*. See Oliver Warner, 'Collingwood and Nelson', p. 318.

17. Dalling to Clinton, 13/8/1779, and Parker's letters of 12 and 18/8/1779, published in the *London Chronicle* of 11–13/1/1780; Dalling to Germain, 6–23/8/1779, CO 137/75; letter of Samuel Joyce, 10/9/1779, Shelburne papers, William L. Clements Library, University of Michigan, Ann Arbor.

18. Dalling to Germain, 28/8 to 9/9/1779, CO 135/75.

19. Nelson to Locker, 12/8/1779, *D&L*, 1, p. 31; Parker to Stephens, 23/8/1779, and Parker, 'Arrangement of the Squadron in Port Royal and Kingston Harbours', ADM 1/241.

20. Nelson to Locker, 12/8/1779, *D&L*, 1, p. 31.

21. Parker to Stephens, 13/9/1779, ADM 1/241; Dalling to Germain, 28/8 to 9/9/1779, CO 137/75.

22. *Hinchingbroke* muster, ADM 36/9510–9511; *Hinchingbroke* pay book, ADM 34/405.

23. *Gentleman's Magazine* (1834), ii, pp. 104–6; Bullen's return of service, 1817, ADM 9/2, no. 22; William O'Byrne, *Naval Biographical Dictionary*, pp. 142–3, 1391.

24. *Hinchingbroke* log, ADM 51/442. Lieutenant Bullen's log, running from 18 January 1780, is filed in NMM: ADM/L/H113. There were ten floggings on board the ship, but one was of a sailor convicted by a court martial of an offence unconnected to the *Hinchingbroke*.

25. Parker to Stephens, 13/9/1779, ADM 1/241.

26. In addition to the log see 'List of Vessels Taken', ADM 1/241, and Nelson to Locker, 23/1/1780, *D&L*, 1, p. 32. Daniel Ross was related to Hercules Ross, the merchant of Jamaica, who unsuccessfully tried to intervene in the subsequent legal proceedings. The log of the *Niger* frigate (ADM 51/637) incorrectly identifies the ships as French.

27. Nelson to Locker, 23/1/1780, *D&L*, 1, p. 32.

28. Nelson to Locker, 23/1/1780, *D&L*, 1, p. 32; Robertson, *Spanish Town Papers*, p. 142.

VIII In the Wake of the Buccaneers (pp. 149–75)

1. Thomas Jefferys, *West Indian Atlas*, p. 10.

2. Dalling to Germain, 4 and 7/2/1780, CO 137/76. See additionally George Metcalf, *Royal Government*, chap. 8, and Andrew Jackson O'Shaughnessy, *An Empire Divided*.

3. Benjamin Moseley, *Treatise on Tropical Diseases*, p. 148.

4. Ernest A. Cruikshank, *Life of Sir Henry Morgan*, pp. 57–8; Lawrie to Dalling, 2/9/1779, CO 137/76.

5. Dalling to Germain, 13/11/1779, 4/2/1780, CO 137/76; Dalling's instructions to John Polson, 1780, CO 137/76:220.

6. Nelson to Locker, 23/1/1780, *D&L*, 1, p. 32.

7. Dalling to Germain, 4/1/1780, 28/1/1780, CO 137/76; Thomas Dancer, *A Brief History*, pp. 7–8; testimony in the 'Report of a Committee' of the Jamaican assembly, 1780, CO 137/79: 177.

8. Nelson, 18/1/1780, NMM: Mon/1; order book of the expedition, 15/2/1780, *Collections of the New York Historical Society* (hereafter *Collections*), p. 68; M. Eyre Matcham, *Nelsons of Burnham Thorpe*, p. 284.

9. Narrative of Robert Hodgson, CO 137/80:322. A political opponent of Lawrie, Hodgson gave a prejudiced assessment of the expedition benefiting from hindsight, but there are valuable details.

10. For the expedition I have principally relied upon reports and correspondence in CO 137/vols 76–81. Particularly useful are Polson to Dalling, 30/4/1780 (the official report), CO 137/77; Polson's journal, the best single source for events between 3 February and 29 April 1780, in CO 137/77:166; various statements in 'Report of a Committee', CO 137/79: 177; Hodgson's narrative, CO 137/80: 322; and Dalling's 'Narrative of the Late Expedition', with its numerous enclosures, CO 137/81: 198. Other major sources are the *Hinchingbroke* log; Dancer, *A Brief History*; various documents in *Collections*, including Polson's order book and Kemble's journal and three sets of papers in the William L. Clements Library, University of Michigan, Ann Arbor: the George Germain papers, the Earl of Shelburne papers, vol. 79, and the Stephen Kemble papers. Nelson made some remarks in 'Sketch of My Life', *D&L*, 1, pp. 7–8, and his memorandum, NMM: STW/2. See also Hist. MSS Commission, *Stopford-Sackville*, 2, pp. 272–96; C. N. Robinson, 'Nelson at Nicaragua'; and C. J. Britton, 'Nelson and the River San Juan'. Secondary accounts have been given by John W. Fortescue, *History of the British Army*, 3, pp. 338–42, and Tom Pocock, *Young Nelson in the Americas*, a comprehensive and well researched account.

11. For the Indians and Sandy Bay blacks see Lawrie, 'General Account of the Mosquito Shore', 1779, CO 137/76: 208; Dalling to Gleadow, CO 137/78: 172; and *The Present State of the West Indies* (1778).

12. Order book, 20/2/1780, 1/3/1780, *Collections*, pp. 71, 75.

13. Dancer, *A Brief History*, p. 10.

14. Kemble journal, *Collections*, p. 5.

15. Dalling to Polson, 17/3/1780, and Dalling to Parker, 17/3/1780, CO 137/77.

16. James Harrison, *Life*, 1, pp. 62–3.

17. Order book, 21/3/1780, *Collections*, p. 76; information of Todd, 25/8/1780, CO 137/78: 239.

18. Details of Bartola and the Spanish fort of San Juan are drawn from the journal of Lieutenant Colonel Kemble, who eventually followed Polson upriver. See his journal, *Collections*, pp. 10, 14.

19. Dancer, *A Brief History*, p. 13; Moseley, *Treatise on Tropical Diseases*, pp. 33–4; James S. Clarke and John McArthur, *Life and Services*, 1. p. 53.

20. List of prisoners, CO 137/77: 154.

21. De Galvez to D'Ayssa, 14/4/1781, CO 137/81: 276; Moseley, *Treatise on Tropical Diseases*, p. 167; Pocock, *Young Nelson in the Americas*, p. 156. Dalling subsequently criticised Polson for not storming the fort. He made no reference to Nelson in this context, but in his 'Narrative of the Late Expedition' (CO 137/81) said that when MacDonald arrived at the fort with the second division of Polson's force he offered to storm it with his volunteers.

22. The army had twenty-four-, twelve-, nine-, six- and four-pounder guns on the expedition (order book, 21/3/1780, *Collections*, pp. 76–8; Dalling's statement, CO 137/81: 349; lists of military stores shipped in the *Superb* and *Penelope*, CO 137/81: 340), but

only the lighter and more manageable four-pounders appear to have gone forward to the siege. This may have influenced gunnery tactics.

23. Polson to Dalling, 30/4/1780, CO 137/77.

24. Return of casualties, 30/4/1780, CO 137/77: 153.

25. For the reduction of rations see order book, *Collections*, p. 83.

26. Moseley, *Treatise on Tropical Diseases*, p. 167.

27. Dancer, *A Brief History*, p. 19; Dalling to Germain, 2 to 20/7/1780, CO 137/78. A messenger who left the fort on the evening of 23 April reported everyone well at that time (*Collections*, p. 5).

28. Dancer, *A Brief History*, pp. 43, 44, 53.

29. Clarke and McArthur, *Life and Services*, 1, p. 54. The nature of the diseases that destroyed the San Juan expedition has aroused such disagreement that it is worth devoting some paragraphs to the subject. A traditional opinion that yellow fever (the notorious 'Yellow Jack') was involved is untenable. Dancer, who was on the spot, understood at the time that his patients were not displaying typical symptoms of yellow fever (*A Brief History*, p. 53), and later distinguished between yellow fever and the type of 'intermittent' disorders he saw in Nicaragua (Dancer, *Medical Assistant*, pp. 65–92, 381–3). Certain defining features of yellow fever, particularly the copious discharges that gave the disease the nickname of 'black vomit', were not reported on the San Juan. Moreover, the course of yellow fever tends to be fairly consistent, with a few days of fever being followed by a three- or four-day remission before relapse with the appearance of severe haemorrhages and other symptoms. Finally, the vectors of malaria, which occur in marshy and estuarine areas, fit the illness of 1780 more comfortably than the jungle vectors of yellow fever.

Dr Anne-Marie Ewart Hills, 'Nelson's Illnesses, 1780–1782', advances the improbable theory that the principal illness was tropical sprue. She argues that the expeditionary force was in a pre-scurvy state at the mouth of the San Juan, and low on folic acid as well as vitamin C. Sprue, an intestinal malfunction, incubates in twenty to thirty days and, though chronic, can progress more swiftly in victims deficient in folic acid. Though Dr Hills is a deservedly respected authority on Nelson's medical history, I do not find this explanation credible at any level. It partly relies upon a statement Nelson later gave Benjamin Moseley, the surgeon general in Jamaica, which said that 'the fever which destroyed the crews of the different vessels [in the mouth of the San Juan] invariably attacked them from twenty to thirty days after their arrival in the harbour' (Moseley, *Treatise on Tropical Diseases*, p. 165). However, though interesting, this account does not constitute strong historical evidence. It appears to have been made a good time after the event, and is at best only third-hand. Nelson was invalided to Jamaica, and did not witness the progress of the disease sweeping the ships. He may have received his information from others who had been present (Collingwood springs to mind), but whether he heard or rendered it accurately is questionable. Moseley himself, presumably on the authority of other witnesses, contradicted Nelson's account by stating that 'few of the Europeans retained their health above sixteen days' (*Treatise on Tropical Diseases*, pp. 162–3).

Dr Hills's belief that the men were in a pre-scorbutic condition, though founded on a reference to scurvy in the log of the *Hinchinbroke*, rests uncomfortably with Dancer's testimony that the expedition arrived at the San Juan 'in general good health and in great spirits' (Dancer, *A Brief History*, p. 10). Moreover, we know from Dancer that at the fort it was the Indians who fell ill first, and enough perished for the British to appropriate nearly £1,000 for the principal purpose of compensating their relatives at a rate of £25 per man (Colville Cairns, proposals of July 1780, Stephen Kemble papers, William L. Clements Library). Yet the Indians had neither been on the ships nor subject to the dietary deficiencies that supposedly primed the sprue. Similarly the immunity of the Bay of Honduras blacks to the disease (Kemble journal, *Collections*, pp. 15, 24) seems consistent with the resistance some native populations develop to malaria.

The typical symptoms of sprue (weakness, a sore tongue, difficulty in swallowing, fatty stools, weight loss, indigestion, anaemia and diarrhoea) would not, I believe, have generated the description of the disease given by Dancer. In sprue, for example, diarrhoea and dysentery are thought to be precipitating factors for the disease, whereas on the San Juan they were associated with its later phases (Dancer, *A Brief History*, p. 44). Finally, sprue is a chronic rather than an acute, rapidly developing and fatal disease. It attacks individuals sporadically, and is not epidemic. Yet the principal disease of 1780 was so general that Dancer thought it contagious. 'In the beginning,' he said, it was 'dependent on climate &c. and affecting only individuals' but later it became 'evidently contagious, and seized almost every one who came within the infection' (Dancer, *A Brief History*, p. 36). Moseley reported that the expedition eventually cost the British fourteen hundred men (Moseley, *Treatise on Tropical Diseases*, p. 163). That sprue could have simultaneously developed in so many and been so swift and destructive is very hard to believe.

James Kemble, *Idols and Invalids*, pp. 117–19, 120–2, had a stronger candidate in typhoid fever, which incubates in seven to twenty one days and is clinically difficult to distinguish from malaria. More than one ailment was probably at work, but malaria fits the full thrust of the evidence best. Both the season (the beginning of the rains) and the environment (the marshy margins of the river and estuary) were tailor-made for malaria. Dr Peter Walsh, who served with Kemble's force, regarded the wet, close weather as 'the principal cause' of the fevers (*Collections*, pp. 15–16). Though at that time mosquitoes were not known to be the agents of malaria and yellow fever, they created serious problems for the men on the San Juan. Indeed, they even featured in the articles of capitulation that led to the surrender of the Spanish fort in May, something that may have been unprecedented in military history. Thus, in the eighth article, the British commander, Captain Polson, undertook 'to do my utmost to keep the mosquitoes within the bounds of moderation' (Robert Beatson, *Naval and Military Memoirs*, 6, p. 230).

In an effort to clarify the matter I submitted the data about the San Juan expedition to experts in the Liverpool School of Tropical Medicine, part of the University of Liverpool. H. M. Gilles, Emeritus Professor of Tropical Medicine, thought 'a combination of malignant tertian malaria and typhoid' a 'reasonable possibility' and added, 'If I were to opt for one single diagnosis' it would be 'malignant tertian malaria in patients debilitated by vitamin deficiencies and under nutrition. It is now well accepted that under nutrition is a risk factor for severe malaria and subsequent death.' Dr. Geoff Gill, Reader in Tropical Medicine, broadly agreed: 'Though it is possible for malaria to cause all these features,' he wrote, 'it would be unusual; and my feeling is that there was worse than one illness . . . I would go for malaria and bacillary (bacterial) dysentery.' For Dr Gill, too, typhoid was a possible suspect, however. On the present evidence this is, perhaps, as far as we can go.

30. Parker to Stephens, 7, 28/4/1780, ADM 1/242; *Janus* muster, ADM 36/8720; and Dalling to Germain, 14/4/1780, CO 137/78.
31. Polson to Kemble, 28/4/1780, *Collections*, p. 208.
32. Polson to Kemble, 1, 12/5/1780, *Collections*, pp. 215, 220.
33. Narrative of Sir Alexander Keith, 1780, CO 137/79: 74; proceedings of a council at Tebuppy, 1/10/1780, CO 137/79: 164; Kemble to Dalling, 19/5 to 11/6/1780, CO 137/78; information of Todd, 25/8/1780, CO 137/78: 239; Polson to Dalling, 30/4/1780, CO 137/77; *Collections*, pp. 14, 31.
34. Forthringham to Parker, 30/4/1780, ADM 1/242.

35. *Hinchingbroke* musters, ADM 36/9510–9511; testimony of Collingwood, 5/12/1780, CO 137/79: 194. Bullen's log (NMM: ADM/L/H113) gives variant details of the fatalities aboard the *Hinchingbroke*.

36. Nelson to Polson, 2/6/1780, *D&L*, 1, p. 33*; Dalling to Nelson, 13/5/1780, Add. MSS 34903. Nelson remained on good terms with the Dalling family, even after the general's death: Louise, Lady Dalling to Nelson, 10/8/1804, NMM: CRK/14.

37. Parker to Stephens, 20/5/1780, ADM 1/242; account of John Tyson, Add. MSS 34990: 36; Nelson to Locker, 23/1/1780, *D&L*, 1, p. 32.

38. Dalling to Germain, 20, 21/5/1780, CO 137/77; Nelson to Paynter, 31/5/1780, Add. MSS 34988.

39. Dalling to Germain, 29/6/1780, CO 137/77.

40. Shaw to Kemble, 27/6/1780, Kemble papers, William L. Clements Library.

41. See Hodgson's narrative, CO 137/80: 322; evidence of William Dalrymple, 6/12/1780, CO 137/79:184; Moseley, *Treatise on Tropical Diseases*, p. 163.

42. Germain to Dalling, 7/12/1780, CO 137/78. For Germain's earlier support of the venture see, for example, his letters to Dalling dated 4 January, 1 March and 5 April 1780 (Germain papers, William L. Clements Library). As late as 1 March, with the rains and their attendant threat of disease looming, Germain urged Dalling to make 'the most vigorous efforts' to implement the plan and reported that three thousand reinforcements were ready to sail from England to Jamaica.

43. *D&L*, 1, p. 7.

44. Joseph and William Brodie Gurney, *Trial of Edward Marcus Despard*, p. 174. Clifford D. Conner has written a biography of Despard.

IX Fighting Back (pp. 176–90)

1. The *Janus* muster (ADM 36/8720) says that Nelson's commission was dated 22 March and that he appeared on 18 May, but I have followed the *Janus* log here (ADM 52/2359).

2. Compare the musters of *Hinchingbroke* (ADM 36/9510–9511) with that of the *Janus*. I did not find a muster for the *Victor*.

3. Nelson to Ross, 12/6/1780, Royal Naval Museum, Portsmouth.

4. James S. Clarke and John McArthur, *Life and Services*, 1, p. 61.

5. Robert Wood, Archibald Bruce and James Melling, 1/9/1780, ADM 1/242; Nelson to Parker, 30/8/1780, ADM 1/242.

6. Parker to Nelson, 1/9/1780, Add. MSS 34903; Parker to Stephens, 5/9/1780, ADM 1/242.

7. Account of the Duke of Clarence, Add. MSS 34990: 54.

8. M. Eyre Matcham, *Nelsons of Burnham Thorpe*, p. 106; Nelson to Fanny, 27/6/1794, Monmouth MSS, E820.

9. Nelson to Fanny, 28/6/1794, Monmouth MSS, E821.

10. Linda Colley, *Britons*, p. 183.

11. Nelson to St Vincent, 23/9/1801, *D&L*, 7, p. ccxxix*; Colin White, 'Nelson and Shakespeare'.

12. Nelson to Ross, 1/9/1780, 12/9/1801, NMM: PST/38, and *D&L*, 4, p. 487.

13. *Lion* muster, ADM 36/9203; *Lion* log books, ADM 51/540 and ADM 52/1847; Cornwallis to Stephens, November 1780, ADM 1/1613; *D&L*, 1, p. 8; Nelson to Cornwallis, 31/1/1799, Hist. MSS Commission, *Various Collections*, 6, p. 392.

14. Nelson to Locker, 5/3/1781, *D&L*, 1, p. 39.

15. R. S. Neale, *Bath*, pp. 17, 22–3.

16. Nelson to Locker, 23/1/1781, *D&L*, 1, p. 35; Louis Hodgkin, *Nelson and Bath*, pp. 11–12.

17. Nelson to Locker, 23/1/1781, 15/2/1781, *D&L*, 1, pp. 35, 38. For the diagnosis see

James Kemble, *Idols and Invalids*, pp. 120–22, and Anne-Marie Ewart Hills in *ND*, 7 (2000), p. 240.

18. Nelson to Locker, 15/2/1781, 5/3/1781, *D&L*, 1, pp. 28, 39; *The Bath Chronicle*, 1/3/1781.

19. Nelson to Locker, 15/2/1781, *D&L*, 1, p. 38.

20. Nelson to Locker, 21/2/1781, *D&L*, 1, p. 39. For Kingsmill (formerly Brice), see *NC*, 5 (1801), pp. 189–212. He was then a senior captain, within hailing distance of achieving flag rank, and therefore a potentially useful patron. Nelson wrote to him regularly in succeeding years, but few of the letters have survived.

21. *Illustrated London News*, 6/6/1846; notes and drawings of James Frederick King (b. 1781), whose father obtained Suckling's house after the latter's death in 1798: George Gater and Walter H. Godfrey, *Old St. Pancras and Kentish Town*, pp. 53–4, pl. 110. The location of the house, long since demolished, is incorrectly identified by Thomas Foley, *Nelson Centenary*, p. 16. It would seem to have been near the junction of present-day Kentish Town and Castle roads.

22. Jenkinson to Sandwich, 12/2/1781, Add. MSS 38308; 'Nelson's Appointment to the Command of the *Albemarle*, 1781'.

23. Account with Robert Winch, 5/5/1781–2/7/1781, Western MSS 3676, Wellcome Library, London.

24. Nelson to Stephens, 23/1/1784, NMM: ADM/C/653; Accounts, 1781, 1784, Western MSS 3676, Wellcome Library, London.

25. Nelson to William, 7/5/1781, Add. MSS 34988; James Harrison, *Life*, 1, p. 66; William Nelson's statement, 1799, NMM: PHB/15.

26. Nelson to William, 24/8/1781, Add. MSS 34988. These paragraphs also depend upon the logs of the *Albemarle*, ADM 51/4110 and ADM 52/2136; Hinton's log, NMM: ADM/L/A72; and the ship's musters, ADM 36/10081–10082.

27. *Norfolk Chronicle*, 8/9/1781; Nelson to William, 19/10/1781, 18/12/1781, Add. MSS 34988.

28. Nelson to Stephens, October 1781, ADM 1/2222; Hinton, passing certificate, 4/2/1779, ADM 107/7; Bromwich, return of service, 1817, ADM 9/6: no. 1800.

29. Nelson to Locker, 21/10/1781, *D&L*, 1, p. 47. Nelson to William, 9/9/1781, 19/10/1781, Add. MSS 34988.

30. Orders of 7, 26/9/1781 and 17/10/1781, ADM 2/111.

31. Nelson to Admiral Robert Roddam, 22/10/1781, Add. MSS 34961; Nelson to Stephens, 3, 6 and 24/9/1781, ADM 1/2222.

32. Nelson to William, 24/8/1781, 18/12/1781, Add. MSS 34988.

33. *D&L*, 1, p. 8; Admiralty to Nelson, 23/10/1781, Add. MSS 34933.

X 'The Poor *Albemarle*' (pp. 191–227)

1. Nelson to Locker, 22/12/1781, *D&L*, 1, p. 49. The *Albemarle* logs (Nelson's in ADM 51/4110; Trail's in ADM 52/2136; and Hinton's and Bromwich's in NMM: ADM/L/A72) are used throughout this chapter. For Bromwich's story of the Danish midshipman see James Stanier Clarke and John McArthur, *Life and Services*, 1, p. 66.

2. Nelson to Locker, 22/12/1781, *D&L*, 1, p. 49; Nelson to Stephens, 18/12/1781, Add. MSS 34961; and Dickson to Stephens, 20, 30/11/1781 and 8, 18/12/1781, ADM 1/1709.

3. Nelson to Locker, 2/1/1781, *D&L*, 1, p. 52; *Albemarle* musters, ADM 36/10081–82. Those who served as midshipmen aboard the *Albemarle* during Nelson's command were George Barlow, James Boyd, David Carnegie, George Dawson, Charles Hardy, John Hughes, George Mitchell, Alexander St Clair, John Williams and John Wright. The captain's servants were John Cussans, Thomas Easton, William Field, James Gregory, John Goodall, Frank Lepee, Samuel Lightfolly, Dennis O'Neal, Samuel Simpkin, Henry Wilson and John Wood.

4. Nelson to William, 25/1/1782, Add. MSS 34988; Dickson to Stephens, 21, 27/12/1781 and 5/1/1782, ADM 1/1709 and ADM 1/1710; Payne to Stephens, 15/1/1782, ADM 1/2307; Hughes to Stephens, 1–3/1/1782, ADM 1/655.

5. *DNB*, 10, pp. 186–7.

6. Nelson to Stephens, 31/1/1782, Add. MSS 34933; report on the *Albemarle*, 1781, ADM 95/30/24.

7. Hughes to Nelson, 11/1/1782, Add. MSS 34961.

8. Nelson to William, 8/2/1782, Add. MSS 34988.

9. Nelson to Hughes, 12/1/1782, Add. MSS 34933.

10. *Albemarle* log, 26/1/1782, ADM 51/4110; Nelson to William, 28/1/1782, Add. MSS 34988; Nelson to Stephens, 20/1/1782, ADM 1/2223; Nelson to Stephens, 31/1/1782, Add. MSS 34933.

11. Clarke and McArthur, *Life and Services*, 1, p. 68.

12. Nelson to William, 25/1/1782, Add. MSS 34988.

13. Nelson to Proby, 21/1/1782, Add. MSS 34961; NMM: SAN/4, p. 15.

14. Nelson to Locker, 5/2/1782, 2/4/1782, *D&L*, 1, pp. 56, 61.

15. Nelson to William, 8/2/1782, Add. MSS 34988.

16. David Cordingley, *Heroines and Harlots*, pp. 13, 14, 201.

17. Tom Pocock, *Sailor King*, p. 71. For a discussion of this subject see N. A. M. Rodger, *Wooden World*, pp. 75–81.

18. Bartholomew Ruspini, *Treatise on Teeth*, p. 64. For an account of mercurial treatments of venereal complaints see William Northcote, *Marine Practice of Physic and Surgery*, 2, chap. 8.

19. Nelson to Locker, 2/4/1782, *D&L*, 1, p. 61; Nelson to his father, 8/3/1782, NMM: STW/1.

20. Nelson to Locker, 1/6/1782, *D&L*, 1, p. 64.

21. Nelson to Locker, 1/6/1782, *D&L*, 1, p. 64; Pringle to Stephens, 25/4/1782, ADM 1/2307; *Daedalus* log, ADM 51/224; Nelson to Worth, 1/7/1782, Add. MSS 34961.

22. Nelson to Ross, 9/8/1783, Royal Naval Museum, Portsmouth.

23. Nelson to Locker, 19/10/1782, *D&L*, 1, p. 66.

24. In addition to the logs and musters of the *Albemarle* see the log of the *Pandora*, ADM 51/668, and Inglis to Stephens, 10/9/1782, ADM 1/998.

25. The logs and muster vary in details. Hinton's seems to have Nelson taking a Cape Cod schooner on 23 August.

26. Testimonial for Carver, 17/8/1782, in Tom Pocock, *Young Nelson in the Americas*, p. 175; Gersham Bradford, 'Nelson in Boston Bay'. Francis William Blagdon, *Orme's Graphic History*, p. 60, gives a variant account of the episode, based on a letter of 21 December 1805, but the details are not borne out by the ships' logs. Some historians (for example Colin White, *Nelson Encyclopaedia*, p. 91) have also dismissed the more traditional story of Carver and the *Harmony*, which appears to have come from Bromwich (Clarke and McArthur, *Life and Services*, 1, pp. 72–3) but it is broadly confirmed by the logs and musters. Hinton's log for 18 August, for instance, reports: 'Brought to a schooner with stock and vegetables that came off from Plymouth on purpose to supply us.' However, I have had to modify it. Carver's name does not appear among the lists of Nelson's prisoners, and he cannot have been aboard the schooner taken in July, as generally represented.

27. For this incident see the logs for 15 August 1782; Nelson to Locker, 19/10/1782, *D&L*, 1, p. 66; *D&L*, 1, p. 8; Clarke and McArthur, *Life and Services*, 1, p. 74; Salter to Digby, 2/8/1782, ADM 1/490; and 'Particulars Respecting the French Fleet Now on the Coast of America', August 1782, ADM 1/490.

28. Nelson to Locker, 19/10/1782, *D&L*, 1, p. 66. For scurvy see Christopher Lloyd and

J. L. S. Coulter, *Medicine in the Navy*. The man who died on the *Albemarle* during this period was a seaman, Robert Wild, but his death on 5 September cannot be positively linked to the scurvy.

29. Clarke and McArthur, *Life and Services*, 1, p. 76. The story is supported by the logs and the pilot's name appears in the muster.

30. Mrs Harrower, daughter of James Thompson, quoted by Henry H. Miles, 'Nelson at Quebec', p. 271; 'Catallus' of 1783, J. M. Le Moine, *Picturesque Quebec*, pp. 232–3. Alexander Davison supplied an account of Nelson's infatuation for a Canadian girl to Clarke and McArthur, *Life and Services*, 1, pp. 76–7, but did not identify her. In the 1860s local Quebec historians interested themselves in the matter and eventually agreed that the object of Nelson's attentions was Mary Simpson. See several works by Le Moine: *Album Canadien*, pp. 57–60; *Chronicles of the St Lawrence*, p. 198; *Picturesque Quebec*, pp. 232–5; and *Historical Notes on Quebec*, pp. 85–6; and particularly the paper by Miles, cited above. Following references to *some* of this material by Walter Sichel, *Emma, Lady Hamilton*, p. 157, and Carola Oman, *Nelson*, pp. 46–7, 684–5, several biographers have alluded to Mary Simpson without making any attempt to verify or amplify the information. For the present account the original Canadian sources were re-evaluated, and additional materials examined, to correct misstatements and shed new light on Mary's circumstances.

The identification of Mary as the girl to whom Nelson lost his heart is highly probable. Davison's profile yields several key facts that fit Mary perfectly: she was North American by birth, unmarried but eligible, became friends with Nelson during his brief visit to Quebec in 1782, and subsequently married and lived in London, England. Moreover, Davison would have been well informed about Mary. He knew her in Canada, and probably also in England. See Haldimand's diary of 1786 for social engagements involving the Davisons and Robert Mathews, later Mary's husband, in London (Douglas Brymner, ed., *Report on Canadian Archives*).

31. It is unclear where or when Mary was born. There appear to be no surviving baptismal records for the Anglican Cathedral of Quebec before 1768. On no known authority Le Moine says Mary was a mere sixteen-year-old in 1782. The only official record of her age that I have found is the certificate of death, dated 30 October 1840. Her age was then given as eighty, probably on the authority of her servant, Elizabeth Newton, who was present at her death. This age was accepted in published obituaries and would have made Mary twenty-three when she met Nelson, a year his junior. It sounds more probable. Had she been sixteen, and therefore underage, Davison would surely have mentioned this among his reasons for objecting to Nelson proposing marriage. See death certificate of Mary Mathews, 1840, subdistrict of St Luke's, General Register Office, London; *Gentleman's Magazine* (1840), p. 671. For her father's service, James Thompson junior's memorandum, James Thompson papers, Archives Nationales du Quebec; Le Moine, *Historical Notes*, p. 86; *Dictionary of Canadian Biography*, 6 (1987), pp. 768–70.

32. *Quebec Gazette*, 5/12/1781, and the diary of James Thompson, 1781, James Thompson papers, Archives Nationales du Quebec, upon which this account is largely based. For Bandon Lodge consult Le Moine, *Historical Notes*, pp. 85–6, who, however, believed the house was occupied by the Prentices in 1781. The details of Bandon Lodge and Freemason's Hall may be confused (Le Moine, *Album Canadien*, p. 58, and *Picturesque Quebec*, p. 234; Miles, 'Nelson at Quebec', pp. 258–9).

33. *Quebec Gazette*, 12/4/1781.

34. James Thompson diary, 29/3/1781, James Thompson papers, Archives Nationales du Quebec. Mary may have had a brother James. Certainly a James Simpson appears several times in the local newspaper, in 1823 becoming a town constable (*Quebec Gazette*, 26/7/1792, 15/10/1801, 25/10/1804, 21/4/1823 and 28/7/1823). However, there was more

than one Simpson family in the town. A Mary Simpson was licensed to sell liquor in Quebec in 1766 (*Quebec Gazette*, 4, 8 and 29/12/1766) and another was married in 1787 (marriage records of the Anglican Cathedral of Quebec, 1768–95, Archives Nationales du Quebec), though this last was illiterate and apparently unrelated to our Mary.

35. Nelson to his father, 19/10/1782, *D&L*, 1, p. 67.

36. *Gentleman's Magazine* (1814), ii, p. 92. A useful sketch of Mathews may be found in *Dictionary of Canadian Biography*, 5 (1983), pp. 584–5.

37. Mary Mathews to Thompson, 9/1/1806, James Thompson papers, Archives Nationales du Quebec; John Sugden, 'Nelson in the St Lawrence', which contains material from the Frederick Haldimand papers; and Nelson to the commissioners of the navy and the Navy Office, 14/10/1782, Add. MSS 34933: 5. The Davisons are treated in *Dictionary of Canadian Biography* and by Jim Saunders in 'A Tribute of Record' and 'Alexander Davison and Horatio Nelson'.

38. The story is recorded by Clarke and McArthur, *Life and Services*, 1, pp. 76–7.

39. John H. Chapman, ed., *Register Book of Marriages*, 2, p. 191; Mathews to Thompson, 9/12/1803, and George Thompson to his father, 5/11/1804, both in James Thompson papers, Archives Nationales du Quebec.

40. George Thompson to his father, 9/1/1806, and Mary Mathews to Thompson, 9/1/1806, James Thompson papers, Archives Nationales du Quebec.

41. Will of Robert Mathews, 6/9/1813, PRO: PROB 11/1559: no. 484; Mary to Mrs Thompson, 6/12/1831, James Thompson papers, Archives Nationales du Quebec. In his will Mathews left £502 to his son, to be added to £998 the boy had already been bequeathed by Mathews's late nephew, Simon Fraser. Mary was an executor.

42. Nelson to Locker, 19/10/1782, *D&L*, 1, p. 66; *Pandora* log, ADM 51/668; Worth to Stephens, 26/11/1782, ADM 1/2676; Nelson to Digby, 11/11/1782, Add. MSS 34961. Mary Simpson has been the heroine of romantic fiction, especially Jean N. McIlwraith's *A Diana of Quebec* (Toronto, 1912) and Anne Hollingworth Wharton's *A Rose of Old Quebec* (Philadelphia, 1913).

43. The Digby–Hood dispute is treated in Pocock, *Sailor King*. For the war off mainland America see John A. Tilley, *British Navy and the American Revolution*, and David Syrett, *Royal Navy in American Waters*.

44. Duke of Clarence account, Add. MSS 34990: 54; Clarke and McArthur, *Life and Services*, 1, pp. 78–9. An interesting letter Nelson is represented to have written to Charles Pilford on 13 November 1782 describes the meeting with William Henry and predicts that the prince would 'make a good sailor' and become a credit to the service. Strangely, there are two copies of this private letter (New York Historical Society; Monmouth MSS, E478), one of them previously owned by a collector of autographs in New York in 1869. A similar Nelson to Pilford letter, dated the following day (Add. MSS 57946) also presages the future: 'my interest at home you know is next to nothing, the name of Nelson being little known. It may be different one of these days. A good chance only is wanting to make it so.' Although published long ago (*Notes and Queries*, 8th series, 11 (1897), p. 201) and congruent with Nelson's thought, it was believed by the British Museum to be the work of Robert Spring, an American forger. The creation of both letters may have been prompted by a study of Nelson to Locker, 17/11/1782, *D&L*, 1, p. 68.

45. Digby made no reference to the disagreement when reporting Nelson's transfer to Stephens, 16/11/1782, ADM 1/490, but Nelson's own letters tell their own story. See also Hood to Digby, 13, 20/11/1782, NMM: Hoo/6.

46. Nelson to Locker, 17/11/1782, *D&L*, 1, p. 68; Digby to Stephens, 13/9/1782, ADM 1/490; *L'Aigle* muster, ADM 36/9638. Peacock had been promoted to post-captain in 1780. A commemorative portrait by Rigaud shows a slim man with a sorrowful expression in a mannered wig and full-dress uniform (NMM).

47. Nelson to Locker, 17/11/1782, *D&L*, 1, p. 68.
48. Clarke and McArthur, *Life and Services*, 1, pp. 77–9; Nelson to Locker, 17/11/1782, *D&L*, 1, p. 68.
49. Kenneth Breen, 'George Bridges, Lord Rodney', p. 240. For Hood see Dorothy Hood, *The Admirals Hood*; Michael Duffy, 'Samuel Hood, First Viscount Hood'; Brian Tunstall and Nicholas Tracy, *Naval Warfare*; and Tilley, *British Navy and the American Revolution*.
50. Hood to Jackson, 16/4/1782, David Hannay, ed., *Letters Written*, p. 101.
51. Hood to Pigot, 22/11/1782, NMM: Hoo/6; Hood to Stephens, 5/12/1782, ADM 1/313.
52. Hood to Jackson, 29/1/1783, *Letters Written*, p. 155; Nelson to Locker, 25/2/1783, *D&L*, 1, p. 71; Hood to Rowley, 17/1/1783, NMM: Hoo/6; Hood to Pigot, 1/2/1783, ADM 1/313; 'Account of Vessels Taken', enclosed in Hood to Stephens, 5/2/1783, ADM 1/313.
53. Nelson to Locker, 25/2/1783, *D&L*, 1, p. 71; Hood to Pigot, 18/2/1793, NMM: Hoo/6.
54. The incident is reconstructed from logs of the *Albemarle*, *Resistance* (ADM 51/777), *Drake* (ADM 51/238) and *Tartar* (ADM 51/973); Nelson to Hood, 9/3/1783, *D&L*, 1, p. 73; Nelson to Cunningham, 8/3/1783, *ND*, 1 (1984), p. 164; Christopher C. Lloyd, ed., *James Trevenen*, p. 56; Clarence's account, Add. MSS 34990: 54; and Nelson to Hood, 6/4/1783, NMM: Hoo/28.
55. The details of these final prizes are variously given, even in the logs. See also the muster; James Harrison, *Life*, 1, pp. 73–5; Clarke and McArthur, *Life and Services*, 1, p. 82; Nelson to Locker, 26/11/1783, *D&L*, 1, p. 88; Nelson to William, 4/12/1783, Add. MSS, 34988; and Nelson to Pigot, 21/4/1783, NMM: Hoo/6.
56. Nelson to Hood, 6/4/1783, NMM: Hoo/28.
57. Hood to Nelson, 6/5/1783, ADM 1/2223.
58. Nelson to Locker, 25/2/1783, *D&L*, 1, p. 71.
59. Robert Huish, *William the Fourth*, pp. 12.–26; Hood to Pigot, 21/4/1783, NMM: Hoo/6.
60. Nelson to Locker, 26/6/1783, *D&L*, 1, p. 75.

XI Love in St-Omer (pp. 228–48)

1. Poor rates, St Martin-in-the-Fields, Westminster Archives Centre, London, F582 and F584 (1783–4).
2. Nelson to Locker, 12/7/1783, *D&L*, 1, p. 76; James Stanier Clarke and John McArthur, *Life and Services*, 1, p. 84; K. S. Cliff, 'Alexander Davison's Chambers'.
3. Nelson to William, 4 and 23/7/1783, NMM: BRP/6 and Add. MSS 34988; Nelson to Locker, 31/7/1783, *D&L*, 1, p. 78.
4. *Albemarle* logs, ADM 51/4110, ADM 52/2136, and NMM: ADM/L/A72.
5. Nelson to Locker, 12/7/1783, *D&L*, 1, p. 76; Nelson to Keppel, 20/8/1783, ADM 1/2223; Bromwich, passing certificate, 7/8/1783, ADM 107/9.
6. Nelson to Stephens, 9/7/1783, 18/10/1783, ADM 1/2223; Nelson to Ross, 9/8/1783, Royal Naval Museum, Portsmouth; *Albemarle* pay book, ADM 34/67.
7. Nelson to Ross, 9/8/1783, Royal Naval Museum, Portsmouth; Nelson to William, 20/8/1783, Add. MSS 34988.
8. Nelson to Stephens, 8/10/1783, ADM 1/2223.
9. James Macnamara died on 1 March 1802. He has often been confused with the officer of the same name who entered the navy in 1782, fought a celebrated duel in Hyde Park in 1803, and died a rear admiral on 15 January 1826. Nelson knew both men and they may have been related. See also Victor Sharman in *ND*, 7 (2002), p. 776.
10. Nelson to Locker, 2/11/1783, *D&L*, 1, p. 82.
11. Nelson to William, 10/11/1783, Add. MSS 34988. This and the letter to Locker cited above are the principal authorities for Nelson's journey.

12. Laurence Sterne, *Life and Opinions of Tristram Shandy*, vol. 7, chap. ix.

13. Carola Oman, *Nelson*, p. 56.

14. John R. Gwyther, 'Nelson at Saint-Omer'. This article contains valuable local research conducted by M. Bernard Level. The actual house Nelson used is unknown, but it could have been either 136 rue de Dunkerque or 5, 7 or 9 rue Hendricq.

15. Barbara E. Rooke, ed., *The Friend*, 1, p. 547.

16. Nelson to Locker, 26/11/1783, *D&L*, 1, p. 88.

17. Joseph Foster, *Alumni Oxonienses*, 1, p. 24; *London Magazine* (1758), p. 315. In his letters Nelson referred only to 'an English clergyman, Mr Andrews', without either naming him fully or indicating his place of origin or habitation in England. His daughter, to whom Nelson proposed marriage, was also unnamed, and biographers called her 'Miss Andrews'. It took me the summers of 1992 and 1993 to identify 'Mr Andrews' as the Reverend Robert Andrews, husband of Sarah (née Hawkins), and the father of at least three daughters and four sons, including Elizabeth, Charlotte, George, Henry and Hugh. These findings, with full reference to relevant naval, military, parish and probate records, were published in a series of articles: John Sugden, 'Captain George Andrews'; John Sugden, 'Looking for Bess'; and John Sugden and Raymond and Ann Evans, 'More Light on George and Elizabeth Andrews'. Raymond and Ann Evans generously allowed me to use their investigations into George's later life in Devonshire. To these must now be added John R. Gwyther, 'Nelson at Saint-Omer', pp. 114–15, which supplies details of Robert Andrews's earlier stay in St-Omer.

   Tom Pocock kindly contributed two portraits to the last of my papers, both given him by a Vincent Lawford. Neither sitter is identified, though Mr Lawford felt sure that one, showing a post-captain, depicted George Andrews. He is less unequivocal about the accompanying portrait, but guessed it might have been a sister of Andrews. Though the last portrait has been published as a likeness of Elizabeth Andrews (Sugden, 'Looking For Bess', p. 388; Tom Pocock, *Nelson's Women*) there is no real evidence to support the identification, and it is in many respects most unlikely. If the post-captain is George Andrews, the matching portrait probably showed his lady, Ann Andrews.

   There are pieces of the puzzle for future Nelson scholars to find, including the baptismal records of the Andrews children, which would provide a full listing of the family, their ages and birthplaces. Although Kelston in Somerset was the family seat of the Hawkins side of the family, I incline to the view that Elizabeth Andrews was probably born in London. Her father seems to have been a Londoner, and the pay book of the *Boreas* (ADM 35/242) gives London as the birthplace of George Andrews.

18. *DNB*, 9, pp. 206–9, 211; B. and A. P. Burke, *Peerage and Baronetage*, pp. 1113–15; will of Sir Caesar Hawkins, June 1785, PRO: PROB 11/1140.

19. This paragraph revises John Sugden, 'Captain George Andrews', in the light of his passing certificate, 4/10/1787, ADM 107/10. See also his memorials to the Admiralty, 26/2/1806, April 1808, and 20/5/1810, ADM 1/1451, 1/1452 and 1/1453.

20. Nelson to Locker, 26/11/1783, *D&L*, 1, p. 88; Nelson to William, 4/12/1783, Add. MSS 34988. The other older daughter has not yet been identified. I suspect that she was named Sarah, after her mother, but there is no satisfactory evidence of this.

21. For Ann Nelson's character see M. Eyre Matcham, *Nelsons of Burnham Thorpe*, p. 105. Her letters from Nelson are mentioned in Nelson to his father, 8/3/1783, NMM: STW/1. Her death was noticed in the *Bath Chronicle and Weekly Gazette*, 20/11/1783; Nelson to Locker, 26/11/1783, *D&L*, 1, p. 88; Ron C. Fiske, *Notices of Nelson*, p. 7; and NMM: GIR/6. In the event of the death of her father, Ann bequeathed Horatio and Susanna £200 each; Edmund and Suckling £100 each; and Catherine £500, with the balance to be divided between all five: will of Ann Nelson, 2/11/1783, PRO: PROB 11/1111, no. 631. There is no explanation of her omission of William and Maurice, but

after the Reverend Edmund's death, William seems to have forgotten that his siblings shared unequally in Ann's legacy (William to Nelson, 14/5/1802, Alfred Morrison, *Hamilton and Nelson Papers*, 2, p. 189). Additional details and documentation relating to Ann can be found in John Sugden, 'Tragic and Tainted? The Mystery of Ann Nelson' and John Sugden, 'New Light on Ann Nelson'. The posthumous elaboration of Ann's tomb and the adjacent interment of a relative, Elizabeth Matcham, suggest she was affectionately remembered by the family.

22. Nelson to Locker, 26/11/1783, *D&L*, 1, 88; Nelson to William, 4/12/1783, Add. MSS 34988.

23. Nelson to Locker, 26/11/1783, *D&L*, 1, p. 88; Count de Deux Ponts to Nelson, 23/3/1784, Add. MSS 34903.

24. Nelson to William, 28/12/1783 to 3/1/1784, Add. MSS 34988.

25. Nelson to Suckling, 14/1/1784, *D&L*, 1, p. 93.

26. Nelson to William, 31/1/1784, Add. MSS 34988.

27. Wills of Elizabeth Warne, 1836, and Roger Warne, 2/3/1842, PRO: PROB 11/1893 and 2026; death certificates of Elizabeth Warne, 25/10/1837, and Roger Warne, 22/7/1845, Central Registry Office, London; *Gentleman's Magazine* (1837), ii, p. 659, and (1845), ii, p. 324; and *Bath Journal*, 23, 30/10/1837.

28. Nelson to William, 20/1/1784, Add. MSS 34988.

29. Nelson to William, 20/1/1784, Add. MSS 34988.

30. Hood to Jackson, 29/1/1783, David Hannay, ed., *Letters Written*, p. 155; Nelson to William, 20/1/1784, 2/4/1784, Add. MSS 34988.

31. Nelson to William, 8/2/1782, 31/1/1784, 2/4/1784, Add. MSS 34988, and Nelson to Locker, 23/1/1784, *D&L* 1, p. 97; Esther Hallam Moorhouse, *Nelson in England*, p. 34. Fox held one of the two Westminster seats, although he ran in second to Hood, and his vote and influence were much reduced.

32. Nelson to William, 31/1/1784, Add. MSS 34988; *Bath Chronicle*, 5/2/1784.

33. Poor rates, St Martin-in-the-Fields, Westminster Archives Centre, London, F 582 and F 584 (1783-4).

34. Orders of 19/3/1784, 6/5/1784, ADM 2/115.

35. Nelson to William, 29/3/1784, Add. MSS 34988.

36. Howe to Hood, 2/7/1787, NMM: Hoo/2; Hood to Nelson, 26/8/1784, Add. MSS 34937. Hood had been made an Irish peer two years before. Boyle, whom Nelson thought a 'charming' young man, was a native of Somerset and the second son of the seventh Earl of Cork. He claimed to have been inspired to join the service by a visit to his father at Plymouth. Officially Boyle had entered the navy at ten, as captain's servant to John Carter Allen of the *Gibraltar*, served Hyde Parker in the same capacity in the *Latona* and *Goliath*, and gone through a naval academy at Greenwich. Talbot was the son of Richard Talbot of Malahide Castle, County Dublin, one of the Irish gentry. Although Tatham was a twenty-year-old Londoner, he also enjoyed Hood's patronage. After Nelson's ship was paid off in 1787, both Talbot and Tatham were transferred to Hood's *Barfleur*, while Boyle went to the flagship of Admiral Peyton. Boyle and Talbot rose to flag rank, but while Tatham was popular and competent his career was damaged by a court martial. In 1803 he commanded a brig in the English Channel. Charles Lock of Exeter, who joined Nelson at Portsmouth on 27 April 1784, may also have been a Hood man. For all of the above see Nelson to Cork, 22/7/1787, Monmouth MSS, E28; ADM 9/2: no. 54 (Boyle); 'Biographical Memoir of the Hon. Captain Courtenay Boyle'; John Marshall, *Royal Navy Biography*, 2, pt I, pp. 104–7; William O'Byrne, *Naval Biographical Dictionary*, pp. 1156–7; J. W. Norie, *Naval Gazetteer*, p. 382; Marsh to Nelson, 3/12/1788, Add. MSS 34903; Richard Vesey Hamilton and John Knox Laughton, ed., *Above and Under Hatches*, p. 116; Hood to Alexander Hood, 8/11/1790, Add. MSS

35194; and *United Service Journal* 45 (1844), p. 320 (an obituary of Boyle, who died 21 May 1844 at the age of seventy-four).

37. Account for tableware, 20/3/1784, Western MSS 3676, Wellcome Library, London. My account of the manning of the *Boreas* depends throughout on its muster (ADM 36/10525) and pay book (ADM 35/242). Consult also Rupert Willoughby, 'Nelson and the Dents', and Nelson to Stephens, 14/4/1787, ADM 1/2223.

38. For Jameson, ADM 1/5315, and Power, ADM 107/17: no. 77.

39. Nelson to Stephens, 26/12/1788, *D&L*, 1, p. 277, and Nelson to the Navy Board, 5/12/1788, Add. MSS 34903.

40. For Robert Parkinson, Stansbury, Nowell and Bishop, see their passing certificates, 4/6/1794, 3/12/1789, 5/12/1786 and 3/9/1788, filed in ADM 6/93, ADM 6/90, ADM 6/89 and ADM 107/11.

There is a serious paper to be written about the 'young gentlemen' ('children', as Nelson called them) of the *Albemarle*, *Boreas* and *Agamemnon*, with a view to establishing the patronage behind the appointments and the extent to which Nelson's 'nursery' fulfilled his ambition of furnishing capable officers. Because protégés were enlisted under various ratings they are not always easy to identify from musters and pay books. Some were entered on the *Boreas* muster on the same day as their captain. Of these, Boyle, Talbot and Tatham were probably preferments of Hood; William Standway Parkinson of London was a recommendation of Captain Pole; and Hardy and Andrews came through other Nelson associates. Hardy, along with Robert Mansell, Andrew Baynton and William Oliver, were transferred to other vessels, the first three within a few months of Nelson taking command.

In time Nelson accommodated other hopefuls, some recommended by colleagues or friends, but a few young men without influence who impressed him. To incorporate the influx and ensure fair play, Nelson juggled the ratings of his young gentlemen creatively, remarking that he had to 'stand friend' to those with no powerful patrons. Some who failed to make the grade had to be disrated. 'The poor ones I only disrated with their own consent,' Nelson said, 'and the younger[s] rated in their room were bound in honour to make their pay as good as before. [The] Honourable Courtenay Boyle, I have understood, did make Mr [Edmund] Bishop, in whose room he was rated, a present when the ship was paid off' (Nelson to Navy Office, 5/12/1788, Add. MSS 34903). Bishop was one of the unsuccessful aspirants, although he remained on the *Boreas* throughout Nelson's command. Promoted midshipman from able seaman, he eventually stepped down to vacate a position for Boyle. Though Bishop subsequently passed his examination for lieutenant on 3 September 1788 he was never commissioned.

Among others slotted in after the first wave were: William Batty, who started as Lieutenant Wallis's servant; Robert Parkinson; eighteen-year-old Alexander R. Kerr of Greenwich, who had begun his career with Captain E. J. Smith of the *Endymion* in 1781, recently been with Captain Charles Cotton on the *Alarm*, and joined the *Boreas* as a supernumerary before Nelson's arrival; twenty-year-old Joshua Beale, who was transferred to Nelson's ship on 23 April 1784; Maurice William Suckling; William Nowell, sent by the captain of the *Scipio*; Charles Lock, who soon moved elsewhere; Thomas Stansbury; Stephen Perdrian, recruited in 1785; and William Warden Shirley, the only son of the governor of the Leeward Islands, who was rated captain's servant on 1 August 1786 at the supposed age of fifteen. In addition to the sources listed in n. 40 above, see Nelson to Stephens, 29/4/1784, ADM 1/2223; Bowyer to Stephens, 5 and 9/5/1784, ADM 1/723; passing certificates in ADM 107/10, p. 231 (Kerr) and 107/17, p. 48 (Suckling); ADM 9/2: no. 312 (Kerr); ADM 9/6: no. 1817 (Suckling); and Marshall, *Royal Navy Biography*, Supplement I, p. 34.

With respect to subsequent performances, the 'class' of the *Boreas* was far more distinguished than that of the *Albermarle*. Eleven individuals populated the latter, but apart from Bromwich none made lieutenant. By comparison, the aspirants of the *Boreas* were under full sail. Two (Boyle and Talbot) became admirals; three (Kerr, Andrews and William Parkinson) post-captains; one, Lock, made commander; and eight (Bromwich, Nowell, Perdrian, Power, Shirley, Stansbury, Suckling and Tatham) became lieutenants. Two, Robert Parkinson and Bishop, passed their lieutenant's examination but never got their commissions confirmed. Some also acquitted themselves well under fire. Andrews, Suckling and Boyle served under Nelson with some success, and Talbot distinguished himself on several occasions, notably in the destruction of a Turkish squadron in 1807, and the taking of the eighty-gun *Rivoli*. He died a GCB. Nelson would have been pleased by Kerr's part in the defeat of the French squadron in the Basque roads in 1809, but not his testimony in extenuation of an incompetent commander-in-chief during the subsequent court martial (John Sugden, 'Lord Cochrane', chap. 6). The impressive record of the 'class' of the *Boreas*, as opposed to that of the *Albermarle*, reflects the greater social standing of its members, as well as any differences in ability.

41. Nelson to William, 19, 29/3/1784, 23/4/1784, Add. MSS 34988; Nelson to Locker, 23/3/1784, *D&L*, 1, p. 100.
42. Nelson to Stephens, 14/4/1784, ADM 1/2223; Stephens to Nelson, 15/4/1784, Add. MSS 34961.
43. Nelson to Locker, 21/4/1784, *D&L*, 1, p. 104.
44. Nelson to William, 25/9/1785, Add. MSS 34988.

XII Hurricane Harbour (pp. 249–81)

1. The dockyard commissioner appears once to have occupied the house used in 1784 by the naval commander of the Leeward Islands station. Presumably when Windsor became available the commissioner released his former habitation. It is not exactly clear where Windsor was situated, other than that it occupied a hill near the dockyard. It may have been on the west side of the strait between the outer and inner anchorages at English Harbour, on the rising ground to the rear of the dockyard storehouses. However, I incline to the view that it occupied Mount Prospect on the eastern side of the strait, above old careening wharves that predated the development of the naval dockyard. A drawing made by Walter Tremenheere (*NC*, 3 [1800], pp. 469–70), showing a house on Mount Prospect flying a flag, may depict Windsor, or another property built on the same site. My description of English Harbour and attempts to resolve the problem of Windsor depend also upon state papers; ADM 140/1173 (a map of 1727); Thomas Jefferys, *West Indian Atlas*, p. 21; George Louis Le Rouge, *Pilote Americain Septentrional*; various materials in Vere Langford Oliver, *History of the Island of Antigua*, especially the letters of Thomas Shirley, 3/11/1781, and John Luffman, 7/10/1786, and the map of 1818, 1, pp. cxxv, cxxx, and facing p. xviii; *Political Magazine*, 3 (1782), p. 39; engraving of the *Boreas* in English Harbour, Lily Lambert McCarthy collection, Royal Naval Museum, Portsmouth; and John Luffman, *Antigua in the West Indies*, a map surveyed in 1787–8.
2. Nelson to Locker, 7/6/1784, 24/9/1784, *D&L*, 1, pp. 109, 110; Nelson to William, 3/5/1785, Add. MSS 34988; Nelson to the Navy Board, 5/12/1788, Add. MSS 34903.
3. Narrative of James Wallis, Add. MSS 34990, published in Geoffrey Rawson, ed., *Letters from the Leeward Islands*, p. 49. Wallis supplied the narrative to Nelson's biographers, Clarke and McArthur, but died in Bath in 1808 before the publication of their book.
4. Hughes to Matcham, 24/6/1806, Add. MSS 34990.
5. Hughes to Matcham, 24/6/1806, Add. MSS 34990; McIntosh to Nelson, 7/6/1784, Add. MSS 34961.
6. Court martial of Thomas Johnston, 7/8/1784, ADM 1/5324.

7. Court martial of John Nairns, 17/8/1784, ADM 1/5324.

8. Nelson to Locker, 7/6/1784, *D&L*, 1, p. 109; Nelson to the governor of St Eustatius, 20/6/1785, Add. MSS 34961.

9. Rawson, *Letters from the Leeward Islands*, p. 49; Hughes to Nelson, 30/6/1784, Add. MSS 34961; Hughes to Stephens, ADM 1/312.

10. The logs of the *Boreas* (ADM 51/125, ADM 51/120 [captain's], ADM 52/2179 [master's] and NMM: ADM/L/B136 [lieutenants']) are used throughout this and the succeeding three chapters. See also Nelson to Damas, 24/7/1784, Add. MSS 34961.

11. Johnston court martial, 7/8/1784, ADM 1/5324.

12. Nairns court martial, 17/8/1784, ADM 1/5324.

13. Richard Vesey Hamilton and John Knox Laughton, ed., *Above and Under Hatches*, pp. 164, 169; court martial of James Wallis, 22,23/9/1784, ADM 1/5324.

14. Nelson to Hughes, 8/9/1784, Add. MSS 34961; Bromwich, return of service, 1817, ADM 9/6: no. 1800. Once confirmed, Bromwich served as a lieutenant on several ships, including the *Terpsichore, Nonsuch* and *Barfleur*. He benefited from the support of John Holloway, one of Nelson's officers, and in 1800–1 was his flag lieutenant on the *Gladiator* in Portsmouth harbour. In 1801 Nelson secured him a post as warden of Portsmouth dockyard through his influence with Earl St Vincent. 'Always happy that I can be useful to an old friend,' Nelson wrote (Nelson to Bromwich, 9/8/1801, NMM: TRN/48). Despite the good opinions of significant officers such as Christopher Parker, Nelson and Holloway, Bromwich died a lieutenant in 1829.

15. Nelson to Locker, 24/9/1784, *D&L*, 1, 110; Nelson to Cornwallis, 25/10/1784, NMM: COR/58.

16. Nelson to Locker, 24/9/1784, 23/11/1784, 16/3/1785, *D&L*, 110, 112, 127; Nelson to Cornwallis, 25/10/1784, NMM: COR/58.

17. Collingwood to Moutray, 17/2/1807, in G. L. Newnham Collingwood, ed., *Correspondence*, 2, 7; Nelson to Locker, 23/11/1784, *D&L*, 1, 112. A scholarly account of Collingwood is still awaited, but the best of several popular biographies is Oliver Warner, *Life and Letters of Vice-Admiral Lord Collingwood*.

18. Nelson to Fanny Nisbet, 13/12/1785, 19/8/1786, Monmouth MSS, E795, and *NLTHW*, 33; Nelson to Locker, 24/9/1784, *D&L*, 1, p. 110; A. M. W. Stirling, ed., *Pages and Portraits*, 1, p. 27; letter of Thomas Luffman, 6/12/1786, Oliver, *History of the Island of Antigua*, 1, p. cxxx.

19. Nelson to Cornwallis, 25/10/1784, NMM: COR/58.

20. John Charnock, *Biographia Navalis*, 6, pp. 331–3; Moutray to Stephens, 13/12/1782, ADM 1/2123, and other correspondence of Moutray in ADM 1/2123–2124.

21. Several of Pemble's letters are filed with the captain's in-letters in ADM 1/2307, but see also his passing certificate, 7/2/1744, ADM 107/3; the marriage registers for Belford, Berwick-upon-Tweed Record Office; and *Gentleman's Magazine* (1784), i, pp. 475–6. Mary's baptism has not yet been found, but her brief obituary in the *Northern Whig* for 1 June 1841 indicates that she was born in 1750 or 1751. Mary died at the Archdeaconry House at Kells, County Meath, in Ireland on 19 May 1841 in her ninety-first year, and thus appears to have been twenty-seven or twenty-eight years younger than her husband, John Moutray (1723–85).

22. Marriage registers of Berwick-upon-Tweed, 1771, Berwick-upon-Tweed Record Office, which describes Mary as 'of this parish'; Augustus J. C. Hare, *Life and Letters*, 1, p. 234; Christina Colvin, ed., *Maria Edgeworth*, p. 356. I am following Edgeworth's biographers in presuming her references were to our Mary Moutray and not the younger namesake of Favour Royal, County Tyrone. Mary was misidentified in John Armstrong Moutray, 'Notes on the Name of Moutray', and errors continue to be made about her in Nelson literature. Eric Bodger of Formby, Liverpool, never published his pioneering

research on the subject, but his files in the Nelson Museum, Monmouth, remain the essential starting point. See also Tom Pocock, 'Captain Nelson and Mrs Moutray' and '"My Dear Sweet Friend"'.

Fortuitously three portraits of Mary Moutray survived until recent times. A chalk and wash half-length profile, made by John Downman in 1781, was formerly in the collection of Sir Henry Ponsonby and recently published by Tom Pocock (Pocock, 'Captain Nelson and Mrs Moutray' and '"My Dear Sweet Friend"'). Sadly the other two portraits, one showing Mary when young and the other in her later years, have been lost. Some time before 1942 a Miss Colston of Ranelagh, Dublin, donated them with related papers and relics to the National Museum of Ireland in Dublin, apparently in the belief that the family line had been extinguished and another safe haven was needed. In 1942 a separate branch of the Moutray family attempted to repossess the portraits, but the Museum declined to part with them, and only allowed copies to be made. Twenty-six years later Eric Bodger, researching a book on Mary Moutray, acquired coloured photographs of both portraits from the Museum. 'The better portrait shows her in her later years,' he wrote, 'and the expression is one of great humour and intelligence; it is evident that, as a girl, she would be [have been] lovely rather than beautiful' (Bodger to Kathleen Moutray, 14/5/1968, and Moutray to Bodger, 23/1/1968, Monmouth MSS, Bodger file). Unfortunately, since 1968 the Museum appears to have lost the Colston–Moutray deposit, including the portraits, and my several efforts over a six-month period to induce a sustained search have been unsuccessful. The National Gallery of Ireland has assured me that the portraits are not in its custody, and I continue to believe that they are somewhere in the National Museum.

23. Collingwood, *Correspondence*, 1, pp. 11–12, and 2, p. 278; and Pigot to Collingwood, 21/7/1783, Add. MSS 14272.

24. Nelson to Locker, 24/9/1784, *D&L*, 1, p. 110; Nelson to William, 16/3/1785, 3/5/1785, Add. MSS 34988. Dorothea, the only daughter of John F. Scrivener of Suffolk, eventually married Dr J. Fisher, Bishop of Salisbury, who may have been a better catch than William Nelson.

25. Collingwood, *Correspondence*, 1, p. 13. These portraits were first reproduced in Oliver Warner, *Portrait of Lord Nelson*. Comparing the logs of the *Boreas* and *Mediator* (ADM 51/589) it is possible to suggest when these interesting experiments were made. The two ships were both in English Harbour on 3–5 December 1784 and 7–11 March 1785. It was most likely on the latter occasion, just before Mary left Antigua, that the incident happened, though Nelson was also at English Harbour on occasions when Collingwood was at nearby St John's: 24 December 1784–3 January 1785 and 5–9 February 1785.

26. Nelson to William, 24/10/1784, Add. MSS 34988.

27. Hughes to Stephens, 23/9/1784, ADM 1/312. Basic manuscript sources for this chapter are filed in CO 152/64, ADM 1/312, ADM 1/2223, Add. MSS 34961 (Nelson letter book), and Add. MSS 14272 (Collingwood papers). Useful published sources are *D&L*, vol. 1, and Rawson, *Letters from the Leeward Islands*.

28. Certificate, 23/4/1785, Western MSS 3668. Wellcome Library, London. For personnel see the *Boreas* muster and pay book: ADM 36/10525 and ADM 35/242. Oliver was discharged to the *Union* on 1 May 1785 and Stansbury to the *Whitby* on 22 June following.

29. Andrew Jackson O'Shaughnessy, *Empire Divided*, p. 246.

30. Brian S. Kirby, 'Nelson and American Merchantmen', p. 139.

31. Collingwood to Hughes, 21/8/1784, Add. MSS 14272.

32. Nelson to Locker, 5/3/1786, *D&L*, 1, p. 156; Hughes to his officers, 12/11/1784, Add. MSS 14272. For this controversy see also Nelson's account of his proceedings, 1786, William L. Clements Library, University of Michigan, Ann Arbor.

33. Nelson to William, 20/2/1785, Add. MSS 34988. Nelson's map (PRO: MPI 1/95) shows his frigate's anchorage as Boreas Cove.

34. Nelson to Hughes, 8/9/1784, Add. MSS 34961.

35. Collingwood to Martin, 1784, Add. MSS 14272; Collingwood to Shirley, 16/12/1784, Add. MSS 14272. Collingwood's interpretation of these two early cases was flatly contradicted by the customs house at St John's. 'I know of no breach of the laws of trade committed by the masters of these vessels,' Samuel Martin, the collector of customs, informed Collingwood on 14 February 1785.

36. Burton to Shirley, 17/12/1784, CO 152/64.

37. Martin to Collingwood, 27/12/1784 and Shirley to Collingwood, 20/12/1784, Add. MSS 14272; Shirley to Hughes, 18/12/1784, CO 152/64.

38. Hughes to the fleet, 30/12/1784, CO 152/64.

39. Council minutes, St Kitts, 7, 8/1/1785, CO 241/18; Kirby, 'Nelson and American Merchantmen', p. 141; statement of June 1785, D&L, 1, p. 136; account of the proceedings of Captain Nelson, 1786, William L. Clements Library.

40. Nelson to Hughes, 9/1/1785, Add. MSS 34961.

41. Collingwood to Hughes, 13/1/1785, Add. MSS 14272.

42. Nelson to Locker, 15/1/1785, D&L, 1, p. 113.

43. Hughes to captains, 29/12/1784; Hughes to Moutray, 29/12/1784, ADM 1/312.

44. DNB, 10, pp. 186–7.

45. Collingwood to Hughes, 13/1/1785, Add. MSS 14272.

46. Nelson to Hughes, 9/1/1785, Add. MSS 34961.

47. Nelson to Sandys and Nelson to Moutray, 6/2/1785, Add. MSS 34961; Moutray to Nelson, 6/2/1785, ADM 1/312.

48. This follows the Boreas log.

49. Nelson to Locker, 5/3/1786, D&L, 1, p. 156.

50. Nelson to Stephens, 17/2/1785, ADM 1/2223; Nelson to Hughes, 12/2/1785, Add. MSS 34961.

51. Moutray to Hughes, 8/2/1785, ADM 1/312; Nelson to William, 24/10/1784, Add. MSS 34988.

52. Hughes to Nelson, 14/2/1785, Add. MSS 34961.

53. Nelson to Hughes, 15/2/1785 and February 1785, Add. MSS 34961; Hughes to Stephens, 14/2/1785, ADM 1/312.

54. A photocopy of the Admiralty's 'instructions for John Moutray, Esq.,' is in Monmouth MSS, Bodger file.

55. Collingwood to his sister, 2/1/1785, E. Hughes, ed., Private Correspondence, p. 16.

56. Nelson to William, 20/2/1785, Add. MSS 34988.

57. Nelson to William, 16/3/1785, Add. MSS 34988.

58. Collingwood, Correspondence, 1, p. 13.

59. Nelson to Locker, 16/3/1785, D&L, 1, p. 127.

60. Nelson to William, 3/5/1785, Add. MSS 34988.

61. Nelson to Collingwood, 28/9/1785, D&L, 1, p. 143; Moutray's correspondence with the Admiralty in ADM 1/2124.

62. Nelson to Fanny, 17/4/1786, Monmouth MSS, E750; marriage settlement, 21/8/1771, Monmouth MSS, Bodger file; will of John Moutray, 16/8/1779, PRO: PROB 11/136, no. 611. The properties concerned were Roxobie, Manor Place, Bowlies farm, Redcraigs and Weddergrowing in the parish of Dunfermline, Fife.

63. Kate Moutray married De Lacey at Westbourne, Sussex, on 29 February 1806.

64. Nelson to Fanny, 25/12/1795, Monmouth MSS, E880; photocopy of Nelson to Moutray, 22/8/1803, in Monmouth MSS, Bodger file.

65. Collingwood to Moutray, 1/11/1808, Collingwood, Correspondence, 2, p. 278. See also 2, pp. 7, 366, and Collingwood to Nelson, 13/14/1797, Add. MSS 34906.

XIII Old Officers and Young Gentlemen (pp. 282–307)

1. Shirley's petition for a baronetcy (granted 1786), CO 152/64; address to Shirley, 1785, CO 152/64; Arthur P. Watts, ed., *Nevis and St Christopher's*. Coincidentally, the absentee lieutenant governor of Antigua was then Major Robert Mathews, a Canadian acquaintance of Nelson who later married Mary Simpson.

2. Shirley to Lord North, 27/7/1783, CO 152/63; Shirley, 3/11/1781, Vere Langford Oliver, *History of the Island of Antigua*, 1, p. cxxv; Andrew Jackson O'Shaughnessy, *Empire Divided*, p. 197.

3. For the pre-revolutionary trade of the West Indian islands see Richard Pares, *Yankees and Creoles*.

4. Thomas Jarvis and Rowland Burton for the assembly, 28/7/1783, CO 152/63.

5. John Luffman, 15/2/1787, Oliver, *History of the Island of Antigua*, 1, p. cxxxi.

6. Burton for the assembly, 9/10/1783, CO 152/63.

7. Shirley to Sydney, 9/2/1784, enclosing petition of St Kitts, CO 152/63; Shirley to Sydney, May and 30/7/1784, CO 152/63.

8. Shirley to Sydney, January 1785, CO 152/64; Sydney to Shirley, 7/11/1784, CO 152/63.

9. Shirley to Nelson, 15/1/1785, Add. MSS 34961.

10. Shirley to Presidents of Councils, 15/1/1785, CO 152/64.

11. Collingwood to Bennett, 15/1/1785 (two letters), Bennett to Collingwood, 15/1/1785, and other documents relating to the *Nancy* in Add. MSS 34961; Nelson to Stephens, 18/1/1785, ADM 1/2223. For the admission that Collingwood's interpretation of the law was correct, see customs officers at St John's, Antigua, to the collector of customs at Nevis, 3/2/1786, CO 152/64.

12. Collingwood to Shirley, 11/1/1785, Add. MSS 14272; Nelson to Shirley, 29/1/1785, Add. MSS 34961.

13. Nelson to Shirley, 29/1/1785, Add. MSS 34961.

14. Shirley to Nelson, 5 and 9/2/1785, Add. MSS 34961.

15. Nelson to Shirley, 1/3/1785, Add. MSS 34961.

16. Shirley to Nelson, 1/3/1785, Add. MSS 34961.

17. Nelson to Shirley, undated, Add. MSS 34961.

18. Sydney to Shirley, 9/4/1785, CO 152/64; Parry to Sydney, 2/4/1785, CO 28/60.

19. Nelson to William, 20/2/1785, 16/3/1785, 13/12/1785 and 29/12/1786, Add. MSS 34988; *Boreas* pay book, ADM 35/242. William's servant, William Kirby, was also kept on the roll. Nelson's ruse was unsuccessful, even though he visited the Navy Office on 20 December 1787 to persuade the government to pay the fictitious wages. He was told that William would not be paid from the day he sailed to England. See Nelson to William, 20/12/1787, NMM: BRP/6.

20. Nelson to Locker, 5/3/1786, *D&L*, 1, p. 156.

21. The case of the *Friends/Polly* can be explored in Wilfred Collingwood's correspondence with the customs officials of St Kitts, April 1785, filed in ADM 1/312: 460–3.

22. Nelson to Sydney, 20/3/1785, *D&L*, 1, p. 129.

23. Martin to Collingwood, 9/5/1785, Add. MSS 14272. Collingwood had intercepted the *Pollies*, built in 1782. Martin argued the owners were 'suffering Loyalists' and accepted the (erroneous) view of Rowland Burton, the king's counsel, that American ships built before 1783 should be deemed British. For this see the correspondence between Collingwood and Martin in the above letter book. In March 1785 Nelson found a Spanish ship unloading illegal cargo, but could not interest the customs in preventing it: Nelson to customs, 23/3/1785, Add. MSS 34961.

24. Printed sources may be found in *D&L*, vol. 1 and Geoffrey Rawson, ed., *Letters from the Leeward Islands*, but see additionally Nelson's representation, 5/5/1785, and Nelson

to the attorney general, 2 and 3/5/1785, Add. MSS 34961; and (for this and the next paragraph) 'List of Vessels Seized', ADM 1/312: 464.

25. For Adye's petition see the council minutes of St Kitts, 8/1/1785, CO 241/18.

26. Hughes to Stephens, 25/5/1785, 20/10/1785, ADM 1/312.

27. Nelson to Stephens, 14/11/1785, Add. MSS 34961; Nelson, 'account of the proceedings of Captain Nelson', 1786, William L. Clements Library, University of Michigan, Ann Arbor; and the Wallis narrative in Rawson, *Letters from the Leeward Islands*, p. 53.

28. Nelson to Adye, 12/9/1785, Monmouth MSS, E497; Ward deposition, 23/6/1786, CO 152/64.

29. Nelson to Stephens, 14/11/1785, Add. MSS 34961.

30. Nelson to Locker, 5/3/1786, *D&L*, 1, p. 156.

31. The ships Collingwood sent in were the *Hazard*, *Little Tom* and *Neptune*. Wilfred Collingwood's prize was the *St. George*. See Bush to Shirley, 30/11/1785, CO 152/64; Collingwood to Martin, 2/7/1785 and Martin to Collingwood, 3/7/1785, Add. MSS 14272.

32. Captain's log of the *Boreas* for 19–21 June 1785; Hughes to Stephens, 25/6/1785, ADM 1/312; Rawson, *Letters from the Leeward Islands*, p. 50.

33. Gill and Menzies to Nelson, 22/7/1785, Add. MSS 34961.

34. Collingwood to Niccolls, 8/10/1785, Add. MSS 14272. The ships were the *Speedwell*, *Maria*, *Lovely Fanny* and *Friendship*. See also Wilfred Collingwood's correspondence with Grenada in 1786, enclosed in Nelson's letters to the Admiralty, ADM 1/2223. For opinions in Barbados see the assembly meeting of 18/1/1786 (including the petition of John Brathwaite, 29/10/1785), CO 31/43.

35. Collingwood's letter book (Add. MSS 14272) is the best source for the case of the *Dolphin*, especially Brandford to Collingwood, 30/7/1785; Collingwood to Brandford, 29/7/1785; Collingwood to Forbes, 12/9/1785; Hughes to Collingwood, 7/10/1785; and Collingwood to Hughes, 9/10/1785. Eventually Collingwood got his expenses for prosecuting the suit, but the appeal against the judgement failed because it was not made within the stipulated time period, and the damages and costs therefore also fell upon him: see Heseltine's letters to Collingwood in 1788, Add. MSS 14272. Also consult ADM 1/312: 499–509, 520–3, and Collingwood's correspondence in ADM 1/1616.

36. Sydney to Nelson, 4/8/1785, Add. MSS 34961; Sydney to Shirley, 4/8/1785, CO 152/64.

37. Nelson to Collingwood, 28/9/1785, *D&L*, 1, p. 143; Hughes to Collingwood, 7/10/1785 (second letter of that date), Add. MSS 14272.

38. Hughes to Stephens, 29/6/1785, ADM 1/312.

39. Nelson, 'account of the proceedings of Captain Nelson', 1786, William L. Clements Library; Nelson to Suckling, 14/11/1785, *D&L*, 1, p. 144.

40. Nelson to Sydney, 17/11/1785, CO 152/64.

41. Sidney to Shirley, 2/6/1785, CO 152/64; Shirley to Sidney, 24/6/1785 and 1/10/1785, CO 152/64; Holloway to Stephens, 23/5/1787, ADM 1/1908.

42. Oath of Seth Warner, 28/5/1784 and customs officers, Antigua, to collector of customs, Nevis, 3/2/1786, CO 152/64.

43. Nelson to Sydney, 4/2/1786, CO 152/64.

44. Shirley to Sydney, 23/7/1785, 2/10/1785, CO 152/64. Shirley's son remained with Nelson until April of the following year when he was transferred to the *Maidstone*.

45. Rawson, *Letters from the Leeward Islands*, p. 66; Rose to Stephens, 24/8/1785, enclosed in Hughes to Collingwood, 16/1/1786, Add. MSS 14272. Indeed, in a curious epilogue we find Hughes writing from retirement in Stoke House, near Cobham, Surrey, in 1796. Learning from Wallis, formerly of the *Boreas*, that some of the prize money was still waiting to be distributed by a 'Mr Nesbitt' of Nevis, he asked Nelson's 'kind assistance' in getting 'my share . . . as Commander in Chief . . .' (Hughes to Nelson, 8/9/1796, NMM: CRK/7).

46. Nelson, 'account of the proceedings of Captain Nelson', 1786, William L. Clements Library; Nelson to Locker, 5/3/1786, D&L, 1, p. 156.

47. Nelson to Fanny Nisbet, 29/3/1786, 23/4/1786, Monmouth MSS, E748, E751.

48. Council minutes of St Kitts with a petition to Shirley, 10/3/1786, CO 241/18.

49. See for example Shirley to Sydney, 7/6/1787, 24/7/1787, CO 152/65.

50. James S. Clarke and John McArthur, Life and Services, 1, p. 113.

51. Nelson to William 12/5/1785, Add. MSS 34988. The captain's log of the Boreas shows the ship anchoring in Nevis Road on 9 May 1785 and moving to St Kitts three days later. I presume this was the occasion Nelson and Fanny met.

XIV Dearest Fanny (pp. 308–37)

1. Carola Oman, Nelson, p. 686, takes the birth date of 1758 from Fanny's sarcophagus, but I prefer the baptism record in the register of Nevis (Vere Langford Oliver, History of the Island of Antigua, 2, p. 71). See also Oliver, 2, pp. 70–1, 301–308, and 3, pp. 443–4, and Edith M. Keate, Nelson's Wife. In view of G. P. B. Naish, Nelson's Letters to His Wife, and the newly discovered collection of Fanny's letters purchased by the National Maritime Museum in 2002 a fresh biography of Lady Nelson is needed.

2. For the Nisbets see also Gentleman's Magazine (1781), p. 491; Hilda Gamlin, Nelson's Friendships, 1, pp. 137–9; John A. Inglis, The Nisbets of Carfin, pp. 2–5; and Terry Coleman, Nelson, p. 72.

3. Richard Pares, West India Fortune, p. 102.

4. Pares, West India Fortune, p. 81; Shirley to Sydney, 12/5/1787, CO 152/65; Nelson to Suckling, 14/11/1785, 9/3/1786, Monmouth MSS, E413, D&L, 1, p. 160.

5. James S. Clarke and John McArthur, Life and Services, 1, pp. 113–14; recollections of Lionel Goldsmid, quoted in Godfrey L. Green, Royal Navy and Anglo-Jewry, p. 87.

6. William Henry to Hood, 15/3/1787, NLTHW, p. 58; A. M. W. Stirling, ed., Pages and Portraits, 1, p. 27, and 2, p. 217; Richard Vesey Hamilton, ed., Sir Thomas Byam Martin, 1, p. 67; and Elliot to his wife, 3/10/1797, NLS, 11051, p. 122.

7. Nelson to William, 28/6/1785, Add. MSS 34988: 65.

8. Nelson to Fanny, 19/8/1785, Monmouth MSS, E743.

9. Nelson to Fanny, 11/9/1785, Monmouth MSS, E744.

10. Nelson to Suckling, 14/11/1785, Monmouth MSS, E413.

11. Nelson to Suckling, 14/11/1785, Monmouth MSS, E413. In fact, Nelson was already befriending two members of the family, descendants of William's uncle, Robert Suckling: Maurice, midshipman of the Boreas, and his brother Robert of the Royal Artillery, then also in the West Indies. See Nelson to Robert Suckling, 15/4/1786, Monmouth MSS, E26.

12. Geoffrey Rawson, ed., Letters from the Leeward Islands, p. 66; accounts in Western MSS 3676, Wellcome Library, London; Nelson to the postmaster general, 10/10/1785, Add. MSS 34961.

13. Nelson to William, 29/12/1786, Add. MSS 34988; Foley, Nelson Centenary, p. 25.

14. Nelson to Fanny, 13/12/1785, Monmouth MSS, E745.

15. Nelson to William, 1/1/1786, Add. MSS 34988.

16. Nelson to Fanny, 3/3/1786, Monmouth MSS, E747.

17. Nelson to Suckling, 9/3/1786, NMM: MON/1.

18. Nelson to Fanny, 3–10/3/1786, Monmouth MSS, E747.

19. Nelson to Fanny, 15/3/1786, 4/5/1786, Monmouth MSS, E748, E752.

20. Nelson to Fanny, 4/5/1786, Monmouth MSS, E752.

21. Holloway to Stephens, 23/5/1787, ADM 1/1908.

22. Hughes to Sydney, 20/10/1785, 7/2/1786, 10/3/1786, ADM 1/312.

23. Parry to Sydney, 28/4/1784, 22/1/1785, 19/8/1785, CO 28/60.

24. For the *Jane and Elizabeth* see also Nelson's letter of 12/11/1790, Add. MSS 34902.

25. Nelson to Hughes, March 1786, Add. MSS 34961; Nelson's narrative, beginning 1 May 1786, Add. MSS 34961; and legal papers Nelson forwarded to the Admiralty, including his journal of the affair, ADM 1/2223. The incident also runs through the published letters and dispatches in *D&L* and *NLTHW*.

26. Brandford to Nelson, 11/4/1786, 14/4/1786, ADM 1/2223.

27. Nelson to Parry, 15/4/1786, Add. MSS 34961. Parry may have been related to the Nisbets. A daughter of one Robert Parry married Walter Nisbet of Mount Pleasant, Josiah's brother (Inglis, *Nisbets of Carfin*).

28. This version of the incident comes from Nelson's deposition before John Horsford, 28/8/1786, Nelson to Sir Charles Middleton, 28/8/1786, and Hughes to Stephens, 14/9/1786, filed in ADM 1/3682. See also the muster and pay books of the *Boreas*, ADM 36/19525 and ADM 35/242, and the 'account of provisions, cask[s], iron hoops', 1783–5, William L. Clements Library, University of Michigan, Ann Arbor.

29. The depositions of McCormick and Mitchell, with other evidence given at the inquest, 16/4/1786, are in CO 28/60: 295–8.

30. Hughes to captains, 21/4/1786, Add. MSS 14272.

31. These depositions dated 22/4/1786 are in CO 28/60: 297.

32. Attempts to apprehend Scotland between 20 and 23 April are described in Parry to Sydney, 31/5/1786, CO 28/60, with its enclosures.

33. Sydney to Parry, 15/9/1786, CO 28/60; Nelson to Fanny, 23/4/1786, Monmouth MSS, E751. Further light might be shed on this affair by numbers of the *Barbados Mercury*, but I could not trace the relevant issues in London or Barbados.

34. *Boreas* muster, ADM 36/10525.

35. Deposition of Daniel Mills and Parry to Stephens, 31/5/1786, ADM 1/3682; lieutenants' logs of the *Boreas*, NMM: ADM/L/B136; Sandys to Stephens, 11/6/1786, ADM 1/2486. The muster of the *Cyrus* contains the name of only one person taken on board at this time. 'Richard Crapnell', entered as a supernumerary on 16 March 1786, may have been John Scotland. See ADM 36/10381. Lieutenant John Johnson and John Callender, commander and master of the *Cyrus*, were found guilty of negligence, but the ship's other officers were acquitted (courts martial, 22/4/1786, ADM 1/5325).

36. Depositions of James Jameson and James Balentine, 28/8/1786, ADM 1/3682.

37. N. A. M. Rodger, *Wooden World*, pp. 225–6. It is worth remembering that during Nelson's lifetime the English penal code gathered in severity, and was known as 'the bloody code'. Whereas less than twenty offences could earn the death penalty under naval discipline, the number of capital statutes in England rose from about fifty in 1688 to some two hundred by 1820. In theory, it was possible to be sentenced to hang for picking pockets of goods worth more than a shilling, for damaging Westminster or London Bridge, or impersonating a pensioner of Greenwich Hospital with a view to falsely obtaining an out-pension. Though, as at sea, there was considerable latitude in applying such statutes, and acquittals and pardons were used to spare malefactors execution in the majority of cases, the penal code still made naval discipline seem lenient. Moreover, it was not uncommon for English quarter-sessions courts to sentence women as well as men to be publicly flogged at the cart's tail for petty larceny, or the theft of goods worth less than one shilling. The public flogging of women remained legal until 1817.

38. Nelson to Parry, 7/10/1786, Parry to Nelson, 18/10/1786, and Nelson to Sydney, 17/1/1787, CO 152/66.

39. Nelson to Parry, May 1786, Add. MSS 34961.

40. Nelson affidavit, 26/6/1786, *D&L*, 1, p. 181; Nelson to Hughes, 4/5/1786 and Nelson to Parry, 1/5/1786, Add. MSS 34961.

41. Nelson narrative, 1 May following, Add. MSS 34961; Brandford to Nelson, 20/5/1786, ADM 1/2223.

42. Solicitors' opinions, 2/8/1786, ADM 7/301.

43. Council minutes of Barbados, 29/8/1786, CO 31/43.

44. Parry to Hughes, 20/5/1786, D&L, 1, p. 185; Parry to Sydney, 20/7/1786, CO 28/60.

45. Council minutes of Barbados, 4/7/1786, CO 31/43; Parry to Nepean, 22, 25/12/1787, CO 28/61; Brandford to Parry, 29/1/1787, CO 28/61; solicitors' opinions, 5/7/1787, ADM 7/301; and legal papers in ADM 2/1062: 272, 275, 305, 427.

46. Nelson to Suckling, 5/7/1786, D&L, 1, p. 186; Nelson to Locker, 27/9/1786, D&L, 1, p. 197; Rawson, Letters from the Leeward Islands, p. 72.

47. Proctor's bill, Nevis, 1786, and 'an account of the difference of charges of the King's Advocate and Proctor at Barbados', 1786, William L. Clements Library.

48. Nelson to Stephens, 9/2/1787, ADM 1/2223; John Sugden, 'Lord Cochrane', pp. 194–205. For attacks on prize courts see also 'A Friend of the Navy', Appeal . . . Against a Late Rejection of the Petition of the Captains; John Frederick Pott, Observations on Matters of Prize; John Frederick Pott, Letter to Samuel Whitbread; Lord Cochrane, Statement Delivered by Lord Cochrane; and J. Richard Hill, Prizes of War, pp. 100–2.

49. The extortionate fees of public servants were being widely criticised at the time, partly on account of a Whig belief that the ability to offer appointments linked to lucrative fees constituted a means by which the king's government achieved undue control of the political process. In 1785 a government 'Commission to Enquire into the Fees, Gratuities, Perquisites and Emoluments Received in Publick Offices' was established, reporting in 1788. Even so, it was not until 1800 that the remuneration of Admiralty clerks was shifted from its reliance upon fees and perquisites to a recognised salary structure. For the commission's effects upon the administration of the Royal Navy see P. K. Crimmin, 'Admiralty Relations with the Treasury'; P. K. Crimmin, 'Financial and Clerical Establishment of the Admiralty Office'; and Bernard Pool, Navy Board Contracts. In addition, the extravagance of many fees was outraging public opinion, even in Antigua. John Luffman, for example, wrote in 1786 that 'the [St Johns] custom-house is a good building near the bottom of St Mary's Street, and the fees exacted there are enormous', and the same year the home government began considering new legislation to introduce 'proper regulations' (Oliver, History of the Island of Antigua, 1, p. cxxix; council minutes of St Kitts, 9/8/1786, CO 241/18).

50. Nelson to Stephens, 27/8/1786, ADM 1/2223; Nelson to William, 25/9/1786, Add. MSS 34988.

51. Nelson to Swedish warship, c. 1785, Add. MSS 34961; Rayalin to Shirley, 14/7/1786 and 26/9/1786, CO 152/65.

52. Nelson to Stephens, 3/11/1786, ADM 1/2223.

53. Lewis to Collingwood, 27/8/1786, and other documents on the matter are filed in ADM 1/2223.

54. Nelson to Locker, 27/9/1786, D&L, 1, p. 197.

55. Nelson to Fanny, 17/4/1786, Monmouth MSS, E750.

56. Nelson to Fanny, 19–23/8/1786, NLTHW, p. 33.

57. Nelson to William, 3/2/1786, NMM: BRP/6; Gentleman's Magazine (1787), i, pp. 89, 274; R. C. Fiske, Notices of Nelson, p. 26.

58. Nelson to William, 29/12/1786, Add. MSS 34988.

XV The Prince and the Post-Captain (pp. 338–72)

1. Admiralty to Hughes, 27/5/1786, ADM 2/1342; Nelson to Fanny, 27/11/1786, Monmouth MSS, E756.

2. Sketches of Holloway may be found in NC, 19 (1808), p. 353–73; John Watkins, William the Fourth, pp. 152–4; and Dictionary of Canadian Biography 6 (1987), pp. 323–4.

3. Nelson's account of his meeting with William Henry (Add. MSS 34902:1) is a foundation for these paragraphs. The Admiralty botched its instructions about the prince. Howe apparently intended William Henry to winter in the Leeward Islands in 1786–7, return north for the summer and spend the winter of 1787–8 in Jamaica. This was the thrust of the instructions to Hughes and Sawyer. However, the same day the orders assigning the prince to the Leeward Islands in 1786 were drafted, Howe told Gardner, who commanded in Jamaica, that William Henry would be spending that time 'at and about Jamaica'. To add to the confusion, in 1786 Sawyer seems to have given the prince leave to go wherever he pleased in the West Indies. See the Admiralty's letters to Hughes, Sawyer and Gardner, all dated 27 May 1786, in ADM 2/1342.

4. Richard Vesey Hamilton, ed., Sir Thomas Byam Martin, 1, p. 25.

5. William Henry, 3/1/1787, in A. Aspinall, ed., Later Correspondence, 1, p. 268; Tom Pocock, Sailor King, pp. 69, 122. For a different view of the prince's acceptability see the letter of April 1789 published in Hilda Gamlin, Nelson's Friendships, 1, p. 147.

6. Nelson to Fanny, 12/12/1786, Monmouth MSS, E578. Nelson's drinking habits are mentioned in the account of William Henry (the Duke of Clarence), Add. MSS 34990: 54.

7. NLTHW, p. 15; William Henry to Hood, 18/4/1787, NLTHW, p. 58.

8. Hamilton, Sir Thomas Byam Martin, 1, p. 67.

9. William Henry to George III, 20/5/1787, Aspinall, Later Correspondence, 1, p. 290; Nelson to William, 29/12/1786, Add. MSS 34988.

10. Nelson to William, 9/2/1787, Add. MSS 34988.

11. Nelson to Locker, 29/12/1786, D&L, 1, p. 205; Nelson to Stephens, 4/7/1787, ADM 1/2223.

12. Nelson to Fanny, 24/12/1786, Monmouth MSS, E759.

13. Stephens to Nelson, 28/3/1787, Add. MSS 34933.

14. William Henry to George III, 7/1/1787, Aspinall, Later Correspondence, 1, p. 266.

15. Nelson to Fanny, 12/12/1786, 11/2/1787, Monmouth MSS, E758, E763; Nelson to William, 9/2/1787, Add. MSS 34988; Clarence to Nelson, 3/10/1796, D&L, 2, p. 246.

16. William Henry said that the captains formed a mess in the house and caused resentment by excluding lieutenants: William Henry to Hood, 9/2/1787, B. McL. Ranft, 'Prince William', p. 270. However, Nelson's account contradicts this, and the prince himself told the king on 20 May 1787 (Aspinall, Later Correspondence, 1, p. 290) that 'I did not ask them to my table, for I had made . . . this rule, that whenever two captains or any strangers dine with me to have that day no officer of the ship at my table'. I have, therefore, attributed the exclusion of the junior officers to William Henry.

17. James Stanier Clarke and John McArthur, Life and Services, 1, p. 129; Wallis, in Geoffrey Rawson, ed., Letters from the Leeward Islands, p. 54; William Henry to the Prince of Wales, 8/2/1787, A. Aspinall, ed., George, Prince of Wales, 1, p. 276; William Henry to Hood, 9/2/1787, Ranft, 'Prince William', p. 270.

18. Nelson to Fanny, 12 and 24/12/1786, 1/1/1787, Monmouth MSS, E758–E760; John Luffman, 16/1/1787, in Vere Langford Oliver, History of the Island of Antigua, 1, p. cxxx.

19. Nelson's account of his meeting with William Henry: Add. MSS 34902:1.

20. Brian Lavery, ed., Shipboard Life, p. 106 (reprints William Henry's order book); Schomberg to William Henry, 13/1/1787, Ranft, 'Prince William', p. 274.

21. William Henry's narrative, Ranft, 'Prince William', p. 281.

22. Nelson to Locker, 13/2/1787, D&L, 1, p. 214.

23. Nelson to his officers, 28/1/1787, Lavery, Shipboard Life, p. 105; William Henry to Hood, 9/2/1787, Ranft, 'Prince William', p. 270.

24. William Henry to Hood, 9/2/1787, Ranft, 'Prince William', p. 270; William Henry to George III, 20/5/1787, Aspinall, *Later Correspondence*, 1, p. 290; Lavery, *Shipboard Life*, pp. 108, 110–11; Hamilton, *Sir Thomas Byam Martin*, 1, pp. 68–9.

25. Schomberg to William Henry, 12/2/1787, Ranft, 'Prince William', p. 283.

26. William Henry to Hood, 15/3/1787, *NLTHW*, p. 58.

27. Nelson to Fanny, 13/1/1787, Monmouth MSS, E761.

28. Richard Pares, *West-India Fortune*, p. 74.

29. Nelson to Fanny, 25/2/1787, Monmouth MSS, E766. According to the contemporary sketch of Nelson in *Public Characters*, pp. 2–3, Fanny eventually married without Herbert's consent, which hardly seems to be true.

30. Nelson to Fanny, 28/2/1787, Monmouth MSS, E768.

31. Marriage certificate, 11/3/1787, Add. MSS 28333.

32. Nelson to Locker, 21/3/1787, *D&L*, 1, p. 219.

33. Rawson, *Letters from the Leeward Islands*, p. 53; William Henry to Hood, 15/3/1787, *NLTHW*, p. 58; Edith M. Keate, *Nelson's Wife*, pp. 67–8; and Carola Oman, *Nelson*, pp. 92–3.

34. The published documents in *D&L*, vol. 1, and the manuscripts in Add. MSS 34902 and 34903 are major sources for this affair. See Nelson, 4/5/1787, Add. MSS 34902, Wilkinson and Higgins to Nelson, 19/4/1787, and John Burke to Nelson, 16/4/1787, Add. MSS 34903.

35. Higgins to William Henry, 13/4/1787, Add. MSS 34903.

36. Nelson's letters to the Admiralty between October 1786 and February 1787 are printed in *D&L*, but the originals filed in ADM 1/2223 contain essential enclosures, including Collingwood to Nelson, 13/9/1786, 19/10/1786 and 19/1/1787. See also Holloway to Stephens, 23/5/1787, ADM 1/1908.

37. Nelson to the dockyards: *Notes and Queries* 150 (1926), p. 55.

38. The figure was actually £543 19s. 0d. but I have rounded this and other figures to the nearest pound.

39. For sample cases see Add. MSS 34903: 13–17, 21; Higgins and Wilkinson to the Navy Board, 18/1/1788, Add. MSS 34903.

40. Nelson to Middleton, 2/5/1787, Add. MSS 34902.

41. Nelson to Howe, c. May 1787, Add. MSS 34902.

42. Nelson to William Henry, 7/5/1787, *D&L*, 1, p. 233.

43. Wilkinson and Higgins, memorial to the king, 1788, Add. MSS 34903: 162.

44. Stephens to Nelson, 9/3/1787, Add. MSS 34933.

45. William Henry to Hood, 9/2/1787, Ranft, 'Prince William', p. 270.

46. John D. Byrn, *Crime and Punishment*, pp. 108, 111–12, 115. Following social science, historians are fond of statistical techniques, but often use them inaccurately, sometimes because their material is neither complete nor accurate enough to support the generalisations they want to make. As far as Byrn's comparison of punishment rates on different ships is concerned, leaving aside the question of log book reliability one would need to control such variables as the duration of stay on station, the amount of time spent in port and ship size and circumstance to make a close comparison of one captain or company with another. Nevertheless, Byrn's figures do indicate that the punishment rate on the *Boreas* was high.

A more spiteful contribution was made by Terry Coleman, *Nelson*, pp. 5, 90, who estimated that Nelson flogged 'almost half his people' in the eighteen months after April 1786. This was a misuse of statistics designed to shock and smear. Coleman made no reference to the punishment rates on any of Nelson's other ships, though he could, for example, have referred to the low rates aboard the *Badger* and *Hinchingbroke* to offer readers a more even-handed analysis. He should certainly have pointed out that the rate on the *Boreas* was the worst of any ship he captained, and therefore unrepresentative of the whole. Instead, he not only gave the *Boreas* statistic in isolation, repeating it twice for emphasis, but even failed to represent that command fairly. By confining his figures to a selected eighteen-month period when punishments were exceptionally common, he almost doubled the flogging rate for the *Boreas* command in its entirety.

Similarly, Coleman's allusions to the rule that men could not be given more than twelve lashes without the authority of a court martial are misleading. It was a rule, he admits, that was 'often broken, but not in a happy ship' (p. 85), thereby implying that Nelson's commands were unhappy ones. The allegation indicts not only Nelson's spell aboard the *Boreas*, but also, for example, his command of the *Agamemnon*, which was notable for the loyalty it inspired in crews. In fact, naval logs of the time show that it was customary to give up to thirty-six lashes without a court martial, probably because officers felt a need to differentiate between the gravity of various offences and the captains necessary to form court martials were seldom readily available. Even captains noted for their humanity resorted to the practice, among them Ralph Willett Miller, whose Christian charity was famous. As one of Miller's officers remarked, 'the person who feels himself uncomfortable under his command . . . must be miserable indeed under that of any other' (Harriet Hoste, ed., *Hoste*, 1, p. 82).

As a commodore and admiral, from 1796, Nelson left discipline to his flag-captains. He did not interfere, even when served by a severe disciplinarian, such as Thomas Masterman Hardy: Oliver Warner, *Nelson*, pp. 163, 165, 172.

47. I have extrapolated punishments from the different logs cited in chap. 12, n. 10. No one log gives a complete list of the floggings aboard the *Boreas*; hence my use of the word 'about'.

48. The trials of Holland, Wilson, Philip McKay, William Pidgeon, Alexander and Edward Pakenham between 1 and 9 July 1784 are filed in ADM 1/5324. See also NMM: AGC/18/1.

49. In addition to the cases mentioned, see those of Thomas Walker, 14/9/1784, James Wallis, 22–23/9/1784, William Richards, 20/10/1784, John Fitzmaurice, 17/6/1785, James Alexander, 17/8/1785, James Harding, 20/4/1786, and John Johnson and John Callender, both 22/4/1786. The trials up to July 1785 can be found in ADM 1/5324 and the balance in ADM 1/5325. For Clark, see also the logs of the *Boreas* and the log of the *Rattler* (ADM 51/770). Clark's second trial was published in Rawson, *Letters from the Leeward Islands*, pp. 56–63, for which reason it is the only one of these cases to be noticed by historians.

50. Nelson to Stephens, 17/8/1787, Add. MSS 34902.

51. Nelson to Collingwood, 3/5/1787, *D&L*, 1, p. 230.

52. Nelson to William Henry, 26/4/1787, *D&L*, 1, p. 224; William Henry to Hood, 18/4/1787, and William Henry to Stephens, 17/5/1787, both in NMM: Hoo/2; documents in Aspinall, *George, Prince of Wales*, 1, pp. 216, 278, 311; Hughes to Stephens, 12/3/1785, ADM 1/312.

53. Nelson to Stephens, 15/3/1787, ADM 1/2223.

54. Nelson to Stephens, 16/4/1787, ADM 1/2223; Nelson to dockyard shipwrights, 17/3/1787, Royal Naval Museum, Portsmouth; Nelson to Gardner, 13/5/1787, Monmouth MSS, E498; William Henry to Nelson, 11/5/1787, 3/12/1787, Ranft, 'Prince William', pp. 284, 285; William Henry to the king, 20/5/1787, Aspinall, *Later Correspondence*, 1, p. 290; William Henry to the Prince of Wales, 20/5/1787, Aspinall, *George, Prince of Wales*, 1, p. 311. The suggestion surfaces in Nelson to William Henry, 7/5/1787, *D&L*, 1, p. 233, but William Henry both claimed to have got the idea from Nelson in March and to have conceived it himself.

55. Nelson to Gardner, 13/5/1787, Monmouth MSS, E498; Nelson to Stephens, 10/7/1787, ADM 1/2223.

56. Nelson to William Henry, 7/5/1787, *D&L*, 1, p. 233.

57. Howe to Hood, 2/7/1787, NMM: Hoo/2; William Henry to Hood, 20/5/1787, NMM: Hoo/2.

58. Parker to Stephens, 3/6/1787, 15/9/1787, ADM 1/315.

59. A. M. W. Stirling, ed., *Pages and Portraits*, 1, p. 27; Hamilton, *Sir Thomas Byam Martin*, 1, p. 66.

60. See the trials on 9 and 19/7/1787 and 9/8/1787, ADM 1/5326.

61. Nelson to William Henry, 27/7/1787, Add. MSS 34902.

62. William Henry to Nelson, 3/12/1787, NMM: STW/7.

63. Nelson to William, 20/12/1787, NMM: BRP/6. Andrews had passed his examination for lieutenant on 4 October 1787 (ADM 107/10, p. 224) and been posted elsewhere two days later.

64. Nelson to Stephens, 29/8/1787, 21/9/1787, 30/9/1787, ADM 1/2223; Nelson to the Navy Board, 30/9/1787, ADM 106/1290.

65. Wallis was promoted commander on 20 January 1794 and post-captain in 1797. He died in 1808. In addition to *D&L*, 1, see Nelson to Adye, 4/9/1787, Monmouth MSS, E29.

66. Nelson to Stephens, 18/7/1787, ADM 1/2223.

67. Nelson to Locker, 12/8/1787, *D&L*, 1, p. 251.

68. Hood to Stephens, 17 and 19/8/1787, NMM: Hoo/7.

69. M. Eyre Matcham, *Nelsons of Burnham Thorpe*, p. 45.

70. Fanny's recollections, *NLTHW*, p. 61; Clarke and McArthur, *Life and Services*, 1, pp. 149–50.

71. Clarke and McArthur, *Life and Services*, 1, pp. 148–9; Edwards to Nelson, 20/10/1787, Western MSS 3668, Wellcome Library, London. I have not yet confirmed this story from contemporary sources.

72. Nelson to Ross, 6/5/1788, Add. MSS 34903.

XVI Beachcombing (pp. 373–412)

1. Nelson to William, 20/12/1787, 3/1/1788, NMM: BRP/6 and Add. MSS 34988. Many letters for this chapter are published in *D&L*, and Add. MSS 34902, 34903 and 34988 are the most important manuscript sources. M. Eyre Matcham, *Nelsons of Burnham Thorpe*, has essential selections from the correspondence between the Reverend Edmund Nelson and his daughter, Kitty Matcham.

2. Nelson to Long, 7/8/1793, Add. MSS 34902; Nelson to Stephens, 26/12/1788, Add. MSS 34902; and Nelson to William, 20/12/1787, NMM: BRP/6.

3. Nelson to Stephens, 29/12/1787, ADM 1/2223.

4. For this episode see *Gentleman's Magazine* (1787), ii, pp. 1188–90; *Morning Chronicle* (London), 18/12/1787; *Whole Proceedings on the King's Commission of the Peace, Oyer and Terminer, and Gaol Delivery for the City of London*; H. L. Cryer, 'Horatio Nelson and the Murderous Cooper' (which drew it to modern attention); M. Ramsay, 'Nelson, Carse and Eighteenth-Century Justice'; and Chatham to Nelson, enclosing Nepean to Chatham, both 11/4/1789, Add. MSS 34903.

5. Nelson to Locker, 27/1/1788, *D&L*, 1, p. 266.

6. Nelson to Ross, 6/5/1788, Add. MSS 34903.

7. Letters of Wilkinson and Higgins to Nelson and the Sick and Hurt Board, both 30/1/1788, Add. MSS 34903.

8. Ordnance Board to Wilkinson and Higgins, 11/6/1788, and Richmond to Nelson, 27/12/1788, Add. MSS 34933.

9. Nelson to Wilkinson and Higgins, 26/4/1788, Add. MSS 34902.

10. Letters to Wilkinson and Higgins from the Victualling Board (30/4/1788), Sick and Hurt Board (6/5/1788) and the Ordnance Board (11/6/1788), all in Add. MSS 34903; Sick and Hurt Board to Nelson, 22/4/1788, Add. MSS 34933; Nelson, 30/4/1788, and Nelson to Sick and Hurt Board, April 1788, D&L, 1, pp. 271, 272.

11. Middleton note, 2/6/1788, Add. MSS 34933: 10, and Nelson to William Henry, 2/6/1788, D&L, 1, p. 275.

12. Fanny's recollections, NLTHW, p. 61.

13. James Harrison, Life, 1, p. 95; Public Characters, p. 7; and, for this and the following paragraph, Matcham, Nelsons of Burnham Thorpe, pp. 37, 46, 53, 57, 59, 66–7, 74, 76. In addition to the sources for family history listed in chap. 2, n. 1, see various documents in Alfred Morrison, Hamilton and Nelson Papers, vol. 2.

14. Matcham, Nelsons of Burnham Thorpe, pp. 45, 55, 57.

15. Marriage settlement, 20/7/1780, NMM: PHB/P/24. Thomas Foley, Nelson Centenary, 30.

16. Matcham is discussed in Foley, Nelson Centenary, p. 25; Matcham, Nelsons of Burnham Thorpe, pp. 30–6; and DNB, 13, p. 27.

17. Norfolk Chronicle, 1/3/1788, and, for Charlotte's early years, Tom Pocock, Nelson's Women, ch. 9.

18. Matcham, Nelsons of Burnham Thorpe, pp. 60–1. Nelson also used his London visits to renew naval friendships by dining at the 'Royal Naval Club of 1765' and the 'Navy Club of 1785'. He attended two such dinners in 1788 and one in 1789: Oliver Warner, Nelson, p. 47.

19. Lady Nelson's account, NLTHW, p. 61.

20. Matcham, Nelsons of Burnham Thorpe, pp. 77, 79–81, 88–9, 108; Martin to Lettsom, 1801, in James Hooper, Nelson's Homeland, p. 69; Nelson to Katy, 13/10/1792, NMM: MAM.

21. Nelson to Cornwallis, 8/10/1788, NMM: COR/58; D&L, 1, p. 277; Chatham to Nelson, March 1789, Add. MSS 34903.

22. Nelson to Locker, 10/9/1789, D&L, 1, p. 281.

23. G. E. Mingay, The Gentry, p. 138. Among useful social histories of the period, I have particularly consulted John Rule, Albion's People, and J. C. D. Clark, English Society.

24. William Faden, Map of Norfolk.

25. Harrison, Life, 1, pp. 97–8, and Clarke and McArthur, Life and Services, 1, pp. 158–60, give details of Nelson's domestic life drawn from people close to him. See also Matcham, Nelsons of Burnham Thorpe, p. 63.

26. Marsh and Creed accounts in Morrison, Hamilton and Nelson Papers, 2, p. 382–99, and Geoffrey Rawson, ed., Letters from the Leeward Islands, pp. 67–9; Nelson and William to the Bank of England, 19/11/1788, Warren R. Dawson, ed., Nelson Collection, p. 289; Nelson to William, 31/10/1792, NMM: BRP/6; Boreas pay book, ADM 35/242; and Nelson to Fanny, 12/3/1793, Monmouth MSS, E776.

27. Land tax records, 1796–7, and the parish registers of Burnham Thorpe, both in the Norfolk Record Office.

28. Matcham, Nelsons of Burnham Thorpe, pp. 72, 77. Maurice Nelson's letters to Sukey date from 24 December 1793 to 3 June 1794, and were written from Exeter, Cowes and Southampton. Sukey was a short form for Susannah in the eighteenth century. Maurice asked to be remembered to Susannah/Susan and Colin (?), the former a child learning her letters and both presumably Sukey's children. Maurice also indicated that Sukey had prevailed upon Andrews 'to let her [Susannah] stay with you', which suggests he was the father. The letters, filed in NMM: CRK/22, also refer to Maurice's dealings with Horatio's old companion, Alexander Davison. For Maurice's appointment as a commissary see J. M. Collinge, Navy Board Officials, p. 125.

29. R. C. Fiske, *Notices of Nelson*, p. 26; Matcham, *Nelsons of Burnham Thorpe*, pp. 64–5, 77, 107. I have not discovered the fate of Sophia Nelson, Suckling's wife. She does not appear in the burials at North Elmham for that period, but as her husband was contemplating marriage to a 'young woman . . . decently brought forward in a line of mediocrity' in 1796 she must have died: Edmund to Nelson, 5/8/1796, Monmouth MSS, E622.

30. Matcham, *Nelsons of Burnham Thorpe*, pp. 76–7; *NLTHW*, p. 64; *D&L*, 1, p. 290.

31. Matcham, *Nelsons of Burnham Thorpe*, p. 86; A. M. W. Stirling, ed., *Coke of Norfolk*, 1, p. 346; Gillian Ford, 'Nelson References in Holkham Game Books'; Gillian Ford, 'Coke and Nelson'; *The Poll For Knights of the Shire for the County of Norfolk*, p. 203.

32. Matcham, *Nelsons of Burnham Thorpe*, p. 87; Nelson to Kitty, 15/12/1792, NMM: MAM; Nelson to Bolton, 23 and 30/4/1792, NMM: GIR/1; accounts with Bolton, Western MSS 3676, Wellcome Library, London; and Nelson to William, 5/2/1792, Add. MSS 34988.

33. Nelson to Bolton, 11/12/1791, NMM: GIR/1; Nelson to William, 20/4/1792, NMM: BRP/6; and Nelson to Kate Matcham, NMM: MAM. If these references were to Kitty Crowe, she eventually married a surgeon named Helsham in 1795 (Edmund to Nelson, 5/8/1794, 5/10/1795, Monmouth MSS, E610, E613).

34. Accounts with Bolton, Western MSS 3676, Wellcome Library, Nelson to Bolton, 11/12/1791, 23/4/1792, 30/4/1792, NMM: GIR/1; Nelson to Bolton, 7/5/1792, NMM: TRA/12; and Nelson to William, 18/11/1788, NMM: BRP/6.

35. Nelson to Kitty, 13/10/1792, NMM: MAM; Matcham, *Nelsons of Burnham Thorpe*, p. 65; will of Mary Nelson, 6/8/1769, PROB 11/1183: 467; and *Norfolk Chronicle*, 28/7/1789.

36. Matcham, *Nelsons of Burnham Thorpe*, p. 69, and Nelson to Bolton, 14/12/1789, NMM: GIR/1.

37. Nelson to William, 5/2/1792, Add. MSS 34988.

38. Cochrane devised a method to increase the rate of fire aboard the *Pallas* when double-shotting his guns, and Broke experimented with non-recoil systems for his artillery: John Sugden, 'Lord Cochrane', pp. 87–91; Peter Padfield, *Broke of the Shannon*; and Peter Padfield, *Guns at Sea*. For the development of fleet tactics John Creswell, *British Admirals*; Brian Tunstall and Nicholas Tracy, *Naval Warfare*; Nicholas Tracy, *Nelson's Battles*; and Peter Le Fevre and Richard Harding, eds, *Precursors of Nelson*, are particularly recommended.

39. Collingwood to Moutray, 10/3/1806, G. L. Newnham Collingwood, ed., *Correspondence*, 1, p. 277.

40. Oliver Warner, 'Collingwood and Nelson', p. 318.

41. Council minutes, Antigua, 4/6/1788, CO 152/68, and Wilkinson and Higgins to Nelson, 24/4/1789, Add. MSS 34903. Documents relating to this affair are scattered through Add. MSS 34903 and 34933, only some of which were selected by Clarke and McArthur, *Life and Services*, pp. 161–7, and *D&L*, 1, pp. 278–80, 283–4. The minutes of the Navy Board are disappointing on the subject, though there are occasional references (for example, 21/1/1789 in ADM 106/2629 and 3/11/1789 and 22/12/1789 in ADM 106/2631).

42. Nelson to Wilkinson and Higgins, 24/1/1789, *D&L*, 1, p. 278. The letters from the Victualling and Sick and Hurt Boards and Ordnance Office to Nelson are filed in Add. MSS 34933: 6, 14, 16.

43. Richmond to Nelson, 16/1/1789, Add. MSS 34933; Alison Gilbert Olson, *The Radical Duke*, chaps 5, 6.

44. Nelson to Wilkinson and Higgins, 28/11/1789, Add. MSS 34933; Clarke and McArthur, *Life and Services*, 1, pp. 166–7; Nelson's sketch of his services, 1790s, NMM: STW/2; and Wilkinson petition, 27/6/1797, ADM 106/1653.

45. Victualling Board to Nelson, 19, 23/6/1789, Add. MSS 34933. The board offered to receive observations in writing if Nelson was unable to travel to London, but it appears that he did make the journey.

46. Nelson to Wilkinson, 7/3/1798, enclosed in Wilkinson to Hamond, 24/3/1798, ADM 106/1653; Gentleman's Magazine, 61 (1791), p. 1235, and 68 (1798), p. 730.

47. Nelson to Adye, 4/9/1787, Monmouth MSS, E29, and Venables, Buggin and Bleasdale to Nelson, 5/3/1790, ADM 1/2223. Nelson's trip to London is revealed by a letter from 23 Norfolk Street, Strand (Nelson to Stephens, 11/2/1790, ADM 1/2223) regarding the deduction of an overpayment of £17 for his services with the Hinchingbroke and Janus. Nelson's comparative penury is evident in his request that, since his half-pay was to be docked, he be paid for his command of the fort at Port Royal in 1779, although that service was not the strict responsibility of the Admiralty.

48. Venables, Buggin and Bleasdale writ, 26/4/1790, enclosed in Nelson's letter of the same date to Stephens, ADM 1/2223.

49. Pole to Nelson, 29/4/1790, Add. MSS 34903; D&L, 1, p. 287. Clarke and McArthur, Life and Services, 1, pp. 160–1, embroidered the account of Lady Nelson (NLTHW, p. 61) but neither is entirely consistent with the contemporary documents.

50. Nelson to Graham, 8/6/1790, Huntington Library, San Marino, California; Nelson, 12/11/1790, Add. MSS 34902.

51. Nelson to William Henry, 24/6/1790, 10/12/1790, Add. MSS 34902; Nelson to Stephens, 8/5/1790, ADM 1/2223; Nelson to Graham, 8/6/1790, Huntington Library; Edmund Nelson to Nelson, 11/10/1790, NMM: BRP/5; and Edmund Nelson to Sarah Nelson, 21/10/1790, in Foley, Nelson Centenary, p. 26. For the international crisis itself see Paul Webb, 'Naval Aspects of the Nootka Sound Crisis'.

52. Hood to Nelson, 9/7/1790, J. H. Godfrey, ed., 'Corsica, 1794', p. 364.

53. Suckling to Nelson, 1/10/1790, Add. MSS 34988; Nelson to Chatham, 26/9/1790, and Mulgrave to Nelson, 17/11/1790, D&L, 1, p. 289; Foley, Nelson Centenary, p. 25; and Clarence to Nelson, Add. MSS 34902: 31.

54. Nelson, 'Sketch', D&L, 1, p. 10; Nelson to Clarence, 10/12/1792, Add. MSS 34902; Nelson to William, 5/2/1792, Add. MSS 34988.

55. Nelson to Cornwallis, 4/4/1791, Hist. MSS Comm., Various Collections, 6, p. 365; Matcham, Nelsons of Burnham Thorpe, p. 83.

56. Nelson to Navy Board, 14/3/1791, ADM 106/1392, and Matcham, Nelsons of Burnham Thorpe, pp. 88, 90. The Trail affair is another episode missed by biographers. Nelson's father mentions the trial without identifying it.

57. Add. MSS 34902: 148.

58. For these trials see HCA 1/25/138–212 (indictments); HCA 1/61, pp. 166–72 (Kimber), 173–6 (Trail) (minutes); The Times, 8–11/6/1792; Norfolk Chronicle, 9/6/1792; Trial of Captain John Kimber. Trail was apparently a Londoner, and his wife, who accompanied her husband aboard the Neptune, subsequently knew Maurice Nelson and his partner: Maurice to Sukey, 27/3/1794, NMM: CRK/22.

59. Harrison, Life, 1, p. 102.

60. Oliver Warner, Portrait of Lord Nelson, p. 191.

61. Nelson's sea journal, NLTHW, pp. 138–9.

62. H. T. Dickinson, Politics of the People, p. 285. After decades of research on English radicalism, conservatism is beginning to attract more attention. See also Harold Perkin, Origins of Modern British Society, for controversial but illuminating discussions of the aristocratic and entrepreneurial 'ideals' and A. P. Thornton, The Habit of Authority; A. D. Harvey, Britain in the Early Nineteenth Century; Ian R. Christie, Stress and Stability; and Clark, English Society.

63. Collingwood to Nelson, 14/11/1792, Add. MSS 34903.

64. Nelson to Hoste, 22/6/1795, Monmouth MSS, E297.

65. Nelson to Clarence, 10/12/1792, Add. MSS 34902, and Clarke and McArthur, *Life and Services*, 1, p. 291. Though insufficiently engaged with the social problems of the poorer classes to develop his thinking, and singularly blind to many of them, Nelson here displayed the rudiments of the outraged paternalism that later led Tory radicals such as Richard Oastler and the Earl of Shaftesbury to become reformers.

66. Roy Porter, *English Society*, p. 104. Among the burgeoning literature of riots a sound survey is John Stevenson, *Popular Disturbances in England*.

67. Nelson to Clarence, 26/5/1797, NMM: AGC/27; Nelson to Hoste, 30/6/1797, *D&L*, 2, p. 401.

68. The literature of radicalism is enormous. M. H. R. Bonwick, 'Radicalism of Sir Francis Burdett', distinguishes between the traditions of Painite, Burdettite and philosophical radicalism. For the struggle at Westminster see Philip Harling, *Waning of 'Old Corruption'* and John Cannon, *Parliamentary Reform*. E. P. Thompson, *Making of the English Working Class*, is still a magnificent and contentious quarry for radical movements afield, for which see also Albert Goodwin, *Friends of Liberty*. D. G. Wright, *Popular Radicalism*, is a brief but sensible survey.

69. For an example of Nelson's willingness to countenance internal continental reform, see Colin White, '"More Enlarged Ideas Than in Former Times"', p. 114.

70. Nelson to Fanny, 11/8/96, Monmouth MSS, E901. For a challenging view of the French Revolution see Simon Schama, *Citizens*.

71. Nelson to Fanny, 13/2/1794, Monmouth MSS, E808, and Nelson to Clarence, 9/11/1799, *D&L*, 4, p. 94.

72. Warner, *Portrait of Lord Nelson*, p. 154.

73. Countess of Minto, ed., *Sir Gilbert Elliot*, 2, p. 165.

74. Nelson to Clarence, 3/11/1792, Add. MSS 34902.

75. Collingwood to Nelson, 14/11/1792, Add. MSS 34903.

76. Nelson to Fanny, 7/1/1793, Monmouth MSS, E774.

77. Matcham, *Nelsons of Burnham Thorpe*, p. 99.

XVII Captain of the *Agamemnon* (pp. 415–57)

1. Warrant, 10/2/1793, Western MSS 3677, Wellcome Library, London. Principal sources for this chapter are *D&L*, p. 1; *NLTHW*; and NMM: Hoo/2–3. For the British plan of campaign see Jennifer Mori, *William Pitt*, and Peter Jupp, *Lord Grenville*.

2. I do not agree with Anthony Deane, *Nelson's Favourite*, p. 29, that the ship was equipped with carronades at this time. I have found no references to these in contemporary documents, and Nelson's own statement of his armament (*NLTHW*, p. 138) seems decisive. However, on 17 April 1795 Nelson's log speaks of shifting two carronades of the French prize *Censeur* to the forecastle, thereby displacing a couple of nine-pounders which were restationed on the quarterdeck. I am not clear whether Nelson was repositioning guns in the prize, or arming *Agamemnon* with guns from the *Censeur* (log, 16–18 April 1795). Logs for the *Agamemnon*, essential for the following chapters, are filed in Add. MSS 36604–36607 (captain's), ADM 52/2707, 2710 and 2632 (master's), and NMM: ADM/L/A51 (lieutenant's). For the ship's sailing qualities see ADM 95/38/148.

3. *Agamemnon* muster, ADM 36/11358; Thomas Foley, *Nelson Centenary*, pp. 27, 30; Walpole to Nelson, 8/3/1793, Add. MSS 34903; Nelson to Fanny, 2/4/1797, Monmouth MSS, E294; Fanny's endorsement to a letter of John McArthur, 1807, Monmouth MSS, E678; Harriet Hoste, ed., *Hoste*, 1, p. 5; Nelson to William, 27/12/1793, Add. MSS 34988; ADM 9/2, no. 317. There is a comparatively recent life of Hoste by Tom Pocock.

4. For Fellows see ADM 9/6, no. 1868. The best account of the manning of the *Agamemnon*

is Edward Fraser, *Sailors Nelson Led*, pp. 1–2. For the Marine Society boys see NMM: MSY/O/7, and John Sugden, 'Forgotten *Agamemnons*'.

5. Richard Vesey Hamilton and John Knox Laughton, eds, *Above and Below Hatches*, p. 176; Allison's passing certificate, 5/3/1788, ADM 6/89. The surgeon of the *Agamemnon* was John Roxburgh. The ship's marines under Sergeant James Luck were reinforced at Spithead by a detachment of the 69th (South Lincolnshire) Regiment of Foot under Captain John Clark.

6. Enclosures with Nelson to Stephens, 26/2/1793, ADM 1/2224.

7. Nelson to William, 10/2/1793, Add. MSS 34988; Nelson to Locker, 21/2/1793, *D&L*, 1, p. 301.

8. In addition to the published sources in n. 1 see Nelson's accounts with David Thomson and others in Western MSS 3667 and 3676, Wellcome Library, London, and with Thomas Fellows in NMM: 75/102.

9. Nelson to Gaskin, 4/3/1793, NMM: AGC/17/1; *ND*, 7 (2001), p. 446; David Shannon, 'Two Missing Nelson Letters Reconstructed'; *DNB*, 21, p. 742; *United Service Journal*, 1843, pt ii, p. 640. Withers died at North Walsham on 4 July 1843, aged seventy-three, leaving a wife and daughter.

10. Nelson to Fanny, 12/3/1793, Monmouth MSS, E776; Edith M. Keate, *Nelson's Wife*, pp. 67–8.

11. Fanny sold her consols for £76 5s. 0d. on 30 March 1793: Western MSS 3676, Wellcome Library.

12. Nelson to Fanny, 14 and 18/4/1793, Monmouth MSS, E780–81; Nelson to William, 18/4/1793, Add. MSS 34988.

13. Nelson to Fanny, 29/4/1793, Monmouth MSS, E783.

14. *Agamemnon* captain's log, 1/5/1793; Hoste to his father, 4 and 11/5/1793, NMM: MRF/88/1.

15. Hoste to his father, 11/5/1793, NMM: MRF/88/1.

16. Nelson to Fanny, 11/5/1793, Monmouth MSS, E786.

17. Nelson to Fanny, 4/8/1793, Monmouth MSS, E792.

18. Nelson to Fanny, 18/5/1793, Monmouth MSS, E787. We lack a satisfactory operational history of the navy during these years, but works supplying useful details include Edward Pelham Brenton, *Naval History*; William James, *Naval History*; William Laird Clowes, ed., *Royal Navy*, vols 4–6; A. T. Mahan, *Influence of Sea Power*; and Geoffrey Marcus, *Age of Nelson*. For this campaign see also John Holland Rose, *Lord Hood*.

19. Nelson to Fanny, 6/6/1793, Monmouth MSS, E788.

20. Nelson to Fanny, 14/6/1793, Monmouth MSS, E789.

21. Nelson to Fanny, 23/6/1793, Monmouth MSS, E790.

22. Nelson to Clarence, 14/7/1793, Add. MSS 34902. Nelson's journal (*NLTHW*, p. 128 following) is relevant for this, and the rest of the chapter. For the Spanish navy see J. D. Harbron, *Trafalgar and the Spanish Navy*, chap. 4, and Jose Ignacio Gonzalez-Aller and Hugo O'Donnell, 'The Spanish Navy in the Eighteenth Century'.

23. Journal, *NLTHW*, p. 128.

24. Hoste to his father, 5/8/1793 and 27/11/1793, NMM: MRF/88/1; Nelson to Dixon Hoste, 3/5/1794, Monmouth MSS, E302; Nelson to Fanny, 4/8/1793, Monmouth MSS, E792.

25. Nelson to Locker, 20/8/1793, *D&L*, 1, p. 319; Hoste, *Hoste*, 1, p. 17; list of captures, Add. MSS 34903: 239; journal, *NLTHW*, p. 130.

26. Nelson to William, 20/8/1793, Add. MSS 34988; Nelson to his father, 20/8/1793, *D&L*, 1, p. 319; Nelson to Fanny, 20/8/1793, Monmouth MSS, E795.

27. Hood to Hamilton, 25/8/1793, NMM: CRK/7. For the French navy in Toulon see William S. Cormack, *Revolution and Political Conflict*, chap. 7.

28. Conway to Nelson, 30/8/1793, *D&L*, 1, p. 323 n.

29. Nelson to Fanny, 7/9/1793, Monmouth MSS, E797.

30. Nelson to Fanny, 7/9/1793, Monmouth MSS, E797.

31. Nelson to Fanny, 7/9/1793, Monmouth MSS, E797. Nelson's journal, *NLTHW*, pp. 132–5, is the main source for the visit to Naples.

32. Harold Acton, *Bourbons of Naples*, is the best study of the Neapolitan background in English, but among older works J. C. Jeaffreson, *The Queen of Naples*, and Constance Giglio, *Naples in 1799*, have interest.

33. Journal, *NLTHW*, p. 133.

34. For Hamilton see Brian Fothergill, *Sir William Hamilton*; Jack Russell, *Nelson and the Hamiltons*; Vittorio Accardi, ed., *Hamilton Papers*; and David Constantine, *Fields of Fire*.

35. Hamilton to Hood, 20/8/1793, NMM: Hoo/2, and Hamilton to Grenville, 10 and 17/9/1793, FO 70/6.

36. Hamilton to Hood, 17/9/1793, NMM: Hoo/2, and Hood to Hamilton, 23/9/1793, NMM: CRK/7. The early meetings in Naples are also referred to in Acton's note and Hamilton to Hood, 12/9/1793, NMM: Hoo/2.

37. For the Palazzo Sessa see Flora Fraser, *Beloved Emma*, chap. 5.

38. Nelson to Fanny, 14/9/1793, Monmouth MSS, E798.

39. The anonymous *Memoirs of Lady Hamilton* was evidently written by Francis Oliver, Sir William's secretary, but must be used with caution. Of the older biographies, J. C. Jeaffreson, *Lady Hamilton and Lord Nelson* and Hilda Gamlin, *Emma, Lady Hamilton* have antiquarian interest, but the publication of Alfred Morrison's collection of *Hamilton and Nelson Papers* paved the way for more reliable accounts, of which by far the best, based on this and other sources, is still Walter Sichel, *Emma, Lady Hamilton*. This, which suggested Emma's important political role in Neapolitan affairs, and both Mollie Hardwick, *Emma, Lady Hamilton* and Flora Fraser, *Beloved Emma* are sympathetic portraits, while Edmund B. F. D'Auvergne, *The Dear Emma*, Jack Russell's *Nelson and the Hamilton* and Winifred Gerin's *Horatia Nelson* offer less endearing views. For the quotations given here, see Fraser, *Beloved Emma*, pp. 149, 160.

40. Fraser, *Beloved Emma*, pp. 121, 131, 149, 163.

41. Fraser, *Beloved Emma*, p. 128.

42. Countess of Minto, ed., *Sir Gilbert Elliot*, 2, p. 364; Cecil Aspinall-Oglander, ed., *Freshly Remembered*, p. 60.

43. Fraser, *Beloved Emma*, p. 270.

44. A. M. Broadley and R. G. Bartelot, *Nelson's Hardy*, p. 94.

45. Hamilton to Nelson, 3/4/1794, Add. MSS 34903. Nelson normally wrote to Sir William, but he did send Emma an account of one of his martial successes in 1796: Nelson to William Hamilton, 27/12/1796, Huntington Library, San Marino, California.

46. Acton's invitation is in Add. MSS 34932: 5.

47. Nelson to William, 24/9/1793, Add. MSS 34988; Nelson's journal, *NLTHW*, p. 135; Acton to Prince Castelcicala, 17/9/1793, FO 70/6; Hamilton to Hood, 17/9/1793, NMM: Hoo/2.

48. Nelson's journal, *NLTHW*, p. 135.

49. Fraser, *Beloved Emma*, p. 126.

50. Nelson journal, *NLTHW*, p. 135.

51. *Agamemnon* logs, 19/9/1793; list of captures, Add. MSS 34903: 239; Udny to McArthur, 3/1/1794, Add. MSS, 34903.

52. Nelson to William, 24/9/1793, Add. MSS 34988.

53. Hervey to Grenville, 1/10/1793, FO 79/9; Nelson to Hamilton, 27/9/1793, Morrison, *Hamilton and Nelson Papers*, 1, p. 180.

54. Nelson to Fanny, 12/10/1793, Monmouth MSS, E801; Minto, *Sir Gilbert Elliot*, 2,

p. 190. The Neapolitan reinforcements arrived at Toulon in three divisions of two thousand men on 28 September, 6 October and 5 December (Hood journal, Rose, *Lord Hood*, p. 102; Hood to Hamilton, 1 and 11/10/1793, NMM: CRK/7).

55. The ship was sailing from Bastia to Leghorn. At Cagliari one of its passengers, Giacomo Monticelli, who claimed to be Milanese but was believed to be a Corsican, deposed that Nelson 'took all his money, and for so doing he was a sea thief'. Outraged, the British consul (Michael Ghillini) counter-complained, and Monticelli first withdrew his charge and then fled to Leghorn on a gondola: Ghillini to Hood, 8/11/1793, NMM: Hoo/3.

56. Hood to Stephens, 9/8/1794, ADM 1/392. For this engagement see the ship's logs; record of works spoken on the quarterdeck, Add. MSS 34988: 112; *D&L*, 1, pp. 334, 337; journal, *NLTHW*, pp. 138–9; Hoste to his father, 27/11/1793, NMM: MRF/88/1; Nelson to Maurice, 8/11/1793, Monmouth MSS, E602; and O. Troude and P. Levot, *Batailles Navales*, 2, p. 313.

57. Nelson summed his five opponents as 170 guns and 1,600 men, against his own 64 guns and 345 men (Nelson to Maurice, 8/11/1793, Monmouth MSS, E602) but this ignores the fact that the *Agamemnon* engaged only one vessel, the *Melpomene*. He also made the *Melpomene* a forty-four-gun ship. As Hoste admitted this was 'a fine forty-gun frigate', and it had only eighteen-pounders to deploy against the British twenty-fours. All the French ships were later captured by the British, and I have taken their armaments from reports made at that time (list of prizes, ADM 1/391, enclosed with no. 145a; Hood to Stephens, 2/6/1794, 9/8/1794, ADM 1/392; Hood to Dundas, 2/6/1794, NMM: Hoo/9; *NLTHW*, p. 169; and letter of Nicholas Hardinge, 1794, in William Henry Wyndham-Quin, *Sir Charles Tyler*, p. 44).

58. *The Times*, 13/12/1793; Matcham, *Nelsons of Burnham Thorpe*, p. 108.

59. Nelson to Fanny, 16/1/1794, Monmouth MSS, E806; Linzee to Hood, 24/10/1793, 9/11/1793, ADM 1/391; Udny to Grenville, 5/12/1793, FO 79/9.

60. Journal, *NLTHW*, p. 138.

61. Journal, *NLTHW*, pp. 139–40; Nelson to Fanny, 1/12/1793, Monmouth MSS, E802; Nelson to Maurice, 8/11/1793, Monmouth MSS, E602; Nelson to Clarence, 2/12/1793, NMM: AGC/27; Nelson to Suckling, 5/12/1793, *D&L*, 1, p. 340. The main accounts of this mission are Linzee to Hood, 9/11/1793 and Perkins Magra to Hood, 10/11/1793, ADM 1/391.

62. Nelson to Fanny, 25/3/1796, Monmouth MSS, E888.

63. Hamilton and Laughton, *Above and Below Hatches*, pp. 130–2.

64. Nelson to Locker, 1/12/1793, *D&L*, 1, p. 337.

65. Hood to Nelson, November 1793, Add. MSS 34937; Nelson to Fanny, 1/12/1793, Monmouth MSS, E802; Linzee to Hood, 7/10/1793, Rose, *Lord Hood*, p. 141; Drake to Grenville, 22/12/1793, FO 28/6.

66. For these activities the *Agamemnon* logs are supported by those of the *Lowestoffe* (ADM 51/535), *Mermaid* (ADM 51/597) and *Tartar* (ADM 51/1123). On the captains see Wyndham-Quin, *Sir Charles Tyler*; Campbell to Nelson, 18/7/1804, NMM: CRK/3; Mary C. Innes, *William Wolseley*; and Wolseley to Nelson, 18/3/1794, Add. MSS 34903.

67. Hood to Linzee, 15/12/1793, NMM: Hoo/9.

68. Nelson to Clarence, 2/12/1793, NMM: AGC/27.

69. Edmund Nelson to Fanny, 13/12/1793, NMM: AGC/18/2; *NLTHW*, p. 175; and Matcham, *Nelsons of Burnham Thorpe*, pp. 100, 102, 103.

70. Fremantle to William Fremantle, 1794 and 13/4/1794, CBS, D-FR/45/2/97 and D-FR/45/2.

71. Nelson to William, 27/12/1793, Add. MSS 34988, and Nelson to Fanny, 27/12/1793, Monmouth MSS, E804.

72. Nelson to Clarence, 2/12/1793, NMM: AGC/27; Nelson to Locker, 1/12/1793, *D&L*,

1, p. 337; Nelson to Fanny, 27/12/1793, Monmouth MSS, E804; and Fanny to Nelson, 10/12/1794, *NLTHW*, p. 261.

73. Nelson to Clarence, 27/12/1793, NMM: AGC/27.

74. Udny to Grenville, 29/12/1793, and Udny to Nelson, 29/12/1793, FO 79/9; Nelson to Stephens, 26–27/12/1793, ADM 1/2224; Udny to Drake, 27 and 28/12/1793, Add. MSS 46826.

75. Hood to Nelson, 15/12/1793, Add. MSS 94937; Hervey to Grenville, 3/1/1794, FO 79/10.

XVIII Corsica (pp. 458–93)

1. Nelson to Fanny, 13/2/1794, Monmouth MSS, E808.

2. Nelson to Fanny, 28/2/1794, Monmouth MSS, E809. Desmond Gregory, *Ungovernable Rock*, surveys the history of the British Corsican protectorate. For Paoli see Peter Adam Thrasher, *Paoli*.

3. Reports of Edward Cooke and Thomas Nepean, 7, 8/1/1794, FO 20/2.

4. Moore's report, January 1794, in J. F. Maurice, ed., *Diary of Moore*, 1, p. 48, and Elliot to Henry Dundas, 14/2/1794, FO 20/2.

5. Hood to Elliot, 26/1/1794, NMM: ELL/140; Hood to Nelson, 4/2/1794, Add. MSS 34937; and *Tartar* log, ADM 52/3104.

6. Nelson to Locker, 17/1/1794, *D&L* 1, p. 347; Nelson to Fanny, 16/1/1794, Monmouth MSS, E806; Hood to Nelson, 7/1/1794, Add. MSS 34937; Nelson journal, *NLTHW*, p. 144.

7. Nelson to Fanny, 16/1/1794, Monmouth MSS, E806; Hood to Stephens, 22/2/1794, ADM 1/392; St Michel to the French Convention, 22/1/1794, in Maurice Jollivet, 'Revolution Française', p. 209.

8. The logs of the *Agamemnon* (chap. 17, n. 2) are relevant for the whole of this chapter, but Nelson's blockade is also illustrated by the logs of the *Leda* (ADM 51/1163), *Amphitrite* (ADM 51/21) and *Lowestoffe* (ADM 51/4470).

9. British sources say that eight boats carried a thousand French soldiers through the shallows from St Fiorenzo, but St Michel, commanding at Bastia, reported (n. 7 above) that an armed felucca and a sloop from St Fiorenzo took troops to the mill, while additional grenadiers arrived from Bastia.

10. Nelson journal, *NLTHW*, p. 145; David to Henry Dundas, 21/2/1794, HO 50/456.

11. Nelson to Suckling, 1/3/1794, *D&L*, 1, p. 362.

12. Nelson's journal and letters contain several allusions to the fortifications of Bastia, for example Nelson to Hoste, 3/5/1794, Monmouth MSS, E302. Among valuable visual pieces of evidence are a contemporary printed French map in NMM, reproduced in Anthony Deane, *Nelson's Favourite*, p. 104; D'Aubant's view of Bastia from the hills, 26/2/1794, and Koehler's map and views, March 1794, in HO 50/456: 180, 181; and the British map in HO 28/15: 313.

13. Hood to Nelson, 20/2/1794, Add. MSS 34937; Hood to Sutton, 20/2/1794, NMM: Hoo/9; McArthur to Nelson, 21/2/1794, Add. MSS 34937; Hood to Henry Dundas, 22/2/1794, HO 28/15. The logs of the ships, such as that of the *Romulus*, 5/2/1794, ADM 51/1151, supply details, but Nelson's journal (*NLTHW*, p. 128 following) is the best source of information on this phase.

14. Nelson to Hood, 8/2/1794, Add. MSS 70948; Nelson to Hood, 19/2/1794, *D&L*, 1, p. 356; *Tartar* log, ADM 52/3104.

15. Nelson to Udny, 12/2/1794, Monmouth MSS, E194.

16. Nelson journal, *NLTHW*, p. 147; Nelson to Udny, 24/2/1794, NMM: AGC/18/3.

17. Udny, 7/3/1794, NMM: AGC/18/3.

18. Nelson to Hood, 19/2/1794, *D&L*, 1, p. 356.

19. This account of the February attacks on Bastia largely depends upon Nelson's journal; Nelson to Hood, 22/2/1794, Monmouth MSS, E500; Nelson to Udny, 24/2/1794, NMM: AGC/18/3; and Anne Fremantle, ed., *Wynne Diaries* (1952), p. 252.

20. Dundas to Hood, 23/2/1794, HO 28/15; Nelson to Fanny, 28/2/1794, Monmouth MSS, E809.

21. Nelson to Fanny, 28/2/1794, Monmouth MSS, E809.

22. Nelson journal, *NLTHW*, p. 148. The main printed sources for the Corsican sieges are the letters and journals in *D&L*, vols 1 and 2; *NLTHW*; J. H. Godfrey, ed., 'Corsica, 1794'; Countess of Minto, ed., *Sir Gilbert Elliot*, 2, chaps 6–7; *The Times*, 3/9/1794 (Hood and Stuart's dispatches covering the fall of Calvi); and Maurice, *Diary of Moore*. The manuscript materials are richer, and include the logs of the *Agamemnon* and other relevant ships; ADM 1/392 (Hood's correspondence with the Admiralty); HO 28/15 (correspondence between Hood and Henry Dundas); NMM: Hoo/3–4, 9 (Hood letters); NMM: CRK/7 (Hood's letters to Sir William Hamilton); FO 20/2 (Elliot's official dispatches); NMM: ELL/138, 140, 149 and 162 (respectively Elliot's correspondence with Nelson, Hood, the military, and his journal of March 1794); the Minto (Elliot) papers, National Library of Scotland, Edinburgh, MSS 11209–11214, 11221; WO 1/302 and HO 50/456 (military dispatches); Add. MSS 34902–34903, 34937, 34941 (Nelson papers); Add. MSS 20107 (the diary of an army officer eager to expose any 'misman-agement of the navy'); Add. MSS 22688 (Paoli papers); and Add. 57320 and 57325 (Moore's journal and letters). For reports from Bastia, written by Lacombe St Michel on 14/3/1794 and 20/4/1794, see Archives Nationales, Paris, AF/II/94, dossier 693: 26, and AF/II/252, dossier 2141: 2. Other sources are plentiful and cited as used.

The secondary accounts have reproduced contemporary divisions. Nelson's biog-raphers have generally repeated his (and the navy's) viewpoint without considering it necessary to consult other official letters and dispatches, although in recent years a new orthodoxy – the uncritical reproduction of Moore's opinions – appears to be developing. John W. Fortescue, a man notorious in some quarters for his prejudices, shows contempt for any but military opinions in his *History of the British Army*, 4, pt I, chap. 8, and both James Carrick Moore (Moore's brother), *Life of Sir John Moore*, vol. 1, chaps 4–5, and Maurice, *Diary of Moore*, follow their subject, in the latter case with considerable cogency. It needs to be understood, however, that there were different army opinions about the practicability of attacking Bastia, though relatively few have survived in extensive form. As I have argued here, the detailed history of the siege reveals the corrosive interplay of powerful personalities and serious flaws in all the major participants. Somewhat less narrowly partisan assessments are Carola Oman, *Sir John Moore*, chap. 3, and Gregory, *Ungovernable Rock*. Maurice Jollivet, '*Revolution Française*', pp. 213–23, uses French sources to produce a laudatory descrip-tion of the defence of Bastia.

Corsica features strongly in considerations of Nelson's operations on shore, though assessments continue to vary. Nelson's failure to grasp essential differences between mili-tary and naval operations needed more attention in Colin White's admiring 'Nelson Ashore, 1780–1797', but Joel Hayward's *For God and Glory*, which appeared as the present book was being prepared for the press, overstates the weaknesses in Nelson's amphibious operations. Indeed, in this respect Hayward's otherwise not inconsiderable account comes close to disparagement. His description of Nelson's service on the San Juan expedition as 'merely adequate' (p. 205) would have astonished Captain Polson, while the analysis of the Corsican campaign uncritically follows Moore and Fortescue. His statement that Nelson's 'relations with army officers were seldom collegial, often tense, and sometimes bad and counterproductive' (p. 164) is untrue and greatly underrates his diplomatic abilities. Nelson's relations with Polson and Villettes, with whom he conducted his first two sieges, were exemplary, and those with Duncan and De Burgh, with whom he principally cooperated in 1794 to 1797, were also good. Nelson even managed to remain on reasonable terms with Stuart at Calvi, though that general was difficult enough to drive the emollient Elliot close to distraction. In Corsica, Nelson disliked Moore precisely because he considered the lieutenant colonel divisive and detrimental to interservice relations, and he had no more respect for Generals Dundas and D'Aubant than Moore did himself. The singular breach in the relations between the services that occurred at that time was due to Hood and Dundas, not Nelson. A detailed study of Nelson's actual and projected joint and shore-based operations between 1780 and 1800 would be welcome.

23. Hood to Nelson, 8 and 9/3/1794, Add. MSS 34937.
24. Elliot to his wife, 13/3/1794, Minto, *Sir Gilbert Elliot*, 2, p. 232; Hood to Henry Dundas, 24/5/1794, HO 28/15; Henry to David Dundas, 20/12/1793, Fortescue, *British Army*, 4, p. 176.
25. T. A. Thorp, 'George Thorp', p. 187; Bowen to Hamilton, 18/2/1794, Warren R. Dawson, ed., *Nelson Collection*, p. 49.
26. Elliot journal, NMM: ELL/162; Fremantle to William Fremantle, 13/4/1794, CBS, D-FR/45/2; Hood to Dundas, 8/3/1794, and Elliot to Hood, 9/3/1794, HO 50/456.
27. Maurice, *Diary of Moore*, I, p. 66.
28. Hood to Dundas, 23/2/1794, Dundas to Hood, 23/2/1794, and Dundas to Hood, 26/2/1794, HO 28/15. Copies of many of these letters are also filed in NMM: Hoo/3 and Hoo/9.
29. Hood to Dundas, 2/3/1794, and Dundas to Hood, 5/3/1794, HO 28/15; Hood to Dundas, 6/3/1794, HO 50/456.
30. Dundas to Hood, 7/3/1794, NMM: Hoo/3; Drake to Grenville, 10/3/1794, with enclosures, *Dropmore MSS*, 2, p. 523; Hood to Hamilton, 28/2/1794, NMM: CRK/7.
31. McArthur to Nelson, 3/3/1794 and Hood to Nelson, 5, 9/3/1794, Add. MSS 34937; Hood to Drake, 3/3/1794, Godfrey, 'Corsica, 1794', p. 368; Hood to Dundas, 6/3/1794, HO 50/456; Nelson to Hood, 5/3/1794, *D&L*, 1, p. 368; intelligence, 26/2/1794, NMM: CRK/7.
32. Elliot journal, NMM: ELL/162; Maurice, *Diary of Moore*, I, p. 68; Hood to Dundas, 9/3/1794, NMM: Hoo/9; Moore to Hood, 15/3/1794, NMM: Hoo/3.
33. Hood to Dundas, 6, 7/3/1794, HO 50/456.
34. Dundas to Hood, 8/3/1794, NMM: Hoo/3; Dundas to Hood, 9/3/1794, HO 28/15; Dundas to Dundas, 10/3/1794, HO 50/456; Elliot journal, NMM: ELL/162. Interestingly, this same David Dundas would head a procession of ten thousand soldiers at Nelson's funeral in 1806.
35. Oman, *Sir John Moore*, p. 119; Elliot to his wife, 28/3/1794, Minto, *Sir Gilbert Elliot*, 2, p. 234.
36. Maurice, *Diary of Moore*, I, p. 71; Elliot journal, NMM: ELL/162.
37. For the use of small boats see the logs of the *Agamemnon*; Hood to Nelson, 9, 16, 22/3/1794, Add. MSS 34903; and Hood to Nelson, 8/3/1794, and McArthur to Nelson, 11/3/1794, Add. MSS 34937.
38. Nelson to Paoli, 6/3/1794, Add. MSS 22688; Nelson to Fanny, 4/3/1794, Monmouth MSS, E810.
39. Nelson to Hood, 18/3/1794, *D&L*, 1, p. 358; Elliot to Henry Dundas, 5/4/1794, FO 20/2.
40. Log of the *Romney*, ADM 51/1143.
41. Elliot journal, NMM: ELL/162; Hood to D'Aubant, 12 and 14/3/1794, NMM: Hoo/9 and HO 28/15.

42. Report of Moore and Koehler, 18/3/1794, HO 28/15: 191; Hood to Henry Dundas, 18 and 19/3/1794, HO 28/15.

43. Elliot journal, NMM: ELL/162; Nelson journal, *NLTHW*, p. 150.

44. Report of the council of war, 20/3/1794, HO 28/15: 187; Maurice, *Diary of Moore*, 1, pp. 72–7; Nelson journal, *NLTHW*, p. 150; Elliot journal, NMM: ELL/162; Elliot and Hood to D'Aubant, 14/3/1794, FO 20/2.

45. Hood to D'Aubant, 21/3/1794, NMM: Hoo/9; Hood to Villettes and Brereton, 22/3/1794, NMM: Hoo/9; Elliot journal, NMM: ELL/162.

46. Hood to D'Aubant, 24/3/1794, NMM: Hoo/9.

47. Hood to Dundas, 27/5/1794, HO 28/15; Elliot journal, NMM: ELL/162; David Dundas memorandum, 30/1/1794, HO 50/456: 80.

48. Elliot journal, NMM: ELL/162; Elliot to his wife, 7/4/1794, Minto, *Sir Gilbert Elliot*, 2, p. 237; Elliot to Dundas, 5/4/1794, FO 20/2. The correspondence about the Light Dragoons is in FO 20/2, HO 28/15 and NMM: ELL/149.

49. Elliot journal, NMM: ELL/162; Hood to Hamilton, 15, 24, 25/3/1794, NMM: CRK/7; Nelson to Hamilton, 27/3/1794, Add. MSS 34902; list of equipment and stores requested from Naples, 26/3/1794, NMM: CRK/14. Not all the supplies from Naples arrived in time, and Hood particularly felt the want of mortar and gunboats (Hood to Hamilton, 21/4/1794, 6/5/1794, NMM: CRK/7).

50. Nelson to Fanny, 22/3/1794, Monmouth MSS, E811; Nelson to Hamilton, 27/3/1794, Add. MSS 34902.

51. Elliot to his wife, 7/4/1794, Minto, *Sir Gilbert Elliot*, 2, p. 237; Elliot journal, NMM: ELL/162. The true opinion of Villettes is unknown. He supported the Moore–Koehler report of 18 March, but perhaps out of mere loyalty to the army and his superior officer. Later he also dutifully landed at Bastia, and joined Nelson in directing a siege under Hood's orders. Captain Fremantle said that Villettes was in favour of an attack upon Bastia: Fremantle to William Fremantle, 13/4/1794, CBS, D-FR/45/2.

52. D'Aubant to Henry Dundas, 2/4/1794, HO 50/456; Maurice, *Diary of Moore*, 1, pp. 74–6, 80, 82, 85; Elliot's journal, 21 and 23/3/1794, NMM: ELL/162.

53. Thrasher, *Paoli*, pp. 285–6.

54. Nelson to Hoste, 3/5/1794, and Nelson to Hamilton, 19/12/1794, Alfred Morrison, *Hamilton and Nelson Papers*, 1, pp. 190, 197. Villettes subsequently became the governor of Bastia and lieutenant governor and commander-in-chief of Jamaica. He died in Jamaica in 1808. See 'Anecdotes of the Late Lieutenant-General Villettes' in *Gentleman's Magazine*.

55. Nelson to Suckling, 7/2/1795, *D&L*, 2, p. 4; Hood to Nelson, 16/3/1794, Add. MSS 34937.

56. Maurice, *Diary of Moore*, I, p. 80.

57. Nelson to William, 26/3/1794, Add. MSS 34988.

58. For the ships see Hood to Dundas, 5/4/1794, HO 28/15. Nelson's journals for the siege of Bastia, from which quotations in the following pages have been taken, are published in *D&L*, vol. 1, and more satisfactorily in *NLTHW*, p. 154 following.

59. *Scout* log, ADM 51/836; Hood to Stephens, 24/5/1794, ADM 1/392; Hood to Wolseley, 28/4/1794, NMM: Hoo/9.

60. Nelson to Hood, 24, 25/4/1794, Add. MSS 34902; Nelson to Suckling, 6/4/1794, *D&L*, 1, p. 381.

61. Hood had offered Villettes five or six hundred seamen to support his soldiers, haul guns and fight batteries (Hood to Villettes, 24/4/1794, NMM: Hoo/9). The fact that Villettes accepted half that number suggests his relative sense of security.

62. Elliot to Henry Dundas, 5/4/1794, FO 20/2; Hood to Alexander Hood, 5/4/1794, Add. MSS 35194.

63. Nelson to Fanny, 22/4/1794, Monmouth MSS, E814.

64. Nelson journal, *NLTHW*, p. 155. Vice Admiral Hotham's nephew, who gave an account of the siege long afterwards, seems to have erred in saying that Hood was ashore when the British batteries opened. He remembered that the French were 'not a little astonished' at the number of guns Nelson and Villettes brought to bear (A. M. W. Stirling, ed., *Pages and Portraits*, 1, pp. 59–60). See also Hood to Henry Dundas, 14/4/1794, NMM: Hoo/9. For Corsican tactics see the journal of George Mundy of the *Juno*, NMM: 85/015.

65. Hood to Stephens, 14/4/1794, ADM 1/392.

66. I have modified some of Nelson's details by reference to the map of the siege in HO 28/15: 313.

67. Elliot to Paoli, 22/4/1794, Add. MSS 22688.

68. Returns of losses enclosed in ADM 1/392, no. 34; Fremantle, *Wynne Diaries*, p. 252; Hood to Nelson, 20/4/1794, Add. MSS 34937; Stirling, *Pages and Portraits*, 1, p. 60.

69. Hood to Henry Dundas, 25/4/1794, NMM: Hoo/9, Nelson to Hood, 3/5/1794, Add. MSS 34937.

70. Fremantle, *Wynne Diaries*, p. 252; Nelson journal, *NLTHW*, p. 156; Hood to Stephens, 25/4/1794, ADM 1/392; Hood to Henry Dundas, 25/4/1794, NMM: Hoo/9; Hood to Nelson, 20/4/1794 and 13/5/1794, Add. MSS 34937; Nelson journal, *D&L*, 1, p. 398. The British were directing most of their fire at military targets, but the damage suggests some indiscriminate bombardment of the town with consequent civilian casualties.

71. Hood to Nelson, 10, 16/4/1794, Add. MSS 34937; Nelson to Hood, 18/3/1794, *D&L*, 1, p. 373; Elliot to his wife, 30/5/1794, Minto, *Sir Gilbert Elliot*, 2, p. 253; log of the *Meleager*, ADM 51/1210. Hood's emphasis on the blockade runs through his correspondence in the Paoli papers (Add. MSS 22688).

72. Nelson journal, *D&L*, 1, p. 388; Udny to Wyndham, 26/3/1794, FO 79/10, Thrasher, *Paoli*, pp. 286–7.

73. Nelson to Hood, 26/4/1794, *D&L*, 1, p. 388; Nelson to Hoste, 3/5/1794, Morrison, *Hamilton and Nelson Papers*, 1, p. 190. Hoste's letter to his father, 7/5/1794 (Harriet Hoste, ed., *Hoste*, 1, p. 26), also reflects the increasing doubts in Nelson's camp. It refers to the inadequacy of their force, the relative inefficacy of their bombardment and the resistance of Bastia's stone buildings to fire. Hoste believed they were no nearer taking Bastia on 7 May than in April. The establishment of the new batteries on 8 May can also be taken as a comment on the inadequacy of the earlier batteries.

74. Hood to Nelson, 21/4/1794, Add. MSS 34937; Hood to Dundas, 25/4/1794, HO 28/15; Elliot to Dundas, 5/4/1794, FO 20/2. According to the contemporary British map (HO 28/15: 313) the French had six hundred and fifty men scattered between eight hill forts or redoubts to the rear of Bastia. The lower hill forts were manned by between twenty-six and sixty-four men each, and the upper camps by between twenty and two hundred men each.

75. Elliot to Dundas, 5/4/1794, FO 20/2; Dundas to Elliot, 25/4/1794, FO 20/2.

76. Hood and Elliot to Dundas, 18/4/1794, FO 20/2.

77. Maurice, *Diary of Moore*, I, p. 82; D'Aubant to Hood and Elliot, 23/4/1794, FO 20/2; Hood to D'Aubant, 1/5/1794, NMM: Hoo/9; D'Aubant to Hood, 2/5/1794, NMM: ELL/140.

78. Hood to Nelson, 13/5/1794, Godfrey, 'Corsica, 1794', p. 393; Nelson journal, *NLTHW*, p. 157.

79. Nelson to Suckling, 6/4/1794, *D&L*, 1, p. 381; James Stanier Clarke and John McArthur, *Life and Services*, 1, pp. 246–7.

XIX A Long and Hazardous Service (pp. 494–519)

1. Nelson journal, *NLTHW*, p. 158.
2. In addition to Nelson's journals see Nelson to William, 30/5/1794, Add. MSS 34988, and several documents in NMM: Hoo/9, including casualty returns; Hood to Nelson, 17/5/1794 and Hood to Stuart, 29/5/1794. Udny reported three thousand six hundred prisoners being shipped to Toulon, but may have excluded Corsican allies of the French (Udny to Drake, 26/5/1794, Add. MSS 46826).
3. Hood to Boyd, 25/5/1794, NMM: Hoo/9; documents referring to the reserves of powder at Gibraltar, especially Rainsford to Henry Dundas, 26/6/1794, in WO 1/288.
4. J. F. Maurice, ed., *Diary of Moore*, 1, p. 89.
5. D'Aubant to Dundas, 23/5/1794, HO 50/456; Hood to d'Aubant, 21/5/1794 (two letters), NMM: Hoo/9.
6. Nelson to Fanny, 20/5/1794, Monmouth MSS, E816. Nelson's tendency to underrate opposition would be noticed again, and Moore's caution earned him some criticism during his later campaign in the Spanish peninsula. Both seem to have been embedded as much in personality as in professional evaluations of particular situations.
7. Nelson to Suckling, 16/7/1794, Monmouth MSS, E44; Hood to Stephens, 24/5/1794, ADM 1/392; Nelson to Fanny, 8/7/1794, Monmouth MSS, E822; Fremantle to William Fremantle, 13/4/1794, CBS, D-FR/45/2. The same injustice was done to Nelson in Hood to Dundas, 24/5/1794, NMM: Hoo/9.
8. Nelson to Fanny, 1 to 4/5/1794, Monmouth MSS, E815; Nelson to Suckling, 16/7/1794, *D&L*, 1, p. 441.
9. J. H. Godfrey, ed., 'Corsica, 1794', p. 400.
10. Desmond Gregory, *Unconquerable Rock*, p. 89.
11. Nelson to Fanny, 7/6/1794, Monmouth MSS, E818; Hood to Hippersley, 15/6/1794, Monmouth MSS, E25; Hood to Stephens, 15/6/1794, ADM 1/392; Nelson to Elliot, 1794, NMM: ELL/138; Hood to Dundas, 15/6/1794, WO 1/302.
12. Stuart to Elliot, 14/6/1794, NMM: ELL/149; Villettes to Nelson, 10/5/1795, Add. MSS 34904; logs of the *Lutine* (Captain James Macnamara) and *Gorgon*, ADM 51/1103 and ADM 51/1152. I have used the manuscript copies of Nelson's Calvi journal in ADM 1/2224; ADM 1/392; and WO 1/302, and the published version, *NLTHW*, p. 160 following, taken from the Monmouth manuscripts. There are minor but significant differences between some of these copies. Nelson's journal gives the figure of fourteen hundred and fifty officers and men embarked. A return of 30/5/1794 (NMM: Hoo/3) lists the number as 1,392. It included detachments of the Royal Artillery and Royal Engineers and men of the 50th and 51st regiments of foot.
13. A plan in NMM: Hoo/3 shows the *Agamemnon* eventually found an anchorage in Alusa Bay, south of Port Agro. For a French account of the siege of Calvi see Maurice Jollivet, *Anglais dans La Mediterranée*, pp. 53–60, but see also the letter of Barthelemi Arna, 8/8/1794, in *Gazette Nationale*, 24/8/1794.
14. Nelson to the agents of victuallers and transports, 17/6/1794, Monmouth MSS, E33. Accounts informed by personal inspection of the ground include J. D. Spinney, 'Nelson at Port Agro'; Tom Pocock, *Horatio Nelson*, chap. 5; and David Shannon, 'Nelson at Calvi'. Among additional logs that illuminate the doings offshore is that of *L'Aigle* (ADM 51/1103).
15. Nelson to Fanny, 27/6/1794, Monmouth MSS, E820. Nelson's journal says that two hundred and fifty seamen were landed on 19 June, but army officers speak of one hundred and fifty. See also Hood to Nelson, 21/6/1794, NMM: Hoo/3.
16. Diary of Hudson Lowe, 19 and 20/6/1794, Add. MSS 20107.
17. Nelson journal, *NLTHW*, p. 165.

18. Stuart to Hood, 28/6/1794, NMM: Hoo/3; Stuart to Elliot, 25/6/1794, NMM: ELL/149; Hood to Elliot, 23/6/1794, NMM: ELL/140; Hood to Dundas, 5/8/1794, WO 1/302.

19. Stuart to Elliot, 25/6/1794, NMM: ELL/149.

20. Hood to Nelson, 23 and 30/6/1794, NMM: Hoo/3; Hood to Stephens, 14/3/1794, 3/5/1794, ADM 1/392; Elliot to Stuart, 30/6/1794, NMM: ELL/152; Fremantle to William Fremantle, 17/5/1794, CBS, D-FR/45/2.

21. Nelson's journal, ADM 1/2224; Nelson to Hood, 11/7/1794, NMM: Hoo/3.

22. A. M. W. Stirling, ed., *Pages and Portraits*, 1, p. 240.

23. Nelson to Hood, 18, 20/7/1794, *D&L* 1, pp. 448, 451. Compare Maurice, *Diary of Moore*, I, pp. 103, 110, and Stuart to Elliot, 25/6/1794, NMM: ELL/149.

24. Stuart to Elliot, 25/6/1794, NMM: ELL/149; Hood to Elliot, 3/7/1794, NMM: ELL/140; Hood to Nelson, 16, 17/7/1794, NMM: Hoo/3 and Hoo/4; Nelson to Hood, 16/7/1794, NMM: Hoo/3; Nelson to Hood, July 1794, Add. MSS 34937; Hood to Nepean, 17/8/1794, WO1/302.

25. Nelson to Hood, 20/7/1794, Add. MSS 34904; Hood to Stephens, 5/8/1794, ADM 1/392.

26. Hood to Nelson, 24/7/1794, 28/12/1796, Add. MSS 34937; Stuart to Nelson, 25/6/1794, Add. MSS 34903.

27. Nelson's journal, ADM 1/2224; Lowe diary, Add. MSS 20107.

28. Stuart's dispatch of 10/8/1794, *The Times*, 3/9/1794.

29. Hood to Nelson, 11/7/1794, NMM: Hoo/3; *D&L*, 2, p. 178; *The Times*, 3/9/1794.

30. Nelson to Hood, 8/7/1794, NMM: Hoo/3.

31. Nelson to Fanny, 18/8/1794, 1/9/1794, Monmouth MSS, E826, E828; Hood to Stephens, 27/8/1794, ADM 1/392. Moutray's promotion to second lieutenant indirectly owed something to Nelson. Boyle, who created the vacancy aboard the *Speedy*, was recalled to England to serve on the *Egmont* at the express wish of the Duke of Clarence. Clarence had met Boyle in the West Indies when both served under Nelson's command. In the *Speedy*, Moutray had also met another graduate of Nelson's *Boreas*, Lieutenant William Tatham.

32. Nelson journal, *NLTHW*, pp. 163, 165; Nelson's journal, ADM 1/2224; Joseph Allen, 'England's Wooden Walls', pp. 348–50. Hallowell was the son of the last surviving commissioner of the American board of customs. There are sketches of him in *Gentleman's Magazine*, 2, new series (1834), pp. 537–9; *DNB*, 3, pp. 956–8; and W. H. Fitchett, *Nelson and His Captains*, chap. 7. Fifty-five Hallowell papers exist at Duke University, Durham, North Carolina.

33. Maurice, *Diary of Moore*, 1, p. 108; Nelson journal, *NLTHW*, p. 165.

34. The shifting of guns receives a high profile in Nelson's journal and in his correspondence with Hood. See, for example, Hood to Nelson, 8, 10, 15/7/1794, NMM: Hoo/3.

35. Nelson to Elliot, 17/7/1794, NMM: ELL/138; certificates of Harness, Jefferson and Chambers dated 9 and 11/8/1794, *D&L*, 1, p. 493, and Add. MSS 35060, Maurice, *Diary of Moore*, 1, p. 110; Thomas Pettigrew, *Memoirs*, 1, pp. 58–9.

36. Nelson to Hood, 12/7/1794, *D&L*, 1, p. 435; Nelson to Suckling, 16/7/1794, Monmouth MSS, E44; Nelson to Fanny, 1/8/1794, Monmouth MSS, E824.

37. Hood to Elliot, 15/7/1794, *NLTHW*, p. 172. The medical debate about Nelson's injury is engaged in James Kemble, *Idols and Invalids*, pp. 128–31; T. C. Barras, 'Vice-Admiral Nelson's Lost Eye'; T. C. Barras, 'I Have a Right to be Blind Sometimes'; Milo Keynes, 'Horatio Nelson Never Was Blind'; Daniel Duldig, 'Nelson a Malingerer?'; Anne-Marie E. Hills, 'His Eye in Corsica'; Anne-Marie E. Hills, 'Nelson: War Pensioner'; and Peter J. Gray, 'Turning a Blind Eye'.

38. Hood to Nelson, 14/7/1794, NMM: Hoo/3; Lowe diary, Add. MSS 20107.

39. Nelson journal, *NLTHW*, p. 167. Publishing Stuart's dispatch, *The Times*, 3/9/1794, misprinted the name of the army officer who helped Nelson establish the battery. Reference to the War Office lists identifies him as Wauchope.

40. For Hood's suspicions see Hood to Elliot, 28/7/1794, NMM: ELL/140. Some historians have emphasised the British lack of powder and shot, but though Hood grew concerned as the siege progressed (Hood to Nelson, 18/7/1794, NMM: Hoo/9) supplies continued to arrive. On 5 August, for example, two ships brought over ten thousand shells and shot and two hundred barrels of powder (Hood to Elliot, 5/8/1794, NMM: ELL/140). These replenishments probably came from Naples or Sardinia (Hood to Hamilton, 24/7/1794, NMM: HML/12, and Hamilton to Hood, 2/8/1794, NMM: HML/10A). At the end of the siege Stuart's complaint, which had lately been the dwindling supplies of powder and shot, became the temporary inability of the ships to land fresh supplies because of gales (Stuart to Elliot, 10/8/1794, NMM: ELL/140).

41. For the arrival of French supplies see Nelson to Elliot, 30/7/1794, NMM: ELL/138, and Hood to Dundas, 5/8/1794, WO 1/302.

42. Hoste to his father, 24/8/1794, Harriet Hoste, ed., *Hoste*, 1, p. 34.

43. Nelson to Fanny, 18, 25/8/1794, 31/1/1795, Monmouth MSS, E826–827, E845.

44. I have discarded the second-hand report in *The Times* of 4 October 1804 that Nelson eventually recovered the sight in his right eye. No first-hand evidence to support this remarkable statement has been found.

45. Hood to Stephens, 31/8/1794, ADM 1/392; *The Times*, 3/9/1794; Nelson to Elliot, 10/8/1794, NMM: ELL/138. The number of French defenders is uncertain. In his journal Nelson said that three hundred French troops and 247 Corsicans surrendered their arms, and that another 313 previously armed men were in the hospital. He made no reference to the numbers of seamen from the frigates and gunboat in the harbour. However, the statement of a French inspector of roads and bridges, made on the *Victory* on 11 August (WO1/302: 165), listed the defenders as three hundred regulars, including the sick, and some six hundred Corsicans and seamen. Hood's flag-captain claimed that four hundred of seven hundred armed defenders in Calvi were in the hospital (Knight to Elliot, 12/8/1794, NMM: ELL/138).

46. Nelson to Elliot, 4/8/1794, NMM: ELL/138; terms of capitulation, WO 1/302: 145 f.

47. Knight to Elliot, 29, 30/7/1794, 4, 12/8/1794, NMM: ELL/138; Hood to Stephens, 9/8/1794, Add. MSS 35195; Hood to Nepean, 17/8/1794, enclosing the statement of the French engineer, WO1/302.

48. Nelson journal, *NLTHW*, p. 169; *Diary of Moore*, I, p. 115; Wemyss to Nelson, 8/8/1794, NMM: Hoo/4; Hood to Nelson, 8/8/1794, NMM: Hoo/4; Nelson to Elliot, 5/8/1794, NMM: ELL/140. Nelson's claim that only four hundred soldiers were fit for duty when Calvi surrendered is exaggerated; Stuart reported the figure as six hundred (Stuart to Elliot, 10/8/1794, NMM: ELL/140). Sickness was also rife among the French, and on that account Stuart delayed occupying the works until they had been evacuated. On 8 August, John Udny wrote to Grenville that the French were suffering from scurvy and a malignant fever (FO 79/11).

49. Nelson to Hood, Monmouth MSS, E510; Nelson to Clarence, 6, 10/8/1794, NMM: AGC/27.

50. Nelson to Sainthill, 14/8/1794, *United Service Journal* (1830), pt i, p. 36; Stuart to Hood, 9/8/1794, ADM 1/392.

51. Master's log of *Agamemnon*, 11 to 12/8/1794, ADM 52/2707; Mary C. Innes, *William Wolseley*, p. 99.

52. Nelson to Fanny, 1/8/1794, Monmouth MSS, E824; Fanny to Nelson, 16/12/1794, *NLTHW*, p. 262; Hamilton to Nelson, 9/12/1794, Add. MSS 34903.

53. Hood to Stephens, 5/8/1794, ADM 1/392; Hood to Dundas, 5/8/1794, NMM: Hoo/9; *The Times*, 3/9/1794.

54. A. T. Mahan, *Life of Nelson*, p. 130; Nelson to Locker, 4/5/1795, *D&L*, 2, p. 34; James Harrison, *Life*, 1, p. 27.

55. Hood to Nelson, 12/8/1794, NMM: Hoo/4.
56. Hood to Stephens, 27/8/1794, ADM 1/392; Add. MSS 34902: 53.

XX Two Meetings with French Gentry (pp. 520–63)

1. *Agamemnon* muster, ADM 36/11539. Principal sources for this chapter are Add. MSS 34902–34904; *D&L*, vols 1 and 2; and *NLTHW*.
2. Nelson to Suckling, 20/9/1794, *D&L*, 1, p. 489.
3. Nelson to Fanny, 18/8/1794, 12/9/1794, 17/1/1795, Monmouth MSS, E826, E829, E843. The Hood–Stuart spat, focusing on transport and the use of soldiers as marines, can be found in WO 1/302 and WO 1/686.
4. Hood to Nelson, 18/9/1794, Add. MSS 34903.
5. Drake to Grenville, 7, 20, 27/9/1794, FO 28/9.
6. Nelson to Fanny, 20/9/1794, Monmouth MSS, E830; letter of Hood, 27/9/1794, FO 28/9; Brame to Stephens, 20/9/1794, ADM 1/3841.
7. Drake to Grenville, 27/9/1794, FO 28/9.
8. Nelson to Fanny, 12/9/1794, Monmouth MSS, E829; Hood to Nelson, 23/2/1796, NMM: CRK/6; Hood to Nelson, 23/8/1795, Add. MSS 34937.
9. Spencer to Hotham, 3/5/1795, Add. MSS, 75780; Elliot to Windham, 2/4/1795, Add. MSS 37852; A. M. W. Stirling, *The Hothams*, vol. 2.
10. Nelson to Locker, 21/3/1795, 4/5/1795, *D&L*, 2, pp. 20, 34.
11. Nelson to Fanny, 1/9/1794, Monmouth MSS, E828; Nelson to Clarence, 13/11/1794, NMM: AGC/27; Nelson to Hamilton, 21/11/1794, Alfred Morrison, ed., *Hamilton and Nelson Papers*, 1, p. 196.
12. According to Elliot, the captains described their fleet as 'going fast to leeward', comparing its increasing disrepair to the position of a crippled ship being driven helplessly upon a lee shore by the wind: Elliot to Dundas, 11/11/1794, FO 20/6.
13. Nelson to Clarence, 7/11/1794, NMM: AGC/27, Nelson's report on the fleet in Toulon, 5/11/1794, ADM 1/2224.
14. Nelson to Elliot, 10/11/1794, NMM: ELL/138; Nelson to Suckling, 7/2/1795, *D&L*, 2, p. 4; Nelson to Hamilton, 21/11/1794, Morrison, *Hamilton and Nelson Papers*, 1, p. 196.
15. Nelson to William, 26/10/1794, Add. MSS 34988.
16. Nelson to William, 26/10/1794, Add. MSS 34988.
17. Nelson to Fanny, 15/11/1794, Monmouth MSS, E838.
18. Nelson to Clarence, 28/11/1794, NMM: AGC/27; Nelson to Fanny, 10, 11/10/1794, 5/12/1794, Monmouth MSS, E833, E836, E840; Fanny to Nelson, 30/9/1794, 10/12/1794, *NLTHW*, pp. 252, 261; will of Nelson, 21/3/1798, *NLTHW*, p. 405. In 1794 Lepee was discharged to Mr Polhill, the surgeon at Leghorn, but on 20 October 1795 he joined the *Zealous* and in 1796 was rated able seaman aboard the *Diadem*: NMM: ADM/L/A51 (certificates and tickets); ADM 36/11362 (*Zealous*); and ADM 36/11823 (*Diadem*).
19. Nelson to Suckling, 31/10/1794, *D&L*, 1, p. 499.
20. Nelson to Suckling, 7/2/1795, *D&L*, 2, p. 4; Nelson to Fanny, 7/2/1795, Monmouth MSS, E846.
21. Nelson to McArthur, 28/11/1794, 10/4/1797, Monmouth MSS, E514, E518. John McArthur, Hood's secretary, acted as prize agent for the captors. Sir William Scott, the great authority on prize law, understood the distinctions between ships 'originally one of the [task] force and being employed by this force in purposes of indispensable necessity', and those 'coming there with provisions or stores and going away immediately or shortly afterwards' (Add. MSS 34905: 197–200), but in Nelson's view admitted too

many unjustified claims. Considering the Calvi claims, for example, Scott made no distinctions between the store ship *Inflexible*, which remained at St Fiorenzo but routinely issued supplies to ships involved in the siege and lent them a few men; the *Sincere*, which ferried supplies back and forth; the *St Fiorenzo* which spent two days at the siege; and the *Britannica* which remained off Calvi throughout, until blown away a few days before the surrender ('Cases of Officers and Men Belonging to the Ships . . . Claiming to Share Prize Money for the Captures made at Calvi', Benjamin Hallowell Carew papers, Duke University, Durham, North Carolina). Nelson's own suggestion, that prize money ought to have been awarded according to the number of days a ship was materially involved, was a sensible basis for the arbitration of such cases. His arguments were not entirely selfish. 'Why is Captain [Benjamin] Hallowell omitted?' he complained. 'He rendered more service than almost any other officer. If these share, I insist he does.'

22. Hood to Nelson, 1/12/1794, *D&L*, 1, p. 506; Hood to Nelson, 27/1/1795, Add. MSS 34937.

23. Spencer to Hood, 27/3/1795, Add. MSS 34937.

24. Details about Leghorn can be found in Thomas Fremantle's journal, published in Anne Fremantle, ed., *Wynne Diaries* (1952), and in *Nautical Magazine*, 3 (1834), pp. 684–9. I have not succeeded in locating the original of Fremantle's diary. It was not deposited with his personal papers in Aylesbury.

25. Fremantle, *Wynne Diaries*, pp. 254–6, 259. For Fremantle see Ann Parry, *The Admirals Fremantle*, and Ludovic Kennedy, *Nelson and His Captains*.

26. Fremantle, *Wynne Diaries*, p. 254; Tom Pocock, *Horatio Nelson*, pp. ix–x; Tom Pocock, *Nelson's Women*, p. 85.

27. Udny to Nelson, July 1796, Add. MSS 34904: 231; Udny to Nelson, 11/4/1797, Add. MSS 34906; Cockburn to Nelson, 24/7/1797, Add. MSS 34906; Brame to Nelson, 21/8/1796, Add. MSS 34904. The publication of the 1952 edition of the Wynne diaries alerted scholars to Nelson's Italian mistress, but it was Pocock, *Nelson and his World*, p. 45, who used the only surviving letter between the two (Nelson to Adelaide, undated, Huntington Library, San Marino, California) to name her. Nelson addressed his letter to 'Signora Adelaide Correglia', while Udny, who also knew her well, forwarded a letter for Nelson to 'Signora Adelaide Carellia'. Carellia was a phonetic rendering of Correglia. Little is known about Adelaide, and Pocock's inference that she was 'an opera singer' (*Horatio Nelson*, p. 124) appears to have no foundation. Research for the present work trebled the previously known number of documents referring to Adelaide, and considerably sharpens the focus upon her circumstances and relationship to Nelson, but the picture still remains misty.

28. Richard Walker, *Nelson Portraits*, pp. 15–17, 19, 195.

29. Fremantle to William Fremantle, undated, CBS, D-FR/45/2/112A; Fremantle, *Wynne Diaries*, p. 254.

30. Nelson to Adelaide, undated, Huntington Library. It is impossible to decide when this note was written. The reference to the ship leaving for Leghorn does not necessarily imply that Nelson himself was going there; it could have meant that he was taking advantage of a ship going to Leghorn to send her a letter. There is a finality in the tone of the note that suggests that it was penned late in 1796 or 1797, when circumstances were ending their relationship.

31. Fremantle, *Wynne Diaries*, p. 255.

32. Nelson sat on the trials of Lieutenant William Walker of the *Rose*, acquitted at Leghorn of illicit profiteering, 13 September 1794; the officers of the *Windsor Castle*, acquitted of tyranny at St Fiorenzo on 11 November 1794; a man of the *Dolphin* accused of fatally wounding a sailmaker; and a seaman of the *Princess Royal*, convicted at Leghorn on 18–19 December 1794 for assaulting his master-of-arms. For details see ADM 1/5331.

33. Jervis to Nelson, 13/7/1796, NMM: CRK/11.

34. Nelson to Fanny, 1/9/1794, 24/10/1794, Monmouth MSS, E828, E835.

35. Fanny to Nelson, 30/9/1794, 2/11/1794, Add. MSS 34988.

36. Nelson to Fanny, 12/10/1794, Monmouth MSS, E834; Fanny to Nelson, 7/11/1794, Add. MSS 34988; Edmund Nelson to Nelson, 3/9/1795, Monmouth MSS, E612.

37. Nelson to Fanny, 17/1/1795, Monmouth MSS, E843.

38. Nelson to Drake, 28/4/1796, Monmouth MSS, E987.

39. Edmund Nelson to Fanny, 13/12/1793, NMM: AGC/18/2; Edmund to Nelson, 5/8/1795, 3/12/1795, Monmouth MSS, E611, E615; Edmund to Fanny, 9/6/1793, undated 1793, 29/7/1794, 19/8/1796, Monmouth MSS, E635, E637, E640–E641; M. Eyre Matcham, *Nelsons of Burnham Thorpe*, pp. 105, 108, 118.

40. Edmund to Nelson, 5/8/1795, Monmouth MSS, E611; Fanny to Nelson, 2/11/1794, 17/12/1794, Add. MSS 34988.

41. Fanny to Nelson, 10, 16/12/1794, Add. MSS 34988.

42. Edmund Nelson to Nelson, 1/1/1795, in James Stanier Clarke and John McArthur, *Life and Services*, 1, p. 291; Nelson to Marsh and Creed, 28/10/1794, *Sotheby's Catalogue*, 29/2/1971. Enmeshed in the riviera campaign Nelson accidentally missed his gift to the Burnham poor in 1795. See also Nelson to his father, 19/8/1796, *D&L*, 2, p. 244, and *Public Characters*, p. 7.

43. Fanny to Nelson, 2/11/1794, 10, 17/12/1794, Add. MSS 34988

44. Nelson to Clarence, 19/1/1795, NMM: AGC/27; Nelson to Pollard, 6/2/1795, *D&L*, 2, p. 4; Nelson to Fanny, 23/1/1795, Monmouth MSS, E844; court martial, 21–28/1/1795, ADM 1/5332.

45. Nelson to Fanny, 25/2/1795, Monmouth MSS, E847; Nelson to Hamilton, 26/2/1795, Morrison, *Hamilton and Nelson Papers*, 1, p. 202; Nelson to Hood, 25/2/1795, Monmouth MSS, E277.

46. Elliot to Portland, 5/4/1795, FO 20/7.

47. For Caraccioli see Hotham to Hamilton, 2/3/1795, NMM: HML/13, and Hamilton to Hotham, 19/2/1795, 23/7/1795, NMM: HML/10B.

48. Nelson to Fanny, 10/3/1795, Monmouth MSS, E850.

49. Nelson to Goodall, 12/3/1795, *D&L*, 2, p. 18.

50. Nelson's journal (Add. MSS 34902: 54–9), 55, which, with the logs of the *Agamemnon*, is the principal source for his part in the battle, but another view from the same ship is given by Hoste to his father, 20/3/1795, NMM: MRF/88/1. Hotham to Stephens, 16/3/1795, ADM 1/393, is the official dispatch. On the French side, see Letourneur's report to the Committee of Public Safety, 16/3/1795, in Maurice Jollivet, *Anglais dans La Mediterranée*, pp. 118–21. Secondary accounts of this and Hotham's subsequent engagement are given by William James, *Naval History*, vol. 1; A. T. Mahan, *Life of Nelson*, chap. 5; and (for the battle off Genoa) E. Chevalier, *Histoire de la Marine Française*, pp. 171–82. My narrative of the action in March is also based upon logs of the *Bedford* (ADM 51/1116), *Britannia* (ADM 51/1155), *Captain* (ADM 51/1107 and NMM: ADM/L/C51), *Courageux* (ADM 51/1103), *Diadem* (ADM 51/1111), *Illustrious* (ADM 51/1124), *Inconstant* (ADM 51/1179), *Princess Royal* (ADM 51/1113), and *St George* (ADM 51/1119).

51. The older studies of the French navy by Jurien de la Gravière and Chevalier need to be reconsidered in light of recent studies by Jonathan R. Dull and William S. Cormack.

52. Nelson to William, 25/3/1795, Add. MSS 34988. Statements of the strength of the *Ça Ira* vary. The day after her eventual capture her captain (Coudé) seems to have given her strength as eighty guns and thirteen hundred men (Hotham dispatch). Nelson was inconsistent. He variously claimed that the *Ça Ira* had eighty-four guns, and formerly eighty-four but now ninety-two guns. For statements, see the journal (n. 50 above),

which exaggerates the weight of the French against the English pound, and Nelson to Fanny, 14/3/1795, 1/4/1795, Monmouth MSS, E851, E855. John Gibson of the *Fox*, who was with the British prizes until 17 March, said the *Ça Ira* actually mounted ninety long guns and four carronades and housed thirteen hundred men (Gibson to Elliot, 18/3/1795, NMM: ELL/138). To complicate matters, a prize court attempted to establish the numbers of men on board the *Ça Ira* because head money, based on the complement of a prize warship, was due the captors. For these proceedings Captain Coudé deposed on 22 April that his ship had been manned by one thousand and sixty (HCA 32/550).

53. The contribution of Fremantle's *Inconstant* is largely taken from his ship's log. It has attracted little comment in secondary sources, but contemporaries justly rated it with Nelson's achievement in the same battle. French prisoners spoke 'with great admiration' of the conduct of both captains, and Augustus Montgomery of the *Courageux* noted that the *Ça Ira* 'was fired at in a very gallant manner by Captain Fremantle of the *Inconstant*, and Captain Nelson also exchanged a few broadsides with her'. See Elliot to Windham, 2/4/1795, Add. MSS 37852, and Montgomery to Udny, 18/3/1795, Add. MSS 39793; and Montgomery to Elliot, 20/3/1795, NMM: ELL/138. Fremantle, like Nelson, considered Hotham's own contributions timid, and wrote that the admiral had 'grown too old, and has not nerves sufficient for the situation in which he is placed' (Fremantle to William Fremantle, 24/3/1795, CBS, D-FR/45/2).

54. Add. MSS 34902: 56; Nelson to Elliot, 5/4/1795, *D&L*, 2, p. 27.

55. Nelson to Locker, 21/3/1795, *D&L*, 2, p. 20.

56. Nelson to William, 25/3/1795, Add. MSS 34988.

57. Elliot to Portland, 19/3/1795, 5/4/1795, FO 20/7; A. M. W. Stirling, ed., *Pages and Portraits*, 2, p. 318.

58. Journal, Add. MSS 34902.

59. Journal, Add. MSS 34902.

60. Nelson to William, 25/3/1795, Add. MSS 34988. The distinguished French naval historian Jean-Pierre Baptiste Edmond Jurien de la Gravière, *Sketches*, p. 93, admits the French dismasting fire to have been 'a vicious [deplorably inefficient] system of gunnery'. For useful discussions of the subject see *NC*, 4 (1800), pp. 143–8, 222–6; Michael Lewis, *Social History of the Navy*, pp. 369–70; and Peter Padfield, *Guns at Sea*, pp. 90–2, 121.

61. Nelson to Fanny, 12/4/1795, Monmouth MSS, E856; Nelson to Suckling, 22/3/1795, Add. MSS 22130.

62. Journal, Add. MSS 34902. Others also noted French gun tactics. The captain's log of the *Princess Royal* (ADM 51/1113) reported the French 'firing hot shot and otherwise very high to disable our ships'.

63. Jollivet, *Anglais dans La Mediterranée*, p. 120. For the last point see Brame to Grenville, 14, 16/3/1795, FO 28/11; and Udny to Hamilton, 20/3/1795, Add. MSS 39793.

64. Nelson to Fanny, 14/3/1795, Monmouth MSS, E851; Edward Pelham Brenton, *Naval History*, 1, pp. 310–11; Montgomery to Udny, 18/3/1795, Add. MSS 39793; Nelson to Clarence, 15/3/1795, NMM: AGC/27. Nelson and Hotham gave the total complements of the prizes as two thousand three hundred, but Gibson put the figure at two thousand one hundred and the French captains themselves as low as 1,981 (Gibson to Elliot, 18/3/1795, NMM: ELL/138; HCA 32/550). However, Hotham also said that thirteen hundred French prisoners were taken, including three hundred sick and wounded (Hotham to Elliot, 26/3/1795, NMM: ELL/140), which, working from his figure for the total complement, implies that one thousand French had been killed on board the *Ça Ira* and *Censeur*. Such a figure is far too high. The highest direct estimates of the French casualties, in killed and wounded, are those of Lieutenant Gibson, who said the *Ça Ira* lost four hundred and fifty and her consort three hundred

and fifty. Thirty-one British prisoners from the *Berwick* were found on the *Ça Ira* and liberated.

65. Nelson to Fanny, 14/3/1795, Monmouth MSS, E851. Figures for British casualties given in the ships' logs, Hotham's dispatch and by James vary. The *Princess Royal* log, for instance, listed her casualties as twenty-two, twice as many as those counted by James. James's list of British casualties for the two days of battle totals seventy-four killed and 284 wounded.

66. Nelson to Fanny, 14/3/1795, Monmouth MSS, E851.

67. Elliot to Windham, 2/4/1795, Add. MSS 37852.

68. Nelson to Fanny, 1/4/1795, Monmouth MSS, E855.

69. Hotham to the fleet, 18/3/1795, Add. MSS 34904; Tyler to Margaret Tyler, 28/3/1795, in William Henry Wyndham-Quin, *Sir Charles Tyler*, p. 67; *Diadem* log, ADM 51/1111; Nelson to Suckling, 22/3/1795, Add. MSS 22130; Nelson to Hamilton, 24/3/1795, Monmouth MSS, E39.

70. Nelson to Goodall, 15/3/1795, NMM: XAGC/8. I attach no importance to the other alleged post-battle exchange between Nelson and Hotham. According to Hotham's nephew, who was not in the fleet at the time, Nelson complained that the Neapolitan *Tancredi* had got in his way during the engagement and asked that Captain Caraccioli be reprimanded (Stirling, *Pages and Portraits*, 1, pp. 74–5). It was unlike Nelson to begrudge gallant conduct, and not long before he had expressed his great affection for the Italian officer (Nelson to Hamilton, 19/12/1794, Morrison, *Hamilton and Nelson Papers*, 1, p. 197). There are no other references to the *Tancredi* impeding *Agamemnon* in the battle, and during the decisive stage of the action the Neapolitan ship was two vessels astern of Nelson, behind Hotham's own *Britannia*. Moreover, no adverse comments about Caraccioli appear elsewhere. Although the *Tancredi* sustained six casualties in the battle, Montgomery said that Caraccioli 'did his best, and . . . if circumstances had permitted . . . would have done himself honour', which suggests that the Italian had little opportunity to get into the fight. Hotham reported that Caraccioli behaved with 'activity and spirit' (Udny to Hamilton, 20/3/1795, Add. MSS 39793; Hotham to Hamilton, 16/3/1795, NMM: HMI/13; Hamilton to Hood, 4/4/1795, NMM: HML/10B). I believe that the story of Nelson's reproof, written long afterwards, was an inaccurate reflection of the tragic subsequent relationship between the two men.

71. Nelson to Fanny, 1/4/1795, Monmouth MSS, E855.

72. Nelson to Suckling, 22/3/1795, Add. MSS 22130; Jurien de la Gravière, *Sketches*, p. 96; Elliot to Portland, 5/4/1795, FO 20/7.

73. Nelson to Hamilton, 7/4/1795, Monmouth MSS, E40.

74. Nelson to Fanny, 1/4/1795, Monmouth MSS, E855; Goodall to Nelson, 8/11/1795, Add. MSS 34904.

75. Nelson to Fanny, 7/6/1795, Monmouth MSS, E862.

76. Nelson to Pollard, 2/7/1795, NMM: 75/102; Nelson to Fanny, 28/4/1795, Monmouth MSS, E860; Nelson to Clarence, 16/4/1795, Add. MSS 46356.

77. Nelson to Suckling, 7/6/1795, *D&L*, 2, p. 40; Nelson to William, 8/6/1795, Add. MSS 34988; Spencer to Hood, 20/3/1796, Add. MSS 75793.

78. Sketches of Troubridge are given in W. H. Fitchett, *Nelson and His Captains*, and Kennedy, *Nelson and His Captains*.

79. Nelson to his father, 24/4/1795, Add. MSS 34988; Nelson to Locker, 4/5/1795, *D&L*, 2, p. 34.

80. Nelson to Suckling, 20/6/1795, *D&L*, 2, p. 44.

81. For the trial see ADM 1/5333, and Wyndham-Quin, *Sir Charles Tyler*, pp. 73–7.

82. Udny to Drake, 8/7/1795, Add. MSS 46826; Nelson to Fanny, 9/7/1795, Monmouth MSS, E866; Hotham to Nepean, 14/7/1795, ADM 1/393; Hoste to his mother, 24/9/1795,

NMM: MRF/88/1; logs of the *Agamemnon, Ariadne* (ADM 51/1128), *Meleager* (ADM 51/1210) and *Moselle* (ADM 52/3236).

83. Nelson to Locker, 8, 14/7/1795, *D&L*, 2, p. 49.
84. Elliot to his wife, 28/7/1795, NLS, 11050: 31; Collingwood to Blackett, 31/8/1795, Edward Hughes, ed., *Private Correspondence*, p. 69; Hood to Nelson, 13/8/1795, Add. MSS 34937; account of a lieutenant of the *Victory* in James, *Naval History*, 1, pp. 269–70. For Hotham's dispatch see Hotham to Nepean, 14/7/1795, ADM 1/393.
85. Elliot to his wife, 28/7/1795, NLS, 11050: 31; Nelson to Fanny, 9/7/1795, Monmouth MSS, E866; Nelson to William, 29/7/1795, Add. MSS 34988.
86. Nelson to Clarence, 15/7/1795, NMM: AGC/27; James, *Naval History*, 1, p. 270; James Greig, ed., *Farington Diary*, 1, pp. 198–9 n. In addition to sources already mentioned, refer also to the logs of the *Britannia* (ADM 51/1119), *Victory* (ADM 51/1105), *Defence* (ADM 51/1131), *Culloden* (51/1130), *Cumberland* (ADM 51/1108), *Princess Royal,* (ADM 51/1125) and *Agamemnon*.
87. Hotham to Nepean, 15/7/1795, ADM 1/393; Add. MSS 34933: 45.
88. Nelson to Elliot, 27/7/1795, NMM: ELL/138. Cornwall Reynolds had succeeded John Roxburgh as surgeon of the *Agamemnon* after the former had been discharged an invalid.
89. Nelson to Dixon Hoste, 22/6/1795, Monmouth MSS, E297.
90. Fremantle to William Fremantle, 1/7/1794, CBS, D-FR/45/2.
91. Nelson to Fanny, 31/10/1794, 12/11/1794, 17/1/1795, Monmouth MSS, E836–E837, E843; Michael Duffy, 'Samuel Hood, First Viscount Hood', p. 272.
92. Nelson to Hamilton, 1/2/1795, Morrison, *Hamilton and Nelson Papers*, 1, p. 201; Nelson to Clarence, 19/1/1795, NMM: AGC/27; Nelson to Fanny, 16/4/1795, *NLTHW*, p. 206; Nelson to Locker, 18/6/1795, *D&L*, 2, p. 43; Hood to Stephens, 29/3/1794, ADM 1/392. The logs of the period contain numerous references to the issue of citrus fruits. For example, the *Leda* brought sixteen cases of oranges and lemons from Naples to the fleet in December 1793. Admiral Jervis, who eventually succeeded Hood as commander-in-chief in the Mediterranean in 1795, has sometimes been credited with maintaining a high level of health in his ships, but it is debatable whether he added anything to the regimen that already existed. The Brame papers of 1795–6, for instance, show that Nelson was already relying heavily upon lemons and onions as well as fresh provisions to keep his men healthy (SRRC, 112/16/33). Moreover, it was Nelson who first raised the issue between the two, writing in May 1796 that he supposed the admiral 'must be interested in whatever concerns the health of seamen' and reporting his acquisition of thousands of fresh lemons (Nelson to Jervis, 30/5/1796, NMM: JER/1–2a). For Nelson's later interest in the health of seamen, see James Watt, 'Naval Surgery in the Time of Nelson', p. 26.
93. Discussions of the line of battle are given in Brian Tunstall and Nicholas Tracy, *Naval Warfare*; John Creswell, *British Admirals*; Nicholas Tracy, *Nelson's Battles*; and Michael Duffy and Roger Morriss, eds, *Glorious First of June 1794*.

XXI Drifting to Leeward (pp. 564–604)

1. Nelson to Trevor, 28/4/1796, Monmouth MSS, E987. The Honourable John Trevor, then in his mid-forties and married to a clergyman's daughter, later succeeded his brother to become third Viscount Hampden.
    Very few of the extensive sources for this chapter have been previously explored. For Nelson's own papers, see Add. MSS 34962 (Nelson letter book); Add. MSS 34902 and 34933 (miscellaneous Nelson correspondence); Add. MSS 34904 and 34952 (Nelson's correspondence for 1795–6, although some documents in the last file are damaged and unreadable even under ultraviolet light); Add. MSS 34941 (letters of De Vins, Beaulieu

and others); Monmouth MSS, E987 (Nelson letter book, 1796); *D&L*, vols 1 and 7; *NLTHW*; various documents in NMM: CRK/14; and the log books of the *Agamemnon* (see chap. 17, n. 2). Nelson's relations with the fleet were also traced through ADM 1/393–394; Add. MSS 34938 and NMM: CRK/11 (Jervis's letters to Nelson); NMM: JER/1–2a (Jervis papers); Add. MSS 31159 (Jervis's letter book), which supplied some of the documents to Edward P. Brenton, *John, Earl of St Vincent*, vol. 1; and papers of George Cockburn in NMM: MRF/D/6 and MRF/D/9. The diplomatic context has been supplied by FO 28/11–15; FO 67/17–21; NMM: CRK/4 (Francis Drake's letters to Nelson); Joseph Brame's letter book and papers in SRRC, 112/16/31 and 112/16/33; and Add. MSS 46822–30 (Drake papers). Among the latter, volumes 46826 (Udny correspondence), 46827 (letters from De Vins and Wallis) and 46828 (letters and complaints of Castiglione) contain the most documents relating to naval operations. The Elliot papers in the National Maritime Museum (NMM/ELL) are also essential sources for the campaign, especially volumes 101 (Trevor), 124 (Brame), 125 (Drake), 138 (Nelson) and 141 (Jervis). Drake's letters to Sir William Hamilton may be found in Add. MSS 39793, and other papers relevant to the Neapolitan contribution can be found in NMM: HML.

2. Nelson to Fanny, 2/12/1795, 19/4/1796, Monmouth MSS, E878, E892; Anthony Brett-James, *General Graham*, p. 66.

3. Nelson's arrival in Genoa was reported in Brame to Nepean, 18/7/1795, SRRC, 112/16/31.

4. For the convoy, see Drake to Elliot, 25/7/1795, NMM: ELL/125.

5. Hotham to Nelson, 17/5/1795, enclosed in Drake to Grenville, 8/8/1795, FO 28/12.

6. Nelson to Collingwood, 31/8/1795, *D&L*, 2, p. 77; Nelson to Suckling, 27/7/1795, *D&L*, 2, p. 61; Nelson to Fanny, 25/8/1795, Monmouth MSS, E870.

7. Nelson, 12/11/1795, NMM: CRK/14; Nelson statement, November 1795, NMM: CRK/14; Drake to Nelson, 23, 25/7/1795, 18/9/1795 and 7/1/1796, NMM: CRK/4; Nelson to Cockburn, 19/7/1795, NMM: MRF/D/9. For the Genoese reaction see also Nelson to Drake, 22/8/1795, NMM: AGC/17/2; Drake to Nelson, 1 and 8 (2 letters)/9/1795, 7/1/1796, NMM: CRK/4; and Nelson to Cockburn, 12/9/1795, NMM: MRF/D/9. Although Nelson contravened Hotham's orders, he had interim authority from Drake, who told him that it was 'extremely beneficial to the king our master's service that you should to the utmost of your power stop all trade and communications between neutral places and France and places occupied by the armies of France until you receive further instructions from the Commander in Chief' (Drake to Nelson, 18/7/1795, NMM: CRK/4). From the beginning of the campaign Nelson formed a close partnership with Drake, who learned on 19 September that he had been appointed to represent Britain at the Austrian headquarters at Vado. The two coordinated their movements and opinions. 'I hope you will be at Vado when I get there, as we must make another attack on the general [De Vins],' Drake wrote (Drake to Nelson, 19/9/1795, NMM: CRK/4).

8. Drake and Trevor to Hotham, 22/7/1795, enclosed in Hotham to Nepean, 29/7/1795, ADM 1/393; Nelson to Hotham, 28/7/1795, Add. MSS 34902; Hotham to Cockburn, 21/7/1795, NMM: MRF/D/9; Hotham to Spencer, 4/6/1795 and August 1795, Add. 75780.

9. Nelson to Hotham, 22/7/1795, Add. MSS 34962; Drake to Grenville, 25/7/1795, FO 28/11; Trevor to Grenville, 24/7/1795, FO 67/17; Drake to Nelson, 29/7/1795, NMM: CRK/4; Brame to Grenville, 23/7/1795, SRRC, 112/16/31. The application for the Neapolitan flotilla can be followed in Trevor to Hotham, 2/7/1795, NMM: HML/11; Hotham to Hamilton, 16/7/1795, 17/8/1795, NMM: HML/13; Hamilton to Hotham, 23/7/1795, 29/8/1795, NMM: HML/10B; Nelson to the Neapolitan commander, 1/10/1795, NMM: JER/1–2a; and Add. MSS 39793: 104, 106, 131.

10. Nelson to Drake, 3/8/1795, Add. MSS 34962; Drake to Nelson, 25, 29/7/1795, 4, 7,

10/8/1795, 7/11/1795, NMM: CRK/4. The logs of Nelson's ships give the most comprehensive day-by-day picture of the naval campaign. They were the frigates *Ariadne* (ADM 51/1128), *Meleager* (ADM 51/1210), *Southampton* (ADM 51/1125 and 1131), *Inconstant* (ADM 51/1179), *Lowestoffe* (ADM 51/1121 and 1133), *Flora* (ADM 51/1167), *Romulus* (ADM 51/1130) and *Tartar* (ADM 52/3509); the brigs and sloops *Moselle* (ADM 51/4475 and ADM 52/3236), *Speedy* (ADM 51/1243) and *Tarleton*; and the *Resolution* (ADM 51/4492) and *Mutine* (ADM 52/3240) cutters. I have not traced a log for the *Tarleton*.

11. Genoa's complaints may be sampled in Nelson to Drake, 30/9/1795, *ND*, 7 (2001), p. 534; Castiglione to Hotham, 31/7/1795, and Hotham to Castiglione, 22/8/1795, both enclosed in ADM 1/393; correspondence enclosed by Drake in FO 28/12: no. 23; Grenville to Drake, 3/9/1795, FO 28/12; 'Abstract of the different points . . . between . . . Great Britain and the Republic of Genoa since . . . 1793', FO 28/16: no. 77; Drake to Nelson, 27/9/1795, with enclosures, NMM: CRK/4; and Add. MSS 46828: 27–83. Details of the *Meleager*'s prizes are from Cockburn to Drake, 7/8/1795, Cockburn to McArthur and Pollard, 8/9/1795, and Cockburn to McArthur, Pollard and Udny, 11/2/1796, all in NMM: MRF/D/6; Drake to Grenville, 28/7/1795, 8, 27/8/1795, with their enclosures, FO 28/11, FO 28/12; and Roger Morriss, *Cockburn*, pp. 23–6.

12. Nelson to Fanny, 5/10/1795, Monmouth MSS, E874.

13. Nelson to Firpo, 7/8/1795, SRRC, 112/16/33: 331; Fellows to Firpo, 30/8/1795, SRRC, 112/16/33: 359; Aliberti to Firpo, 10/9/1795, 12/1/1796, SRRC, 112/16/33: 367, 414.

14. Anne Fremantle, ed., *Wynne Diaries* (1952), p. 255; Brame to Nelson, 29/8/1795, SRRC, 112/16/31. While at Vado Adelaide may have communicated with her mother in Genoa through Nelson's letters to Brame, the British consul in that town. Brame regularly informed Nelson that his enclosures had been carefully forwarded: Brame to Aliberti, 18/8/1795, SRRC, 112/16/33: 348, and Brame to Nelson, 5/9/1795, SRRC, 112/16/31.

15. Brame to Nelson, 5/3/1796, SRRC, 112/16/31.

16. Account by Andrews, 20/8/1795, Add. MSS 34962; log of the *Mutine* (n. 10 above).

17. Nelson's letters to Fremantle and Cockburn, both dated 26/8/1795, are filed in Add. MSS 34962.

18. Nelson's summons, 26/8/1795, Add. MSS 34902; Nelson to Hotham, 27/8/1795, ADM 1/393.

19. Nelson to Hotham, 28/8/1795, Add. MSS 34962; Nelson to Drake, 27/8/1795, FO 28/12.

20. Hoste to his brother, 14/9/1795, NMM: MRF/88/1; log book of the *Inconstant*, ADM 51/1179.

21. Complaint of Spinola, 28/10/1795, Add. MSS 34933: 54; Hotham to Nelson, 4/9/1795, NMM: CRK/7; Udny to Drake, 1/9/1795, Add. MSS 46926.

22. Log book of the *Moselle*, ADM 52/3226.

23. Nelson to Fanny, 1/9/1795, Monmouth MSS, E871; Nelson to Jackson, 2/9/1795, Add. MSS 34962; letter of 10/9/1795, Add. MSS 34962: 37.

24. Hamilton to Nelson, 31/10/1796, Add. MSS 34904; Nelson to William, 29/7/1795, Add. MSS 34988; Nelson to Suckling, 27/10/1795, *D&L*, 2, p. 92; Nelson to Drake, 28/4/1796, Monmouth MSS, E987; Nelson to Fanny, 2/8/1796, 24/7/1795, Monmouth MSS, E900, E868; Nelson to Hotham, 30/8/1795, ADM 1/393.

25. Nelson to Clarence, 27/10/1795, NMM: CRK/14; Nelson to Drake, 6, 8/8/1795, Add. MSS 34962; Nelson to Cockburn, 8/8/1795, *D&L*, 2, p. 67; Fellows to Firpo, 10, 13/8/1795, SRRC, 112/16/33: 335, 337; De Vins to Drake, 5/8/1795, Add. MSS 46827.

26. Drake to Grenville, 29/8/1795, FO 28/12; Trevor to Grenville, FO 67/19; Nelson to Drake, 12/11/1795, Monmouth MSS, E37.

27. Drake to Nelson, 15/8/1795, NMM: CRK/14; Nelson to Drake, 16/8/1795, NMM: PST/39; Nelson to Jackson, 17/8/1795, Add. MSS 34962; Jackson to Nelson, 21/8/1795, Add. MSS 34904; Hotham's letters to Nelson in Add. MSS 34904: 44–50, Add. MSS

46835: 134, and NMM: JER/1–2a; Nelson's account of the Vado campaign, NMM: JER/1–2a; De Vins to Drake, 11/8/1795, Add. MSS 46827; Jackson to Eden, 27/8/1795, FO 67/18; Nelson to Fanny, 1/9/1795, Monmouth MSS, E871.

28. Drake to Grenville, 29/8/1795, 14, 22/9/1795, FO 28/12.

29. Nelson to Hotham, 17/9/1795, Add. MSS 34962; Eden to Grenville, 5/9/1795, FO 7/42.

30. Of the many studies of Bonaparte, personal favourites are August Fournier, *Life of Napoleon I*, and David G. Chandler, *Campaigns of Napoleon*. The most recent study of the Italian campaign is Martin Boycott-Brown's *The Road to Rivoli*.

31. Trevor to Grenville, 1/8/1795, FO 67/17; Drake to Grenville, 28/8/1795, FO 28/12; Drake to Elliot, 29/8/1795, 11/9/1795, NMM: ELL/25; Eden to Grenville, 13/10/1795, FO 7/43.

32. Nelson to De Vins, 11/9/1795, FO 28/12; Nelson to De Vins, 14/9/1795, NMM: JER/1–2a; De Vins to Drake, 14/9/1795, Add. MSS 46827.

33. Nelson to Hotham, 17/9/1795, Add. MSS 34962; De Vins to Drake, 14, 19/9/1795, Add. MSS 46827.

34. Udny to Drake, 1/9/1795, Add. MSS 46826.

35. Drake to Grenville, 5/9/1795, FO 28/12.

36. For these paragraphs see Hotham to Nelson, 10, 15/9/1795, Add. MSS 34904; Nelson to Hotham, 17, 20/9/1795, Add. MSS 34962 and NMM: JER/1–2a; and Fremantle to William Fremantle, 26/11/1795, CBS, D-FR/45/2.

37. Drake to Grenville, 26/9/1795, FO 28/13; Nelson's account of the Vado campaign, NMM: JER/1–2a (part also in NMM: CRK/14, and the whole reprinted in *D&L*, 7, p. xix); Hotham to Nelson, 9/10/1795, Add. MSS 34904; various documents in NMM: CRK/14.

38. Nelson, undated letter in NMM: CRK/14.

39. Nelson to Nepean, 13/11/1795, ADM 1/2225; Nelson's account of the Vado campaign, NMM: JER/1–2a.

40. Trevor to Elliot, 21/10/1795, NMM: ELL/101; Drake to Grenville, 29/9/1795, and enclosures, FO 28/13; Nelson to Trevor, 6, 7/11/1795, FO 67/19; Nelson to Wallis, 7/11/1795, and Nelson to De Vins, 8/11/1795, both in NMM: JER/1–2a; the *Moselle* log.

41. Drake to Grenville, 5 and 11(with enclosure)/9/1795, 2/11/1795, FO 28/12; FO 28/13; no. 42.

42. Drake to Grenville, 29/9/1795, 1, 3, 9/10/1795, FO 28/13; Nelson to Jackson, 19/9/1795, Add. MSS 34962; Nelson's account of the Vado campaign, NMM: JER/1–2a; Brame to Udny and Trevor, 10/10/1795, SRRC, 112/16/31; log of the *Southampton*, ADM 51/1131.

43. Nelson statement, November 1795, NMM: CRK/14; Drake to Nelson, 7/11/1795, NMM: CRK/4.

44. Nelson to Parker, 20/11/1795, FO 67/19; Goodall to Nelson, 8/11/1795, Add. MSS 34904; Hotham to Spencer, 1/11/1795, Add. MSS 75780. For a favourable view of Parker see Fremantle to William Fremantle, 26/11/1795, CBS, D-FR/45/2.

45. Drake to Nelson, 12, 15/11/1795, NMM: CRK/4. For the *La Brune* affair see Nelson to Nepean, 13/11/1795, *D&L*, 2, p. 98*; Drake to Grenville, 14, 19/11/1795, FO 28/13; Drake to Elliot, 21/11/1795, NMM: ELL/125; Brame to Udny, 14/11/1795, SRRC, 112/16/31.

46. Nelson to Parker, 20/11/1795, 23/12/1795, Add. MSS 34962, and NMM: JER/1–2a.

47. The watering parties are mentioned in Drake to Grenville, 3/12/1795, with enclosures, FO 28/13. Noble, Withers and Newman were taken to Nice and Marseilles before being returned to Genoa, where they were discharged to Brame on 23 February 1796, on the condition that the British would release three French officers of equivalent rank in return: Drake to Nelson, 1/12/1795, NMM: CRK/4; Brame to Noble, 15/12/1795, and Brame to Drake, 24/2/1796, both in SRRC, 112/16/31; Noble to Drake, 20/11/1795, SRRC, 112/16/33: 382; and documents filed at SRRC, 112/16/33: 401, 455. Withers believed

that Nelson had oiled these negotiations by releasing clothes he had captured from the French, but although a valise and personal accoutrements belonging to a French artillery officer were sent to France's minister plenipotentiary in Genoa, this was done afterwards and quite gratuitously. See *United Service Journal*, 1843, ii, p. 640; Brame to Elliot, 11/6/1796, NMM: ELL/124; and Faypoult to Nelson, 23/6/1796, SRRC, 112/16/33: 740. However, Nelson was concerned to effect the release of his officers: Nelson to Brame, 16/12/1795, 27/1/1796, SRRC, 112/16/33: 390, 430. Withers and Noble have already been mentioned. Samuel Newman began his naval career as an able seaman on the *Speedy* in July 1793, and joined the *Agamemnon* as a twenty-year-old midshipman at St Fiorenzo on 4 February 1795. He continued to serve on her till she was paid off in September 1796. Newman passed for lieutenant on 7 May 1800 (ADM 6/98) but never received his commission.

48. Drake to Grenville, 7/12/1795, Add. MSS 39793; Nelson to Hoste, 12/12/1795, Monmouth MSS, E298; Nelson to the commanding officer at Leghorn, 25/11/1795, NMM: ELL/125.

49. Drake to Nelson, 7/1/1796, and other letters in NMM: CRK/4; Eden to Drake, 21/12/1795, Add. MSS 46825.

50. Nelson to Nepean, 26/11/1795, ADM 1/2225; Trevor to Nelson, 23/12/1795, Add. MSS 34904.

51. Spencer to Nelson, 15/1/1796, NMM: CRK/11; Nelson letter, 6/11/1795, Add. MSS 21506: 151; Nelson to Lloyd, 29/1/1798, facsimile in the John Rylands Library, Manchester, MAM PLP78.52.1.

52. Nelson to Fanny, 2, 7/12/1795, Monmouth MSS, E878; Jervis to Nelson, 29/9/1796, Add. MSS 31166; James Harrison, *Life*, 1, p. 140.

53. Nelson to Jervis, 21/12/1795, NMM: CRK/14.

54. Edmund Nelson to Nelson, 3/12/1795, Monmouth MSS, E615.

55. Jervis to James, 28/6/1797, Add. MSS 31160.

56. Jervis to Bowen, 23/8/1797, Add. MSS 31160.

57. Jervis to Aylmer, 31/8/1797, Add. MSS 31160.

58. Jedediah S. Tucker, *St Vincent*, 2, p. 390; Geoffrey Marcus, *Age of Nelson*, p. 66. More recent studies of Jervis include Evelyn Berckman, *Nelson's Dear Lord*; the hyperbolic Charles B. Arthur, *Remaking of the English Navy*; Ruddock F. Mackay, 'Lord St Vincent's Early Years'; and P. K. Crimmin, 'John Jervis'. A new biography, written by someone willing to confront a heterogeneous mass of primary material with a cool head, is needed.

59. Fremantle to William Fremantle, CBS, D-FR/45/2/117.

60. Jervis's record on health was also questioned in Christopher C. Lloyd and J. L. S. Coulter, *Medicine in the Navy*.

61. Lady Elliot to Elliot, 6/12/1795, NLS, 11072: 160.

62. Jervis to Nelson, 13/1/1796, NMM: CRK/11; Nelson to William, 26/12/1795, Add. MSS 34988; Jervis to Spencer, 13/1/1796, 24/1/1796, Add. MSS 75799.

63. Anne Fremantle, ed., *Wynne Diaries* (1935–40), 2, p. 112.

64. Trevor to Jervis, 27/1/1796, FO 67/20; Nelson to Fanny, 20/1/1796, Monmouth MSS, E883.

65. Jervis to Trevor, 11/2/1796, Add. MSS 31166; Nelson to Fanny, 27/1/1796, Monmouth MSS, E884; Jervis to Nelson, 21/1/1796, Add. MSS 34938; Jervis to Nepean, 24/1/1796, Add. MSS 31171; Udny to Macartney, 4/1/96, Add. MSS 46825; Nelson to Drake, 27/1/1796, Houghton Library, Harvard University, Cambridge, Massachusetts. Nelson's letter book for 1796, Monmouth MSS, E987, and the logs of the *Diadem* (ADM 51/1167), *Blanche* (ADM 51/1140), *Meleager* (ADM 51/1210), and *Peterel* (ADM 51/1137) have also been used for the 1796 campaign.

66. Nelson to Fanny, 12/2/1796, Monmouth MSS, E885.

67. Nelson to Fanny, 17, 28/2/1796, Monmouth MSS, E886.

68. Nelson to Drake, 6/4/1796, D&L, 2, p. 142; Jervis to Nepean, 18/4/1796, ADM 1/394; Jervis to Elliot, 3/4/1796, NMM: ELL/141; Nelson to Drake, 19/4/1796, and Nelson to Jervis, 18/4/1796, both in NMM: JER/1–2a; Nelson to Drake, 19/4/1796, Monmouth MSS, E987; Nelson to Brame, 14/4/1796, SRRC, 112/16/33: 551.

69. Jervis to Nelson, 21/3/1796, Add. MSS 31166; Add. MSS 31175: 83; Jervis to Spencer, 28/3/1796, 31/5/1796, Add. MSS 75799, 75793.

70. Nelson to Jervis, 8/4/1796, NMM: JER/1–2a; Macartney to Drake, 10/1/1796, Add. MSS 46825; Brame to Drake, 11/4/1796, FO 28/14.

71. The correspondence on this subject is extensive, but see Nelson to Trevor, 24/2/1796, 2/3/1796, FO 67/20; Nelson to Hamilton, 11/3/1796, NMM: JER/1 2a; Nelson to Drake, 15/3/1796, NMM: CRK/14; Hamilton to Jervis, 22/3/1796, 17/5/1796, NMM: HML/10C; Hamilton to Drake, 11, 30/4/1796, FO 28/14, FO 28/15; Hamilton to Trevor, 26/4/1796, NMM: HML/10D; Trevor to Hamilton, 13/4/1796, NMM: HML/11; Trevor to Grenville, 31/3/1796 and Brame to Trevor, 30/3/1796, FO 67/20; and correspondence in Add. MSS 31159: 43; Add. MSS 31175: 105; Add. MSS 39793: 139, 143; Add. MSS 46826: 159; and Egerton MSS 2639: 269, 283.

72. Drake to Nelson, 6, 12, 29/3/1796, 21/4/1796, NMM: CRK/4; Jervis to Elliot, 3/4/1796, NMM: ELL/141; Jervis to Nelson, 26/4/1796, NMM: CRK/11; Acton to Hamilton, 9/4/1796, Egerton MSS 2639. Several proposals for amphibious operations off the coast appear to have been made. One, of uncertain origin, suggested that Jervis use two or three frigates, some gun launches, a few hundred soldiers and the seamen to destroy enemy batteries and supplies at Vado, Savona and Finale (memorandum, 18/6/1796, SRRC, 112/16/33: 725).

73. Nelson to Fanny, 9/4/1796, Monmouth MSS, E890; Nelson to Drake, 6/4/1796, Monmouth MSS, E515; Nelson's proposals to Beaulieu, April 1796, Monmouth MSS, E987; Brame memoranda, NMM: ELL/124.

74. Brame, 11/4/1796, FO 67/21: 29; Nelson to Trevor, 11/4/1796, FO 67/21.

75. Nelson to Trevor, 11/4/1796, Monmouth MSS, E987; Eden to Greville, 20/4/1796, FO 7/45; Nelson to Drake, 11/4/1796, FO 28/14; Trevor to Grenville, 13/4/1796, 16/4/1796, FO 67/21.

76. Trevor to Nelson, 23/5/1796, Add. MSS 34904.

77. Jervis to Nelson, 11/5/1796, NMM: CRK/11; Jervis to Nepean, 11/5/1796, Add. MSS 31171.

78. Nelson to Jervis, 8/4/1796, ADM 1/394.

79. 'Disposition of the frigates between Toulon and Cape del Mele', FO 67/21, p. 110; Nelson to Trevor, 19/4/1796, FO 67/21; Nelson to Drake, 19/4/1796, Add. MSS 46835.

80. Nelson to Jervis, 25/4/1796, ADM 1/394; Nelson to Drake, 28/4/1796, Monmouth MSS, E987; DNB, 14, pp. 515–6; logs cited in n. 65 above.

81. Acton to Hamilton, 3/5/1796, Egerton MSS 2639; Spencer to Nelson, 26/4/1796, 4/5/1796, NMM: CRK/11.

82. John C. Dann, ed., Nagle Journal, pp. 200–3, contains the sometimes inaccurate memories of a sailor serving aboard the Blanche in these raids.

83. Nelson to Jervis, 1/6/1796, 24/6/1796, ADM 1/394; Nelson to Jervis, 2/6/1796, NMM: JER/1–2a; Nelson to Graham, 19/6/1796, Monmouth MSS, E987; Nelson draft to Genoa, 22/6/1796, NMM: CRK/14; ship's logs; Edward P. Brenton, Naval History, 1, p. 337; Jervis to Coffin, 29/6/1796, Add. MSS 31159; Morriss, Cockburn, p. 28.

84. Jervis to Drake, 11/5/1796, Tucker, St Vincent, 1, p. 181; Nelson to Jervis, 14/5/1796, Monmouth MSS, E987; Nelson to Elliot, 16/5/1796, NMM: ELL/138.

85. Nelson to Jervis, 18/5/1796, NMM: JER/1–2a; Nelson to Drake, 14/5/1796, Monmouth MSS, E987; Drake to Nelson, 24/5/1796, NMM: CRK/4.

86. Nelson to Jervis, 3/6/1796, NMM: JER/1–2a. James Kemble, Idols and Invalids, p. 133,

suggests that these symptoms indicate arteriosclerosis of the coronary arteries (producing angina) or spondylitis deformans, involving arthritis, but at thirty-eight Nelson would seem to have been young for either condition. Moreover, for many years he had complained of chest pains, which may have been related to his tropical disorders.

87. Jervis to Nelson, 29/6/1796, Add. MSS 34938; Jervis to Nelson, 5/9/1796, *NLTHW*, p. 337.

88. Nelson to Jervis, 5/6/1796, NMM: JER/1–2a.

89. Nelson to Fanny, 2/8/1796, Monmouth MSS, E900; Jervis to Nepean, 22/6/1796, ADM 1/394; Jervis to Nelson, 22/5/1796, 1, 7, 8/6/1796, NMM: CRK/11 and Add. MSS 34938: 31, 32.

90. Jervis to Spencer, 18/7/1796, Add. MSS 75793.

XXII From Flag Captain to Ship-Boy (pp. 605–34)

1. Barbara E. Rooke, ed., *The Friend*, 1, p. 572; Richard Holmes, *Coleridge*, chap. 1.

2. Nelson to Jervis, 28/6/1796, *D&L*, 7, p. lxxxix. The number of transfers mentioned in Jervis to Nelson, 10/6/1796, Add. MSS 31175, is incomplete. This chapter rests heavily on the musters of the *Agamemnon* (ADM 36/11358–62) and *Captain* (ADM 36/11799).

3. Florence Marryat, *Captain Marryat*, 1, pp. 19–20.

4. Edward Fraser, *Sailors Nelson Led*, pp. 54–5.

5. The quotation is from the master's log for 10/5/1795 (ADM 52/2632). The number and severity of the floggings and the names of the offenders are sometimes given differently in the logs, making precise figures impossible. For example, two soldiers punished for fighting in October 1793 received six lashes each according to one log, and a dozen each in another. Moreover, the severity of the punishment is unrecorded for about 24 per cent of the floggings noted. See also BL: John to Ann Brock, 10/5/1793.

6. Nelson to the Marine Society, 6/2/1793, Monmouth MSS, E328.

7. E. G. Thomas, 'Old Poor Law', p. 58; R. Leslie-Melville, *Sir John Fielding*, pp. 114–25; James Stephen Taylor, *Jonas Hanway*.

8. Minutes of the Marine Society, 21/2/1793, NMM: MSY/B/5. For a discussion of boys at sea see Michael Lewis, *Social History of the Navy*, pp. 86–90, 149–55.

9. The register of the Marine Society, 19 to 21/2/1793, NMM: MSY/o/7, contains the names of twenty boys sent to Nelson, but one never enlisted on the *Agamemnon*, and his place was taken by another originally destined for the *Ramilles*. Of these, three were discharged before the ship left for the Mediterranean, and seventeen sailed. However, the *Agamemnon* muster (ADM 36/11358) lists three additional boys as having been acquired from the Marine Society, though only one actually sailed. One deserted and another requested a discharge in April 1793. As none of the additional boys appear on the Marine Society register, they may have been entered in the muster as charity boys by mistake. John Sugden, 'Forgotten *Agamemnons*', addresses these contradictions and gives fuller information. For the Marine Society training ship, see their minutes, 17/1/1793, NMM: MSY/B/5.

10. Another two boys received two dozen lashes each for theft on 19 October 1794, but they are not identified in the logs, and may not have belonged to the Marine Society contingent.

11. Of the seventeen Marine Society boys known to have sailed to the Mediterranean, two deserted and one, Thomas Paling, disappears from the musters in 1794, after being disrated a captain's servant on 11 November 1794, in compliance with the new Admiralty order abolishing that rating. Other boys similarly disrated reappear on the ship's books as 'boys', but Paling seems to have transferred to another ship.

12. Brian Lavery, *Nelson's Navy*, p. 134.

13. BL: John to Ann Brock, 10/5/1793.

14. Joseph Allen, 'England's Wooden Walls', pp. 346–7. The quotation does not appear in the manuscript version of Allen's interview with Wilkinson, 15/2/1840, NMM: BGY/W/3. See also Robinson to Nelson, 16/8/1805, and Romano to Nelson, 17/1/1804, Western MSS 3676, Wellcome Library, London; Archibald Johnston petition, 22/9/1802, Monmouth MSS, E122; Nelson to St Vincent, 8/9/1801, D&L, 4, p. 486; and ADM 107/5, p. 184 (Collett's passing certificate). Isaac Collett was about thirteen years old when he joined the *Agamemnon* as a volunteer in November 1794. Nelson rated him midshipman, and he became a lieutenant in 1801, but died without further advancement nineteen years later.

15. King to Nelson, 15/9/1797, 28/2/1798, Monmouth MSS, E541, and Add. MSS 24906; Add. MSS 31176: 39; and Nelson to King, 9/11/1804, D&L, 7, p. ccxix. Remarkably, King's account book as a petty officer of the *Captain* has survived: BL: A. M. Broadley, 'Nelsoniana', p. 3, facing p. 2.

16. The prize money accounts (Western MSS 3676, Wellcome Library, London) contain the names of some of Nelson's closest followers. Among the literate were Sykes, Lovell, Thompson and Fearney, though the latter spelt his name phonetically, 'Fairnie'. Cook, Cooper, Cross, Hagan and Levett signed with crosses. This paragraph also depends upon Lovell, interviewed by Allen, 1840, NMM: BGY/W/3; Matthew H. Barker, *Life of Nelson*, pp. 165–6; D&L, 2, p. 405; Sykes to Nelson, 27/9/1797, Add. MSS 34906; Nelson to Hannah Huddlestone, 23/9/1797, NMM: AGC/18/5; and E. H. Fairbrother, 'John Sykes'.

17. Villettes to Nelson, 7/7/1795, Add. MSS 34904.

18. Nelson to Hamilton, 31/8/1794, Houghton Library, Harvard University, Cambridge, Massachusetts.

19. Nelson to Jervis, 3/6/1796, 7/4/1796, 22/5/1796, NMM: JER/1–2a and NMM: CRK/11; Peirson to Nelson, 17/3/1797, Add. MSS 34905; Hood to Hamilton, 6/5/1794, NMM: CRK/7; and documents in Alfred Morrison, ed., *Hamilton and Nelson Papers*, 1, p. 193, and 2, pp. 312, 332, 335, 336. Thomas Foley, *Nelson Centenary*, p. 45, identifies Peirson as the son of Marmaduke Langdale Lepinder (later Peirson) by Anne, daughter of William Robinson of Tottenham, which would make him the nephew of the William Robinson posthumously alleged to have seduced Ann Nelson. Nelson was not uncritical of Peirson. 'I should not have approved of him for a son-in-law, although I believe him to be a very good young man,' he told Fanny, 'but I don't think he will make a pleasant husband. He is too *nice* in his dress and fidgety, and has not the knack of being contented with his situation' (Nelson to Fanny, 12/7/1797, Monmouth MSS, E935).

20. Nelson to Jervis, 13/9/1796, Add. MSS 75799; Suckling to Nelson, 22/3/1797, Add. MSS 34988; return of service, 1817, ADM 9/6: no. 1817.

21. Jervis to Nelson, 7/6/1796, 29/9/1796, NMM: CRK/11 and Add. MSS 31166.

22. For Bullen see his record of service, 1817, ADM 9/2: no. 22; William O'Byrne, *Naval Biographical Dictionary*, pp. 142–3, 1391; and sources listed in chap. 1, n. 10.

23. Andrews to Elliot, 16/3/1794, 10/11/1794, NMM: ELL/138; Nelson to Elliot, 5 and 8/4/1795, NMM: ELL/138; Nelson to Fanny, 22/6/1795, Monmouth MSS, E864.

24. List of appointments, 1793, ADM 1/391; O'Byrne, *Naval Biographical Dictionary*, pp. 1132–3 (Cheetham). The three stand-ins, all supplied in September 1793 and lasting between two and five days, were John Hall, Mungo Weir and John Gourly. Another short-stay lieutenant aboard *Agamemnon* was James McArthur, who stood in for Noble (then a prisoner of the French) from February to April 1796.

25. Nelson to Fanny, 22/5/1795, 2/8/1795, Monmouth MSS, E858, E869.

26. Survey on Allison's health, 1/7/1795, and other documents in ADM 1/2739; *Agamemnon* log, 4/7/1795; and Nelson to Locker, 8/7/1795, D&L, 2, p. 49.

27. John Sugden, 'Captain George Andrews'; John Sugden and Ray F. and Ann Evans, 'More

Light on George and Elizabeth Andrews'; Culverhouse to Nelson, 23/3/1797, Add. MSS 34905; Andrews to Nelson, 13/9/1801, 22/8/1805, NMM: CRK/1 and Add. MSS 34930.

28. Return of service, 1817, ADM 9/2: no. 219. Spicer gave his age as twenty-nine in a statement of 7 March 1797 (HCA 32/845), but he seems to have been older. According to a certificate from his home parish of St Stephen's, Saltash, he was baptised on 22 September 1765: see the documents enclosed with his passing certificate, 4/5/1791, ADM 107/15.

29. Return of service, 1817, ADM 9/2: no. 214; O'Byrne, *Naval Biographical Dictionary*, pp. 818–19; Hoste to his father, 9/12/1795, in Harriet Hoste, ed., *Hoste*, 1, p. 49; *DNB*, 14, pp. 525–6; and Noble to Nelson, undated, NMM: CRK/9.

30. O'Byrne, *Naval Biographical Dictionary*, pp. 220–1.

31. Return of service, 1817, ADM 9/2: no. 39; Nelson to Fanny, 20/5/1796, Monmouth MSS, E895; *DNB*, 2, pp. 396–7; Ludovic Kennedy, *Nelson and His Captains*; Nelson to Jervis, 13/9/1796, Add. MSS 75799.

32. Jervis to Nepean, 18/7/1796, ADM 1/394; W. H. Fitchett, *Nelson and His Captains*, p. 66.

33. The identified quarterdeck aspirants of the *Agamemnon* were William Bolton, John Page Brandon, Isaac Charles Smith Collett, Thomas Eager, Thomas Bourdon Fellows, Samuel Gamble, Thomas Hall, William Hoste, David Lindsey, Thomas Lund, Samuel Newman, Josiah Nisbet, Christopher Schroder, Maurice William Suckling, John Weatherhead, Charles David Williams, Richard Williams, William D. Williams, Thomas Withers, John Wood and Ralph Woodman. For Wood see Linzee to Nepean, 27/8/1796, ADM 1/395. Subsequently, on the *Captain* and *Theseus*, Nelson also made midshipmen of other old *Agamemnons*, including Israel Coulson, Samuel Shillingford, William Fearney and Francis Cook, but I have excluded these from the analysis.

34. Thomas Foley, *Nelson Centenary*, pp. 30–1; Nelson to Fanny, 18/12/1795, 25/8/1795, 23/8/1796, Monmouth MSS, E879, E870, E902; Josiah to Fanny, 20/8/1793, Monmouth MSS, E675; Jervis to Nelson, 29/3/1798, Add. MSS 34939. Nelson was apparently trying to avoid offending Fanny, and Jervis, who supervised Josiah after Nelson left the fleet, similarly sugared the pill. 'Though young and a wild boy, [Josiah] has a great deal of stuff in him,' he wrote to Nelson on 23 October 1797 (Add. MSS 34939).

35. Nelson to Hoste, 3/5/1794, Monmouth MSS, E302.

36. Hoste to his brother, 14/9/1795, NMM: MRF/88/1.

37. Hoste to his father, 5/6/1796, 26/11/1796, NMM: MRF/88/1. Gardiner to Dixon Hoste, 3/6/1796, Hoste, *Hoste*, 1, p. 54; and Nelson to Dixon Hoste, 25/11/1796, *D&L*, 2, p. 304.

38. Nelson to Fanny, 24/4/1796, Monmouth MSS, E893; Tom Pocock, *Remember Nelson*, pp. 53–4.

39. Nelson to Hotham, 17/10/1794, ADM 1/392; Nelson, 19/6/1797, NMM: AGC/N/13; Nelson to Pollard, 17/2/1796, NMM: MON/1; Nelson to Daniel Williams, 27/2/1795, 5/5/1795, *D&L*, 2, pp. 9, 38; Daniel Williams to Nelson, 29/12/1794, Add. MSS 34903; note by Nelson and others, ADM 36/11359. The petty officers transferring with Nelson were Weatherhead, Hoste, Nisbet, Bolton, Eager, Lindsey, Schroder, Collett, Charles Williams, Lund and Withers. Eager left the *Captain* for the *Belette* on 7 October 1796. Among officers who did not follow Nelson to the *Captain* were Wilson, the master, who wanted to return to his large family in England, and Reynolds the surgeon, who swapped berths with his opposite number in the *Nemesis*.

40. Jervis to Nepean, 28/9/1796, ADM 1/395; Jervis to Nelson, 30/11/1796, Add. MSS 34938.

41. Allen, 'England's Wooden Walls', p. 351 (Spicer).

42. Fellows, return of service, 1817, ADM 9/6: no. 1868.

43. Fanny to Nelson, 28/5/1797, and Maurice Nelson to Fanny, 10/5/1797, Add. MSS 34988, and Monmouth MSS, E664.

44. Andrews to Nelson, 22/8/1805, Add. MSS 34930; Spicer to Nelson, 2/9/1805, Add. MSS 34931; Noble to Nelson, 23/8/1805, Add. MSS 34930; Bullen, 1845, in BL: A. M. Broadley, 'Nelsoniana', 2, facing p. 160; and Withers to Nelson, 2/12/1800, NMM: CRK/13.

45. Betsy Wynne's opinions of the captains of the fleet can be read in Anne Fremantle, ed., *Wynne Diaries* (1935–40), 2, pp. 101, 103, 106, 121–3.

46. David Spinney, *Rodney*, is a competent biography but for an excellent résumé of that officer's difficult personality consult N. A. M. Rodger, *The Wooden World*, pp. 323–7. For Cochrane: Brian Vale, 'Lord Cochrane in Chile', pp. 59–68. Sir Francis Drake's highly individual style of leadership contributed to similar difficulties in 1577–87, though these were also rooted in Elizabethan beliefs about command and inherited social status. Drake's 'low' birth was resented by some junior officers who thought themselves his social superiors. For more on Nelson's leadership style see chap. 26, below.

47. Nelson to Walker, 25/4/179(4?), Monmouth MSS, E202; Anne Fremantle, ed., *Wynne Diaries* (1952), p. 253; and Frederick to Nelson, 11/8/1796, NMM: CRK/5.

48. Hood to Stephens, 21/1/1794, ADM 1/392; Nelson to William, 20/6/1796, Add. MSS 34988; Elliot to Windham, 22/11/1795, Add. MSS 37852; Edward P. Brenton, *John, Earl of St Vincent*, 1, pp. 197, 209.

49. Hoste to his father, October 1797, in Hoste, *Hoste*, 1, p. 82, and Miller's account of 9/7/1797 in Kirstie Buckland, ed., *Miller Papers*, p. 14. There is a fine account of Miller in Kennedy, *Nelson and his Captains*.

50. Miller to Elliot, 14/11/1795, 16/12/1795, 17/12/1795, Add. MSS 37852, p. 262, and NMM: ELL/138; Nelson to Jervis, 4/6/1796, NMM: JER/1–2a; and Miller to Ward, 1797, J. G. Bullocke, ed., *Tomlinson Papers*, p. 381. When he returned from the Mediterranean in 1797 Nelson visited one of Miller's daughters, who was then in the care of a Taylor family (Nelson to Miller, 11/12/1797, NMM: XAGC/8).

51. Courts martial of Hugh Griffith and John Gourly, 29/10/1796, ADM 1/5337. Among the captains forming the court were Collingwood, Troubridge and Samuel Hood. Gourly himself died a 'retired' rear admiral in 1854.

52. Nelson to Jervis, 19/9/1796, NMM: JER/2B.

53. Court martial proceedings at St Fiorenzo, October 1796, ADM 1/5337, and Jervis to Nelson, 29/9/1796, Add. MSS 31166.

54. Jervis to Nelson, 19/10/1796, NMM: CRK/11; Add. MSS 31175: 226–8. Sawyer's counter charges against three lieutenants, a lieutenant of marines, a master and a purser were all dismissed.

55. Sawyer to Nelson, 1796, Add. MSS 34905, and Nelson to Jervis, 30/9/1796, NMM: JER/2B. The book Nelson loaned was probably *The Works of Flavius Josephus* (1777), a set of two volumes bound together. At least Nelson later gave a copy of the book to his daughter, Horatia: TC, 5 (1995), p. 20. Payments of prize money to Sawyer are shown in Western MSS 3676, Wellcome Library.

56. John Barrow, *Auto-Biographical Memoir*, p. 463.

57. Cockburn to Nelson, 24/7/1797, Add. MSS 34906; Roger Morriss, *Cockburn*, pp. 28, 33; Maurice Nelson to Nelson, 4/8/1797, NMM: BRP/5.

XXIII Commodore Nelson (pp. 635–83)

1. Nelson to Hamilton, 20/5/1796, Alfred Morrison, ed., *Hamilton and Nelson Papers*, 1, p. 219; SRRC, 112/16/33: 660. Major published sources for this chapter are *D&L*, vols 2 and 7, and *NLTHW*.

2. Anne Fremantle, ed., *Wynne Diaries* (1935–40), 2, pp. 95, 97. For details of the flight of the British community see FO 79/15; Udny to Drake, 25/6/1796, FO 28/15; Elliot to Jervis, 26/6/1796, NMM: ELL/159; and James Greig, *Farington Diary*, 1, pp. 239–40.

3. Accounts enclosed in Pollard to Nelson, 7/1/1797, NMM: CRK/10; Udny to Nelson, July 1796, Add. MSS 34904.

4. Anne Fremantle, ed., *Wynne Diaries* (1952), p. 256. The 1796 references to Adelaide in Fremantle's diary have been missed by previous Nelson scholars, and mis-indexed by its editor.

5. Nelson to Jervis, 25/6/1796, NMM: JER/1–2a; Jervis to Nelson, 18/6/1796, 31/7/1796, Add. MSS 31175, and Add. MSS 31166; Jervis to Drake, 17/9/1796, Add. MSS 31166; Nelson to Jervis, 24/6/1796, ADM 1/394; Jervis to Elliot, 29/6/1796, NMM: ELL/141; Jervis to Brame, 26/8/1796, SRRC, 112/16/33: 838.

6. Jervis summarily dismissed the Genoese charges. 'I pay no regard to the complaints of the Secretary of State, your answer being quite sufficient,' he wrote (Jervis to Nelson, 29/6/1796, Add. MSS 31159). Nelson's explanation went to the Admiralty, and, on his request, Drake also submitted a copy to Lord Grenville, the foreign secretary. Judge William Scott, to whom Grenville forwarded the documents in turn on 17 August, concluded that Nelson's answer 'contains a satisfactory vindication of his conduct, founded upon facts, which in point of legal effect would justify much stronger and more direct measures of hostile activity than any to which the commodore has ventured to resort'. Further charges, sent to Scott for a legal opinion in September, were found to be equally vague and poorly sustained. See Nelson to Drake, 25/6/1796, FO 28/15; Scott to Grenville, 22/8/1796, 7/9/1796, FO 28/15; Brame to Nelson (25/3/1796), Trevor (July 1796) and Drake (25/6/1796), SRRC, 112/16/31; and Nelson to Castiglione, 22/6/1796, SRRC, 112/16/33: 735.

7. Fremantle, 22/6/1796, Add. MSS 34904: 183; Brame to Grenville, 28/6/1796, FO 67/21. This chapter depends upon the logs of the *Captain* throughout: Add. MSS 36607; ADM 51/1174, ADM 51/1194 and ADM 52/2825; and NMM: ADM/L/C51.

8. Nelson to Elliot, 1/7/1796, with enclosure, NMM: ELL/138; Nelson to Jervis, 28/6/1796, NMM: JER/1–2a; Fremantle to Jervis, 30/6/1796, ADM 1/394; Udny to Elliot, 27/6/1796, NMM: ELL/132; Bonaparte to the Directory, 2/7/1796, *Correspondance de Napoléon*, 1, p. 445; Udny to Drake, 25/6/1796, SRRC, 112/16/33: 746.

9. Fremantle to William Fremantle, 13/7/1796, CBS, D-FR/45/2.

10. Bonaparte to Vaubois, 29/6/1796, *Correspondance de Napoléon*, 1, p. 442; Elliot to Windham, 3/7/1796, NMM: ELL/159.

11. Elliot to Jervis, 15/5/1796, 26, 27/6/1796, NMM: ELL/159; Elliot to Garlies, 1/7/1796, NMM: ELL/159.

12. Jervis to Nelson, 25/7/1796, Add. MSS 31159; Nelson to Fanny, 22/11/1796, 13/1/1797, Monmouth MSS, E910, E915; Hood to Nelson, 28/12/1796, Add. MSS 34937; Elliot to Nelson, 4/7/1796, NMM: ELL/159.

13. Though Jervis said he had ordered Nelson 'to blockade the port in the closest manner' (Jervis to Gregory, 1/7/1796, Add. MSS 31166), his instructions (Jervis to Nelson, 30/6/1796, and 1/7/1796, Add. MSS 34938) mention nothing about the severity of the blockade, which was raised in Nelson to Jervis, 3/7/1796, Add. MSS 34904. Hence my statement that Nelson and Jervis's views converged and that Nelson did not merely implement the orders of his commander-in-chief. See also Jervis to Nelson, 31/7/1796, Add. MSS 31166 and Nelson to Brame, 6/7/1796, ADM 1/394.

14. Elliot to Nelson, 2, 6/7/1796, NMM: ELL/159 and CRK/5; Elliot to Garlies, 1/7/1796, NMM: ELL/159; Trevor to Nelson, 30/6/1796, Add. MSS 34904.

15. Elliot to Portland, 11/7/1796, FO 20/11.

16. James Macnamara of the *Southampton* should not be confused with the officer of the

same name Nelson had known in the West Indies and France. 'Mac' died in 1802, a superannuated rear admiral. The captain of the *Southampton* was not made post until 1795, and died a rear admiral in 1826.

17. Elliot to Jervis, 14/7/1796, and Elliot to Duncan, 17/7/1796, NMM: ELL/159; Fremantle, *Wynne Diaries* (1952), p. 257.

18. Sources for the taking of Porto Ferraio are Elliot to Portland, 11/7/1796, enclosing Nelson to Elliot, 10/7/1796, and Duncan to Elliot, 10/7/1796, FO 20/11; Nelson to Wyndham, 11/7/1796, Add. MSS 34904; Nelson to Elliot and Jervis, both 9/7/1796, Add. MSS 34904; Nelson to Jervis, 10/7/1796, ADM 1/394; Elliot to Duncan, 6/7/1796, and other documents in Elliot's letter book, NMM: ELL/159; military journal and plan of Porto Ferraio in NMM: ELL/135; Fremantle, *Wynne Diaries* (1935–40), 2, p. 105; ships' logs, including those of *Southampton* (ADM 51/1131) and *Inconstant* (ADM 51/1179); statement of prize money, 27/12/1796, NMM: CRK/1; and Pietro Vigo, *Nelson a Livorno*, chap. 3.

19. For Jervis's reaction to the peace: Jervis to Nelson, 15/7/1796, Add. MSS 31159.

20. Jackson to Grenville, 27/8/1796, FO 67/22.

21. Nelson to Jervis, 3/7/1796, Add. MSS 34904; Jervis to Nelson, 8, 11, 19/8/1796, Add. MSS 31159, and NMM: CRK/11; Jervis to Nepean, 11/8/1796, ADM 1/395; Jervis to Elliot, 12/8/1796, NMM: ELL/141.

22. Nelson to Spencer, 20/8/1796, Add. MSS 75795; Elliot to Hamilton, 29/9/1796, FO 20/5; documents enclosed in Jervis to Nepean, 2/1/1796, ADM 1/395, and in NMM: JER/2b and NMM: ELL/159; Nelson's letter in Add. MSS 34902: 106.

23. Graham to Jervis, 13/6/1796, Add. MSS 34908.

24. Trevor to Grenville, 27/7/1796, FO 67/22; Jervis to Nelson, 14, 23/8/1796, NMM: CRK/11; Jervis to Elliot, 14, 15/7/1796, NMM: ELL/141.

25. Nelson to Elliot, 1/8/1796, *D&L*, 2, p. 227, Elliot to Nelson, 30/7/1796, 26/8/1796, 2/9/1796, NMM: CRK/11, NMM: ELL/159 and NMM: CRK/5; De Silva to Nelson, 2/8/1796, NMM: CRK/12.

26. Nelson to Lavillette, 22/8/1796, Monmouth MSS, E987.

27. Nelson to Elliot, 3/8/1796, NMM: ELL/138; Jervis to Bute, 18/7/1796, Add. MSS 31166. Some intelligences are in Add. MSS 34941. For Nelson's payment of spies, defrayed by Jervis, see Jervis to Nelson, 15/7/1796, Add. MSS 34938.

28. Nelson to Elliot, 3/8/1796, NMM: ELL/138; Caffarena to Nelson, 3/8/1796, NMM: ELL/138. Nelson's letter to Elliot has hitherto been taken from the printed version in Nicolas (*D&L*, 2, p. 232), where it is incorrectly transcribed to read 'One *old* lady tells me [sic] all she hears.' The original 'us' instead of 'me' was less personal, and reinforces suspicions that he was not alluding to Adelaide.

29. Udny to Nelson, July and 23/7/1796, Add. MSS 34904; letter to Nelson, 28/7/1796, Add. MSS 34904: 262.

30. Brame to Nelson, 21, 22/8/1796, Add. MSS 34904.

31. Nelson to Jervis, 2 and 3/8/1796, *D&L*, 2, p. 225; Nelson to Collingwood, 1/8/1796, Morrison, *Hamilton and Nelson Papers*, 1, p. 221; Drake to Grenville, 8/7/1796, FO 28/15; Jackson to Grenville, 17/8/1796, FO 67/22; Bonaparte to the Directory, 2/7/1796, *Correspondance de Napoléon*, 1, p. 445.

32. Lavillette to Nelson, 24/8/1796, NMM: JER/2b.

33. Nelson to Trevor, 28/4/1796, Monmouth MSS, E987; Jervis to Hamilton, 26/4/1796, Add. MSS 31166.

34. Elliot to O'Hara, 22/7/1796, and Elliot to Jervis, 31/7/1796, both in NMM: ELL/159.

35. Nelson to Elliot, 5, 11/8/1796, NMM: ELL/138; Elliot to Jervis, 31/7/1796, NMM: ELL/159.

36. Elliot to Nelson, 6/8/1796, NMM: CRK/5; De Burgh to Elliot, 12/8/1796, and undated,

NMM: ELL/148; Elliot to Windham, 10/8/1796, NMM: ELL/159; Elliot to Portland, 19/7/1796, 8/8/1796, FO 20/11.

37. Duncan to Elliot, 13/8/1796, NMM: ELL/135.

38. Jervis to Nelson, 31/7/1796, Add. MSS 31166; Jervis to Elliot, 25/7/1796, 6, 15, 22/8/1796, Add. MSS 31166: 70, 79, 80, and Add. MSS 31196: 84.

39. Nelson to William, 18/8/1796, Add. MSS 34988; Nelson to Collingwood, 18, 20/8/1796, E. Hughes, ed., *Private Correspondence of Admiral Lord Collingwood*, p. 75.

40. For the failure of the Leghorn expedition I have depended upon Elliot to Nelson, 12, 15, 16, 30/8/1796, NMM: CRK/5; Jackson to Grenville, 24, 27/8/1796, FO 67/22; Elliot to Portland, 28/8/1796, FO 20/11; Drake to Grenville, 27/7/1796 and Drake to Elliot, 30/8/1796, FO 28/15; and several documents in NMM: ELL/159, particularly Elliot's letters to Nelson (10, 13/8/1796), De Burgh (13, 15/8/1796), Graham (15/8/1796), Duncan (15, 25/8/1796), Windham (15/8/1796) and Jervis (17, 19/8/1796).

41. Nelson to Jervis, 3/8/1796, *D&L*, 2, p. 226; Nelson to Fanny, 23/8/1796, Monmouth MSS, E902; Jervis to Nelson, 15, 25/8/1796, Add. MSS 34938; Jervis to Elliot, 15/8/1796, Add. MSS 31166; Jervis to Graham, 17/8/1796, Add. MSS 31166.

42. Madame Caffarena to Nelson, 20, 21 22/8/1796, 5/10/1796, NMM: CRK/3; Madame Caffarena to Nelson, 14/8/1796, NMM: ELL/138; Joseph Caffarena to Nelson, 15/8/1796, and Daniels to Elliot, 16/9/1796, NMM: ELL/124; Elliot to Windham, 24/6/1796, NMM: ELL/159; Jervis to Nepean, 27/8/1796, Add. MSS 31171; Jervis to Bute, 30/8/1796, Add. MSS 31166; Jervis to Nelson, 25 and 28/8/1796, NMM: CRK/11; Garlies to Elliot, 1/9/1796, NMM: ELL/137; Nelson to Spencer, 20/8/1796, Add. MSS 75795. Details of the blockade of Leghorn are preserved in the log books of *La Minerve* (NMM: ADM/L/M292), *Lively* (ADM 51/1186 and ADM 52/2926), *Sardine* (ADM 51/1181) and *Blanche* (ADM 51/1140).

43. Caffarena to Nelson, 30/8/1796, 4/9/1796, Add. MSS 34904; Nelson to Genoa, 22/6/1796, NMM: CRK/14; Elliot to Nelson, 17/7/1796, NMM: ELL/159; Add. MSS 34904: 164, 223, 224, 335, 359; Harriman to Nelson, 3/9/1796, NMM: CRK/6; Drake to Nelson, 16/8/1796, NMM: CRK/4; Drake to Grenville, 10/8/1796, FO 28/15.

44. Heatly to Elliot, 20/9/1796, NMM: ELL/137; Drake's letters to Nelson and Brame, 19/9/1796, NMM: CRK/4; documents filed in FO 28/15.

45. Brame to Jervis, 9/9/1796, with enclosures, ADM 1/395; Brame to Drake, 9/9/1796, with enclosures, FO 28/16; Nelson's notes to Genoa, and the record of his interview with the doge, SRRC, 112/16/33: 858, 863, 999.

46. NMM: ADM/L/C51; log of *L'Eclair* (ADM 51/1173).

47. For Genoese responses see Castiglione to Brame, 11, 12 September 1796, enclosed in Brame to Drake, 13/9/1796, FO 28/16; statement of 17/9/1796, enclosed in FO 28/16, no. 72; complaint of Spinola, 7/10/1796, FO 28/16; FO 67/23: 32; and Castiglione's answers, 15/10/1796, FO 67/23: 98. The merchant's account can be found in Jackson to Grenville, 14/9/1796, FO 67/22: 216. Many sources for the Genoa affair are duplicated in different files. Scholars should begin with FO 28/16, which contains Nelson to Brame, 11/9/1796, his 'statement of facts', Compton's account, and Brame to Drake, 13/9/1796 (all enclosed in Drake to Grenville, 20/9/1796); Drake to Grenville, 5, 8/10/1796, with their enclosures; and Drake to Jervis, 21/9/1796. In FO 20/12 several documents, including the depositions of Berry and Noble, 11/9/1796, Nelson to Drake, 12/9/1796 and Elliot to Jervis, 20/9/1796, are enclosed in Elliot to Portland, 20/11/1796. Jackson sent some of these and other documents home from Turin: see Brame to Castiglione, 12/9/1796, FO 67/22; Brame to Jackson, 13/9/1796, FO 67/22; and Jackson to Grenville, 14, 17, 24/9/1796, FO 67/22. In addition to these, I have used Brame's letters to Nelson, Jackson and Drake in his letter book (SRRC, 112/16/31); several papers in SRRC, 112/16/33, and NMM: ELL/138; ADM 1/395: nos 155–6; Countess of Minto,

Sir Gilbert Elliot, 2, p. 352; Add. MSS 34904: 382 (letters of Brame and Bird); Add. MSS 34941: 157 following (letters to Nelson); and James Stanier Clarke and John McArthur, *Life and Services*, 1, pp. 460–8.

48. Elliot to Nelson, 17/7/1796, NMM: CRK/5.

49. Nelson to Brame, 24/3/1796, and Castiglione to Brame, 14/8/1796, SRRC, 112/16/33: 503, 815; Brame to Nelson, 25/3/1796 and Nelson's note of 28/4/1796, SRRC, 112/16/31.

50. For the French complaints about the Genoese battery see letters between Sucy and Bediani, 12/9/1796, *Annual Register*, 1796, pt ii, pp. 199, 200. The amount of ammunition expended by the *Captain* is given in the list of gunner's stores, 1796–7, Houghton Library, Harvard University, Cambridge, Massachusetts.

51. Nelson to Brame, 11/9/1796, SRRC, 112/16/33: 873, and other documents in the same collection.

52. Brame to Jervis, 16/9/1796, SRRC, 112/16/31.

53. Elliot to Jervis, 20/9/1796, FO 20/12; Jervis to Nelson, 17, 20/9/1796, Add. MSS 31166; Jervis to Brame, 25/9/1796, Add. MSS 31166; and Jervis to Nepean, 28/3/1797, ADM 1/396.

54. Drake's letters to Genoa (September 1796), Brame (30/8/1796, 4/9/1796) and Jervis (30/8/1796), SRRC, 112/16/33: 899, 844, 831A, 843.

55. Vouchers for provisions received by Nelson in Genoa, 5 to 11/9/1796, are filed in SRRC, 112/16/33: 853–5, 860.

56. Elliot to Nelson, 15/9/1796, ADM 1/395; Elliot to Nelson, 3/10/1796, Add. MSS 34904.

57. Nelson to Jervis, 14 to 15/9/1796, Monmouth MSS, E987.

58. Elliot to Jervis, 21/9/1796, NMM: ELL/159; Logan to Elliot, 20/9/1796, NMM: ELL/124. The capture of Capraia can be studied in Nelson to Jervis, 19/9/1796, Elliot to Nelson, 15/9/1796, and other enclosures in ADM 1/395, no. 156; Nelson to Elliot, 19/9/1796 and Nelson to De Burgh, 25/9/1796, Monmouth MSS, E988; Logan to Elliot, 19, 20, 22/9/1796, 6/10/1796, NMM: ELL/124; return of the Genoese garrison, NMM: ELL/124; Add. MSS 34904: 390; FO 20/12: no. 121 and enclosures; Elliot to Logan, 15/9/1796, and other letters in NMM: ELL/159; documents in NMM: JER/2b; logs of the *Captain* (ADM 52/2825) and *La Minerve* (NMM: ADM/L/M292); and Clarke and McArthur, *Life and Services*, 1, pp. 468–72.

59. Logan to Elliot, 22/9/1796, NMM: ELL/124.

60. Summons, 18/9/1796, and Nelson and Logan to Aynolo, 18/9/1796, NMM: ELL/124.

61. Nelson to Towry, Preston, Garlies and Tyrrell, September 1796, Add. MSS 34904; Nelson to Udny, 24/9/1796, NMM: ELL/132; Nelson to Bolton, 1796, Monmouth MSS, E988.

62. Letters from Genoa, 30/9/1796, 8/10/1796, FO 67/23: 32, 37; Genoese protest, 4/10/1796, SRRC, 112/16/33: 915.

63. Nelson, 1/9/1796, Monmouth MSS, E987; Nelson to Jervis, 30/9/1796, NMM: JER/2b, Jervis to Nelson, 25/9/1796, Add. MSS 31166.

64. For Nelson's officers and the switch to *Diadem* see Jervis to Elliot, 12/9/1796, NMM: ELL/141; Add. MSS 31175: 213; Jervis to Nelson, 8/10/1796, NMM: CRK/11; and *Diadem* muster, ADM 36/11823. The lieutenants on the *Diadem* were John Leckie, H. E. R. Baker, William Bennett, William B. Ryder and Joshua Rowe.

65. Drake to Grenville, 1/10/1796, FO 28/16; Nelson, 1, 3/10/1796, NMM: CRK/14; Elliot's instructions, 3/10/1796, Add. MSS 34904: 403; papers in SRRC, 112/16/33: 905, 912, 919; and several letters of Jervis to Elliot and Brame, 18 September to 7 October, in NMM: ELL/141 and Add. MSS 31166: 97, 100.

66. Documents enclosed in Drake to Grenville, 19, 26/10/1796, FO 28/16, including Nelson to Genoese government, 9/10/1796, and in NMM: JER/2b and CRK/14; Trevor to Grenville, 12, 15/10/1796, FO 67/23; Nelson to Brame, 8, 9/10/1796, FO 67/23; *Diadem* logs in ADM 51/1167 and NMM: ADM/L/D93.

67. Letters of Logan and Brame, 15/10/1796, FO 28/16 enclosed in no. 91; Trevor to Grenville, 21/10/1796, FO 67/23; Castiglione's response, 15/10/1796, FO 67/23: 98.

68. Grenville to Admiralty, 2/2/1796, D&L, 2, p. 311; Grenville to Drake, 18/10/1796, FO 28/16; Nelson to Brame, 4/11/1796, SRRC, 112/16/33: 959.

69. Jervis to Elliot, 13/10/1796 (two letters), NMM: ELL/141.

70. Minutes of Committee of Thirty, 12, 13/10/1796, FO 67/23: 114.

71. Elliot to Portland, 19, 26/10/1796, FO 20/12; Elliot to his wife, 24/10/1796, NLS, 11050: 125. Elliot told Portland that Jervis had 'misapprehended several points relative to the affairs of Bastia', but it was the naval officers, from whom Jervis obtained his information, not Elliot, who supervised the evacuation.

72. Nelson to Fanny, 7/11/1796, Monmouth MSS, E909; De Burgh to Elliot, 13/10/1796, NMM: ELL/148.

73. Jervis to Elliot, 15/10/1796, NMM: ELL/141.

74. Nelson to Clarence, 11/11/1796, Add. MSS 34902.

75. Nelson to Jervis, 15/10/1796, NMM: JER/2b; Jervis to Nelson, 16/10/1796, Add. MSS 31159; logs of the *Captain, Diadem, Excellent, Southampton* and *Egmont*, respectively filed in ADM 52/2825 and ADM 51/1167, 1169, 1189 and 1223. For lieutenants' logs of the *Diadem* see n. 66 above. Nelson's brief official report of the evacuation of Bastia, addressed to Jervis and dated 21 October, is filed in ADM 1/395. Additional details come from Hoste to his father, 26/11/1796, NMM: MRF/88/1.

76. 'Nelson at Bastia, by an old *Agamemnon*', p. 217. I have reservations about using this source, which contains vivid and exaggerated vignettes of the last days in Corsica. The anonymous author ('M.C.') may have been Mark Cooper from Norfolk, an ordinary seaman of twenty-six in 1796. Cooper was illiterate but could have dictated the material. Most of the few seamen named by M.C. could not be identified from the musters of the *Captain* and *Diadem*, though reference is made to John (Jack) Thompson, who is represented as having used his fists to drive local looters from the house of a Corsican woman (pp. 216–17). Thompson, a quartermaster's mate from Preston in Lancashire, was then in his mid-twenties and one of Nelson's most devoted followers.

77. For Casalta's march see Saliceti to the French Directory, 11/11/1796, in Maurice Jollivet, *Anglais dans La Mediterranée*, p. 282.

78. Elliot to his wife, 24/10/1796, NLS, 11050: 125; note of instructions by De Burgh in NMM: ELL/148.

79. Elliot to Portland, 26/10/1796, FO 20/12; Jervis to Nepean, 6/11/1796, Add. MSS 31171. Saliceti incorrectly reported that the British left fifty soldiers behind.

80. Nelson to Hamilton, 18, 19/10/1796, Morrison, *Hamilton and Nelson Papers*, 1, p. 225. See also Add. MSS 31159: 142 (two letters of Jervis to Coffin); Add. MSS 31166: 108–9; Add. MSS 34904: 441; Add. MSS 34938: 153; ADM 1/395: 174. After the disembarkations Porto Ferraio had detachments of the 18th, 50th and 51th British regiments; two battalions of Dillon's regiment; a Swiss regiment; and a corps of French and Maltese gunners (Edward P. Brenton, *John, Earl of St Vincent*, 1, p. 289).

81. The unsuccessful attempt to reoccupy Capraia emerges from Nelson to Collingwood, and Collingwood to Macnamara, both 20/10/1796, NMM: COL/2; *Excellent* log, NMM: ADM/L/E159; and the unsigned account of 29/10/1796, and Nelson to Brame, 26/10/1796, SRRC, 112/16/33: 957, 959.

82. Jervis to Nepean, 29/10/1796, Add. MSS 31171; Jervis to Cockburn, 21/10/1796, Add. MSS 31159. Though disappointed in Man, Nelson still regarded him as 'my old friend and worthy' (Nelson to Clarence, 23/11/1796, NMM: AGC/27).

83. Nelson to Fanny, 13/10/1796, Monmouth MSS, E906.

84. Nelson to Locker, 5/11/1796, D&L, 2, p. 298; Nelson to Jervis, 30/9/1796, NMM:

JER/2b (two letters); Drake to Nelson, 29/10/1796, Add. MSS 34904; Nelson to Hamilton, 1/12/1796, Morrison, *Hamilton and Nelson Papers*, 1, p. 226.

85. Nelson to Brame, 26/10/1796, SRRC, 112/16/33: 959.

86. Nelson lost two lieutenants with the captured prize crew, and on 12 January 1797 promoted Charles Gill to fill one of the vacancies on *La Minerve*: Nelson to Gill, 12/1/1797, Houghton Library, Harvard University, Cambridge, Massachusetts.

87. Nelson to Elliot, 24/12/1796, *D&L*, 2, p. 318; Fremantle, *Wynne Diaries* (1935–40), 2, pp. 144–6, 164; Nelson to Hamilton, 27/12/1796, Morrison, *Hamilton and Nelson Papers*, 1, p. 226.

88. Jervis to Elliot, 11/11/1796, Add. MSS 31166; Jervis to De Burgh, 10/12/1796, Add. MSS 31166; Jervis to O'Hara, 13/2/1797, Add. MSS 31159; Nelson to Spencer, 16/1/1797, Add. 75808.

89. De Burgh to Nelson, 28/12/1796, NMM: JER/2b (two letters); Elliot to Nelson, 1/1/1797, Add. MSS 34905; De Burgh's letters to Nelson and Jervis, 23/1/1797, ADM 1/396, enclosed in no. 19; De Burgh to Portland, 13, 24/1/1797, and Elliot's letters to Portland, especially 24/1/1797, all in FO/12; De Burgh to Windham, 3/1/1797, FO 79/15; De Burgh to Elliot, January 1797 (two letters), NMM: ELL/148.

90. Jervis to O'Hara, 13/2/1797, Add. MSS 31159; Fremantle to William Fremantle, 10/12/1796, CBS, D-FR/45/2.

91. De Burgh to Nelson, undated, Add. MSS 34905: 108; Fremantle to William Fremantle, 10/12/1796, 21/3/1797, CBS, D-FR/45/2.

92. These cases involved John Clark and Richard Parke (June 1796), Alexander Ross (August), Hugh Griffiths and John Gourly (October), and John Seymour, James Wilson, Thomas Upton and Edward Tyrrell (December). See ADM 1/5336–37, and Jervis to Nelson, 18/6/1796, 6/8/1796, Add. MSS 31175.

93. Jervis to Nelson, 10/9/1796, Add. MSS 31176.

94. Court martial records, ADM 1/5337–38 and Add. MSS 34905; Jervis to Nelson, 14/12/1796, Add. MSS 31159; petition of Robert Major, 10/1/1797, Western MSS 3676, Wellcome Library, London. A useful discussion of the *Dromedary* case is Nick Slope, 'The Trials of Nelson: Nelson's Camel'.

95. De Burgh to Hamilton, 29/1/1797, BL: A. M. Broadley, 'Nelsoniana', 3, facing p. 340.

96. Nelson to Jervis, 25/1/1797, ADM 1/396; John Drinkwater-Bethune, *Narrative of the Battle*, p. 8. Letters relating to the evacuation of Porto Ferraio, with sailing directions for convoys, are contained in Monmouth MSS, E988.

97. Jervis to Nelson, 13/1/1797, Add. MSS 31159; Jervis to Parker, 14/1/1797, Add. MSS 31159.

98. Nelson to Pollard, 25/1/1797, William L. Clements Library, University of Michigan, Ann Arbor.

XXIV The Happy Moment (pp. 684–718)

1. John Drinkwater-Bethune, *Narrative of the Battle*, p. 13. For this voyage see Drinkwater-Bethune, *Narrative of the Battle*, pp. 12–15, and the logs of *La Minerve*, ADM 51/1204, ADM 52/3223 and NMM: ADM/L/M292.

2. Jervis to Nepean, 9/6/1797, Add. MSS 31171.

3. The logs of the ships of the fleet supply many of the details in this account, but for the *Victory* see also Jervis's journal, Add. MSS 31186: 159–61, and for the *Captain* the log of Oliver Davis, NMM: WAL/21B.

4. G. S. Parsons, *Nelsonian Reminiscences*, pp. 168–9. Jervis's dispatches of the battle (ADM 1/396: no. 21) are in *D&L*, 2, pp. 333–6, and many of the British logs were published in T. Sturgis-Jackson, ed., *Logs*, 1, pp. 197–254. Cordoba's dispatch, and some analogous

documents, were given in Julian S. Corbett, ed., *Spencer*, 1, pp. 340 ff. The historiography of the battle of Cape St Vincent may be traced in John Drinkwater (later Drinkwater-Bethune), *Proceedings of the British Fleet*, the original unadorned version of this most valuable of contemporary accounts; Charles Ekins, *Naval Battles*, pp. 239–50; William James, *Naval History*, 2, pp. 29–53; A. T. Mahan, *Life of Nelson*, chap. 8; 'Battle of Cape St Vincent', *Journal of the Royal United Service Institution*, which contains the papers of Lt William Bryan Wyke and other documents; A. H. Taylor, 'Battle of Cape St Vincent', which considers Spanish evidence; Russell Grenfell, *Horatio Nelson*, chap. 5; Christopher Lloyd, *St Vincent and Camperdown*; John Creswell, *British Admirals*, pp. 214–28; M. A. J. Palmer, 'Sir John's Victory'; Brian Tunstall and Nicholas Tracy, *Naval Warfare*, pp. 216–19; David Davies, *Fighting Ships*, chap. 5; Colin White, *1797*; and Stephen Howarth, ed., *Battle of Cape St Vincent*. Of these, Palmer and White are particularly instructive.

5. Colin White, 'The Midshipman and the Commodore', argues that the *Captain* took her place between the *Barfleur* and *Namur*, and was fourth from the end of the line, but both Nelson and Miller, among other important witnesses, are clear that their ship was third from the rear. Evidence exists for both positions. Compare, for example, the note in the Spencer papers, Add. MSS 75802, with the contemporary plan of the battle in NMM: MKH/102.

6. John Wilkie's account, 'Battle of Cape St Vincent', p. 334; Drinkwater, *Proceedings of the British Fleet*, p. 22; Corbett, *Spencer*, 1, p. 346.

7. Reminiscences of John Griffiths, first lieutenant of *Culloden*, in Jedediah S. Tucker, *St Vincent*, 1, pp. 256–7.

8. Drinkwater, *Proceedings of the British Fleet*, p. 26.

9. Clear statements of the repulse of the Spanish leeward division can be found in the admiral's journal, Add. MSS 31186: 160; the narrative of Lieutenant Lewis Stephen Davis, NMM: HIS/35; and Mundy's journal from the *Blenheim*, NMM: 85/015.

10. The story about Jervis on the poop (Tucker, *St Vincent*, 1, p. 259) may have come from the admiral's secretary, father of the author.

11. I do not accept James's view (2, p. 37) that Nelson wore out of line in response to Jervis's signal no. forty-one, flown at 12.51. James may have been misled by the log of the *Prince George*, which erroneously interpreted signal forty-one as an instruction to 'form the line as was most convenient' (Sturgis-Jackson, *Logs*, 1, p. 218). The correct meaning – that ships were to 'take suitable stations and engage as arrive up in succession' – shows that it supplemented signal eighty, flown immediately before and directed to the *Britannia*. Together, the signals directed captains in the rear of the fleet to tack to starboard in succession, and then to use discretion in placing their ships as they came up with the enemy. They did not authorise Nelson to wear his ship out of line to larboard, 'without waiting our turn' (Miller to his father, 3/3/1797, in White, *1797*, p. 152). White's *1797* gives a convincing reconstruction of this phase of the battle.

12. Wilkie's account, p. 335, records Nelson's position a little to windward of the British line.

13. Nelson to Spencer, 28/3/1797, *D&L*, 7, p. cxxxi. For Nelson's willingness to modify Jervis's orders see Jervis to Nelson, 8, 19/8/1796, Add. MSS 31159.

14. Tunstall and Tracy, *Naval Warfare*, pp. 213–14.

15. Nelson's own statement ('Remarks Relative to Myself in the *Captain*') that he first engaged 'the headmost, and of course leeward-most' of the Spaniards, and that these ships 'from not wishing (I suppose) to have a decisive battle, hauled to the wind . . . which brought the ships afore-mentioned to be the leewardmost and sternmost ships in their fleet' (Add. MSS 34902: 119) may have fathered the legend of the *Captain* being thrown across the path of the Spanish van, instead of attacking the ships towards their

centre or rear. A contemporary map of uncertain origin in the Samuel Hood papers also has Nelson attacking the enemy van (NMM: MKH/102). This contradicts Drinkwater (*Proceedings of the British Fleet*, p. 13), who had a perfect view of that quarter and located Nelson's attack at the sixth ship from the Spanish rear; Miller (NMM: ADM/L/C51), who has the *Captain* crossing enemy bows to reach the Spanish flagship ninth from the rear; and Cordoba himself. The latter's flagship, *Santissima Trinidad*, which Nelson attacked, was a slow sailer, and in bearing up had already fallen to the rear before Nelson engaged (Corbett, *Spencer*, pp. 343, 345). The subsequent action certainly enveloped the rearmost Spaniards, including *Santissima Trinidad* (130 guns), *San Josef*, *Salvador del Mundo* and *Mexicano* (all 112 guns), *San Nicolas* (eighty-four guns), and *San Ysidro* and *Soberano* (both seventy-four guns).

16. Drinkwater-Bethune, *Narrative of the Battle*, p. 79; Collingwood to his wife, 17/2/1797, G. L. Newnham Collingwood, ed., *Correspondence*, 1, p. 37; Foote, enclosed in ADM 1/396: no. 25. There is doubt about whether the *Captain* or the *Culloden* opened fire first. Nelson said that *Culloden* 'immediately' supported him astern ('Remarks Relative' Add. MSS 34902: 119), while Miller thought Troubridge might actually have began firing on the hindmost Spaniards 'about two minutes before' (NMM: ADM/L/C51). Other evidence is inconclusive. Saumarez of the *Orion* described the *Captain* as 'the leading ship' and the *Culloden* and others 'the next that came up' (Saumarez to his brother, 15/2/1797, in Sir John Ross, *Saumarez*, 1, p. 170). The 'Journal of the Proceedings of H.M. Fleet on the 14th of February 1797, by an Officer on Board one of the Ships' (Ekins, *Naval Battles*, p. 245) adopted the popular course of bracketing the ships together: 'the *Captain* took her station in the van, ahead of the *Culloden*, and both engaged the centre of the enemy . . .'. However, the *Prince George* has both the *Culloden* and the *Blenheim* engaging before the *Captain*. Her log reports the *Culloden* firing at one-twenty or one-twenty-five, the *Blenheim* at about one thirty and the *Captain* 'a few minutes after' (*Prince George* log, ADM 51/1197). This, like other comments from the *Prince George*, seems ill sustained. While the *Culloden* probably opened fire at about the same time as the *Captain*, the *Blenheim* certainly entered the action later. Mundy's *Blenheim* journal reports that his ship fell half a mile behind the *Culloden* after tacking at the head of the British line, and that Troubridge had been 'closely engaged by five or six of the enemy for fifteen minutes before we arrived up with her'. However, the *Captain* had come under the *Culloden*'s lee bow and 'in some measure assisted her tho' at random shot'. Mundy's view of the *Captain* was probably obscured by the *Culloden*, which was firing between them, but it establishes that she engaged before the *Blenheim*. Miller's log also records that the *Culloden* and *Captain* alone deflected the Spaniards from bearing up, 'the rest of our van being very considerably astern of the *Culloden*'. See Mundy journal, NMM: 85/015, and Miller log, NMM: ADM/L/C51. On the other hand, Nelson and Miller's belief that the *Captain* and *Culloden* were unsupported for up to an hour was greatly exaggerated.

17. Drinkwater, *Proceedings of the British Fleet*, pp. 13–14; *The Times*, 13/3/1797; Geoffrey Marcus, *Age of Nelson*, p. 78; Collingwood to Nelson, 15/2/1797, Add. MSS 34905; Add. MSS 31186: 160; Palmer, 'Sir John's Victory', p. 42; Oliver Davis to his parents, 2/6/1797, NMM: WAL/21A; and the logs of the *Victory* (ADM 51/1187), *Southampton* (ADM 51/1189) and *Captain* (ADM 52/2825 and ADM 51/1194). In another letter Collingwood wrote that 'a skilful manoeuvre, which was led to by Commodore Nelson, turned most of our force to the greater part where their admiral was' (Collingwood to Carlyle, 22/2/1797, E. Hughes, ed., *Private Correspondence*, p. 79).

18. For Troubridge giving way to the *Blenheim* see Mundy's journal, NMM: 85/105. In a somewhat crabbed contribution the log of the *Prince George* complained that 'by backing her main top sail [the *Captain*] kept the followers from closing up so fast with the enemy

as might have been done' (ADM 51/1197), but ships so placed almost inevitably backed to maintain their station. The *Prince George*, *Orion*, *Captain* and *Culloden* all did so. See also 'Journal of the Proceedings', Ekins, *Naval Battles*, p. 245.

19. Master's log of *Captain*, ADM 52/2825.

20. The armament of the *San Nicolas* became known after she fell into the hands of the Royal Navy. Jervis described her as an eighty-four-gun ship, but only eighty guns were mounted (statements of Culverhouse and Frederick in HCA 32/845). That the *Captain* carried one or two sixty-eight-pound carronades is evident from the fact that she fired one hundred and five sixty-eight-pound round shot and twelve sixty-eight-pound grape and case shot during the battle (William Collett and Ralph W. Miller, gunner's expenditure of stores, 14/2/1797, Houghton Library, Harvard University, Cambridge, Massachusetts). Whether these carronades had replaced or supplemented long guns is not clear.

21. 'Remarks Relative', Add. MSS 34902: 119. For *Excellent*'s role see the account from that ship in 'Battle of Cape St Vincent', p. 329.

22. Collingwood to his wife, 17/2/1797, in Collingwood, *Correspondence*, 1, p. 37.

23. Sturgis-Jackson, *Logs*, 1, p. 224.

24. Miller to his father, 3/3/1797, in White, *1797*, p. 152.

25. Muster of the *Captain*, ADM 36/14801. Culverhouse (HCA 32/845) probably put the manpower of the *San Nicolas* a little too high at about seven hundred.

26. Davis to his parents, 2/6/1707, NMM: WAL/21A.

27. Parsons, *Nelsonian Reminiscences*, p. 170; James, *Naval History*, 2, p. 45; Drinkwater, *Proceedings of the British Fleet*, p. 26; Add. MSS 34902: 149; 'dimensions' of the *San Josef*, Western MSS 3676, Wellcome Library, London.

28. 'Remarks Relative', Add. MSS 34902: 119. Francis William Blagdon, *Orme's Graphic History*, pp. iii, 13, was confused as to whether the ship's commander, Brigadier Don Pedro Piñeda, or a subordinate, Don José Delkenna, surrendered the ship to Nelson. This book also appears to have been the source of the popular legend that Nelson boarded one of the Spanish ships with the cry, 'Westminster Abbey or a glorious victory!' (p. 12). Blagdon claimed to have used 'the minutes of an officer in one of the repeating frigates' (p. 10), which may have given rise to the idea that the authority for Nelson's war cry was John Drinkwater. It does not, however, appear in Drinkwater's own account.

29. Davis to his parents, 2/6/1797, NMM: WAL/21A.

30. Elliot to Nelson, 15/2/1797, NMM: ELL/138; Elliot to his wife, 1/3/1797, NLS, 11050: 162.

31. Nelson to Clarence, 22/3/1797, NMM: AGC/27. On the state of the Spanish flagship compare Foote's report (ADM 1/396: no. 25), which minimises her injuries, with the statement of 8/3/1797 from Cadiz (ADM 1/396: enclosed in no. 41) which describes her as 'entirely dismasted'.

32. Nelson to William, 6/4/1797, Add. MSS 34988; Jervis to Nelson, 25/2/1797, Add. MSS 34938; Collingwood to Edward Collingwood, 22/2/1797, Add. MSS 52780; Mundy journal, NMM: 85/015. Nevertheless, Jervis remained sure that he had been right to call off the action because of 'the certainty of losing our trophies, and which [what] would have been infinitely more painful, the *Captain*' (Jervis to Elliot, 16/2/1797, NMM: ELL/141).

33. Collingwood to Carlyle, 22/2/1797, Hughes, *Private Correspondence*, p. 79. The casualties of the *San Nicolas* have variously been given as 129 killed and wounded and 143 killed and ninety-seven wounded, and those of the *San Josef* as fifty-six killed and forty to fifty wounded and thirty-nine killed and twenty wounded: Corbett, *Spencer*, 1, pp. 353–4; ADM 1/396, enclosures in no. 21; Hoste to his father, 16/2/1797, NMM: MRF/88/1.

34. Collingwood to Carlyle, 22/2/1797, Hughes, *Private Correspondence*, p. 79.

35. The first version of 'Remarks Relative to Myself in the *Captain*', filed in Add. MSS 34902: 116–18.

36. Elliot to Nelson, 15/2/1797, NMM: ELL/138; James Harrison, *Life*, 1, pp. 175–6.

37. Tucker, *St Vincent*, 1, p. 262.

38. William Collett and Ralph W. Miller, expenditure of gunner's stores, 14/2/1797, Houghton Library.

39. Davis to his parents, 2/6/1797, NMM: WAL/21A. The muster of the *Captain* details her casualties.

40. Nelson to Elliot, 15/2/1797, NMM: ELL/138; Nelson to Suckling, 23/2/1797, NMM: XAGC/8, Anne-Marie E. Hills, 'His Belly off Cape St Vincent'; court martial of Hallowell, 17/2/1797, ADM 1/5338; Nelson to Thompson, 17/2/1797, Monmouth MSS, E41; Angerstein to Nelson, 5/6/1801, NMM: CRK/1.

41. Nelson to McArthur, 10/4/1797, *D&L*, 2, p. 371; Jervis to Nepean, 22/2/1797, ADM 1/396. An unofficial report of 18 March gave the Spanish casualties on the prizes as 261 killed and 342 wounded (SRRC, 112/16/33: 1033).

42. Drinkwater-Bethune, *Narrative of the Battle*, pp. 88–9.

43. Nelson to Clarence, 2/4/1797, NMM: AGC/27.

44. Add. MSS 34902: 116–20, 119–20; *NLTHW*, p. 317. Nelson told Elliot that Miller was at work on 'two sketches of the action' (Nelson to Elliot, 16/2/1797, NMM: ELL/138).

45. Nelson to Locker, 21/2/1797, *D&L* 2, p. 353.

46. Jervis to Seymour, 17/2/1797, Tucker, *St Vincent*, 1, p. 265.

47. Maurice to Nelson, 8/3/1797, Add. MSS 34988; Fanny to Nelson, 17/4/1797, *NLTHW*, p. 361.

48. Jervis to Spencer, 16/2/1797, *D&L*, 2, p. 335.

49. Nelson to Clarence, 22/2/1797, NMM: AGC/27; Add. MSS 27845: 154; Mrs Henry Baring, ed., *William Windham*, 354; Windham to Nelson, 16/1/1797, NMM: CRK/13; Locker to Nelson, 17, 26/3/1797, Add. MSS 34905; *The Times*, 13/3/1797; Marianne Czisnik, 'Nelson and The Nile'.

50. *The Times*, 2, 9/3/1797. The account Miller gave his father (White, 1797, p. 152) is echoed in differently worded fragments published in *The Times* 13/3/1797, and elsewhere, suggesting that Miller wrote letters to different people in a similar style.

51. Drinkwater, *Proceedings of the British Fleet*, pp. 5–6; Drinkwater-Bethune, *Narrative of the Battle*, pp. iii, 1, 82–5. Nelson's own version of the battle was being fine-tuned by Miller as early as 22 February (Nelson to Fanny, 22/2/1797, Monmouth MSS, E919; *D&L*, 2, p. 350) and it does not appear that he instigated Drinkwater's publication. Indeed, Fanny had to purchase a copy of it when printed (*NLTHW*, p. 366).

52. Parker to Nelson, 25/7/1797; Parker's narrative, and Nelson to Parker, 19/8/1797, *D&L*, 2, pp. 471, 473. The papers of the prize courts, which arbitrated competing claims to captured ships, contain no reference to the *Prince George* with respect to the *San Nicolas* and *San Josef*. They do record the interest of Captain Frederick, whose *Blenheim* may have fired on the Spanish ships earlier in the action (HCA 32/845). However, this evidence is not decisive, because presumably all British ships in the battle were entitled to a share of the head money generated by the prizes. Laying aside Parker's statements, the other accounts from the *Prince George* establish that the ship had cannonaded Nelson's opponents from astern of the *Captain* before interrupting her fire to work forward, around the latter's lee. Having done so, the *Prince George* resumed firing, concentrating upon the bows of the enemy ships, only to be hailed from the *Captain* and told they had struck. This much is consistent with Nelson's account, but stops short of corroborating Parker's grievance. Furthermore, the records of the *Prince George* sometimes conflict with other evidence. For example, they assert that after the intervention of the *Excellent*

the *Captain* temporarily advanced to re-engage the *Santissima Trinidad*, though this appears in no other source. The 'fog of war' was undoubtedly a factor. Wilkie, the master of the *Prince George*, admitted 'that our observation . . . could not be extensive or very accurate' because of the smoke ('Battle of Cape St Vincent', p. 337). Parker's credibility is also undermined by his long-standing jealousy of Nelson. In 1787 he had accused Nelson of stealing his patronage; in 1798 he would complain of Nelson's receipt of the command of another detached squadron. The early history of their relationship has escaped previous Nelson biographers.

53. Spencer to Nelson, 8/3/1797, Add. MSS 75808; Nelson to Hamilton, 27/4/1797, Huntington Library, San Marino, California; Portland to St Vincent, 22/6/1797, Add. MSS 34933.

54. Miller to his father, 3/3/1797, White, *1797*, p. 152; Miller, will, 17/1/1798, Kirstie Buckland, ed., *Miller Papers*, p. 33.

55. Berry to Nelson, 18/2/1797, Add. MSS 34905.

56. Nelson to Collingwood, 15/2/1797, *D&L*, 2, p. 347.

57. Jervis to Spencer, 16/2/1797, *D&L*, 2, p. 335.

58. Noble and Spicer returned home to seek appointments as commanders: Noble to Nepean, 1/6/1797, ADM 1/226. For Withers see Withers to Nelson, 4/10/1797, enclosed in Nelson to Nepean, 9/10/1797, ADM 1/396; Withers to Nelson, 4/9/1801, Alfred Morrison, *Hamilton and Nelson Papers*, 2, p. 163; Jervis to Nelson, 2/6/1797, Add. MSS 34938.

59. Peirson to Nelson, 11/3/1797, 10/1/1800, Add. MSS 34905 and 34916; Windham to Nelson, 1797, Add. MSS 34906; War Office, *List*, volumes for 1795–1800; Morrison, *Hamilton and Nelson Papers*, 2, pp. 85, 208, 299, 300; James Stanier Clarke and John McArthur, *Life and Services*, 1, p. 514; Thomas Foley, *Nelson Centenary*, pp. 38, 45, 50. Peirson died returning from Honduras in 1800 at the age of twenty-seven. His daughter Caroline was said to have resembled her father.

60. Parker to Nelson, 15/3/1797, Add. MSS 34905; Collingwood to Nelson, 13/4/1797, Add. MSS 34906; Nelson to Fanny, 28/2/1797, Monmouth MSS, E920. The freedom of London was presented in a box of chased gold with an enamelled lid showing the battle of Cape St Vincent: Leslie Southwick, 'Tokens of Victory'.

61. Fanny to Nelson, 26/3/1797, *NLTHW*, p. 355; Edmund Nelson to Nelson, 6/3/1797, Monmouth MSS, E625.

62. Fanny to Nelson, 11/3/1797, Add. MSS 34988 (italics hers).

63. Fanny to Nelson, 23/2/1797, 20/3/1797 and 3/4/1797, Add. MSS 34988.

64. Fanny to Nelson, 10/4/1797, Add. MSS 34988.

XXV Who will not Fight for Dollars? (pp. 719–49)

1. Nelson to Katy Matcham, 31/3/1797, NMM: MAM.

2. Nelson to Fanny, 30/6/1797, Monmouth MSS, E932.

3. Fanny to Nelson, 3/4/1797, Add. MSS 34988.

4. Nelson to Fanny, 14/3/1797, Monmouth MSS, E922.

5. Fanny to Nelson, 17/4/1797, Add. MSS 34988; Nelson to Scrivener, 15/6/1797, Ron C. Fiske, *Notices of Nelson*, p. 13.

6. Nelson to William, 10/11/1783, Add. MSS 34988; William to Nelson, 3/5/1802, Alfred Morrison, *Hamilton and Nelson Papers*, 2, p. 188; Nelson to Fanny, 17/2/1796, 20/5/1796, Monmouth MSS, E886, E895.

7. Nelson to his father, 19/8/1796, Add. MSS 34988; Henry Gunning, *Reminiscences*, 2, p. 232; J. A. Venn, *Alumni Cantabrigienses*, 2, pt 4, p. 524.

8. Nelson to Fanny, 6/1/1796, 9/4/1796, 20/5/1796, Monmouth MSS, E881, E890, E895; pay books of *Agamemnon* and *Captain*, ADM 35/69, ADM 35/401; Nelson to Nepean, 6/10/1797, 28/11/1797, ADM 1/396; Marsh and Creed accounts in Morrison, *Hamilton*

and Nelson Papers, 2, pp. 382–99, and (for 1797) in Western MSS 3676, Wellcome Library, London.

9. Accounts of Daniel Shelds, Turnbull and Company, and William Dickman in Western MSS 3676, Wellcome Library; Nelson to Fellowes, 2/10/1797, Huntington Library, San Marino, California.

10. Nelson to William, 4/3/1796, Add. MSS 34933. Prize and head money, the latter payable on captured warships, could yield large returns. Nelson netted £381 for the capture of the *Vierge de la Mercie* in 1793, while in 1794 three small ships and some bales of cotton gave the *Agamemnon* £758, of which the captain's share (two-eighths in this instance) would have been £190 (McArthur to Nelson, 15/7/1795, Western MSS 3676, Wellcome Library; Udny to Nelson, 18/6/1794, with accounts, NMM: 75/102). The total amount Nelson made in this way is difficult to assess. One list (Add. MSS 34902: 104; *D&L*, 2, p. 178) suggests that Nelson earned £2,745 from prize and head money up to 11 May 1796, but additional sums were being paid as court proceedings and prize-taking continued. Two cargoes taken in April and May 1796 eventually yielded the *Agamemnon* 2,840 Spanish dollars, probably giving Nelson £172, and the following January he received £226 on account of a Genoese corn polacre brought into Porto Ferraio (prize list, 1796, and accounts of Udny and Ogle, 1797, Western MSS 3676, Wellcome Library). Final receipts for the riviera campaign were still unclear in 1802 (*D&L*, 5, pp. 11, 13).

11. Nelson to Jervis, 10/7/1797, NMM: JER/3–4; Jervis to Elliot, 14/7/1796, Add. MSS 31166.

12. Mary C. Innes, *William Wolseley*, pp. 99–100; Nelson to Pollard, 27/6/1794, in Warren R. Dawson, ed., *Nelson Collection*, p. 51; Plampin to Nelson, 1795, Add. MSS 34905; log of the *Romulus*, ADM 51/1130.

13. Saumarez to his brother, 6/3/1797, in Sir John Ross, *Saumarez*, 1, p. 177.

14. Jervis to Nelson, 2/3/1797, Add. MSS 31176; Jervis to Nepean, 5/3/1797, ADM 1/396; Nelson to Connell, 28/3/1797, Huntington Library; notes of Sir Robert Chambers, Monmouth MSS, E378. The officers of the *Irresistible* were Lieutenants William Bevians, Andrew Thomson, George Seaton, Arthur Maxwell and Robert Forbes, and surgeon Richard Burke (ADM 36/11775). For her movements see the logs, ADM 51/1194 and ADM 52/3128.

15. Jervis to Nelson, 3, 4, 10/4/1797, Add. MSS 31176; Nelson to his captains, 11/4/1797, ADM 1/396.

16. Collingwood to Nelson, 13/4/1797, Add. MSS 34906.

17. Nelson to Jervis, 12/4/1797, *D&L*, 2, p. 378.

18. Nelson to Jervis, 14/3/1797, 11/4/1797, *D&L*, 7, p. cxxix, and 2, p. 376.

19. Jervis to Nelson, 12/4/1797, Add. MSS 31176; Jervis to Fremantle, 14/3/1797, Add. MSS 31166; Sutton to Pole, 28/4/1797, NMM: WYN/101.

20. Nelson to Jervis, 1/5/1797, Monmouth MSS, E988. For Fremantle's voyage see the log of the *Inconstant*, ADM 51/1179.

21. Anne Fremantle, ed., *Wynne Diaries* (1935–40), 2, p. 176, which also contains a journal of Nelson's return journey; Nelson to Jervis, 21/4/1797, 1/5/1797, ADM 1/396; Spencer to Jervis, 8/7/1797, Add. MSS 75812.

22. Cockburn to Nelson, 24/7/1797, Add. MSS 34906.

23. Udny to Nelson, 11/4/1797, Add. MSS 34906.

24. Ogle to Nelson, 22/3/1797, Add. MSS 34905; Nelson accounts in Morrison, *Hamilton and Nelson Papers*, 2, pp. 382–99.

25. For the missing ship see De Burgh to Elliot, 21/5/1797, 6/7/1797, NMM: ELL/148; Nelson to Jervis, 5/5/1797, Monmouth MSS, E988.

26. Sutton to Pole, 28/4/1797, NMM: WYN/101; Nelson to Spencer, 28/5/1797, BL: A. M. Broadley, 'Nelsoniana', 1, facing p. 24.

27. Nelson to Clarence, 26/5/1797, NMM: AGC/27; Nelson to Calder, 17/6/1797, Monmouth

MSS, E988; Nelson to Hoste, 30/6/1797, *D&L*, 2, p. 401. The first complaint of the mutineers, as given in the *Queen Charlotte* petition of 18/4/1797, concerned pay: G. E. Manwaring and Bonamy Dobree, *Floating Republic*, p. 265.

28. Court martial, 20/5/1797, ADM 1/5339; Jervis to Nepean, 21/5/1797, ADM 1/396; Fremantle, *Wynne Diaries*, 2, p. 184.

29. Nelson to Miller, 24/5/1797, Historical Society of Pennsylvania, Philadelphia. Nelson to McArthur, 1/6/1797, Rosenbach Museum and Library, Philadelphia, Pennsylvania.

30. Weatherhead was made acting lieutenant on 2 April 1797, filling the place of the promoted Noble, and Nisbet received a similar commission two days later, although in his case it was regularised in May (Add. MSS 31176: 117; muster, ADM 36/14801; Nisbet's return of service, 1817, ADM 9/2: no. 94). The other transferring lieutenants were Summers and Compton, and two recruits to the *Captain*, John Davies and Richard Hawkins, originally recruited from the *Lively* and *Egmont* respectively. The seven petty officers included Bolton, Hoste and Schroder of the *Agamemnon*, and Joseph Peraldi, a nineteen-year-old Corsican from Ajaccio. The important posts retained by *Theseus* men were those of captain of marines (Thomas Oldfield), master (Thomas Atkinson) and purser (John Hopper).

   Among the ratings following Nelson into his new ship were nineteen *Agamemnons*: Tom Allen, Francis Cook, Mark Cooper, John Cross, Charles Fenwick, William Fearney, John Hagan, Arthur Johnson, George Jones, William Levett, George Logan, John Lovell, Thomas Ramsay, Michael Riley, Samuel Shillingford, William Short, William Sparks (a boy), John Sykes and John (Jack) Thompson (muster of the *Theseus*, ADM 36/12648). Lovell, Short and Cook later served under William Hoste, when he eventually got a command of his own. Francis Cook lost his hand in a boat action and became a cook on Hoste's *Mutine*. See Joseph Allen, 'England's Wooden Walls', pp. 348–9.

31. Report of the *Theseus*, 30/5/1797, enclosed in ADM 1/396: no. 107.

32. Hoste to his father, 27/5/1797, NMM: MRF/88/1; logs of the *Theseus*, ADM 51/1173 (Aylmer), 51/1221 and 52/2993, and NMM: ADM/L/T87A.

33. Nelson to Clarence, 15/6/1797, NMM: AGC/27. For the more usual wording see Nelson to Fanny, 15/6/1797, Monmouth MSS, E930.

34. Nelson to Jervis, 9/6/1797, 10/6/1797, *D&L*, 2, pp. 393, 395; Jervis to Nelson, 10/6/1797, Add. MSS 34938. The original of the first of these letters, written by Nelson on 9 June (filed in NMM: JER/3–4) does not include the quotation about the two prisoners. Nicolas took his version (cited here) from Clarke and McArthur, but they reproduced documents inaccurately, and sometimes put material from two or more original letters together, publishing them under one date as if they belonged to a single communication. Probably Clarke and McArthur took the description of the prisoners from another Nelson letter, and incorporated it into the 9 June document in that way.

35. Nelson's letters to Jervis and Calder, 9/7/1797, *D&L*, 2, pp. 408, 409.

36. Nick Slope, 'The Trials of Nelson: Nelson and the *Emerald*'.

37. In addition to musters of the *Theseus*, see Jervis to Nelson, 2/6/1797, Add. MSS 34938, in which the commander-in-chief reports issuing a warrant as second master of the *Ville de Paris* to satisfy Nelson.

38. Nelson to Fanny, 9/3/1797, 2/4/1797, Monmouth MSS, E923–924.

39. Letter to Tyson, 1800, Add. MSS 34916: 187; Nelson to Fanny, 9/3/1797, 12/4/1797, Monmouth MSS, E923, E926; Nisbet's return of service, 1817, ADM 9/2: no. 94. Nisbet may even have avoided taking his lieutenants' examination. Spencer complained that lieutenants were being made in the Mediterranean fleet without certificates being forwarded, specifically mentioning Nisbet: Spencer to Jervis, 1/7/1797, Add. MSS 75812.

40. Maurice to Nelson, 16/5/1797, 4/8/1797, Add. MSS 34988, and NMM: BRP/5; Add. MSS 31176: 159; Jervis to Nelson, 17 and 19/6/1797, Add. MSS 34938; Nelson to Jervis, 18/9/1797, NMM: JER/3–4; Nelson to Fanny, 2/4/1797 and 30/6/1797, Monmouth

MSS, E924, E932. Later Bolton served under Nelson again and received a knighthood through the association.

41. Nelson to Hoste, 30/6/1797 and September 1797, *D&L*, 2, pp. 401, 442; Fanny to Nelson, 3/4/1797, Add. MSS 34988.

42. Nelson to Clarence, 15/6/1797, NMM: AGC/27. Nelson to McArthur, 1/6/1797, Rosenbach Museum and Library.

43. For the disposition of the ships see the map by a British officer, 18/5/1797, Add. MSS 34906: 124, and the drawings made by Thomas Buttersworth, NMM. The Spanish side of the blockade was described by Augusto Conte y Lacave, *Ataque de Cadiz*. Jervis's letters to Nelson can be read in Add. MSS 34938–34939, but his journal may be consulted in Add. MSS 31186: 189 following.

44. Nelson to Saumarez, 9/6/1797, Ross, *Saumarez*, 1, p. 180; Nelson to Mazzaredo, 30/6/1797, Monmouth MSS, E988.

45. Information of Duff, 29/5/1797, FO 72/45; Jervis to Nepean, 30/6/1797, ADM 1/396; map of Cadiz harbour, NC, 21 (1809), facing p. 476.

46. Plan to attack Cadiz, April 1797, Add. MSS 75812.

47. Nelson to Jervis, 7/6/1797, 6/6/1797, NMM: JER/3–4, and *D&L*, 2, p. 392; Ross, *Saumarez*, 1, p. 180; Add. MSS 34906: 135; Jervis to Nelson, Add. MSS 34938: 710; Jervis to O'Hara, 18/6/1797, Add. MSS 31166.

48. Jervis to Nelson, 10/7/1797, Add. MSS 34939.

49. Mazzaredo's letters to Nelson, Add. MSS 34941: 176–86, and Nelson letter book, Monmouth MSS, E988.

50. Nelson to Inglefield, 11/7/1797, *D&L*, 2, p. 411; Nelson to Jervis, 13/6/1797, Add. MSS 75812; Nelson to Fanny, 11/7/1797, Monmouth MSS, E934.

51. Jervis to Walpole, 6/7/1797, Add. MSS 31160.

52. Nelson to Clarence, 28/6/1797, NMM: AGC/27.

53. Jervis to Nelson, 3/6/1797, Add. MSS 34938; Nelson to Jervis, 3/7/1797, NMM: JER/3–4; Jervis to Nepean, 5/7/1797, ADM 1/396; Jervis to Nelson, 3/7/1797, Add. MSS 34939; Jervis to Spencer, 15/6/1797, Add. MSS 75812. The most useful account of the bombardments of Cadiz was given by Miller and dated 9/7/1797. It was rediscovered and published by Kirstie Buckland, ed., *Miller Papers*, pp. 8–15.

54. Nelson to Jervis, 3/7/1797, NMM: JER/3–4. In addition to the logs of the *Theseus*, I have used those of the *Goliath* (ADM 51/1205), *Terpsichore* (ADM 51/4507), *Emerald* (51/1166) and *Seahorse* (51/1190). Jervis thought Nelson's dispatch covering the attack (Nelson to Jervis, 4/7/1797, enclosed in ADM 1/396: no. 124) 'characteristic of your noble soul, and cannot be improved by the ablest pen in Europe' (Jervis to Nelson, 5/7/1797, Add. MSS 34939).

55. Buckland, *Miller Papers*, p. 9.

56. *Guiana Chronicle*, 21/3/1836, which contains a statement supposed to have been made by a participant.

57. Allen, 'England's Wooden Walls', pp. 348–9; *D&L*, p. 11; *Guiana Chronicle*, 21/3/1836; James Stanier Clarke and John McArthur, *Life and Services*, 2, p. 39; medical journal of the *Theseus*, ADM 101/123/2. Nelson referred to Sykes in his dispatch, and offered to pay his ongoing medical expenses. Prompted by Maurice Nelson, Fanny also sent him an inscribed small cased silver watch, which, with related relics, is preserved at Monmouth. Sykes recovered and returned to duty on 23 July. Fanny and Peirson were able to serve him in England, and through Nelson's influence he was transferred to Jervis's *Ville de Paris* and in October appointed a gunner of the *Andromache*. Unfortunately, he was accidentally killed when a gun burst on 1 May 1798; his estate, valued at under £300, went to his mother, Hannah. Consult Nelson to Huddlestone, 23/9/1797, NMM: AGC/18/5; Maurice Nelson to Nelson, 4/8/1797, NMM: BRP/5; Jervis

to Nelson, 30/10/1797, Add. MSS 34939; Matthew H. Barker, *Life of Nelson*, pp. 165–6; E. H. Fairbrother, 'John Sykes'. The story of Sykes's saving of Nelson seems to have become so popular that other sailors attempted to appropriate it for themselves: *NC*, 30 (1813), p. 120.

58. Fremantle to William Fremantle, 4/7/1797, CBS, D-FR/45/2; Nelson to Jervis, 7/7/1797, *D&L*, 2, p. 407; Fremantle, *Wynne Diaries*, 2, p. 183; report enclosed in ADM 1/396: no. 124. I dismiss the Spanish claim that six British boats attacked the *San Pablo* (Conte y Lacave, *Ataque de Cadiz*, 68). Nelson mentioned Miller and Fremantle in his dispatch, but exaggerated his own exploit in 'Sketch of My Life' by implying that his boat's crew captured the Spanish barge unaided. The other vessels taken were the *Pelayo*, under Don Juan Cabaleri, who was killed in the fight, and the *Glorioso*, under Don Pedro Ferriz, who was wounded.

59. Buckland, *Miller Papers*, pp. 10–11. A witness aboard the *Goliath* wrote frankly of 'the ridiculous bombardment' (NMM: 85/015).

60. Return of casualties enclosed in ADM 1/396: no. 124; medical journal of the *Theseus*, ADM 101/123/2.

61. Jervis to Nelson, 4, 5/7/1797, Add. MSS 34939.

62. Buckland, *Miller Papers*, p. 12.

63. Jervis to Walpole, 6/7/1797, Add. MSS 31160; Buckland, *Miller Papers*, p. 13; the *Theseus* log; Oliver Davis narrative, NMM: WAL/21B. Nelson was rowed forward to the bomb vessel during the action, returning to the *Theseus* at about three-thirty to four in the morning.

64. Jervis to Nepean, 10/7/1797, ADM 1/396; Nelson to Fanny, 11/7/1797, Monmouth MSS, E934; Buckland, *Miller Papers*, pp. 14–15; Jervis to Spencer, 9/7/1797, Add. MSS 75812.

65. Nelson to Mazzaredo, 8/7/1797, Monmouth MSS, E988; Nelson to Scrivener, 15/6/1797, Fiske, *Notices of Nelson*, p. 13.

66. Nelson to McArthur, 16/3/1797, Add. MSS 34905.

67. Jervis to Nelson, 4/4/1797, Add. MSS 34938.

68. Nelson to Jervis, 21/4/1797, NMM: JER/3–4.

69. Jervis to Nelson, 17/6/1797, Add. MSS 34938; Elliott to his wife, 27/6/1797, NLS, 11051: 73.

70. Jervis to Spencer, 10/4/1796, Add. MSS 75793; Hood to Nelson, 4/7/1797, Add. MSS 34906. Tom Wareham, *Star Captains*, pp. 172–4, discusses Bowen.

71. Nelson to Commandant General of the Canaries, 20/7/1797, Add. MSS 34906; instructions of Jervis, 14/7/1797, Add, MSS 34939: 42.

72. Nelson to Sykes, 14/7/1797, Historical Society of Pennsylvania, Philadelphia.

73. Nelson to Jervis, 6, 7/6/1797, NMM: JER/3–4, and *D&L*, 2, p. 392.

74. Jervis to Nelson, 15/7/1797, Add. MSS 34939.

XXVI More Daring Intrepidity was Never Shown (pp. 750–77)

1. Waller journal, enclosed in ADM 1/396: no. 151.

2. Miller's account in Kirstie Buckland, ed., *Miller Papers*, p. 16.

3. The issue is a theme in Russell F. Weigley, *Age of Battles*.

4. John Knox Laughton, ed., *Letters and Despatches of Horatio, Viscount* Nelson, p. 150. For the development of Nelson's system see M. A. J. Palmer, 'Lord Nelson', and Brian Lavery, *Nelson and the Nile*.

5. Francisco Lanuza Cano, *Ataque*, chaps 4–7, with appended plans and illustrations, gives a comprehensive picture of the defences of Santa Cruz.

   The principal British sources for the attack on Tenerife are the log books in ADM 51/1166, 1190, 1199, 1201–2, 1221, 4507, and NMM: ADM/L/C246 and ADM/L/S224; ADM 1/396: no. 151, which contains the public dispatches, Waller's journal, and other documents; Add. MSS 34906; Add. MSS 34938–9 (St Vincent letters); *D&L*, vols 2 and 7; Miller's account, written soon afterwards, and cited in note 2 above; John McDougall to his parents, 8/9/1797, in Pedro Ontorio Oquillas, Luis Cola Benitez and Daniel Garcia Pulido, eds, *Fuentes Documentales*, p. 348; Oliver Davis narrative, NMM: WAL/21B; and William McPherson's account in Sydney Fremantle, 'Nelson's First Writing', p. 210. Two solid secondary accounts from the British side are J. D. Spinney, 'Nelson at Santa Cruz', and Colin White, *1797*.

British and Spanish accounts of the Tenerife affair are often widely disparate. The Spanish documents are comprehensively gathered in Lanuza Cano, *Ataque*, and the exemplary Oquillas, Benitez and Pulido, *Fuentes Documentales*, but English-speaking readers may consult the translation of Bernardo Cologan's account in 'Nelson at Tenerife', *Daily Telegraph*, 18/8/1896; Michael Nash, *Santa Cruz*; and the garbled translations in Add. MSS 34906: 215, 218. Spanish historians have shown more interest in the engagement than their British counterparts: Don Jose de Monteverde, *Relación*; Leopoldo Pedreira, Mario Arozena, et al., *Recuerdo del Centenario*; and Agustin Guimera, *Nelson at Tenerife*.

6. Nelson to Troubridge, 20/7/1797, Add. MSS 34902; Christopher C. Lloyd, ed., *Keith Papers*, 2, p. 91; Buckland, *Miller Papers*, pp. 17–18.

7. I am following Lanuza Cano, *Ataque*, p. 59, for the strength of the Paso Alto battery.

8. 'Remarks on board H.M. Ship *Theseus*', ADM 1/396. This is Nelson's record between 14 July and 16 August. A variation, entitled 'Detail of the Proceedings', is in Add. MSS, 34906: 200.

9. Spanish account, Add. MSS 34906: 215; Davis account, NMM: WAL/21B; Buckland, *Miller Papers*, p. 19.

10. Davis account, NMM: WAL/21A; Buckland, *Miller Papers*, p. 26; Fremantle, *Wynne Diaries* (1935–40), 2, p. 184.

11. Antonio to Alvarez, 27/7/1797, Add. MSS 34906: 218

12. Saumarez to Richard Saumarez, 6/3/1797, Sir John Ross, *Saumarez*, 1, p. 177.

13. Fremantle, *Wynne Diaries*, 2, pp. 184–5; Buckland, *Miller Papers*, pp. 21–2. The German informant is also mentioned in Waller's journal, ADM 1/396.

14. Nelson to Hamond, 8/9/1797, NMM: MON/1.

15. Jervis to O'Hara, 13/2/1797, Add. MSS 31159; Elliot to Jervis, 29/6/1796, NMM: ELL/159.

16. G. L. Newnham Collingwood, ed., *Correspondence*, 1, p. 61; Thorp, 24/7/1797, in T. A. Thorp, 'George Thorp', pp. 182, 190.

17. Buckland, *Miller Papers*, p. 23.

18. Nelson to Jervis, 24/7/1797, Add. MSS 34906.

19. Lady Nelson's account, 1806, Monmouth MSS, E676a. This account is reprinted with minor transcription errors in *NLTHW*, p. 374.

20. Buckland, *Miller Papers*, p, 24; Add. MSS 31176: 117.

21. The log of the *Leander* (ADM 51/1201) says that the boats drew some fire from the forts as they passed, but whether this preceded the outbreak of fighting at the mole is unclear.

22. Journal, Add. MSS 34906: 185.

23. Hoste to his father, 15/8/1797, Nash, *Santa Cruz*, p. v.

24. Cologan's account in Oquillas, Benitez and Pulido, *Fuentes Documentales*, p. 87; Guimera, *Nelson at Tenerife*, p. 29.

25. Lady Nelson's account, 1806, Monmouth MSS, E676a; Buckland, *Miller Papers*, p. 31.

26. The story about Maurice Suckling's sword comes from the earliest sketch of Nelson (*Public Characters*, p. 7), which appears to draw upon family information.

27. Spanish account, Add. MSS 34906: 215.

28. Buckland, *Miller Papers*, p. 26.

29. Buckland, *Miller Papers*, p. 27. Both British and Spanish accounts of the Tenerife affair betray ready exaggeration. Juan Guinther's claim that 742 invading Britons survived to benefit from the ceasefire on 25 July (Oquillas, Benitez and Pulido, *Fuentes Documentales*, p. 114) would seem to be absurd. Less than that number participated in the attack, and more than three hundred either lost their lives or failed to land. On the other hand Captain Waller's claim that the British were opposed by seven hundred regulars, three hundred French and six or seven thousand militia was a gross overstatement fed by the inflated claims the Spaniards made to intimidate their opponents during negotiations.

30. Fanny's endorsement on McArthur to Fanny, 22/1/1807, Monmouth MSS, E678; Lady Nelson's account, 1806, Monmouth MSS, E676a.

31. Hoste to his father, 15/8/1797, Nash, *Santa Cruz*, p. v. A story that Nelson doffed his hat with his left hand to return the salute of his officers is contained in what appears to be a later (and possibly less reliable) insertion into Lady Nelson's account. I know of no credible source at all for the popular legend that Nelson was first taken to the *Seahorse*, but declined to go aboard for fear of alarming Mrs Fremantle.

32. Fremantle, *Wynne Diaries*, 2, p. 189; James Stanier Clarke and John McArthur, *Life and Services*, 3, p. 214. For Nelson's operation see the medical journal of the *Theseus*, ADM 101/123/2; D'Arcy Power, 'Some Bygone Operations in Surgery'; James Kemble, *Idols and Invalids*, pp. 134–42; H. T. A. Bosanquet, 'Lord Nelson'; L. P. Lequesne, 'Nelson's Wounds'; Jessie Dobson, 'Lord Nelson'; P. D. Gordon Pugh, *Nelson and His Surgeons*; Beatus Ruettimann, 'How Nelson Lost his Arm'; and James Watt, 'Naval Surgery in the Time of Nelson'. For contemporary surgical procedures I have relied upon William Northcote, *Marine Practice of Physic and Surgery*, 1, pp. 179–98, and William Turnbull, *Naval Surgeon*, pp. 303–5, 380–7. I am grateful to Surgeon Vice Admiral Sir James Watt, the foremost authority on historical naval surgery, for sending me his observations on this subject.

33. Clarence's account is in Add. MSS 34990: 54.

34. Nelson's wound continued to cause him unusual pain but scholars have disagreed about its origin. One of the ligatures proved remarkably tenacious and refused to come away, and before the end of 1797 physicians in London were blaming Eshelby for trapping the median nerve with the bound artery. Some scholars have followed, condemning the operation as a botched job, but this is unfair. As I have said, the inclusion of the nerve in a ligature seems to have been a commonly accepted practice at that time. Sir James Watt has also drawn my attention to the difficulties faced by Eshelby as he tried to secure bleeding arteries deep inside the wound in a poor light. He believes that Eshelby found an artery bleeding higher up the wound, near the median nerve. In applying forceps and ligaturing the artery he accidentally caught up the median nerve, causing post-operative pain that was later sustained by infection. This disappeared when the ligature eventually fell away. Kemble, *Idols and Invalids*, pp. 140–1, also gave infection a role in perpetuating Nelson's pain, believing that it developed when the obstinate ligature kept the wound open. However, Kemble dismissed the role of the median nerve too readily. He contended that fixing the median nerve to the ligature would not in itself have occasioned pain, a theory he partly based upon his view that Nelson's pain was not 'nervous in origin'. Had it been so, Kemble argued, Nelson would have felt 'phantom' pains in his amputated limb. In fact, contrary to what Kemble supposed, Nelson *did* report phantom pains in his amputated right hand (William to Nelson, 7/10/1797, Monmouth MSS, E653).

35. Terms, 25/7/1797, Add. MSS 34906: 181.

36. Buckland, *Miller Papers*, p. 30; Troubridge to Nelson, 25/7/1797, Add. MSS 34906; Jervis to Mazarredo, 18/8/1797, Add. MSS 31160.

37. Hoste to his father, 15/8/1797, Nash, *Santa Cruz*, p. v; Oquillas, Benitez and Pulido, *Fuentes Documentales*, p. 84; medical journal of the *Theseus*, ADM 101/123/2.

38. Details of individual casualties here and elsewhere are drawn from the medical journal of the *Theseus*, ADM 101/123/2, and the *Theseus* muster, ADM 36/12648.

39. Miller's return in Buckland, *Miller Papers*, p. 32, gives similar but slightly higher casualties than the official return enclosed in ADM 1/396: no. 151. For the Spanish and French losses see Lanuza Cano, *Ataque*, chap. 17 and p. 607.

40. Miller to Thompson, 26/7/1797, Add. MSS 46119; Fremantle, 'Nelson's First Writing', p ?07; Wentworth to Lee, Monmouth MSS, E248.

41. Nelson to Gutierrez, 26/7/1797, Oquillas, Benitez and Pulido, *Fuentes Documentales*, p. 32.

42. Nash, *Santa Cruz*, p. 17.

43. Nelson to St Vincent, 27/7/1797, ADM 1/396.

44. Hoste to his father, 15/8/1797, Nash, *Santa Cruz*, p. v; Harriet Hoste, ed., *Hoste*, 1, p. 86.

45. Nelson to St Vincent, 27/7/1797, ADM 1/396.

46. Nelson to Jervis, 16/8/1797, Add. MSS 34902.

XXVII Useless to my Country (pp. 778–88)

1. Logs of the *Seahorse*, ADM 51/1190, ADM 52/3416; Elliot to his wife, 27/6/1797, NLS, 11051: 73; De Burgh to Elliot, 21/5/1797, NMM: ELL/148.

2. Medical journal of the *Seahorse*, ADM 101/120/6; Elliot to his wife, 3/10/1797, NLS. 11051: 122; Anne Fremantle, ed., *The Wynne Diaries* (1935–40), 2, pp. 188–9; Jervis to Nelson, 23/10/1797, Add. MSS 34939.

3. Jervis to Nelson, 16/8/1797, Add. MSS 34939.

4. Jervis to Nepean, 16/8/1797, ADM 1/396; the *Seahorse* muster, ADM 36/13125; G. L. Newnham Collingwood, ed., *Correspondence*, 1, p. 61. Other officers of the *Seahorse* included Lieutenants Archibald Dickson and Edward Galway and the master, Michael Spratt. An interesting name on the muster was that of a twenty-seven-year-old Londoner John Spurling, master's mate. He would distinguish himself as a master of the *Imperieuse* under Lord Cochrane in 1806–9.

5. Jervis to Nisbet, 16/8/1797, ADM 1/2226; Add. MSS 31176: 228; Nelson to Hoste, September 1797, *D&L*, 2, p. 442; Harriet Hoste, ed., *Hoste*, 1, p. 86.

6. Nelson to Fanny, 5/8/1797, *NLTHW*, p. 332.

7. Grenville to Fremantle, 1/9/1797, and Betsy to William Fremantle, 2, 6/9/1797, CBS, D-FR/45/2; Ramsay to Nelson, 26/11/1802, NMM: CRK/10.

8. Weatherhead to Nelson, 26/10/1797, Add. MSS 34906; Nelson to Weatherhead, 31/10/1797, 27/1/1798, *D&L*, 2, p. 451, and Royal Naval Museum, Portsmouth.

9. The literature of this engagement is discussed in Pedro Ontorio Oquillas, Luis Cola Benitez and Daniel Garcia Pulido, eds, *Fuentes Documentales*, pt vi.

10. George III to Spencer, 2/9/1797, A. Aspinall, ed., *Later Correspondence*, 2, p. 619.

11. Add. MSS 29232: 314.

12. David White, 'Heralds and Their Clients'.

13. Nelson to his father, 1/1/1797, Monmouth MSS, E599; Nelson to Suckling, 30/8/1797, Monmouth MSS, E43.

14. Some insight into Jervis's ideas is given by his signal book, 31/1/1796, NMM: CRK/14.

15. Collingwood to Edward Collingwood, 23/1/1795, Add. MSS 52780.

16. Nelson to Fanny, 2/8/1796, Add. MSS 34988.

17. Nelson to his father, 1/1/1797, Monmouth MSS, E599.

18. Nelson to Charles Long, 7/8/1793, Add. MSS 34902.

19. *NLTHW*, p. 465.

20. Russell Grenfell, *Nelson the Sailor*, p. 213.

ABBREVIATIONS

Published sources are cited by short titles that key to the select bibliography. Abbreviations commonly used are as follows:

Add. MSS	Additional Manuscripts at the British Library
ADM	Admiralty papers, Public Record Office
BL	British Library, London
CBS	Centre for Buckinghamshire Studies, Aylesbury
CO	Colonial Office papers, PRO
D&L	Nicolas, ed., *Dispatches and Letters . . . of Nelson*
DNB	*Dictionary of National Biography*
FO	Foreign Office papers, PRO
HCA	High Court of Admiralty papers, PRO
MM	*Mariner's Mirror* (Journal of the Society of Nautical Research)
Monmouth MSS	Manuscripts at the Nelson Museum, Monmouth
NC	Clarke and McArthur, eds, *The Naval Chronicle*
ND	*Nelson Dispatch* (Journal of the Nelson Society)
NLS	National Library of Scotland, Edinburgh
NMM	National Maritime Museum, Greenwich
NLTHW	Naish, ed., *Nelson's Letters to his Wife*
PRO	Public Record Office, Kew
SRRC	Shropshire Records and Research Centre, Shrewsbury
TC	*Trafalgar Chronicle* (Yearbook of the 1805 Club)
WO	War Office papers, PRO

SELECT BIBLIOGRAPHY

A: Manuscripts

Centre for Buckinghamshire Studies, Aylesbury
Fremantle papers (D-FR/32/2/3; D-FR/41/6; D-FR/45/2)

Berwick-upon-Tweed Record Office
Parish registers of Berwick-upon-Tweed and Belford

National Library of Scotland, Edinburgh
Copies of Collingwood papers (NLS 1811)
Lynedoch papers (NLS 3596)
Minto papers (NLS 9819, 11049–51, 11072, 11083, 11111, 11139, 11193, 11209–14, 11221)

Norfolk Nelson Museum, Great Yarmouth
Ben Burgess Collection

National Maritime Museum, Greenwich
Admiralty Correspondence (ADM/C)
Admiralty Lieutenants' Logs (ADM/L) A51, A72, B5, B97, B136, B175A, C51, C246, D93, E159, H113, J121, L220, M292, P406, S222–4, T87A, T268, W180
Administration and Law papers (ADL)
Agamemnon interviews (BGY/W/3)
Autograph Collections (AGC)
Autograph Collections/Nelson (AGC/N)
Bridport papers (BRP)
Thomas Buttersworth paintings
George Cockburn papers (MRF/D)
Cuthbert Collingwood papers (COL)
William Cornwallis papers (COR)

Lewis Stephen Davis narrative (HIS/35)
Alexander Davison Collection
Gilbert Elliot papers (ELL)
Facsimiles (FAC)
Thomas Foley papers (FOL)
Girdlestone papers (GIR)
William Hamilton papers (HML)
Samuel Hood papers (MKH)
Viscount Hood papers (HOO)
William Hoste papers (MRF/88)
John Jervis papers (JER)
Marine Society papers (MSY)
Matcham papers (MAM)
Monserrat collection (MON)
George Mundy diary (85/015)
Nelson accounts (75/102)
Nelson letters to Clarence (AGC/27)
Nelson–Ward papers (NWD)
Phillipps–Croker collection (RCL, PHB and CRK)
Photographs (PGR)
Photostats (PST)
Charles Pole papers (WYN)
Sandwich papers (SAN)
Ship draught plans
Stewart collection (STW)
Sutcliffe-Smith collection (SUT)
Trafalgar House collection (TRA)
Transcripts (TRN)
Walter collection (WAL)
Xerox autograph collections [Spiro collection of Nelson letters] (XAGC)

Public Record Office, Kew

ADM [Admiralty] 1/164 (East Indies)
ADM 1/240–2 (Jamaica)
ADM 1/312–13, 315 (Leeward Islands)
ADM 1/391–6 (Mediterranean)
ADM 1/490 (North America)
ADM 1/579 (admirals' in-letters)
ADM 1/655, 665 (Downs)
ADM 1/723 (Nore)
ADM 1/952–3, 998 (Portsmouth)
ADM 1/1451–3, 1613, 1616, 1620, 1622–3, 1709–10, 1789, 1791, 1908,
    1911–12, 1998, 2053–4, 2123–34, 2222–6, 2303, 2307, 2389–90, 2481–2,
    2486, 2490, 2676 (captains' in-letters)

ADM 1/2739 (lieutenants' in-letters)

ADM 1/3820 (plantations)

ADM 1/3841–2 (consul's intelligence)

ADM 1/3682–3 (solicitors' opinions)

ADM 1/5306–8, 5310, 5315, 5324–6, 5330–41 (courts martial)

ADM 2/102, 111–17 (Admiralty orders and instructions)

ADM 2/1062 (legal correspondence)

ADM 2/1342 (secret out-letters)

ADM 6/89, 90, 93–4, 98, 107 (lieutenants' passing certificates)

ADM 7/301 (law officers' opinions)

ADM 9/1–2, 6 (returns of service)

ADM 12 (digests of correspondence)

ADM 33/509, 635, 676, 696 (pay books)

ADM 34/67, 116, 137, 463, 467, 749, 835–6 (pay books)

ADM 35/69, 242, 401, 492, 843, 1103, 1657, 1856 (pay books)

ADM 36/5402–3, 7523, 7567, 7583, 7669, 7688–90, 8117–18, 8677, 8720,
9203, 9390, 9510–11, 9882–3, 10047, 10081–2, 10381, 10525, 11358–62,
11539, 11775, 11799, 11823, 12648, 13125, 13135, 14801, 19525 (musters)

ADM 50/9, 11, 79, 100, 117, 125 (admirals' journals)

ADM 51/21, 78, 120, 125, 137, 167, 224, 238, 259, 442, 476, 513, 535,
540, 557, 589, 597, 637, 668, 757, 763, 777, 836, 973, 1015, 1085,
1103–5, 1107–8, 1111, 1113, 1116, 1119, 1121, 1123–5, 1128, 1130–1,
1133, 1137, 1140, 1143, 1150–2, 1155, 1163–6, 1167–9, 1172–4, 1179,
1180–1, 1186–7, 1189, 1190–1, 1194, 1197, 1199, 1201–2, 1204–5,
1209–10, 1212, 1223, 1243, 1267, 1369, 4110, 4247, 4470, 4475, 4492,
4507 (captains' logs)

ADM 52/1416, 1591, 1639, 1701, 1847, 1991, 2002, 2054, 2095, 2136,
2179, 2359, 2632, 2707, 2710, 2825, 2926, 2993, 3104, 3128, 3223,
3236, 3240, 3509 (masters' logs)

ADM 55/12 (Lutwidge journal)

ADM 95/30 (24), 37 (15), 38 (148), 39 (80, 116), 41 (110) (ship sailing qualities)

ADM 101/120/6 (medical journal of the *Seahorse*)

ADM 101/123/2 (medical journal of the *Theseus*)

ADM 106/1290, 1392, 1653 (Navy Board in-letters)

ADM 106/2624–35 (Navy Board minutes)

ADM 107/3, 6–13, 15–18, 21, 25, 41 (lieutenants' passing certificates)

ADM 140/1173 (map of English Harbour)

CO [Colonial Office] 7/1 (Antigua)

CO 28/60–1 (Barbados)

CO 31/43 (Barbados council and assembly)

CO 116/1 (newspaper of 21/3/1836)

CO 137/75–82 (Jamaica)

CO 152/63–71 (Leeward Islands)
CO 184 (Nevis)
CO 241/18 (St Kitts sessional papers)
FO [Foreign Office] 7/42–7 (Vienna)
FO 20/1–12 (Corsica)
FO 28/6–17 (Genoa)
FO 67/17–23 (Sardinia)
FO 70/6–10 (Naples)
FO 72/44–5 (Spain)
FO 79/8–15 (Tuscany)
FO 90/1 (America)
HCA [High Court of Admiralty] 1/25/138–412 (oyer and terminer indictments)
HCA 1/61 (oyer and terminer minutes)
HCA 32/550, 845 (prize courts)
HO [Home Office] 28/14–15 (Hood)
HO 50/456 (military dispatches)
IR 1/28 (Internal Revenue)
MPI 1/95 (Nelson's map of St John, Virgin Islands)
Pitcairn-Jones, C. G. 'Sea Officers List'
PROB (Probate) 11/936, 1031, 1044, 1111, 1136, 1140, 1183, 1518, 1559, 1893, 2026 (wills)
WO [War Office] 1/288 (Gibraltar)
WO 1/302 (Corsica)
WO 1/683 (America and the West Indies)
WO 1/686 (Admiralty)

British Library, London

Add. MSS 14272–80, 52780 (Collingwood papers)
Add. MSS 20080, 21506, 22130, 70948 (miscellaneous autographs)
Add. MSS 20107 (Hudson Lowe papers)
Add. MSS 21800 (Frederick Haldimand papers)
Add. MSS 22688 (Pasquale de Paoli papers)
Add. MSS 28333, 34902–2, 36604–13, 46356 (Knightley) (Nelson papers)
Add, MSS 29232 (Miscellaneous personal papers)
Add. MSS 29893 (George Manby recollections)
Add. MSS 31158–93 (St Vincent papers)
Add. MSS 35191–202 (Bridport papers)
Add. MSS 37845, 37852, 37877 (William Windham papers)
Add. MSS 38308 (Liverpool papers)
Add. MSS 39793 (William Hamilton papers)
Add. MSS 46119 (Thomas Boulden Thompson papers)
Add. MSS 46822–38 (Francis Drake papers)
Add. MSS 57320, 57325 (John Moore papers)
Add. MSS 56486, 57946 (forgeries)

Add. MSS 75777–814 (Althorp papers)
King's MSS 224 (Phipps journal)
Egerton MSS 1614–23 (Hamilton/Nelson papers)
Egerton MSS 2240–1 (Nelson papers)
Egerton MSS 2638–9 (William Hamilton papers)
A. M. Broadley Collection, 'Nelsoniana,' 8 vols (Printed Books C.136.e.1)
John to Ann Brock, 1793 (Printed Books C.45.h.5)

British Museum, London
Sketches and annotations of Philip James de Loutherbourg, 1797.

Goldsmiths' Company, London
Apprentice Books

Guildhall Library, Aldermanbury, London
Parish registers, St Luke's Old Street; St Leonard's, Shoreditch
London trade directories

Wellcome Library for the History and Understanding of Medicine, London
Western MSS 3667–81, 7362 (Nelson papers)

Westminster Archives Centre, London
Poor rates, F 582, F584

John Rylands Library, Manchester
Nelson facsimile (MAM PLP78.52.1)

Nelson Museum, Monmouth
Nelson Manuscripts (E series)
Nelson artefacts, illustrations and memorabilia
E. C. Bodger files

Norfolk Heritage Centre, Norwich
Census records for Burnham Thorpe and Brancaster, Norfolk

Norfolk Record Office, Norwich
Parish registers of Burnham Thorpe, North Walsham, North Elmham, Burton Norton
Land tax records, 1796–7
Faculty book (diocesan records), DN/FCB/1
Recognisances and index of licencees (MF/RO/610/3)
Hilborough papers
Rolfe papers
Bulwer papers (MF/RO/334/1 and 3)
Gawdy photocopies (FX 254)
'Nelsoniana' photocopies
Paston school papers (MC 20/27)

'A Particular Survey and Valuation of the Manors of Burnham Lexham and
Burnham Polstead Hall, and of Several Other Estates' (post 1803)

City Museums and Record Service, Portsmouth
Madden papers

Royal Naval Museum, Portsmouth
Hercules Ross papers
Lily L. McCarthy collection
Miscellaneous Nelson papers

Shropshire Records and Research Centre, Shrewsbury
Papers of William Hill, Baron Berwick, Attingham Collection, 112/16/31
(Brame Letter book) and 112/16/33 (Brame papers)

General Register Office, Southport
Register of Births, Marriages and Deaths

William L. Clements Library, University of Michigan, Ann Arbor
Nelson papers
Stephen Kemble papers
D'Auvergne: charts and views from Arctic expedition, 1773
George Germain papers
Earl of Shelburne papers, vol. 79.

Houghton Library, Harvard University, Cambridge, Massachusetts
Joseph Husband Collection of Nelson and Hamilton papers

Duke University, Durham, North Carolina
Benjamin Hallowell Carew papers

The Morgan Library, New York City
Miscellaneous Nelson papers

New York Historical Society, New York City
Miscellaneous Nelson papers.

Historical Society of Pennsylvania, Philadelphia
Nelson papers

Rosenbach Museum and Library, Philadelphia
John McArthur papers

John Hay Library, Brown University, Providence, Rhode Island
Napoleon collection

Huntington Library, San Marino, California
Nelson papers

Archives Nationales du Quebec
James Thompson papers

Registers of the Anglican Cathedral, Quebec

University of Victoria, Victoria, British Columbia
Brown collection

Centre Historique des Archives Nationales, Paris
AA/15, dossier 751, 754
Comité de Salut Public (AF/II/94, dossier 693; AF/II/182–5; AF/II/252, dossier 2140–1)

B: Published Sources

(Works are published in London unless otherwise stated)

ABRAHAMS, ALECK, and ARDAGH, JOHN, *The Life and Works of William Robinson* (1925)

ACCARDI, VITTORIO, ed., *The Hamilton Papers* (Napoli, 1999)

ACTON, HAROLD, *The Bourbons of Naples* (1956)

ALBION, ROBERT G., *Forests and Sea Power: The Timber Problem of the Royal Navy, 1652–1862* (Cambridge, Massachusetts, 1926)

ALLEN, JOSEPH, 'England's Wooden Walls', *United Service Magazine* (1839), pt iii, pp. 346–51

—*Life of Lord Viscount Nelson, K.B., Duke of Bronte* (1853)

'Anecdotes of the Late Lieutenant-General Villettes', *Gentleman's Magazine,* 79 (1809), I, pp. 297–301, and II, pp. 798–9

Annual Register

ARTHUR, CHARLES B., *The Remaking of the English Navy by Admiral St Vincent – Key to the Victory over Napoleon* (Lanham, Maryland, 1986)

ASPINALL, A., ed., *The Correspondence of George, Prince of Wales, 1770–1812* (1963–71, 8 vols)

—ed., *The Later Correspondence of George III* (Cambridge, 1966–70, 5 vols)

ASPINALL-OGLANDER, CECIL, ed., *Freshly Remembered: The Story of Thomas Graham, Lord Lynedoch* (1956)

BALLEINE, G. R., *The Tragedy of Philippe d'Auvergne* (1973)

BARING, Mrs HENRY, ed., *The Diary of the Rt Hon. William Windham* (1866)

BARKER, JULIET, *Wordsworth: A Life* (2000)

BARKER, MATTHEW H. ('The Old Sailor'), *The Life of Nelson* (1836)

BARRAS, T. C. 'Vice-Admiral Nelson's Lost Eye', *Transactions of the Ophthalomological Society of the United Kingdom* (1986), pp. 351–5

—'I Have a Right to be Blind Sometimes', *ND*, 2 (1987), pp. 163–8

BARROW, JOHN, *An Auto-Biographical Memoir of Sir John Barrow, Bart.* (1847)

Bath Chronicle and Weekly Gazette

Bath Journal

'The Battle of Cape St Vincent', *Journal of the Royal United Service Institution*, 59 (1914), pp. 321–41

BAUGH, DANIEL A., *British Naval Administration in the Age of Walpole* (Princeton, New Jersey, 1965)

BEATSON, ROBERT, *Naval and Military Memoirs of Great Britain* (1804, 6 vols)

BENNETT, GEOFFREY, *Nelson the Commander* (1972)

BERCKMAN, EVELYN, *Nelson's Dear Lord: A Portrait of the Earl of St Vincent* (1962)

BERESFORD, CHARLES, LORD, and WILSON, H. W., *Nelson and His Times* (1897)

'Biographical Memoir of the Right Honourable Lord Nelson of the Nile, K.B.', *NC*, 3 (1800), pp. 157–91

'Biographical Memoir of Philip d'Auvergne, Duke of Bouillon', *NC*, 13 (1805), pp. 169–91

'Biographical Memoir of Captain William Johnstone Hope, of the Royal Navy', *NC*, 18 (1807), pp. 269–75

'Biographical Memoir of the Honourable Captain Courtenay Boyle', *NC*, 30 (1813), pp. 1–41

'Biographical Memoir of the Late Charles Boyles, Esq., Vice-Admiral of the Blue', *NC*, 38 (1817), pp. 265–9

BLACK, JEREMY, 'Anglo-Spanish Naval Relations in the Eighteenth Century', *MM*, 77 (1991), pp. 235–58

BLAGDON, FRANCIS WILLIAM, *Orme's Graphic History of the Life, Exploits, and Death of Horatio Nelson* (1806)

BLOMEFIELD, FRANCIS, and PARKIN, CHARLES, *An Essay Towards A Topographical History of the County of Norfolk* (1805–10, 11 vols)

BONWICK, M. H. R., 'The Radicalism of Sir Francis Burdett (1770–1844) and Early Nineteenth-Century Radicalisms' (Ph.D., Cornell University, 1967)

BOSANQUET, H. T. A. 'Lord Nelson and the Loss of his Arm', *MM*, 38 (1952), pp. 184–94

BOURGUIGNON, HENRY J., *Sir William Scott, Lord Stowell* (Cambridge, 1987)

BOYCOTT-BROWN, MARTIN, *The Road to Rivoli* (2001)

BOYLE, JOHN, *Letters from Italy* (1774)

BOYLE, P., *The Fashionable Court Guide or Town Visiting Directions of the Year 1792* (1792)

BRADFORD, GERSHAM, 'Nelson in Boston Bay', *American Neptune*, 11 (1951), pp. 239–44

BREEN, KENNETH, 'George Bridges, Lord Rodney', in Le Fèvre, Peter, and Harding, Richard, eds, *Precursors of Nelson* (2000), pp. 225–46, 413

BRENTON, EDWARD PELHAM, *The Naval History of Great Britain* (1823–5; revised edn, 1837, 2 vols)

—*Life and Correspondence of John, Earl of St Vincent* (1838, 2 vols)

BRETT-JAMES, ANTHONY, *General Graham, Lord Lynedoch* (1959)

BRITTON, CHARLES J., 'Nelson and the River San Juan', *MM*, 28 (1942), pp. 213–21

—*New Chronicles of the Life of Lord Nelson* (Birmingham, 1947)

BROADLEY, A. M., and BARTELOT, R. G., *Nelson's Hardy* (1909)

BROOMFIELD, J. H., 'Lord Sandwich at the Admiralty Board: Politics and the British Navy, 1771–1778', *MM*, 51 (1965), pp. 7–17

BROWNE, GEORGE LATHOM, *Nelson: The Public and Private Life of Horatio, Viscount Nelson* (1890)

BRYMNER, DOUGLAS, ed., *Report on the Canadian Archives, 1889* (Ottawa, 1890)

BUCKLAND, KIRSTIE, ed., *The Miller Papers* (Shelton, Notts, 1999)

BULLOCKE, J. G., ed., *The Tomlinson Papers* (1935)

BURGESS, BEN, 'Who First Painted the Parsonage?' *ND*, 4 (1993), pp. 169–75

BURKE, B. and A. P., *Peerage and Baronetage* (1921 edn ed. A. W. Thorpe)

BYRN, JOHN D., *Crime and Punishment in the Royal Navy. Discipline on the Leeward Islands Station, 1784–1812* (Aldershot, 1989)

CALLO, JOSEPH F., *Nelson in the Caribbean: The Hero Emerges, 1784–1787* (Annapolis, Maryland, 2003)

CAMPBELL, R., *The London Tradesman* (1747)

CANNON, JOHN, *Parliamentary Reform, 1640–1832* (Cambridge, 1972)

—*Aristocratic Century: The Peerage of Eighteenth-Century England* (Cambridge, 1984)

CANO, FRANCISCO LANUZA, *Ataque y Derrota de Nelson en Santa Cruz de Tenerife* (Madrid, 1955)

CHANDLER, DAVID G., *The Campaigns of Napoleon* (1967)

CHAPMAN, JOHN H., ed., *The Register Book of Marriages Belonging to the Parish of St George, Hanover Square, in the County of Middlesex* (1888, 2 vols)

CHARNOCK, JOHN, *Biographia Navalis* (1794–8, 6 vols)

—*Biographical Memoirs of Lord Viscount Nelson* (1806)

CHEVALIER, E., *Histoire de la Marine Française sous la Première République* (Paris, 1886)

CHRISTIE, IAN R., *Stress and Stability in Late Eighteenth-Century Britain* (Oxford, 1984)

CLARK, J. C. D. *English Society, 1688–1832* (Cambridge, 1985)

CLARKE, JAMES STANIER, and MCARTHUR, JOHN, eds, *The Naval Chronicle* (1799–1819, 40 vols)

—*The Life of Admiral Lord Nelson, K.B., From His Lordship's Manuscripts* (1809, 2 vols)

—*The Life and Services of Horatio, Viscount Nelson, Duke of Bronte, Vice-Admiral of the White, K.B.* (1840, 3 vols)

CLIFF, K. S., 'Alexander Davison's Chambers – A Mystery Solved', *ND*, 7 (2000), pp. 41–3

CLOWES, WILLIAM LAIRD, et al., *The Royal Navy, A History* (1897–1903, 7 vols)

COCHRANE, THOMAS, *Statement Delivered by Lord Cochrane in . . . Defence of the Rights of the Navy in Matters of Prize* (1810)

—(and EARP, GEORGE BUTLER), *Autobiography of a Seaman* (1859–60, 2 vols)

COLEMAN, TERRY, *Nelson: The Man and the Legend* (2001; rev. edn, 2002)

Collections of the New York Historical Society for the Year 1884 (New York, 1885)

COLLEDGE, JAMES J., *Ships of the Royal Navy* (Newton Abbot, 1969–80, 2 vols)

COLLEY, LINDA, *Britons* (New Haven, 1992)

COLLINGE, J. M., *Navy Board Officials, 1660–1832* (1978)

COLLINGWOOD, G. L. NEWNHAM, ed., *A Selection from the Public and Private Correspondence of Vice-Admiral Lord Collingwood* (1827; reprinted 1837, 2 vols)

COLVIN, CHRISTINA, ed., *Maria Edgeworth: Letters from England, 1813–1844* (Oxford, 1971)

COMFORT, SIM, 'Some Notes on Naval Signals and Collecting Signal Books', *TC*, 3 (1993), pp. 16–26

Commissioned Sea Officers of the Royal Navy, 1660–1815 (1954, 3 vols)

CONNER, CLIFFORD D. *Colonel Despard, the Life and Times of an Anglo-Irish Rebel* (Conshohocken, Pennsylvania, 2000)

CONSTANTINE, DAVID, *Fields of Fire: A Life of Sir William Hamilton* (2001)

CORBETT, JULIAN STAFFORD, ed., *Fighting Instructions* (1905)

—and RICHMOND, H. W., eds, *Private Papers of George, Second Earl Spencer* (1913–24, 4 vols)

CORDINGLEY, DAVID, *Heroines and Harlots* (2001)

CORMACK, WILLIAM S., *Revolution and Political Conflict in the French Navy, 1789–1794* (Cambridge, 1995)

CORNWALLIS-WEST, G., *The Life and Letters of Admiral Cornwallis* (1927)

Correspondance de Napoléon I (Paris, 1858–69, 32 vols)

COWIE, LEONARD W., *Lord Nelson, 1758–1805, A Bibliography* (Westport, Connecticut, 1990)

CRESWELL, JOHN, *British Admirals of the Eighteenth Century: Tactics in Battle* (1972)

CRIMMIN, P. K., 'Admiralty Relations with the Treasury, 1783–1806: The Preparation of Naval Estimates and the Beginnings of Treasury Control', *MM*, 53 (1967), pp. 63–72

—'The Financial and Clerical Establishment of the Admiralty Office, 1783–1806', *MM*, 55 (1969), pp. 299–309

—'Letters and Documents Relating to the Service of Nelson's Ships, 1780–1805', *Historical Research*, 70 (1997), pp. 52–69

—'John Jervis, Earl of St Vincent, 1735–1823', in Le Fèvre, Peter, and Harding, Richard, eds, *Precursors of Nelson* (2000), pp. 324–50, 418–20

CROSS, FREDERICK J., *The Birthplace of Nelson* (1904)

CRUIKSHANK, ERNEST A., *The Life of Sir Henry Morgan* (Toronto, 1935)

CRYER, H. L., 'Horatio Nelson and the Murderous Cooper', *MM*, 60 (1974), pp. 3–7

CZISNIK, MARIANNE, 'Nelson and the Nile: The Creation of Admiral Nelson's Public Image', *MM*, 88 (2002), pp. 41–60

DANCER, THOMAS, *A Brief History of the Late Expedition Against Fort San Juan* (Kingston, Jamaica, 1781)

—*The Medical Assistant: or Jamaica Practice of Physic* (Kingston, Jamaica, 1801)

DANN, JOHN C., ed., *The Nagle Journal* (New York, 1988)

D'AUVERGNE, EDMUND B. F., *The Dear Emma* (1936)

DAVIES, DAVID, *A Brief History of Fighting Ships* (1996; reprinted 2002)

DAWSON, WARREN R., *Memoir of Thomas Joseph Pettigrew* (1931)

—ed., *The Nelson Collection at Lloyds* (1932)

DEAN, GRAHAM, and EVANS, KEITH, *Nelson's Heroes* (Norwich, 1994)

DEANE, ANTHONY, *Nelson's Favourite: HMS Agamemnon at War, 1781–1809* (1996)

DEUTSCH, OTTO ERICH, *Admiral Nelson and Joseph Haydn* (Slinfold, West Sussex, 2000)

DICKINSON, H. T., *The Politics of the People in Eighteenth-Century Britain* (1995)

Dictionary of Canadian Biography, vols 5 and 6 (Toronto, 1983, 1987)

Dictionary of National Biography (1885–90; reprinted 1908–9, 22 vols)

DOBSON, JESSIE, 'Lord Nelson and the Expenses of His Cure', *Annals of the Royal College of Surgeons*, 21 (1957), pp. 119–22

DRINKWATER (afterwards Drinkwater-Bethune), JOHN, *A Narrative of the Proceedings of the British Fleet . . . in the Late Action with the Spanish Fleet . . . off Cape St Vincent* (1797)

DRINKWATER-BETHUNE, JOHN, *A Narrative of the Battle of St Vincent with Anecdotes of Nelson, Before and After That Battle* (1840)

DUFFY, MICHAEL, 'Samuel Hood, First Viscount Hood, 1724–1816', in Le Fèvre, Peter, and Harding, Richard, eds, *Precursors of Nelson* (2000), pp. 249–77, 413–16

—'Contested Empires, 1756–1815', in Paul Langford, ed., *The Eighteenth-Century* (Oxford, 2002), pp. 213–42

—and MORRISS, ROGER, eds, *The Glorious First of June: A Naval Battle and Its Aftermath* (Exeter, 2001)

DULDIG, DANIEL, 'Nelson a Malingerer?', TC, 8 (1998), pp. 74–9

DULL, JONATHAN R., The French Navy and American Independence (Princeton, 1975)

DUPIN, C., A Tour Through the Naval and Military Establishments of Great Britain, 1816–1820 (1822)

EASTWOOD, DAVID, 'Patriotism Personified: Robert Southey's Life of Nelson Reconsidered', MM, 77 (1991), pp. 143–9

EDINGER, GEORGE A., and NEEP, E. J. C., Horatio Nelson (1930)

EKINS, CHARLES, Naval Battles of Great Britain (1824; reprinted 1828)

EMSLEY, CLIVE, British Society and the French Wars, 1793–1815 (1979)

FADEN, WILLIAM, Map of Norfolk (1797)

FAIRBROTHER, E. H., 'John Sykes, Nelson's Coxswain', Notes and Queries, 12th series, 5 (1919), pp. 257–8

FAWCETT, NIGEL, 'Did Nelson Ever Come Ashore in Simon's Town?', ND, 2 (1985), pp. 35–7

FENWICK, KENNETH, HMS Victory (1962)

FISKE, RON C., 'A New View of Woodton Hall, Norfolk', ND, 2 (1987), pp. 212–14

—Notices of Nelson Extracted from 'Norfolk and Norwich Notes and Queries' (Nelson Society, 1989)

—'Nelson, Levett Hanson and the Order of St Joachim', ND, 7 (2002), pp. 649–58

FITCHETT, W. H., Nelson and his Captains (1902)

FOLEY, THOMAS (Florence Horatia Suckling), The Nelson Centenary (Norwich, 1905)

FORD, GILLIAN, 'Nelson References in Holkham Game Books', ND, 1 (1982), pp. 51–2

—'Coke and Nelson: Grand Fete at Holkham. Why Did Nelson Refuse To Go?', ND, 1 (1983), pp. 83–5

FORDER, C. R., A History of the Paston Grammar School, North Walsham (North Walsham, 1934)

FORTESCUE, JOHN W., A History of the British Army (1899–1933, 13 vols)

FOSTER, JOSEPH, Alumni Oxonienses (1887–8; reprinted New York 1968, 4 vols)

FOTHERGILL, BRIAN, Sir William Hamilton, Envoy Extraordinary (1969)

FOURNIER, AUGUST, Life of Napoleon I (1911, 2 vols)

FRASER, EDWARD, The Sailors Whom Nelson Led (1913)

FRASER, FLORA, Beloved Emma (1986)

—'If You Seek His Monument', in Colin White, ed., The Nelson Companion (1995), pp. 128–51

FREMANTLE, ANNE, ed., The Wynne Diaries (1935–40, 3 vols)

—The Wynne Diaries (1952)

FREMANTLE, SYDNEY, 'Nelson's First Writing With The Left Hand', *MM*, 36 (1950), pp. 205–11

'A Friend of the Navy': *An Appeal . . . Against a Late Rejection of the Petition of the Captains of the Royal Navy for an Augmentation of Pay* (1809)

GAMLIN, HILDA, *Emma, Lady Hamilton* (Liverpool, 1891)

—*Nelson's Friendships* (1899, 2 vols)

GATER, GEORGE, and GODFREY, WALTER H., *Old St Pancras and Kentish Town* (1938)

Gazette Nationale, ou le Moniteur Universal (Paris)

Gentleman's Magazine

GERIN, WINIFRED, *Horatia Nelson* (1970)

GIGLIO, CONSTANCE, *Naples in 1799* (1903)

GODFREY, J. H., ed., 'Corsica, 1794', in Christopher Lloyd, ed., *The Naval Miscellany*, IV (1952), pp. 359–422

GONZALEZ ALLER, JOSE IGNACIO, and O'DONNELL, HUGO, 'The Spanish Navy in the Eighteenth Century', in Stephen Howarth, ed., *Battle of Cape St Vincent* (1998), pp. 67–83

GOODWIN, ALBERT, *The Friends of Liberty: The English Democratic Movement in the Age of the French Revolution* (1979)

GOODWIN, PETER, *Nelson's Ships: A History of the Vessels in Which He Served, 1771–1805* (2002)

GORE, JOHN, *Nelson's Hardy and His Wife* (1935)

GOULTY, GEORGE A., 'Lord Nelson and the Goulty Connection', *Genealogists' Magazine*, 21 (1985), pp. 399–402

GRAY, PETER J., 'Turning a Blind Eye', *TC*, 11 (2001), pp. 38–51

GREEN, GEOFFREY L., *The Royal Navy and Anglo-Jewry, 1740–1820* (1989)

GREGORY, DESMOND, *The Ungovernable Rock* (Cranbury, 1985)

GREIG, JAMES, ed., *The Farington Diary* (1922–8, 8 vols)

GRENFELL, RUSSELL, *Nelson the Sailor* (1949; reprinted as *Horatio Nelson*, 1968)

GUNNING, HENRY, *Reminiscences of the University, Town and County of Cambridge* (1854, 2 vols)

GURNEY, JOSEPH and WILLIAM, *The Trial of Edward Marcus Despard, Esquire, for High Treason* (1803)

GWYTHER, JOHN R., 'Nelson at Saint-Omer', *TC*, 9 (1999), pp. 112–16

HALEVY, ELIE, *England in 1815* (1937; reprinted 1961)

HAMILTON, RICHARD VESEY, ed., *Letters and Papers of Admiral of the Fleet Sir Thomas Byam Martin, G.C.B.* (1898–1903, 3 vols)

—and LAUGHTON, JOHN KNOX, eds, *Above and Under Hatches. The Recollections of James Anthony Gardner* (1906; reprinted 2000)

HANNAY, DAVID, ed., *Letters Written by Sir Samuel Hood* (1895)

HARBRON, JOHN D., *Trafalgar and the Spanish Navy* (1988)

HARDWICK, MOLLIE, *Emma, Lady Hamilton* (1969)

HARE, AUGUSTUS J. C., *The Life and Letters of Maria Edgeworth* (1894, 2 vols)

HARLAND, JOHN, *Seamanship in the Age of Sail* (1984)

HARLING, PHILIP, *The Waning of 'Old Corruption'* (Oxford, 1996)

HARRIES, RICHARD, CATTERMOLE, PAUL, and MACKINTOSH, PETER, *A History of Norwich School* (Norwich, 1991)

HARRISON, JAMES, *Life of the Rt Honourable Horatio, Lord Viscount Nelson* (1806, 2 vols)

HARVEY, A. D., *Britain in the Early Nineteenth Century* (1978)

HAYWARD, JOEL, *For God and Glory. Lord Nelson and His Way of War* (Annapolis, Maryland, 2003)

HIBBERT, CHRISTOPHER, *Nelson: A Personal History* (1994)

HILL, J. RICHARD, *Prizes of War: The Naval Prize System in the Napoleonic Wars, 1793–1815* (Stroud, Glos, 1998)

HILLS, ANNE-MARIE EWART, 'His Eye in Corsica', *ND*, 6 (1998–9), pp. 294–9

—'Nelson: War Pensioner', *ND*, 6 (1998–9), pp. 427–31

—'Nelson's Illnesses, 1780–1782', *TC*, 12 (2002), pp. 128–39

HISTORICAL MANUSCRIPTS COMMISSION: *Report on the Manuscripts of Mrs Stopford-Sackville* (1904–10, 2 vols)

—*Report on the Manuscripts in Various Collections* (1909)

—*The Manuscripts of J. B. Fortescue at Dropmore* (1892–1915, 9 vols)

HODGKIN, LOUIS, *A Brief Guide to Nelson and Bath* (Corsham, 1991)

HOLMES, RICHARD, *Coleridge. Darker Reflections* (1998)

HOOD, DOROTHY, *The Admirals Hood* (1941)

HOOPER, JAMES, *Nelson's Homeland* (1905)

HOSTE, HARRIET, ed., *Memoirs and Letters of Captain Sir William Hoste* (1833, 2 vols)

HOWARTH, STEPHEN, ed., *Battle of Cape St Vincent* (Shelton, Nottinghamshire, 1998)

—and DAVID, *Nelson: The Immortal Memory* (1988)

HUGHES, EDWARD, ed., *The Private Correspondence of Admiral Lord Collingwood* (1957)

HUISH, ROBERT: *The History of the Life and Reign of William the Fourth* (1837)

Illustrated London News

INGLIS, JOHN A., *The Nisbets of Carfin* (1916)

INNES, MARY C., *A Memoir of William Wolseley, Admiral of the Red Squadron* (1895)

JACKSON, PETER, ed., *John Tallis's London Street Views, 1838–1840* (Richmond, 2002)

JAMES, WILLIAM, *The Naval History of Great Britain* (1822–4; reprinted 1837, 6 vols)

JEAFFRESON, JOHN CORDY, *Lady Hamilton and Lord Nelson* (1888, 2 vols)
—*The Queen of Naples and Lord Nelson* (1889, 2 vols)
JEFFERYS, THOMAS, *The West Indian Atlas, or a Compendious Description of the West-Indies* (1775)
JENKINS, E. H., *A History of the French Navy* (1973)
JENNINGS, LOUIS J., ed., *Correspondence and Diaries of John Wilson Croker* (1884, 3 vols)
JOLLIVET, MAURICE, *La 'Revolution Française' en Corse* (Paris, 1892)
—*Les Anglais dans La Mediterranée (1794–1797)* (Paris, 1896)
Journal of a Voyage Undertaken by Order of His Present Majesty, for Making Discoveries Towards the North Pole, published in *An Historical Account of all the Voyages Round the World Performed by English Navigators*, 4 (1773)
JUPP, PETER, *Lord Grenville, 1759–1834* (Oxford, 1985)
JURIEN DE LA GRAVIÈRE, JEAN-PIERRE BAPTISTE EDMOND, *Sketches of the Last Naval War* (1848)
'J.W.B.', 'Nelson's Sister Anne', *Notes and Queries*, 10th series, 1 (1904), p. 170
KEATE, EDITH MURRAY, *Nelson's Wife. The First Biography of Frances Herbert, Viscountess Nelson* (1939)
KEMBLE, JAMES, *Idols and Invalids* (1933)
KEMP, PETER, ed., *Oxford Companion to Ships and the Sea* (1976)
KENNEDY, LUDOVIC, *Nelson's Band of Brothers* (1951; revised as *Nelson and His Captains*, 1975)
KENNEDY, PAUL M., *The Rise and Fall of British Naval Mastery* (1976)
Kent's Directory
Kentish Gazette (Canterbury)
KEYNES, MILO, 'Horatio Nelson Never Was Blind: His Woundings and His Frequent Ill-Health', *Journal of Medical Biography*, 6 (1998), pp. 114–19
KIRBY, BRIAN S., 'Nelson and American Merchantmen in the West Indies, 1784–1787', *MM*, 75 (1989), pp. 137–47
KNIGHT, CORNELIA, *Autobiography of Miss Cornelia Knight* (1861, 2 vols)
KNIGHT, R. J. B., 'Sandwich, Middleton, and Dockyard Appointments', *MM*, 57 (1971), pp. 175–92
LACAVE, AUGUSTO CONTE Y, *El Ataque de Cadiz* (Madrid, 1976)
LAMBERT, ANDREW, *The Foundations of Naval History. John Knox Laughton, the Royal Navy and the Historical Profession* (1998)
—ed., *Letters and Papers of Professor Sir John Knox Laughton, 1830–1915* (2002)
LAUGHTON, JOHN KNOX, ed., *Letters and Despatches of Horatio, Viscount Nelson, K.B.* (1886)
—*Nelson* (1895)
—*The Nelson Memorial: Nelson and His Companions-at-Arms* (1896)

LAVERY, BRIAN, ed., *Shipboard Life and Organisation, 1731–1815* (1998)
—*Nelson's Navy* (1989)
—*Nelson and the Nile* (1998)
LE FÈVRE, PETER, and HARDING, RICHARD, eds, *Precursors of Nelson* (2000)
LE MOINE, JAMES M., *Album Canadien, Histoire, Archaeologie-Ornithologie* (Quebec, 1870)
—*The Chronicles of the St Lawrence* (Montreal, 1878)
—*Picturesque Quebec* (Montreal, 1882)
—*Historical Notes on Quebec and its Environs* (Quebec, 1890)
LEQUESNE, L. P., 'Nelson's Wounds', *Middlesex Hospital Journal*, 55 (1955), pp. 182–7
LE ROUGE, GEORGE LOUIS, *Pilote American Septentrional* (Paris, 1778)
LESLIE-MELVILLE, R., *The Life and Work of Sir John Fielding* (1935)
LEWIS, MICHAEL, *England's Sea-Officers* (1939)
—*A Social History of the Navy, 1793–1815* (London, 1960)
LEWIS, SAMUEL, *A Topographical Dictionary of England* (1833, 4 vols)
LEWIS, WILMARTH S., et al., eds, *Horace Walpole's Correspondence* (New Haven, Connecticut, 1937–83, 48 vols)
LINDSAY-MACDOUGALL, K. F., 'Nelson Manuscripts at the National Maritime Museum', *MM*, 41 (1955), pp. 227–32
LIVEZEY, WILLIAM EDMUND, *Mahan on Sea Power* (Norman, Oklahoma, 1947)
LLOYD, C. C., ed., *The Keith Papers* (1927–55, 3 vols)
—*A Memoir of James Trevenen* (1959)
—*St Vincent and Camperdown* (1963)
—and COULTER, J. L. S., *Medicine and the Navy, 1714–1815* (1961)
Lloyds List
LOADS, W., 'Reminiscences of a Pastonian of 1864', *Pastonian* 52 (1925), p. 18
London Magazine
LUCAS, E. V., ed., *The Letters of Charles Lamb* (1935, 3 vols)
LUFFMAN, JOHN, *Antigua in the West Indies, America* (1793)
LYON, D., *The Sailing Navy List* (1993)
MCCARTHY, LILY LAMBERT, and LEA, JOHN, *Remembering Nelson* (Portsmouth, 1995)
MACE, RODNEY, *Trafalgar Square: Emblem of an Empire* (1976)
MACKAY, RUDDOCK F., 'Lord St Vincent's Early Years (1735–1755)', *MM*, 76 (1990), pp. 51–63
MAHAN, A. T., *The Influence of Sea Power Upon the French Revolution and Empire, 1793–1812* (1892, 2 vols)
—*The Life of Nelson* (1898; revised edn 1899)

MANWARING, G. E., and DOBREE, BONAMY, *The Floating Republic* (1935; reprinted 1966)

MARCUS, GEOFFREY, J., *The Age of Nelson* (1971)

—*Heart of Oak: A Survey of British Sea Power in the Georgian Era* (1975)

Mariner's Mirror (Journal of the Society for Nautical Research)

MARKHAM, ALBERT H., ed., *Northward Ho!* (1879)

MARRIOTT, LEO, *What's Left of Nelson* (Littlehampton, 1995)

MARRYAT, FLORENCE, *Life and Letters of Captain Marryat* (1872, 2 vols)

MARSHALL, JOHN, *Royal Navy Biography* (1823–35, 8 vols)

MASEFIELD, JOHN, *Sea Life in Nelson's Time* (1905)

MATCHAM, MARY EYRE, *The Nelsons of Burnham Thorpe* (1911)

MAURICE, J. F., ed., *The Diary of Sir John Moore* (1904, 2 vols)

Memoirs of Lady Hamilton (1815; reprinted with corrections 1891)

METCALF, GEORGE, *Royal Government and Political Conflict in Jamaica, 1729–1783* (1965)

MILES, HENRY H., 'Nelson at Quebec. An Episode in the Life of the Great British Admiral', *Rose-Belford's Canadian Monthly and National Review*, 2 (1879), pp. 257–75

MINGAY, G. E., *The Gentry. The Rise and Fall of a Ruling Class* (1976)

MINTO, COUNTESS OF, ed., *Life and Letters of Sir Gilbert Elliot, First Earl of Minto* (1874, 3 vols)

MONTEVERDE, DON JOSE DE, *Relación Circunstanciada de la Defensa que hizo la Plaza de Santa Cruz de Tenerife* (Madrid, 1798)

MOORE, JAMES CARRICK, *The Life of Sir John Moore* (1834, 2 vols)

MOORHOUSE, ESTHER HALLAM, *Nelson in England* (1913)

MORI, JENNIFER, *William Pitt and the French Revolution, 1785–1795* (1997)

Morning Chronicle

MORRISON, ALFRED, ed., *The Hamilton and Nelson Papers* (1893–4, 2 vols)

MORRISS, ROGER, *The Royal Dockyards During the Revolutionary and Napoleonic Wars* (Leicester, 1983)

—*Cockburn and the British Navy in Transition* (Exeter, 1997)

MOSELEY, BENJAMIN, *A Treatise on Tropical Diseases; Military Operations; and On the Climate of the West Indies* (1803)

MOUTRAY, JOHN ARMSTRONG, 'Notes on the Name of Moutray', *Genealogist*, 7 (1883), pp. 24–7

NAISH, GEORGE P. B., ed., *Nelson's Letters to his Wife and Other Documents, 1785–1831* (1958)

NAMIER, LEWIS, and BROOKE, JOHN, eds, *The History of Parliament: The House of Commons, 1754–1790* (1964)

NASH, MICHAEL, *Santa Cruz, 1797* (North Walsham, 1984)

Nautical Magazine

NEALE, R. S., *Bath, 1680–1850, A Social History* (1981)

The Nelson Dispatch (vols 1–8, 1982 et seq.)

NELSON, THOMAS, *Genealogical History of the Nelson Family* (King's Lynn, 1908)

'Nelson at Bastia, by an old *Agamemnon*', *United Service Magazine*, 1841, pt I, pp. 212–18

'Nelson at Tenerife', *Daily Telegraph*, 18 August 1896

Nelson, the Alexander Davison Collection (2002)

'Nelson's Appointment to the Command of the Albemarle, 1781', *MM*, 62 (1976), pp. 133–4

New Lloyds List

NICOLAS, NICHOLAS HARRIS, ed., *The Dispatches and Letters of Vice-Admiral Lord Viscount Nelson* (1844–6, 7 vols)

Norfolk Chronicle (Norwich)

NORIE, J. W., *The Naval Gazetteer, Biographer and Chronologist* (1827)

NORTHCOTE, WILLIAM, *The Marine Practice of Physic and Surgery* (1770, 2 vols)

Notes and Queries

Nouvelle Biographie Générale (Paris, 1852–66, 46 vols)

O'BYRNE, WILLIAM, *A Naval Biographical Dictionary* (1849, 2 vols)

O'SHAUGHNESSY, ANDREW JACKSON, *An Empire Divided. The American Revolution and The British Caribbean* (Philadelphia, 2000)

OLIVER, VERE LANGFORD, *The History of the Island of Antigua* (1894–9, 3 vols)

OLSON, ALISON GILBERT, *The Radical Duke. The Career and Correspondence of Charles Lennox, Third Duke of Richmond* (1961)

OMAN, CAROLA, *Nelson* (1947)

—*Sir John Moore* (1953)

—*An Oxford Childhood* (1976)

OQUILLAS, PEDRO ONTORIO, BENITEZ, LUIS COLA, and PULIDO, DANIEL GARCIA, eds, *Fuentes Documentales del 25 de Julio de 1797* (Santa Cruz, 1997)

PADFIELD, PETER, *Broke of the Shannon* (1968)

—*Guns at Sea* (1973)

PALMER, M. A. J., 'Lord Nelson: Master of Command', *Naval War College Reviews*, 41 (1988), pp. 105–16

—'Sir John's Victory: The Battle of Cape St Vincent Reconsidered', *MM*, 77 (1991), pp. 31–46

PARES, RICHARD, *A West India Fortune* (1950)

—*Yankees and Creoles* (1956)

PARKINSON, CYRIL NORTHCOTE, *Edward Pellew, Viscount Exmouth, Admiral of the Red* (1934)

PARRY, ANN, *The Admirals Fremantle* (1971)

PARSONS, GEORGE SAMUEL, *Nelsonian Reminiscences: Leaves from Memory's Log* (1843; reprinted 1998)

PEDREIRA, LEOPOLDO, and AROZENA, MARIO, et al., *Recuerdo del Centenario* (Santa Cruz, 1897)

PERKIN, HAROLD, *The Origins of Modern British Society* (1969)

PETTIGREW, THOMAS JOSEPH, *Memoirs of the Life of Vice-Admiral Lord Viscount Nelson* (1849, 2 vols)

PHIPPS, CONSTANTINE JOHN, *A Voyage Towards the North Pole, Undertaken by His Majesty's Command, 1773* (Dublin, 1775)

POCOCK, TOM, *Nelson and His World* (1968)

—*Remember Nelson. The Life of Captain Sir William Hoste* (1977)

—*The Young Nelson in the Americas* (1980)

—'Captain Nelson and Mrs Moutray', *ND*, 1 (1982), pp. 54–7

—'"My Dear, Sweet Friend." Mrs Moutray and Captain Nelson', *Country Life*, 22 September 1983

—*Sailor King. The Life of King William IV* (1991)

—*Horatio Nelson* (1987; revised edn 1995)

—*Nelson's Women* (1999)

Political Magazine, and Parliamentary, Naval, Military and Literary Journal

Poll for the Knights of the Shire for the County of Norfolk; Taken March 23, 1768 (Norwich, 1768)

POND, FRANK and JEAN, 'The Rolfe Tombs', *ND*, 4 (1992), pp. 103–5

POOL, BERNARD, *Navy Board Contracts, 1660–1832* (1966)

PORTER, ROY, *English Society in the Eighteenth Century* (1982; revised edn 1991)

POTT, JOHN FREDERICK, *Observations on Matters of Prize and the Practice of the Admiralty Prize Courts* (1810)

—*A Letter to Samuel Whitbread, M.P., in Defence of the Navy* (1810)

POWER, D'ARCY, 'Some Bygone Operations in Surgery: Amputation, the Operation on Nelson in 1797', *British Journal of Surgery*, 19 (1931), pp. 171–5, 351–5

The Present State of the West Indies (1778)

PRYCE-LEWIS, O., 'Horatio Nelson and Simon's Bay', *MM*, 72 (1986), pp. 355–9

Public Advertiser

Public Characters, or Contemporary Biography (1805)

Public Ledger

PUGH, P. D. GORDON, *Nelson and His Surgeons* (1968)

PULESTON, WILLIAM DILWORTH, *Mahan* (1939)

Quebec Gazette

RAMSAY, MALCOLM, 'Nelson, Carse and Eighteenth-Century Justice', *MM*, 65 (1979), p. 177

RANFT, B. MCL., ed., 'Prince William and Lieutenant Schomberg', in C. C. Lloyd, ed., *The Naval Miscellany*, IV (1952), pp. 267–93

RAVINA, AGUSTIN GUIMERA, *Nelson at Tenerife* (Shelton, Nottinghamshire, 1999)

RAWSON, GEOFFREY, ed., *Nelson's Letters from the Leeward Islands* (1953)
—*Letters from Lord Nelson* (1960)

REYNOLDS, C. G., *Command of the Sea: The History and Strategy of Maritime Empires* (New York, 1974)

RICHARDSON, PATRICIA, 'Captain William Locker, Royal Navy', *ND*, 3 (1988), pp. 52–8

RICHMOND, H. W., *Statesmen and Sea Power* (Oxford, 1947)

ROBERTSON, EILEEN ARNOT, *The Spanish Town Papers* (London, 1959)

ROBINSON, C. N., 'Nelson at Nicaragua', *MM*, 10 (1924), pp. 78–89

RODGER, N. A. M., *The Admiralty* (Lavenham, 1979)
—*The Wooden World. An Anatomy of the Georgian Navy* (1986; reprinted 1988)
—'Lieutenants' Sea-Time and Age', *MM*, 75 (1989), pp. 269–72
—*The Insatiable Earl. A Life of John, Fourth Earl of Sandwich, 1718–1792* (1993)

ROOKE, BARBARA E., ed., *The Friend* by Samuel Taylor Coleridge (1969, 2 vols)

ROSCOE, E. S., *Lord Stowell: His Life and the Development of English Prize Law* (1916)

ROSE, JOHN HOLLAND, *Life of Napoleon I* (1901–2, 2 vols)
—*Lord Hood and the Defence of Toulon* (Cambridge, 1922)

ROSEBERY, LORD, ed., *The Windham Papers* (1913, 2 vols)

ROSS, JOHN, *Memoirs and Correspondence of Admiral Lord de Saumarez* (1838, 2 vols)

The Royal Kalendar, or Complete and Correct Annual Register for England, Scotland, Ireland and America for the Year 1787 (1787) (Nelson's copy at Monmouth)

RUETTIMANN, BEATUS, 'How Nelson Lost His Arm: The History and Age Old Problems of Amputation Surgery', *ND*, 2 (1985), pp. 63–8

RULE, JOHN, *Albion's People. English Society, 1714–1815* (1992)

RUSPINI, BARTHOLOMEW, *A Treatise on Teeth* (1797)

RUSSELL, JACK, *Nelson and the Hamiltons* (1969; revised edn New York, 1969)

SAINTY, J. C., *Admiralty Officials, 1660–1870* (1974)

SAUNDERS, H. W., *A History of Norwich Grammar School* (Norwich, 1932)

SAUNDERS, JIM, 'A Tribute of Record', *ND*, 3 (1989), pp. 111–13
—'Alexander Davison and Horatio Nelson', *ND*, 8 (2003), pp. 81–105

SAVOURS, ANN, 'The Younger Cleverley and the Arctic, 1773–1774', *MM*, 69 (1983), pp. 301–4

—'"A Very Interesting Point in Geography": The 1773 Phipps Expedition Towards the North Pole', *Arctic*, 37 (1984), pp. 402–28

SCHAMA, SIMON, *Citizens: A Chronicle of the French Revolution* (New York, 1990)

Service Afloat, or the Naval Career of Sir William Hoste (1887)

SHANNON, DAVID, 'Nelson at Calvi: Hard Work and Heroism', *ND*, 2 (1987), pp. 230–3

—'Two Missing Nelson Letters Reconstructed', *ND*, 7 (2002), pp. 595–8

SHARMAN, VICTOR, 'Nelson's Sea-Daddy', *ND*, 8 (2003), pp. 55–64, 118–22, 194–200

SICHEL, WALTER, *Emma, Lady Hamilton* (1905; revised edn 1907)

SITWELL, SACHEVERELL, *Conversation Pieces* (1936)

SKAGGS, DAVID C., and ALTHOFF, GERALD T., *A Signal Victory: The Lake Erie Campaign, 1812–1813* (Annapolis, Maryland, 1997)

'Sketch of the Life of Admiral Lord Nelson of the Nile', *Lady's Magazine*, 29 (1798), pp. 483–5

SLOPE, NICK, 'The Trials of Nelson: Nelson's Camel', *ND*, 7 (2001), pp. 436–45

—'The Trials of Nelson: Nelson and the *Emerald*', *ND*, 7 (2002), pp. 612–17

SMYTH, W. H., *Life and Services of Captain Philip Beaver* (1829)

SOUTHEY, ROBERT, *Life of Nelson* (1813; reprinted 1903)

SOUTHWICK, LESLIE, 'Tokens of Victory', *TC*, 7 (1997), pp. 32–46

SPINNEY, J. D., 'Nelson at Santa Cruz', *MM*, 45 (1959), pp. 207–23

—*Rodney* (1969)

—'Nelson at Port Agro', *MM*, 65 (1979), pp. 90–1

STAMMERS, MICHAEL, 'The Hand-Maiden and Victim of Agriculture, the Port of Wells-Next-the-Sea, Norfolk, in the Eighteenth and Nineteenth Centuries', *MM*, 86 (2000), pp. 60–5

Statutes at Large (Cambridge and London, 1762–1865, 106 vols)

Steel's Navy List

STERNE, LAURENCE, *The Life and Opinions of Tristram Shandy, Gentleman*, ed. Ian Cameron Ross (1983)

STEVENSON, JOHN, *Popular Disturbances in England, 1700–1870* (1979)

STIRLING, A. M. W., ed., *Coke of Norfolk and His Friends* (1908, 2 vols)

—*Pages and Portraits from the Past. Being the Private Papers of Sir William Hotham, G.C.B., Admiral of the Red* (1909, 2 vols)

—*The Hothams* (1918, 2 vols)

STOREY, MARK, *Robert Southey: A Life* (Oxford, 1997)

STURGIS-JACKSON, T., ed., *Logs of Great Sea Fights* (1899–1900, 2 vols)

SUGDEN, JOHN, 'Lord Cochrane, Naval Commander, Radical and Inventor, 1775–1860' (Ph.D., Sheffield University, 1981)

—'Lord Nelson and the Film Industry', *ND*, 2 (1986–7), pp. 83–8, 179

—'Nelson in the St Lawrence', *ND*, 4 (1991), pp. 7–8

—'Captain George Andrews, 1767–1810, a Protégé of Nelson', *MM*, 81 (1995), pp. 85–8

—'Looking For Bess', *ND*, 5 (1995–6), pp. 219–22, 260–4, 387–9

— and EVANS, RAYMOND and ANN, 'More Light on George and Elizabeth Andrews', *ND*, 5 (1996), pp. 288–90

—'Tragic or Tainted? The Mystery of Ann Nelson', *ND*, 8 (2003), pp. 47–54

—'New Light on Ann Nelson', *ND*, 8 (2003), pp. 155–7

—'Forgotten *Agamemnons*: Nelson's Marine Society Boys' (forthcoming in *ND*, 8) (2004).

SULLIVAN, J. A., 'Nelson and Influence', *MM*, 62 (1976), pp. 385–6

SYRETT, DAVID, *The Royal Navy in American Waters, 1775–1783* (1989)

—'Nelson's Uncle: Captain Maurice Suckling, R.N.', *MM*, 88 (2002), pp. 33–40

—and DINARDO, R. L., *The Commissioned Sea Officers of the Royal Navy, 1660–1815* (Aldershot, 1994)

TALBOTT, JOHN E., *The Pen and Ink Sailor* (1998)

TAYLOR, A. H., 'The Battle of Cape St Vincent', *MM*, 40 (1954), pp. 228–30

TAYLOR, JAMES STEPHEN, *Jonas Hanway, Founder of the Marine Society* (1985)

The Times

THOMAS, E. G., 'The Old Poor Law and Maritime Apprenticeship', *MM*, 63 (1977), pp. 153–61

THOMPSON, E. P., *The Making of the English Working Class* (1963; revised edn Harmondsworth, 1968)

THORNTON, A. P., *The Habit of Authority: Paternalism in British History* (1966)

THORP, T. A., 'George Thorp, 1790–1797', *Blackwood's Magazine*, 254 (1943), pp. 182–90

THRASHER, PETER ADAM, *Pasquale Paoli, an Enlightened Hero, 1725–1807* (1907)

TILLEY, JOHN A., *The British Navy and the American Revolution* (Columbia, South Carolina, 1987)

TRACY, NICHOLAS, 'The Falkland Islands Crisis of 1770: Use of Naval Force', *English Historical Review*, 90 (1975), pp. 40–75

—*Nelson's Battles: The Art of Victory in the Age of Sail* (1996)

Trafalgar Chronicle (pts 1–14, 1991 et seq.)

The Trial of Captain John Kimber for the Murder of an African Girl (1792)

TROUDE, O., and LEVOT, P., *Batailles Navales de la France* (Paris, 1867, 4 vols)

TUCKER, JEDEDIAH S., *Memoirs of Admiral, the Right Honourable the Earl of St Vincent* (1844, 2 vols)

TUNSTALL, BRIAN, and TRACY, NICHOLAS, *Naval Warfare in the Age of Sail* (1990)

TURNBULL, WILLIAM, *The Naval Surgeon* (1806)

United Service Journal

VALE, BRIAN, *Independence or Death!* (1996)

—'Lord Cochrance in Chile: Heroism, Plots and Paranoia', in Nicholas Tracy, ed., *The Age of Sail* (2002), pp. 59–68

VENN, J. A., *Alumni Cantabrigienses* (Cambridge, 1922–54, 6 vols)

VIGO, PIETRO, *Nelson a Livorno* (Siena, Italy, 1903)

VINCENT, EDGAR, *Nelson, Love and Fame* (New Haven, Connecticut, 2003)

WALKER, RICHARD, *The Nelson Portraits* (Portsmouth, 1998)

WALTHEW, KENNETH, *From Rock and Tempest: The Life of Captain George William Manby* (1971)

WAR OFFICE, *A List of the Officers of the Army and Marines*

WAREHAM, TOM, *The Star Captains* (2001)

WARNER, OLIVER, *Lord Nelson: A Guide to Reading* (1955)

—*A Portrait of Lord Nelson* (1958; revised 1959)

—*Nelson's Battles* (1965)

—'Admiral Page's Comments on *The Naval Chronicle*', MM, 53 (1967), pp. 376–9

—*The Life and Letters of Vice-Admiral Lord Collingwood* (1968)

—*Nelson* (1975)

—'Collingwood and Nelson', ND, 7 (2001), pp. 318–26

WATKINS, JOHN, *The Life and Times of William the Fourth* (1831)

WATSON, J. STEVEN, *The Age of George III, 1760–1815* (Oxford, 1960)

WATT, JAMES, 'Naval Surgery in the Time of Nelson', in Nicholas Tracy, ed., *The Age of Sail* (2002), pp. 25–33

WATTS, ARTHUR P., ed., *Nevis and St Christopher's, 1782–1784* (Paris, 1925)

WEBB, PAUL, 'The Naval Aspects of the Nootka Sound Crisis', MM, 61 (1975), pp. 133–54

WEIGLEY, RUSSELL F., *The Age of Battles* (1991)

WHITE, COLIN, ed., *The Nelson Companion* (Portsmouth, 1995)

—*1797: Nelson's Year of Destiny* (Stroud, 1997)

—'The Midshipman and the Commodore', ND, 6 (1997), pp. 55–7

—'Nelson and Shakespeare', ND, 7 (2000), pp. 145–50

—'The Nelson Letters Project', MM, 87 (2001), pp. 476–8

—*The Nelson Encyclopaedia* (2002)

—'Nelson Ashore, 1780–1797', in Peter Hore, ed., *Seapower Ashore* (2001), pp. 53–78

—'The Nelson Letters Project', MM, 89 (2003), pp. 464–6

—'"More Enlarged Ideas Than in Former Times": New Insights from the Nelson Letters Project,' TC, 13 (2003), pp. 112–17

WHITE, DAVID, 'Heralds and their Clients: The Arms of Nelson', TC, 8 (1998), pp. 56–73

The Whole Proceedings on the King's Commission of the Peace, Oyer and Terminer, and Gaol Delivery for the City of London (1787) reprinted in *TC*, 3 (1993), pp. 56–69

WILKINSON, CLENNELL, *Nelson* (1931)

WILLOUGHBY, RUPERT, 'Nelson and the Dents', *ND*, 1 (1984), pp. 152–6

WRIGHT, D. G., *Popular Radicalism, 1780–1880* (1988)

WYNDHAM-QUIN, WILLIAM HENRY, *Sir Charles Tyler, G.C.B., Admiral of the White* (1912)

YARRINGTON, ALISON, 'Nelson the Citizen Hero: State and Public Patronage of Monumental Sculpture, 1805–1818', *Art History*, 6 (1983), pp. 315–29

—*The Commemoration of the Hero, 1800–1864* (New York, 1988)

GLOSSARY

ABLE SEAMAN In theory, a rating given to a prime seaman

ABOUT, GO To change tacks

ADMIRAL An officer eligible to command a fleet and fly a distinguishing flag. In descending order of seniority the three grades were admiral, vice admiral and rear admiral. See also BLUE

ADMIRALTY The senior naval board, whose first lord was a cabinet minister

ADVOCATE An attorney presenting a case

AFT Towards the rear or stern of a ship

ARTICLES OF WAR A statutory disciplinary code, regularly read to the ship's company

BACK To brace a sail so that the wind blows directly onto the front of it and retards the ship's progress

BEAM The width of a boat or ship or a frame supporting the decks

BENDING SAILS Attaching sails to yards, gaffs or stays

BITTS A frame to which mooring cables are attached

BLUE, THE The junior of three groups (red, white and blue) across which flag ranks were distributed. They recalled seventeenth-century squadronal colours

BOATSWAIN A warrant officer responsible for much of the routine working of a ship

BOMB VESSEL A vessel reinforced to carry heavy mortars to fire explosive shells. The noun bombard apparently refers to a similar vessel

BOW CHASERS Guns mounted in the bows of a ship

BOWER An anchor on the bow of a ship

BOWSPRIT A spar extending forward from the bows of a ship

BRIG A two-masted, square-rigged vessel, weaker than a frigate but used for similar duties

BULKHEAD An internal partition in a ship

BUMPKIN A short boom used to extend the lower edges of the principal sails on the masts

CABLE'S LENGTH Two hundred yards

CABLE TIER/SCUTTLE An area on the orlop deck used to store cables

CANISTER/CASE SHOT Cased shot designed to scatter among opponents

CAPSTAN A man-powered winch to work anchors, weights or heavy sails

CARRONADE A heavy gun used for close-quarter action

CARTOUCHE BOX A case for ammunition

CASEMATE/BOMBPROOF A place secure from bombardment

CATHEAD A timber projection near the bows of a ship to hold anchors

CHAINS Platforms on the outside of a ship from which the shrouds and ratlines lead to the masts

CHAIN SHOT Shot linked by a bar or chain, used to clear decks of men or bring down sails, spars and rigging

CHASE A ship being pursued

CLERK OF THE CHEQUE A dock-yard official responsible for accounts

CLEW UP To draw up the lower edges of a square sail for furling, using the clew and clew-lines

COCKPIT The place below the lower gun deck, near the aft hatchway, used by surgeons in a battle

COMMANDER A 'rank' between lieutenant and post-captain, enti-tling its holder to command a ship no larger than a sixth-rate

COMMISSIONED OFFICER An officer of the rank of lieutenant or above, holding the king's commis-sion from the Admiralty

COMMODORE A temporary post held by a senior captain, usually one given the command of a squadron; entitled to fly a broad pendant

CORVETTE A French sloop

COXSWAIN The helmsman and commander of a a ship's boat

CROSS JACKYARD The lower yard of the mizzen

CROW A crowbar used in handling guns

CUTTER A small single-master

DOCKYARD COMMISSIONER The officer in charge of a dockyard, usually by a civil appointment

DOG WATCH Two two-hour watches between 4 and 8 p.m.

DORY A small flat-bottomed Ameri-can boat

DOUBLE SHOTTING The loading of two round shot within a single charge to increase short-range velocity

DRIVER An additional sail for the mizzen

FASCINE Bundles of brush to pack military defences

FATHOM Six feet

FELUCCA A small, oared vessel, sometimes also equipped with a lateen sail

FIFTY An increasingly obsolete war-ship of fifty long guns

FIGHTING INSTRUCTIONS Code for tactical signals and movements, frequently elaborated by individual admirals

FISH To strengthen or splint a broken spar

FLAG RANK Loosely, an admiral with the right to fly his flag at the masthead

FOREMAST The mast nearest the bow of a ship, extended by the fore topmast and carrying the foresail, fore topsail and fore topgallant sail

FORECASTLE An area beneath the short raised forward deck of a ship; loosely, the living quarters of a crew, distinguished from those of officers aft

FREIGHT MONEY Money received by captains for shipping freight

FRIGATE A three-masted, square-rigged warship mounting between twenty-four and forty-four guns; light and fast, frigates cruised against enemy merchantmen and small warships and gathered intelligence, but were too weak to stand in the line of battle

GAFF The spar on the after side of a mast, used to suspend a supplementary sail

GALLERIES Stern or quarter walkways

GALLEY An oared fighting ship; a rowing boat, usually with one or two masts

GALLIOT A small single-masted galley

GIG A narrow, light, fast ship's boat

GRAPE Anti-personnel shot that scatters

GUARDA COSTA A Spanish guard boat

GUARDSHIP A warship stationed to protect a harbour or anchorage

GUNBOAT A small, lightly armed boat

GUNWALE Timbers covering the upper edge of a ship's side

HALYARDS Tackle for raising sails, spars or yards

HAUL UP To turn closer to the direction from which the wind is blowing

HAWSE The space between a ship's bow and the ground in which her anchor was fastened

HEAD MONEY Money paid to the captors of warships, based on the sizes of their crews

HELM Originally the steering tiller but latterly the wheel

HOWITZER A short, heavy siege gun

IMPRESS SERVICE The service for raising men, operating in and out of ports under the command of a regulating captain

INDIAMAN A merchantman trading with the East or West Indies

JIB An extension of the bowsprit

JOLLY BOAT A small, general-purpose boat

JURY MAST A temporary mast

KEDGE ANCHOR A small anchor used to haul grounded ships towards deeper water or to move ships when they are becalmed in shallows

KEELSON An internal keel to strengthen a frame

KETCH A vessel with main and mizzen masts, sometimes used as a bomb vessel

LARBOARD The left-hand side of a ship, looking forward to the bow

LARBOARD TACK To sail with the wind coming over the larboard side of a ship

LATEEN A triangular sail suspended on a yard at an angle of some forty-five degrees to the mast

LEE An area sheltered from the wind

LEEWARD The direction to which the wind is blowing. A vessel to leeward is on the sheltered side of a ship. A lee shore faces an onshore wind. A ship adopting the leeward position in battle places the enemy between herself and the wind. If crippled, such a ship can escape by running to leeward before the wind

LEVANTER A strong easterly or northeasterly Mediterranean wind

LIEUTENANT A commissioned officer, eligible to command unrated ships but usually supporting a commander or post-captain

LINE OF BATTLE The regular battle formation of fleets was line ahead, so that each ship presented a broadside towards the enemy

LOWER DECK Deck of a ship above the orlop; colloquially, ordinary ratings were not allowed use of the quarterdeck

LUFF To change course into the wind

MAINMAST The middle mast of a three-masted ship, extended by the main topmast and carrying the mainsail, main topsail and main topgallant

MASTER-AT-ARMS Warrant officer responsible for discipline, also known as corporal

MASTER'S MATE Technically an assistant to the sailing master, but often a trainee commissioned officer analogous to a midshipman

MERCHANTMAN A merchant ship

MERLON A military parapet between embrasures

MIDSHIPMAN A petty officer, generally presumed to be training to become a lieutenant, and usually a boy or youth

MIZZEN MAST In a three-masted ship the rearmost mast, extended by the mizzen topmast

NAVY BOARD A civil body, primarily responsible for the building and maintenance of ships and supplies

ORDINARY SEAMAN A rating given to a seaman superior to a landman but inferior to an able seaman

ORDNANCE BOARD A board, independent of the Admiralty, supplying guns, ordnance stores and ammunition to the armed services

ORLOP The lowest deck of a ship, above the hold

PANGA A small Central American boat

PASSING CERTIFICATE A certificate attesting to a candidate's success in an examination for lieutenant

PINNACE Oared ship's boat, sometimes able to raise a temporary mast

PITPAN A long, flat-bottomed canoe, used in Central America

POLACRE A three-masted Mediterranean vessel, generally possessing square sails on the mainmast and lateen sails on the fore and mizzen masts

POOP DECK A short, high deck at the rear of a ship

POST-CAPTAIN An officer eligible to command any size of warship and entered on an official list according to the date of his first captain's commission.

POWDER MONKEY A boy employed to carry powder from the magazine to the gundeck

PRIVATEER A private man-of-war authorised to attack enemy commerce in wartime

PRIZE AGENT An agent to whom prizes were entrusted, responsible for overseeing cases and handling pay and prize money

PRIZE CREW A skeleton crew put on a prize to conduct her to port

PROCTOR An official of the vice-admiralty courts responsible for preparing a case for an advocate

QUARTER After parts of a ship on either side of the stern; the direction from which the wind blows

QUARTERDECK A raised part of the upper deck to the rear of the mainmast, reserved for the use of officers

QUARTERMASTER A petty officer who assisted the master and his mates

RATE Six categories of warship, based on the number of guns, excluding carronades. First rates (one hundred guns or more), second rates (eighty-four or more) and third rates (seventy or more) were the principal ships of the line

RIGGING The network of ropes supporting a ship's masts. Standing rigging refers to fixed ropes, and running rigging to ropes managing sails

ROUNDSHOT Fired from smooth-bore cannons, the calibres used were of 4, 6, 9, 12, 18, 24 and 32 lbs

ROYALS Auxiliary sails raised above the topgallants

SCHOONER A two- or three-masted vessel rigged fore and aft

SEA FENCIBLES A maritime militia raised after 1798 to defend Britain from invasion

SEA TIME The six years of sea-going experience necessary to become a lieutenant.

SEVENTY-FOUR The classic ship of the line, with seventy-four guns

SHALLOP A large, heavy boat with fore and aft sails or lug sails, or a shallow-draught boat using oars or a sail

SHEET Ropes manipulating a sail

SHEET ANCHOR An anchor supporting the bower

SHEER-HULK A decommissioned ship equipped with sheers to lift heavy weights. Ships needing masts lifting in or out were brought alongside a sheer-hulk

SHIP OF THE LINE A capital ship, usually of sixty-four or more long guns, strong enough to stand in the line of battle

SHIPS IN ORDINARY Laid up or decommissioned ships

SHROUDS Standing rigging from masts to the ship sides

SICK AND HURT BOARD A subsidiary of the Admiralty, responsible for ships' surgeons, naval hospitals and (until 1796) prisoners of war

SLING The middle part of a yard, encircled by a sling hoop from which it is suspended from the mast and hoisted or lowered

SLOOP Loosely used in the Navy to describe a warship smaller than a frigate, possibly a two-masted brig or a three-master

SLOPS Clothing supplied by the Navy Board, obtained from a ship's purser, who deducted the cost from due wages. A slop ship was used to store such clothing

SNOW A two-masted merchantman

SPANKER A supplementary sail raised on a boom attached to the mizzen

SPARS A generic term for masts, yards, booms and gaffs

SPOKE The word used to report an exchange of information between two vessels; this could be by hailing or by a boat from one going alongside the other

SPRINGS Supplementary ropes connected to an anchor, used to manoeuvre a moored ship more adeptly

SPRITSAIL A small sail suspended from the bowsprit

SQUADRON A number of warships too small to constitute a fleet

SQUARE RIG Four-sided sails placed across the yards

STARBOARD Right-hand side of a ship, looking forward to the bows

STARBOARD TACK To sail with the wind coming from starboard

STAYS Fore and aft ropes supporting a mast

STAYSAILS Triangular sails suspended from the stays

STERN CHASERS Guns mounted on the stern

STUDDING SAILS Sails set out upon booms from the square sails in good weather

SUPERNUMERARY A passenger, carried on the books for victuals, but not a member of the regular ship's company

SWIVEL A light anti-personnel gun that turned on a pivot

TACK To turn a ship by putting her head against the direction of the wind

TARTAN A Mediterranean vessel, generally with one mast, a large lateen sail and a foresail

THREE/TWO DECKER Terms referring to the number of gundecks on a warship

TOPGALLANTS Sails above the principal sails on the masts of a square rigger

TOPMAST Extension to a fore-, main- or mizzen mast

TOPSAIL The sail above the principal sail on a mast of a square rigger

VAN The front of a fleet

VICE-ADMIRALTY COURT An overseas branch of the High Court of the Admiralty

VICTUALLING BOARD A subsidiary of the Navy Board responsible for the provision of victuals and slop clothing

WAD A bundle of rags rammed down the muzzle of a cannon to prevent the shot rolling out

WARD ROOM A mess for commissioned officers

WARRANT OFFICER An officer appointed by a warrant of the Navy Board, such as a master, surgeon or purser

WATCH A period of duty on a ship, usually four hours long; one of two contingents into which the crew is divided, so that some seamen rest while others handle the ship

WEAR To turn a ship by putting the bow away from the wind

WEATHER To pass to windward of a ship or land form

WEATHER GAUGE A ship in the windward position was said to have the weather gauge. Thus situated, it had advantages over an opponent to leeward. Ships with the weather gauge could manoeuvre more easily than those to leeward, which attacked against the wind

WINDWARD Anything to windward of a ship is between that ship and the wind. In a naval action a ship with her enemy to leeward is said to have the windward position or the weather gauge and the advantage of the wind

XEBEC A small, three-masted vessel with both square and lateen sails

YARD A spar across a mast, supporting a sail

YAWL A yacht or small sailing boat

YEOMAN OF THE POWDER ROOM A petty officer with responsibility for the magazine

INDEX

Clark, John 89, 679
Clark, Captain John 488
Clark, William 49
Clark, William 170
Clark, William 361–2
Clarke, James Stanier 4–5
  on the *Albermarle* 197–8
  the encounter with the polar bear 75
  and the evacuation of the *Glasgow* 139–40
  Nelson's appearance 215–6
  Nelson's thoughts of leaving the service 371–2
Clarke, John 780
Clerke, Captain John 100, 103
Clive, Robert 51
Cochran, Sergeant John 252, 256
Cochrane, Thomas, Lord 628, 753
Cockburn, Captain George
  action against the *Santa Sabina* 19, 20, 25
  and Adelaide Correglia 530
  and the *Belvedere* 569–70
  escape from Gibraltar 684–6
  evacuation of Elba 15, 677
  Jervis on 625
  move to *La Minerve* 641
  naval career 16
  Nelson presents with sword 26
  Nelson's support for 633–4
  raid on Alassio 572–3
  and Sawyer 631, 632
  at Torre del l'Arma 600–1
Codrington, Lieutenant Charles Pusick 177
Coke, Thomas William 386–7, 417
Coleman, Terry 9
Coleridge, Samuel Taylor 2, 605
Collett, Isaac Charles Smith 623, 627, 861n14
Colley, Linda 180
Collier, Captain George 86–7
Collingwood, Cuthbert 142, 142–3, 168, 254
  attempt to reoccupy Capraia 673–4
  at Cape St Vincent 392, 690, 697, 698–9
  on Cape St Vincent 705
  character 258–9
  comparison with Nelson 258–9, 392
  decisiveness 784

and the *Dolphin* 298–9
enforcement of the navigation laws 265–9, 286, 288, 294, 297–300, 825n23, 826n35
and the evacuation of Corsica 671
and Mary Moutray 261, 281
and the Moutrays return to England 277, 278
on Nelson 392–3
on Nelson and Jervis 726–7
Nelson thanks for action at Cape St Vincent 714
portrait of Nelson 262–3
protest to Hughes 271
protests Moutray's especial commission 273
Collingwood, Wilfred
  command of the *Kite* 197
  command of the *Rattler* 254
  comparison with Nelson 258
  death of 362–3
  enforcement of the navigation laws 265–72, 287–8, 293, 297, 353
  and William Lewis 334–5
Colossus, HMS
  at Cadiz 725
  at Cape St Vincent 691, 692
  and the Elba convoy 728
  at Toulon 426, 427
  voyage to Toulon 422
command control 751–2, 787
commanders 129, 133
Compton, Lieutenant Henry
  at Genoa 659–60, 661
  naval career 621, 626, 735
  and the Tenerife expedition 775
  transfer to the *Captain* 616
  transfer to the *Seahorse* 779
  transfer to the *Theseus* 876n30
Concepción, the 664
Conference, the 147
convoy work 96–8, 109–11
Cook, Christopher 416
Cook, Francis 701, 703, 733
Cook, Captain James 63, 86
Cook, John 50
Cooke, Captain Edward 460, 470–1, 501
Cooper, John 230
Cooper, John 780
Cordoba y Ramos, Vice Admiral Jose de 688, 690, 693, 697